Lecture Notes in Computer Science 11206

Commenced Publication in 1973
Founding and Former Series Editors:
Gerhard Goos, Juris Hartmanis, and Jan van Leeuwen

Editorial Board

More information about this series at http://www.springer.com/series/7412

Vittorio Ferrari · Martial Hebert
Cristian Sminchisescu · Yair Weiss (Eds.)

Computer Vision – ECCV 2018

15th European Conference
Munich, Germany, September 8–14, 2018
Proceedings, Part II

 Springer

Editors
Vittorio Ferrari
Google Research
Zurich
Switzerland

Cristian Sminchisescu
Google Research
Zurich
Switzerland

Martial Hebert
Carnegie Mellon University
Pittsburgh, PA
USA

Yair Weiss
Hebrew University of Jerusalem
Jerusalem
Israel

ISSN 0302-9743   ISSN 1611-3349   (electronic)
Lecture Notes in Computer Science
ISBN 978-3-030-01215-1   ISBN 978-3-030-01216-8   (eBook)
https://doi.org/10.1007/978-3-030-01216-8

Library of Congress Control Number: 2018955489

LNCS Sublibrary: SL6 – Image Processing, Computer Vision, Pattern Recognition, and Graphics

This Springer imprint is published by the registered company Springer Nature Switzerland AG
The registered company address is: Gewerbestrasse 11, 6330 Cham, Switzerland

Foreword

It was our great pleasure to host the European Conference on Computer Vision 2018 in Munich, Germany. This constituted by far the largest ECCV event ever. With close to 2,900 registered participants and another 600 on the waiting list one month before the conference, participation more than doubled since the last ECCV in Amsterdam. We believe that this is due to a dramatic growth of the computer vision community combined with the popularity of Munich as a major European hub of culture, science, and industry. The conference took place in the heart of Munich in the concert hall Gasteig with workshops and tutorials held at the downtown campus of the Technical University of Munich.

One of the major innovations for ECCV 2018 was the free perpetual availability of all conference and workshop papers, which is often referred to as open access. We note that this is not precisely the same use of the term as in the Budapest declaration. Since 2013, CVPR and ICCV have had their papers hosted by the Computer Vision Foundation (CVF), in parallel with the IEEE Xplore version. This has proved highly beneficial to the computer vision community.

We are delighted to announce that for ECCV 2018 a very similar arrangement was put in place with the cooperation of Springer. In particular, the author's final version will be freely available in perpetuity on a CVF page, while SpringerLink will continue to host a version with further improvements, such as activating reference links and including video. We believe that this will give readers the best of both worlds; researchers who are focused on the technical content will have a freely available version in an easily accessible place, while subscribers to SpringerLink will continue to have the additional benefits that this provides. We thank Alfred Hofmann from Springer for helping to negotiate this agreement, which we expect will continue for future versions of ECCV.

September 2018

Horst Bischof
Daniel Cremers
Bernt Schiele
Ramin Zabih

Preface

Welcome to the proceedings of the 2018 European Conference on Computer Vision (ECCV 2018) held in Munich, Germany. We are delighted to present this volume reflecting a strong and exciting program, the result of an extensive review process. In total, we received 2,439 valid paper submissions. Of these, 776 were accepted (31.8%): 717 as posters (29.4%) and 59 as oral presentations (2.4%). All oral presentations were presented as posters as well. The program selection process was complicated this year by the large increase in the number of submitted papers, +65% over ECCV 2016, and the use of CMT3 for the first time for a computer vision conference. The program selection process was supported by four program co-chairs (PCs), 126 area chairs (ACs), and 1,199 reviewers with reviews assigned.

We were primarily responsible for the design and execution of the review process. Beyond administrative rejections, we were involved in acceptance decisions only in the very few cases where the ACs were not able to agree on a decision. As PCs, and as is customary in the field, we were not allowed to co-author a submission. General co-chairs and other co-organizers who played no role in the review process were permitted to submit papers, and were treated as any other author is.

Acceptance decisions were made by two independent ACs. The ACs also made a joint recommendation for promoting papers to oral status. We decided on the final selection of oral presentations based on the ACs' recommendations. There were 126 ACs, selected according to their technical expertise, experience, and geographical diversity (63 from European, nine from Asian/Australian, and 54 from North American institutions). Indeed, 126 ACs is a substantial increase in the number of ACs due to the natural increase in the number of papers and to our desire to maintain the number of papers assigned to each AC to a manageable number so as to ensure quality. The ACs were aided by the 1,199 reviewers to whom papers were assigned for reviewing. The Program Committee was selected from committees of previous ECCV, ICCV, and CVPR conferences and was extended on the basis of suggestions from the ACs. Having a large pool of Program Committee members for reviewing allowed us to match expertise while reducing reviewer loads. No more than eight papers were assigned to a reviewer, maintaining the reviewers' load at the same level as ECCV 2016 despite the increase in the number of submitted papers.

Conflicts of interest between ACs, Program Committee members, and papers were identified based on the home institutions, and on previous collaborations of all researchers involved. To find institutional conflicts, all authors, Program Committee members, and ACs were asked to list the Internet domains of their current institutions. We assigned on average approximately 18 papers to each AC. The papers were assigned using the affinity scores from the Toronto Paper Matching System (TPMS) and additional data from the OpenReview system, managed by a UMass group. OpenReview used additional information from ACs' and authors' records to identify collaborations and to generate matches. OpenReview was invaluable in refining conflict definitions and in generating quality matches. The only glitch is that, once the matches were generated, a small percentage of papers were unassigned because of discrepancies between the OpenReview conflicts and the conflicts entered in CMT3. We manually assigned these papers. This glitch is revealing of the challenge of using multiple systems at once (CMT3 and OpenReview in this case), which needs to be addressed in future.

After assignment of papers to ACs, the ACs suggested seven reviewers per paper from the Program Committee pool. The selection and rank ordering were facilitated by the TPMS affinity scores visible to the ACs for each paper/reviewer pair. The final assignment of papers to reviewers was generated again through OpenReview in order to account for refined conflict definitions. This required new features in the OpenReview matching system to accommodate the ECCV workflow, in particular to incorporate selection ranking, and maximum reviewer load. Very few papers received fewer than three reviewers after matching and were handled through manual assignment. Reviewers were then asked to comment on the merit of each paper and to make an initial recommendation ranging from definitely reject to definitely accept, including a borderline rating. The reviewers were also asked to suggest explicit questions they wanted to see answered in the authors' rebuttal. The initial review period was five weeks. Because of the delay in getting all the reviews in, we had to delay the final release of the reviews by four days. However, because of the slack included at the tail end of the schedule, we were able to maintain the decision target date with sufficient time for all the phases. We reassigned over 100 reviews from 40 reviewers during the review period. Unfortunately, the main reason for these reassignments was reviewers declining to review, after having accepted to do so. Other reasons included technical relevance and occasional unidentified conflicts. We express our thanks to the emergency reviewers who generously accepted to perform these reviews under short notice. In addition, a substantial number of manual corrections had to do with reviewers using a different email address than the one that was used at the time of the reviewer invitation. This is revealing of a broader issue with identifying users by email addresses that change frequently enough to cause significant problems during the timespan of the conference process.

The authors were then given the opportunity to rebut the reviews, to identify factual errors, and to address the specific questions raised by the reviewers over a seven-day rebuttal period. The exact format of the rebuttal was the object of considerable debate among the organizers, as well as with prior organizers. At issue is to balance giving the author the opportunity to respond completely and precisely to the reviewers, e.g., by including graphs of experiments, while avoiding requests for completely new material or experimental results not included in the original paper. In the end, we decided on the two-page PDF document in conference format. Following this rebuttal period, reviewers and ACs discussed papers at length, after which reviewers finalized their evaluation and gave a final recommendation to the ACs. A significant percentage of the reviewers did enter their final recommendation if it did not differ from their initial recommendation. Given the tight schedule, we did not wait until all were entered.

After this discussion period, each paper was assigned to a second AC. The AC/paper matching was again run through OpenReview. Again, the OpenReview team worked quickly to implement the features specific to this process, in this case accounting for the existing AC assignment, as well as minimizing the fragmentation across ACs, so that each AC had on average only 5.5 buddy ACs to communicate with. The largest number was 11. Given the complexity of the conflicts, this was a very efficient set of assignments from OpenReview. Each paper was then evaluated by its assigned pair of ACs. For each paper, we required each of the two ACs assigned to certify both the final recommendation and the metareview (aka consolidation report). In all cases, after extensive discussions, the two ACs arrived at a common acceptance decision. We maintained these decisions, with the caveat that we did evaluate, sometimes going back to the ACs, a few papers for which the final acceptance decision substantially deviated from the consensus from the reviewers, amending three decisions in the process.

We want to thank everyone involved in making ECCV 2018 possible. The success of ECCV 2018 depended on the quality of papers submitted by the authors, and on the very hard work of the ACs and the Program Committee members. We are particularly grateful to the OpenReview team (Melisa Bok, Ari Kobren, Andrew McCallum, Michael Spector) for their support, in particular their willingness to implement new features, often on a tight schedule, to Laurent Charlin for the use of the Toronto Paper Matching System, to the CMT3 team, in particular in dealing with all the issues that arise when using a new system, to Friedrich Fraundorfer and Quirin Lohr for maintaining the online version of the program, and to the CMU staff (Keyla Cook, Lynnetta Miller, Ashley Song, Nora Kazour) for assisting with data entry/editing in CMT3. Finally, the preparation of these proceedings would not have been possible without the diligent effort of the publication chairs, Albert Ali Salah and Hamdi Dibeklioğlu, and of Anna Kramer and Alfred Hofmann from Springer.

September 2018

Vittorio Ferrari
Martial Hebert
Cristian Sminchisescu
Yair Weiss

Organization

General Chairs

Horst Bischof	Graz University of Technology, Austria
Daniel Cremers	Technical University of Munich, Germany
Bernt Schiele	Saarland University, Max Planck Institute for Informatics, Germany
Ramin Zabih	CornellNYCTech, USA

Program Committee Co-chairs

Vittorio Ferrari	University of Edinburgh, UK
Martial Hebert	Carnegie Mellon University, USA
Cristian Sminchisescu	Lund University, Sweden
Yair Weiss	Hebrew University, Israel

Local Arrangements Chairs

Björn Menze	Technical University of Munich, Germany
Matthias Niessner	Technical University of Munich, Germany

Workshop Chairs

Stefan Roth	TU Darmstadt, Germany
Laura Leal-Taixé	Technical University of Munich, Germany

Tutorial Chairs

Michael Bronstein	Università della Svizzera Italiana, Switzerland
Laura Leal-Taixé	Technical University of Munich, Germany

Website Chair

Friedrich Fraundorfer	Graz University of Technology, Austria

Demo Chairs

Federico Tombari	Technical University of Munich, Germany
Joerg Stueckler	Technical University of Munich, Germany

Publicity Chair

Giovanni Maria   University of Catania, Italy
  Farinella

Industrial Liaison Chairs

Florent Perronnin   Naver Labs, France
Yunchao Gong   Snap, USA
Helmut Grabner   Logitech, Switzerland

Finance Chair

Gerard Medioni   Amazon, University of Southern California, USA

Publication Chairs

Albert Ali Salah   Boğaziçi University, Turkey
Hamdi Dibeklioğlu   Bilkent University, Turkey

Area Chairs

Kalle Åström   Lund University, Sweden
Zeynep Akata   University of Amsterdam, The Netherlands
Joao Barreto   University of Coimbra, Portugal
Ronen Basri   Weizmann Institute of Science, Israel
Dhruv Batra   Georgia Tech and Facebook AI Research, USA
Serge Belongie   Cornell University, USA
Rodrigo Benenson   Google, Switzerland
Hakan Bilen   University of Edinburgh, UK
Matthew Blaschko   KU Leuven, Belgium
Edmond Boyer   Inria, France
Gabriel Brostow   University College London, UK
Thomas Brox   University of Freiburg, Germany
Marcus Brubaker   York University, Canada
Barbara Caputo   Politecnico di Torino and the Italian Institute
                          of Technology, Italy
Tim Cootes   University of Manchester, UK
Trevor Darrell   University of California, Berkeley, USA
Larry Davis   University of Maryland at College Park, USA
Andrew Davison   Imperial College London, UK
Fernando de la Torre   Carnegie Mellon University, USA
Irfan Essa   GeorgiaTech, USA
Ali Farhadi   University of Washington, USA
Paolo Favaro   University of Bern, Switzerland
Michael Felsberg   Linköping University, Sweden

Sanja Fidler	University of Toronto, Canada
Andrew Fitzgibbon	Microsoft, Cambridge, UK
David Forsyth	University of Illinois at Urbana-Champaign, USA
Charless Fowlkes	University of California, Irvine, USA
Bill Freeman	MIT, USA
Mario Fritz	MPII, Germany
Jürgen Gall	University of Bonn, Germany
Dariu Gavrila	TU Delft, The Netherlands
Andreas Geiger	MPI-IS and University of Tübingen, Germany
Theo Gevers	University of Amsterdam, The Netherlands
Ross Girshick	Facebook AI Research, USA
Kristen Grauman	Facebook AI Research and UT Austin, USA
Abhinav Gupta	Carnegie Mellon University, USA
Kaiming He	Facebook AI Research, USA
Martial Hebert	Carnegie Mellon University, USA
Anders Heyden	Lund University, Sweden
Timothy Hospedales	University of Edinburgh, UK
Michal Irani	Weizmann Institute of Science, Israel
Phillip Isola	University of California, Berkeley, USA
Hervé Jégou	Facebook AI Research, France
David Jacobs	University of Maryland, College Park, USA
Allan Jepson	University of Toronto, Canada
Jiaya Jia	Chinese University of Hong Kong, SAR China
Fredrik Kahl	Chalmers University, USA
Hedvig Kjellström	KTH Royal Institute of Technology, Sweden
Iasonas Kokkinos	University College London and Facebook, UK
Vladlen Koltun	Intel Labs, USA
Philipp Krähenbühl	UT Austin, USA
M. Pawan Kumar	University of Oxford, UK
Kyros Kutulakos	University of Toronto, Canada
In Kweon	KAIST, South Korea
Ivan Laptev	Inria, France
Svetlana Lazebnik	University of Illinois at Urbana-Champaign, USA
Laura Leal-Taixé	Technical University of Munich, Germany
Erik Learned-Miller	University of Massachusetts, Amherst, USA
Kyoung Mu Lee	Seoul National University, South Korea
Bastian Leibe	RWTH Aachen University, Germany
Aleš Leonardis	University of Birmingham, UK
Vincent Lepetit	University of Bordeaux, France and Graz University of Technology, Austria
Fuxin Li	Oregon State University, USA
Dahua Lin	Chinese University of Hong Kong, SAR China
Jim Little	University of British Columbia, Canada
Ce Liu	Google, USA
Chen Change Loy	Nanyang Technological University, Singapore
Jiri Matas	Czech Technical University in Prague, Czechia

Yasuyuki Matsushita	Osaka University, Japan
Dimitris Metaxas	Rutgers University, USA
Greg Mori	Simon Fraser University, Canada
Vittorio Murino	Istituto Italiano di Tecnologia, Italy
Richard Newcombe	Oculus Research, USA
Minh Hoai Nguyen	Stony Brook University, USA
Sebastian Nowozin	Microsoft Research Cambridge, UK
Aude Oliva	MIT, USA
Bjorn Ommer	Heidelberg University, Germany
Tomas Pajdla	Czech Technical University in Prague, Czechia
Maja Pantic	Imperial College London and Samsung AI Research Centre Cambridge, UK
Caroline Pantofaru	Google, USA
Devi Parikh	Georgia Tech and Facebook AI Research, USA
Sylvain Paris	Adobe Research, USA
Vladimir Pavlovic	Rutgers University, USA
Marcello Pelillo	University of Venice, Italy
Patrick Pérez	Valeo, France
Robert Pless	George Washington University, USA
Thomas Pock	Graz University of Technology, Austria
Jean Ponce	Inria, France
Gerard Pons-Moll	MPII, Saarland Informatics Campus, Germany
Long Quan	Hong Kong University of Science and Technology, SAR China
Stefan Roth	TU Darmstadt, Germany
Carsten Rother	University of Heidelberg, Germany
Bryan Russell	Adobe Research, USA
Kate Saenko	Boston University, USA
Mathieu Salzmann	EPFL, Switzerland
Dimitris Samaras	Stony Brook University, USA
Yoichi Sato	University of Tokyo, Japan
Silvio Savarese	Stanford University, USA
Konrad Schindler	ETH Zurich, Switzerland
Cordelia Schmid	Inria, France and Google, France
Nicu Sebe	University of Trento, Italy
Fei Sha	University of Southern California, USA
Greg Shakhnarovich	TTI Chicago, USA
Jianbo Shi	University of Pennsylvania, USA
Abhinav Shrivastava	UMD and Google, USA
Yan Shuicheng	National University of Singapore, Singapore
Leonid Sigal	University of British Columbia, Canada
Josef Sivic	Czech Technical University in Prague, Czechia
Arnold Smeulders	University of Amsterdam, The Netherlands
Deqing Sun	NVIDIA, USA
Antonio Torralba	MIT, USA
Zhuowen Tu	University of California, San Diego, USA

Tinne Tuytelaars   KU Leuven, Belgium
Jasper Uijlings   Google, Switzerland
Joost van de Weijer   Computer Vision Center, Spain
Nuno Vasconcelos   University of California, San Diego, USA
Andrea Vedaldi   University of Oxford, UK
Olga Veksler   University of Western Ontario, Canada
Jakob Verbeek   Inria, France
Rene Vidal   Johns Hopkins University, USA
Daphna Weinshall   Hebrew University, Israel
Chris Williams   University of Edinburgh, UK
Lior Wolf   Tel Aviv University, Israel
Ming-Hsuan Yang   University of California at Merced, USA
Todd Zickler   Harvard University, USA
Andrew Zisserman   University of Oxford, UK

Technical Program Committee

Hassan Abu Alhaija	Peter Anderson	Arunava Banerjee
Radhakrishna Achanta	Juan Andrade-Cetto	Atsuhiko Banno
Hanno Ackermann	Mykhaylo Andriluka	Aayush Bansal
Ehsan Adeli	Anelia Angelova	Yingze Bao
Lourdes Agapito	Michel Antunes	Md Jawadul Bappy
Aishwarya Agrawal	Pablo Arbelaez	Pierre Baqué
Antonio Agudo	Vasileios Argyriou	Dániel Baráth
Eirikur Agustsson	Chetan Arora	Adrian Barbu
Karim Ahmed	Federica Arrigoni	Kobus Barnard
Byeongjoo Ahn	Vassilis Athitsos	Nick Barnes
Unaiza Ahsan	Mathieu Aubry	Francisco Barranco
Emre Akbaş	Shai Avidan	Adrien Bartoli
Eren Aksoy	Yannis Avrithis	E. Bayro-Corrochano
Yağız Aksoy	Samaneh Azadi	Paul Beardlsey
Alexandre Alahi	Hossein Azizpour	Vasileios Belagiannis
Jean-Baptiste Alayrac	Artem Babenko	Sean Bell
Samuel Albanie	Timur Bagautdinov	Ismail Ben
Cenek Albl	Andrew Bagdanov	Boulbaba Ben Amor
Saad Ali	Hessam Bagherinezhad	Gil Ben-Artzi
Rahaf Aljundi	Yuval Bahat	Ohad Ben-Shahar
Jose M. Alvarez	Min Bai	Abhijit Bendale
Humam Alwassel	Qinxun Bai	Rodrigo Benenson
Toshiyuki Amano	Song Bai	Fabian Benitez-Quiroz
Mitsuru Ambai	Xiang Bai	Fethallah Benmansour
Mohamed Amer	Peter Bajcsy	Ryad Benosman
Senjian An	Amr Bakry	Filippo Bergamasco
Cosmin Ancuti	Kavita Bala	David Bermudez

Jesus Bermudez-Cameo
Leonard Berrada
Gedas Bertasius
Ross Beveridge
Lucas Beyer
Bir Bhanu
S. Bhattacharya
Binod Bhattarai
Arnav Bhavsar
Simone Bianco
Adel Bibi
Pia Bideau
Josef Bigun
Arijit Biswas
Soma Biswas
Marten Bjoerkman
Volker Blanz
Vishnu Boddeti
Piotr Bojanowski
Terrance Boult
Yuri Boykov
Hakan Boyraz
Eric Brachmann
Samarth Brahmbhatt
Mathieu Bredif
Francois Bremond
Michael Brown
Luc Brun
Shyamal Buch
Pradeep Buddharaju
Aurelie Bugeau
Rudy Bunel
Xavier Burgos Artizzu
Darius Burschka
Andrei Bursuc
Zoya Bylinskii
Fabian Caba
Daniel Cabrini Hauagge
Cesar Cadena Lerma
Holger Caesar
Jianfei Cai
Junjie Cai
Zhaowei Cai
Simone Calderara
Neill Campbell
Octavia Camps

Xun Cao
Yanshuai Cao
Joao Carreira
Dan Casas
Daniel Castro
Jan Cech
M. Emre Celebi
Duygu Ceylan
Menglei Chai
Ayan Chakrabarti
Rudrasis Chakraborty
Shayok Chakraborty
Tat-Jen Cham
Antonin Chambolle
Antoni Chan
Sharat Chandran
Hyun Sung Chang
Ju Yong Chang
Xiaojun Chang
Soravit Changpinyo
Wei-Lun Chao
Yu-Wei Chao
Visesh Chari
Rizwan Chaudhry
Siddhartha Chaudhuri
Rama Chellappa
Chao Chen
Chen Chen
Cheng Chen
Chu-Song Chen
Guang Chen
Hsin-I Chen
Hwann-Tzong Chen
Kai Chen
Kan Chen
Kevin Chen
Liang-Chieh Chen
Lin Chen
Qifeng Chen
Ting Chen
Wei Chen
Xi Chen
Xilin Chen
Xinlei Chen
Yingcong Chen
Yixin Chen

Erkang Cheng
Jingchun Cheng
Ming-Ming Cheng
Wen-Huang Cheng
Yuan Cheng
Anoop Cherian
Liang-Tien Chia
Naoki Chiba
Shao-Yi Chien
Han-Pang Chiu
Wei-Chen Chiu
Nam Ik Cho
Sunghyun Cho
TaeEun Choe
Jongmoo Choi
Christopher Choy
Wen-Sheng Chu
Yung-Yu Chuang
Ondrej Chum
Joon Son Chung
Gökberk Cinbis
James Clark
Andrea Cohen
Forrester Cole
Toby Collins
John Collomosse
Camille Couprie
David Crandall
Marco Cristani
Canton Cristian
James Crowley
Yin Cui
Zhaopeng Cui
Bo Dai
Jifeng Dai
Qieyun Dai
Shengyang Dai
Yuchao Dai
Carlo Dal Mutto
Dima Damen
Zachary Daniels
Kostas Daniilidis
Donald Dansereau
Mohamed Daoudi
Abhishek Das
Samyak Datta

Achal Dave
Shalini De Mello
Teofilo deCampos
Joseph DeGol
Koichiro Deguchi
Alessio Del Bue
Stefanie Demirci
Jia Deng
Zhiwei Deng
Joachim Denzler
Konstantinos Derpanis
Aditya Deshpande
Alban Desmaison
Frédéric Devernay
Abhinav Dhall
Michel Dhome
Hamdi Dibeklioğlu
Mert Dikmen
Cosimo Distante
Ajay Divakaran
Mandar Dixit
Carl Doersch
Piotr Dollar
Bo Dong
Chao Dong
Huang Dong
Jian Dong
Jiangxin Dong
Weisheng Dong
Simon Donné
Gianfranco Doretto
Alexey Dosovitskiy
Matthijs Douze
Bruce Draper
Bertram Drost
Liang Du
Shichuan Du
Gregory Dudek
Zoran Duric
Pınar Duygulu
Hazım Ekenel
Tarek El-Gaaly
Ehsan Elhamifar
Mohamed Elhoseiny
Sabu Emmanuel
Ian Endres

Aykut Erdem
Erkut Erdem
Hugo Jair Escalante
Sergio Escalera
Victor Escorcia
Francisco Estrada
Davide Eynard
Bin Fan
Jialue Fan
Quanfu Fan
Chen Fang
Tian Fang
Yi Fang
Hany Farid
Giovanni Farinella
Ryan Farrell
Alireza Fathi
Christoph Feichtenhofer
Wenxin Feng
Martin Fergie
Cornelia Fermuller
Basura Fernando
Michael Firman
Bob Fisher
John Fisher
Mathew Fisher
Boris Flach
Matt Flagg
Francois Fleuret
David Fofi
Ruth Fong
Gian Luca Foresti
Per-Erik Forssén
David Fouhey
Katerina Fragkiadaki
Victor Fragoso
Jan-Michael Frahm
Jean-Sebastien Franco
Ohad Fried
Simone Frintrop
Huazhu Fu
Yun Fu
Olac Fuentes
Christopher Funk
Thomas Funkhouser
Brian Funt

Ryo Furukawa
Yasutaka Furukawa
Andrea Fusiello
Fatma Güney
Raghudeep Gadde
Silvano Galliani
Orazio Gallo
Chuang Gan
Bin-Bin Gao
Jin Gao
Junbin Gao
Ruohan Gao
Shenghua Gao
Animesh Garg
Ravi Garg
Erik Gartner
Simone Gasparin
Jochen Gast
Leon A. Gatys
Stratis Gavves
Liuhao Ge
Timnit Gebru
James Gee
Peter Gehler
Xin Geng
Guido Gerig
David Geronimo
Bernard Ghanem
Michael Gharbi
Golnaz Ghiasi
Spyros Gidaris
Andrew Gilbert
Rohit Girdhar
Ioannis Gkioulekas
Georgia Gkioxari
Guy Godin
Roland Goecke
Michael Goesele
Nuno Goncalves
Boqing Gong
Minglun Gong
Yunchao Gong
Abel Gonzalez-Garcia
Daniel Gordon
Paulo Gotardo
Stephen Gould

Venu Govindu
Helmut Grabner
Petr Gronat
Steve Gu
Josechu Guerrero
Anupam Guha
Jean-Yves Guillemaut
Alp Güler
Erhan Gündoğdu
Guodong Guo
Xinqing Guo
Ankush Gupta
Mohit Gupta
Saurabh Gupta
Tanmay Gupta
Abner Guzman Rivera
Timo Hackel
Sunil Hadap
Christian Haene
Ralf Haeusler
Levente Hajder
David Hall
Peter Hall
Stefan Haller
Ghassan Hamarneh
Fred Hamprecht
Onur Hamsici
Bohyung Han
Junwei Han
Xufeng Han
Yahong Han
Ankur Handa
Albert Haque
Tatsuya Harada
Mehrtash Harandi
Bharath Hariharan
Mahmudul Hasan
Tal Hassner
Kenji Hata
Soren Hauberg
Michal Havlena
Zeeshan Hayder
Junfeng He
Lei He
Varsha Hedau
Felix Heide

Wolfgang Heidrich
Janne Heikkila
Jared Heinly
Mattias Heinrich
Lisa Anne Hendricks
Dan Hendrycks
Stephane Herbin
Alexander Hermans
Luis Herranz
Aaron Hertzmann
Adrian Hilton
Michael Hirsch
Steven Hoi
Seunghoon Hong
Wei Hong
Anthony Hoogs
Radu Horaud
Yedid Hoshen
Omid Hosseini Jafari
Kuang-Jui Hsu
Winston Hsu
Yinlin Hu
Zhe Hu
Gang Hua
Chen Huang
De-An Huang
Dong Huang
Gary Huang
Heng Huang
Jia-Bin Huang
Qixing Huang
Rui Huang
Sheng Huang
Weilin Huang
Xiaolei Huang
Xinyu Huang
Zhiwu Huang
Tak-Wai Hui
Wei-Chih Hung
Junhwa Hur
Mohamed Hussein
Wonjun Hwang
Anders Hyden
Satoshi Ikehata
Nazlı Ikizler-Cinbis
Viorela Ila

Evren Imre
Eldar Insafutdinov
Go Irie
Hossam Isack
Ahmet İşcen
Daisuke Iwai
Hamid Izadinia
Nathan Jacobs
Suyog Jain
Varun Jampani
C. V. Jawahar
Dinesh Jayaraman
Sadeep Jayasumana
Laszlo Jeni
Hueihan Jhuang
Dinghuang Ji
Hui Ji
Qiang Ji
Fan Jia
Kui Jia
Xu Jia
Huaizu Jiang
Jiayan Jiang
Nianjuan Jiang
Tingting Jiang
Xiaoyi Jiang
Yu-Gang Jiang
Long Jin
Suo Jinli
Justin Johnson
Nebojsa Jojic
Michael Jones
Hanbyul Joo
Jungseock Joo
Ajjen Joshi
Amin Jourabloo
Frederic Jurie
Achuta Kadambi
Samuel Kadoury
Ioannis Kakadiaris
Zdenek Kalal
Yannis Kalantidis
Sinan Kalkan
Vicky Kalogeiton
Sunkavalli Kalyan
J.-K. Kamarainen

Martin Kampel
Kenichi Kanatani
Angjoo Kanazawa
Melih Kandemir
Sing Bing Kang
Zhuoliang Kang
Mohan Kankanhalli
Juho Kannala
Abhishek Kar
Amlan Kar
Svebor Karaman
Leonid Karlinsky
Zoltan Kato
Parneet Kaur
Hiroshi Kawasaki
Misha Kazhdan
Margret Keuper
Sameh Khamis
Naeemullah Khan
Salman Khan
Hadi Kiapour
Joe Kileel
Chanho Kim
Gunhee Kim
Hansung Kim
Junmo Kim
Junsik Kim
Kihwan Kim
Minyoung Kim
Tae Hyun Kim
Tae-Kyun Kim
Akisato Kimura
Zsolt Kira
Alexander Kirillov
Kris Kitani
Maria Klodt
Patrick Knöbelreiter
Jan Knopp
Reinhard Koch
Alexander Kolesnikov
Chen Kong
Naejin Kong
Shu Kong
Piotr Koniusz
Simon Korman
Andreas Koschan

Dimitrios Kosmopoulos
Satwik Kottur
Balazs Kovacs
Adarsh Kowdle
Mike Krainin
Gregory Kramida
Ranjay Krishna
Ravi Krishnan
Matej Kristan
Pavel Krsek
Volker Krueger
Alexander Krull
Hilde Kuehne
Andreas Kuhn
Arjan Kuijper
Zuzana Kukelova
Kuldeep Kulkarni
Shiro Kumano
Avinash Kumar
Vijay Kumar
Abhijit Kundu
Sebastian Kurtek
Junseok Kwon
Jan Kybic
Alexander Ladikos
Shang-Hong Lai
Wei-Sheng Lai
Jean-Francois Lalonde
John Lambert
Zhenzhong Lan
Charis Lanaras
Oswald Lanz
Dong Lao
Longin Jan Latecki
Justin Lazarow
Huu Le
Chen-Yu Lee
Gim Hee Lee
Honglak Lee
Hsin-Ying Lee
Joon-Young Lee
Seungyong Lee
Stefan Lee
Yong Jae Lee
Zhen Lei
Ido Leichter

Victor Lempitsky
Spyridon Leonardos
Marius Leordeanu
Matt Leotta
Thomas Leung
Stefan Leutenegger
Gil Levi
Aviad Levis
Jose Lezama
Ang Li
Dingzeyu Li
Dong Li
Haoxiang Li
Hongdong Li
Hongsheng Li
Hongyang Li
Jianguo Li
Kai Li
Ruiyu Li
Wei Li
Wen Li
Xi Li
Xiaoxiao Li
Xin Li
Xirong Li
Xuelong Li
Xueting Li
Yeqing Li
Yijun Li
Yin Li
Yingwei Li
Yining Li
Yongjie Li
Yu-Feng Li
Zechao Li
Zhengqi Li
Zhenyang Li
Zhizhong Li
Xiaodan Liang
Renjie Liao
Zicheng Liao
Bee Lim
Jongwoo Lim
Joseph Lim
Ser-Nam Lim
Chen-Hsuan Lin

Shih-Yao Lin
Tsung-Yi Lin
Weiyao Lin
Yen-Yu Lin
Haibin Ling
Or Litany
Roee Litman
Anan Liu
Changsong Liu
Chen Liu
Ding Liu
Dong Liu
Feng Liu
Guangcan Liu
Luoqi Liu
Miaomiao Liu
Nian Liu
Risheng Liu
Shu Liu
Shuaicheng Liu
Sifei Liu
Tyng-Luh Liu
Wanquan Liu
Weiwei Liu
Xialei Liu
Xiaoming Liu
Yebin Liu
Yiming Liu
Ziwei Liu
Zongyi Liu
Liliana Lo Presti
Edgar Lobaton
Chengjiang Long
Mingsheng Long
Roberto Lopez-Sastre
Amy Loufti
Brian Lovell
Canyi Lu
Cewu Lu
Feng Lu
Huchuan Lu
Jiajun Lu
Jiasen Lu
Jiwen Lu
Yang Lu
Yujuan Lu

Simon Lucey
Jian-Hao Luo
Jiebo Luo
Pablo Márquez-Neila
Matthias Müller
Chao Ma
Chih-Yao Ma
Lin Ma
Shugao Ma
Wei-Chiu Ma
Zhanyu Ma
Oisin Mac Aodha
Will Maddern
Ludovic Magerand
Marcus Magnor
Vijay Mahadevan
Mohammad Mahoor
Michael Maire
Subhransu Maji
Ameesh Makadia
Atsuto Maki
Yasushi Makihara
Mateusz Malinowski
Tomasz Malisiewicz
Arun Mallya
Roberto Manduchi
Junhua Mao
Dmitrii Marin
Joe Marino
Kenneth Marino
Elisabeta Marinoiu
Ricardo Martin
Aleix Martinez
Julieta Martinez
Aaron Maschinot
Jonathan Masci
Bogdan Matei
Diana Mateus
Stefan Mathe
Kevin Matzen
Bruce Maxwell
Steve Maybank
Walterio Mayol-Cuevas
Mason McGill
Stephen Mckenna
Roey Mechrez

Christopher Mei
Heydi Mendez-Vazquez
Deyu Meng
Thomas Mensink
Bjoern Menze
Domingo Mery
Qiguang Miao
Tomer Michaeli
Antoine Miech
Ondrej Miksik
Anton Milan
Gregor Miller
Cai Minjie
Majid Mirmehdi
Ishan Misra
Niloy Mitra
Anurag Mittal
Nirbhay Modhe
Davide Modolo
Pritish Mohapatra
Pascal Monasse
Mathew Monfort
Taesup Moon
Sandino Morales
Vlad Morariu
Philippos Mordohai
Francesc Moreno
Henrique Morimitsu
Yael Moses
Ben-Ezra Moshe
Roozbeh Mottaghi
Yadong Mu
Lopamudra Mukherjee
Mario Munich
Ana Murillo
Damien Muselet
Armin Mustafa
Siva Karthik Mustikovela
Moin Nabi
Sobhan Naderi
Hajime Nagahara
Varun Nagaraja
Tushar Nagarajan
Arsha Nagrani
Nikhil Naik
Atsushi Nakazawa

P. J. Narayanan
Charlie Nash
Lakshmanan Nataraj
Fabian Nater
Lukáš Neumann
Natalia Neverova
Alejandro Newell
Phuc Nguyen
Xiaohan Nie
David Nilsson
Ko Nishino
Zhenxing Niu
Shohei Nobuhara
Klas Nordberg
Mohammed Norouzi
David Novotny
Ifeoma Nwogu
Matthew O'Toole
Guillaume Obozinski
Jean-Marc Odobez
Eyal Ofek
Ferda Ofli
Tae-Hyun Oh
Iason Oikonomidis
Takeshi Oishi
Takahiro Okabe
Takayuki Okatani
Vlad Olaru
Michael Opitz
Jose Oramas
Vicente Ordonez
Ivan Oseledets
Aljosa Osep
Magnus Oskarsson
Martin R. Oswald
Wanli Ouyang
Andrew Owens
Mustafa Özuysal
Jinshan Pan
Xingang Pan
Rameswar Panda
Sharath Pankanti
Julien Pansiot
Nicolas Papadakis
George Papandreou
N. Papanikolopoulos

Hyun Soo Park
In Kyu Park
Jaesik Park
Omkar Parkhi
Alvaro Parra Bustos
C. Alejandro Parraga
Vishal Patel
Deepak Pathak
Ioannis Patras
Viorica Patraucean
Genevieve Patterson
Kim Pedersen
Robert Peharz
Selen Pehlivan
Xi Peng
Bojan Pepik
Talita Perciano
Federico Pernici
Adrian Peter
Stavros Petridis
Vladimir Petrovic
Henning Petzka
Tomas Pfister
Trung Pham
Justus Piater
Massimo Piccardi
Sudeep Pillai
Pedro Pinheiro
Lerrel Pinto
Bernardo Pires
Aleksis Pirinen
Fiora Pirri
Leonid Pischulin
Tobias Ploetz
Bryan Plummer
Yair Poleg
Jean Ponce
Gerard Pons-Moll
Jordi Pont-Tuset
Alin Popa
Fatih Porikli
Horst Possegger
Viraj Prabhu
Andrea Prati
Maria Priisalu
Véronique Prinet

Victor Prisacariu
Jan Prokaj
Nicolas Pugeault
Luis Puig
Ali Punjani
Senthil Purushwalkam
Guido Pusiol
Guo-Jun Qi
Xiaojuan Qi
Hongwei Qin
Shi Qiu
Faisal Qureshi
Matthias Rüther
Petia Radeva
Umer Rafi
Rahul Raguram
Swaminathan Rahul
Varun Ramakrishna
Kandan Ramakrishnan
Ravi Ramamoorthi
Vignesh Ramanathan
Vasili Ramanishka
R. Ramasamy Selvaraju
Rene Ranftl
Carolina Raposo
Nikhil Rasiwasia
Nalini Ratha
Sai Ravela
Avinash Ravichandran
Ramin Raziperchikolaei
Sylvestre-Alvise Rebuffi
Adria Recasens
Joe Redmon
Timo Rehfeld
Michal Reinstein
Konstantinos Rematas
Haibing Ren
Shaoqing Ren
Wenqi Ren
Zhile Ren
Hamid Rezatofighi
Nicholas Rhinehart
Helge Rhodin
Elisa Ricci
Eitan Richardson
Stephan Richter

Gernot Riegler
Hayko Riemenschneider
Tammy Riklin Raviv
Ergys Ristani
Tobias Ritschel
Mariano Rivera
Samuel Rivera
Antonio Robles-Kelly
Ignacio Rocco
Jason Rock
Emanuele Rodola
Mikel Rodriguez
Gregory Rogez
Marcus Rohrbach
Gemma Roig
Javier Romero
Olaf Ronneberger
Amir Rosenfeld
Bodo Rosenhahn
Guy Rosman
Arun Ross
Samuel Rota Bulò
Peter Roth
Constantin Rothkopf
Sebastien Roy
Amit Roy-Chowdhury
Ognjen Rudovic
Adria Ruiz
Javier Ruiz-del-Solar
Christian Rupprecht
Olga Russakovsky
Chris Russell
Alexandre Sablayrolles
Fereshteh Sadeghi
Ryusuke Sagawa
Hideo Saito
Elham Sakhaee
Albert Ali Salah
Conrad Sanderson
Koppal Sanjeev
Aswin Sankaranarayanan
Elham Saraee
Jason Saragih
Sudeep Sarkar
Imari Sato
Shin'ichi Satoh

Torsten Sattler
Bogdan Savchynskyy
Johannes Schönberger
Hanno Scharr
Walter Scheirer
Bernt Schiele
Frank Schmidt
Tanner Schmidt
Dirk Schnieders
Samuel Schulter
William Schwartz
Alexander Schwing
Ozan Sener
Soumyadip Sengupta
Laura Sevilla-Lara
Mubarak Shah
Shishir Shah
Fahad Shahbaz Khan
Amir Shahroudy
Jing Shao
Xiaowei Shao
Roman Shapovalov
Nataliya Shapovalova
Ali Sharif Razavian
Gaurav Sharma
Mohit Sharma
Pramod Sharma
Viktoriia Sharmanska
Eli Shechtman
Mark Sheinin
Evan Shelhamer
Chunhua Shen
Li Shen
Wei Shen
Xiaohui Shen
Xiaoyong Shen
Ziyi Shen
Lu Sheng
Baoguang Shi
Boxin Shi
Kevin Shih
Hyunjung Shim
Ilan Shimshoni
Young Min Shin
Koichi Shinoda
Matthew Shreve

Tianmin Shu
Zhixin Shu
Kaleem Siddiqi
Gunnar Sigurdsson
Nathan Silberman
Tomas Simon
Abhishek Singh
Gautam Singh
Maneesh Singh
Praveer Singh
Richa Singh
Saurabh Singh
Sudipta Sinha
Vladimir Smutny
Noah Snavely
Cees Snoek
Kihyuk Sohn
Eric Sommerlade
Sanghyun Son
Bi Song
Shiyu Song
Shuran Song
Xuan Song
Yale Song
Yang Song
Yibing Song
Lorenzo Sorgi
Humberto Sossa
Pratul Srinivasan
Michael Stark
Bjorn Stenger
Rainer Stiefelhagen
Joerg Stueckler
Jan Stuehmer
Hang Su
Hao Su
Shuochen Su
R. Subramanian
Yusuke Sugano
Akihiro Sugimoto
Baochen Sun
Chen Sun
Jian Sun
Jin Sun
Lin Sun
Min Sun

Qing Sun
Zhaohui Sun
David Suter
Eran Swears
Raza Syed Hussain
T. Syeda-Mahmood
Christian Szegedy
Duy-Nguyen Ta
Tolga Taşdizen
Hemant Tagare
Yuichi Taguchi
Ying Tai
Yu-Wing Tai
Jun Takamatsu
Hugues Talbot
Toru Tamak
Robert Tamburo
Chaowei Tan
Meng Tang
Peng Tang
Siyu Tang
Wei Tang
Junli Tao
Ran Tao
Xin Tao
Makarand Tapaswi
Jean-Philippe Tarel
Maxim Tatarchenko
Bugra Tekin
Demetri Terzopoulos
Christian Theobalt
Diego Thomas
Rajat Thomas
Qi Tian
Xinmei Tian
YingLi Tian
Yonghong Tian
Yonglong Tian
Joseph Tighe
Radu Timofte
Massimo Tistarelli
Sinisa Todorovic
Pavel Tokmakov
Giorgos Tolias
Federico Tombari
Tatiana Tommasi

Chetan Tonde
Xin Tong
Akihiko Torii
Andrea Torsello
Florian Trammer
Du Tran
Quoc-Huy Tran
Rudolph Triebel
Alejandro Troccoli
Leonardo Trujillo
Tomasz Trzcinski
Sam Tsai
Yi-Hsuan Tsai
Hung-Yu Tseng
Vagia Tsiminaki
Aggeliki Tsoli
Wei-Chih Tu
Shubham Tulsiani
Fred Tung
Tony Tung
Matt Turek
Oncel Tuzel
Georgios Tzimiropoulos
Ilkay Ulusoy
Osman Ulusoy
Dmitry Ulyanov
Paul Upchurch
Ben Usman
Evgeniya Ustinova
Himanshu Vajaria
Alexander Vakhitov
Jack Valmadre
Ernest Valveny
Jan van Gemert
Grant Van Horn
Jagannadan Varadarajan
Gul Varol
Sebastiano Vascon
Francisco Vasconcelos
Mayank Vatsa
Javier Vazquez-Corral
Ramakrishna Vedantam
Ashok Veeraraghavan
Andreas Veit
Raviteja Vemulapalli
Jonathan Ventura

Matthias Vestner
Minh Vo
Christoph Vogel
Michele Volpi
Carl Vondrick
Sven Wachsmuth
Toshikazu Wada
Michael Waechter
Catherine Wah
Jacob Walker
Jun Wan
Boyu Wang
Chen Wang
Chunyu Wang
De Wang
Fang Wang
Hongxing Wang
Hua Wang
Jiang Wang
Jingdong Wang
Jinglu Wang
Jue Wang
Le Wang
Lei Wang
Lezi Wang
Liang Wang
Lichao Wang
Lijun Wang
Limin Wang
Liwei Wang
Naiyan Wang
Oliver Wang
Qi Wang
Ruiping Wang
Shenlong Wang
Shu Wang
Song Wang
Tao Wang
Xiaofang Wang
Xiaolong Wang
Xinchao Wang
Xinggang Wang
Xintao Wang
Yang Wang
Yu-Chiang Frank Wang
Yu-Xiong Wang

Zhaowen Wang
Zhe Wang
Anne Wannenwetsch
Simon Warfield
Scott Wehrwein
Donglai Wei
Ping Wei
Shih-En Wei
Xiu-Shen Wei
Yichen Wei
Xie Weidi
Philippe Weinzaepfel
Longyin Wen
Eric Wengrowski
Tomas Werner
Michael Wilber
Rick Wildes
Olivia Wiles
Kyle Wilson
David Wipf
Kwan-Yee Wong
Daniel Worrall
John Wright
Baoyuan Wu
Chao-Yuan Wu
Jiajun Wu
Jianxin Wu
Tianfu Wu
Xiaodong Wu
Xiaohe Wu
Xinxiao Wu
Yang Wu
Yi Wu
Ying Wu
Yuxin Wu
Zheng Wu
Stefanie Wuhrer
Yin Xia
Tao Xiang
Yu Xiang
Lei Xiao
Tong Xiao
Yang Xiao
Cihang Xie
Dan Xie
Jianwen Xie

Jin Xie
Lingxi Xie
Pengtao Xie
Saining Xie
Wenxuan Xie
Yuchen Xie
Bo Xin
Junliang Xing
Peng Xingchao
Bo Xiong
Fei Xiong
Xuehan Xiong
Yuanjun Xiong
Chenliang Xu
Danfei Xu
Huijuan Xu
Jia Xu
Weipeng Xu
Xiangyu Xu
Yan Xu
Yuanlu Xu
Jia Xue
Tianfan Xue
Erdem Yörük
Abhay Yadav
Deshraj Yadav
Payman Yadollahpour
Yasushi Yagi
Toshihiko Yamasaki
Fei Yan
Hang Yan
Junchi Yan
Junjie Yan
Sijie Yan
Keiji Yanai
Bin Yang
Chih-Yuan Yang
Dong Yang
Herb Yang
Jianchao Yang
Jianwei Yang
Jiaolong Yang
Jie Yang
Jimei Yang
Jufeng Yang
Linjie Yang

Michael Ying Yang
Ming Yang
Ruiduo Yang
Ruigang Yang
Shuo Yang
Wei Yang
Xiaodong Yang
Yanchao Yang
Yi Yang
Angela Yao
Bangpeng Yao
Cong Yao
Jian Yao
Ting Yao
Julian Yarkony
Mark Yatskar
Jinwei Ye
Mao Ye
Mei-Chen Yeh
Raymond Yeh
Serena Yeung
Kwang Moo Yi
Shuai Yi
Alper Yılmaz
Lijun Yin
Xi Yin
Zhaozheng Yin
Xianghua Ying
Ryo Yonetani
Donghyun Yoo
Ju Hong Yoon
Kuk-Jin Yoon
Chong You
Shaodi You
Aron Yu
Fisher Yu
Gang Yu
Jingyi Yu
Ke Yu
Licheng Yu
Pei Yu
Qian Yu
Rong Yu
Shoou-I Yu
Stella Yu
Xiang Yu

Yang Yu
Zhiding Yu
Ganzhao Yuan
Jing Yuan
Junsong Yuan
Lu Yuan
Stefanos Zafeiriou
Sergey Zagoruyko
Amir Zamir
K. Zampogiannis
Andrei Zanfir
Mihai Zanfir
Pablo Zegers
Eyasu Zemene
Andy Zeng
Xingyu Zeng
Yun Zeng
De-Chuan Zhan
Cheng Zhang
Dong Zhang
Guofeng Zhang
Han Zhang
Hang Zhang
Hanwang Zhang
Jian Zhang
Jianguo Zhang
Jianming Zhang
Jiawei Zhang
Junping Zhang
Lei Zhang
Linguang Zhang
Ning Zhang
Qing Zhang

Quanshi Zhang
Richard Zhang
Runze Zhang
Shanshan Zhang
Shiliang Zhang
Shu Zhang
Ting Zhang
Xiangyu Zhang
Xiaofan Zhang
Xu Zhang
Yimin Zhang
Yinda Zhang
Yongqiang Zhang
Yuting Zhang
Zhanpeng Zhang
Ziyu Zhang
Bin Zhao
Chen Zhao
Hang Zhao
Hengshuang Zhao
Qijun Zhao
Rui Zhao
Yue Zhao
Enliang Zheng
Liang Zheng
Stephan Zheng
Wei-Shi Zheng
Wenming Zheng
Yin Zheng
Yinqiang Zheng
Yuanjie Zheng
Guangyu Zhong
Bolei Zhou

Guang-Tong Zhou
Huiyu Zhou
Jiahuan Zhou
S. Kevin Zhou
Tinghui Zhou
Wengang Zhou
Xiaowei Zhou
Xingyi Zhou
Yin Zhou
Zihan Zhou
Fan Zhu
Guangming Zhu
Ji Zhu
Jiejie Zhu
Jun-Yan Zhu
Shizhan Zhu
Siyu Zhu
Xiangxin Zhu
Xiatian Zhu
Yan Zhu
Yingying Zhu
Yixin Zhu
Yuke Zhu
Zhenyao Zhu
Liansheng Zhuang
Zeeshan Zia
Karel Zimmermann
Daniel Zoran
Danping Zou
Qi Zou
Silvia Zuffi
Wangmeng Zuo
Xinxin Zuo

Contents – Part II

Poster Session

Contextual-Based Image Inpainting:
Infer, Match, and Translate

Yuhang Song[1](✉)📧, Chao Yang[1]📧, Zhe Lin[2]📧, Xiaofeng Liu[3]📧,
Qin Huang[1]📧, Hao Li[1,4,5]📧, and C.-C. Jay Kuo[1]📧

[1] University of Southern California, 3740 McClintock Ave, Los Angeles, USA
{yuhangso,chaoy,qinhuang}@usc.edu, cckuo@sipi.usc.edu
[2] Adobe Research, 345 Park Ave, San Jose, USA
zlin@adobe.com
[3] Carnegie Mellon University, 5000 Forbes Ave, Pittsburgh, USA
liuxiaofeng@cmu.edu
[4] Pinscreen, 525 Broadway, Santa Monica, USA
hao@hao-li.com
[5] USC Institute for Creative Technologies,
12015 E Waterfront Dr, Los Angeles, USA

Abstract. We study the task of image inpainting, which is to fill in the missing region of an incomplete image with plausible contents. To this end, we propose a learning-based approach to generate visually coherent completion given a high-resolution image with missing components. In order to overcome the difficulty to directly learn the distribution of high-dimensional image data, we divide the task into inference and translation as two separate steps and model each step with a deep neural network. We also use simple heuristics to guide the propagation of local textures from the boundary to the hole. We show that, by using such techniques, inpainting reduces to the problem of learning two image-feature translation functions in much smaller space and hence easier to train. We evaluate our method on several public datasets and show that we generate results of better visual quality than previous state-of-the-art methods.

Keywords: Image inpainting · GANs · Feature manipulation

1 Introduction

The problem of generating photo-realistic images from sampled noise or conditioning on other inputs such as images, texts or labels has been heavily investigated. In spite of recent progress of deep generative models such as Pixel-CNN [26], VAE [20] and GANs [12], generating high-resolution images remains a difficult task. This is mainly because modeling the distribution of pixels is difficult and the trained models easily introduce blurry components and artifacts when the dimensionality becomes high. Several approaches have been proposed

---

Y. Song and C. Yang—Equal contributions.

© Springer Nature Switzerland AG 2018
V. Ferrari et al. (Eds.): ECCV 2018, LNCS 11206, pp. 3–18, 2018.
https://doi.org/10.1007/978-3-030-01216-8_1

to alleviate the problem, usually by leveraging multi-scale training [6, 36] or incorporating prior information [24].

(a)   (b)   (c)   (d)   (e)   (f)

Fig. 1. Our result comparing with GL inpainting [14]. (a) & (d) The input image with missing hole. (b) & (d) Inpainting result given by GL inpainting [14]. (c) & (f) Final inpainting result using our approach. The size of images are 512 × 512.

In addition to the general image synthesis problem, the task of image inpainting can be described as: given an incomplete image as input, how do we fill in the missing parts with semantically and visually plausible contents. We are interested in this problem for several reasons. First, it is a well-motivated task for a common scenario where we may want to remove unwanted objects from pictures or restore damaged photographs. Second, while purely unsupervised learning may be challenging for large inputs, we show in this work that the problem becomes more constrained and tractable when we train in a multi-stage self-supervised manner and leverage the high-frequency information in the known region.

Context-encoder [27] is one of the first works that apply deep neural networks for image inpainting. It trains a deep generative model that maps an incomplete image to a complete image using reconstruction loss and adversarial loss. While adversarial loss significantly improves the inpainting quality, the results are still quite blurry and contain notable artifacts. In addition, we found it fails to produce reasonable results for larger inputs like 512 × 512 images, showing it is unable generalize to high-resolution inpainting task. More recently, [14] improved the result by using dilated convolution and an additional local discriminator. However it is still limited to relatively small images and holes due to the spatial support of the model.

Yang *et al.* [34] proposes to use style transfer for image inpainting. More specifically, it initializes the hole with the output of context-encoder, and then improves the texture by using style transfer techniques [21] to propagate the high-frequency textures from the boundary to the hole. It shows that matching the neural features not only transfers artistic styles, but can also synthesize real-world images. The approach is optimization-based and applicable to images of arbitrary sizes. However, the computation is costly and it takes long time to inpaint a large image.

Our approach overcomes the limitation of the aforementioned methods. Being similar to [34], we decouple the inpainting process into two stages: inference and translation. In the inference stage, we train an *Image2Feature* network that initializes the hole with coarse prediction and extract its features. The prediction is blurry but contains high-level structure information in the hole. In the translation stage, we train a *Feature2Image* network that transforms the feature back into a complete image. It refines the contents in the hole and outputs a complete image with sharp and realistic texture. Its main difference with [34] is that, instead of relying on optimization, we model texture refinement as a learning problem. Both networks can be trained end-to-end and, with the trained models, the inference can be done in a single forward pass, which is much faster than iterative optimizations.

To ease the difficulty of training the Feature2Image network, we design a "patch-swap" layer that propagates the high-frequency texture details from the boundary to the hole. The patch-swap layer takes the feature map as input, and replaces each neural patch inside the hole with the most similar patch on the boundary. We then use the new feature map as the input to the Feature2Image network. By re-using the neural patches on the boundary, the feature map contains sufficient details, making the high-resolution image reconstruction feasible.

We note that by dividing the training into two stages of Image2Feature and Feature2Image greatly reduces the dimensionality of possible mappings between input and output. Injecting prior knowledge with patch-swap further guides the training process such that it is easier to find the optimal transformation. When being compared with the GL inpainting [14], we generate sharper and better inpainting results at size 256×256. Our approach also scales to higher resolution (i.e. 512×512), which GL inpainting fails to handle. As compared with neural inpainting [34], our results have comparable or better visual quality in most examples. In particular, our synthesized contents blends with the boundary more seamlessly. Our approach is also much faster.

The main contributions of this paper are: (1) We design a learning-based inpainting system that is able to synthesize missing parts in a high-resolution image with high-quality contents and textures. (2) We propose a novel and robust training scheme that addresses the issue of feature manipulation and avoids under-fitting. (3) We show that our trained model can achieve performance comparable with state-of-the-art and generalize to other tasks like style transfer.

2   Related Work

Image generation with generative adversarial networks (GANs) has gained remarkable progress recently. The vanilla GANs [12] has shown promising performance to generate sharp images, but training instability makes it hard to scale to higher resolution images. Several techniques have been proposed to stabilize the training process, including DCGAN [28], energy-based GAN [38], Wasserstein GAN (WGAN) [1,30], WGAN-GP [13], BEGAN [4], LSGAN [23] and the more recent Progressive GANs [19]. A more relevant task to inpainting is conditional image generation. For example, Pix2Pix [17], Pix2Pix HD [32] and Cycle-GAN [40] translate images across different domains using paired or unpaired data. Using deep neural network for image inpainting has also been studied in [14, 27, 33–35].

Our patch-swap can be related to recent works in neural style transfer. Gatys et al. [10] first formulates style transfer as an optimization problem that combines

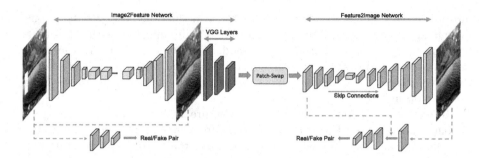

Fig. 2. Overview of our network architecture. We use Image2Feature network as coarse inference and use VGG network to extract a feature map. Then patch-swap matches neural patches from boundary to the hole. Finally the Feature2Image network translates to a complete, high-resolution image.

texture synthesis with content reconstruction. As an alternative, [8,9,26] use neural-patch based similarity matching between the content and style images for style transfer. Li and Wand [21] optimize the output image such that each of the neural patch matches with a similar neural patch in the style image. This enables arbitrary style transfer at the cost of expensive computation. [5] proposes a fast approximation to [21] where it constructs the feature map directly and uses an inverse network to synthesize the image in feed-forward manner.

Traditional non-neural inpainting algorithms [2,3] mostly work on the image space. While they share similar ideas of patch matching and propagation, they are usually agnostic to high-level semantic and structural information.

3 Methodology

3.1 Problem Description

We formalize the task of image inpainting as follows: suppose we are given an incomplete input image I_0, with R and $\bar{R}$ representing the missing region (the hole) and the known region (the boundary) respectively. We would like to fill in R with plausible contents I_R and combine it with I_0 as a new, complete image I. Evaluating the quality of inpainting is mostly subject to human perception but ideally, I_R should meet the following criteria: 1. It has sharp and realistic-looking textures; 2. It contains meaningful content and is coherent with $I_{\bar{R}}$ and 3. It looks like what appears in the ground truth image I_{gt} (if available). In our context, R can be either a single hole or multiple holes. It may also come with arbitrary shape, placed on a random location of the image.

3.2 System Overview

Our system divides the image inpainting tasks into three steps:

Inference: We use an Image2Feature network to fill an incomplete image with coarse contents as inference and extract a feature map from the inpainted image.

Matching: We use patch-swap on the feature map to match the neural patches from the high-resolution boundary to the hole with coarse inference.

Translation: We use a Feature2Image network to translate the feature map to a complete image.

The entire pipeline is illustrated in Fig. 2.

3.3   Training

We introduce separate steps of training the Image2Feature and Feature2Image network. For illustration purpose, we assume the size of I_0 is $256 \times 256 \times 3$ and the hole R has size 128×128.

Inference: Training   Image2Feature   Network.   The goal of the Image2Feature network is to fill in the hole with coarse prediction. During training, the input to the Image2Feature translation network is the $256 \times 256 \times 3$ incomplete image I_0 and the output is a feature map F_1 of size $64 \times 64 \times 256$. The network consists of an FCN-based module G_1, which consists of a down-sampling front end, multiple intermediate residual blocks and an up-sampling back end. G_1 is followed by the initial layers of the 19-layer VGG network [31]. Here we use the filter pyramid of the VGG network as a higher-level representation of images similar to [10]. At first, I_0 is given as input to G_1 which produces a coarse prediction I_1^R of size 128×128. I_1^R is then embedded into R forming a complete image I_1, which again passes through the VGG19 network to get the activation of *relu3_1* as F_1. F_1 has size $64 \times 64 \times 256$. We also use an additional PatchGAN discriminator D_1 to facilitate adversarial training, which takes a pair of images as input and outputs a vector of true/fake probabilities.

For G_1, the down-sampling front-end consists of three convolutional layers, and each layer has stride 2. The intermediate part has 9 residual blocks stacked together. The up-sampling back-end is the reverse of the front-end and consists of three transposed convolution with stride 2. Every convolutional layer is followed by batch normalization [16] and ReLu activation, except for the last layer which outputs the image. We also use dilated convolution in all residual blocks. Similar architecture has been used in [32] for image synthesis and [14] for inpainting. Different from [32], we use dilated layer to increase the size of receptive field. Comparing with [14], our receptive field is also larger given we have more down-sampling blocks and more dilated layers in residual blocks.

During training, the overall loss function is defined as:

$$L_{G_1} = \lambda_1 L_{perceptual} + \lambda_2 L_{adv}. \tag{1}$$

The first term is the perceptual loss, which is shown to correspond better with human perception of similarity [37] and has been widely used in many tasks [5, 7,11,18]:

$$L_{perceptual}(F, I_g t) = \| \, \mathcal{M}_F \circ (F_1 - vgg(I_{gt})) \, \|_1 . \tag{2}$$

Here $\mathcal{M}_F$ are the weighted masks yielding the loss to be computed only on the hole of the feature map. We also assign higher weight to the overlapping pixels between the hole and the boundary to ensure the composite is coherent. The weights of VGG19 network are loaded from the ImageNet pre-trained model and are fixed during training.

The adversarial loss is based on Generative Adversarial Networks (GANs) and is defined as:

$$L_{adv} = \max_{D_1} E[\log(D_1(I_0, I_{gt})) + \log(1 - D_1(I_0, I_1))]. \tag{3}$$

We use a pair of images as input to the discriminator. Under the setting of adversarial training, the real pair is the incomplete image I_0 and the original image I_{gt}, while the fake pair is I_0 and the prediction I_1.

To align the absolute value of each loss, we set the weight $\lambda_1 = 10$ and $\lambda_2 = 1$ respectively. We use Adam optimizer for training. The learning rate is set as $lr_G = 2e-3$ and $lr_D = 2e-4$ and the momentum is set to 0.5.

Match: Patch-Swap Operation. Patch-swap is an operation which transforms F_1 into a new feature map F_1'. The idea is that the prediction I_1^R is blurry, lacking many of the high-frequency details. Intuitively, we would like to propagate the textures from $I_1^{\bar{R}}$ onto I_1^R but still preserves the high-level information of I_1^R. Instead of operating on I_1 directly, we use F_1 as a surrogate for texture propagation. Similarly, we use r and $\bar{r}$ to denote the region on F_1 corresponding to R and $\bar{R}$ on I_1. For each 3×3 neural patch $p_i (i = 1, 2, ..., N)$ of F_1 overlapping with r, we find the closest-matching neural patch in $\bar{r}$ based on the following cross-correlation metric:

$$d(p, p') = \frac{<p, p'>}{\| p \| \cdot \| p' \|} \tag{4}$$

Suppose the closest-matching patch of p_i is q_i, we then replace p_i with q_i. After each patch in r is swapped with its most similar patch in $\bar{r}$, overlapping patches are averaged and the output is a new feature map F_1'. We illustrate the process in Fig. 3.

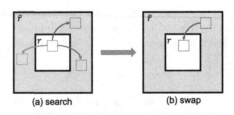

(a) search   (b) swap

Fig. 3. Illustration of patch-swap operation. Each neural patch in the hole r searches for the most similar neural patch on the boundary $\bar{r}$, and then swaps with that patch.

Measuring the cross-correlations for all the neural patch pairs between the hole and boundary is computationally expensive. To address this issue, we follow similar implementation in [5] and speed up the computation using paralleled convolution. We summarize the algorithm as following steps. First, we normalize and stack the neural patches on $\bar{r}$ and view the stacked vector as a convolution filter. Next, we apply the convolution filter on r. The result is that at each location of r we get a vector of values which is the cross-correlation between the neural patch centered at that location and all patches in $\bar{r}$. Finally, we replace the patch in r with the patch in $\bar{r}$ of maximum cross-correlation. Since the whole process can be parallelized, the amount of time is significantly reduced. In practice, it only takes about 0.1 s to process a $64 \times 64 \times 256$ feature map.

Translate: Training Feature2Image Translation Network. The goal of the Feature2Image network is to learn a mapping from the swapped feature map to a complete and sharp image. It has a U-Net style generator G_2 which is similar to G_1, except the number of hidden layers are different. The input to G_2 is a feature map of size $64 \times 64 \times 256$. The generator has seven convolution blocks and eight deconvolution blocks, and the first six deconvolutional layers are connected with the convolutional layers using skip connection. The output is a complete $256 \times 256 \times 3$ image. It also consists of a Patch-GAN based discriminator D_2 for adversarial training. However different from the Image2Feature network which takes a pair of images as input, the input to D_2 is a pair of image and feature map.

A straightforward training paradigm is to use the output of the Image2Feature network F_1 as input to the patch-swap layer, and then use the swapped feature F_1' to train the Feature2Image model. In this way, the feature map is derived from the coarse prediction I_1 and the whole system can be trained end-to-end. However, in practice, we found that this leads to poor-quality reconstruction I with notable noise and artifacts (Sect. 4). We further observed that using the ground truth as training input gives rise to results of significantly improved visual quality. That is, we use the feature map $F_{gt} = \text{vgg}(I_{gt})$ as input to the patch-swap layer, and then use the swapped feature $F_{gt}' = \text{patch\_swap}(F_{gt})$ to train the Feature2Image model. Since I_{gt} is not accessible at test time, we still use $F_1' = \text{patch\_swap}(F_1)$ as input for inference. Note that now the Feature2Image model trains and tests with different types of input, which is not a usual practice to train a machine learning model.

Here we provide some intuition for this phenomenon. Essentially by training the Feature2Image network, we are learning a mapping from the feature space to the image space. Since F_1 is the output of the Image2Feature network, it inherently contains a significant amount of noise and ambiguity. Therefore the feature space made up of F_1' has much higher dimensionality than the feature space made up of F_{gt}'. The outcome is that the model easily under-fits F_1', making it difficult to learn a good mapping. Alternatively, by using F_{gt}', we are selecting a clean, compact subset of features such that the space of mapping is much smaller, making it easier to learn. Our experiment also shows that the model trained with ground truth generalizes well to noisy input F_1' at test time. Similar to [39], we can further improve the robustness by sampling from both the ground truth and Image2Feature prediction.

The overall loss for the Feature2Image translation network is defined as:

$$L_{G_2} = \lambda_1 L_{perceptual} + \lambda_2 L_{adv}. \tag{5}$$

The reconstruction loss is defined on the entire image between the final output I and the ground truth I_{gt}:

$$L_{perceptual}(I, I_{gt}) = \| vgg(I) - vgg(I_{gt}) \|_2 . \tag{6}$$

The adversarial loss is given by the discriminator D_2 and is defined as:

$$L_{adv} = \max_{D_2} E[\log(D_2(F_{gt}', I_{gt})) + \log(1 - D_2(F_{gt}', I))]. \tag{7}$$

The real and fake pair for adversarial training are (F_{gt}', I_{gt}) and (F_{gt}', I).

When training the Feature2Image network we set $\lambda_1 = 10$ and $\lambda_2 = 1$. For the learning rate, we set $lr_G = 2e{-}4$ and $lr_D = 2e{-}4$. Same as the Image2Feature network, the momentum is set to 0.5.

3.4   Multi-scale Inference

Given the trained models, inference is straight-forward and can be done in a single forward pass. The input I_0 successively passes through the Image2Feature network to get I_1 and $F_1 = vgg(I_1)$, then the patch-swap layer (F_1'), and then finally the Feature2Image network (I). We then use the center of I and blend with I_0 as the output.

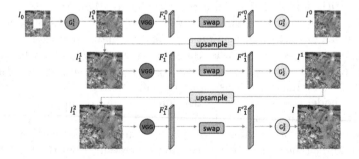

Fig. 4. Multi-scale inference.

Our framework can be easily adapted to multi-scale. The key is that we directly upsample the output of the lower scale as the input to the Feature2Image network of the next scale (after using VGG network to extract features and apply patch-swap). In this way, we will only need the Image2Feature network at the smallest scale s_0 to get I_1^0 and F_1^0. At higher scales $s_i (i > 0)$ we simply set $I_1^{s_i} = \text{upsample}(I^{s_{i-1}})$ and let $F_1^{s_i} = \text{vgg}(I_1^{s_i})$ (Fig. 4). Training Image2Feature network can be challenging at high resolution. However by using the multi-scale approach we are able to initialize from lower scales instead, allowing us to handle large inputs effectively. We use multi-scale inference on all our experiments.

4   Experiments

4.1   Experiment Setup

We separately train and test on two public datasets: COCO [22] and ImageNet CLS-LOC [29]. The number of training images in each dataset are: 118,287 for COCO and 1,281,167 for ImageNet CLS-LOC. We compare with content aware fill (CAF) [2], context encoder (CE) [27], neural patch synthesis (NPS) [34] and global local inpainting (GLI) [14]. For CE, NPS, and GLI, we used the public available trained model. CE and NPS are trained to handle fixed holes, while GLI and CAF can handle arbitrary holes. To fairly evaluate, we experimented on both settings of fixed hole and random hole. For fixed hole, we compare with CAF, CE, NPS, and GLI on image size 512×512 from ImageNet test set. The hole is set to be 224×224 located at the image center. For random hole, we compare with CAF and GLI, using COCO test images resized to 256×256. In the case of random hole, the hole size ranges from 32 to 128 and is placed anywhere on the image. We observed that for small holes on 256×256 images, using patch-swap and Feature2Image network to refine is optional as our Image2Feature network already generates satisfying results most of the time. While for 512×512 images, it is necessary to apply multi-scale inpainting, starting from size 256×256. To address both sizes and to apply multi-scale, we train the Image2Feature network at 256×256 and train the Feature2Image network at both 256×256 and 512×512. During training, we use early stopping, meaning we terminate the training when the loss on the held-out validation set converges. On our NVIDIA GeForce GTX 1080Ti GPU, training typically takes one day to finish for each model, and test time is around 400ms for a 512×512 image.

4.2   Results

Quantitative Comparison. Table 1 shows numerical comparison result between our approach, CE [27], GLI [14] and NPS [34]. We adopt three quality measurements: mean ℓ_1 error, SSIM, and inception score [30]. Since context encoder only inpaints 128×128 images and we failed to train the model for larger inputs, we directly use the 128×128 results and bi-linearly upsample them to 512×512. Here we also compute the SSIM over the hole area only. We see that although our mean ℓ_1 error is higher, we achieve the best SSIM and inception score among all the methods, showing our results are closer to the ground truth by human perception. Besides, mean ℓ_1 error is not an optimal measure for inpainting, as it favors averaged colors and blurry results and does not directly account for the end goal of perceptual quality.

Table 1. Numerical comparison on 200 test images of ImageNet.

Method	Mean ℓ_1 error	SSIM	Inception score
CE [27]	15.46%	0.45	9.80
NPS [34]	**15.13%**	0.52	10.85
GLI [14]	15.81%	0.55	11.18
Our approach	15.61%	**0.56**	**11.36**

Visual Result. Figure 9 shows our comparison with GLI [1] in random hole cases. We can see that our method could handle multiple situations better, such as object removal, object completion and texture generation, while GLIs results are noisier and less coherent. From Fig. 10, we could also find that our results are better than GLI most of the time for large holes. This shows that directly training a network for large hole inpainting is difficult, and it is where our "patch-swap" can be most helpful. In addition, our results have significantly fewer artifacts than GLI. Comparing with CAF, we can better predict the global structure and fill in contents more coherent with the surrounding context. Comparing with CE, we can handle much larger images and the synthesized contents are much sharper. Comparing with NPS whose results mostly depend on CE, we have similar or better quality most of the time, and our algorithm also runs much faster. Meanwhile, our final results improve over the intermediate output of Image2Feature. This demonstrates that using patch-swap and Feature2Image transformation is beneficial and necessary.

User Study. To better evaluate and compare with other methods, we randomly select 400 images from the COCO test set and randomly distribute these images to 20 users. Each user is given 20 images with holes together with the inpainting results of NPS, GLI, and ours. Each of them is asked to rank the results in non-increasing order (meaning they can say two results have similar quality). We collected 399 valid votes in total found our results are ranked best most of the time: in 75.9% of the rankings our result receives highest score. In particular, our results are overwhelmingly better than GLI, receiving higher score 91.2% of the time. This is largely because GLI does not handle large holes well. Our results are also comparable with NPS, ranking higher or the same 86.2% of the time.

4.3   Analysis

Comparison. Comparing with [34], not only our approach is much faster but also has several advantages. First, the Feature2Image network synthesizes the entire image while [34] only optimizes the hole part. By aligning the color of the boundary between the output and the input, we can slightly adjust the tone to make the hole blend with the boundary more seamlessly and naturally (Fig. 10). Second, our model is trained to directly model the statistics of real-world images and works well on all resolutions, while [34] is unable to produce sharp results when the image is small. Comparing with other learning-based inpainting methods, our approach is more general as we can handle larger inputs like 512×512. In contrast, [27] can only inpaint 128×128 images while [14] is limited to 256×256 images and the holes are limited to be smaller than 128×128.

Ablation Study. For the Feature2Image network, we observed that replacing the deconvolutional layers in the decoder part with resize-convolution layers resolves the checkerboard patterns as described in [25] (Fig. 5 left). We also tried only using ℓ_2 loss instead of perceptual loss, which gives blurrier inpainting (Fig. 5 middle). Additionally, we experimented different activation layers of VGG19 to extract features and found that *relu3_1* works better than *relu2_1* and *relu4_1*.

We may also use iterative inference by running Feature2Image network multiple times. At each iteration, the final output is used as input to VGG and patch-swap, and then again given to Feature2Image network for inference. We found iteratively applying Feature2Image improves the sharpness of the texture but sometimes aggregates the artifacts near the boundary.

For the Image2Feature network, an alternative is to use vanilla context encoder [27] to generate I_0^0 as the initial inference. However, we found our model produces better results as it is much deeper, and leverages the fully convolutional network and dilated layer.

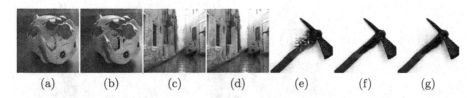

(a)   (b)   (c)   (d)   (e)   (f)   (g)

Fig. 5. Left: using deconvolution (a) vs resize-convolution (b). Middle: using ℓ_2 reconstruction loss (c) vs using perceptual loss (d). Right: Training Feature2Image network using different input data. (e) Result when trained with the Image2Feature prediction. (f) Result when trained with ground truth. (g) Result when fine-tuned with ground truth and prediction mixtures.

As discussed in Sect. 3.3, an important practice to guarantee successful training of the Feature2Image network is to use ground truth image as input rather than using the output of the Image2Feature network. Figure 5 also shows that training with the prediction from the Image2Feature network gives very noisy results, while the models trained with ground truth or further fine-tuned with ground-truth and prediction mixtures can produce satisfying inpainting.

Our framework can be easily applied to real-world tasks. Figure 6 shows examples of using our approach to remove unwanted objects in photography. Given our network is fully convolutional, it is straight-straightforward to apply it to photos of arbitrary sizes. It is also able to fill in holes of arbitrary shapes, and can handle much larger holes than [15].

Fig. 6. Arbitrary shape inpainting of real-world photography. (a), (d): Input. (b), (e): Inpainting mask. (c), (f): Output.

Fig. 7. Arbitrary style transfer. (a), (d): Content. (b), (e): Style. (c), (f): Result.

Fig. 8. Failure cases. (a), (c) and (e): Input. (b), (d) and (f): Output.

Fig. 9. Visual comparisons of ImageNet results with random hole. Each example from top to bottom: input image, GLI [14], our result. All images have size 256×256.

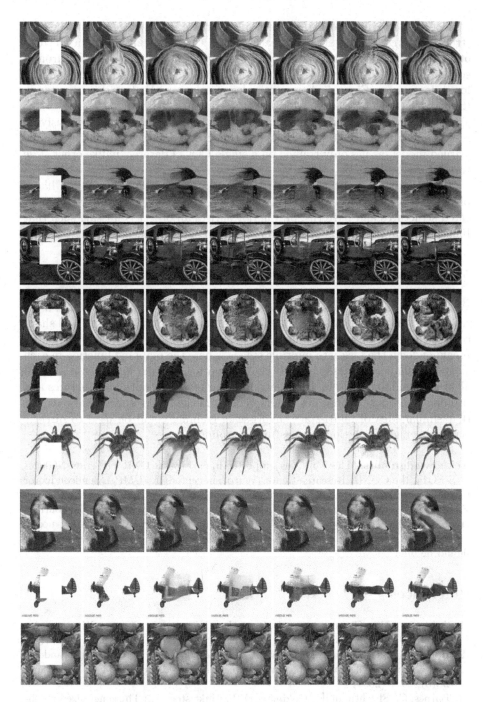

Fig. 10. Visual comparisons of ImageNet and COCO results. Each example from left to right: input image, CAF [2], CE [27], NPS [34], GLI [14], our result w/o Feature2Image, our final result. All images have size 512×512.

The Feature2Image network essentially learns a universal function to reconstruct an image from a swapped feature map, therefore can also be applied to other tasks. For example, by first constructing a swapped feature map from a content and a style image, we can use the network to reconstruct a new image for style transfer. Figure 7 shows examples of using our Feature2Image network trained on COCO towards arbitrary style transfer. Although the network is agnostic to the styles being transferred, it is still capable of generating satisfying results and runs in real-time. This shows the strong generalization ability of our learned model, as it's only trained on a single COCO dataset, unlike other style transfer methods.

Our approach is very good at recovering a partially missing object like a plane or a bird (Fig. 10). However, it can fail if the image has overly complicated structures and patterns, or a major part of an object is missing such that Image2Feature network is unable to provide a good inference (Fig. 8).

5   Conclusion

We propose a learning-based approach to synthesize missing contents in a high-resolution image. Our model is able to inpaint an image with realistic and sharp contents in a feed-forward manner. We show that we can simplify training by breaking down the task into multiple stages, where the mapping function in each stage has smaller dimensionality. It is worth noting that our approach is a meta-algorithm and naturally we could explore a variety of network architectures and training techniques to improve the inference and the final result. We also expect that similar idea of multi-stage, multi-scale training could be used to directly synthesize high-resolution images from sampling.

Acknowledgments. This work was supported in part by the ONR YIP grant N00014-17-S-FO14, the CONIX Research Center, one of six centers in JUMP, a Semiconductor Research Corporation (SRC) program sponsored by DARPA, the Andrew and Erna Viterbi Early Career Chair, the U.S. Army Research Laboratory (ARL) under contract number W911NF-14-D-0005, Adobe. The content of the information does not necessarily reflect the position or the policy of the Government, and no official endorsement should be inferred.

References

1. Arjovsky, M., Chintala, S., Bottou, L.: Wasserstein gan. arXiv preprint arXiv:1701.07875 (2017)
2. Barnes, C., Shechtman, E., Finkelstein, A., Goldman, D.B.: Patchmatch: a randomized correspondence algorithm for structural image editing. ACM Trans. Graph. **28**(3), 24–1 (2009)
3. Barnes, C., Shechtman, E., Goldman, D.B., Finkelstein, A.: The generalized patchmatch correspondence algorithm. In: Daniilidis, K., Maragos, P., Paragios, N. (eds.) ECCV 2010. LNCS, vol. 6313, pp. 29–43. Springer, Heidelberg (2010). https://doi.org/10.1007/978-3-642-15558-1_3

4. Berthelot, D., Schumm, T., Metz, L.: Began: boundary equilibrium generative adversarial networks. arXiv preprint arXiv:1703.10717 (2017)
5. Chen, T.Q., Schmidt, M.: Fast patch-based style transfer of arbitrary style. arXiv preprint arXiv:1612.04337 (2016)
6. Denton, E.L., Chintala, S., Fergus, R., et al.: Deep generative image models using a Laplacian pyramid of adversarial networks. In: Advances in Neural Information Processing Systems, pp. 1486–1494 (2015)
7. Dosovitskiy, A., Brox, T.: Generating images with perceptual similarity metrics based on deep networks. In: Advances in Neural Information Processing Systems, pp. 658–666 (2016)
8. Elad, M., Milanfar, P.: Style transfer via texture synthesis. IEEE Trans. Image Process. **26**(5), 2338–2351 (2017)
9. Frigo, O., Sabater, N., Delon, J., Hellier, P.: Split and match: example-based adaptive patch sampling for unsupervised style transfer. In: Proceedings of the IEEE Conference on Computer Vision and Pattern Recognition, pp. 553–561 (2016)
10. Gatys, L.A., Ecker, A.S., Bethge, M.: A neural algorithm of artistic style. arXiv preprint arXiv:1508.06576 (2015)
11. Gatys, L.A., Ecker, A.S., Bethge, M.: Image style transfer using convolutional neural networks. In: 2016 IEEE Conference on Computer Vision and Pattern Recognition (CVPR), pp. 2414–2423. IEEE (2016)
12. Goodfellow, I., et al.: Generative adversarial nets. In: Advances in Neural Information Processing Systems, pp. 2672–2680 (2014)
13. Gulrajani, I., Ahmed, F., Arjovsky, M., Dumoulin, V., Courville, A.: Improved training of Wasserstein GANs. arXiv preprint arXiv:1704.00028 (2017)
14. Iizuka, S., Simo-Serra, E., Ishikawa, H.: Globally and locally consistent image completion. ACM Trans. Graph. **36**(4), 107:1–107:14 (2017). (Proceedings of SIGGRAPH 2017)
15. Iizuka, S., Simo-Serra, E., Ishikawa, H.: Globally and locally consistent image completion. ACM Trans. Graph. (TOG) **36**(4), 107 (2017)
16. Ioffe, S., Szegedy, C.: Batch normalization: accelerating deep network training by reducing internal covariate shift. arXiv preprint arXiv:1502.03167 (2015)
17. Isola, P., Zhu, J.Y., Zhou, T., Efros, A.A.: Image-to-image translation with conditional adversarial networks. arXiv preprint arXiv:1611.07004 (2016)
18. Johnson, J., Alahi, A., Fei-Fei, L.: Perceptual losses for real-time style transfer and super-resolution. In: Leibe, B., Matas, J., Sebe, N., Welling, M. (eds.) ECCV 2016. LNCS, vol. 9906, pp. 694–711. Springer, Cham (2016). https://doi.org/10.1007/978-3-319-46475-6_43
19. Karras, T., Aila, T., Laine, S., Lehtinen, J.: Progressive growing of GANs for improved quality, stability, and variation. arXiv preprint arXiv:1710.10196 (2017)
20. Kingma, D.P., Welling, M.: Auto-encoding variational Bayes. arXiv preprint arXiv:1312.6114 (2013)
21. Li, C., Wand, M.: Combining Markov random fields and convolutional neural networks for image synthesis. In: Proceedings of the IEEE Conference on Computer Vision and Pattern Recognition, pp. 2479–2486 (2016)
22. Lin, T.-Y., et al.: Microsoft COCO: common objects in context. In: Fleet, D., Pajdla, T., Schiele, B., Tuytelaars, T. (eds.) ECCV 2014. LNCS, vol. 8693, pp. 740–755. Springer, Cham (2014). https://doi.org/10.1007/978-3-319-10602-1_48
23. Mao, X., Li, Q., Xie, H., Lau, R.Y., Wang, Z., Smolley, S.P.: Least squares generative adversarial networks. arXiv preprint ArXiv:1611.04076 (2016)

24. Nguyen, A., Yosinski, J., Bengio, Y., Dosovitskiy, A., Clune, J.: Plug & play generative networks: conditional iterative generation of images in latent space. arXiv preprint arXiv:1612.00005 (2016)
25. Odena, A., Dumoulin, V., Olah, C.: Deconvolution and checkerboard artifacts. Distill (2016). https://doi.org/10.23915/distill.00003, http://distill.pub/2016/deconv-checkerboard
26. van den Oord, A., Kalchbrenner, N., Espeholt, L., Vinyals, O., Graves, A., et al.: Conditional image generation with PixelCNN decoders. In: Advances in Neural Information Processing Systems, pp. 4790–4798 (2016)
27. Pathak, D., Krahenbuhl, P., Donahue, J., Darrell, T., Efros, A.A.: Context encoders: feature learning by inpainting. In: Proceedings of the IEEE Conference on Computer Vision and Pattern Recognition, pp. 2536–2544 (2016)
28. Radford, A., Metz, L., Chintala, S.: Unsupervised representation learning with deep convolutional generative adversarial networks. arXiv preprint arXiv:1511.06434 (2015)
29. Russakovsky, O., et al.: Imagenet large scale visual recognition challenge. Int. J. Comput. Vis. **115**(3), 211–252 (2015)
30. Salimans, T., Goodfellow, I., Zaremba, W., Cheung, V., Radford, A., Chen, X.: Improved techniques for training GANs. In: Advances in Neural Information Processing Systems, pp. 2234–2242 (2016)
31. Simonyan, K., Zisserman, A.: Very deep convolutional networks for large-scale image recognition. arXiv preprint arXiv:1409.1556 (2014)
32. Wang, T.C., Liu, M.Y., Zhu, J.Y., Tao, A., Kautz, J., Catanzaro, B.: High-resolution image synthesis and semantic manipulation with conditional GANs. arXiv preprint arXiv:1711.11585 (2017)
33. Wang, W., Huang, Q., You, S., Yang, C., Neumann, U.: Shape inpainting using 3D generative adversarial network and recurrent convolutional networks. In: Proceedings of the IEEE Conference on Computer Vision and Pattern Recognition, pp. 2298–2306 (2017)
34. Yang, C., Lu, X., Lin, Z., Shechtman, E., Wang, O., Li, H.: High-resolution image inpainting using multi-scale neural patch synthesis. In: The IEEE Conference on Computer Vision and Pattern Recognition (CVPR), July 2017
35. Yeh, R.A., Chen, C., Lim, T.Y., Schwing, A.G., Hasegawa-Johnson, M., Do, M.N.: Semantic image inpainting with deep generative models. In: Proceedings of the IEEE Conference on Computer Vision and Pattern Recognition, pp. 5485–5493 (2017)
36. Zhang, H., et al.: Stackgan: text to photo-realistic image synthesis with stacked generative adversarial networks. arXiv preprint arXiv:1612.03242 (2016)
37. Zhang, R., Isola, P., Efros, A.A., Shechtman, E., Wang, O.: The unreasonable effectiveness of deep features as a perceptual metric. arXiv preprint arXiv:1801.03924 (2018)
38. Zhao, J., Mathieu, M., LeCun, Y.: Energy-based generative adversarial network. arXiv preprint arXiv:1609.03126 (2016)
39. Zheng, S., Song, Y., Leung, T., Goodfellow, I.: Improving the robustness of deep neural networks via stability training. In: Proceedings of the IEEE Conference on Computer Vision and Pattern Recognition, pp. 4480–4488 (2016)
40. Zhu, J.Y., Park, T., Isola, P., Efros, A.A.: Unpaired image-to-image translation using cycle-consistent adversarial networks. arXiv preprint arXiv:1703.10593 (2017)

TextSnake: A Flexible Representation for Detecting Text of Arbitrary Shapes

Shangbang Long[1,2] ⓘ, Jiaqiang Ruan[1,2], Wenjie Zhang[1,2], Xin He[2],
Wenhao Wu[2], and Cong Yao[2(✉)] ⓘ

[1] Peking University, Beijing, China
{longlongsb,jiaqiang.ruan,zhang_wen_jie}@pku.edu.cn
[2] Megvii (Face++) Technology Inc., Beijing, China
{hexin,wwh}@megvii.com, yaocong2010@gmail.com

Abstract. Driven by deep neural networks and large scale datasets, scene text detection methods have progressed substantially over the past years, continuously refreshing the performance records on various standard benchmarks. However, limited by the representations (axis-aligned rectangles, rotated rectangles or quadrangles) adopted to describe text, existing methods may fall short when dealing with much more free-form text instances, such as curved text, which are actually very common in real-world scenarios. To tackle this problem, we propose a more flexible representation for scene text, termed as *TextSnake*, which is able to effectively represent text instances in horizontal, oriented and curved forms. In TextSnake, a text instance is described as a sequence of ordered, overlapping disks centered at symmetric axes, each of which is associated with potentially variable radius and orientation. Such geometry attributes are estimated via a Fully Convolutional Network (FCN) model. In experiments, the text detector based on TextSnake achieves state-of-the-art or comparable performance on Total-Text and SCUT-CTW1500, the two newly published benchmarks with special emphasis on curved text in natural images, as well as the widely-used datasets ICDAR 2015 and MSRA-TD500. Specifically, TextSnake outperforms the baseline on Total-Text by more than 40% in F-measure.

Keywords: Scene text detection · Deep neural network · Curved text

1 Introduction

In recent years, the community has witnessed a surge of research interest and effort regarding the extraction of textual information from natural scenes, a.k.a. scene text detection and recognition [48]. The driving factors stem from both application prospect and research value. On the one hand, scene text detection and recognition have been playing ever-increasingly important roles in a wide range of practical systems, such as scene understanding, product search, and autonomous driving. On the other hand, the unique traits of scene text, for instance, significant variations in color, scale, orientation, aspect ratio and

© Springer Nature Switzerland AG 2018
V. Ferrari et al. (Eds.): ECCV 2018, LNCS 11206, pp. 19–35, 2018.
https://doi.org/10.1007/978-3-030-01216-8_2

pattern, make it obviously different from general objects. Therefore, particular challenges are posed and special investigations are required.

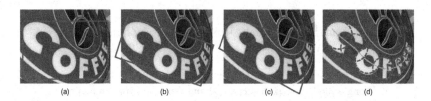

Fig. 1. Comparison of different representations for text instances. (a) Axis-aligned rectangle. (b) Rotated rectangle. (c) Quadrangle. (d) TextSnake. Obviously, the proposed TextSnake representation is able to effectively and precisely describe the geometric properties, such as location, scale, and bending of curved text with perspective distortion, while the other representations (axis-aligned rectangle, rotated rectangle or quadrangle) struggle with giving accurate predictions in such cases.

Text detection, as a prerequisite step in the pipeline of textual information extraction, has recently advanced substantially with the development of deep neural networks and large image datasets. Numerous innovative works [6,9,10, 17,22,28–31,34,36,39,40,46,47] are proposed, achieving excellent performances on standard benchmarks.

However, most existing methods for text detection shared a strong assumption that text instances are roughly in a linear shape and therefore adopted relatively simple representations (axis-aligned rectangles, rotated rectangles or quadrangles) to describe them. Despite their progress on standard benchmarks, these methods may fall short when handling text instances of irregular shapes, for example, curved text. As depicted in Fig. 1, for curved text with perspective distortion, conventional representations struggle with giving precise estimations of the geometric properties.

In fact, instances of curved text are quite common in real life [15,43]. In this paper, we propose a more flexible representation that can fit well text of arbitrary shapes, i.e., those in horizontal, multi-oriented and curved forms. This representation describes text with a series of ordered, overlapping disks, each of which is located at the center axis of text region and associated with potentially variable radius and orientation. Due to its excellent capability in adapting for the complex multiplicity of text structures, just like a snake changing its shape to adapt for the external environment, the proposed representation is named as TextSnake. The geometry attributes of text instances, i.e., central axis points, radii and orientations, are estimated with a single Fully Convolutional Network (FCN) model. Besides ICDAR 2015 and MSRA-TD500, the effectiveness of TextSnake is validated on Total-Text and SCUT-CTW1500, which are two newly-released benchmarks mainly focused on curved text. The proposed algorithm achieves state-of-the-art performance on the two curved text datasets, while at the same time outperforming previous methods on horizontal and multi-oriented text, *even in the single-scale testing mode.* Specifically, TextSnake achieves significant improvement over the baseline on Total-Text by 40.0% in F-measure.

In summary, the major contributions of this paper are three-fold: (1) We propose a flexible and general representation for scene text of arbitrary shapes; (2) Based on this representation, an effective method for scene text detection is proposed; (3) The proposed text detection algorithm achieves state-of-the-art performance on several benchmarks, including text instances of different forms (horizontal, oriented and curved).

2   Related Work

In the past few years, the most prominent trend in the area of scene text detection is the transfer from conventional methods [3,24] to deep learning based methods [12,13,17,29,47]. In this section, we look back on relevant previous works. For comprehensive surveys, please refer to [41,48]. Before the era of deep learning, SWT [3] and MSER [24] are two representative algorithms that have influenced a variety of subsequent methods [11,42]. Modern methods are mostly based on deep neural networks, which can be coarsely classified into two categories: regression based and segmentation based.

Regression based text detection methods [17] mainly draw inspirations from general object detection frameworks. TextBoxes [17] adopted SSD [19] and added "long" default boxes and filters to handle the significant variation of aspect ratios of text instances. Based on Faster-RCNN [26], Ma *et al.* [23] devised Rotation Region Proposal Networks (RRPN) to detect arbitrary-Oriented text in natural images. EAST [47] and Deep Regression [8] both directly produce the rotated boxes or quadrangles of text, in a per-pixel manner.

Segmentation based text detection methods cast text detection as a semantic segmentation problem and FCN [21] is often taken as the reference framework. Yao *et al.* [39] modified FCN to produce multiple heatmaps corresponding various properties of text, such as text region and orientation. Zhang *et al.* [46] first use FCN to extract text blocks and then hunt character candidates from these blocks with MSER [24]. To better separate adjacent text instances, the method of [36] distinguishes each pixel into three categories: non-text, text border and text. These methods mainly vary in the way they separate text pixels into different instances.

The methods reviewed above have achieved excellent performances on various benchmarks in this field. However, most works, except for [6,15,39], have not payed special attention to curved text. In contrast, the representation proposed in this paper is suitable for text of arbitrary shapes (horizontal, multi-oriented and curved). It is primarily inspired by [6,39] and the geometric attributes of text are also estimated via the multiple-channel outputs of an FCN-based model. Unlike [39], our algorithm does not need character level annotations. In addition, it also shares a similar idea with SegLink [29], by successively decomposing text into local components and then composing them back into text instances. Analogous to [45], we also detect linear symmetry axes of text instances for text localization.

Another advantage of the proposed method lies in its ability to reconstruct the precise shape and regional strike of text instances, which can largely facilitate the subsequent text recognition process, because all detected text instances could be conveniently transformed into a canonical form with minimal distortion and background (see the example in Fig. 9).

3   Methodology

In this section, we first introduce the new representation for text of arbitrary shapes. Then we describe our method and training details.

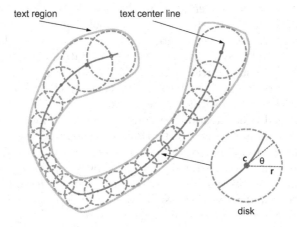

Fig. 2. Illustration of the proposed TextSnake representation. Text region (in yellow) is represented as a series of ordered disks (in blue), each of which is located at the center line (in green, a.k.a symmetric axis or skeleton) and associated with a radius r and an orientation θ. In contrast to conventional representations (e.g., axis-aligned rectangles, rotated rectangles and quadrangles), TextSnake is more flexible and general, since it can precisely describe text of different forms, regardless of shapes and lengths. (Color figure online)

3.1   Representation

As shown in Fig. 1, conventional representations for scene text (e.g., axis-aligned rectangles, rotated rectangles and quadrangles) fail to precisely describe the geometric properties of text instances of irregular shapes, since they generally assume that text instances are roughly in linear forms, which does not hold true for curved text. To address this problem, we propose a flexible and general representation: TextSnake. As demonstrated in Fig. 2, TextSnake expresses a text instance as a sequence of overlapping disks, each of which is located at the center line and associated with a radius and an orientation. Intuitively, TextSnake is able to change its shape to adapt for the variations of text instances, such as rotation, scaling and bending.

Mathematically, a text instance t, consisting of several characters, can be viewed as an ordered list $S(t)$. $S(t) = \{D_0, D_1, \cdots, D_i, \cdots, D_n\}$, where D_i stands for the ith disk and n is the number of the disks. Each disk D is associated with a group of geometry attributes, i.e. $D = (c, r, \theta)$, in which c, r and θ are the center, radius and orientation of disk D, respectively. The radius r is defined as half of the local width of t, while the orientation θ is the tangential direction of the center line around the center c. In this sense, text region t can be easily reconstructed by computing the union of the disks in $S(t)$.

Note that the disks do not correspond to the characters belonging to t. However, the geometric attributes in $S(t)$ can be used to rectify text instances of irregular shapes and transform them into rectangular, straight image regions, which are more friendly to text recognizers.

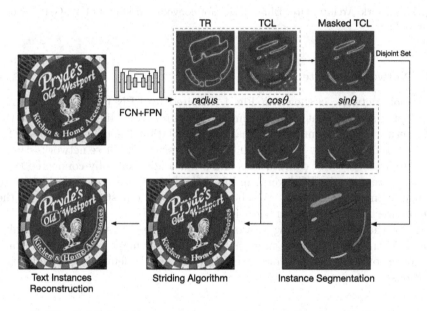

Fig. 3. Method framework: network output and post-processing

3.2 Pipeline

In order to detect text with arbitrary shapes, we employ an FCN model to predict the geometry attributes of text instances. The pipeline of the proposed method is illustrated in Fig. 3. The FCN based network predicts score maps of text center line (TCL) and text regions (TR), together with geometry attributes, including r, $\cos\theta$ and $\sin\theta$. The TCL map is further masked by the TR map since TCL is naturally part of TR. To perform instance segmentation, disjoint set is utilized, given the fact that TCL does not overlap with each other. A striding algorithm is used to extract the central axis point lists and finally reconstruct the text instances.

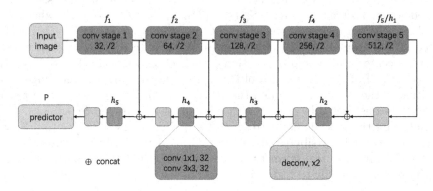

Fig. 4. Network Architecture. Blue blocks are convolution stages of VGG-16. (Color figure online)

3.3   Network Architecture

The whole network is shown in Fig. 4. Inspired by FPN [18] and U-net [27], we adopt a scheme that gradually merges features from different levels of the stem network. The stem network can be convolutional networks proposed for image classification, e.g. VGG-16/19 [33] and ResNet [7]. These networks can be divided into 5 stages of convolutions and a few additional fully-connected (FC) layers. We remove the FC layers, and feed the feature maps after each stage to the feature merging network. We choose VGG-16 as our stem network for the sake of direct and fair comparison with other methods.

As for the feature merging network, several stages are stacked sequentially, each consisting of a merging unit that takes feature maps from the last stage and corresponding stem network layer. Merging unit is defined by the following equations:

$$h_1 = f_5 \tag{1}$$

$$h_i = conv_{3\times3}(conv_{1\times1}[f_{6-i}; UpSampling_{\times2}(h_{i-1})]), \text{ for } i = 2, 3, 4, 5 \tag{2}$$

where f_i denotes the feature maps of the i-th stage in the stem network and h_i is the feature maps of the corresponding merging units. In our experiments, upsampling is implemented as deconvolutional layer as proposed in [44].

After the merging, we obtain a feature map whose size is $\frac{1}{2}$ of the input images. We apply an additional upsampling layer and 2 convolutional layers to produce dense predictions:

$$h_{final} = UpSampling_{\times2}(h_5) \tag{3}$$

$$P = conv_{1\times1}(conv_{3\times3}(h_{final})) \tag{4}$$

where $P \in \mathcal{R}^{h \times w \times 7}$, with 4 channels for logits of TR/TCL, and the last 3 respectively for r, $cos\theta$ and $sin\theta$ of the text instance. As a result of the additional upsampling layer, P has the same size as the input image. The final predictions are obtained by taking softmax for TR/TCL and regularizing $cos\theta$ and $sin\theta$ so that the squared sum equals 1.

3.4 Inference

After feed-forwarding, the network produces the TCL, TR and geometry maps. For TCL and TR, we apply thresholding with values T_{tcl} and T_{tr} respectively. Then, the intersection of TR and TCL gives the final prediction of TCL. Using disjoint-set, we can efficiently separate TCL pixels into different text instances.

Finally, a striding algorithm is designed to extract an ordered point list that indicates the shape and course of the text instance, and also reconstruct the text instance areas. Two simple heuristics are applied to filter out false positive text instances: (1) The number of TCL pixels should be at least 0.2 times their average radius; (2) At least half of pixels in the reconstructed text area should be classified as TR.

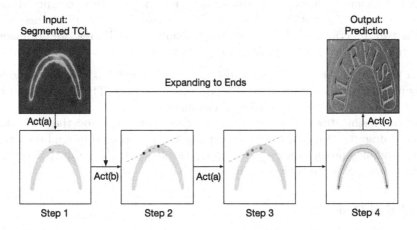

Fig. 5. Framework of post-processing algorithm. Act(a) centralizing: relocate a given point to the central axis; Act(b) striding: a directional search towards the ends of text instances; Act(c) sliding: a reconstruction by sliding a circle along the central axis.

The procedure for the striding algorithm is shown in Fig. 5. It features 3 main actions, denoted as Act(a), Act(b), and Act(c), as illustrated in Fig. 6. Firstly, we randomly select a pixel as the starting point, and centralize it. Then, the search process forks into two opposite directions, striding and centralizing until it reaches the ends. This process would generates 2 ordered point list in two opposite directions, which can be combined to produce the final central axis list that follows the course of the text and describe the shape precisely. Details of the 3 actions are shown below.

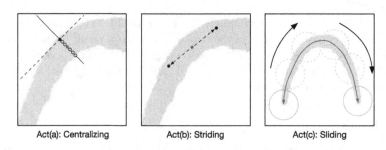

Act(a): Centralizing   Act(b): Striding   Act(c): Sliding

Fig. 6. Mechanisms of centralizing, striding and sliding

Act(a) Centralizing. As shown in Fig. 6, given a point on the TCL, we can draw the tangent line and the normal line, respectively denoted as dotted line and solid line. This step can be done with ease using the geometry maps. The midpoint of the intersection of the normal line and the TCL area gives the centralized point.

Act(b) Striding. The algorithm takes a stride to the next point to search. With the geometry maps, the displacement for each stride is computed and represented as $(\frac{1}{2}r \times cos\theta, \frac{1}{2}r \times sin\theta)$ and $(-\frac{1}{2}r \times cos\theta, -\frac{1}{2}r \times sin\theta)$, respectively for the two directions. If the next step is outside the TCL area, we decrement the stride gradually until it's inside, or it hits the ends.

Act(c) Sliding. The algorithm iterates through the central axis and draw circles along it. Radii of the circles are obtained from the r map. The area covered by the circles indicates the predicted text instance.

In conclusion, taking advantage of the geometry maps and the TCL that precisely describes the course of the text instance, we can go beyond detection of text and also predict their shape and course. Besides, the striding algorithm saves our method from traversing all pixels that are related.

3.5   Label Generation

Extracting Text Center Line. For triangles and quadrangles, it's easy to directly calculate the TCL with algebraic methods, since in this case, TCL is a straight line. For polygons of more than 4 sides, it's not easy to derive a general algebraic method.

Instead, we propose a method that is based on the assumption that, text instances are snake-shaped, i.e. that it does not fork into multiple branches. For a snake-shaped text instance, it has two edges that are respectively the *head* and the *tail*. The two edges near the head or tail are running parallel but in opposite direction.

For a text instance t represented by a group of vertexes $\{v_0, v_1, v_2, ..., v_n\}$ in clockwise or counterclockwise order, we define a measurement for each edge $e_{i,i+1}$ as $M(e_{i,i+1}) = \cos\langle e_{i+1,i+2}, e_{i-1,i}\rangle$. Intuitively, the two edges with M nearest to -1, e.g. *AH* and *DE* in Fig. 7, are the head and tail. After that, equal number

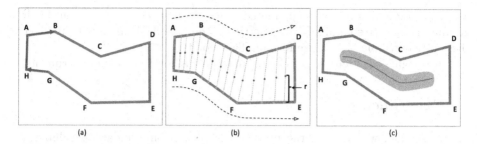

Fig. 7. Label Generation. (a) Determining text head and tail; (b) Extracting text center line and calculating geometries; (c) Expanded text center line.

of anchor points are sampled on the two sidelines, e.g. $ABCD$ and $HGFE$ in Fig. 7. TCL points are computed as midpoints of corresponding anchor points. We shrink the two ends of TCL by $\frac{1}{2}r_{end}$ pixels, so that TCL are inside the TR and makes it easy for the network to learn to separate adjacent text instances. r_{end} denotes the radius of the TCL points at the two ends. Finally, we expand the TCL area by $\frac{1}{5}r$, since a single-point line is prone to noise.

Calculating r and θ. For each points on TCL: (1) r is computed as the distance to the corresponding point on sidelines; (2) θ is computed by fitting a straight line on the TCL points in the neighborhood. For non-TCL pixels, their corresponding geometry attributes are set to 0 for convenience.

3.6 Training Objectives

The proposed model is trained end-to-end, with the following loss functions as the objectives:

$$L = L_{cls} + L_{reg} \tag{5}$$

$$L_{cls} = \lambda_1 L_{tr} + \lambda_2 L_{tcl} \tag{6}$$

$$L_{reg} = \lambda_3 L_r + \lambda_4 L_{sin} + \lambda_5 L_{cos} \tag{7}$$

L_{cls} in Eq. 5 represents classification loss for TR and TCL, and L_{reg} for regression loss of r, $cos\theta$ and $sin\theta$. In Eq. 6, L_{tr} and L_{tcl} are cross-entropy loss for TR and TCL. Online hard negative mining [32] is adopted for TR loss, with the ratio between the negatives and positives kept to 3:1 at most. For TCL, we only take into account pixels inside TR and adopt no balancing methods.

In Eq. 7, regression loss, i.e. L_r L_{sin} and L_{cos}, are calculated as Smoothed-L1 loss [4]:

$$\begin{pmatrix} L_r \\ L_{cos} \\ L_{sin} \end{pmatrix} = SmoothedL1 \begin{pmatrix} \frac{\hat{r}-r}{r} \\ \widehat{cos\theta} - cos\theta \\ \widehat{sin\theta} - sin\theta \end{pmatrix} \tag{8}$$

where $\widehat{r}$, $\widehat{cos\theta}$ and $\widehat{sin\theta}$ are the predicted values, while r, $cos\theta$ and $sin\theta$ are their ground truth correspondingly. Geometry loss outside TCL are set to 0, since these attributes make no sense for non-TCL points.

The weights constants λ_1, λ_2, λ_3, λ_4 and λ_5 are all set to 1 in our experiments.

4   Experiments

In this section, we evaluate the proposed algorithm on standard benchmarks for scene text detection and compare it with previous methods. Analyses and discussions regarding our algorithm are also given.

4.1   Datasets

The datasets used for the experiments in this paper are briefly introduced below:

SynthText [5] is a large sacle dataset that contains about $800K$ synthetic images. These images are created by blending natural images with text rendered with random fonts, sizes, colors, and orientations, thus these images are quite realistic. We use this dataset to pre-train our model.

TotalText [15] is a newly-released benchmark for text detection. Besides horizontal and multi-Oriented text instances, the dataset specially features *curved text*, which rarely appear in other benchmark datasets, but are actually quite common in real environments. The dataset is split into training and testing sets with 1255 and 300 images, respectively.

CTW1500 [43] is another dataset mainly consisting of curved text. It consists of 1000 training images and 500 test images. Text instances are annotated with polygons with 14 vertexes.

ICDAR 2015 is proposed as the Challenge 4 of the 2015 Robust Reading Competition [14] for incidental scene text detection. There are 1000 images for training and 500 images for testing. The text instances from this dataset are labeled as word level quadrangles.

MSRA-TD500 [38] is a dataset with multi-lingual, arbitrary-oriented and long text lines. It includes 300 training images and 200 test images with text line level annotations. Following previous works [22,47], we also include the images from HUST-TR400 [37] as training data when fine-tuning on this dataset, since its training set is rather small.

For experiments on ICDAR 2015 and MSRA-TD500, we fit a minimum bounding rectangle based on the output text area of our method.

4.2   Data Augmentation

Images are randomly rotated, and cropped with areas ranging from 0.24 to 1.69 and aspect ratios ranging from 0.33 to 3. After that, noise, blur, and lightness are randomly adjusted. We ensure that the text on the augmented images are still legible, if they are legible before augmentation.

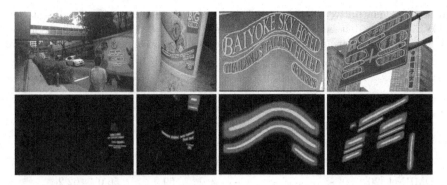

Fig. 8. Qualitative results by the proposed method. Top: detected text contours (in *yellow*) and ground truth annotations (in *green*). Bottom: combined score maps for TR (in *red*) and TCL (in *yellow*). From left to right in column: image from ICDAR 2015, TotalText, CTW1500 and MSRA-TD500. Best viewed in color. (Color figure online)

4.3 Implementation Details

Our method is implemented in Tensorflow 1.3.0 [1]. The network is pre-trained on SynthText for one epoch and fine-tuned on other datasets. We adopt the Adam optimazer [16] as our learning rate scheme. During the pre-training stage, the learning rate is fixed to 10^{-3}. During the fine-tuning stage, the learing rate is set to 10^{-3} initially and decays exponentially with a rate of 0.8 every 5000 iterations. During fine-tuning, the number of iterations is decided by the sizes of datasets. All the experiments are conducted on a regular workstation (CPU: Intel(R) Xeon(R) CPU E5-2650 v3 @ 2.30 GHz; GPU:Titan X; RAM: 384 GB). We train our model with the batch size of 32 on 2 GPUs in parallel and evaluate our model on 1 GPU with batch size set as 1. Hyper-parameters are tuned by grid search on training set.

4.4 Experiment Results

Experiments on Curved Text (Total-Text and CTW1500). Fine-tuning on these two datasets stops at about $5k$ iterations. Thresholds T_{tr}, T_{tcl} are set to $(0.4, 0.6)$ and $(0.4, 0.5)$ respectively on Total-Text and CTW1500. In testing, all images are rescaled to 512×512 for Total-Text, while for CTW1500, the images are not resized, since the images in CTW1500 are rather small (The largest image is merely 400×600). For comparison, we also evaluated the models of EAST [47] and SegLink [29] on Total-Text and CTW1500. The quantitative results of different methods on these two datasets are shown in Table 1.

The superior performances of our method on Total-Text and CTW1500 verify that the proposed representation can handle well curved text in natural images.

Experiments on Incidental Scene Text (ICDAR 2015). Fine-tuning on ICDAR 2015 stops at about $30k$ iterations. In testing, all images are resized to 1280×768. T_{tr}, T_{tcl} are set to $(0.4, 0.9)$. For the consideration that images in

Table 1. Quantitative results of different methods evaluated on Total-Text and CTW1500. Note that EAST and SegLink were not fine-tuned on Total-Text. Therefore their results are included only for reference. Comparative results on CTW1500 are obtained from [43].

Datasets	Total-text			CTW1500		
Method	Precision	Recall	F-measure	Precision	Recall	F-measure
SegLink [29]	30.3	23.8	26.7	42.3	40.0	40.8
EAST [47]	50.0	36.2	42.0	78.7	49.1	60.4
DeconvNet [25]	33.0	40.0	36.0	-	-	-
DMPNet [20]	-	-	-	69.9	56.0	62.2
CTD [43]	-	-	-	74.3	65.2	69.5
CTD+TLOC [43]	-	-	-	**77.4**	69.8	73.4
TextSnake	**82.7**	**74.5**	**78.4**	67.9	**85.3**	**75.6**

ICDAR 2015 contains many unlabeled small texts, predicted rectangles with the shorter side less than 10 pixels or the area less than 300 are filtered out.

The quantitative results of different methods on ICDAR 2015 are shown in Table 2. With only *single-scale* testing, our method outperforms most competitors (including those evaluated in multi-scale). This demonstrates that the proposed representation TextSnake is general and can be readily applied to multi-oriented text in complex scenarios.

Experiments on Long Straight Text Lines (MSRA-TD500). Fine-tuning on MSRA-TD500 stops at about $10k$ iterations. Thresholds for T_{tr}, T_{tcl} are $(0.4, 0.6)$. In testing, all images are resized to 1280×768. Results are shown in Table 2. The F-measure (78.3%) of the proposed method is higher than that of the other methods.

4.5   Analyses and Discussions

Precise Description of Text Instances. What distinguishes our method from others is its ability to predict a precise description of the shape and course of text instances(see Fig. 8).

We attribute such ability to the TCL mechanism. Text center line can be seen as a kind of skeletons that prop up the text instance, and geo-attributes providing more details. Text, as a form of written language, can be seen as a stream of signals mapped onto 2D surfaces. Naturally, it should follows a course to extend.

Therefore we propose to predict TCL, which is much narrower than the whole text instance. It has two advantages: (1) A slim TCL can better describe the course and shape; (2) TCL, intuitively, does not overlaps with each other, so that instance segmentation can be done in a very simple and straightforward way, thus simplifying our pipeline.

Table 2. Quantitative results of different methods on ICDAR 2015 and MSRA-TD500. *stands for multi-scale, †indicates that the base net of the model is not VGG16.

Datasets	ICDAR 2015			MSRA-TD500			FPS
Method	Precision	Recall	F-measure	Precision	Recall	F-measure	
Zhang et al. [46]	70.8	43.0	53.6	83.0	67.0	74.0	0.48
Yao et al. [39]	72.3	58.7	64.8	76.5	**75.3**	75.9	1.61
SegLink [29]	73.1	76.8	75.0	86.0	70.0	77.0	-
EAST [47]	80.5	72.8	76.4	81.7	61.6	70.2	6.52
WordSup * [9]	79.3	77.0	78.2	-	-	-	2
EAST * † [47]	83.3	78.3	80.7	**87.3**	67.4	76.1	**13.2**
He et al. * † [8]	82.0	80.0	81.0	77.0	70.0	74.0	1.1
PixelLink [2]	**85.5**	**82.0**	**83.7**	83.0	73.2	77.8	3.0
TextSnake	84.9	80.4	82.6	83.2	73.9	**78.3**	1.1

Moreover, as depicted in Fig. 9, we can exploit local geometries to sketch the structure of the text instance and transform the predicted curved text instances into canonical form, which may largely facilitate the recognition stage.

Fig. 9. Text instances transformed to canonical form using the predicted geometries.

Generalization Ability. To further verify the generalization ability of our method, we train and fine-tune our model on datasets *without* curved text and evaluate it on the two benchmarks *featuring* curved text. Specifically, we fine-tune our models on ICDAR 2015, and evaluate them on the target datasets. The models of EAST [47], SegLink [29], and PixelLink [2] are taken as baselines, since these two methods were also trained on ICDAR 2015.

As shown in Table 3, our method still performs well on curved text and significantly outperforms the three strong competitors SegLink, EAST and PixelLink, without fine-tuning on curved text. We attribute this excellent generalization ability to the proposed flexible representation. Instead of taking text as a whole, the representation treats text as a collection of local elements and integrates them together to make decisions. Local attributes are kept when formed into a

Table 3. Comparison of cross-dataset results of different methods. The following models are fine-tuned on ICDAR 2015 and evaluated on Total-Text and CTW1500. Experiments for SegLink, EAST and PixelLink are done with the open source code. The evaluation protocol is DetEval [35], the same as Total-Text.

Datasets	Total-text			CTW1500		
Methods	Precision	Recall	F-measure	Precision	Recall	F-measure
SegLink [29]	35.6	33.2	34.4	33.0	2.4	30.5
EAST [47]	49.0	43.1	45.9	46.7	37.2	41.4
PixelLink [2]	53.5	52.7	53.1	50.6	42.8	46.4
TextSnake	**61.5**	**67.9**	**64.6**	**65.4**	**63.4**	**64.4**

whole. Besides, they are independent of each other. Therefore, the final predictions of our method can retain most information of the shape and course of the text. We believe that this is the main reason for the capacity of the proposed text detection algorithm in hunting text instances with various shapes.

5   Conclusion and Future Work

In this paper, we present a novel, flexible representation for describing the properties of scene text with arbitrary shapes, including horizontal, multi-oriented and curved text instances. The proposed text detection method based upon this representation obtains state-of-the-art or comparable performance on two newly-released benchmarks for curved text (Total-Text and SCUT-CTW1500) as well as two widely-used datasets (ICDAR 2015 and MSRA-TD500) in this field, proving the effectiveness of the proposed method. As for future work, we would explore the direction of developing an end-to-end recognition system for text of arbitrary shapes.

References

1. Abadi, M., et al.: TensorFlow: a system for large-scale machine learning. OSDI **16**, 265–283 (2016)
2. Deng, D., Liu, H., Li, X., Cai, D.: PixelLink: detecting scene text via instance segmentation. In: Proceedings of AAAI (2018)
3. Epshtein, B., Ofek, E., Wexler, Y.: Detecting text in natural scenes with stroke width transform. In: Proceedings of The IEEE Conference on Computer Vision and Pattern Recognition (CVPR), pp. 2963–2970. IEEE (2010)
4. Girshick, R.: Fast R-CNN. In: Proceedings of The IEEE International Conference on Computer Vision (ICCV), December 2015
5. Gupta, A., Vedaldi, A., Zisserman, A.: Synthetic data for text localisation in natural images. In: Proceedings of the IEEE Conference on Computer Vision and Pattern Recognition (CVPR), pp. 2315–2324 (2016)

6. He, D., et al.: Multi-scale FCN with cascaded instance aware segmentation for arbitrary oriented word spotting in the wild. In: Proceedings of The IEEE Conference on Computer Vision and Pattern Recognition (CVPR), pp. 474–483. IEEE (2017)
7. He, K., Zhang, X., Ren, S., Sun, J.: Deep residual learning for image recognition. In: Proceedings of The IEEE Conference on Computer Vision and Pattern Recognition (CVPR) (2016)
8. He, W., Zhang, X.Y., Yin, F., Liu, C.L.: Deep direct regression for multi-oriented scene text detection. In: Proceedings of The IEEE International Conference on Computer Vision (ICCV), October 2017
9. Hu, H., Zhang, C., Luo, Y., Wang, Y., Han, J., Ding, E.: WordSup: exploiting word annotations for character based text detection. In: Proceedings of The IEEE International Conference on Computer Vision (ICCV), October 2017
10. Huang, L., Yang, Y., Deng, Y., Yu, Y.: DenseBox: unifying landmark localization with end to end object detection. arXiv preprint arXiv:1509.04874 (2015)
11. Huang, W., Qiao, Y., Tang, X.: Robust scene text detection with convolution neural network induced MSER trees. In: Fleet, D., Pajdla, T., Schiele, B., Tuytelaars, T. (eds.) ECCV 2014. LNCS, vol. 8692, pp. 497–511. Springer, Cham (2014). https://doi.org/10.1007/978-3-319-10593-2_33
12. Jaderberg, M., Simonyan, K., Vedaldi, A., Zisserman, A.: Reading text in the wild with convolutional neural networks. Int. J. Comput. Vis. **116**(1), 1–20 (2016)
13. Jaderberg, M., Vedaldi, A., Zisserman, A.: Deep features for text spotting. In: Fleet, D., Pajdla, T., Schiele, B., Tuytelaars, T. (eds.) ECCV 2014. LNCS, vol. 8692, pp. 512–528. Springer, Cham (2014). https://doi.org/10.1007/978-3-319-10593-2_34
14. Karatzas, D., et al.: ICDAR 2015 competition on robust reading. In: 13th International Conference on Document Analysis and Recognition (ICDAR), pp. 1156–1160. IEEE (2015)
15. Kheng Chng, C., Chan, C.S.: Total-text: a comprehensive dataset for scene text detection and recognition. In: 14th IAPR International Conference on Document Analysis and Recognition (ICDAR) (2017)
16. Kingma, D., Ba, J.: Adam: a method for stochastic optimization. In: Proceedings of ICLR (2015)
17. Liao, M., Shi, B., Bai, X., Wang, X., Liu, W.: TextBoxes: a fast text detector with a single deep neural network. In: Proceedings of AAAI, pp. 4161–4167 (2017)
18. Lin, T.Y., Dollar, P., Girshick, R., He, K., Hariharan, B., Belongie, S.: Feature pyramid networks for object detection. In: Proceedings of The IEEE Conference on Computer Vision and Pattern Recognition (CVPR), July 2017
19. Liu, W., et al.: SSD: single shot MultiBox detector. In: Leibe, B., Matas, J., Sebe, N., Welling, M. (eds.) ECCV 2016. LNCS, vol. 9905, pp. 21–37. Springer, Cham (2016). https://doi.org/10.1007/978-3-319-46448-0_2
20. Liu, Y., Jin, L.: Deep matching prior network: toward tighter multi-oriented text detection (2017)
21. Long, J., Shelhamer, E., Darrell, T.: Fully convolutional networks for semantic segmentation. In: Proceedings of the IEEE Conference on Computer Vision and Pattern Recognition (CVPR), pp. 3431–3440 (2015)
22. Lyu, P., Yao, C., Wu, W., Yan, S., Bai, X.: Multi-oriented scene text detection via corner localization and region segmentation. In: Proceedings of The IEEE Conference on Computer Vision and Pattern Recognition (CVPR) (2018)
23. Ma, J., et al.: Arbitrary-oriented scene text detection via rotation proposals. arXiv preprint arXiv:1703.01086 (2017)

24. Neumann, L., Matas, J.: A method for text localization and recognition in real-world images. In: Kimmel, R., Klette, R., Sugimoto, A. (eds.) ACCV 2010. LNCS, vol. 6494, pp. 770–783. Springer, Heidelberg (2011). https://doi.org/10.1007/978-3-642-19318-7_60

25. Noh, H., Hong, S., Han, B.: Learning deconvolution network for semantic segmentation, pp. 1520–1528 (2015)

26. Ren, S., He, K., Girshick, R., Sun, J.: Faster R-CNN: towards real-time object detection with region proposal networks. In: Advances in Neural Information Processing Systems, pp. 91–99 (2015)

27. Ronneberger, O., Fischer, P., Brox, T.: U-Net: convolutional networks for biomedical image segmentation. In: Navab, N., Hornegger, J., Wells, W.M., Frangi, A.F. (eds.) MICCAI 2015. LNCS, vol. 9351, pp. 234–241. Springer, Cham (2015). https://doi.org/10.1007/978-3-319-24574-4_28

28. Sheng, Z., Yuliang, L., Lianwen, J., Canjie, L.: Feature enhancement network: a refined scene text detector. In: Proceedings of AAAI (2018)

29. Shi, B., Bai, X., Belongie, S.: Detecting oriented text in natural images by linking segments. In: Proceedings of The IEEE Conference on Computer Vision and Pattern Recognition (CVPR), July 2017

30. Shi, B., Bai, X., Yao, C.: An end-to-end trainable neural network for image-based sequence recognition and its application to scene text recognition. IEEE Trans. Pattern Anal. Mach. Intell. **39**(11), 2298–2304 (2017)

31. Shi, B., Yang, M., Wang, X., Lyu, P., Yao, C., Bai, X.: ASTER: an attentional scene text recognizer with flexible rectification. IEEE Trans. Pattern Anal. Mach. Intell. (2018)

32. Shrivastava, A., Gupta, A., Girshick, R.: Training region-based object detectors with online hard example mining, pp. 761–769 (2016)

33. Simonyan, K., Zisserman, A.: Very deep convolutional networks for large-scale image recognition. arXiv preprint arXiv:1409.1556 (2014)

34. Tian, S., Lu, S., Li, C.: WeText: scene text detection under weak supervision. In: Proceedings of The IEEE International Conference on Computer Vision (ICCV) (2017)

35. Wolf, C., Jolion, J.M.: Object count/area graphs for the evaluation of object detection and segmentation algorithms. Int. J. Doc. Anal. Recognit. (IJDAR) **8**(4), 280–296 (2006)

36. Wu, Y., Natarajan, P.: Self-organized text detection with minimal post-processing via border learning. In: Proceedings of The IEEE Conference on Computer Vision and Pattern Recognition (CVPR), pp. 5000–5009 (2017)

37. Yao, C., Bai, X., Liu, W.: A unified framework for multioriented text detection and recognition. IEEE Trans. Image Process. **23**(11), 4737–4749 (2014)

38. Yao, C., Bai, X., Liu, W., Ma, Y., Tu, Z.: Detecting texts of arbitrary orientations in natural images. In: Proceedings of The IEEE Conference on Computer Vision and Pattern Recognition (CVPR), pp. 1083–1090. IEEE (2012)

39. Yao, C., Bai, X., Sang, N., Zhou, X., Zhou, S., Cao, Z.: Scene text detection via holistic, multi-channel prediction. arXiv preprint arXiv:1606.09002 (2016)

40. Yao, C., Bai, X., Shi, B., Liu, W.: Strokelets: a learned multi-scale representation for scene text recognition. In: Proceedings of the IEEE Conference on Computer Vision and Pattern Recognition, pp. 4042–4049 (2014)

41. Ye, Q., Doermann, D.: Text detection and recognition in imagery: a survey. IEEE Trans. Pattern Anal. Mach. Intell. **37**(7), 1480–1500 (2015)

42. Yin, X.C., Yin, X., Huang, K., Hao, H.W.: Robust text detection in natural scene images. IEEE Trans. Pattern Anal. Mach. Intell. **36**(5), 970–983 (2014)

43. Yuliang, L., Lianwen, J., Shuaitao, Z., Sheng, Z.: Detecting curve text in the wild: new dataset and new solution. arXiv preprint arXiv:1712.02170 (2017)

44. Zeiler, M.D., Krishnan, D., Taylor, G.W., Fergus, R.: Deconvolutional networks. In: Proceedings of The IEEE Conference on Computer Vision and Pattern Recognition (CVPR), pp. 2528–2535 (2010)

45. Zhang, Z., Shen, W., Yao, C., Bai, X.: Symmetry-based text line detection in natural scenes. In: Proceedings of the IEEE Conference on Computer Vision and Pattern Recognition, pp. 2558–2567 (2015)

46. Zhang, Z., Zhang, C., Shen, W., Yao, C., Liu, W., Bai, X.: Multi-oriented text detection with fully convolutional networks. In: Proceedings of the IEEE Conference on Computer Vision and Pattern Recognition (CVPR), pp. 4159–4167 (2016)

47. Zhou, X., et al.: EAST: an efficient and accurate scene text detector. In: Proceedings of The IEEE Conference on Computer Vision and Pattern Recognition (CVPR), July 2017

48. Zhu, Y., Yao, C., Bai, X.: Scene text detection and recognition: recent advances and future trends. Front. Comput. Sci. **10**(1), 19–36 (2016)

Graph Adaptive Knowledge Transfer for Unsupervised Domain Adaptation

Zhengming Ding[1,2(✉)], Sheng Li[3], Ming Shao[4], and Yun Fu[5]

[1] Department of Electrical and Computer Engineering, Northeastern University,
Boston, USA
zmding.iupui@gmail.com
[2] Department of CIT, Indiana University-Purdue University Indianapolis,
Indianapolis, USA
[3] Department of Computer Science, University of Georgia, Athens, USA
shengli.uga@gmail.com
[4] Department of CIS, University of Massachusetts Dartmouth, Dartmouth, USA
mshao@umassd.edu
[5] College of Computer and Information Science, Northeastern University,
Boston, USA
yunfu@ece.neu.edu

Abstract. Unsupervised domain adaptation has caught appealing attentions as it facilitates the unlabeled target learning by borrowing existing well-established source domain knowledge. Recent practice on domain adaptation manages to extract effective features by incorporating the pseudo labels for the target domain to better solve cross-domain distribution divergences. However, existing approaches separate target label optimization and domain-invariant feature learning as different steps. To address that issue, we develop a novel Graph Adaptive Knowledge Transfer (GAKT) model to jointly optimize target labels and domain-free features in a unified framework. Specifically, semi-supervised knowledge adaptation and label propagation on target data are coupled to benefit each other, and hence the marginal and conditional disparities across different domains will be better alleviated. Experimental evaluation on two cross-domain visual datasets demonstrates the effectiveness of our designed approach on facilitating the unlabeled target task learning, compared to the state-of-the-art domain adaptation approaches.

Keywords: Domain adaptation · Adaptive graph
Semi-supervised learning

1 Introduction

In the real-world applications, there often exists a challenge that we can get access to the abundant target data but with limited or even no labels [1,2]. However, it would be extremely time-consuming and expensive to manually annotate the data. Domain adaptation has shown appealing performance in handling such

ⓒ Springer Nature Switzerland AG 2018
V. Ferrari et al. (Eds.): ECCV 2018, LNCS 11206, pp. 36–52, 2018.
https://doi.org/10.1007/978-3-030-01216-8_3

a challenge through knowledge transfer from an external well-established source domain, which lies in a different distribution from the target domain [3–12]. The mechanism of domain adaptation is to uncover the common latent factors across source and target domains, and adopt them to reduce both the marginal and conditional mismatch in terms of the feature space between domains. Following this, different domain adaptation techniques have been developed, including feature alignment and classifier adaptation (Fig. 1).

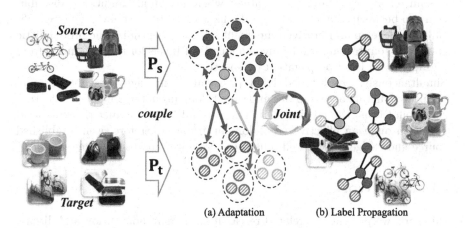

(a) Adaptation   (b) Label Propagation

Fig. 1. Illustration of our proposed algorithm, where source and target domains are lying in different distributions under the original feature space. We jointly seek two coupled projections $P_{s/t}$ to map the original data to a domain-invariant space. (a) A semi-supervised class-wise adaptation strategy is proposed via assigning every target data point with a probabilistic label. (b) When source and target data have smaller domain mismatch, graph-based label propagation strategy could assign target labels more accurately.

Recent research efforts on domain adaptation have already witnessed appealing performance via learning effective domain-invariant features from two different domains, such that source knowledge could be adapted to facilitate the recognition task in target domain [3,5,7,8,10–19]. Among them, Maximum Mean Discrepancy (MMD) [20] is one of the most widely used strategies to measure the distribution difference between source and target domains [3,7,10,16,21]. Later on, many domain adaptation approaches were proposed to design a revised class-wise MMD by incorporating the pseudo labels of target data. Those algorithms target at iteratively assigning temporal labels for the target samples and then further refining the class-wise domain adaptation regularizer. However, all the existing methods optimize the target labels in a separate step along with the domain-invariant feature learning. Thus, they may fail to benefit each other in an effective manner.

In this paper, we develop an effective Graph Adaptive Knowledge Transfer (GAKT) framework by unifying domain-invariant feature learning and target label optimization into a joint learning framework. The key idea is to jointly optimize the probabilistic class-wise adaptation term and the graph-based label propagation in a semi-supervised scheme. Thus, two procedures could benefit each other for promising knowledge transfer. To our best knowledge, this would be the first work to jointly model knowledge transfer and label propagation in a unified framework. To sum up, we have two-fold contributions as follows:

- We attempt to seek a domain-invariant feature space by designing a domain/class-wise adaptation strategy, where marginal/conditional distribution gap between source and target domains could be both leveraged. Specifically, we develop an iterative refinement scheme to optimize the probabilistic class-wise adaptation term by involving the soft labels for target samples from a graph-based label propagation perspective.
- Simultaneously, graph-based label propagation manages to capture more intrinsic structure across source and target domains in the domain-free feature space, and thus, the labeled source data could better predict the unlabeled target through an effective cross-domain graph. Therefore, well-established source knowledge can be well reused to recognize unlabeled target samples.

2   Related Work

In this part, we present the related research on domain adaptation and discuss the difference between our method and others.

Domain adaptation has been shown as an attractive approach in lots of real-world applications when we have sparsely or none label information for the target domain [2]. Specifically, domain adaptation attempts to enhance the target learning by borrowing the labeled source knowledge, which is lying in the different distributions with the target domain. For instance, we tend to take a picture with cellphone and search in the Amazon pool to recognize what is the object. Generally, there is a distribution gap between the cellphone picture (low resolution and complex background) and Amazon gallery images (clear background). Hence, the core challenge turns to adapting any one domain or both domains to reduce the distribution mismatch.

Generally, domain adaptation techniques can be split into two different lines based on the accessibility of labeled information in the target domain, one is semi-supervised domain adaptation, and the other is unsupervised domain adaptation. For semi-supervised scenario [22,23], we are accessible to a small amount of labeled target data, which makes the domain adaptation easier. A more challenge case is unsupervised domain adaptation [3,24], in which we aim to deal with totally unlabeled target domain. Thus, unsupervised domain adaptation attracts more attention. Along this line, domain-invariant feature learning and classifier adaption are two strategies to fight off unsupervised domain adaptation. Specifically, domain-invariant feature learning includes traditional subspace learning [7,8,13,21,25–27] and deep learning methods [5,19,28,29]. Among them, subspace-based domain adaptation approaches have been verified with promising results by aligning two different domains into a domain-invariant low-dimensional feature space. Deep domain adaption methods aim to seek an end-to-end deep architecture to jointly mitigate the domain shift and seek a general classifier. Besides, subspace-based domain adaptation can still improve the adaptation ability over deep domain adaptation with the effective deep features, e.g., DeCAF features.

Hence, we equip subspace learning technique to address marginal/conditional divergences across two different domains. Meanwhile a cross-domain graph built on the source and target would better transfer the label information by capturing the intrinsic structure in the shared space. Specifically, label propagation [30,31] would be jointly unified into the domain-invariant feature learning framework to refine the class-wise adaption term, which would benefit the effective feature learning. That is being said, the soft labels and their probability are not only needed, but also effective. This is the most significant difference compared to the existing works. More interestingly, we can adapt the newly designed loss function to deep architecture to fine-tune the network parameters in a unified deep domain adaption framework [18,32].

3   The Proposed Algorithm

Given a labeled source domain with n_s data points and feature dimension d from C categories: $\{X_s, Y_s\} = \{(x_{s,1}, y_{s,1}), \cdots, (x_{s,n_s}, y_{s,n_s})\}$ in which $x_{s,i} \in \mathbb{R}^d$ is the feature vector while $y_{s,i} \in \mathbb{R}^C$ is its corresponding one-hot label vector. Define X_t as an unlabeled target domain with n_t data points, i.e., $X_t = \{x_{t,1}, \cdots, x_{t,n_t}\}$, in which $x_{t,i} \in \mathbb{R}^d$. In the domain adaptation problem, source and target domains shall have the consistent label information and the goal is to recognize the unlabeled target samples.

Since source and target samples are distributed in different feature spaces, i.e., $X_s \subsetneq \text{span}(X_t)$, we devote to seek a latent common space shared across source and target domains through two coupled projections $P_{s/t} \in \mathbb{R}^{d \times p}$. p is the dimension of the low-dimensional space ($p \ll d$). In this way, the domain shift between source and target could be well addressed, and hence, the discriminative knowledge within well-established source could be reused to facilitate the unlabeled target classification.

3.1   Motivation

Existing transfer subspace learning approaches [3,10,13] iteratively predict pseudo labels of the target data through classifiers, e.g., support vector machines (SVM). Most recently, Hou et al. improved the performance through further refining the pseudo labels using label propagation after initial labels from classifiers [7]. Moreover, Yan et al. explored a weighted MMD to account for class weight bias and enhance domain adaptation performance [12]. However, they built the revised MMD by assigning each target data point with only a single specific label. This could hurt the knowledge transfer since target samples might be predicted wrongly in the beginning. Moreover, when target samples from two classes have overlap distribution, it would easily undermine the intrinsic structure within the data by assigning only one hard label to those samples.

Another phenomenon is that we could acquire better target label prediction performance with more iterations during model optimization. Hence, the label probability to the true class for the unlabeled target samples would be triggered to a higher level. When we predict target data with inaccurate labels, they are unable to contribute during the designed class-wise adaptation term. For those reasons, we consider each target sample could be assigned to the entire label pool but with different probabilities, which we refer to as "soft label". In another word, although the label probability to the true class is a little bit lower in the early stage, it could still benefit the label propagation stage. To further extract effective features, we design an effective probabilistic class-wise adaptation regularizer to convey knowledge transfer by capturing the intrinsic structure of target domain. On the other hand, the label propagation turns out to be more effective with more discriminative domain-invariant features. Finally, these two strategies tend to trigger and benefit each other during the model optimization, which could also be formulated into the unified perspective of multi-view representation [2].

3.2   Probabilistic Class-Wise Domain Adaptation

We first go over the empirical Maximum Mean Discrepancy (MMD) [3], a widely used approach to alleviating marginal distribution disparity. MMD actually contrasts various distributions through the sample mean distance across two domains under the projected feature space, namely

$$\mathcal{M}(P_s, P_t) = \left\| \frac{1}{n_s} \sum_{i=1}^{n_s} P_s^\top x_{s,i} - \frac{1}{n_t} \sum_{j=1}^{n_t} P_t^\top x_{t,j} \right\|_2^2 = \left\| \frac{P_s^\top X_s \mathbf{1}_{n_s}}{n_s} - \frac{P_t^\top X_t \mathbf{1}_{n_t}}{n_t} \right\|_2^2,$$

(1)

in which $x_{s/t,i/j}$ denotes the i/j-th sample of $X_{s/t}$ while $\mathbf{1}_{n_{s/t}}$ is an all one column vector with size of $n_{s/t}$.

Such an MMD strategy in Eq. (1) is capable of reducing the disparity of the marginal distributions, but it fails to approach the conditional distribution divergence of two domains. In classification problems, it is essential to reduce the conditional distribution mismatch between two different domains. When target samples are completely not annotated, alignment of the conditional distributions becomes nontrivial, even through exploring sufficient statistics of the distributions. To that end, we develop a probabilistic class-wise adaptation formula to effectively guide the intrinsic knowledge transfer. In this way, the predicted soft labels for the target samples could also benefit the domain alignment as well even when little knowledge of them can be accessible at the beginning.

Suppose $F_t^j \in \mathbb{R}^c$ as the probabilistic label to the j-th target data point, in which every element $f_t^{(c,j)}$ ($f_t^{(c,j)} \geq 0$ and $\sum_{c=1}^C f_t^{(c,j)} = 1$) means the probability for the j-th unlabeled target data point belonging to the c-th category. In other words, each target sample partially contributes to various classes during label prediction. For instance, the "computer" will be most likely linked to the "monitor", rather than "mug", because computers and monitors look more visually similar. Hence, such probabilities and linkage between different concepts would pave the way for the label propagation.

To promote the usage of soft labels in multiple classes and thus address the conditional distribution divergences across two domains, we bring forward the probabilistic labels to the MMD modeling and design a novel weighted class-wise adaption loss function as follows:

$$
\begin{aligned}
\mathcal{C}(P_s, P_t, F_t) &= \sum_{c=1}^{C} \left\| \frac{1}{n_s^c} \sum_{i=1}^{n_s^c} P_s^\top x_{s,i}^c - \frac{1}{n_t^c} \sum_{j=1}^{n_t} f_t^{(c,j)} P_t^\top x_{t,j} \right\|_2^2, \\
&= \| P_s^\top X_s Y_s N_s - P_t^\top X_t F_t N_t \|_F^2,
\end{aligned}
\tag{2}
$$

in which $\|\cdot\|_F$ indicates the Frobenius norm and n_s^c means the source sample size of the c-th class. n_t^c denotes the target sample size for the c-th category, which is neither an integer nor directly provided (We cannot obtain the true target sample size of each class). Thus, we approximately compute the n_t^c by $n_t^c = \sum_{j=1}^{n_t} f_t^{(c,j)}$. Note, $N_{s/t} \in \mathbb{R}^{C \times C}$ are diagonal matrices with the c-th diagonal element as $\frac{1}{n_{s/t}^c}$. In fact, our probabilistic class-wise adaptation term (Eq. (2)) is able to fight off the impact of class weight bias, by considering prior category distributions.

The above Eqs. (1) and (2) learn two domain-specific projections individually, and we also want to mitigate the discrepancy across different domains via constraining the source and target projections similar. Along with this line, an auxiliary mapping function M was explored to link the source projection with the target one, i.e., $\|P_s - MP_t\|_F^2$ [33,34], while Zhang et al. jointly optimized them and adopted $\|P_s - P_t\|_F^2$ to preserve the source discriminative information and the target variance [35]. However, they ignored the domain-specific parts and focused on the domain-shared projection bases. In this paper, we consider both uncovering more shared bases across source and target domains, and preserving the domain-specific bases, and thus, we explore $l_{2,1}$-norm to constrain two projections, i.e., $\|P_s - P_t\|_{2,1}$. By integrating Eq. (1), Eq. (2), and projection alignment, we have the objective with constraints $P_s^\top X_s H_s X_s^\top P_s = I_p$ and $P_t^\top X_t H_t X_t^\top P_t = I_p$:

$$
\mathcal{D}(P_s, P_t, F) = \| P_s^\top X_s \bar{Y}_s \bar{N}_s - P_t^\top X_t \bar{F}_t \bar{N}_t \|_F^2 + \alpha \| P_s - P_t \|_{2,1}, \tag{3}
$$

where $\bar{Y}_s = [\mathbf{1}_{n_s}, Y_s]$, $\bar{F}_t = [\mathbf{1}_{n_t}, F_t]$, and $\bar{N}_{s/t} = \mathbf{diag}(\frac{1}{n_{s/t}}, N_{s/t})$, $H_{s/t} = I_{n_{s/t}} - \frac{1}{n_{s/t}} \mathbf{I}_{n_{s/t}}$ denotes the centering matrix while $\mathbf{I}_{n_{s/t}}$ means the $n \times n_{s/t}$ matrix of ones. As discussed in [3,7], such a constraint would help keep the data variance after adaptation, which further brings in additional data discriminating ability during the learning of $P_{s/t}$.

3.3   Joint Knowledge Transfer and Label Propagation

Suppose $\mathbf{G}$ is an undirected graph defined on the mixture of the source and target with $n = n_s + n_t$ samples and W is its corresponding weight matrix. We could model a smooth Label Propagation through the graph Laplacian regularization [30,31,36]:

$$\min_F \mathrm{tr}(F^\top L F), \quad \text{s.t.} \quad F_s = Y_s, \quad F \geq 0. \tag{4}$$

where $F = [F_s; F_t] \in \mathbb{R}^{n \times C}$ and $L = W - D \in \mathbb{R}^{n \times n}$ represents the graph Laplacian [31,36–38]. Meanwhile, D denotes a diagonal matrix with the diagonal entries as the column sums of W. Specifically,

$$L = \begin{bmatrix} L_{ss}, L_{st} \\ L_{ts}, L_{tt} \end{bmatrix} = \begin{bmatrix} W_{ss} - D_{ss}, & W_{st} \\ W_{ts}, & W_{tt} - D_{tt} \end{bmatrix},$$

where $W_{st} = W_{ts}^\top \in \mathbb{R}^{n_s \times n_t}$ is a weight matrix across source and target samples.

Note the above graph Laplacian shares the same learning target F_t, and we may merge the two learning problems and formulate the final learning objective for joint knowledge adaption:

$$\min_{P_s, P_t, F} \|P_s^\top X_s \bar{Y}_s \bar{N}_s - P_t^\top X_t \bar{F}_t \bar{N}_t\|_F^2 + \alpha \|P_s - P_t\|_{2,1} + \lambda \mathrm{tr}(F^\top L F),$$
$$\text{s.t.} \quad P_{s/t}^\top X_{s/t} H_{s/t} X_{s/t}^\top P_{s/t} = I_p, \quad F \geq 0, \quad F\mathbf{1}_C = \mathbf{1}_n, \quad F_s = Y_s. \tag{5}$$

To deal with the constraint $F_t \mathbf{1}_C = \mathbf{1}_{n_t}$ efficiently, we relax the equality condition by incorporating a penalty regularizer $\gamma \|F_t \mathbf{1}_C - \mathbf{1}_{n_t}\|_2^2$ into the objective formula (Eq. (5)), in which γ is the positive penalty parameter.

Remark: Our proposed approach joints effective domain-free feature learning and target label propagation in a unified knowledge adaptation framework. Thus, it could benefit each other to improve the recognition for the target domains. With domain/class-wise adaption, the well-established source information is able to boost the target recognition. With domain shift mitigated, an effective graph across source and target could be built so that source labels are able to propagate the unlabeled target data. Meanwhile, when more accurate labels are assigned to the target data, probabilistic class-wise adaptation term could transfer more effective knowledge across two domains. Such an EM-like refinement will facilitate the knowledge transfer.

3.4   Optimization Solution

It is easy to check that P_s, P_t and F_t in Eq. (5) cannot be jointly optimized. To address this optimization problem, we first transform it into the augmented Lagrangian function by relaxing the non-negative constraint as:

$$\mathcal{J} = \|P_s^\top X_s \bar{Y}_s \bar{N}_s - P_t^\top X_t \bar{F}_t \bar{N}_t\|_F^2 + \alpha \|P_s - P_t\|_{2,1} + \lambda \mathrm{tr}(F^\top L F)$$
$$+ \gamma \|F_t \mathbf{1}_C - \mathbf{1}_{n_t}\|_2^2 + \mathrm{tr}(\Phi F_t^\top),$$
$$\text{s.t.} \quad P_{s/t}^\top X_{s/t} H_{s/t} X_{s/t}^\top P_{s/t} = I_p, \quad F_s = Y_s, \tag{6}$$

where Φ is the Lagrange multiplier for constraint $F_t \geq 0$. While it is difficult to jointly optimize F_t, P_s and P_t, it is solvable over each of them in a leave-one-out manner. Specifically, we explore an EM-like optimization scheme to update the variables. For **E-step**, we fix P_s, P_t and update F_t and N_t; while for **M-step**, we update the subspace projections P_s, P_t using the updated F_t, N_t. Hence, we optimize two sub-problems iteratively.

E-step: Label Propagation

Given two subspace projections P_s and P_t, we could insert $F_s = Y_s$ into $\text{tr}(F^\top LF)$ and get $\text{tr}(F_t^\top L_{tt}F_t + 2Y_s^\top L_{st}F_t)$. Thus, we obtain the partial derivative of $\mathcal{J}$ w.r.t. F_t, by setting it to zero as:

$$\frac{\partial \mathcal{J}}{\partial F_t} = 2(Z_t - Z_s) + 2\gamma(F_t \mathbf{1}_C - \mathbf{1}_{n_t})\mathbf{1}_C^\top + 2\lambda Q + \Phi = 0,$$

$$\text{where} \quad \begin{cases} Q = L_{tt}F_t + L_{st}^\top Y_s, \\ Z_s = X_s^\top P_s(P_s^\top X_s Y_s N_s)N_t, \\ Z_t = X_t^\top P_t(P_t^\top X_t F_t N_t)N_t. \end{cases} \tag{7}$$

Using the KKT conditions $\Phi \odot F_t = 0$ [39] ($\odot$ denotes the dot product of two matrices), we achieve the following equations for F_t:

$$\left[(Z_t - Z_s) + \gamma(F_t \mathbf{1}_C - \mathbf{1}_{n_t})\mathbf{1}_C^\top + \lambda Q \right] \odot F_t = -\Psi \odot F_t = 0.$$

Following [37], we obtain the updating rule:

$$F_t = F_t \odot \sqrt{\frac{[Z_t]^+ + [Z_s]^- + \mathcal{F}_W}{[Z_t]^- + [Z_s]^+ + \mathcal{F}_D}}, \tag{8}$$

where $\mathcal{F}_W = \gamma F_t \mathbf{1}_C^\top + \lambda(W_{tt}F_t + W_{st}^\top Y_s)$ and $\mathcal{F}_D = \gamma \mathbf{1}_{n_t}\mathbf{1}_C^\top + \lambda D_{tt}F_t$. Specifically, $[A]^+$ means the negative elements of the matrix A are replaced by 0. Similarly, $[A]^-$ denotes the positive elements of the matrix A are replaced by 0. When we achieve F_t, N_t can be updated accordingly.

M-step: Learning Subspace Projection

When F_t and N_t are optimized, we could update the subspace projection $P = [P_s, P_t]$ with the refined class-wise adaption term. Thus,

$$\begin{aligned} P &= \underset{P^\top SP = I_{2p}}{\arg\min} \; \|P_s^\top X_s \bar{Y}_s \bar{N}_s - P_t^\top X_t \bar{F}_t \bar{N}_t\|_F^2 + \alpha\|P_s - P_t\|_{2,1} \\ &= \underset{P^\top SP = I_{2p}}{\arg\min} \; \text{tr}(P^\top \mathbf{T}P) + \alpha\text{tr}(P^\top \mathbf{G}P), \end{aligned} \tag{9}$$

where

$$\mathbf{S} = \begin{bmatrix} X_s H_s X_s^\top, 0 \\ 0, X_t H_t^\top X_t \end{bmatrix} \mathbf{T} = \begin{bmatrix} X_s \bar{Y}_s \bar{N}_s \bar{N}_s^\top \bar{Y}_s^\top X_s^\top, & X_s \bar{Y}_s \bar{N}_s \bar{N}_t \bar{F}_t^\top X_t \\ X_t \bar{F}_t \bar{N}_t \bar{N}_s^\top \bar{Y}_s^\top X_s^\top, & X_t \bar{F}_t \bar{N}_t \bar{N}_t^\top \bar{F}_t^\top X_t \end{bmatrix} \mathbf{G} = \begin{bmatrix} G, -G \\ -G, G \end{bmatrix}$$

G is a $p \times p$ diagonal matrix with its i-th diagonal element as $G_{ii} = \frac{1}{\|\mathbf{p}_i\|_2}$ if $\mathbf{p}_i \neq 0$, otherwise $G_{ii} = 0$. $\mathbf{p}_i$ is the i-th row vector of $P_s - P_t$. Equation (9) could be addressed by a generalized Eigen-decomposition problem: $(\mathbf{T} + \alpha\mathbf{G})\rho = \eta S\rho$. The vectors ρ_i ($i \in [0, p-1]$) are obtained according to its minimum eigenvalues.

Thus, we achieve updated subspace projection $P = [\rho_0, \cdots, \rho_{p-1}]$. After we achieve P_s and P_t, we could optimize G.

By alternating the **E** and **M** steps detailed above, we will iteratively optimize the problem until the objective function becomes converged. What is noteworthy is that, we could generally obtain a probabilistic labeling for the unlabeled target samples with two effective coupled projections. Thus, if we exploit such a label assignment strategy (Eq. (8)) to improve the projection discriminability (Eq. (9)) in an iterative fashion, we are able to alternatively enhance the labeling quality and feature learning. For initialization of F_t, we adopt Label Propagation (Eq. (4)) from L built on original features of source and target domains. Furthermore, we can further achieve the partial derivatives with respect to X, i.e., $\frac{\partial \mathcal{J}}{\partial X}$, and then conduct the standard back propagation strategy to optimize the convolutional neural network weights.

3.5   Time Complexity

In this section, we analyze the model complexity for our approach. There are two main time-consuming components: (1) Non-negative F_t optimization (Step 1); (2) Subspace projection learning (Step 2).

In detail, the major time-consuming terms in non-negative F_t optimization are matrix multiplications in **Step 1**. Generally, the multiplication for matrix with the size $n_t \times n_t$ could cost $\mathcal{O}(n_t^3)$. Suppose there are l multiplication operations, thus, **Step 1** would cost $\mathcal{O}(l n_t^3)$. **Step 2** could cost $\mathcal{O}(d^3)$ for the generalized Eigen-decomposition of Eq. (9) for matrices with size of $\mathbb{R}^{d \times d}$, which could be reduced to $\mathcal{O}(d^{2.376})$ through the Coppersmith-Winograd method [40]. Furthermore, we can speed up the operations of large matrices through a sparse matrix, and state-of-the-art divide-and-conquer approaches. Meanwhile, we could also store some intermediate computation results which could be reused in every stage.

4   Experiments

In this part, we first illustrate the benchmarks as well as the experimental settings, and then present the comparative evaluations with existing domain adaptation approaches, further with some property analysis.

4.1   Datasets and Experimental Setting

Office-31+Caltech256[1] consists of 10 common categories from Office-31 and Caltech-256 benchmarks, with 3 subsets (Amazon, Webcam, and DSLR) from Office-31 and one from Caltech-256, respectively. Note that Amazon and Caltech-256 images are collected online with a clear background, while Webcam and DSLR images are taken from office environments with different devices. For a

---

[1] http://www-scf.usc.edu/~boqinggo/domainadaptation.html.

fair comparison, we utilize the 4096-dim DeCAF^6 feature and adopt the full-sample protocol provided by [24] in unsupervised domain adaptation.

Office+Home[2] [18] contains 4 domains, each with 65 categories' daily objects. Specifically, Art denotes artistic depictions for object images; Clipart means picture collection of clipart; Product shows object images with a clear background, similar to Amazon category in Office-31; Real-World represents object images collected with a regular camera. We adopt deep features of the fc_7 layer in the VGG-F model, pre-trained using the ImageNet 2012 [18].

We mainly compare with six state-of-the-art shallow domain adaptation approaches to evaluate the effectiveness of our algorithm as follows: Geodesic Flow Kernel (GFK) [24], Joint Distribution Adaptation (JDA) [3], Closest Common Space Learning (CCSL) [16], Label Structural Consistency (LSC) [7], Joint Geometrical and Statistical Alignment (JGSA) [35] and Probabilistic Unsupervised Domain Adaptation (PUnDA) [11]. Moreover, Label Propagation (LP) [30] is adopted as a baseline, which directly builds a graph on original features across source and target domains. For LP and our model, we both adopt k-nearest neighbor graph ($k = 5$ in our experiment) with heat-kernel weight [30]. We further compare to several deep domain adaptation models, i.e., DAN [32], DHN [18] and WDAN [12], to show the superiority of our model. Specifically, we adopt the VGG-F structure for these three methods in terms of fair comparison. Also, we cite the results reported by other publications when the experimental settings are exactly the same, or run available source codes under other settings.

In all our experiments, we adopt k-nearest neighbor graph ($k = 5$ in our experiment) with heat-kernel weight [30]. We set $\lambda = 10$, $\alpha = 0.1$, and $\gamma = 10^4$ in our experiments to guarantee the sum of each soft label to be 1. We adopt the top-1 classification accuracy for the unlabeled target sample as the evaluation metric.

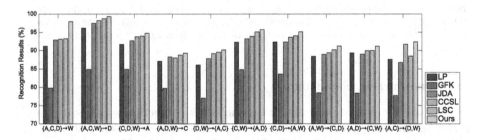

Fig. 2. Recognition rates of 6 approaches on Office-31+Caltech-256, where A = Amazon, C = Caltech-256, D = DSLR and W = Webcam.

---

[2] https://hemanthdv.github.io/officehome-dataset/.

Table 1. Recognition rates (%) of 11 algorithms on Office-31+Caltech-256, where A = Amazon, C = Caltech-256, D = DSLR and W = Webcam.

Methods \S→T	C→W	C→D	C→A	W→C	W→A	W→D	A→C	A→W	A→D	D→C	D→W	D→A
LP [30]	80.34	93.63	92.07	78.63	80.82	97.38	86.62	80.36	93.63	85.49	**100.00**	91.23
GFK [24]	75.08	83.06	87.65	77.38	84.25	99.30	79.07	76.68	79.43	80.41	79.70	84.96
JDA [3]	85.08	90.36	87.65	83.64	87.02	**100.00**	86.33	83.78	88.54	83.88	97.98	90.28
CCSL [16]	82.37	87.90	93.32	82.90	89.98	96.18	87.18	83.05	87.26	84.06	96.27	90.92
LSC [7]	91.18	95.26	94.28	87.97	93.31	**100.00**	87.88	88.81	94.90	86.19	99.32	92.37
RTML [10]	92.46	92.36	90.26	84.65	87.92	**100.00**	86.86	84.68	90.26	84.62	98.26	90.82
JGSA [35]	85.08	92.36	91.75	84.68	91.44	**100.00**	85.04	84.75	85.35	85.75	98.64	92.28
PUnDA [11]	86.76	90.98	93.12	83.28	89.06	99.16	86.64	82.86	85.86	83.48	98.24	89.24
DAN [32]	92.64	90.52	92.03	81.53	92.13	**100.00**	86.05	91.82	91.74	82.04	98.55	90.02
WDAN [12]	93.67	93.48	93.11	84.12	92.87	**100.00**	86.93	**92.26**	92.87	83.92	99.28	91.87
Ours	**95.36**	**96.42**	**95.12**	**88.84**	**93.84**	**100.00**	**88.46**	90.18	**95.48**	86.82	**100.00**	**93.98**

Table 2. Recognition accuracies (%) for cross-domain experiments on Office+Home, where Art (Ar), Product (Pr), Real-World (Rw), and Clipart (Cl).

Config	Ar→Cl	Ar→Pr	Ar→Rw	Cl→Ar	Cl→Pr	Cl→Rw	Pr→Ar	Pr→Cl	Pr→Rw	Rw→Ar	Rw→Cl	Rw→Pr
LP [30]	20.36	36.32	30.24	28.37	36.32	32.28	23.32	28.25	43.23	30.28	30.24	52.38
GFK [24]	21.60	31.72	38.83	21.63	34.94	34.20	24.52	25.73	42.92	32.88	28.96	50.89
JDA [3]	25.34	35.98	42.94	24.52	40.19	40.90	25.96	32.72	49.25	35.10	35.35	55.35
CCSL [16]	23.51	34.12	40.02	22.54	35.69	36.04	24.84	27.09	46.36	34.61	31.75	52.89
LSC [7]	31.81	39.42	50.25	35.46	51.19	51.43	30.46	39.54	59.74	43.98	42.88	62.25
RTML [10]	27.57	36.20	46.09	29.49	44.69	44.66	28.21	36.12	52.99	38.54	40.62	57.80
JGSA [35]	28.81	37.57	48.92	31.67	46.30	46.76	28.72	35.90	54.473	40.61	40.83	59.16
PUnDA [11]	29.99	37.76	50.17	33.90	48.91	48.71	30.31	38.69	56.91	42.25	44.51	61.05
DAN [32]	30.66	42.17	54.13	32.83	47.59	49.78	29.07	34.05	56.70	43.58	38.25	62.73
DHN [18]	31.64	40.75	51.73	34.69	51.93	52.79	29.91	39.63	60.71	44.99	**45.13**	62.54
WDAN [12]	32.26	43.16	54.98	34.28	49.92	50.26	30.82	38.27	56.87	44.32	39.35	63.34
Ours	**34.49**	**43.63**	**55.28**	**36.14**	**52.74**	**53.16**	**31.59**	**40.55**	**61.43**	**45.64**	44.58	**64.92**

4.2   Comparison Experiments

First of all, we evaluate our algorithm and other competitors with source and target as one single subset. Tables 1 and 2 list the comparison results of 12 different cases based on Office-31+Caltech-256 and Office+Home, respectively. From the performance, we notice that our proposed approach works better than other baselines across almost all the cases. Especially in two cases, our model achieves 100% accuracy. Also in several tasks, e.g., $C \to W$, the performance of our proposed algorithm is 3% higher than the state-of-the-art approaches.

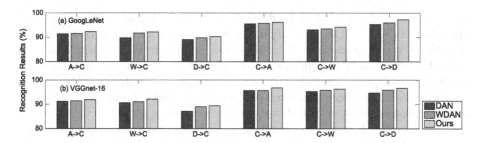

Fig. 3. Recognition rates of 3 approaches on two deep features (a) GoogLeNet and (b) VGGnet-16 from Office-31+Caltech-256, where A = Amazon, C = Caltech-256, D = DSLR, and W = Webcam.

Secondly, we explore the evaluation on knowledge transfer with multiple sub-domains. Figure 2 lists the comparison results from different methods on various imbalanced cross-domain combinations. For x-axis in Fig. 2, either domain consists of multiple sub-domain data, and complete results of different approaches are listed. From these results, we see our approach works favorably against state-of-the-art unsupervised domain adaptation algorithms.

Discussion: LP could work well in some cases when the distribution differences of two domains are not large, e.g., $D \rightarrow W$, $W \rightarrow D$, $A \rightarrow C$ and $C \rightarrow A$. However, it cannot achieve appealing performance in some challenging tasks, e.g., $C \rightarrow W$. While our approach could even improve by 18.9% in $C \rightarrow W$, which verifies the effectiveness of our approach. Another thing is that deep features pre-trained on large-scale dataset could mitigate the domain shift somehow, especially for different resolutions.

CCSL is designed for the imbalanced domain transfer, by associating such data to the capability of keeping discriminative and structural information within and across domains. However, it is too specific and not general. From the performance, we witness that our algorithm is able to consistently outperform CCSL. JDA and RTML both adopt pseudo labels of the target sample from a specific classier to refine the class-wise adaptation term. In this way, every target sample is assigned to a single label, which may bring in problems when they are assigned with wrong labels. RTML further explores the marginal denoising reconstruction, and thus achieves better results than JDA.

Besides, LSC adopts a specific classifier to initialize the pseudo labels of the target, and then refines the labels through label propagation on a cross-domain graph. However, it still considers the hard labels of the target data to build the class-wise adaptation. Most importantly, such label prediction and feature learning are separately learned for JDA, RTML and LSC. Compared with these methods, we manage to conduct joint feature learning and label propagation to benefit each other for more effective knowledge transfer. Compared with [7], while the two models share certain spirits, our method concentrates on building a joint UDA learning model. The model in [7], however, designs a separate label propagation after feature alignment, which may hinder the knowledge transfer.

In addition, [7] still feeds the hard labels back to optimize feature adaption, which strictly follows the conventional semi-supervised learning. However, we introduce the soft labels as well as class-wise adaption strategy which is well integrated with the label propagation framework. That is being said, the soft labels and their probability are not only needed, but also effective. This is the most significant difference compared to the existing works. From the results, we notice that our model performs better in all the cases.

Moreover, JGSA also seeks two linear projections that transform source and target data into a low-dimensional domain-invariant space in which the geometrical and distribution shift are mitigated jointly. However, it does not consider the class-wise adaptation to mitigate the conditional distribution difference. Similarly, PUnDA also seeks linear transformations per domain to project data into a shared space, which jointly reduces the domain mismatch while improving the classifier's discriminability.

Deep domain adaptation methods manage to simultaneously build deep architectures and conduct knowledge transfer. From our results, we notice that such a joint learning strategy could benefit the performance when comparing with several traditional linear transfer learning models. However, our model could further outperform those deep domain adaptation models, i.e., DAN, DHN, WDAN, which indicates that two separate steps in our pipeline can also adapt knowledge across different domains. Specifically, upon advanced deep features, our model is able to further improve the performance, which primarily stems from our probabilistic class-wise adaptation scheme to explore the intrinsic structure of the data during knowledge transfer. Moreover, traditional deep domain adaptation approaches always adopt a pre-trained model, which is similar to the case that we directly work on the deep features. The difference is that we only fine-tune the final layer. From our experimental results, we find knowledge transfer part plays a key role in successful domain adaptation, while fine-tuning deep structure parameters influences slightly on the final performance. To verify this point, we further evaluate our model with deep domain adaptation in different architectures, i.e., GoogLeNet [41] and VGGnet-16 [42]. Our model adopts the features generated from GoogLeNet and VGG-16, and their dimensionality are 1024 and 4096, respectively. The experimental results are provided in Fig. 3, where we witness that the proposed approach still obtains better performance than deep domain adaptation models.

Finally, we notice that the performances of all the algorithms on Office+Home are much lower than Office-31+Caltech256, due to the fact that there are more categories and more samples in Office+Home.

4.3 Empirical Evaluation

In this part, we present the convergence analysis, influence of parameters, and dimensionality of two coupled projections.

First of all, we testify the convergence of our proposed model. The cross-domain task $C \rightarrow A$ on Office-31+Caltech256 is adopted for evaluation. The convergence curve is shown in Fig. 4(a), where we could observe that our approach converges very well.

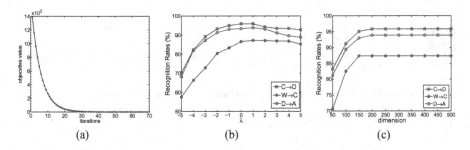

(a)   (b)   (c)

Fig. 4. (a) Convergence curve for our proposed approach. (b) Parameter analysis of λ, where the values of x-axis use log() to rescale the length. (c) The influence of different dimensions for $P_{s/t}$.

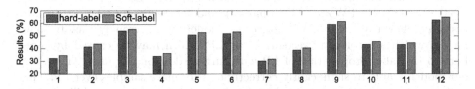

Fig. 5. Recognition accuracies (%) for domain adaptation experiments 12 cross-domain tasks (listed in Table 2) on the Office+Home dataset.

Secondly, we evaluate the influence of parameter λ and show the recognition results at various values in Fig. 4(b), in which we notice that our model generates better performance across three different cases when $\lambda \in [1, 10]$. Generally, we set $\lambda = 10$ as default during the experiments.

Moreover, we verify the dimension property of P_s and P_t. In Fig. 4(c), we obtain an initially significant increase followed by a stable recognition performance, which denotes that our model works very well even when the data are lying in a low-dimensional space. Thus, we could verify that effective projections further enhance the knowledge transferability based on the deep features.

Finally, we aim to show that the proposed soft-label MMD is significantly superior to the hard-label MMD. Specifically, we do a post-processing for each F_t updating by transforming it to a zero-one matrix. We show the results of this variant and our proposed model on 12 cross-domain tasks (Office+Home datasets) in Fig. 5, where we notice that soft-label version could generally improve the performance over hard-label version 1–2%. On the other hand, we can also get a rough idea about the advantage of soft labels over the "hard" ones. For example, our model and LSC [7] used soft-label MMD and hard-label MMD, respectively, although both used label propagation. From the results, we already notice our model works better than LSC.

Furthermore, we visualize the soft labels F_t to show that our model could improve the label prediction through model optimization (An example is shown in Fig. 6). From the results, we notice that our approach could enhance the label prediction based on the original LP. That means our "soft label" would be

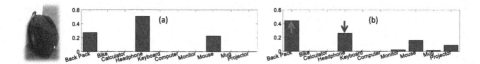

Fig. 6. The predicted soft label for "Back Pack" are learned by (a) original LP and (b) our proposed algorithm, where we notice that the probability of backpack category increases from 0.26 to 0.43 with our model.

optimized during the model training. We also offer statistics summarizing how many images are wrongly classified by LP [30] but are correctly classified by the proposed approach, and vice versa. Specifically, we evaluate on Office+Home database with 4 sets, i.e., Art (2411 samples); Clipart (4325 samples); Product (4341 samples); Real World (4308 samples), and the results for 12 cross-domain tasks are shown in Table 3. We notice our model would wrongly classify some images which are correctly recognized by LP, which may be caused by some hurt to the label propagation of LP with further domain alignment. However, our model is able to significantly correctly classify more samples over LP. This indicates our joint adaptation could enhance the label prorogation ability across different labeled source and unlabeled target domains.

Table 3. Statistics summarization. **Case 1**: how many images are wrongly classified by LP [30] but correctly classified by ours; **Case 2**: vice versa.

	Ar→Cl	Ar→Pr	Ar→Rw	Cl→Ar	Cl→Pr	Cl→Rw	Pr→Ar	Pr→Cl	Pr→Rw	Rw→Ar	Rw→Cl	Rw→Pr
Case 1	638	347	1109	203	739	907	227	533	795	372	624	87
Case 2	27	30	30	16	26	7	28	1	11	2	4	33

5 Conclusion

In this paper, we developed a novel Graph Adaptive Knowledge Transfer framework for unsupervised domain adaption. Specifically, we built a probabilistic class-wise adaptation term by assigning the target samples with multiple labels through graph-based label propagation. Meanwhile, two effective subspace projections were learned via the probabilistic class-wise adaption strategy so that intrinsic information across source and target could be preserved with the graph. In this way, accurate labels could be assigned to target samples with label propagation. These two strategies worked in an EM-like way to improve the unlabeled target recognition. Experiments on two cross-domain visual benchmarks verified the effectiveness of the designed algorithm over other state-of-the-art domain adaptation models, even deep domain adaptation ones.

Acknowledgment. This work is supported in part by the NSF IIS award 1651902, NIJ Graduate Research Fellowship 2016-R2-CX-0013, ONR Young Investigator Award N00014-14-1-0484, and U.S. Army Research Office Young Investigator Award W911NF-14-1-0218.

References

1. Patel, V.M., Gopalan, R., Li, R., Chellappa, R.: Visual domain adaptation: a survey of recent advances. IEEE Sig. Process. Mag. **32**(3), 53–69 (2015)
2. Ding, Z., Shao, M., Fu, Y.: Robust multi-view representation: a unified perspective from multi-view learning to domain adaption. In: IJCAI, pp. 5434–5440 (2018)
3. Long, M., Wang, J., Ding, G., Sun, J., Yu, P.S.: Transfer feature learning with joint distribution adaptation. In: ICCV, pp. 2200–2207 (2013)
4. Baktashmotlagh, M., Harandi, M.T., Lovell, B.C., Salzmann, M.: Unsupervised domain adaptation by domain invariant projection. In: ICCV, pp. 769–776 (2013)
5. Ding, Z., Shao, M., Fu, Y.: Deep low-rank coding for transfer learning. In: IJCAI, pp. 3453–3459 (2015)
6. Shao, M., Ding, Z., Zhao, H., Fu, Y.: Spectral bisection tree guided deep adaptive exemplar autoencoder for unsupervised domain adaptation. In: AAAI, pp. 2023–2029 (2016)
7. Hou, C.A., Tsai, Y.H.H., Yeh, Y.R., Wang, Y.C.F.: Unsupervised domain adaptation with label and structural consistency. IEEE TIP **25**(12), 5552–5562 (2016)
8. Tsai, Y.H.H., Hou, C.A., Chen, W.Y., Yeh, Y.R., Wang, Y.C.F.: Domain-constraint transfer coding for imbalanced unsupervised domain adaptation. In: AAAI, pp. 3597–3603 (2016)
9. Wei, P., Ke, Y., Goh, C.K.: Deep nonlinear feature coding for unsupervised domain adaptation. In: IJCAI, pp. 2189–2195 (2016)
10. Ding, Z., Fu, Y.: Robust transfer metric learning for image classification. IEEE TIP **26**(2), 660–670 (2017)
11. Gholami, B., (Oggi) Rudovic, O., Pavlovic, V.: PUnDA: probabilistic unsupervised domain adaptation for knowledge transfer across visual categories. In: ICCV, pp. 3581–3590 (2017)
12. Yan, H., Ding, Y., Li, P., Wang, Q., Xu, Y., Zuo, W.: Mind the class weight bias: weighted maximum mean discrepancy for unsupervised domain adaptation. In: CVPR, pp. 2272–2281 (2017)
13. Li, J., Zhao, J., Lu, K.: Joint feature selection and structure preservation for domain adaptation. In: IJCAI, pp. 1697–1703 (2016)
14. Liu, H., Shao, M., Ding, Z., Fu, Y.: Structure-preserved unsupervised domain adaptation. IEEE TKDE (2018). https://ieeexplore.ieee.org/document/8370901/
15. Ding, Z., Ming, S., Fu, Y.: Latent low-rank transfer subspace learning for missing modality recognition. In: AAAI, pp. 1192–1198 (2014)
16. Hsu, T.M.H., Chen, W.Y., Hou, C.A., Tsai, Y.H.H., Yeh, Y.R., Wang, Y.C.F.: Unsupervised domain adaptation with imbalanced cross-domain data. In: ICCV, pp. 4121–4129 (2015)
17. Herath, S., Harandi, M., Porikli, F.: Learning an invariant Hilbert space for domain adaptation. In: CVPR, pp. 3956–3965 (2017)
18. Venkateswara, H., Eusebio, J., Chakraborty, S., Panchanathan, S.: Deep hashing network for unsupervised domain adaptation. In: CVPR, pp. 5018–5027 (2017)
19. Zhang, W., Ouyang, W., Li, W., Xu, D.: Collaborative and adversarial network for unsupervised domain adaptation. In: CVPR, pp. 3801–3809 (2018)
20. Gretton, A., Borgwardt, K.M., Rasch, M., Schölkopf, B., Smola, A.J.: A kernel method for the two-sample-problem. In: NIPS, pp. 513–520 (2007)
21. Li, J., Lu, K., Huang, Z., Zhu, L., Shen, H.T.: Transfer independently together: a generalized framework for domain adaptation. IEEE TCYB (2018). https://ieeexplore.ieee.org/document/8337102/

22. Kumar, A., Saha, A., Daume, H.: Co-regularization based semi-supervised domain adaptation. In: NIPS, pp. 478–486 (2010)
23. Saenko, K., Kulis, B., Fritz, M., Darrell, T.: Adapting visual category models to new domains. In: Daniilidis, K., Maragos, P., Paragios, N. (eds.) ECCV 2010. LNCS, vol. 6314, pp. 213–226. Springer, Heidelberg (2010). https://doi.org/10.1007/978-3-642-15561-1_16
24. Gong, B., Shi, Y., Sha, F., Grauman, K.: Geodesic flow kernel for unsupervised domain adaptation. In: CVPR, pp. 2066–2073 (2012)
25. Shekhar, S., Patel, V., Nguyen, H., Chellappa, R.: Generalized domain-adaptive dictionaries. In: CVPR, pp. 361–368 (2013)
26. Shao, M., Kit, D., Fu, Y.: Generalized transfer subspace learning through low-rank constraint. IJCV 109(1–2), 74–93 (2014)
27. Li, S., Song, S., Huang, G., Ding, Z., Wu, C.: Domain invariant and class discriminative feature learning for visual domain adaptation. IEEE TIP 27(9), 4260–4273 (2018)
28. Ding, Z., Nasrabadi, N.M., Fu, Y.: Semi-supervised deep domain adaptation via coupled neural networks. IEEE TIP 27(11), 5214–5224 (2018)
29. Chen, Q., Liu, Y., Wang, Z., Wassell, I., Chetty, K.: Re-weighted adversarial adaptation network for unsupervised domain adaptation. In: CVPR, pp. 7976–7985 (2018)
30. Zhou, D., Bousquet, O., Lal, T.N., Weston, J., Schölkopf, B.: Learning with local and global consistency. NIPS 16(16), 321–328 (2004)
31. Wang, L., Ding, Z., Fu, Y.: Adaptive graph guided embedding for multi-label annotation. In: IJCAI, pp. 2798–2804 (2018)
32. Long, M., Cao, Y., Wang, J., Jordan, M.I.: Learning transferable features with deep adaptation networks. In: ICML, pp. 97–105 (2015)
33. Fernando, B., Habrard, A., Sebban, M., Tuytelaars, T.: Unsupervised visual domain adaptation using subspace alignment. In: ICCV, pp. 2960–2967 (2013)
34. Wang, S., Ding, Z., Fu, Y.: Coupled marginalized auto-encoders for cross-domain multi-view learning. In: IJCAI, pp. 2125–2131 (2016)
35. Zhang, J., Li, W., Ogunbona, P.: Joint geometrical and statistical alignment for visual domain adaptation. In: CVPR, pp. 1859–1867 (2017)
36. Nguyen, C.H., Mamitsuka, H.: Discriminative graph embedding for label propagation. IEEE TNN 22(9), 1395–1405 (2011)
37. Zhao, H., Ding, Z., Fu, Y.: Multi-view clustering via deep matrix factorization. In: AAAI, pp. 2921–2927 (2017)
38. Ding, Z., Shao, M., Fu, Y.: Deep robust encoder through locality preserving low-rank dictionary. In: Leibe, B., Matas, J., Sebe, N., Welling, M. (eds.) ECCV 2016. LNCS, vol. 9910, pp. 567–582. Springer, Cham (2016). https://doi.org/10.1007/978-3-319-46466-4_34
39. Kuhn, H.W.: Nonlinear programming: a historical view. In: Giorgi, G., Kjeldsen, T.H. (eds.) Traces and Emergence of Nonlinear Programming, pp. 393–414. Springer, Basel (2014). https://doi.org/10.1007/978-3-0348-0439-4_18
40. Coppersmith, D., Winograd, S.: Matrix multiplication via arithmetic progressions. In: ACM STOC, pp. 1–6 (1987)
41. Szegedy, C., et al.: Going deeper with convolutions. In: CVPR, pp. 1–9 (2015)
42. Simonyan, K., Zisserman, A.: Very deep convolutional networks for large-scale image recognition. arXiv preprint arXiv:1409.1556 (2014)

Robust Image Stitching with Multiple Registrations

Charles Herrmann[1], Chen Wang[1,2], Richard Strong Bowen[1], Emil Keyder[2],
Michael Krainin[3], Ce Liu[3], and Ramin Zabih[1,2(✉)]

[1] Cornell Tech, New York, NY 10044, USA
{cih,chenwang,rsb,rdz}@cs.cornell.edu
[2] Google Research, New York, NY 10011, USA
wangch@google.com, emilkeyder@google.com, raminz@google.com
[3] Google Research, Cambridge, MA 02142, USA
mkrainin@google.com, celiu@google.com

Abstract. Panorama creation is one of the most widely deployed techniques in computer vision. In addition to industry applications such as Google Street View, it is also used by millions of consumers in smartphones and other cameras. Traditionally, the problem is decomposed into three phases: registration, which picks a single transformation of each source image to align it to the other inputs, seam finding, which selects a source image for each pixel in the final result, and blending, which fixes minor visual artifacts [1,2]. Here, we observe that the use of a single registration often leads to errors, especially in scenes with significant depth variation or object motion. We propose instead the use of *multiple* registrations, permitting regions of the image at different depths to be captured with greater accuracy. MRF inference techniques naturally extend to seam finding over multiple registrations, and we show here that their energy functions can be readily modified with new terms that discourage duplication and tearing, common problems that are exacerbated by the use of multiple registrations. Our techniques are closely related to layer-based stereo [3,4], and move image stitching closer to explicit scene modeling. Experimental evidence demonstrates that our techniques often generate significantly better panoramas when there is substantial motion or parallax.

1 Image Stitching and Parallax Errors

The problem of image stitching, or the creation of a panorama from a set of overlapping images, is a well-studied topic with widespread applications [5–7]. Most modern digital cameras include a panorama creation mode, as do iPhones and Android smartphones. Google Street View presents the user with panoramas stitched together from images taken from moving vehicles, and the overhead views shown in map applications from Google and Microsoft are likewise stitched together from satellite images. Despite this ubiquity, stitching is far from solved. In particular, stitching algorithms often produce parallax errors even in a static

© Springer Nature Switzerland AG 2018
V. Ferrari et al. (Eds.): ECCV 2018, LNCS 11206, pp. 53–69, 2018.
https://doi.org/10.1007/978-3-030-01216-8_4

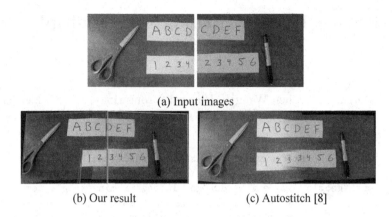

(a) Input images

(b) Our result   (c) Autostitch [8]

Fig. 1. Motion errors example. The strip of papers with numbers has undergone translation between input images. Our result in (b) shows the use of multiple registrations. Green: the reference, Red: registration aligning the number strip, Blue: registration aligning the letter strip. Autostitch result in (c) has visible ghosting on the number strip. (Color figure online)

scene with objects at different depths, or dynamic scene with moving objects. An example of motion errors is shown in Fig. 1.

The stitching problem is traditionally viewed as a sequence of steps that are optimized independently [6,7]. In the first step, the algorithm computes a *single* registration for each input image to align them to a common surface.[1] The warped images are then passed on to the seam finding step; here the algorithm determines the registered image it should draw each pixel from. Finally, a blending procedure [9] is run on the composite image to correct visually unpleasant artifacts such as minor misalignment, or differences in color or brightness due to different exposure or other camera characteristics.

In this paper, we argue that currently existing methods cannot capture the required perspective changes for scenes with parallax or motion in a single registration, and that seam finding cannot compensate for this when the seam must pass through content-rich regions. Single registrations fundamentally fail to capture the background and foreground of a scene simultaneously. This is demonstrated in Fig. 1, where registering the background causes errors in the foreground and vice versa. Several papers [1,2] have addressed this problem by creating a single registration that is designed to produce a high quality stitch. However, as we will show, these still fail in cases of large motion or parallax due to the limitations inherent to single registrations. We instead propose an end-to-end approach where multiple candidate registrations are presented to the seam finding phase as alternate source images. The seam finding stage is then free to choose different registrations for different regions of the composite

---

[1] We use the term registration for an arbitrary (potentially non-rigid) image transformation, and homography for a line-preserving image transformation. We will sometimes refer to the registration process as warping, or creating a warp.

output image. Note that as any registration can serve as a candidate under our scheme, it represents a generalization of methods that attempt to find a single good registration for stitching.

Unfortunately, the classical seam finding approach [5] does not naturally work when given multiple registrations. First, traditional seam finding treats each pixel from the warped image equally. However, by the nature of our multiple registration algorithm, each of them only provides a good alignment for a particular region in the image. Therefore, we need to consider this pixel-level alignment quality in the seam finding phase. Second, seam finding is performed locally by setting up an MRF that tries to place seams where they are not visually obvious. Figure 1 illustrates a common failure; the best seam can cause objects to be duplicated. This issue is made worse by the use of multiple registrations. In traditional image stitching, pixels come from one of two images, so in the worst case scenario, an object is repeated twice. However, if we use n registrations, an object can be repeated as many as $n + 1$ times.

We address this issue by adding several additional terms to the MRF that penalize common stitching errors and encourage image accuracy. Our confidence term encourages pixels to select their value from registrations which align nearby pixels, our duplication term penalizes label sets which select the same object in different locations from different input images, and finally our tear term penalizes breaking coherent regions. While our terms are designed to handle the challenges of multiple registrations, they also provide improvements to the classical single-registration framework.

Our work can be interpreted as a layer-based approach to image stitching, where each registration is treated as a layer and the seam finding stage simultaneously solves for layer assignment and image stitching [3]. Under this view, this paper represents a modest step towards explicit scene modeling in image stitching.

1.1 Motivating Examples

Figure 2 demonstrates the power of multiple registrations. The plant, the floor and the wall each undergo very distinctive motions. Our technique captures all 3 motions. Another challenging example is shown in Fig. 3. Photoshop computes a single registration to align the background buildings, which duplicates the traffic cones and the third car from left. Our technique handles all these objects at different depth correctly.

1.2 Problem Formulation and Our Approach

We adopt the common formulation of image stitching, sometimes called *perspective stitching* [12] or a *flat panorama* [6, Sect. 6.1], that takes one image I_0 as the reference, then warps another candidate image I_1 into the reference coordinate system, and add its content to I_0.

Instead of proposing a single warped $\omega(I_1)$ and sending it to the seam finding phase, we proposed a set of warping $\omega_1(I_1), \ldots, \omega_N(I_1)$, where each $\omega_i(I_1)$ aligns a region in I_1 with I_0. We will detail our approach for multiple registrations in Sect. 3.1. Then we will formalize a multi-label MRF problem for seam finding. We have label set $\mathcal{L} = \{0, 1, \ldots, N\}$, such that label $x_p = 0$ indicates pixel p in the final stitched result will take its color value from I_0, and from $\omega_{x_p}(I_1)$ when $x_p > 0$. We will get the optimal seam by minimizing the energy function $E(x)$ with the new proposed terms to address the challenges we introduced before. We will describe our seam finding energy $E(x)$ in Sect. 3.2. Finally, we adopt Poisson blending [9] to smooth transitions over stitching boundaries when generating the final result.

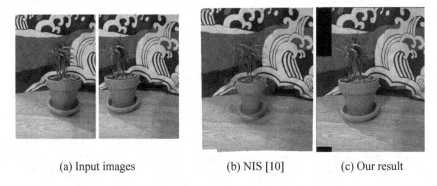

(a) Input images   (b) NIS [10]   (c) Our result

Fig. 2. Motivating example for multiple registrations. Even the sophisticated single registration approach of NIS [10] gives severe ghosting.

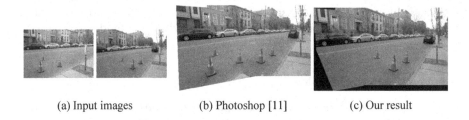

(a) Input images   (b) Photoshop [11]   (c) Our result

Fig. 3. Motivating example for multiple registrations. State of the art commercial packages like Adobe Photoshop [11] duplicate the traffic cones and other objects.

2   Related Work

The presence of visible seams due to parallax and other effects is a long-standing problem in image stitching. Traditionally there have been two avenues for eliminating or reducing these artifacts: improving registrations by allowing more degrees of freedom, or hiding misalignments by selecting better seams. Our algorithm can be seen as employing both of these strategies: the use of multiple registrations allows us to better tailor each registration to a particular region of the panorama, while our new energy terms improve the quality of the final seams.

2.1 Registration

Most previous works take a homography as a starting point and perform additional warping to correct any remaining misalignment. [13] describes a process in which each feature is shifted toward the average location of its matches in other images. The APAP algorithm divides images into grid cells and estimates a separate homography for each cell, with regularization toward a global homography [14].

Instead of solving registration and seam finding independently, another line of work explicitly takes into account the fact that the eventual goal of the registration step is to produce images that can be easily stitched together. ANAP, for instance, can be improved by limiting perspective distortions in regions without overlap and otherwise regularizing to produce more natural-looking mosaics [15]. Another approach is to confine the warping to a minimal region of the input images that is nevertheless large enough for seam selection and blending, which allows the algorithm to handle larger amounts of parallax [2]. Going a step further it is possible to interleave the registration and seam finding phases, as in the SEAGULL system [1]. In this case, the mesh-based warp can be modified to optimize feature correspondences that lie close to the current seam.

2.2 Seam Finding and Other Combination Techniques

The seam finding phase requires determining, for each pixel, which of the two source images contributes its color. [5] observed that this problem can be naturally formulated as a Markov Random Field and solved via graph cuts. This approach tends to give strong results, and the graph cuts method in particular often produces energies that are within a few percent of the global minimum [16]. Further work in this area has focused on taking into account the presence of edges or color gradients in the energy function in order to avoid visible discontinuities [17].

An alternative to seam finding is the use of a multi-band blending [18] phase immediately after registration [8]. This step blends low frequencies over a large spatial range and high frequencies over a short range to minimize artifacts.

2.3 Comparison to Our Technique

Our work clearly generalizes the line of work that optimizes a single registration, as this arises as a special case when only one candidate warp is used. More usefully, existing registration methods can serve as candidate generators in our technique. A single registration algorithm can propose multiple candidates when run with different parameters, or in the case of a randomized algorithm, such as RANSAC, run several times.

Similarly, our algorithm can be viewed as implicitly defining a single registration, given at each pixel by the warp ω_i associated with the candidate registration from which the pixel was drawn in the final output. In theory, this piecewise defined warp is sufficient to obtain the results reported here, but in practice, finding it is difficult. Previous work along these lines has focused on iterative schemes in order to compute the varying warps that are required in different regions of the image [10,15], but this is in general a very computationally challenging problem and the warping techniques used may not be sufficient to produce a good final results. Our technique allows multiple simple registrations to be used instead.

3   Our Multiple Registration Approach

We use a classic three stage image stitching pipeline, composed of registration, seam finding, and blending phases [6,7].

In the registration phase, we propose multiple registrations, each of which attempts to register some part of one of the images with the other. In contrast to previous methods, which only pass a single proposed registration to the seam finding stage, our approach allows all of these proposed registrations to be used. Note that in this phase it is important that the set of registrations we propose be diverse.

In the seam finding stage, we solve an MRF inference problem to find the best way to stitch together the various proposals. We observed that using traditional MRF energy to stitch multiple registrations naively generated poor results, due to the reasons we mentioned in Sect. 1. To address these challenges, we propose the improved MRF energy by adding (1) a new data term that describes our confidence between different warping proposals at pixel p and (2) several new smoothness terms which attempt to prevent duplication or tearing. Although this new energy is proposed primarily for the stitching problem with multiple registrations, it addresses problems observed in the traditional approach (single registration) as well and provides marked improvements in final panorama quality in either framework.

Finally, we adopt Poisson blending [9] to smooth transitions over stitching boundaries when generating the final result.

3.1   Generating Multiple Registrations

There are two common categories of registration methods [7]: *global* transformations, implied by a single motion model over the whole image, such as a homography; and *spatially-varying* transformations, implicitly described by a non-uniform mesh. The candidate registrations we produce are spatially-varying non-rigid transformations. Similar to [2], we first obtain a homography that matches some part of the image well and then refine its mesh representation.

We have a 3 step process: homography finding, filtering, and refinement. In the homography finding step, we generate candidate homographies by running RANSAC on the set of sparse correspondences between features obtained from the two input images. We ensure that the set of homographies is diverse by a filtering step, which removes poor quality homographies and duplicates. In the refinement step, we solve a quadratic program (QP) to obtain an improved local warping mesh for each of the homographies that pass the filtering step.

Homography Finding Step. Given two input images I_0 and I_1, we first compute a set of sparse correspondences $C = \{(p_1^0, p_1^1), \ldots, (p_n^0, p_n^1)\}$, where each $p_i^0 \in I_0$, $p_i^1 \in I_1$ and (p_i^0, p_i^1) is a pair of matched pixels. We run τ_H iterations of a modified RANSAC algorithm to generate a set of potential homographies $\mathcal{H}$. In each iteration t, we randomly choose a pixel p and consider correspondences within a distance r_H; if there are enough nearby correspondences to allow us to estimate a homography H_t we add this to our set of candidates. The homography H_t is estimated using least median of squares as implemented in OpenCV [19].

Filtering Step. In order to simplify the seam finding step, it is desirable to limit the number of candidate homographies. We employ two strategies to achieve this: *screening*, which removes homographies from consideration as soon as they are found, and *deduplication*, which runs on the full set of homographies that remain after screening.

The screening procedure eliminates two kinds of homographies: those that are unlikely to give rise to realistic images, and those that are too close to the identity transformation to be useful in the final result. Homographies of the first type are eliminated by considering two properties: (1) whether the difference between a *similarity* motion that is obtained from the same set of seed points exceeds a fixed threshold [2, Sect. 3.2.1], and (2) whether the magnitude of the scaling parameters of the homography exceed a (different) fixed threshold. The intuition is that real world perspective changes are often close to similarities, and stitchable images are likely to be close to each other in scale. Homographies that are too close to I are eliminated by checking whether the overlap between the area covered by the original image and the area covered by the transformed image exceeds 95%. Finally, we reject homographies where either diagonal is shorter than half the length of the diagonal of the original image.

To determine the set of homographies that are near-duplicates of each other and of which all but one can therefore be safely discarded, we compute a set of inlier correspondences D_t for each H_t that passes screening. D_t is constructed iteratively, starting with all correspondences $(p_i^0, p_i^1) \in C_t'$, where C_t' is the subset of seed points that were chosen in iteration t for which the reprojection error is below a threshold T_H. Correspondences containing points that lie within a distance r_D of some point already in D_t are then added until a fixpoint is reached. This step is a generalization of the strategy introduced in [2, §3.2.1].

Given the sets D_t computed for each H_t, we define a *similarity measure* between homographies $\text{sim}(H_a, H_b) = \cos(V_a, V_b)$, where $\cos$ represents the cosine distance and V_a the 0-1 indicator vector for D_t. Homographies are then considered in descending order of $|D_t|$ and added to the set $\mathcal{H}$ if their similarity to all the elements that have already been added to the set is below a threshold θ_H. We also enforce an upper limit N_H on the number of homographies considered, terminating the procedure early when this limit is reached.

Refinement Step. Our final step is motivated by the observation that our process sometimes produces homographies that cause reprojection errors of several pixels. This may occur even for large planar objects, such as the side of a building, which should be fit exactly by a homography. We make a final adjustment to our homography, then add spatial variation.

To adjust the homography, we define an objective function $f(H) = \sum_{c_i \in C} S(e_{c_i;H})$, where $e_{c_i;H}$ is the reprojection error of correspondence c_i under H, and S is a smoothing function $S(t) = 1 - \frac{1}{1+\exp(-(T_H-t))}$. To generate a *refined* homography $\hat{H}_i$ from an input H_i, we minimize f using Ceres [20], initializing with H_i. The resulting $\hat{H}_i$ is a better-fitting homography that is in some sense near H_i. The smoothing function S is designed to provide gradient in the right direction for correspondences that are close to being inliers while ignoring those that are outliers either because they are incorrect matches or because they are better explained by some other homography.

The homographies $\hat{H}_i \in \mathcal{H}$ often do an imperfect job of aligning I_0 and I_1 in regions that are only mostly flat. In order to address this, we compute a finer-grained non-rigid registration ω_i for each $\hat{H}_i$ using a content-preserving warp (CPW) technique that is better able to capture the transformation between the two images [21]. We start from a uniform grid mesh M_i drawn over $\hat{H}_i(I_1)$, and attempt to use CPW to get a new mesh $\hat{M}_i$ to capture fine-grained local variations between I_0 and $H_i(I_1)$.

Finally, we denote by $\omega_i(I_1)$ the warped candidate image I_1 with $\hat{M}_i$ applied.

3.2 Improved MRF Energy for Seam Finding

The final output of the registration stage is a set of proposed warps $\{\omega_i(I_1)\}$, ($i = 1, 2, \ldots, N$). For notational simplicity, we write $\{I_i^S\}$ where $I_0^S = I_0$, $I_i^S = \omega_i(I_1)$ are the source images in the seam finding stage. These images are used to set up a Markov Random Field (MRF) inference problem, to decide how to combine regions of the different images in order to obtain the final stitched image. The label set for this MRF problem is given by $\mathcal{L} = \{0, 1, \ldots, N\}$, and its purpose is to assign a label $x_p \in \mathcal{L}$ to each pixel p in the stitching space, which indicates that the value of that pixel is copied from $I_{x_p}^S$.

It would be natural to expect that we can use the standard MRF stitching energy function $E^{\text{old}}(x) = \sum_p E_m^{\text{old}}(x_p) + \sum_{p,q \in \mathcal{N}} E_s^{\text{old}}(x_p, x_q)$ introduced by [5] (where $\mathcal{N}$ is the 4-adjacent neighbors). However, we observed that this energy function is not suitable for the case of multiple registrations.

In this formulation, the data term $E_m^{\text{old}}(x_p) = 0$ when pixel p has a valid color value in $I_{x_p}^S$, and λ_m otherwise. This means we will impose a penalty λ_m for out-of-mask pixels but treat all the inside-mask pixels equally (they all have cost 0). However, we found that even state-of-the-art single-registration algorithms [1, 2], cannot align every single pixel. In contrast, our multiple registrations are designed to only capture a single region with each warp. We propose a new mask data term for multiple registrations and a warp data term to address this problem.

The traditional smoothness term is $E_s^{\text{old}}(x_p, x_q) = \lambda_s(\|I_{x_p}^S(p) - I_{x_q}^S(p)\| + \|I_{x_p}^S(q) - I_{x_q}^S(q)\|)$ when $x_p \neq x_q$, and 0 otherwise. It only enforces local similarity across the stitching seam to make it less visible, without any other global constraints. Note that there are a number of nice extensions to this basic idea that improve the smoothness term; for example [6, p. 62] describes several ways to pick better seams and avoid tearing. However, we may still duplicate content in the stitching result with a single registration due to parallax or motion. This problem can be more serious with multiple registrations since we may duplicate content $N + 1$ times instead of just twice. Therefore, we propose a new pairwise term to explicitly penalize duplications.

In sum, we compute the optimal seam by minimizing the energy function $E(x) = \sum_p E_m(x_p) + \sum_p E_w(x_p) + \sum_{p,q \in \mathcal{N}} E_s(x_p, x_q) + E_d(x)$ using expansion moves [22]. We now describe our mask data term E_m, warp data term E_w, smoothness term E_s and duplication term E_d in turn.

Mask Data Term for Multiple Registrations. There is an immediate issue with the standard mask-based data term in the presence of multiple registrations. When one input is significantly larger than the others, the MRF will choose this warping for pixels where its mask is 1 and the other warping masks are 0. Worse, since the MRF itself imposes spatial coherence, this choice of input will be propagated to other parts of the image.

We handle this situation conservatively, by imposing a mask penalty λ_m on pixels that are not in the intersection of all the candidate warpings $\bigcap_i \omega_i(I_1)$ when assigning them to a candidate image (i.e., $x_p \neq 0$). Pixels that lie inside the reference image ($x_p = 0$) are handled normally, in that they have no mask penalty with the reference image mask and λ_m mask penalty out of the mask. Note that this mask penalty is a soft constraint: pixels outside of the intersection $\bigcap_i \omega_i(I_1)$ can be assigned an intensity from a candidate image, if it is promising enough by our other criteria.

Formally we can write our mask data term as

$$E_m(x_p) = \begin{cases} \lambda_m \left(1 - \mathsf{mask}_0(p)\right), & x_p = 0, \\ \lambda_m \left(1 - \prod_{i=1}^{N} \mathsf{mask}_i(p)\right), & x_p \neq 0, \end{cases} \qquad (1)$$

where $\mathsf{mask}_i(p) = 1$ indicates I_i^S has a valid pixel at p, $\mathsf{mask}_i(p) = 0$ otherwise.

Warp Data Term. In the presence of multiple registrations, we need a data term that makes significant distinctions among different proposed warps. There are two natural ways to determine whether a particular warp ω is a good choice at the pixel p. First, we can determine how confident we are that ω actually represents the motion of the scene at p. Second, for pixels in the reference image, we can check intensity/color similarity between $I_0(p)$ and $\omega(I_1)(p)$.

Since our warp is computed using features and RANSAC, we can identify inlier feature points in $\omega_i(I_1)$ when the reprojection error is smaller than a parameter T_H. Denoting these inliers as $\mathcal{I}_i$, we place a Gaussian weight $G(.)$ on each inlier, and define motion quality for pixel p in I_i^S as $Q_m^i(p) = \sum_{q \in \mathcal{I}_i} G(\|p - q\|)$. This makes pixels closer to inliers have greater confidence in the warp.

For color similarity we use the L_2 distance between the local patch around pixel p in the reference I_0^S and our warped image I_i^S: $Q_c^i(p) = \sum_{q \in \mathcal{B}_r(p)} \|I_0^S(p) - I_i^S(p)\|$, where $\mathcal{B}_r(p)$ is the set of pixels within distance r to pixel p. So pixels with better image content alignment become more confident in the warp.

Putting them together, we have $e_w^i(p) = -Q_m^i(p) + \lambda_c Q_c^i(p)$ to be our quality score for pixel p for warp ω_i (lower means better, since we want to minimize the energy). Then we have a normalized score $\hat{e}_w^i(p) \in [-1, 1]$ per warped image, and define the warp data term as: $E_w(x_p) = \lambda_w \hat{e}_w^{x_p}(p)$ when $x_p \neq 0$, and $E_w(x_p) = 0$ otherwise.

Smoothness Terms. We adopt some standard smoothness terms used in state-of-the-art MRF stitching. Following [6,7] these terms include:

1. The color-based seam penalty (introduced in [5,17]) for local patches to encourage seams that introduce invisible transitions between source images,
2. The edge-based seam penalty introduced in [17] to discourage the seam from cutting through edges, hence reduce the "tearing" artifacts where only some part of an object appears in the stitched result,
3. A Potts term to encourage local label consistency.

Duplication Avoidance Term. For stitching tasks with large parallax or motion, it is easy to duplicate scene content in the stitching result. We address this issue by explicitly formalizing a duplication avoidance term in our energy. If pixel p from the reference image I_0^S and q from the candidate image I_i^S form a true correspondence, then they refer to the same point (i.e., scene element) in the real world. Therefore, we penalize a labeling that contains both of them (i.e., $x_p = 0, x_q = i$), as shown in Fig. 4. Since our correspondence is sparse, we also apply this idea to the local region within a radius r of pixels p and q. We reweight the penalty by a Gaussian G since the farther away we are from these corresponding pixels, the more uncertain the correspondence.

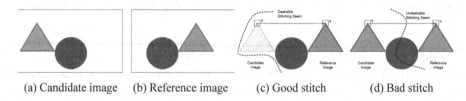

(a) Candidate image   (b) Reference image   (c) Good stitch   (d) Bad stitch

Fig. 4. Illustration of the duplication term. Figure (c) provides a bad stitching result with the green triangles duplicated. The feature point correspondence between pixel p and q suggests duplication, and we introduce a term which penalizes this scenario. (Color figure online)

Formally, our duplication term E_c is defined as

$$E_d(x) = \lambda_d \sum_{i=1}^{N} \sum_{(p,q)\in\mathcal{C}_i} \sum_{\delta\in\mathcal{B}_r} e_r(x_{p+\delta}, x_{q+\delta}; \delta, i) \qquad (2)$$

where $\mathcal{C}_i$ is the pixel correspondence between I_0^S and I_i^S, and $\mathcal{B}_r = \{(dx, dy) \in \mathcal{I}^2 \mid \|(dx, dy)\| \leq r\}$ is a box of radius r. $e_r(x_{p+\delta}, x_{q+\delta}; \delta, i) = G(\|\delta\|)$ when $x_p = 0, x_q = i$, and 0 otherwise.

4   Experimental Results and Implementation Details

Experimental Setup. Our goal is to perform stitching on images whose degree of parallax and motion causes previous methods to fail. Ideally, there would be a standard dataset of images that are too difficult to stitch, along with an evaluation metric. Unfortunately this is not the case, in part due to the difficulty of defining ground truth for image stitching. We therefore had to rely on collecting challenging imagery ourselves, though we found one appropriate example (Fig. 5) whose stitching failures were widely shared on social media.

We implemented or obtained code for a number of alternative methods, as detailed below, and ran them on all of our examples, along with our technique using a single parameter setting. Since our images are so challenging, it was not uncommon for a competing method to return no output ("failing to stitch"). In the entire corpus of images we examined, we found numerous cases where competing techniques produced dramatic artifacts, while our algorithm had minimal if any errors. We have not found any example images where our technique produces dramatic artifacts and a competitor does not. However, we found a few less challenging images that are well handled by competitors but where we produce small artifacts. These examples, along with other data, images, and additional material omitted here are available online,[2] for reasons of space we focus here on images that provide useful insight. However, the images included here are representative of the performance we have observed on the entire corpus of challenging images we collected.

We follow the experimental setup of [2], who (very much like our work) describe a stitching approach that can handle images with too much parallax for previous techniques. The strongest overall competitor turns out to be Adobe Photoshop 2018's stitcher Photomerge [11]. While experimental results reported in [2] compare their algorithm with Photoshop 2014, the 2018 version is substantially better, and does an excellent job of stitching images with too many motions for any other competing methods. Therefore, we take Photoshop's failing on a dataset as a signal that dataset is particularly challenging; in this section, we show several examples in this section where we successfully stitch such datasets. In addition to Photoshop we downloaded and ran APAP [14], Autostitch [8], and NIS [10]. To produce stitching results from APAP we follow the approach of [2], who extended APAP with seam-finding. Results from all methods are shown in Figs. 9 and 10.

---

[2] See https://sites.google.com/view/oois-eccv18.

Implementation Details. For feature extraction and matching, we used Deep-Match [23]. The associated DeepFlow solver was used to generate flows for the optical flow-based warping. We used the Ceres solver [20] for the QP problems that arose when generating multiple registrations, as discussed in Sect. 3.1.

Visual Evaluation. Following [2] we review several images from our test set and highlight the strengths and weaknesses of our technique, as well as those of various methods from the literature. All of our results are shown for a single set of parameters.

We observed two classes of stitching errors: warping errors, where the algorithm fails to generate any candidate image that is well-aligned with the reference image; and stitching errors, where the MRF does not produce good output despite the presence of good candidate warps. An example of our technique making a *warping error* is shown in Fig. 9e, where no warp found by our algorithm continues the parking stall line, causing a visible seam. An example of a *stitching error* is given in Fig. 10e, where the remainder of the car's wheel is available in the warp from which our mosaic draws the front wheelwell. Errors may manifest as a number of different kinds of artifacts, such as: tearing (e.g., the arm in Fig. 5b); wrong perspective (e.g., the tan background building in Fig. 9b); or duplication (e.g., the stop sign in Fig. 7b), ghosting (e.g., the bollards in Fig. 6b), or omission (e.g., the front door of the car in Fig. 10c) of scene content.

Quantitative Evaluation. The only quantitative metric used by previous stitching papers is seam quality (MRF energy). However, as we have shown, local seam quality is not indicative of stitch quality. Also, this technique requires the user to know the seam location, which precludes it from being run on black-box algorithms like Photoshop. Here we attempt to define a metric to address these problems.

We first observe that stitching can be viewed as a form of view synthesis with weaker assumptions regarding the camera placement or type. With this connection in mind, we redefine perspective stitching as extending the field of view of a reference image using the information in the candidate images. This redefintion naturally leads to an evaluation technique. We crop part of the reference image and then stitch the cropped image with the candidate image. This cropped region serves as a ground truth, which we can compare against the appropriate location in the stitch result. Note that in perspective stitching, the reference image's size is not altered so we know the exact area where the cropped region should be. We then calculate MS-SSIM [24] or PSNR.

We report this evaluation for 2 examples in Table 1: 50 pixels are cropped off the edge of the reference images in Stop Sign (left side of first image for Fig. 7) and Graffiti Building (right side of first image for Fig. 8). The stitch results for the cropped images appear almost identical to the stitch results for the whole images. Best score shown inbold. "Ground Truth" compares only the ground truth region to the appropriate location, while "Uncropped Reference" compares the uncropped reference.

(a) Input images

(b) Photoshop [11]   (c) Our result

Fig. 5. "Ski" dataset. Photoshop tears the people and the fence. Our stitch has the fence stop abruptly but keeps the people in place. Note that the candidate provides no information that allows us to extend the fence.

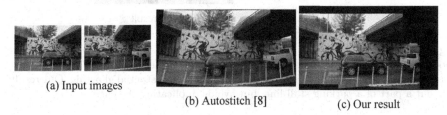

(a) Input images

(b) Autostitch [8]   (c) Our result

Fig. 6. "Bike Mural" dataset. Autostitch has ghosting on the car, bridge, and poles. Our algorithm shortens the truck and deletes a pole, but has no perceptible ghosting or tearing of the objects.

(a) Input images

(b) Photoshop [11]   (c) Our result

Fig. 7. "Stop Sign" dataset. Photoshop duplicates the stop sign. Of all the implementations we tried, ours is the only visually plausible result, successfully avoiding duplicating the foreground.

(a) Input images

(b) APAP [14]   (c) Our result

Fig. 8. "Graffiti-Building" dataset. APAP deletes significant amounts of red graffiti, and introduces noticeable curvature. Our result does not produce tearing, ghosting, or duplication. (Color figure online)

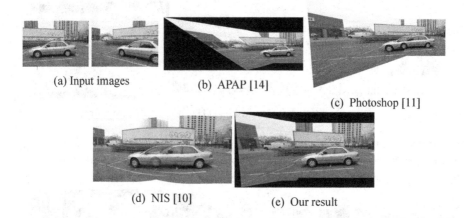

(a) Input images   (b) APAP [14]

(c) Photoshop [11]

(d) NIS [10]   (e) Our result

Fig. 9. "Parking lot" dataset. Autostitch fails to stitch. APAP duplicates the car's hood, tears a background building, and introduces a corner in the roof of the trailer. Photoshop duplicates the front half of the car. NIS has substantial ghosting. Our result cuts out a part of a parking stall line, but avoids duplicating the car.

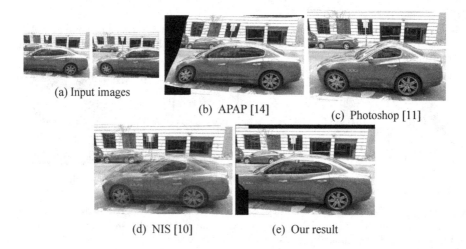

(a) Input images

(b) APAP [14]

(c) Photoshop [11]

(d) NIS [10]   (e) Our result

Fig. 10. "Cars" dataset. Autostitch fails to stitch. APAP and Photoshop shorten the car. APAP also introduces substantial curvature into the background building. NIS has substantial ghosting and shortens the car. Our result deletes part of the hood and front wheel; however, it is the only result which produces an artifact-free car body.

Note that for Stop Sign, all algorithms performed reasonably in Ground Truth Region. However, both APAP and Photoshop include a duplicate of the stop sign that lowers their values for Uncropped Reference.

(a) Input images

(b) Our result

Fig. 11. An example of tearing and duplication produced by our method. "Cars" dataset.

Table 1. Evaluation scores for different algorithms.

Image	Comparison	Metric	Ours	APAP [14]	Photoshop [11]
Stop sign	Ground truth region	MS-SSIM	0.6851	0.6573	**0.6861**
		PSNR	**19.4943**	17.7073	18.9996
	Uncropped reference	MS-SSIM	**0.9354**	0.8981	0.9108
		PSNR	**23.0006**	20.3533	20.9238
Graffiti building	Ground truth region	MS-SSIM	**0.4636**	0.3747	0.1250
		PSNR	**14.9983**	13.1269	9.6520
	Uncropped reference	MS-SSIM	**0.9253**	0.5737	0.8541
		PSNR	**24.7637**	14.8298	18.7102

5 Conclusions, Limitations, and Future Work

We have demonstrated a novel formulation of the image stitching problem in which multiple candidate registrations are used. We have generalized MRF seam finding to this setting and proposed new terms to combat common artifacts such as object duplication. Our techniques outperform existing algorithms in large parallax and motion scenarios.

Our methods naturally generalize to other stitching surfaces such as cylinders or spheres via modifications to the warping function. Three or more input images can be handled by proposing multiple registrations of each candidate image, and letting the seam finder composite them. A potential problem is the presence of undetected sparse correspondences, which can lead to duplications or tears (Fig. 11). The use of dense correspondences may remedy this issue, but our preliminary experiments suggest that optical flows cannot easily capture motion in input images with large disparities, and do not produce correspondences of sufficient quality. A second issue is that it is unclear whether to populate regions of the output mosaic when only data from a single candidate image is present, as the constrained choice of candidate here may conflict with choices made in other regions of the mosaic. This can to some extent be handled with modifications to the data term, but compared to traditional methods, scene content may be lost. One example of this occurs in Fig. 10, where the front wheel of the car is omitted in the final output. These problems remain exciting challenges for future work.

Acknowledgements. This research was supported by NSF grants IIS-1161860 and IIS-1447473 and by a Google Faculty Research Award. We thank Connie Choi for help collecting images.

References

1. Lin, K., Jiang, N., Cheong, L.-F., Do, M., Lu, J.: SEAGULL: seam-guided local alignment for parallax-tolerant image stitching. In: Leibe, B., Matas, J., Sebe, N., Welling, M. (eds.) ECCV 2016. LNCS, vol. 9907, pp. 370–385. Springer, Cham (2016). https://doi.org/10.1007/978-3-319-46487-9_23
2. Zhang, F., Liu, F.: Parallax-tolerant image stitching. In: CVPR, pp. 3262–3269 (2014)
3. Willis, J., Argawal, S., Serge, B.: What went where. In: CVPR, pp. 37–44 (2003)
4. Wang, J., Adelson, E.: Representing moving images with layers. TIP 3(5), 625–638 (1994)
5. Kwatra, V., Schödl, A., Essa, I., Turk, G., Bobick, A.: Graphcut textures: image and videosynthesis using graph cuts. SIGGRAPH 22(3), 277–286 (2003)
6. Szeliski, R.: Image alignment and stitching: a tutorial. Found. Trends Comput. Graph. Vis. 2(1), 1–104 (2007)
7. Szeliski, R.: Computer Vision: Algorithms and Applications. Springer, Berlin (2010). https://doi.org/10.1007/978-1-84882-935-0
8. Brown, M., Lowe, D.G.: Automatic panoramic image stitching using invariant features. IJCV 74(1), 59–73 (2007)
9. Perez, P., Gangnet, M., Blake, A.: Poisson image editing. SIGGRAPH 22, 313–318 (2003)
10. Chen, Y.-S., Chuang, Y.-Y.: Natural image stitching with the global similarity prior. In: Leibe, B., Matas, J., Sebe, N., Welling, M. (eds.) ECCV 2016. LNCS, vol. 9909, pp. 186–201. Springer, Cham (2016). https://doi.org/10.1007/978-3-319-46454-1_12
11. Adobe: Create panoramic images with photomerge. https://helpx.adobe.com/in/photoshop/using/create-panoramic-images-photomerge.html. Accessed 25 July 2018
12. Adobe: Create and edit panoramic images. https://helpx.adobe.com/photoshop/using/create-panoramic-images-photomerge.html. Accessed 25 July 2018
13. Shum, H.Y., Szeliski, R.: Construction of panoramic image mosaics with global and local alignment. In: Benosman, R., Kang, S.B. (eds.) Panoramic Vision. MCS, pp. 227–268. Springer, New York (2001). https://doi.org/10.1007/978-1-4757-3482-9_13
14. Zaragoza, J., Chin, T.J., Brown, M.S., Suter, D.: As-projective-as-possible image stitching with moving DLT. In: CVPR, pp. 2339–2346 (2013)
15. Lin, C.C., Pankanti, S.U., Natesan Ramamurthy, K., Aravkin, A.Y.: Adaptive as-natural-as-possible image stitching. In: CVPR, pp. 1155–1163 (2015)
16. Szeliski, R., et al.: A comparative study of energy minimization methods for Markov random fields. TPAMI 30(6), 1068–1080 (2008)
17. Agarwala, A., et al.: Interactive digital photomontage. SIGGRAPH 23(3), 294–302 (2004)
18. Burt, P., Adelson, E.: A multiresolution spline with application to image mosaics. SIGGRAPH 2(4), 217–236 (1983)
19. Bradski, G.: The OpenCV library. Dr. Dobb's J. Softw. Tools 120, 122–125 (2000)

20. Agarwal, S., Mierle, K.: Others: ceres solver. http://ceres-solver.org/. Accessed 25 July 2018
21. Liu, F., Gleicher, M., Jin, H., Agarwala, A.: Content-preserving warps for 3D video stabilization. SIGGRAPH **28**(3) (2009)
22. Boykov, Y., Veksler, O., Zabih, R.: Fast approximate energy minimization via graph cuts. TPAMI **23**(11), 1222–1239 (2001)
23. Weinzaepfel, P., Revaud, J., Harchaoui, Z., Schmid, C.: Deepflow: large displacement optical flow with deep matching. In: ICCV, pp. 1385–1392 (2013)
24. Wang, Z., Simoncelli, E., Bovik, A.: Multiscale structural similarity for image quality assessment. In: Asilomar Conference on Signals, Systems and Computers, pp. 1398–1402 (2004)

CTAP: Complementary Temporal Action Proposal Generation

Jiyang Gao$^{(\boxtimes)}$, Kan Chen, and Ram Nevatia

University of Southern California, Los Angeles, USA
{jiyangga,kanchen,nevatia}@usc.edu

Abstract. Temporal action proposal generation is an important task, akin to object proposals, temporal action proposals are intended to capture "clips" or temporal intervals in videos that are likely to contain an action. Previous methods can be divided to two groups: sliding window ranking and actionness score grouping. Sliding windows uniformly cover all segments in videos, but the temporal boundaries are imprecise; grouping based method may have more precise boundaries but it may omit some proposals when the quality of actionness score is low. Based on the complementary characteristics of these two methods, we propose a novel Complementary Temporal Action Proposal (CTAP) generator. Specifically, we apply a Proposal-level Actionness Trustworthiness Estimator (PATE) on the sliding windows proposals to generate the probabilities indicating whether the actions can be correctly detected by actionness scores, the windows with high scores are collected. The collected sliding windows and actionness proposals are then processed by a temporal convolutional neural network for proposal ranking and boundary adjustment. CTAP outperforms state-of-the-art methods on average recall (AR) by a large margin on THUMOS-14 and ActivityNet 1.3 datasets. We further apply CTAP as a proposal generation method in an existing action detector, and show consistent significant improvements.

Keywords: Temporal action proposal · Temporal action detection

1 Introduction

We focus on the task of generating accurate temporal action proposals in videos; akin to object proposals for object detection [1], temporal action proposals are intended to capture "clips" or temporal intervals in videos that are likely to contain an action. There has been some previous work in this topic and it has been shown that, as expected and in analogy with object proposals, quality of temporal action proposals has a direct influence on the action detection performance [2,3]. High quality action proposals should reach high Average Recall (AR) with as few number of retrieved proposals as possible.

J. Gao and K. Chen—Equal contribution. Code is in http://www.github.com/jiyanggao/CTAP.

© Springer Nature Switzerland AG 2018
V. Ferrari et al. (Eds.): ECCV 2018, LNCS 11206, pp. 70–85, 2018.
https://doi.org/10.1007/978-3-030-01216-8_5

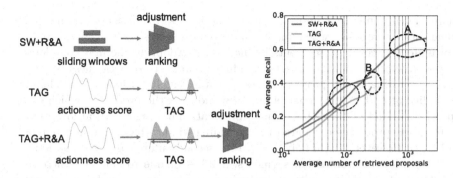

Fig. 1. The architectures of three baseline methods are shown: (1) SW+R&A: sliding windows are processed by a model for proposal ranking and boundary adjustment, *e.g.* TURN [2], SCNN [3]; (2) TAG: TAG [4] generate proposals based on unit-level actionness; (3) TAG+R&A: actionness proposals are processed with proposal ranking and boundary adjustment.

The existing action proposal generation methods can be considered to belong to two main types. The first type is sliding-window based, which takes clips from sliding windows as input, and outputs scores for proposals. SCNN-prop [3] is a representative of this type; it applies a binary classifier to rank the sliding windows. TURN [2] adopts temporal regression in additional to binary classification to adjust the boundary of sliding windows. The architecture of this type is outlined as "SW-R&A" in Fig. 1. Sliding windows uniformly cover all segments in the videos (thus cover every ground truth segment), however the drawback is that the temporal boundaries are imprecise, in spite of the use of boundary adjustment, and thus high AR is reached at large number of retrieved of proposals, as shown in circle A in Fig. 1.

The second type of action proposal generation methods can be summarized as actionness score based. It applies binary classification on a finer level, *i.e.*, unit or snippet (a few contiguous frames) level, to generate actionness scores for each unit. A Temporal Action Grouping (TAG) [4] technique, derived from the watershed algorithm [5], is designed to group continuous high-score regions as proposals. Each proposal's score is calculated as the average of its unit actionness scores. The structure is shown as "TAG" in Fig. 1. This type of method generates high precision boundaries, as long as the quality of actionness scores is high. However, the actionness scores have two common failure cases: having high scores at background segments, and having low scores at action segments. The former case leads to generation of wrong proposals, while the latter case may omit some correct proposals. These lead to the upper bound of AR performance limited at a low value (circle B in Fig. 1).

Based on the above analysis, ranking-sliding-window and grouping-actionness-score methods have two complementary properties: (1) The boundaries from actionness-based proposals are more precise as they are predicted on a finer level, and window-level ranking could be more discriminative as it takes more global contextual information; (2) actionness-based methods may omit some correct proposals when quality of actionness scores is low, sliding windows can uniformly cover all segments in the videos. Adopting the first complementary characteristic helps to resolve the first failure case of actionness proposals (*i.e.*, generating wrong proposals). As shown in Fig. 1, a window-level classifier is applied after TAG to adjust boundaries and rank the proposals, which corresponds to model "TAG+R&A". Such combination has higher AR at low number of retrieved proposals compared to the sliding-window-based method (circle C in Fig. 1). However, it still fails to solve the second failure case, when actionness scores are low at true action segments, TAG is unable to generate these proposal candidates. This results in the limited performance upper bound as shown in circle B, Fig. 1. To address this, we further explore the complementary characteristics, and propose to adaptively select sliding windows to fill the omitted ones in actionness proposals.

We propose a novel Complementary Temporal Action Proposal (CTAP) generator consisting of three modules. The first module is an initial proposal generator, which outputs actionness proposals and sliding-window proposals. The second module is a proposal complementary filter collects missing correct ones from sliding windows (addressing the second failure case of actionness score). Specifically, the complementary filter applies a binary classifier on the initial proposals to generate the probabilities indicating whether the proposals can be detected by actionness and TAG correctly, this classifier is called proposal-level actionness trustworthiness estimator. The third module ranks the proposals and adjusts the temporal boundaries. Specifically, we design a temporal convolutional neural network, rather than simple temporal mean pooling used in TURN [2], to preserve the temporal ordering information.

We evaluated the proposed method on THUMOS-14 and ActivityNet v1.3; experiments show that our method outperforms state-of-the-art methods by a large margin for action proposal generation. We further apply the generated temporal proposals on the action detection task with a standard detector, and show significant performance improvements consistently.

In summary, our contribution are three-fold: (1) We proposed a novel Complementary Temporal Action Proposal (CTAP) generator which uses the complementary characteristics of actionness proposals and sliding windows to generate high quality proposals. (2) We designed a new boundary adjustment and proposal ranking network with temporal convolution which can effectively save the ordering information on the proposal boundaries. (3) We evaluated our method on two large scale datasets (THUMOS-14 and ActivityNet v1.3) and our model outperforms state-of-the-art methods by a large margin.

2   Related Work

In this section, we introduce the related work, which includes temporal action proposal, temporal action detection and online action detection.

Temporal Action Proposal. Temporal action proposal generation has been shown to be an effective step in action detection, and could be useful for many high level video understanding tasks [3,6,7]. Two types of methods have been proposed, the first type of methods formulates it as a binary classification problem on sliding windows. Among them, Sparse-prop [8] uses STIPs [9] and dictionary learning for proposal generation. SCNN-prop [3] is based on training C3D [10] network for binary classification task. TURN [2] cuts the videos to units, and reuse unit-level features for proposals, which improves computational efficiency. TURN [2] also proposes to apply temporal regression to adjust the action boundaries which improves the AR performance. The performance of this type of methods is limited by the imprecise temporal boundaries of sliding windows. The second type of method is based on snippet level actionness score and apply Temporal Action Grouping (TAG) [4] method on the score sequence to group continuous high-score region as proposal. However, TAG may omit the correct proposals when the quality of actionness scores is low. Besides, DAPs [11] and SST [12] are online proposal generators, which could run over the video in a single pass, without the use of overlapping temporal sliding windows.

Temporal Action Detection. This task [3,13–15] focuses on predicting the action categories, and also the start/end times of the action instances in untrimmed videos. S-CNN [3] presents a two-stage action detection model, which first generates proposals and then classifies the proposals. Lin *et al.* propose a Single Shot Action Detector (SSAD) [16], which skips the proposal generation step and directly detects action instances in untrimmed video. Gao *et al.* [6] design a Cascaded Boundary Regression (CBR) network to refine the action boundaries iteratively. SSN [4] presents a mechanism to model the temporal structures of activities, and thus the capability of discriminating between complete and incomplete proposals for precisely detecting actions. R-C3D [17] designs a 3D fully convolutional network, which generates candidate temporal regions and classifies selected regions into specific activities in a two-stage manner. Yuan *et al.* [18] propose to localize actions by searching for the structured maximal sum of frame-wise classification scores. Shou *et al.* [19] design a Convolutional-De-Convolutional (CDC) operation that makes dense predictions at a fine granularity in time to determine precise temporal boundaries. Dai *et al.* [20] propose a temporal context network, which adopts a similar architecture to Faster-RCNN [1], for temporal action detection. Beyond the fixed category action detection, TALL [21] proposes to use natural language as the query to detect the target actions in videos.

Online action detection [22–24] is different from temporal action detection that the whole video is not available at detection time, thus it needs the system to detect actions on the fly. Geest *et al.* [22] built a dataset for online action detection, which consists of 16 hours (27 episodes) of TV series with temporal annotation for 30 action categories. Gao *et al.* [23] propose a Reinforced Encoder Decoder (RED) network for online action detection and action anticipation.

3   Complementary Temporal Action Proposal Generator

In this section, we present the details of the Complementary Temporal Action Proposal (CTAP) generator. There are three stages in the pipeline of CTAP. The first stage is to generate initial proposals, which come from two sources, one is actionness score and TAG [4], the other is sliding windows. The second stage is complementary filtering. As we discussed before, TAG omits some correct proposals when the quality of actionness score is low (*i.e.* low actionness score on action segments), but sliding windows uniformly cover all segments in videos. Thus, we design a complementary filter to collect high quality complementary proposals from sliding windows to fill the omitted actionness proposals. The third stage is boundary adjustment and proposal ranking, which is composed of a temporal convolutional neural network.

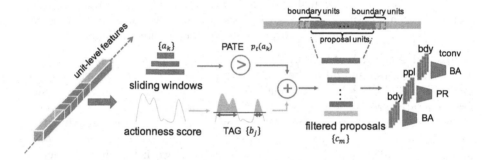

Fig. 2. The architecture of Complementary Temporal Action Proposal (CTAP) generator. "BA" is short for boundary adjustment, "PR" is short for proposal ranking, "ppl" is short for proposal and "bdy" is short for boundary.

3.1   Initial Proposal Generation

In this part, we first introduce video pre-processing, then present the actionness score generation, temporal grouping process and sliding window sampling strategy.

Video Pre-processing. Following previous work [2], a long untrimmed video is first cut into video units or snippets, each unit contains n_u continuous frames. A video unit u is processed by a visual encoder E_v to extract the unit-level representation $\mathbf{x}_u = E_v(u) \in \mathbb{R}^{d_f}$. In our experiments, we use the two-stream CNN model [25,26] as the visual encoder, details are given in Sect. 4.2. Consequently, a long video is converted to a sequence of unit-level features, which are used as basic processing units later.

Actionness Score. Based on unit-level features, we train a binary classifier to generate actionness score for each unit. Specifically, we design a two-layer temporal convolutional neural network, which takes a t_a continuous unit features as input, $\mathbf{x} \in \mathbb{R}^{t_a \times d_f}$, and outputs a probability for each unit indicating whether it is background or action, $\boldsymbol{p}_x \in \mathbb{R}^{t_a}$.

$$\boldsymbol{p}_x = \sigma(t_{conv}(\mathbf{x})), \quad t_{conv}(\mathbf{x}) = \mathcal{F}(\varphi(\mathcal{F}(\mathbf{x}; \mathbf{W}_1)); \mathbf{W}_2) \tag{1}$$

where $\mathcal{F}(.; \mathbf{W})$ denotes a temporal convolution operator, $\mathbf{W}$ is the weight of its convolution kernel. In this network, $\mathbf{W}_1 \in \mathbb{R}^{d_f \times d_m \times k \times k}$, $\mathbf{W}_2 \in \mathbb{R}^{d_m \times 1 \times k \times k}$ (k is the kernel size) are training parameters. $\varphi(.)$ is an non-linear activation function, $\sigma(.)$ is a sigmoid function.

After generating the probability $\boldsymbol{p}_x$ for each continuous unit features $\mathbf{x}$, the loss is calculated as the cross-entropy for each input sample within the batch:

$$\mathcal{L}_{act} = -\frac{1}{N} \sum_{i=1}^{N} [\mathbf{y}_i^\top \log(\boldsymbol{p}_{x_i}) + (1 - \mathbf{y}_i)^\top \log(1 - \boldsymbol{p}_{x_i})] \tag{2}$$

where $\mathbf{y}_i \in \mathbb{R}^{t_a}$ is a binary sequence for each input x_i indicating whether each unit in x_i contains action (label 1) or not (label 0). N is the batch size.

Actionness Proposal Generation Strategy. We follow [4] and implement a watershed algorithm [5] to segment 1-D sequence signals. Given each unit's actionness score, raw proposals are generated whose units all have scores larger than a threshold τ. For some neighbor raw proposals, if the time during ration (*i.e.*, maximum end time minus minimum start time among these raw proposals) is larger than a ratio η of the whole video length, we group them as a proposal candidate. We iterate all possible combinations of τ and η to generate proposal candidates and apply non-maximum suppression (NMS) to eliminate redundant proposals. The output actionness proposals are denoted as $\{b_j\}$.

Sliding Window Sampling Strategy. Unlike actionness proposals which depend on actionness score distribution, sliding windows can uniformly cover all segments in the videos. The goal is to maximum the match with groundtruth segments (high recall), meanwhile maintaining the number of sliding windows as low as possible. In our experiments, different combinations of window size and overlap ratio are tested on validation set. The sliding windows are denoted as $\{a_k\}$. Detail setting is given in Sect. 4.2.

3.2 Proposal Complementary Filtering

As discussed before, actionness proposals could be more precise but less stable, but sliding windows are more stable but less precise. The goal of second stage is to collect proposals, that could be omitted by TAG, from sliding windows. The core of this stage is a binary classifier, whose input is a sequence of unit features (*i.e.* a proposal), and output is the probability that indicates whether this proposal can be correctly detected by the unit-level actionness scores and TAG. This classifier is called Proposal-level Actionness Trustworthiness Estimator (PATE).

PATE Training. The training samples are collected as follows: Given a video, the groundtruth segments $\{g_i\}$ are matched with actionness proposals $\{b_j\}$. For a groundtruth segment g_i, if there exists an actionness proposal b_j that has temporal Intersection over Union (tIoU) with g_i larger than a threshold θ_c, then we label g_i as a positive sample ($y_i = 1$); if no such b_j exists, then g_i is labelled as a negative sample ($y_i = 0$). The unit level features inside g_i are mean pooled to a single proposal-level feature $\mathbf{x}_{g_i} \in \mathbb{R}^{d_f}$. PATE outputs trustworthiness scores indicating the probabilities that whether the proposals can be correctly detected by actionness scores and TAG:

$$s_i = \sigma \left(\mathbf{W}_4(\varphi(\mathbf{W}_3 \mathbf{x}_{g_i} + \mathbf{b}_3)) + \mathbf{b}_4 \right) \tag{3}$$

where $\mathbf{W}_3 \in \mathbb{R}^{d_f \times d_m}$, $\mathbf{W}_4 \in \mathbb{R}^{d_m \times 1}$, $\mathbf{b}_3 \in \mathbb{R}^{d_m}$, $\mathbf{b}_4 \in \mathbb{R}$ are training parameters. Other notations are similar to Eq. 1. The network is trained by a standard cross-entropy loss over training samples from each batch (N is the batch size).

$$\mathcal{L}_{pate} = -\frac{1}{N} \sum_{i=1}^{N} [y_i \log(s_i) + (1 - y_i) \log(1 - s_i)] \tag{4}$$

Complementary Filtering. In test stage, we apply the trustworthiness estimator to every proposal from sliding windows $\{a_k\}$. For an input proposal, the trustworthiness score p_t tells us that "how well the actionness scores are trustworthy on the video content from this proposal". For a sliding window a_k, if $p_t(a_k)$ is lower than a threshold θ_a (means TAG may fail on this segment), this sliding window is collected. The collected proposals from sliding windows and all actionness proposals are denoted as $\{c_m\}$, and are sent to the next stage, which ranks the proposals and adjusts the temporal boundaries. We call this process as complementary filtering and the name derives from somewhat similar processes used in estimation theory[1].

3.3   Proposal Ranking and Boundary Adjustment

The third stage of CTAP is to rank the proposals and adjust the temporal boundaries. TURN [2] does this also, however it uses mean-pooling to aggregate temporal features, which losses the temporal ordering information. Instead, we design a Temporal convolutional Adjustment and Ranking (TAR) network which use temporal conv layers to aggregate the unit-level features.

TAR Architecture. Suppose that the start and end units (*i.e.* temporal boundary) of an input proposal c_m are u_s, u_e, we uniformly sample n_{ctl} unit-level features inside the proposal, called proposal units $\mathbf{x}_c \in \mathbb{R}^{n_{ctl} \times d_f}$. We sample n_{ctx} unit features at the start and end boundaries respectively, which are $[u_s - n_{ctx}/2, u_s + n_{ctx}/2]$ and $[u_e - n_{ctx}/2, u_e + n_{ctx}/2]$, called boundary units (denoted as $\mathbf{x}_s \in \mathbb{R}^{n_{ctx} \times d_f}$, $\mathbf{x}_e \in \mathbb{R}^{n_{ctx} \times d_f}$). Boundary units and proposal units

---

[1] The original use of complementary filtering is to estimate a signal given two noisy measurements, where one of the noise is mostly high-frequency (maybe precise but not stable) and the other noise is mostly low-frequency (stable but not precise).

are illustrated in Fig. 2. These three feature sequences (one sequence for proposal units and two sequences for boundary units) are input to three independent sub-networks. The proposal ranking sub-network outputs probability of action, the boundary adjustment sub-network outputs regression offsets. Each sub-network contains two temporal convolutional layers. Which can be represented as:

$$o_s = t_{conv}(\mathbf{x}_s), \quad p_c = \sigma(t_{conv}(\mathbf{x}_c)), \quad o_e = t_{conv}(\mathbf{x}_e) \tag{5}$$

where o_s, o_e, p_c denote the offsets prediction for start and end boundaries and the action probability for each proposal respectively. Other notations are the same in Eq. 1. Similar to TURN [2], we use non-parameterized regression offsets. The final score for a proposal a_k from sliding windows is multiplied by the PATE score $(p_t(a_k) \cdot p_c(a_k))$. The actionness proposals use $p_c(a_k)$ as the final score.

TAR Training. To collect training samples, we use dense sliding windows to match with groundtruth action segments. A sliding window is assigned to a groundtruth segments if: (1) it has the highest tIoU overlaps with a certain groundtruth segment among all other windows; or (2) it has tIoU larger than 0.5 with any one of the groundtruth segments. We use the standard Softmax cross-entropy loss to train proposal ranking sub-network and the L1 distance loss for boundary adjustment sub-network. Specifically, the regression loss can be expressed as,

$$\mathcal{L}_{reg} = \frac{1}{N_{pos}} \sum_{i=1}^{N_{pos}} l_i^*(|o_{s,i} - o_{s,i}^*| + |o_{e,i} - o_{e,i}^*|) \tag{6}$$

where $o_{s,i}$ is the predicted start offset, $o_{e,i}$ is the predicted end offset, $o_{s,i}^*$ is the groundtruth start offset, $o_{e,i}^*$ is the groundtruth end offset. l_i^* is the label, 1 for positive samples and 0 for background samples. N_{pos} is the number of positive samples in a mini-batch, as the regression loss is calculated only for positive samples. Similar to Eq. 4, a cross entropy objective is calculated to guide the learning of prediction score p_c for each proposal.

4   Experiments

We evaluate CTAP on THUMOS-14 [27] and ActivityNet v1.3 [28] datasets respectively.

4.1   Datasets

THUMOS-14 contains 1010 and 1574 videos for validation and testing purposes from 20 sport classes. Among them, there are 200 and 212 videos are labeled with temporal information in validation and test set respectively. Following the settings of previous work [2,3], we train our model on the validation set and conduct evaluation on the test set.

ActivityNet v1.3 consists of 19,994 videos collected from YouTube labeled in 200 classes. The whole dataset is divided into three disjoint splits: training, validation and test, with a ration of 50%, 25%, 25%, respectively. Since the annotation of the test split is not publicly available for competition purpose, we compare and report performances of different models on the validation set.

4.2   Experiment Setup

Unit-Level Feature Extraction. We use the twostream model [26] as the visual encoder E_v that is pre-trained on ActivityNet v1.3 training set. In each unit, the central frame is sampled to calculate the appearance CNN feature, it is the output of `Flatten_673` layer in ResNet [29]. For the motion feature, we sample 6 consecutive frames at the center of a unit and calculate optical flows between them; these flows are then fed into the pretrained BN-Inception model [30] and the output of `global pool` layer is extracted. The motion features and the appearance features are both 2048-dimensional, and are concatenated into 4096-dimensional vectors ($d_f = 4096$), which are used as unit-level features. On THUMOS-14, we test our model with two settings of unit features Flow-16 and Twostream-6. Flow-16 only uses denseflow CNN features, and the unit size is set to 16, which is the same as [2] ($n_u = 16$), Twostream-6 use twostream features and unit size is 6 ($n_u = 6$). On ActivityNet v1.3, two-stream features are used and unit size is 16 (Twostream-16, $n_u = 16$).

Sliding Window Sampling Strategy. We follow TURN [2] and adopt proposals' length set of {16, 32, 64, 128, 256, 512} with tIOU of 0.75, which achieves the optimal results. On ActivityNet v1.3, we adopt proposals' length set of {64, 128, 256, 512, 768, 1024, 1536, 2048, 2560, 3072, 3584, 4096, 6144} with tIOU = 0.75, which achieves the reported best performance in the submission.

Actionness Score Generation. We set the kernel size for each temporal convolution as 3 ($k = 3$). The stride for temporal convolution is 1. We choose rectified linear unit (ReLU) as the non-linear activation function φ. The first temporal convolution output dimension $d_m = 1024$. t_a is set to be 4. Batch size is 128, learning rate is 0.005, and the model is trained for about 10 epochs.

TAG Algorithm. Following the setting of [4], we set the initial value of τ as 0.085. To enumerate all possible combinations of (τ, η), we first iterate τ in the range of [0.085, 1] with a step of 0.085. In each iteration, we further iterate η in the range of [0.025, 1] with a step of 0.025. The threshold of NMS is set as 0.95 to eliminate redundant proposals.

PATE Setting. We set the first fully-connected layer's output dimension $d_m = 1024$. θ_a is set to be 0.1 on THUMOS-14 and ActivityNet v1.3. Batch size is 128 and learning rate is 0.005. PATE is trained for about 10 epochs.

TAR Setting. On THUMOS-14, we uniformly sample 8 unit features inside each proposal ($n_{ctl} = 4$), and 4 unit features as context ($n_{ctx} = 4$). On ActivityNet v1.3, we set $n_{ctl} = 8$ and $n_{ctx} = 4$. d_m is set to 1024. TAR is optimized using Adam algorithm [31]. Batch size is 128 and learning rate is 0.005. TAR is trained for 10 epoches on THUMOS-14 and 4 epoches on ActivityNet v1.3.

Evaluation Metrics. For temporal action proposal generation task, Average Recall (AR) is usually used as evaluation metrics. Following previous work, we use IoU thresholds set from 0.5 to 1.0 with a step of 0.05 on THUMOS-14 and 0.5 to 0.95 with a step of 0.05 on ActivityNet v1.3. We draw the curve of AR with different Average Number(AN) of retrieved proposals to evaluate the relationship between recall and proposal number, which is called AR-AN curve. On ActivityNet v1.3, we also use area under the AR-AN curve (AUC) as metrics, where AN varies from 0 to 100. For the evaluation of temporal action detection, we follow the traditional mean Average Precision (mAP) metric used in THUMOS-14. A prediction is regarded as positive only when it has correct category prediction and tIoU with ground truth higher than a threshold. We use the official toolkit of THUMOS-14.

4.3   Evaluation on THUMOS-14

In this part, we evaluate our method on THUMOS-14 dataset. First, we compare our proposal ranking and boundary adjustment module TAR with TURN [2]. Second, we evaluate the effectiveness of PATE and the proposal complementary filtering module. Third, we compare our full model with state-of-the-art methods, and finally we apply our proposals on action detection task to verify the its performance advantage.

Table 1. Performance comparison between TAR and TURN [2] on THUMOS-14 test set. Same unit feature (flow-16) and test sliding windows are used on TAR and TURN for fair comparison. Average Recall (AR) at different numbers is reported.

Method	AR@50	AR@100	AR@200
TURN [2]	21.75	31.84	42.96
TAR	**22.99**	**32.21**	**45.08**

TAR vs TURN [2]. As we presented before, TURN [2] uses temporal mean pooling to aggregate features, it losses temporal ordering information, which could be important for boundary adjustment. TAR uses temporal convolution to extract temporal information from unit features, and adopts independent sub-networks for proposal ranking and boundary adjustment. To fairly compare with TURN, we use flow-16 features, and the same test sliding window settings as TURN. As shown in Table 1, we can see that, at AN = 50, 100 and 200, TAR outperforms TURN at all these points, which shows the effectiveness of TAR.

Complementary Filtering. Besides using PATE in the proposal complementary filtering, we design three baseline methods to combine the sliding windows and actionness proposals. The first method is a simple "union", in which

Table 2. Complementary filtering evaluation on THUMOS-14 test set, compared with "Union" and "tIoU-selection". Average Recall (AR) at different numbers is reported.

Method	AR@50	AR@100	AR@200
Union	25.80	34.70	46.19
Union+NMS	28.07	39.71	49.60
tIoU-selection	30.35	38.34	42.41
PATE complementary filtering	**31.03**	**40.23**	**50.13**

we simply put all actionness proposals and all sliding windows together, and send them into TAR module for ranking and adjustment. The second method is "union"+NMS, in which we apply NMS to filter the duplicate proposals from the union set; the threshold of NMS is set to 0.7, which achieves the best performance among {0.5, 0.7, 0.9}. The third method is tIoU-based: all actionness proposals are selected; we calculate the tIoU between the sliding windows and actionness proposals, if there exists a sliding window whose highest tIoU with all actionness proposals is lower than 0.5, then it is selected. We use flow-16 unit features and the same test sliding windows in "TAR vs TURN" experiments.

The results are shown in Table 2. We can see that, complementary filtering achieves the best AR on every AN (50, 100 and 200). The performance of "Union" suffers at low AN, but is higher than "tIoU-selection" at AN = 200. We believe the reason is that simple union method adds too many low quality proposals from sliding windows. Union+NMS improves the performance, however due to the lack of priority of TAG and SW proposals, NMS may select an inaccurate SW proposal with a higher score instead of an accurate TAG proposal with a lower score. In contrast, PATE tries to preserve such priority and focuses on picking out the sliding window proposals that TAG may fail on. tIoU-selection also suffers, as it eliminates some high quality windows simply based on the tIoU threshold. Complementary filtering dynamically generates trustworthiness scores on different windows, which make the selection process more effective.

We also show the AR performance of two sources, actionness proposals and sliding windows, in Fig. 3. Both flow-16 (F16) feature and twostream-6 (TS6) feature are illustrated. It can be seen that the performance of complementary proposals is higher than that of actionness proposals (TAG+TAR) and sliding windows (SW+TAR) at every AN consistently, which shows that our method can effectively select high quality complementary proposals from sliding windows to fill the omitted ones in actionness proposals.

Comparison with State-of-the-Art Methods. We compare our full model with state-of-the-art methods on THUMOS-14 dataset by the Average recall on average number of proposals (AR-AN) curve and recall@100-tIoU curve, as shown in Fig. 4. It can be seen that our model outperforms the state-of-the-art model by a large margin on both curves. Specifically, for AR@100, the performance of CTAP is around 43%, while the state-of-the-art method TURN [2] only achieves about 32%.

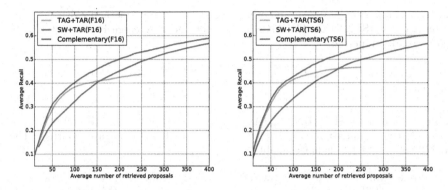

Fig. 3. AR-AN curves of the complementary results with flow-16 feature (F16) and two-stream-6 feature (TS6). Complementary filtering proposals outperform sliding windows (SW+TAR) and actionness proposals (TAG+TAR) consistently.

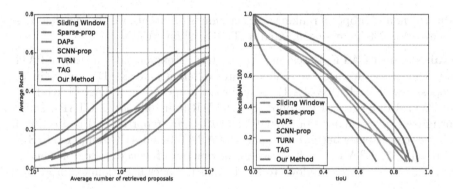

Fig. 4. AN-AR curve and recall@AN = 100 curve of CTAP and state-of-the-art methods on THUMOS-14 test set.

CTAP for Temporal Action Detection. To verify the quality of our proposals, we feed CTAP proposals into SCNN [3], and compare with other proposal generation methods on the same action detector (SCNN). The results are shown in Table 3. We can see that our CTAP-TS6 achieves the best performance, and outperforms the state-of-the-art proposal method TURN [2] and TAG [4] by over 4%, which proves the effectiveness of the proposed method.

4.4 Evaluation on ActivityNet V1.3

Evaluation of TAR. To show the effectiveness of TAR, we report the AR@100 values and area under AR-AN curve for different models in Table 4. For sliding window proposals, we observe that TAR's prediction (SW-TAR) achieves 18.29% and 6.86% improvement in AR@100 and AUC compared to those of TURN [2] (SW-TURN). The results show that TAR is more effective in temporal boundary

Table 3. Comparison of CTAP and other proposal generation methods with the same action detector (SCNN) on THUMOS-14 test set, mean Average Precision (mAP % @tIoU = 0.5) is reported.

Method	Sparse [8]	DAPs [11]	SCNN-prop[3]	TURN [2]	TAG[4]	CTAP-F16	CTAP-TS6
tIoU=0.5	15.3	16.3	19.0	25.6	25.9	27.9	**29.9**

Table 4. Evaluation of TURN [2], TAR, MSAR [32], Prop-SSAD [33] and CTAP on ActivityNet v1.3 validation set. AR@100 and AUC of AR-AN curve are reported. (The AR@100 of MSRA [32] is not available.)

Method	SW-TURN [2]	TAG-TURN [4]	SW- TAR	TAG- TAR	MSRA [32]	Prop-SSAD [33]	CTAP
AR@100	49.73	63.46	68.02	64.01	-	73.01	**73.17**
AUC	54.16	53.92	61.02	64.62	63.12	64.40	**65.72**

adjustment and proposal ranking. For actionness proposals, we observe that TAR achieves 10.70% increase compared to TURN [2] on AUC.

Evaluation of PATE. Based on TAR, we further explore the function of PATE complementary filtering. We evaluate three different models: (1) sliding window proposals with TAR (SW-TAR) (2) actioness proposals with TAR (TAG-TAR) (3) PATE Complementary proposals with TAR (our full model, CTAP). Different models' performances of AR@100 and AUC are reported in Table 4. CTAP achieves consistently better performance of AR@100 and AUC compared to SW-TAR and TAG-TAR, which shows its advantage of selecting complementary proposals from sliding windows to fill the omitted ones in actionness proposals.

Comparison with State-of-the-Art Methods. CTAP is compared with state-of-the-art methods on ActivityNet v1.3 validation set by the Average Recall at top 100 ranked proposals (AR@100) and area under AR-AN curve (AUC). In Table 4, we find CTAP achieves 2.60% and 1.32% increase in AR@100 compared with state-of-the-art methods MSRA [32] and Prop-SSAD [33] respectively.

Table 5. Generalization evaluation of CTAP on Activity Net v1.3 (validation set) in terms of AR@100 and AR-AN under curve area.

	Seen (100 classes)	Unseen (100 classes)
AR@100	74.06	72.51
AR-AN	66.01	64.92

Generalization Ability of Proposals. We evaluate the generalization ability of CTAP on ActivityNet v1.3 validation set. Following the setting of [34], we evaluate the AR@100 and AR-AN under curve area (AUC) for 100 seen classes and unseen classes respectively. In Table 5, we observe that CTAP achieves better

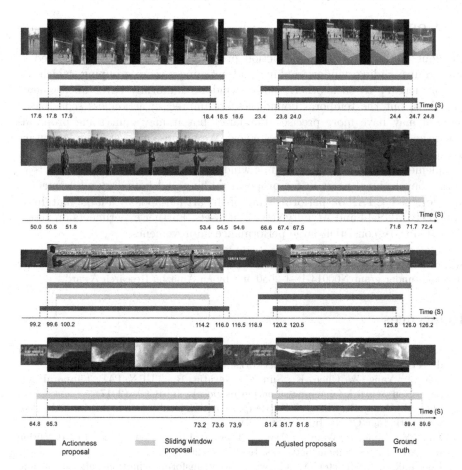

Fig. 5. Visualization of temporal action proposals generated by CTAP. First two rows represent 4 temporal action proposals from 2 videos in THUMOS-14. Last two rows represent 4 temporal action proposals from 2 videos in ActivityNet v1.3.

performance on 100 seen classes. On unseen 100 classes, there is only a slight drop in AR@100 and AUC, which shows the generalizability of CTAP.

4.5   Qualitative Results

We further visualize some temporal action proposals generated by CTAP. As shown in Fig. 5, CTAP is able to select most suitable initial proposals from actionness proposals or sliding windows, and then adjust their temporal boundaries more precisely.

5 Conclusion

Previous methods for temporal action proposal generation can be divided to two groups: sliding window ranking and actionness score grouping, which are complementary to each other: sliding windows uniformly cover all segments in videos, but the temporal boundaries are imprecise; actionness score based method may have more precise boundaries but it may omit some proposals when the quality of actioness scores is low. We propose a novel Complementary Temporal Action Proposal (CTAP) generator, which could collect high quality complementary proposals from sliding windows and actionness proposals. A temporal convolutional network for proposal ranking and boundary adjustment is also designed. CTAP outperforms state-of-the-art methods by a large margin on both THUMOS-14 and ActivityNet 1.3 datasets. Further experiments on action detection show consistent large performance improvements.

Acknowledgements. This research was supported, in part, by the Office of Naval Research under grant N00014-18-1-2050 and by an Amazon Research Award.

References

1. Ren, S., He, K., Girshick, R., Sun, J.: Faster R-CNN: towards real-time object detection with region proposal networks. In: NIPS (2015)
2. Gao, J., Yang, Z., Chen, K., Sun, C., Nevatia, R.: TURN TAP: temporal unit regression network for temporal action proposals. In: ICCV (2017)
3. Shou, Z., Wang, D., Chang, S.F.: Temporal action localization in untrimmed videos via multi-stage CNNs. In: CVPR (2016)
4. Zhao, Y., Xiong, Y., Wang, L., Wu, Z., Tang, X., Lin, D.: Temporal action detection with structured segment networks. In: ICCV (2017)
5. Roerdink, J.B., Meijster, A.: The watershed transform: definitions, algorithms and parallelization strategies. Fundam. Inform. **41**, 187–228 (2000)
6. Gao, J., Yang, Z., Nevatia, R.: Cascaded boundary regression for temporal action detection. In: BMVC (2017)
7. Gao, J., Ge, R., Chen, K., Nevatia, R.: Motion-appearance co-memory networks for video question answering. In: CVPR (2018)
8. Caba Heilbron, F., Carlos Niebles, J., Ghanem, B.: Fast temporal activity proposals for efficient detection of human actions in untrimmed videos. In: CVPR (2016)
9. Laptev, I.: On space-time interest points. IJCV **64**, 107–123 (2005)
10. Tran, D., Bourdev, L., Fergus, R., Torresani, L., Paluri, M.: Learning spatiotemporal features with 3D convolutional networks. In: ICCV (2015)
11. Escorcia, V., Heilbron, F.C., Niebles, J.C., Ghanem, B.: DAPs: deep action proposals for action understanding. In: ECCV (2016)
12. Buch, S., Escorcia, V., Shen, C., Ghanem, B., Carlos Niebles, J.: SST: single-stream temporal action proposals. In: CVPR (2017)
13. Serena, Y., Olga, R., Greg, M., Li, F.F.: End-to-end learning of action detection from frame glimpses in videos. In: CVPR (2016)
14. Sun, C., Shetty, S., Sukthankar, R., Nevatia, R.: Temporal localization of fine-grained actions in videos by domain transfer from web images. In: MM. ACM (2015)

15. Yuan, J., Ni, B., Yang, X., Kassim, A.A.: Temporal action localization with pyramid of score distribution features. In: CVPR (2016)
16. Lin, T., Zhao, X., Shou, Z.: Single shot temporal action detection. In: MM. ACM (2017)
17. Xu, H., Das, A., Saenko, K.: R-C3D: region convolutional 3D network for temporal activity detection. In: ICCV (2017)
18. Yuan, Z., Stroud, J.C., Lu, T., Deng, J.: Temporal action localization by structured maximal sums. In: CVPR (2017)
19. Shou, Z., Chan, J., Zareian, A., Miyazawa, K., Chang, S.F.: CDC: convolutional-de-convolutional networks for precise temporal action localization in untrimmed videos. In: CVPR (2017)
20. Dai, X., Singh, B., Zhang, G., Davis, L.S., Qiu Chen, Y.: Temporal context network for activity localization in videos. In: ICCV (2017)
21. Gao, J., Sun, C., Yang, Z., Nevatia, R.: TALL: temporal activity localization via language query. In: ICCV (2017)
22. De Geest, R., Gavves, E., Ghodrati, A., Li, Z., Snoek, C., Tuytelaars, T.: Online action detection. In: ECCV (2016)
23. Gao, J., Yang, Z., Nevatia, R.: RED: reinforced encoder-decoder networks for action anticipation. In: BMVC (2017)
24. Shou, Z., et al.: Online action detection in untrimmed, streaming videos-modeling and evaluation. CoRR (2018)
25. Simonyan, K., Zisserman, A.: Two-stream convolutional networks for action recognition in videos. In: NIPS (2014)
26. Xiong, Y., et al.: CUHK & ETHZ & SIAT submission to activitynet challenge 2016. CoRR (2016)
27. Jiang, Y.G., et al.: THUMOS challenge: action recognition with a large number of classes. In: CVPR Workshop (2015)
28. Caba Heilbron, F., Escorcia, V., Ghanem, B., Carlos Niebles, J.: ActivityNet: a large-scale video benchmark for human activity understanding. In: CVPR (2015)
29. He, K., Zhang, X., Ren, S., Sun, J.: Deep residual learning for image recognition. In: CVPR (2016)
30. Ioffe, S., Szegedy, C.: Batch normalization: accelerating deep network training by reducing internal covariate shift. In: ICML (2015)
31. Kingma, D., Ba, J.: Adam: a method for stochastic optimization. In: ICLR (2015)
32. Yao, T., et al.: MSR Asia MSM at ActivityNet challenge 2017: trimmed action recognition, temporal action proposals and dense-captioning events in videos. In: CVPR Workshop (2017)
33. Lin, T., Zhao, X., Shou, Z.: Temporal convolution based action proposal: submission to activitynet 2017. In: ICCV Workshop (2017)
34. Xiong, Y., Zhao, Y., Wang, L., Lin, D., Tang, X.: A pursuit of temporal accuracy in general activity detection. CoRR (2017)

Effective Use of Synthetic Data for Urban Scene Semantic Segmentation

Fatemeh Sadat Saleh[1,2]($\boxtimes$) (ID), Mohammad Sadegh Aliakbarian[1,2,3] (ID),
Mathieu Salzmann[4] (ID), Lars Petersson[2] (ID), and Jose M. Alvarez[5] (ID)

[1] ANU, Canberra, Australia
[2] Data61-CSIRO, Canberra, Australia
{fatemehsadat.saleh,mohammadsadegh.aliakbarian,
lars.petersson}@data61.csiro.au
[3] ACRV, Canberra, Australia
[4] CVLab, EPFL, Lausanne, Switzerland
mathieu.salzmann@epfl.ch
[5] NVIDIA, Santa Clara, USA
josea@nvidia.com

Abstract. Training a deep network to perform semantic segmentation requires large amounts of labeled data. To alleviate the manual effort of annotating real images, researchers have investigated the use of synthetic data, which can be labeled automatically. Unfortunately, a network trained on synthetic data performs relatively poorly on real images. While this can be addressed by domain adaptation, existing methods all require having access to real images during training. In this paper, we introduce a drastically different way to handle synthetic images that does not require seeing any real images at training time. Our approach builds on the observation that foreground and background classes are not affected in the same manner by the domain shift, and thus should be treated differently. In particular, the former should be handled in a detection-based manner to better account for the fact that, while their texture in synthetic images is not photo-realistic, their shape looks natural. Our experiments evidence the effectiveness of our approach on Cityscapes and CamVid with models trained on synthetic data only.

Keywords: Synthetic data · Semantic segmentation
Object detection · Instance-level annotation

1 Introduction

As for many other computer vision tasks, deep networks have proven highly effective to perform semantic segmentation. Their main drawback, however, is their requirement for vast amounts of labeled data. In particular, acquiring such data for semantic segmentation is very expensive. For instance, pixel labeling of

---

This work was supported by the Australian Centre of Excellence for Robotic Vision.

V. Ferrari et al. (Eds.): ECCV 2018, LNCS 11206, pp. 86–103, 2018.
https://doi.org/10.1007/978-3-030-01216-8_6

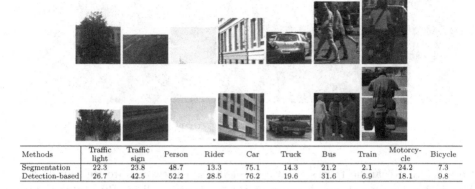

Methods	Traffic light	Traffic sign	Person	Rider	Car	Truck	Bus	Train	Motorcy-cle	Bicycle
Segmentation	22.3	23.8	48.7	13.3	75.1	14.3	21.2	2.1	24.2	7.3
Detection-based	26.7	42.5	52.2	28.5	76.2	19.6	31.6	6.9	18.1	9.8

Fig. 1. Visual comparison of different classes in real Cityscapes images (Top) and synthetic GTA5 ones (Middle). Background classes (first 4 columns) are much less affected by the domain shift than foreground ones (last 3 columns), which present clearly noticeable differences in texture, but whose shape remain realistic. (Bottom) We compare the accuracy of a semantic segmentation network (DeepLab) and of a detection-based model (Mask R-CNN), both trained on synthetic data only, on the foreground classes of Cityscapes. Note that the detection-based approach, by leveraging shape, yields significantly better results than the segmentation one.

one Cityscapes image takes 90 min on average [7]. As a consequence, there has been a significant effort in the community to rely on the advances of computer graphics to generate synthetic datasets [35–37].

Despite the increasing realism of such synthetic data, there remain significant perceptual differences between synthetic and real images. Therefore, the performance of a state-of-the-art semantic segmentation network, such as [4,25,28,52], trained on synthetic data and tested on real images remains disappointingly low. While domain adaptation methods [5,6,19,20,27,51] can improve such performance by explicitly accounting for the domain shift between real and synthetic data, they require having access to a large set of real images, albeit unsupervised, during training. As such, one cannot simply deploy a model trained off-line on synthetic data in a new, real-world environment.

In this paper, we introduce a drastically different approach to addressing the mismatch between real and synthetic data, based on the following observation: Not all classes suffer from the same type and degree of perceptual differences. In particular, as can be seen in Fig. 1, the *texture* of background classes in synthetic images looks more realistic than that of foreground classes[1]. Nevertheless, the *shape* of foreground objects in synthetic images looks very natural. We therefore argue that these two different kinds of classes should be treated differently.

---

[1] We distinguish foreground classes from background ones primarily based on whether they have a well-defined shape and come in instances, or they are shapeless and identified by texture or material property. In essence, this corresponds to the distinction between *things* and *stuff* in [17]. See Fig. 1 for examples.

Fig. 2. Aerial views of our synthetic VEIS environment.

Specifically, we argue that semantic segmentation networks are well-suited to handle background classes because of their texture realism. By contrast, we expect object detectors to be more appropriate for foreground classes, particularly considering that modern detectors rely on generic object proposals. Indeed, when dealing with all possible texture variations of all foreground object classes, the main source of information to discriminate a foreground object from the background is shape.

To empirically sustain our claim that detectors are better-suited for foreground classes, we trained separately a DeepLab [4] semantic segmentation network and a Mask R-CNN [16], performing object detection followed by binary segmentation and class prediction, on synthetic data. At the bottom of Fig. 1, we compare the mean Intersection over Union (mIoU) of these two models on the foreground classes of Cityscapes. Note that, except for *motorcycle*, the detector-based approach outperforms the semantic segmentation network on all classes.

Motivated by this observation, we therefore develop a simple, yet effective semantic segmentation framework that better leverages synthetic data during training. In essence, our model combines the foreground masks produced by Mask R-CNN with the pixel-wise predictions of the DeepLab semantic segmentation network. Our experiments on Cityscapes [7] and CamVid [3] demonstrate that this yields significantly higher segmentation accuracies on real data than only training a semantic segmentation network on synthetic data. Furthermore, our approach outperforms the state-of-the-art domain adaptation techniques [6,19,20,51] without having seen any real images during training, and can be further improved by making use of unsupervised real images.

Furthermore, as a secondary contribution, we introduce a virtual environment created in the Unity3D framework, called **VEIS** (Virtual Environment for Instance Segmentation). This was motivated by the fact that existing synthetic datasets [35–37] do not provide instance-level segmentation annotations for all the foreground classes of standard real datasets, such as CityScapes. VEIS automatically annotates synthetic images with instance-level segmentation for foreground classes. It captures urban scenes, such as those in Fig. 2 shown from an aerial view, using a virtual camera mounted on a virtual car, yielding images such as those of Fig. 6. While not highly realistic, we show that, when used with a detector-based approach, this data allows us to boost semantic segmentation performance, despite it being of only little use in a standard semantic segmentation framework. We will make our data and the VEIS environment publicly available.

2   Related Work

Semantic segmentation, that is, understanding an image at pixel-level, has been widely studied by the computer vision community [4,11,15,25,26,28,33,42,43, 46,52,53]. As for many other tasks, the most recent techniques rely on deep networks [4,25,28,52]. Unfortunately, in contrast with image recognition problems, obtaining fully-supervised data for semantic segmentation, with pixel-level annotations, is very expensive and time-consuming. Two trends have therefore been investigated to overcome this limitation: Weakly-supervised methods and the use of synthetic data.

Weakly-supervised semantic segmentation aims to leverage a weaker form of annotation, such as image tags [23,29,30,32,34,40,41,48,49], bounding boxes [8,21], scribbles [2] and object size statistics [31], which are cheaper to obtain. While great progress has been made in this area, most existing methods focus only on foreground object classes and treat the background as one single entity. However, having detailed information about the different background classes is crucial in many practical scenarios, such as automated driving, where one needs to differentiate, e.g., the road from a grass field. To the best of our knowledge, [39] constitutes the only method that considers multiple background classes for weakly-supervised semantic segmentation. This is achieved by leveraging both appearance and motion via a two-stream architecture trained using a loss based on classifier heatmaps. While this method is reasonably effective at segmenting background classes, there is still a huge gap compared to fully-supervised methods, especially in the foreground classes.

With the advance of computer graphics, generating fully-supervised synthetic data has become an attractive alternative to weakly-supervised learning. This has led to several datasets, such as SYNTHIA [37], GTA5 [36] and VIPER [35], as well as virtual environments to generate data [9]. Unfortunately, despite the growing realism of such synthetic data, simply training a deep network on synthetic images to apply it to real ones still yields disappointing results. This problem is due to the domain shift between real and synthetic data, and has thus been tackled by domain adaptation methods [5,6,19,20,27,51], which, in essence, aim to reduce the gap between the feature distributions of the two domains. In [20], this is achieved by a domain adversarial training strategy inspired by the method of [12,13]. This is further extended in [5] to align not only global, but also class-specific statistics. Domain adversarial training is combined in [6] with a feature regularizer based on the notion of distillation [18]. In [51], a curriculum style learning is introduced to align the label distribution over both entire images and superpixels. By contrast, [19] and [27] rely on a generative approach with cycle consistency to adapt the pixel-level and feature-level representations. While these methods outperform simply training a network on the synthetic data, without any form of adaptation, they all rely on having access to real images, without supervision, during training. As such, they cannot be directly deployed in a new environment without undergoing a new training phase.

Here, we follow an orthogonal approach to leverage synthetic data, based on the observation that foreground and background classes are subject to different perceptual mismatches between synthetic and real images. We therefore propose to rely on a standard semantic segmentation network for background classes, whose textures look quite realistic, and on a detection-based strategy for foreground objects because, while their textures look less natural, their shapes are realistic. Our experiments evidence that this outperforms state-of-the-art domain adaptation strategies. However, being orthogonal to domain adaptation, our method could also be used in conjunction with domain adaptation techniques. As a matter of fact, [45], which also argues that modern detectors rely on shape and discard the background texture, introduces a domain adaptation approach for the task of object detection, which could potentially be leveraged to deal with the foreground classes in our approach. We believe, however, that this goes beyond the scope of this paper.

3   Method

In this section, we introduce our approach to effectively use synthetic data for semantic segmentation in real driving scenarios. Note that, while we focus on driving scenarios, our approach generalizes to other semantic segmentation problems. However, synthetic data is typically easier to generate for urban scenes. Below, we first consider the case where we do not have access to any real images during training. We then introduce a simple strategy to leverage the availability of unsupervised real images.

3.1   Detection-Based Semantic Segmentation

As discussed above, and illustrated by Fig. 1, the perceptual differences of foreground and background classes in synthetic and real images are different. In fact, background classes in synthetic images look quite realistic, presenting very natural textures, whereas the texture of foreground classes does look synthetic, but their shape is realistic. We therefore propose to handle the background classes with a semantic segmentation network, but rather make use of a detection-based technique for the foreground classes. Below, we describe this in more detail, and then discuss how we perform semantic segmentation on a real image.

Dealing with Background Classes. To handle the background classes, we make use of the VGG16-based DeepLab model, depicted in Fig. 3. Specifically, we use DeepLab with a large field of view and dilated convolution layers [4]. We train this model on the GTA5 dataset [36] in which the background classes look photo-realistic. The choice of this dataset above others was also motivated by the fact that it contains all the classes of the commonly used real datasets, such as Cityscapes and CamVid. To train our model, we use the cross-entropy loss

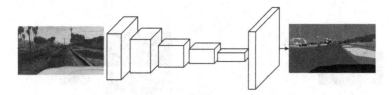

Fig. 3. Dealing with background classes. We make use of the DeepLab semantic segmentation framework trained on synthetic GTA5 [36] frames with corresponding per-pixel annotations.

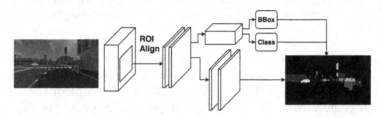

Fig. 4. Dealing with foreground classes. We rely on the detection-based Mask R-CNN framework trained on our synthetic VEIS data with instance-level annotations. Note that these annotations were obtained automatically.

between the network's predictions and the ground-truth pixel-wise annotations of the synthetic images. Note that the network is trained on all classes, both foreground and background, but, as explained later, the foreground predictions are mostly discarded by our approach.

Dealing with Foreground Classes. For foreground classes, our goal is to make use of a detection-based approach, which, as argued in Sect. 1, relies more strongly on object shape than on texture, thus making texture realism of the synthetic data less crucial. Since our final goal is to produce a pixel-wise segmentation of the objects, we propose to rely on a detection-based instance-level semantic segmentation technique. Note that, once an object has been detected, segmenting it from the background within its bounding box is a comparatively easier task than semantic segmentation of an entire image. Therefore, texture realism is also not crucial here. To address this task, we make use of Mask R-CNN [16], which satisfies our criteria: As illustrated in Fig. 4, it relies on an initial object detection stage, followed by a binary mask extraction together with object classification. Since existing synthetic datasets do not provide instance-level segmentations for all foreground classes of standard real datasets, we train Mask R-CNN using our own synthetic data, discussed in Sect. 4. We make use of the standard architecture described in [16], as well as of the standard loss, which combines detection, segmentation, classification and regression terms.

Prediction on Real Images. The two networks described above are trained using synthetic data only. At test time, we can then feed a real image to each network to obtain predictions. However, our goal is to obtain a single,

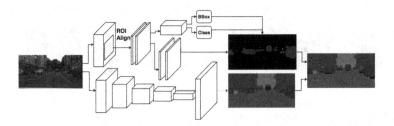

Fig. 5. Fusing foreground and background predictions. Our approach combines the detection-based foreground predictions with the results of the semantic segmentation approach. Note that we do *not* require seeing any real images during training.

pixel-wise semantic segmentation, not two separate kinds of outputs. To achieve this, as illustrated in Fig. 5, we fuse the two kinds of predictions, starting from the Mask R-CNN ones. Specifically, given the Mask R-CNN predictions, we follow a strategy inspired by the panoptic segmentation procedure of [22], which constitutes an NMS-like approach to combine instance segments. More precisely, we first sort the predicted segments according to their confidence scores, and then iterate over this sorted list, starting from the most confident segment. If the current segment candidate overlaps with a previous segment, we remove the pixels in the overlapping region. The original procedure of [22] relies on two different thresholds: One to discard the low-scoring segments and the other to discard non-overlapping yet too small segment regions. The values of these thresholds were obtained by grid search on real images. Since we do not have access to the ground-truth annotations of the real images, and in fact not even access to the real images during training, we ignore these two heuristics to discard segments, and thus consider all segments and all non-overlapping segment regions when combining the Mask R-CNN predictions.

Combining the Mask R-CNN predictions yield a semantic segmentation map that only contains foreground classes and has a large number of holes, where no foreground objects were found. To obtain our final semantic segmentation map, we fill these holes with the predictions obtained by the DeepLab network. That is, every pixel that is not already assigned to a foreground class takes the label with highest probability at that pixel location in the DeepLab result.

3.2 Leveraging Unsupervised Real Images

The method described in Sect. 3.1 uses only synthetic images during training. In some scenarios, however, it is possible to have access to unlabeled real images at training time. This is in fact the assumption made by domain adaptation techniques. To extend our approach to this scenario, we propose to treat the predictions obtained by the method of Sect. 3.1 as pseudo ground-truth labels for the real images. To be precise, we make a small change to these predictions: In the holes left after combining the Mask R-CNN predictions, we assign the pixels that are predicted as foreground classes by the DeepLab model to an *ignore*

Fig. 6. Example images and corresponding instance-level annotations, obtained automatically, from our synthetic VEIS dataset.

label, so that they are not used for training. This is motivated by the fact that, as discussed above, the predictions of foreground classes by a standard semantic segmentation network are not reliable. We then use the resulting pseudo-labels as ground-truth to train a DeepLab semantic segmentation network from real images. As will be shown in our results, thanks to the good quality of our initial predictions, this helps further boost segmentation accuracy.

4   The VEIS Environment and Dataset

In this section, we introduce our Virtual Environment for Instance Segmentation (VEIS) and the resulting dataset used in our experiments. While there are already a number of synthetic datasets for the task of semantic segmentation in urban scenes [35–37], they each suffer from some drawbacks. In particular, GTA5 [36] does not have instance-level annotations, and is thus not suitable for our purpose. By contrast, SYNTHIA [37] and VIPER [35] do have instance-level annotations, but not for all foreground classes of commonly-used real datasets, such as Cityscapes. For instance, *train, truck, traffic light* and *traffic sign* are missing in SYNTHIA, and *rider, traffic sign, train* and *bicycle* in VIPER. Furthermore, [35,36] were acquired using the commercial game engine Grand Theft Auto V (GTAV), which only provides limited freedom for customization and control over the scenes to be captured, thus making it difficult to obtain a large diversity and good balance of classes. Obtaining ground-truth instance-level annotations in the GTAV game also involves a rather complicated procedure [35].

Environment. To alleviate these difficulties, we used the Unity3D [47] game engine, in which one can manually design scenes with common urban structures and add freely-available 3D objects, representing foreground classes, to the scene. Example 3D scenes are shown in Fig. 2. Having access to the source code and manually constructing the scenes both facilitate generating annotations such as instance-level pixel-wise labels automatically. Specifically, before starting to generate the frames, our framework counts the number of instances of each class, and then assigns a unique ID to each instance. These unique IDs then automatically create unique textures and shaders for their corresponding instances. When data generation starts, both the original textures and shaders and the automatically created ones are rendered, thus allowing us to capture the synthetic image and the instance-level semantic segmentation map at the same time and in real time. Creating VEIS took 1 day to 1 person. This is very little effort, considering that VEIS allows us to have access to a virtually unlimited number of annotated images with the object classes of standard real urban scene datasets, such as CamVid and CityScapes.

As can be seen from the samples shown in Fig. 6, the images generated by VEIS look less photo-realistic than those of [35,36]. Therefore, as evidenced by our experiments, using them to train a semantic segmentation network does not significantly help improve accuracy on real images compared to using existing synthetic datasets. However, using these images within our proposed detection-based framework allows us to significantly improve semantic segmentation quality. This is due to the fact that, while not realistic in texture, the foreground objects generated by VEIS are realistic in shape, and our environment allowed us to cover a wide range of shape and pose variations.

Note that, in principle, we could have used other open source frameworks to generate our data, such as CARLA [9], implemented as an open-source layer of the Unreal Engine 4 (UE4) [10]. However, CARLA is somewhat too advanced for the purpose of our investigation. It targets the complete autonomous driving pipeline, with three different approaches covering a standard modular pipeline, an end-to-end approach based on imitation learning, and an end-to-end approach based on reinforcement learning. Since our goal was only to generate synthetic images covering a large diversity of foreground objects, we found Unity3D to be sufficient and easier to deploy.

The VEIS Dataset. Using our VEIS environment, we generated images from two different types of scenes: (1) A multi-class, complex scene, where a city-like environment was synthesized with various objects of different classes. (2) A single-class, simple scene, where one or multiple objects of a single class were placed in a single road with background items (e.g., road, sidewalk, building, tree, sky), and images from multiple views were captured. Our VEIS dataset then contains 30180 frames from the multi-class scene and 31125 frames from the single-class scene, amounting to a total of 61305 frames with corresponding instance-level semantic segmentation. Note that the instance-level annotations were obtained with no human intervention. Some statistics of this dataset are shown in Table 1. In particular, we used a small amount of unique 3D objects for most of the classes and just repeated them in the scenes but with varying pose and articulation where applicable.

5   Experiments

In this section, we first describe the datasets used in our experiments and provide details about our learning and inference procedures. We then present the results

Table 1. Some statistics of our synthetic data

Class	T. light	T. sign	Person	Rider	Car	Truck	Bus	Train	M. bike	Bicycle
#unique instances	3	69	31	1	13	6	3	3	7	4
#instances in dataset	101771	261015	176552	67073	148760	26847	45082	12071	50687	67672

of our model and compare it to state-of-the-art weakly-supervised semantic segmentation and domain adaptation methods.

5.1 Datasets

To train our model and the baseline, we make use of the synthetic GTA5 dataset [36] and of our new VEIS dataset introduced in Sect. 4. Furthermore, we also provide results of fully-supervised models trained on the synthetic SYN-THIA [37] and VIPER [35] datasets. At test time, we evaluate the models on the real images of the CityScapes [7] and CamVid [3] road scene datasets. Below, we briefly discuss the characteristics of these datasets.

GTA5 [36] was captured using the Grand Theft Auto V video game and contains 24966 photo-realistic images with corresponding pixel-level annotations. The resolution of the images is 1920 × 1080 and the class definitions of the semantic categories are compatible with those in the Cityscapes dataset.

VIPER [35] is a slightly more recent dataset than GTA5, also acquired using the Grand Theft Auto V video game, but covering a wider range of weather conditions. It contains more than 250K high-resolution (1920 × 1080) video frames, all annotated with ground-truth labels for both low-level and high-level vision tasks, including optical flow, semantic instance segmentation, object detection and tracking, object-level 3D scene layout, and visual odometry. In our experiments, the model exploiting VIPER was trained using the training and validation sets of this dataset (over 180K frames). While VIPER is larger than GTA5, its labels are not really compatible with Cityscapes. For example, the classes *rider* and *wall* are missing; the class *pole* has been incorporated into *infrastructure*[2]; the windows of the cars are not labeled as *car* unlike in Cityscapes. This explains why most of our experiments rather rely on GTA5.

SYNTHIA [37] is another dataset of synthetic images, with a subset called SYNTHIA-RAND-CITYSCAPES meant to be compatible with Cityscapes. This subset contains 9,400 images with pixel-level semantic annotations. However, some classes, such as *train*, *truck* and *terrain*, have no annotations. As for VIPER, we show the performance of a fully-supervised method trained on SYNTHIA. This is for the sake of completeness, even though we favor GTA5 since it contains all the classes of Cityscapes.

Cityscapes [7] is a large-scale dataset of real images, containing high-quality pixel-level annotations for 5000 images collected in street scenes from 50 different cities. There is also another set of images with coarse level annotations. We

---

[2] To evaluate the *pole* class, we considered any *infrastructure* prediction as *pole*, which is the dominant label in this slightly broader class.

report the results of all models on the 500 validation images. Furthermore, the methods that rely on unsupervised real images during training, including ours, were trained using the 22971 train/train-extra RGB frames of this dataset.

CamVid [3] consists of over 10 min of high quality 30 Hz footage. The videos were captured at 960×720 resolution with a camera mounted inside a car. Three of the four sequences were shot in daylight, and the fourth one was captured at dusk. This dataset contains 32 categories. In our experiments, following [3], we used a subset of 11 classes. The dataset is split into 367 training, 101 validation and 233 test images. Note that, as for the Cityscapes dataset, we evaluate on the test set and, when training on unsupervised data, used the RGB frames of training+validation without any type of annotation.

5.2 Implementation Details

As discussed in Sect. 3, our approach makes use of two types of networks: DeepLab (Large FOV) [4] for semantic segmentation and Mask R-CNN [16] for instance-level segmentation. Below, we briefly discuss these models.

DeepLab. To train our semantic segmentation networks, using either the synthetic GTA5 dataset or real images with pseudo ground truth, we used a DeepLab model with a large field of view and dilated convolution layers. We relied on stochastic gradient descent with a learning rate starting at 25×10^{-5}, with a decrease factor of 10 every $40k$ iterations, a momentum of 0.9, a weight decay of 0.0005, and mini-batches of size 1. Similarly to recent methods [4,25,39,52], the weights of our semantic segmentation network were initialized with those of the VGG-16 classifier [44] pre-trained on ImageNet [38]. Note that, because of limited GPU memory, we down-sampled the high resolution images of Cityscapes, GTA5, VIPER, and SYNTHIA by a factor 2 when using them for training.

Mask R-CNN. To train a Mask R-CNN network, we make use of the implementation provided by the "Detectron" framework [14]. We train an end-to-end Mask R-CNN model with a $64 \times 4d$ ResNeXt-101-FPN backbone, pre-trained on ImageNet, on our synthetic VEIS dataset. We use mini-batches of size 1 and train the model for 200k iterations, starting with a learning rate of 0.001 and reducing it to 0.0001 after 100k iterations.

5.3 Evaluated Methods

In our experiments, we report the results of the following methods:
GTA5 [6]: This baseline denotes a DeepLab model trained on GTA5 by the authors of [6]. We directly report the numbers as provided in [6].
GTA5: This corresponds to our replication of the baseline above. We found our implementation to yield an average accuracy 9.4% higher than the one reported in [6]. As such, this constitutes our true baseline.
SYNTHIA: This refers to a DeepLab model trained on the SYNTHIA [37] dataset instead of GTA5.

VIPER: This baseline denotes a DeepLab model trained on the VIPER dataset.
VEIS: This corresponds to training a DeepLab model on our new dataset. Note that here we considered all the classes, both foreground and background ones, for semantic segmentation, ignoring the notion of instances.
GTA5+VEIS: This denotes a DeepLab model trained jointly on GTA5 and our new dataset for semantic segmentation.
GTA5+VEIS and Pseudo-GT: For this baseline, we used the results of the GTA5+VEIS baseline to generate pseudo-labels on the real images. We then trained another DeepLab network using these pseudo-labels as ground-truth. In essence, this corresponds to the approach discussed in Sect. 3.2, but without handling the foreground classes in a detection-based manner.
Ours: This corresponds to our method in Sect. 3.1, which relies on the GTA5 synthetic data and uses a detection-based model for foreground classes combined with a DeepLab semantic segmentation network for the background ones.
Ours and Pseudo-GT: This consists of using the method above (Ours) to generate pseudo-labels on the real images, and training a DeepLab model from these pseudo-labels, as introduced in Sect. 3.2.

5.4   Experimental Results

We now compare the results of the different methods discussed above on the real images of Cityscapes and CamVid. Furthermore, we also compare our approach to the state-of-the-art weakly supervised semantic segmentation and domain adaptation methods on Cityscapes.

In Table 2, we provide the results of the methods described above on Cityscapes. The foreground classes are highlighted. In essence, we can see that GTA5 performs better than training DeepLab on the datasets {SYNTHIA,VIPER,VEIS} alone, because these datasets either do not contain all the Cityscapes classes {SYNTHIA,VIPER}, or because they are less realistic {VEIS}. Complementing GTA5 with VEIS {GTA5+VEIS} improves the results by only a small margin, again because of the non-photo-realistic VEIS images. By contrast, using GTA5 and VEIS jointly within our approach (Ours) yields a significant improvement. This is because our detection-based way of dealing with foreground classes is less sensitive to photo-realism, but focuses on shape, which does look natural in our VEIS data. As a matter of fact, our improvement is particularly marked for foreground classes. Finally, while using pseudo-labels from the {GTA5+VEIS} baseline only yields a minor improvement, their use within our framework gives a significant accuracy boost. Some qualitative results are shown in Fig. 7.

In Table 3, we compare our approach with the state-of-the-are weakly-supervised method of [39] and with state-of-the-art domain adaptation methods. The results for these methods were directly taken from their respective papers. Note that, even without seeing the Cityscapes images at all, our approach (Ours) outperforms all these baselines. Using unsupervised Cityscapes images (Ours+pseudo-GT) helps to further improve over the baselines. To also show that our approach generalizes to the situation where there is no domain shift,

Table 2. Comparison of models trained on synthetic data. All the results are reported on the Cityscapes validation set. Note that ps-GT (pseudo-GT) indicates the use of unlabeled real images during training.

	road	side.	buil.	wall	fence	pole	light	sign	Vege.	terr.	sky	person	rider	car	truck	bus	train	motor	bike	mIOU
GTA5 [6]	29.8	16.0	56.6	9.2	17.3	13.5	13.6	9.8	74.9	6.7	54.3	41.9	2.9	45.0	3.3	13.1	1.3	6.0	0.0	21.9
GTA5	80.5	26.0	74.7	23.0	9.8	9.1	13.4	7.3	79.4	28.6	72.1	40.4	5.1	77.8	23.0	18.6	1.2	5.3	0.0	31.3
SYNTHIA	36.7	22.7	51.0	0.3	0.1	16.6	0.1	9.5	72.5	0.0	78.4	47.5	5.6	61.4	0.0	13.0	0.0	3.2	3.1	22.1
VIPER	36.9	19.0	74.7	0.0	5.3	7.1	10.0	10.1	78.7	13.6	69.6	43.0	0.0	41.2	20.8	13.9	0.0	9.1	0.0	23.9
VEIS	70.8	9.5	50.9	0.0	0.0	0.3	15.6	26.8	66.8	12.7	52.3	44.0	14.2	60.6	10.2	8.2	3.2	5.5	11.8	24.4
GTA5+VEIS	66.2	21.6	72.3	15.7	18.3	12.3	22.3	23.8	78.4	11.3	74.6	48.7	13.3	75.1	14.3	21.2	2.1	24.2	7.3	32.8
GTA5+VEIS&ps-GT	77.6	26.8	75.5	19.4	19.5	4.8	18.7	19.8	79.5	21.7	78.9	47.3	8.7	77.6	23.1	16.1	2.2	15.6	0.0	33.3
Ours	71.9	23.8	75.5	23.4	14.9	9.3	26.7	42.5	80.1	34.0	76.3	52.2	28.5	76.2	19.6	31.6	6.9	18.1	9.8	38.0
Ours&ps-GT	79.8	29.3	77.8	24.2	21.6	6.9	23.5	44.2	80.5	38.0	76.2	52.7	22.2	83.0	32.3	41.3	27.0	19.3	27.7	42.5

Table 3. Comparison to domain adaptation and weakly-supervised methods. All methods were trained on GTA5, except for [39] which does not use synthetic images and Ours which uses GTA5 for background classes and VEIS for foreground. The domain adaptation methods and Ours+Pseudo-GT make use of unlabeled real images during training. The results are reported on the Cityscapes validation set. Note that all the models below use the same backbone architecture as us (DeepLab or FCN8).

Methods	road	side.	buil.	wall	fence	pole	light	sign	Vege.	terr.	sky	person	rider	car	truck	bus	train	motor	bike	mIOU
Fully Sup.	95.8	70.4	85.4	42.7	41.0	21.2	33.7	44.8	86.2	51.4	88.4	58.1	30.1	86.4	43.8	56.7	42.8	33.9	54.8	56.2
Fully Sup. Ours	95.6	70.1	86.1	43.8	41.4	16.6	31.3	43.3	85.9	52.0	89.6	67.0	29.9	87.7	61.8	72.7	53.1	50.8	60.5	60.0
Weakly-Sup. [39]	75.9	1.5	41.7	14.1	15.3	6.3	4.4	7.7	58.4	12.6	56.2	16.2	6.1	41.2	22.7	16.6	20.4	15.7	14.9	23.6
FCNs in Wld [20]	70.4	32.4	62.1	14.9	5.4	10.9	14.2	2.7	79.2	21.3	64.6	44.1	4.2	70.4	8.0	7.3	0.0	3.5	0.0	27.1
Curriculum [51]	74.8	22.0	71.7	6.0	11.9	8.4	16.3	11.1	75.7	13.3	66.5	38.0	0.3	55.2	18.8	18.9	0.0	16.8	14.6	28.9
ROAD [6]	85.4	31.2	78.6	27.9	22.2	21.9	23.7	11.4	80.7	29.3	68.9	48.5	14.1	78.0	19.1	23.8	9.4	8.3	0.0	35.9
CYCADA [19]	85.2	37.2	76.5	21.8	15.0	23.8	22.9	21.5	80.5	31.3	60.7	50.5	9.0	76.9	17.1	28.2	4.5	9.8	0.0	35.4
Ours	71.9	23.8	75.5	23.4	14.9	9.3	26.7	42.5	80.1	34.0	76.3	52.2	28.5	76.2	19.6	31.6	6.9	18.1	9.8	38.0
Ours+Pseudo-GT	79.8	29.3	77.8	, 24.2	21.6	6.9	23.5	44.2	80.5	38.0	76.2	52.7	22.2	83.0	32.3	41.3	27.0	19.3	27.7	42.5

we trained its two components on Cityscapes and evaluated it on the Cityscapes validation set (Fully Sup. Ours in Table 3). This significantly improves the segmentation accuracy of foreground classes (e.g., person, car, truck, bus, train, motorbike, bike).

The results on CamVid in Table 4, where we compare our method to fully-supervised techniques that make use of CamVid images and annotations to train a model, GTA5-based baselines, and the state-of-the-art weakly-supervised method, show a similar trend. Our approach clearly outperforms the weakly-supervised method of [39] and a DeepLab semantic segmentation network trained on synthetic data. In fact, on this dataset, it event outperforms some of the fully supervised methods that rely on annotated CamVid images for training.

5.5   Shape vs. Texture in the Presence of Domain Shift

In addition to Fig. 1, we experimentally show that shape is more representative than texture for foreground classes when dealing with the domain shift. To this end, first, we trained a binary VGG-16 classifier to determine whether a

Table 4. Comparison with fully- and weakly-supervised methods on CamVid.

Methods	build.	vege.	sky	car	sign	road	ped.	fence	pole	side.	cyclist	mIOU
SegNet [1]	68.7	52.0	87.0	58.5	13.4	86.2	25.3	17.9	16.0	60.5	24.8	46.4
Liu and He [24]	66.8	66.6	90.1	62.9	21.4	85.8	28.0	17.8	8.3	63.5	8.5	47.2
FCN 8 [25]	n/a											52.0
DeepLab-LargeFOV [4,50]	81.5	74.6	89.0	82.2	42.3	92.2	48.4	27.2	14.3	75.4	50.1	61.6
Dilation8 [50]	82.6	76.2	89.9	84.0	46.9	92.2	56.3	35.8	23.4	75.3	55.5	65.3
Weakly Sup. [39]	58.9	46.4	83.8	26.5	12.0	64.4	8.0	11.3	3.1	1.1	11.0	29.7
GTA5	66.6	53.9	61.4	70.4	32.8	80.9	28.2	24.4	14.6	57.1	0.0	44.6
GTA5+VEIS	73.6	54.2	77.9	66.2	33.6	77.3	26.1	16.0	3.3	48.4	11.9	44.4
Ours	66.3	55.0	61.9	73.4	37.4	82.7	41.4	23.9	9.2	57.7	14.9	47.6
Ours+Pseudo-GT	72.3	55.2	72.6	73.1	37.4	83.9	39.9	33.2	1.2	55.5	12.8	48.8

Fig. 7. Qualitative results on Cityscapes.

silhouette of a foreground object comes from real or synthetic data. We used synthetic data from our VEIS dataset and real data from Cityscapes. We found that such a classifier was unreliable to distinguish these two classes, achieving an accuracy of 70.0% despite our best effort to train it. Note that this is better than chance because the synthetic silhouettes are perfect whereas the real ones were obtained manually. We performed the same experiment with textured foreground objects (but no background) and found that the same classifier was then successful, with an accuracy of 95.1%. This shows that texture is indeed much more indicative of the data domain than shape, and thus supports our claim. As a second experiment, we trained a multi-class classifier on silhouettes of synthetic foreground VEIS objects and tested it on silhouettes of real Cityscapes objects. The resulting classifier achieved an accuracy of 81.0% on the real data, vs 89.2% on a validation set of synthetic samples. Training the same classifier on textured silhouettes yielded an accuracy of 83.7% on real data and 94.2% on synthetic data. In other words, there is a larger accuracy gap between the real and synthetic domains when training on textured data, thus further showing that shape is more robust to the domain shift.

6   Conclusion

We have introduced an approach to effectively leveraging synthetic training data for semantic segmentation in urban scenes, by handling the foreground classes in a detection-based manner. Our experiments have demonstrated that this outperforms training a standard semantic segmentation network from synthetic data and state-of-the-art domain adaptation techniques. Nevertheless, our approach is orthogonal to domain adaptation. As such, in the future we will investigate how domain adaptation can be incorporated into our framework.

References

1. Badrinarayanan, V., Handa, A., Cipolla, R.: SegNet: a deep convolutional encoder-decoder architecture for robust semantic pixel-wise labelling. arXiv preprint arXiv:1505.07293 (2015)
2. Bearman, A., Russakovsky, O., Ferrari, V., Fei-Fei, L.: What's the point: semantic segmentation with point supervision. In: Leibe, B., Matas, J., Sebe, N., Welling, M. (eds.) ECCV 2016. LNCS, vol. 9911, pp. 549–565. Springer, Cham (2016). https://doi.org/10.1007/978-3-319-46478-7_34
3. Brostow, G.J., Fauqueur, J., Cipolla, R.: Semantic object classes in video: a high-definition ground truth database. Pattern Recognit. Lett. **30**(2), 88–97 (2009)
4. Chen, L.C., Papandreou, G., Kokkinos, I., Murphy, K., Yuille, A.L.: DeepLab: semantic image segmentation with deep convolutional nets, atrous convolution, and fully connected CRFs. arXiv preprint arXiv:1606.00915 (2016)
5. Chen, Y.H., Chen, W.Y., Chen, Y.T., Tsai, B.C., Wang, Y.C.F., Sun, M.: No more discrimination: cross city adaptation of road scene segmenters. In: 2017 IEEE International Conference on Computer Vision (ICCV), pp. 2011–2020. IEEE (2017)
6. Chen, Y., Li, W., Van Gool, L.: ROAD: reality oriented adaptation for semantic segmentation of urban scenes. arXiv preprint arXiv:1711.11556 (2017)
7. Cordts, M., et al.: The cityscapes dataset for semantic urban scene understanding. In: Proceedings of the IEEE Conference on Computer Vision and Pattern Recognition, pp. 3213–3223 (2016)
8. Dai, J., He, K., Sun, J.: Boxsup: Exploiting bounding boxes to supervise convolutional networks for semantic segmentation. In: The IEEE International Conference on Computer Vision (ICCV) (2015)
9. Dosovitskiy, A., Ros, G., Codevilla, F., López, A., Koltun, V.: CARLA: an open urban driving simulator. arXiv preprint arXiv:1711.03938 (2017)
10. Epic-Games: Unreal Engine 4 (2018)
11. Farabet, C., Couprie, C., Najman, L., LeCun, Y.: Learning hierarchical features for scene labeling. IEEE Trans. Pattern Anal. Mach. Intell. **35**(8), 1915–1929 (2013)
12. Ganin, Y., Lempitsky, V.: Unsupervised domain adaptation by backpropagation. In: International Conference on Machine Learning, pp. 1180–1189 (2015)
13. Ganin, Y., et al.: Domain-adversarial training of neural networks. J. Mach. Learn. Res. **17**(1), 2096–2030 (2016)
14. Girshick, R., Radosavovic, I., Gkioxari, G., Dollár, P., He, K.: Detectron (2018). https://github.com/facebookresearch/detectron

15. Gould, S., Rodgers, J., Cohen, D., Elidan, G., Koller, D.: Multi-class segmentation with relative location prior. Int. J. Comput. Vis. **80**(3), 300–316 (2008)
16. He, K., Gkioxari, G., Dollár, P., Girshick, R.: Mask R-CNN. In: 2017 IEEE International Conference on Computer Vision (ICCV), pp. 2980–2988. IEEE (2017)
17. Heitz, G., Koller, D.: Learning spatial context: using stuff to find things. In: Forsyth, D., Torr, P., Zisserman, A. (eds.) ECCV 2008. LNCS, vol. 5302, pp. 30–43. Springer, Heidelberg (2008). https://doi.org/10.1007/978-3-540-88682-2_4
18. Hinton, G., Vinyals, O., Dean, J.: Distilling the knowledge in a neural network. arXiv preprint arXiv:1503.02531 (2015)
19. Hoffman, J., et al.: CYCADA: cycle-consistent adversarial domain adaptation. arXiv preprint arXiv:1711.03213 (2017)
20. Hoffman, J., Wang, D., Yu, F., Darrell, T.: FCNs in the wild: pixel-level adversarial and constraint-based adaptation. arXiv preprint arXiv:1612.02649 (2016)
21. Khoreva, A., Benenson, R., Hosang, J., Hein, M., Schiele, B.: Weakly supervised semantic labelling and instance segmentation. arXiv preprint arXiv:1603.07485 (2016)
22. Kirillov, A., He, K., Girshick, R., Rother, C., Dollár, P.: Panoptic segmentation. arXiv preprint arXiv:1801.00868 (2018)
23. Kolesnikov, A., Lampert, C.H.: Seed, expand and constrain: three principles for weakly-supervised image segmentation. CoRR abs/1603.06098 (2016). http://arxiv.org/abs/1603.06098
24. Liu, B., He, X.: Multiclass semantic video segmentation with object-level active inference. In: Proceedings of the IEEE Conference on Computer Vision and Pattern Recognition, pp. 4286–4294 (2015)
25. Long, J., Shelhamer, E., Darrell, T.: Fully convolutional networks for semantic segmentation. In: Proceedings of the IEEE Conference on Computer Vision and Pattern Recognition, pp. 3431–3440 (2015)
26. Mottaghi, R., et al.: The role of context for object detection and semantic segmentation in the wild. In: Proceedings of the IEEE Conference on Computer Vision and Pattern Recognition, pp. 891–898 (2014)
27. Murez, Z., Kolouri, S., Kriegman, D., Ramamoorthi, R., Kim, K.: Image to image translation for domain adaptation. arXiv preprint arXiv:1712.00479 (2017)
28. Noh, H., Hong, S., Han, B.: Learning deconvolution network for semantic segmentation. In: Proceedings of the IEEE International Conference on Computer Vision, pp. 1520–1528 (2015)
29. Oh, S.J., Benenson, R., Khoreva, A., Akata, Z., Fritz, M., Schiele, B.: Exploiting saliency for object segmentation from image level labels. In: Conference on Computer Vision and Pattern Recognition (CVPR) (2017)
30. Papandreou, G., Chen, L.C., Murphy, K.P., Yuille, A.L.: Weakly- and semi-supervised learning of a deep convolutional network for semantic image segmentation. In: The IEEE International Conference on Computer Vision (ICCV) (2015)
31. Pathak, D., Krahenbuhl, P., Darrell, T.: Constrained convolutional neural networks for weakly supervised segmentation. In: The IEEE International Conference on Computer Vision (ICCV) (2015)
32. Pathak, D., Shelhamer, E., Long, J., Darrell, T.: Fully convolutional multi-class multiple instance learning. In: ICLR Workshop (2015)
33. Pinheiro, P., Collobert, R.: Recurrent convolutional neural networks for scene labeling. In: International Conference on Machine Learning, pp. 82–90 (2014)
34. Pinheiro, P.O., Collobert, R.: From image-level to pixel-level labeling with convolutional networks. In: The IEEE Conference on Computer Vision and Pattern Recognition (CVPR) (2015)

35. Richter, S.R., Hayder, Z., Koltun, V.: Playing for benchmarks. In: International Conference on Computer Vision (ICCV) (2017)
36. Richter, S.R., Vineet, V., Roth, S., Koltun, V.: Playing for data: ground truth from computer games. In: Leibe, B., Matas, J., Sebe, N., Welling, M. (eds.) ECCV 2016. LNCS, vol. 9906, pp. 102–118. Springer, Cham (2016). https://doi.org/10.1007/978-3-319-46475-6_7
37. Ros, G., Sellart, L., Materzynska, J., Vazquez, D., Lopez, A.: The SYNTHIA dataset: a large collection of synthetic images for semantic segmentation of urban scenes. In: The IEEE International Conference on Computer Vision (ICCV), vol. 2, p. 6 (2017)
38. Russakovsky, O., et al.: ImageNet large scale visual recognition challenge. Int. J. Comput. Vis. (IJCV) 115(3), 211–252 (2015)
39. Sadat Saleh, F., Sadegh Aliakbarian, M., Salzmann, M., Petersson, L., Alvarez, J.M.: Bringing background into the foreground: making all classes equal in weakly-supervised video semantic segmentation. In: Proceedings of the IEEE International Conference on Computer Vision, pp. 2106–2116 (2017)
40. Saleh, F., Ali Akbarian, M.S., Salzmann, M., Petersson, L., Gould, S., Alvarez, J.M.: Built-in foreground/background prior for weakly-supervised semantic segmentation. In: Leibe, B., Matas, J., Sebe, N., Welling, M. (eds.) ECCV 2016. LNCS, vol. 9912, pp. 413–432. Springer, Cham (2016). https://doi.org/10.1007/978-3-319-46484-8_25
41. Saleh, F., Aliakbarian, M.S., Salzmann, M., Petersson, L., Alvarez, J.M., Gould, S.: Incorporating network built-in priors in weakly-supervised semantic segmentation. IEEE Trans. Pattern Anal. Mach. Intell. 40(6), 1382–1396 (2017)
42. Sharma, A., Tuzel, O., Jacobs, D.W.: Deep hierarchical parsing for semantic segmentation. In: 2015 IEEE Conference on Computer Vision and Pattern Recognition (CVPR), pp. 530–538. IEEE (2015)
43. Shotton, J., Winn, J., Rother, C., Criminisi, A.: *TextonBoost*: joint appearance, shape and context modeling for multi-class object recognition and segmentation. In: Leonardis, A., Bischof, H., Pinz, A. (eds.) ECCV 2006. LNCS, vol. 3951, pp. 1–15. Springer, Heidelberg (2006). https://doi.org/10.1007/11744023_1
44. Simonyan, K., Zisserman, A.: Very deep convolutional networks for large-scale image recognition. arXiv preprint arXiv:1409.1556 (2014)
45. Sun, B., Saenko, K.: From virtual to reality: Fast adaptation of virtual object detectors to real domains. In: BMVC, vol. 1, p. 3 (2014)
46. Tighe, J., Lazebnik, S.: SuperParsing: scalable nonparametric image parsing with superpixels. In: Daniilidis, K., Maragos, P., Paragios, N. (eds.) ECCV 2010. LNCS, vol. 6315, pp. 352–365. Springer, Heidelberg (2010). https://doi.org/10.1007/978-3-642-15555-0_26
47. Unity3D: Unity Technologies. Unity Development Platform (2018)
48. Wei, Y., Feng, J., Liang, X., Cheng, M.M., Zhao, Y., Yan, S.: Object region mining with adversarial erasing: a simple classification to semantic segmentation approach. In: IEEE CVPR (2017)
49. Wei, Y., et al.: STC: a simple to complex framework for weakly-supervised semantic segmentation. IEEE Trans. Pattern Anal. Mach. Intell. 39(11), 2314–2320 (2016)
50. Yu, F., Koltun, V.: Multi-scale context aggregation by dilated convolutions. arXiv preprint arXiv:1511.07122 (2015)
51. Zhang, Y., David, P., Gong, B.: Curriculum domain adaptation for semantic segmentation of urban scenes. In: The IEEE International Conference on Computer Vision (ICCV), vol. 2, p. 6 (2017)

52. Zhao, H., Shi, J., Qi, X., Wang, X., Jia, J.: Pyramid scene parsing network. In: IEEE Conf. on Computer Vision and Pattern Recognition (CVPR), pp. 2881–2890 (2017)
53. Zheng, S., et al.: Conditional random fields as recurrent neural networks. In: Proceedings of the IEEE International Conference on Computer Vision, pp. 1529–1537 (2015)

Open-World Stereo Video Matching
with Deep RNN

Yiran Zhong[1,3,4(✉)], Hongdong Li[1,3], and Yuchao Dai[2]

[1] Australian National University, Canberra, Australia
[2] Northwestern Polytechnical University, Xi'an, China
{yiran.zhong,hongdong.li}@anu.edu.au, daiyuchao@nwpu.edu.cn
[3] Australian Centre for Robotic Vision, Canberra, Australia
[4] Data61 CSIRO, Canberra, Australia

Abstract. Deep Learning based stereo matching methods have shown great successes and achieved top scores across different benchmarks. However, like most data-driven methods, existing deep stereo matching networks suffer from some well-known drawbacks such as requiring large amount of labeled training data, and that their performances are fundamentally limited by the generalization ability. In this paper, we propose a novel Recurrent Neural Network (RNN) that takes a continuous (possibly previously unseen) stereo video as input, and directly predicts a depth-map at each frame without a pre-training process, and without the need of ground-truth depth-maps as supervision. Thanks to the recurrent nature (provided by two convolutional-LSTM blocks), our network is able to memorize and learn from its past experiences, and modify its inner parameters (network weights) to adapt to previously unseen or unfamiliar environments. This suggests a remarkable generalization ability of the net, making it applicable in an *open world* setting. Our method works robustly with changes in scene content, image statistics, and lighting and season conditions *etc.* By extensive experiments, we demonstrate that the proposed method seamlessly adapts between different scenarios. Equally important, in terms of the stereo matching accuracy, it outperforms state-of-the-art deep stereo approaches on standard benchmark datasets such as KITTI and Middlebury stereo.

Keywords: Stereo video matching · Open world
Recurrent neural network · Convolutional LSTM

1 Introduction

Stereo matching is a classic problem in computer vision, and it has been extensively studied in the literature for decades. Recently, deep learning based

Electronic supplementary material The online version of this chapter (https://doi.org/10.1007/978-3-030-01216-8_7) contains supplementary material, which is available to authorized users.

© Springer Nature Switzerland AG 2018
V. Ferrari et al. (Eds.): ECCV 2018, LNCS 11206, pp. 104–119, 2018.
https://doi.org/10.1007/978-3-030-01216-8_7

stereo matching methods are taking over, becoming one of the best performing approaches. As an evidence, they occupy the leader-boards for almost all the standard stereo matching benchmarks (e.g., KITTI [1], Middlebury stereo [2]).

However, there exists a considerable gap between the success of these "deep stereo matching methods" on somewhat artificially created benchmark datasets and their real-world performances when being employed "in the wild" (open world), probably for the following reasons:

(1) Most of the existing deep stereo matching methods are supervised learning based methods, for which the training process demands massive annotated training samples. In the context of stereo matching, getting large amount of training data (i.e. ground-truth disparity/depth maps) is an extremely expensive task.

(2) The performance of existing deep stereo matching methods and their applicability in real-world scenarios are fundamentally limited by their generalization ability: like most data-driven methods, they only work well on testing data that are sufficiently similar to the training data. Take autonomous driving for example, a deep stereo matching network trained in one city, under one traffic condition, might not work well in another city, under different lighting conditions.

(3) So far, most deep stereo matching methods exclusively focus on processing single pair of stereo images in a frame-by-frame manner, while in real world stereo camera captures continuous video. The rich temporal information contained in the stereo video has not been exploited to improve the stereo matching performance or robustness.

In this paper, we tackle all the above drawbacks with current deep stereo matching methods. We propose a novel deep Recurrent Neural Network (RNN) that computes a depth/disparity map continuously from stereo video, without any pre-training process. Contrary to conventional stereo matching methods (e.g., [3,4]) which focus on processing a single pair of stereo images individually, this work is capitalized on explicitly exploiting the temporally dynamic nature of stereo video input.

Our deep stereo video matching network, termed as "OpenStereoNet" is not fixed, but changes its inner parameters continuously as long as new stereo frames being fed into the network. This enables our network to adapt to changing situations (e.g. changing lighting condition, changing image contents, etc.), allowing it to work in unconstrained open world environments. OpenStereoNet is made of a convolutional Feature-Net for feature extraction, a Match-Net for depth prediction, and two recurrent Long Short-Term Memory (LSTM) blocks to encode and to exploit temporal dynamics in the video. Importantly and in contrast to existing deep stereo matching methods, our network does not need any ground-truth disparity map as supervision, yet it naturally generalizes well to unseen datasets. As new videos are processed, the network is able to memorize, and to learn from, its past experiences. Without needing ground-truth disparity maps, our network is able to tune its parameters after seeing more images from stereo videos, simply by minimizing image-domain warping errors. Also, to better leverage the sequential information in the stereo video, we apply the Long Short-Term Memory (LSTM) module to the bottleneck of feature extraction and feature matching part of our network. In the later part of this paper, we demonstrate that our method can be applied to vary open-world scenarios such as indoor/outdoor scenes, different weather/light conditions and different camera settings with superior performance. Also ablation study concerning the effect of the LSTM modules is conducted. Another novelty of this work is that: we adopt convolutional-LSTM [5] (cLSTM) as the recurrent feedback module, and use it directly on a continuous video sequence harnessing the temporal dynamics of the video. To our knowledge, while RNN-LSTM has been applied to other video processing tasks (such as sequence captions, or human action recognition), it has not been used for stereo matching for video sequences.

2 Related Work

Stereo matching is a classic problem in computer vision, and has been researched for several decades. There have been significant number of papers published on this topic (The reader is referred to some survey papers *e.g.*, [2,6]). Below we only cite a few most recent deep-learning based stereo methods that we consider most closely related to the method to be described.

Supervised Deep Stereo Matching. In this category, a deep network (often based on CNN, or Convolutional Neural Networks) is often trained to benefit the task of stereo matching in one of the following aspects: (i) to learn better image features and a tailored stereo matching metrics (*e.g.*, [7,8]); (ii) to learn better regularization terms in a loss function [9]; and (iii) to predict dense disparity map in an end-to-end fashion (*e.g.*, [4,10]). The learned deep features replace handcrafted features, resulting in more distinctive features for matching. End-to-end deep stereo methods often formulate the task as either depth values regression, or multiple (discrete) class classification. DispNetC [10] is a new development, which directly computes the correspondence field between stereo images by minimizing a regression loss. Another example is the GC-Net [4], which explicitly learns feature cost volume, and regularization function in a network structure. Cascade residual learning (CRL) [11] adopted a multi-stage cascade CNN architecture, following a coarse-to-fine or residual learning principle [12].

Unsupervised Deep Stereo Matching. Recently, there have been proposed deep net based single-image depth recovery methods which do not require ground-truth depth maps. Instead, they rely on minimizing photometric warping error to drive the network in an unsupervised way (see *e.g.*, [13–17]). Zhou *et.al.* [15] proposed an unsupervised method which is iteratively trained via warping error propagating matches. The authors adopted TV (total variation) constraint to select training data and discard uninformative patches. Inspired by recent advances in direct visual odometry (DVO), Wang *et.al.* [18] argued that the depth CNN predictor can be learned without a pose CNN predictor.

Luo *et. al.* [19] reformulated the problem of monocular depth estimation as two sub-problems, namely a view synthesis procedure followed by standard stereo matching. However, extending these monocular methods to stereo matching is non-trivial. When feeding the networks with stereo pairs, their performances are even not comparable with traditional stereo matching methods [14].

Recurrent Neural Net and LSTM. Our method is based on RNN (with cLSTM as the feedback module), and directly applied to sequence input of stereo video harnessing the temporal dynamic nature of a continuous video. To the best of our knowledge, where RNN-LSTM has been applied to other video based tasks (such as a sequence captions, action recognition), it has not been directly used for stereo video matching, especially to exploit the temporal smoothness feature for improving stereo matching performance.

3   Network Architecture

In this section, we describe our new "open-world" stereo video matching deep neural network (for ease of reference, we call it *OpenStereoNet*). The input to the network is a live continuous stereo video sequence of left and right image frames of I_L^t, I_R^t, for $t = 1, 2, ...$ The output is the predicted depth-map (disparity map) at each time step t. We assume the input stereo images are already rectified.

Our network does not require ground-truth depth-maps as supervision. Instead, the stereo matching task is implemented by searching a better depth map which results in minimal photometric warping error between the stereo image pair. By continuously feeding in new stereo image frames, our network is able to automatically adapt itself to new inputs (could be new visual scenes never seen before) and produce accurate depth map estimations. More technical details will be explained in the sequel of the paper.

3.1   Overall Network Architecture

The overall structure of our OpenStereoNet is illustrated in Fig. 1, which consists of the following major parts (or sub-Nets): (1) Feature-Net, (2) Match-Net, (3) LSTM blocks, and (4) a loss function block.

Information Flow. Starting from inputted left and right images at time t, the information processing flow in our network is clear: (1) The Feature-Net acts as a convolutional feature extractor which extracts features from the left and right images individually. Note, Feature-Net for the left image and Feature-Net for the right image share the weights. (2) The obtained feature maps are concatenated (with certain interleave pattern) into a 4D feature-volume. (3) The Match-Net takes the 4D feature volume as input, and learns an encoder-decoder representation of the features. A projection layer (based on soft-argmin [4]) within the Match-Net is applied to produce the 2D disparity map prediction. Finally, the loss function block employs the current estimated disparity map to warp the right image to the left view and compare the photometric warping

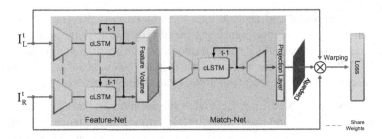

Fig. 1. Overall network structure of our OpenStereoNet. It consists of a convolutional Feature-Net, an encoder-decoder type Match-Net and two recurrent (convolutional) LSTM units to learn temporal dynamics of the video input. Given a stereo pair I_L^t, I_R^t at time t, the Feature-Net produces feature maps which are subsequently aggregated to form a feature-volume. The Match-Net first learns a representation of the feature volume then projects it to obtain disparity estimation. Our loss function is based on image warping error evaluated on raw image inputs by the current disparity map.

loss as well as other regularization term, which is used to refine the network via *backprop*.

3.2 Feature-Net

Conventional stereo matching methods often directly compare the raw pixel values in the left image with that in the right image. Recent advance in deep learning show that using learned convolutional features can be more robust for various vision tasks. For stereo matching, to learn a feature map that is more robust to photometric variations (such as occlusion, non-lambertian, lighting effects and perspective effects) will be highly desirable.

In this paper, we design a very simple convolutional feature-net with 18 convolutional layers (including RELU) using 3×3 kernels and skip connections in between. The output feature has a dimensionality of 32. We run feature extraction on both images in a symmetric weight-sharing manner.

3.3 Feature-Volume Construction

We use the learned features to construct a feature volume. Instead of constructing a cost volume by concatenating all costs with their corresponding disparities, we concatenate the learned features from the left and right images. Specifically, we concatenate each learned feature with their corresponding feature from the opposite stereo image across each disparity level in a preset disparity range D as illustrated in Fig. 2. All the features are packed to form a 4D feature volume with dimensionality $H \times W \times (D+1) \times 2F$ for the left-to-right and right-to-left feature volume correspondingly, where H, W, D, F represent the height, width, disparity range, and feature dimensionality respectively.

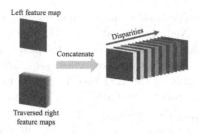

Fig. 2. Feature Volume Construction. We collect the two feature maps computed by the Feature-Net, and assemble them together to a Feature-Volume in the way as illustrated here: the blue rectangle represents a feature map from the left image, the stacked orange rectangles represent traversed the right feature at different disparities in the range $[0, D]$. Note that the left feature map is duplicated $D + 1$ times to match the traversed right feature maps. (Color figure online)

3.4   Match-Net

Taking the assembled Feature-Volume as input, our Match-Net is constituted of an encoder-decoder as the front-end, followed by a single last layer which projects the output of the encoder-decoder to a 2D disparity-map.

Encoder-Decoder Front-End. The denoising Encoder-Decoder is an hourglass-shaped deep-net. Between the encoder and decoder there is a bottleneck, as shown in Fig. 1. Since the input feature-volume is of 4 dimensions, H (height) $\times$ W (width) $\times$ (D + 1)(disparity range) $\times$ 2F(feature dim.), we use 3D-convolutional kernels and the underlying CNNs in the Encoder-Decoder are in fact 3D-CNNs.

Projection Layer. The output of the preceding encoder-decoder is still a 4D feature-volume. The last layer of our Match-Net first projects the 4D volume to a 3D *cost-volume–i.e.*an operation commonly used in conventional stereo matching methods, then applies the soft-argmin operation (*c.f.* [4]) to predict a disparity $\delta = \sum_{d=0}^{D} [d \times \sigma(-c_d)]$, where c_d is the matching cost at disparity d and $\sigma(\cdot)$ denotes the softmax operator.

3.5   Convolutional-LSTM

Since our goal is to develop a deep-net focusing on stereo video processing (as opposed to individual images), in order to capture the inherent temporal dynamics (*e.g.*, temporal smoothness) existed in a video, we leverage the internal representations obtained by our two sub-networks (*i.e.*, Feature-Net and Match-Net), and model these internal representation's dynamic transitions as an *implicit* model for the video sequence. Specifically, given a continuous video, we consider the image content (as well as the disparity) in each frame changes smoothly to the next frame. To capture such dynamic changes, we adopt the structure of LSTM-based Recurrent Neural Networks (RNN). The LSTMs act as memory of the net, by which the network memorizes its past experiences. This gives our network the ability to learn the stereo video sequence's temporal dynamics encoded in the inner states of the LSTMs. As shown in Fig. 3, the output of our Feature-Net, and the encoder-decoder in our Match-Net, are each passed to an LSTM unit. Briefly, LSTM units are a particular type of hidden unit that improve the training of RNNs [20]. An LSTM unit contains a cell, which can be thought of as a memory state. Access to the cell is controlled through an input gate and a forget gate. The final output of the LSTM unit is a function of the cell state and an output gate (c.f. [21]).

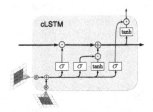

Fig. 3. A convolutional-LSTM.

We realize that for stereo matching it is desirable to use spatially-invariant operator such as convolutional kernels, in the same spirit of the CNN. In light of this, we propose to use the convolutional LSTM architecture (or cLSTM in short, c.f. [5]) as the recurrent unit for our stereo video matching task. This way, the relative spatial layout information of the feature representation–which is essential for the task of depth map computation–is preserved. In our experiments we used very small kernels for the cLSTM (e.g. 3×3, or 5×5). This leads to compact LSTM units, and greatly simplifies the computation cost and GPU-RAM consumption. The encoder–LSTM–decoder architecture is also similar to the Encoder-Recurrent-Decoder architecture proposed in [22]. Our entire network works end-to-end to combine feature representation learning with the learning of temporal dynamics via the two LSTM blocks.

4   Self-adapting Learning and Loss Function

4.1   Self-adapting Training and Testing

Recall that the ultimate goal of this work is to develop a deep network that can automatically adapt itself to new (previously unseen) stereo video inputs. In this sense, the network is not fixed static, but is able to dynamically evolve in time. This is achieved by two mechanisms:

– The network has memory units (i.e. the two LSTM blocks), which enable the network to adjust its current behavior (partly) based its past experiences;

- We always run an online back-propagation (*backprop*) updating procedure after any feed-forward process.

The latter actually eliminates the separation between a network's training stage and testing stage. In other words, our OpenStereoNet is constantly performing both operations all the time. This gives the network self-adaption ability, allows it to self-adapt by continuously fine-tuning its parameters based on new stereo image inputs (possibly seen in a new environment). Thus, our OpenStereoNet can "automatically" generalize to unseen images.

Since we do not require ground-truth depth-maps as supervision, input stereo pairs themselves serve as self-supervision signals, and the network is able to update automatically, by self-adapting learning.

4.2 Overall Loss Function

The overall loss function for our OpenStereoNet is a weighted summation of a data term and a regularization term, as in $Loss = L_{\text{data}} + \mu L_{\text{reg}}$.

Data Term: Image Warping Error. We directly measure the warping error evaluated on the input stereo images, based on the estimated disparity map. Specifically, given the left image I_L^t and the disparity map for the right image $d_R^t = g(I_R^t, I_L^t, h_R^{t-1}, h_L^{t-1})$, the right image I_R^t can be reconstructed by warping the left image with d_R^t, $I_R^{t'}(u,v) = I_L^t(u+d,v)$, where $I_R^{t'}$ is the warped right image. We use the discrepancy between $I_R^{t'}$ and the observed right image I_R^t as the supervision signal. Our data loss is derived as: $L_{\text{data}} = \sum(\lambda_1(1 - \mathcal{S}(I_L, I_L'))/2 + \lambda_2(\left|I_L - I_L'\right| + \left|\nabla I_L - \nabla I_L'\right|))/N$. The data term consists of S, which is the structural similarity SSIM as defined in [23], pixel value difference and image gradient difference. The trade-off parameters were chosen empirically in our experiments at $\mu = 0.05, \lambda_1 = 0.8, \lambda_2 = 0.1$.

Regularization Term: Priors on Depth-Map. We enforce a common prior that depth-maps are piecewise smooth or piecewise linear. This is implemented by penalizing the second-order derivative of the estimated disparity map. To exploit correlations between depth map values and pixel colors, we weight this term by image color gradient, *i.e.*: $L_{\text{reg}} = \sum(e^{-\left|\nabla_u^2 I_L\right|}\left|\nabla_u^2 d_L\right| + e^{-\left|\nabla_v^2 I_L\right|}\left|\nabla_v^2 d_L\right|)/N$, where ∇ is gradient operator.

5 Experiments

We implement our OpenStereoNet in TensorFlow. Since the network runs in an online fashion (with batch-size one), *i.e.*, there is no clear distinction between training and testing, we start from randomly initialized weights for both the Feature-Net and the Match-Net, and allow the network to evolve as new stereo images being fed in. All images have been rescaled to 256×512 for easy comparison. Typical processing time of our net is about 0.8–1.6 s per frame tested on a regular PC of 2017 equipped with a GTX 1080Ti GPU. We use the RMSProp optimizer with a constant learning rate of 0.001. We have evaluated our network on several standard benchmark datasets for stereo matching, including KITTI [1], Middlebury [24,25], Synthia [26], and Frieburg SceneFlow [10] (e.g. FlyingThings3D). These experiments are reported below.

5.1   KITTI Visual Odometry (VO) Stereo Sequences

In this set of experiments on KITTI dataset [1], we simply feed a KITTI VO stereo video sequence to our network, and start to produce a depth map prediction, as well as update the network weights frame by frame by backproping the error signal of the loss function. In all our experiments we observe that: soon after about a few hundreds of input frames have been processed (usually about 10 s video at 30 fps) the network already starts to produce sensible depth maps, and the loss function appears to converge. We call this process of training on the first a few hundred frames the *network prime* process, and we believe its purpose is to teach the network to learn useful convolutional features for typical visual scenes. Once the network has been "primed", it can be applied to new previously unseen stereo videos.

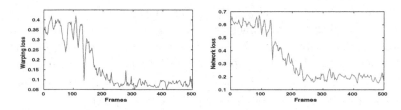

Fig. 4. Typical network convergence curves from random initialization.

| (a) Left frame | (b) Sparse LIDAR | (c) Ours (3.44%) |
| (d) SPS-st (5.61%) | (e) MC-CNN (4.75%) | (f) DispNet (25.98%) |

Fig. 5. Our qualitative results on KITTI VO dataset: results are reported on the $D1\_all$ error metric. Disparities are transformed to log space for better visualization.

Figure 4 shows typical converge curves for a network during the prime stage. After the prime stage, we randomly select 5 KITTI VO sequences, test our network on them, and compare its performance with three state-of-the-art stereo methods, including the DispNet [10], MC-CNN [7], and SPS-ST [27]. The first two are deep stereo matching methods, and the last one a traditional (non-deep) stereo method. Quantitative comparison of their performances are reported in Table 1, from which one can clearly see that our OpenStereoNet achieves the best performance throughout all the metrics evaluated. For deep MC-CNN we use a model which was firstly trained on Middlebury dataset for the sake of fair comparison. For SPS-ST, its meta-parameters was also tuned on KITTI dataset. Figure 5 gives some sample visual results for comparison. Note that our method obtains sharp and clean depth discontinuity for cars and trees, better than the other methods. Dispnet, on the other hand, is affected by shadows on road, with many artifacts on the road surface. A quantitative comparison is provided in Table 1. Our method outperforms all baseline methods with a large margin.

Table 1. Quantitative results on KITTI VO dataset.

Methods	Abs Rel	Sq Rel	RMSE	RMSE log	D1_all	$\delta < 1.25$
Dispnet [10]	0.122	1.938	8.844	0.189	32.045	0.877
MC-CNN [7]	0.069	1.229	6.002	0.264	8.018	0.932
SPS-st [27]	0.060	1.341	5.521	0.159	4.970	0.957
Ours	**0.053**	**0.540**	**4.451**	**0.137**	**4.403**	**0.959**

5.2 Synthia Dataset

The Synthia dataset [26] contains 7 sequences with different scenarios under different seasons and lighting conditions. Our primary aim for experimenting on Synthia is to analyze our network's generalization (self-adaption) ability. We create a long video sequence by combining together three Synthia sequences of the same scene but under different seasons and lighting conditions. For example, Fig. 6 shows some sample frames of *Spring, Dawn and Night*. We simply run our network model on this video, and display the disparity error as a function of frames. We run our network on this long sequence. For each condition, we report our quantitative and qualitative results based on the first 250 frames of that sequence.

As shown in Fig. 6, our network recovers consistently high quality disparity maps regardless the lighting conditions. This claim is further proved by the qualitative results in Fig. 7. In term of disparity accuracy, our method achieves a Mean Absolute Error (MAE) of 0.958 pixels on the *Spring* scene while the *Dawn* sequence has reached an MAE of 0.7991 pixels and 1.2415 pixels for the *Night* sequence.

5.3 Ablation Studies: Effects of the LSTMs and Backprop

There are two mechanisms that contribute to the self-adaptive ability of our OpenStereoNet, *i.e.*, the cLSTMs recurrent blocks and the backprop refinement

Fig. 6. Our qualitative results on Synthia: top to bottom: input left image, ground truth disparity, our result. The first column is taken from the *Spring* subset, the middle column is from *Dawn*, and the last column is from *Night*. Our method performs uniformly on different sequences.

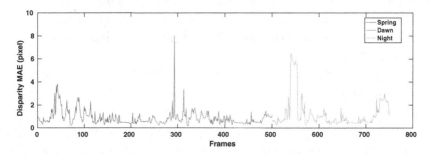

Fig. 7. We run our method on a continuous video sequence consisting of the same scene under three different season/lighting conditions (spring, dawn, night). The curve shows the final disparity error as a function of the stereo frame. From this curve it is clear that our network is able to adapt to new scenarios automatically.

process. To understand their respective effects on the final performance of our network, we conduct ablation studies by isolating their operations. To be precise, we have tested the following four types of variants of our full networks: (type-1) remove LSTMs and also disable the backprop process (*i.e.*, the *baseline* network); (type-2) remove LSTMs, but keep backprop on; (type-3) with LSTMs on, without backprop, and (type-4) with both LSTMs on and backprop on (*i.e.*, our full network).

Results by these four types of networks are given in the following curves in Fig. 8. One can clearly see the positive effects of the LSTM units and the backprop. In particular, adding LSTMs has reduced the loss function of the baseline network significantly. In another ablation test, we run the above type-3

Table 2. Ablation study on LSTM module on KITTI.

Methods	Abs Rel	Sq Rel	RMSE	RMSE log	D1_all	$\delta < 1.25$
Type-3 net (without LSTMs)	0.066	1.580	5.332	0.167	5.089	0.957
Type-4 net (with LSTMs)	**0.053**	**0.540**	**4.451**	**0.137**	**4.403**	**0.959**

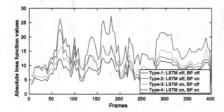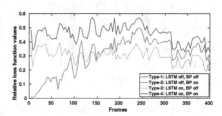

Fig. 8. We run our method on a continuous video sequence. The left figure shows the comparison of absolute losses for the 4 types (note: the lower, the better), while the right figure gives comparison of the relative loss against the the (type-1) baseline network (note: the higher, the better). The y-axis indicates the final disparity errors, and x-axis the input frame-Ids.

network on the previous selected KITTI VO sequence, and list their accuracy in Table 2. From this, one can see that by applying the LSTM module, we have achieved better performance across all error metrics.

5.4 Middlebury Stereo Dataset

The stereo pairs in the Middlebury stereo dataset [24, 25] are indoor scenes with multiple handcrafted layouts. The ground truth disparities are captured by structured light with higher density and precision than KITTI dataset. We report our results on selected stereo pairs from Middlebury 2005 [24] and 2006 [25] and compare with other baseline methods. In order to evaluate our method on these images, we augmented each stereo pair to a stereo video sequence by simply repeating the stereo pair.

We use *bad-pixel-ratio* as our error metrics used in this experiment, and all results are reported with 1-pixel thresholding. As shown in Fig. 9, our method achieves superior performance than all baseline methods. Other deep learning based methods have even worse performance than the conventional method SPS-st when there is no fine tuning.

5.5 Other Open World Stereo Sequences

To further demonstrate the generalization ability of our OpenStereoNet, we test it on a number of other freely downloaded stereo video datasets from the Internet. Note that our network had never seen these test data before. Below we give some sample results, obtained by our method and by the DispNet, on the Freiburg Sceneflow Dataset [10] and on RDS-Random Dot Stereo.

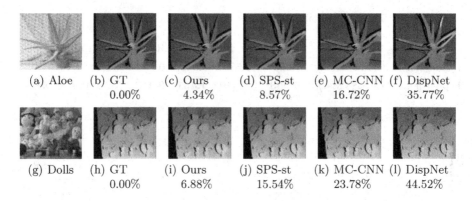

(a) Aloe   (b) GT   (c) Ours   (d) SPS-st   (e) MC-CNN   (f) DispNet
            0.00%   4.34%   8.57%   16.72%   35.77%

(g) Dolls   (h) GT   (i) Ours   (j) SPS-st   (k) MC-CNN   (l) DispNet
            0.00%   6.88%   15.54%   23.78%   44.52%

Fig. 9. Our results on Middlebury: left to right: left image, ground-truth disparity, our result, SPS-st result, MC-CNN result and DispNet result. We report the *bad-pixel-ratio* at 1-pixel threshold.

Freiburg Sceneflow Dataset. We select two stereo videos from the Monkaa and FlyingThings3D dataset [10] and directly feed them into our network. Qualitative results are shown in Figs. 10 and 11 correspondingly. Our network produces very accurate disparity maps when compared with the ground truth disparity maps. Furthermore, the reconstructed color images with the estimated disparity map further prove the effectiveness of our model.

Random Dot Stereo. We test the behavior of our OpenStereoNet on random dot stereo images where there is no semantic content in the images. Our network works well, however the DispNet fails miserably as shown in Fig. 12.

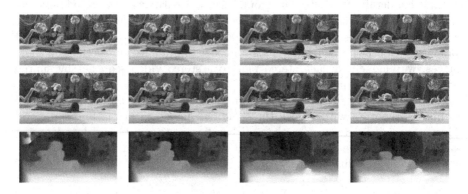

Fig. 10. Our qualitative results on Monkaa: from top to bottom: left image, reconstructed left image, recovered disparity map. From left to right: frame 11, frame 15, frame 133, frame 143. (Color figure online)

Fig. 11. Our qualitative results on FlyingThings3D: from left to right: left image, reconstructed left image, estimated disparity map, and ground truth. (Color figure online)

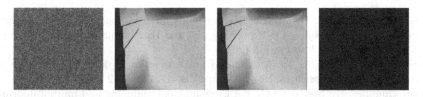

Fig. 12. Test results on RDS (Random dot stereo) images: left to right: input stereo (left image), ground-truth disparity (color coded), our result, result by Dispnet. Our method successfully recovers the correct disparity map, demonstrating its superior generalibility on unseen images. (Color figure online)

6 Conclusions and Discussions

This paper addresses a practical demand of deploying stereo matching technique to unconstrained real-world environments with previously unseen or unfamiliar "open-world" scenarios. We envisage such a stereo matching method that is able to take a continuous live stereo video as input, and automatically predict the corresponding disparity maps. To this end, this paper has proposed a deep Recurrent Neural Network (RNN) based stereo video matching method–*OpenStereoNet*. It consists of a CNN Feature-Net, a Match-Net and two convolutional-LSTM recurrent blocks to learn temporal dynamics in the scene. We do notice that finding optical flow (or scene flow) between image frames is yet another feasible paradigm to encode and to exploit temporal dynamics existed in a video sequence. However, we argue optical flow itself is a significant research topic in itself, no less challenging than stereo matching, and a comparison between the two approaches deserves to be a valuable future work.

Our OpenStereoNet does not need ground-truth disparity maps for training. In fact, there is even no clear distinction between training and testing as the network is able to learn on-the-fly, and to adapt itself to never-seen-before imageries rapidly. We have conducted extensive experiments on various datasets in order to validate the effectiveness of our network. Importantly, we have found that our network generalizes well to new scenarios. Evaluated based on absolute performance metrics for stereo, our method outperforms state-of-the-art competing methods by a clear margin.

Acknowledgements. Y. Zhong's PhD scholarship is funded by CSIRO Data61. H. Li's work is funded in part by Australia ARC Centre of Excellence for Robotic Vision (CE140100016). Y. Dai is supported in part by National 1000 Young Talents Plan of China, Natural Science Foundation of China (61420106007, 61671387), and ARC grant (DE140100180). The authors are very grateful to NVIDIA's generous gift of GPUs to ANU used in this research.

References

1. Geiger, A., Lenz, P., Urtasun, R.: Are we ready for autonomous driving? The kitti vision benchmark suite. In: Proceedings of the IEEE Conference on Computer Vision and Pattern Recognition (2012)
2. Scharstein, D., Szeliski, R.: A taxonomy and evaluation of dense two-frame stereo correspondence algorithms. Int. J. Comp. Vis. **47**(1–3), 742 (2002)
3. Hirschmuller, H.: Stereo processing by semiglobal matching and mutual information. IEEE Trans. Pattern Anal. Mach. Intell. **30**(2), 328341 (2008)
4. Kendall, A., et al: End-to-end learning of geometry and context for deep stereo regression. In: Proceedings of the IEEE International Conference on Computer Vision, October 2017
5. Shi, X., Chen, Z., Wang, H., Yeung, D.Y., Wong, W., Woo, W.: Convolutional LSTM network: a machine learning approach for precipitation nowcasting. In: Proceedings of the Advances in Neural Information Processing Systems, NIPS 2015, Cambridge, MA, USA, pp. 802–810. MIT Press (2015)
6. Janai, J., Gney, F., Behl, A., Geiger, A.: Computer vision for autonomous vehicles: problems, datasets and state-of-the-art. Arxiv (2017)
7. Zbontar, J., LeCun, Y.: Stereo matching by training a convolutional neural network to compare image patches. J. Mach. Learn. Res. **17**(1), 22872318 (2016)
8. Luo, W., Schwing, A.G., Urtasun, R.: Efficient deep learning for stereo matching. In: Proceedings of the IEEE Conference on Computer Vision and Pattern Recognition, pp. 5695–5703, June 2016
9. Seki, A., Pollefeys, M.: SGM-Nets: semi-global matching with neural networks. In: Proceedings of the IEEE Conference on Computer Vision and Pattern Recognition (2017)
10. Mayer, N., et al.: A large dataset to train convolutional networks for disparity, optical OW, and scene OW estimation. In: Proceedings of the IEEE Conference on Computer Vision and Pattern Recognition, June 2016
11. Pang, J., Sun, W., Ren, J.S., Yang, C., Yan, Q.: Cascade residual learning: a two-stage convolutional neural network for stereo matching. In: International Conference on Computer Vision - Workshop on Geometry Meets Deep Learning (2017)
12. He, K., Zhang, X., Ren, S., Sun, J.: Deep residual learning for image recognition. In: Proceedings of the IEEE Conference on Computer Vision and Pattern Recognition, pp. 770–778, June 2016
13. Garg, R., Vijay Kumar, B.G., Carneiro, G., Reid, I.: Unsupervised CNN for single view depth estimation: geometry to the rescue. In: Leibe, B., Matas, J., Sebe, N., Welling, M. (eds.) ECCV 2016. LNCS, vol. 9912, pp. 740–756. Springer, Cham (2016). https://doi.org/10.1007/978-3-319-46484-8_45

14. Godard, C., Mac Aodha, O., Brostow, G.J.: Unsupervised monocular depth esti-
    mation with left-right consistency. In: Proceedings of the IEEE Conference on
    Computer Vision and Pattern Recognition (2017)
15. Zhou, T., Brown, M., Snavely, N., Lowe, D.G.: Unsupervised learning of depth
    and ego-motion from video. In: Proceedings of the IEEE Conference on Computer
    Vision and Pattern Recognition (2017)
16. Xie, J., Girshick, R., Farhadi, A.: Deep3D: fully automatic 2D-to-3D video con-
    version with deep convolutional neural networks. In: Leibe, B., Matas, J., Sebe,
    N., Welling, M. (eds.) ECCV 2016. LNCS, vol. 9908, pp. 842–857. Springer, Cham
    (2016). https://doi.org/10.1007/978-3-319-46493-0_51
17. Zhong, Y., Dai, Y., Li, H.: Self-supervised learning for stereo matching with self-
    improving ability. arXiv:1709.00930 (2017)
18. Wang, C., Buenaposada, J.M., Zhu, R., Lucey, S.: Learning Depth from Monocular
    Videos using Direct Methods. ArXiv e-prints, November 2017
19. Luo, Y., et al.: Single View Stereo Matching. ArXiv e-prints, March 2018
20. Bengio, Y., Simard, P., Frasconi, P.: Learning long-term dependencies with gradient
    descent is difficult. Trans. Neural Netw. 5(2), 157166 (1994)
21. Hochreiter, S., Schmidhuber, J.: Long short-term memory. Neural Comput. 9(8),
    17351780 (1997)
22. Fragkiadaki, K., Levine, S., Felsen, P., Malik, J.: Recurrent network models for
    human dynamics. In: Proceedings of the IEEE International Conference on Com-
    puter Vision, Washington, D.C., USA, pp. 4346–4354. IEEE Computer Society
    (2015)
23. Wang, Z., Bovik, A.C., Sheikh, H.R., Simoncelli, E.P.: Image quality assessment:
    from error visibility to structural similarity. IEEE Trans. Image Process. 13(4),
    600612 (2004)
24. Scharstein, D., Pal, C.: Learning conditional random fields for stereo. In: Proceed-
    ings of the IEEE Conference on Computer Vision and Pattern Recognition, p. 18,
    June 2007
25. Hirschmller, H., Scharstein, D.: Evaluation of cost functions for stereo matching. In:
    Proceedings of the IEEE Conference on Computer Vision and Pattern Recognition.
    IEEE Computer Society (2007)
26. Ros, G., Sellart, L., Materzynska, J., Vazquez, D., Lopez, A.: The SYNTHIA
    dataset: a large collection of synthetic images for semantic segmentation of urban
    scenes. In: Proceedings of the IEEE Conference on Computer Vision and Pattern
    Recognition (2016)
27. Yamaguchi, K., McAllester, D., Urtasun, R.: Efficient joint segmentation, occlu-
    sion labeling, stereo and flow estimation. In: Fleet, D., Pajdla, T., Schiele, B.,
    Tuytelaars, T. (eds.) ECCV 2014. LNCS, vol. 8693, pp. 756–771. Springer, Cham
    (2014). https://doi.org/10.1007/978-3-319-10602-1_49

Deep High Dynamic Range Imaging
with Large Foreground Motions

Shangzhe Wu[1,3(✉)] ⓘ, Jiarui Xu[1] ⓘ, Yu-Wing Tai[2] ⓘ, and Chi-Keung Tang[1] ⓘ

[1] The Hong Kong University of Science and Technology, Kowloon, Hong Kong
{swuai,jxuat}@connect.ust.hk, cktang@cs.ust.hk
[2] Tencent Youtu, Shanghai, China
yuwingtai@tencent.com
[3] University of Oxford, Oxford, UK

Abstract. This paper proposes the first non-flow-based deep framework for high dynamic range (HDR) imaging of dynamic scenes with **large-scale foreground motions**. In state-of-the-art deep HDR imaging, input images are first aligned using optical flows before merging, which are still error-prone due to occlusion and large motions. In stark contrast to flow-based methods, we formulate HDR imaging as an image translation problem **without optical flows**. Moreover, our simple translation network can automatically hallucinate plausible HDR details in the presence of total occlusion, saturation and under-exposure, which are otherwise almost impossible to recover by conventional optimization approaches. Our framework can also be extended for different reference images. We performed extensive qualitative and quantitative comparisons to show that our approach produces excellent results where color artifacts and geometric distortions are significantly reduced compared to existing state-of-the-art methods, and is robust across various inputs, including images without radiometric calibration.

Keywords: High dynamic range imaging
Computational photography

1 Introduction

Off-the-shelf digital cameras typically fail to capture the entire dynamic range of a 3D scene. In order to produce high dynamic range (HDR) images, custom captures and special devices have been proposed [8,24,25]. Unfortunately, they are usually too heavy and/or too expensive for capturing fleeting moments to cherish, which are typically photographed using cellphone cameras. The other more practical approach is to merge several low dynamic range (LDR) images captured at different exposures. If the LDR images are perfectly aligned, in other words no camera motion or object motion is observed, the merging problem is considered almost solved [1,17]. However, foreground and background misalignments

---

This work was partially done when Shangzhe Wu was an intern at Tencent Youtu.

V. Ferrari et al. (Eds.): ECCV 2018, LNCS 11206, pp. 120–135, 2018.
https://doi.org/10.1007/978-3-030-01216-8_8

EV -2.0   EV 0.0   EV +2.0

Kalantari [14] HDRCNN [3]   Sen [23]

Input LDRs   Our Result   Input LDRs Optical Flow   Hu [10]   Oh [19]   Ours

Fig. 1. Our goal is to produce an HDR image from a stack of LDR images that can be corrupted by large foreground motions, such as images shown on the left. Our resulted HDR image is displayed after tonemapping. On the right, the first two columns show that the optical flow alignment used by Kalantari [14] introduces severe geometric distortions and color artifacts, which are unfortunately preserved in the final HDR results. The last three columns compare the results produced by other state-of-the-art methods and ours where no optical flow alignment is used. Our simple network produces high quality ghost-free HDR image in the presence of large-scale saturation and foreground motions.

are unavoidable in the presence of large-scale foreground motions in addition to small camera motions. While the latter can be resolved to a large extent by homography transformation [26], foreground motions, on the other hand, will make the composition nontrivial. Many existing solutions tackling this issue are prone to introducing artifacts or ghosting in the final HDR image [14,15,31], or fail to incorporate misaligned HDR contents by simply rejecting the pixels in misaligned regions as outliers [9,16,19], see Fig. 1.

Recent works have been proposed to learn this composition process using deep neural networks [14]. In [14], they first used optical flow to align input LDR images, followed by feeding the aligned LDRs into a convolutional neural network (CNN) to produce the final HDR image. Optical flows are often unreliable, especially for images captured with different exposure levels, which inevitably introduce artifacts and distortions in the presence of large object motions. Although in [14] it was claimed that the network is able to resolve these issues in the merging process, failure cases still exist as shown in Fig. 1, where color artifacts and geometry distortions are quite apparent in the final results.

In contrast, we regard merging multiple exposure shots into an HDR image as an image translation problem, which have been actively studied in recent years. In [11] a powerful solution was proposed to learn a mapping between images in two domains using a Generative Adversarial Network (GAN). Meanwhile, CNNs have been demonstrated to have the ability to learn misalignment [2] and hallucinate missing details [30]. Inspired by these works, we believe that optical flow may be an overkill for HDR imaging. In this paper, we propose a simple end-to-end network that can learn to translate multiple LDR images into a ghost-free HDR image even in the presence of large foreground motions.

In summary, our method has the following advantages. First, unlike [14], our network is trained end-to-end without optical flow alignment, thus intrinsically avoiding artifacts and distortions caused by erroneous flows. In stark contrast to prevailing flow-based HDR imaging approaches [14], this provides a novel perspective and significant insights for HDR imaging, and is much faster and more practical. Second, our network can hallucinate plausible details that are totally missing or their presence is extremely weak in all LDR inputs. This is particularly desirable when dealing with large foreground motions, because usually some contents are not captured in all LDRs due to saturation and occlusion. Finally, the same framework can be easily extended to more LDR inputs, and possibly with any specified reference image. We perform extensive qualitative and quantitative comparisons, and show that our simple network outperforms the state-of-the-art approaches in HDR synthesis, including both learning based or optimization based methods. We also show that our network is robust across various kinds of input LDRs, including images with different exposure separations and images without correct radiometric calibration.

2 Related Work

Over the past decades, many research works have been dedicated to the problem of HDR imaging. As mentioned above, one practical solution is to compose an HDR image from a stack of LDR images. Early works such as [1,17] produce excellent results for static scenes and static cameras.

To deal with camera motions, previous works [12,15,26] register the LDR images before merging them into the final HDR image. Since many image registration algorithms depend on the brightness consistence assumptions, the brightness changes are often addressed by mapping the images to another domain, such as luminance domain or gradient domain, before estimating the transformation.

Compared to camera motions, object motions are much harder to handle. A number of methods reject the moving pixels using weightings in the merging process [9,16]. Another approach is to detect and resolve ghosting after the merging [4,21]. Such methods simply ignore the misaligned pixels, and fail to fully utilize available contents to generate an HDR image.

There are also more complicated methods [15,31] that rely on optical flow or its variants to address dense correspondence between image pixels. However, optical flow often results in artifacts and distortions when handling large displacements, introducing extra complication in the merging step. Among the works in this category, [14] produces perhaps the best results, and is highly related to our work. The authors proposed a CNN that learns to merge LDR images aligned using optical flow into the final HDR image. Our method is different from theirs in that we do not use optical flow for alignment, which intrinsically avoids the artifacts and distortions that are present in their results. We provide concrete comparisons in the later sections.

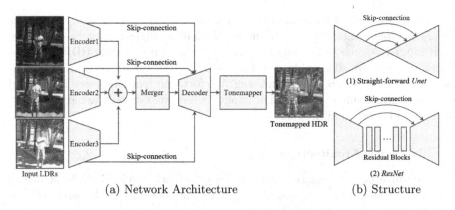

(a) Network Architecture   (b) Structure

Fig. 2. Our framework is composed of three components: encoder, merger and decoder. Different exposure inputs are passed to different encoders, and concatenated before going through the merger and the decoder. We experimented with two structures, *Unet* and *ResNet*. We use skip-connections between the mirrored layers. The output HDR of the decoder is tonemapped before it can be displayed.

Another approach to address the dense correspondence is patch-based system [10,23]. Although these methods produce excellent results, the running time is much longer, and often fail in the presence of large motions and large saturated regions.

A more recent work [3] attempts to reconstruct a HDR image from one single LDR image using CNN. Although their network can hallucinate details in regions where input LDRs exhibit only very weak response, one intrinsic limitation of their approach is the total reliance on one single input LDR image, which often fails in highly contrastive scenes due to large-scale saturation. Therefore, we intend to explore better solutions to merge HDR contents from multiple LDR images, which can easily be captured in a burst, for instance, using cellphone cameras.

Typically, to produce an HDR image also involves other processing, including radiometric calibration, tone-mapping and dynamic range compression. Our work is focused on the merging process. Besides, there are also more expensive solutions that use special devices to capture a higher dynamic range [8,24,25] and directly produce HDR images. For a complete review of the problem, readers may refer to [5].

3   Approach

We formulate the problem of HDR imaging as an image translation problem. Similar to [14], given a set of LDR images $\{I_1, I_2, ..., I_k\}$, we define a reference image I_r. In our experiments, we use three LDRs, and set the middle exposure shot as reference. The same network can be extended to deal with more LDR inputs, and possibly with any specified reference image. We provide results in Sect. 5.3 to substantiate such robustness.

Specifically, our goal is to learn a mapping from a stack of LDR images $\{I_1, I_2, I_3\}$ to a ghost-free HDR image H that is aligned with the reference LDR input I_r (same as I_2), and contains the maximum possible HDR contents. These contents are either obtained directly from LDR inputs, or from hallucinations when they are completely missing. We focus on handling large foreground motions, and assume the input LDR images, which are typically taken in a burst, have small background motions.

3.1   Network Architecture

We capitalize on a translation network to learn such a mapping. As shown in Fig. 2, our framework is essentially a symmetric encoder-decoder architecture, with two variants, *Unet* and *ResNet*.

Unet [22] is a common tool for translation learning. It is essentially an encoder-decoder architecture, with skip-connections that forward the output of the encoder layer (conv) directly to the input of the corresponding decoder layer (deconv) through channel-wise concatenation. In recent image translation works, such as [11], *Unet* has been demonstrated to be powerful in a wide range of tasks. However, unlike [11] where *Unet* was used in an adversarial setting, we may not need a discriminator network in HDR imaging, because the mapping from LDR to HDR is relatively easy to learn, compared to other scenarios in [11], where the two images domains are much more distinct, such as *edge* ↔ *photo*.

In addition to simple *Unet*, we also experimented with another structure, *ResNet*, similar to *Image Transformation Networks* proposed in [13], which simply replaces the middle layers with residual blocks [7]. Similar structure is also used in recent translation works [29]. In this paper, we name the this structure *ResNet*, as opposed to the previous one, *Unet*. We compare their performance in later sections.

The overall architecture can be conceptually divided into three components: encoder, merger and decoder. Since we have multiple exposure shots, intuitively we may have separate branches to extract different types of information from different exposure inputs. Instead of duplicating the whole network, which may defer the merging, we separate the first two layers as encoders for each exposure inputs. After extracting the features, the network learns to merge them, mostly in the middle layers, and to decode them into an HDR output, mostly in the last few layers.

3.2   Processing Pipeline and Loss Function

Given a stack of LDR images, if they are not in RAW format, we first linearize the images using the estimated inverse of Camera Response Function (CRF) [6], which is often referred to as radiometric calibration. We then apply gamma correction to produce the input to our system.

Although this process is technically important in order to recover the accurate radiance map, in practice, our system could also produce visually plausible approximation without radiometric calibration, such as examples shown in

Fig. 10. This is because the gamma function can be a rough approximation of the CRF.

We denote the set of input LDRs by $\mathcal{I} = \{I_1, I_2, I_3\}$, sorted by their exposure biases. We first map them to $\mathcal{H} = \{H_1, H_2, H_3\}$ in the HDR domain. We use simple gamma encoding for this mapping:

$$H_i = \frac{I_i^\gamma}{t_i}, \gamma > 1 \tag{1}$$

where t_i is the exposure time of image I_i. Note that we use H to denote the target HDR image, and H_i to denote the LDR inputs mapped to HDR domain. The values of I_i, H_i and H are bounded between 0 and 1.

We then concatenate $\mathcal{I}$ and $\mathcal{H}$ channel-wise into a 6-channel input and feed it directly to the network. This is also suggested in [14]. The LDRs facilitate the detection of misalignments and saturation, while the exposure-adjusted HDRs improve the robustness of the network across LDRs with various exposure levels. Our network f is thus defined as:

$$\hat{H} = f(\mathcal{I}, \mathcal{H}) \tag{2}$$

where $\hat{H}$ is the estimated HDR image, and is also bounded between 0 and 1.

Since HDR images are usually displayed after tonemapping, we compute the loss function on the tonemapped HDR images, which is more effective than directly computed in the HDR domain. In [14] the author proposed to use μ-law, which is commonly used for range compression in audio processing:

$$T(H) = \frac{\log(1 + \mu H)}{\log(1 + \mu)} \tag{3}$$

where H is an HDR image, and μ is a parameter controlling the level of compression. We set μ to 5000. Although there are other powerful tonemappers, most of them are typically complicated and not fully differentiable, which makes them not suitable for training a neural network.

Finally, our loss function is defined as:

$$\mathcal{L}_{Unet} = \|T(\hat{H}) - T(H)\|_2 \tag{4}$$

where H is the ground truth HDR image.

4   Datasets

We used the dataset provided by [14] for training and testing. Although other HDR datasets are available, many of them either do not have ground truth HDR images, or contain only a very limited number of scenes. This dataset contains 89 scenes with ground truth HDR images. As described in [14], for each scene, 3 different exposure shots were taken while object was moving, and another 3 shots were taken while object remained static. The static sets are used to

Table 1. Comparison of average running time on the test set under CPU environment.

	Sen [23]	Hu [10]	Kalantari [14]	HDRCNN [3]	Ours *Unet*	Ours *ResNet*
Time (s)	261	137	72.1	12.6	11.9	14.7

Table 2. Quantitative comparisons of the results on Kalantari's test set [14]. The first two rows are PSNR/SSIM computed using tonemapped outputs and ground truth, and the following two rows are PSNR/SSIM computed using linear images and ground truth. The last row is HDR-VDP-2 [18] sores. All values are the average across 15 testing images in the original test set.

	Sen [23]	Hu [10]	Kalantari [14]	Ours *Unet*	Ours *ResNet*
PSNR-T	40.80	35.79	**42.70**	40.81	41.65
SSIM-T	0.9808	0.9717	**0.9877**	0.9844	0.9860
PSNR-L	38.11	30.76	**41.22**	40.52	40.88
SSIM-L	0.9721	0.9503	0.9845	0.9837	**0.9858**
HDR-VDP-2	59.38	57.05	63.98	64.88	**64.90**

produce ground truth HDR with reference to the medium exposure shot. This medium exposure reference shot then replaces the medium exposure shot in the dynamic sets. All images are resized to 1000×1500. Each set consists of LDR images with exposure biases of $\{-2.0, 0.0, +2.0\}$ or $\{-3.0, 0.0, +3.0\}$. We also tested our trained models on Sen's dataset [23] and Tursun's dataset [27,28].

4.1 Data Preparation

To focus on handling foreground motions, we first align the background using simple homography transformation, which does not introduce artifacts and distortions. This makes the learning more effective than directly trained without background alignment. Comparison and discussion are provided in Sect. 5.4.

4.2 Data Augmentation and Patch Generation

The dataset was split into 74 training examples and 15 testing examples by [14]. For the purpose of efficient training, instead of feeding the original full-size image into our model, we crop the images into 256×256 patches with a stride of 64, which produces around 19000 patches. We then perform data augmentation (flipping and rotation), further increasing the training data by 8 times.

In fact, a large portion of these patches contain only background regions, and exhibit little foreground motions. To keep the training focused on foreground motions, we detect large motion patches by thresholding the structural similarity between different exposure shots, and replicate these patches in the training set.

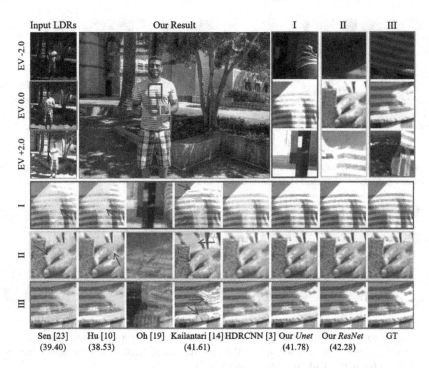

Fig. 3. Comparison against several state-of-the-art methods. In the upper half of the figure, the left column shows in the input LDRs, the middle is our tonemapped HDR result, and the last three columns show three zoomed-in LDR regions marked in the HDR image. The lower half compares the zoomed-in HDR regions of our results against others. The numbers in brackets at the bottom indicate the PSNR of the tonemapped images. Images are obtained from the Kalantari's test set [14].

5   Experiments and Results

5.1   Implementation Details

We first perform radiometric calibration and map the input LDRs to HDR domain. Each of the resulted radiance maps is channel-wise concatenated with the LDR image respectively, and then separately fed into different encoders. After 2 layers, all feature maps are then concatenated channel-wise for merging.

The encoding layers are convolution layers with a stride of 2, while the decoding layers are deconvolution layers kernels with a stride of 1/2. The output of the last deconvolution layer is connected to a flat-convolution layer to produce the final HDR. All layers use 5×5 kernels, and are followed by batch normalization (except the first layer and the output layer) and leaky ReLU (encoding layers) or ReLU (decoding layers). The channel numbers are doubled each layer from 64 to 512 during encoding and halved from 512 to 64 during decoding.

For *Unet* structure, 256×256 input patches are passed through 8 encoding layers to produce a $1 \times 1 \times 512$ block, followed by 8 decoding layers plus an

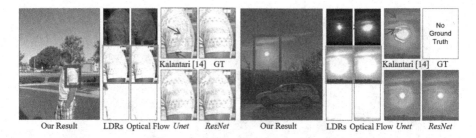

Fig. 4. Comparison against flow-based method [14]. Images are obtained from the Kalantari's dataset [14] and Tursun's dataset [27,28].

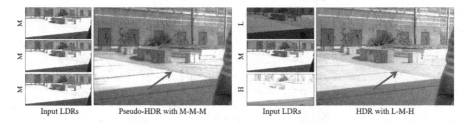

Fig. 5. Example of hallucination. The left is generated using only medium exposure shot, and the right is generated using low, medium and high exposure shots. Images are obtained from the Kalantari's dataset [14].

output layer to produce a 256×256 HDR patch. Our *ResNet* is different only in that after 3 encoding layers, the $32 \times 32 \times 256$ block is passed through 9 residual blocks with 3×3 kernels, followed by 3 decoding layers and an output layer.

5.2   Running Time

We report running time comparison with other methods in Table 1. Although our network is trained with GPU, other conventional optimization methods are optimized with CPU. For fair comparison, we evaluated all methods under CPU environment, on a PC with i7-4790K (4.0 GHz) and 32 GB RAM. We tested all methods using 3 LDR images of size 896×1408 as input. Note that the optical flow alignment used in [14] takes 59.4 s on average. When run with GPU (Titan X Pascal), our *Unet* and *ResNet* take 0.225 s and 0.239 s respectively.

5.3   Evaluation and Comparison

We perform quantitative and qualitative evaluations, and compare results with the state-of-the-art methods, including two patch-based methods [10,23], motion rejection method [19], the flow-based method with CNN merger [14], and the single image HDR imaging [3]. For all methods, we used the codes provided by the authors. Note that all the HDR images are displayed after tonemapping using *Photomatix* [20], which is different from the tonemapper used in training.

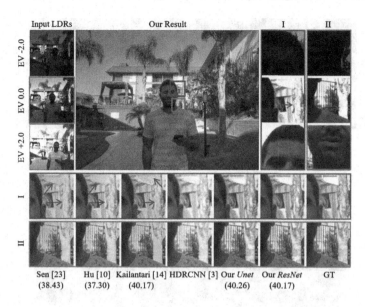

Fig. 6. Comparison of hallucinated details. Our network hallucinates the missing trunk texture, while others may fail. Images are obtained from the Kalantari's dataset [14].

Quantitative Comparison. We compute the PSNR and SSIM scores between the generated HDR and the ground truth HDR, both before and after tonemapping using μ-law. We also compute the HDR-VDP-2 [18], a metric specifically designed for measuring the visual quality of HDR images. For the two parameters used to compute the HDR-VDP-2 scores, we set the diagonal display size to 24 in., and the viewing distance to 0.5 m. We did not compare with [19] and [3] quantitatively, since the former is optimized for more than 5 LDR inputs and the latter produces unbounded HDR results.

Table 2 shows quantitative comparison of our networks against the state-of-the-art methods. Note that all results are calculated on the Kalantari's test set [14]. While [14] results in slightly higher PSNR scores, our methods result in comparable SSIM scores and slightly higher HDR-VDP-2 scores. Besides, *ResNet* seems to yield higher scores than *Unet*.

Qualitative Comparison. Figure 3 compares the testing results against state-of-the-art methods. In regions with no object motions, all methods produce decent results. However, when large object motion is present in saturated regions, [10,14,23] tend to produce unsightly artifacts. Flow-based method [14] also produces geometric distortions. Because Oh's method [19] uses rank minimization, which generally requires more inputs, it results in ghosting artifacts when applied with 3 inputs. Since HDRCNN [3] estimates the HDR image using only one single reference LDR image, it does not suffer from object motions, but tends to produce less sharp results and fail in large saturated regions, as shown

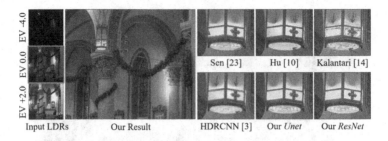

Fig. 7. Comparison of highlight regions. Examples come from the Sen's dataset [23].

Fig. 8. Results with different reference images. The first row shows three LDR inputs, and the second row shows the corresponding HDR results with reference to each input.

in Fig. 1. Our two networks produce comparably good results, free of obvious artifacts and distortions. In general, *ResNet* seems to consistently outperform *Unet*.

Comparison Against Flow-Based Method. In addition to Figs. 1 and 3, Fig. 4 illustrates our advantages over Kalantari's method [14], where optical flow alignment introduces severe distortions and color artifacts. Our method does not rely on erroneous optical flow, which intrinsically avoids such distortions, and is also much more efficient computationally.

Hallucination. One important feature of our method is the capability of hallucinating missing details that are nearly impossible to recover using conventional optimization approaches. As shown in Fig. 5, when given only the medium exposure, our network is able to properly hallucinate the grass texture in the saturated regions. When given also two other exposure shots, our network is able to incorporate the additional information such as the ground texture.

In Fig. 6, we examine the effectiveness of hallucination, by comparing our results to others with no hallucination. Hallucination can be very useful in

Input LDRs   Our Result   HDRCNN (1) Kalantari (3) Sen (3)   Sen (5)   *ResNet* (3) *ResNet* (5)

Fig. 9. Results with more input LDRs. The integers in the parentheses indicate the number of LDR images used to generate produce the HDR.

(a) Samsung Galaxy S5   (b) Huawei Mate 9   (c) iPhone 6s

Fig. 10. HDR results without radiometric calibration. All examples are novel images taken using cellphones with different CRFs.

dynamic scenes, since contents in over-exposed or under-exposed regions are often missing in all LDRs due to total occlusions caused by object motions.

Highlight. In addition to Fig. 4, where we show that our method outperforms [14] in highlight regions, Fig. 7 compares our highlight details against others. While other methods often fail to recover details in highlight regions and introduce artifacts and distortions, our method generally works well. Specifically, Hu's method [10] performs poorly in general at highlight regions, and other methods can only partially recover the details. Kalantari's method [14] tends to introduce evident distortions and color artifacts as shown in Fig. 7.

Different Reference Image. Figure 8 illustrates another advantage of our image translation formulation: the flexibility in choosing different reference images. Currently this is achieved by re-arranging the input LDRs. For example, using only low and high exposure shots and feeding them to the network in the order of {Low-Low-Medium} will result in a pseudo-HDR image with reference to the low exposure shot. Technically, this output does not represent the accurate radiance values, but is perceptually compelling and similar to real HDR images.

Fig. 11. This example illustrates the effect of background alignment.

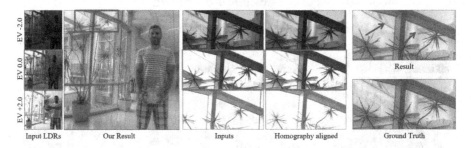

Fig. 12. Blurry results caused by parallax effects, which cannot be resolved by homography transformation.

Our framework may be extended to directly output multiple HDR images with different reference images, if trained in such a fashion, although we do not have appropriate datasets to corroborate this.

More Input LDRs. Our framework can potentially be extended for supporting more than 3 input LDRs. This is useful, because more LDRs capture more contents and improve the robustness. Although we do not have a suitable dataset to fully explore this, we decided to conduct a brief experiment using Sen's dataset [23]. We used their produced HDR images as ground truth for training, which are yet to be perfect to be used as ground truth, but sufficient for our purpose of testing such extensibility. Using this dataset, we tested our framework using 5 LDR inputs. Figure 9 compares our results with others. Interestingly, while Sen's [23] results using 5 inputs do not seem to be clearly better than those using 3 inputs, in our results, the details in saturated and under-exposed regions are markedly improved by using more input LDRs.

Cellphone Example. We also tested our model on novel cellphone images for proof of practicality, shown in Fig. 10. Our network produces good results in various kinds of settings. The input images were captured using different cellphones with different camera response functions. It is worth noting that when producing these pseudo-HDR examples, we did not perform radiometric calibration. This again demonstrates the robustness of our network.

5.4   Discussion on Background Alignment

In all our experiments and comparisons, since we are focused on handling large foreground motions, we align the backgrounds of the LDR inputs using homography transformation. Without background alignment, we found that our network tends to produce blurry edges where background is largely misaligned, as shown in Fig. 11. This can be due to the confusion caused by the background motion, which CNN is generally weak at dealing with. However, such issues can be easily resolved using simple homography transformation that almost perfectly aligns the background in most cases. Recall that in practice, the LDR inputs can be captured in a burst within a split second using nowadays handheld devices.

Nevertheless, homography is not always perfect. One particular case where homography may not produce perfect alignment is the existence of parallax effects in saturated regions. The final HDR output may be blurry. See Fig. 12.

6   Conclusion and Future Work

In this paper, we demonstrate that the problem of HDR imaging can be formulated as an image translation problem and tackled using deep CNNs. We conducted extensive quantitative and qualitative experiments to show that our non-flow-based CNN approach outperforms the state-of-the-arts, especially in the presence of large foreground motions. In particular, our simple translation network intrinsically avoids distortions and artifacts produced by erroneous optical flow alignment, and is computationally much more efficient. Furthermore, our network can hallucinate plausible details in largely saturated regions with large foreground motions, and recovers highlight regions better than other methods. Our system can also be easily extended with more inputs, and with different reference images, not limited to the medium exposure LDR. It is also robust across different inputs, including images that are not radiometrically calibrated.

While our advantages are clear, it is yet to be a perfect solution. We also observe challenges of recovering massive saturated regions with minimal number of input LDRs. In the future, we would attempt to incorporate high-level knowledge to facilitate such recovery, and devise a more powerful solution.

Acknowledgement. This work was supported in part by Tencent Youtu.

References

1. Debevec, P.E., Malik, J.: Recovering high dynamic range radiance maps from photographs. In: Proceedings of the 24th Annual Conference on Computer Graphics and Interactive Techniques, SIGGRAPH 1997, pp. 369–378. ACM Press/Addison-Wesley Publishing Co., New York (1997). https://doi.org/10.1145/258734.258884
2. Dosovitskiy, A., et al.: FlowNet: learning optical flow with convolutional networks. In: IEEE ICCV (2015). http://lmb.informatik.uni-freiburg.de/Publications/2015/DFIB15
3. Eilertsen, G., Kronander, J., Denes, G., Mantiuk, R., Unger, J.: HDR image reconstruction from a single exposure using deep CNNs. ACM TOG 36(6), 178 (2017)
4. Gallo, O., Gelfandz, N., Chen, W.C., Tico, M., Pulli, K.: Artifact-free high dynamic range imaging. In: 2009 IEEE International Conference on Computational Photography (ICCP), pp. 1–7, April 2009. https://doi.org/10.1109/ICCPHOT.2009.5559003
5. Gallo, O., Sen, P.: Stack-based algorithms for HDR capture and reconstruction. In: Dufaux, F., Callet, P.L., Mantiuk, R.K., Mrak, M. (eds.) High Dynamic Range Video, pp. 85–119. Academic Press (2016). https://doi.org/10.1016/B978-0-08-100412-8.00003-6
6. Grossberg, M.D., Nayar, S.K.: Determining the camera response from images: what is knowable? IEEE Trans. Pattern Anal. Mach. Intell. 25(11), 1455–1467 (2003). https://doi.org/10.1109/TPAMI.2003.1240119
7. He, K., Zhang, X., Ren, S., Sun, J.: Deep Residual Learning for Image Recognition. CoRR abs/1512.03385 (2015). http://arxiv.org/abs/1512.03385
8. Heide, F., et al.: FlexISP: a flexible camera image processing framework. ACM TOG 33(6), 231 (2014)
9. Heo, Y.S., Lee, K.M., Lee, S.U., Moon, Y., Cha, J.: Ghost-free high dynamic range imaging. In: Kimmel, R., Klette, R., Sugimoto, A. (eds.) ACCV 2010. LNCS, vol. 6495, pp. 486–500. Springer, Heidelberg (2011). https://doi.org/10.1007/978-3-642-19282-1_39
10. Hu, J., Gallo, O., Pulli, K., Sun, X.: HDR deghosting: how to deal with saturation? In: IEEE CVPR (2013)
11. Isola, P., Zhu, J.Y., Zhou, T., Efros, A.A.: Image-to-image translation with conditional adversarial networks. In: IEEE CVPR (2017)
12. Jacobs, K., Loscos, C., Ward, G.: Automatic high-dynamic range image generation for dynamic scenes. IEEE Comput. Graph. Appl. 28(2), 84–93 (2008). https://doi.org/10.1109/MCG.2008.23
13. Johnson, J., Alahi, A., Fei-Fei, L.: Perceptual losses for real-time style transfer and super-resolution (2016)
14. Kalantari, N.K., Ramamoorthi, R.: Deep high dynamic range imaging of dynamic scenes. ACM TOG 36(4), 1–14 (2017)
15. Kang, S.B., Uyttendaele, M., Winder, S., Szeliski, R.: High dynamic range video. ACM TOG 22(3), 319–325 (2003). https://doi.org/10.1145/882262.882270
16. Khan, E.A., Akyuz, A.O., Reinhard, E.: Ghost removal in high dynamic range images. In: 2006 International Conference on Image Processing, pp. 2005–2008, October 2006. https://doi.org/10.1109/ICIP.2006.312892
17. Mann, S., Picard, R.W.: On being 'undigital' with digital cameras: extending dynamic range by combining differently exposed pictures. In: Proceedings of Imaging Science and Technology, pp. 442–448 (1995)

18. Mantiuk, R., Kim, K.J., Rempel, A.G., Heidrich, W.: HDR-VDP-2: a calibrated visual metric for visibility and quality predictions in all luminance conditions. ACM TOG **30**(4), 40:1–40:14 (2011). https://doi.org/10.1145/2010324.1964935
19. Oh, T.H., Lee, J.Y., Tai, Y.W., Kweon, I.S.: Robust high dynamic range imaging by rank minimization. IEEE Trans. Pattern Anal. Mach. Intell. **37**(6), 1219–1232 (2015). https://doi.org/10.1109/TPAMI.2014.2361338
20. Photomatix: Photomatix (2017). https://www.hdrsoft.com
21. Raman, S., Chaudhuri, S.: Reconstruction of high contrast images for dynamic scenes. Vis. Comput. **27**(12), 1099–1114 (2011). https://doi.org/10.1007/s00371-011-0653-0
22. Ronneberger, O., Fischer, P., Brox, T.: U-net: convolutional networks for biomedical image segmentation. In: Navab, N., Hornegger, J., Wells, W.M., Frangi, A.F. (eds.) MICCAI 2015. LNCS, vol. 9351, pp. 234–241. Springer, Cham (2015). https://doi.org/10.1007/978-3-319-24574-4_28
23. Sen, P., Kalantari, N.K., Yaesoubi, M., Darabi, S., Goldman, D.B., Shechtman, E.: Robust patch-based HDR reconstruction of dynamic scenes. ACM TOG **31**(6), 203:1–203:11 (2012)
24. Serrano, A., Heide, F., Gutierrez, D., Wetzstein, G., Masia, B.: Convolutional sparse coding for high dynamic range imaging. Comput. Graph. Forum **35**(2), 153–163 (2016)
25. Tocci, M.D., Kiser, C., Tocci, N., Sen, P.: A versatile HDR video production system. ACM TOG **30**(4), 41:1–41:10 (2011). https://doi.org/10.1145/2010324.1964936
26. Tomaszewska, A., Mantiuk, R.: Image registration for multi-exposure high dynamic range image acquisition. In: International Conference in Central Europe on Computer Graphics and Visualization, WSCG 2007 (2007). http://wscg.zcu.cz/wscg2007/Papers_2007/full/B13-full.pdf
27. Tursun, O.T., Akyüz, A.O., Erdem, A., Erdem, E.: The state of the art in HDR deghosting: a survey and evaluation. Comput. Graph. Forum **34**(2), 683–707 (2015). https://doi.org/10.1111/cgf.12593
28. Tursun, O.T., Akyüz, A.O., Erdem, A., Erdem, E.: An objective deghosting quality metric for HDR images. Comput. Graph. Forum **35**(2), 139–152 (2016). https://doi.org/10.1111/cgf.12818
29. Zhu, J.Y., Park, T., Isola, P., Efros, A.A.: Unpaired image-to-image translation using cycle-consistent adversarial networks. In: IEEE ICCV (2017)
30. Zhu, S., Liu, S., Loy, C.C., Tang, X.: Deep cascaded bi-network for face hallucination. In: Leibe, B., Matas, J., Sebe, N., Welling, M. (eds.) ECCV 2016. LNCS, vol. 9909, pp. 614–630. Springer, Cham (2016). https://doi.org/10.1007/978-3-319-46454-1_37
31. Zimmer, H., Bruhn, A., Weickert, J.: Freehand HDR imaging of moving scenes with simultaneous resolution enhancement. Comput. Graph. Forum **30**(2), 405–414 (2011). https://doi.org/10.1111/j.1467-8659.2011.01870.x

Linear Span Network for Object Skeleton Detection

Chang Liu, Wei Ke, Fei Qin, and Qixiang Ye$^{(\boxtimes)}$

University of Chinese Academy of Sciences, Beijing, China
{liuchang615,kewei11}@mails.ucas.ac.cn, {fqin1982,qxye}@ucas.ac.cn

Abstract. Robust object skeleton detection requires to explore rich representative visual features and effective feature fusion strategies. In this paper, we first re-visit the implementation of HED, the essential principle of which can be ideally described with a linear reconstruction model. Hinted by this, we formalize a Linear Span framework, and propose Linear Span Network (LSN) which introduces Linear Span Units (LSUs) to minimizes the reconstruction error. LSN further utilizes subspace linear span besides the feature linear span to increase the independence of convolutional features and the efficiency of feature integration, which enhances the capability of fitting complex ground-truth. As a result, LSN can effectively suppress the cluttered backgrounds and reconstruct object skeletons. Experimental results validate the state-of-the-art performance of the proposed LSN.

Keywords: Linear span framework · Linear span unit
Linear span network · Skeleton detection

1 Introduction

Skeleton is one of the most representative visual properties, which describes objects with compact but informative curves. Such curves constitute a continuous decomposition of object shapes [13], providing valuable cues for both object representation and recognition. Object skeletons can be converted into descriptive features and spatial constraints, which enforce human pose estimation [22], semantic segmentation [20], and object localization [8].

Researchers have been exploiting the representative CNNs for skeleton detection and extraction [5,17,18,24] for years. State-of-the-art approaches root in effective multi-layer feature fusion, with the motivation that low-level features focus on detailed structures while high-level features are rich in semantics [5]. As a pioneer work, the holistically-nested edge detection (HED) [24] is computed as a pixel-wise classification problem, without considering the complementary

---

C. Liu and W. Ke—Equal contributions.
The source code is publicly available at https://github.com/LinearSpanNetwork.

© Springer Nature Switzerland AG 2018
V. Ferrari et al. (Eds.): ECCV 2018, LNCS 11206, pp. 136–151, 2018.
https://doi.org/10.1007/978-3-030-01216-8_9

among multi-layer features. Other state-of-the-art approaches, *e.g.*, fusing scale-associated deep side-outputs (FSDS) [17,18] and side-output residual network (SRN) [5] investigates the multi-layer association problem. FSDS requires intensive annotations of the scales for each skeleton point, while SRN struggles to pursuits the complementary between adjacent layers without complete mathematical explanation. The problem of how to principally explore and fuse more representative features remains to be further elaborated.

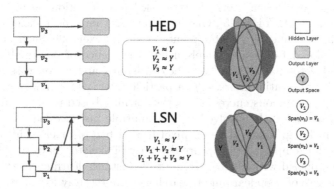

Fig. 1. A comparison of holistically-nested edge detection (HED) network [24] and linear span network (LSN). HED uses convolutional features without considering their complementary. The union of the output spaces of HED is small, denoted as the pink area. As an improved solution, LSN spans a large output space.

Through the analysis, it is revealed that HED treats the skeleton detection as a pixel-wise classification problem with the side-output from convolutional network. Mathematically, this architecture can be equalized with a linear reconstruction model, by treating the convolutional feature maps as linear bases and the 1×1 convolutional kernel values as weights. Under the guidance of the linear span theory [6], we formalize a linear span framework for object skeleton detection. With this framework, the output spaces of HED could have intersections since it fails to optimize the subspace constrained by each other, Fig. 1. To ease this problem, we design Linear Span Unit (LSU) according to this framework, which will be utilized to modify convolutional network. The obtained network is named as Linear Span Network (LSN), which consists feature linear span, resolution alignment, and subspace linear span. This architecture will increase the independence of convolutional features and the efficiency of feature integration, which is shown as the smaller intersections and the larger union set, Fig. 1. Consequently, the capability of fitting complex ground-truth could be enhanced. By stacking multiple LSUs in a deep-to-shallow manner, LSN captures both rich object context and high-resolution details to suppress the cluttered backgrounds and reconstruct object skeletons. The contributions of the paper include:

– A linear span framework that reveals the essential nature of object skeleton detection problem, and proposes that the potential performance gain could be achieved with both the increased independence of spanning sets and the enlarged spanned output space.

- A Linear Span Network (LSN) can evolve toward the optimized architecture for object skeleton detection under the guidance of linear span framework.

2   Related Work

Early skeleton extraction methods treat skeleton detection as morphological operations [7,9,11,12,14,23,25]. One hypothesis is that object skeletons are the subsets of lines connecting center points of super-pixels [9]. Such line subsets could be explored from super-pixels using a sequence of deformable discs to extract the skeleton path [7]. In [23], The consistence and smoothness of skeleton are modeled with spatial filters, *e.g.*, a particle filter, which links local skeleton segments into continuous curves. Recently, learning based methods are utilized for skeleton detection. It is solved with a multiple instance learning approach [21], which picks up a true skeleton pixel from a bag of pixels. The structured random forest is employed to capture diversity of skeleton patterns [20], which can be also modeled with a subspace multiple instance learning method [15].

With the rise of deep learning, researchers have recently formulated skeleton detection as image-to-mask classification problem by using learned weights to fuse the multi-layer convolutional features in an end-to-end manner. HED [24] learns a pixel-wise classifier to produce edges, which can be also used for skeleton detection. Fusing scale-associated deep side-outputs (FSDS) [18] learns multi-scale skeleton representation given scale-associated ground-truth. Side-output residual network (SRN) [5] leverages the output residual units to fit the errors between the object symmetry/skeleton ground-truth and the side-outputs of multiple convolutional layers.

The problem about how to fuse multi-layer convolutional features to generate an output mask, *e.g.*, object skeleton, has been extensively explored. Nevertheless, existing approaches barely investigate the problem about the linear independence of multi-layer features, which limits their representative capacity. Our approach targets at exploring this problem from the perspective of linear span theory by feature linear span of multi-layer features and subspace linear span of the spanned subspaces.

3   Problem Formulation

3.1   Re-thinking HED

In this paper, we re-visit the implementation of HED, and reveal that HED as well as its variations can be all formulated by the linear span theory [6].

HED utilizes fully convolutional network with deep supervision for edge detection, which is one of the typical low-level image-to-mask task. Denoting

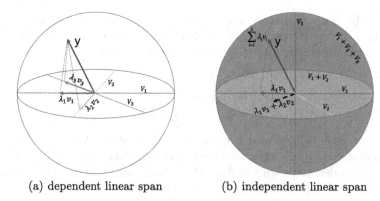

(a) dependent linear span   (b) independent linear span

Fig. 2. Schematic of linear span with a set of dependent vectors (a) and independent vectors (b).

the convolutional feature as C with m maps and the classifier as w, HED is computed as a pixel-wise classification problem, as

$$\hat{y}_j = \sum_{k=1}^{m} w_k \cdot c_{k,j}, j = 1, 2, \cdots, |\hat{Y}|, \tag{1}$$

where $c_{k,j}$ is the feature value of the j-th pixel on the k-th convolutional map and $\hat{y}_j$ is the classified label of the j-th pixel in the output image $\hat{Y}$.

Not surprisingly, this can be equalized as a linear reconstruction problem, as

$$Y = \sum_{k=1}^{m} \lambda_k v_k, \tag{2}$$

where λ_k is linear reconstruction weight and v_k is the k-th feature map in C.

We treat each side-output of HED as a feature vector in the linear spanned subspace $V_i = span(v_1^i, v_2^i, \cdots, v_m^i)$, in which i is the index of convolutional stages. Then HED forces each subspace V_i to approximate the ground-truth space $\mathcal{Y}$. We use three convolutional layers as an example, which generate subspaces V_1, V_2, and V_3. Then the relationship between the subspaces and the ground-truth space can be illustrated as lines in a 3-dimension space in Fig. 2(a).

As HED does not optimize the subspaces constrained by each other, it fails to explore the complementary of each subspace to make them decorrelated. The reconstructions can be formulated as

$$\begin{cases} V_1 \approx \mathcal{Y} \\ V_2 \approx \mathcal{Y}. \\ V_3 \approx \mathcal{Y} \end{cases} \tag{3}$$

When v_1, v_2, and v_3 are linearly dependent, they only have the capability to reconstruct vectors in a plane. That is to say, when the point Y is out of the plane, the reconstruction error is hardly eliminated, Fig. 2(a).

Obviously, if v_1, v_2, and v_3 are linearly independent, *i.e.*, not in the same plane, Fig. 2(b), the reconstruction could be significantly eased. To achieve this target, we can iteratively formulate the reconstruction as

$$\begin{cases} V_1 \approx \mathcal{Y} \\ V_1 + V_2 \approx \mathcal{Y} \\ V_1 + V_2 + V_3 \approx \mathcal{Y} \end{cases}. \tag{4}$$

It s observed that V_2 is refined with the constraint of V_1. And V_3 is optimized in the similar way, which aims for vector decorrelation. The sum of subspaces, *i.e.*, $V_1 + V_2$ is denoted with the dark blue plane, and $V_1 + V_2 + V_3$ is denoted with the light blue sphere, Fig. 2(b).

Now, it is very straightforward to generalize Eq. (4) to

$$\sum_{k=1}^{l} V_k \approx \mathcal{Y}, l = 1, 2, \cdots, n. \tag{5}$$

One of the variations of HED, *i.e.*, SRN, which can be understand as a special case of Eq. (5) with $\sum_{k=l-1}^{l} V_k \approx \mathcal{Y}$, has already shown the effectiveness.

3.2   Linear Span View

Based on the discussion of last section, we can now strictly formulate a mathematical framework based on linear span theory [6], which can be utilized to guide the design of Linear Span Network (LSN) toward the optimized architecture.

In linear algebra, linear span is defined as a procedure to construct a linear space by a set of vectors or a set of subspaces.

Definition 1. $\mathcal{Y}$ is a linear space over $\mathbb{R}$. The set $\{v_1, v_2, \ldots, v_m\} \subset \mathcal{Y}$ is a spanning set for $\mathcal{Y}$ if every y in $\mathcal{Y}$ can be expressed as a linear combination of $v_1, v_2, \ldots, v_m$, as

$$y = \sum_{k=1}^{m} \lambda_k v_k, \ \lambda_1, \ldots, \lambda_m \in \mathbb{R}, \tag{6}$$

and $\mathcal{Y} = span(\{v_1, v_2, \ldots, v_m\})$.

Theorem 1. Let $v_1, v_2, \ldots, v_m$ be vectors in $\mathcal{Y}$. Then $\{v_1, v_2, \ldots, v_m\}$ spans $\mathcal{Y}$ if and only if, for the matrix $F = [v_1, v_2, \ldots, v_m]$, the linear system $F\lambda = y$ is consistent for every y in $\mathcal{Y}$.

Remark 1. According to *Theorem* 1, if the linear system is consistent for almost every vector in a linear space, the space can be approximated by the linear spanned space. This theorem uncovers the principle of LSN, which pursues a linear system as mentioned above setting up for as many as ground-truth.

Definition 2. A finite set of vectors, which span $\mathcal{Y}$ and are linearly independent, is called a basis for $\mathcal{Y}$.

Theorem 2. Every linearly independent set of vectors $\{v_1, v_2, \ldots, v_m\}$ in a finite dimensional linear space $\mathcal{Y}$ can be completed to a basis of $\mathcal{Y}$.

Theorem 3. Every subspace U has a complement in $\mathcal{Y}$, that is, another subspace V such that vector y in $\mathcal{Y}$ can be decomposed uniquely as

$$y = u + v, u \text{ in } U, v \text{ in } V. \tag{7}$$

Definition 3. $\mathcal{Y}$ is said to be the sum of its subspaces $V_1, \ldots, V_m$ if every y in Y can be expressed as

$$y = v_1 + \ldots + v_m, v_j \text{ in } V_j. \tag{8}$$

Remark 2. We call the spanning of feature maps to a subspace as feature linear span, and the sum of subspaces as subspace linear span. From *Theorems* 2 and 3, it is declared that the union of the spanning sets of subspaces is the spanning set of the sum of the subspaces. That is to say, in the subspace linear span we can merge the spanning sets of subspaces step by step to construct a larger space.

Theorem 4. Supposing $\mathcal{Y}$ is a finite dimensional linear space, U and V are two subspaces of $\mathcal{Y}$ such that $\mathcal{Y} = U + V$, and W is the intersection of U and V, *i.e.*, $W = U \cap V$. Then

$$\dim \mathcal{Y} = \dim U + \dim V - \dim W. \tag{9}$$

Remark 3. From *Theorem* 4, the smaller the dimension of the intersection of two subspaces is, the bigger the dimension of the sum of two subspaces is. Then, successively spanning the subspaces from deep to shallow with supervision increases independence of spanning sets and enlarges the sum of subspaces. It enfores the representative capacity of convolutional features and integrates them in a more effective way.

4   Linear Span Network

With the help of the proposed framework, the Linear Span Network (LSN) is designed for the same targets with HED and SRN, *i.e.*, the object skeleton detection problem. Following the linear reconstruction theory, a novel architecture named Linear Span Unit (LSU) has been defined first. Then, LSN is updated from VGG-16 [17] with LSU and hints from *Remarks* 1–3. VGG-16 has been chosen for the purpose of fair comparison with HED and SRN. In what follows, the implementation of LSU and LSN are introduced.

4.1   Linear Span Unit

The architecture of Linear Span Unit (LSU) is shown in Fig. 3, where each feature map is regarded as a feature vector. The input feature vectors are unified with a concatenation (concat for short) operation, as

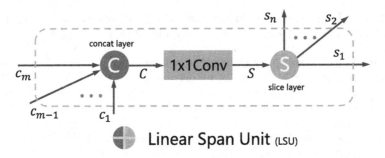

Fig. 3. Linear Span Unit, which is used in both feature linear span and subspace linear span. In LSU, the operation of linear reconstruction is implemented by a concatenation layer and a 1×1 convolutional layer.

$$C = \underset{k=1}{\overset{m}{concat}}(c_k), \tag{10}$$

where c_k is the k-th feature vector. In order to compute the linear combination of the feature vectors, a convolution operation with $1 \times 1 \times m$ convolutional kernels is employed:

$$s_i = \sum_{k=1}^{m} \lambda_{k,i} \cdot c_k, i = 1, 2, \cdots, n, \tag{11}$$

where $\lambda_{k,i}$ is the convolutional parameter with k elements for the i-th reconstruction output. The LSU will generate n feature vectors in the subspace spanned by the input feature vectors. A slice layer is further utilized to separate them for different connections, which is denoted as

$$\bigcup_{i=1}^{n} s_i = slice(S). \tag{12}$$

4.2   Linear Span Network Architecture

The architecture of LSN is shown in Fig. 4, which is consisted of three components, *i.e.*, feature linear span, resolution alignment, and subspace linear span are illustrated. The VGG-16 network with 5 convolutional stages [19] is used as the backbone network.

In feature linear span, LSU is used to span the convolutional feature of the last layer of each stage according to Eq. 11. The supervision is added to the output of LSU so that the spanned subspace approximates the ground-truth space, following *Remark* 1. If only feature linear span is utilized, the LSN is degraded to HED [24]. Nevertheless, the subspaces in HED separately fit the ground-truth space, and thus fail to decorrelate spanning sets among subspaces. According to *Remarks* 2 and 3, we propose to further employ subspace linear span to enlarge the sum of subspaces and deal with the decorrelation problem.

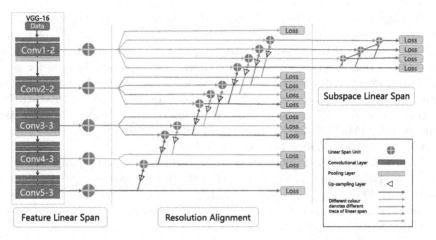

Fig. 4. The architecture of the proposed Linear Span Network (LSN), which leverages Linear Span Units (LSUs) to implement three components of the feature linear span, the resolution alignment, and the subspace linear span. The feature linear span uses convolutional features to build subspaces. The LSU is re-used to unify the resolution among multi-stages in resolution alignment. The subspace linear span summarizes the subspaces to fit the ground-truth space.

As the resolution of the vectors in different subspaces is with large variation, simple up-sampling operation will cause the Mosaic effect, which generates noise in subspace linear span. Without any doubt, the resolution alignment is necessary for LSN. Thus, in Fig. 4, LSUs have been laid between any two adjacent layers with supervision. As a pre-processing component to subspace linear span, it outputs feature vectors with same resolution.

The subspace linear span is also implemented by LSUs, which further concatenates feature vectors from deep to shallow layers and spans the subspaces with Eq. (5). According to *Remark* 3, a step-by-step strategy is utilized to explore the complementary of subspaces. With the loss layers attached on LSUs, it not only enlarges the sum of subspaces spanned by different convolutional layers, but also decorrelates the union of spanning sets of different subspaces. With this architecture, LSN enforces the representative capacity of convolutional features to fit complex ground-truth.

5   Experiments

5.1   Experimental Setting

Datasets: We evaluate the proposed LSN on pubic skeleton datasets including SYMMAX [21], WH-SYMMAX [15], SK-SMALL [18], SK-LARGE [17], and Sym-PASCAL [5]. We also evaluate LSN to edge detection on the BSDS500 dataset [1] to validate its generality.

SYMMAX is derived from BSDS300 [1], which contains 200/100 training and testing images. It is annotated with local skeleton on both foreground and background. WH-SYMMAX is developed for object skeleton detection, but contains only cropped horse images, which are not comprehensive for general object skeleton. SK-SMALL involves skeletons about 16 classes of objects with 300/206 training and testing images. Based on SK-SMALL, SK-LARGE is extended to 746/745 training and testing images. Sym-PASCAL is derived from the PASCAL-VOC-2011 segmentation dataset [4] which contains 14 object classes with 648/787 images for training and testing.

The BSDS500 [1] dataset is used to evaluate LSN's performance on edge detection. This dataset is composed of 200 training images, 100 validation images, and 200 testing images. Each image is manually annotated by five persons on average. For training images, we preserve their positive labels annotated by at least three human annotators.

Evaluation Protocol: Precision recall curve (PR-curve) is use to evaluate the performance of the detection methods. With different threshold values, the output skeleton/edge masks are binarized. By comparing the masks with the ground-truth, the precision and recall are computed. For skeleton detection, the F-measure is used to evaluate the performance of the different detection approaches, which is achieved with the optimal threshold values over the whole dataset, as

$$F = \frac{2PR}{P+R}. \tag{13}$$

To evaluate edge detection performance, we utilize three standard measures [1]: F-measures when choosing an optimal scale for the entire dataset (ODS) or per image (OIS), and the average precision (AP).

Hyper-Parameters: For both skeleton and edge detection, we use VGG16 [19] as the backbone network. During learning we set the mini-batch size to 1, the loss-weight to 1 for each output layer, the momentum to 0.9, the weight decay to 0.002, and the initial learning rate to 1e-6, which decreases one magnitude for every 10,000 iterations.

5.2   LSN Implementation

We evaluate four LSN architectures for subspace linear span and validate the iterative training strategy.

LSN Architectures. If there is no subspace linear span, Fig. 4, LSN is simplified to HED [24], which is denoted as LSN_1. The F-measure of LSN_1 is 49.53%. When the adjacent two subspaces are spanned, it is denoted as LSN_2, which is the same as SRN [5]. LSN_2 achieve significant performance improvement over HED which has feature linear span but no subspace span. We compare LSNs with different number of subspaces to be spanned, and achieve the best F-measure of 66.82%. When the subspace number is increased to 4, the skeleton detection performance drops. The followings explained why LSN_3 is the best choice.

If the subspaces to be spanned are not enough, the complementary of convolutional features from different layers could not be effectively explored. On the contrary, if a LSU fuses feature layers that have large-scale resolution difference, it requires to use multiple up-sampling operations, which deteriorate the features. Although resolution alignment significantly eases the problem, the number of adjacent feature layers to be fused in LSU remains a practical choice. LSN_3 reported the best performance by fusing a adjacent layer of higher resolution and a adjacent layer of lower resolution. On one hand, the group of subspaces in LSN_3 uses more feature integration. On the other hand, there is not so much information loss after an 2× up-sampling operation (Table 1).

Table 1. The performance of different LSN implementations on the SK-LARGE dataset. LSN_3 that fuses an adjacent layer of higher resolution and an adjacent layer of lower resolution reported the best performance.

Architecture	F-measure (%)
LSN_1 (HED, feature linear span only)	49.53
LSN_2 (SRN, feature and 2-subspace linear span)	65.88
LSN_3 (LSN, feature and 3-subspace linear span)	**66.15**
LSN_4 (LSN, feature and 4-subspace linear span)	65.89

Table 2. The performance for different training strategies.

	w/o RA	end-to-end	iter1	iter2	iter3
F-measure(%)	66.15	66.63	**66.82**	66.74	66.68

Training Strategy. With three feature layers spanned, LSN needs up-sampling the side-output feature layers from the deepest to the shallowest ones. We use the supervised up-sampling to unify the resolution of feature layers.

During training, the resolution alignment is also achieved by stacking LSUs. We propose a strategy that train the two kinds of linear span, i.e., feature linear span with resolution alignment and subspace linear span, iteratively. In the first iteration, we tune the LSU parameters for feature linear span and resolution alignment using the pre-trained VGG model on ImageNet, as well as update the convolutional parameters. Keeping the LSU parameters for resolution alignment unchanged, we tune LSU parameters for feature linear span and subspace linear span using the new model. In other iteration, the model is fine-tuned on the snap-shot of the previous iteration. With this training strategy, the skeleton detection performance is improved from 66.15% to 66.82%, Table 2. The detection performance changes marginally when more iterations are used. We therefore use the single iteration (iter1) in all experiments.

LSU Effect. In Fig. 5, we use a giraffe's skeleton from SK-LARGE as an example to compare and analyze the learned feature vectors (bases) by HED [24], SRN [24], and LSN. In Fig. 5(a) and (c), we respectively visualize the feature vectors learned by HED [24] and the proposed LSN. It can be seen in the first column that the HED's results incorporate more background noise and mosaic effects. This shows that the proposed LSN can better span an output feature space. In Fig. 5(b) and (d), we respectively visualize the subspace vectors learned by SRN [5] and the proposed LSN. It can be seen in the first column that the SRN's results incorporate more background noises. It requires to depress such noises by using a residual reconstruction procedure. In contrast, the subspace vectors of LSN is much clearer and compacter. This fully demonstrates that LSN can better span the output space and enforce the representative capacity of convolutional features, which will ease the problems of fitting complex outputs with limited convolutional layers (Fig. 6).

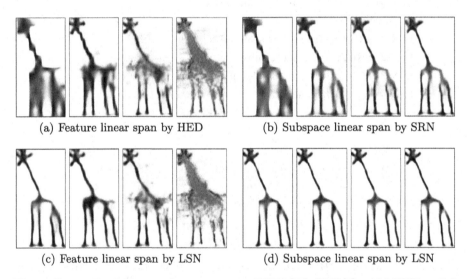

(a) Feature linear span by HED   (b) Subspace linear span by SRN

(c) Feature linear span by LSN   (d) Subspace linear span by LSN

Fig. 5. Comparison of output feature vectors of HED [24], SRN [5], and LSN(From left to right results are listed in a deep-to-shallow manner). By comparing (a) and (c), (b) and (d), one can see that LSN can learn better feature vectors and subspaces(basis) to span the output space. It enforces the representative capacity of convolutional features to fit complex outputs with limited convolutional layers.

5.3   Performance and Comparison

Skeleton Detection. The proposed LSN is evaluated and compared with the state-of-the-art approaches, and the performance is shown in Fig. 5 and Table 3. The result of SRN [5] is obtained by running authors' source code on a Tesla K80 GPU, and the other results are provided by [17].

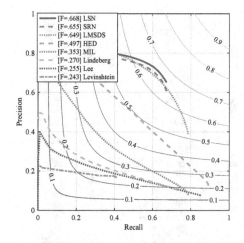

Fig. 6. The PR-curve on SK-LARGE.

Table 3. Performance comparison on SK-LARGE dataset. † GPU time.

Mehods	F-measure	Runtime/s
Lindeberg [11]	0.270	4.05
Levinshtein [9]	0.243	146.21
Lee [7]	0.255	609.10
MIL [21]	0.293	42.40
HED [24]	0.495	**0.05†**
SRN [5]	0.655	0.08†
LMSDS [17]	0.649	**0.05†**
LSN (ours)	**0.668**	0.09†

The conventional approaches including Lindeberg [11], Levinshtein [9], and Lee [7], produce the skeleton masks without using any learning strategy. They are time consuming and achieve very low F-measure of 27.0%, 24.3%, and 25.5%, respectively. The typical learning approach, *i.e.*, multiple instance learning (MIL) [21], achieves F-measure of 29.3%. It extractes pixel-wised feature with multi-orientation and multi-scale, and averagely uses 42.40 s to distinguish skeleton pixels from the backgrounds in a single image.

The CNN based approaches achieve huge performance gain compared with the conventional approaches. HED [24] achieves the F-measure of 49.5% and uses 0.05 s to process an images, while SRN [5] achieves 64.9% and uses 0.08 s. The scale-associated multi-task method, LMSDS [17], achieves the performance of 64.9%, which is built on HED with the pixel-level scale annotations. Our proposed LSN reportes the best detection performance of 66.8% with a little more runtime cost compared with HED and SRN.

The results show that feature linear span is efficient for skeleton detection. As discussed above, HED and SRN are two special case of LSN. LSN that used three spanned layers in each span unit is a better choice than the state-of-the art SRN. Some skeleton detection results are shown in Fig. 7. It is illustrated that HED produces lots of noise while the FSDS is not smooth. Comparing SRN with LSN, one can see that LSN rectifies some false positives as shown in column one and column three and reconstruct the dismiss as shown in column six.

The proposed LSN is also evaluated on other four commonly used datasets, including WH-SYMMAX [15], SK-SMALL [18], SYMMAX [21], and Sym-PASCAL [5]. The F-measure are shown in Table 4. Similar with SK-LARGE, LSN achieves the best detection performance on WH-SYMMAX, SK-SMALL, and SYMMAX, with the F-measure 79.7%, 63.3% and 48.0%. It achieves 5.4%, 8.1%, and 5.3% performance gain compared with HED, and 1.7%, 0.1%, and

HED

FSDS

SRN

LSN
(ours)

GT

Fig. 7. Skeleton detection examples by state-of-the-art approaches including HED [24], FSDS [18], SRN [5], and LSN. The red boxes are false positive or dismiss in SRN, while the blue ones are correct reconstruction skeletons in LSN at the same position. (Best viewed in color with zoon-in.)

Table 4. Performance comparison of the state-of-the-art approaches on the public WH-SYMMAX [15], SK-SMALL [18], SYMMAX [21], and Sym-PASCAL [5] datasets.

	WH-SYMMAX	SK-SMALL	SYMMAX	Sym-PASCAL
Levinshtein [9]	0.174	0.217	–	0.134
Lee [7]	0.223	0.252	–	0.135
Lindeberg [11]	0.277	0.227	0.360	0.138
Particle Filter [23]	0.334	0.226	–	0.129
MIL [21]	0.365	0.392	0.362	0.174
HED [24]	0.743	0.542	0.427	0.369
FSDS [18]	0.769	0.623	0.467	0.418
SRN [5]	0.780	0.632	0.446	**0.443**
LSN (ours)	**0.797**	**0.633**	**0.480**	0.425

2.4% gain compared with SRN. On Sym-PASCAL, LSN achieves comparable performance of 42.5% vs. 44.3% with the state-of-the art SRN.

Edge Detection. Edge detection task has similar implementation with skeleton that discriminate whether a pixel belongs to an edge. It also can be reconstructed by the convolutional feature maps. In this section, we compare the edge detection

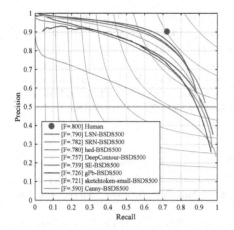

Fig. 8. The PR-curve on the BSDS500 edge detection dataset.

Table 5. Performance comparison on the BSDS500 edge detection dataset. † GPU time.

Mehods	ODS	OIS	AP	FPS
Canny [2]	0.590	0.620	00578	15
ST [10]	0.721	0.739	0.768	1
gPb [1]	0.726	0.760	0.727	1/240
SE [16]	0.739	0.759	0.792	2.5
DC [16]	0.757	0.776	0.790	1/30†
HED [24]	0.780	0.797	0.814	2.5†
SRN [5]	0.782	0.800	0.779	2.3†
LSN (ours)	**0.790**	**0.806**	0.618	2.0†
Human	0.800	0.800	–	–

result of the proposed LSN with some other state-of-the-art methods, such as Canny [2], Sketech Tokens [10], Structured Edge (SE) [3], gPb [1], DeepContour [16], HED [24], and SRN [5], Fig. 8 and Table 5.

In Fig. 8, it is illustrated that the best conventional approach is SE with F-measure (ODS) of 0.739 and all the CNN based approaches achieve much better detection performance. HED is one of the baseline deep learning method, which achieved 0.780. The proposed LSN reportes the highest F-measure of 0.790, which has a very small gap (0.01) to human performance. The F-measure with an optimal scale for the per image (OIS) was 0.806, which was even higher than human performance, Table 5. The good performance of the proposed LSN demonstrates its general applicability to image-to-mask tasks.

6 Conclusion

Skeleton is one of the most representative visual properties, which describes objects with compact but informative curves. In this paper, the skeleton detection problem is formulated as a linear reconstruction problem. Consequently, a generalized linear span framework for skeleton detection has been presented with formal mathematical definition. We explore the Linear Span Units (LSUs) to learn a CNN based mask reconstruction model. With LSUs we implement three components including feature linear span, resolution alignment, and subspace linear span, and update the Holistically-nested Edge Detection (HED) network to Linear Span Network (LSN). With feature linear span, the ground truth space can be approximated by the linear spanned output space. With subspace linear span, not only the independence among spanning sets of subspaces can be increased, but also the spanned output space can be enlarged. As a result, LSN will have better capability to approximate the ground truth space, *i.e.*, against the cluttered background and scales. Experimental results validate the state-of-the-art performance of the proposed LSN, while we provide a principled way to learn more representative convolutional features.

Acknowledgement. This work was partially supported by the National Nature Science Foundation of China under Grant 61671427 and Grant 61771447, and Beijing Municipal Science & Technology Commission under Grant Z181100008918014.

References

1. Arbelaez, P., Maire, M., Fowlkes, C.C., Malik, J.: Contour detection and hierarchical image segmentation. IEEE Trans. Pattern Anal. Mach. Intell. **33**(5), 898–916 (2011)
2. Canny, J.F.: A computational approach to edge detection. IEEE Trans. Pattern Anal. Mach. Intell. **8**(6), 679–698 (1986)
3. Dollár, P., Zitnick, C.L.: Fast edge detection using structured forests. IEEE Trans. Pattern Anal. Mach. Intell. **37**(8), 1558–1570 (2015)
4. Everingham, M., Gool, L.J.V., Williams, C.K.I., Winn, J.M., Zisserman, A.: The pascal visual object classes (VOC) challenge. Int. J. Comput. Vis. **88**(2), 303–338 (2010)
5. Ke, W., Chen, J., Jiao, J., Zhao, G., Ye, Q.: SRN: side-output residual network for object symmetry detection in the wild. In: IEEE Conference on Computer Vision and Pattern Recognition, pp. 302–310 (2017)
6. Lax, P.: Linear Algebra and Its Applications, vol. 2. Wiley, Hobken (2007)
7. Lee, T.S.H., Fidler, S., Dickinson, S.J.: Detecting curved symmetric parts using a deformable disc model. In: IEEE International Conference on Computer Vision, pp. 1753–1760 (2013)
8. Lee, T.S.H., Fidler, S., Dickinson, S.J.: Learning to combine mid-level cues for object proposal generation. In: IEEE International Conference on Computer Vision, pp. 1680–1688 (2015)
9. Levinshtein, A., Sminchisescu, C., Dickinson, S.J.: Multiscale symmetric part detection and grouping. Int. J. Comput. Vis. **104**(2), 117–134 (2013)
10. Lim, J.J., Zitnick, C.L., Dollár, P.: Sketch tokens: a learned mid-level representation for contour and object detection. In: IEEE Conference on Computer Vision and Pattern Recognition, pp. 3158–3165 (2013)
11. Lindeberg, T.: Edge detection and ridge detection with automatic scale selection. Int. J. Comput. Vis. **30**(2), 117–156 (1998)
12. Saha, P.K., Borgefors, G., di Baja, G.S.: A survey on skeletonization algorithms and their applications. Pattern Recogn. Lett. **76**, 3–12 (2016)
13. Sebastian, T.B., Klein, P.N., Kimia, B.B.: Recognition of shapes by editing their shock graphs. IEEE Trans. Pattern Anal. Mach. Intell. **26**(5), 550–571 (2004)
14. Shen, W., Bai, X., Hu, R., Wang, H., Latecki, L.J.: Skeleton growing and pruning with bending potential ratio. Pattern Recogn. **44**(2), 196–209 (2011)
15. Shen, W., Bai, X., Hu, Z., Zhang, Z.: Multiple instance subspace learning via partial random projection tree for local reflection symmetry in natural images. Pattern Recogn. **52**, 306–316 (2016)
16. Shen, W., Wang, X., Wang, Y., Bai, X., Zhang, Z.: Deepcontour: a deep convolutional feature learned by positive-sharing loss for contour detection. In: IEEE Conference on Computer Vision and Pattern Recognition, pp. 3982–3991 (2015)

17. Shen, W., Zhao, K., Jiang, Y., Wang, Y., Bai, X., Yuille, A.L.: DeepSkeleton: learning multi-task scale-associated deep side outputs for object skeleton extraction in natural images. IEEE Trans. Image Process. **26**(11), 5298–5311 (2017)
18. Shen, W., Zhao, K., Jiang, Y., Wang, Y., Zhang, Z., Bai, X.: Object skeleton extraction in natural images by fusing scale-associated deep side outputs. In: IEEE Conference on Computer Vision and Pattern Recognition, pp. 222–230 (2016)
19. Simonyan, K., Zisserman, A.: Very deep convolutional networks for large-scale image recognition. arXiv abs/1409.1556 (2014)
20. Teo, C.L., Fermüller, C., Aloimonos, Y.: Detection and segmentation of 2D curved reflection symmetric structures. In: IEEE International Conference on Computer Vision, pp. 1644–1652 (2015)
21. Tsogkas, S., Kokkinos, I.: Learning-based symmetry detection in natural images. In: Fitzgibbon, A., Lazebnik, S., Perona, P., Sato, Y., Schmid, C. (eds.) ECCV 2012. LNCS, vol. 7578, pp. 41–54. Springer, Heidelberg (2012). https://doi.org/10.1007/978-3-642-33786-4_4
22. Wei, S., Ramakrishna, V., Kanade, T., Sheikh, Y.: Convolutional pose machines. In: IEEE Conference on Computer Vision and Pattern Recognition, pp. 4724–4732 (2016)
23. Widynski, N., Moevus, A., Mignotte, M.: Local symmetry detection in natural images using a particle filtering approach. IEEE Trans. Image Process. **23**(12), 5309–5322 (2014)
24. Xie, S., Tu, Z.: Holistically-nested edge detection. In: IEEE International Conference on Computer Vision5, pp. 1395–1403 (2015)
25. Yu, Z., Bajaj, C.L.: A segmentation-free approach for skeletonization of gray-scale images via anisotropic vector diffusion. In: IEEE Computer Society Conference on Computer Vision and Pattern Recognition, pp. 415–420 (2004)

SaaS: Speed as a Supervisor
for Semi-supervised Learning

Safa Cicek$^{(\boxtimes)}$, Alhussein Fawzi, and Stefano Soatto

University of California, Los Angeles, USA
{safacicek,fawzi,soatto}@ucla.edu

Abstract. We introduce the SaaS Algorithm for semi-supervised learning, which uses learning speed during stochastic gradient descent in a deep neural network to measure the quality of an iterative estimate of the posterior probability of unknown labels. Training speed in supervised learning correlates strongly with the percentage of correct labels, so we use it as an inference criterion for the unknown labels, without attempting to infer the model parameters at first. Despite its simplicity, SaaS achieves competitive results in semi-supervised learning benchmarks.

1 Introduction

The key idea of our approach is to *use speed of convergence as an inference criterion for the value of the unknown labels* for semi-supervised learning (SSL). Figure 1 explicitly shows the relation between label corruption and training speed.

In SSL, one is given some labeled and some unlabeled data to train (infer the parameters of) a classifier, in hope of it performing better than if trained on the labeled data alone [1]. This is an important problem in vision where annotations are costly but unlabeled data are aplenty.

To measure learning speed, we use a small number of epochs as the unit of time, and compute the decrease of the loss in that interval when following a standard optimization procedure (stochastic gradient descent or Langevin dynamics). The main idea of our SSL algorithm is then to optimize the labels of unlabeled data (or more precisely, the posterior distribution of the unlabeled data) to maximize the loss decrease.

The resulting SaaS Algorithm is composed of an *outer loop*, which updates the distribution of unknown labels, and an *inner loop* which simulates the optimization procedure over a small number of epochs.

The proposed algorithm is unusual, as the posterior distribution of the unknown labels is initially inferred *independently of the model parameters* (weights), rather than along with them as customary in SSL.

Electronic supplementary material The online version of this chapter (https://doi.org/10.1007/978-3-030-01216-8_10) contains supplementary material, which is available to authorized users.

V. Ferrari et al. (Eds.): ECCV 2018, LNCS 11206, pp. 152–166, 2018.
https://doi.org/10.1007/978-3-030-01216-8_10

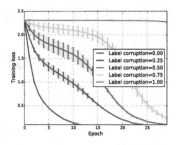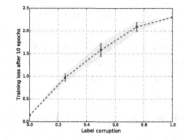

Fig. 1. Supervision quality affects learning speed. During training, the loss decreases rapidly when most labels provided are correct, and slows down significantly as the percentage of correct labels decreases. The left plot shows the loss when training a Resnet18 on CIFAR10 for different percentages of corrupted labels. The error bars show mean and standard deviation over 3 runs with random initial weights. The right panel shows the loss as a function of the percentage of incorrect labels for a unit of time corresponding to ten epochs. All the results use a fixed learning rate of 0.1, with no data augmentation or weight decay.

Despite its simplicity, SaaS achieves competitive results, reported in Sect. 3. In the next section we formalize our method, and in Sect. 4 we discuss our contributions in relation to the prior art, and highlight its features and limitations.

1.1   Description of the Method

We are given some labeled data $\mathbf{x}^l \doteq \{x_i^l\}_{i=1}^{N^l}$ with labels $\mathbf{y}^l \doteq \{y_i^l\}_{i=1}^{N^l}$ and some unlabeled data, $\mathbf{x}^u \doteq \{x_i^u\}_{i=1}^{N^u}$. The unknown labels $\mathbf{Y}^u \doteq \{Y_i^u\}_{i=1}^{N^u}$ are hidden variables whose "true values" y_i^u are not of interest *per se*, but must be dealt with (nuisance variables). Most SSL approaches attempt to infer or marginalize the unknown labels along with the model parameters, for us the weights w of a neural network, only to discard the former and keep the weights.

Unlike most SSL approaches, in our approach we *estimate the posterior distribution of the unknown labels* $P_i^u \doteq P(Y_i^u | X_i^u = x_i^u)$. The outer loop of the algorithm updates the estimates of the posterior P_i^u, while the inner loop optimizes over the weights (for the fixed estimate of the posterior) to estimate the loss decrease over the time interval. It is important to note that we are *not attempting to infer the weights* (but only the posterior distribution of the unknown labels), which are resampled at each (outer) iteration.[1] By design, the weights do not converge, yet empirically we observe that the posterior distribution of the unknown labels does. We then use the maximum a-posteriori estimate of the labels $\hat{y}_i^u = \arg\max_i P_i^u$ to infer a point-estimate of the weights $\hat{w}$ in a standard supervised training session. This procedure is described in the SaaS algorithm in Sect. 2, where ℓ is a loss function described in Sect. 2, $N = N^u + N^l$ is the

---

[1] We have tested both drawing the weights from a Gaussian distribution, or resetting them to their initial value, which yields similar results.

total number of samples and η are suitable learning rates for a batch size $|B|$ in SGD.

In Sect. 3 we test the SaaS algorithm on SSL benchmarks, and in Sect. 4 we place our contribution in the context of related literature. Next, we describe the algorithm in greater detail.

2 Derivation of the Model

We represent a deep neural network with parameters (weights) w, trained for classification into one of K classes, as a function $f_w(x) \in \mathbb{R}^K$ where x is the input (test) datum, and the k-th component of the output approximates the posterior probability $f_{w_t}(x_i)[k] \simeq P(y_i = k|x_i)$. Stochastic gradient descent (SGD) performs incremental updates of the unknown parameters with each iteration t computing the loss by summing on a random subset of the training set called "mini-batch" B_t. The number of iterations needed to sample all the dataset is called an epoch. We represent SGD as an operator $G(\cdot) : w_t \rightarrow w_{t+1}$, which maps the current estimate of the weights to the next one. Note that G depends on the given (true) labels, and the hypothesized ones for the unlabeled data.

To quantify *learning speed* we use the cumulative loss in a fixed time (epoch) interval: For a given training set $\{\mathbf{x}, \mathbf{y}\}$, it is the aggregated loss during T optimization steps, *i.e.*, the area under the learning curve

$$\mathcal{L}_T = \frac{1}{T} \sum_{t=1}^{T} \frac{1}{|B_t|} \sum_{i=1}^{|B_t|} \ell(x_i, y_i; w_t) \qquad (1)$$

where $|B_t|$ denotes the cardinality of the mini-batch, composed of samples $(x_i, y_i) \sim P(x, y)$; ℓ denotes the classification loss corresponding to weights w_t. Computing the loss above over all the data points requires the labels being known. Alternatively, it can be interpreted as a loss for a joint hypothesis for the weights w_t *and* the label y_i. We use the cross-entropy loss, which is the sampled version of $H_{P,Q}(y|x) = \mathbb{E}_{P(x)}\mathbb{E}_{P(y|x)} - \log Q(y|x)$ where $Q(y = k|x) = f_w(x)[k]$ is the kth coordinate of the output of the network.

The true joint distribution $P(x)P(y|x) = P(x, y)$ is not known, but the dataset is sampled from it. In particular, if $y_i = k$ is the true label for x_i, we have $P(y_i|x_i) = \delta(y_i - k)$ where δ is Dirac's Delta. Otherwise, we represent it as an unknown K-dimensional probability vector P_i^u with k-th component $P_i^u[k] = P(y_i = k|x_i)$, $k = 1, \ldots, K$, to be inferred along with the unknown weights w. We can write the sum $\sum_{k=1}^{K} P_i[k]P_j[k]$ as an inner product between the probability vectors $\langle P_i, P_j \rangle = P_i^T P_j$, so that the *cumulative loss* can be written as

$$\mathcal{L}_T(P^u) = \frac{1}{T} \sum_{t=1}^{T} \frac{1}{|B_t^u|} \sum_{i=1}^{|B_t^u|} \underbrace{- \langle \log f_{w_t}(x_i^u), P_i^u \rangle}_{\ell(x_i^u, P_i^u; w_t)} \qquad (2)$$

where B_t^u is mini-batch of unlabeled samples at iteration t. Note that cross-entropy depends on the *posterior distribution* of the unknown labels, P_i^u, rather than their sample value y_i^u. The loss depends on the posterior for the entire unlabeled set, which we indicate as an $N^u \times K$ matrix P^u, and the entire set of weights $w = \{w_1, \ldots, w_T\}$.

We also add as an explicit regularizer the entropy of the network outputs for the unlabeled samples: $-\mathbb{E}_Q \log Q(y^u|x^u)$, as common in SSL [2], which we approximate with the unlabeled samples as

$$H_Q(w) = \sum_{i=1}^{N^u} \underbrace{- \langle f_w(x_i^u), \log f_w(x_i^u) \rangle}_{q(x_i^u;w)} \tag{3}$$

We further incorporate data augmentation by averaging over group transformations $g(x) \in \mathbb{G}$, such as translation and horizontal flipping, sampled uniformly $g_i \sim \mathcal{U}(\mathbb{G})$. Let us define the following shorthand notations: $\ell(B_t^u, P^u; w_{t-1}) = \frac{1}{|B_t^u|} \sum_{i=1}^{|B_t^u|} \ell(g_i(x_i^u), P_i^u; w_{t-1})$ and $q(B_t^u; w_{t-1}) = \frac{1}{|B_t^u|} \sum_{i=1}^{|B_t^u|} q(g_i(x_i^u); w_{t-1})$. Similarly for labeled set, $\ell(B_t^l, P^l; w_{t-1}) = \frac{1}{|B_t^l|} \sum_{i=1}^{|B_t^l|} \ell(g_i(x_i^l), P_i^l; w_{t-1})$ where $P_i^l = \delta_{i,k}$ is the Kronecker Delta with k the true label associated to x_i^l. The overall learning can be framed as the following optimization

$$P^u = \arg\min_{P^u} \frac{1}{T} \sum_{t=1}^{T} \ell(B_t^u, P^u; w_{t-1}) \tag{4}$$

$$\text{subject to } w_{t-\frac{1}{2}} = w_{t-1} - \eta_w \nabla_{w_{t-1}} \left(\ell(B_t^u, P^u; w_{t-1}) + \beta q(B_t^u; w_{t-1}) \right)$$

$$w_t = w_{t-\frac{1}{2}} - \eta_w \nabla_{w_{t-\frac{1}{2}}} \ell(B_t^l, P^l; w_{t-\frac{1}{2}}) \ \forall \ t = 1 \ldots T$$

$$P^u \in \mathcal{S}$$

where the last constraint imposes that the rows of P^u be in the probability simplex of $\mathbb{R}^K$. The objective of the above optimization is to find the posterior of the unlabeled data that leads to the fastest learning curve, when using stochastic gradient descent to train the weights w on both labeled and unlabeled data. The update of the weights is specifically decomposed into two steps: the first step is an update equation for the weights with *unlabeled* samples and posterior P^u, while the second step updates the weights using the labeled samples and ground truth labels. We stress that the latter update is crucial in order to fit the weights to the available training data, and hence prevents from learning trivial solutions of P^u that lead to a fast convergence rate, but does not fit the data properly. We also note that the entropy term is only minimized for unlabeled samples. We set $\beta = 1$ in all the experiments.

It is customary to regularize the labels in SSL using entropy or a proxy [2–6], including mutual exclusivity [7,8]. [9] uses mutual exclusivity adaptively by not forcing it in the early epochs for similar categories. All these losses force decision boundaries to be in the low-density region, a desired property under cluster assumptions. [5,6] also maximize the entropy of the marginal label distribution to balance the classes. Together with entropy minimization, balancing classes is equivalent to maximizing the mutual information between estimates and the data if the label prior is uniform. However, we did not apply this loss to not restrict ourselves to balanced datasets or to the settings where we have prior knowledge on the label distributions.

2.1 Implementation

To solve the optimization problem in Eq. (4), we perform gradient descent over the unknowns P^u, where P^u is the unknown-label posterior initialized randomly. Starting from w_0 sampled from a Gaussian distribution, the inner loop performs a few epochs of SGD to measure learning speed (cumulative loss) $\mathcal{L}_T$ *while keeping the label posterior fixed*. The outer loop then applies a gradient step to update the unknown-label posterior P^u. After each update, the weights are either reset to w_0, or resampled from the Gaussian. In the beginning of each outer epoch, label estimates $P^u \in \mathbb{R}^{N^u \times K}$ are projected with operation $\Pi(P^u)$ to the closest point on the probability simplex of dimension $N^u \times K$.

After the label posterior converges (the weights never do, by design, in the first phase), we select the maximum a-posteriori estimate $\hat{y}_i^u = \arg\max_i P_i^u$, and proceed with training as if fully supervised in the second phase. We call the resulting algorithm, described in Algorithm 1, SaaS.

Algorithm 1. SaaS Algorithm

1: $P^u \sim \mathcal{N}(0, I)$
2: Select learning rates η for the weights η_w and label posteriors η_{P^u}
3: **Phase I**: Estimate P^u
4: **while** P^u has not stabilized **do**
5:     $P^u = \Pi(P^u)$ (project posterior onto the probability simplex)
6:     $w_1 \sim \mathcal{N}(0, I)$
7:     $\Delta P^u = 0$
8:     // Run SGD for T steps (on the weights) to estimate loss decrease
9:     **for** $t = 1 : T$ **do**
10:         $w_{t-\frac{1}{2}} = w_{t-1} - \eta_w \nabla_{w_{t-1}} \left(\ell(B_t^u, P^u; w_{t-1}) + \beta q(B_t^u; w_{t-1}) \right)$
11:         $w_t = w_{t-\frac{1}{2}} - \eta_w \nabla_{w_{t-\frac{1}{2}}} \ell(B_t^l, P^l; w_{t-\frac{1}{2}})$
12:         $\Delta P^u = \Delta P^u + \nabla_{P^u} \ell(B_t^u, P^u; w_t)$
13:     // Update the posterior distribution
14:     $P^u = P^u - \eta_{P^u} \Delta P^u$
15: **Phase II**: Estimate the weights.
16: $\hat{y}_i^u = \arg\max_i P_i^u \ \forall i = 1, \ldots, N^u$
17: $w_1 \sim \mathcal{N}(0, I)$
18: **while** w has not stabilized **do**
19:     $w_{t-\frac{1}{2}} = w_{t-1} - \eta_w \nabla_{w_{t-1}} \frac{1}{|B_t^u|} \sum_{i=1}^{|B_t^u|} \ell(x_i^u, \hat{y}_i^u; w_{t-1})$
20:     $w_t = w_{t-\frac{1}{2}} - \eta_w \nabla_{w_{t-\frac{1}{2}}} \frac{1}{|B_t^l|} \sum_{i=1}^{|B_t^l|} \ell(x_i^l, y_i^l; w_{t-\frac{1}{2}})$

It should be noted that the computation of the gradient $\nabla_{P^u} \ell(B_t^u, P^u; w_t)$ is not straightforward, as w_t is, in general, a (complex) function of P^u. In the computation of the gradient, we omit here the dependence of w_t on P^u, and use the approximation $\nabla_{P_i^u} \ell(w_t, x_i^u, P_i^u) \approx -\log f_{w_t}(x_i^u)$. This approximation is exact whenever each data point is visited once (i.e., $T = 1$ epoch); as T is chosen to be relatively small here, we assume that this approximation holds.

It is important to note that, with the SaaS algorithm, we are not attempting to solve the optimization problem: $\min_{w, P^u} \sum_{i=1}^{N} \ell(x_i, P_i^u; w)$. This problem has many trivial solutions, as observed by [10], as deep neural networks can easily fit random labels when trained long enough. Thus, for many posteriors P^u, there are weights w achieving zero loss on this objective. One of many such trivial solutions is setting the label posterior P^u to the outputs of the network trained only with the labeled samples. This would result in the same test performance as that of a supervised baseline and does not utilize the unlabeled samples at all. On the other hand, SaaS uses the cumulative loss up to a *fixed*, small iteration T as an inference criterion for label posterior P^u.

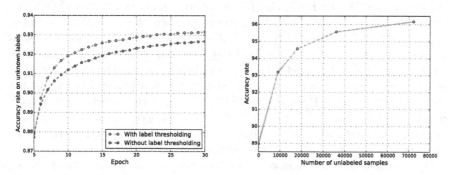

Fig. 2. (Left) Effect of label thresholding. We project P^u to the closest probability simplex with minimum probability for a class being 0.05. Plot is given for unlabeled accuracy as label thresholding used in the first phase of the SaaS. The plot is given from epoch 5 to epoch 30. (Right) Test accuracy vs. number of unlabeled samples. Accuracy on the test data versus number of unlabeled samples for the SVHN dataset using ResNet18. As the number of unlabeled samples increases, performance improves significantly, as expected in a semi-supervised learning scheme. Results are averaged over three random labeled sets, but error bars are not visible because deviations are smaller than the line-width.

Finally, instead of projecting P^u onto the probability simplex $\mathcal{S}$, we have found that the projection onto a slightly modified set $\mathcal{S}_\alpha = \{x \in \mathbb{R}^K : \sum_i x_i = 1, x_i \geq \alpha\}$ (with $\alpha \geq 0$ chosen to be small) lead to better optimization results for P^u. This is in line with recent work in supervised classification, where this technique is used in order to improve the accuracy of deep neural networks [11,12]. Figure 2 (left) illustrates the effect of this approach for SaaS, and shows a clear improvement in SVHN dataset.

3   Empirical Evaluation

We test the SaaS algorithm against the state-of-the-art in the most common benchmarks, described next.

Datasets. SVHN [13] consists of images of house numbers. We use $73,257$ samples for training, rather than the entire $600,000$ images; $26,032$ images are separated for evaluation. CIFAR-10 [14] has $60,000$ images, of which $50,000$ are used for training and $10,000$ for testing. We choose labeled samples randomly. We also choose them to be uniform over the classes as it is done in previous works [3]. For both datasets, 10% of the training set used for hyper-parameter tuning.

Training. As pointed out by [10], deep networks can easily (over)fit random labels. We set T small enough (40 epochs for CIFAR10 and 5 epochs for SVHN) so that simulated weights cannot fit randomly initialized posterior estimates in the early epochs. We use ResNet18 [15] as our architecture and vanilla SGD with momentum 0.9 as an optimizer. We perform random affine transformations as data augmentations both in SVHN and CIFAR10. We additionally use horizontal flip and color jitter in CIFAR10. Learning rates for w and P^u are chosen as $\eta_w = 0.01$ and $\eta_{P^u} = 1$ respectively. We keep these rates fixed when learning P^u. We fixed the number of outer epochs as well for the first phase of the algorithm by setting it to 75 for SVHN and 135 for CIFAR10. For the second phase of SaaS (supervised part), training is not limited to a small epoch T. Instead, learning rate initialized as 0.1 and halved after 50 epochs unless accuracy in validation is increasing. We stop when the learning rate reaches 0.001.

The baseline for comparison is performance on the same datasets using only the labeled set (i.e. 4K samples for CIFAR10 and 1K samples for SVHN) (Table 1). When training the (supervised) baseline, we employ the same learning parameters, architecture and augmentations as Phase II of SaaS. As expected, SaaS substantially improves baseline results, which is indicative that unlabeled data being effectively exploited by the algorithm (Table 1).

In Table 2, we compare SaaS with state-of-the-art SSL methods on standard SSL benchmarks. In CIFAR-10, algorithms are trained with 4,000 labeled and 46,000 unlabeled samples. In SVHN, they are trained with 1,000 labeled and 72,257 unlabeled samples. The means and deviations of the test errors are reported by averaging over three random labeled sets. The state-of-the-art methods we compare include input smoothing algorithms [3], ensembling models [16,17], generative models [18] and models employing problem specific prior [19]. SaaS is comparable to state-of-the-art methods. Specifically, SaaS achieves the best performance in SVHN and second best result in CIFAR10 after VAT. Considering that VAT does input smoothing by adversarial training, our performance can be improved by combining with it.

An SSL algorithm is expected to be more accurate when the number of unlabeled data increases. As it can be seen in Fig. 2 (right), we consistently get better results with more unlabeled samples.

Table 1. Baseline error rates. Error rates on the benchmark test set for the baseline system trained with 4K labeled samples on CIFAR10 and 1K labeled samples on SVHN. **Error rate on unknown labels.** SaaS performance on the *unlabeled* set. **Error rate on test data.** SaaS performance on the *test* set. Results are averaged over three random labeled sets. As it can be seen, results of SaaS on test data are significantly better than that of baseline supervised algorithm.

Dataset	CIFAR10-4k	SVHN-1k
Error rate by supervised baseline on test data	17.64 ± 0.58	11.04 ± 0.50
Error rate by SaaS on unlabeled data	12.81 ± 0.08	6.22 ± 0.02
Error rate by SaaS on test data	10.94 ± 0.07	3.82 ± 0.09

Table 2. Comparison with the state-of-the-art. Error rates on the test set are given for CIFAR10 and SVHN. NR stands for "not reported." CIFAR10 is trained using 4K labels, SVHN using 1K. Results are averaged over three random labeled sets. Despite its simplicity, SaaS performs at the state-of-the-art. It could be combined with adversarial examples (VAT) but here we report the naked results to highlight the role of speed as a proxy for learning in a semi-supervised setting while maintaining a simple learning scheme.

Method-Dataset	CIFAR10-4k	SVHN-1k
VAT+EntMin [3]	**10.55**	3.86
Stochastic Transformation [19]	11.29	NR
Temporal Ensemble [17]	12.16	4.42
GAN+FM [18]	15.59	5.88
Mean Teacher [16]	12.31	3.95
SaaS	10.94 ± 0.07	$\mathbf{3.82 \pm 0.09}$

We motivated SaaS as a method finding labels for which training decrease in a fix small number of epochs (e.g. 10) is the maximum. To verify that our algorithm actually does what is intended to do, we train networks on the pseudo-labels generated by SaaS. One can see in Fig. 3 (left) that as SaaS iterates more (i.e. as the number of updates for P^u increases), resulting pseudo-labels leads to larger training loss decrease (faster training) in the early epochs. This experiment verifies that SaaS gives pseudo-labels on which training would be faster.

The results reported in Table 1 are with ResNet18 and affine augmentations. Our method uses augmentation, but for direct comparison with some of the previous papers, we also report results with the convolutional network "conv-large" and translational augmentations as used in [3, 16] in Table 3. Additionally,

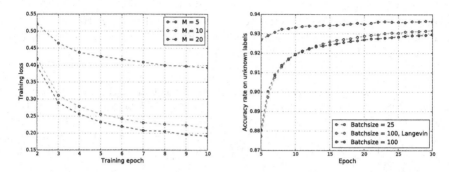

Fig. 3. (Left) SaaS finds pseudo-labels on which training is faster. Training loss for a network trained with given P^u, as estimated by the first phase of our algorithm with different numbers of outer epochs M. M is the number of epoch at which outer iteration stopped in the SaaS. Label hypotheses generated by our algorithm lead to faster training as the iteration count increases. Losses are plotted starting from epoch 2. This plot verifies that our algorithm finds labels on which training is faster. (Right) Effect of Langevin. Performance improves with smaller batch size, albeit at a significant computational cost: algorithm is about three times slower for $|B| = 25$ (plots shown for SVHN). We therefore choose $|B| = 100$ and add zero-mean Gaussian noise to the weight updates for comparable results (Langevin). The results converge to those of $|B| = 25$ when we train longer. Plot is given for unlabeled accuracy because Langevin is only used in the first phase of SaaS. The plot is given from epoch 5 to epoch 30.

horizontal flipping is used in CIFAR10. Moreover, we applied pre-processing by centering relative to the Mahalanobis metric (known as ZCA) as in [3,16].

Table 3. For direct comparison, we implement SaaS with the "conv-large" architecture of [3] and the same augmentation scheme. Baseline performance (supervised) is also shown. SaaS improves both on the unlabeled set and test set. Results are averaged over three random labeled sets.

Dataset	CIFAR10-4k	SVHN-1k
Error rate by supervised baseline on test data	17.88 ± 0.19	12.72 ± 1.13
Error rate by SaaS on unlabeled data	14.26 ± 0.30	7.26 ± 0.19
Error rate by SaaS on test data	13.22 ± 0.31	4.77 ± 0.27

Small Batch-Size and Langevin Dynamics. Finally, we discuss a method we use to reduce the training time for SaaS. We achieve better performance with smaller batch size $|B| = 25$ for both labeled and unlabeled data. When $|B| = 100$, generalization performance degrades as expected [20]. Unfortunately, small batch-size slows down training, so we use $|B| = 100$ for both labeled and unlabeled data and add zero-mean Gaussian noise to the weight updates, a process known as stochastic gradient Langevin dynamics (SGLD) [21–23], with variance $10^{-5}\eta_w$ for all the datasets. Comparison of small and large batches without noise and large batches with noise can be seen in Fig. 3 (right). With this, first phase of the algorithm (getting the estimates of unknown labels) takes about 1 day for SVHN and 4 days for CIFAR10 using GeForce GTX 1080 when we use ResNet18.

Failure Case. As we have shown, our algorithm performs well even with few augmentations (e.g. only translation). However, when we do not use any augmentation at all, our method does not perform as well. With no augmentation and ResNet18, our algorithm suffers a very large drop in performance, achieving error rates of 40.19 ± 3.89 for SVHN and 64.05 ± 1.79 for CIFAR10 on unlabeled data. We next explain this substantial change in the performance.

Figure 1 suggests that there is a strong correlation between label accuracy and training speed. However, note that this plot is an average over different realizations of labels and initial weights. This does not suggest that for every realization of random labels, this correlation would hold. A simple example is having constant labeling on all the samples for which training would be immediate. In this case, most of the labels would be incorrect for a balanced dataset meaning that correlation between training speed and label accuracy does not hold for every single realization. Hence, we need to have a way of eliminating the degenerate solutions. While the first constraint we put to eliminate these solutions is to impose a small training loss on labeled examples, this might not be enough in many semi-supervised settings. Data augmentation further puts constraints on the desired unknown label posterior: labels of images have to remain constant with respect to image transformations. This constraint hence guides the algorithm to the desired label posterior, and leads to significant performance gains on SaaS.

4 Discussion and Related Work

The key idea of our approach to SSL is to leverage on training speed as a proxy to measure the quality of putative labels as they are iteratively refined in a differentiable manner.

That speed of convergence relates to generalization is implicit in the work of [24], who derive an upper bound on generalization error as a function of a constant times the sum of step sizes, suggesting that faster training correlates with better generalization.

Another way of understanding our method is via shooting algorithms used to solve boundary value problems (BVP). In a BVP with second order dynamics, a trajectory is found by simulating it with a guess of initial state; then, the initial state is refined iteratively such that the target error would be minimized. In our problem, dynamics are given by SGD. Assuming that we use SGD without momentum, we have a first order differential equation. The first boundary condition is the initialization of weights and the second boundary condition is a small cumulative loss. The latter one is used to refine P^u which is a parameter of the dynamics instead of the initial state.

In the next paragraphs we discuss our contribution in relation to the vast and growing literature on SSL.

Ensemble Methods include teacher-student models, that use a combination of estimates (or weights) of classifiers trained under stochastic transformations. Although we train only one network, our method resembles the teachers-student models: Our P^u update is similar to a teacher classifier in the teacher-student models. However, we randomly start a student model at each outer epoch. In [17] the prediction of the network over the training epochs are averaged, whereby in each epoch a different augmentation is applied. [16] minimize the consistency cost, which is the distance between two network outputs. Hence, the student network minimizes classification and consistency costs with labeled data and only consistency with the unlabeled data. The weights of the teacher model are the running average of the weights of the student network.

Cluster Assumption. The cluster assumption posits that inputs with the same class are in the same cluster under an appropriate metric. It takes many forms (max-margin, low-density separation, smoothness, manifold). In general, it could be framed as $\int ||\nabla_x f_w(x)||^2 d\mu_x$ being small where μ_x is the probability distribution over some manifold. VAT [3,25] is a recent application of this idea to deep networks, realized by adding a regularization term to minimize the difference between the network outputs for clean and adversarial noise-added-inputs. This state-of-the-art method is similar to the adversarial training of [26], the main difference being that it does not require label information, and thus can be applied to SSL. Our method is orthogonal to VAT and can be improved by combining with it.

Self-training is an iterative process where confident labels from previous iterations are used as ground truth. In [27], disjoint subsets of features of labeled samples are used to produce different hypotheses on randomly selected subsets of the unlabeled data. Labeled data are extended with the most confident estimates on this subset. This approach fails to enlarge the sigma-algebra generated by the labeled samples and generally fails if the classifier does not give correct estimates for at least one feature subset. We maintain an estimate of the posterior probability of each label, and only force a point estimate in the refinement (second) phase of the algorithm.

Encoding Priors. In image classification one can enforce invariance of labels to some transformations. This is achieved by minimizing the difference between network outputs under different transformations. In [19], transformations are affine (translation, rotation, flipping, stretching and shearing). Although they achieve good results, their improvement on baseline supervised performance (using only labeled data) is marginal. *E.g.*, in CIFAR-10 supervised error is 13.6% while semi-supervised error is 11.29%. Similarly, [28] suggests minimizing the norm of directional derivatives of the network with respect to small transformations. We also employ augmentations like most SSL papers on image classification.

Generative Models used to be the standard for SSL, but the high dimensionality of problems in vision presents a challenge. Adversarial methods like GANs have been recently applied, whereby an additional $C + 1$-th (fake) class is used. The loss function is designed to force the discriminator output to be low for the fake class for the unlabeled samples while making it high for the generated samples. [18] suggested a regularizer for the generator, called feature matching (FM), whereby the generator tries to match the first-order statistics of the generated sample features to those of the real data. According to [4], the discriminator benefits the generator if it has samples within the data manifold, but around subspaces in which the density of samples is low. Unlike feature matching, they match the inverse distribution in non-zero density areas rather than their means. Instead of one generator network, [29] uses an encoder-decoder network generating images and labels from which the discriminator tries to differentiate.

Graph Based Methods. [30] assumes that an affinity matrix of size $N \times N$ is given, which has information independent from the one in the features of the data. In the loss function, they have a term penalizing different labels assigned to similar samples based on this similarity matrix. [31,32] finds a sparse clustering using the ℓ_1-norm. [33] propagates pairwise *must* and *cannot* constraints in an efficient way. [34] uses the current hypothesis for the unknown labels in learning as in our algorithm. They update the affinity matrix and estimates of the unknown labels iteratively. [35] suggests a dictionary learning method which can be used for SSL. Recent graph based methods [36–39] exploit deep networks for function approximation in a manner that can be used for SSL.

Within this rich and multi-faceted context, our approach provides one more element to consider: The fact that the speed of convergence when optimizing with respect to the probability of unknown labels is highly dependent on their correctness, even when starting from a random initial condition. This frees us from having to jointly optimized the parameters and the posterior on the labels, which would blow up the dimensionality, and allows us to focus sequentially on first estimating the unknown label distribution – irrespective of the model parameters/weight – and then retrieve the weights using the maximum a-posteriori estimate of the labels.

Our method can be combined with other ideas recently introduced in SSL, including using adversarial examples. We do not do so in our experiments, to isolate the contribution of our algorithm. Nevertheless, just the method alone, with some data augmentation but without sophisticated tricks, achieves promising performance.

Acknowledgment. Research supported by ONR N00014-13-1-0563 and ARO W911NF-17-1-0304.

References

1. Chapelle, O., Scholkopf, B., Zien, A.: Semi-supervised learning (Chapelle, O., et al. (eds.) 2006) [book reviews]. IEEE Trans. Neural Netw. **20**(3), 542 (2009)
2. Grandvalet, Y., Bengio, Y.: Semi-supervised learning by entropy minimization. In: Advances in Neural Information Processing Systems, pp. 529–536 (2005)
3. Miyato, T., Maeda, S.I., Koyama, M., Ishii, S.: Virtual adversarial training: a regularization method for supervised and semi-supervised learning. arXiv preprint arXiv:1704.03976 (2017)
4. Dai, Z., Yang, Z., Yang, F., Cohen, W.W., Salakhutdinov, R.R.: Good semi-supervised learning that requires a bad gan. In: Advances in Neural Information Processing Systems, pp. 6513–6523 (2017)
5. Krause, A., Perona, P., Gomes, R.G.: Discriminative clustering by regularized information maximization. In: Advances in Neural Information Processing Systems, pp. 775–783 (2010)
6. Springenberg, J.T.: Unsupervised and semi-supervised learning with categorical generative adversarial networks. arXiv preprint arXiv:1511.06390 (2015)
7. Sajjadi, M., Javanmardi, M., Tasdizen, T.: Mutual exclusivity loss for semi-supervised deep learning. In: 2016 IEEE International Conference on Image Processing (ICIP), pp. 1908–1912. IEEE (2016)
8. Xu, J., Zhang, Z., Friedman, T., Liang, Y., Van den Broeck, G.: A semantic loss function for deep learning with symbolic knowledge. arXiv preprint arXiv:1711.11157 (2017)
9. Shrivastava, A., Singh, S., Gupta, A.: Constrained semi-supervised learning using attributes and comparative attributes. In: Fitzgibbon, A., Lazebnik, S., Perona, P., Sato, Y., Schmid, C. (eds.) ECCV 2012. LNCS, vol. 7574, pp. 369–383. Springer, Heidelberg (2012). https://doi.org/10.1007/978-3-642-33712-3_27
10. Zhang, C., Bengio, S., Hardt, M., Recht, B., Vinyals, O.: Understanding deep learning requires rethinking generalization. arXiv preprint arXiv:1611.03530 (2016)
11. Pereyra, G., Tucker, G., Chorowski, J., Kaiser, L., Hinton, G.: Regularizing neural networks by penalizing confident output distributions. arXiv preprint arXiv:1701.06548 (2017)
12. Szegedy, C., Vanhoucke, V., Ioffe, S., Shlens, J., Wojna, Z.: Rethinking the inception architecture for computer vision. In: Proceedings of the IEEE Conference on Computer Vision and Pattern Recognition, pp. 2818–2826 (2016)
13. Netzer, Y., Wang, T., Coates, A., Bissacco, A., Wu, B., Ng, A.Y.: Reading digits in natural images with unsupervised feature learning. In: NIPS Workshop on Deep Learning and Unsupervised Feature Learning, vol. 2011, p. 5 (2011)
14. Krizhevsky, A., Hinton, G.: Learning multiple layers of features from tiny images (2009)
15. He, K., Zhang, X., Ren, S., Sun, J.: Identity mappings in deep residual networks. In: Leibe, B., Matas, J., Sebe, N., Welling, M. (eds.) ECCV 2016. LNCS, vol. 9908, pp. 630–645. Springer, Cham (2016). https://doi.org/10.1007/978-3-319-46493-0_38
16. Tarvainen, A., Valpola, H.: Mean teachers are better role models: weight-averaged consistency targets improve semi-supervised deep learning results. In: Advances in Neural Information Processing Systems, pp. 1195–1204 (2017)
17. Laine, S., Aila, T.: Temporal ensembling for semi-supervised learning. arXiv preprint arXiv:1610.02242 (2016)
18. Salimans, T., Goodfellow, I., Zaremba, W., Cheung, V., Radford, A., Chen, X.: Improved techniques for training GANs. In: Advances in Neural Information Processing Systems, pp. 2234–2242 (2016)

19. Sajjadi, M., Javanmardi, M., Tasdizen, T.: Regularization with stochastic transformations and perturbations for deep semi-supervised learning. In: Advances in Neural Information Processing Systems, pp. 1163–1171 (2016)
20. Keskar, N.S., Mudigere, D., Nocedal, J., Smelyanskiy, M., Tang, P.T.P.: On large-batch training for deep learning: generalization gap and sharp minima. arXiv preprint arXiv:1609.04836 (2016)
21. Welling, M., Teh, Y.W.: Bayesian learning via stochastic gradient langevin dynamics. In: Proceedings of the 28th International Conference on Machine Learning (ICML-11), pp. 681–688 (2011)
22. Raginsky, M., Rakhlin, A., Telgarsky, M.: Non-convex learning via stochastic gradient langevin dynamics: a nonasymptotic analysis. In: Proceedings of the 30th Conference on Learning Theory, COLT 2017, Amsterdam, The Netherlands, July 7–10 2017, pp. 1674–1703 (2017)
23. Chaudhari, P., Choromanska, A., Soatto, S., LeCun, Y.: Entropy-SGD: biasing gradient descent into wide valleys. arXiv preprint arXiv:1611.01838 (2016)
24. Hardt, M., Recht, B., Singer, Y.: Train faster, generalize better: Stability of stochastic gradient descent. In: Proceedings of the 33nd International Conference on Machine Learning, ICML 2016, New York City, NY, USA, June 19–24 2016, pp. 1225–1234 (2016)
25. Miyato, T., Maeda, S.i., Koyama, M., Nakae, K., Ishii, S.: Distributional smoothing with virtual adversarial training. arXiv preprint arXiv:1507.00677 (2015)
26. Goodfellow, I.J., Shlens, J., Szegedy, C.: Explaining and harnessing adversarial examples. arXiv preprint arXiv:1412.6572 (2014)
27. Blum, A., Mitchell, T.: Combining labeled and unlabeled data with co-training. In: Proceedings of the eleventh annual conference on Computational learning theory, pp. 92–100. ACM (1998)
28. Simard, P., Victorri, B., LeCun, Y., Denker, J.: Tangent prop-a formalism for specifying selected invariances in an adaptive network. In: Advances in Neural Information Processing Systems, pp. 895–903 (1992)
29. Dumoulin, V., et al.: Adversarially learned inference. arXiv preprint arXiv:1606.00704 (2016)
30. Yang, Z., Cohen, W.W., Salakhutdinov, R.: Revisiting semi-supervised learning with graph embeddings. In: Proceedings of the 33nd International Conference on Machine Learning, ICML 2016, New York City, NY, USA, June 19–24 2016, pp. 40–48 (2016)
31. Nie, F., Wang, H., Huang, H., Ding, C.: Unsupervised and semi-supervised learning via 1-norm graph. In: 2011 IEEE International Conference on Computer Vision (ICCV), pp. 2268–2273. IEEE (2011)
32. Su, H., Zhu, J., Yin, Z., Dong, Y., Zhang, B.: Efficient and robust semi-supervised learning over a sparse-regularized graph. In: Leibe, B., Matas, J., Sebe, N., Welling, M. (eds.) ECCV 2016. LNCS, vol. 9912, pp. 583–598. Springer, Cham (2016). https://doi.org/10.1007/978-3-319-46484-8_35
33. Lu, Z., Ip, H.H.S.: Constrained Spectral clustering via exhaustive and efficient constraint propagation. In: Daniilidis, K., Maragos, P., Paragios, N. (eds.) ECCV 2010. LNCS, vol. 6316, pp. 1–14. Springer, Heidelberg (2010). https://doi.org/10.1007/978-3-642-15567-3_1
34. Li, C.G., Lin, Z., Zhang, H., Guo, J.: Learning semi-supervised representation towards a unified optimization framework for semi-supervised learning. In: Proceedings of the IEEE International Conference on Computer Vision, pp. 2767–2775 (2015)

35. Wang, X., Guo, X., Li, S.Z.: Adaptively unified semi-supervised dictionary learning with active points. In: Proceedings of the IEEE International Conference on Computer Vision, pp. 1787–1795 (2015)
36. Haeusser, P., Mordvintsev, A., Cremers, D.: Learning by association-a versatile semi-supervised training method for neural networks. In: Proceedings of IEEE Conference on Computer Vision and Pattern Recognition (CVPR) (2017)
37. Gaunt, A., Tarlow, D., Brockschmidt, M., Urtasun, R., Liao, R., Zemel, R.: Graph partition neural networks for semi-supervised classification (2018)
38. Kipf, T.N., Welling, M.: Semi-supervised classification with graph convolutional networks. arXiv preprint arXiv:1609.02907 (2016)
39. Weston, J., Ratle, F., Mobahi, H., Collobert, R.: Deep learning via semi-supervised embedding. In: Montavon, G., Orr, G.B., Müller, K.-R. (eds.) Neural Networks: Tricks of the Trade. LNCS, vol. 7700, pp. 639–655. Springer, Heidelberg (2012). https://doi.org/10.1007/978-3-642-35289-8_34

Attention-GAN for Object Transfiguration in Wild Images

Xinyuan Chen[1,2,3(✉)], Chang Xu[3], Xiaokang Yang[1], and Dacheng Tao[3]

[1] MoE Key Lab of Artificial Intelligence, AI Institute,
Shanghai Jiao Tong University, Shanghai, China
{xychen91,xkyang}@sjtu.edu.cn
[2] Centre for Artificial Intelligence, SIT, FEIT, University of Technology Sydney,
Sydney, Australia
[3] UBTECH Sydney AI Centre, SIT, FEIT, University of Sydney, Sydney, Australia
{c.xu,dacheng.tao}@sydney.edu.au

Abstract. This paper studies the object transfiguration problem in wild images. The generative network in classical GANs for object transfiguration often undertakes a dual responsibility: to detect the objects of interests and to convert the object from source domain to another domain. In contrast, we decompose the generative network into two separated networks, each of which is only dedicated to one particular sub-task. The attention network predicts spatial attention maps of images, and the transformation network focuses on translating objects. Attention maps produced by attention network are encouraged to be sparse, so that major attention can be paid on objects of interests. No matter before or after object transfiguration, attention maps should remain constant. In addition, learning attention network can receive more instructions, given the available segmentation annotations of images. Experimental results demonstrate the necessity of investigating attention in object transfiguration, and that the proposed algorithm can learn accurate attention to improve quality of generated images.

Keywords: Generative adversarial networks · Attention mechanism

1 Introduction

The task of image-to-image translation aims to translate images from a source domain to another target domain, e.g., greyscale to color and image to semantic label. A lot of researches on image-to-image translation have been produced in the supervised setting, where ground truths in the target domain are available. [1] learns a parametric translation function using CNNs by minimizing the discrepancy between generated images and the corresponding target images. [2]

Electronic supplementary material The online version of this chapter (https://doi.org/10.1007/978-3-030-01216-8_11) contains supplementary material, which is available to authorized users.

uses conditional GANs to learn a mapping from input to output images. Similar ideas have been applied to various tasks such as generating photographs from sketch or from semantic layout [3,4], and image super-resolution [5].

To achieve image-to-image translation in the absence of paired examples, a series of works has emerged by combining classical adversarial training [6] with different carefully designed constraints, e.g., circularity constraint [7–9], f-consistency constraint [10], and distance constraints [11]. Although there is no paired data, these constraints are able to establish the connections between two domains so that meaningful analogs are obtained. Circularity constraint [7–9] requires a sample from one domain to the other that can be mapped back to produce the original sample. f-consistency requires both input and output in each domain should be consistent with each other in intermediate space of a neural network. [11] learns the image translation mapping in a one-sided unsupervised way by enforcing high cross-domain correlation between matching pairwise distances computed in source and target domains.

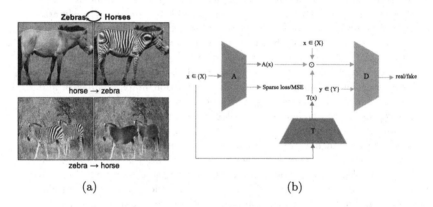

Fig. 1. (a): Object transfiguration of horse $\leftrightarrow$ zebra. (b): an illustration of Attention-GAN. A, T, D respectively represent the attention network, the transformation network and the discriminative network. Sparse loss denotes the sparse regularization for the predicted attention map. MSE denotes mean square error loss for supervised learning. $A(x)$ denotes the attention map predicted by the attention network. $T(x)$ denotes the transformed images. $\odot$ denotes the layered operation.

Object transfiguration is a special task in the image-to-image translation problem. Instead of taking the image as a whole to accomplish the transformation, object transfiguration aims to transform a particular type of object in an image to another type of object without influencing the background regions. For example, in the top line of Fig. 1(a), horses in the image are transformed into zebras, and zebras are transformed into horses, but the grassland and the trees are expected to be constant. Existing methods [7,11] used to tackle object transfiguration as a general image-to-image task, without investigating unique insights of the problem. In such a one-shot generation, a generative network actually takes two distinct roles: detecting the region of interests and converting object from source domain to target domain. However, incorporating these two functionalities in a single network would confuse the aims of the generative network. In iterations, it could be unclear whether the generative network should improve its detection of the objects of interests or boost its transfiguration of the objects. The quality of generated images is often seriously influenced as a result, e.g. some background regions might be taken into transformation by mistake.

In this paper, we propose an attention-GAN algorithm for the object transfiguration problem. The generative network in classical GANs has been factorized as two separated networks: an attention network to predict where the attention should be paid, and a transformation network that actually carries out the transformation of objects. A sparse constraint is applied over the attention map, so that limited attention energy can be focused on regions of priority rather than spreaded on the whole image at random. A layered operation is adopted to finalize the generated images by combining the transformed objects and the original background regions with the help of the learned sparse attention mask. A discriminative network is employed to distinguish real images from these synthesized images, while attention network and transformation network cooperate to generate synthesized images that can fool the discriminative network. Cycle-consistent loss [7–9] was adopted to handle unpaired data. Moreover, if segmentation results of images are available, the attention network can be learned in a supervised manner and the performance of the proposed algorithm can be improved accordingly. Experimental results on three object transfiguration tasks, i.e. horse ↔ zebra, tiger ↔ leopard, and apple ↔ orange [12], suggest the advantages of investigating attention in object transfiguration, and the quantitative and the qualitative performance improvement of the proposed algorithm over state-of-the-art methods.

2   Related Work

Generative Adversarial Networks. Generative adversarial networks (GANs) [6] have achieved impressive results in image generation [13–15] by way of a two-player minimax game: a discriminator aims to distinguish the generated images from real images while a generator aims to generate realistic images to fool the discriminator. A series of multi-stage generative models has been proposed to generate more realistic images [16–18]. [17] proposes composite generative adversarial network (CGAN) that disentangles complicated factors of images by employing multiple generators to generate different parts of the image. The layered recursive GANs [18] learns to generate image background and foregrounds separately and recursively. GANs have shown a great success on a variety of conditional image generation applications, e.g., image-to-image translation [7–9,19], text-to-image generation [20,21]. Different from the original GANs that generate images from noise variables, conditional GANs synthesize images based on the input information (e.g., category, image and text). [22] proposes a mask-conditional contrast-GAN architecture to disentangle image background with object semantic changes by exploiting the semantic annotations in both train and test phases. However, it is hard to collect segmentation mask for a large number of images, especially in test phase.

Attention Model in Networks. Motivated by human attention mechanism theories [23], attention mechanism has been successfully introduced in computer vision and natural language processing tasks, e.g. image classification [24–26], image captioning [27], visual question answering [28], image segmentation [29]. Rather than compressing an entire image or a sequence into a static representation, attention allows the model to focus on the most relevant part of images or features as needed. Mnih et al. [24] propose a recurrent network model that is capable of only processing a sequence of regions or locations of an image or video. Bahdanau et al. [30] propose an attention model that softly weights the importance of input words in a source sentence when predicting a target word for machine translation. Following this, Xu et al. [27] and Yao et al. [31] use attention models for image captioning and video captioning respectively. The model automatically learns to fix its gaze on salient objects while generates the corresponding words in the output sequence. In visual question answering, [28] uses the question to choose relevant regions of the images for computing the answer. In image generation, Gregor et al. [32] proposes a generative network combined attention mechanism with a sequential variational auto-encoding framework. The generator attends a smaller region of an input image guided by the ground truth image, and generates a few pixels for an image at a time. Differently, our method combine the attention mechanism with GANs framework and produce region of interest in absence of ground truth images in target domain.

3   Preliminaries

In the task of image-to-image translation, we have two domains X and Y with training samples $\{x_i\}_i^N \in X$ and $\{y_i\}_i^N \in Y$. The goal is to learn mapping from one domain to the other $\mathcal{G} : X \rightarrow Y$, (e.g. horse→zebra). The discriminator D_Y aims to distinguish real image y from translated images $\mathcal{G}(x)$. On the contrary, the mapping function $\mathcal{G}$ tries to generate images $\mathcal{G}(x)$ that looks similar to images in Y domain to fool the discriminator. The objective of *adversarial loss* in LSGAN [33] is expressed as:

$$\mathcal{L}_{GAN}(\mathcal{G}, D_Y, X, Y) = \mathbb{E}_{y \in Y}\left[D_Y^2(y)\right] + \mathbb{E}_{x \in X}\left[(D_Y(\mathcal{G}(x)) - 1)^2\right], \quad (1)$$

The mapping function $\mathcal{F} : Y \rightarrow X$, in the same way, tries to fool the discriminator D_X:

$$\mathcal{L}_{GAN}(\mathcal{F}, D_X, X, Y) = \mathbb{E}_{x \in X}\left[D_X^2(x)\right] + \mathbb{E}_{y \in Y}\left[(D_X(\mathcal{F}(y)) - 1)^2\right]. \quad (2)$$

The discriminators D_X and D_Y try to maximize the loss while mapping functions $\mathcal{G}$ and $\mathcal{F}$ try to minimize the loss. However, a network of sufficient capacity can map the set of input images to any random permutation of images in the target domain. To guarantee that the learned function maps an individual input x to a desired output y, the *cycle consistency loss* is proposed to measure the discrepancy occurred when the translated image is brought back to the original image space:

$$\mathcal{L}_{cyc}(G, F) = \mathbb{E}_{x \in X} \left[\|\mathcal{F}(\mathcal{G}(x)) - x\|_1 \right] + \mathbb{E}_{y \in Y} \left[\|\mathcal{G}(\mathcal{F}(y)) - y\|_1 \right]. \quad (3)$$

Taking advantages of adversarial loss and cycle consistency loss, the model achieves a one-to-one correspondence mapping, and discovers the cross-domain relation [8]. The full objective is:

$$\begin{aligned} \mathcal{L}(\mathcal{G}, \mathcal{F}, D_X, D_Y) &= \mathcal{L}_{GAN}(\mathcal{G}, D_Y, X, Y) \\ &+ \mathcal{L}_{GAN}(\mathcal{F}, D_X, Y, X) + \lambda \mathcal{L}_{cyc}(\mathcal{G}, \mathcal{F}), \end{aligned} \quad (4)$$

where λ controls the relative importance of the two objectives. However, the generative mapping functions $\mathcal{G}$ and $\mathcal{F}$ actually takes a dual responsibility for object transfiguration: to detect the objects of interest and to transfigure the object, which confuse the aims of the generative network.

On the other hand, we notice that the model can be viewed as two 'autoencoders': $\mathcal{F} \circ \mathcal{G} : X \to X$ and $\mathcal{G} \circ \mathcal{F} : Y \to Y$, where the translated image $\mathcal{G}(x)$ and $\mathcal{F}(y)$ can be viewed as intermediate representations trained by adversarial loss. In object transfiguration task, the generative mappings $\mathcal{G}$ and $\mathcal{F}$ are trained to generate objects to fool the discriminator. Therefore, the image background can be coded as any representation so long as it can be decoded back to the original, which does not guarantee background consistency before and after transformation. As a result, the proposed Attention-GAN that decomposes the generative network into two separated network: an attention network to predict the object of interests and a transformation network focuses on transforming object.

4 Model

The proposed model consists of three players: an attention network, a transformation network, and a discriminative network. The attention network predicts the region of interest from the original image x. The transformation network focuses on transforming the object from one domain to the other. The resulting image is therefore a combination of the transformed object and the background of original image with a layered operator. Finally, the discriminator aims to distinguish the real image $y \in Y$ and the generated image. The overview of the proposed model is illustrated in Fig. 1(b). For notation simplicity, we only show the forward process that transforms images from domain X to domain Y, and the backward process from domain Y back to the domain X can be easily obtained in the similar approach.

4.1 Formulations

The architecture of the proposed model is shown in Fig. 2. Given an input image x in domain X, the attention network A_X outputs a spatial score map $A_X(x)$,

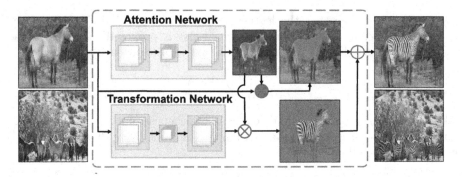

Fig. 2. The proposed Attention-GAN for object transfiguration from one class to another. The attention network predicts the attention maps. The transformation network synthesizes the target object. A layered operation is applied on the background and transformed images to output the resulting image.

whose size is the same as the original image x. The element value of score map is from 0 to 1. The attention network assigns higher scores of visual attention to the region of interest while suppressing background. In another branch, the transformation network T outputs the transformed image $T(x)$ that looks similar to those in the target domain Y. Then we adopt a layered operation to construct the final image. Given transformed region $A_X(x)$, a transformed image $T_X(x)$ and image background from original image x are combined as:

$$\mathcal{G}(x) \equiv A_X(x) \odot T_X(x) + (1 - A_X(x)) \odot x, \tag{5}$$

where $\odot$ denotes the element-wise multiplication operator. Another mapping function $\mathcal{F}$ is introduced to bring transformed images $\mathcal{G}(x)$ back to the original space $\mathcal{F}(\mathcal{G}(x)) \approx x$. The mapping from an image y in target domain Y to the source domain follows:

$$\mathcal{F}(y) \equiv A_Y(y) \odot T_Y(y) + (1 - A_Y(y)) \odot y. \tag{6}$$

Followed by Sect. 3, the *adversarial loss* (Eqs. (1) and (2)) and the *cycle consistency loss* (Eq. (3)) are introduced to learn the overall mappings $\mathcal{G}$ and $\mathcal{F}$. In classical GANs [7–9], the generative mapping $\mathcal{G}$ transforms the whole image to target domain and then the generative mapping $\mathcal{F}$ is required to bring the transformed image back to original image $\mathcal{F}(\mathcal{G}(x)) \approx x$. However, in practice, the background of the generated image appears to be unreal and significantly different from the original image background, so that the cycle consistency loss can hardly reach 0. In our method, the attention network outputs a mask that separates the image into region of interest and background. The background part will not be transformed, so that the cycle consistency loss in the background reaches 0.

4.2 Attention Losses

Similar to cycle consistency, the attention map of object x in domain X predicted by attention network A_X should be consistent with the attention map of the transformed object by attention network A_Y. For example, if a horse is transformed into a zebra, the region of the zebra should be brought back to the horse as a cycle. That is to say, the regions of interest in the original image and the transformed image should be the same: $A_X(x) \approx A_Y(\mathcal{G}(x))$. Similarly, for each image y from domain Y, attention network A_Y and A_X should satisfy consistency: $A_Y(y) \approx A_X(\mathcal{F}(y))$. To that end, we propose an attention cycle-consistent loss:

$$\mathcal{L}_{A_{cyc}}(A_X, A_Y) = \mathbb{E}_{x \in X}\left[\|A_X(x) - A_Y(\mathcal{G}(x))\|_1\right] + \mathbb{E}_{y \in Y}\left[\|A_Y(y) - A_X(\mathcal{F}(y))\|_1\right] \tag{7}$$

In addition, we introduce a sparse loss to encourage the attention network to pay attention to a small region related to the object instead of the whole image:

$$\mathcal{L}_{sparse}(A_X, A_Y) = \mathbb{E}_{x \in X}\left[\|A_X(x)\|_1\right] + \mathbb{E}_{y \in Y}\left[\|A_Y(y)\|_1\right]. \tag{8}$$

Considering Eq. (7), the attention maps of $A_X(\mathcal{F}(y))$ and $A_Y(\mathcal{G}(x))$ should be consistent to $A_Y(y)$ and $A_X(x)$, so they do not include additional sparse loss on $A_X(\mathcal{F}(y))$ and $A_Y(\mathcal{G}(x))$.

Hence, by combining Eqs. (1–3), (7) and (8), our full objective is:

$$\mathcal{L}(T_X, T_Y, D_X, D_Y, A_X, A_Y) = \mathcal{L}_{GAN}(\mathcal{G}, D_Y, X, Y) + \mathcal{L}_{GAN}(\mathcal{F}, D_X, X, Y)$$
$$+ \lambda_{cyc}\mathcal{L}_{cyc}(\mathcal{G}, \mathcal{F}) + \lambda_{A_{cyc}}\mathcal{L}_{A_{cyc}}(A_X, A_Y) + \lambda_{sparse}\mathcal{L}_{sparse}(A_X, A_Y), \tag{9}$$

where λ_{sparse} and λ_{cyc} balance the relative importance of different terms. Attention network, transformation network and discriminative network in both X domain and Y domain can be solved in the following min-max game:

$$\arg \min_{T_X, T_Y, A_X, A_Y} \max_{D_X, D_Y} \mathcal{L}(T_X, T_Y, D_X, D_Y, A_X, A_Y), \tag{10}$$

the optimization algorithm is described in the supplementary material.

4.3 Extra Supervision

In some cases, segmentation annotations can be collected and used as attention map. For example, our horse $\rightarrow$ zebra image segmentation of horse is exactly the region of interest. We therefore supervise the training of the attention network by segmentation label. Given a training set $\{(x_1, m_1), \cdots, (x_N, m_N)\}$ of N examples, where m_i indicates the binary labels of segmentation, we minimize the discrepancy between predicted attention maps $A(x_i)$ and segmentation label m_i. To learn the attention maps for both X domain and Y domain, the total attention loss can be written as:

$$\mathcal{L}_{A_{sup}}(A_X, A_Y) = \sum_{i=1}^{N_X} \|m_i - A_X(x_i)\|_1 + \sum_{j=1}^{N_Y} \|m_j - A_Y(y_j)\|_1. \tag{11}$$

The full objective thus becomes:

$$\mathcal{L}(T_X, T_Y, D_X, D_Y, A_X, A_Y) = \mathcal{L}_{GAN}(\mathcal{G}, D_Y, X, Y) + \mathcal{L}_{GAN}(\mathcal{F}, D_X, X, Y)$$
$$+ \lambda_{cyc}\mathcal{L}_{cyc}(\mathcal{G}, \mathcal{F}) + \lambda_{A_{sup}}\mathcal{L}_{A_{sup}}(A_X, A_Y),$$

(12)

where λ_{cyc} and $\lambda_{A_{sup}}$ control the relative importance of the objectives. As the attention maps are supervised by semantic annotations, we do not incorporate the constraints of Eqs. (7) and (8).

5   Experiments

In this section, we first introduce two metrics to evaluate the quality of generated images. We then compare unsupervised Attention-GAN against CycleGAN [7]. Next, we study the importance of the *attention sparse loss*, and compare our method against some variants. Lastly, we demonstrate empirical results of supervised Attention-GAN.

We first evaluated the proposed Attention-GAN on three tasks: horse ↔ zebra, tiger ↔ leopard and apple ↔ orange (Fig. 3). The images for horse, zebra, apple and orange were provided by CycleGAN [7]. The images for tiger and leopards are from ImageNet [12], which consists of 1,444 images for tiger, 1,396 for leopard. We randomly selected 60 images for test, and the rest for training set. In supervised experiment, we performed horse ↔ zebra task where images and annotations can be obtained from MSCOCO dataset [34]. For each object category, images in MSCOCO training set were used for training and those in MSCOCO val set were for testing. For all experiments, the training samples were first scaled as 286×286, and then randomly flipped and cropped as 256×256. In test phase, we scaled input images to the size of 256×256.

For all experiments, the networks were trained with an initial learning rate of 0.0002 for the first 100 epoch and a linearly decaying rate that goes to zero over the next 100 epochs. We used the Adam solver [35] with batch size of 1. We updated the discriminative networks using a randomly selected sample from a buffer of previously generated images followed by [36]. The training process is shown in supplementary material. The architectures of transformation networks and attention networks are based on Johnson *et al.* [37]. The discriminators are adapted from the Markovian Patch-GAN [2,7,9,38]. Details are listed in the supplementary material.

5.1   Assessment of Image Quality

Since object transiguration is required to predict the region of interest and transform the object while preserve the background, we introduce metrics to estimate quality of transformed image.

To assess the background consistency of transformation, we compute PSNR and SSIM between generated image background and original image background. PSNR is an approximation to human perception of reconstruction

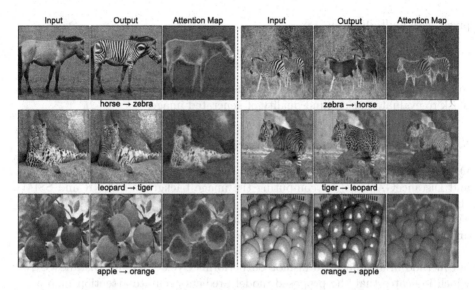

Fig. 3. Results of object transfiguration on different tasks: horse ↔ zebra, leopard ↔ tiger and apple ↔ orange. In each case, the first image is the original images, the second image is the synthesized image, and the third image is the predicted attention map. Our proposed model only manipulates the attention parts of image and preserves the background consistency. (Color figure online)

Table 1. Background consistency performance of different object transfiguration tasks for background PSNR and SSIM.

	Task	CycleGAN	DistanceGAN	Ours (unsupervised)	Ours (supervised)
PSNR	horse → zebra	18.1875	11.1896	22.2629	24.589
	zebra → horse	18.1021	10.1153	21.5360	23.9330
SSIM	horse → zebra	0.6725	0.2630	0.9003	0.9482
	zebra → horse	0.7155	0.3627	0.8988	0.9534

quality, which is defined via mean squared error (MSE). Given testing samples $\{(x_1, m_1), \cdots, (x_N, m_N)\}$, we use pixels-wise multiplication $\odot$ by the segmentation mask to compute image background PSNR:

$$\frac{1}{N} \sum_{i=1}^{N} PSNR\left(x_i \odot (1 - m_i), \mathcal{G}(x_i) \odot (1 - m_i)\right), \qquad (13)$$

where x_i indicates original image, $\mathcal{G}(x_i)$ indicates the resulting image, $(1 - m_i)$ indicates the image background, the pixels-wise multiplication $x_i \odot (1 - m_i)$ indicates the background of original image, and $\mathcal{G}(x_i) \odot (1 - m_i)$ indicates the background of generated image. Similarly, we use SSIM to assess the structural similarity between background of original image and composited output by using pixels-wise multiplication:

$$\frac{1}{N} \sum_{i=1}^{N} SSIM \left(x_i \odot (1 - m_i), y_i \odot (1 - m_i) \right). \tag{14}$$

In experiment, we use MSCOCO [34] dataset's test images and segmentation mask to evaluate background quality of generated image.

5.2 Unsupervised Results Comparisons to State-of-the-Art

Quantitative Comparison. We compare our method with CycleGAN [7] and DistanceGAN [11] by computing the image background PSNR and SSIM (Eqs. (13) and (14)). The test dataset is from MSCOCO dataset [34]. As MSCOCO dataset does not have the classes of tiger or leopard, and apples and oranges in images are too small, we only compare the results of horse $\leftrightarrow$ zebra. Results are shown in Table 1. As can be seen, for both PSNR and SSIM, our method in unsupervised fashion outperforms CycleGAN and DistanceGAN, which indicates that the proposed model predicts accurate attention map and achieves a better performance of transformation quality. Since our method outperforms DistanceGAN by a large margin, we only explore qualitative quality and human perceptual study with CycleGAN.

Fig. 4. Comparison with CycleGAN on horse $\leftrightarrow$ zebra. In each case, the first image is the input image, the second is the result of CycleGAN [7], and the third is the result of our Attention-GAN. (Color figure online)

Qualitative Comparison. Results of horse $\leftrightarrow$ zebra are shown in Fig. 4. We observed that our method provides translation results of higher visual quality on test data compared to those of CycleGAN. For example, in the horse $\rightarrow$ zebra task, CycleGAN mistakes some parts of background as target and transforms

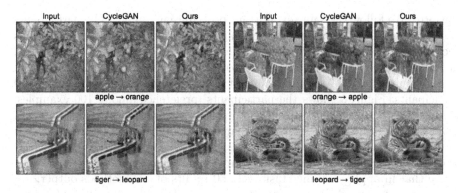

Fig. 5. Comparison with CycleGAN on apple ↔ orange and tiger ↔ leopard. In each case: input image (left), result of CycleGAN [7] (middle), and result of our Attention-GAN (right). (Color figure online)

them into black and white stripes. In second column of Fig. 4, CycleGAN translates the green grass and trees into brown in the zebra → horse task. In contrast, our method generates zebra in the correct location and preserves background consistency. Comparison results on tiger ↔ leopard and apple ↔ orange are shown in Fig. 5. The results of Attention-GAN are more visually pleasing than those of CycleGAN. In most cases, CycleGAN can not preserve background consistency, e.g., the blue jeans in the first image are transformed to yellow, the blue water in third image is transformed to yellow and the yellow weeds in the last image is transformed to green. One possible reason is that our Attention-GAN disentangles the background and object of interests by the attention network and only transforms the object, while the compared method only uses one generative network that manipulate the whole image.

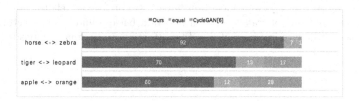

Fig. 6. The stacked bar chart of participants' preferences for our methods compared to CycleGAN [21]. The blue bar indicates the number of images that more participants prefer our results. The gray bar indicates the number of images that more participants prefer CycleGAN's results. The orange bar indicates the number of images where two methods get a equal number of votes from 10 participants. (Color figure online)

Human Perceptual Study. We further evaluate our algorithm via a human study. We perform pairwise A/B tests deployed on the Amazon Mechanical Turk platform. We follow the same experiment procedure in [39,40]. The participants are asked to select the more realistic image from each pair. Each pair contains two images translated from the same source image by two approaches. We test the tasks of horse $\leftrightarrow$ zebra, tiger $\leftrightarrow$ leopard and apple $\leftrightarrow$ orange. In each task, we randomly select 100 images from test set. Each image are compared by 10 participants. Figure 6 shows the participants' preference among 100 examples. We observe that 92 results of our methods outperforms results of CycleGAN in horse $\leftrightarrow$ zebra task. In tiger $\leftrightarrow$ leopard, still only 17% results of compared method beat ours, which indicates that qualitative assessments obtained by our proposed approaches are better than those obtained by existing methods. We also notice that in apple $\leftrightarrow$ orange task, only 60 results of our methods outperform the compared method. We consider the reason is that a large portion of images in apple and orange dataset are close-up images whose background is simple so that CycleGAN could reach a competitive result.

Fig. 7. Generation results of our model on horse $\rightarrow$ zebra. From left to right: Inputs, attention maps, outputs of transformation network, background images factorized by attention maps, object of images factorized by attention maps, final composite images.

5.3   Model Analysis

We perform model analysis on the horse $\rightarrow$ zebra task. Figure 7 shows the generated images, along with the intermediate generation results of model. In the second column, the attention maps with are shown. As can be seen, while being completely unsupervised, the attention network of model is able to successfully disentangle the objects of our interests and the background from input image. The third column is the output of the transformation network, where the transformed zebra are visually pleasing while the background parts of images are meaningless. It demonstrates that the transformation network only focuses on transforming the object of interests. Moreover, Fig. 7 shows that the final output images in the last column are combined by the background parts in the forth column and the objects of interests in the fifth column.

Table 2. Performance of horse → zebra for different losses.

	$\lambda_{attn} = 0$	$\lambda_{attn} = 1$	$\lambda_{attn} = 5$
PSNR	19.8621	22.2629	24.2173
SSIM	0.8291	0.9003	0.9367

Figure 8 shows the qualitative results of variants of our model on horse → zebra. It can be seen that without the sparse loss ($\lambda_{sparse} = 0$ in Eq. (8)), the attention network would predict some parts of image background as regions of interests. When λ_{sparse} was set to 5, the attention mask shrinked too much to cover the whole object of interests. It is because if we emphasize too much on the relative importance of sparse loss, the attention network can not comprehensively predict the object location. We find $\lambda_{sparse} = 1$ is an appropriate choice, which makes a good balance to pay enough attention on the objects of interests. In Table 2, we observe that with the value of λ_{sparse} becoming larger, the performance of background consistency is better. However, the qualities of transformed object decrease if λ_{sparse} is set too large. This indicates that the λ_{sparse} can be viewed as a parameter that balance the performance of background consistency and transformation quality.

Fig. 8. The effect of sparse loss with different parameters λ_{sparse} for mapping horse → zebra. From left to right: input, output and attention map without sparse loss, input and attention map when $\lambda_{sparse} = 1$, input and attention map when $\lambda_{sparse}=5$.

5.4 Comparisons of Supervised Results

We compute PSRN, SSIM of background region between generated and original images in horse ↔ zebra task. In Table 1, the Attention-GAN with supervision outperforms unsupervised Attention-GAN and CycleGAN from the perspective of background consistency. This demonstrates that the attention network predicts the object of interests more accurately with the segmentation mask. In Fig. 9, CycleGAN and unsupervised Attention-GAN predict some parts of the person as region of interests and transform them into texture of zebra (see the first row of Fig. 9). We also notice that the attention maps with supervision tend to be dark red or dark blue, which indicates the supervised attention network predicts with higher confidence, and disentangles the background and object of interests more clearly.

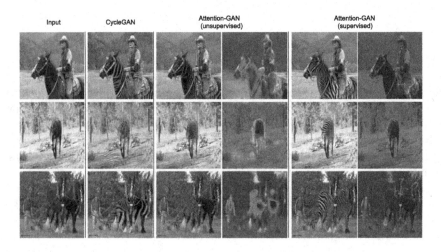

Fig. 9. Comparison of horse ↔ zebra between CycleGAN [7], unsupervised Attention-GAN and supervised Attention-GAN.

We evaluate the foreground mask of horse in terms of UoI and mAPr@0.5. The unsupervised Attention-GAN got 28.1% of UoI and 20.3% of mAPr@0.5. On the other hand, the supervised Attention-GAN got 37.8% of UoI score and 30.5% of mAPr@0.5. Although our algorithm is not particularly designed for semantic segmentation, the proposed attention network is able to learn the object of interests in an unsupervised way and achieve a reasonable performance.

5.5 Global Image Transformation

Both local and global image transformation are important. We study object transfiguration, and evaluate it on horse ↔ zebra, apple ↔ orange and tiger ↔ leopard. More applications include virtual try-on [41] with regard to a desired clothing item of a person, and face attributes (e.g. mustache and glass) changing [42]. The proposed attention GAN is effective to identify important regions in object transfiguration problems, and it can also lead to some interesting observations in global image transformation. In summer ↔ winter, there is no explicit object of interests, but the algorithm does recognize some regions with more attention, e.g. grass and trees in Fig. 10, which are usually green in summer and brown in winter. Meanwhile, regions without distinctive characteristics, e.g., blue sky would not be attended.

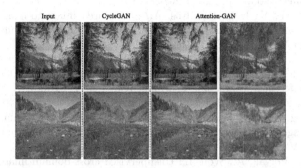

Fig. 10. Results of Summer → Winter comparing with CycleGAN (Color figure online)

6   Conclusion

This paper introduces attention mechanism into the generative adversarial nets considering image context and structure information on object transfiguration task. We develop a three-player model that consists of an attention network, a transformation network and a discriminative network. The attention network predicts the regions of interest whilst the transformation network transforms the object from one class to another. We show that our model has advantages over the one-shot generation method [7] in preserving background consistency and transformation quality.

Acknowledgment. This work was supported in part by State Key Research and Development Program (2016YFB1001003), NSFC (61527804, 61521062), in part by Australian Research Council Projects FL-170100117, DE-180101438, DP-180103424 and LP-150100671, and in part by USyd-SJTU Partnership Collaboration Award.

References

1. Long, J., Shelhamer, E., Darrell, T.: Fully convolutional networks for semantic segmentation. In: Proceedings of the IEEE Conference on Computer Vision and Pattern Recognition, pp. 3431–3440 (2015)
2. Isola, P., Zhu, J.Y., Zhou, T., Efros, A.A.: Image-to-image translation with conditional adversarial networks. arXiv preprint arXiv:1611.07004 (2016)
3. Karacan, L., Akata, Z., Erdem, A., Erdem, E.: Learning to generate images of outdoor scenes from attributes and semantic layouts. arXiv preprint arXiv:1612.00215 (2016)

4. Sangkloy, P., Lu, J., Fang, C., Yu, F., Hays, J.: Scribbler: controlling deep image synthesis with sketch and color. arXiv preprint arXiv:1612.00835 (2016)

5. Dong, C., Loy, C.C., He, K., Tang, X.: Image super-resolution using deep convolutional networks. IEEE Trans. Pattern Anal. Mach. Intell. **38**(2), 295–307 (2016)

6. Goodfellow, I., et al.: Generative adversarial nets. In: Advances in neural information processing systems, pp. 2672–2680 (2014)

7. Zhu, J.Y., Park, T., Isola, P., Efros, A.A.: Unpaired image-to-image translation using cycle-consistent adversarial networks. In: The IEEE International Conference on Computer Vision (ICCV), October 2017

8. Kim, T., Cha, M., Kim, H., Lee, J.K., Kim, J.: Learning to discover cross-domain relations with generative adversarial networks. In: Proceedings of the 34th International Conference on Machine Learning, ICML 2017, Sydney, NSW, Australia, 6–11 August 2017, pp. 1857–1865 (2017)

9. Yi, Z., Zhang, H., Tan, P., Gong, M.: DualGAN: unsupervised dual learning for image-to-image translation. In: The IEEE International Conference on Computer Vision (ICCV), October 2017

10. Taigman, Y., Polyak, A., Wolf, L.: Unsupervised cross-domain image generation. CoRR abs/1611.02200 (2016)

11. Benaim, S., Wolf, L.: One-sided unsupervised domain mapping. In: Advances in Neural Information Processing Systems 30: Annual Conference on Neural Information Processing Systems 2017, Long Beach, CA, USA, 4–9 December 2017, pp. 752–762 (2017)

12. Deng, J., Dong, W., Socher, R., Li, L.J., Li, K., Fei-Fei, L.: ImageNet: a large-scale hierarchical image database. In: IEEE Conference on Computer Vision and Pattern Recognition, CVPR 2009. IEEE, pp. 248–255 (2009)

13. Denton, E.L., Chintala, S., Fergus, R., et al.: Deep generative image models using a Laplacian pyramid of adversarial networks. In: Advances in Neural Information Processing Systems, pp. 1486–1494 (2015)

14. Radford, A., Metz, L., Chintala, S.: Unsupervised representation learning with deep convolutional generative adversarial networks. arXiv preprint arXiv:1511.06434 (2015)

15. Wang, C., Wang, C., Xu, C., Tao, D.: Tag disentangled generative adversarial network for object image re-rendering. In: Proceedings of the Twenty-Sixth International Joint Conference on Artificial Intelligence, IJCAI 2017, pp. 2901–2907 (2017)

16. Im, D.J., Kim, C.D., Jiang, H., Memisevic, R.: Generating images with recurrent adversarial networks. arXiv preprint arXiv:1602.05110 (2016)

17. Kwak, H., Zhang, B.T.: Generating images part by part with composite generative adversarial networks. arXiv preprint arXiv:1607.05387 (2016)

18. Yang, J., Kannan, A., Batra, D., Parikh, D.: LR-GAN: layered recursive generative adversarial networks for image generation. In: 5th International Conference on Learning Representations (ICLR) (2017)

19. Wang, C., Xu, C., Wang, C., Tao, D.: Perceptual adversarial networks for image-to-image transformation. IEEE Trans. Image Process. **27**(8), 4066–4079 (2018)

20. Balcan, M., Weinberger, K.Q. (eds.): Proceedings of the 33nd International Conference on Machine Learning, ICML 2016, JMLR Workshop and Conference Proceedings, New York City, NY, USA, 19–24 June 2016, vol. 48. JMLR.org (2016)

21. Zhang, H., et al.: StackGAN: text to photo-realistic image synthesis with stacked generative adversarial networks. In: The IEEE International Conference on Computer Vision (ICCV), October 2017

22. Liang, X., Zhang, H., Xing, E.P.: Generative semantic manipulation with contrasting GAN. arXiv preprint arXiv:1708.00315 (2017)
23. Rensink, R.A.: The dynamic representation of scenes. Vis. Cognit. **7**(1–3), 17–42 (2000)
24. Mnih, V., Heess, N., Graves, A., et al.: Recurrent models of visual attention. In: Advances in Neural Information Processing Systems, pp. 2204–2212 (2014)
25. Zhou, B., Khosla, A., Lapedriza, A., Oliva, A., Torralba, A.: Learning deep features for discriminative localization. In: Proceedings of the IEEE Conference on Computer Vision and Pattern Recognition, pp. 2921–2929 (2016)
26. Xiao, T., Xu, Y., Yang, K., Zhang, J., Peng, Y., Zhang, Z.: The application of two-level attention models in deep convolutional neural network for fine-grained image classification. In: Proceedings of the IEEE Conference on Computer Vision and Pattern Recognition, pp. 842–850 (2015)
27. Xu, K., et al.: Show, attend and tell: neural image caption generation with visual attention. In: International Conference on Machine Learning, pp. 2048–2057 (2015)
28. Xu, H., Saenko, K.: Ask, attend and answer: exploring question-guided spatial attention for visual question answering. In: Leibe, B., Matas, J., Sebe, N., Welling, M. (eds.) ECCV 2016 Part VII. LNCS, vol. 9911, pp. 451–466. Springer, Cham (2016). https://doi.org/10.1007/978-3-319-46478-7_28
29. Chen, L.C., Yang, Y., Wang, J., Xu, W., Yuille, A.L.: Attention to scale: scale-aware semantic image segmentation. In: Proceedings of the IEEE Conference on Computer Vision and Pattern Recognition, pp. 3640–3649 (2016)
30. Bahdanau, D., Cho, K., Bengio, Y.: Neural machine translation by jointly learning to align and translate. In: 3th International Conference on Learning Representations (ICLR), April 2015
31. Yao, L., et al.: Describing videos by exploiting temporal structure. In: Proceedings of the IEEE International Conference on Computer Vision, pp. 4507–4515 (2015)
32. Gregor, K., Danihelka, I., Graves, A., Rezende, D., Wierstra, D.: DRAW: a recurrent neural network for image generation. In Bach, F., Blei, D. (eds.): Proceedings of the 32nd International Conference on Machine Learning, Proceedings of Machine Learning Research, Lille, France, PMLR, 07–09 July 2015, vol. 37, 1462–1471 (2015)
33. Mao, X., Li, Q., Xie, H., Lau, R.Y., Wang, Z., Paul Smolley, S.: Least squares generative adversarial networks. In: The IEEE International Conference on Computer Vision (ICCV), October 2017
34. Lin, T.-Y., et al.: Microsoft COCO: common objects in context. In: Fleet, D., Pajdla, T., Schiele, B., Tuytelaars, T. (eds.) ECCV 2014 Part V. LNCS, vol. 8693, pp. 740–755. Springer, Cham (2014). https://doi.org/10.1007/978-3-319-10602-1_48
35. Kingma, D., Ba, J.: Adam: a method for stochastic optimization. arXiv preprint arXiv:1412.6980 (2014)
36. Shrivastava, A., Pfister, T., Tuzel, O., Susskind, J., Wang, W., Webb, R.: Learning from simulated and unsupervised images through adversarial training. In: The IEEE Conference on Computer Vision and Pattern Recognition (CVPR), July 2017
37. Johnson, J., Alahi, A., Fei-Fei, L.: Perceptual losses for real-time style transfer and super-resolution. In: Leibe, B., Matas, J., Sebe, N., Welling, M. (eds.) ECCV 2016 Part II. LNCS, vol. 9906, pp. 694–711. Springer, Cham (2016). https://doi.org/10.1007/978-3-319-46475-6_43

38. Li, C., Wand, M.: Precomputed real-time texture synthesis with markovian generative adversarial networks. In: Leibe, B., Matas, J., Sebe, N., Welling, M. (eds.) ECCV 2016 Part III. LNCS, vol. 9907, pp. 702–716. Springer, Cham (2016). https://doi.org/10.1007/978-3-319-46487-9_43
39. Chen, Q., Koltun, V.: Photographic image synthesis with cascaded refinement networks. In: The IEEE International Conference on Computer Vision (ICCV), vol. 1 (2017)
40. Wang, T.C., Liu, M.Y., Zhu, J.Y., Tao, A., Kautz, J., Catanzaro, B.: High-resolution image synthesis and semantic manipulation with conditional GANs. arXiv preprint arXiv:1711.11585 (2017)
41. Han, X., Wu, Z., Wu, Z., Yu, R., Davis, L.S.: VITON: an image-based virtual try-on network. In: The IEEE Conference on Computer Vision and Pattern Recognition (CVPR), June 2018
42. Upchurch, P., et al.: Deep feature interpolation for image content changes. In: The IEEE Conference on Computer Vision and Pattern Recognition (CVPR), July 2017

Exploring the Limits of Weakly Supervised Pretraining

Dhruv Mahajan, Ross Girshick[✉], Vignesh Ramanathan, Kaiming He,
Manohar Paluri, Yixuan Li, Ashwin Bharambe, and Laurens van der Maaten

Facebook, Menlo Park, USA
rbg@fb.com

Abstract. State-of-the-art visual perception models for a wide range of tasks rely on supervised pretraining. ImageNet classification is the de facto pretraining task for these models. Yet, ImageNet is now nearly ten years old and is by modern standards "small". Even so, relatively little is known about the behavior of pretraining with datasets that are multiple orders of magnitude larger. The reasons are obvious: such datasets are difficult to collect and annotate. In this paper, we present a unique study of transfer learning with large convolutional networks trained to predict hashtags on *billions* of social media images. Our experiments demonstrate that training for large-scale hashtag prediction leads to excellent results. We show improvements on several image classification and object detection tasks, and report the highest ImageNet-1k single-crop, top-1 accuracy to date: 85.4% (97.6% top-5). We also perform extensive experiments that provide novel empirical data on the relationship between large-scale pretraining and transfer learning performance.

1 Introduction

Nearly all state-of-the-art visual perception algorithms rely on the same formula: (1) pretrain a convolutional network on a large, manually annotated image classification dataset and (2) finetune the network on a smaller, task-specific dataset. This formula [1–3] has been in wide use for several years and led to impressive improvements on numerous tasks. Examples include: object detection [1,4], semantic segmentation [5,6], human pose estimation [7,8], video recognition [9], monocular depth estimation [10], and so on. In fact, it is so effective that it would now be considered foolhardy *not* to use supervised pretraining.

The ImageNet dataset [11] is the de facto pretraining dataset. While there are studies analyzing the effects of various ImageNet pretraining factors on transfer learning (e.g., [12,13]) or the use of different datasets that are of the same size magnitude as ImageNet (e.g., [14,15]), relatively little is known about pretraining on datasets that are *multiple* orders of magnitude larger ([16,17] are the largest

Electronic supplementary material The online version of this chapter (https://doi.org/10.1007/978-3-030-01216-8_12) contains supplementary material, which is available to authorized users.

V. Ferrari et al. (Eds.): ECCV 2018, LNCS 11206, pp. 185–201, 2018.
https://doi.org/10.1007/978-3-030-01216-8_12

studies to date). The reasons for this are numerous: few such datasets exist, building new datasets is labor intensive, and large computational resources are needed to conduct experiments. Yet, given the central role of pretraining it is important to expand our scientific knowledge in this domain.

This paper tries to address this complex issue by studying an unexplored data regime: *billions of images "labeled" in the wild with social media hashtags*. This data source has the advantage of being large and continuously growing, as well as "free", from an annotation perspective, because no manual labeling is required. However, the data source also has potential disadvantages: hashtags may be too noisy to serve as an effective supervisory signal and the image distribution might be biased in ways that harm transfer learning. It is not a priori obvious that training on this data will yield good transfer learning results.

The main result of this paper is that without manual dataset curation or sophisticated data cleaning, models trained on billions of Instagram images using thousands of distinct hashtags as labels exhibit excellent transfer learning performance. For example, we observe improvements over the state-of-the-art for image classification and object detection, where we obtain a single-crop, top-1 accuracy of 85.4% on the ImageNet-1k image-classification dataset and 45.2% AP on the COCO object-detection dataset [18], compared to 79.8% and 43.7%, respectively, when training (or pretraining) the same models on ImageNet-1k. Our primary goal, however, is to contribute novel experimental data about this previously unexplored regime. To that end, we conduct numerous experiments that reveal interesting trends. For example, we find that "hashtag engineering" (i.e., collecting images tagged with a specific subset of hashtags) is a promising new direction for improving transfer learning results, that training on large-scale hashtag data is unexpectedly robust to label noise, and that the features learned allow a simple linear classifier to achieve state-of-the-art ImageNet-1k top-1 accuracy of 83.6% without any finetuning (compared to 84.2% with finetuning).

2   Scaling up Supervised Pretraining

In our experiments, we train standard convolutional network architectures to predict hashtags on up to 3.5 billion public Instagram images. To make training at this scale practical, we adopt a distributed synchronous implementation of stochastic gradient descent with large (8k image) minibatches, following Goyal et al. [19]. We experiment on a variety of datasets, which we describe next.

2.1   Instagram Datasets

We use a simple data collection pipeline: (1) We select a set of hashtags. (2) We download images that are tagged with at least one of these hashtags. (3) Then, because multiple hashtags may refer to the same underlying concept, we apply a simple process that utilizes WordNet [20] synsets to merge some hashtags into a single canonical form (e.g., #brownbear and #ursusarctos are merged). (4)

Finally, for each downloaded image, we replace each hashtag with its canonical form and discard any hashtags that were not in the selected set. The canonical hashtags are used as labels for training and evaluation.

By varying the selected hashtags and the number of images to sample, we can construct a variety of datasets of different sizes and visual distributions. Table 1 summarizes the datasets used in our experiments. Each dataset is named by completing a template, *role-source-I-L*, that indicates its role (training, validation, testing), source (IG for Instagram, IN for ImageNet, etc.), number of images I, and number of labels L. We use approximate image and label counts for convenience, for example "train-IG-940M-1.5k" is an Instagram dataset for training with ~940e6 images and ~1,500 labels. We omit the role and image count when it is clear from context or not useful to present.

We design three hashtag sets for the Instagram data: (1) A ~1.5k set with hashtags from the standard 1,000 IN-1k synsets (each synset contains at least one synonym, hence there are more hashtags than synsets). (2) A ~17k set with hashtags that are synonyms in any of the noun synsets in WordNet. And (3) an ~8.5k set with the most frequent hashtags from the 17k set. The hashtag set sizes are measured after merging the hashtags into their canonical forms. We hypothesize that the first set has a visual distribution similar to IN-1k, while the other two represent more general visual distributions covering fine-grained visual categories. Details of how these hashtags are selected and how the merging process works are given in supplemental material.

Table 1. Summary of image classification datasets. Each dataset is named with a template, *role-source-I-L*, that indicates its role (training, validation, testing), source, number of images I, and number of labels L.

Name template	Description
train-IG-I-1.5k	Instagram training set of I images and ~1.5k hashtags from ImageNet-1k
train-IG-I-8.5k	Instagram training set of I images and ~8.5k hashtags from WordNet
train-IG-I-17k	Instagram training set of I images and ~17k hashtags from WordNet
train-IN-1M-1k	The standard ImageNet-1k ILSVRC training set with 1.28M images
val-IN-50k-1k	The standard ImageNet-1k ILSVRC validation set with 50k images
train-IN-I-L	Extended ImageNet training set of I images and $L \in \{5k, 9k\}$ labels
val-IN-I-L	Extended ImageNet validation set of I images and $L \in \{5k, 9k\}$ labels
train-CUB-6k-200	The Caltech-UCSD Birds-200-2011 training set
val-CUB-6k-200	The Caltech-UCSD Birds-200-2011 validation set
train-Places-1.8M-365	The Places365-Standard training set (high-resolution version)
val-Places-37k-365	The Places365-Standard validation set (high-resolution version)
train-COCO-115k-80	The standard COCO detection training set (2017 version)
val-COCO-5k-80	The standard COCO detection validation set (2017 version)
test-COCO-20k-80	The standard COCO detection test-dev set (2017 version)

Image Deduplication. When performing transfer learning, it is essential to understand and properly address overlap between training and test sets. Overlap can exists because images may come from the same underlying sources (e.g., Wikipedia, Flickr, Google). For instance, ~5% of the images in the val-CUB-6k-200 set [21] also appear in train-IN-1M-1k, and 1.78% of images in val-IN-50k-1k set are in the JFT-300M training set [17]. To address this issue, we performed the following deduplication procedure: we compute R-MAC features [22,23] for all candidate images using a ResNet-50 model, and use these features to find the $k = 21$ nearest neighbors for each of the images in our test sets (additional details are in the supplemental material). Subsequently, we manually inspected all images and their nearest neighbors to identify duplicates. While it is difficult to know the true recall of our duplicate detection system, this procedure uncovered 150 val-IN-50k-1k (0.30%), 10 val-CUB-6k-200 (0.17%), 151 val-Places-37k-365 (0.41%), and 6 val-COCO-5k-80 (0.12%) duplicates; we will continue to improve this system and, as a result, the estimated number of duplicates may increase. In our results, we report the observed accuracy of our models; in the supplemental material, we report a conservative lower bound on accuracy by marking all duplicates as incorrect. Given the small percentage of duplicates, they do not impact our findings.

Discussion. Our datasets have two nice properties: public visibility and simplicity. By using publicly accessible images, the data used in our experiments is visible to everyone. To see what it looks like, the images are browsable by hashtag at https://www.instagram.com/explore/tags/ followed by a specific hashtag; for example https://www.instagram.com/explore/tags/brownbear shows images tagged with #brownbear. Our data is also taken from the "wild", essentially as-is, with minimal effort to sanitize it. This makes the dataset construction process particularly simple and transparent.

We contrast these properties with the JFT-300M dataset [17], which is not publicly visible and is the result of a proprietary collection process ("The [JFT-300M] images are labeled using an algorithm that uses a complex mixture of raw web signals, connections between web-pages and user feedback."). Additional details describing the collection of JFT-300M have not been publicly disclosed.

Despite our efforts to make the dataset content and collection process transparent, we acknowledge that, similar to JFT-300M, it is not possible for other research groups to know exactly which images we used nor to download them en masse. Hence it is not possible for others to replicate our results at this time. However, we believe that it is better if we undertake this study and share the results with the community than to not publish the results.

2.2   ImageNet Datasets

In addition to the standard IN-1k dataset, we experiment with larger subsets of the full ImageNet 2011 release that contains 14.2M images and 22k labels. We construct training and validation sets that include 5k and 9k labels. For the 5k set, we use the now standard IN-5k proposed in [15] (6.6M training images). For the 9k label set, we follow the same protocol used to construct IN-5k, which involves taking the next most frequent 4k labels and all of the associated images (10.5M training images). In all cases, we use 50 images per class for validation.

2.3 Models

We use residual networks with grouped convolutional layers, called ResNeXt [15]. Our experiments use ResNeXt-101 $32 \times C$d, which has 101 layers, 32 groups, and group widths C of: 4 (8B multiply-add FLOPs, 43M parameters), 8 (16B, 88M), 16 (36B, 193M), 32 (87B, 466M), and 48 (153B, 829M). Our implementation matches [19]. We believe our results will generalize to other architectures [24–26].

Loss Function. In contrast to ImageNet, our Instagram datasets may contain multiple labels per image (because a user specified multiple hashtags). The average number of hashtags per image varies depending on the dataset; for instance, train-IG-1B-17k contains ∼2 hashtags per image. Our model computes probabilities over all hashtags in the vocabulary using a softmax activation and is trained to minimize the cross-entropy between the predicted softmax distribution and the target distribution of each image. The target is a vector with k non-zero entries each set to $1/k$ corresponding to the $k \geq 1$ hashtags for the image.

We have also experimented with per-hashtag sigmoid outputs and binary logistic loss, but obtained significantly worse results. While counter-intuitive given the multi-label data, these findings match similar observations in [16]. The successful application of sigmoid activations and logistic loss may require sophisticated label completion techniques [17] and more hyper-parameter search.

2.4 Pretraining Details

Our models are trained by synchronous stochastic gradient descent (SGD) on 336 GPUs across 42 machines with minibatches of 8,064 images. Each GPU processes 24 images at a time and batch normalization (BN) [27] statistics are computed on these 24 image sets. The length of the training schedule, measured in units of number-of-images-processed (i.e., minibatch size × total SGD updates), is determined by a heuristic: we choose two training extremes (for instance, 120 epochs on 1.2e6 images and 2 epochs on 3.5e9 images) and linearly interpolate the schedule between them to set the number-of-images-processed for each experiment. Schedules for each experiment are in the supplemental material. Our ResNeXt-101 32 × 16d networks took ∼22 days to train on 3.5B images.

To set the learning rate, we follow the linear scaling rule with gradual warm-up described in [19]. We use a warm-up from 0.1 up to $0.1/256 \times 8064$, where 0.1 and 256 are canonical learning rate and minibatch sizes [28]. After the warm-up, the learning rate is multiplied by 0.5 at equally spaced steps, such that the total number of learning rate reductions is 20 over the course of training. The same settings are used when training on ImageNet and Instagram data, except that when training on ImageNet we use 128 GPUs in 16 machines (for a minibatch size of 3,072) due to the smaller dataset size and we use the standard learning rate schedule that involves three equally spaced reductions by a factor of 0.1. All other initialization and training details match [19] and are summarized in the supplemental material.

3   Experiments

In our experiments, we pretrain convolutional networks for hashtag prediction and transfer those networks to a variety of tasks. There are two established protocols for judging the quality of a pretrained model (see [29] Sect. 3 for a discussion). Both analyze how pretraining on a *source task*, e.g. IN-1k classification, leads to gains (or losses) on a *target task*, e.g. bird recognition or object detection.

Full network finetuning views pretraining as sophisticated weight initialization: the success of pretraining is judged by its impact on the target task after further training the network weights in a task-specific manner (i.e. finetuning). By contrast, *feature transfer* uses the pretrained network as a feature extractor: it judges the quality of the network by how effective its features are on other tasks, without updating any of the network parameters. These protocols are two extremes of a spectrum along which the proportion of pretrained weights that are finetuned varies from all to none. We employ both protocols in our experiments; at times one is more appropriate than the other.

Full network finetuning is performed by removing the hashtag-specific fully connected classification layer from the network and replacing it with a randomly initialized classification layer with one output per class in the target task. This modified network is then trained using SGD with momentum. We select the finetuning learning rate and schedule by grid search on a proper validation set for each target task. To do this, we randomly hold out a small portion of the *training* set (see supplemental material). This practice ensures that our results on the standard validation sets are clean.

Feature transfer is performed by training an L2-regularized linear logistic regressor on the training data for the target task using SGD. The features produced by the pretrained network are used as input into the classifier. We train the classifier until convergence to the global optimum.

3.1   Image Classification Experiments

We evaluate Instagram pretraining by measuring classification accuracies on three classification target tasks: ImageNet [30], CUB2011 [21], and Places365 [14]. We perform inference on 224×224 center-cropped images, and study the effects of (1) the hashtag vocabulary size, (2) the training set size, (3) the amount of noise in the hashtag targets, and (4) the hashtag sampling strategy.

How Does the Instagram Hashtag Set Impact Accuracy? Our first experiment varies the Instagram hashtag sets used in pretraining (1.5k, 8.5k, vs. 17k) whilst keeping other factors constant. We compute transfer learning results as top-1 classification accuracy on five target datasets: val-IN-1k, val-IN-5k, val-IN-9k, val-CUB-200, val-Places-365. For baseline models, we use ImageNet classification as a source task: we train networks on train-IN-1k, train-IN-5k, and train-IN-9k, and evaluate them on the corresponding validation sets (finetuning is not needed in these cases). For val-CUB-200 and val-Places-365, we use train-IN-1k as the baseline source task and finetune on train-CUB-200 and train-Places-365. Full network finetuning of ResNeXt-101 32 × 16d is used for all source-target pairs in which source and target are not the same.

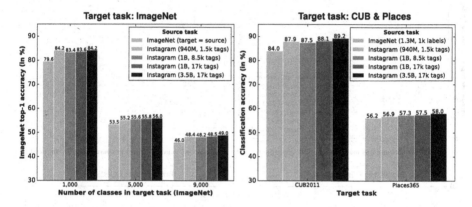

Fig. 1. small Classification accuracy of ResNeXt-101 32×16d pretrained on IG-1B with different hashtag vocabularies (purple bars) on IN-{1k, 5k, 9k} (left) and CUB2011, Places365 (right). Baseline models (gray bars) are trained on IN-{1k, 5k, 9k} (left) and IN-1k (right), respectively. Full network finetuning is used. Higher is better. (Color figure online)

Figure 1 shows that pretraining for hashtag prediction substantially improves target task accuracy: on the standard IN-1k benchmark set, a network pretrained on nearly 1B Instagram images with 1.5k hashtags achieves a state-of-the-art accuracy of 84.2%—an improvement of 4.6% over the same model architecture trained on IN-1k alone and a 1.5% boost over the prior state-of-the-art [31], which uses an optimized network architecture. The performance improvements due to Instagram pretraining vary between ImageNet tasks: on the 1k class task, the model pretrained with the IN-1k-aligned 1.5k hashtag set outperforms source networks trained on larger hashtag sets. This trend reverses as the number of target ImageNet classes increases: on 9k ImageNet target classes, the model pretrained with 17k hashtags strongly outperforms the 1.5k hashtag model. On the CUB2011 and Places365 target tasks, source models trained with the largest hashtag sets perform the best, likely, because the 17k hashtags span more objects, scenes, and fine-grained categories. These patterns are intuitive and suggest that alignment between the source and target label sets is an important factor.

We also show results in Fig. 1 using a larger 3.5B image set with 17k hashtags (dark purple bars), which performs best across all target tasks. Furthermore, following [32], we measure the *rectified* classification accuracy of this model on val-IN-1k. We present all incorrect classifications to five human annotators, asking whether or not the prediction is correct: if at least four annotators answer this question affirmatively the model's prediction is considered correct. Whereas the IN-1M-1k model obtained a rectified top-1 accuracy of 87.5% on val-IN-1k, our IG-3.5B-17k pretrained model achieved 90.4%.

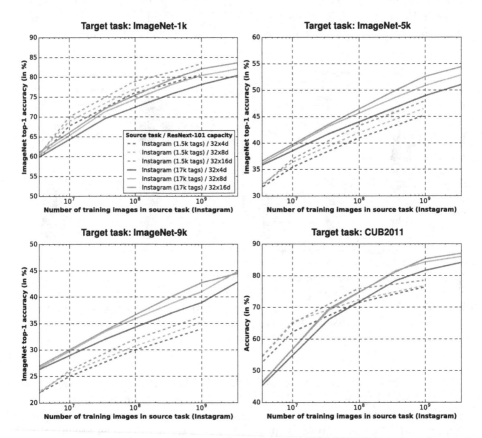

Fig. 2. Classification accuracies on IN-{1k, 5k, 9k} and CUB2011 target tasks as a function of the number of Instagram images used for pretraining for three network architectures (colors) and two hashtag vocabularies (dashed/solid lines). Only the linear classifier is trained on the target task. Higher is better. (Color figure online)

How Does the Pretraining Image Set Size Impact Accuracy? This experiment studies the relationship between the number of images used in Instagram pretraining and classification accuracy on the target task. For these experiments, when transferring to the target task we keep the pretrained network weights fixed and only train a linear classifier for the target task. We make this choice because when the number of pretraining images is small relative to the number of target task images (e.g., 1M vs. 7M), the effect of pretraining is masked by the large amount of finetuning data (this was not the case in the previous experiment where the source task had orders of magnitude more images).

Figure 2 shows the classification accuracy on ImageNet validation sets (y-axis) as a function of the number of Instagram training images (x-axis; note the log scale) ranging from 3.5M to 3.5B images. The figure shows results for models pretrained to predict 1.5k hashtags (dashed lines) or 17k hashtags (solid lines) for ResNeXt-101 models with three different capacities (represented by different colors).[1] The four panels correspond to ImageNet target tasks with three different number of classes (1k, 5k, 9k) and CUB2011.

In line with prior results [16,17], we observe near log-linear behavior: each time we multiply the amount of training data by a factor of x, we observe a fixed increase y in classification accuracy. While the scaling behavior is consistent across hashtag vocabulary sizes and models, the accuracy increase y is larger for higher-capacity networks: across all figures, the lines corresponding to ResNeXt-101 32 × 16d networks (purple) are steeper than those corresponding to 32 × 8d and 32 × 4d models. This result suggests that when training convolutional networks on billions of training images, current network architectures are prone to underfitting. We also observe log-linear scaling break down in two regimes: (1) because accuracy is bounded, endless log-linear scaling is not possible. On datasets like IN-1k and CUB2011 the ceiling effect necessarily creates sub-log-linear scaling. (2) We observe a deviation from log-linear scaling in the 1B to 3.5B image regime even without apparent ceiling effects on IN-{5k, 9k}.

These plots also illustrate an interesting effect of the hashtag vocabulary on the transfer task accuracy. On IN-1k, networks pretrained on the target-task-aligned 1.5k hashtags outperform those trained using a larger hashtag vocabulary, because the 1.5k hashtags were selected to match the ImageNet synsets. However, as the matching between hashtag vocabulary and target classes disappears and the visual variety in the transfer task increases, networks pretrained to recognize a larger number of hashtags increasingly outperform networks pretrained on fewer hashtags: on the IN-9k transfer task, the difference in accuracy between networks trained on 1.5k and those trained on 17k hashtags is ∼7%. In the supplemental material, we analyze the effect of weakly supervised pretraining on recognizing individual IN-1k classes in more detail.

The highest accuracies on val-IN-1k are 83.3% (source: IG-940M-1k) and 83.6% (source: IG-3.5B-17k), both with ResNeXt-101 32 × 16d. *These results are obtained by training a linear classifier on fixed features and yet are nearly as good as full network finetuning, demonstrating the effectiveness of the feature representation learned from hashtag prediction.* These results also have low variance: we pretrained the ResNeXt-101 32 × 16d architecture of two different random samples of 1B images and then trained linear classifiers on IN-{1k, 5k, 9k} finding a difference in top-1 accuracy of less than 0.1% in all cases.

---

[1] The maximum number of images available for the 1.5k hashtag set is 940M.

To test whether the above observations generalize to fine-grained classification, we repeated the experiments on the CUB2011 dataset, and show the results in Fig. 2, bottom right. The curves reveal that when training data is limited, the 1.5k hashtag dataset is better, but once the number of training images surpasses ~100M, the larger 17k hashtag dataset prevails, presumably because it represents a more diverse visual distribution with more fine-grained concepts.

What is the Effect of Hashtag Label Noise on Model Accuracy? A major difference between hashtag supervision and the labels provided in datasets such as ImageNet is that hashtag supervision is inherently *noisy*: users may apply hashtags that are irrelevant to the visual content of the image, or they may have left out hashtags that would have been visually relevant [33–35]. Because an exact characterization of this label noise is difficult, instead, we investigate the effect of injecting additional label noise on the accuracy of our networks. To do so, we pretrain ResNeXt-101 32×16d networks on a version of IG-1B-17k in which we randomly replaced $p\%$ of the hashtags by hashtags sampled from the marginal distribution over hashtags (excluding the tag to be replaced).

Figure 3 shows the ImageNet classification accuracy of the resulting networks for different numbers of classes at three levels, p, of artificial label noise as well as for a baseline in which no artificial label noise was added during pretraining. We only train the final linear classifier on the target task, because full finetuning may mask the damage caused by pretraining noise. *The results suggest that the networks are remarkably resilient against label noise:* a noise level of $p = 10\%$ leads to a loss of less than 1% in classification accuracy, and at $p = 25\%$ label noise, the reduction in accuracy is around 2%. These results suggest that label noise may be a limited issue if networks are trained on billions of images.

How Does the Sampling of Pretraining Data Impact Accuracy? Another difference between hashtag and ImageNet supervision is that, like in language modeling, hashtags are governed by a Zipfian distribution. Prior studies in language modeling found that resampling Zipfian distributions reduces the impact of the head of the word distribution on the overall training loss [36]. Motivated by this work, we perform experiments in which we evaluate three different types of data sampling in the Instagram pretraining: (1) a *natural* sampling in which we sample images and hashtags according to the distribution by which they appear on Instagram; (2) *square-root* sampling [36] in which we take the square-root of the head of the hashtag distribution, renormalize, and sample according to the resulting distribution (due to practical considerations, our implementation is slightly different; see supplemental material); and (3) *uniform* sampling in which we sample a hashtag uniformly at random, and then sample an image that has this hashtag associated to it uniformly at random [16]. (Aside from this experiment, we always pretrain on Instagram data using square-root sampling.) As before, we only train the final linear classifier on the target task.

Figure 4 displays classification accuracy as a function of the number of ImageNet classes for networks that were pretrained on IG-1B-17k using the three

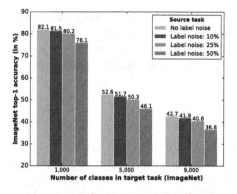

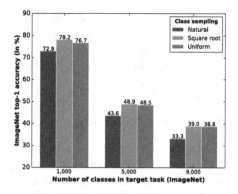

Fig. 3. Classification accuracy of ResNeXt-101 32 × 16d, pretrained on IG-1B-17k, on val-IN-{1k, 5k, 9k} at three levels of injected label noise. The no-label-noise baseline is trained on the original hashtags. Only the linear classifier is trained on the target task.

Fig. 4. Classification accuracy of ResNeXt-101 32 × 4d, pretrained on IG-1B-17k, on val-IN-{1k, 5k, 9k} for three different hashtag sampling strategies: natural sampling, uniform sampling, and square-root sampling. Only the linear classifier is trained on the target task.

sampling strategies. The results show that resampling of the hashtag distribution is important in order to obtain good transfer to ImageNet image-classification tasks: using uniform or square-root sampling leads to an accuracy improvement of 5 to 6% irrespective of the number of ImageNet classes in the transfer task. In line with prior results, the figure also shows that larger hashtag vocabularies lead to increasing accuracy improvements as the number of target classes grows.

With Billions of Images, is Transfer Learning Model-Capacity Bound? ow, we look at what happens when we train convolutional networks that are substantially larger than those typically used in recent studies (and our experiments so far). In particular, we use IG-940M-1.5k to pretrain ResNeXt-101 32 × 32d and ResNeXt-101 32×48d, which have 2.4× and 4.3× more add-mult FLOPs than ResNeXt-101 32 × 16d, respectively. Using these "super-sized" models improves val-IN-1k results over the 32 × 16d model from 84.2% top-1 accuracy to 85.1% and 85.4%, respectively (top-5 accuracy: from 97.2% to 97.5% and 97.6%).

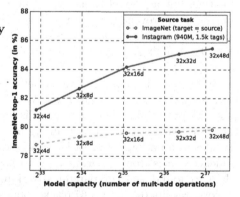

Fig. 5. Classification accuracy on val-IN-1k using ResNeXt-101 32×{4, 8 16, 32, 48}d with and without pretraining on the IG-940M-1.5k dataset.

By comparison, when training from scratch on IN-1k, top-1 accuracy saturates at around 79.6% with the 32×16d model and does not meaningfully increase by using larger models. These results, plotted in Fig. 5, indicate that with large-scale Instagram hashtag training, transfer-learning performance appears bottlenecked by model capacity.

3.2   Object Detection

We have looked at target tasks that require image classification, but we are also interested in observing if pretraining on Instagram hashtag data can improve object detection and instance segmentation tasks by finetuning networks on the COCO dataset [18]. We use Mask R-CNN [4,37] and experiment with ResNeXt-101 FPN [38] backbones of three different capacities (see Fig. 6).

We compare performance on the 2017 test-dev set using several different pre-trained networks. As baselines, we use IN-{1k, 5k} pretraining (IN-9k performs no better than IN-5k) and compare them to IG-940M-1k and IG-1B-17k. For the largest model (32×16d) we also include results for IG-3.5B-17k. We use standard settings [37] for end-to-end Mask R-CNN training with one exception: for the Instagram pretrained models we found it necessary to perform grid search for the finetuning learning rate on the validation set. We found that models pretrained on the Instagram data require finetuning learning rates that are $\sim$4–10$\times$ lower than ImageNet pretrained models (see supplemental material). This finding illustrates that finetuning recipes developed for ImageNet pretrained models do not transfer to new pretraining sets: a larger amount of pretraining data implies the need for lower finetuning learning rates.

Figure 6 shows two interesting trends. First, we observe that *when using large amounts of pretraining data, detection is model capacity bound:* with the lowest capacity model (32×4d), the gains from larger datasets are small or even negative, but as model capacity increases the larger pretraining datasets yield consistent improvements. We need even larger models to take advantage of the large-scale pretraining data. The second trend we observe comes from comparing COCO's default AP metric (average precision averaged over intersection-over-union (IoU) overlap thresholds 0.5:0.95) to AP@50 (average precision computed at IoU threshold 0.5 only). The former emphasizes precise localization while the later allows for looser localization. We observe that the improvement over IN-{1k, 5k} pretraining from IG-1B-1k is much larger in terms of AP@50. Thus, the gains from Instagram pretraining may be primarily due to improved object classification performance, rather than spatial localization performance. Further evidence comes from experiments with keypoint detection using Mask R-CNN, where we found that compared to IN-1k pretraining, IG-1B-1k pretraining leads to worse results (65.3% vs. 67.0% keypoint AP). These two findings suggest that pretraining for Instagram hashtag classification may reduce spatial localization performance while improving classification.

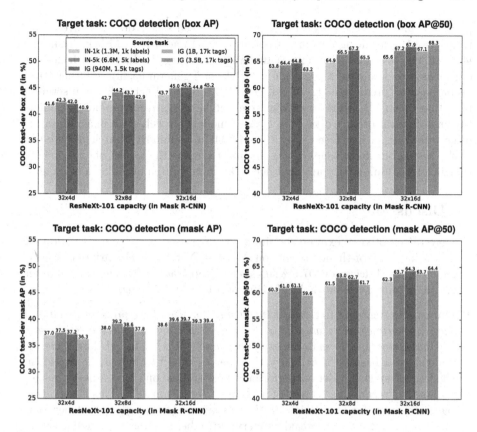

Fig. 6. Transfer to object detection and instance segmentation with Mask R-CNN. We compare ResNeXt-101 FPN backbones of three different capacities using a variety of source pretraining tasks. Higher is better.

4 Related Work

Our study is part of a larger body of work on training convolutional networks on large, weakly supervised image datasets. Sun et al. [17] train convolutional networks on the JFT-300M of 300 million weakly supervised images. Our Instagram datasets are an order of magnitude larger than JFT-300M, and collecting them required much less manual annotation work (see Sect. 2.1). Due to the larger training set size and the use of better network architectures, we obtain substantially higher accuracies on transfer tasks: e.g., we obtain 85.4% top-1 accuracy on ImageNet-1k, compared to 79.2% reported in [17].

Other prior studies [16,39] trained convolutional networks to predict words or n-grams in comments on a collection of 100 million Flickr photos and corresponding comments [40]. Word or n-gram supervision is weaker than hashtag supervision because it is less structured, as reflected in the poor transfer of features to ImageNet reported in [16]. Other work [33,35] also trained networks to predict hashtags on the Flickr dataset but, unlike our study, does not investigate transfer of the resulting networks to other tasks. In addition to Flickr hashtags, [41] trained hard mixture of expert models on food-related Instagram hashtags; our focus is on standard recognition networks and general hashtags. Other studies on hashtag prediction [42] do not train convolutional networks from scratch, but train linear classifiers to predict relevant hashtags from pre-defined image features. Several other works have trained models on web-scale image data for other purposes, such as face recognition [43,44] and similarity search [45,46], but to the best of our knowledge, we are the first to report the results of experiments that involve training convolutional networks from scratch on billions of images.

5   Discussion

We have attempted to explore the limits of supervised pretraining. In addition to producing state-of-the-art results on the ImageNet-1k benchmark task (85.4% single-crop, top-1 accuracy; 97.6% single-crop, top-5 accuracy) and several other vision tasks, our study has led to four important observations:

1. Our results suggests that, *whilst increasing the size of the pretraining dataset may be worthwhile, it may be at least as important to select a label space for the source task to match that of the target task.* We found that networks trained on a hashtag vocabulary that was designed to match the classes in the ImageNet-1k dataset outperformed those trained on twice as many images without such careful selection of hashtags (Fig. 2, top left). This observation paves the way for the design of "label-space engineering" approaches that aim to optimally select (weakly supervised) label sets for a particular target task. Such label-space engineering may be much more fruitful than further increasing the scale of the data on which models are trained.

2. In line with prior work [16,17], *we observe that current network architectures are underfitting when trained on billions of images.* Whilst such underfitting does lead to very high robustness to noise in our hashtag targets (Fig. 3), our results do suggest that accuracy improvements on target tasks may be obtained by further increases of the capacity of our networks (Fig. 2). Capacity may be increased, for instance, by increasing the number of layers and the number of filters per layer of existing architectures or by mixtures-of-experts [41] (using model parallelization across GPUs). However, it is not unthinkable that some of the design choices that were made in current network architectures are too tailored to ImageNet-1k classification, and need to be revisited when training on billions of images with hashtag supervision.

3. Our results also underline the importance of increasing the visual variety that we consider in our benchmark tasks. They show that *the differences in the quality of visual features become much more pronounced if these features are evaluated on tasks with a larger visual variety.* For instance, we find that the accuracy difference between models pretrained using two different vocabularies increases as the number of target classes increases (Fig. 2): if we would have only evaluated our models on ImageNet-1k, we would have concluded

they learned visual features of similar quality, whereas results on ImageNet-9k show that one model learns substantially better features than the other. We believe evaluation on more ImageNet classes is a good step towards a more comprehensive assessment of visual recognition models.

4. Results from transferring our models to object detection, instance segmentation, and keypoint detection tasks suggestion that *training for large-scale hashtag prediction improves classification while at the same time possibly harming localization performance*. This opens a future direction of modifying large-scale, weakly supervised pretraining tasks to better suit the localization needs of important target tasks like detection and human pose estimation.

In closing, we reflect on the remarkable fact that training for hashtag prediction, *without the need for additional manual annotation or data cleaning*, works at all. We believe our study illustrates the potential of natural or "wild" data compared to the traditional approach of manually designing and annotating datasets.

Acknowledgements. We thank Matthijs Douze, Aapo Kyrola, Andrew Dye, Jerry Pan, Kevin Wilfong, Martin Englund, and Zeki Yalniz for helpful discussions and support.

References

1. Girshick, R., Donahue, J., Darrell, T., Malik, J.: Rich feature hierarchies for accurate object detection and semantic segmentation. In: CVPR (2014)
2. Donahue, J., et al.: DeCAF: a deep convolutional activation feature for generic visual recognition. arXiv:1310.1531 (2013)
3. Zeiler, M.D., Fergus, R.: Visualizing and understanding convolutional neural networks. In: ECCV (2014)
4. He, K., Gkioxari, G., Dollar, P., Girshick, R.: Mask R-CNN. In: ICCV (2017)
5. Long, J., Shelhamer, E., Darrell, T.: Fully convolutional networks for semantic segmentation. In: CVPR (2015)
6. Zhao, H., Shi, J., Qi, X., Wang, X., Jia, J.: Pyramid scene parsing network. In: CVPR (2017)
7. Cao, Z., Simon, T., Wei, S.E., Sheikh, Y.: Realtime multi-person 2D pose estimation using part affinity fields. In: CVPR (2017)
8. Papandreou, G., et al.: Towards accurate multi-person pose estimation in the wild. In: CVPR (2017)
9. Carreira, J., Zisserman, A.: Quo vadis, action recognition? a new model and the kinetics dataset. In: CVPR (2017)
10. Eigen, D., Fergus, R.: Predicting depth, surface normals and semantic labels with a common multi-scale convolutional architecture. In: ICCV (2015)
11. Russakovsky, O., et al.: ImageNet large scale visual recognition challenge. IJCV **115**, 211–252 (2015)
12. Agrawal, P., Girshick, R., Malik, J.: Analyzing the performance of multilayer neural networks for object recognition. In: Fleet, D., Pajdla, T., Schiele, B., Tuytelaars, T. (eds.) ECCV 2014 Part VII. LNCS, vol. 8695, pp. 329–344. Springer, Cham (2014). https://doi.org/10.1007/978-3-319-10584-0_22
13. Huh, M., Agrawal, P., Efros, A.: What makes ImageNet good for transfer learning? arXiv:1608.08614 (2016)

14. Zhou, B., Lapedriza, A., Khosla, A., Oliva, A., Torralba, A.: Places: a 10 million image database for scene recognition. PAMI **40**, 1452–1464 (2017)
15. Xie, S., Girshick, R., Dollar, P., Tu, Z., He, K.: Aggregated residual transformations for deep neural networks. In: CVPR (2017)
16. Joulin, A., van der Maaten, L., Jabri, A., Vasilache, N.: Learning visual features from large weakly supervised data. In: Leibe, B., Matas, J., Sebe, N., Welling, M. (eds.) ECCV 2016 Part VII. LNCS, vol. 9911, pp. 67–84. Springer, Cham (2016). https://doi.org/10.1007/978-3-319-46478-7_5
17. Sun, C., Shrivastava, A., Singh, S., Gupta, A.: Revisiting unreasonable effectiveness of data in deep learning era. In: Proceedings of ICCV (2017)
18. Lin, T.-Y., et al.: Microsoft COCO: common objects in context. In: Fleet, D., Pajdla, T., Schiele, B., Tuytelaars, T. (eds.) ECCV 2014 Part V. LNCS, vol. 8693, pp. 740–755. Springer, Cham (2014). https://doi.org/10.1007/978-3-319-10602-1_48
19. Goyal, P., et al.: Accurate, large minibatch SGD: training ImageNet in 1 hour. In: arXiv:1706.02677 (2017)
20. WordNet: About WordNet (2010). http://wordnet.princeton.edu
21. Welinder, P., et al.: Caltech-UCSD Birds 200. Technical report, Caltech (2010)
22. Gordo, A., Almazan, J., Revaud, J., Larlus, D.: Deep image retrieval: learning global representations for image search. In: arXiv:1604.01325 (2016)
23. Tolias, G., Sicre, R., Jegou, H.: Particular object retrieval with integral max-pooling of CNN activations. In: ICLR (2016)
24. He, K., Zhang, X., Ren, S., Sun, J.: Deep residual learning for image recognition. In: CVPR (2016)
25. Huang, G., Liu, Z., Weinberger, K., van der Maaten, L.: Densely connected convolutional networks. In: CVPR. (2017)
26. Szegedy, C., Ioffe, S., Vanhoucke, V., Alemi, A.: Inception-V4, inception-ResNet and the impact of residual connections on learning. In: arXiv:1602.07261 (2016)
27. Ioffe, S., Szegedy, C.: Batch normalization: accelerating deep network training by reducing internal covariate shift. In: ICML (2015)
28. He, K., Zhang, X., Ren, S., Sun, J.: Delving deep into rectifiers: surpassing human-level performance on ImageNet classification. In: ICCV (2015)
29. Pathak, D., Girshick, R., Dollár, P., Darrell, T., Hariharan, B.: Learning features by watching objects move. In: CVPR (2017)
30. Deng, J., Dong, W., Socher, R., Li, L.J., Li, K., Fei-Fei, L.: ImageNet: a large-scale hierarchical image database. In: CVPR (2009)
31. Zoph, B., Vasudevan, V., Shlens, J., Le, Q.: Learning transferable architectures for scalable image recognition. In: arXiv:1707.07012 (2017)
32. Stock, P., Cisse, M.: Convnets and ImageNet beyond accuracy: explanations, bias detection, adversarial examples and model criticism. In: arXiv:1711.11443 (2017)
33. Izadinia, H., Russell, B., Farhadi, A., Hoffman, M., Hertzmann, A.: Deep classifiers from image tags in the wild. In: Multimedia COMMONS (2015)
34. Misra, I., Zitnick, C.L., Mitchell, M., Girshick, R.: Seeing through the human reporting bias: visual classifiers from noisy human-centric labels. In: CVPR (2016)
35. Veit, A., Nickel, M., Belongie, S., van der Maaten, L.: Separating self-expression and visual content in hashtag supervision. In: arXiv 1711.09825 (2017)
36. Mikolov, T., Sutskever, I., Chen, K., Corrado, G., Dean, J.: Distributed representations of words and phrases and their compositionality. In: NIPS (2013)
37. Girshick, R., Radosavovic, I., Gkioxari, G., Dollár, P., He, K.: Detectron (2018). https://github.com/facebookresearch/detectron

38. Lin, T.Y., Dollár, P., Girshick, R., He, K., Hariharan, B., Belongie, S.: Feature pyramid networks for object detection. In: CVPR (2017)
39. Li, A., Jabri, A., Joulin, A., van der Maaten, L.: Learning visual n-grams from web data. In: Proceedings of ICCV (2017)
40. Thomee, B., et al.: YFCC100M: the new data in multimedia research. Commun. ACM **59**(2), 64–73 (2016)
41. Gross, S., Ranzato, M., Szlam, A.: Hard mixtures of experts for large scale weakly supervised vision. In: CVPR (2017)
42. Denton, E., Weston, J., Paluri, M., Bourdev, L., Fergus, R.: User conditional hashtag prediction for images. In: Proceedings of KDD, pp. 1731–1740 (2015)
43. Schroff, F., Kalenichenko, D., Philbin, J.: FaceNet: a unified embedding for face recognition and clustering. In: CVPR (2015)
44. Taigman, Y., Yang, M., Ranzato, M., Wolf, L.: Web-scale training for face identification. In: CVPR (2015)
45. Johnson, J., Douze, M., Jégou, H.: Billion-scale similarity search with GPUs. arXiv preprint arXiv:1702.08734 (2017)
46. Stewénius, H., Gunderson, S.H., Pilet, J.: Size matters: exhaustive geometric verification for image retrieval accepted for ECCV 2012. In: Fitzgibbon, A., Lazebnik, S., Perona, P., Sato, Y., Schmid, C. (eds.) ECCV 2012 Part II. LNCS, pp. 674–687. Springer, Heidelberg (2012). https://doi.org/10.1007/978-3-642-33709-3_48

Egocentric Activity Prediction via Event Modulated Attention

Yang Shen, Bingbing Ni[⊠], Zefan Li, and Ning Zhuang

SJTU-UCLA Joint Center for Machine Perception and Inference,
Shanghai Jiao Tong University, Shanghai, China
{cohakuel,bingbingni,leezf,ningzhuang}@sjtu.edu.cn

Abstract. Predicting future activities from an egocentric viewpoint is of particular interest in assisted living. However, state-of-the-art egocentric activity understanding techniques are mostly NOT capable of predictive tasks, as their synchronous processing architecture performs poorly in either modeling event dependency or pruning temporal redundant features. This work explicitly addresses these issues by proposing an asynchronous gaze-event driven attentive activity prediction network. This network is built on a gaze-event extraction module inspired by the fact that gaze moving in/out of a certain object most probably indicates the occurrence/ending of a certain activity. The extracted gaze events are input to: (1) an asynchronous module which reasons about the temporal dependency between events and (2) a synchronous module which softly attends to informative temporal durations for more compact and discriminative feature extraction. Both modules are seamlessly integrated for collaborative prediction. Extensive experimental results on egocentric activity prediction as well as recognition well demonstrate the effectiveness of the proposed method.

Keywords: Egocentric video · Prediction · Event · Gaze · Attention Asynchronous

1 Introduction

Egocentric (first-person viewpoint) activity analysis [8,28,32] is of particular interest for assisted living. Previous methods [9,19,22] mainly focus on activity recognition (*i.e.,* to classify those already occurred activities into different classes); however, for a realistic application, being able to predict an activity before its occurrence is more important, especially in the smart home scenario. For a certain task, the occurrence of activities is usually in order, so modeling the relationship between continuous activities can help to predict the future activity. However, the task of egocentric activity prediction is challenging for most of the existing egocentric methods mainly due to their synchronous processing architecture's limitation in both modeling event dependency and pruning temporal redundant features. On the one hand, the dependency between activities are

© Springer Nature Switzerland AG 2018
V. Ferrari et al. (Eds.): ECCV 2018, LNCS 11206, pp. 202–217, 2018.
https://doi.org/10.1007/978-3-030-01216-8_13

usually of temporal dependency (and asynchronous). For instance, an incoming activity such as scoop peanut (with) knife might depend on the occurrence of the other activities such as open peanut or "take knife", which might occur several seconds (100 frames) ago. However, current methods such as LSTM-based approaches [2, 4, 29] (*i.e.*, they usually model the dependency no longer than 10 frames) cannot model such a long time dependency. In other words, to predict an egocentric activity, a good model should make use of the previously occurred related events with very long range temporal contexts (i.e., asynchronous dependency). In this paper, inspired by the fact that gaze moving in/out of a certain object closely corresponds to the occurrence/ending of a certain activity, the event is defined as gaze moving in/out of a certain object. On the other hand, most video data recorded by the egocentric camera are redundant which not only convey no useful information for predicting the subsequent event but also induce harmful noise for the task. For example, given a sequence including put cereal, take milk and open milk, the next activity is pour milk (to) bowl, in this case, put cereal has little correlation with the activity to be predicted. So it is redundant and should be omitted. In this sense, a mechanism is required to temporally *attend to* those informative frame features for a higher performance activity predictor.

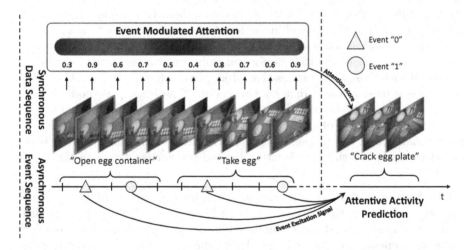

Fig. 1. Motivation overview. Long term asynchronous dependency is of great importance in activity prediction task. Thus we propose a two-branch architecture to deal with both asynchronous event's mutual excitation and synchronous action information. Moreover, each video sequence contains both important and redundant frames. The event modulated attention module is designed to prune redundant features and get a better representation of the sequence.

To explicitly address these issues, this work proposes an asynchronous gaze-event driven attentive activity prediction framework, as illustrated in Fig. 1. We construct a two-stream asynchronous/synchronous mixed network driven by gaze event. The asynchronous sub-network is constructed based on a Hawkes process model [12], which directly models inter-relationship between different events situated with arbitrary temporal distance. The synchronous sub-network extracts frame-wise deep object and gaze features, and is instantly triggered by gaze events, to output the attended temporal span of informative object/gaze features, yielding discriminative local feature representations for event prediction. Both sub-networks seamlessly collaborate with each other for future activity prediction, and are also trained end-to-end. Extensive experimental results on egocentric activity prediction as well as recognition well demonstrate the effectiveness of the proposed method.

2   Related Work

Egocentric Video Analysis: Currently, egocentric video analysis mainly focuses on activity recognition [8,28,32]. CNN was used as an appearance feature extractor in [26,27], similar to third-person vision activity recognition research. [22] proposed a two-stream network using CNN to analyze appearance and motion information separately. Gaze location is an important cue in egocentric video analysis. Gaze allocation models were usually derived from static picture viewing studies. This has led to methods for computation of image saliency [14] which use low-level image features such as color contrast or motion to provide a good explanation of how humans orient their attention. However, those low-level saliency models performed worse in fixation location prediction compared with those methods based on object-level information [3,6]. Gaze location was first used as a feature in [9]. Fathi et al. [8] proposed a method modeling the spatio-temporal relationship between gaze, object and activity label by capturing the distribution of visual features and objects in the vicinity of the gaze point. Zhang et al. [31] proposed a generative adversarial neural network based model to anticipate the gaze location beyond the current frame to the future frame.

Event Sequence Analysis: Recurrent neural network [7] was proposed to process sequential data with correlation. Long Short-Term Memory recurrent network (LSTM) is the most successful recurrent neural network architecture which learns the dependency among frames by its special unit structure and it solves the difficulty of training RNN such as explosion and descent vanishing. LSTM was firstly proposed in [13] to comply long-range learning. LSTM was utilized to learn features of 9-frame video clips to realize action classification [2]. LSTM was combined with convolutional neural network (CNN) to further realize video classification [25]. Besides standard time series modeling and prediction of RNN, asynchronous series is also an input to RNN to encode long-range event dependency. Du et al. [5] used the asynchronous event sequence with timestamps about event occurrence as the input to RNNs. Xiao et al. [30] took an RNN perspective to point process, which is an effective mathematical tool to model event data, on the failure prediction for ATMs maintenance. Our work is the first work to integrate both time series and asynchronous series to egocentric video analysis.

Attention Mechanism: The attention mechanism has a great role in sequence learning by adding a model in encoding/decoding section to change the weight of the targeted data. Mnih et al. [23] used an attention-based RNN model to extract information from an image or video only with a sequence of regions selected. Jang et al. [15] proposed a dual-LSTM based method with both spatial and temporal attention, extended Visual Question Answering to the video domain. Liu et al. [21] added the quality score learning to the set-level person re-identification. In this paper, we propose a new event modulated attention triggered by gaze event to deal with the redundant frames.

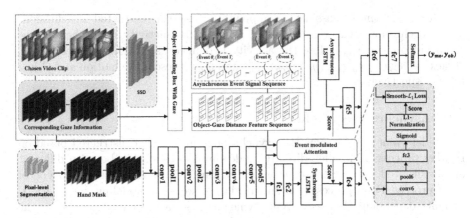

Fig. 2. Overview of our approach. We propose to combine the time-varying features and long-range dependency to predict the future activity. Time series sequence (the lower part) and event sequence (the upper part) can be modeled synergically. Besides, the Temporal Attention Module outputs a sequence of attention scores to decide which frames to attend. Finally, both attentive synchronous and asynchronous features are sent to a softmax classifier to predict the ensuing activity $\mathbf{y}_{\hat{act}} = (y_{mo}, y_{ob})$.

3 Methodology

State-of-the-art egocentric activity researches, mostly focusing on classification tasks [8,9,19,22], are not capable of predictive tasks, as their synchronous processing architecture performs poorly in modeling event dependency. Another drawback is that, synchronous frames contain lots of redundant information and harmful noise.

Motivated by above limitations, we propose an asynchronous gaze-event driven attentive activity prediction network. More specifically, given a short video clip of N frames $X = \{x_1, x_2, \ldots, x_N\}$, our network predicts the ensuing activity: $\mathbf{y}_{\hat{act}}$. The architecture of the entire network is illustrated in Fig. 2.

The proposed network extracts both synchronous and asynchronous information. Also, the attention mechanism is applied, to focus on the more informative frame features for a higher performance activity predictor. The whole structure mainly consists of three modules:

- **The Asynchronous Module**, using a gaze-event driven LSTM, taking sequences of event data as the input triggered by gaze, deals with temporal dependency between events with arbitrary distance.
- **The Synchronous Module**, using a time series LSTM, taking the hand mask and gaze location information as the input, deals with synchronous frame information, i.e., instant feature-event relationship.
- **Event Modulated Attention**, designed as a convolutional network, learns soft attention scores to temporally attend to those informative frame features.

Then a softmax classifier is applied to fuse the extracted synchronous and asynchronous features to predict the ensuring activity (right behind the given video clip): $\hat{\mathbf{y}_{act}}$. Here the activity is defined as motion + objects (e.g., "crack" + "egg"). $\hat{\mathbf{y}_{act}} = (y_{mo}, y_{ob})$, y_{mo} and y_{ob} represent the motion and object label, respectively.

3.1   Asynchronous Module

To model event dependency, the asynchronous module is constructed based on Hawkes process [12], which directly models inter-relationship between different events situated with arbitrary temporal distance. Hawkes process is a type of point process. Point process is a principled framework for modeling event data [1] and interdependency between events, which lies with arbitrary distance along the temporal axis. The conditional intensity function is originally defined as follow:

$$\lambda(t) = \lim_{\Delta t \to 0} \frac{E(N(t + \Delta t) - N(t)|H_t)}{\Delta t} = \frac{E(dN(t)|H_t)}{dt}, \tag{1}$$

where $\lambda(t)$ is the rate of the occurrence of a new event conditioned on the history H_t, for a short time interval $[t, t + dt)$. $E(dN(t)|H_t)$ represents the expectation of the number of events happened in the interval $[t, t + dt)$ given the historical observations H_t.

In Hawkes process, the conditional intensity function is defined by a specific parameterization:

$$\lambda_{Hawkes}(t) = \mu(t) + \sum_{t_i < t} \delta(t, t_i), \tag{2}$$

where $\delta(t, t_i)$ is the time-decaying kernel. $\mu(t)$ represents the background effect. $\sum_{t_i < t} \delta(t, t_i)$ is the excitation effect from history events, modeled by a trigger term. Hawkes process can help to model the excitation relationship of the happened events and the coming events, which is important for our prediction task.

Gaze information is significant in egocentric video analysis, for eyes usually lead to the next activity before the hands. Gaze movement is an important cue for the ensuing activity analysis. Thus, we define the asynchronous events triggered by gaze (examples can be seen in Fig. 3):

- Event '**0**' occurs when the gaze point moves into the target object in a certain frame of the video clip.
- Event '**1**' occurs when the gaze point leaves the target object in a certain frame of the video clip.

As can be seen in the upper part of Fig. 2, these two types of events are captured to get an asynchronous event signal sequence. To capture these asynchronous events, following steps are adopted:

Firstly, for an egocentric video dataset, a single shot multibox detector (SSD) [20] is trained to give bounding boxes for all the objects in the dataset. Secondly, sliding windows are used to incept small video clips from the whole dataset, with each clip consisting of 90–120 frames. Clips contain too few or too many events should be removed because too few events cannot provide enough information for prediction while those containing too many events indicates the excessively high moving frequency of the gaze point, which also has a negative influence in prediction. The rest video clips constitute the training sets. For each video clip, the detected object bounding box information is combined with the corresponding gaze information to generate the asynchronous event signal sequence:

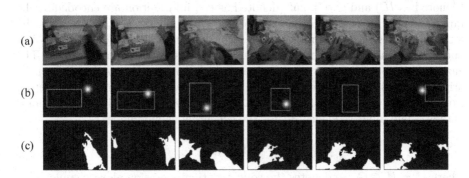

Fig. 3. Data examples of GTEA Gaze dataset. (a) Original video images; (b) the relationship between gaze movement and the object being manipulated, gaze moving in/out is signed as '0/1'; (c) the hand masks we get from the pixel-level segmentation network [33].

$$Z = \{z_i\}_{i=1}^{N} = \{z_1, z_2, \ldots, z_N\}, \tag{3}$$

where $z_i \in \{-1, 0, 1\}$ denotes the event type in the i-th frame:

$$z_i = \begin{cases} 0 & \text{event '0' occurs in the i-th frame;} \\ 1 & \text{event '1' occurs in the i-th frame;} \\ -1 & \text{neither event '0' or '1' occurs.} \end{cases} \tag{4}$$

Suppose there are precisely m types objects in the dataset, labeled from 1 to m. For the i-th frame in a video clip, with object and gaze-point information, we define the object-gaze distance feature sequence:

$$d_i = \begin{bmatrix} d_{i1}, d_{i2}, ..., d_{im} \end{bmatrix}^T, \tag{5}$$

where d_i denotes the euclidean distance between the gaze point and the center of the i-th object. $d_i = -1$ when the i-th object fails to be detected in this frame.

For a chosen video clip with N frames: $X = \{x_1, x_2, ..., x_N\}$, the corresponding input sequence X^a for the asynchronous module is:

$$X^a = \{x_i^a\}_{i=1}^N, \tag{6}$$

where $x_i^a = \begin{bmatrix} z_i \\ d_i \end{bmatrix} = \begin{bmatrix} z_i, d_{i1}, d_{i2}, ..., d_{im} \end{bmatrix}^T.$

3.2   Synchronous Sequence Module

As shown in Eq. 2, besides history event excitation, the background excitation $\mu(t)$ is also an important cue for event modeling. In our method, the background excitation is modeled by a time series LSTM (the synchronous module). The lower part of Fig. 2 detailedly describes the structure of the synchronous module.

For each frame x_i in a chosen video clip ($X = \{x_1, x_2, ..., x_N\}$), the hand mask (denoted as H_i) and gaze point (denoted as G_i) information are encoded as the input features for the synchronous module. The hand mask H_i is extracted by a pixel-level segmentation network [33], which adopts a low resolution FCN32-s and uses the sum of per-pixel two-class softmax losses as the loss function. The gaze-point information is a 2D coordinate which denotes the gaze location in the original frames. To enhance the gaze information, we map a normal distribution (mean value $\mu = 0$ and variance $\sigma^2 = 0.2$) to the gaze point, and get a gaze-point map G_i. The input sequence X^s for the synchronous module is:

$$X^s = \{x_i^s\}_{i=1}^N, \tag{7}$$

where $x_i^s = H_i \oplus G_i$, $\oplus$ denotes the concatenation operation along channel axis.

3.3   Temporal Attention for Two-Stream LSTM

Event Modulated Attention: For a video clip, some frames may have little correlation with the activity to be predicted, which include harmful noise and should be omitted. Our hypothesis is that frames between event '0' and event '1' deserve more attention (frames start from event '0' and end in event '1'). For example, as shown in Fig. 1, the asynchronous event signal sequence is $Z = \{-1, 0, -1, 1, -1, 0, -1, -1, 1, -1\}$. We can generate the binary attention mask: $M = \{0, 1, 1, 1, 0, 1, 1, 1, 1, 0\}$, which highlights the useful information (signed as '1') and drops the useless frames (signed as '0').

However, directly applying binary attention mask leads to numerical problems in latter LSTM cells. Thus we propose **Event Modulated Attention** (in Fig. 2) to learn a soft attention score. This module is a convolutional network with input features extracted from the pool5 layer of AlexNet. The output spatial is $256 \times 6 \times 6$. The convolution part contains a convolutional layer with kernel size 3×3, stride 1, 256 output-channels and a mean-pooling layer with the stride of 2 and kernel size of 2×2. Then a fully connected layer follows to generate a $N \times 1$ raw score $\tilde{q} = [\tilde{q}_1, \tilde{q}_2, \ldots, \tilde{q}_N]$. $\tilde{q}$ is activated and normalized by a sigmoid layer and a group L1-normalization layer to get the final attention score $q = [q_1, q_2, \ldots, q_N]$. We use the binary attention mask M generated from the corresponding asynchronous event signal sequence Z as the supervised signal for this modular. To avoid gradient vanishing problem of $L1$-Loss, we apply the smooth $L1$-Loss [10]:

$$smooth_{L1}(x) = \begin{cases} 0.5x^2 & |x| < 1 \\ |x| & |x| \geqslant 1. \end{cases} \tag{8}$$

Finally, the attention score q functions as a feature score to determine the importance of different frame features.

LSTM Block: LSTM [13] is a powerful tool in dealing with the sequential input. Having input sequence: $X = \{x_1, x_2, \ldots, x_N\}$, LSTM generates the hidden states $\{h_1, h_2, \ldots, h_N\}$ and output a sequence [7]. A basic LSTM block include three gates, the input gate i_t, the forget gate f_t and the output gate o_t, it updates as follows [11]:

$$\begin{aligned} i_t &= \sigma(W_i x_t + U_i h_{t-1} + V_i c_{t-1} + b_i) \\ f_t &= \sigma(W_f x_t + U_f h_{t-1} + V_f c_{t-1} + b_f) \\ c_t &= f_c c_{t-1} + i_t * tanh(W_c x_t + U_c h_{t-1} + b_c) \\ o_t &= \sigma(W_o x_t + U_o h_{t-1} + V_o c_{t-1} + b_o) \\ h_t &= o_t * tanh(c_t) \end{aligned} \tag{9}$$

where c_t is a single memory cell. σ means sigmoid function and $*$ represents the element-wise multiplication operator. W, U, V are the weighted matrices and b is the bias vector. x_t and h_t represent the input feature vector and the hidden output vector. The update equation of c_t is composed of two parts: a fraction of the previous cell state c_{t-1} and a new input state created.

Two-Stream LSTM: In the proposed framework, we design two individual LSTM modules: the synchronous module, with its units aligned with the timestamps of a time series, and the asynchronous module, whose units are aligned with events. As shown in Fig. 2, two LSTM modules are designed as follow:

- To capture the long-range dependency over history with arbitrary time intervals, the asynchronous part takes the object-gaze distance and event signal as its input.
- The synchronous part takes the hand mask and gaze-point information as its input and is designed to timely track the temporal information.

Two fully connected layers are established after LSTM. The whole network is supervised by a Softmax Loss:

$$L_{class} = \frac{1}{N} \sum_{i=1}^{N} -\boldsymbol{y}_i \log \hat{\boldsymbol{y}}_i - (1 - \boldsymbol{y}_i) \log(1 - \hat{\boldsymbol{y}}_i), \tag{10}$$

where N is the number of training samples, $\boldsymbol{y}_i$ represents the ground truth and $\hat{\boldsymbol{y}}_i$ is our predicted label.

4   Experiments

In this section we briefly introduce the datasets (Sect. 4.1), then analyze the temporal dependency between activities (Sect. 4.2) and present experimental results of three tasks of activity prediction (Sect. 4.3), recognition (Sect. 4.4) and robustness analysis (Sect. 4.5).

4.1   Datasets

In our work, we use two public datasets: GTEA Gaze [9] and GTEA Gaze+ [8]: Both of them contain the subjects' gaze location in each frame and the activity labels.

- GTEA Gaze (Gaze): This dataset contains 17 sequences of meal preparation activities performed by 14 different subjects, with the resolution of 640×480.
- GTEA Gaze+ (Gaze+): This dataset contains 37 sequences performed by 6 subjects of preparing 7 types of meals, with a higher resolution of 960×720.

4.2   Temporal Dependency Between Activities

We extend the typical egocentric activity recognition task to a future activity prediction task, for there exists strong relevance between the neighboring activities (for example, after the activities take milk and open milk, there is a great possibility that pour milk will happen).

To statistically analyze the temporal dependency between neighbouring activities, we collect 6 sequences of making north American breakfast in Gaze+ and 5 sequences of making sandwich in Gaze. Neighboring activity distribution is shown in Fig. 4, the vertical coordinate denotes the current activity and the horizontal coordinate denotes the next activity. Each row of this matrix represents the occurrence probability percentage of the next activity after the current activity. Our hypothesis is that there exists temporal dependency between neighbouring activities. To verify this, we apply the Spearman Correlation Analysis. The Spearman correlation coefficient is defined as the Pearson correlation coefficient between the ranked variables, and it is appropriate for both continuous and

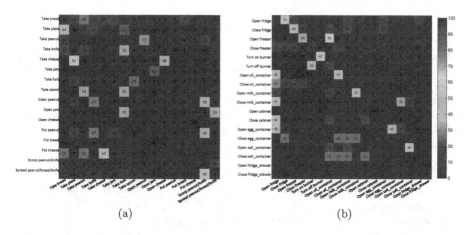

(a)   (b)

Fig. 4. Statistics on neighboring activities, best viewed in color. (a) Gaze 16 classes; (b) Gaze+ 18 classes. The vertical coordinate denotes the current activity and the horizontal coordinate denotes the next activity. Each row of this matrix represents the occurrence probability percentage of the next activity after the current activity.

discrete ordinal variables [18]. The Spearman correlation coefficient is computed as follows:

$$\rho = \frac{\sum_i (x_i - \overline{x})(y_i - \overline{y})}{\sqrt{\sum_i (x_i - \overline{x})^2 (y_i - \overline{y})^2}}, i = 1, 2, ..., N, \tag{11}$$

where x_i and y_i are the original data, $\overline{x}$ and $\overline{y}$ are the mathematical expectation. The Spearman correlation coefficient for Gaze+ is 0.43 and the corresponding p-value is $6.97 \times 10^{-7} \ll 0.05$. According to Hypothesis Testing theory, we can strongly believe that there exists moderate dependency between neighboring activities. Thus it is reasonable for us to model the dependency between neighbouring activities to predict the future activity.

4.3 Activity Prediction

We use 13 sequences for training and 4 sequences for test on GTEA Gaze, 30 sequences for training and 7 sequences for test on GTEA Gaze+. The test set includes each type of meal preparation. As we discussed in Sect. 3.1, we use sliding windows to extract small video clips (1528 for Gaze, 4151 for Gaze+) as our training samples, with each containing 90–120 frames. Also, we get the hand mask, event signal sequence and object-gaze distance feature sequence during data preparation. The training stage includes the following steps: (i) train the synchronous branch separately (Time series LSTM, lower part in Fig. 2, with pre-trained AlexNet [17].) without attention scores and asynchronous features. (ii) train the asynchronous branch separately (Event sequence LSTM, upper part in Fig. 2) without attention scores and synchronous features. (iii) train the whole network with attention module and both branches.

Table 1. Performance for activity prediction and recognition. (a) Results from Fathi et al. [8] using the observed gaze; (b) Two-stream CNN results with object-cnn, SVM-fusion and joint training [22]; (c) 2D and 3D Ego ConvNet results (**H**: Hand mask, **C**: Camera/Head motion, **M**: Saliency map) [28]. (d) Results of our method, for activity recognition, we use the adjusted network with two synchronous models. Gaze (RB) and Gaze+ (RB) represent the sub-datasets re-annotated by the Rubicon Boundaries labeling method.

	Methods	Prediction		Recognition			
		Gaze	Gaze+	Gaze	Gaze+	Gaze(RB)	Gaze+(RB)
[8]	Observed gaze	-	-	0.47	0.51	0.48	0.52
[22]	Object-cnn	0.442	0.438	0.471	0.464	0.487	0.473
	Motion+object-svm	0.192	0.264	0.284	0.347	0.305	0.352
	Motion+object-joint	0.576	0.601	**0.624**	0.664	0.636	0.668
[28]	H+C+M(2D)	0.437	0.462	0.508	0.534	0.523	0.538
	H+C+M(3D)	0.492	0.504	0.525	0.542	0.536	0.553
	H+C+M(2D+3D)	0.514	0.537	0.549	0.581	0.560	0.589
Ours	Time series LSTM	0.581	0.614	0.619	**0.671**	**0.654**	**0.686**
	Event sequence LSTM	0.612	0.659	-	-	-	-
	Fusion LSTMs	0.632	0.674	-	-	-	-
	Attention based LSTMs	**0.648**	**0.687**	-	-	-	-

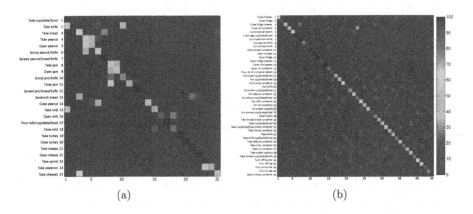

(a)   (b)

Fig. 5. Confusion matrix of our proposed method for activity prediction, best viewed in color. (a) Gaze 25 classes; (b) Gaze+ 44 classes.

For each state, we use the same training strategy: stochastic gradient descent with momentum $= 0.9$, weight decay $= 0.0005$. We apply exponential decay to learning rate, with initial learning rate 0.0001 for Alexnet and 0.001 for two LSTM modules. We conduct our experiments on the open source Caffe framework [16]. For prediction baselines, most related works focus on the activity recognition task. Thus we adjust two state-of-the-art works [22,28] to activity prediction task, with each containing three different methods. To do so, we simply replace the recognition label with the prediction label. For our own methods, we test four different network versions as follows: **(1) Time series LSTM:** without attention and asynchronous information; **(2) Event sequence LSTM:** without attention and synchronous information; **(3) Fusion LSTMs:** concatenating both asynchronous and synchronous features; **(4) Attention based LSTMs:** concatenating both asynchronous and synchronous features with soft attention scores. The reproduced experiment results are shown in the prediction part of Table 1.

The event sequence LSTM outperforms time series LSTM, which suggests that history event effects are important for future activity occurrence. The proposed two-stream LSTM without attention outperforms [22,28] by 5.6% (7.3%) and 11.8% (13.7%) on Gaze (Gaze+) respectively. The reason for this improvement is that previous methods only utilize synchronous information while our network makes use of event triggered asynchronous information. Moreover, event modulated attention enhances the prediction accuracy by 1.6% and 1.3% on Gaze and Gaze+ respectively. This is because the temporal attention mechanism largely reduces negative impact of redundant and noise frames. The confusion matrices (using two-stream LSTM with attention) are shown in Fig. 5.

To further show the importance of gaze movement to the activity, we also test the accuracy of single motion prediction. Shown in the left part of Table 2, our results outperform our baseline [22]. The reason is that the sequence of the gaze movement information is the most important cue for motion prediction. The traditional method [22] to use optical flow/CNN to analyze motion is easily influenced by the camera and subjects' shake, while our attention mechanism can solve the problem.

4.4 Activity Recognition

We apply our prediction framework to a set level activity recognition task. We extract new video clips (3568 for Gaze, 10624 for Gaze+) as our training samples, with each video clip containing 7 frames of the same label. We adjust the asynchronous branch to another synchronous branch by removing the event signal sequence, with the original synchronous branch remaining the same. Thus our activity recognition network (containing two synchronous branches) consists of two time series LSTM modules. The train strategy is similar to activity prediction task.

For contrast experiments, we train three different methods on Gaze and Gaze+ [8,22,28]. Observed gaze method is adopted by Faith et al. [8], modeling the spatio-temporal relationship between gaze, object and activity label

Table 2. Performance of motion prediction and recognition. (a) Two-stream CNN results of joint training from Ma et al. [22]; (b) Results of our method, attention based LSTMs for motion prediction and time series LSTM for motion recognition.

	Methods	Prediction		Recognition	
		Gaze	Gaze+	Gaze	Gaze+
[22]	Joint training CNNs	0.308	0.576	0.363	0.651
Ours	Time series LSTM	-	-	**0.526**	**0.788**
	Attention based LSTMs	**0.612**	**0.842**	-	-

by capturing the distribution of visual features and objects in the vicinity of the gaze point. The other two models [22,28] achieve state-of-the-art results, which are our baselines. Results are shown in the recognition part of Table 1. Our method outperforms the state-of-the-art methods in Gaze+ and is slightly inferior to the joint training method of [22] in Gaze. One reason is that our method is set level recognition while baselines are all frame level recognition. Frames in a sequence are complementary and using the features extracted from the frame sequence can hopefully lead to higher accuracy in action recognition. Another reason is that Gaze and Gaze+ contain many transition frames (between neighboring activities), resulting ambiguous labeling problems among these frames. Thus we use the Rubicon Boundaries labeling method proposed by [24] to re-annotate the labels of Gaze and Gaze+ (denoted as Gaze (RB) and Gaze+ (RB)). We only use the sub-segment of activity phases as our sub-dataset and drop the sub-segment of pre-activity and concatenation phases. Results are shown in Table 1. Our method outperforms all other methods by a large margin. We also test the accuracy of motion recognition, our method outperforms the baseline [22], which shows the gaze movement can bring more information of motion than optical flow, because optical flow to analyze motion is easily influence by the camera shake.

4.5   Robustness Analysis

To test the robustness of our network, we randomly add Gaussian noise with different variances on the features before they are sent into LSTM on the activity prediction task (using two-stream LSTM with/without attention mechanism). For the synchronous module, we randomly add noise on the concatenation of hand mask and gaze. For the asynchronous module, we add noise on the bounding box scores after object localization network. For our baselines, we add the same random noise on the hand mask, saliency map and optical flow.

Results from Fig. 6 show that our methods outperform our baselines after adding Gaussian noise of different variances. Accuracy of our two-stream LSTM without attention drops 14.5% (15.5%) on Gaze (Gaze+), while the declines are 19.7% (19.8%) of Ma et al. [22] and 24.9% (21.0%) of Singh et al. [28] on Gaze (Gaze+). We conclude that it is mainly due to different feature representations. Our methods use sequence information as the input and mainly focus

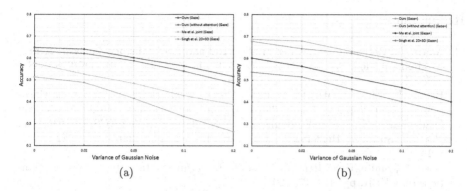

Fig. 6. Results of activity prediction by adding Gaussian noise on our method and baselines of both datasets (a) Gaze; (b) Gaze+, best viewed in color. The dashed and solid lines are results on Gaze and Gaze+ respectively. The methods we show are fusion LSTMs of our method, motion-object joint training of Ma et al. [22] and Ego ConvNet with 2D and 3D of Singh et al. [28]. Note that noise has the least effect on our method.

on long-term context features which are not sensitive to the single frame noise, while our baselines focus on frame level recognition, more sensitive to single frame noise. The declines are 13.1% (13.9%) on Gaze (Gaze+) after adding the event modulated attention module on two-stream LSTM, which shows that the soft attention scores we obtain from the temporal attention module can further reduce the impact of single frame noise. That is because the temporal attention module can attend to those frames that are more important and our baselines take all the frames equally.

5   Conclusion

We extend the typical egocentric activity recognition task to a future activity prediction task, as we prove that there exists moderate relevance between the neighboring activities. We have developed a gaze-event driven attentive activity prediction network to integrate both synchronous and asynchronous information, modeled as background and event excitation. The asynchronous event is defined as gaze moving in/out of the manipulated. We believe that our work will certainly help advance the field of egocentric activity analysis.

Acknowledgments. This work was supported by National Science Foundation of China (U161146161502301, 61521062). This work was supported by SJTU-UCLA Joint Center for Machine Perception and Inference. The work was also partially supported by China's Thousand Youth Talents Plan, STCSM 18DZ2270700 and MoE Key Lab of Artificial Intelligence, AI Institute, Shanghai Jiao Tong University, China. This work was supported in part by NSFC 61671298, STCSM 17511105400.

References

1. Aalen, O., Borgan, O., Gjessing, H.: Survival and Event History Analysis: A Process Point of View. Springer, New York (2008). https://doi.org/10.1007/978-0-387-68560-1
2. Baccouche, M., Mamalet, F., Wolf, C., Garcia, C., Baskurt, A.: Action classification in soccer videos with long short-term memory recurrent neural networks. In: Diamantaras, K., Duch, W., Iliadis, L.S. (eds.) ICANN 2010. LNCS, vol. 6353, pp. 154–159. Springer, Heidelberg (2010). https://doi.org/10.1007/978-3-642-15822-3_20
3. Borji, A., Sihite, D.N., Itti, L.: Probabilistic learning of task-specific visual attention. In: CVPR, pp. 470–477 (2012)
4. Cho, K., van Merrienboer, B., Bahdanau, D., Bengio, Y.: On the properties of neural machine translation: encoder-decoder approaches. In: Proceedings of SSST@EMNLP, pp. 103–111 (2014). http://aclweb.org/anthology/W/W14/W14-4012.pdf
5. Du, N., Dai, H., Trivedi, R., Upadhyay, U., Gomez-Rodriguez, M., Song, L.: Recurrent marked temporal point processes: embedding event history to vector. In: Proceedings of the 22nd ACM SIGKDD International Conference, pp. 1555–1564 (2016)
6. Einhauser, W., Spain, M., Perona, P.: Objects predict fixations better than early saliency. J. Vis. **8**(14), 18:1–18:26 (2008)
7. Elman, J.L.: Finding structure in time. Cogn. Sci. **14**(2), 179–211 (1990)
8. Fathi, A., Li, Y., Rehg, J.M.: Learning to recognize daily actions using gaze. In: Fitzgibbon, A., Lazebnik, S., Perona, P., Sato, Y., Schmid, C. (eds.) ECCV 2012. LNCS, vol. 7572, pp. 314–327. Springer, Heidelberg (2012). https://doi.org/10.1007/978-3-642-33718-5_23
9. Fathi, A., Ren, X., Rehg, J.M.: Learning to recognize objects in egocentric activities. In: CVPR, pp. 3281–3288 (2011)
10. Girshick, R.B.: Fast R-CNN. CoRR abs/1504.08083 (2015). http://arxiv.org/abs/1504.08083
11. Graves, A.: Generating sequences with recurrent neural networks. CoRR abs/1308.0850 (2013). http://arxiv.org/abs/1308.0850
12. Hawkes, A.G.: Spectra of some self-exciting and mutually exciting point processes. Biometrika **58**(1), 83–90 (1971). https://doi.org/10.2307/2334319
13. Hochreiter, S., Schmidhuber, J.: Long short-term memory. Neural Comput. **9**(8), 1735–1780 (1997)
14. Itti, L., Koch, C., Niebur, E.: A model of saliency-based visual attention for rapid scene analysis. IEEE Trans. Pattern Anal. Mach. Intell. **20**(11), 1254–1259 (1998)
15. Jang, Y., Song, Y., Yu, Y., Kim, Y., Kim, G.: TGIF-QA: toward spatio-temporal reasoning in visual question answering. In: CVPR, pp. 1359–1367 (2017)
16. Jia, Y., et al.: Caffe: convolutional architecture for fast feature embedding. In: ACMMM, pp. 675–678 (2014). http://doi.acm.org/10.1145/2647868.2654889
17. Krizhevsky, A., Sutskever, I., Hinton, G.E.: Imagenet classification with deep convolutional neural networks. In: NIPS, pp. 1106–1114 (2012)
18. Lehman, A., O'Rourke, N., Hatcher, L., Stepanski, E.: JMP for Basic Univariate and Multivariate Statistics: Methods for Researchers and Social Scientists, 2nd edn, p. 123. SAS Institute Inc., Cary (2005)
19. Li, Y., Ye, Z., Rehg, J.M.: Delving into egocentric actions. In: CVPR, pp. 287–295 (2015)

20. Liu, W., et al.: SSD: single shot multibox detector. In: Leibe, B., Matas, J., Sebe, N., Welling, M. (eds.) ECCV 2016. LNCS, vol. 9905, pp. 21–37. Springer, Cham (2016). https://doi.org/10.1007/978-3-319-46448-0_2

21. Liu, Y., Yan, J., Ouyang, W.: Quality aware network for set to set recognition. In: CVPR, pp. 4694–4703 (2017)

22. Ma, M., Fan, H., Kitani, K.M.: Going deeper into first-person activity recognition. In: CVPR, pp. 1894–1903 (2016)

23. Mnih, V., Heess, N., Graves, A., Kavukcuoglu, K.: Recurrent models of visual attention. In: NIPS, pp. 2204–2212 (2014). http://papers.nips.cc/paper/5542-recurrent-models-of-visual-attention

24. Moltisanti, D., Wray, M., Mayol-Cuevas, W.W., Damen, D.: Trespassing the boundaries: labeling temporal bounds for object interactions in egocentric video. In: ICCV, pp. 2905–2913 (2017)

25. Ng, J.Y., Hausknecht, M.J., Vijayanarasimhan, S., Vinyals, O., Monga, R., Toderici, G.: Beyond short snippets: deep networks for video classification. In: CVPR, pp. 4694–4702 (2015)

26. Poleg, Y., Ephrat, A., Peleg, S., Arora, C.: Compact CNN for indexing egocentric videos. In: WACV, pp. 1–9 (2016)

27. Ryoo, M.S., Rothrock, B., Matthies, L.H.: Pooled motion features for first-person videos. In: CVPR, pp. 896–904 (2015)

28. Singh, S., Arora, C., Jawahar, C.V.: First person action recognition using deep learned descriptors. In: CVPR, pp. 2620–2628 (2016)

29. Sutskever, I., Vinyals, O., Le, Q.V.: Sequence to sequence learning with neural networks. In: NIPS, pp. 3104–3112 (2014). http://papers.nips.cc/paper/5346-sequence-to-sequence-learning-with-neural-networks

30. Xiao, S., Yan, J., Yang, X., Zha, H., Chu, S.M.: Modeling the intensity function of point process via recurrent neural networks. In: AAAI, pp. 1597–1603 (2017). http://aaai.org/ocs/index.php/AAAI/AAAI17/paper/view/14391

31. Zhang, M., Ma, K.T., Lim, J., Zhao, Q., Feng, J.: Deep future gaze: gaze anticipation on egocentric videos using adversarial networks. In: CPVR, pp. 3539–3548 (2017)

32. Zhou, Y., Ni, B., Hong, R., Yang, X., Tian, Q.: Cascaded interactional targeting network for egocentric video analysis. In: CVPR, pp. 1904–1913 (2016)

33. Zhu, X., Jia, X., Wong, K.-Y.K.: Pixel-level hand detection with shape-aware structured forests. In: Cremers, D., Reid, I., Saito, H., Yang, M.-H. (eds.) ACCV 2014. LNCS, vol. 9006, pp. 64–78. Springer, Cham (2015). https://doi.org/10.1007/978-3-319-16817-3_5

How Good Is My GAN?

Konstantin Shmelkov$^{(\boxtimes)}$, Cordelia Schmid, and Karteek Alahari

Univ. Grenoble Alpes, Inria, CNRS, Grenoble INP, LJK, 38000 Grenoble, France
konstantin.shmelkov@inria.fr

Abstract. Generative adversarial networks (GANs) are one of the most popular methods for generating images today. While impressive results have been validated by visual inspection, a number of quantitative criteria have emerged only recently. We argue here that the existing ones are insufficient and need to be in adequation with the task at hand. In this paper we introduce two measures based on image classification—GAN-train and GAN-test, which approximate the recall (diversity) and precision (quality of the image) of GANs respectively. We evaluate a number of recent GAN approaches based on these two measures and demonstrate a clear difference in performance. Furthermore, we observe that the increasing difficulty of the dataset, from CIFAR10 over CIFAR100 to ImageNet, shows an inverse correlation with the quality of the GANs, as clearly evident from our measures.

1 Introduction

Generative Adversarial Networks (GANs) [19] are deep neural net architectures composed of a pair of competing neural networks: a generator and a discriminator. This model is trained by alternately optimizing two objective functions so that the generator G learns to produce samples resembling real images, and the discriminator D learns to better discriminate between real and fake data. Such a paradigm has huge potential, as it can learn to generate any data distribution. This has been exploited with some success in several computer vision problems, such as text-to-image [56] and image-to-image [24,59] translation, super-resolution [31], and realistic natural image generation [25].

Since the original GAN model [19] was proposed, many variants have appeared in the past few years, for example, to improve the quality of the generated images [12,15,25,36], or to stabilize the training procedure [7,9,20,34, 36,40,57]. GANs have also been modified to generate images of a given class by conditioning on additional information, such as the class label [16,35,37,41].

This work was supported in part by the ERC advanced grant ALLEGRO, gifts from Amazon, Facebook and Intel, and the Indo-French project EVEREST (no. 5302-1) funded by CEFIPRA.

Electronic supplementary material The online version of this chapter (https:// doi.org/10.1007/978-3-030-01216-8_14) contains supplementary material, which is available to authorized users.

V. Ferrari et al. (Eds.): ECCV 2018, LNCS 11206, pp. 218–234, 2018.
https://doi.org/10.1007/978-3-030-01216-8_14

There are a number of ways to do this: ranging from concatenation of label y to the generator input $\mathbf{z}$ or intermediate feature maps [16,35], to using conditional batch normalization [37], and augmenting the discriminator with an auxiliary classifier [41]. With several such variants being regularly proposed in the literature, a critical question is *how these models can be evaluated and compared to each other.*

Evaluation and comparison of GANs, or equivalently, the images generated by GANs, is challenging. This is in part due to the lack of an explicit likelihood measure [51], which is commonplace in comparable probabilistic models [27, 47]. Thus, much of the previous work has resorted to a mere subjective visual evaluation in the case of images synthesized by GANs. As seen from the sample images generated by a state-of-the-art GAN [36] in Fig. 1, it is impossible to judge their quality precisely with a subjective evaluation. Recent work in the past two years has begun to target this challenge through quantitative measures for evaluating GANs [22,25,32,46].

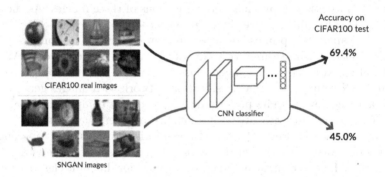

Fig. 1. State-of-the-art GANs, e.g., SNGAN [36], generate realistic images, which are difficult to evaluate subjectively in comparison to real images. Our new image classification accuracy-based measure (GAN-train is shown here) overcomes this issue, showing a clear difference between real and generated images.

Inception score (IS) [46] and Fréchet Inception distance (FID) [22] were suggested as ad-hoc measures correlated with the visual quality of generated images. Inception score measures the quality of a generated image by computing the KL-divergence between the (logit) response produced by this image and the marginal distribution, i.e., the average response of all the generated images, using an Inception network [50] trained on ImageNet. In other words, Inception score does not compare samples with a target distribution, and is limited to quantifying the diversity of generated samples. Fréchet Inception distance compares Inception activations (responses of the penultimate layer of the Inception network) between real and generated images. This comparison however approximates the activations of real and generated images as Gaussian distributions (cf. Eq. (2)), computing their means and covariances, which are too crude to capture subtle details. Both these measures rely on an ImageNet-pretrained Inception network, which is far from ideal for other datasets, such as faces and biomedical imaging. Overall, IS and FID are useful measures to evaluate how training advances, but they guarantee no correlation with performance on real-world tasks. As we discuss in Sect. 5, these measures are insufficient to finely separate state-of-the-art GAN models, unlike our measures (see SNGAN vs WPGAN-GP (10M) in Table 2 for example).

An alternative evaluation is to compute the distance of the generated samples to the real data manifold in terms of precision and recall [32]. Here, high precision implies that the generated samples are close to the data manifold, and high recall shows that the generator outputs samples that cover the manifold well. These measures remain idealistic as they are impossible to compute on natural image data, whose manifold is unknown. Indeed, the evaluation in [32] is limited to using synthetic data composed of gray-scale triangles. Another distance suggested for comparing GAN models is sliced Wasserstein distance (SWD) [25]. SWD is an approximation of Wasserstein-1 distance between real and generated images, and is computed as the statistical similarity between local image patches extracted from Laplacian pyramid representations of these images. As shown in Sect. 5, SWD is less-informative than our evaluation measures.

In this paper, we propose new evaluation measures to compare class-conditional GAN architectures with GAN-train and GAN-test scores. We rely on a neural net architecture for image classification for both these measures. To compute GAN-train, we train a classification network with images generated by a GAN, and then evaluate its performance on a test set composed of real-world images. Intuitively, this measures the difference between the learned (i.e., generated image) and the target (i.e., real image) distributions. We can conclude that generated images are similar to real ones if the classification network, which learns features for discriminating images generated for different classes, can correctly classify real images. In other words, GAN-train is akin to a recall measure, as a good GAN-train performance shows that the generated samples are diverse enough. However, GAN-train also requires a sufficient precision, as otherwise the classifier will be impacted by the sample quality.

Our second measure, GAN-test, is the accuracy of a network trained on real images and evaluated on the generated images. This measure is similar to precision, with a high value denoting that the generated samples are a realistic approximation of the (unknown) distribution of natural images. In addition to these two measures, we study the utility of images generated by GANs for augmenting training data. This can be interpreted as a measure of the diversity of the generated images. The utility of our evaluation approach, in particular, when a subjective inspection is insufficient, is illustrated with the GAN-train measure in Fig. 1. We will discuss these measures in detail in Sect. 3.

As shown in our extensive experimental results in Sect. 5 and the appendix in the supplementary material and technical report [5], these measures are much more informative to evaluate GANs, compared to all the previous measures discussed, including cases where human studies are inconclusive. In particular, we evaluate two state-of-the-art GAN models: WGAN-GP [20] and

SNGAN [36], along with other generative models [45,47] to provide baseline comparisons. Image classification performance is evaluated on MNIST [30], CIFAR10, CIFAR100 [28], and the ImageNet [14] datasets. Experimental results show that the quality of GAN images decreases significantly as the complexity of the dataset increases.

2   Related Work

We present existing quantitative measures to evaluate GANs: scores based on an Inception network, i.e., IS and FID, a Wasserstein-based distance metric, precision and recall scores, and a technique built with data augmentation.

2.1   Inception Score

One of the most common ways to evaluate GANs is the Inception score [46]. It uses an Inception network [50] pre-trained on ImageNet to compute logits of generated images. The score is given by:

$$\text{IS}(G) = \exp(\mathbb{E}_{\mathbf{x} \sim p_g}[D_{\text{KL}}(p(y|\mathbf{x}) \parallel p(y))]), \tag{1}$$

where $\mathbf{x}$ is a generated image sampled from the learned generator distribution p_g, $\mathbb{E}$ is the expectation over the set of generated images, D_{KL} is the KL-divergence between the conditional class distribution $p(y|\mathbf{x})$ (for label y, according to the Inception network) and the marginal class distribution $p(y) = \mathbb{E}_{\mathbf{x} \sim p_g} [p(y|\mathbf{x})]$. By definition, Inception score does not consider real images at all, and so cannot measure how well the generator approximates the real distribution. This score is limited to measuring only the diversity of generated images. Some of its other limitations, as noted in [8], are: high sensitivity to small changes in weights of the Inception network, and large variance of scores.

2.2   Fréchet Inception Distance

The recently proposed Fréchet Inception distance (FID) [22] compares the distributions of Inception embeddings (activations from the penultimate layer of the Inception network) of real $(p_r(\mathbf{x}))$ and generated $(p_g(\mathbf{x}))$ images. Both these distributions as modeled as multi-dimensional Gaussians parameterized by their respective mean and covariance. The distance measure is defined between the two Gaussian distributions as:

$$d^2((\mathbf{m}_r, \mathbf{C}_r), (\mathbf{m}_g, \mathbf{C}_g)) = \|\mathbf{m}_r - \mathbf{m}_g\|^2 + \text{Tr}(\mathbf{C}_r + \mathbf{C}_g - 2(\mathbf{C}_r \mathbf{C}_g)^{\frac{1}{2}}), \tag{2}$$

where $(\mathbf{m}_r, \mathbf{C}_r)$, $(\mathbf{m}_g, \mathbf{C}_g)$ denote the mean and covariance of the real and generated image distributions respectively. FID is inversely correlated with Inception score, and suffers from the same issues discussed earlier.

The two Inception-based measures cannot separate image quality from image diversity. For example, low IS or FID values can be due to the generated images being either not realistic (low image quality) or too similar to each other (low diversity), with no way to analyze the cause. In contrast, our measures can distinguish when generated images become less diverse from worse image quality.

2.3   Other Evaluation Measures

Sliced Wasserstein distance (SWD) [25] was used to evaluate high-resolution GANs. It is a multi-scale statistical similarity computed on local image patches extracted from the Laplacian pyramid representation of real and generated images. A total of 128 7×7 local patches for each level of the Laplacian pyramid are extracted per image. While SWD is an efficient approximation, using randomized projections [44], of the Wasserstein-1 distance between the real and generated images, its utility is limited when comparing a variety of GAN models, with not all of them producing high-resolution images (see our evaluation in Sect. 5).

Precision and recall measures were introduced [32] in the context of GANs, by constructing a synthetic data manifold. This makes it possible to compute the distance of an image sample (generated or real) to the manifold, by finding its distance to the closest point from the manifold. In this synthetic setup, precision is defined as the fraction of the generated samples whose distance to the manifold is below a certain threshold. Recall, on the other hand, is computed by considering a set of test samples. First, the latent representation $\tilde{z}$ of each test sample x is estimated, through gradient descent, by inverting the generator G. Recall is then given by the fraction of test samples whose L2-distance to $G(\tilde{z})$ is below the threshold. High recall is equivalent to the GAN capturing most of the manifold, and high precision implies that the generated samples are close to the manifold. Although these measures bring the flavor of techniques used widely to evaluate discriminative models to GANs, they are impractical for real images as the data manifold is unknown, and their use is limited to evaluations on synthetic data [32].

2.4   Data Augmentation

Augmenting training data is an important component of learning neural networks. This can be achieved by increasing the size of the training set [29] or incorporating augmentation directly in the latent space [54]. A popular technique is to increase the size of the training set with minor transformations of data, which has resulted in a performance boost, e.g., for image classification [29]. GANs provide a natural way to augment training data with the generated samples. Indeed, GANs have been used to train classification networks in a semi-supervised fashion [13,52] or to facilitate domain adaptation [10]. Modern GANs generate images realistic enough to improve performance in applications, such as, biomedical imaging [11,18], person re-identification [58] and image enhancement [55]. They can also be used to refine training sets composed of synthetic images for applications such as eye gaze and hand pose estimation [49]. GANs are also used to learn complex 3D distributions and replace computationally intensive simulations in physics [39,42] and neuroscience [38]. Ideally, GANs should be able to recreate the training set with different variations. This can be used to compress datasets for learning incrementally, without suffering from catastrophic forgetting as new classes are added [48]. We will study the utility of GANs for training image classification networks with data augmentation (see Sect. 5.4), and analyze it as an evaluation measure.

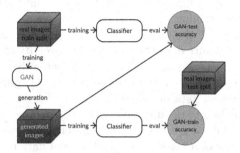

Fig. 2. Illustration of GAN-train and GAN-test. GAN-train learns a classifier on GAN generated images and measures the performance on real test images. This evaluates the diversity and realism of GAN images. GAN-test learns a classifier on real images and evaluates it on GAN images. This measures how realistic GAN images are.

In summary, evaluation of generative models is not a easy task [51], especially for models like GANs. We bring a new dimension to this problem with our GAN-train and GAN-test performance-based measures, and show through our extensive analysis that they are complementary to all the above schemes.

3   GAN-train and GAN-test

An important characteristic of a conditional GAN model is that generated images should not only be realistic, but also recognizable as coming from a given class. An optimal GAN that perfectly captures the target distribution can generate a new set of images S_g, which are indistinguishable from the original training set S_t. Assuming both these sets have the same size, a classifier trained on either of them should produce roughly the same validation accuracy. This is indeed true when the dataset is simple enough, for example, MNIST [48] (see also Sect. 5.2). Motivated by this optimal GAN characteristic, we devise two scores to evaluate GANs, as illustrated in Fig. 2.

GAN-train is the accuracy of a classifier trained on S_g and tested on a validation set of real images S_v. When a GAN is not perfect, GAN-train accuracy will be lower than the typical validation accuracy of the classifier trained on S_t. It can happen due to many reasons, e.g., (i) mode dropping reduces the diversity of S_g in comparison to S_t, (ii) generated samples are not realistic enough to make the classifier learn relevant features, (iii) GANs can mix-up classes and confuse the classifier. Unfortunately, GAN failures are difficult to diagnose. When GAN-train accuracy is close to validation accuracy, it means that GAN images are high quality and as diverse as the training set. As we will show in Sect. 5.3, diversity varies with the number of generated images. We will analyze this with the evaluation discussed at the end of this section.

GAN-test is the accuracy of a classifier trained on the original training set S_t, but tested on S_g. If a GAN learns well, this turns out be an easy task because both the sets have the same distribution. Ideally, GAN-test should be close to the validation accuracy. If it significantly higher, it means that the GAN overfits, and simply memorizes the training set. On the contrary, if it is significantly lower, the GAN does not capture the target distribution well and the image quality is poor. Note that this measure does not capture the diversity of samples because a model that memorizes exactly one training image perfectly will score very well. GAN-test accuracy is related to the precision score in [32], quantifying how close generated images are to a data manifold.

To provide an insight into the diversity of GAN-generated images, we measure GAN-train accuracy with generated sets of different sizes, and compare it with the validation accuracy of a classifier trained on real data of the corresponding size. If all the generated images were perfect, the size of S_g where GAN-train is equal to validation accuracy with the reduced-size training set, would be a good estimation of the number of distinct images in S_g. In practice, we observe that GAN-train accuracy saturates with a certain number of GAN-generated samples (see Figs. 4(a) and (b) discussed in Sect. 5.3). This is a measure of the diversity of a GAN, similar to recall from [32], measuring the fraction of the data manifold covered by a GAN.

4   Datasets and Methods

Datasets. For comparing the different GAN methods and PixelCNN++, we use several image classification datasets with an increasing number of labels: MNIST [30], CIFAR10 [28], CIFAR100 [28] and ImageNet1k [14]. CIFAR10 and CIFAR100 both have 50k 32×32 RGB images in the training set, and 10k images in the validation set. CIFAR10 has 10 classes while CIFAR100 has 100 classes. ImageNet1k has 1000 classes with 1.3M training and 50k validation images. We downsample the original ImageNet images to two resolutions in our experiments, namely 64×64 and 128×128. MNIST has 10 classes of 28×28 grayscale images, with 60k samples for training and 10k for validation.

We exclude the CIFAR10/CIFAR100/ImageNet1k validation images from GAN training to enable the evaluation of test accuracy. This is not done in a number of GAN papers and may explain minor differences in IS and FID scores compared to the ones reported in these papers.

4.1   Evaluated Methods

Among the plethora of GAN models in literature, it is difficult to choose the best one, especially since appropriate hyperparameter fine-tuning appears to bring all major GANs within a very close performance range, as noted in a study [32]. We choose to perform our analysis on Wasserstein GAN (WGAN-GP), one of the most widely-accepted models in literature at the moment, and SNGAN, a very recent model showing state-of-the-art image generation results on ImageNet. Additionally, we include two baseline generative models, DCGAN [45] and PixelCNN++ [47]. We summarize all the models included in our experimental analysis below, and present implementation details in the appendix [5].

Wasserstein GAN. WGAN [7] replaces the discriminator separating real and generated images with a critic estimating Wasserstein-1 (i.e., earth-mover's) distance between their corresponding distributions. The success of WGANs in comparison to the classical GAN model [19] can be attributed to two reasons. Firstly, the optimization of the generator is easier because the gradient of the critic function is better behaved than its GAN equivalent. Secondly, empirical observations show that the WGAN value function better correlates with the quality of the samples than GANs [7].

In order to estimate the Wasserstein-1 distance between the real and generated image distributions, the critic must be a K-Lipschitz function. The original paper [7] proposed to constrain the critic through weight clipping to satisfy this Lipschitz requirement. This, however, can lead to unstable training or generate poor samples [20]. An alternative to clipping weights is the use of a gradient penalty as a regularizer to enforce the Lipschitz constraint. In particular, we penalize the norm of the gradient of the critic function with respect to its input. This has demonstrated stable training of several GAN architectures [20].

We use the gradient penalty variant of WGAN, conditioned on data in our experiments, and refer to it as WGAN-GP in the rest of the paper. Label conditioning is an effective way to use labels available in image classification training data [41]. Following ACGAN [41], we concatenate the noise input $\mathbf{z}$ with the class label in the generator, and modify the discriminator to produce probability distributions over the sources as well as the labels.

SNGAN. Variants have also analyzed other issues related to training GANs, such as the impact of the performance control of the discriminator on training the generator. Generators often fail to learn the multimodal structure of the target distribution due to unstable training of the discriminator, particularly in high-dimensional spaces [36]. More dramatically, generators cease to learn when the supports of the real and the generated image distributions are disjoint [6]. This occurs since the discriminator quickly learns to distinguish these distributions, resulting in the gradients of the discriminator function, with respect to the input, becoming zeros, and thus failing to update the generator model any further.

SNGAN [36] introduces spectral normalization to stabilize training the discriminator. This is achieved by normalizing each layer of the discriminator (i.e., the learnt weights) with the spectral norm of the weight matrix, which is its largest singular value. Miyato *et al.* [36] showed that this regularization outperforms other alternatives, including gradient penalty, and in particular, achieves state-of-the-art image synthesis results on ImageNet. We use the class-conditioned version of SNGAN [37] in our evaluation. Here, SNGAN is conditioned with projection in the discriminator network, and conditional batch normalization [17] in the generator network.

DCGAN. Deep convolutional GANs (DCGANs) is a class of architecture that was proposed to leverage the benefits of supervised learning with CNNs as well as the unsupervised learning of GAN models [45]. The main principles behind DCGANs are using only convolutional layers and batch normalization for the generator and discriminator networks. Several instantiations of DCGAN are possible with these broad guidelines, and in fact, many do exist in literature [20,36,41]. We use the class-conditioned variant presented in [41] for our analysis.

PixelCNN++. The original PixelCNN [53] belongs to a class of generative models with tractable likelihood. It is a deep neural net which predicts pixels sequentially along both the spatial dimensions. The spatial dependencies among pixels are captured with a fully convolutional network using masked convolutions. PixelCNN++ proposes improvements to this model in terms of regularization, modified network connections and more efficient training [47].

5 Experiments

5.1 Implementation Details of Evaluation Measures

We compute Inception score with the WGAN-GP code [1] corrected for the 1008 classes problem [8]. The mean value of this score computed 10 times on 5k splits is reported in all our evaluations, following standard protocol.

We found that there are two variants for computing FID. The first one is the original implementation [2] from the authors [22], where all the real images and at least 10k generated images are used. The second one is from the SNGAN [36] implementation, where 5k generated images are compared to 5k real images. Estimation of the covariance matrix is also different in both these cases. Hence, we include these two versions of FID in the paper to facilitate comparison in the future. The original implementation is referred to as FID, while our implementation [4] of the 5k version is denoted as FID-5K. Implementation of SWD is taken from the official NVIDIA repository [3].

5.2 Generative Model Evaluation

MNIST. We validate our claim (from Sect. 3) that a GAN can perfectly reproduce a simple dataset on MNIST. A four-layer convnet classifier trained on real MNIST data achieves 99.3% accuracy on the test set. In contrast, images generated with SNGAN achieve a GAN-train accuracy of 99.0% and GAN-test accuracy of 99.2%, highlighting their high image quality as well as diversity.

CIFAR10. Table 1 shows a comparison of state-of-the-art GAN models on CIFAR10. We observe that the relative ranking of models is consistent across different metrics: FID, GAN-train and GAN-test accuracies. Both GAN-train and GAN-test are quite high for SNGAN and WGAN-GP (10M). This implies that both the image quality and the diversity are good, but are still lower than that of real images (92.8 in the first row). Note that PixelCNN++ has low diversity because GAN-test is much higher than GAN-train in this case. This is in line with its relatively poor Inception score and FID (as shown in [32] FID is quite sensitive to mode dropping).

Table 1. CIFAR10 experiments. IS: higher is better. FID and SWD: lower is better. SWD values here are multiplied by 10^3 for better readability. GAN-train and GAN-test are accuracies given as percentage (higher is better).

Model	IS	FID-5K	FID	GAN-train	GAN-test	SWD 16	SWD 32
Real images	11.33	9.4	2.1	92.8	-	2.8	2.0
SNGAN	8.43	18.8	11.8	82.2	87.3	3.9	24.4
WGAN-GP (10M)	8.21	21.5	14.1	79.5	85.0	3.8	6.2
WGAN-GP (2.5M)	8.29	22.1	15.0	76.1	80.7	3.4	6.9
DCGAN	6.69	42.5	35.6	65.0	58.2	6.5	24.7
PixelCNN++	5.36	121.3	119.5	34.0	47.1	14.9	56.6

Fig. 3. First column: SNGAN-generated images. Other columns: 5 images from CIFAR10 "train" closest to GAN image from the first column in feature space of baseline CIFAR10 classifier.

Note that SWD does not correlate well with other metrics: it is consistently smaller for WGAN-GP (especially SWD 32). We hypothesize that this is because SWD approximates the Wasserstein-1 distance between patches of real and generated images, which is related to the optimization objective of Wasserstein GANs, but not other models (e.g., SNGAN). This suggests that SWD is unsuitable to compare WGAN and other GAN losses. It is also worth noting that WGAN-GP (10M) shows only a small improvement over WGAN-GP (2.5M) despite a four-fold increase in the number of parameters. In Fig. 3 we show SNGAN-generated images on CIFAR10 and their nearest neighbors from the training set in the feature space of the classifier we use to compute the GAN-test measure. Note that SNGAN consistently finds images of the same class as a generated image, which are close to an image from the training set.

To highlight the complementarity of GAN-train and GAN-test, we emulate a simple model by subsampling/corrupting the CIFAR10 training set, in the spirit of [22]. GAN-train/test now corresponds to training/testing the classifier on modified data. We observe that GAN-test is insensitive to subsampling unlike GAN-train (where it is equivalent to training a classifier on a smaller split). Salt and pepper noise, ranging from 1% to 20% of replaced pixels per image, barely affects GAN-train, but degrades GAN-test significantly (from 82% to 15%).

Through this experiment on modified data, we also observe that FID is insufficient to distinguish between the impact of image diversity and quality. For example, FID between CIFAR10 train set and train set with Gaussian noise ($\sigma = 5$) is 27.1, while FID between train set and its random 5k subset with the same noise is 29.6. This difference may be due to lack of diversity or quality or both. GAN-test, which measures the quality of images, is identical (95%) in both these cases. GAN-train, on the other hand, drops from 91% to 80%, showing that the 5k train set lacks diversity. Together, our measures, address one of the main drawbacks of FID.

CIFAR100. Our results on CIFAR100 are summarized in Table 2. It is a more challenging dataset than CIFAR10, mainly due to the larger number of classes and fewer images per class; as evident from the accuracy of a convnet for classification trained with real images: 92.8 vs 69.4 for CIFAR10 and CIFAR100 respectively. SNGAN and WGAN-GP (10M) produce similar IS and FID, but very different GAN-train and GAN-test accuracies. This makes it easier to conclude that SNGAN has better image quality and diversity than WGAN-GP (10M). It is also interesting to note that WGAN-GP (10M) is superior to WGAN-GP (2.5M) in all the metrics, except SWD. WGAN-GP (2.5M) achieves reasonable IS and FID, but the quality of the generated samples is very low, as evidenced by GAN-test accuracy. SWD follows the same pattern as in the CIFAR10 case: WGAN-GP shows a better performance than others in this measure, which is not consistent with its relatively poor image quality. PixelCNN++ exhibits an interesting behavior, with high GAN-test accuracy, but very low GAN-train accuracy, showing that it can generate images of acceptable quality, but they lack diversity. A high FID in this case also hints at significant mode dropping. We also analyze the quality of the generated images with t-SNE [33] in the appendix [5].

Random Forests. We verify if our findings depend on the type of classifier by using random forests [23,43] instead of CNN for classification. This results in GAN-train, GAN-test scores of 15.2%, 19.5% for SNGAN, 10.9%, 16.6% for WGAN-GP (10M), 3.7%, 4.8% for WGAN-GP (2.5M), and 3.2%, 3.0% for DCGAN respectively. Note that the relative ranking of these GANs remains identical for random forests and CNNs.

Human Study. We designed a human study with the goal of finding which of the measures (if any) is better aligned with human judgement. The subjects were asked to choose the more realistic image from two samples generated for a particular class of CIFAR100. Five subjects evaluated SNGAN vs one of the following: DCGAN, WGAN-GP (2.5M), WGAN-GP (10M) in three separate tests. They made 100 comparisons of randomly generated image pairs for each test, i.e., 1500 trials in total. All of them found the task challenging, in particular for both WGAN-GP tests.

We use Student's t-test for statistical analysis of these results. In SNGAN vs DCGAN, subjects chose SNGAN 368 out of 500 trials, in SNGAN vs WGAN-GP (2.5M), subjects preferred SNGAN 274 out of 500 trials, and in SNGAN vs WGAN-GP (10M), SNGAN was preferred 230 out of 500. The preference of SNGAN over DCGAN is statistically significant ($p < 10^{-7}$), while the preference over WGAN-GP (2.5M) or WGAN-GP (10M) is insignificant ($p = 0.28$ and $p = 0.37$ correspondingly). We conclude that the quality of images generated needs to be significantly different, as in the case of SNGAN vs DCGAN, for human studies to be conclusive. They are insufficient to pick out the subtle, but performance-critical, differences, unlike our measures.

Table 2. CIFAR100 experiments. Refer to the caption of Table 1 for details.

Model	IS	FID-5K	FID	GAN-train	GAN-test	SWD 16	SWD 32
Real images	14.9	10.8	2.4	69.4	-	2.7	2.0
SNGAN	9.30	23.8	15.6	45.0	59.4	4.0	15.6
WGAN-GP (10M)	9.10	23.5	15.6	26.7	40.4	6.0	9.1
WGAN-GP (2.5M)	8.22	28.8	20.6	5.4	4.3	3.7	7.7
DCGAN	6.20	49.7	41.8	3.5	2.4	9.9	20.8
PixelCNN++	6.27	143.4	141.9	4.8	27.5	8.5	25.9

Table 3. ImageNet experiments. SNGAN* refers to the model provided by [36], trained for 850k iterations. Refer to the caption of Table 1 for details.

Res	Model	IS	FID-5K	FID	GAN-train top-1	GAN-train top-5	GAN-test top-1	GAN-test top-5
64px	Real images	63.8	15.6	2.9	55.0	78.8	-	-
	SNGAN	12.3	44.5	34.4	3	8.4	12.9	28.9
	WGAN-GP	11.3	46.7	35.8	0.1	0.7	0.1	0.5
128px	Real images	203.2	17.4	3.0	59.1	81.9	-	-
	SNGAN*	35.3	44.9	33.2	9.3	21.9	39.5	63.4
	WGAN-GP	11.6	91.6	79.5	0.1	0.5	0.1	0.5

ImageNet. On this dataset, which is one of the more challenging ones for image synthesis [36], we analyzed the performance of the two best GAN models based on our CIFAR experiments, i.e., SNGAN and WGAN-GP. As shown in Table 3, SNGAN achieves a reasonable GAN-train accuracy and a relatively high GAN-test accuracy at 128×128 resolution. This suggests that SNGAN generated images have good quality, but their diversity is much lower than the original data. This may be partly due to the size of the generator (150 Mb) being significantly smaller in comparison to ImageNet training data (64 Gb for 128×128). Despite this difference in size, it achieves GAN-train accuracy of 9.3% and 21.9% for top-1 and top-5 classification results respectively. In comparison, the performance of WGAN-GP is dramatically poorer; see last row for each resolution in the table.

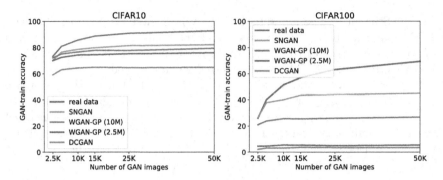

Fig. 4. The effect of varying the size of the generated image set on GAN-train accuracy. For comparison, we also show the result (in blue) of varying the size of the real image training dataset. (Best viewed in pdf.) (Color figure online)

In the case of images generated at 64×64 resolution, GAN-train and GAN-test accuracies with SNGAN are lower than their 128×128 counterparts. GAN-test accuracy is over four times better than GAN-train, showing that the generated images lack in diversity. It is interesting to note that WGAN-GP produces Inception score and FID very similar to SNGAN, but its images are insufficient to train a reasonable classifier and to be recognized by an ImageNet classifier, as shown by the very low GAN-train and GAN-test scores.

5.3   GAN Image Diversity

We further analyze the diversity of the generated images by evaluating GAN-train accuracy with varying amounts of generated data. A model with low diversity generates redundant samples, and increasing the quantity of data generated in this case does not result in better GAN-train accuracy. In contrast, generating more samples from a model with high diversity produces a better GAN-train score. We show this analysis in Fig. 4, where GAN-train accuracy is plotted with respect to the size of the generated training set on CIFAR10 and CIFAR100.

In the case of CIFAR10, we observe that GAN-train accuracy saturates around 15–20k generated images, even for the best model SNGAN (see Fig. 4a). With DCGAN, which is weaker than SNGAN, GAN-train saturates around 5k images, due to its relatively poorer diversity. Figure 4b shows no increase in GAN-train accuracy on CIFAR100 beyond 25k images for all the models. The diversity of 5k SNGAN-generated images is comparable to the same quantity of real images; see blue and orange plots in Fig. 4b. WGAN-GP (10M) has very low diversity beyond 5k generated images. WGAN-GP (2.5M) and DCGAN perform poorly on CIFAR100, and are not competitive with respect to the other methods.

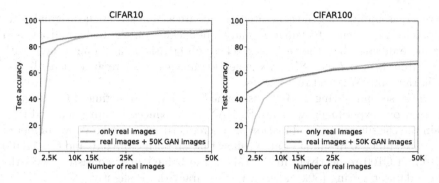

Fig. 5. The impact of training a classifier with a combination of real and SNGAN generated images.

5.4 GAN Data Augmentation

We analyze the utility of GANs for data augmentation, i.e., for generating additional training samples, with the best-performing GAN model (SNGAN) under two settings. First, in Figs. 5a and b, we show the influence of training the classifier with a combination of real images from the training set and 50k GAN-generated images on the CIFAR10 and CIFAR100 datasets respectively. In this case, SNGAN is trained with all the images from the original training set. From both the figures, we observe that adding 2.5k or 5k real images to the 50k GAN-generated images improves the accuracy over the corresponding real-only counterparts. However, adding 50k real images does not provide any noticeable improvement, and in fact, reduces the performance slightly in the case of CIFAR100 (Fig. 5b). This is potentially due to the lack of image diversity.

Table 4. Data augmentation when SNGAN is trained with reduced real image set. Classifier is trained either on this data (real) or a combination of real and SNGAN generated images (real+GAN). Performance is shown as % accuracy.

Num real images	real C10	real+GAN C10	real C100	real+GAN C100
2.5k	73.4	67.0	25.6	23.9
5k	80.9	77.9	40.0	33.5
10k	85.8	83.5	51.5	45.5

This experiment provides another perspective on the diversity of the generated set, given that the generated images are produced by a GAN learned from the entire CIFAR10 (or CIFAR100) training dataset. For example, augmenting 2.5k real images with 50k generated ones results in a better test accuracy than the model trained only on 5k real images. Thus, we can conclude that the GAN model generates images that have more diversity than the 2.5k real ones. This is however, assuming that the generated images are as realistic as the original data. In practice, the generated images tend to be lacking on the realistic front, and are more diverse than the real ones. These observations are in agreement with those from Sect. 5.3, i.e., SNGAN generates images that are at least as diverse as 5k randomly sampled real images.

In the second setting, SNGAN is trained in a low-data regime. In contrast to the previous experiment, we train SNGAN on a reduced training set, and then train the classifier on a combination of this reduced set, and the same number of generated images. Results in Table 4 show that on both CIFAR10 and CIFAR100 (C10 and C100 respectively in the table), the behaviour is consistent with the whole dataset setting (50k images), i.e., accuracy drops slightly.

6 Summary

This paper presents steps towards addressing the challenging problem of evaluating and comparing images generated by GANs. To this end, we present new quantitative measures, GAN-train and GAN-test, which are motivated by precision and recall scores popularly used in the evaluation of discriminative models. We evaluate several recent GAN approaches as well as other popular generative models with these measures. Our extensive experimental analysis demonstrates that GAN-train and GAN-test not only highlight the difference in performance of these methods, but are also complementary to existing scores.

References

1. https://github.com/igul222/improved_wgan_training
2. https://github.com/bioinf-jku/TTUR
3. https://github.com/tkarras/progressive_growing_of_gans
4. Source code. http://thoth.inrialpes.fr/research/ganeval
5. Supplementary material, also available in arXiv Technical report. https://arxiv.org/abs/1807.09499
6. Arjovsky, M., Bottou, L.: Towards principled methods for training generative adversarial networks. In: ICLR (2017)
7. Arjovsky, M., Chintala, S., Bottou, L.: Wasserstein generative adversarial networks. In: ICML (2017)
8. Barratt, S., Sharma, R.: A note on the inception score. arXiv preprint arXiv:1801.01973 (2018)
9. Berthelot, D., Schumm, T., Metz, L.: BEGAN: boundary equilibrium generative adversarial networks. arXiv preprint arXiv:1703.10717 (2017)
10. Bousmalis, K., Silberman, N., Dohan, D., Erhan, D., Krishnan, D.: Unsupervised pixel-level domain adaptation with generative adversarial networks. In: CVPR (2017)
11. Calimeri, F., Marzullo, A., Stamile, C., Terracina, G.: Biomedical data augmentation using generative adversarial neural networks. In: Lintas, A., Rovetta, S., Verschure, P.F.M.J., Villa, A.E.P. (eds.) ICANN 2017. LNCS, vol. 10614, pp. 626–634. Springer, Cham (2017). https://doi.org/10.1007/978-3-319-68612-7_71

12. Chen, X., Duan, Y., Houthooft, R., Schulman, J., Sutskever, I., Abbeel, P.: Info-GAN: interpretable representation learning by information maximizing generative adversarial nets. In: NIPS (2016)
13. Dai, Z., Yang, Z., Yang, F., Cohen, W.W., Salakhutdinov, R.R.: Good semi-supervised learning that requires a bad GAN. In: NIPS (2017)
14. Deng, J., Dong, W., Socher, R., Li, L.J., Li, K., Fei-Fei, L.: ImageNet: a large-scale hierarchical image database. In: CVPR (2009)
15. Denton, E.L., Chintala, S., Szlam, A., Fergus, R.: Deep generative image models using a Laplacian pyramid of adversarial networks. In: NIPS (2015)
16. Dumoulin, V., et al.: Adversarially learned inference. In: ICLR (2017)
17. Dumoulin, V., Shlens, J., Kudlur, M.: A learned representation for artistic style. In: ICLR (2017)
18. Frid-Adar, M., Klang, E., Amitai, M., Goldberger, J., Greenspan, H.: Synthetic data augmentation using GAN for improved liver lesion classification. In: ISBI (2018)
19. Goodfellow, I., et al.: Generative adversarial nets. In: NIPS (2014)
20. Gulrajani, I., Ahmed, F., Arjovsky, M., Dumoulin, V., Courville, A.C.: Improved training of wasserstein GANs. In: NIPS (2017)
21. He, K., Zhang, X., Ren, S., Sun, J.: Identity mappings in deep residual networks. In: Leibe, B., Matas, J., Sebe, N., Welling, M. (eds.) ECCV 2016. LNCS, vol. 9908, pp. 630–645. Springer, Cham (2016). https://doi.org/10.1007/978-3-319-46493-0_38
22. Heusel, M., Ramsauer, H., Unterthiner, T., Nessler, B., Hochreiter, S.: GANs trained by a two time-scale update rule converge to a local Nash equilibrium. In: NIPS (2017)
23. Ho, T.K.: Random decision forests. In: ICDAR (1995)
24. Isola, P., Zhu, J.Y., Zhou, T., Efros, A.A.: Image-to-image translation with conditional adversarial networks. In: CVPR (2017)
25. Karras, T., Aila, T., Laine, S., Lehtinen, J.: Progressive growing of GANs for improved quality, stability, and variation. In: ICLR (2018)
26. Kingma, D., Ba, J.: Adam: a method for stochastic optimization. In: ICLR (2015)
27. Kingma, D.P., Welling, M.: Auto-encoding variational Bayes. In: ICLR (2014)
28. Krizhevsky, A.: Learning multiple layers of features from tiny images. Technical report, University of Toronto (2009)
29. Krizhevsky, A., Sutskever, I., Hinton, G.E.: ImageNet classification with deep convolutional neural networks. In: NIPS (2012)
30. LeCun, Y., Bottou, L., Bengio, Y., Haffner, P.: Gradient-based learning applied to document recognition. Proc. IEEE **86**(11), 2278–2324 (1998)
31. Ledig, C., et al.: Photo-realistic single image super-resolution using a generative adversarial network. In: CVPR (2017)
32. Lucic, M., Kurach, K., Michalski, M., Gelly, S., Bousquet, O.: Are GANs created equal? A large-scale study. arXiv preprint arXiv:1711.10337 (2017)
33. van der Maaten, L., Hinton, G.: Visualizing data using t-SNE. JMLR **9**(Nov), 2579–2605 (2008)
34. Mao, X., Li, Q., Xie, H., Lau, R.Y., Wang, Z., Smolley, S.P.: Least squares generative adversarial networks. In: ICCV (2017)
35. Mirza, M., Osindero, S.: Conditional generative adversarial nets. arXiv preprint arXiv:1411.1784 (2014)
36. Miyato, T., Kataoka, T., Koyama, M., Yoshida, Y.: Spectral normalization for generative adversarial networks. In: ICLR (2018)
37. Miyato, T., Koyama, M.: cGANs with projection discriminator. In: ICLR (2018)

38. Molano-Mazon, M., Onken, A., Piasini, E., Panzeri, S.: Synthesizing realistic neural population activity patterns using generative adversarial networks. In: ICLR (2018)
39. Mosser, L., Dubrule, O., Blunt, M.J.: Reconstruction of three-dimensional porous media using generative adversarial neural networks. Phys. Rev. E **96**(4), 043309 (2017)
40. Nowozin, S., Cseke, B., Tomioka, R.: f-GAN: training generative neural samplers using variational divergence minimization. In: NIPS (2016)
41. Odena, A., Olah, C., Shlens, J.: Conditional image synthesis with auxiliary classifier GANs. In: ICML (2017)
42. Paganini, M., de Oliveira, L., Nachman, B.: Accelerating science with generative adversarial networks: an application to 3D particle showers in multilayer calorimeters. Phys. Rev. Lett. **120**(4), 042003 (2018)
43. Pedregosa, F., et al.: Scikit-learn: machine learning in Python. JMLR **12**, 2825–2830 (2011)
44. Rabin, J., Peyré, G., Delon, J., Bernot, M.: Wasserstein barycenter and its application to texture mixing. In: Bruckstein, A.M., ter Haar Romeny, B.M., Bronstein, A.M., Bronstein, M.M. (eds.) SSVM 2011. LNCS, vol. 6667, pp. 435–446. Springer, Heidelberg (2012). https://doi.org/10.1007/978-3-642-24785-9_37
45. Radford, A., Metz, L., Chintala, S.: Unsupervised representation learning with deep convolutional generative adversarial networks. In: ICLR (2016)
46. Salimans, T., Goodfellow, I., Zaremba, W., Cheung, V., Radford, A., Chen, X.: Improved techniques for training GANs. In: NIPS (2016)
47. Salimans, T., Karpathy, A., Chen, X., Kingma, D.P.: PixelCNN++: improving the PixelCNN with discretized logistic mixture likelihood and other modifications. In: ICLR (2017)
48. Shin, H., Lee, J.K., Kim, J., Kim, J.: Continual learning with deep generative replay. In: NIPS (2017)
49. Shrivastava, A., Pfister, T., Tuzel, O., Susskind, J., Wang, W., Webb, R.: Learning from simulated and unsupervised images through adversarial training. In: CVPR (2017)
50. Szegedy, C., et al.: Going deeper with convolutions. In: CVPR (2015)
51. Theis, L., van den Oord, A., Bethge, M.: A note on the evaluation of generative models. In: ICLR (2016)
52. Tran, T., Pham, T., Carneiro, G., Palmer, L., Reid, I.: A Bayesian data augmentation approach for learning deep models. In: NIPS (2017)
53. Van Den Oord, A., Kalchbrenner, N., Kavukcuoglu, K.: Pixel recurrent neural networks. In: ICML (2016)
54. Wang, Y.X., Girshick, R., Hebert, M., Hariharan, B.: Low-shot learning from imaginary data. In: CVPR (2018)
55. Yun, K., Bustos, J., Lu, T.: Predicting rapid fire growth (flashover) using conditional generative adversarial networks. arXiv preprint arXiv:1801.09804 (2018)
56. Zhang, H., et al.: StackGAN: text to photo-realistic image synthesis with stacked generative adversarial networks. In: ICCV (2017)
57. Zhao, J., Mathieu, M., LeCun, Y.: Energy-based generative adversarial networks. In: ICLR (2017)
58. Zhong, Z., Zheng, L., Zheng, Z., Li, S., Yang, Y.: Camera style adaptation for person re-identification. In: CVPR (2018)
59. Zhu, J.Y., Park, T., Isola, P., Efros, A.A.: Unpaired image-to-image translation using cycle-consistent adversarial networks. In: ICCV (2017)

3D-CODED: 3D Correspondences by Deep Deformation

Thibault Groueix[1]([✉]), Matthew Fisher[2], Vladimir G. Kim[2], Bryan C. Russell[2], and Mathieu Aubry[1]

[1] LIGM (UMR 8049), École des Ponts, UPE, Champs-sur-Marne, France
thibault.groueix.2012@polytechnique.org
[2] Adobe Research, San Francisco, USA
http://imagine.enpc.fr/~groueixt/3D-CODED/

Abstract. We present a new deep learning approach for matching deformable shapes by introducing *Shape Deformation Networks* which jointly encode 3D shapes and correspondences. This is achieved by factoring the surface representation into (i) a template, that parameterizes the surface, and (ii) a learnt global feature vector that parameterizes the transformation of the template into the input surface. By predicting this feature for a new shape, we implicitly predict correspondences between this shape and the template. We show that these correspondences can be improved by an additional step which improves the shape feature by minimizing the Chamfer distance between the input and transformed template. We demonstrate that our simple approach improves on state-of-the-art results on the difficult FAUST-inter challenge, with an average correspondence error of 2.88 cm. We show, on the TOSCA dataset, that our method is robust to many types of perturbations, and generalizes to non-human shapes. This robustness allows it to perform well on real unclean, meshes from the SCAPE dataset.

Keywords: 3D deep learning · Computational geometry
Shape matching

1 Introduction

There is a growing demand for techniques that make use of the large amount of 3D content generated by modern sensor technology. An essential task is to establish reliable 3D shape correspondences between scans from raw sensor data or between scans and a template 3D shape. This process is challenging due to low sensor resolution and high sensor noise, especially for articulated shapes, such as humans or animals, that exhibit significant non-rigid deformations and shape variations (Fig. 1).

Electronic supplementary material The online version of this chapter (https://doi.org/10.1007/978-3-030-01216-8_15) contains supplementary material, which is available to authorized users.

© Springer Nature Switzerland AG 2018
V. Ferrari et al. (Eds.): ECCV 2018, LNCS 11206, pp. 235–251, 2018.
https://doi.org/10.1007/978-3-030-01216-8_15

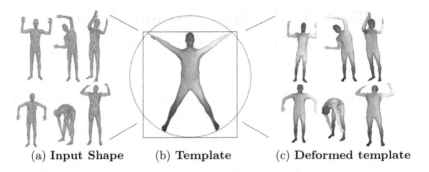

(a) **Input Shape**   (b) **Template**   (c) **Deformed template**

Fig. 1. Our approach predicts shape correspondences by learning a consistent mesh parameterization with a shared template. Colors show correspondences. (Color figure online)

Traditional approaches to estimating shape correspondences for articulated objects typically rely on intrinsic surface analysis either optimizing for an isometric map or leveraging intrinsic point descriptors [39]. To improve correspondence quality, these methods have been extended to take advantage of category-specific data priors [9]. Effective human-specific templates and registration techniques have been developed over the last decade [45], but these methods require significant effort and domain-specific knowledge to design the parametric deformable template, create an objective function that ensures alignment of salient regions and is not prone to being stuck in local minima, and develop an optimization strategy that effectively combines a global search for a good heuristic initialization and a local refinement procedure.

In this work, we propose *Shape Deformation Networks*, a comprehensive, all-in-one solution to template-driven shape matching. A Shape Deformation Network learns to deform a template shape to align with an input observed shape. Given two input shapes, we align the template to both inputs and obtain the final map between the inputs by reading off the correspondences from the template.

We train our Shape Deformation Network as part of an encoder-decoder architecture, which jointly learns an encoder network that takes a target shape as input and generates a global feature representation, and a decoder Shape Deformation Network that takes as input the global feature and deform the template into the target shape. At test time, we improve our template-input shape alignment by optimizing locally the Chamfer distance between target and generated shape over the global feature representation which is passed in as input to the Shape Deformation Network. Critical to the success of our Shape Deformation Network is the ability to learn to deform a template shape to targets with varied appearances and articulation. We achieve this ability by training our network on a very large corpus of shapes.

In contrast to previous work [45], our method does not require a manually designed deformable template; the deformation parameters and degrees of freedom are implicitly learned by the encoder. Furthermore, while our network can take advantage of known correspondences between the template and the example shapes, which are typically available when they have been generated using some parametric model [6,41], we show it can also be trained without correspondence supervision. This ability allows the network to learn from a large collection of shapes lacking explicit correspondences.

We demonstrate that with sufficient training data this simple approach achieves state-of-the-art results and outperforms techniques that require complex multi-term objective functions instead of the simple reconstruction loss used by our method.

2   Related Work

Registration of non-rigid geometries with pose and shape variations is a long standing problem with extensive prior work. We first provide a brief overview of generic correspondence techniques. We then focus on category specific and template matching methods developed for human bodies, which are more closely related to our approach. Finally, we present an overview of deep learning approaches that have been developed for shape matching and more generally for working with 3D data.

Generic Shape Matching. To estimate correspondence between articulated objects, it is common to assume that their intrinsic structure (e.g., geodesic distances) remains relatively consistent across all poses [27]. Finding point-to-point correspondences that minimize metric distortion is a non-convex optimization problem, referred to as generalized multi-dimensional scaling [11]. This optimization is typically sensitive to an initial guess [10], and thus existing techniques rely on local feature point descriptors such as HKS [39] and WKS [5], and use hierarchical optimization strategies [14,34]. Some relaxations of this problem have been proposed such as: formulating it as Markov random field and using linear programming relaxation [13], optimizing for soft correspondence [20,37,38], restricting correspondence space to conformal maps [21,22], heat kernel maps [29], and aligning functional bases [30].

While these techniques are powerful generic tools, some common categories, such as humans, can benefit from a plethora of existing data [6] to leverage stronger class-specific priors.

Template-Based Shape Matching. A natural way to leverage class-specific knowledge is through the explicit use of a shape model. While such template-based techniques provide the best correspondence results they require a careful parameterization of the template, which took more than a decade of research to reach the current level of maturity [1–3,24,45]. For all of these techniques, fitting this representation to an input 3D shape requires also designing an objective function that is typically non-convex and involves multiple terms to guide the optimization to the right global minima. In contrast, our method only relies on a single template 3D mesh and surface reconstruction loss. It leverages a neural network to learn how to parameterize the human body while optimizing for the best reconstruction.

Deep Learning for Shape Matching. Another way to leverage priors and training data is to learn better point-wise shape descriptors using human models with ground truth correspondence. Several neural network based methods have recently been developed to this end to analyze meshes [7,26,28,33] or depth maps [42]. One can further improve these results by leveraging global context, for example, by estimating an inter-surface functional map [23]. These methods still rely on hand-crafted point-wise descriptors [40] as input and use neural networks to improve results. The resulting functional maps only align basis functions and additional optimization is required to extract consistent point-to-point correspondences [30]. One would also need to optimize for template deformation to use these matching techniques for surface reconstruction. In contrast our method does not rely on hand-crafted features (it only takes point coordinates as input) and implicitly learns a human body representation. It also directly outputs a template deformation.

Deep Learning for 3D Data. Following the success of deep learning approaches for image analysis, many techniques have been developed for processing 3D data, going beyond local descriptor learning to improve classification, segmentation, and reconstruction tasks. Existing networks operate on various shape representations, such as volumetric grids [17,43], point clouds [16,31,32], geometry images [35,36], seamlessly parameterized surfaces [25], by aligning a shape to a grid via distance-preserving maps [15], by folding a surface [44] or by predicting chart representations [18]. We build on these works in several ways. First, we process the point clouds representing the input shapes using an architecture similar to [31]. Second, similar to [35], we learn a surface representation. However, we do not explicitly encode correspondences in the output of a convolution network, but implicitly learn them by optimizing for parameters of the generation network as we optimize for reconstruction loss.

3   Method

Our goal is, given a reference shape $\mathcal{S}_r$ and a target shape $\mathcal{S}_t$, to return a set of point correspondences $\mathcal{C}$ between the shapes. We do so using two key ideas. First, we learn to predict a transformation between the shapes instead of directly learning the correspondences. This transformation, from 3D to 3D can indeed be represented by a neural network more easily than the association between variable and large number of points. The second idea is to learn transformations only from one template $\mathcal{A}$ to any shape. Indeed, the large variety of possible poses of humans makes considering all pairs of possible poses intractable during training. We instead decouple the correspondence problem into finding two sets

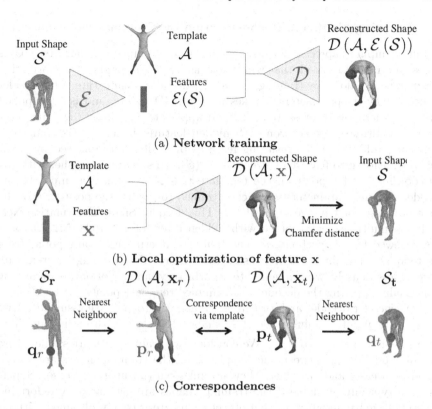

(a) **Network training**

(b) **Local optimization of feature x**

(c) **Correspondences**

Fig. 2. Method overview. (a) A feed-forward pass in our autoencoder encodes input point cloud $\mathcal{S}$ to latent code $\mathcal{E}(\mathcal{S})$ and reconstruct $\mathcal{S}$ using $\mathcal{E}(\mathcal{S})$ to deform the template $\mathcal{A}$. (b) We refine the reconstruction $\mathcal{D}(\mathcal{A}, \mathcal{E}(\mathcal{S}))$ by performing a regression step over the latent variable $\mathbf{x}$, minimizing the Chamfer distance between $\mathcal{D}(\mathcal{A}, \mathbf{x})$ and $\mathcal{S}$. (c) Finally, given two point clouds $\mathcal{S}_r$ and $\mathcal{S}_t$, to match a point $\mathbf{q}_r$ on $\mathcal{S}_r$ to a point $\mathbf{q}_t$ on $\mathcal{S}_t$, we look for the nearest neighbor $\mathbf{p}_r$ of $\mathbf{q}_r$ in $\mathcal{D}(\mathcal{A}, \mathbf{x}_r)$, which is by design in correspondence with $\mathbf{p}_t$; and look for the nearest neighbor $\mathbf{q}_t$ of $\mathbf{p}_t$ on $\mathcal{S}_t$. Red indicates what is being optimised. (Color figure online)

of correspondences to a common template shape. We can then form our final correspondences between the input shapes via indexing through the template shape. An added benefit is during training we simply need to vary the pose for a single shape and use the known correspondences to the template shape as the supervisory signal.

Our approach has three main steps which are visualized Fig. 2. First, a feedforward pass through our encoder network generates an initial global shape descriptor (Sect. 3.1). Second, we use gradient descent through our decoder Shape Deformation Network to refine this shape descriptor to improve the reconstruction quality (Sect. 3.2). We can then use the template to match points between any two input shapes (Sect. 3.3).

3.1   Learning 3D Shape Reconstruction by Template Deformation

To put an input shape S in correspondence with a template $\mathcal{A}$, our first goal is to design a neural network that will take S as input and predict transformation parameters. We do so by training an encoder-decoder architecture. The encoder $\mathcal{E}_\phi$ defined by its parameters ϕ takes as input 3D points, and is a simplified version of the network presented in [31]. It applies to each input 3D point coordinate a multi-layer perceptron with hidden feature size of 64, 128 and 1024, then maxpooling over the resulting features over all points followed by a linear layer, leading to feature of size 1024 $\mathcal{E}_\phi(S)$. This feature, together with the 3D coordinates of a point on the template $\mathbf{p} \in \mathcal{A}$, are taken as input to the decoder $\mathcal{D}_\theta$ with parameters θ, which is trained to predict the position $\mathbf{q}$ of the corresponding point in the input shape. This decoder Shape Deformation Network is a multi-layer perceptron with hidden layers of size 1024, 512, 254 and 128, followed by a hyperbolic tangent. This architecture maps any points from the template domain to the reconstructed surface. By sampling the template more or less densely, we can generate an arbitrary number of output points by sequentially applying the decoder over sampled template points.

This encoder-decoder architecture is trained end-to-end. We assume that we are given as input a training set of N shapes $\left\{S^{(i)}\right\}_{i=1}^N$ with each shape having a set of P vertices $\{\mathbf{q}_j\}_{j=1}^P$. We consider two training scenarios: one where the correspondences between the template and the training shapes are known (supervised case) and one where they are unknown (unsupervised case). Supervision is typically available if the training shapes are generated by deforming a parametrized template, but real object scans are typically obtained without correspondences.

Supervised Loss. In the supervised case, we assume that for each point $\mathbf{q}_j$ on a training shape we know the correspondence $\mathbf{p}_j \leftrightarrow \mathbf{q}_j$ to a point $\mathbf{p}_j \in \mathcal{A}$ on the template $\mathcal{A}$. Given these training correspondences, we learn the encoder $\mathcal{E}_\phi$ and decoder $\mathcal{D}_\theta$ by simply optimizing the following reconstruction losses,

$$\mathcal{L}^{\mathrm{sup}}(\theta, \phi) = \sum_{i=1}^N \sum_{j=1}^P |\mathcal{D}_\theta\left(\mathbf{p}_j; \mathcal{E}_\phi\left(S^{(i)}\right)\right) - \mathbf{q}_j^{(i)}|^2 \tag{1}$$

where the sums are over all P vertices of all N example shapes.

Unsupervised Loss. In the case where correspondences between the exemplar shapes and the template are not available, we also optimize the reconstructions, but also regularize the deformations toward isometries. For reconstruction, we use the Chamfer distance $\mathcal{L}^{\mathrm{CD}}$ between the inputs S_i and reconstructed point clouds $\mathcal{D}_\theta\left(\mathcal{A}; \mathcal{E}_\phi\left(S^{(i)}\right)\right)$. For regularization, we use two different terms. The first term $\mathcal{L}^{\mathrm{Lap}}$ encourages the Laplacian operator defined on the template and the deformed template to be the same (which is the case for isometric deformations of the surface). The second term $\mathcal{L}^{\mathrm{edges}}$ encourages the ratio between edges length in the template and its deformed version to be close to 1. More details on these different losses are given in supplementary material. The final loss we optimize is:

$$\mathcal{L}^{unsup} = \mathcal{L}^{CD} + \lambda_{Lap}\mathcal{L}^{Lap} + \lambda_{edges}\mathcal{L}^{edges} \tag{2}$$

where λ_{Lap} and λ_{edges} control the influence of regularizations against the data term $\mathcal{L}^{CD}$. They are both set to 5.10^{-3} in our experiments.

We optimize the loss using the Adam solver, with a learning rate of 10^{-3} for 25 epochs then 10^{-4} for 2 epochs, batches of 32 shapes, and 6890 points per shape.

One interesting aspect of our approach is that it learns jointly a parameterization of the input shapes via the decoder and to predict the parameters $\mathcal{E}_\phi(\mathcal{S})$ for this parameterization via the encoder. However, the predicted parameters $\mathcal{E}_\phi(\mathcal{S})$ for an input shape $\mathcal{S}$ are not necessarily optimal, because of the limited power of the encoder. Optimizing these parameters turns out to be important for the final results, and is the focus of the second step of our pipeline.

3.2 Optimizing Shape Reconstruction

We now assume that we are given a shape $\mathcal{S}$ as well as learned weights for the encoder $\mathcal{E}_\phi$ and decoder $\mathcal{D}_\theta$ networks. To find correspondences between the template shape and the input shape, we will use a nearest neighbor search to find correspondences between that input shape and its reconstruction. For this step to work, we need the reconstruction to be accurate. The reconstruction given by the parameters $\mathcal{E}_\phi(\mathcal{S})$ is only approximate and can be improved. Since we do not know correspondences between the input and the generated shape, we cannot minimize the loss given in Eq. (1), which requires correspondences. Instead, we minimize with respect to the global feature $\mathbf{x}$ the Chamfer distance between the reconstructed shape and the input:

$$\mathcal{L}^{CD}(\mathbf{x}; \mathcal{S}) = \sum_{\mathbf{p} \in \mathcal{A}} \min_{\mathbf{q} \in \mathcal{S}} |\mathcal{D}_\theta(\mathbf{p}; \mathbf{x}) - \mathbf{q}|^2 + \sum_{\mathbf{q} \in \mathcal{S}} \min_{\mathbf{p} \in \mathcal{A}} |\mathcal{D}_\theta(\mathbf{p}; \mathbf{x}) - \mathbf{q}|^2. \tag{3}$$

Starting from the parameters predicted by our first step $\mathbf{x} = \mathcal{E}_\phi(\mathcal{S})$, we optimize this loss using the Adam solver for 3,000 iterations with learning rate $5 * 10^{-4}$. Note that the good initialization given by our first step is key since Eq. (3) corresponds to a highly non-convex problem, as shown in Fig. 6.

3.3 Finding 3D Shape Correspondences

To recover correspondences between two 3D shapes $\mathcal{S}_r$ and $\mathcal{S}_t$, we first compute the parameters to deform the template to these shapes, $\mathbf{x}_r$ and $\mathbf{x}_t$, using the two steps outlined in Sects. 3.1 and 3.2. Next, given a 3D point $\mathbf{q}_r$ on the reference shape $\mathcal{S}_r$, we first find the point $\mathbf{p}$ on the template $\mathcal{A}$ such that its transformation with parameters $\mathbf{x}_r$, $\mathcal{D}_\theta(\mathbf{p}; \mathbf{x}_r)$ is closest to $\mathbf{q}_r$. Finally we find the 3D point $\mathbf{q}_t$ on the target shape $\mathcal{S}_t$ that is the closest to the transformation of $\mathbf{p}$ with parameters $\mathbf{x}_t$, $\mathcal{D}_\theta(\mathbf{p}; \mathbf{x}_t)$. Our algorithm is summarized in Algorithm 1 and illustrated in Fig. 2.

Algorithm 1. Algorithm for finding 3D shape correspondences

Input   : Reference shape $\mathcal{S}_r$ and target shape $\mathcal{S}_t$
Output: Set of 3D point correspondences $\mathcal{C}$
1 #Regression steps over latent code to find best reconstruction of $\mathcal{S}_r$ and $\mathcal{S}_t$
2 $\mathbf{x}_r \leftarrow arg\,min_{\mathbf{x}}\mathcal{L}^{\mathrm{CD}}(\mathbf{x}; \mathcal{S}_r)$ #detailed in equation (3)
3 $\mathbf{x}_t \leftarrow arg\,min_{\mathbf{x}}\mathcal{L}^{\mathrm{CD}}(\mathbf{x}; \mathcal{S}_t)$ #detailed in equation (3)
4 $\mathcal{C} \leftarrow \varnothing$
5 # Matching of $\mathbf{q}_r \in \mathcal{S}_r$ to $\mathbf{q}_t \in \mathcal{S}_t$
6 **foreach** $\mathbf{q}_r \in \mathcal{S}_r$ **do**
7      $\mathbf{p} \leftarrow arg\,min_{\mathbf{p}' \in \mathcal{A}}|\mathcal{D}_\theta(\mathbf{p}'; \mathbf{x}_r) - \mathbf{q}_r|^2$
8      $\mathbf{q}_t \leftarrow arg\,min_{\mathbf{q}' \in \mathcal{S}_t}|\mathcal{D}_\theta(\mathbf{p}; \mathbf{x}_t) - \mathbf{q}'|^2$
9      $\mathcal{C} \leftarrow \mathcal{C} \cup \{(\mathbf{q}_r, \mathbf{q}_t)\}$
10 **end**
11 **return** $\mathcal{C}$

---

4   Results

4.1   Datasets

Synthetic Training Data. To train our algorithm, we require a large set of shapes. We thus rely on synthetic data for training our model.

For human shapes, we use SMPL [6], a state-of-the-art generative model for synthetic humans. To obtain realistic human body shape and poses from the SMPL model, we sampled 2.10^5 parameters estimated in the SURREAL dataset [41]. One limitation of the SURREAL dataset is it does not include any humans bent over. Without adapted training data, our algorithm generalized poorly to these poses. To overcome this limitation, we generated an extension of the dataset. We first manually estimated 7 key-joint parameters (among 23 joints in the SMPL skeletons) to generate bent humans. We then sampled randomly the 7 parameters around these values, and used parameters from the SURREAL dataset for the other pose and body shape parameters. Note that not all meshes generated with this strategy are realistic as shown in Fig. 3. They however allow us to better cover the space of possible poses, and we added $3 \cdot 10^4$ shapes generated with this method to our dataset. Our final dataset thus has $2.3 \cdot 10^5$ human meshes with a large variety of realistic poses and body shapes.

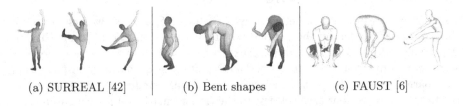

(a) SURREAL [42]   (b) Bent shapes   (c) FAUST [6]

Fig. 3. Examples of the different datasets used in the paper.

For animal shapes, we use the SMAL [47] model, which provides the equivalent of SMPL for several animals. Recent papers estimate model parameters from images, but no large-scale parameter set is yet available. For training we thus generated models from SMAL with random parameters (drawn from a Gaussian distribution of *ad-hoc* variance 0.2). This approach works for the 5 categories available in SMAL. In SMALR [46], Zuffi et al. showed that the SMAL model could be generalized to other animals using only an image dataset as input, demonstrating it on 17 additional categories. Note that since the templates for two animals are in correspondences, our method can be used to get inter-category correspondences for animals. We qualitatively demonstrate this on hippopotamus/horses in the appendix [19].

Testing Data. We evaluate our algorithm on the FAUST [6], TOSCA [12] and SCAPE [4] datasets.

The FAUST dataset consists of 100 training and 200 testing scans of approximately 170,000 vertices. They may include noise and have holes, typically missing part of the feet. In this paper, we never used the training set, except for a single baseline experiment, and we focus on the test set. Two challenges are available, focusing on intra- and inter-subject correspondences. The error is the average Euclidean distance between the estimated projection and the ground-truth projection. We evaluated our method through the online server and are the best public results on the 'inter' challenge at the time of submission[1].

The SCAPE [4] dataset has two sets of 71 meshes: the first set consists of real scans with holes and occlusions and the second set are registered meshes aligned to the first set. The poses are different from both our training dataset and FAUST.

TOSCA is a dataset produced by deforming 3 template meshes (human, dog, and horse). Each mesh is deformed into multiple poses, and might have various additional perturbations such as random holes in the surface, local and global scale variations, noise in vertex positions, varying sampling density, and changes in topology.

Shape Normalization. To be processed and reconstructed by our network, the training and testing shapes must be normalized in a similar way. Since the vertical direction is usually known, we used synthetic shapes with approximately the same vertical axis. We also kept a fixed orientation around this vertical axis, and at test time selected the one out of 50 different orientations which leads to the smaller reconstruction error in term of Chamfer distance. Finally, we centered all meshes according to the center of their bounding box and, for the training data only, added a random translation in each direction sampled uniformly between -3 cm and 3 cm to increase robustness.

---

[1] http://faust.is.tue.mpg.de/challenge/Inter-subject_challenge.

4.2   Experiments

In this part, we analyze the key components of our pipeline. More results are available in the appendix [19].

Results on FAUST. The method presented above leads to the best results to date on the FAUST-inter dataset: 2.878 cm: **an improvement of 8% over state of the art**, 3.12 cm for [45] and 4.82 cm for [23]. Although it cannot take advantage of the fact that two meshes represent the same person, our method is also the second best performing (average error of 1.99 cm) on FAUST-intra challenge.

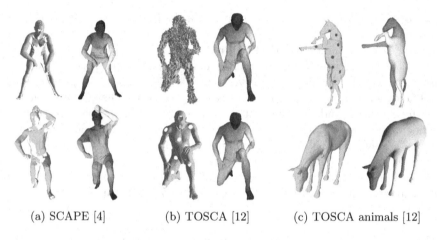

(a) SCAPE [4]   (b) TOSCA [12]   (c) TOSCA animals [12]

Fig. 4. Other datasets. Left images show the input, right images the reconstruction with colors showing correspondences. Our method works with real incomplete scans **(a)**, strong synthetic perturbations **(b)**, and on non-human shapes **(c)**. (Color figure online)

Results on SCAPE: Real and Partial Data. The SCAPE dataset provides meshes aligned to real scans and includes poses different from our training dataset. When applying a network trained directly on our SMPL data, we obtain satisfying performance, namely 3.14 cm average Euclidean error. Quantitative comparison of correspondence quality in terms of geodesic error are given in Fig. 5. We outperform all methods except for Deep Functional Maps [23]. SCAPE also allows evaluation on real partial scans. Quantitatively, the error on these partial meshes is 4.04 cm, similar to the performance on the full meshes. Qualitative results are shown in Fig. 4a.

Results on TOSCA: Robustness to Perturbations. The TOSCA dataset provides several versions of the same synthetic mesh with different perturbations. We found that our method, still trained only on SMPL or SMAL data, is

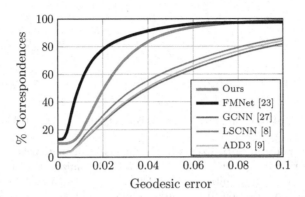

Fig. 5. Comparison with learning-based shape matching approaches on the SCAPE dataset. Our method is trained on synthetic data, FMNet was trained on FAUST data, and all other methods on SCAPE. We outperform all methods except FMNet even though our method was trained on a different dataset.

robust to all perturbations (isometry, noise, shotnoise, holes, micro-holes, topology changes, and sampling), except scale, which can be trivially fixed by normalizing all meshes to have consistent surface area. Examples of representative qualitative results are shown Fig. 4 and quantitative results are reported in appendix [19].

Table 1. Importance of the reconstruction optimization step. Optimizing the latent feature is key to our results. Regular point sampling for training and high resolution for the nearest neighbor step provide an additional boost.

Method	Faust error (cm)
Without regression	6.29
With regression	3.255
With regression + regular sampling	3.048
With regression + regular sampling + high-res template	**2.878**

Reconstruction Optimization. Because the nearest neighbors used in the matching step are sensitive to small errors in alignment, the second step of our pipeline which finds the optimal features for reconstruction, is crucial to obtain high quality results. This optimization however converges to a good optimum only if it is initialized with a reasonable reconstruction, as visualized in Fig. 6. Since we optimize using Chamfer distance, and not correspondences, we also rely on the fact that the network was trained to generate humans in correspondence and we expect the optimized shape to still be meaningful.

Table 1 reports the associated quantitative results on FAUST-inter. We can see that: (i) optimizing the latent feature to minimize the Chamfer distance

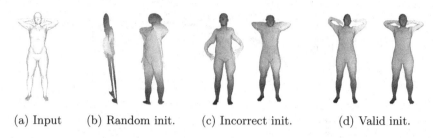

(a) Input   (b) Random init.   (c) Incorrect init.   (d) Valid init.

Fig. 6. Reconstruction optimization. The quality of the initialization (i.e. the first step of our algorithm) is crucial for the deformation optimization. For a given target shape (a) and for different initializations (left of (b), (c) and (d)) the figure shows the results of the optimization. If the initialization is random (b) or incorrect (c), the optimization converges to bad local minima. With a reasonable initialization (d) it converges to a shape very close to the target ((d), right).

between input and output provides a strong boost; (ii) using a better (more uniform) sampling of the shapes when training our network provided a better initialization; (iii) using a high resolution sampling of the template (~200k vertices) for the nearest-neighbor step provide an additional small boost in performance.

Table 2. FAUST-inter results when training on different datasets. Adding synthetic data reduce the error by a factor of 3, showing its importance. The difference in performance between the basic synthetic dataset and its augmented version is mostly due to failure on specific poses, as in Fig. 3.

Training data	Faust error (cm)
FAUST training set	18.22
Non-augmented synthetic dataset 2×10^5 shapes	5.63
Augmented synthetic data, 10^3 shapes	5.76
Augmented synthetic data, 10^4 shapes	4.70
Augmented synthetic data, 2.3×10^5 shapes	**3.26**

Necessary Amount of Training Data. Training on a large and representative dataset is also crucial for our method. To analyze the effect of training data, we ran our method without re-sampling FAUST points regularly and with a low resolution template for different training sets: FAUST training set, 2×10^5 SURREAL shapes, and 2.3×10^5, 10^4 and 10^3 shapes from our augmented dataset. The quantitative results are reported Table 2 and qualitative results can be seen in Fig. 7. The FAUST training set only include 10 different poses and is too small to train our network to generalize. Training on many synthetic shapes from the SURREAL dataset [41] helps overcome this generalization problem. However, if the synthetic dataset does not include any pose close to test poses (such as

(a) Input   (b) FAUST training data   (c) Augm. synth. training data

Fig. 7. Importance of the training data. For a given target shape (a) reconstructed shapes when the network is trained on FAUST training set (b) and on our augmented synthetic training set (c), before (left) and after (right) the optimization step.

bent-over humans), the method will fail on these poses (4 test pairs of shapes out of 40). Augmenting the dataset as described in Sect. 4.1 overcomes this limitation. As expected the performance decreases with the number of training shapes, respectively to 5.76 cm and 4.70 cm average error on FAUST-inter.

Table 3. Results with and without supervised correspondences. Adding regularization helps the network find a better local minimum in terms of correspondences.

Loss	Faust error (cm)
Chamfer distance, Eq. 3 (unsupervised)	8.727
Chamfer distance + Regularization, Eq. 2 (unsupervised)	4.835
Correspondences, Eq. 1 (supervised)	**2.878**

Unsupervised Correspondences. We investigate whether our method could be trained without correspondence supervision. We started by simply using the reconstruction loss described in Eq. (3). One could indeed expect that an optimal way to deform the template into training shapes would respect correspondences. However, we found that the resulting network did not respect correspondences between the template and the input shape, as visualized Fig. 8. However, these results improve with adequate regularization such as the one presented in Eq. (2), encouraging regularity of the mapping between the template and the reconstruction. We trained such a network with the same training data as in the supervised case but **without any correspondence supervision** and obtained a 4.88 cm of error on the FAUST-inter data, i.e. similar to Deep Functional Map [23] which had an error of 4.83 cm. This demonstrates that our method can be efficient even without correspondence supervision. Further details on regularization losses are given in the appendix [19] Table 3.

Rotation Invariance. We handled rotation invariance by rotating the shape and selecting the orientation for which the reconstruction is optimal. As an alternative, we tried to learn a network directly invariant to rotations around

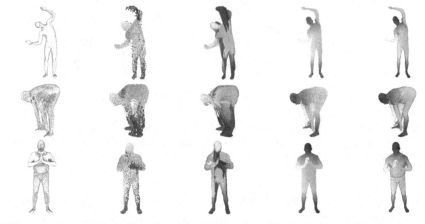

(a)   Input (b) P.C. after (c) Mesh after (d) P.C. after (e) Mesh after
(FAUST)   optim.   optim.   optim + Regul   optim + Regul

Fig. 8. Unsupervised correspondences. We visualize for different inputs (a), the point clouds (P.C.) predicted by our approach (b, d) and the corresponding meshes (c, e). Note that without regularization, because of the strong distortion, the meshes appear to barely match to the input, while the point clouds are reasonable. On the other hand surface regularization creates reasonable meshes.

the vertical axis. It turned out the performances were slightly worse on FAUST-inter (3.10 cm), but still better than the state of the art. We believe this is due to the limited capacity of the network and should be tried with a larger network. However, interestingly, this rotation invariant network seems to have increased robustness and provided slightly better results on SCAPE.

5   Conclusion

We have demonstrated an encoder-decoder deep network architecture that can generate human shape correspondences competitive with state-of-the-art approaches and that uses only simple reconstruction and correspondence losses. Our key insight is to factor the problem into an encoder network that produces a global shape descriptor, and a decoder Shape Deformation Network that uses this global descriptor to map points on a template back to the original geometry. A straightforward regression step uses gradient descent through the Shape Deformation Network to significantly improve the final correspondence quality.

Acknowledgments. This work was partly supported by ANR project EnHerit ANR-17-CE23-0008, Labex Bézout, and gifts from Adobe to École des Ponts. We thank Gül Varol, Angjoo Kanazawa, and Renaud Marlet for fruitful discussions.

References

1. Allen, B., Curless, B., Popovic, Z.: Articulated body deformation from range scan data. In: SIGGRAPH (2002)
2. Allen, B., Curless, B., Popovic, Z.: The space of human body shapes: reconstruction and parameterization from range scans. In: SIGGRAPH (2003)
3. Allen, B., Curless, B., Popovic, Z.: Learning a correlated model of identity and pose-dependent body shape variation for real-time synthesis. In: Symposium on Computer Animation (2006)
4. Anguelov, D., Srinivasan, P., Koller, D., Thrun, S., Rodgers, J., Davis, J.: SCAPE: shape completion and animation of people. ACM Trans. Graph. (TOG) **24**(3), 408–416 (2005)
5. Aubry, M., Schlickewei, U., Cremers, D.: The wave kernel signature: a quantum mechanical approach to shape analysis. In: IEEE International Conference on Computer Vision (ICCV) - Workshop on Dynamic Shape Capture and Analysis (4DMOD) (2011)
6. Bogo, F., Romero, J., Loper, M., Black, M.J.: FAUST: dataset and evaluation for 3D mesh registration. In: Proceedings of the IEEE Conference on Computer Vision and Pattern Recognition (CVPR), June 2014
7. Boscaini, D., Masci, J., Rodola, E., Bronstein, M.M.: Learning shape correspondence with anisotropic convolutional neural networks. In: NIPS (2016)
8. Boscaini, D., Masci, J., Melzi, S., Bronstein, M.M., Castellani, U., Vandergheynst, P.: Learning class-specific descriptors for deformable shapes using localized spectral convolutional networks. Comput. Graph. Forum **34**(5), 13–23 (2015)
9. Boscaini, D., Masci, J., Rodolà, E., Bronstein, M.M., Cremers, D.: Anisotropic diffusion descriptors. Comput. Graph. Forum **35**(2), 431–441 (2016)
10. Bronstein, A.M., Bronstein, M.M., Kimmel, R.: Efficient computation of isometry-invariant distances between surfaces. SIAM J. Sci. Comput. **28**(5), 1812–1836 (2006)
11. Bronstein, A.M., Bronstein, M.M., Kimmel, R.: Generalized multidimensional scaling: a framework for isometry-invariant partial surface matching. In: Proceedings of the National Academy of Sciences (PNAS) (2006)
12. Bronstein, A.M., Bronstein, M.M., Kimmel, R.: Numerical Geometry of Non-Rigid Shapes. MCS. Springer Science & Business Media, New York (2009). https://doi.org/10.1007/978-0-387-73301-2
13. Chen, Q., Koltun, V.: Robust nonrigid registration by convex optimization. In: International Conference on Computer Vision (ICCV) (2015)
14. Raviv, D., Dubrovina, A., Kimmel, R.: Hierarchical framework for shape correspondence. Numer. Math. Theory Methods Appl. (2013)
15. Ezuz, D., Solomon, J., Kim, V.G., Ben-Chen, M.: GWCNN: a metric alignment layer for deep shape analysis. In: SGP (2017)
16. Fan, H., Su, H., Guibas, L.: A point set generation network for 3D object reconstruction from a single image. In: Proceedings of IEEE Conference on Computer Vision and Pattern Recognition (CVPR) (2017)
17. Girdhar, R., Fouhey, D.F., Rodriguez, M., Gupta, A.: Learning a predictable and generative vector representation for objects. In: Leibe, B., Matas, J., Sebe, N., Welling, M. (eds.) ECCV 2016. LNCS, vol. 9910, pp. 484–499. Springer, Cham (2016). https://doi.org/10.1007/978-3-319-46466-4_29
18. Groueix, T., Fisher, M., Kim, V.G., Russell, B., Aubry, M.: AtlasNet: a Papier-Mâché approach to learning 3D surface generation. In: Proceedings of the IEEE Conference on Computer Vision and Pattern Recognition (CVPR) (2018)

19. Groueix, T., Fisher, M., Kim, V.G., Russell, B., Aubry, M.: Supplementary material (appendix) for the paper (2018). http://imagine.enpc.fr/~groueixt/3D-CODED/index.html
20. Kim, V.G., Li, W., Mitra, N.J., DiVerdi, S., Funkhouser, T.: Exploring collections of 3D models using fuzzy correspondences. Trans. Graph. $31(4)$, 54:1–54:11 (2012). (Proc. of SIGGRAPH)
21. Kim, V.G., Lipman, Y., Funkhouser, T.: Blended intrinsic maps. Trans. Graph. $30(4)$ (2011). (Proc. of SIGGRAPH)
22. Lipman, Y., Funkhouser, T.: Mobius voting for surface correspondence. ACM Trans. Graph. $28(3)$ (2009). (Proc. SIGGRAPH)
23. Litany, O., Remez, T., Rodola, E., Bronstein, A.M., Bronstein, M.M.: Deep functional maps: structured prediction for dense shape correspondence. In: ICCV (2017)
24. Loper, M., Mahmood, N., Romero, J., Pons-Moll, G., Black, M.J.: SMPL: a skinned multi-person linear model. In: SIGGRAPH Asia (2015)
25. Maron, H., et al.: Convolutional neural networks on surfaces via seamless toric covers. In: SIGGRAPH (2017)
26. Masci, J., Boscaini, D., Bronstein, M.M., Vandergheynst, P.: Geodesic convolutional neural networks on riemannian manifolds. In: Proceedings of the IEEE International Conference on Computer Vision (ICCV) Workshops, pp. 37–45 (2015)
27. Mémoli, F., Sapiro, S.: A theoretical and computational framework for isometry invariant recognition of point cloud data. Found. Comput. Math. $5(3)$, 313–347 (2005)
28. Monti, F., Boscaini, D., Masci, J., Rodola, E., Svoboda, J., Bronstein, M.M.: Geometric deep learning on graphs and manifolds using mixture model CNNs. In: CVPR (2017)
29. Ovsjanikov, M., Mérigot, Q., Mémoli, F., Guibas, L.: One point isometric matching with the heat kernel. Comput. Graph. Forum 29, 1555–1564 (2010). (Proc. of SGP)
30. Ovsjanikov, M., Ben-Chen, M., Solomon, J., Butscher, A., Guibas, L.: Functional maps: a flexible representation of maps between shapes. ACM Trans. Graph. (2012)
31. Qi, C.R., Su, H., Mo, K., Guibas, L.J.: PointNet: deep learning on point sets for 3D classification and segmentation. In: Proceedings of IEEE Conference on Computer Vision and Pattern Recognition (CVPR) (2017)
32. Qi, C.R., Yi, L., Su, H., Guibas, L.J.: PointNet++: deep hierarchical feature learning on point sets in a metric space. In: Advances in Neural Information Processing Systems (NIPS) (2017)
33. Rodola, E., Rota Bulo, S., Windheuser, T., Vestner, M., Cremers, D.: Dense non-rigid shape correspondence using random forests. In: CVPR (2014)
34. Sahillioglu, Y., Yemez, Y.: Coarse-to-fine combinatorial matching for dense isometric shape correspondence. Comput. Graph. Forum 30, 1461–1470 (2011)
35. Sinha, A., Unmesh, A., Huang, Q., Ramani, K.: SurfNet: generating 3D shape surfaces using deep residual networks. In: Proceedings of IEEE Conference on Computer Vision and Pattern Recognition (CVPR) (2017)
36. Sinha, A., Bai, J., Ramani, K.: Deep learning 3D shape surfaces using geometry images. In: Proceedings of IEEE Conference on Computer Vision and Pattern Recognition (CVPR) (2016)
37. Solomon, J., Nguyen, A., Butscher, A., Ben-Chen, M., Guibas, L.: Soft maps between surfaces. In: SGP (2012)
38. Solomon, J., Peyre, G., Kim, V.G., Sra, S.: Entropic metric alignment for correspondence problems. Trans. Graph. 35, 1–13 (2016). (Proc. of SIGGRAPH)

39. Sun, J., Ovsjanikov, M., Guibas, L.: A concise and provably informative multi-scale signature-based on heat diffusion. Comput. Graph. Forum **28**, 1383–1392 (2009). (Proc. of SGP)
40. Tombari, F., Salti, S., Di Stefano, L.: Unique signatures of histograms for local surface description. In: Daniilidis, K., Maragos, P., Paragios, N. (eds.) ECCV 2010. LNCS, vol. 6313, pp. 356–369. Springer, Heidelberg (2010). https://doi.org/10. 1007/978-3-642-15558-1_26
41. Varol, G., et al.: Learning from synthetic humans. In: CVPR (2017)
42. Wei, L., Huang, Q., Ceylan, D., Vouga, E., Li, H.: Dense human body correspondences using convolutional networks. In: Computer Vision and Pattern Recognition (CVPR) (2016)
43. Wu, Z., et al.: 3D ShapeNets: a deep representation for volumetric shapes. In: Proceedings of the IEEE Conference on Computer Vision and Pattern Recognition, pp. 1912–1920 (2015)
44. Yang, Y., Feng, C., Shen, Y., Tian, D.: FoldingNet: point cloud auto-encoder via deep grid deformation. In: CVPR (2018)
45. Zuffi, S., Black., M.J.: The stitched puppet: a graphical model of 3D human shape and pose. In: Proceedings of the IEEE Conference on Computer Vision and Pattern Recognition (CVPR) (2015)
46. Zuffi, S., Kanazawa, A., Black, M.J.: Lions and tigers and bears: capturing non-rigid, 3D, articulated shape from images. In: IEEE Conference on Computer Vision and Pattern Recognition (CVPR) (2018)
47. Zuffi, S., Kanazawa, A., Jacobs, D., Black, M.J.: 3D menagerie: modeling the 3D shape and pose of animals. In: CVPR (2017)

Audio-Visual Event Localization in Unconstrained Videos

Yapeng Tian$^{(\boxtimes)}$ ⓘ, Jing Shi ⓘ, Bochen Li ⓘ, Zhiyao Duan ⓘ,
and Chenliang Xu ⓘ

University of Rochester, Rochester, USA
yapengtian@rochester.edu

Abstract. In this paper, we introduce a novel problem of audio-visual event localization in unconstrained videos. We define *an audio-visual event* as an event that is both visible and audible in a video segment. We collect an *Audio-Visual Event* (AVE) dataset to systemically investigate three temporal localization tasks: supervised and weakly-supervised audio-visual event localization, and cross-modality localization. We develop an audio-guided visual attention mechanism to explore audio-visual correlations, propose a dual multimodal residual network (DMRN) to fuse information over the two modalities, and introduce an audio-visual distance learning network to handle the cross-modality localization. Our experiments support the following findings: joint modeling of auditory and visual modalities outperforms independent modeling, the learned attention can capture semantics of sounding objects, temporal alignment is important for audio-visual fusion, the proposed DMRN is effective in fusing audio-visual features, and strong correlations between the two modalities enable cross-modality localization.

Keywords: Audio-visual event · Temporal localization · Attention Fusion

1 Introduction

Studies in neurobiology suggest that the perceptual benefits of integrating visual and auditory information are extensive [9]. For computational models, they reflect in lip reading [5,12], where correlations between speech and lip movements provide a strong cue for linguistic understanding; in music performance [32], where vibrato articulations and hand motions enable the association between sound tracks and the performers; and in sound synthesis [41], where physical interactions with different types of material give rise to plausible sound patterns. Albeit these advances, these models are limited in their constrained domains.

Indeed, our community has begun to explore marrying computer vision with audition *in-the-wild* for learning a *good* representation [2,6,42]. For example, a

Electronic supplementary material The online version of this chapter (https://doi.org/10.1007/978-3-030-01216-8_16) contains supplementary material, which is available to authorized users.

ⓒ Springer Nature Switzerland AG 2018
V. Ferrari et al. (Eds.): ECCV 2018, LNCS 11206, pp. 252–268, 2018.
https://doi.org/10.1007/978-3-030-01216-8_16

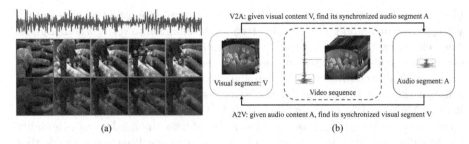

(a)   (b)

Fig. 1. (a) illustrates audio-visual event localization. The first two rows show a 5 s video sequence with both audio and visual tracks for an audio-visual event *chainsaw* (event is temporally labeled in yellow boxes). The third row shows our localization results (in red boxes) and the generated audio-guided visual attention maps. (b) illustrates cross-modality localization for V2A and A2V (Color figure online)

sound network is learned in [6] by a visual teacher network with a large amount of unlabeled videos, which shows better performance than learning in a single modality. However, they have all assumed that the audio and visual contents in a video are matched (which is often not the case as we will show) and they are yet to explore whether the joint audio-visual representations can facilitate understanding unconstrained videos.

In this paper, we study a family of audio-visual event temporal localization tasks (see Fig. 1) as a proxy to the broader audio-visual scene understanding problem for unconstrained videos. We pose and seek to answer the following questions: (Q1) Does inference jointly over auditory and visual modalities outperform inference over them independently? (Q2) How does the result vary under noisy training conditions? (Q3) How does knowing one modality help model the other modality? (Q4) How do we best fuse information over both modalities? (Q5) Can we locate the content in one modality given its observation in the other modality? Notice that the individual questions might be studied in the literature, but we are not aware of any work that conducts a systematic study to answer these collective questions as a whole.

In particular, we define an *audio-visual event* as an event that is both visible and audible in a video segment, and we establish three tasks to explore aforementioned research questions: (1) supervised audio-visual event localization, (2) weakly-supervised audio-visual event localization, and (3) event-agnostic cross-modality localization. The first two tasks aim to predict which temporal segment of an input video has an audio-visual event and what category the event belongs to. The weakly-supervised setting assumes that we have no access to the temporal event boundary but an event tag at video-level for training. Q1–Q4 will be explored within these two tasks. In the third task, we aim to locate the corresponding visual sound source temporally within a video from a given sound segment and vice versa, which will answer Q5.

We propose both baselines and novel algorithms to solve the above three tasks. For the first two tasks, we start with a baseline model treating them as a sequence labeling problem. We utilize CNN [31] to encode audio and visual inputs, adapt LSTM [26] to capture temporal dependencies, and apply Fully

Connected (FC) network to make the final predictions. Upon this baseline model, we introduce an audio-guided visual attention mechanism to verify whether audio can help attend visual features; it also implies spatial locations for sounding objects as a side output. Furthermore, we investigate several audio-visual feature fusion methods and propose a novel dual multimodal residual fusion network that achieves the best fusion results. For weakly-supervised learning, we formulate it as a Multiple Instance Learning (MIL) [35] task, and modify our network structure via adding a MIL pooling layer. To address the harder cross-modality localization task, we propose an audio-visual distance learning network that measures the relativeness of any given pair of audio and visual content.

Observing that there is no publicly available dataset directly suitable for our tasks, we collect a large video dataset that consists of 4143 10-s videos with both audio and video tracks for 28 audio-visual events and annotate their temporal boundaries. Videos in our dataset are originated from YouTube, thus they are unconstrained. Our extensive experiments support the following findings: modeling jointly over auditory and visual modalities outperforms modeling independently over them, audio-visual event localization in a noisy condition can still achieve promising results, the audio-guided visual attention can well capture semantic regions covering sounding objects and can even distinguish audio-visual unrelated videos, temporal alignment is important for audio-visual fusion, the proposed dual multimodal residual network is effective in addressing the fusion task, and strong correlations between the two modalities enable cross-modality localization. These findings have paved a way for our community to solve harder, high-level understanding problems in the future, such as video captioning [56] and movieQA [53], where the auditory modality plays an important role in understanding video but lacks effective modeling.

Our work makes the following contributions: (1) a family of three audio-visual event localization tasks; (2) an audio-guided visual attention model to adaptively explore the audio-visual correlations; (3) a novel dual multimodal residual network to fuse audio-visual features; (4) an effective audio-visual distance learning network to address cross-modality localization; (5) a large audio-visual event dataset containing more than 4K unconstrained and annotated videos, which to the best of our knowledge, is the largest dataset for sound event detection. Dataset, code, and supplementary material are available on our webpage: https://sites.google.com/view/audiovisualresearch.

2   Related Work

In this section, we first describe how our work differs from closely-related topics: sound event detection, temporal action localization and multimodal machine learning, then discuss relations to recent works in modeling vision-and-sound.

Sound event detection considered in the audio signal processing community aims to detect and temporally locate sound events in an acoustic scene. Approaches based on Hidden Markov Models (HMM), Gaussian Mixture Models (GMM), feed-forward Deep Neural Networks (DNN), and Bidirectional Long Short-Term Memory (BLSTM) [46] are developed in [10,23,36,43]. These methods focus on audio signals, and visual signals have not been explored. Corresponding datasets, e.g., TUT [36], for sound event detection only contain sound tracks, and are not suitable for audio-visual scene understanding.

Temporal action localization aims to detect and locate actions in videos. Most works cast it as a classification problem and utilize a temporal sliding window approach, where each window is considered as an action candidate subject to classification [39]. Escorcia et al. [14] present a deep action proposal network that is effective in generating temporal action proposals for long videos and can speed up temporal action localization. Recently, Shou et al. [48] propose an end-to-end Segment-based 3D CNN method (S-CNN), Zhao et al. [60] present a structured segment network (SSN), and Lea et al. [30] develop an Encoder-Decoder Temporal Convolutional Network (ED-TCN) to hierarchically model actions. Different from these works, an audio-visual event in our consideration may contain multiple actions or motionless sounding objects, and we model over both audio and visual domains. Nevertheless, we extend the ED-TCN and SSN methods to address our supervised audio-visual event localization task and compare them in Sect. 6.3.

Multimodal machine learning aims to learn joint representations over multiple input modalities, e.g., speech and video, image and text. Feature fusion is one of the most important part for multimodal learning [8], and many different fusion models have been developed, such as statistical models [15], Multiple Kernel Learning (MKL) [19,44], Graphical models [20,38]. Although some mutimodal deep networks have been studied in [27,28,37,38,50,51,58], which mainly focus on joint audio-visual representation learning based on Autoencoder or deep Boltzmann machines [51], we are interested in investigating the best models to fuse learned audio and visual features for localization purpose.

Recently, some inspiring works are developed for modeling vision-and-sound [2,6,22,41,42]. Aytar et al. [6] use a visual teacher network to learn powerful sound representations from unlabeled videos. Owens et al. [42] leverage ambient sounds as supervision to learn visual representations. Arandjelovic and Zisserman [2] learn both visual and audio representations in an unsupervised manner through an audio-visual correspondence task, and in [3], they further locate sound source spatially in an image based on an extended correspondence network. Aside from works in representation learning, audio-visual cross-modal synthesis is studied in [11,42,61], and associations between natural image scenes and accompanying free-form spoken audio captions are explored in [22]. Concurrently, some interesting and related works on sound source separation, localization and audio-visual representation learning are explored in [13,16,40,47,59]. Unlike the previous works, in this paper, we systematically investigate audio-visual event localization tasks.

3 Dataset and Problems

AVE: The *Audio-Visual Event* Dataset. To the best of our knowledge, there is no publicly available dataset directly suitable for our purpose. Therefore, we

Fig. 2. The AVE dataset. Some examples in the dataset are shown. The distribution of videos in different categories and the distribution of event lengths are illustrated

introduce the *Audio-Visual Event* (AVE) dataset, a subset of AudioSet [18], that contains 4143 videos covering 28 event categories and videos in AVE are temporally labeled with audio-visual event boundaries. Each video contains at least one 2 s long *audio-visual event*. The dataset covers a wide range of audio-visual events (*e.g.*, man speaking, woman speaking, dog barking, playing guitar, and frying food *etc.*) from different domains, e.g., human activities, animal activities, music performances, and vehicle sounds. We provide examples from different categories and show the statistics in Fig. 2. Each event category contains a minimum of 60 videos and a maximum of 188 videos, and 66.4% videos in the AVE contain audio-visual events that span over the full 10 s. Next, we introduce three different tasks based on the AVE to explore the interactions between auditory and visual modalities.

Fully and Weakly-Supervised Event Localization. The goal of event localization is to predict the event label for each video segment, which contains both audio and visual tracks, for an input video sequence. Concretely, for a video sequence, we split it into T non-overlapping segments $\{V_t, A_t\}_{t=1}^T$, where each segment is 1 s long (since our event boundary is labeled at second-level), and V_t and A_t denote the visual content and its corresponding audio counterpart in a video segment, respectively. Let $\boldsymbol{y}_t = \{y_t^k | y_t^k \in \{0,1\}, k = 1, \ldots, C, \sum_{k=1}^C y_t^k = 1\}$ be the event label for that video segment. Here, C is the total number of AVE events plus one background label.

For the supervised event localization task, the event label $\boldsymbol{y}_t$ of each visual segment V_t or audio segment A_t is known during training. We are interested in event localization in audio space alone, visual space alone and the joint audio-visual space. This task explores whether or not audio and visual information can help each other improve event localization. Different than the supervised setting, in the weakly-supervised manner we have only access to a video-level event tag, and we still aim to predict segment-level labels during testing. The weakly-supervised task allows us to alleviate the reliance on well-annotated data for modelings of audio, visual and audio-visual.

Cross-Modality Localization. In the cross-modality localization task, given a segment of one modality (auditory/visual), we would like to find the position of its synchronized content in the other modality (visual/auditory). Concretely, for visual localization from audio (A2V), given a l-second audio segment $\hat{A}$ from

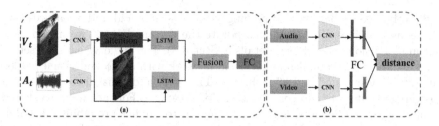

Fig. 3. (a) Audio-visual event localization framework with audio-guided visual attention and multimodal fusion. One timestep is illustrated, and note that the fusion network and FC are shared for all timesteps. (b) Audio-visual distance learning network

$\{A_t\}_{t=1}^T$, where $l < T$, we want to find its synchronized l-second visual segment within $\{V_t\}_{t=1}^T$. Similarly, for audio localization from visual content (V2A), given a l-second video segment $\hat{V}$ from $\{V_t\}_{t=1}^T$, we would like to find its l-second audio segment within $\{A_t\}_{t=1}^T$. This task is conducted in the event-agnostic setting such that the models developed for this task are expected to work for general videos where the event labels are not available. For evaluation, we only use short-event videos, in where the lengths of audio-visual event are all shorter than 10 s.

4   Methods for Audio-Visual Event Localization

First, we present the overall framework that treats the audio-visual event localization as a sequence labeling problem in Sect. 4.1. Upon this framework, we propose our audio-guided visual attention in Sect. 4.2 and a novel dual multimodal residual fusion network in Sect. 4.3. Finally, we extend this framework to work in weakly-supervised setting in Sect. 4.4.

4.1   Audio-Visual Event Localization Network

Our network mainly consists of five modules: feature extraction, audio-guided visual attention, temporal modeling, multimodal fusion and temporal labeling (see Fig. 3(a)). The feature extraction module utilizes pre-trained CNNs to extract visual features $v_t = [v_t^1, \ldots, v_t^k] \in \mathbb{R}^{d_v \times k}$ and audio features $a_t \in \mathbb{R}^{d_a}$ from each V_t and A_t, respectively. Here, d_v denotes the number of CNN visual feature maps, k is the vectorized spatial dimension of each feature map, and d_a denotes the dimension of audio features. We use an audio-guided visual attention model to generate a context vector $v_t^{att} \in \mathbb{R}^{d_v}$ (see details in Sect. 4.2). Two separate LSTMs take v_t^{att} and a_t as inputs to model temporal dependencies in the two modalities respectively. For an input feature vector F_t at time step t, the LSTM updates a hidden state vector h_t and a memory cell state vector c_t:

$$h_t, c_t = \text{LSTM}(F_t, h_{t-1}, c_{t-1}), \tag{1}$$

where F_t refers to v_t^{att} or a_t in our model. For evaluating the performance of the proposed attention mechanism, we compare to models that do not use attention;

we directly feed global average pooling visual features and audio features into LSTMs as baselines. To better incorporate the two modalities, we introduce a multimodal fusion network (see details in Sect. 4.3). The audio-visual representation h_t^* is learned by a multimodal fusion network with audio and visual hidden state output vectors h_t^v and h_t^a as inputs. This joint audio-visual representation is used to output event category for each video segment. For this, we use a shared FC layer with the Softmax activation function to predict probability distribution over C event categories for the input segment and the whole network can be trained with a multi-class cross-entropy loss.

4.2   Audio-Guided Visual Attention

Psychophysical and physiological evidence shows that sound is not only informative about its source but also its location [17]. Based on this, Hershey and Movellan [24] introduce an exploratory work on localizing sound sources utilizing audio-visual synchrony. It shows that the strong correlations between the two modalities can be used to find image regions that are highly correlated to the audio signal. Recently, [3,42] show that sound indicates object properties even in unconstrained images or videos. These works inspire us to use audio signal as a means of guidance for visual modeling.

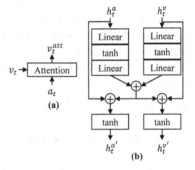

Fig. 4. (a) Audio-guided visual attention mechanism. (b) Dual multimodal residual network for audio-visual feature fusion

Given that attention mechanism has shown superior performance in many applications such as neural machine translation [7] and image captioning [34,57], we use it to implement our audio-guided visual attention (see Fig. 3(a) and Fig. 4(a)). The attention network will adaptively learn which visual regions in each segment of a video to look for the corresponding sounding object or activity.

Concretely, we define the attention function f_{att} and it can be adaptively learned from the visual feature map v_t and audio feature vector a_t. At each time step t, the visual context vector v_t^{att} is computed by:

$$v_t^{att} = f_{att}(a_t, v_t) = \sum_{i=1}^{k} w_t^i v_t^i, \qquad (2)$$

where w_t is an attention weight vector corresponding to the probability distribution over k visual regions that are attended by its audio counterpart. The attention weights can be computed based on MLP with a Softmax activation function:

$$w_t = Softmax(x_t), \qquad (3)$$

$$x_t = W_f \sigma(W_v U_v(v_t) + (W_a U_a(a_t)) \mathbb{1}^T), \qquad (4)$$

where U_v and U_a, implemented by a dense layer with nonlinearity, are two transformation functions that project audio and visual features to the same dimension d, $W_v \in \mathbb{R}^{k \times d}$, $W_a \in \mathbb{R}^{k \times d}$, $W_f \in \mathbb{R}^{1 \times k}$ are parameters, the entries in $\mathbb{1} \in \mathbb{R}^k$ are all 1, $\sigma(\cdot)$ is the hyperbolic tangent function, and $w_t \in \mathbb{R}^k$ is the computed attention map. The attention map visualization results show that the audio-guided attention mechanism can adaptively capture the location information of sound source (see Fig. 5), and it can also improve temporal localization accuracy (see Table 1).

4.3 Audio-Visual Feature Fusion

Our fusion method is designed based on the philosophy in [51], which processes multiple features separately and then learns a joint representation using a middle layer. To combine features coming from visual and audio modalities, inspired by the Mutimodal Residual Network (MRN) in [29] (which works for text-and-image), we introduce a Dual Multimodal Residual Network (DMRN). The MRN adopts a textual residual branch and feeds transformed visual features into different textual residual blocks, where only textual features are updated. In contrary, the proposed DMRN shown in Fig. 4(b) updates both audio and visual features simultaneously.

Given audio and visual features h_t^a and h_t^v from LSTMs, the DMRN will compute the updated audio and visual features:

$$h_t^{a'} = \sigma(h_t^a + f(h_t^a, h_t^v)), \tag{5}$$

$$h_t^{v'} = \sigma(h_t^v + f(h_t^a, h_t^v)), \tag{6}$$

where $f(\cdot)$ is an additive fusion function, and the average of $h_t^{a'}$ and $h_t^{v'}$ is used as the joint representation h_t^* for labeling the video segment. Here, the update strategy in DMRN can both preserve useful information in the original modality and add complimentary information from the other modality. Simply, we can stack multiple residual blocks to learn a deep fusion network with updated $h_t^{a'}$ and $h_t^{v'}$ as inputs of new residual blocks. However, we empirically find that it does not improve performance by stacking many blocks for both MRN and DMRN. We argue that the network becomes harder to train with increasing parameters and one block is enough to handle this simple fusion task well.

We would like to underline the importance of fusing audio-visual features after LSTMs for our task. We empirically find that late fusion (fusion after temporal modeling) is much better than early fusion (fusion before temporal modeling). We suspect that the auditory and visual modalities are not temporally aligned. Temporal modeling by LSTMs can implicitly learn certain alignments which can help make better audio-visual fusion. The empirical evidences will be shown in Table 2.

4.4 Weakly-Supervised Event Localization

To address the weakly-supervised event localization, we formulate it as a MIL problem and extend our framework to handle noisy training condition. Since only video-level labels are available, we infer label of each audio-visual segment pair in the training phase, and aggregate these individual predictions into a video-level prediction by MIL pooling as in [55]:

$$\hat{m} = g(m_1, m_2, \ldots, m_T) = \frac{1}{T} \sum_{t=1}^{T} m_t, \tag{7}$$

where $m_1, \ldots, m_T$ are predictions from the last FC layer of our audio-visual event localization network, and $g(\cdot)$ averages over all predictions. The probability distribution of event category for the video sequence can be computed using $\hat{m}$ over the Softmax. During testing, we can predict the event category for each segment according to computed m_t.

5   Method for Cross-Modality Localization

To address the cross-modality localization problem, we propose an audio-visual distance learning network (AVDLN) as illustrated in Fig. 3(b); we notice similar networks are studied in concurrent works [3,52]. Our network can measure the distance $D_\theta(V_i, A_i)$ for a given pair of V_i and A_i. At test time, for visual localization from audio (A2V), we use a sliding window method and optimize the following objective:

$$t^* = \arg\min_t \sum_{s=1}^{l} D_\theta(V_{s+t-1}, \hat{A}_s), \tag{8}$$

where $t^* \in \{1, \ldots, T - l + 1\}$ denotes the start time when visual and audio content synchronize, T is the total length of a testing video sequence, and l is the length of the audio query $\hat{A}$. This objective function computes an optimal matching by minimizing the cumulative distance between the audio segments and the visual segments. Therefore, $\{V_i\}_{i=t^*}^{t^*+l-1}$ is the matched visual content. Similarly, we can define audio localization from visual content (V2A); we omit it here for a concise writing. Next, we describe the network used to implement the matching function.

Let $\{V_i, A_i\}_{i=1}^{N}$ be N training samples and $\{y_i\}_{i=1}^{N}$ be their labels, where V_i and A_i are a pair of 1 s visual and audio segments, $y_i \in \{0, 1\}$. Here, $y_i = 1$ means that V_i and A_i are synchronized. The AVDLN will learn to measure distances between these pairs. The network encodes them using pre-trained CNNs, and then performs dimensionality reduction for encoded audio and visual representations using two different two-layer FC networks. The outputs of final FC layers are $\{R_i^v, R_i^a\}_{i=1}^{N}$. The distance between V_i and A_i is measured by the Euclidean distance between R_i^v and R_i^a:

$$D_\theta(V_i, A_i) = ||R_i^v - R_i^a||_2. \tag{9}$$

To optimize the parameters θ of the distance metric D_θ, we introduce the contrastive loss proposed by Hadsell $et\ al.$ [21]. The contrastive loss function is:

$$L_C = y_i D_\theta^2(V_i, A_i) + (1 - y_i)(\max(0, th - D_\theta(V_i, A_i)))^2, \tag{10}$$

where $th > 0$ is a margin. If a dissimilar pair's distance is less than th, the loss will make the distance D_θ bigger; if their distance is bigger than the margin, it will not contribute to the loss.

6   Experiments

First, we introduce the used visual and audio representations in Sect. 6.1. Then, we describe the compared baseline models and evaluation metrics in Sect. 6.2. Finally, we show and analyze experimental results of different models in Sect. 6.3.

6.1   Visual and Audio Representations

It has been suggested that CNN features learned from a large-scale dataset (*e.g.* ImageNet [45], AudioSet [18]) are highly generic and powerful for other vision or audition tasks. So, we adopt pre-trained CNN models to extract features for visual segments and their corresponding audio segments.

For each 1 s visual segment, we extract *pool*5 feature maps from sampled 16 RGB video frames by VGG-19 network [49], which is pre-trained on ImageNet, and then utilize global average pooling [33] over the 16 frames to generate one $512 \times 7 \times 7$-D feature map. We also explore the temporal visual features extracted by C3D [54], which is capable of learning spatio-temporal visual features. But we do not observe significant improvements when combining C3D features. We extract a 128-D audio representation for each 1 s audio segment via a VGG-like network [25] pre-trained on AudioSet.

6.2   Baselines and Evaluation Metrics

To validate the effectiveness of the joint audio-visual modeling, we use single-modality models as baselines, which only use audio-alone or visual-alone features and share the same structure with our audio-visual models. To evaluate the audio-guided visual attention, we compare our V-att and A+V-att models with V and A+V models in fully and weakly supervised settings. Here, V-att models adopt audio-guided visual attention to pool visual feature maps, and the other V models use global average pooling to compute visual feature vectors. We visualize generated attention maps for subjective evaluation. To further demonstrate the effectiveness of the proposed networks, we also compare them with a state-of-the-art temporal labeling network: ED-TCN [30] and proposal-based SSN [60].

We compare our fusion method: DMRN with several network-based multi-modal fusion methods: Additive, Maxpooling (MP), Gated, Multimodal Bilinear (MB), and Gated Multimodal Bilinear (GMB) in [28], Gated Multimodal Unit (GMU) in [4], Concatenation (Concat), and MRN [29]. Three different fusion strategies: early, late and decision fusions are explored. Here, early fusion methods directly fuse audio features from pre-trained CNNs and attended visual features; late fusion methods fuse audio and visual features from outputs of two LSTMs; and decision fusion methods fuse the two modalities before

Fig. 5. Qualitative visualization of audio-guided visual attention. The semantic regions containing many different sound sources, such as barking dog, crying boy/babies, speaking woman, horning bus, guitar *etc*, can be adaptively captured by our attention model

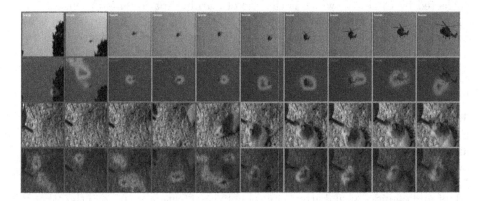

Fig. 6. Visualization of visual attention maps on two **challenging** examples. The first and third rows are 10 video frames uniformly extracted from two 10 s videos, and the second and fourth rows are generated attention maps. The **yellow** box (groundtruth label) denotes that the frame contain audio-visual event in which sounding object is visible and sound is audible. If there is no audio-visual event in a frame, random background regions will be attended (5th frame of the second example); otherwise, the attention will focus on sounding sources (Color figure online)

Softmax layer. To further enhance the performance of DMRN, we also introduce a variant model of DMRN called dual multimodal residual fusion ensemble (DMRFE) method, which feeds audio and visual features into two separated blocks and then use average ensemble to combine the two predicted probabilities.

Table 1. Event localization prediction accuracy (%) on AVE dataset. A, V, V-att, A+V, A+V-att denote that these models use audio, visual, attended visual, audio-visual and attended audio-visual features, respectively. W-models are trained in a weakly-supervised manner. Note that audio-visual models all fuse features by concatenating the outputs of LSTMs

Models	A	V	V-att	A+V	A+V-att	W-A	W-V	W-V-att	W-A+V	W-A+V-att
Accuracy	59.5	55.3	58.6	71.4	**72.7**	53.4	52.9	55.6	63.7	66.7

For supervised and weakly-supervised event localization, we use overall accuracy as an evaluation metric. For cross-modality localization, e.g., V2A and A2V, if a matched audio/visual segment is exactly the same as its groundtruth, we regard it as a good matching; otherwise, it will be a bad matching. We compute the percentage of good matchings over all testing samples as prediction accuracy to evaluate the performance of cross-modality localization. To validate the effectiveness of the proposed model, we also compare it with deep canonical correlation analysis (DCCA) method [1].

6.3 Experimental Comparisons

Table 1 compares different variations of our proposed models on supervised and weakly-supervised audio-visual event localization tasks. Table 2 shows event localization performance of different fusion methods. Figures 5 and 6 illustrate generated audio-guided visual attention maps.

To benchmark our models with state-of-the-art temporal action localization methods, we extend the SSN [60] and ED-TCN [30] to address the supervised audio-visual event localization, and train them on AVE. The SSN and ED-TCN achieve 26.7% and 46.9% overall accuracy, respectively. For comparison, our V model with the same features achieves 55.3%.

Audio and Visual. From Table 1, we observe that A outperforms V and W-A is also better than W-V. It demonstrates that audio features are more powerful to address audio-visual event localization task on the AVE dataset. However, when we look at each individual event, using audio is not always better than using visual. We observe that V is better than A for some events (*e.g.* car, motocycle, train, bus). Actually, most of these events are outdoor. Audios in these videos can be very noisy: several different sounds may be mixed together (*e.g.* people cheers with a racing car), and may have very low intensity (*e.g.* horse sound from far distance). For these conditions, visual information will give us more discriminative and accurate information to understand events in videos. A is much better than V for some events (*e.g.* dog, man and woman speaking, baby crying). Sounds will provide clear cues for us to recognize these events. For example, if we hear barking sound, we know that there may be a dog. We also observe that A+V is better than both A and V, and W-A+V is better than W-A and W-V. From the above results and analysis, we can conclude that auditory and visual modalities will provide complementary information for us to

Table 2. Event localization prediction accuracy (%) of different feature fusion methods on AVE dataset. These methods all use same audio and visual features as inputs. Top-2 results in each line are highlighted

Methods	Additive	MP	Gated	MB	GMU	GMB	Concat	MRN	DMRN	DMRFE
Early fusion	59.9	67.9	67.9	69.2	**70.5**	**70.2**	61.0	69.8	68.0	-
Late fusion	71.3	71.4	70.5	70.5	71.6	71.0	72.7	70.8	**73.1**	**73.3**
Decision fusion	**70.5**	64.5	65.2	64.6	67.6	67.3	69.7	63.8	**70.4**	-

understand events in videos. The results also demonstrate that our AVE dataset is suitable for studying audio-visual scene understanding tasks.

Audio-Guided Visual Attention. The quantitative results (see Table 1) show that V-att is much better than V (a 3.3% absolute improvement) and A+V-att outperforms A+V by 1.3%. We show qualitative results of our attention method in Fig. 5. We observe that a range of semantic regions in many different categories and examples can be attended by sound, which validates that our attention network can learn which visual regions to look at for sounding objects. An interesting observation is that the audio-guided visual attention tends to focus on sounding regions, such as man's mouth, head of crying boy *etc*, rather than whole objects in some examples. Figure 6 illustrates two challenging cases. For the first example, the sounding helicopter is quite small in the first several frames but our attention model can still capture its locations. For the second example, the first five frames do not contain an audio-visual event; in this case, attentions are spread on different background regions. When the rat appears in the 5th frame but is not making any sound, the attention does not focus on the rat. When the rat sound becomes audible, the attention focuses on the sounding rat. This observation validates that the audio-guided attention mechanism is helpful to distinguish audio-visual unrelated videos, and is not just to capture a saliency map with objects.

Audio-Visual Fusion. Table 2 shows audio-visual event localization prediction accuracy of different multimodal feature fusion methods on AVE dataset. Our DMRN model in the late fusion setting can achieve better performance than all compared methods, and our DMRFE model can further improve performance. We also observe that late fusion is better than early fusion and decision fusion. The superiority of late fusion over early fusion demonstrates that temporal modeling before audio-visual fusion is useful. We know that auditory and visual modalities are not completely aligned, and temporal modeling can implicitly learn certain alignments between the two modalities, which is helpful for the audio-visual feature fusion task. The decision fusion can be regard as a type of late fusion but using lower dimension (same as the category number) features. The late fusion outperforms the decision fusion, which validates that processing multiple features separately and then learning joint representation using a middle layer rather than the bottom layer is an efficient fusion way.

Full and Weak Supervision. Obviously, supervised models are better than weakly supervised ones, but quantitative comparisons show that weakly-supervised approaches achieve promising event localization performance, which demonstrates the effectiveness of the MIL frameworks, and validates that the audio-visual event localization task can be addressed even in a noisy condition. Notice that W-V-att achieves slightly better performance than V, which suggests that the audio-guided visual attention is effective in selecting useful features.

Cross-Modality Localization. Table 3 reports the prediction accuracy of our method and DCCA [1] on cross-modality localization task. Our AVDL outperforms DCCA over a large margin both on A2V and V2A tasks. Even using the strict evaluation metric (which counts only the exact matches), our models on both subtasks: A2V and V2A, show promising results, which further demonstrates that there are strong correlations between audio and visual modalities, and it is possible to address the cross-modality localization for unconstrained videos.

Table 3. Accuracy on cross-modality localization. A2V: visual localization from audio segment query; V2A: audio localization from visual segment query

Models	AVDLN	DCCA
A2V	**44.8**	34.8
V2A	**35.6**	34.1

7   Conclusion

In this work, we study a suit of five research questions in the context of three audio-visual event localization tasks. We propose both baselines and novel algorithms to address each of the three tasks. Our systematic study well supports our findings: modeling jointly over auditory and visual modalities outperforms independent modeling, audio-visual event localization in a noisy condition is still tractable, the audio-guided visual attention is able to capture semantic regions of sound sources and can even distinguish audio-visual unrelated videos, temporal alignments are important for audio-visual feature fusion, the proposed dual residual network is capable of audio-visual fusion, and strong correlations existing between the two modalities enable cross-modality localization.

Acknowledgement. This work was supported by NSF BIGDATA 1741472. We gratefully acknowledge the gift donations of Markable, Inc., Tencent and the support of NVIDIA Corporation with the donation of the GPUs used for this research. This article solely reflects the opinions and conclusions of its authors and neither NSF, Markable, Tencent nor NVIDIA.

References

1. Andrew, G., Arora, R., Bilmes, J., Livescu, K.: Deep canonical correlation analysis. In: Proceedings of ICML, pp. 1247–1255. PMLR (2013)
2. Arandjelovic, R., Zisserman, A.: Look, listen and learn. In: Proceedings of ICCV. IEEE (2017)

3. Arandjelović, R., Zisserman, A.: Objects that sound. In: Ferrari, V., Hebert, M., Sminchisescu, C., Weiss, Y. (eds.) Computer Vision – ECCV 2018. Springer, Heidelberg (2018)

4. Arevalo, J., Solorio, T., Montes-y Gómez, M., González, F.A.: Gated multimodal units for information fusion. In: Proceedings of ICLR Workshop (2017)

5. Assael, Y.M., Shillingford, B., Whiteson, S., de Freitas, N.: LipNet: sentence-level lipreading. CoRR abs/1611.01599 (2016)

6. Aytar, Y., Vondrick, C., Torralba, A.: SoundNet: learning sound representations from unlabeled video. In: Proceedings of NIPS. Curran Associates, Inc. (2016)

7. Bahdanau, D., Cho, K., Bengio, Y.: Neural machine translation by jointly learning to align and translate. In: Proceedings of ICLR (2015)

8. Baltrušaitis, T., Ahuja, C., Morency, L.P.: Multimodal machine learning: a survey and taxonomy. IEEE TPAMI (2018)

9. Bulkin, D.A., Groh, J.M.: Seeing sounds: visual and auditory interactions in the brain. Curr. Opin. Neurobiol. **16**(4), 415–419 (2006)

10. Cakir, E., Heittola, T., Huttunen, H., Virtanen, T.: Polyphonic sound event detection using multi label deep neural networks. In: Proceedings of IJCNN. IEEE (2015)

11. Chen, L., Srivastava, S., Duan, Z., Xu, C.: Deep cross-modal audio-visual generation. In: Proceedings of ACMMM Workshop. ACM (2017)

12. Chung, J.S., Senior, A., Vinyals, O., Zisserman, A.: Lip reading sentences in the wild. In: Proceedings of CVPR. IEEE (2017)

13. Ephrat, A., et al.: Looking to listen at the cocktail party: a speaker-independent audio-visual model for speech separation. arXiv preprint arXiv:1804.03619 (2018)

14. Escorcia, V., Caba Heilbron, F., Niebles, J.C., Ghanem, B.: DAPs: deep action proposals for action understanding. In: Leibe, B., Matas, J., Sebe, N., Welling, M. (eds.) ECCV 2016. LNCS, vol. 9907, pp. 768–784. Springer, Cham (2016). https://doi.org/10.1007/978-3-319-46487-9_47

15. Fisher III., J.W., Darrell, T., Freeman, W.T., Viola, P.A.: Learning joint statistical models for audio-visual fusion and segregation. In: Proceedings of NIPS. Curran Associates, Inc. (2001)

16. Gao, R., Feris, R., Grauman, K.: Learning to separate object sounds by watching unlabeled video. In: Ferrari, V., Hebert, M., Sminchisescu, C., Weiss, Y. (eds.) Computer Vision – ECCV 2018. Springer, Heidelberg (2018)

17. Gaver, W.W.: What in the world do we hear?: An ecological approach to auditory event perception. Ecol. Psychol. **5**(1), 1–29 (1993)

18. Gemmeke, J.F., et al.: Audio set: an ontology and human-labeled dataset for audio events. In: Proceedings of ICASSP. IEEE (2017)

19. Gönen, M., Alpaydın, E.: Multiple kernel learning algorithms. JMLR **12**(Jul), 2211–2268 (2011)

20. Gurban, M., Thiran, J.P., Drugman, T., Dutoit, T.: Dynamic modality weighting for multi-stream HMMs in audio-visual speech recognition. In: Proceedings of ICMI. ACM (2008)

21. Hadsell, R., Chopra, S., LeCun, Y.: Dimensionality reduction by learning an invariant mapping. In: Proceedings of CVPR. IEEE (2006)

22. Harwath, D., Torralba, A., Glass, J.: Unsupervised learning of spoken language with visual context. In: Proceedings of NIPS. Curran Associates, Inc. (2016)

23. Heittola, T., Mesaros, A., Eronen, A., Virtanen, T.: Context-dependent sound event detection. EURASIP J. Audio Speech Music Process. **2013**(1), 1 (2013)

24. Hershey, J.R., Movellan, J.R.: Audio vision: Using audio-visual synchrony to locate sounds. In: Proceedings of NIPS. Curran Associates, Inc. (2000)

25. Hershey, S., et al.: CNN architectures for large-scale audio classification. In: Proceedings of ICASSP. IEEE (2017)
26. Hochreiter, S., Schmidhuber, J.: Long short-term memory. Neural Comput. **9**(8), 1735–1780 (1997)
27. Hu, D., Li, X., et al.: Temporal multimodal learning in audiovisual speech recognition. In: Proceedings of CVPR. IEEE (2016)
28. Kiela, D., Grave, E., Joulin, A., Mikolov, T.: Efficient large-scale multi-modal classification. In: Proceedings of AAAI. AAAI Press (2018)
29. Kim, J.H., et al.: Multimodal residual learning for visual QA. In: Proceedings of NIPS. Curran Associates, Inc. (2016)
30. Lea, C., et al.: Temporal convolutional networks for action segmentation and detection. In: Proceedings of CVPR. IEEE (2017)
31. LeCun, Y., Bottou, L., Bengio, Y., Haffner, P.: Gradient-based learning applied to document recognition. Proc. IEEE **86**(11), 2278–2324 (1998)
32. Li, B., Xu, C., Duan, Z.: Audio-visual source association for string ensembles through multi-modal vibrato analysis. In: Proceedings of SMC (2017)
33. Lin, M., Chen, Q., Yan, S.: Network in network. arXiv preprint arXiv:1312.4400 (2013)
34. Lu, J., Xiong, C., Parikh, D., Socher, R.: Knowing when to look: adaptive attention via a visual sentinel for image captioning. In: Proceedings of CVPR. IEEE (2017)
35. Maron, O., Lozano-Pérez, T.: A framework for multiple-instance learning. In: Proceedings of NIPS. Curran Associates, Inc. (1998)
36. Mesaros, A., Heittola, T., Virtanen, T.: TUT database for acoustic scene classification and sound event detection. In: Proceedings of EUSIPCO. IEEE (2016)
37. Mroueh, Y., Marcheret, E., Goel, V.: Deep multimodal learning for audio-visual speech recognition. In: Proceedings of ICASSP. IEEE (2015)
38. Ngiam, J., Khosla, A., Kim, M., Nam, J., Lee, H., Ng, A.Y.: Multimodal deep learning. In: Proceedings of ICML. PMLR (2011)
39. Oneata, D., Verbeek, J., Schmid, C.: Action and event recognition with fisher vectors on a compact feature set. In: Proceedings of ICCV. IEEE (2013)
40. Owens, A., Efros, A.A.: Audio-visual scene analysis with self-supervised multisensory features. In: Ferrari, V., Hebert, M., Sminchisescu, C., Weiss, Y. (eds.) Computer Vision – ECCV 2018. Springer, Heidelberg (2018)
41. Owens, A., Isola, P., McDermott, J., Torralba, A., Adelson, E.H., Freeman, W.T.: Visually indicated sounds. In: Proceedings of CVPR. IEEE (2016)
42. Owens, A., Wu, J., McDermott, J.H., Freeman, W.T., Torralba, A.: Ambient sound provides supervision for visual learning. In: Leibe, B., Matas, J., Sebe, N., Welling, M. (eds.) ECCV 2016. LNCS, vol. 9905, pp. 801–816. Springer, Cham (2016). https://doi.org/10.1007/978-3-319-46448-0_48
43. Parascandolo, G., Huttunen, H., Virtanen, T.: Recurrent neural networks for polyphonic sound event detection in real life recordings. In: Proceedings of ICASSP. IEEE (2016)
44. Poria, S., Cambria, E., Gelbukh, A.: Deep convolutional neural network textual features and multiple kernel learning for utterance-level multimodal sentiment analysis. In: Proceedings of EMNLP. Association for Computational Linguistics (2015)
45. Russakovsky, O., et al.: ImageNet large scale visual recognition challenge. IJCV **115**(3), 211–252 (2015)
46. Schuster, M., Paliwal, K.K.: Bidirectional recurrent neural networks. IEEE TSP **45**(11), 2673–2681 (1997)
47. Senocak, A., Oh, T.H., Kim, J., Yang, M.H., Kweon, I.S.: Learning to localize sound source in visual scenes. In: Proceedings of CVPR. IEEE (2018)

48. Shou, Z., Wang, D., Chang, S.F.: Temporal action localization in untrimmed videos via multi-stage CNNs. In: Proceedings of CVPR. IEEE (2016)
49. Simonyan, K., Zisserman, A.: Very deep convolutional networks for large-scale image recognition. In: Proceedings of ICLR (2015)
50. Srivastava, N., Salakhutdinov, R.: Learning representations for multimodal data with deep belief nets. In: Proceedings of ICML Workshop. PMLR (2012)
51. Srivastava, N., Salakhutdinov, R.R.: Multimodal learning with deep Boltzmann machines. In: Proceedings of NIPS. Curran Associates, Inc. (2012)
52. Surís, D., Duarte, A., Salvador, A., Torres, J., Giró-i Nieto, X.: Cross-modal embeddings for video and audio retrieval. arXiv preprint arXiv:1801.02200 (2018)
53. Tapaswi, M., Zhu, Y., Stiefelhagen, R., Torralba, A., Urtasun, R., Fidler, S.: MovieQA: understanding stories in movies through question-answering. In: Proceedings of CVPR. IEEE (2016)
54. Tran, D., Bourdev, L., Fergus, R., Torresani, L., Paluri, M.: Learning spatiotemporal features with 3D convolutional networks. In: Proceedings of ICCV. IEEE (2015)
55. Wu, J., Yu, Y., Huang, C., Yu, K.: Deep multiple instance learning for image classification and auto-annotation. In: Proceedings of CVPR. IEEE (2015)
56. Xu, J., Mei, T., Yao, T., Rui, Y.: MSR-VTT: a large video description dataset for bridging video and language. In: Proceedings of CVPR. IEEE (2016)
57. Xu, K., et al.: Show, attend and tell: neural image caption generation with visual attention. In: Proceedings of ICLR (2015)
58. Yang, X., Ramesh, P., Chitta, R., Madhvanath, S., Bernal, E.A., Luo, J.: Deep multimodal representation learning from temporal data. In: Proceedings of CVPR. IEEE (2017)
59. Zhao, H., Gan, C., Rouditchenko, A., Vondrick, C., McDermott, J., Torralba, A.: The sound of pixels. In: Ferrari, V., Hebert, M., Sminchisescu, C., Weiss, Y. (eds.) Computer Vision – ECCV 2018. Springer, Heidelberg (2018)
60. Zhao, Y., Xiong, Y., Wang, L., Wu, Z., Tang, X., Lin, D.: Temporal action detection with structured segment networks. In: Proceedings of ICCV. IEEE (2017)
61. Zhou, Y., Wang, Z., Fang, C., Bui, T., Berg, T.L.: Visual to sound: generating natural sound for videos in the wild. In: CVPR. IEEE (2018)

Grounding Visual Explanations

Lisa Anne Hendricks[1]([⊠]) [iD], Ronghang Hu[1] [iD], Trevor Darrell[1] [iD],
and Zeynep Akata[2] [iD]

[1] UC Berkeley, Berkeley, USA
{lisa_anne,ronghang,trevor}@eecs.berkeley.edu
[2] University of Amsterdam, Amsterdam, The Netherlands
z.akata@uva.nl

Abstract. Existing visual explanation generating agents learn to fluently justify a class prediction. However, they may mention visual attributes which reflect a strong class prior, although the evidence may not actually be in the image. This is particularly concerning as ultimately such agents fail in building trust with human users. To overcome this limitation, we propose a phrase-critic model to refine generated candidate explanations augmented with flipped phrases which we use as negative examples while training. At inference time, our phrase-critic model takes an image and a candidate explanation as input and outputs a score indicating how well the candidate explanation is grounded in the image. Our explainable AI agent is capable of providing counter arguments for an alternative prediction, i.e. counterfactuals, along with explanations that justify the correct classification decisions. Our model improves the textual explanation quality of fine-grained classification decisions on the CUB dataset by mentioning phrases that are grounded in the image. Moreover, on the FOIL tasks, our agent detects when there is a mistake in the sentence, grounds the incorrect phrase and corrects it significantly better than other models.

Keywords: Explainability · Counterfactuals · Grounding
Phrase correction

1 Introduction

Modern neural networks are good at localizing objects [6], predicting object categories [7] and describing scenes with natural language [32]. However, the reasoning behind the decision of neural networks are often hidden from the user. Therefore, in order to interpret and monitor neural networks, providing explanations of network decisions has gained interest [8,13,22].

Ideally, an agent that accurately explains a classifier's decision via natural language, as depicted in Fig. 1, is expected to generate explanations such as "This

Electronic supplementary material The online version of this chapter (https://doi.org/10.1007/978-3-030-01216-8_17) contains supplementary material, which is available to authorized users.

ⓒ Springer Nature Switzerland AG 2018
V. Ferrari et al. (Eds.): ECCV 2018, LNCS 11206, pp. 269–286, 2018.
https://doi.org/10.1007/978-3-030-01216-8_17

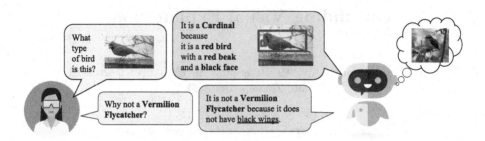

Fig. 1. Our phrase-critic agent considers grounded visual evidence to determine if candidate explanations are image relevant. In this example, as many cardinals are red and have a black patch on their faces, mentioning and grounding those properties constitutes an effective factual explanation, i.e. rationalization. Furthermore, in our framework, informing the user of why an image does not belong to another class via the absence of certain attributes constitutes a counterfactual explanation. (Color figure online)

is a *Cardinal* because it is a red bird with a red beak and a black face" where the phrases should be both *class discriminative*, i.e. a red beak is discriminative for cardinals, and *image relevant*, i.e. the image indeed contains a red beak. Moreover, an explainable AI agent should be capable of arguing why the image was not classified as another class such as *Vermilion Flycatcher* by mentioning a class-specific property such as "black wings" that differentiates a cardinal from a vermilion flycatcher. Contrasting two concepts via class-specific attributes provides an additional means of model interpretation.

Often class and image relevance are in opposition. For example, if one attribute frequently occurs within a class, an agent may learn to justify its prediction by mentioning this attribute without even looking at the image. We aim to resolve such conflicts through a phrase-critic which explicitly determines if an explanatory sentence is image relevant by visually grounding discriminative object parts mentioned in an explanation.

One way to design such an agent is to use densely labeled data with ground truth part annotations. However, it can be time consuming to collect densely labeled data for every task. On the other hand, large, diverse datasets such as the Visual Genome [11] with densely labeled out-of-domain data do exist. Detecting visual evidence in a sentence via off-the-shelf grounding models can be unreliable, especially when applied to new domains. Nevertheless, integrating a natural language grounding model [10] trained on auxiliary data and an LSTM-based explanation model [8] via our proposed *phrase-critic* effectively grounds discriminative phrases in generated explanations.

Our phrase-critic integrates a ranking-loss to the explanation model and builds a set of mismatching part-attribute pairs by flipping attributes in the explanation, inspired by a relative attribute paradigm for recognition and retrieval [19]. By positing that a bird with a black beak can not also be a bird with a red beak, our model learns to score the correct attribute higher than automatically generated mutually-exclusive attributes.

We quantitatively and qualitatively show that our *phrase-critic* generates image relevant explanations more accurately than a strong baseline of mean-pooled scores from a natural language grounding model. Furthermore, our framework can easily be extended to other tasks beyond textual explanations. We also show that our phrase-critic framework effectively discerns whether a sentence contains a mistake, points out where the mistake is and fixes it, leading to an impressive performance on FOIL tasks [24].

2   Related Work

In this section, we review recent papers in the context of explanations, mainly focusing on textual and visual explanations and finally we discuss pragmatics oriented language generation papers that are relevant to ours.

Explainability. The importance of explanations for humans has been studied in the field of psychology [14,15], showing that humans use explanations as a guide for learning and understanding by building inferences and seeking propositions or judgments that enrich their prior knowledge. Humans usually seek explanations that fill the requested gap depending on prior knowledge and goal in question. Moreover, explanations are typically contrastive. Much of these ideas are built with careful empirical work, i.e. with human subjects on a specific aspect of explanations [18]. Since explanations are intended for a human understander, we emphasize the importance of human evaluation in evaluating the relevance of textual explanations to the image as well as looking for the criteria for what makes an explanation good, with the goal of training a "critic" that could evaluate explanations automatically.

Textual and Visual Explanation. In [26], trust is regarded as a primary reason to explore explainable intelligent systems. We argue a system which outputs discriminative features of an object class without being image relevant is likely to lose the trust of users. Consequently, we seek to explicitly enforce image relevance with our model. Like [2], we aim to generate *rationalizations* explaining the evidence for a decision as opposed to introspective explanations which aim to explain the intermediate activations of neural networks.

Early textual explanation models are applied to medical images [25] and developed as a feedback for teaching programs [3,12,27]. These systems are mainly template based. Recently, [8] proposed a deep model to generate natural language justifications of a fine-grained object classifier. However, it does not ground the relevant object parts in the sentence or the image. In [20], although an attention based explanation system is proposed, there are no constraints to ensure the actual presence of the mentioned attributes or entities in the image. Consequentially, albeit generating convincing textual explanations, [8,20] do not

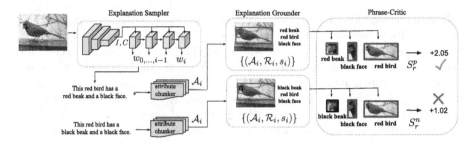

Fig. 2. Our phrase-critic model ensures that generated explanations are both class discriminative and image relevant. We first sample a set of explanations generated by [8], chunk the sentences into noun phrases and visually ground constituent nouns using [10]. Our model assigns a score to each noun phrase-bounding box pair and selects the sentence with the highest cumulative score judging it as the most relevant explanation. (Color figure online)

include a process for networks to correct themselves if their textual explanation is not well-grounded visually. In contrast, we propose a general process to first check whether explanations are accurately aligned with image input and then improve textually explanations by selecting a better-aligned candidate.

Other work has considered *visual explanations* which visualize which regions of an image are important for a decision [5,23,33,34]. Our model produces bounding boxes around regions which correspond to discriminative features, and is thus visual in nature. However, in contrast to visual explanation work, our goal is to rank generated explanatory phrases based on how well they are grounded in an image.

Pragmatics-Oriented Language Generation. Our work is also related to the recent work of pragmatics-oriented language generation [1] where a describer produces a set of sentences, then a choice ranker chooses which sentence best fulfills a specific goal, e.g. distinguishing one image from another. Similarly, image descriptions are generated to make the target image distinguishable from a similar image in [28], and referential expressions are generated on objects in a discriminative way such that one can correctly localize the mentioned object from the generated expression in [17]. In this work, we generate textual explanation to maximize both class-specificity and image-relevance. Though similar in spirit, part of our novelty lies in how we learn to rank sentences.

3   Visual Explanation Critic

Our model consists of three main components. First, we train a textual explanation model [8] with a discriminative loss to encourage sentences to mention class specific attributes. Next, we train a phrase grounding model [10] to ground phrases in the generated textual explanations. Finally, our proposed phrase-critic model ranks textual explanations based on how well they are grounded in the image. As shown in Fig. 2, our system first generates possible explanations (e.g., "This red bird has a red beak and a black face"), grounds constituent phrases (e.g., "red bird", "red beak", "black face") in the image, and then assigns a score to the noun phrase-bounding box pairs based on how well constituent phrases are grounded in the image. The explanation with the highest cumulative score gets selected as the correct explanation.

Phrase-Critic. The phrase-critic model constitutes our core innovation. Given a set $\{(\mathcal{A}_i, \mathcal{R}_i, s_i)\}$, where $\mathcal{A}_i$ is an attribute phrase, $\mathcal{R}_i$ is the corresponding region (more precisely, visual features extracted from the region), and s_i the region score, our phrase-critic model, $f_{critic}(\{(\mathcal{A}_i, \mathcal{R}_i, s_i)\})$, maps them into a single image relevance score S_r. For a given attribute phrase A_i such as "black beak", we ground (localize) it into a corresponding image region R_i and obtain its localization score s_i, using an off-the-shelf localization model from [10]. It is worth noting that the scores directly produced by the grounding model can not be directly combined with other metrics, such as sentence fluency, because these scores are difficult to normalize across different images and different visual parts. For example, a correctly grounded phrase "yellow belly" may have a much smaller score than the correctly grounded phrase "yellow eye" because a bird belly is less well defined than a bird eye. Henceforth, our phrase-critic model plays an essential role in producing normalized, utilizable and comparable scores. More specifically, given an image I, the phrase-critic model processes the list of $\{(\mathcal{A}_i, \mathcal{R}_i, s_i)\}$ by first encoding each $(\mathcal{A}_i, \mathcal{R}_i, s_i)$ into a fixed-dimensional vector x_{enc} with an LSTM and then applying a two-layer neural network to regress the final score S_r which reflects the overall image relevance of an explanation.

We construct ten negative explanation sentences for each image as we explain in the next section. Each negative explanation sentence (not image relevant) gets paired with a positive explanation (image-relevant). We then train our explanation critic using the following margin-based ranking loss $\mathcal{L}_{\text{rank}}$ on each pair of positive and negative explanations, to encourage the model to give higher scores to positive explanations than negative explanations:

$$\mathcal{L}_{\text{rank}} = \max(0, \underbrace{f_{critic}(\{A_i^n\}, I; \theta)}_{S_r^n} - \underbrace{f_{critic}(\{A_i^p\}, I; \theta)}_{S_r^p} + 1) \tag{1}$$

where A_i^p are matching noun phrase whereas A_i^n are mismatching noun phrases respectively, therefore S_r^p and S_r^m are the scores of the positive and the negative explanations. In the following, we discuss how we construct our negative image-sentence pairs.

Mining and Augmenting Negative Sentences. The simplest way to sample a negative pair is to consider a mismatching ground truth image and sentence pair. However, we find that mismatching sentences are frequently either too different from ground truth sentences (and thus do not provide a useful training signal) or too similar to ground truth sentences, such that both the positive and negative sentence are image relevant. Hence, inspired by a relative attribute paradigm for recognition and retrieval [19], we create negative sentences by flipping attributes corresponding to color, size and objects in attribute phrases. For example, if a ground truth sentence mentions a "yellow belly" and "red head" we might change the attribute phrase "yellow belly" to "yellow beak" and "red head" to "black head". This means the negative sentence still mentions some attributes present in the image, but is not completely correct. We find that creating hard negatives is important when training our self-verification model.

Ranking Explanations. After generating a set of candidate explanations and computing an explanation score, we choose the best explanation based on the score for each explanation. In practice, we find it is important to rank sentences based on both the relevance score S_r and a fluency score S_f (defined as the $\log P(w_{0:T})$). However, we find that first discarding sentences which have a low fluency score, and then choosing the sentence with the highest relevance works better:

$$S = \mathbb{1}\underbrace{\left(\sum_i \log P(w_i|w_{0,\dots,i-1}) > T \right)}_{S_f} \underbrace{f_{critic}(\{A_i\}, I; \theta)}_{S_r} \tag{2}$$

where S_r is the relevance score and S_f is the log probability of a sentence based on the trained explanation model. $\mathbb{1}(\cdot)$ is the indicator function and T is a fluency threshold. Including S_f is important because otherwise the explanation scorer will rank "This is a bird with a long neck, long neck, and red beak" high (if a long neck and red beak are present) even though mentioning "long neck" twice is clearly ungrammatical. Based on experiments on our validation set, we set T equal to negative five.

Grounding Visual Features. Our framework for grounding visual features involves three steps: generating visual explanations, factorizing the sentence into smaller chunks, and localizing each chunk with a grounding model. Visual explanations are generated with a recurrent neural network (specifically an LSTM [9]) over the image. Unlike standard visual description models, e.g. [4], the visual explanation generation model [8] is conditioned on the class C predicted by the visual model as well as the image I itself. The explanation model relies on two losses: a relevance loss

$$\mathcal{L}_{rel} = \frac{1}{N} \sum_{n=0}^{N-1} \sum_{t=0}^{T-1} \log p(w_{t+1}|w_{0:t}, I, C) \tag{3}$$

which corresponds to the standard word level softmax cross entropy loss used to train sentence generation models, and a discriminative loss

$$\mathcal{L}_{discr} = \mathbb{E}_{\tilde{w} \sim p(w|I,C)} [R(\tilde{w})] \tag{4}$$

which assigns a high reward (R) to class discriminative features sentences. REIN-FORCE [30] is used to backpropagate through the sampling mechanism required to generate sentences for the discriminative loss. The visual explanation generation loss ($\mathcal{L}_{\mathrm{VEG}}$) is the linear combination of these two losses:

$$\mathcal{L}_{\mathrm{VEG}} = \mathcal{L}_{\mathrm{rel}} - \lambda\mathcal{L}_{\mathrm{discr}}. \tag{5}$$

In order to verify that explanations are image relevant, for each explanation we extract a list of i attribute phrases ($\mathcal{A}_i$) using a rule-based attribute phrase chunker. Our chunker works as follows: we first use a POS tagger, then extract attribute phrases by finding phrases which syntactically match the structure of attribute phrases. We find that attribute phrases have two basic types of syntactic structure: a noun followed by a verb and an adjective, e.g. "bird is black" or "feathers are speckled", or an adjective (or list of adjectives) followed by a noun, e.g. "red and orange head" or "colorful body". Though this syntactic structure is specific to the bird data, similar methods could be used to extract visual phrases for other applications. Attribute phrases are ordered based on the order in which they occur in the generated visual explanation.

Once we have extracted attribute phrases $\mathcal{A}_i$, we ground each of them to a visual region $\mathcal{R}_i$ in the original image by using [10] pre-trained on the Visual Genome dataset [11] without any access to task-specific ground truth. For a given attribute phrase $\mathcal{A}_i$, the grounding model localizes the phrase into an image region, returning a bounding box $\mathcal{R}_i$ and a score s_i of how likely the returned bounding box matches the phrase. The grounding model works in a retrieval manner. It first extracts a set of candidate bounding boxes from the image, and embeds the attribute phrase into a vector. Then the embedded phrase vector is compared with the visual features of each candidate bounding box to get a matching score (s_i). Finally the bounding box with the highest matching score is returned as the grounded image region. The attribute phrase, the corresponding region, and the region score form an attribute phrase grounding ($\mathcal{A}_i, \mathcal{R}_i, s_i$). This attribute phrase grounding is used as an input to our phrase-critic.

Whereas visual descriptions are encouraged to discuss attributes which are relevant to a specific class, the grounding model is only trained to determine whether a natural language phrase is in an image. Being discriminative rather than generative, the critic model does not have to learn to generate fluent, grammatically correct sentences, and can thus focus on checking whether the mentioned attribute phrases are image-relevant. Consequently, the models are complementary, allowing one model to catch the mistakes of the other.

4 Experiments

In this section, we first detail the datasets we use in our experiments. We then present a comparison between different methods to rank sampled sentences. We compare our model to baselines both qualitatively and through a human evaluation. Additionally, we discuss how our model enables *counterfactual* explanations.

CUB. We validate our approach on the CUB dataset [29] which contains 200 classes of fine-grained bird species with approximately 60 images each and a total of 11,788 images of birds. Recently, [21] collected 10 sentences for each image with a detailed description of the bird. This dataset is suitable for our task as every sentence as well as every image is associated with a single label. Note that CUB does not contain ground truth part bounding boxes, however it contains keypoints that roughly fall on each body part. We use them only to evaluate the precision of our detected bounding boxes. To generate sentences, we use random sampling [4] to sample 100 sentences from the baseline model proposed by [8]. We use the set of 100 sentences generated via random sampling as candidate sentences for phrase-critic. As a "Baseline" model, we select sentences based only on the fluency score S_f. In addition to our phrase-critic, we also consider a strong baseline which only considers the score from a grounding model (without the phrase critic), i.e. we call it "Grounding model". In this case, we first ground noun phrases, then rank sentences by the average score of the grounded noun phrases in the image.

FOIL. Our phrase-critic model is flexible and can also be applied to other relevant tasks. To show the generality of our approach, we also consider the dataset proposed in [24] which consists of sentences and corresponding "FOIL" sentences which have exactly one error. [24] proposes three tasks: (1) classifying whether a sentence is image relevant or not, (2) determining which word in a sentence is not image relevant and (3) correcting the sentence error. To use our phrase-critic for (1), we employ a standard binary classification loss. For (2), we follow [24] and determine which words are not image relevant by holding out one word at a time from the sentence. When we remove an irrelevant word, the score from the classifier should increase. Thus, we can determine the least relevant word in a sentence by observing which word (upon removal) leads to the largest score from our classifier. Also following [24], for the third task we replace the foiled word with words from a set of target words and choose a target word based on which one maximizes the score of the classifier. To train our phrase critic, we use the positive and negative samples as defined by [24]. As is done across all experiments, we extract phrases with our noun phrase chunker and use this as input to the phrase-critic.

4.1   Fine-Grained Bird Species Explanation Experiments

In this section, we conduct detailed bird species explanation experiments on the CUB dataset. We first present comparison with baselines qualitatively both for successful and failure cases as well as quantitatively through human judgement. We then present results illustrating the accuracy of the detected bounding boxes. We finally discuss our counterfactual explanation results.

Baseline Comparison. Our aim here is to compare our phrase-critic model with the baseline visual explanation model [8] and the grounding model [10].

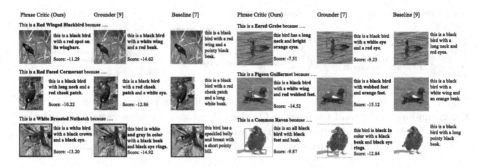

Fig. 3. Our phrase-critic model generates more image-relevant explanations compared to [8] justified by the grounding of the noun phrases. Compared to grounder [10], our phrase-critic generates more class-specific explanations. The numbers indicate the cumulative score of the explanation computed by our phrase-critic ranker. (Color figure online)

In Fig. 3, the results on the left are generated by our phrase critic model, the ones in the middle by the grounding model [10] and the ones on the right are by the baseline model [8]. Note that [8] does not contain an attribute phrase grounder, therefore we cannot localize the evidence for the given explanation here. As a general observation, our model improves over both baselines in the following ways. Our critic model (1) grounds attribute phrases both in the image and in the sentence, (2) is in favor of accurate and class-specific noun phrases and (3) provides the cumulative score of each explanatory sentence.

To further emphasize the importance of visual and textual grounding of the noun phrases in evaluating the accuracy of the visual explanation model, let us more closely examine the second row of Fig. 3. We note that all models mention a "black bird" and "red cheek patch". As the "Red Faced Cormorant" has these properties, these attributes are accurate. However, the explanation sentence is more trustable when the visual evidence of the noun phrase properly localized, which is not done by the baseline explanation model. To verify our intuition that grounded explanations are more trustable, we ask Amazon Mechanical Turke workers to evaluate whether our explanations with or without bounding boxes are more informative. Our results indicate that bounding boxes are informative (41.9% of the time bounding boxes lead to more informative explanations and 49.3% of the time explanations with and without bounding boxes are equally informative). Therefore, we emphasize that visual and textual grounding is beneficial and important for evaluating the accuracy of the visual explanation model.

Again examining the "Red Faced Cormorant" in the second row of Fig. 3, although "red cheek patch" is correctly grounded both by our phrase critic and the baseline phrase grounder, our phrase critic also mentions and grounds an important class-specific attribute of "long neck" while the grounding model mentions a missing "white eye" attribute which it cannot grounded. Thus, the score

This is a **Northern Flicker** because ...

... this is a **black and white spotted bird** with red beak.

... this bird has a speckled belly and breast with a long pointy bill.

This is a **Pigeon Guillemot** because ...

... this is a **black bird with white on the wingbars** and red feet.

... this is a black bird with a white wing and an orange beak.

This is a **Pileated Woodpecker** because ...

... this is a **black bird with a long white neck and a red crown**.

... this is a black bird with a white nape and a red crown

Fig. 4. Failure cases: In some cases our model predicts an incorrect noun phrase and the grounding may reveal the reason. On the other hand, in some cases although the explanation sentences are accurate, the phrases are not grounded well, i.e. the bounding boxes are off. Top: Our phrase-critic, bottom: baseline [8]. (Color figure online)

based ranking of noun phrase and region pairs lead to more accurate and visually grounded visual explanations.

Thanks to the integrated visual grounding capability and phrase ranking mechanism, the critic is able to detect the mistakes of the baseline model and correct them. Some detailed observations from Fig. 3 are as follows. "Red Winged Blackbird" having a "red spot on its wingbars" is one of the most discriminative properties of this bird which is mentioned by our critic and also grounded accurately. Similarly, the most important property of "Eared Grebe" is its "red eyes". We see that for "Pigeon Guillermot" our model talks about its "white wing" and "red webbed feet" whereas the grounding model does not mention the "white wing" property and the baseline model does not only ground the phrase but also it does not mention the "red feet". Our model does not only qualitatively generate more accurate explanations, these sentences also get higher cumulative phrase scores as shown beside each image in the figure providing another level of confidence.

Failure Cases. In Fig. 4 we present some typical failure cases of our model. In some cases such as the first example, the nouns, i.e. bird and beak, are correctly grounded however the attribute is wrong. Although the bird has a black beak, due to the red color of the fruit it is holding, our model thinks it is a red beak. Another failure case is when the noun phrases are semantically accurate however they are not correctly grounded. For instance, in the second example, both "black bird with white on the wingbars" and "red feet" are correctly identified, however the bounding box of the feet is off. Note that in CUB dataset, the ground truth part bounding box annotations are not available, hence our model figures out the location of a "red feet" by adapting the grounding model trained on Visual Genome, which may not include similar box-phrase combinations. Similarly, in the third example, the orientation of the bounding box of the phrase "long white neck" is inaccurate since the bird is perching on the tree trunk vertically although most of the birds perch on tree branches in a horizontal manner.

Human Evaluation. In this section we discuss the effectiveness of our explanation ranker via human evaluation. We sample 2000 random images from the test set and ask Amazon Mechanical Turkers to annotate whether a noun phrase

Table 1. Human evaluations comparing baseline explanation model [8], grounding model [10], and our phrase-critic model. CNP: the percentage of correct noun phrases predicted by each model, CS: the percentage of correct sentences where all the phrases are semantically accurate.

Method	% Correct noun phrases	% Correct sentences
Baseline [8]	76.64	52.10
Grounding model [10]	76.32	49.85
Our phrase critic	**77.96**	**61.97**

selected by a model is observed in the image or not. We run this human study three times to eliminate the annotator bias. In this study, we measure the percentage of correct noun phrases, i.e. CNP, and the correct sentences, i.e. CS, that are agreed by at least the two out of three annotators. Our results are presented in Table 1. We first compare our phrase-critic method to the baseline explanation generator [8]. We find that sentences chosen with our phrase critic have improved CNP score (77.96% vs 76.64%) in contrast to our baseline. Next, we find that attributes mentioned by our critic model reflect the images more accurately than the grounding only baseline [10] (77.96% image relevant attributes vs. 76.32%). This result shows that our phrase critic model generates phrases that are more accurate than the baselines as well as being visible in the image.

We also compute the percentage of correct sentences (CS), i.e. all noun phrases appearing in the sentence correctly match the given image, for each model. We observe the same ordering trend between the three models as the CNP scores, i.e. Grounding model < Baseline < Phrase Critic with the phrase-critic producing correct sentences 59.67% of the time in comparison to 51.49% and 47.74% for the baseline and grounder respectively. We note that the performance gain of our phrase-critic model is larger when considering entire sentences, perhaps because our phrase-critic is specifically optimized to discriminate between sentences. These results indicate that our phrase critic model leads to fewer mistakes overall.

Bounding Box Accuracy. As the CUB dataset does not contain ground-truth bounding boxes, we cannot evaluate the precision of our detected part bounding boxes w.r.t. a ground truth. However, the dataset contains keypoints for 15 body parts, e.g. bill, throat, left eye, nape, etc. and utilizing these keypoint annotations that roughly correspond to "beak", "head", "belly" and "eye" regions, provides us a good proxy for this task. We measure how frequently a keypoint falls into the detected bounding box of the corresponding body part to determine the accuracy of the bounding boxes. In addition, we measure the distance of the corresponding keypoint to the center of the bounding box to determine the precision of the bounding boxes. Note that for the results in the first row, we take the explanation generated by [8] and ground the phrases using the off-the-shelf grounding model [10].

Table 2. Evaluating the grounding accuracy for four commonly mentioned bird parts. As we have no have access to ground truth boxes, we measure how frequently the ground truth keypoints fall within a detected bounding box, measuring the % of the keypoints that fall inside the bounding box (left) and the distance between the keypoint and the center of the bounding box (right). The baseline [8] does not include noun phrase grounding, so we apply [10] to noun phrases extracted from [8]

Explanations	% Accuracy				Euclidean distance			
	Beak	Head	Belly	Eye	Beak	Head	Belly	Eye
Baseline [8]	93.50	58.74	65.58	55.11	24.16	57.56	56.80	76.90
Grounding model [10]	94.30	60.60	65.40	**60.78**	**22.66**	46.31	**52.69**	**57.55**
Phrase critic	**95.88**	**74.06**	**66.65**	56.72	23.74	**20.26**	52.75	69.83

Our results in Table 2 show that while "beak", "head" and "belly" regions are detected with high accuracy (95.88%, 74.06% and 66.65% resp.), "eye" detections are weaker (56.72%). When we look at the distance between the bounding box center and the keypoint, we observe a similar trend. The head region gets detected by our model significantly better than others, i.e. 20.26 vs 46.31 with [10] and 57.56 with [8]. The belly and the beak distances are close to the ones measured by the grounding model whereas the eye region gets detected with a lower precision with our model compared to the grounding model.

We closely investigate the accuracy of the predicted noun phrases that fall into the eye region and observe that although the eye regions get detected with a higher precision with the baseline grounding model, the semantic meaning of the attribute gets predicted more accurately with our phrase critic. For instance, our model mentions "red eye" more accurately than the grounding model although the part box is more accurately localized by the grounding model. One example of this can be seen in Fig. 3 (top right) where the grounder selects the sentences "... this is a black bird with a white eye and a red eye." Here, the grounding model has selected a sentence which cannot be true (the bird cannot have white eye as well as a red eye). Even though the bounding box around the eye is accurate, the modifying attributes are not both correct.

Counterfactual Explanations. Another way of explaining a visual concept is through generating *counterfactual* explanations that indicate why the classifier does not predict another class label. To construct counterfactual explanations, we posit that if an attribute is discriminative for another class, i.e. a class that is different from the class that the query image belongs to, but not present in the query image, then this attribute is a *counterfactual* evidence. To discuss counterfactual evidence for a classification decision, we first hypothesize which visual evidence might indicate that the bird belongs to another class. We do so by considering explanations produced by our phrase-critic for visually most similar examples from a different, i.e. counterfactual, classes. Our phrase-critic determines which attributes are most class specific for the counterfactual class

Fig. 5. Our phrase-critic is able to generate factual and counterfactual explanations. Factual explanations mention the characteristic properties of the correct class (left image) and counterfactual explanations mention the properties that are not visible in the image, i.e. non-groundable properties, for the negative class (right image). (Color figure online)

and most image relevant for the query image while generating factual explanations. While generating counterfactual explanations, our model determines the counterfactual evidence by searching for the attributes of the counterfactual class which lead to the lowest phrase-critic score for the query image. We then construct a sentence by negating counterfactual phrases. For instance, "bird has a long flat bill" is negated to "bird does not have a long flat bill" where the counterfactual phrase is the "long flat bill". Alternatively, we can use the same evidence to rephrase the sentence "If this bird had been a (counterfactual class), it would have had a long flat bill."

To illustrate, we present our results in Fig. 5. Note that the figures show two images for each result where the first image is the query image. The second image is the counterfactual image, i.e. the most similar image to the query image from the counterfactual class, that we show only for reference purposes. The counterfactual explanation is generated for this image just for determining the most class-specific noun phrase. Once a list of counterfactual noun phrases is determined, those noun phrases are grounded in the query image and the noun phrase that gets the lowest score is determined as the counterfactual evidence. To illustrate, let us consider an image of a *Crested Auklet* and a nearest neighbor image from another class, e.g., *Red Faced Cormorant*. The attributes "black bird" and "long flat bill" are possible counterfactual attributes for the original crested auklet image. We use our phrase-critic to select the attribute which produces the *lowest* score for the Crested Auklet image.

Figure 5 shows our final counterfactual explanation for why the *Crested Auklet* image is not a *Red Faced Cormorant* (it does not have a long flat bill). On the other hand, when the query image is a *Parakeet Auklet*, the factual explanation talks about "red eyes" which are present for *Horned Grebe* but not for *Parakeet Auklet*. Similarly, a *Least Auklet* is correctly determined to be a "black and white spotted bird" with a "small beak" while a *Belted Kingfisher* is a has

Table 3. Quantitative FOIL results: our phrase critic significantly outperforms the state-of-the-art [16,31] reported in [24] and the grounding model [10] on all three FOIL tasks.

	Classification	Word detection	Word correction
IC - Wang [31]	42.21	27.59	22.16
HieCoAtt [16]	64.14	38.79	4.21
Grounding model [10]	56.68	39.80	8.80
Phrase critic (ours)	**87.00**	**73.72**	**49.60**

Fig. 6. Qualitative FOIL results: We present the image with foil sentence (top) and correct sentence (bottom) as determined by our phrase-critic model. The numbers indicate our phrase-critic score of the given sentence. By design our model grounds all the phrases in the sentence, including the foil phrases. (Color figure online)

a "long pointy bill" which is the counterfactual attribute for *Least Auklet*. On the other hand, a *Cardinal* is classified as a cardinal because of the "red bird" and "black face" attributes while not as a *Scarlet Tanager* because of the lack of "black wings". These results show that our counterfactual explanations do not always generate the same phrases for the counterfactual classes. Our counterfactual explanations talk about properties of the counterfactual class that are not relevant to the particular query image, whose evidence is clearly visible in both the counterfactual and the query images.

In conclusion, counterfactual explanations go one step further in language-based explanation generation. Contrasting a class with another closely related class helps the user build a more coherent cognitive representation of a particular object of interest.

4.2   FOIL Experiments

Table 3 shows the performance of our phrase critic on the FOIL tasks compared to the best performing models evaluated in [24]. IC-Wang [31] is an image captioning model whereas HieCoAtt [16] is an attention based VQA model. As described above, we follow the protocol of [24] when evaluating our model on the FOIL tasks. To apply the grounding model to the classification task, we determine a threshold score on the train set (i.e., any sentence with an average grounding score above a certain threshold is classified as image relevant).

Our results show that the phrase critic is able to effectively adapt a grounding model in order to determine whether or not sentences are image relevant. We see that our grounding model baseline performs competitively when compared to prior work, indicating that grounding noun phrases is a promising step to determine if sentences are image relevant. However, our phrase critic model outperforms all baselines by a wide margin, outperforming the next best model by over 20 points on the classification task, over 30 points on the word identification task, and close to 30 points on the word correction task. The large gap between the grounding model baseline and the phrase-critic highlights the importance of our phrase-critic in learning how to properly adapt outputs from a grounding model to our final task.

Figure 6 shows example negative and positive sentences from the FOIL dataset, the grounding determined by our phrase-critic, and the score output by our phrase-critic model. Our general observation is that our phrase critic gives a significantly lower score to FOIL sentences which are not image relevant. In addition, it accurately grounds mentioned objects and accurately scores sentences based on if they are image relevant.

Some detailed observations are as follows. For the first example the score of the FOIL sentence is 0.25 as the sentence contains "a boat" phrase that is inaccurate whereas the sentence with the correct phrase, i.e. "a train", gets the score 0.71 which clearly indicates that this is the correct sentence. Our model is able to ground more than two phrases accurately as well. For the last image in the first row, the phrases "an older man", "green sports coat" and "flower" are correctly predicted and grounded whereas "blue backpack" gets grounded close to the shoulder, which is a sensible region to consider even though there is no backpack in the image. This FOIL sentence gets the score 0.22 whereas the correct sentence that gets the score 0.98 grounds "blue tie" correctly while also correctly grounding all other phrases in the sentence.

When the FOIL object is one of the many objects in the sentence and occupies a small region in the image, our phrase-critic is also successful. For instance in the third image in the first row, "an suitcase" is grounded in an arbitrary location on the side of an image which leads to an extremely low sentence score, 0.06. In the image relevant sentence, "an umbrella" is grounded correctly leading to a high sentence score, 0.99. In conclusion, our phrase critic accurately grounds the phrases when they are present and assigns scores to the matching phrases and bounding boxes that helps us further understand why a model has taken such a decision.

5 Conclusions

We propose a phrase-critic model which measures the image-relevance of a generated explanation sentence. In this framework, we first generate alternative natural language explanations of a fine-grained visual classification decision, then factorize the explanation sentences into a set of visual attributes and visually ground them. Our phrase critic model (1) assigns normalized scores to noun phrases measuring how well they are grounded in the image, (2) ranks the sentences based on the cumulative score, (3) selects the best explanation that is both image and class relevant.

Our experiments on the CUB dataset shows that this grounding approach forces our explanations to refer to the elements that are present in the image and are class-specific. We evaluate our model on the fine-grained bird explanation task both qualitatively and quantitatively. An intuitive alternative for factual explanations, i.e. explaining the correct class, is counterfactual explanations, i.e. explaining why a certain image is not classified as another class. We show that our model is able to generate accurate counterfactual explanations. Our experiments on the FOIL tasks illustrates that our model is able to determine an inaccurate phrase in the sentence, point to the evidence in the image and also correct it significantly better than the competing models.

Acknowledgments. This work was supported by DARPA XAI program.

References

1. Andreas, J., Klein, D.: Reasoning about pragmatics with neural listeners and speakers. arXiv preprint arXiv:1604.00562 (2016)
2. Biran, O., McKeown, K.: Justification narratives for individual classifications. In: Proceedings of the AutoML Workshop at ICML, vol. 2014 (2014)
3. Core, M.G., Lane, H.C., Van Lent, M., Gomboc, D., Solomon, S., Rosenberg, M.: Building explainable artificial intelligence systems. In: NCAI (2006)
4. Donahue, J.: Long-term recurrent convolutional networks for visual recognition and description. TPAMI **39**(4), 677–691 (2017)
5. Fong, R.C., Vedaldi, A.: Interpretable explanations of black boxes by meaningful perturbation. arXiv preprint arXiv:1704.03296 (2017)
6. Girshick, R.: Fast R-CNN. In: ICCV (2015)
7. He, K., Zhang, X., Ren, S., Sun, J.: Deep residual learning for image recognition. In: Proceedings of the IEEE Conference on Computer Vision and Pattern Recognition, pp. 770–778 (2016)
8. Hendricks, L.A., Akata, Z., Rohrbach, M., Donahue, J., Schiele, B., Darrell, T.: Generating visual explanations. In: ECCV (2016)
9. Hochreiter, S., Schmidhuber, J.: Long short-term memory. Neural Comput. **9**(8), 1735–1780 (1997)
10. Hu, R., Rohrbach, M., Andreas, J., Darrell, T., Saenko, K.: Modeling relationships in referential expressions with compositional modular networks. In: Proceedings of the IEEE Conference on Computer Vision and Pattern Recognition (2017)
11. Krishna, R., et al.: Visual genome: connecting language and vision using crowd-sourced dense image annotations. arXiv preprint arXiv:1602.07332 (2016)

12. Lane, H.C., Core, M.G., Van Lent, M., Solomon, S., Gomboc, D.: Explainable artificial intelligence for training and tutoring. Technical report, DTIC Document (2005)
13. Letham, B., Rudin, C., McCormick, T.H., Madigan, D.: Interpretable classifiers using rules and Bayesian analysis: building a better stroke prediction model. Ann. Appl. Stat. **9**(3), 1350–1371 (2015)
14. Lombrozo, T.: Explanation and abductive inference. In: Oxford Handbook of Thinking and Reasoning (2012)
15. Lombrozo, T.: The structure and function of explanations. Trends Cogn. Sci. **10**(10), 464–470 (2006)
16. Lu, J., Yang, J., Batra, D., Parikh, D.: Hierarchical question-image co-attention for visual question answering. In: Advances in Neural Information Processing Systems, pp. 289–297 (2016)
17. Mao, J., Huang, J., Toshev, A., Camburu, O., Yuille, A.L., Murphy, K.: Generation and comprehension of unambiguous object descriptions. In: Proceedings of the IEEE Conference on Computer Vision and Pattern Recognition, pp. 11–20 (2016)
18. Pacer, M., Williams, J., Chen, X., Lombrozo, T., Griffiths, T.: Evaluating computational models of explanation using human judgments. In: Proceedings of the Twenty-Ninth Conference on Uncertainty in Artificial Intelligence (2013)
19. Parikh, D., Grauman, K.: Relative attributes. In: ICCV (2011)
20. Park, D.H., Hendricks, L.A., Akata, Z., Schiele, B., Darrell, T., Rohrbach, M.: Multimodal explanations: justifying decisions and pointing to the evidence. In: CVPR (2018)
21. Reed, S., Akata, Z., Lee, H., Schiele, B.: Learning deep representations of fine-grained visual descriptions. In: CVPR (2016)
22. Ribeiro, M.T., Singh, S., Guestrin, C.: Why should i trust you? Explaining the predictions of any classifier. arXiv preprint arXiv:1602.04938 (2016)
23. Selvaraju, R.R., Cogswell, M., Das, A., Vedantam, R., Parikh, D., Batra, D.: Grad-CAM: visual explanations from deep networks via gradient-based localization. https://arxiv.org/abs/1610.02391 v3 **7**(8) (2016)
24. Shekhar, R., et al.: Foil it! Find one mismatch between image and language caption. arXiv preprint arXiv:1705.01359 (2017)
25. Shortliffe, E.H., Buchanan, B.G.: A model of inexact reasoning in medicine. Math. Biosci. **23**(3), 351–379 (1975)
26. Teach, R.L., Shortliffe, E.H.: An analysis of physician attitudes regarding computer-based clinical consultation systems. Comput. Biomed. Res. **14**(6), 542–558 (1981)
27. Van Lent, M., Fisher, W., Mancuso, M.: An explainable artificial intelligence system for small-unit tactical behavior. In: NCAI (2004)
28. Vedantam, R., Bengio, S., Murphy, K., Parikh, D., Chechik, G.: Context-aware captions from context-agnostic supervision. arXiv preprint arXiv:1701.02870 (2017)
29. Welinder, P., et al.: Caltech-UCSD birds 200. Technical report, California Institute of Technology (2010)
30. Williams, R.J.: Simple statistical gradient-following algorithms for connectionist reinforcement learning. Mach. Learn. **8**(3–4), 229–256 (1992)
31. Wu, Q., Teney, D., Wang, P., Shen, C., Dick, A., van den Hengel, A.: Visual question answering: a survey of methods and datasets. Comput. Vis. Image Underst. **163**, 21–40 (2017)
32. Xu, K., et al.: Show, attend and tell: neural image caption generation with visual attention. In: International Conference on Machine Learning, pp. 2048–2057 (2015)

33. Zeiler, M.D., Fergus, R.: Visualizing and understanding convolutional networks. In: Fleet, D., Pajdla, T., Schiele, B., Tuytelaars, T. (eds.) ECCV 2014. LNCS, vol. 8689, pp. 818–833. Springer, Cham (2014). https://doi.org/10.1007/978-3-319-10590-1_53
34. Zintgraf, L.M., Cohen, T.S., Adel, T., Welling, M.: Visualizing deep neural network decisions: prediction difference analysis. arXiv preprint arXiv:1702.04595 (2017)

Adversarial Open-World Person Re-Identification

Xiang Li[1], Ancong Wu[1], and Wei-Shi Zheng[1,2,3(✉)] (iD)

[1] Sun Yat-sen University, Guangzhou, China
{lixiang47,wuancong}@mail2.sysu.edu.cn, wszheng@ieee.org
[2] Inception Institute of Artificial Intelligence, Abu Dhabi, United Arab Emirates
[3] Key Laboratory of Machine Intelligence and Advanced Computing, MOE,
Guangzhou, China

Abstract. In a typical real-world application of re-id, a watch-list
(gallery set) of a handful of target people (*e.g.* suspects) to track around
a large volume of non-target people are demanded across camera views,
and this is called the open-world person re-id. Different from conventional
(closed-world) person re-id, a large portion of probe samples are not from
target people in the open-world setting. And, it always happens that a
non-target person would look similar to a target one and therefore would
seriously challenge a re-id system. In this work, we introduce a deep open-
world group-based person re-id model based on adversarial learning to
alleviate the attack problem caused by similar non-target people. The
main idea is learning to attack feature extractor on the target people by
using GAN to generate very target-like images (imposters), and in the
meantime the model will make the feature extractor learn to tolerate
the attack by discriminative learning so as to realize group-based verification. The framework we proposed is called the adversarial open-world
person re-identification, and this is realized by our Adversarial PersonNet
(APN) that jointly learns a generator, a person discriminator, a target
discriminator and a feature extractor, where the feature extractor and
target discriminator share the same weights so as to makes the feature
extractor learn to tolerate the attack by imposters for better group-based
verification. While open-world person re-id is challenging, we show for
the first time that the adversarial-based approach helps stabilize person
re-id system under imposter attack more effectively.

1 Introduction

Person re-identification (re-id), which is to match a pedestrian across disjoint
camera views in diverse scenes, is practical and useful for many fields, such as
public security applications and has gained increasing interests in recent years
[3,4,6,10,11,21,33,35,36,39,41,44]. Rather than re-identifying every person in
a multiple camera network, a typical real-world application is to re-identify or
track only a handful of target people on a watch list (gallery set), which is called
the open-world person re-id problem [4,41,45]. While target people will reappear
in the camera network at different views, a large volume of non-target people,

© Springer Nature Switzerland AG 2018
V. Ferrari et al. (Eds.): ECCV 2018, LNCS 11206, pp. 287–303, 2018.
https://doi.org/10.1007/978-3-030-01216-8_18

some of which could be very similar to target people, would appear as well. This contradicts to the conventional closed-world person re-id setting that all probe queries are belonging to target people on the watch list. In comparison, the open-world person re-id is extremely challenging because both target and non-target (irrelevant) people are included in the probe set.

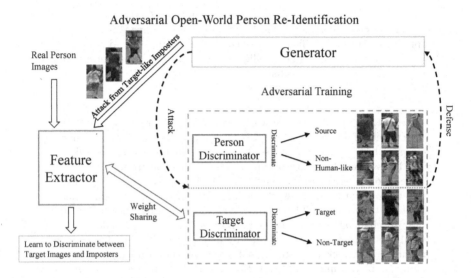

Fig. 1. Overview of adversarial open-world person re-identification. The goal for the generator is to generate target-like images, while we have two discriminators here. The person discriminator is to discriminate whether the generated images are from source dataset (*i.e.* being human-like). And the target discriminator is to discriminate whether the generated images are of target people. By the adversarial learning, we aim to generate images beneficial for training a better feature extractor for telling target person images apart from non-target ones.

However, the majority of current person re-identification models are designed for the closed-world setting [6,32,35–37,39,42,44] rather than the open-world one. Without consideration of discriminating target and non-target people during learning, these approaches are not stable and could often fail to reject a query image whose identity is not included in the gallery set. Zheng *et al.* [41] considered this problem and proposed open-world group-based verification model. Their model is based on hand-crafted feature and transfer-learning-based metric learning with auxiliary data, but the results are still far from solving this challenge. More importantly, the optimal feature representation and target-person-specific information for open-world setting have not been learned.

In this work, we present an adversarial open-world person re-identification framework for (1) learning features that are suitable for open-world person re-id, and (2) learning to attack the feature extractor by generating very target-like imposters and make person re-id system learn to tolerate it for better verification.

An end-to-end deep neural network is designed to realize the above two objectives, and an overview of this pipeline is shown in Fig. 1. The feature learning and the adversarial learning are mutually related and learned jointly, meanwhile the generator and the feature extractor are learned from each other iteratively to enhance both the efficiency of generated images and the discriminability of the feature extractor. To use the unlabeled images generated, we further incorporate a label smoothing regularization for imposters (LSRI) for this adversarial learning process. LSRI allocates equal probabilities of being any non-target people and zero probabilities of being target people to the generated target-like imposters, and it would further improve the discrimination ability of the feature extractor for distinguishing real target people from fake ones (imposters).

While GAN has been attempted in Person re-id models recently in [8,42,43] for generating images adapted from source dataset so as to enrich the training dataset on target task. However, our objective is beyond this conventional usage. By sharing the weights between feature extractor and target discriminator (see Fig. 2), our adversarial learning makes the generator and feature extractor interact with each other in an end-to-end framework. This interaction not only makes the generator produce imposters look like target people, but also more importantly makes the feature extractor learn to tolerate the attack by imposters for better group-based verification.

In summary, our contributions are more on solving the open-world challenge in person re-identification. It is the first time to formulate the open-world group-based person re-identification under an adversarial learning framework. By learning to attack and learning to defend, we realize four progresses in a unified framework, including generating very target-like imposters, mimicking imposter attacking, discriminating imposters from target images and learning re-id feature to represent. Our investigation suggests that adversarial learning is a more effective way for stabilizing person re-id system undergoing imposters.

2   Related Work

Person Re-Identification: Since person re-identification targets to identify different people, better feature representations are studied by a great deal of recent research. Some of the research try to seek more discriminative/reliable hand-crafted features [10,17,21,22,24,25,36]. Except that, learning the best matching metric [5,6,14,18,26,32,39] is also widely studied for solving the cross-view change in different environments. With the rapid development of deep learning, learning to represent from images [1,7,9,20] is attracted for person re-id, and in particular Xiao et al. [37] came up with domain guided drop out model for training CNN with multiple domains so as to improve the feature learning procedure. Also, recent deep approaches in person re-identification are found to unify feature learning and metric learning [1,30,35,44]. Although these deep learning methods are expressive for large-scale datasets, they tend to be resistless for noises and incapable of distinguishing non-target people apart from the target ones, and thus becomes unsuitable for the open-world setting. In comparison, our deep model aims to model the effect of non-target people during training and optimize the person re-id in the open-world setting.

Towards Open-World Person Re-Identification: Although the majority of works on person re-id are focusing on the closed-world setting, a few works have been reported on addressing the open-world setting. The work of Candela *et al.* [4] is based on Conditional Random Field (CRF) inference attempting to build connections between cameras towards open-world person re-identification. But their work lacks the ability to distinguish very similar identities, and with some deep CNN models coming up, features from multiple camera views can be well expressed by joint camera learning. Wang *et al.* [33] worked out an approach by proposing a new subspace learning model suitable for open-world scenario. However, group-based setting and interference defense is not considered. Also, their model requires a large volume of extra unlabeled data. Zhu *et al.* [45] proposed a novel hashing method for fast search in the open-world setting. However, Zhu *et al.* aimed at large scale open-world re-identification and efficiency is considered primarily. Besides, noiseproof ability is not taken into account. The most correlated work with this paper is formulated by Zheng *et al.* [40,41], where the group-based verification towards open-world person re-identification was proposed. They came up with a transfer relative distance comparison model (t-LRDC), learning a distance metric and transferring non-target data to target data in order to overcome data sparsity. Different from the above works, we present the first end-to-end learning model to unify feature learning and verification modeling to address the open-world setting. Moreover, our work does not require extra auxiliary datasets to mimic attack of imposters, but integrates an adversarial processing to make re-id model learn to tolerate the attack.

Adversarial Learning: In 2014, Szegedy *et al.* [31] have found out that tiny noises in samples can lead deep classifiers to mis-classify, even if these adversarial samples can be easily discriminated by human. Then many researchers have been working on adversarial training. Seyed-Mohsen *et al.* [27] proposed DeepFool, using the gradient of an image to produce a minimal noise that fools deep networks. However, their adversarial samples are towards individuals and the relation between target and non-target groups is not modelled. Thus, it does not well fit into the group-based setting. Papernot *et al.* [28] formulated a class of algorithms by using knowledge of deep neural networks (DNN) architecture for crafting adversarial samples. However, rather than forming a general algorithm for DNNs, our method is more specific for group-based person verification and the imposter samples generated are more effective to this scenario. Later, SafetyNet by Lu *et al.* [23] was proposed with an RBF-SVM in full-connected layer to detect adversarial samples. However, we perform the adversarial learning at feature level to better attack the learned features.

3   Adversarial PersonNet

3.1   Problem Statement

In this work, we concentrate on open-world person re-id by group-based verification. The group-based verification is to ensure a re-id system to identify whether a query person image comes from target people on the watch list. In this scenario, people out of this list/group are defined as non-target people.

Our objective is to unify feature learning by deep convolution networks and adversarial learning together so as to make the extracted feature robust and resistant to noise for discriminating between target people and non-target ones. The adversarial learning is to generate target-like imposter images to attack the feature extraction process and simultaneously make the whole model learn to distinguish these attacks. For this purpose, we propose a novel deep learning model called Adversarial PersonNet (APN) that suits open-world person re-id.

To better express our work under this setting in the following sections, we suppose that N_T target training images constitute a target sample set X_T sampled from C_T target people. Let $\boldsymbol{x}_i^T$ indicate the ith target image and $y_i^T \in Y_T$ represents the corresponding person/class label. The label set Y_T is denoted by $Y_T = \{y_1^T, ..., y_{N_T}^T\}$ and there are C_T target classes in total. Similarly, we are given a set of C_S non-target training classes containing N_S images, denoted as $X_S = \{\boldsymbol{x}_1^S, ..., \boldsymbol{x}_{N_S}^S\}$, where $\boldsymbol{x}_i^S \in X_S$ is the ith non-target image. y_i^S is the class of $\boldsymbol{x}_i^S$ and $Y_S = \{y_1^S, ..., y_{N_S}^S\}$. Note that there is no identity overlap between target people and non-target people. Under open-world setting, $N_S \gg N_T$. The problem is to better determine whether a person is on the target-list; that is for a given image $\boldsymbol{x}$ without knowing its class y, determine if $y \in Y_T$. We use $f(\boldsymbol{x}, \boldsymbol{\theta})$ to represent the extracted feature from image $\boldsymbol{x}$, and $\boldsymbol{\theta}$ is the weight of the feature extraction part of the CNN.

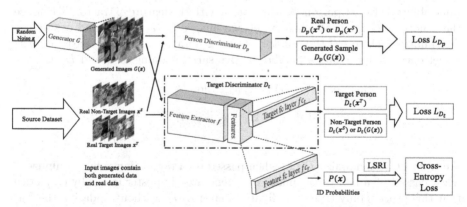

Fig. 2. Adversarial PersonNet structure. Two discriminators D_p and D_t accept samples from both datasets and generator G. Since D_t shares the same weights with feature extractor f, we represent them as the same cuboid in this figure.

3.2   Learning to Attack by Adversarial Networks

Always, GANs are designed to generate images similar to those in the *source set*, which is constituted by both target and non-target image sets. A generator G and a discriminator D_p are trained adversarially. However the generator G normally only generates images looking like the ones in the source set and the discriminator D_p discriminates the generated images from the source ones. In this case, our source datasets are all pedestrian images, so we call such D_p the *person discriminator* in response to its ability of determining whether an image is of pedestrian-like images. D_p is trained by minimizing the following loss function:

$$L_{D_p} = -\frac{1}{m} \sum_{i=1}^{m} [\log D_p(\boldsymbol{x}) + \log (1 - D_p(G(\boldsymbol{z})))], \tag{1}$$

where m is the number of samples, $\boldsymbol{x}$ represents image from source dataset and $\boldsymbol{z}$ is a noise randomly generated.

Suppose that there is a pre-trained feature extractor for person re-id task and in an attempt to steer generator G to produce not only pedestrian-like but also feature attacking images towards this feature extractor, we design a paralleled discriminator D_t with the following definition:

$$D_t(\boldsymbol{x}) = f c_t(f(\boldsymbol{x}, \boldsymbol{\theta})). \tag{2}$$

The discriminator D_t is to determine whether an image will be regarded as target image by feature extractor. $f(\boldsymbol{x}, \boldsymbol{\theta})$ indicates that part of D_t has the same network structure as feature extractor f and shares the same weights $\boldsymbol{\theta}$ (Actually, the feature extractor can be regarded as a part of D_t.). $f c_t$ means a full-connected layer following the feature extractor apart from the one connected to original CNN (with a fc layer used to pre-train the feature extractor). So D_t shares the same ability of target person discrimination with the feature extractor. To induce the generator G for producing target-like images for attacking and ensure the discriminator D_t to tell the non-target and generated imposters apart from the target ones, we formulate a paralleled adversarial training of G and D_t as

$$\min_{G} \max_{D_t} V_t(D_t, G) = \mathbb{E}_{\boldsymbol{x}^T \sim X_T}[\log D_t(\boldsymbol{x}^T)]$$
$$+ \mathbb{E}_{\boldsymbol{x}^S \sim X_S}[\log (1 - D_t(\boldsymbol{x}^S))] \tag{3}$$
$$+ \mathbb{E}_{\boldsymbol{z} \sim p_z(\boldsymbol{z})}[\log (1 - D_t(G(\boldsymbol{z})))].$$

We train D_t to maximize $D_t(\boldsymbol{x})$ when passed by a target image but minimize it when passed by a non-target image or a generated imposter image by G. Notice that this process only trains the final $f c_t$ layer of D_t without updating the feature extractor weights $\boldsymbol{\theta}$, to prevent the feature extractor from being affected by discriminator learning when the generated images are not good enough.

We call D_t the *target discriminator*. And we propose the loss function L_{D_t} for the training process of target discriminator D_t:

$$\begin{cases} L_{D_t} = -\frac{1}{m} \sum_{i=1}^{m} [\log Q_t(\boldsymbol{x}) + \log (1 - D_t(G(\boldsymbol{z})))], \\ Q_t(\boldsymbol{x}) = \begin{cases} D_t(\boldsymbol{x}), & \boldsymbol{x} \in X_T; \\ 1 - D_t(\boldsymbol{x}), & \boldsymbol{x} \in X_S. \end{cases} \end{cases} \quad (4)$$

We integrate the above into a standard GAN framework as follows:

$$\min_{G} \max_{D_p} \max_{D_t} V'(D_p, D_t, G) =$$

$$\mathbb{E}_{\boldsymbol{x}^T \sim X_T} [\log D_p(\boldsymbol{x}^T) + \log D_t(\boldsymbol{x}^T)]$$

$$+ \mathbb{E}_{\boldsymbol{x}^S \sim X_S} [\log D_p(\boldsymbol{x}^S) + \log (1 - D_t(\boldsymbol{x}^S))] \quad (5)$$

$$+ \mathbb{E}_{\boldsymbol{z} \sim p_z(\boldsymbol{z})} [\log (1 - D_p(G(\boldsymbol{z}))) + \log (1 - D_t(G(\boldsymbol{z})))].$$

The collaboration of generator and couple discriminators is illustrated in Fig. 2. While GAN with only person discriminator will force the generator G to produce source-like person images, with the incorporation of the loss of target discriminator D_t, G is more guided to produce very much target-like imposter images. The target-like imposters, generated based on the discriminating ability of feature extractor, satisfy the usage of attacking the feature extractor. Examples of images generated by APN are shown in Fig. 3 together with the target images and the images generated by controlled groups (APN without target discriminator D_t and APN without person discriminator D_p) to indicate that our network indeed has the ability to generate target-like images. The generator G is trained to fool the target discriminator in the feature space, so that the generated adversarial images can attack the re-id system. While the target discriminator D_t is mainly to tell these attack apart from the target people so as to defend the re-id system.

3.3 Joint Learning of Feature Representation and Adversarial Modelling

We finally aim to learn robust person features that are tolerant to imposter attack for open-world group-based person re-id. For further utilizing the generated person images to enhance the performance, we jointly learn feature representation and adversarial modelling in a semi-supervised way.

Although the generated images look similar to target images, they are regarded as imposter samples, and we wish to incorporate unlabeled generated imposter samples. Inspired by the smoothing regularization [42], we modify the LSRO [42] in order to make it more suitable for group-based verification by setting the probability of an unlabeled generated imposter sample $G(\boldsymbol{z})$ belonging to an existing known class k as follows:

$$q_{LSRI}(k)(G(\boldsymbol{z})) = \begin{cases} \frac{1}{C_S}, & k \in Y_S; \\ 0, & k \in Y_T, \end{cases} \quad (6)$$

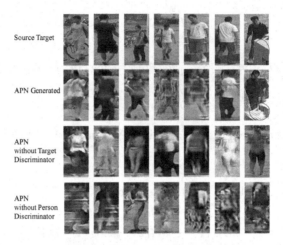

Fig. 3. Examples of generated images. Although images produced by the generator are based on random noises, we can tell that the imposters generated by APN are very similar to targets. These similarities are mostly based on clothes, colors and postures (*e.g.* the fifth column). Moreover, surroundings are learned by APN as shown in the seventh column in the red circle. (Color figure online)

Compared to LSRO, we do not allocate a uniform distribution on each unlabeled data sample over all classes (including both target and non-target ones), but only allocate a uniform distribution on non-target classes. This is significant because we attempt to separate imposter samples from target classes. The modification is exactly for the defense towards the attack of imposter samples. By using this regularization, the generated imposters are more trending to be far away from target classes and have equal chances of being non-target. We call the modified regularization in Eq. (6) as label smoothing regularization for imposters (LSRI).

Hence for each input sample x_i, we set its ground truth class distribution as:

$$q(k) = \begin{cases} 1, & k = y_i \text{ and } x_i \in X_T \cup X_S; \\ 0, & k \neq y_i \text{ and } x_i \in X_T \cup X_S, \text{ or } x_i \in X_G \text{ and } k \in Y_T; \\ \frac{1}{C_S}, & x_i \in X_G, \text{ and } k \in Y_S; \end{cases} \quad (7)$$

where y_i is the corresponding label of x_i, and we let x_i^G be the ith generated image and denote $X_G = \{x_1^G, ..., x_{N_G}^G\}$ as the set of generated imposter samples. With Eq. (7), we can now learn together with our feature extractor (*i.e.* weights θ). By such a joint learning, the feature learning part will become more discriminative between target and target-like imposter images.

3.4   Network Structure

We now detail the network structure. As shown in Fig. 2, our network consists of two parts: (1) learning robust feature representation, and (2) learning to attack by adversarial networks. For the first part, we train the feature extractor from source datasets and generated attacking samples. In this part, features are trained to be robust and resistant to imposter samples. LSRI is applied in this part to differentiate imposters from target people. Here, a full-connected layer fc_r is connected to feature extractor f at this stage, and we call it the *feature fc layer*. For the second part, as shown in Fig. 2, our learning attack by adversarial networks is a modification of DCGAN [35]. We combine modified DCGAN with couple discriminators to form an adversarial network. The generator G here is modified to produce target-like imposters specifically as an attacker. And the target discriminator D_t defends as discriminating target from non-target people. Of course, in this discriminator, a new fc layer is attached to the tail of feature extractor f, and we mark it fc_t, also called *target fc layer*, used to discriminate target from non-target images at the process of learning to attack by adversarial networks. By Eq. (2), D_t is the combination of f and target fc layer fc_t.

4   Experiments

4.1   Group-Based Verification Setting

We followed the criterion defined in [41] for evaluation of open-world group-based person re-id. The performance of how well a true target can be verified correctly and how badly a false target can be verified as true incorrectly is indicated by true target rate (TTR) and false target rate (FTR), which are defined as follows:

$$\textbf{True Target Rate (TTR)} = \#TTQ/\#TQ, \quad \textbf{False Target Rate (FTR)} = \#FNTQ/\#NTQ,$$
$$(8)$$

where TQ is the set of query target images from target people, NTQ is the set of query non-target images from non-target people, TTQ is the set of query target images that are verified as target people, and $FNTQ$ is the set of query non-target images that are verified as target people.

To obtain TTR and FTR, we follow the two steps below: (1) For each target person, there is a set of images S (single-shot or multi-shot) in gallery set. Given a query sample x, the distance between sample x and a set S is the minimal distance between that sample and any target sample of that set; (2) Whether a query image is verified as a target person is determined by comparing the distance to a threshold r. By changing the threshold r, a set of TTR and FTR values can be obtained. A higher TTR value is preferred when FTR is small.

In our experiments, we conducted two kinds of verification as defined in [41] namely Set Verification (*i.e.* whether a query is one of the persons in the target set, where the target set contains all target people.) and Individual Verification (*i.e.* whether a query is the true target person. For each target query image, the target set contains only this target person). In comparison, Set Verification is more difficult. Although determining whether a person image belongs to a group of target people seems easier, it also gives more chances for imposters to cheat the classifier, producing more false matchings [41].

4.2 Datasets and Settings

We evaluated our method on three datasets including Market-1501 [38], CUHK01 [19], and CUHK03 [20]. For each dataset, we randomly selected 1% people as target people and the rest as non-target. Similar to [41], for target people, we separated images of each target people into training and testing sets by half. Since only four images are available in CUHK01, we chose one for training, two for gallery (reduce to one in single-shot case) and one for probe. Our division guaranteed that probe and gallery images are from diverse cameras for each person. For non-target people, they were divided into training and testing sets by half in person/class level to ensure there is no overlap on identity. In testing phase, two images of each target person in testing set were randomly selected to form gallery set, and the remaining images were selected to form query set. In the default setting, all images of non-target people in testing set were selected to form query set. The data split was kept the same for all evaluations on our and the compared methods. Specifically, the data split is summarized below:

CUHK01 CUHK01 contains 3,884 images of 971 identities from two camera views. In our experiment, 9 people were marked as target and 1,888 images of 472 people were selected to form the non-target training set. The testing set of non-target people contains 1,960 images of 490 people.

CUHK03 CUHK03 is larger than CUHK01 and some images were automatically detected. A total of 1,360 identities were divided into 13 target people, 667 training non-target people and 693 testing non-target people. The numbers of training and testing non-target images were 6,247 and 6,563 respectively.

Market-1501 Market-1501 is a large-scale dataset containing a total of 32,668 images of 1,501 identities. We randomly selected 15 people as target and 728 people as non-target to form the training set containing a total of 12,433 images, and the testing non-target set contains 758 identities with 13,355 images.

Under the above settings, we evaluated our model together with selected popular re-id models. Since APN is based on ResNet-50 and our evaluations attempt to show our improvement on ResNet-50, metric learning methods such as t-LRDC [41], XICE [45], XQDA [21] and CRAFT [6] are also applied to the feature extracted by ResNet-50.

4.3 Implementation Details

In our APN, we used ResNet-50 [12] as the feature extractor in the target discriminator. The generator and person discriminator is based on DCGAN [29]. At the first step of our procedure, we pre-trained the feature extractor using auxiliary datasets, 3DPeS [2], iLIDS [34], PRID2011 [13] and Shinpuhkan [15]. These datasets were only used in the pre-training stage for the feature extractor. In pre-training, we used stochastic gradient descent with momentum 0.9. The learning rate was 0.1 at the beginning and multiplied by 0.1 every 10 epochs.

Then, the adversarial part of APN was trained using ADAM optimizer [16] with parameters $\beta_1 = 0.5$ and $\beta_2 = 0.99$. Using the target dataset for evaluation, the person discriminator D_p and generator G were pre-trained for 30 epochs. Then, the target discriminator D_t together with the person discriminator D_p, and the generator G were trained jointly for $k_1 = 15$ epochs, where G is optimized twice in each iteration to prevent losses of discriminators from going to zero. Finally, the feature extractor was trained again for $k_2 = 20$ epochs with a lower learning rate starting from 0.001 and multiplied by 0.1 every 10 epochs. The above procedure was executed repeatedly as an adversarial process.

Table 1. Comparison with typical person re-identification: TTR (%) against FTR

Evaluation	Market-1501						CHUK01						CUHK03					
FTR	0.1%	1%	5%	10%	20%	30%	0.1%	1%	5%	10%	20%	30%	0.1%	1%	5%	10%	20%	30%
Dataset	Set Verification																	
APN	9.01	22.32	46.78	63.34	73.82	81.12	16.67	33.33	88.89	88.89	94.44	100	22.18	41.14	52.02	58.87	73.68	80.24
ResNet-50 [12]	3.43	20.79	43.35	57.43	71.24	79.83	0	11.11	33.33	55.56	72.22	83.33	9.27	18.95	30.65	39.52	47.98	58.47
DCGAN+LSRO [43]	6.77	20.60	42.06	58.80	72.49	80.11	3.14	22.22	66.67	72.22	88.89	94.44	11.75	23.02	35.15	43.77	50.04	63.46
ResNet+t-LRDC [42]	3.00	18.88	42.06	51.07	65.24	75.54	5.56	5.56	16.67	44.44	72.22	72.22	7.74	19.35	33.01	38.81	49.18	59.45
ResNet+XICE [46]	3.28	15.75	41.63	51.07	69.53	78.11	0	11.11	16.67	44.44	72.22	81.09	5.77	13.18	20.16	37.19	45.91	57.43
ResNet+XQDA [22]	3.86	21.89	44.64	62.23	74.68	81.12	0	5.56	22.22	44.44	72.22	83.33	6.05	15.32	27.02	36.29	46.37	59.68
ResNet+CRAFT [6]	1.29	15.02	34.76	46.35	64.81	79.83	5.56	5.56	27.78	55.56	72.22	88.89	9.27	20.97	31.45	39.92	47.58	59.27
JSTL-DGD [38]	6.67	18.03	35.62	60.52	73.09	79.39	16.67	27.53	44.44	66.67	77.78	94.44	19.35	34.67	45.22	53.64	58.25	68.23
DeepFool [28]	10.78	21.89	45.05	59.23	69.53	85.41	16.67	22.22	33.33	44.44	61.11	77.78	19.35	31.45	42.74	46.37	56.05	65.32
Dataset	Individual Verification																	
APN	32.71	63.18	80.32	87.68	95.54	97.30	41.67	72.22	97.22	100	100	100	43.13	58.58	76.14	83.09	90.08	93.65
ResNet-50 [12]	30.15	61.23	77.09	85.47	91.32	97.12	33.33	44.44	72.22	86.11	97.22	100	39.19	53.22	70.76	77.55	86.11	92.86
DCGAN+LSRO [43]	28.14	62.77	77.29	84.09	92.96	95.11	36.11	67.56	72.22	88.89	100	100	40.72	51.18	74.91	80.58	86.36	92.06
ResNet+t-LRDC [42]	10.70	25.41	44.31	57.26	66.29	80.32	5.56	16.67	20.14	55.56	80.56	91.67	16.57	32.86	45.73	53.22	68.23	83.68
ResNet+XICE [46]	11.71	39.64	53.10	68.74	77.29	90.21	36.11	48.51	79.23	81.72	91.67	97.22	23.51	39.19	51.18	64.93	77.85	82.54
ResNet+XQDA [22]	31.03	59.10	74.51	79.39	87.63	91.42	11.11	38.89	69.44	83.33	88.89	97.22	31.89	45.36	59.15	64.38	76.44	84.87
ResNet+CRAFT [6]	22.66	62.08	78.53	83.74	91.42	97.16	11.11	33.33	63.89	80.56	88.89	97.22	30.43	43.35	57.29	68.65	80.88	84.08
JSTL-DGD [38]	27.60	52.84	70.15	77.00	87.10	90.29	25.00	50.00	86.11	91.67	97.22	100	37.97	50.45	67.58	76.19	82.54	87.57
DeepFool [28]	31.30	64.43	83.31	91.89	95.85	96.73	33.82	48.51	79.23	95.71	98.15	100	32.86	53.22	68.23	75.10	83.68	89.88

4.4 Comparison with Open-World Re-Id Methods

Open-world re-id is still under studied, and t-LRDC [41] and XICE [45] are two represented existing methods designed for the open-world setting in person re-id. Since the original works of these two existing open-world methods use traditional hand-crafted features, which are not comparable with deep learning models, we applied these two methods to ResNet-50 features for better comparison. The results are reported in Table 1. Our APN outperformed t-LRDC and XICE in all cases, and the margin is especially large on CUHK03. Compared to t-LRDC and XICE, our APN is an end-to-end learning framework and takes adversarial learning into account for feature learning, so that APN is more tolerant to the attack of samples of non-target people.

4.5 Comparison with Closed-World Re-id Methods

We compared our method with related popular re-id methods developed for closed-world person re-identification. We mainly evaluated ResNet-50 [12], XQDA [21], CRAFT [6], and JSTL-DGD [37] for comparison. These methods were all evaluated by following the same setting as our APN, where the deep features extracted by ResNet-50 were applied for all non-deep-learning methods. As shown in Table 1, these approaches optimal for closed-world scenario cannot well adapt to the open-world setting. In all cases, the proposed APN achieved overall better performance, especially when tested on Set Verification and when FTR is 1% as compared to the others. On Market-1501, APN obtained 4.29 more matching rate than the second place JSTL-DGD, a favorable deep model for re-id, when FTR is 1% on Set Verification, and as well outperformed JSTL-DGD on all conditions on Individual Verification. On CUHK01, APN gained 5.8 more matching rate as compared to JSTL-DGD when FTR is 1% and 45 matching rate more when FTR is 5% on Set Verification. The compared closed-world models were designed with the assumption that the same identities hold between gallery and probe sets, while the relation between target and non-target people is not modelled. Meanwhile our APN is designed for the open-world group-based verification for discriminating target from non-target people.

Table 2. Different generated imposter sources

Dataset	Market-1501						CUHK01						CUHK03					
FTR	0.1%	1%	5%	10%	20%	30%	0.1%	1%	5%	10%	20%	30%	0.1%	1%	5%	10%	20%	30%
Evaluation	Set Verification																	
APN	**9.01**	**22.32**	**46.78**	**63.34**	**73.82**	**81.12**	**16.67**	**33.33**	**88.89**	**88.89**	**94.44**	**100**	**22.18**	41.14	**52.02**	**58.87**	**73.68**	**80.24**
APN w/o D_t	8.58	20.60	43.78	58.80	70.82	77.68	5.56	27.78	77.78	77.78	94.44	94.44	17.34	**43.15**	49.19	55.24	67.34	78.23
APN w/o D_p	7.13	18.21	39.65	56.65	68.49	75.54	3.14	17.34	50.00	66.67	83.33	94.44	16.53	41.14	47.98	54.03	65.32	75.41
APN w/o WS	3.43	19.30	40.52	50.18	65.24	73.22	0	13.85	37.12	53.20	77.78	86.33	16.53	32.49	39.01	46.15	55.24	64.31
No Imposter	8.58	20.60	45.05	56.65	69.53	78.97	0	22.22	77.78	77.78	88.89	94.44	16.53	38.71	48.39	54.03	69.76	78.23
Evaluation	Individual Verification																	
APN	**32.71**	**63.18**	**80.32**	**87.68**	**95.54**	**97.30**	**41.67**	**72.22**	**97.22**	**100**	**100**	**100**	**43.13**	**58.58**	**76.14**	**83.09**	**90.08**	**93.65**
APN w/o D_t	**32.71**	61.13	75.68	85.25	90.17	95.11	35.79	70.02	95.66	**100**	**100**	**100**	41.23	55.33	75.50	81.23	87.89	92.06
APN w/o D_p	28.62	53.37	75.68	83.81	88.05	94.65	33.21	68.76	94.44	**100**	**100**	**100**	37.18	55.33	69.64	79.44	85.08	89.21
APN w/o WS	25.32	50.74	72.14	81.26	87.63	93.10	21.42	57.69	79.44	96.51	**100**	**100**	32.86	47.29	68.23	72.15	79.42	90.10
No Imposter	26.20	57.03	77.11	84.63	91.48	93.71	38.89	69.72	94.44	**100**	**100**	**100**	40.87	56.57	75.50	82.09	89.29	92.06

4.6 Comparison with Related Adversarial Generation

We compared our model with fine-tuned ResNet-50 with adversarial samples generated by DeepFool [27], which is also a method using extra generated samples. DeepFool produced adversarial samples to fool the network by adding noise computed by gradient. As shown in Table 1, our APN performed much better than DeepFool especially on CUHK01 and CUHK03. DeepFool cannot adapt to open-world re-id well because the adversarial samples generated are produced with a separate learning from the classifier learning and thus the relation between the generated samples and target set is not modelled for group-based verification, while in our APN we aim to generate target-like samples so as to make adversarial learning facilitate learning better features.

We also evaluated ResNet-50 trained with samples generated by DCGAN and using LSRO as done in [42]. And APN outperformed it in all cases. The work of [42] only used generated samples to enlarge the dataset and the group-based verification for open-world re-id is not taken into consideration.

Table 3. Number of shots on Set Verification

Method	APN						ResNet-50					
FTR	0.1%	1%	5%	10%	20%	30%	0.1%	1%	5%	10%	20%	30%
Dataset	Market-1501											
Single-shot	5.15	15.45	41.63	51.93	64.38	72.10	3.00	13.73	32.19	42.49	61.37	66.09
Multi-shot	9.01	22.32	46.78	63.34	73.82	81.12	3.43	20.79	43.35	57.43	71.24	79.83
Dataset	CUHK01											
Single-shot	11.11	33.33	66.67	77.78	88.89	100	0	22.22	38.89	77.78	88.89	94.44
Multi-shot	16.67	33.33	88.89	88.89	94.44	100	0	22.22	77.78	77.78	88.89	94.44
Dataset	CUHK03											
Single-shot	20.97	38.31	45.56	52.42	63.31	69.76	16.53	36.29	44.35	50.63	61.69	66.53
Multi-shot	22.18	41.14	52.02	58.87	73.68	80.24	16.53	38.71	48.39	54.03	69.76	78.23

Table 4. Number of shots on Individual Verification

Method	APN						ResNet-50					
FTR	0.1%	1%	5%	10%	20%	30%	0.1%	1%	5%	10%	20%	30%
Dataset	Market-1501											
Single-shot	20.20	55.07	76.50	85.00	91.42	94.28	15.60	39.19	62.00	71.73	82.11	88.57
Multi-shot	32.71	63.18	80.32	87.68	95.54	97.30	30.15	61.23	77.09	85.47	91.32	97.12
Dataset	CUHK01											
Single-shot	39.61	72.22	91.67	100	100	100	31.11	44.44	68.45	85.14	97.22	100
Multi-shot	41.67	72.22	97.22	100	100	100	33.33	44.44	72.22	86.11	97.22	100
Dataset	CUHK03											
Single-shot	38.69	53.27	70.44	80.56	88.89	92.86	38.39	50.84	66.96	77.38	85.31	90.87
Multi-shot	43.13	58.58	76.14	83.09	90.08	93.65	39.19	53.32	70.76	77.55	86.11	92.86

Table 5. Different target proportion of Market-1501 on Set Verification (TP. stands for Target Proportion)

Method	APN						ResNet-50					
FTR	0.1%	1%	5%	10%	20%	30%	0.1%	1%	5%	10%	20%	30%
TP. 0.5%	25.35	43.74	66.39	77.89	86.54	93.79	14.48	37.96	61.25	73.50	82.85	90.62
TP. 1%	9.01	22.32	46.78	59.23	73.82	81.12	3.43	18.79	40.35	57.43	70.24	77.83
TP. 3%	5.66	17.31	35.11	46.76	59.55	69.58	4.50	15.34	31.63	44.50	58.22	67.55
TP. 5%	5.38	15.77	31.36	42.11	56.43	68.09	5.02	12.31	30.08	39.02	53.97	64.99

Table 6. LSRI vs. LSRO

Evaluation	Set verification						Individual verification					
FTR	0.1%	1%	5%	10%	20%	30%	0.1%	1%	5%	10%	20%	30%
Dataset	Market-1501											
LSRI	9.01	22.32	46.78	63.34	73.82	81.12	32.71	63.18	80.32	87.68	95.54	97.30
LSRO [42]	8.15	20.60	45.92	57.51	72.53	79.83	28.42	61.66	78.80	84.61	90.56	92.54
Dataset	CUHK01											
LSRI	16.67	33.33	88.89	88.89	94.44	100	41.67	72.22	97.22	100	100	100
LSRO [42]	16.67	27.78	77.78	88.89	88.89	94.44	36.11	68.23	97.22	100	100	100
Dataset	CUHK03											
LSRI	22.18	41.14	52.02	58.87	73.68	80.24	43.13	58.58	76.14	83.09	90.08	93.65
LSRO [42]	17.34	39.52	49.60	55.24	69.76	79.03	39.01	52.53	71.50	80.13	88.49	91.27

4.7 Further Evaluation of Our Method

Effect of Generated Imposters. We compared to the case without using the generated imposters. We trained our network in the same way without inputting the generated images in the training of feature extractor. The results are shown in the rows indicated by "No Imposters" in Table 2. It can be observed that, training with the imposters generated by APN can achieve large improvement as compared to the case without it, because these imposters are target-like and can improve the discriminating ability of the features. In details, on Set Verification, APN outperformed an average of 2.15 matching rate on Market-1501 and 3.23 matching rate on CUHK03, and for CUHK01 APN outperformed 16.67% when FTR is 0.1%. On Individual Verification, APN outperformed an average of 4.43 matching rate on Market-1501 and has better performance on all other cases.

Effect of Weight Sharing. The weight sharing between the target discriminator and the feature extractor aims to ensure that the generator can learn from the feature extractor and generate more target-like attack samples. Without the sharing, there is no connection between generation and feature extraction. Taking Individual Verification on Market for instance, ours degrades from 63.18% to 50.74% (no sharing indicated by "APN w/o WS") when FTR = 1% in Table 2.

Effect of Person Discriminator and Target Discriminator. Our APN is based on GAN consisting of generator, person discriminator D_p and target discriminator D_t. To further evaluate them, we compared with APN without person discriminator (APN w/o D_p) and APN without target discriminator (APN w/o D_t). APN without target discriminator can be regarded as two independent components DCGAN and feature extraction network. To fairly compare these cases, LSRI was also applied as in APN for the generated samples. The results are reported in Table 2. It is obvious that our full APN is the most effective one among the compared cases. Sometimes generating imposters by APN without person discriminator D_p or target discriminator D_t even degrade the performance as compared to the case of no imposter. When target discriminator is discarded, although person-like images can be generated, they are not similar to target people and thus are not serious attacks to the features for group-based verification. In the case without person discriminator, the generator even fails to generate person-like images (see Fig. 3) so that the performance is largely degraded. This indicates that the person discriminator plays an important role in generating person-like images, and the target discriminator is significant for helping the generator to generate better target-like imposters, so that the feature extractor can benefit more from distinguishing these imposters.

LSRI vs LSRO. We verified that the modification of LSRO, namely LSRI in Eq. (6) is more suitable for optimizing the open-world re-id. The performance of comparing our LSRI with the original LSRO is reported in Table 6. It shows that the feature extractor is more likely to correctly discriminate target people under the same FTR using LSRI on. It is proved that our modification LSRI is more appropriate for open-world re-id scenario, since the imposters are allocated equal probabilities of being non-target for group-based towards modelling, so they are more likely to be far away from target person samples, leading to more discriminative feature representation for target people, while in LSRO, the imposters are allocated equal probabilities of being non-target as well as target.

Effect of Target Proportion. The evaluation results on different target proportion are reported in Table 5. We used different percentages of people marked as target. This verification was conducted on Market-1501, and we used original ResNet-50 for comparison. While TTR declines with the growth of target proportion due to more target people to verify, our APN can still outperformed the original ResNet-50 in all cases.

Effect of the Number of Shots. The performance under multi-shot and single-shot settings were also compared in our experiments. For multi-shot setting, we randomly selected two images of each target person as gallery set, while for single-shot setting, we only selected one. As shown in Tables 3 and 4, on both single-shot and multi-shot settings, our APN outperformed ResNet-50 on all conditions of Market-1501, CUHK01, and CUHK03. Especially on Set Verification, for CUHK01, when FTR is 0.1%, APN outperformed ResNet-50 11.11% under single-shot setting and 16.67% under multi-shot setting.

5   Conclusion

For the first time, we demonstrate how adversarial learning can be used to solve the open-world group-based person re-id problem. The introduced adversarial person re-id enables a mutually related and cooperative progress among learning to represent, learning to generate, learning to attack, and learning to defend. In addition, this adversarial modelling is also further improved by a label smoothing regularization for imposters under semi-supervised learning.

Acknowledgment. This work was supported partially by the National Key Research and Development Program of China (2016YFB1001002) and the NSFC (61522115, 61472456), Guangdong Programme (2016TX03X157), and the Royal Society Newton Advanced Fellowship (NA150459). The corresponding author for this paper is Wei-Shi Zheng.

References

1. Ahmed, E., Jones, M.J., Marks, T.K.: An improved deep learning architecture for person re-identification. In: CVPR. IEEE Computer Society (2015)
2. Baltieri, D., Vezzani, R., Cucchiara, R.: 3DPeS: 3D people dataset for surveillance and forensics. In: Proceedings of the 1st International ACM Workshop on Multimedia access to 3D Human Objects, Scottsdale, Arizona, USA, pp. 59–64, November 2011
3. Bedagkar-Gala, A., Shah, S.K.: A survey of approaches and trends in person re-identification. Image Vis. Comput. **32**(4), 270–286 (2014)

4. Cancela, B., Hospedales, T.M., Gong, S.: Open-world person re-identification by multi-label assignment inference. In: Valstar, M.F., French, A.P., Pridmore, T.P. (eds.) BMVC. BMVA Press (2014)

5. Chen, Y.C., Zheng, W.S., Lai, J.H., Yuen, P.C.: An asymmetric distance model for cross-view feature mapping in person reidentification. IEEE Trans. Circuits Syst. Video Technol. **27**(8), 1661–1675 (2017)

6. Chen, Y.C., Zhu, X., Zheng, W.S., Lai, J.H.: Person re-identification by camera correlation aware feature augmentation. CoRR abs/1703.08837 (2017)

7. Cheng, D., Gong, Y., Zhou, S., Wang, J., Zheng, N.: Person re-identification by multi-channel parts-based CNN with improved triplet loss function. In: CVPR. IEEE Computer Society (2016)

8. Deng, W., Zheng, L., Ye, Q., Kang, G., Yang, Y., Jiao, J.: Image-image domain adaptation with preserved self-similarity and domain-dissimilarity for person reidentification. In: CVPR, p. 6. IEEE Computer Society (2018)

9. Ding, S., Lin, L., Wang, G., Chao, H.: Deep feature learning with relative distance comparison for person re-identification. CoRR abs/1512.03622 (2015)

10. Farenzena, M., Bazzani, L., Perina, A., Murino, V., Cristani, M.: Person re-identification by symmetry-driven accumulation of local features. In: CVPR. IEEE Computer Society (2010)

11. Gong, S., Cristani, M., Yan, S., Loy, C.C. (eds.): Person Re-Identification. ACVPR. Springer, London (2014). https://doi.org/10.1007/978-1-4471-6296-4

12. He, K., Zhang, X., Ren, S., Sun, J.: Deep residual learning for image recognition. In: CVPR. IEEE Computer Society (2016)

13. Hirzer, M., Beleznai, C., Roth, P.M., Bischof, H.: Person re-identification by descriptive and discriminative classification. In: Heyden, A., Kahl, F. (eds.) SCIA 2011. LNCS, vol. 6688, pp. 91–102. Springer, Heidelberg (2011). https://doi.org/10.1007/978-3-642-21227-7_9

14. Hirzer, M., Roth, P.M., Köstinger, M., Bischof, H.: Relaxed pairwise learned metric for person re-identification. In: Fitzgibbon, A., Lazebnik, S., Perona, P., Sato, Y., Schmid, C. (eds.) ECCV 2012. LNCS, vol. 7577, pp. 780–793. Springer, Heidelberg (2012). https://doi.org/10.1007/978-3-642-33783-3_56

15. Kawanishi, Y., Wu, Y., Mukunoki, M., Minoh, M.: Shinpuhkan 2014: a multi-camera pedestrian dataset for tracking people across multiple cameras (2014)

16. Kingma, D.P., Ba, J.: Adam: a method for stochastic optimization. CoRR abs/1412.6980 (2014)

17. Kviatkovsky, I., Adam, A., Rivlin, E.: Color invariants for person reidentification. IEEE Trans. Pattern Anal. Mach. Intell. **35**(7), 1622–1634 (2013)

18. Köstinger, M., Hirzer, M., Wohlhart, P., Roth, P.M., Bischof, H.: Large scale metric learning from equivalence constraints. In: CVPR. IEEE Computer Society (2012)

19. Li, W., Zhao, R., Wang, X.: Human reidentification with transferred metric learning. In: ACCV (2012)

20. Li, W., Zhao, R., Xiao, T., Wang, X.: DeepReID: deep filter pairing neural network for person re-identification. In: CVPR. IEEE Computer Society (2014)

21. Liao, S., Hu, Y., Zhu, X., Li, S.Z.: Person re-identification by local maximal occurrence representation and metric learning. In: CVPR, pp. 2197–2206. IEEE Computer Society (2015)

22. Liu, C., Gong, S., Loy, C.C.: On-the-fly feature importance mining for person re-identification. Pattern Recognit. **47**(4), 1602–1615 (2014)

23. Lu, J., Issaranon, T., Forsyth, D.A.: SafetyNet: detecting and rejecting adversarial examples robustly. CoRR abs/1704.00103 (2017)

24. Ma, B., Su, Y., Jurie, F.: BiCov: a novel image representation for person re-identification and face verification. In: BMVC (2012)
25. Ma, B., Su, Y., Jurie, F.: Covariance descriptor based on bio-inspired features for person re-identification and face verification. Image Vis. Comput. **32**(6–7), 379–390 (2014). https://doi.org/10.1016/j.imavis.2014.04.002
26. Mignon, A., Jurie, F.: PCCA: a new approach for distance learning from sparse pairwise constraints. In: CVPR. IEEE Computer Society (2012)
27. Moosavi-Dezfooli, S.M., Fawzi, A., Frossard, P.: DeepFool: a simple and accurate method to fool deep neural networks. In: CVPR. IEEE Computer Society (2016)
28. Papernot, N., McDaniel, P.D., Jha, S., Fredrikson, M., Celik, Z.B., Swami, A.: The limitations of deep learning in adversarial settings. CoRR abs/1511.07528 (2015)
29. Radford, A., Metz, L., Chintala, S.: Unsupervised representation learning with deep convolutional generative adversarial networks. CoRR abs/1511.06434 (2015)
30. Subramaniam, A., Chatterjee, M., Mittal, A.: Deep neural networks with inexact matching for person re-identification. In: Lee, D.D., Sugiyama, M., von Luxburg, U., Guyon, I., Garnett, R. (eds.) NIPS (2016)
31. Szegedy, C., et al.: Intriguing properties of neural networks. CoRR abs/1312.6199 (2013)
32. Tao, D., Jin, L., Wang, Y., Yuan, Y., Li, X.: Person re-identification by regularized smoothing KISS metric learning. IEEE Trans. Circuits Syst. Video Technol. **23**(10), 1675–1685 (2013)
33. Wang, H., Zhu, X., Xiang, T., Gong, S.: Towards unsupervised open-set person re-identification. In: ICIP. IEEE (2016)
34. Wang, T., Gong, S., Zhu, X., Wang, S.: Person re-identification by discriminative selection in video ranking. IEEE Trans. Pattern Anal. Mach. Intell. **38**(12), 2501–2514 (2016)
35. Wu, L., Shen, C., van den Hengel, A.: PersonNet: person re-identification with deep convolutional neural networks. CoRR abs/1601.07255 (2016)
36. Wu, S., Chen, Y.C., Li, X., Wu, A., You, J., Zheng, W.S.: An enhanced deep feature representation for person re-identification. CoRR abs/1604.07807 (2016)
37. Xiao, T., Li, H., Ouyang, W., Wang, X.: Learning deep feature representations with domain guided dropout for person re-identification. In: CVPR. IEEE Computer Society (2016)
38. Zheng, L., Shen, L., Tian, L., Wang, S., Wang, J., Tian, Q.: Scalable person re-identification: a Benchmark. In: ICCV (2015)
39. Zheng, W.S., Gong, S., Xiang, T.: Person re-identification by probabilistic relative distance comparison. In: CVPR. IEEE Computer Society (2011)
40. Zheng, W.S., Gong, S., Xiang, T.: Transfer re-identification: from person to set-based verification. In: CVPR. IEEE Computer Society (2012)
41. Zheng, W.S., Gong, S., Xiang, T.: Towards open-world person re-identification by one-shot group-based verification. IEEE Trans. Pattern Anal. Mach. Intell. **38**(3), 591–606 (2016)
42. Zheng, Z., Zheng, L., Yang, Y.: Unlabeled samples generated by GAN improve the person re-identification baseline in vitro. CoRR abs/1701.07717 (2017)
43. Zhong, Z., Zheng, L., Zheng, Z., Li, S., Yang, Y.: Camera style adaptation for person re-identification. In: CVPR, pp. 5157–5166. IEEE Computer Society (2018)
44. Zhu, J., Zeng, H., Liao, S., Lei, Z., Cai, C., Zheng, L.: Deep hybrid similarity learning for person re-identification. CoRR abs/1702.04858 (2017)
45. Zhu, X., Wu, B., Huang, D., Zheng, W.S.: Fast open-world person re-identification. IEEE Trans. Image Process. **PP**(99), 1 (2017). https://doi.org/10.1109/TIP.2017.2740564

Generative Domain-Migration Hashing for Sketch-to-Image Retrieval

Jingyi Zhang[1,2], Fumin Shen[1(✉)], Li Liu[2], Fan Zhu[2], Mengyang Yu[3], Ling Shao[2], Heng Tao Shen[1], and Luc Van Gool[3]

[1] Center for Future Media and School of Computer Science and Engineering, University of Electronic Science and Technology of China, Chengdu, China
fumin.shen@gmail.com
[2] Inception Institute of Artificial Intelligence, Abu Dhabi, UAE
[3] Computer Vision Lab, ETH Zurich, Zürich, Switzerland

Abstract. Due to the succinct nature of free-hand sketch drawings, sketch-based image retrieval (SBIR) has abundant practical use cases in consumer electronics. However, SBIR remains a long-standing unsolved problem mainly because of the significant discrepancy between the sketch domain and the image domain. In this work, we propose a Generative Domain-migration Hashing (GDH) approach, which for the first time generates hashing codes from synthetic natural images that are migrated from sketches. The generative model learns a mapping that the distributions of sketches can be indistinguishable from the distribution of natural images using an adversarial loss, and simultaneously learns an inverse mapping based on the cycle consistency loss in order to enhance the indistinguishability. With the robust mapping learned from the generative model, GDH can migrate sketches to their indistinguishable image counterparts while preserving the domain-invariant information of sketches. With an end-to-end multi-task learning framework, the generative model and binarized hashing codes can be jointly optimized. Comprehensive experiments of both category-level and fine-grained SBIR on multiple large-scale datasets demonstrate the consistently balanced superiority of GDH in terms of efficiency, memory costs and effectiveness (Models and code at https://github.com/YCJGG/GDH).

Keywords: Domain-migration · Hash function · SBIR

1 Introduction

The prevalence of touchscreen in consumer electronics (range from portable devices to large home appliance) facilitates human-machine interactions free-hand drawings. The input of sketches is succinct, convenient and efficient for

Electronic supplementary material The online version of this chapter (https://doi.org/10.1007/978-3-030-01216-8_19) contains supplementary material, which is available to authorized users.

© Springer Nature Switzerland AG 2018
V. Ferrari et al. (Eds.): ECCV 2018, LNCS 11206, pp. 304–321, 2018.
https://doi.org/10.1007/978-3-030-01216-8_19

visually recording ideas, and can beat hundreds of words in some scenarios. As an extended application based on sketches, sketch-based image retrieval (SBIR) [1,9,39,40,48,55,56] has attracted increasing attention.

The primary challenge in SBIR is that free-hand sketches are inherently abstract and iconic, which magnifies cross-domain discrepancy between sketches and real-world images. Recent works attempt to employ cross-view learning methods [4,9,13,14,29,32,34,37–39] to address such a challenge, where the common practice is to reduce the domain discrepancy by embedding both sketches and natural images to a common space and use the projected features for retrieval. The most critical deficiency of this line of approaches is the learned mappings within each domain cannot be well-generalized to the test data, especially for categories with large variance. Similar to other image-based retrieval problems, the query time grows increasingly with the database size and exponentially with the dimension of sketch/image representations. To this end, Deep Sketch Hashing (DSH) [29] is introduced to replace the full-precision sketch/image representations with binary vectors. However, the quantization error introduced by the binarization procedure can destroy both domain-invariant information and the semantic consistency across domains.

In this work, our primary goal is to improve deficiencies in aforementioned works and provide a practical solution to the scalable SBIR problem. We propose a Generative Domain-migration Hashing (GDH) method that improves the generalization capability by migrating sketches into the natural image domain, where the distribution migrated sketches can be indistinguishable from the distribution of natural images. Additionally, we introduce an end-to-end multi-task learning framework that jointly optimizes the cycle consistent migration as well as the hash codes, where the adversarial loss and the cycle consistency loss can simultaneously preserve the semantic consistency of the hashing codes. GDH also integrates an attention layer that guides the learning process to focus on the most representative regions.

While SBIR aims to retrieve natural images that shares identical category labels with the query sketch, fine-grained SBIR aims to preserve the intra-category instance-level consistency in addition to the category-level consistency. For the consistency purpose, we refer to standard SBIR as category-level SBIR and the fine-grained version as fine-grained SBIR respectively throughout the paper. Since the bidirectional mappings learned in GDH are highly under-constrained (*i.e.*, does not require the pixel-level alignment [15] between sketches and natural images), GDH can naturally provide an elegant solution for preserving the geometrical morphology and detailed instance-level characteristic between sketches and natural images. In addition, a triplet ranking loss is introduced to enhance the fine-grained learning based on visual similarities of intra-class instances. The pipeline of the proposed GDH method for both category-level and fine-grained SBIR tasks is illustrated in Fig. 1. Extensive experiments on various large-scale datasets for both category-level and fine-grained SBIR tasks demonstrate the consistently balanced superiority of GDH in terms of memory cost, retrieval time and accuracy. The main contributions of this work are as follows:

- We for the first time propose a generative model GDH for the hashing-based SBIR problem. Comparing to existing methods, the generative model can essentially improve the generalization capability by migrating sketches into their indistinguishable counterparts in the natural image domain.
- Guided by an adversarial loss and a cycle consistency loss, the optimized binary hashing codes can preserve the semantic consistency across domains. Meanwhile, training GDH does not require the pixel-level alignment across domains, and thus allows generalized and practical applications.
- GDH can improve the category-level SBIR performance over the state-of-the-art hashing-based SBIR method DSH [29] by up to 20.5% on the TU-Berlin Extension dataset, and up to 26.4% on the Sketchy dataset respectively. Meanwhile, GDH can achieve comparable performance with real-valued fine-grained SBIR methods, while significantly reduce the retrieval time and memory cost with binary codes.

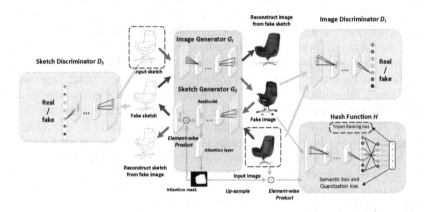

Fig. 1. Illustration of our deep model for the domain-migration networks and compact binary codes learning. The domain-migration module consists of G_I, G_S, D_I and D_S. The bottom right module is the hashing network H. The red arrows represent the cycle between real sketches and fake natural while the purple arrows represent the cycle between real natural images and fake sketches.

2   Related Work

In this section, we discuss the following four directions of related works.

Category-Level SBIR: The majority of existing category-level SBIR methods [4,9,13,14,22,29,32,34,37–39] rely on learning a common feature space for both sketches and natural images. However, learning such a common feature space based on that can end up with an overfitting solution to the training data.

Hashing-Based SBIR: If the learned common feature space is real-valued, the retrieval time depends on the database size, and the scalability of the algorithms can be consequently restrained. In order to to improve the efficiency, hashing-based methods [26,28,30,31,36,42–46,51,61] are introduced to solve the SBIR problem. The state-of-the-art hashing-based SBIR method DSH [28] employed an end-to-end semi-heterogeneous CNNs to learn binarized hashing codes for retrieval. However, the generalization issue remains in DSH since the learned semi-heterogeneous CNNs are also non-linear mappings across the two domains.

Generative Adversarial Networks: The success of Generative Adversarial Networks (GANs) [10] in various image generation [6] and representation learning [33] tasks is inspiring in a way that sketches can be migrated into the natural image domain using the adversarial loss, where the migrated sketches cannot be distinguished from natural images. Image-to-image translation methods [16,41] can serve this purpose and are capable of migrating sketches into natural images, however, the pixel-level alignment between each sketch and image pair required for training are impractical. In order to address such an issue, Zhu et al. [62] introduced a cycle consistency loss. In this work, we employ such a cycle consistency loss and force the bidirectional mappings to be consistent with each other. Benefiting from the highly under-constrained cycled learning, sketches can be migrated to their indistinguishable counterparts in the natural image domain.

Fine-Grained SBIR: Among a limited number of fine-grained SBIR methods [3,20,21,35,40,48,53–55], Yu et al. [55] proposed the multi-branch networks with triplet ranking loss, which preserved the visual similarities of intra-class sketch and natural image instances. In our work, we also exploit the triplet ranking loss for preserving the visual similarity of intra-class instances. With improved generalization capability to the test data and the binarized hashing codes, the proposed GDH method can achieve comparable performance with [55] on the fine-grained SBIR task, while requiring much less memory and retrieval time.

3   Generative Domain-Migration Hash

3.1   Preliminary

Given n_1 training images $I = \{I_i\}_{i=1}^{n_1}$ and n_2 training sketches $S = \{S_i\}_{i=1}^{n_2}$, the label vectors (row vectors) for all the training instances are $Y^I = \{\mathbf{y}_i^I\}_{i=1}^{n_1} \in \{0,1\}^{n_1 \times c}$ and $Y^S = \{\mathbf{y}_i^S\}_{i=1}^{n_2} \in \{0,1\}^{n_2 \times c}$, respectively, where $\mathbf{y}_i^I$ and $\mathbf{y}_i^S$ are one-hot vectors and c is the number of classes. We aim to learn the migration from sketches to natural images, and simultaneously learn the hashing function $\mathbf{H} : \{I, I_{fake}\} \to \{-1, +1\}^K$, where K is the length of hash codes. Such that the semantic consistency can be preserved between the extracted hashing codes of both authentic and generated natural images.

3.2   Network Architecture

To serve the above purposes, we simultaneously optimize a pair of generative and discriminative networks and a hashing network.

Generative Networks: Let G_I and G_S be two parallel generative CNNs for migrating sketches to the natural images and vice versa: $G_I : S \rightarrow I$ and $G_S : I \rightarrow S$. Considering natural images contain much more information than their sketch counterparts, migrating sketches to natural images is essentially an upsampling process and potentially requires more parameters.

In order to suppress the background information and guide the learning process to concentrate on the most representative regions, we integrate an attention module [47,60] in G_S. The attention module contains a convolutional layer with 1×1 kernel size, where a softmax function with a threshold is applied to the output for obtaining a binary attention mask. Element-wise $\odot$ multiplication can be performed between the binary attention mask and the feature map from ResBlocks.

Discriminative Networks: Along with two generators, two discriminative networks are correspondingly integrated in GDH, where D_I aims to distinguish the images with its mask ($I \odot mask$) and the generated images $G_I(S)$, and D_S aims to distinguish the real sketches S and the generated sketches $G_S(I)$.

Hashing Network: The hashing network $\mathbf{H}$ aims to generate binary hashing codes of both real images I and generated images $G_I(S)$, and can be trained based on both real image with its mask ($I \odot mask$) and generated image $G_I(S)$ from the domain-migration network. The hashing network $\mathbf{H}$ is modified from the 18-layer Deep Residual Network (Resnet) [12] by replacing the softmax layer with a fully-connected layer with a binary constraint on the values, where the dimension of the fully-connected layer equals to the length of the hashing codes.

We denote the parameters of the shared-weight hashing network as $\boldsymbol{\theta}_H$. For natural images and sketches, we formulate the deep hash function (*i.e., the Hashing network*) as $\mathbf{B}^I = \mathrm{sgn}(\mathbf{H}(I \odot mask; \boldsymbol{\theta}_H)) \in \{0, 1\}^{n_1 \times K}$ and $\mathbf{B}^S = \mathrm{sgn}(\mathbf{H}(G_I(S); \boldsymbol{\theta}_H)) \in \{0, 1\}^{n_2 \times K}$, respectively, where $\mathrm{sgn}(\cdot)$ is the sign function. Note that we use the row vector of the output for the convenience of computation. In the following section, we will introduce the deep generative hashing objective of joint learning of binary codes and hash functions.

We denote the parameters of the shared-weight hashing network as $\boldsymbol{\theta}_H$. For natural images and sketches, we formulate the deep hash function (*i.e., the Hashing network*) as $\mathbf{B}^I = \mathrm{sgn}(\mathbf{H}(I \odot mask; \boldsymbol{\theta}_H)) \in \{0, 1\}^{n_1 \times K}$ and $\mathbf{B}^S = \mathrm{sgn}(\mathbf{H}(G_I(S); \boldsymbol{\theta}_H)) \in \{0, 1\}^{n_2 \times K}$, respectively, where $\mathrm{sgn}(\cdot)$ is the sign function. Note that we use the row vector of the output for the convenience of computation. In the following section, we will introduce the deep generative hashing objective of joint learning of binary codes and hash functions.

3.3   Objective Formulation

There are five losses in our objective function. The adversarial loss and the cycle consistency loss guide the learning of the domain-migration network.

The semantic and triplet losses preserve the semantic consistency and visual similarity of intra-class instances across domains. The quantization loss and unification constraint can preserve the feature space similarity of pair instances. Detailed discussion of each loss is provided in following paragraphs.

Adversarial and Cycle Consistency Loss: Our domain-migration networks are composed of four parts: G_I, G_S, D_I and D_S [62]. We denote the parameters of G_I, G_S, D_I and D_S as $\boldsymbol{\theta}_C$. Specifically, $\boldsymbol{\theta}_C|_{G_I}$ is the parameter of G_I and so forth. Note that the inputs of domain-migration networks should be image-sketch pairs and usually we have $n_1 \gg n_2$. Thus we reuse the sketches from same category to match the images. Sketches from the same category are randomly repeated and S will be expanded to $\hat{S} = \{S_1, \cdots, S_1, S_2 \cdots, S_2, \cdots, S_{n_2}, \cdots, S_{n_2}\}$ to make sure $|\hat{S}| = |I|$. Suppose the data distributions are $I \sim p_I$ and $\hat{S} \sim p_{\hat{S}}$. For the generator $G_I : \hat{S} \to I$ and its discriminator D_I, the adversarial loss can be written as

$$\min_{\boldsymbol{\theta}_C|_{G_I}} \max_{\boldsymbol{\theta}_C|_{D_I}} \mathcal{L}_G(G_I, D_I, \hat{S}, I) := \mathbf{E}_{I \sim p_I}[\log D_I(I \odot mask, \boldsymbol{\theta}_C|_{D_I})]$$
$$+ \mathbf{E}_{\hat{S} \sim p_{\hat{S}}}[\log(1 - D_I(G_I(\hat{S}, \boldsymbol{\theta}_C|_{G_I}), \boldsymbol{\theta}_C|_{D_I})], \tag{1}$$

where the generator and the discriminator compete in a two-player minimax game: the generator tries to generate images $G_I(\hat{S})$ that look similar to the images from domain I and its corresponding $mask$, while the discriminator tries to distinguish between real images and fake images. The adversarial loss of the other mapping function $G_S : I \to \hat{S}$ is defined in the similar way. The Cycle Consistency Loss can prevent the learned mapping function G_I and G_S from conflicting against each other, which can be expressed as

$$\min_{\boldsymbol{\theta}_C|_{G_I}, \boldsymbol{\theta}_C|_{G_S}} \mathcal{L}_{cyc}(G_I, G_S) := \mathbf{E}_{I \sim p_I}\|G_S(G_I(\hat{S}, \boldsymbol{\theta}_C|_{G_I}), \boldsymbol{\theta}_C|_{G_S}) - \hat{S}\|$$
$$+ \mathbf{E}_{\hat{S} \sim p_{\hat{S}}}\|G_I(G_S(I, \boldsymbol{\theta}_C|_{G_S}), \boldsymbol{\theta}_C|_{G_I}) - I \odot mask\|. \tag{2}$$

where $\|\cdot\|$ is the Frobenius norm. The full optimization problem for domain-migration networks is

$$\min_{\substack{\boldsymbol{\theta}_C|_{G_I} \, \boldsymbol{\theta}_C|_{D_I} \\ \boldsymbol{\theta}_C|_{G_S} \, \boldsymbol{\theta}_C|_{D_S}}} \mathcal{L}_{gan} := \mathcal{L}_G(G_I, D_I, \hat{S}, I) + \mathcal{L}_G(G_S, D_S, I, \hat{S}) + \upsilon \mathcal{L}_{cyc}(G_I, G_S). \tag{3}$$

We set the balance parameter $\upsilon = 10$ in the experiment according to the previous work [62].

Semantic Loss: The label vectors of images and sketches are Y^I and Y^S. Inspired by Fast Supervised Discrete Hashing [11], we consider the following semantic factorization problem with the projection matrix $\mathbf{D} \in \mathbb{R}^{c \times K}$:

$$\min_{\mathbf{B}^I, \mathbf{B}^S, \mathbf{D}} \mathcal{L}_{sem} := \left\|\mathbf{B}^I - Y^I\mathbf{D}\right\|^2 + \left\|\mathbf{B}^S - Y^S\mathbf{D}\right\|^2 + \|\mathbf{D}\|^2,$$
$$\text{s.t. } \mathbf{B}^I \in \{-1, +1\}^{n_1 \times K}, \mathbf{B}^S \in \{-1, +1\}^{n_2 \times K}. \tag{4}$$

$\mathcal{L}_{sem}$ aims to minimize the distance between the binary codes of the same category, and maximize the distance between the binary codes of different categories.

Quantization Loss: The quantization loss is introduced to preserve the intrinsic structure of the data, and can be formulated as follows:

$$\min_{\boldsymbol{\theta}_H} \mathcal{L}_q := \left\| \mathbf{H}\left(I; \boldsymbol{\theta}_H\right) - \mathbf{B}^I \right\|^2 + \left\| \mathbf{H}\left(G_I\left(S, \boldsymbol{\theta}_C | _{G_I}\right); \boldsymbol{\theta}_H\right) - \mathbf{B}^S \right\|^2. \quad (5)$$

Triplet Ranking Loss: For the fine-grained retrieval task, we integrate the triplet ranking loss into the objective function for preserving the similarity of paired cross-domain instances within an object category. For a given triplet $\left(S_i, I_i^+, I_i^-\right)$, specifically, each triplet contains a query sketch S_i and a positive image sample I_i^+ and a negative image sample I_i^-. We define the triplet ranking loss function as follow:

$$\min_{\boldsymbol{\theta}_H} \mathcal{L}_{tri} := \sum_i \max \left(0, \Delta + \left\| \mathbf{H}\left(G_I\left(S_i, \boldsymbol{\theta}_C | _{G_I}\right); \boldsymbol{\theta}_H\right) - \mathbf{H}\left(I_i^+; \boldsymbol{\theta}_H\right) \right\|^2 \right.$$
$$\left. - \left\| \mathbf{H}\left(G_I\left(S_i, \boldsymbol{\theta}_C | _{G_I}\right); \boldsymbol{\theta}_H\right) - \mathbf{H}\left(I_i^-; \boldsymbol{\theta}_H\right) \right\|^2 \right), \quad (6)$$

where the parameter Δ represents the margin between the similarities of the outputs of the two pairs (S_i, I_i^+) and (S_i, I_i^-). In other words, the hashing network ensures that the Hamming distance between the outputs of the negative pair (S_i, I_i^-) is larger than the Hamming distance between the outputs of the positive pair (S_i, I_i^+) by at least a margin of Δ. In this paper, we let Δ equal to half of the code length (*i.e.*, $\Delta = 0.5K$).

Full Objective Function: We also desire the binary codes of a real natural image and a generated image to be close to each other. Thus, we employ a unification constraint $\mathcal{L}_c = \|\mathbf{H}(I; \boldsymbol{\theta}_H) - \mathbf{H}(G_I(\hat{S}, \boldsymbol{\theta}_C | _{G_I}); \boldsymbol{\theta}_H)\|^2$ is added to the final objective function which is formulated as follows:

$$\min_{\mathbf{B}^I, \mathbf{B}^S, \mathbf{D}, \boldsymbol{\theta}_C, \boldsymbol{\theta}_H} \mathcal{L}_{total} := \mathcal{L}_{gan} + \mathcal{L}_{sem} + \lambda \mathcal{L}_{tri} + \alpha \mathcal{L}_q + \beta \mathcal{L}_c,$$
$$\text{s.t. } \mathbf{B}^I \in \{-1, +1\}^{n_1 \times K}, \mathbf{B}^S \in \{-1, +1\}^{n_2 \times K}, \quad (7)$$

where λ is a control parameter, which equals 1 for fine-grained task and equals 0 for semantic-level SBIR only, The hyper-parameters α and β control the contributions of the two corresponding terms.

3.4   Joint Optimization

Due to the non-convexity of the joint optimization and **NP**-hardness to output the discrete binary codes, it is infeasible to find the global optimal solution. Inspired by [11], we propose an optimization algorithm based on alternating iteration and sequentially optimize one variable while the others are fixed. In this way, variables $\mathbf{D}$, $\mathbf{B}^I$, $\mathbf{B}^S$, parameter $\boldsymbol{\theta}_C$ of the domain-migration networks, and parameter $\boldsymbol{\theta}_H$ of the hash function will be iteratively updated.

D-*Step*. By fixing all the variables except **D**, Eq. (7) can be simplified as a classic quadratic regression problem:

$$\min_{\mathbf{D}} \left\| \mathbf{B}^I - Y^I \mathbf{D} \right\|^2 + \left\| \mathbf{B}^S - Y^S \mathbf{D} \right\|^2 + \left\| \mathbf{D} \right\|^2$$

$$= \min_{\mathbf{D}} tr \left(\mathbf{D}^\top \left(Y^{I^\top} Y^I + Y^{S^\top} Y^S + \mathbf{I} \right) \mathbf{D} \right) - 2tr \left(\mathbf{D}^\top \left(Y^{I^\top} \mathbf{B}^I + Y^{S^\top} \mathbf{B}^S \right) \right), \tag{8}$$

where **I** is the identity matrix. Taking the derivative of the above function with respect to **D** and setting it to zero, we have the analytical solution to Eq. (8):

$$\mathbf{D} = \left(Y^{I^\top} Y^I + Y^{S^\top} Y^S + \mathbf{I} \right)^{-1} \left(Y^{I^\top} \mathbf{B}^I + Y^{S^\top} \mathbf{B}^S \right). \tag{9}$$

B^I-*Step*. When all the variables are fixed except **B**^{I}, we rewrite Eq. (7) as

$$\min_{\mathbf{B}^I} \left\| \mathbf{B}^I - Y^I \mathbf{D} \right\|^2 + \alpha \left\| \mathbf{H} \left(I; \boldsymbol{\theta}_H \right) - \mathbf{B}^I \right\|^2. \tag{10}$$

Since $tr \left(\mathbf{B}^{I^\top} \mathbf{B}^I \right)$ is a constant, Eq. (10) is equivalent to the following problem:

$$\min_{\mathbf{B}^I} -tr \left(\mathbf{B}^{I^\top} \left(Y^I \mathbf{D} + \alpha \mathbf{H} \left(I; \boldsymbol{\theta}_H \right) \right) \right). \tag{11}$$

For $\mathbf{B}^I \in \{-1, +1\}^{n_1 \times K}$, $\mathbf{B}^I$ has a closed-form solution as follows:

$$\mathbf{B}^I = \text{sgn} \left(Y^I \mathbf{D} + \alpha \mathbf{H} \left(I; \boldsymbol{\theta}_H \right) \right). \tag{12}$$

B^S-*Step*. Considering all the terms related to **B**^{S}, it can be learned by a similar formulation as Eq. (12):

$$\mathbf{B}^S = \text{sgn} \left(Y^S \mathbf{D} + \alpha \mathbf{H} \left(G_I \left(S, \boldsymbol{\theta}_C |_{G_I} \right); \boldsymbol{\theta}_H \right) \right). \tag{13}$$

$(\boldsymbol{\theta}_C, \boldsymbol{\theta}_H)$-*Step*. After the optimization for **D**, **B**^{I} and **B**^{S}, we update the network parameters $\boldsymbol{\theta}_C$ and $\boldsymbol{\theta}_H$ according to the following loss:

$$\min_{\boldsymbol{\theta}_C, \boldsymbol{\theta}_H} \mathcal{L} := \mathcal{L}_{gan} + \lambda \mathcal{L}_{tri} + \alpha \mathcal{L}_q + \beta \mathcal{L}_c. \tag{14}$$

We train our networks on I and $\hat{S}$, where the sketch-image pairs are randomly select to compose of the mini-batch, and then backpropagation algorithm with SGD is adopted for optimizing two networks. In practice, we use deep learning frameworks (*e.g.*, Pytorch) to achieve all the steps. We iteratively update $\mathbf{D} \rightarrow \mathbf{B}^I \rightarrow \mathbf{B}^S \rightarrow \{\boldsymbol{\theta}_C, \boldsymbol{\theta}_H\}$ in each epoch. As such, GDH can be finally optimized within L epochs, where $20 \leq L \leq 30$ in our experiment. The algorithm of GDH is illustrated in Algorithm 1.

Once GDH model is learned, for a given query sketch s_q, we can infer its binary code $\mathbf{b}^{s_q} = \text{sgn} \left(\mathbf{H} \left(G_I \left(S_q, \boldsymbol{\theta}_C |_{G_I} \right); \boldsymbol{\theta}_H \right) \right)$ through the G_I network and the hash network **H**. For the image gallery, the hash codes $\mathbf{b}^I = \text{sgn} \left(\mathbf{H} \left(I \odot mask; \boldsymbol{\theta}_H \right) \right)$ of each image is computed through the hash network, where $mask$ can be easily obtained by $G_S \left(I; \boldsymbol{\theta}_C |_{G_S} \right)$. Note that fake images generated by $G_I \left(S_q, \boldsymbol{\theta}_C |_{G_I} \right)$ are non-background and thus they don't need multiply $mask$ before feed into the hashing network.

Algorithm 1. Generative Domain-migration Hash (GDH)

Input: Training natural images $I = \{I_i\}_{i=1}^{n_1}$ and the corresponding sketches $S = \{S_i\}_{i=1}^{n_2}$; the label information Y^I and Y^S; the code length K; the number of training epochs L; the balance parameters α, β, λ.

Output: Generative models G_I and G_S; deep hash function **H**.

1: Randomly initialize $\mathbf{B}^I \in \{-1, +1\}^{n_1 \times K}$ and $\mathbf{B}^S \in \{-1, +1\}^{n_2 \times K}$;

2: **For** $l = 1, 2, \cdots, L$ **do**

3:    Update **D** according to Eq. (9);

4:    Update $\mathbf{B}^I$ according to Eq. (12);

5:    Update $\mathbf{B}^S$ according to Eq. (13);

6:    Update the network parameters $\boldsymbol{\theta}_C$ and $\boldsymbol{\theta}_H$ according to Eq. (14) by training with the l-th epoch data;

7: **End**

8: **Return** the network parameters $\boldsymbol{\theta}_C$ and $\boldsymbol{\theta}_H$.

---

4 Experiments and Results

In the experiment section, we aim to address the following three questions:

- How does GDH perform as compared to other state-of-the-art binary or real-valued methods for category-level SBIR?
- How does GDH perform as compared to other state-of-the-art real-valued methods for fine-grained SBIR?
- How does each component or constraint contribute to the overall performance of GDH?

4.1 Datasets and Settings

Category-Level Retrieval. GDH is evaluated on two largest SBIR datasets: Sketchy [40] and TU-Berlin [8] Extension. The Sketchy database contains 125 categories with 75,471 sketches of 12,500 object images. We additionally utilize another 60,502 natural images [29] collected from ImageNet [5]. Hence, the whole image database contains 73,002 images in total. TU-Berlin is a sketch dataset with 250 object categories, where each category contains 80 sketches. An additional 204,489 natural images associated with TU-Berlin provided by [59] are used to construct the image database. Similar to previous hashing experiments [29], 50 and 10 sketches are respectively selected as the query sets for TU-Berlin and Sketchy, where the remaining are used as the gallery for training.

We compare GDH with 8 existing category-level SBIR methods, including 4 hand-crafted methods: LSK [38], SEHLO [37], GF-HOG [13] and HOG [4]; and 4 deep learning based methods: 3D shape [50], Sketch-a-Net (SaN) [56], GN Triplet [40] and Siamese CNN [35]. Furthermore, we also compare GDH with 7 state-of-the-art cross-modality hashing methods: Collective Matrix Factorization Hashing (CMFH) [7], Cross-Model Semi-Supervised Hashing (CMSSH) [2], Cross-View Hashing(CVH) [19], Semantic Correlation Maximization (SCMSeq and SCM-Orth) [57], Semantics-Preserving Hashing(SePH) [25], Deep Cross-Modality Hashing (DCMH) [17] and Deep Sketch Hash (DSH) [29]. Finally, we also compare our method to other four cross-view feature embedding methods: CCA [49], PLSR [27], XQDA [24] and CVFL [52]. The implementation details and experimental results of above methods are reported in [29].

We use the Adam solver [18] with a batch size of 32. Our balance parameters are set to $\alpha = 10^{-5}, \beta = 10^{-5}$ and $\lambda = 0$ for both datasets. All networks are trained with an initial learning rate $lr = 0.0002$. After 25 epochs, we decrease the learning rate of the hashing network $lr \rightarrow 0.1lr$ and terminate the optimization after 30 epochs for both datasets. Our method is implemented by Pytorch with dual 1080Ti GPUs and an i7-4790K CPU.

Table 1. Comparison with previous SBIR methods w.r.t. MAP, retrieval time per query (s) and memory cost (MB) on TU-Berlin Extension and Sketchy.

Methods	Dimension	TU-Berlin Extension			Sketchy		
		MAP	Retrieval time per query (s)	Memory cost (MB) (204,489 images)	MAP	Retrieval time per query (s)	Memory cost (MB) (73,002 images)
HOG [4]	1296	0.091	1.43	2.02×10^3	0.115	0.53	7.22×10^2
GF-HOG [13]	3500	0.119	4.13	5.46×10^3	0.157	1.41	1.95×10^3
SHELO [37]	1296	0.123	1.44	2.02×10^3	0.182	0.50	7.22×10^2
LKS [38]	1350	0.157	0.204	2.11×10^3	0.190	0.56	7.52×10^2
Siamese CNN [35]	64	0.322	7.70×10^{-2}	99.8	0.481	2.76×10^{-2}	35.4
SaN [56]	512	0.154	0.53	7.98×10^2	0.208	0.21	2.85×10^2
GN Triplet* [40]	1024	0.187	1.02	1.60×10^3	0.529	0.41	5.70×10^2
3D shape* [50]	64	0.072	7.53×10^{-2}	99.8	0.084	2.64×10^{-2}	35.6
Siamese-AlexNet	4096	0.367	5.35	6.39×10^3	0.518	1.68	2.28×10^3
Triplet-AlexNet	4096	0.448	5.35	6.39×10^3	0.573	1.68 s	2.28×10^3
GDH (Proposed)	32 (bits)	0.563	5.57×10^{-4}	0.78	0.724	2.55×10^{-4}	0.28
	64 (bits)	**0.690**	7.03×10^{-4}	1.56	**0.810**	2.82×10^{-4}	0.56
	128 (bits)	0.659	1.05×10^{-3}	3.12	0.784	3.53×10^{-4}	1.11

"*" denotes that we directly use the public models provided by the original papers without any fine-tuning on the TU-Berlin Extension and Sketchy datasets.

Fine-Grained Retrieval. We conduct experiments of GDH on the QMUL-Shoes and QMUL-Chairs datasets [55]. The two datasets are fine-grained instance-level SBIR datasets which contain 419 shoes sketch-photo pairs and 297 chairs sketch-photo pairs, respectively.

We compare our proposed GDH method with several fine-grained methods including 2 hand-crafted methods: HOG+BoW+RankSVM [23] and Dense HOG+RankSVM [55], and 3 deep feature baselines: Improved Sketch-a-Net (ISN) [56], 3D shape (3DS) [50] and Triplet Sketch-a-Net (TSN) [55]. All of these algorithms are real-valued methods. It is noteworthy that the networks in TSN [55] are heavily pre-trained and the data have been processed by complex augmentation. However, to emphasize the ability of our domain-migration model, data augmentation is not included in our experiment.

Note that, QMUL-Shoes and QMUL-Chairs are unique fine-grained datasets, in which only contains one category for each of them. Therefore, it is unnecessary to optimize the semantic loss in Eq. (7). To better fit the task of fine-grained retrieval, we skip the first five steps in Algorithm 1 and directly update the parameters of θ_C and θ_H. Our balance parameters are set to $\lambda = 1$. The implementation details are the same as the settings for category-level retrieval.

4.2   Results and Discussions

Comparison with Category-Level SBIR Baselines. We compare our GDH method with the 10 baseline methods in terms of Mean Average Precision (MAP), retrieval time and memory cost on two datasets. The code lengths of outputs are 32, 64 and 128 bits. As reported in Table 1, GDH consistently achieves the best performance with much faster query time and much lower memory cost compared to other SBIR methods on both datasets. Also, GDH largely improves the state-of-the-art performance of Triplet-AlexNet by 24.2% and 23.7% on the TU-Berlin and Sketchy datasets, respectively. The performance of 128 bits is lower than the performance of 64 bits can be explained with the quantization error accumulation [44]. We also notice that the performance of compared methods on both datasets is much lower than reported in previous papers [50,55]. The reason is that the data they previously used are all well-aligned with perfect background removal and the edge of objects can almost fit the sketches. Meanwhile, our experiments adopt realistic images with complicated background, which are greatly different from sketches.

Comparison with Cross-Modality Hashing. In Table 2, we compare our GDH method with cross-modality hashing/feature learning methods with 32, 64 and 128 bits binary codes. We use the learned deep features as the inputs for non-end-to-end learning methods for a fair comparison with GDH. GDH achieves the best performance compared to all the cross-modality baselines on both datasets. Specifically, GDH can outperform the best-performing hashing-based SBIR method DSH [29] by 20.5%/7.1%, 16.9%/10% and 8.1%/0.1% at different code lengths on both datasets, respectively.

Comparison for Fine-Grained SBIR. In Table 3, we report the top-1 and top-10 accuracies of GDH over other five methods on the Shoes and Chairs datasets for fine-grained SBIR. Compared to the state-of-the-art real-valued TSN (without data augmentation), the 128-bit GDH achieves 2.7%/2.7% and 2.6%/3.4% improvements in terms of top-1 and top-10 accuracies on both the Shoes and Chairs datasets respectively. Specifically, the top-10 accuracy on the Chairs dataset reaches 99%, which is even higher than the performance of TSN with data augmentation.

Remark. For fine-grained SBIR, despite binary hashing codes are used, comparable or even improved performance over the real-valued state-of-the-art methods

Table 2. MAP comparison with different cross-modality retrieval methods for category-level SBIR on TU-Berlin Extension and Sketchy.

Method		TU-Berlin extension			Sketchy		
		32 bits	64 bits	128 bits	32 bits	64 bits	128 bits
Cross-modality hashing methods (binary codes)	CMFH [7]	0.149	0.202	0.180	0.320	0.490	0.190
	CMSSH [2]	0.121	0.183	0.175	0.206	0.211	0.211
	SCM-Seq [57]	0.211	0.276	0.332	0.306	0.417	0.671
	SCM-Orth [57]	0.217	0.301	0.263	0.346	0.536	0.616
	CVH [19]	0.214	0.294	0.318	0.325	0.525	0.624
	SePH [25]	0.198	0.270	0.282	0.534	0.607	0.640
	DCMH [17]	0.274	0.382	0.425	0.560	0.622	0.656
	DSH [29]	0.358	0.521	0.570	0.653	0.711	0.783
Cross-view feature learning methods (real-valued vectors)	CCA [49]	0.276	0.366	0.365	0.361	0.555	0.705
	XQDA [27]	0.191	0.197	0.201	0.460	0.557	0.550
	PLSR [24]	0.141 (4096-d)			0.462 (4096-d)		
	CVFL [52]	0.289 (4096-d)			0.675 (4096-d)		
Proposed	**GDH**	**0.563**	**0.690**	**0.651**	**0.724**	**0.811**	**0.784**

For end-to-end deep methods, raw natural images and sketches are used. For others, 4096-d AlexNet *fc7* image features and 512-d SaN *fc7* sketch features are used. PLSR and CVFL are both based on reconstructing partial data to approximate full data, so the dimensions are fixed to 4096-d.

Table 3. Accuracy comparison with different real-valued methods for fine-grained SBIR on QMUL-shoes and QMUL-chairs.

Methods		QMUL-shoes.acc@1	QMUL-shoes.acc@10	QMUL-chairs.@1	QMUL-chairs.@10
Real-valued vectors	BoW-HOG + rankSVM [23]	0.174	0.678	0.289	0.670
	Dense-HOG + rankSVM [55]	0.244	0.652	0.526	0.938
	ISN Deep + rankSVM [56]	0.200	0.626	0.474	0.825
	3DS Deep + rankSVM [50]	0.052	0.217	0.061	0.268
	TSN without data aug. [55]	0.330	0.817	0.644	0.956
	TSN with data aug. [55]	0.391	0.878	0.691	0.979
Binary codes	GDH @ 32-bit	0.286	0.720	0.392	0.876
	GDH @ 64-bit	0.323	0.783	0.556	0.959
	GDH @ 128-bit	0.357	0.843	0.671	0.990

To emphasize the ability of our domain-migration model, data augmentation [55] is not included. Even so, our binary results are competitive and promising compared to other real-valued methods.

can be observed in Table 3. On the other side, the binary codes in GDH allow much reduced memory costs and retrieval time than the real-valued approaches. However, GDH generally shows degraded performance on the fine-grained SBIR when comparing to its performance on category-level SBIR. Our explanation towards such a phenomenon is that the geometrical morphology and detailed instance-level characteristic within a category can be much more difficult to capture with binary hashing codes than the inter-category discrepancies. In Fig. 2, some examples based on the retrieval results of GDH are illustrated. More illustrations and experiments can be found in the **Supplementary Material**.

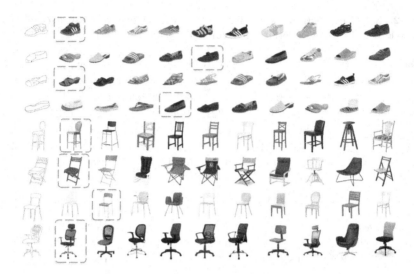

Fig. 2. Example query sketches with their top-10 retrieval accuracies on the Sketchy dataset by using 128-bit GDH codes. Orange boxes indicate the groundtruth results. (Color figure online)

4.3 Ablation Study

We demonstrate the effectiveness of each loss component of GDH in Table 4. The detailed descriptions of the unification constraint $\mathcal{L}_c$, the quantization loss $\mathcal{L}_q$ and the adversarial and cycle consistent loss $\mathcal{L}_{gan}$ are provided in Sect. 3.3. It can be observed that all these components are complementary and beneficial to the effectiveness of GDH. Especially, the adversarial and cycle consistent loss $\mathcal{L}_{gan}$ and the quantization loss $\mathcal{L}_q$ are equivalently critical for category-level SBIR, and he triplet ranking loss $\mathcal{L}_{tri}$ is essential for fine-grained SBIR. It can also be observed that the attention layer is consistently effective for improving the overall performance with a stable margin.

Inspired by the mix-up operation [58], in order to further reduce the domain discrepancy, we propose a feature fusion method that employs a linear mix-up of two types of hashing binary codes: (1) $\text{sgn}(\frac{1}{2}\mathbf{H}(G_I(G_S(I_i, \boldsymbol{\theta}_C|_{G_I}), \boldsymbol{\theta}_C|_{G_S}); \boldsymbol{\theta}_H) + \frac{1}{2}\mathbf{H}(I_i; \boldsymbol{\theta}_H))$ and (2) $\text{sgn}(\mathbf{H}(G_I(S_i, \boldsymbol{\theta}_C|_{G_I}); \boldsymbol{\theta}_H))$. Besides the linear embedding, we also evaluated other fusion strategies such as concatenation and the Kronecker product. However, none of these fusion methods is helpful. In Fig. 3, we illustrate that the generated sketches of GDH can well represent corresponding natural images. It is obviously observed that using sketches to generate fake natural images are more difficult than the inverse generation. Additionally, we conduct another experiment in the sketch domain rather than the natural image domain. By using a similar hashing technique in the sketch domain, all the sketches S and the corresponding generated fake sketches $G_S(I)$ are embedded into the Hamming space as $\mathbf{H}(S_i) = \mathbf{H}(S_i; \boldsymbol{\theta}_H)$ and $\mathbf{H}(I_i) = \mathbf{H}(G_S(I_i); \boldsymbol{\theta}_H)$. However,

Table 4. Effectiveness (MAP/accuracy with 128-bit) of different components (Sketchy for category-level SBIR and QMUL-Shoes for fine-grained SBIR).

Methods	Category-level MAP (Sketchy)	Fine-grained acc. (QMUL-Shoes)	
		top-1	top-10
Without $\mathcal{L}_c$	0.727	–	–
Without $\mathcal{L}_q$	0.104	–	–
Without $\mathcal{L}_{gan}$	0.221	0.226	0.671
Without attention layer	0.798	0.335	0.823
Linear mix-up	0.782	0.282	0.744
Concatenation mix-up	0.642	0.182	0.654
Kronecker product mix-up	0.735	0.242	0.704
Embed images into sketch domain	0.310	0.263	0.791
Our model GDH @ 128-bit (binary)	**0.811**	**0.357**	**0.843**

Fig. 3. Visualization of our domain-migration networks. The first two rows are sketch-to-image results and the last two rows are image-to-sketch results, which indicates that our domain-migration networks are capable to transfer domains from both directions.

it resulted in a dramatically decreased performance, especially when handling images that have complex backgrounds.

5   Conclusion

In this paper, we proposed a Generative Domain-migration Hashing method for both category-level and fine-grained SBIR tasks. Instead of mapping sketches and natural images into a common space, GDH for the first time employs a generative model that migrates sketches to their indistinguishable counterparts in the natural image domain. Guided by the adversarial loss and the cycle consistency loss, robust hashing codes for both real and synthetic images (*i.e., migrated from sketches*) can be obtained with an end-to-end multi-task learning framework that does not rely on the pixel-level alignment between cross-domain pairs. We additionally integrated an attention layer to effectively suppress the background information and guide the learning process of GDH to concentrate on the most critical regions. Extensive experiments on large-scale datasets demonstrated the consistently balanced superiority of GDH in terms of efficiency, memory costs and performance on both category-level and fine-grained SBIR tasks. GDH also outperformed the best-performing hashing-based SBIR method DSH [29] by up to 20.5% on the TU-Berlin Extension dataset, and up to 26.4% on the Sketchy dataset respectively.

Acknowledgment. This work was supported in part by the National Natural Science Foundation of China under Project 61502081 and Project 61632007, the Fundamental Research Funds for the Central Universities under Project ZYGX2014Z007.

References

1. Bozas, K., Izquierdo, E.: Large scale sketch based image retrieval using patch hashing. In: Bebis, G., et al. (eds.) ISVC 2012. LNCS, vol. 7431, pp. 210–219. Springer, Heidelberg (2012). https://doi.org/10.1007/978-3-642-33179-4_21
2. Bronstein, M.M., Bronstein, A.M., Michel, F., Paragios, N.: Data fusion through cross-modality metric learning using similarity-sensitive hashing. In: The Twenty-Third IEEE Conference on Computer Vision and Pattern Recognition, CVPR 2010, San Francisco, CA, USA, 13–18 June 2010, pp. 3594–3601 (2010)
3. Bui, T., Ribeiro, L., Ponti, M., Collomosse, J.P.: Generalisation and sharing in triplet convnets for sketch based visual search. CoRR abs/1611.05301 (2016)
4. Dalal, N., Triggs, B.: Histograms of oriented gradients for human detection. In: 2005 IEEE Computer Society Conference on Computer Vision and Pattern Recognition (CVPR 2005), San Diego, CA, USA, 20–26 June 2005, pp. 886–893 (2005)
5. Deng, J., Dong, W., Socher, R., Li, L.J., Li, K., Fei-Fei, L.: ImageNet: a large-scale hierarchical image database. In: Proceedings of CVPR, pp. 248–255 (2009)
6. Denton, E.L., Chintala, S., Fergus, R., et al.: Deep generative image models using a Laplacian pyramid of adversarial networks. In: Advances in Neural Information Processing Systems, pp. 1486–1494 (2015)
7. Ding, G., Guo, Y., Zhou, J.: Collective matrix factorization hashing for multimodal data. In: 2014 IEEE Conference on Computer Vision and Pattern Recognition, CVPR 2014, Columbus, OH, USA, 23–28 June 2014, pp. 2083–2090 (2014)
8. Eitz, M., Hays, J., Alexa, M.: How do humans sketch objects? ACM Trans. Graph. **31**(4), 44:1–44:10 (2012)
9. Eitz, M., Hildebrand, K., Boubekeur, T., Alexa, M.: An evaluation of descriptors for large-scale image retrieval from sketched feature lines. Comput. Graph. **34**(5), 482–498 (2010)
10. Goodfellow, I., et al.: Generative adversarial nets. In: Advances in Neural Information Processing Systems, pp. 2672–2680 (2014)
11. Gui, J., Liu, T., Sun, Z., Tao, D., Tan, T.: Fast supervised discrete hashing. IEEE Trans. Pattern Anal. Mach. Intell. **40**(2), 490–496 (2018)
12. He, K., Zhang, X., Ren, S., Sun, J.: Deep residual learning for image recognition. In: 2016 IEEE Conference on Computer Vision and Pattern Recognition, CVPR 2016, Las Vegas, NV, USA, 27–30 June 2016, pp. 770–778 (2016)
13. Hu, R., Barnard, M., Collomosse, J.P.: Gradient field descriptor for sketch based retrieval and localization. In: Proceedings of the International Conference on Image Processing, ICIP 2010, Hong Kong, China, 26–29 September 2010, pp. 1025–1028 (2010)

14. Hu, R., Collomosse, J.P.: A performance evaluation of gradient field HOG descriptor for sketch based image retrieval. Comput. Vis. Image Underst. **117**(7), 790–806 (2013)

15. Isola, P., Zhu, J., Zhou, T., Efros, A.A.: Image-to-image translation with conditional adversarial networks. In: 2017 IEEE Conference on Computer Vision and Pattern Recognition, CVPR 2017, Honolulu, HI, USA, 21–26 July 2017, pp. 5967–5976 (2017)

16. Isola, P., Zhu, J.Y., Zhou, T., Efros, A.A.: Image-to-image translation with conditional adversarial networks (2017)

17. Jiang, Q., Li, W.: Deep cross-modal hashing. In: 2017 IEEE Conference on Computer Vision and Pattern Recognition, CVPR 2017, Honolulu, HI, USA, 21–26 July 2017, pp. 3270–3278 (2017)

18. Kingma, D.P., Ba, J.: Adam: a method for stochastic optimization. CoRR abs/1412.6980 (2014)

19. Kumar, S., Udupa, R.: Learning hash functions for cross-view similarity search. In: Proceedings of the 22nd International Joint Conference on Artificial Intelligence, IJCAI 2011, Barcelona, Catalonia, Spain, 16–22 July 2011, pp. 1360–1365 (2011)

20. Li, K., Pang, K., Song, Y., Hospedales, T.M., Xiang, T., Zhang, H.: Synergistic instance-level subspace alignment for fine-grained sketch-based image retrieval. IEEE Trans. Image Process. **26**(12), 5908–5921 (2017)

21. Li, K., Pang, K., Song, Y., Hospedales, T.M., Zhang, H., Hu, Y.: Fine-grained sketch-based image retrieval: the role of part-aware attributes. In: 2016 IEEE Winter Conference on Applications of Computer Vision, WACV 2016, Lake Placid, NY, USA, 7–10 March 2016, pp. 1–9 (2016)

22. Li, Y., Hospedales, T.M., Song, Y., Gong, S.: Intra-category sketch-based image retrieval by matching deformable part models. In: British Machine Vision Conference, BMVC 2014, Nottingham, UK, 1–5 September 2014 (2014)

23. Li, Y., Hospedales, T.M., Song, Y., Gong, S.: Free-hand sketch recognition by multi-kernel feature learning. Comput. Vis. Image Underst. **137**, 1–11 (2015)

24. Liao, S., Hu, Y., Zhu, X., Li, S.Z.: Person re-identification by local maximal occurrence representation and metric learning. In: IEEE Conference on Computer Vision and Pattern Recognition, CVPR 2015, Boston, MA, USA, 7–12 June 2015, pp. 2197–2206 (2015)

25. Lin, Z., Ding, G., Hu, M., Wang, J.: Semantics-preserving hashing for cross-view retrieval. In: IEEE Conference on Computer Vision and Pattern Recognition, CVPR 2015, Boston, MA, USA, 7–12 June 2015, pp. 3864–3872 (2015)

26. Liong, V.E., Lu, J., Wang, G., Moulin, P., Zhou, J.: Deep hashing for compact binary codes learning. In: Proceedings of CVPR, pp. 2475–2483 (2015)

27. Liu, H., Ma, Z., Han, J., Chen, Z., Zheng, Z.: Regularized partial least squares for multi-label learning. Int. J. Mach. Learn. Cybern. **9**(2), 335–346 (2018)

28. Liu, L., Shao, L., Shen, F., Yu, M.: Discretely coding semantic rank orders for image hashing. In: Proceedings of CVPR, pp. 1425–1434 (2017)

29. Liu, L., Shen, F., Shen, Y., Liu, X., Shao, L.: Deep sketch hashing: fast free-hand sketch-based image retrieval. In: 2017 IEEE Conference on Computer Vision and Pattern Recognition, CVPR 2017, Honolulu, HI, USA, 21–26 July 2017, pp. 2298–2307 (2017)

30. Liu, W., Mu, C., Kumar, S., Chang, S.F.: Discrete graph hashing. In: Proceedings of NIPS, pp. 3419–3427 (2014)

31. Liu, W., Wang, J., Ji, R., Jiang, Y.G., Chang, S.F.: Supervised hashing with kernels. In: Proceedings of CVPR, pp. 2074–2081 (2012)

32. Lowe, D.G.: Object recognition from local scale-invariant features. In: ICCV, pp. 1150–1157 (1999)
33. Mathieu, M.F., Zhao, J.J., Zhao, J., Ramesh, A., Sprechmann, P., LeCun, Y.: Disentangling factors of variation in deep representation using adversarial training. In: Advances in Neural Information Processing Systems, pp. 5040–5048 (2016)
34. Parui, S., Mittal, A.: Similarity-invariant sketch-based image retrieval in large databases. In: Fleet, D., Pajdla, T., Schiele, B., Tuytelaars, T. (eds.) ECCV 2014, Part VI. LNCS, vol. 8694, pp. 398–414. Springer, Cham (2014). https://doi.org/10.1007/978-3-319-10599-4_26
35. Qi, Y., Song, Y., Zhang, H., Liu, J.: Sketch-based image retrieval via Siamese convolutional neural network. In: 2016 IEEE International Conference on Image Processing, ICIP 2016, Phoenix, AZ, USA, 25–28 September 2016, pp. 2460–2464 (2016)
36. Qin, J., et al.: Binary coding for partial action analysis with limited observation ratios. In: Proceedings of CVPR, pp. 146–155 (2017)
37. Saavedra, J.M.: Sketch based image retrieval using a soft computation of the histogram of edge local orientations (S-HELO). In: 2014 IEEE International Conference on Image Processing, ICIP 2014, Paris, France, 27–30 October 2014, pp. 2998–3002 (2014)
38. Saavedra, J.M., Barrios, J.M.: Sketch based image retrieval using learned keyshapes (LKS). In: Proceedings of the British Machine Vision Conference 2015, BMVC 2015, Swansea, UK, 7–10 September 2015, pp. 164.1–164.11 (2015)
39. Saavedra, J.M., Bustos, B.: An improved histogram of edge local orientations for sketch-based image retrieval. In: Goesele, M., Roth, S., Kuijper, A., Schiele, B., Schindler, K. (eds.) DAGM 2010. LNCS, vol. 6376, pp. 432–441. Springer, Heidelberg (2010). https://doi.org/10.1007/978-3-642-15986-2_44
40. Sangkloy, P., Burnell, N., Ham, C., Hays, J.: The sketchy database: learning to retrieve badly drawn bunnies. ACM Trans. Graph. **35**(4), 119:1–119:12 (2016)
41. Sangkloy, P., Lu, J., Fang, C., Yu, F., Hays, J.: Scribbler: controlling deep image synthesis with sketch and color. In: IEEE Conference on Computer Vision and Pattern Recognition (CVPR), vol. 2 (2017)
42. Shen, F., Gao, X., Liu, L., Yang, Y., Shen, H.T.: Deep asymmetric pairwise hashing. In: Proceedings of the 2017 ACM on Multimedia Conference, MM 2017, Mountain View, CA, USA, 23–27 October 2017, pp. 1522–1530 (2017)
43. Shen, F., Liu, W., Zhang, S., Yang, Y., Shen, H.T.: Learning binary codes for maximum inner product search. In: The IEEE International Conference on Computer Vision (ICCV), pp. 4148–4156, December 2015
44. Shen, F., Shen, C., Liu, W., Shen, H.T.: Supervised discrete hashing. In: Proceedings of CVPR, pp. 37–45 (2015)
45. Shen, F., Xu, Y., Liu, L., Yang, Y., Huang, Z., Shen, H.T.: Unsupervised deep hashing with similarity-adaptive and discrete optimization. IEEE Trans. Pattern Anal. Mach. Intell. (TPAMI) (2018)
46. Shen, F., Yang, Y., Liu, L., Liu, W., Dacheng Tao, H.T.S.: Asymmetric binary coding for image search. IEEE TMM **19**(9), 2022–2032 (2017)
47. Song, J., Qian, Y., Song, Y.Z., Xiang, T., Hospedales, T.: Deep spatial-semantic attention for fine-grained sketch-based image retrieval. In: ICCV (2017)
48. Song, J., Yu, Q., Song, Y., Xiang, T., Hospedales, T.M.: Deep spatial-semantic attention for fine-grained sketch-based image retrieval. In: IEEE International Conference on Computer Vision, ICCV 2017, Venice, Italy, 22–29 October 2017, pp. 5552–5561 (2017)

49. Vía, J., Santamaría, I., Pérez, J.: Canonical correlation analysis (CCA) algorithms for multiple data sets: application to blind SIMO equalization. In: 13th European Signal Processing Conference, EUSIPCO 2005, Antalya, Turkey, 4–8 September 2005, pp. 1–4 (2005)
50. Wang, F., Kang, L., Li, Y.: Sketch-based 3D shape retrieval using convolutional neural networks. In: IEEE Conference on Computer Vision and Pattern Recognition, CVPR 2015, Boston, MA, USA, 7–12 June 2015, pp. 1875–1883 (2015)
51. Weiss, Y., Torralba, A., Fergus, R.: Spectral hashing. In: Proceedings of NIPS, pp. 1753–1760 (2008)
52. Xie, W., Peng, Y., Xiao, J.: Cross-view feature learning for scalable social image analysis. In: Proceedings of the Twenty-Eighth AAAI Conference on Artificial Intelligence, Québec City, Québec, Canada, 27–31 July 2014, pp. 201–207 (2014)
53. Xu, P., et al.: Cross-modal subspace learning for fine-grained sketch-based image retrieval. Neurocomputing **278**, 75–86 (2018)
54. Xu, P., et al.: Instance-level coupled subspace learning for fine-grained sketch-based image retrieval. In: Hua, G., Jégou, H. (eds.) ECCV 2016, Part I. LNCS, vol. 9913, pp. 19–34. Springer, Cham (2016). https://doi.org/10.1007/978-3-319-46604-0_2
55. Yu, Q., Liu, F., Song, Y., Xiang, T., Hospedales, T.M., Loy, C.C.: Sketch me that shoe. In: 2016 IEEE Conference on Computer Vision and Pattern Recognition, CVPR 2016, Las Vegas, NV, USA, 27–30 June 2016, pp. 799–807 (2016)
56. Yu, Q., Yang, Y., Liu, F., Song, Y., Xiang, T., Hospedales, T.M.: Sketch-a-Net: a deep neural network that beats humans. Int. J. Comput. Vis. **122**(3), 411–425 (2017)
57. Zhang, D., Li, W.: Large-scale supervised multimodal hashing with semantic correlation maximization. In: Proceedings of the Twenty-Eighth AAAI Conference on Artificial Intelligence, Québec City, Québec, Canada, 27–31 July 2014, pp. 2177–2183 (2014)
58. Zhang, H., Cissé, M., Dauphin, Y.N., Lopez-Paz, D.: mixup: beyond empirical risk minimization. CoRR abs/1710.09412 (2017)
59. Zhang, H., Liu, S., Zhang, C., Ren, W., Wang, R., Cao, X.: SketchNet: sketch classification with web images. In: 2016 IEEE Conference on Computer Vision and Pattern Recognition, CVPR 2016, Las Vegas, NV, USA, 27–30 June 2016, pp. 1105–1113 (2016)
60. Zhang, X., et al.: HashGAN: attention-aware deep adversarial hashing for cross modal retrieval. CoRR abs/1711.09347 (2017)
61. Zhang, Z., Chen, Y., Saligrama, V.: Efficient training of very deep neural networks for supervised hashing. In: Proceedings of CVPR, pp. 1487–1495 (2016)
62. Zhu, J., Park, T., Isola, P., Efros, A.A.: Unpaired image-to-image translation using cycle-consistent adversarial networks. In: IEEE International Conference on Computer Vision, ICCV 2017, Venice, Italy, 22–29 October 2017, pp. 2242–2251 (2017)

TBN: Convolutional Neural Network with Ternary Inputs and Binary Weights

Diwen Wan[1,2], Fumin Shen[1(✉)], Li Liu[2], Fan Zhu[2], Jie Qin[3], Ling Shao[2],
and Heng Tao Shen[1]

[1] Center for Future Media and School of Computer Science and Engineering,
University of Electronic Science and Technology of China, Chengdu, China
funmin.shen@gmail.com
[2] Inception Institute of Artificial Intelligence, Abu Dhabi, UAE
[3] Computer Vision Lab, ETH Zurich, Zurich, Switzerland

Abstract. Despite the remarkable success of Convolutional Neural Networks (CNNs) on generalized visual tasks, high computational and memory costs restrict their comprehensive applications on consumer electronics (*e.g.*, portable or smart wearable devices). Recent advancements in binarized networks have demonstrated progress on reducing computational and memory costs, however, they suffer from significant performance degradation comparing to their full-precision counterparts. Thus, a highly-economical yet effective CNN that is authentically applicable to consumer electronics is at urgent need. In this work, we propose a Ternary-Binary Network (TBN), which provides an efficient approximation to standard CNNs. Based on an accelerated ternary-binary matrix multiplication, TBN replaces the arithmetical operations in standard CNNs with efficient **XOR, AND** and **bitcount** operations, and thus provides an optimal tradeoff between memory, efficiency and performance. TBN demonstrates its consistent effectiveness when applied to various CNN architectures (*e.g., AlexNet and ResNet*) on multiple datasets of different scales, and provides ∼32× memory savings and 40× faster convolutional operations. Meanwhile, TBN can outperform XNOR-Network by up to 5.5% (top-1 accuracy) on the ImageNet classification task, and up to 4.4% (mAP score) on the PASCAL VOC object detection task.

Keywords: CNN · TBN · Acceleration · Compression
Binary operation

1 Introduction

Along with the overwhelming success of deep learning, convolutional neural networks (CNNs) have demonstrated their capabilities in various computer vision

Electronic supplementary material The online version of this chapter (https://doi.org/10.1007/978-3-030-01216-8_20) contains supplementary material, which is available to authorized users.

© Springer Nature Switzerland AG 2018
V. Ferrari et al. (Eds.): ECCV 2018, LNCS 11206, pp. 322–339, 2018.
https://doi.org/10.1007/978-3-030-01216-8_20

tasks [8,13,14,18,29,31,37–39,41,43,45–47,49]. Effective CNNs normally contain millions of weight parameters, and require billions of high precision operations to be performed for a single classification task. Consequently, either training a CNN model with large-scale data or deploying a CNN model for real-time prediction task has rigid hardware demands (such as GPUs and TPUs) for the overheads in both storage and computing. However, such rigid hardware demands restrict CNNs' comprehensive applications on consumer electronics, such as virtual reality (VR), augmented reality (AR), smart wearable devices and self-driving cars. Significant research efforts have been paid on how to reduce the computational and memory costs of CNNs. Existing CNN lightweighting techniques include pruning [16,17,53], quantization [5,15,35,36,48,54,56], factorization [2,21,23,26,30,51,55], network binarization [7,42], distilling [19] and others [10,54]. Since network binarization can lower 32-bit full-precision values down to 1-bit binary values and allow efficient convolution operations, it has the most potentials in lightweighting the network for practical usages on portable devices. Recent progresses in binarized CNNs [7,42] have provided evidences of successfully reducing the computational and memory costs with the binary replacement. In CNNs, two types of values can be binarized: (1) network weights in the convolutional layers and the fully-connected layers, and (2) input signals to the convolutional layers and the fully-connected layers. Binarizing the network weights can directly result in ∼32× memory saving over the real-valued counterparts, and meanwhile bring ∼2× computational efficiency by avoiding the multiplication operation in convolutions. On the other hand, simultaneously binarizing both weights and the input signals can result in 58× computational efficiency by replacing the arithmetical operations in convolutions with XNOR and bitcount operations. Despite the significant cost reduction, noticeable accuracy degradation of the binarized CNNs introduced new performance issues for practical usages. Undoubtedly, such performance degradation is due to the quantization errors when brutally binarizing real-values in both network weights and layer-wise inputs.

In this work, we aim to improve the performance of binarized CNNs with ternary inputs to the convolutional and fully-connected layers. The ternary inputs constrain input signal values into -1, 0, and 1, and can essentially reduce the quantization error when binarizing full-precision input signals. By incorporating ternary layer-wise inputs with binary network weights, we propose a Ternary-Binary Network (TBN) that provides an optimal tradeoff between the performance and computational efficiency. The illustration of the pipeline of proposed TBN approach can be found in Fig. 1. In addition, an efficient threshold-based approximated solution is introduced to minimize the quantization error between the full-precision network weights and the binary weights along with a scaling factor, and an accelerated ternary-binary dot product method is introduced using simple bitwise operations (*i.e.*, **XOR** and **AND**) and the **bitcount** operation. Specifically, TBN can provide ∼32× memory saving and 40× speedup over its real-valued CNN counterparts. Comparing to XNOR-Network [42], with an identical memory cost and slightly sacrificed efficiency, TBN can outperform

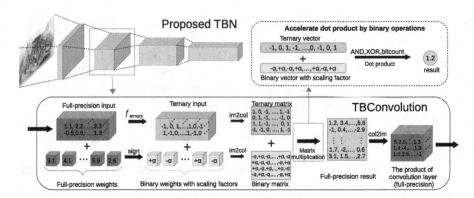

Fig. 1. The illustration of TBN, which is an efficient variation of convolutional neural networks. The weight filters of TBN have binary values and its inputs contain ternary values. The binary operations is used to accelerate the convolution operation. Our TBN is not only efficient in terms of memory and computation but also has good performance. This helps to use CNNs on resource-limited portable devices.

XNOR-Network on both image classification task and object detection task. The main contributions of this paper can be summarized as follows:

- We propose a Ternary-Binary Network, which for the first time elegantly incorporates the ternary layer-wise inputs with binary weights and provides an optimal tradeoff between the performance and computational efficiency.
- We introduce an accelerated ternary-binary dot product method that employs simple **XOR**, **AND** and **bitcount** operations. As a result, TBN can provide $\sim 32\times$ memory saving and $40\times$ speedup over its real-valued CNN counterparts.
- By incorporating with various CNN architectures (including *LeNet-5*, *VGG-7*, *AlexNet*, *ResNet-18* and *ResNet-34*), TBN can achieve the promising image classification and object detection performance on multiple datasets among quantized neural networks. Particularly, TBN outperforms XNOR-Network [42] by up to 5.5% (top-1 accuracy) on the ImageNet classification task, and up to 4.4% (mAP score) on the PASCAL VOC object detection task.

2   Related Work

Abundant research efforts have been paid on how to lightweight standard full-precision CNNs through quantization. In this section, we list some recent relevant work along such a research line, and discuss how they relate to the proposed TBN. We roughly divide these work into the following two categories: (1) quantized weights with real-value inputs and (2) quantized weights and inputs.

Quantized Weights with Real-Value Inputs: Networks with quantized weights can result in a direct reduction in network sizes, however, the efficiency

Table 1. Comparisons between TBN and its closely related methods in terms of input and weight types, numbers of multiply-accumulate operations (MACs) and binary operations required by matrix multiplication, speedup ratios and operation types. More detailed statistical analysis can be found in Sect. 4.3.

Methods		Inputs	Weights	MACs	Binary operations	Speedup	Operations
	Full-precision	$\mathbb{R}$	$\mathbb{R}$	$n \times m \times q$	0	1×	+, ×
Quantize weights	TTQ [58]	$\mathbb{R}$	$\{-\alpha^n, 0 + \alpha^p\}$	$n \times m \times q$	0	~ 2×	+, −
	TWN [33]	$\mathbb{R}$	$\{-\alpha, 0, -\alpha\}$	$n \times m \times q$	0	~ 2×	+, −
	BWN [42]	$\mathbb{R}$	$\{-\alpha, +\alpha\}$	$n \times m \times q$	0	~ 2×	+, −
	BC [6]	$\mathbb{R}$	$\{-1, +1\}$	$n \times m \times q$	0	~ 2×	+, −
Quantize inputs and weights	TNN [1]	$\{-1, 0, 1\}$	$\{-1, 0, 1\}$	0	$8 \times n \times m \times q$	15×	AND, bitcount
	GXNOR [9]	$\{-1, 0, 1\}$	$\{-1, 0, 1\}$	0	$5 \times n \times m \times q$	15×	AND, bitcount
	BNN [7]	$\{-1, +1\}$	$\{-1, +1\}$	0	$2 \times n \times m \times q$	64×	XOR, bitcount
	XNOR [42]	$\{-\beta, +\beta\}$	$\{-\alpha, +\alpha\}$	$2 \times n \times m$	$2 \times n \times m \times q$	58×	XOR, bitcount
	HORQ [34]	$\{-\beta, +\beta\} \times 2$	$\{-\alpha, +\alpha\}$	$4 \times n \times m$	$4 \times n \times m \times q$	29×	XOR, bitcount
	DoReFa* [57]	$\{0, 1\} \times 2$	$\{0, 1\}$	0	$4 \times n \times m \times q$	30×	AND, bitcount
	TBN	$\{-1, 0, +1\}$	$\{-\alpha, +\alpha\}$	$n \times m$	$3 \times n \times m \times q$	40×	AND, XOR, bitcount

*We adopt DoReFa Network with 1-bit weight, 2-bit activation.

improvement, which is achieved by avoiding the multiplication operation, is limited if the input signals remain real-valued. The most basic forms of weight quantization either directly constrains the weight values into the binary space $\{-1, 1\}$, e.g., BinaryConnect (BC [6]), or constrain the weight values along with a scaling factor $\{-\alpha, \alpha\}$, e.g., Binary-Weight-Networks(BWNs [42]). Beyond the binary weights, ternary weights are introduced to reduce the quantization error. Ternary Weight Networks (TWNs [33]) quantize the weights into $\{-\alpha, 0, \alpha\}$, while Trained Ternary Quantization (TTQ [58]) achieves better performance by constraining the weights to asymmetric ternary values $\{-\alpha^n, 0, \alpha^p\}$.

Quantized Weights and Inputs: Comparing to the storage, the computational efficiency is a more critical demand for real-time predictions in resource-constrained environments. Since quantizing input signals can potentially replace arithmetical operations with XNOR and bitcount operations and improve the efficiency, networks that attempted to quantize both network weights and layer-wise input signals are proposed. Expectation BackPropagation (EBP [48]), Binarized Neural Networks (BNNs [7]), Bitwise Neural Networks [25] and XNOR-Networks [42] have explored to brutally binarize input signals in addition to the binary weights. Targeting at lessening the quantization errors, high-order quantization methods, e.g., High-Order Residual Quantization (HORQ [34]), multi-bit quantization methods, *e.g.*, DoReFa-Net [57] and ternary quantization methods, *e.g.*, Gated XNOR Networks (GXNOR [9]).

The proposed TBN also falls in the type of networks that quantize both weights and inputs. Comparing to aforementioned work that aim to compensate the effectiveness of binarized networks with degraded efficiency, TBN for the first time provides an elegant integration between the binary weights and ternary inputs, so as to provide an optimal tradeoff between memory, efficiency and performance. We illustrate comparisons of these measurements between TBN and aforementioned method in Table 1.

There are other kinds of methods to compress and accelerate CNNs, *e.g.* pretrained based methods, distillation and so on. Fixed-point Factorized Networks (FFN [52]) decomposed the weight matrix of pretrained models into two ternary matrices and a non-negative diagonal matrix so that both the computational complexity and the storage requirement of networks are reduced. Ternary neural networks (TNNs [1]) used the teacher networks containing high-precision weights and ternary inputs, to teach the student networks which both weights and inputs are ternary-valued. LBCNN [24] used pre-defined binary convolutional filters to reduce the number of learnable parameters.

3   Ternary-Binary Networks

In this section, we introduce our proposed TBN in detail. Firstly, we present some notations and show how to implement the convolutional operation by matrix multiplication. Secondly, we explain how to obtain the binary weights and ternary inputs by approximating their full-precision counterparts. Given the binary weights and ternary inputs, we further illustrate the multiplication between them. Finally, the whole training procedure of our TBN is elaborated.

3.1   Convolution with Matrix Multiplication

A convolutional layer can be represented by a triplet $\langle \mathbf{I}, \mathcal{W}, * \rangle$. $\mathbf{I} \in \mathbb{R}^{c \times h_{in} \times w_{in}}$ is the input tensor, where (c, h_{in}, w_{in}) represents *channels, heights* and *widths*, respectively. $\mathbf{W} \in \mathbb{R}^{c \times h \times w} = \mathcal{W}_{i(i=1,...,n)}$ is the ith weight filter in $\mathcal{W}$, where n is the number of weight filters, and (h, w) represents the filter size. $*$ represents the convolution operation between $\mathbf{I}$ and $\mathbf{W}$ and the product is $\mathbf{C} \in \mathbb{R}^{n \times h_{out} \times w_{out}}$, where $h_{out} = (h_{in} + 2 \cdot p - w)/s + 1$ and $w_{out} = (w_{in} + 2 \cdot p - w)/s + 1$, and (p, s) represent the pad and stride parameter respectively. We refer to the inner product layer as the convolution layer, which is same to XNOR-Network [42].

As adopted in the popular Caffe package [22], we use matrix multiplication to implement the convolution layer $\langle \mathbf{I}, \mathcal{W}, * \rangle$. Specifically, by flattening each filter $\mathbf{W}$ to a row vector of shape $1 \times q$ ($q = c \times h \times w$), the set of weight filters $\mathcal{W}$ can be reshaped to a matrix $\widetilde{\mathbf{W}} \in \mathbb{R}^{n \times q}$. We use function *ten2mat* to represent this step, *i.e.* $\widetilde{\mathbf{W}} = ten2mat(\mathcal{W})$. Similarly, transforming each sub-tensor in the input tensor $\mathbf{I}$ with the same size as the filter to a column vector, we get the matrix $\widetilde{\mathbf{I}} \in \mathbb{R}^{q \times m}$ ($m = h_{out} \times w_{out}$) after accumulating these vectors, *i.e.*

$\widetilde{\mathbf{I}} = ten2mat(\mathbf{I})$. Let we denote the product of the matrix multiplication with $\widetilde{\mathbf{I}}$ and $\widetilde{\mathbf{W}}$ as its operands as $\widetilde{\mathbf{C}} \in \mathbb{R}^{n \times m}$, $i.e.$ $\widetilde{\mathbf{C}} = \widetilde{\mathbf{W}}\widetilde{\mathbf{I}}$. Finally, we reshape the matrix $\widetilde{\mathbf{C}}$ back to output tensor $\mathbf{C}$. This step is the inverse operation of $ten2mat$, denoted it by $mat2ten$. This is the entire process of implementing a convolutional layer using matrix multiplication, which can be summarized as:

$$\mathbf{C} = mat2ten(\widetilde{\mathbf{W}}\widetilde{\mathbf{I}}), \widetilde{\mathbf{W}} = ten2mat(\mathcal{W}), \widetilde{\mathbf{I}} = ten2mat(\mathbf{I}) \tag{1}$$

3.2 Binary Weights

Following XNOR-Networks [42], we adopt the similar paradigm to estimate the binary weights. Concretely, we use a binary filter $\mathbf{B} \in \{-1, +1\}^{c \times h \times w}$ and a scaling factor $\alpha \in \mathbb{R}^{+}$ to approximate a full-precision weight filter $\mathbf{W} \in \mathcal{W}$ such that $\mathbf{W} \approx \alpha\mathbf{B}$. The optimal approximation is obtained by solving the optimization problem of minimizing the ℓ_2 distance between full-precision and binary weight filters, $i.e.$ $\alpha, \mathbf{B} = \arg\min_{\alpha, \mathbf{B}} \|\mathbf{W} - \alpha\mathbf{B}\|_2^2$. The optimal solution is

$$\mathbf{B} = sign(\mathbf{W}), \ \alpha = \frac{1}{c \times h \times w}\|\mathbf{W}\|_1. \tag{2}$$

The binary weight filters obtained by this simple strategy can reduce the storage of a convolutional layer by $\sim32\times$ compared to single-precision filters.

3.3 Ternary Inputs

In XNOR-Networks, the strategy to quantize the inputs of a convolutional layer to binary become quite complex. They taken the sign of input values to get binary input and calculated a matrix $\mathbf{A}$ by averaging the absolute values of elements in the input $\mathbf{I}$ across the channels, $i.e.$, $\mathbf{A} = \frac{\sum \|\mathbf{I}_{:,:,i}\|}{c}$. Then the scaling matrix $\mathbf{K}$ for the input was obtained by convolving the matrix $\mathbf{A}$ by a kernel $\mathbf{k} \in \mathbb{R}^{h \times w}$ with $\mathbf{k}_{ij} = \frac{1}{h \times w}$. However, the scaling factors of the binary inputs does not affect the performance of XNOR-Networks. Indicated by this, we abandon the scaling factors for the inputs to reduce unnecessary computation. On the other hand, TWN [33] with ternary weights has better performance than BWN [42] with binary weights. In order to improve the performance of binarized CNNs, we quantize each element of input tensor $\mathbf{I}$ into a ternary value $\{-1, 0, 1\}$ without the scaling factor.

We propose following threshold-based ternary function $f_{ternary}$ to obtain ternary input tensor $\mathbf{T} \in \{-1, 0, +1\}^{c \times h_{in} \times w_{in}}$:

$$\mathbf{T}_i = f_{ternary}(\mathbf{I}_i, \Delta) = \begin{cases} +1, \mathbf{I}_i > \Delta; \\ 0, |\mathbf{I}_i| \leq \Delta; \\ -1, \mathbf{I}_i < -\Delta; \end{cases} \tag{3}$$

where $\Delta \in \mathbb{R}^{+}$ is an positive threshold parameter. The value of Δ controls the numbers of -1, 0 and 1 in $\mathbf{T}$, which will highly affect the final accuracy. When

Δ is equal to 0, the function $f_{ternary}$ degenerates to the sign function. So that, a same performance as XNOR-Network will be obtained. However, when Δ is too big, each element in $\mathbf{T}$ will be zero according to Eq. (3), and we will get the worst result. Thus, an appropriate value of Δ is necessary. However, it is hard to obtain optimal Δ. Similar to TWN [33], we use following formula to calculate Δ:

$$\Delta = \delta \times \mathrm{E}(|\mathbf{I}|) \approx \frac{\delta}{c \times h_{in} \times w_{in}} \|\mathbf{I}\|_1 \tag{4}$$

where δ is a constant factor for all layers. We set $\delta = 0.4$ in the experiments. By this means, it is fast and easy to quantize a real-valued input tensor into a ternary architecture.

3.4 Ternary-Binary Dot Product

Once we obtain the binary weights and ternary inputs, how to achieve effective ternary-binary multiplication is our next target. As we know, the matrix multiplication is based on the dot product. That is to say, the entry $C_{ij} \in \widetilde{\mathbf{C}}$ is the result of dot product between the ith row of weight matrix $\widetilde{\mathbf{W}}$ and the jth column of input matrix $\widetilde{\mathbf{I}}$. I.e., $C_{ij} = \widetilde{\boldsymbol{W}}_i \cdot \widetilde{\boldsymbol{I}}_j$ where $\cdot$ is the dot product, $\widetilde{\boldsymbol{W}}_i = [\widetilde{W}_{i1}, \ldots, \widetilde{W}_{iq}]$ and $\widetilde{\boldsymbol{I}}_j = [\widetilde{I}_{1j}, \ldots, \widetilde{I}_{qj}]$. We can use binary operations to accelerate the dot product with a binary vector and a ternary vector as its operands. Let us use $\alpha \boldsymbol{b}$ to denote the binary filter $\mathbf{B}$ corresponding to $\widetilde{\boldsymbol{W}}_i$, where $\widetilde{\boldsymbol{W}}_i \approx \alpha \boldsymbol{b}, \boldsymbol{b} = ten2mat(\mathbf{B}) \in \{-1, 1\}^q$ and α is the scaling factor. Similarly, the ternary vector $\boldsymbol{t} \in \{-1, 0, +1\}^q$ corresponds to $\widetilde{\boldsymbol{I}}_j$. So we can implement this special dot product efficiently with the following formula:

$$C_{ij} = \alpha(c_t - 2 \times \mathbf{bitcount}((\boldsymbol{b}\ \mathbf{XOR}\ \boldsymbol{t'})\ \mathbf{AND}\ \boldsymbol{t''})), \tag{5}$$

where we decompose vector $\boldsymbol{t}$ into two vector $\boldsymbol{t'} \in \{-1, 1\}^q$ and $\boldsymbol{t''} \in \{0, 1\}^q$ as follows:

$$t'_i = \begin{cases} 1, & t_i = 1 \\ -1, & \text{otherwise} \end{cases}, \quad t''_i = \begin{cases} 0, & t_i = 0 \\ 1, & \text{otherwise} \end{cases}, \quad i = 1, \ldots, q \tag{6}$$

so that $t_i = t'_i \times t''_i$. $c_t = \mathbf{bitcount}(\boldsymbol{t''}) = \|\boldsymbol{t}\|_1$ is a constant which is independent of $\boldsymbol{b}$. In Eq. (5), the operation $\mathbf{bitcount}$ return the count of number of bits set to 1 and $\mathbf{XOR}, \mathbf{AND}$ are the logic operations. It should be noted that 1 in $\boldsymbol{b}, \boldsymbol{t'}, \boldsymbol{t''}$ is considered to be logic true, and the others (i.e. $0, -1$) are regard as logic false. So we can implement the efficient matrix multiplication.

3.5 Training TBN

With above strategies, we can get an very fast convolutional layer with ternary inputs and binary weights (TBConvolution), and Algorithm 1 demonstrates how TBConvolution works. In the TBN, there is a batch normalization layer [20] to normalize the inputs before each TBConvolution, so that the number of -1, 0, 1 for ternary inputs is more balanced. A non-linear activation layer (e.g. ReLU)

Algorithm 1. TBConvolution($\mathcal{W}, \mathbf{I}$)

Input: A set of weight filters $\mathcal{W} \in \mathbb{R}^{n \times c \times h \times w}$, the input tensor $\mathbf{I} \in \mathbb{R}^{c \times h_{in} \times w_{in}}$ and convolutional parameters including the stride s and pad p
Output: The convolutional result $\mathbf{C} \in \mathbb{R}^{n \times h_{out} \times w_{out}}$
1: **for** i^{th} filter $\mathbf{W}$ in $\mathcal{W}$ **do**
2:    $\alpha = \frac{1}{c \times h \times w} \|\mathbf{W}\|_1$ // calculate the scaling factor w.r.t. Eq. (2)
3:    $\mathbf{B} = sign(\mathbf{W})$ // get the binary filter w.r.t. Eq. (2)
4:    $\mathbf{W} \approx \alpha \mathbf{B}$
5: **end for**
6: $\Delta = \frac{\delta}{c \times h_{in} \times w_{in}} \|\mathbf{I}\|_1$ // calculate the threshold parameter w.r.t. Eq. (4)
7: $\mathbf{T} = f_{ternary}(\mathbf{I}, \Delta)$ // get the ternary input w.r.t. Eq. (3)
8: $\widetilde{\mathbf{W}} = ten2mat(\mathcal{W})$ and $\widetilde{\mathbf{I}} = ten2mat(\mathbf{T})$ // covert weights and input tensors to matrices w.r.t. Eq. (1)
9: $\widetilde{\mathbf{C}} = \widetilde{\mathbf{W}}\widetilde{\mathbf{I}}$ // accelerate matrix multiplication w.r.t. Eq. (5)
10: $\mathbf{C} = mat2ten(\widetilde{\mathbf{C}})$ // convert the product to the tensor w.r.t. Eq. (1)

Algorithm 2. Training an L-layer TBN

Input: A minibatch of inputs and targets $(\mathbf{X}_0, \mathbf{Y})$, cost function $C(\mathbf{Y}, \hat{\mathbf{Y}})$, current weights $\widehat{\mathcal{W}}(t) = \{\mathcal{W}_l(t)\}_{l=1}^L$, and current learning rate $\eta(t)$
Output: updated weight $\widehat{\mathcal{W}}(t+1)$ and updated learning rate $\eta(t+1)$
1: **for** $l = 1$ to L **do**
2:    $\mathbf{I}_l = \text{BatchNormalization}(\mathbf{X}_{l-1})$
3:    $\mathbf{X}_l = \text{TBConvolution}(\mathcal{W}_l(t), \mathbf{I}_l)$
4: **end for**
5: $\frac{\partial C}{\partial \mathcal{W}} = \text{Backward}(\frac{\partial C}{\partial \mathbf{X}_L}, \widehat{\mathcal{W}}(t))$ // standard backward propagation with Eq. (7)

6: $\widehat{\mathcal{W}}(t+1) = \text{UpdateParameters}(\widehat{\mathcal{W}}(t), \frac{\partial C}{\partial \mathcal{W}}, \eta(t))$ // Any optimizer (e.g. ADAM)
7: $\eta(t+1) = \text{UpdateLearningRate}(\eta(t), t)$ // Any learning rate scheduling function
Note: $\mathcal{W}_l$ here is identical to the lth layer TBN weights $\mathcal{W}$ (mentioned in Section 3.1)

---

after each TBConvolution is optional because ternary quantization can play the role of the non-linear activation function. Other layers (*e.g.* pooling and dropout) can be inserted after TBConvolution (or before the batch normalization layer). To train TBN, the full-precision gradient is adopted and we use straight-through estimator [4] to compute the gradient of binary and ternary quantization function, *i.e.*

$$\frac{\partial sign}{\partial r} = \frac{\partial f_{ternary}}{\partial r} = 1_{|r|<1} = \begin{cases} 1, & |r| < 1 \\ 0, & \text{otherwise} \end{cases} \quad (7)$$

Similar to the strategy used in BNN [7], XNOR-Networks [42] and HORQ [34], we do not apply our approach on the first or last layer. Algorithm 2 demonstrates the procedure for training an L-layer Ternary-Binary Network. We can use any optimizer (*e.g.* ADAM [27]) to train TBNs.

4   Experiments

As the proposed TBN uses ternary inputs with binary weights to simultaneously reduce the approximation error caused by quantization but maintain the reasonable performance to some extend, the goal of our experiments is mainly to answer the following three research questions:

- **Q1:** How does TBN perform compared to other quantized/squeezed deep networks (*i.e.*, XNOR-Networks, HORQ) in different tasks (*i.e.*, image recognition and object detection)?
- **Q2:** How fast can TBN accelerate compared to other quantized networks?
- **Q3:** How is the performance of TBN influenced by different components (*e.g.* the sparsity of ternary inputs, the usage of activation functions)?

4.1   Image Classification

Datasets and Configurations: We evaluate the performance of our proposed approach on four different datasets, *i.e.* MNIST [32], CIFAR-10 [28], SVHN [40], ImageNet (ILSVRC2012) [44], and compare it with other methods. As previously mentioned, our TBN can accommodate any network architectures. Hence,

Table 2. The classification accuracies of different CNNs trained with various models on the four datasets. Both "top-1/top-5" accuracies are presented for the ImageNet dataset. "-" indicates that the results are not provided in their original papers.

Dataset models		MNIST LeNet-5	CIFAR-10 VGG-7	SVHN VGG-7	ImageNet AlexNet	ImageNet ResNet-18	ImageNet ResNet-34
	Full-precision	99.48	92.88	97.68	57.2/80.2	69.3/89.2	73.3/91.4
Quantize weights	BC [6]	98.82	91.73	97.85	35.5/61.0	-	-
	BWN [42]	99.38	92.58	97.46	56.8/79.4	60.8/83.0	-
	TWN [33]	99.38	92.56	-	54.5/76.8	65.3/86.2	-
	TTQ [58]	-	-	-	57.5/79.7	66.6/87.2	-
Other methods	FFN [52]	-	-	-	55.5/79.0	-	-
	LCNN-fast [3]	-	-	-	44.3/68.7	51.8/76.8	-
	LCNN-accurate [3]	-	-	-	55.1/78.1	62.2/84.6	-
	LBCNN [24]	99.51	92.66	94.50	54.9/-	-	-
Quantize inputs and weights	TNN [1]	98.33	87.89	97.27	-	-	-
	GXNOR [9]	99.32	92.50	97.37	-	-	-
	BNN [7]	98.60	89.85	97.47	27.9/50.42	-	-
	DoReFa-Net* [57]	-	-	97.6	47.7/-	-	-
	BinaryNet [50]	-	-	-	46.6/71.1	-	-
	HORQ [34]	99.38	91.18	97.41	-	55.9/78.9	-
	XNOR-Network [42]	99.21	90.02	96.96	44.2/69.2	51.2/73.2	55.9/79.1
	TBN	99.38	90.85	97.27	49.7/74.2	55.6/79.0	58.2/81.0

*We adopt DoReFa-Net with 1-bit weight, 2-bit activation and 32-bit gradient for fair comparison.

we performance the following evaluations with different networks on the above datasets. Note that we adopt the Adam optimizer with Batch Normalization to speed up the training, and ReLU is adopted as the activation function in all the following experiments. In addition, all the deep networks used in this section are training from the scratch.

Results on MNIST with LeNet-5: The LeNet-5 [32] architecture we used is "32-C5 + MP2 + 64-C5 + MP2 + 512-FC + 10-FC + SVM". It is composed of two convolutional layers with size 5×5, a fully connected layer and a SVM classifier with 10 labels. Specifically, there is no pre-processing, data-augmentation or pre-training skills to remain the challenge. The learning rate starts at 0.001 and is divided by 10 at epoch 15, 30, 45 with the mini-batch size 200. We report the best accuracy on the testing set. From the results shown in Table 2, we observe that our TBN has the same performance as HORQ but outperforms XNOR-Network by 0.17%. In fact, on the MNIST dataset, there are subtle difference between those methods (less than 1%).

Results on CIFAR-10 with VGG-7: To train the networks on CIFAR-10 dataset, we follow the same data augmentation scheme in ResNet [18]. In detail, we use the VGG inspired architecture, denoted as VGG-7, by: "$2 \times (128\text{-}C3) + MP2 + 2 \times (256\text{-}C3) + MP2 + 2 \times (512\text{-}C3) + MP2 + 1024\text{-}FC + 10\text{-}FC + Softmax$", where C3 is a 3×3 convolutional block, MP2 is a max-pooling layer with kernel size 2 and stride 2, and Softmax is a softmax loss layer. We train this model for 200 epochs with a mini-batch of 200. The learning rate also starts at 0.001 and is scaled by 0.5 every 50 epochs. The results are given in Table 2. The accuracy of our TBN on CIFAR-10 is higher than XNOR-Network's and BNNs. However, compared with HORQ, and GXNOR, the performance of TBN is slightly worse since more quantization for both inputs and weights are adopted in our methods.

Results on SVHN with VGG-7: We also use VGG-7 networks for SVHN. Because SVHN is a much larger dataset than CIFAR-10, we only train VGG-7 for 60 epochs. From, results presented in Table 2, it is easily discovered that the performances between TBN, HORQ, XNOR-Networks, BNN, GXNOR and TNN is almost at the same level (Fig. 2).

Results on ImageNet with AlexNet: In this experiment, we report our classification performance in terms of top-1 and top-5 accuracies using AlexNet. Specifically, AlexNet is with 5 convolutional layers and two fully-connected layers. We train the network for 100 epochs. The learning rate starts at 0.001 and is divided by 0.1 every 25 epochs. Figures 2(a) and (b) demonstrate the classification accuracy for training and inference along with the training epochs. The solid lines represent training and validation accuracy of TBN, and dashed lines show the accuracy of XNOR-Network. The final accuracy of AlexNet is showed

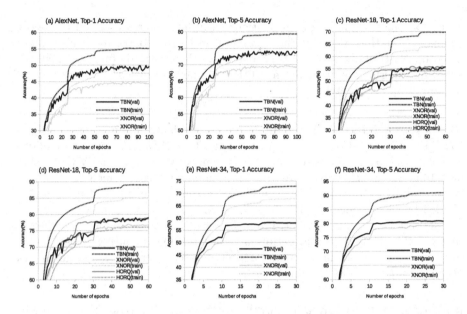

Fig. 2. (a) and (b) Compare the top-1 and top-5 accuracies between TBN and XNOR-Networks on AlexNet; (c) and (d) compare the top-1 and top-5 accuracies between TBN, HORQ and XNOR-Networks on ResNet-18; (e) and (f) compare the top-1 and top-5 accuracies between TBN and XNOR-Networks on ResNet-34.

in Table 2, which illustrates our TBN outperforms XNOR-Network by the large margin (5.5% on top-1 accuracy and 5.0% on top-5 accuracy) (Table 3).

Results on ImageNet with ResNet: In addition to the AlexNet, we also train two Ternary-Binary Networks for both ResNet-18 and ResNet-34 [18] architectures on the ImageNet dataset. We run the training algorithm for 60 epochs with a mini-batch size of 128. The learning rate starts at 0.001 and is scaled by 0.1 every 20 epochs. ResNet-34 adopts the same training strategy, but is only trained with 30 epochs in total and the learning rate is decayed every 10 epochs. Figures 2(c)–(f) demonstrate the classification accuracies (top-1 and top-5) of ResNet-18 and ResNet-34 respectively, along with the epochs for training and inference. The final results are reported in Table 2, which show that Ternary-Binary Network is better than XNOR-Networks (ResNet-18: by 4.4%/4.8% on top-1/top-5, ResNet-34: by 2.3%/1.9% on top-1/top-5). Meanwhile, the performance of our TBN is competitive to that of HORQ (top1: 55.6% vs. 55.9%; top-5 79.0% vs. 78.9% on ResNet-18).

4.2 Object Detection

We also evaluate the performance of TBN on the object detection task. Various modified network architectures are used, including Faster-RCNN [43], and

Table 3. The performance (in mAP) comparison of TBN, XNOR-Networks and full-precision CNN models for object detection. All methods are trained on the combination of VOC2007 and VOC2012 `trainval` sets and tested on the VOC2007 `test` set.

Method base network	Full-precision VGG-16	Full-precision ResNet-34	XNOR-Networks ResNet-34	TBN ResNet-34
Faster R-CNN	73.2	75.6	54.7	59.0
SSD 300	74.3	75.5	55.1	59.5

Single Shot Detector (SSD [38]). We change the base network of these architectures to the TBN with ResNet-34. We compare the performance with XNOR-Networks and full-precision networks. We evaluate all methods on the PASCAL VOC dataset [11,12], which is a standard recognition benchmark with detection and semantic segmentation challenges. We train our models on the combination of VOC2007 `trainval` and VOC2012 `trainval` (16,551 images) and test on VOC2007 `test` (4,952 images).

The comparison results for object detection are illustrated in Table 4(b). As can be seen from the table, the models based on ResNet-34 can achieve better performance both on Faster R-CNN and SSD. Our TBN with ResNet achieves up to 4.4% higher than XNOR-Networks in terms of mAP, although there is a large margin compared to full-precision networks.

4.3 Efficiency

In this section, we will illustrate the efficiency comparison between different methods. Suppose matrix multiplication $\widetilde{\mathbf{C}} = \widetilde{\mathbf{W}}\widetilde{\mathbf{I}}$, where $\widetilde{\mathbf{W}} \in \mathbb{R}^{n \times q}$, $\widetilde{\mathbf{I}} \in \mathbb{R}^{q \times m}$ and $\widetilde{\mathbf{C}} \in \mathbb{R}^{n \times m}$. To calculate $\widetilde{\mathbf{C}}$, there are $n \times m \times q$ multiply-accumulate operations (MACs) required. If the matrix $\widetilde{\mathbf{I}}$ is quantized to ternary values and the matrix $\widetilde{\mathbf{W}}$ is binary-valued, matrix multiplication requires $n \times m$ multiplications and $n \times m \times q$ **AND**, **XOR** and **bitcount** operations respectively, according to Eq. (5). We provide a comparison between our approach and the related works using quantized inputs and weights in Table 1. Compared with XNOR-Networks, our approach increases $n \times m \times q$ binary operations and saves $n \times m$ MACs, while HORQ needs twice the number of MACs and binary operations as XNOR networks.

The general computation platform (*i.e.*, CPU, GPU, ARM) can perform an L-bits binary operation in one clock cycle ($L = 64$ typical[1]). Assume the ratio between the speed of performing an L-bits binary operation and a multiply-accumulate operation is γ, *i.e.*

$$\gamma = \frac{\text{average time required by MAC}}{\text{average time required by } L\text{-bits binary operation}} \tag{8}$$

---

[1] An Intel SSE(, AVX, AVX-512) instruction can perform 128(, 256, 512) bits binary operation.

Therefore, the speedup ratio of Ternary-Binary Networks is:

$$S = \frac{\gamma nmq}{\gamma nm + 3nm\lceil\frac{q}{L}\rceil} = \frac{\gamma q}{\gamma + 3\lceil\frac{q}{L}\rceil} \tag{9}$$

It shows that speedup ratio depends on q, L, while γ is determined by machine. For a convolutional layer, $q = c \times h \times w$, that is to say, S is independent of the input size. According to the speedup ratio achieved by XNOR-Network, we can safely assume $\gamma = 1.91$. To maximize the speedup, q should be several times of L. In Fig. 3, we illustrate the relationship between the speedup ratio and q, L. It shows that we can obtain higher speedup ratio by increasing q or L.

Table 1 compares the speedup ratio achieved by different methods, in which parameters are fixed as: $\gamma = 1.91, L = 64$ and $q = c \times h \times w = 2304^2$. When real-valued inputs with either binary or ternary weight, the MAC operation can be replaced by only addition and subtraction, and achieving ~2× speedup [42]. While, the methods which both weights and inputs are quantized achieve high speedup ($\geq 15\times$) by using binary operation. Specifically, more bits used by weights or inputs, the lower speedup ratio is but getting the lower the approximation error. Using our approach, we gain 40× theoretical speedup ratio, which is 11× higher than HORQ. See **Supplementary Material** for more details.

Remark. Why Not Use Ternary Weights with Binary Inputs: Actually, a ternary (2-bit) weights network with binary inputs uses the same scheme as TBN to accelerate CNN, but requires twice as much storage space as TBN. Since TBN has higher compression rate, we choose the TBN from these two equivalent approaches.

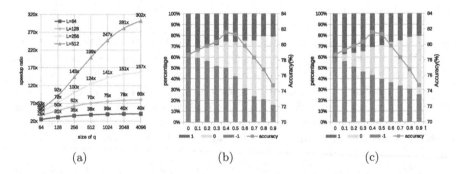

| (a) | (b) | (c) |

Fig. 3. (a) The relationship between speedup ratio and q under different L; (b) the classification accuracy with varying δ in Eq. (4), *i.e.* sparsity of ternary inputs. The percentage stacked histogram shows the percentage of the average number of $-1, 0, 1$ w.r.t. the inputs of the second convolutional layer; (c) the classification accuracy and percentage stacked histogram w.r.t. the inputs of the third convolutional layer.

---

2 For the majority of convolutional layer in ResNet [18] architecture, it's kernel size is 3×3 and input channel size is 256, so we fix $q = 256 \times 3^2 = 2304$.

4.4   Analysis of TBN Components

Sparsity of Ternary Inputs: To explore the relationship between sparsity and accuracy, we vary δ in Eq. (4) and train a **Simple Network** structure on CIFAR-10: "32-C5 + MP3 + 32-C5 + MP3 + 64-C5 + AP3 + 10FC + Softmax". We adopt this kind of structure because of its simplicity and flexibility for the performance comparison. The learning strategy is the same as VGG-7 in Sect. 4.1. The classification accuracies with different degrees of sparsities are shown in Fig. 3(b) and (c). As can been seen from the two figures, when δ grows from 0 (which is the case of XNOR-Networks) to 0.4, both the number of zeros and accuracy increase accordingly. However, when δ further increases, the model capacity is reduced and the error rate is increased quickly. Therefore, we set $\delta = 0.4$ in our experiments.

Table 4. (a) The classification performance of TBN while using non-linear layers with different activation functions (on the CIFAR-10 dataset). "None" denotes that we don't use non-linear layer; (b) the comparison of accuracies (%) on CIFAR-10 after quantizing the inputs of first/last convolutional layers. ✓ indicates that we quantize the first/last layers, and ✗ indicates that we use full-precision inputs and weights.

(a)

Base Networks	Non-Linear Layers			
	None	ReLU	Sigmoid	PReLU
ResNet-20	81.36	82.15	79.12	84.34
VGG-7	89.49	90.85	89.78	90.10
Simple Network	75.92	81.21	78.67	81.14

(b)

First	Last	XNOR	TBN	BWN	HORQ
✗	✗	79.11	81.21	82.66	81.12
✗	✓	71.64	76.88	81.86	76.64
✓	✗	62.85	65.57	76.61	68.69
✓	✓	52.41	58.86	73.66	62.55
Full-Precision		85.51			

Effect of Activation Function: Here, we explore the influence of different activation functions on our TBN framework. Specifically, we incorporate three non-linear activation functions, *i.e.* ReLU, Sigmoind and PReLU. 'Simple Network' in the table indicates the simple base network architecture used in the above paragraph. As shown in Table 4(a), the accuracy can be improved when using the non-linear activation functions, and using PReLU could achieve the best performance. However, the improvement is subtle, mainly because the ternary quantization function in our TBN already plays the role of activation function.

Quantizing the First/Last Layer? As shown in our framework, we avoid the quantization step on the first and last layers of the networks. The reasons are two-fold: Firstly, the inputs of the first layer have much fewer channels (*i.e.* $c = 3$), thus the speedup ratio in efficiency is not considerably high. Secondly, if the inputs of the first or last layer are quantized, the performance will drop significantly, which can be seen from Table 4(b). Note that all the results here are obtained based on the previously mentioned Simple Network. As we can see from the table, the accuracies of the four networks decrease consistently by a large margin after quantizing their first/last layers, and the performance drop is especially obvious when the first layer is quantized.

5 Conclusion

In this paper, we for the first time incorporated binary network weights and ternary layer-wise inputs as a lightweighted approximation to standard CNNs. We claim the ternary inputs along with the binary weights can provide an optimal tradeoff between memory, efficiency and performance. An accelerated ternary-binary matrix multiplication that employs highly efficient **XOR, AND** and **bitcount** operations was introduced in TBN, which achieved ∼32× memory saving and 40× speedup over its full-precision CNN counterparts. TBN demonstrated its consistent effectiveness when applied to various CNN architectures on multiple datasets of different scales, and it also outperformed the XNOR-Network by up to 5.5% (top-1 accuracy) on the ImageNet classification task, and up to 4.4% (mAP score) on the PASCAL VOC object detection task.

Acknowledgments. This work was supported in part by the National Natural Science Foundation of China under Project 61502081 and Project 61632007, the Fundamental Research Funds for the Central Universities under Project ZYGX2014Z007.

References

1. Alemdar, H., Leroy, V., Prost-Boucle, A., Pétrot, F.: Ternary neural networks for resource-efficient AI applications. In: 2017 International Joint Conference on Neural Networks (IJCNN), pp. 2547–2554. IEEE (2017)
2. Ambai, M., Matsumoto, T., Yamashita, T., Fujiyoshi, H.: Ternary weight decomposition and binary activation encoding for fast and compact neural network. In: Proceedings of International Conference on Learning Representations (2017)
3. Bagherinezhad, H., Rastegari, M., Farhadi, A.: LCNN: lookup-based convolutional neural network. In: Proceedings of IEEE Conference on Computer Vision and Pattern Recognition (2017)
4. Bengio, Y., Léonard, N., Courville, A.: Estimating or propagating gradients through stochastic neurons for conditional computation. arXiv preprint arXiv:1308.3432 (2013)
5. Courbariaux, M., Bengio, Y., David, J.: Low precision arithmetic for deep learning. CoRR, abs/1412.7024 **4** (2014)
6. Courbariaux, M., Bengio, Y., David, J.P.: Binaryconnect: training deep neural networks with binary weights during propagations. In: Proceedings of Advances in Neural Information Processing Systems, pp. 3123–3131 (2015)
7. Courbariaux, M., Hubara, I., Soudry, D., El-Yaniv, R., Bengio, Y.: Binarized neural networks: training deep neural networks with weights and activations constrained to +1 or −1. In: Proceedings of Advances in Neural Information Processing Systems, pp. 4107–4115 (2016)
8. Dai, J., Li, Y., He, K., Sun, J.: R-FCN: Object detection via region-based fully convolutional networks. In: Proceedings of Advances in Neural Information Processing Systems, pp. 379–387 (2016)

9. Deng, L., Jiao, P., Pei, J., Wu, Z., Li, G.: Gated XNOR networks: deep neural networks with ternary weights and activations under a unified discretization framework. arXiv preprint arXiv:1705.09283 (2017)

10. Denil, M., Shakibi, B., Dinh, L., De Freitas, N., et al.: Predicting parameters in deep learning. In: Proceedings of Advances in Neural Information Processing Systems, pp. 2148–2156 (2013)

11. Everingham, M., Van Gool, L., Williams, C.K.I., Winn, J., Zisserman, A.: The PASCAL Visual Object Classes Challenge 2007 (VOC 2007) Results. http://www.pascal-network.org/challenges/VOC/voc2007/workshop/index.html

12. Everingham, M., Van Gool, L., Williams, C.K.I., Winn, J., Zisserman, A.: The PASCAL Visual Object Classes Challenge 2012 (VOC 2012) Results. http://www.pascal-network.org/challenges/VOC/voc2012/workshop/index.html

13. Girshick, R.: Fast R-CNN. In: Proceedings of IEEE Conference on Computer Vision, pp. 1440–1448 (2015)

14. Girshick, R., Donahue, J., Darrell, T., Malik, J.: Rich feature hierarchies for accurate object detection and semantic segmentation. In: Proceedings of IEEE Conference on Computer Vision and Pattern Recognition, pp. 580–587 (2014)

15. Gupta, S., Agrawal, A., Gopalakrishnan, K., Narayanan, P.: Deep learning with limited numerical precision. In: Proceedings of International Conference on Machine Learning, pp. 1737–1746 (2015)

16. Han, S., Mao, H., Dally, W.J.: Deep compression: compressing deep neural networks with pruning, trained quantization and Huffman coding. In: Deep compression: compressing deep neural networks with pruning, trained quantization and Huffman coding (2016)

17. Han, S., Pool, J., Tran, J., Dally, W.: Learning both weights and connections for efficient neural network. In: Proceedings of Advances in Neural Information Processing Systems, pp. 1135–1143 (2015)

18. He, K., Zhang, X., Ren, S., Sun, J.: Deep residual learning for image recognition. In: Proceedings of IEEE Conference on Computer Vision and Pattern Recognition, pp. 770–778 (2016)

19. Hinton, G., Vinyals, O., Dean, J.: Distilling the knowledge in a neural network. In: NIPS 2014 Deep Learning and Representation Learning Workshop (2014)

20. Ioffe, S., Szegedy, C.: Batch normalization: accelerating deep network training by reducing internal covariate shift. In: Proceedings of International Conference on Machine Learning, pp. 448–456 (2015)

21. Jaderberg, M., Vedaldi, A., Zisserman, A.: Speeding up convolutional neural networks with low rank expansions. In: BMVC (2014)

22. Jia, Y., et al.: Caffe: convolutional architecture for fast feature embedding. arXiv preprint arXiv:1408.5093 (2014)

23. Jin, J., Dundar, A., Culurciello, E.: Flattened convolutional neural networks for feedforward acceleration. arXiv preprint arXiv:1412.5474 (2014)

24. Juefei-Xu, F., Boddeti, V.N., Savvides, M.: Local binary convolutional neural networks. In: Proceedings of IEEE Conference on Computer Vision and Pattern Recognition (2017)

25. Kim, M., Smaragdis, P.: Bitwise neural networks. CoRR abs/1601.06071 (2015)

26. Kim, Y.D., Park, E., Yoo, S., Choi, T., Yang, L., Shin, D.: Compression of deep convolutional neural networks for fast and low power mobile applications. arXiv preprint arXiv:1511.06530 (2015)

27. Kingma, D., Ba, J.: Adam: a method for stochastic optimization. In: Proceedings of International Conference on Learning Representations (2015)

28. Krizhevsky, A., Hinton, G.: Learning multiple layers of features from tiny images (2009)
29. Krizhevsky, A., Sutskever, I., Hinton, G.E.: ImageNet classification with deep convolutional neural networks. In: Proceedings of Advances in Neural Information Processing Systems, pp. 1097–1105 (2012)
30. Lebedev, V., Ganin, Y., Rakhuba, M., Oseledets, I., Lempitsky, V.: Speeding-up convolutional neural networks using fine-tuned CP-decomposition. In: Proceedings of International Conference on Learning Representations (2015)
31. LeCun, Y., Bengio, Y., Hinton, G.: Deep learning. Nature **521**(7553), 436–444 (2015)
32. LeCun, Y., Bottou, L., Bengio, Y., Haffner, P.: Gradient-based learning applied to document recognition. Proc. IEEE **86**(11), 2278–2324 (1998)
33. Li, F., Zhang, B., Liu, B.: Ternary weight networks. In: The 1st International Workshop on Efficient Methods for Deep Neural Networks (2016)
34. Li, Z., Ni, B., Zhang, W., Yang, X., Gao, W.: Performance guaranteed network acceleration via high-order residual quantization. In: Proceedings of IEEE Conference on Computer Vision (2017)
35. Lin, D., Talathi, S., Annapureddy, S.: Fixed point quantization of deep convolutional networks. In: Proceedings of International Conference on Machine Learning, pp. 2849–2858 (2016)
36. Lin, Z., Courbariaux, M., Memisevic, R., Bengio, Y.: Neural networks with few multiplications. In: Proceedings of International Conference on Learning Representations (2016)
37. Liu, L., Shao, L., Shen, F., Yu, M.: Discretely coding semantic rank orders for image hashing. In: Proceeding of the IEEE Conference on Computer Vision and Pattern Recognition (CVPR), pp. 2862–2871 (2017)
38. Liu, W., et al.: SSD: single shot multibox detector. In: Leibe, B., Matas, J., Sebe, N., Welling, M. (eds.) ECCV 2016. LNCS, vol. 9905, pp. 21–37. Springer, Cham (2016). https://doi.org/10.1007/978-3-319-46448-0_2
39. Long, J., Shelhamer, E., Darrell, T.: Fully convolutional networks for semantic segmentation. In: Proceedings of IEEE Conference on Computer Vision and Pattern Recognition, pp. 3431–3440 (2015)
40. Netzer, Y., Wang, T., Coates, A., Bissacco, A., Wu, B., Ng, A.Y.: Reading digits in natural images with unsupervised feature learning. In: NIPS Workshop on Deep Learning and Unsupervised Feature Learning, vol. 2011, p. 5 (2011)
41. Pinheiro, P.O., Collobert, R., Dollár, P.: Learning to segment object candidates. In: Proceedings of Advances in Neural Information Processing Systems, pp. 1990–1998 (2015)
42. Rastegari, M., Ordonez, V., Redmon, J., Farhadi, A.: XNOR-Net: ImageNet classification using binary convolutional neural networks. In: Leibe, B., Matas, J., Sebe, N., Welling, M. (eds.) ECCV 2016. LNCS, vol. 9908, pp. 525–542. Springer, Cham (2016). https://doi.org/10.1007/978-3-319-46493-0_32
43. Ren, S., He, K., Girshick, R., Sun, J.: Faster R-CNN: towards real-time object detection with region proposal networks. In: Proceedings of Advances in Neural Information Processing Systems, pp. 91–99 (2015)
44. Russakovsky, O., Deng, J., Su, H., Krause, J., Satheesh, S., Ma, S., Huang, Z., Karpathy, A., Khosla, A., Bernstein, M.: Imagenet large scale visual recognition challenge. Int. J. Comput. Vis. **115**(3), 211–252 (2015)
45. Shen, F., Gao, X., Liu, L., Yang, Y., Shen, H.T.: Deep asymmetric pairwise hashing. In: Proceedings of the 2017 ACM on Multimedia Conference, pp. 1522–1530. ACM (2017)

46. Shen, F., Xu, Y., Liu, L., Yang, Y., Huang, Z., Shen, H.T.: Unsupervised deep hashing with similarity-adaptive and discrete optimization. IEEE Trans. Pattern Anal. Mach. Intell. (2018)

47. Simonyan, K., Zisserman, A.: Very deep convolutional networks for large-scale image recognition. In: Proceedings of International Conference on Learning Representations (2015)

48. Soudry, D., Hubara, I., Meir, R.: Expectation backpropagation: parameter-free training of multilayer neural networks with continuous or discrete weights. In: Proceedings of Advances in Neural Information Processing Systems, pp. 963–971 (2014)

49. Szegedy, C., Liu, W., Jia, Y., Sermanet, P., Reed, S., Anguelov, D., Erhan, D., Vanhoucke, V., Rabinovich, A.: Going deeper with convolutions. In: Proc. IEEE Conf. Comp. Vis. Patt. Recogn. pp. 1–9 (2015)

50. Tang, W., Hua, G., Wang, L.: How to train a compact binary neural network with high accuracy? In: Proceedings of AAAI Conference on Artificial Intelligence, pp. 2625–2631 (2017)

51. Wang, P., Cheng, J.: Accelerating convolutional neural networks for mobile applications. In: Proceedings of the 2016 ACM on Multimedia Conference, pp. 541–545. ACM (2016)

52. Wang, P., Cheng, J.: Fixed-point factorized networks. In: Proceedings of IEEE Conference on Computer Vision and Pattern Recognition (2017)

53. Wen, W., Wu, C., Wang, Y., Chen, Y., Li, H.: Learning structured sparsity in deep neural networks. In: Proceedings of Advances in Neural Information Processing Systems, pp. 2074–2082 (2016)

54. Wu, J., Leng, C., Wang, Y., Hu, Q., Cheng, J.: Quantized convolutional neural networks for mobile devices. In: Proceedings of IEEE Conference on Computer Vision and Pattern Recognition, pp. 4820–4828 (2016)

55. Zhang, X., Zou, J., He, K., Sun, J.: Accelerating very deep convolutional networks for classification and detection. IEEE Trans. Pattern Anal. Mach. Intell. $38(10)$, 1943–1955 (2016)

56. Zhou, A., Yao, A., Guo, Y., Xu, L., Chen, Y.: Incremental network quantization: towards lossless CNNs with low-precision weights. In: Proceedings of International Conference on Learning Representations (2017)

57. Zhou, S., Wu, Y., Ni, Z., Zhou, X., Wen, H., Zou, Y.: Dorefa-Net: training low bitwidth convolutional neural networks with low bitwidth gradients. In: Proceedings of IEEE Conference on Computer Vision and Pattern Recognition (2016)

58. Zhu, C., Han, S., Mao, H., Dally, W.J.: Trained ternary quantization. In: Proceedings of International Conference on Learning Representations (2017)

End-to-End View Synthesis for Light Field Imaging with Pseudo 4DCNN

Yunlong Wang[1,2], Fei Liu[2], Zilei Wang[1], Guangqi Hou[2],
Zhenan Sun[2(✉)], and Tieniu Tan[1,2]

[1] University of Science and Technology of China, Hefei, China
zlwang@ustc.edu.cn
[2] Center for Research on Intelligent Perception and Computing,
National Laboratory of Pattern Recognition,
Institute of Automation, Chinese Academy of Sciences, Beijing, China
{yunlong.wang,fei.liu}@cripac.ia.ac.cn, {gqhou,znsun,tnt}@nlpr.ia.ac.cn

Abstract. Limited angular resolution has become the main bottleneck of microlens-based plenoptic cameras towards practical vision applications. Existing view synthesis methods mainly break the task into two steps, *i.e.* depth estimating and view warping, which are usually inefficient and produce artifacts over depth ambiguities. In this paper, an end-to-end deep learning framework is proposed to solve these problems by exploring Pseudo 4DCNN. Specifically, 2D strided convolutions operated on stacked EPIs and detail-restoration 3D CNNs connected with angular conversion are assembled to build the Pseudo 4DCNN. The key advantage is to efficiently synthesize dense 4D light fields from a sparse set of input views. The learning framework is well formulated as an entirely trainable problem, and all the weights can be recursively updated with standard backpropagation. The proposed framework is compared with state-of-the-art approaches on both genuine and synthetic light field databases, which achieves significant improvements of both image quality (*+2* dB *higher*) and computational efficiency (*over 10X faster*). Furthermore, the proposed framework shows good performances in real-world applications such as biometrics and depth estimation.

Keywords: View synthesis · Light Field · End-to-end
Pseudo 4DCNN

1 Introduction

As a revolutionary imaging technology, Light Field (LF) imaging [1,11,14,23] has attracted extensive attention from both academia and industry, especially with the emergence of commercial plenoptic cameras [16] and recent dedication in the field of Virtual Reality (VR) and Augmented Reality (AR) [8]. With additional optical components like the microlens array inserted between the main lens and the image sensor, plenoptic cameras are capable of capturing both intensity and direction information of rays from real-world scenes, which enables

© Springer Nature Switzerland AG 2018
V. Ferrari et al. (Eds.): ECCV 2018, LNCS 11206, pp. 340–355, 2018.
https://doi.org/10.1007/978-3-030-01216-8_21

applications such as refocusing and 3D display. However, the inherent tradeoff between angular and spatial resolution is inevitable due to the limited sensor resolution, which restricts LF imaging in many practical vision applications.

One possible solution to this problem is view synthesis, which synthesizes novel views from a sparse set of input views. Inspired by traditional view synthesis approaches and recent success of data-driven methods, Kalantari et al. [9] break down the goal of view synthesis into the disparity estimator and color predictor modeled by convolutional neural network (CNN). Since disparities are implicitly inferred from the first CNN, it obtains better results than other state-of-the-art (SOTA) methods [12,21,22] that require explicit depth[1] information as priors for view warping. However, this framework is quite limited in reconstructing challenging LF scenes, such as occluded regions, non-Lambertian surfaces, etc. Actually, depth-dependent view synthesis methods inevitably rely on the accuracy of depth information, which tends to produce artifacts where inaccurate depth estimation usually happens. Moreover, they mostly generate a single novel view so that it is rather inefficient to synthesize all the in-between views.

Recently, Wu et al. [24] firstly model view synthesis as learning-based angular detail restoration on 2D Epipolar Plane Images (EPIs). They propose a "blur-restoration-deblur" framework without estimating the geometry of the scene. It achieves superior results than Kalantari et al. [9] on a variety of scenes, even in the occluded regions, non-Lambertian surfaces and transparent regions. However, their framework still has some shortcomings. Firstly, the full LF data is underused since EPIs are just 2D slices of 4D LF. Secondly, it is quite time-consuming because the operations of "blur-restoration-deblur" on EPIs loop numerous times before all the in-between views are synthesized.

In fact, 4D LF data are highly correlated in ray space, which record abundant information of the scene. The key insight of view synthesis for light field imaging is to make full use of the input views. Unlike 2D array or 3D volume, it is proved to be a tough problem working on the high dimensional data with CNN currently. Therefore, there scarcely exist approaches that address the problem of view synthesis in this way. In this paper, we propose an end-to-end learning framework that efficiently synthesizes dense 4D LF from sparse input views. Specifically, the learnable interpolation using 2D strided convolutions is applied on stacked EPIs to initially upsample 3D volumes extracted from LF data. Then, 3D CNNs are employed to recover high-frequency details of volumes in the row or column pattern. The angular conversion is introduced as the joint component to transform from receiving output of row network to giving input of column network. Moreover, a prior sensitive loss function is proposed to measure the errors of synthesized views according to the level of received prior knowledge. The learning framework is well formulated as an entirely trainable problem and all the weights can be recursively updated with standard backpropagation.

Experimental results on a variety of challenging scenes, including depth variations, complex light conditions, severe occlusions, non-Lambertian surfaces and

---

[1] depth and disparity are used interchangeably throughout the paper, since they are closely related in structured light fields.

so on, demonstrate that the proposed framework significantly outperforms other SOTA approaches with higher numerical quality and better visual effect. By directly operating on 4D LF data, the proposed framework also greatly accelerates the process of view synthesis, over one order of magnitude faster than other SOTA methods.

1.1 Depth-Dependent View Synthesis

Generally, depth-dependent view synthesis approaches synthesize novel views of a scene in a two-step process [3,5], *i.e.* estimating disparities of the input views and warping to the novel views based on the disparities, then combining warped images in a specific way (*e.g.* weighted summation) to obtain the final novel views.

Wanner and Goldluecke [22] propose the optimization framework to synthesize novel views with explicit geometry information, which only performs well for synthetic scenes with ground truth disparities, but produces significant artifacts for real-world scenes. The phase-based approach by Zhang *et al.* [28] reconstructs LF from a micro-baseline stereo pair. However, it is quite time-consuming for refining the disparity iteratively. The patch-based synthesis method by Zhang *et al.* [27] decomposes the disparity map into different layers and requires user interactions for various LF editing goals. Note that even state-of-the-art LF depth estimation methods are not specifically designed to be suitable for pixel warping. Thus view synthesis approaches that take explicit depth as priors usually fail to reconstruct plausible results for real-world scenes.

To alleviate the need of explicit depth information for view-warping, another strategy aims to synthesize novel views along with implicitly estimating the geometry of the scene. Kalantari *et al.* [9] propose the first deep learning system for view synthesis. Inspired by aforementioned methods, they factorize view synthesis into the disparity estimator and color predictor modeled by CNNs. Both networks are trained simultaneously by minimizing the error between the synthesized view and the ground truth. Thus, the disparity for view-warping is implicitly produced by the first CNN, which is more suitable for view synthesis application. However, this method is quite limited in reconstructing challenging LF scenes due to the insufficient information of warped images. Srinivasan *et al.* [18] build on the pipeline similar to Kalantari *et al.* [9], and synthesize a 4D RGBD LF from a single 2D RGB image. Overall, depth-dependent view synthesis strongly depends on the depth information. For challenging scenes that contain significant depth variations, complex lighting conditions, occlusions, non-Lambertian surfaces, *etc*, where inaccurate depth estimation usually happens, these methods tend to fail since the warped images are not able to provide sufficient information to synthesize high-quality views.

1.2 Depth-Independent View Synthesis

Alternative approaches for view synthesis are to upsample the angular dimensions without any geometry information of the scene. Some depth-independent methods are designed to process the input LF sampled in specific patterns. For example, Levin and Durand [10] exploit dimensionality gap priors to synthesize novel views from a set of images sampled in a circular pattern. Shi *et al.* [17] sample a small number of 1D viewpoint trajectories formed by a box and two diagonals to recover 4D LF. To capture input views in such specific pattern is rather difficult, and thus these methods are still far from practical applications.

Many learning-based methods working on angular SR of LF have been proposed recently. Yoon *et al.* [26] propose a deep learning framework called LFCNN, in which two adjacent views are employed to generate the in-between view. In the successive work [25], some modifications are applied to the network structure but with the same input organization strategy as [26]. These methods can not make full use of the angular domain as only a couple of sub-aperture images around the novel view are fed into the network. Besides, it can only generate novel views at 2X upsampling factor.

Wu *et al.* [24] model view synthesis as learning-based angular detail restoration on 2D EPIs. A "blur-restoration-deblur" framework is presented that consists of three steps: firstly, the input EPI is convolved with a predefined blur kernel; secondly, a CNN is applied to restore the angular detail of the EPI damaged by the undersampling; finally, a non-blind deconvolution is operated to recover the spatial detail suppressed by the EPI blur. It achieves promising results on a variety of scenes, but there are still some shortcomings: the potential of the full LF data is underused; the operations of "blur-restoration-deblur" loop numerous times before all the in-between views are synthesized.

To sum up, the key insight of view synthesis is to make full use of the input views. To reduce the difficulty of collecting data, it is appropriate that the input views are regularly spaced on a grid. Besides, it is rather difficult to work on the high dimensional data with current CNN frameworks. In this paper, an end-to-end framework called Pseudo 4DCNN is proposed to efficiently synthesize novel views of densely sampled LF from sparse input views.

2 Methodology

2.1 Problem Formulation

In this paper, 4D LF data are denoted as $L(x, y, s, t)$ decoded from the LF raw image as depicted in Fig. 1. Each light ray is illustrated by the interactions with two parallel planes, travelling from the angular coordinate (s, t) on the main lens plane to the spatial coordinate (x, y) on the microlens array plane.

Given $n \times n$ sparse input views on a grid at the spatial resolution of $H \times W$, the goal of view synthesis for LF imaging is to restore a more densely sampled LF at the resolution of (H, W, N, N), where $N = f \times (n - 1) + 1$ and f is the upsampling factor in the angular dimension.

As shown in Fig. 1, EPI is a 2D slice of 4D LF by fixing one angular dimension and one spatial dimension. The framework proposed by Wu *et al.* [24] is based on restoration of 2D EPIs, enhancing one angular dimension s or t. 3D volume from 4D LF like $V_{t^*}(x, y, s)$ can be extracted by fixing one angular dimension $(t = t^*)$, which consists of stacked 2D EPIs. To directly process 4D LF, we assemble 2D strided convolutions on stacked EPIs and sequential 3D CNNs connected with angular conversion to build Pseudo 4DCNN. The proposed framework is well formulated to be entirely differentiable, which makes the learning process more tractable. In the next section, the proposed framework is described in detail.

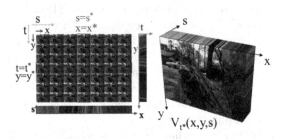

Fig. 1. 4D light fields $L(x, y, s, t)$. A horizontal EPI is a 2D (x, s) slice $L(x, y^*, s, t^*)$ by setting $y = y^*$ and $t = t^*$, and a vertical EPI (y, t) by setting $x = x^*$ and $s = s^*$. By analogy, 3D volume $V_{t^*}(x, y, s)$ can be extracted by setting $t = t^*$.

2.2   Proposed Framework

Overview. Given input sparse views $L_0(x, y, s, t)$ with the resolution of (H, W, n, n) depicted as Fig. 2, we fix one angular dimension $t = t^*, t^* \in \{1, 2, \ldots, n\}$ to extract 3D volume with the resolution of (H, W, n) as

$$V_{t^*}(x, y, s) = L_0(x, y, s, t^*) \tag{1}$$

$V_{t^*}(x, y, s)$ are interpolated as $V_{t^*}(x, y, s) \uparrow$ to the desired resolution (H, W, N) given the upsampling factor. The high-frequency details of $V_{t^*}(x, y, s) \uparrow$ are restored by the row network modeling as $F_r(\cdot)$, and then form the intermediate LF as

$$L_{inter}(x, y, s, t^*) = F_r(V_{t^*}(x, y, s) \uparrow) \tag{2}$$

Next, we perform angular conversion to transform from the angular dimension t to dimension s. By fixing $s = s^*, s^* \in \{1, 2, \ldots, N\}$, $V_{s^*}(x, y, t)$ are extracted from $L_{inter}(x, y, s^*, t)$ as

$$V_{s^*}(x, y, t) = L_{inter}(x, y, s^*, t) \tag{3}$$

with the resolution of (H, W, n), which is also interpolated to $V_{s^*}(x, y, t) \uparrow$ at the same resolution as $V_{t^*}(x, y, s) \uparrow$. The column network is then employed to recover details of $V_{s^*}(x, y, t) \uparrow$, modeling as $F_c(\cdot)$. Finally, the output $L_{out}(x, y, s, t)$ with the resolution of (H, W, N, N) are formed as

$$L_{out}(x, y, s^*, t) = F_c(V_{s^*}(x, y, t) \uparrow) \tag{4}$$

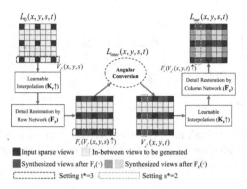

Fig. 2. Overview of the proposed framework Pseudo 4DCNN. Take reconstructing 7×7 LF data from 3×3 sparse views for example ($n = 3, N = 7, t^* = 3, s^* = 2$).

Learnable Interpolation on 3D Volumes. Volumes $V_{t^*}(x, y, s)$ and $V_{s^*}(x, y, t)$ consist of two spatial dimensions and one angular dimension as Fig. 1. Take $V_{t^*}(x, y, s)$ as an example, they can be regarded as n sub-aperture images with the resolution of (H, W), and are also composed of W stacked EPIs with the resolution of (H, n). Long et al. [13] state that upsampling can be performed using fractionally strided convolution. By reversing the forward and backward passes of convolution, the interpolation kernel for upsampling can be learned through end-to-end training with backpropagation. Rather than fixed interpolation on a single EPI, we introduce the learnable interpolation on stacked EPIs in 3D volumes using a deconvolutional layer as

$$V_{t^*}(x, y^*, s) \uparrow = deconv(V_{t^*}(x, y^*, s), f, K_r) \tag{5}$$

where $V_{t^*}(x, y^*, s)$ is a 2D EPI slice inside the 3D volume $V_{t^*}(x, y, s)$ by fixing $y = y^*$, f is the desired upsampling factor and K_r is the learnable kernel.

Another deconvolutional layer is employed to upsample $V_{s^*}(x, y, t)$ as

$$V_{s^*}(x^*, y, t) \uparrow = deconv(V_{s^*}(x^*, y, t), f, K_c) \tag{6}$$

As deconvolutional layers are differentiable, the learnable interpolation enables the proposed framework to be trained in an end-to-end strategy.

Detail Restoration Using 3D CNNs. 3D Convolutional Neural networks [15,19] are mostly applied to extract spatio-temporal features among frames for video analysis. Instead, we employ 3D CNNs and the residual learning [6] to recover high-frequency details of 3D volumes extracted from 4D LF.

In order to ensure efficiency, the proposed network $F_r(\cdot)$ and $F_c(\cdot)$ are of the same structure, which is lightweight and simple. As depicted in Fig. 3, both networks consist of two hidden layers followed by the sum of the predicted residual $\Re(V)$ and the input volume V as $F(V) = V + \Re(V)$. The first 3D convolutional layer comprises 64 channels with the kernel $5 \times 5 \times 3$, where each kernel operates

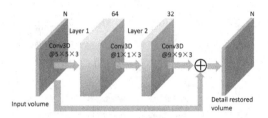

Fig. 3. Structure of the network for recovering details of 3D volumes. Layer 1 and layer 2 are followed by a rectified linear unit (ReLU). The final detail restored volume is the sum of the predicted residual and the input.

on 5×5 spatial region across 3 adjacent views inside V. Therefore, the size of filters W_1 in the first layer is $64 \times N \times 5 \times 5 \times 3$ and the size of bias b_1 is 64. Similarly, the second 3D convolutional layer comprises 32 channels with the kernel $1 \times 1 \times 3$, where each kernel operates on 1×1 spatial region (*i.e.* single pixel) across 3 adjacent slices of feature maps of the first layer. The size of filters W_2 in the second layer is $32 \times 64 \times 1 \times 1 \times 3$ and the size of bias b_2 is 32. The output layer of the network for the residual prediction utilizes $9 \times 9 \times 3$ filter, and thus the size of filters W_o in this layer is $N \times 32 \times 9 \times 9 \times 3$ and the size of bias b_o is N. Note that the first and second layers are activated by the rectified linear unit (ReLU), *i.e.* $\sigma(x) = \max(0, x)$, while the output layer is not followed by any activation layer. The residual prediction is formulated as

$$\Re(V) = W_o * \sigma(W_2 * \sigma(W_1 * V + b_1) + b_2) + b_o \tag{7}$$

where $*$ denotes the 3D convolution operation. To avoid border effects, we appropriately pad the input and feature maps before every convolution operations to maintain the input and output at the same size.

Prior Sensitive Loss Function. The proposed framework is designed to directly reconstruct the desired 4D LF. Rather than minimizing the L_2 distance between a pair of synthesized and ground truth images in [9] or between a pair of detail restored and ground truth EPIs in [24], the prior sensitive loss function is specifically formulated as follows:

$$E = \frac{1}{2N^2} \sum_{s^*=1, t^*=1}^{N} w_{s^* t^*} \| L_{gt}(s^*, t^*) - L_{out}(s^*, t^*) \|^2 \tag{8}$$

where the loss E is a weighted average over the entire mean squared errors (MSE) between the reconstructed L_{out} and ground truth L_{gt}.

Novel views generated in the later stage of the pipeline receive less prior information from the sparse input views as shown in Fig. 2. For instance, synthesized views after the row network $F_r(\cdot)$ are inferred from the input views, while a portion of those views synthesized after the column network $F_c(\cdot)$ only receive prior information propagated from earlier synthesized views. Hence, we design a prior sensitive scheme which pays more attention to the errors of the later synthesized views by using larger weights. According to the order that views are generated and the level of received prior knowledge, all the synthesized views are divided into four groups and their MSE against the ground truth are summed up with corresponding weights. The weighting coefficient $w_{s^*t^*}$ for the synthesized view at (s^*, t^*) is particularly set as

$$
w_{s^*t^*} = \begin{cases} \lambda_1 & s^* \in [1 : f : N], t^* \in [1 : f : N] \\ \lambda_2 & s^* \in [1 : f : N], t^* \notin [1 : f : N] \\ \lambda_3 & s^* \notin [1 : f : N], t^* \in [1 : f : N] \\ \lambda_4 & s^* \notin [1 : f : N], t^* \notin [1 : f : N] \end{cases} \tag{9}
$$

Empirically, $\lambda_1, \lambda_2, \lambda_3, \lambda_4$ are set to 0.1, 1, 1 and 2 relatively.

Derivation on End-to-End Training. As the proposed system comprises 2D strided convolutions and detail-restoration 3D CNNs connected with angular conversion, it is non-trivial to train the networks with standard backpropagation. We analyze in detail that the proposed framework is entirely differentiable and all the weights can be recursively updated with standard backpropagation.

Firstly, we calculate the partial derivative of the loss E with respect to the intermediate LF $L_{inter}(x, y, s, t)$ using chain rule as

$$
\frac{\partial E}{\partial L_{inter}(x, y, s, t)} = \frac{\partial E}{\partial L_{out}(x, y, s, t)} \cdot \frac{\partial L_{out}(x, y, s, t)}{\partial L_{inter}(x, y, s, t)} \tag{10}
$$

according to Eq. 8, the first term on the right-hand side of Eq. 10 is derivable. The second term can be derived as

$$
\frac{\partial L_{out}(x, y, s, t)}{\partial L_{inter}(x, y, s, t)} = \sum_{s^*=1}^{N} \frac{\partial L_{out}(x, y, s^*, t)}{\partial V_{s^*}(x, y, t) \uparrow} \cdot \frac{\partial V_{s^*}(x, y, t) \uparrow}{\partial V_{s^*}(x, y, t)} \tag{11}
$$

The partial derivative of $L_{out}(x, y, s, t)$ with respect to $L_{inter}(x, y, s, t)$ is the sum of N partial derivatives of $L_{out}(x, y, s^*, t)$ with respect to $V_{s^*}(x, y, t)$. The first term on the right-hand side of Eq. 11 is apparently differentiable since it is the partial derivative of the output of the column network $F_c(\cdot)$ with respect to its input as Eq. 4. Further, the second term can be derived as

$$
\frac{\partial V_{s^*}(x, y, t) \uparrow}{\partial V_{s^*}(x, y, t)} = \sum_{x^*=1}^{H} \frac{\partial V_{s^*}(x^*, y, t) \uparrow}{\partial V_{s^*}(x^*, y, t)} \tag{12}
$$

the term on the right-hand side attributes its partial derivative to upsampling on EPIs using the learnable interpolation as Eq. 6. At this point, we have proved that the term on the left-hand side of Eq. 10 is differentiable.

The angular conversion operates on $L_{inter}(x, y, s, t)$ to transform from receiving output of the row network $F_r(V_{t^*}(x, y, s) \uparrow)$ to giving input of the column network $V_{s^*}(x, y, t)$, and thus there are no parameters in this component. Next, we calculate the partial derivative of $L_{inter}(x, y, s, t)$ with respect to the input sparse LF $L_0(x, y, s, t)$ as

$$\frac{\partial L_{inter}(x, y, s, t)}{\partial L_0(x, y, s, t)} = \sum_{t^*=1}^{n} \frac{\partial L_{inter}(x, y, s, t^*)}{\partial V_{t^*}(x, y, s) \uparrow} \cdot \frac{\partial V_{t^*}(x, y, s) \uparrow}{\partial V_{t^*}(x, y, s)} \qquad (13)$$

Similarly, it can be deduced that the first term on the right-hand side of Eq. 13 is differentiable because the numerator and the denominator of this term correspond exactly to the output and input of the row network $F_r(\cdot)$ as Eq. 2. The second term can be further derived as

$$\frac{\partial V_{t^*}(x, y, s) \uparrow}{\partial V_{t^*}(x, y, s)} = \sum_{y^*=1}^{W} \frac{\partial V_{t^*}(x, y^*, s) \uparrow}{\partial V_{t^*}(x, y^*, s)} \qquad (14)$$

the term on the right-hand side of Eq. 14 is also differentiable since $V_{t^*}(x, y^*, s)$ is upsampled to $V_{t^*}(x, y^*, s) \uparrow$ by the learnable interpolation as Eq. 5. Overall, the partial derivative of the loss E with respect to the input $L_0(x, y, s, t)$ is derived as

$$\frac{\partial E}{\partial L_0(x, y, s, t)} = \frac{\partial E}{\partial L_{inter}(x, y, s, t)} \cdot \frac{\partial L_{inter}(x, y, s, t)}{\partial L_0(x, y, s, t)} \qquad (15)$$

Considering Eqs. 10 and 13, it can be concluded that the proposed framework is entirely differentiable. Due to space limitations, formulations about the gradients of upsampling kernels and weights in the row or column network are not presented here.

2.3 Training Details

To train the proposed framework, we take over 300 LF samples with various lighting conditions, texture properties and depth variations through Lytro Illum and the lab-developed LF camera under indoor and outdoor environment. The LF raw images are decoded via Light Field Toolbox v0.4 [4]. LF images captured by Lytro Illum are with the spatial resolution 625×434 and angular resolution 9×9, while 729×452 and 11×11 respectively by the lab-developed LF camera.

Specifically, small patches in the same position of each view are extracted to formulate the training LF data. The spatial patch size is 48×48 and the stride is 20. If the angular upsampling factor is $3X$, we remove the border views and crop the original LF data to 7×7 views as ground truth, and then downsample to 3×3 views as the input. For $2X$ angular upsampling, the original LF data are just downsampled to 5×5 views. We cascade the proposed framework trained for $2X$ to deal with $4X$ angular upsampling.

In total, over 10^5 training samples are collected. Similar to other SR methods, we only process the luminance Y channel in the YCrcb color space. Since the proposed framework comprises two detail-restoration 3D CNNs connected with angular conversion, operating firstly in row or column pattern is prone to influence the accuracy of the final output. To alleviate such effect, we double the training datasets by adding a copy of each LF sample with permuted angular dimensions.

The optimization of end-to-end training is conducted by the mini-batch momentum Stochastic Gradient Descent (SGD) method with a batch size of 64, momentum of 0.9 and weight decay of 0.001. The kernels of the learnable interpolation are initialized exactly like the bilinear upsampling. The filters of 3D CNNs are initialized from a zero-mean Gaussian distribution with standard deviation 0.01 and all the bias are initialized to zero. The learning rate is initially set to 10^{-4} and then decreased by a factor of 0.1 every 10 epochs until the validation loss converges. The proposed framework is implemented using Theano package [2] and proceeded on a workstation with an Intel 3.6 GHz CPU and a TiTan X GPU. Training takes within 8 h to converge.

3   Experimental Results and Applications

To validate the efficiency and effectiveness of the proposed framework, we compare with two recent state-of-the-art approaches, *i.e.* the depth-dependent method by Kalantari *et al.* [9] and depth-independent method by Wu *et al.* [24]. Experiments are carried out on various datasets for evaluating the robustness, including real-world scenes, synthetic scenes and biometrics data. The peak signal-to-noise ratio (PSNR), the gray-scale structural similarity (SSIM) and elapsed time per synthesized view are utilized to evaluate the algorithms numerically.

3.1   Real-World Scenes

As to experiments on real-world scenes, we follow the protocols in [24] to reconstruct 7×7 LF from 3×3 sparse views on *30 Scenes* captured by Lytro Illum in [9]. The performances of comparative methods [9,24] are obtained via implementing source codes released by respective authors, and the parameters are carefully tuned to maximize performances. For fair comparisons, all methods run in the GPU mode and are proceeded on the same workstation.

Figure 4 depicts quantitative comparisons of the average PSNR and elapsed time on *30 scenes* [9]. It is easy to find out that the proposed framework performs significantly better than other approaches: (1) greatly accelerates the process of view synthesis (0.28 s), (2) strongly improves the image quality of reconstructed 4D LF (43.28 dB). As demonstrated by numerical results, the proposed framework gains huge advantages in terms of both efficiency and effectiveness. Moreover, we conduct ablation experiments on *30 Scenes* with variants of Pseudo 4DCNN. As shown in Table 1, if F_c equals to F_r, the results decrease 0.38dB on average. Also, the results decrease 0.94 dB on average without prior sensitive loss. It can be demonstrated that each component of Pseudo 4DCNN definitely contributes to improving the performance.

For qualitative comparisons, we select two challenging outdoor scenes (*Rock, Flower*) containing complex depth variations and occlusions as shown in Fig. 5.

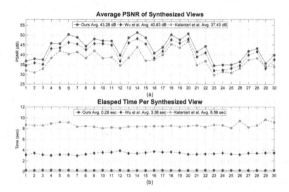

Fig. 4. Quantitative comparisons on real-world scenes (*30 scenes* [9]). The lateral axis represents scene No. from 1 to 30. (a) Average PSNR statistics. The proposed framework achieves **43.28** dB per LF scene on average, **5.85** dB higher than Kalantari *et al.* [9] (**37.43** dB) and **2.45** dB higher than Wu *et al.* [24] (**40.83** dB). (b) Elapsed time statistics. The proposed framework takes **0.28** s per synthesized view on average to reconstruct 7 × 7 LF from 3 × 3 views (angular upsampling factor 3X) at the spatial resolution of 625 × 434, nearly **30X** faster than Kalantari *et al.* [9] (**8.59** s) and **12X** faster than Wu *et al.* [24] (**3.38** s). So the proposed framework greatly improves the accuracy and accelerates the process of view synthesis for LF imaging.

The depth-dependent method in [9] is not sensitive to depth changes in small areas, leading to large errors around object boundaries and depth discontinuities. The "blur-restore-deblur" scheme in [24] fails to reconstruct plausible details for small objects at a far distance, *e.g.* the white car in *Rock*, the background tree in *Flower*. As shown in the last column, our results are closer to ground truth. **Enlarge and view these figures on screen for better comparisons. See more comparisons in the supplement.**

Table 1. Quantitative comparisons on *30 Scenes* with variants of Pseudo 4DCNN.

	PSNR (dB)	SSIM
Pseudo-4DCNN full	**43.28**	**0.9916**
Same sub-networks ($F_r = F_c$)	42.90	0.9907
Without prior sensitive loss	42.34	0.9901
Without 2D learnable interpolation	40.15	0.9885
Without 3D detail-restoration CNN	39.01	0.9876

3.2   Synthetic Scenes

The synthetic experimental results are shown in Table 2, including two challenging scenes *Kitchen* and *Museum* from the LF datasets by Honauer *et al.* [7]. The spatial resolution is 512 × 512 and angular resolution 9 × 9. The central 7 × 7 views are extracted as ground truth, and 3 × 3 sparse views are taken as input.

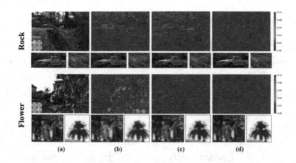

Fig. 5. Qualitative comparisons on *30 scenes* [9]. The ground truth view, error maps in the Y channel, and close-ups of image patches are presented. (a) Ground Truth. (b) Kalantari *et al.* [9] (c) Wu *et al.* [24] (d) Ours.

Transparent glasses in *Museum* and highlights in *Kitchen* are extremely difficult for view synthesis. The disparity estimator network in [9] fails to estimate reasonable disparities for non-Lambertian surfaces, especially at the boundaries. Significant artifacts are produced at the boundaries and geometry structures of transparent surfaces can not be preserved (Fig. 6). The method in [24] reconstructs better photo-realistic details than [9]. The proposed framework achieves the best performance, which is quite robust to specular reflection properties.

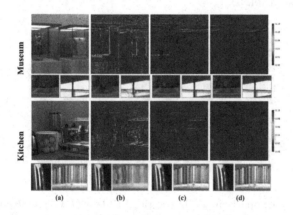

Fig. 6. Qualitative Comparisons on synthetic scenes. (*Kitchen* and *Museum*) (a) Ground Truth. (b) Kalantari *et al.* [9] (c) Wu *et al.* [24] (d) Ours.

Table 2. Quantitative comparisons on synthetic scenes (*Kitchen* and *Museum*).

	Kitchen		Museum	
	PSNR	SSIM	PSNR	SSIM
Kalantari *et al.* [9]	32.13	0.9156	30.45	0.9097
Wu *et al.* [24]	35.57	0.9360	34.98	0.9344
Ours	**38.12**	**0.9621**	**37.92**	**0.9559**

3.3   Application for Biometrics LF Data

For potential applications on biometrics, we capture a midsize LF dataset with over 200 face scenes (*Face*) and 100 iris scenes (*Iris*). *Face* is captured using Lytro Illum under natural lighting. Each scene contains 3 persons standing 0.2 m, 1 m, 3 m, and the faces are roughly 200 × 200, 100 × 100, 60 × 60 pixels on each sub-aperture image. *Iris* is captured under near infrared lighting with our lab-developed LF camera. Our LF camera is microlens-based and equipped with *240* um/*f4* microlens and a *135* mm/*f5.6* main lens. By setting the capturing distance 0.8 m, the iris on each sub-aperture image is around 90 pixels. We reconstruct 9 × 9 light fields from 5 × 5 sparse views on these biometrics LF data.

The bottleneck of view synthesis on *Face* is that severe defocus blur arises on the face outside depth of field (DOF). In Fig. 7, large errors around the eyes are occurred by [9] and the eyelid area are over-smoothed by [24]. Although LF cameras gain advantages in extending DOF that is beneficial for iris recognition, to obtain a LF iris image is greatly influenced by the specular reflection of the cornea region. Besides, the depth range of iris varies relatively small while the textures are very rich. As a consequence, [9] produces over-smoothed results without enough texture details on iris, and [24] recovers better textures of the iris but can not preserve details on the glossy area of the face. In contrast, the proposed framework obtains superior performances in both terms of efficiency and effectiveness (Table 3).

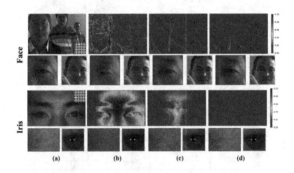

Fig. 7. Qualitative comparisons on biometrics LF data (*Face* and *Iris*). (a) Ground Truth. (b) Kalantari *et al.* [9] (c) Wu *et al.* [24] (d) Ours.

Table 3. Quantitative comparisons on biometrics LF data (*Face* and *Iris*).

	Face			Iris		
	PSNR	SSIM	Time (sec)	PSNR	SSIM	Time (sec)
Kalantari *et al.* [9]	29.50	0.8660	724.48	25.17	0.8235	904.02
Wu *et al.* [24]	40.04	0.9624	262.38	34.98	0.9344	339.71
Ours	**42.36**	**0.9869**	**23.49**	**40.14**	**0.9851**	**30.42**

3.4   Application for Depth Enhancement

We evaluate the accuracy and robustness of the proposed framework for depth enhancement. Table 4 shows quantitative comparisons on various scenes as well as challenging parts. It is observed that the depth maps with our reconstructed LF are roughly the same as depth maps with ground truth LF. The proposed framework will effectively contribute to depth enhancement of LF imaging.

Table 4. MSE statistics of depth estimation on the 4D LF benchmark [7] using the algorithm of Wang *et al.* [20].

Scenes		Wu *et al.* [24]	GT LF	**Ours**
Backgammon	Overall	0.1471	0.1307	**0.1181**
	Foreground fattening	0.1947	0.1680	**0.1601**
Pyramids	Overall	0.0214	**0.0191**	0.0193
	Pyramids	0.0117	0.0116	**0.0111**
Boxes	Overall	0.0512	**0.0497**	0.0507
	Fine surrounding	0.0312	**0.0287**	0.0303
Dino	Overall	0.0186	**0.0159**	**0.0159**
	Discontinuities	0.0174	**0.0161**	0.0163

4   Conclusion

In this paper, an end-to-end learning framework is proposed to directly synthesize novel views of dense 4D LF from sparse input views. To directly process high dimensional LF data, we assemble 2D strided convolutions operated on stacked EPIs and two detail-restoration 3D CNNs connected with angular conversion to build Pseudo 4DCNN. The proposed framework is well formulated to be entirely differentiable that can be trained with standard backpropagation. The proposed framework outperforms other SOTA approaches on various LF scenes. What's more, it greatly accelerates the process of view synthesis for LF imaging.

Acknowledgement. This work is funded by National Natural Science Foundation of China (Grant No. 61427811, 61573360) and National Key Research and Development Program of China (Grant No. 2016YFB1001000, No. 2017YFB0801900).

References

1. Adelson, E.H., Bergen, J.R.: The plenoptic function and the elements of early vision. In: Computational Models of Visual Processing, pp. 3–20. MIT Press (1991)
2. Al-Rfou, R., et al.: Theano: a Python framework for fast computation of mathematical expressions. arXiv preprint (2016)

3. Chaurasia, G., Duchene, S., Sorkine-Hornung, O., Drettakis, G.: Depth synthesis and local warps for plausible image-based navigation. ACM Trans. Graph. (TOG) **32**(3), 30 (2013)
4. Dansereau, D.G., Pizarro, O., Williams, S.B.: Decoding, calibration and rectification for lenselet-based plenoptic cameras. In: Proceedings of the IEEE Conference on Computer Vision and Pattern Recognition, pp. 1027–1034 (2013)
5. Eisemann, M., et al.: Floating textures. In: Computer Graphics Forum, vol. 27, pp. 409–418. Wiley Online Library (2008)
6. He, K., Zhang, X., Ren, S., Sun, J.: Deep residual learning for image recognition. In: Proceedings of the IEEE Conference on Computer Vision and Pattern Recognition, pp. 770–778 (2016)
7. Honauer, K., Johannsen, O., Kondermann, D., Goldluecke, B.: A dataset and evaluation methodology for depth estimation on 4D light fields. In: Lai, S.-H., Lepetit, V., Nishino, K., Sato, Y. (eds.) ACCV 2016. LNCS, vol. 10113, pp. 19–34. Springer, Cham (2017). https://doi.org/10.1007/978-3-319-54187-7_2
8. Huang, F.C., Chen, K., Wetzstein, G.: The light field stereoscope: immersive computer graphics via factored near-eye light field displays with focus cues. ACM Trans. Graph. (TOG) **34**(4), 60 (2015)
9. Kalantari, N.K., Wang, T.C., Ramamoorthi, R.: Learning-based view synthesis for light field cameras. ACM Trans. Graph. (TOG) **35**(6), 193 (2016)
10. Levin, A., Durand, F.: Linear view synthesis using a dimensionality gap light field prior. In: 2010 IEEE Conference on Computer Vision and Pattern Recognition, CVPR, pp. 1831–1838. IEEE (2010)
11. Levoy, M., Hanrahan, P.: Light field rendering. In: Proceedings of the 23rd Annual Conference on Computer Graphics and Interactive Techniques, pp. 31–42 (1996)
12. Liu, F., Hou, G., Sun, Z., Tan, T.: High quality depth map estimation of object surface from light-field images. Neurocomputing **252**, 3–16 (2017)
13. Long, J., Shelhamer, E., Darrell, T.: Fully convolutional networks for semantic segmentation. In: Proceedings of the IEEE Conference on Computer Vision and Pattern Recognition, pp. 3431–3440 (2015)
14. Ng, R., Levoy, M., Brédif, M., Duval, G., Horowitz, M., Hanrahan, P.: Light field photography with a hand-held plenoptic camera. Computer Science Technical report CSTR, vol. 2, no. 11, pp. 1–11 (2005)
15. Qi, C.R., Su, H., Nießner, M., Dai, A., Yan, M., Guibas, L.J.: Volumetric and multi-view CNNs for object classification on 3D data. In: Proceedings of the IEEE Conference on Computer Vision and Pattern Recognition, pp. 5648–5656 (2016)
16. Raytrix: 3D light field camera technology. http://www.raytrix.de/
17. Shi, L., Hassanieh, H., Davis, A., Katabi, D., Durand, F.: Light field reconstruction using sparsity in the continuous Fourier domain. ACM Trans. Graph. (TOG) **34**(1), 12 (2014)
18. Srinivasan, P.P., Wang, T., Sreelal, A., Ramamoorthi, R., Ng, R.: Learning to synthesize a 4D RGBD light field from a single image. In: International Conference on Computer Vision, ICCV, pp. 2262–2270 (2017)
19. Tran, D., Bourdev, L., Fergus, R., Torresani, L., Paluri, M.: Learning spatiotemporal features with 3D convolutional networks. In: Proceedings of the IEEE International Conference on Computer Vision, pp. 4489–4497 (2015)
20. Wang, T.C., Efros, A., Ramamoorthi, R.: Occlusion-aware depth estimation using light-field cameras. In: IEEE International Conference on Computer Vision, ICCV, pp. 3487–3495 (2015)

21. Wang, T.C., Efros, A.A., Ramamoorthi, R.: Depth estimation with occlusion modeling using light-field cameras. IEEE Trans. Pattern Anal. Mach. Intell. (TPAMI) **38**(11), 2170–2181 (2016)
22. Wanner, S., Goldluecke, B.: Variational light field analysis for disparity estimation and super-resolution. IEEE Trans. Pattern Anal. Mach. Intell. **36**(3), 606–619 (2014)
23. Wu, G., et al.: Light field image processing: an overview. IEEE J. Sel. Top. Signal Process. (JSTSP) **11**, 926–954 (2017)
24. Wu, G., Zhao, M., Wang, L., Dai, Q., Chai, T., Liu, Y.: Light field reconstruction using deep convolutional network on EPI. In: IEEE Conference on Computer Vision and Pattern Recognition, CVPR, pp. 1638–1646 (2017)
25. Yoon, Y., Jeon, H.G., Yoo, D., Lee, J.Y., Kweon, I.S.: Light-field image super-resolution using convolutional neural network. IEEE Signal Process. Lett. **24**(6), 848–852 (2017)
26. Yoon, Y., Jeon, H.G., Yoo, D., Lee, J.Y., So Kweon, I.: Learning a deep convolutional network for light-field image super-resolution. In: Proceedings of the IEEE International Conference on Computer Vision Workshops, pp. 24–32 (2015)
27. Zhang, F.L., Wang, J., Shechtman, E., Zhou, Z.Y., Shi, J.X., Hu, S.M.: Plenopatch: patch-based plenoptic image manipulation. IEEE Trans. Vis. Comput. Graph. **23**(5), 1561–1573 (2017)
28. Zhang, Z., Liu, Y., Dai, Q.: Light field from micro-baseline image pair. In: Proceedings of the IEEE Conference on Computer Vision and Pattern Recognition, pp. 3800–3809 (2015)

DeepPhys: Video-Based Physiological Measurement Using Convolutional Attention Networks

Weixuan Chen[1]([✉]) [ID] and Daniel McDuff[2] [ID]

[1] MIT Media Lab, Cambridge, MA 02139, USA
cvx@media.mit.edu
[2] Microsoft Research, Redmond, WA 98052, USA

Abstract. Non-contact video-based physiological measurement has many applications in health care and human-computer interaction. Practical applications require measurements to be accurate even in the presence of large head rotations. We propose the first end-to-end system for video-based measurement of heart and breathing rate using a deep convolutional network. The system features a new motion representation based on a skin reflection model and a new attention mechanism using appearance information to guide motion estimation, both of which enable robust measurement under heterogeneous lighting and major motions. Our approach significantly outperforms all current state-of-the-art methods on both RGB and infrared video datasets. Furthermore, it allows spatial-temporal distributions of physiological signals to be visualized via the attention mechanism.

1 Introduction

Subtle changes in the human body, "hidden" to the unaided eye, can reveal important information about the health and wellbeing of an individual. Computer analysis of videos and images can be used to recover these signals [3,24,30] and magnify them [14,40]. Non-contact video-based physiological measurement is a fast growing research domain as it offers the potential for unobtrusive, concomitant measurement and visualization of important vital signs using ubiquitous sensors (e.g. low-cost webcams or smartphone cameras) [20].

Imaging Photoplethysmography (iPPG) is a set of techniques for recovering the volumetric change in blood close to the surface of the skin, the resulting signal is known as the blood volume pulse (BVP). The principle is based on measurement of subtle changes in light reflected from the skin. In a similar fashion, Imaging Ballistocardiography (iBCG) uses motion information extracted from videos to recover the Ballistocardiogram [3]. These small motions of the body, due to the mechanical flow of blood, provide complementary cardiac information

Electronic supplementary material The online version of this chapter (https://doi.org/10.1007/978-3-030-01216-8_22) contains supplementary material, which is available to authorized users.

V. Ferrari et al. (Eds.): ECCV 2018, LNCS 11206, pp. 356–373, 2018.
https://doi.org/10.1007/978-3-030-01216-8_22

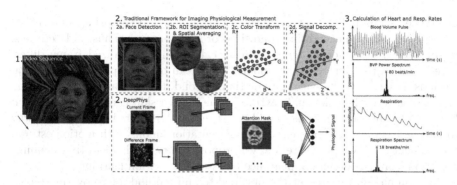

Fig. 1. We present DeepPhys a novel approach to video-based physiological measurement using convolutional attention networks that significantly outperforms the state-of-the-art and allows spatial-temporal visualization of physiological information in video. DeepPhys is an end-to-end network that can accurately recover heart rate and breathing rate from RGB or infrared videos.

to the PPG signal. Respiratory signals (breathing) can also be recovered using color [25] and motion-based [31] analyses. If the physiological parameters (i.e., heart and/or breathing rate) of an individual are known, magnification of the color change and/or motion can be performed [14,40], which provides a very intuitive visualization of the physiological changes.

Based on the techniques above, a number of algorithms have been proposed to enable recovering vital signs from only a webcam video. However, early solutions among them were either not amenable to computation [30,35] or lacked rigorous evaluation across a range of motion and ambient lighting conditions [1,24]. Recent approaches that have presented improved results under such video conditions are often complex multi-stage methods that are hard to tune and implement. Almost all methods require face tracking and registration, skin segmentation, color space transformation, signal decomposition and filtering steps.

In computer vision end-to-end deep neural models have out-performed traditional multi-stage methods that require hand-crafted feature manipulation. An end-to-end learning framework for recovering physiological signals would be desirable. However, to date convolution neural networks (CNNs) have only been applied to skin segmentation in iPPG [5] and not for recovering vital signs. This motivated our design of DeepPhys - a novel convolutional attention network (CAN) for video-based physiological measurement, which significantly outperforms the state-of-the-art and allows spatial-temporal visualization of physiological signal distributions (e.g., blood perfusion) from RGB videos. Figure 1 shows how DeepPhys compares to traditional methods.

An end-to-end network for video-based physiological measurement should be a model that reads motion information from video frames, discriminates different motion sources and synthesizes a target motion signal. However, no existing deep learning models are suited to this task. First, deep neural networks used in similar tasks commonly rely on motion representations such as optical flow or frame difference as input, but they are either contradictory to the principle of iPPG or sensitive to different lighting conditions or skin contours. Thus, in DeepPhys, we propose a new motion representation calculating normalized frame difference based on the skin reflection model, which can better capture physiological motions under heterogeneous illumination. Second, the appearance information in video such as the color and texture of the human skin can guide where and how the physiological motions should be estimated, but there is currently no way to jointly learn auxiliary appearance representations along with motion estimators in neural networks. Therefore, we propose a new mechanism that acquires attention from the human appearance to assist the motion learning.

To summarize, we present the first end-to-end method for recovering physiological signals (HR, BR) from videos. DeepPhys is a novel convolutional attention network that simultaneously learns a spatial mask to detect the appropriate regions of interest and recovers the BVP and respiration signals. Below we describe the theoretical underpinning of our approach, the model, and validation on four datasets each recorded with different devices, of different subjects, and under different lighting configurations. We perform a thorough comparison against the state-of-the-art approaches, the results of which illustrate the benefits of our proposed model.

2   Related Work

2.1   Remote Physiological Measurement

Minute variations in light reflected from the skin can be used to extract human physiological signals (e.g., heart rate (HR) [30] and breathing rate (BR) [25]). A digital single reflex camera (DSLR) is sufficient to measure the subtle blood volume pulse signal (BVP) [30,35]. The simplest method involves spatially averaging the image color values for each frame within a time window, this is highly susceptible to noise from motion, lighting and sensor artifacts. Recent advancements have led to significant improvements in measurement under increasingly challenging conditions. Figure 1 shows a traditional approach to remote physiological measurement that involves skin segmentation, color space transformation and signal decomposition.

Color Space Transforms: The optical properties of the skin under ambient illumination mean that the green color channel tends to give the strongest PPG signal and this was used in initial work [17,35]. However, the color channels can be weighted and combined to yield better results. The CHROM [13] method uses a linear combination of the chrominance signals by assuming a standardized skin color profile to white-balance the video frames. The Pulse Blood Vector (PBV) method [12] leverages the characteristic blood volume changes in different parts of the frequency spectrum to weight the color channels.

Signal Decomposition: It has been demonstrated that blind-source separation can be used to improve the signal-to-noise ratio of the PPG signal from webcam videos [24]. Leveraging information from all three color channels and multiple spatial locations makes the approach more robust to changes in illumination with head motion. More rigorous evaluation demonstrated it was possible to recover heart rate variability (HRV) and breathing rate (BR) estimates [25]. A majority of the work on video-based physiological measurement has relied on unsupervised learning. Independent component analysis (ICA) [19,24,25] and principal component analysis (PCA) [37] are two common approaches for combining multiple color or location channels. More advanced signal decomposition methods have resulted in improved heart rate measurement, even in the presence of large head motions and lighting variation [16,34,38,39].

Supervised Learning Approaches: Few approaches have made use of supervised learning for video-based physiological measurement. Formulating the problem is not trivial. Template matching and Support Vector approaches [23] have obtained modest results. Linear regression and Nearest Neighbor (NN) techniques have been combined with signal decomposition methods [21] to solve the problem of selecting the appropriate source signal. However, these are still limited by the performance of the decomposition method (e.g., ICA or PCA).

2.2 Deep Learning

Motion Analysis plays a significant role in deep-learning-based video processing. First, deep learning has achieved remarkable successes in explicit motion analysis tasks, such as optical flow estimation [9,15] and motion prediction [11,43]. Different from images, videos have both spatial information (appearance) and temporal dynamics (motion). Therefore, solving any video-related problem using machine learning should benefit from implicit motion modeling. In contemporary techniques, both appearance and motion representations can be learned in parallel (two-stream methods [27]), in cascade (CNN connected with RNN [4,8]) or in a mixed way (3D CNN [33]). Commonly, for more efficient learning, several motion representations are manually calculated from videos to serve as the input of learning models, including optical flow [22,27] and frame difference [43].

Attention Mechanisms in neural networks are inspired by the human visual system, which can focus on a certain region of an image with high resolution while perceiving the surrounding image in low resolution. To put it simply, they confer more weight on a subset of features. As one of the latest advancements in deep learning, attention mechanisms have been widely used in machine translation [2], image captioning [41] and many other tasks. In learning-based video analytics, attention mechanisms also show great power, either by temporally focusing on different frames of a video [44] or by spatially focusing on different parts of a frame [26]. It has been shown that attention can be derived from motions to guide appearance representation learning [18,32]. In this work, we do exactly the opposite, acquiring attention from appearance to guide motion representation learning, which has never been done before to our knowledge.

3   Skin Reflection Model

Video-based physiological measurement involves capturing both subtle color changes (iPPG) and small motions (iBCG and respiratory movement) of the human body using a camera. For modeling lighting, imagers and physiology, previous works used the Lambert-Beer law (LBL) [16,42] or Shafer's dichromatic reflection model (DRM) [38]. We build our learning model on top of the DRM as it provides a better framework for modeling both color changes and motions. Assume the light source has a constant spectral composition but varying intensity. We can define the RGB values of the k-th skin pixel in an image sequence by a time-varying function:

$$\boldsymbol{C}_k(t) = I(t) \cdot (\boldsymbol{v}_s(t) + \boldsymbol{v}_d(t)) + \boldsymbol{v}_n(t) \tag{1}$$

where $\boldsymbol{C}_k(t)$ denotes a vector of the RGB values; $I(t)$ is the luminance intensity level, which changes with the light source as well as the distance between the light source, skin tissue and camera; $I(t)$ is modulated by two components in the DRM: specular reflection $\boldsymbol{v}_s(t)$, mirror-like light reflection from the skin surface, and diffuse reflection $\boldsymbol{v}_d(t)$, the absorption and scattering of light in skin-tissues; $\boldsymbol{v}_n(t)$ denotes the quantization noise of the camera sensor. $I(t)$, $\boldsymbol{v}_s(t)$ and $\boldsymbol{v}_d(t)$ can all be decomposed into a stationary and a time-dependent part through a linear transformation [38]:

$$\boldsymbol{v}_d(t) = \boldsymbol{u}_d \cdot d_0 + \boldsymbol{u}_p \cdot p(t) \tag{2}$$

where $\boldsymbol{u}_d$ denotes the unit color vector of the skin-tissue; d_0 denotes the stationary reflection strength; $\boldsymbol{u}_p$ denotes the relative pulsatile strengths caused by hemoglobin and melanin absorption; $p(t)$ denotes the BVP.

$$\boldsymbol{v}_s(t) = \boldsymbol{u}_s \cdot (s_0 + \Phi(m(t), p(t))) \tag{3}$$

where $\boldsymbol{u}_s$ denotes the unit color vector of the light source spectrum; s_0 and $\Phi(m(t), p(t))$ denote the stationary and varying parts of specular reflections; $m(t)$ denotes all the non-physiological variations such as flickering of the light source, head rotation and facial expressions.

$$I(t) = I_0 \cdot (1 + \Psi(m(t), p(t))) \tag{4}$$

where I_0 is the stationary part of the luminance intensity, and $I_0 \cdot \Psi(m(t), p(t))$ is the intensity variation observed by the camera. The interaction between physiological and non-physiological motions, $\Phi(\cdot)$ and $\Psi(\cdot)$, are usually complex nonlinear functions. The stationary components from the specular and diffuse reflections can be combined into a single component representing the stationary skin reflection:

$$\boldsymbol{u}_c \cdot c_0 = \boldsymbol{u}_s \cdot s_0 + \boldsymbol{u}_d \cdot d_0 \tag{5}$$

where $\boldsymbol{u}_c$ denotes the unit color vector of the skin reflection and c_0 denotes the reflection strength. Substituting (2), (3), (4) and (5) into (1), produces:

$$\boldsymbol{C}_k(t) = I_0 \cdot (1 + \Psi(m(t), p(t))) \cdot$$
$$(\boldsymbol{u}_c \cdot c_0 + \boldsymbol{u}_s \cdot \Phi(m(t), p(t)) + \boldsymbol{u}_p \cdot p(t)) + \boldsymbol{v}_n(t) \tag{6}$$

As the time-varying components are much smaller (i.e., orders of magnitude) than the stationary components in (6), we can neglect any product between varying terms and approximate $\boldsymbol{C}_k(t)$ as:

$$\boldsymbol{C}_k(t) \approx \boldsymbol{u}_c \cdot I_0 \cdot c_0 + \boldsymbol{u}_c \cdot I_0 \cdot c_0 \cdot \Psi(m(t), p(t)) +$$
$$\boldsymbol{u}_s \cdot I_0 \cdot \Phi(m(t), p(t)) + \boldsymbol{u}_p \cdot I_0 \cdot p(t) + \boldsymbol{v}_n(t) \; (7)$$

For any of the video-based physiological measurement methods, the task is to extract $p(t)$ from $\boldsymbol{C}_k(t)$. To date, all iPPG works have ignored $p(t)$ inside $\Phi(\cdot)$ and $\Psi(\cdot)$, and assumed a linear relationship between $\boldsymbol{C}_k(t)$ and $p(t)$. This assumption generally holds when $m(t)$ is small (i.e., the skin ROI is stationary under constant lighting conditions). However, $m(t)$ is not small in most realistic situations. Thus, a linear assumption will harm measurement performance. This motivates our use of a machine learning model to capture the more general and complex relationship between $\boldsymbol{C}_k(t)$ and $p(t)$ in (7).

4   Approach

4.1   Motion Representation

We developed a new type of normalized frame difference as our input motion representation. Optical flow, though commonly used, does not fit our task, because it is based on the brightness constancy constraint, which requires the light absorption of objects to be constant. This obviously contradicts the existence of a varying physiological signal $p(t)$ in (2). The first step of computing our motion representation is spatial averaging of pixels, which has been widely used for reducing the camera quantization error $\boldsymbol{v}_n(t)$ in (7). We implemented this by downsampling every frame to L pixels by L pixels using bicubic interpolation. Selecting L is a trade-off between suppressing camera noise and retaining spatial resolution ([37] found that $L = 36$ was a good choice for face videos.) The downsampled pixel values will still obey the DRM model only without the camera quantization error:

$$\boldsymbol{C}_l(t) \approx \boldsymbol{u}_c \cdot I_0 \cdot c_0 + \boldsymbol{u}_c \cdot I_0 \cdot c_0 \cdot \Psi(m(t), p(t)) +$$
$$\boldsymbol{u}_s \cdot I_0 \cdot \Phi(m(t), p(t)) + \boldsymbol{u}_p \cdot I_0 \cdot p(t) \; (8)$$

where $l = 1, \cdots, L^2$ is the new pixel index in every frame.

Then we need to reduce the dependency of $\boldsymbol{C}_l(t)$ on the stationary skin reflection color $\boldsymbol{u}_c \cdot I_0 \cdot c_0$, resulting from the light source and subject's skin tone. In unsupervised learning approaches, the frames processed usually come from a short time window, in which the term $\boldsymbol{u}_c \cdot I_0 \cdot c_0$ is relatively constant. However, in a supervised learning data cohort, the term will vary between subjects and lighting conditions, which will explain the majority of the variance in $\boldsymbol{C}_l(t)$. This will not only make it harder to learn to discriminate the real variance of interest $p(t)$, but also depend the learned model on specific skin tones and lamp spectra in the training data. In (8) $\boldsymbol{u}_c \cdot I_0 \cdot c_0$ appears twice. It is impossible to eliminate

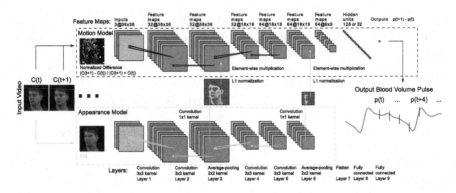

Fig. 2. The architecture of our end-to-end convolutional attention network. The current video frame at time t and the normalized difference between frames at $t+1$ and t are given as inputs to the appearance and motion models respectively. The network learns spatial masks, that are shared between the models, and features important for recovering the BVP and respiration signals.

the second term as it interacts with $\Psi(\cdot)$. However, the first time-invariant term, which is usually dominant, can be removed by taking the first order derivative of both sides of (8) with respect to time:

$$C_l'(t) \approx \boldsymbol{u}_c \cdot I_0 \cdot c_0 \cdot (\frac{\partial \Psi}{\partial m}m'(t) + \frac{\partial \Psi}{\partial p}p'(t)) +$$

$$\boldsymbol{u}_s \cdot I_0 \cdot (\frac{\partial \Phi}{\partial m}m'(t) + \frac{\partial \Phi}{\partial p}p'(t)) + \boldsymbol{u}_p \cdot I_0 \cdot p'(t) \quad (9)$$

One problem with this frame difference representation is that the stationary luminance intensity level I_0 is spatially heterogeneous due to different distances to the light source and uneven skin contours. The spatial distribution of I_0 has nothing to do with physiology, but is different in every video recording setup. Thus, $C_l'(t)$ was normalized by dividing it by the temporal mean of $C_l(t)$ to remove I_0:

$$\frac{C_l'(t)}{\overline{C_l(t)}} \approx \mathbf{1} \cdot (\frac{\partial \Psi}{\partial m}m'(t) + \frac{\partial \Psi}{\partial p}p'(t)) + diag^{-1}(\boldsymbol{u}_c)\boldsymbol{u}_p \cdot \frac{1}{c_0} \cdot p'(t) +$$

$$diag^{-1}(\boldsymbol{u}_c)\boldsymbol{u}_s \cdot \frac{1}{c_0} \cdot (\frac{\partial \Phi}{\partial m}m'(t) + \frac{\partial \Phi}{\partial p}p'(t)) \quad (10)$$

where $\mathbf{1} = [1\ 1\ 1]^T$. In (10), $\overline{C_l(t)}$ needs to be computed pixel-by-pixel over a short time window to minimize occlusion problems and prevent the propagation of errors. We found it was feasible to compute it over two consecutive frames so that (10) can be expressed discretely as:

$$D_l(t) = \frac{C_l'(t)}{\overline{C_l(t)}} \sim \frac{C_l(t + \Delta t) - C_l(t)}{C_l(t + \Delta t) + C_l(t)} \quad (11)$$

which is the normalized frame difference we used as motion representation (Δt is the sampling interval). In the computed $\boldsymbol{D}_l(t)$, outliers are usually due to large $m'(t)$ or occlusion. To diminish these outliers, we clipped $\boldsymbol{D}_l(t)$ by three standard deviations over each video and all color channels. To summarize, the clipped $\boldsymbol{D}_l(t)$ will be the input of our learning model, and the first order derivative of a gold-standard physiological signal $p'(t) = p(t + \Delta t) - p(t)$ will be the training label. To align $\boldsymbol{D}_l(t)$ and $p'(t)$, the physiological signals were interpolated to the video sampling rate beforehand using piecewise cubic Hermite interpolation. For higher convergence speed of stochastic gradient descent, $\boldsymbol{D}_l(t)$ and $p'(t)$ were also scaled to unit standard deviation over each video.

4.2 Convolutional Neural Network

The foundation of our learning model is a VGG-style CNN for estimating the physiological signal derivative from the motion representation, as shown in Fig. 2 (motion model). The last layer has linear activation units and a mean square error (MSE) loss, so the outputs will form a continuous signal $\widetilde{p'(t)}$. Since most physiological signals are frequency-bounded, the output was band-pass filtered to remove noise outside the frequency range of interest. Finally, the power spectrum was computed from the filtered signal with the location of the highest peak taken as the estimated HR or BR.

Different from classical CNN models deigned for object recognition, we used average pooling layers instead of max pooling. The reasoning was that for physiological measurement, combining an important feature with a less important feature can often produce a higher signal-to-noise ratio than using the more important feature alone. We also compared multiple activation functions and found the symmetry seemed to help with performance. Thus, we used hyperbolic tangent (tanh) instead of rectified linear units (ReLU) as hidden layer activation functions. Besides, our attention mechanism uses gating schemes similar to those in long short-term memory (LSTM) networks, which help prevent the main problem with tanh, vanishing gradients.

The loss function of our model is the MSE between the estimated and gold-standard physiological signal derivative, but our final goal is to compute the dominant frequency of the estimated signal (i.e., HR or BR). Though the temporal error and frequency error generally have high correlation, a small temporal error does not guarantee a small frequency error. It is also hard to directly use the frequency error as the loss function of a CNN, because the calculation of the dominant frequency involves a non-differentiable operation $argmax$. Thus we adopted ensemble learning over training checkpoints. Specifically, we trained CNN models for an extra 16 epochs after convergence. These models were applied to the training data with frequency errors computed, and the model with the smallest error was chosen. We found that this strategy consistently achieved smaller frequency errors than simply using the last checkpoint model.

4.3   Attention Mechanism

Naively our motion representation in (10) and (11) assumes every pixel l is part of a body, and more specifically skin. Using normalized frame difference helps reduce the impact of background pixels; however, any movement will add noise. To reduce this effect, previous methods usually reply on preprocessing such as skin segmentation to select a region of interest (ROI). In our end-to-end model, a new attention mechanism can be added to achieve similar functionality. Also, the distribution of physiological signals is not uniform on the human body, so learning soft-attention masks and assigning higher weights to skin areas with stronger signals should improve the measurement accuracy.

Whether a pixel patch belongs to the skin and exhibits strong physiological signals can be partly inferred from its visual appearance. However, the derivation and normalization operations in (10) removed appearance information. To provide a basis for learning attention, we created a separate appearance model (see Fig. 2). This model has the same architecture as the motion model without the last three layers, and has the raw frames (centered to zero mean and scaled to unit standard deviation) as input. Soft-attention masks were estimated using a 1×1 convolution filter right before every pooling layer so that masks were synthesized from different levels of appearance features. Let $x_m^j \in \mathbb{R}^{C_j \times H_j \times W_j}$ and $x_a^j \in \mathbb{R}^{C_j \times H_j \times W_j}$ be the feature maps of convolution layer j right before pooling in the motion model and the appearance model respectively, with C_j, H_j and W_j being the number of channels, height and width. The attention mask $q^j \in \mathbb{R}^{1 \times H_j \times W_j}$ can be computed as:

$$q^j = \frac{H_j W_j \cdot \sigma(w^{j^T} x_a^j + b^j)}{2\|\sigma(w^{j^T} x_a^j + b^j)\|_1} \tag{12}$$

where $w^j \in \mathbb{R}^{C_j}$ is the 1×1 convolution kernel, b^j is the bias, and $\sigma(\cdot)$ is a sigmoid function. Different from softmax functions commonly used for generating soft-attention probability maps, we used a sigmoid activation followed by l_1 normalization, which is even softer than softmax and produces less extreme masks. Finally, the mask was multiplied with the motion model feature map to output:

$$z_m^j = (\mathbf{1} \cdot q^j) \odot x_m^j \tag{13}$$

where $z_m^j \in \mathbb{R}^{C_j \times H_j \times W_j}$ is the masked feature map passed on to the next layer, $\mathbf{1} \in \mathbb{R}^{C_j}$ is a vector with all ones, and $\odot$ is element-wise multiplication. The motion model and the appearance model were learned jointly to find the best motion estimator and the best ROI detector simultaneously.

5   Datasets

We tested our method on four datasets, each featuring participants of both genders, different ages, a wide range of skin tones (Asians, Africans and Caucasians) and some had thick facial hair and/or glasses.

RGB Video I [10]. Videos were recorded with a Scout scA640-120gc GigE-standard, color camera, capturing 8-bit, 658×492 pixel images, 120 fps. The camera was equipped with 16 mm fixed focal length lenses. Twenty-five participants (17 males) were recruited to participate for the study. Gold-standard physiological signals were measured using a research-grade biopotential acquisition unit.

Each participant completed six (each against two background screens) 5-minute tasks. The tasks were designed to capture different levels of head motion.

Task 1: Participants placed their chin on a chin rest (normal to the camera) in order to limit head motion.

Task 2: Participants repeated Task 1 without the aid of the chin rest, allowing for small natural motions.

Task 3: Participants performed a 120-degree sweep centered about the camera at a speed of 10 degrees/sec.

Task 4: As Task 3 but with a speed of $20°/s$.

Task 5: As Task 3 but with a speed of $30°/s$.

Task 6: Participants were asked to reorient their head position once per second to a randomly chosen imager in the array. Thus simulating random head motion.

Fig. 3. Example frames from the four datasets: (a) RGB Video I, (b) RGB Video II, (c) MAHNOB-HCI, (d) Infrared Video. The yellow bounding boxes indicate the areas cropped as the input of our models. (e) shows exemplary attention weights of the left frame in (a) for HR measurement, and of the right frame in (a) for BR measurement. (Color figure online)

RGB Video II [7]. Videos were recorded with an Intel RealSense Camera VF0800 and 18 participants (16 males, 2 females, 23–50 years) were recruited (data from 3 participants were eliminated due to high collection error). Participant was seated still at a desk under ambient light for 30 s. All videos were recorded in color (24-bit RGB with 3 channels $\times$ 8 bits/channel) at a floating frame rate around 24 fps with pixel resolution of 1920×1080. Gold-standard physiological signals were measured with a FlexComp Infiniti that recorded Blood Volume Pulse (BVP) from a finger probe at a constant sampling frequency of 256 Hz. Respiration was not recorded in this study.

MAHNOB-HCI [28]. A multimodal dataset with videos of subjects participating in two experiments: (i) emotion elicitation and (ii) implicit tagging. It contains 27 subjects (12 males and 15 females) in total, and all videos are in 61 fps with a 780 × 580 resolution. Following [17], we used a 30-second clip (frames from 306 through 2135) of 527 sequences. To compute the ground truth heart rate we used the second channel (EXG2) of the corresponding ECG waveforms.

Infrared Video [6]. To show that our·approach generalizes to other datasets collected using different imagers we performed similar analysis on a dataset of IR videos. Twelve participants (8 males, 4 females) between the ages of 23–34 years were recruited for this study. Participants were seated at a desk and a Leap Motion controller was placed on the edge of the desk, parallel with it, and facing upward. 640 × 240 pixel near-IR frames were recorded at a floating frame rate around 62 fps. Gold-standard physiological signals were measured with a FlexComp Infiniti that simultaneously recorded BVP from a finger probe and respiration from a chest belt at a constant sampling frequency of 256 Hz. Each experiment consisted of two 1 min recordings: (1) in a well-lit room (184 lux at the camera), (2) in a completely dark room (1 lux at the camera).

6   Results and Discussion

For our experiments, we used Adadelta [45] to optimize the models across a computing cluster. All the optimizer parameters were copied from [45], and a batch size of 128 examples was used. To overcome overfitting, three dropout layers [29] were inserted between layers 3 and 4, layers 6 and 7, and layers 8 and 9 in Fig. 2 with dropout rates d_1, d_2 and d_3 respectively. Along with n_8 the number of hidden units in layer 8 and N_e the number of training epochs, the five parameters were chosen differently to adapt to different model complexities and different generalization challenges (values can be found in Supplemental Materials).

Apart from the proposed CAN model, we also implemented a standalone CNN motion model (top portion of Fig. 2) to verify the effectiveness of the attention mechanism. The input of the model was either the normalized frame difference (Motion-only CNN) or the normalized frame difference stacked with the raw frame (Stacked CNN). A 6th-order Butterworth filter was applied to the model outputs (cut-off frequencies of 0.7 and 2.5 Hz for HR, and 0.08 and 0.5 Hz for BR). The filtered signals were divided into 30-second windows with 1-second stride and four standard metrics were computed over all windows of all the test videos in a dataset: mean absolute error (MAE), root mean square error (RMSE), Pearson's correlation coefficient (r) between the estimated HR/BR and the ground truth HR/BR, and signal-to-noise ratio (SNR) of the estimated physiological signals [13] averaged among all windows. The SNR is calculated in the frequency domain as the ratio between the energy around the first two harmonics (0.2 Hz frequency bins around the gold-standard HR, and 0.05 Hz frequency bins around the gold-standard BR) and remaining frequencies within

Table 1. Performance of heart rate and breathing rate measurement for RGB Video I. Participant dependent (p.-dep.) and participant independent results are shown, as are task independent results for the six tasks with varying levels of head rotation

Heart Rate	Mean Absolute Error/BPM							Signal-To-Noise Ratio/dB						
Methods	1	2	3	4	5	6	Avg.	1	2	3	4	5	6	Avg.
Estepp et al. [10]	3.48	3.95	3.80	6.55	11.8	13.4	7.16	6.06	4.82	3.77	−0.10	−4.72	−9.63	0.03
McDuff et al. [19]	1.17	1.70	1.70	4.00	5.22	11.8	4.29	10.9	9.55	6.69	3.08	0.08	−6.93	3.90
Balakrishnan et al. [3]	4.99	5.16	12.7	17.4	18.7	14.2	12.2	−1.08	−0.34	−8.83	−12.6	−14.2	−12.1	−8.19
De Haan et al. [13]	4.53	4.59	4.35	4.84	6.89	10.3	5.92	1.72	1.38	3.97	3.63	2.02	−2.47	1.71
Wang et al. [38]	1.50	1.53	1.50	1.84	2.05	6.11	2.42	6.84	6.21	4.80	2.97	0.77	−4.33	2.88
Tulyakov et al. [34]	1.76	2.14	14.9	19.0	15.7	22.0	12.6	4.32	2.29	−11.8	−14.3	−12.3	−15.3	−7.85
Ours: Part. Dep.														
Motion-only CNN	1.17	1.29	1.29	1.66	2.04	2.95	1.73	10.2	9.28	7.02	4.18	1.95	−1.00	5.28
Stacked CNN	1.18	1.30	1.26	1.51	1.82	2.62	1.61	10.7	9.60	8.28	5.59	2.84	0.29	6.22
CAN	1.17	1.26	1.16	1.61	2.04	1.78	1.50	10.9	9.66	8.20	5.69	3.57	1.33	6.55
Ours: Part. Ind.														
Motion-only CNN	1.17	1.41	1.33	1.91	3.57	6.41	2.63	9.60	8.62	6.25	2.73	−0.15	−4.02	3.84
Stacked CNN	1.12	1.66	1.30	1.65	2.33	6.25	2.38	9.26	8.18	7.27	3.81	1.14	−2.84	4.47
CAN	1.16	1.45	1.23	1.72	2.42	5.59	2.26	9.52	8.82	7.36	3.90	1.10	−2.72	4.66
CAN (task 1)	1.16	3.01	3.43	4.85	7.92	13.9	5.70	9.52	5.74	2.01	−2.13	−5.77	−9.70	−0.06
CAN (task 2)	1.12	1.45	1.67	3.35	7.51	12.9	4.66	10.1	8.82	4.25	−0.90	−5.33	−8.96	1.33
CAN (task 3)	1.18	1.41	1.23	1.78	2.73	9.23	2.93	9.75	8.79	7.36	4.33	0.55	−5.88	4.15
CAN (task 4)	1.13	1.57	1.24	1.72	2.79	8.98	2.91	9.95	8.72	7.06	3.90	0.37	−5.68	4.05
CAN (task 5)	1.16	1.38	1.30	1.54	2.42	7.05	2.48	9.86	8.98	7.68	4.40	1.10	−4.15	4.65
CAN (task 6)	1.14	1.32	1.22	1.47	2.17	5.59	2.15	10.4	9.62	8.21	5.15	1.83	−2.72	5.41
CAN (all tasks)	1.13	1.34	2.45	1.64	1.83	6.32	2.45	9.88	7.21	1.46	8.48	4.11	−3.23	4.65
Breath. Rate	Mean Absolute Error/BPM							Signal-To-Noise Ratio/dB						
Methods	1	2	3	4	5	6	Avg.	1	2	3	4	5	6	Avg.
Tarassenko et al. [31]	2.51	2.53	3.19	4.85	4.22	4.78	3.68	−1.29	−1.82	−6.32	−8.55	−8.79	−10.6	−6.22
Ours: Part. Dep.														
Motion-only CNN	2.03	2.47	3.21	3.04	3.11	4.27	3.02	−0.33	−1.91	−5.28	−4.83	−5.33	−9.64	−4.55
Stacked CNN	1.74	2.27	2.98	2.79	3.03	5.33	3.02	1.84	−0.93	−6.31	−5.18	−5.70	−11.2	−4.58
CAN	1.70	2.19	3.24	3.05	3.06	3.96	2.86	2.73	−0.02	−4.39	−4.47	−4.36	−7.97	−3.08
Ours: Part. Ind.														
Motion-only CNN	1.70	2.31	4.09	4.85	4.60	4.06	3.60	0.75	−0.17	−6.03	−9.19	−9.05	−9.06	−5.46
Stacked CNN	2.00	2.10	5.67	5.55	6.34	5.76	4.57	0.19	−0.25	−12.0	−11.5	−12.7	−13.0	−8.20
CAN	1.28	1.64	4.15	4.37	3.77	4.37	3.26	4.45	2.96	−5.05	−6.72	−6.70	−8.93	−3.33
CAN (task 1)	1.28	1.72	6.34	7.28	6.28	4.01	4.48	4.45	2.37	−10.0	−13.5	−13.9	−9.02	−6.60
CAN (task 2)	1.21	1.64	5.73	5.65	4.92	3.82	3.83	4.39	2.96	−7.97	−12.3	−11.7	−8.54	−5.52
CAN (task 3)	1.62	1.71	4.15	4.57	4.16	3.56	3.30	3.38	2.74	−5.05	−7.05	−6.71	−6.23	−3.15
CAN (task 4)	1.74	1.85	3.80	4.37	4.60	3.42	3.30	2.69	2.56	−5.10	−6.72	−7.86	−6.63	−3.51
CAN (task 5)	1.65	1.74	4.37	4.45	3.77	3.37	3.22	2.90	3.18	−6.20	−7.02	−6.70	−5.69	−3.25
CAN (task 6)	2.06	1.76	5.89	5.92	5.21	4.37	4.20	1.11	1.54	−9.72	−11.9	−10.1	−8.93	−6.33
CAN (all tasks)	1.54	4.69	3.71	2.14	5.27	3.33	3.45	3.09	−6.45	−7.09	0.21	−10.7	−7.36	−4.71

a range of [0.5 4] Hz for HR, and a range of [0.05 1] Hz for BR. Due to limited space, the metrics RMSE and r are shown in Supplemental Materials.

6.1 RGB Video I

Every video frame was center-cropped to 492×492 pixels to remove the lateral blank areas before being fed into our processing pipeline. We compare our proposed approach to six other methods [3,10,13,19,34,37] for recovering the blood volume pulse. For recovering the respiration, we compare to the approach proposed by Tarassenko et al. [31]. The details about the implementation of these methods are included in Supplemental Materials.

Participant-Dependent Performance. Each five-minute video was divided into five folds of one minute duration. We trained and tested via cross-validation on the concatenated five folds within each task, in which case every participant appeared in both the training set and the test set. The evaluation metrics MAE and SNR are averaged over five folds and shown in Table 1. Table 1 shows that our motion-only CNN, stacked CNN and CAN all outperform the prior methods for HR measurement over task two to task six, both in terms of MAE and SNR. The benefit is particularly strong for the tasks involving high velocity head motions. On task one, our MAE and SNR are very close to the best results achieved by previous methods using hand-crafted features, probably because task one simulates an ideal situation and there is nearly no space for improvement. Within each of our three approaches, CAN shows superior performance on average and obvious advantages for task six, which can be explained by the effectiveness of the attention mechanism in dealing with the frequently changing ROI. The breathing rate results (Table 1) follow a similar pattern.

Participant-Independent Performance. All the 25 participants were randomly divided into five folds of five participants each. The learning models were trained and tested via five-fold cross-validation within each task to evaluate how our models can be generalized to new participants. The evaluation metrics MAE and SNR are also averaged over five folds and shown in Table 1. Compared with the participant-dependent results, the participant-independent results have lower performance to varying degrees. However, for heart rate measurement the Stacked CNN and CAN still outperform all the previous methods. For breathing rate measurement, though motion-only CNN and the stacked CNN have accuracies similar or inferior to Tarassenko et al. [31], the CAN still shows improvement in five tasks and overall.

Task-Independent Performance. Both the participant-dependent and participant-independent results are from training and testing models within tasks. Next, we present task-independent performance where the CAN model was trained on a specific task and then tested on other tasks. The training set and test set were again participant-independent. In the HR results shown in Table 1, there is a clear pattern that a model trained on tasks with less motion performs badly on tasks with greater motion. Models trained on tasks with greater motion generalize very well across all tasks. The CAN model trained on task six even has lower MAE and higher SNR than the model trained and tested within each single task. This also explains why the model trained on all the tasks achieves moderate performance, slightly better than the task five model but much worse than the task six model. On the other hand, for breathing rate measurement, a model trained on one task usually performs best on the same task, and does not generalize well to different tasks. As a result, the distributions of the average MAE and SNR in Table 1 exhibit a symmetric pattern from the task one model to the task six model.

Table 2. RGB Video II, MAHNOB-HCI and Infrared Video dataset results. (MAE = Mean Absolute Error, SNR = Signal-To-Noise Ratio)

DATASET	RGB VIDEO II		MANHOB-HCI	
	Heart Rate		Heart Rate	
Methods	MAE /BPM	SNR /dB	MAE /BPM	SNR /dB
Estepp et al. [10]	14.7	-13.2	-	-
McDuff et al. [19]	0.25	-4.48	10.5	-10.4
Balakrishnan et al. [3]	11.3	-9.17	17.7	-12.9
De Haan et al. [13]	0.30	-2.30	5.09	-9.12
Wang et al. [38]	0.26	1.50	-	-
Tulyakov et al. [34]	2.27	-0.20	4.96	-8.93
Ours (transfer learning):				
CAN	0.14	0.03	4.57	-8.98

DATASET	IR Video			
	Heart Rate		Breath. Rate	
Methods	MAE /BPM	SNR /dB	MAE /BPM	SNR /dB
Chen et al. [6]	0.65	3.15	0.27	5.71
Ours (part. ind.):				
Motion-only CNN	1.44	9.55	0.49	8.95
Stacked CNN	0.87	10.9	0.14	10.4
CAN	0.55	13.2	0.14	10.8

6.2   RGB Video II and MAHNOB-HCI

As shown in Fig. 3, the video frames in the two datasets have complicated backgrounds, and the facial ROI only occupies a small area. To ensure a sufficient number of physiology-related pixels after downsampling, a face detector based on OpenCV's Haar-like cascades [36] was applied to the first frame of each video, and a square region with 160% width and height of the detected bounding box was cropped as the input to our approach.

Transfer Learning. To test whether our model can be generalized to videos with a different resolution, background, lighting condition and sampling frequency, we tried transfer learning without any fine-tuning. We trained the models on Task 2 of RGB Video I (the most similar task to RGB Video II and MAHNOB-HCI) and applied them directly to these datasets. Since RGB Video II only has blood volume pulse ground truth, we compare our approach with only the HR measurement methods. For MAHNOB-HCI, as it is public, we evaluated our approach against only those methods reported in previous studies on the dataset. The results are presented in Table 2. Without any prior knowledge about the two datasets, our CAN model still attains the lowest MAE compared with any previous method, and its SNR is only second to Wang et al. [37] on RGB Video II and Tulyakov et al. [34] on MAHNOB-HCI.

6.3   Infrared Video

For these videos we cropped a fixed 130×130 pixels bounding box against the lower boundary of the frame as our model input (see Fig. 3d). Since the frames in the dataset are monochromatic, all the previous methods we implemented for the RGB datasets are not applicable. We compare our approach with a PCA-based algorithm [6], which has achieved the highest accuracy on the dataset, for both HR and BR measurement.

Participant-independent Performance. In the dataset, each video is one minute in length, which is too short to be split into multiple folds for participant-dependent evaluation. Thus we only ran experiments in a participant-independent way: The 13 participants were randomly divided into five folds, and the learning models were trained and tested via five-fold cross-validation. The results are averaged over five folds and shown in Table 2. For both heart rate and breathing rate measurement, the CAN model not only beats the previous best results but also beats the other learning-based methods without an attention mechanism.

6.4 Visualization of Attention Weights

An advantage of utilizing the proposed attention mechanism is that the spatial-temporal distributions of physiological signals can be revealed by visualizing the attention weights. As shown in Fig. 3e, the attention of the heart rate model is commonly focused on the forehead, the earlobe and the carotid arteries. The earlobe has a large blood supply and the carotid arteries have the most significant pulse-induced motions. For BR measurement, the attention maps are more scattered, because respiration movement can transmit to any body part even including the hair. We also found high attention weights around the nose on many subjects, which suggests our CAN model uses subtle nasal flaring as a feature for respiratory tracking (see Supplemental Materials).

7 Conclusions

We have proposed the first end-to-end network for non-contact measurement of HR and BR. Our convolutional attention network allows spatial-temporal visualization of physiological distributions whilst learning color and motion information for recovering the physiological signals. We evaluated our method on three datasets of RGB videos and a dataset of IR videos. Our method outperformed all the prior state-of-the-art approaches that we compared against. The performance improvements were especially good for the tasks with increasing range and angular velocities of head rotation. We attribute this improvement to the end-to-end nature of the model which is able to learn an improved mapping between the video color and motion information. The participant dependent vs. independent performance as well as the transfer learning results shows that our supervised method does indeed generalize to other people, skin types and illumination conditions.

References

1. Aarts, L.A., et al.: Non-contact heart rate monitoring utilizing camera photoplethysmography in the neonatal intensive care unit - a pilot study. Early Hum. Dev. **89**(12), 943–948 (2013)
2. Bahdanau, D., Cho, K., Bengio, Y.: Neural machine translation by jointly learning to align and translate. arXiv preprint arXiv:1409.0473 (2014)
3. Balakrishnan, G., Durand, F., Guttag, J.: Detecting pulse from head motions in video. In: IEEE Conference on Computer Vision and Pattern Recognition (CVPR), pp. 3430–3437. IEEE (2013)
4. Ballas, N., Yao, L., Pal, C., Courville, A.: Delving deeper into convolutional networks for learning video representations. In: International Conference on Learning Representations (ICLR), pp. 1–11 (2016)
5. Chaichulee, S., et al.: Multi-task convolutional neural network for patient detection and skin segmentation in continuous non-contact vital sign monitoring. In: 12th IEEE International Conference on Automatic Face & Gesture Recognition (FG), pp. 266–272. IEEE (2017)
6. Chen, W., Hernandez, J., Picard, R.W.: Non-contact physiological measurements from near-infrared video of the neck. arXiv preprint arXiv:1805.09511 (2017)
7. Chen, W., Picard, R.W.: Eliminating physiological information from facial videos. In: 12th IEEE International Conference on Automatic Face & Gesture Recognition (FG), pp. 48–55. IEEE (2017)
8. Donahue, J., et al.: Long-term recurrent convolutional networks for visual recognition and description. In: IEEE Conference on Computer Vision and Pattern Recognition (CVPR), pp. 2625–2634 (2015). https://doi.org/10.1109/CVPR.2015.7298878
9. Dosovitskiy, A., et al.: FlowNet: learning optical flow with convolutional networks. In: IEEE International Conference on Computer Vision (ICCV), pp. 2758–2766 (2015)
10. Estepp, J.R., Blackford, E.B., Meier, C.M.: Recovering pulse rate during motion artifact with a multi-imager array for non-contact imaging photoplethysmography. In: IEEE International Conference on Systems, Man and Cybernetics (SMC), vol. 940, pp. 1462–1469. IEEE (2014)
11. Finn, C., Goodfellow, I., Levine, S.: Unsupervised learning for physical interaction through video prediction. In: Advances in Neural Information Processing Systems (NIPS), pp. 64–72 (2016)
12. de Haan, G., van Leest, A.: Improved motion robustness of remote-PPG by using the blood volume pulse signature. Physiol. Measur. **35**(9), 1913 (2014)
13. de Haan, G., Jeanne, V.: Robust pulse rate from chrominance-based rPPG. IEEE Trans. Biomed. Eng. **60**(10), 2878–2886 (2013)
14. Hurter, C., McDuff, D.: Cardiolens: remote physiological monitoring in a mixed reality environment. In: ACM SIGGRAPH 2017 Emerging Technologies, p. 6. ACM (2017)
15. Ilg, E., Mayer, N., Saikia, T., Keuper, M., Dosovitskiy, A., Brox, T.: FlowNet 2.0: evolution of optical flow estimation with deep networks. In: IEEE Conference on Computer Vision and Pattern Recognition (CVPR), vol. 2, p. 6. IEEE (2017). https://doi.org/10.1109/CVPR.2017.179
16. Lam, A., Kuno, Y.: Robust heart rate measurement from video using select random patches. In: IEEE International Conference on Computer Vision (ICCV), pp. 3640–3648. IEEE (2015)

17. Li, X., Chen, J., Zhao, G., Pietikainen, M.: Remote heart rate measurement from face videos under realistic situations. In: IEEE Conference on Computer Vision and Pattern Recognition (CVPR), pp. 4264–4271. IEEE (2014). https://doi.org/10.1109/CVPR.2014.543
18. Li, Z., Gavrilyuk, K., Gavves, E., Jain, M., Snoek, C.G.: Videolstm convolves, attends and flows for action recognition. Comput. Vis. Image Underst. **166**, 41–50 (2018)
19. McDuff, D., Gontarek, S., Picard, R.: Improvements in remote cardio-pulmonary measurement using a five band digital camera. IEEE Trans. Biomed. Eng. **61**(10), 2593–2601 (2014)
20. McDuff, D.J., Estepp, J.R., Piasecki, A.M., Blackford, E.B.: A survey of remote optical photoplethysmographic imaging methods. In: 37th Annual International Conference of the IEEE Engineering in Medicine and Biology Society (EMBC), pp. 6398–6404. IEEE (2015)
21. Monkaresi, H., Calvo, R.A., Yan, H.: A machine learning approach to improve contactless heart rate monitoring using a webcam. IEEE J. Biomed. Health Inf. **18**(4), 1153–1160 (2014)
22. Ng, J.Y.H., Hausknecht, M., Vijayanarasimhan, S., Vinyals, O., Monga, R., Toderici, G.: Beyond short snippets: deep networks for video classification. In: IEEE Conference on Computer Vision and Pattern Recognition (CVPR), pp. 4694–4702 (2015). https://doi.org/10.1109/CVPR.2015.7299101
23. Osman, A., Turcot, J., El Kaliouby, R.: Supervised learning approach to remote heart rate estimation from facial videos. In: 11th IEEE International Conference and Workshops on Automatic Face and Gesture Recognition (FG), vol. 1, pp. 1–6. IEEE (2015)
24. Poh, M.Z., McDuff, D.J., Picard, R.W.: Non-contact, automated cardiac pulse measurements using video imaging and blind source separation. Opt. Express **18**(10), 10762–10774 (2010)
25. Poh, M.Z., McDuff, D.J., Picard, R.W.: Advancements in noncontact, multiparameter physiological measurements using a webcam. IEEE Trans. Biomed. Eng. **58**(1), 7–11 (2011)
26. Sharma, S., Kiros, R., Salakhutdinov, R.: Action recognition using visual attention. arXiv preprint arXiv:1511.04119 (2015)
27. Simonyan, K., Zisserman, A.: Two-stream convolutional networks for action recognition in videos. In: Advances in Neural Information Processing Systems (NIPS), pp. 568–576 (2014). https://doi.org/10.1017/CBO9781107415324.004
28. Soleymani, M., Lichtenauer, J., Pun, T., Pantic, M.: A multimodal database for affect recognition and implicit tagging. IEEE Trans. Affect. Comput. **3**(1), 42–55 (2012)
29. Srivastava, N., Hinton, G., Krizhevsky, A., Sutskever, I., Salakhutdinov, R.: Dropout: a simple way to prevent neural networks from overfitting. J. Mach. Learn. Res. **15**, 1929–1958 (2014). https://doi.org/10.1214/12-AOS1000
30. Takano, C., Ohta, Y.: Heart rate measurement based on a time-lapse image. Med. Eng. Phys. **29**(8), 853–857 (2007)
31. Tarassenko, L., Villarroel, M., Guazzi, A., Jorge, J., Clifton, D., Pugh, C.: Non-contact video-based vital sign monitoring using ambient light and auto-regressive models. Physiol. Measur. **35**(5), 807 (2014)
32. Tran, A., Cheong, L.F.: Two-stream flow-guided convolutional attention networks for action recognition. arXiv preprint arXiv:1708.09268 (2017)

33. Tran, D., Bourdev, L., Fergus, R., Torresani, L., Paluri, M.: Learning spatiotemporal features with 3D convolutional networks. In: IEEE Conference on Computer Vision and Pattern Recognition (CVPR), pp. 675–678. IEEE (2014). https://doi.org/10.1109/CVPR.2014.223

34. Tulyakov, S., Alameda-Pineda, X., Ricci, E., Yin, L., Cohn, J.F., Sebe, N.: Self-adaptive matrix completion for heart rate estimation from face videos under realistic conditions. In: IEEE Conference on Computer Vision and Pattern Recognition (CVPR), pp. 2396–2404. IEEE (2016)

35. Verkruysse, W., Svaasand, L.O., Nelson, J.S.: Remote plethysmographic imaging using ambient light. Opt. Express $16(26)$, 21434–21445 (2008)

36. Viola, P., Jones, M.: Rapid object detection using a boosted cascade of simple features. In: IEEE Conference on Computer Vision and Pattern Recognition (CVPR), vol. 1, p. I-511. IEEE (2001)

37. Wang, W., Stuijk, S., de Haan, G.: Exploiting spatial redundancy of image sensor for motion robust rPPG. IEEE Trans. Biomed. Eng. $62(2)$, 415–425 (2015)

38. Wang, W., den Brinker, A.C., Stuijk, S., de Haan, G.: Algorithmic principles of remote PPG. IEEE Trans. Biomed. Eng. $64(7)$, 1479–1491 (2017). https://doi.org/10.1109/TBME.2016.2609282

39. Wang, W., Stuijk, S., De Haan, G.: A novel algorithm for remote photoplethysmography: spatial subspace rotation. IEEE Trans. Biomed. Eng. $63(9)$, 1974–1984 (2016)

40. Wu, H.Y., Rubinstein, M., Shih, E., Guttag, J.V., Durand, F., Freeman, W.T.: Eulerian video magnification for revealing subtle changes in the world. ACM Trans. Graph. $31(4)$, 65 (2012)

41. Xu, K., et al.: Show, attend and tell: neural image caption generation with visual attention. In: International Conference on Machine Learning (ICML), pp. 2048–2057 (2015)

42. Xu, S., Sun, L., Rohde, G.K.: Robust efficient estimation of heart rate pulse from video. Biomed. Opt. Express $5(4)$, 1124 (2014). https://doi.org/10.1364/BOE.5.001124

43. Xue, T., Wu, J., Bouman, K., Freeman, B.: Visual dynamics: probabilistic future frame synthesis via cross convolutional networks. In: Advances in Neural Information Processing Systems (NIPS), pp. 91–99 (2016)

44. Yao, L., et al.: Video description generation incorporating spatio-temporal features and a soft-attention mechanism. arXiv preprint arXiv:1502.08029 (2015)

45. Zeiler, M.D.: ADADELTA: an adaptive learning rate method. arXiv preprint arXiv:1212.5701 (2012)

Deep Video Generation, Prediction and Completion of Human Action Sequences

Haoye Cai[1,3], Chunyan Bai[1,4(✉)], Yu-Wing Tai[2], and Chi-Keung Tang[1]

[1] Hong Kong University of Science and Technology, Clear Water Bay, Hong Kong
{hcaiaa,cbai}@connect.ust.hk, cktang@cs.ust.hk
[2] Tencent Youtu, Shenzhen, China
yuwingtai@tencent.com
[3] Stanford University, Stanford, CA 94305, USA
[4] Carnegie Mellon University, Pittsburgh, PA 15213, USA
https://iamacewhite.github.io/supp

Abstract. Current video generation/prediction/completion results are limited, due to the severe ill-posedness inherent in these three problems. In this paper, we focus on human action videos, and propose a general, two-stage deep framework to generate human action videos with no constraints or arbitrary number of constraints, which uniformly addresses the three problems: video generation given no input frames, video prediction given the first few frames, and video completion given the first and last frames. To solve video generation from scratch, we build a two-stage framework where we first train a deep generative model that generates human pose sequences from random noise, and then train a skeleton-to-image network to synthesize human action videos given the human pose sequences generated. To solve video prediction and completion, we exploit our trained model and conduct optimization over the latent space to generate videos that best suit the given input frame constraints. With our novel method, we sidestep the original ill-posed problems and produce for the first time high-quality video generation/prediction/completion results of much longer duration. We present quantitative and qualitative evaluations to show that our approach outperforms state-of-the-art methods in all three tasks.

Keywords: Video generation · Generative models

1 Introduction

In this paper we propose a general, two-stage deep framework for human video generation (i.e. generating video clips directly from latent vectors), prediction

---

H. Cai and C. Bai—Equal Contribution.

Electronic supplementary material The online version of this chapter (https://doi.org/10.1007/978-3-030-01216-8_23) contains supplementary material, which is available to authorized users.

© Springer Nature Switzerland AG 2018
V. Ferrari et al. (Eds.): ECCV 2018, LNCS 11206, pp. 374–390, 2018.
https://doi.org/10.1007/978-3-030-01216-8_23

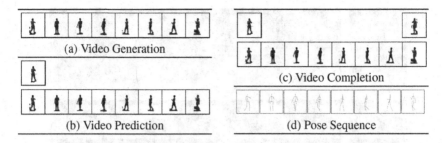

Fig. 1. (a) Video generation, (b) prediction and (c) completion of human action videos using our general two-stage deep framework. (d) In all cases, a complete human pose skeleton sequence is generated in the first stage

(i.e. predicting future frames of a short clip or single frame), and completion (i.e. completing the intermediate content given the beginning and the ending), where each problem was previously addressed as separate problems (Fig. 1). Previous video generation capitalizing state-of-the-art deep convolutional neural network (CNN), such as [35], has demonstrated the significant difficulty of the problem, where their first results were still far from photorealism. Current future prediction [19] in the form of video prediction [34,37] generates a short video from a given frame to predict future actions in a very limited scope with blurry results. Lastly, while there exist deep learning works on image completion [45], there is no known representative deep learning work on video completion.

To better address the general video synthesis problem, we need to understand how pixels change to generate a full temporal object action. With a higher level of uncertainty in the exact movement between frames of the moving object on pixel level, as observed in [34,37], the problem is more tractable by modeling the uncertainty with underlying structure of the moving objects. Hence, we utilize this idea and conduct our experiments on human action videos, which is a well-studied and useful class of videos in various computer vision applications, and in this case the natural choice of underlying structure is human poses (or skeletons). Thus we divide the video generation task into human pose sequence generation (pose space) followed by image generation (pixel space) from the generated human pose sequences. Then, for the prediction and completion problems, we can solve them using the same model by regarding them as constrained generation.

Specifically, our general deep framework for video generation has two stages: first, a new conditional generative adversarial network (GAN) to generate plausible pose sequences that perform a given category of actions; second, a supervised reconstruction network with feature matching loss to transfer pose sequences to the pixel space. Our general video generation framework can be specialized to video prediction/completion (i.e. constrained generation) by optimizing in the latent space to generate video results closest to the given input constraints. Hence our approach can either generate videos from scratch, or complete/predict a video with arbitrary number of input frames available given the action class. We

Fig. 2. Real-world examples. We use reference images in the first column (arbitrary unrelated actions) to generate *Direction/Greeting* actions. 1st and 2nd row: UCF-101 results. 3rd row: Forrest Gump results. See full videos in supplemental material

provide extensive qualitative and quantitative experimental results to demonstrate that our model is able to generate and complete natural human motion videos. We also test our model on real-world videos (Fig. 2).

2 Related Work

We review here recent representative state-of-the-art works related to this paper.

Video Prediction/Generation. In video prediction, research has been done to model uncertain human motion in pose space [34,37]. Attempts have also been made to learn the deep feature representation [16,19,36,43]. For video generation, work has been done to generate videos directly in pixel space [18,35] or generate from caption [18]. While these works shed light on how to model the uncertain temporal information in videos, the results are suboptimal. Our proposed method achieves higher quality, and more importantly, aims at a higher goal: video completion, prediction and generation in the same framework.

Image/Video Completion. Much work has been focusing on image completion with Generative Models [45], but video completion with deep learning has remain unexplored despite its importance [13,42]. If the temporal distance to be completed is small, e.g., [23] then video frame interpolation can be performed to fill in the in-between frames. However, we are dealing with a different problem where input frames are far apart from each other. The modeling of such uncertainty increases the difficulty of this task. In our paper, we aim to perform video completion by optimizing the latent space under the constraint of input frames.

Human Pose Estimation. Various research efforts [4,6,22,33,41] have been made to produce state-of-the-art human pose estimation results, providing us with reliable human pose extractor. In our paper, we leverage the reliable human pose estimation results by [4,22] as input to our completion pipeline.

Generative Models. Our work is based on Generative Adversarial Networks (GAN). Goodfellow et al. [10] first proposed GAN that can implicitly generate any probabilistic distribution. Then conditional GAN [20] was proposed to enable generation under constraint. Subsequent works include usage of convolution neural networks [26], improvement of training stability [28] followed by WGAN [1] and Improved WGAN [11] which further made GAN reliable. In our paper, we first train a conditional WGAN to generate single frame human pose, then we train a conditional sequence GAN to generate latent vector sequences for the single frame model to output human action sequences.

Optimization over Input Data. To specialize to video prediction and completion, we model them as constrained video generation and update input latent vector to find the motion sequence that best matches the input frames. Recently, back-propagation on input data is performed on image inpainting [45] to generate the best match of corrupted image. Zhu et al. [48] utilized such method to enable generative visual manipulation. Google DeepDream [21] also used optimization on latent manifold to generate dream-like images. Earlier, similar method has been employed to perform texture synthesis and style transfer [8,9,15].

Skeleton to Image Transformation. Our two-stage model involves a second stage that transforms human poses to pixel level images, which has been attempted by various deep learning methods. Recent works [17,34,37,44,46] utilize GAN or multi-stage method to complete this task. We propose a simple yet effective supervised learning framework comparable to state-of-the-arts.

3   Methodology

We present a general generative model that uniformly addresses video generation, prediction and completion problems for human motions. The model itself is originally designed for video generation, i.e., generating human action videos from random noise. We split the generation process into two stages: first, we generate human skeleton sequences from random noise, and then we transform from the skeleton images to the real pixel-level images (Fig. 3). In Sect. 3.1 we will elaborate the model and methods we use to generate human skeleton motion sequences, and in Sect. 3.2 we will present our novel method for solving the skeleton-to-image transformation problem. Lastly, in Sect. 3.3, we will show that we can specialize this model without modification to accomplish video prediction and completion by regarding them as constrained video generation.

3.1   General Generative Model

We propose a two-step generation model that generates human skeleton motion sequences from random noise.

Let J be the number of joints of human skeleton, and we represent each joint by its (x, y) location in image space. We formulate a skeleton motion sequence V as a collection of human skeletons across T consecutive frames in total, i.e., $V \in \mathbb{R}^{T \times 2J}$, where each skeleton frame $V_t \in \mathbb{R}^{2J}, t \in \{1 \cdots T\}$ is a vector containing all (x, y) joint locations. Our goal is to learn a function

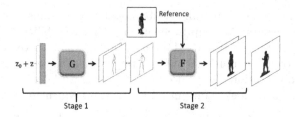

Fig. 3. Overview of our two-stage video generation. In the first stage we generate skeleton motion sequences by G from random noise, while in the second stage we use our skeleton-to-image transformer F to transform skeleton sequence to image space

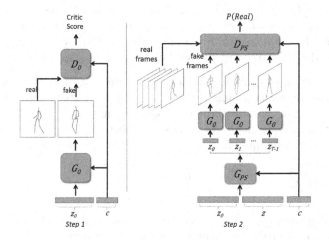

Fig. 4. Illustration of our two-step generation pipeline. In step one (left) G_0 takes a random noise vector and outputs the generated pose vector. The D_0 then differentiate between real and fake pose vectors. Both inputs to G_0 and D_0 are concatenated with conditional class vector. In step two (right), G_{PS} takes the random noise z conditioned on the latent vector of the first frame and the class vector, and generates a sequence of latent vectors which can be transformed to pose vectors via G_0. Then D_{PS} takes as input real/fake frames to determine $P(Real)$

$G : \mathbb{R}^n \to \mathbb{R}^{T \times 2J}$ which maps an n-dimensional noise vector to a joint location vector sequence.

To find this mapping, our experiments showed that human pose constraints are too complicated to be captured by an end-to-end model trained from direct GAN method [10]. Therefore, we switch to our novel two-step strategy, where we first train a *Single Pose Generator* $G_0 : \mathbb{R}^m \to \mathbb{R}^{2J}$ which maps a m-dimensional latent vector to a single-frame pose vector, and then train a *Pose Sequence Generator* $G_{PS} : \mathbb{R}^n \to \mathbb{R}^{T \times m}$ which maps the input random noise to the latent vector sequences, the latter of which can be transformed into human pose vector sequences through our *Single Pose Generator* in a frame-by-frame manner.

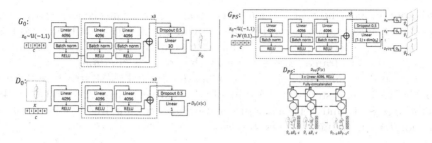

Fig. 5. Two-step generation architecture. Detailed architecture configuration of step one (on the left) and step two (on the right) are shown respectively. Here $\oplus$ stands for element wise addition and $\bigcirc$ stands for an LSTM cell

Figure 4 shows the overall pipeline and the results for each step. The advantage of adopting this two-step method is that by training the single-frame generator, we enforce human pose constraints on each frame, which alleviate the difficulty compared to end-to-end training and thus enable the model to generate longer sequences. Additionally, in order to generate different types of motions, we employ the Conditional GAN [20] method and concatenate an one-hot class vector indicating the class of motion to the input of our generators.

Single Pose Generator. In the first step, we employ the improved WGAN [11] method with gradient penalty for our adversarial training. We build a multilayer perceptron for both our generator and critic with similar structures and add condition to the input of both of them according to Conditional GAN [20]. Our generator G_0 takes as input an m-dimensional latent vector z_0 concatenated with a one-hot class vector c and outputs a pose vector $G_0(z_0|c)$. Our critic D_0 takes as input a real pose vector x_0 or a generated one, concatenated with c, yielding a critic score. The detailed architecture configurations are shown in Fig. 5, and are detailed in supplementary materials. Thus the WGAN objective is:

$$\min_{G_0} \max_{D_0 \in \mathcal{D}} \mathbb{E}_{c \sim p_c}[\mathbb{E}_{x_0 \sim p_{pose}}[D_0(x_0|c)] - \mathbb{E}_{z_0 \sim p_{z_0}}[D_0(G_0(z_0|c)|c)]] \qquad (1)$$

where $\mathcal{D}$ is the set of 1-Lipschitz functions, p_c is the distribution of different classes, p_{pose} is the distribution of the real pose data, and p_{z_0} is the uniform noise distribution.

Pose Sequence Generator. In the second step, we use the normal GAN [10] method instead for training our *Pose Sequence Generator*, since in our experiments normal GAN performs better than WGAN for this specific task. The generator G_{PS} generates a sequence of latent vectors, which are then fed into the *Single Pose Generator* resulting in a sequence of pose vectors $\hat{V}$, from a random noise vector z conditioned on z_0 and c. Note that z_0 is a random noise vector describing the initial condition of the generated pose.

In our implementation we generate latent vector sequences by generating the shifts between two consecutive frames, namely, the output of the network is $s_0, s_1, ..., s_{T-2}$ where $z_{t+1} = s_t + z_t$ for all $t \in \{0...T-2\}$ and z_t is the latent vector for the t-th frame (z_0 is given from the noise distribution).

For the discriminator, we employ a bi-directional LSTM structure, whose input of each time step t is the shift of consecutive frames $\Delta \hat{V}_t = \hat{V}_{t+1} - \hat{V}_t$ conditioned on $\hat{V}_t$ and c. The structural details are shown in Fig. 5. The objective function for the training in this step is:

$$\min_{G_{PS}} \max_{D_{PS}} \mathbb{E}_{c \sim p_c}[\mathbb{E}_{V \sim p_{video}}[\log D_{PS}(V|c)] +$$
$$\mathbb{E}_{z_0 \sim p_{z_0}, z \sim p_z}[\log(1 - D_{PS}(G_{PS}(z_0|z, c)|c))]] \tag{2}$$

where $\mathcal{P}_c$ is the distribution of different classes, p_{video} is the distribution of the real video sequence data, p_{z_0} is the uniform noise distribution and p_z is the Gaussian noise distribution. We also add an L2 regularization term on the generated latent vector shifts for temporal smoothness.

3.2   Skeleton to Image Transformation

In this stage, we train a skeleton-to-image transformation to convert pose space to image space. Formally, given an input pose vector $x \in \mathbb{R}^{2J}$ and a reference image $y_0 \in \mathbb{R}^{w \times h \times 3}$ where h and w are the width and height of images, we need to transform x to a pixel-level image $y \in \mathbb{R}^{w \times h \times 3}$. In order to make the dimensions of inputs well-aligned, we first convert the pose vector x to a set of heat maps $S = (S_1, S_2, ..., S_J)$, where each heat map $S_j \in \mathbb{R}^{w \times h}, j \in \{1...J\}$ is a 2D representation of the probability that a particular joint occurs at each pixel location. Specifically, let $\mathbf{l_j} \in \mathbb{R}^2, (\mathbf{l_j} = (x_{2j}, x_{2j+1}))$ be the 2D position for joint j. The value at location $\mathbf{p} \in \mathbb{R}^2$ in the heat map S_j is then defined as,

$$S_j(\mathbf{p}) = \exp(-\frac{\|\mathbf{p} - \mathbf{l_j}\|_2^2}{\sigma^2}) \tag{3}$$

where σ controls the variance. Then our goal is to learn a function $F : \mathbb{R}^{w \times h \times J} \rightarrow \mathbb{R}^{w \times h \times 3}$ that transforms joint heat maps into pixel-level human images, conditioned on the input reference image. We train a supervised network here.

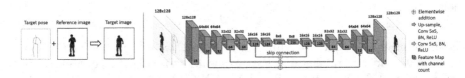

Fig. 6. Left: transferring target pose to a real image. Right: skeleton-to-image network. Image sizes and feature dimensions are shown in the figure. Note that the input has 18 channels, which consist of 3 RGB channels of reference image and 15 joint heat maps

Skeleton-to-Image Network. To learn our function F, we employ a U-Net like network [17,27] (i.e., convolutional autoencoder with skip connections as shown in Fig. 6) that takes, as input, a set of joint heat maps S and a reference image y_0 and produces, as output, a human image $\hat{y}$. For the encoder part, we employ a convolutional network which is adequately deep so that the final receptive field covers the entire image. For the decoder part, we use symmetric structure to gradually generate the image. To avoid inherit checkerboard artifact in transposed convolution layers, there has been several papers proposing solutions including sub-pixel convolution, resize and convolution etc [7,24,29]. In our case we apply nearest neighbor up-sampling followed by convolution layer in decoder.

Loss Function. To train our skeleton-to-image network, we compare the output image with the corresponding ground truth image by binary cross entropy loss. We calculate the binary cross entropy loss for intensity values at each pixel, i.e.

$$\mathcal{L}_{bce} = -\frac{1}{k} \sum (1-y) \log(1 - F(\mathbf{x}|y_0)) + y \log(F(\mathbf{x}|y_0)) \tag{4}$$

where y is the ground truth image, x is pixel and k is the number of pixels. Our experiments show that only using binary cross entropy loss tends to produce blurry results. Hence, in order to enforce details in the produced images, we further employ a feature-matching loss (in some papers also referred as perceptual loss), as suggested in [5,14]. We match the activations in a pre-trained visual perception network that is applied to the ground truth image and the generated image respectively. Different layers in the network represent different levels of abstraction, providing comprehensive guidance towards more realistic images. Specifically, let Φ be the visual perception network (VGG-19 [30]), and Φ_l be the activations in the l-th layer. Our feature-matching loss is defined as,

$$\mathcal{L}_2 = \sum_l \lambda_l \|\Phi_l(F(\mathbf{x}|y_0)) - \Phi_l(y)\|_1 \tag{5}$$

where λ_l is the weight for the l-th layer, which are manually set to balance the contribution of each term. For layers Φ_l, we use 'conv1_2', 'conv2_2', 'conv3_2', 'conv4_2' and 'conv5_2' in VGG-19 [30].

The overall loss for our skeleton-to-image network is therefore defined as

$$\mathcal{L} = \mathcal{L}_1 + \lambda\mathcal{L}_2 \tag{6}$$

where λ denotes the regularization factor of feature matching loss.

3.3   Prediction and Completion

To uniformly address video completion and video prediction, we model them as constrained video generation, which is ready to be defined by the general generative model. We optimize on the latent space to achieve our goal. For simplicity, the optimization is conducted on generated pose sequence, and we

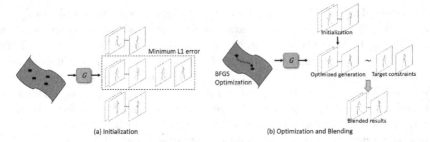

Fig. 7. Our completion/prediction pipeline. (a) initialization: we randomly sample from the latent space and compare L1 error with the constraint frames. Dashed box shows the best initialization chosen. (b) We run BFGS optimization algorithms starting at our initialization, then finally blend the constraints and the generated results

can transform to complete video by our skeleton-to-image transformer using the completed pose sequence. We utilize state-of-the-art human pose estimator like [22] to obtain pose sequences.

Video Completion. To fill in missing frames of a video, our method utilizes the generator G trained with full-length human pose sequence. The learned latent space $\mathbf{z}$ is effective in representing p_{data}. We perform video completion by finding the latent vector $\hat{\mathbf{z}}$ on the manifold that best fits the input frames constraint. As illustrated in Fig. 7, we can generate the missing content using the trained generative model G. The constraints can be arbitrary number of frames.

Objective Function: We regard this problem as an optimization problem. Let $\mathbf{I} \in \mathbb{R}^{t \times 2J}$ be the input frame constraints and $\mathbf{z}$ denote the learned latent space of G. We define the optimal completion encoding $\hat{\mathbf{z}}$ by:

$$\hat{\mathbf{z}} = \arg\min_{\mathbf{z}}\{\mathcal{L}_c(\mathbf{z}|\mathbf{I}) + \alpha \times \mathcal{L}_p(\mathbf{z})\}, \tag{7}$$

where $\mathcal{L}_c$ denotes the contextual L1 loss between the constrained frames and corresponding generated frames and $\mathcal{L}_p$ denotes the perceptual loss of generated frames, i.e. "realness" of the pose sequence. α denotes a regularization factor of the perceptual loss. $\mathcal{L}_c$ and $\mathcal{L}_p$ are defined as follows:

$$\mathcal{L}_c(\mathbf{z}|\mathbf{I}) = \sum_{i \in I} |G(\mathbf{z})_i - \mathbf{I}_i| \tag{8}$$

$$\mathcal{L}_p(\mathbf{z}) = -\log(D(G(\mathbf{z}))) \tag{9}$$

where $\mathbf{I}$ is the set of constrained frames, z is latent vector, i denotes the index of frames in $\mathbf{I}$; i can be arbitrary numbers subject to the given constraints. By optimizing Eq. (7), we obtain a full generated sequence $G(\hat{\mathbf{z}}) \in \mathbb{R}^{T \times 2J}$ which is the "closest" match to the input frames.

Two-Step Optimization: In order to optimize Eq. (7), we employ a two-step method illustrated in Fig. 7. To address the optimization of such highly non-convex latent space, we first randomly sample from the latent space and compare the loss of Eq. (7) to find the best initialization, namely $\mathbf{z}_0$.

As proposed in [48], taking the initialization $\mathbf{z}_0$ as the starting point, we apply Limited Broyden-Fletcher-Goldfarb-Shanno optimization (L-BFGS-B) [3] on the $(n + m)$-dimension latent space to find the optimal completion result $\hat{\mathbf{z}}$.

Video Blending: Ideally, $G(\hat{\mathbf{z}})$ should be the result. However, slight shift and distortion from input constraints are observed as our method does not guarantee perfect alignment with the input. To address this, we use Poisson blending [25] to make our final pose sequence consistent with the input constraints. The key idea is to maintain the gradients on the temporal direction of $G(\hat{\mathbf{z}})$ to preserve motion smoothness while shifting the generated frames to match the input constraint. Our final solution, $\hat{\mathbf{x}}$, can be obtained by

$$\hat{\mathbf{x}} = \arg\min_{\mathbf{x}} \|\nabla_t \mathbf{x} - \nabla_t G(\hat{\mathbf{z}})\|_2^2, \text{ s.t. } \mathbf{x}_i = \mathbf{I}_i \text{ for } i \in \mathbb{R}^{t \times 2J} \tag{10}$$

where ∇_t is the gradient operator on the temporal dimension. This blending preserves the naturalness of the videos while better aligning with the input frame constraints.

Video Prediction. Video prediction can be solved under the same general framework (same as in Fig. 7) as it can be essentially interpreted as video generation with first few frames as constraints.

Formally, let $I \in \mathbb{R}^{t \times 2J}$ be consecutive frames at time step 0 to t as input, we generate future frames $G_t, G_{t+1}, \cdots G_T$ so that $I_0, I_1, \cdots, I_t, G_{t+1}, \cdots G_T$ form a natural and semantically meaningful video. To achieve such goal, we model video prediction as video generation with first few frames as constraint. In other words, we perform the same steps as in the previous section with the input described above to obtain a completed video sequence.

4 Experiments

4.1 Dataset

We evaluate our model primarily on Human3.6m dataset [12]. The dataset provides ground truth 2D human poses. In our experiments, in order to reduce redundant frames and encourage larger motion variations, we subsample the video frames to 16 fps. The action classes we select are 'Direction', 'Greeting', 'Sitting', 'Sitting Down', 'Walking', all of which contain large human motions.

For our skeleton sequence generation task, we randomly select 5 subjects as training set and reserve 2 subjects as test set. For our skeleton-to-image transformation task, we treat the unchosen action classes as training set, and our chosen 5 action classes as test set.

Since our major concern is human motion, we thus subtract all the backgrounds and generate the foreground human figure only for this dataset. To test our method under real-world setting with background, we further train our networks on UCF-101 [32] training set, and test the model using UCF-101 [32] test set as well as real-world movie footages from Forrest Gump (1995).

4.2 Evaluation

Evaluating the quality of synthesized videos is a difficult problem for video generation due to no corresponding ground truth. For video prediction and completion, one can measure the difference from the ground truth frames by Peak Signal-to-Noise Ratio (PSNR) and Structural Similarity Index (SSIM) [40], but we argue that, since videos tend to have multiple possible futures, it is not advisable to compare predicted results against one ground truth. Furthermore, they do not measure the temporal smoothness and human-likeness.

In order to evaluate the visual quality of our results, we measure whether our generated videos are adequately realistic such that a pre-trained recognition network can recognize the object and action in the generated video. This method is inherently similar to Inception Score in [28,37], object detection evaluation in [39] and Semantic Interpretability in [47]. Though Inception Score has its limitations [2], it remains the best systematic metric for video generation. Current state-of-the-art video action recognition model is the two-stream network proposed by Yan et al. [31] and improved by Wang et al. [38]. We employ [38] and fine-tune it on our dataset, and evaluate the following two scores measuring the visual quality of generated image frames and video sequences respectively:

Inception Score for Frames. One criterion for video evaluation score is that they should reflect if the video contains natural images along the sequence. Thus we calculate the inception score [28] based on the output classification result of the RGB stream [38] for each frame generated as the evaluation metric. The average score across the whole video should reflect the overall image quality. Additionally, we also show the Inception Score obtained at each time step, which gives us a detailed snapshot of how the quality of video vary over time.

Inception Score for Videos. As proposed in [37], we evaluate the inception score [28] based on the fused classification results from our two-stream action classifier. By taking in to consideration the motion flow across the whole video, the output classes serve as an accurate indicator of the actions perceived in the video. Thus such score can give an overall quality of the full video sequence.

4.3 Baselines

We present several baseline methods to provide comparisons of our results with results from previous methods.

For Video Generation, our baseline is *Video-GAN* (VGAN) [35]. This approach trains a GAN that generates videos in pixel space. It is first successful attempt on video generation with deep learning methods.

For Video Prediction, the first baseline is *PredNet* [16], one of the latest results in video prediction. The second baseline is *Multi-Scale GAN* (MS-GAN) proposed by Mathieu et al. [19]. This approach has been successful in various video prediction tasks including human action videos. The third baseline is *Pose-VAE*, a sequential model proposed in [37], which utilized pose representation and have produced state-of-the-art results.

For Video Completion, our baseline is *Conditional Video-GAN* (cond-VGAN) [35]. The model can predict next frames given input as in the paper, therefore we adapt it to video completion by changing its input to the first and last frame.

5   Results

For video generation, we generate videos from random noise vectors with dimensions consistent with the proposed models. For video prediction, we feed the first 4 frames as inputs, i.e. the baselines make prediction based on the input 4 frames, and our model generates videos with the first 4 frames as constraints. For video completion, we fix the first and the last frames as constraints. In order to calculate the proposed metrics, we randomly generate 320 50-frame video samples for each method (except for the Video-GAN method [35] which is fixed by architecture to generate only 32 frames).

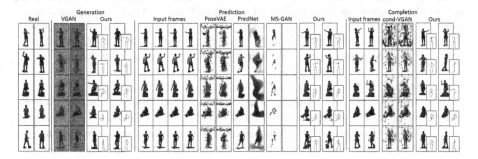

Fig. 8. Qualitative comparisons. Each image-pair column corresponds to a generation method (the first column is real data), and columns are grouped together in the order of generation, prediction and completion, respectively. Each row corresponds to an action class, from top to bottom: Direction, Greeting, Sitting, Sitting Down, Walking. For each method we show the 10th and the 40th frames. For our method we also show the generated pose results

5.1   Qualitative Results

In Fig. 8 we show the qualitative results of our model on Human3.6m dataset [12], in comparison with other state-of-the-art methods. Since the results are videos, we strongly suggest readers to check our supplementary materials. The baseline methods are all fine-tuned/re-trained on our Human3.6m dataset [12]. We show generated results for each of our selected classes. Due to the page limit, we only show the beginning and the middle frames in the result videos.

By examining the results, we find that our model is capable of generating plausible human motion videos with high visual quality. In terms of image

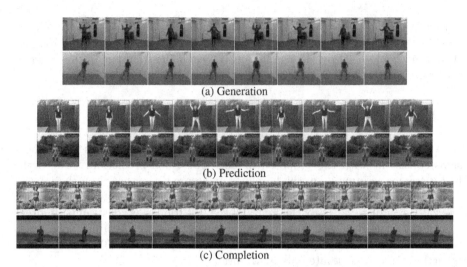

(a) Generation

(b) Prediction

(c) Completion

Fig. 9. Real-world results on UCF-101. For each task, we display 8 frames of our generated videos for the *JumpingJack* (1st row) and *TaiChi* (2nd row) actions. (a) is generated from random noise, (b) is generated given the first four frames (we only show the first frame in the first column), and (c) is generated given the first and last frames (shown in the first two columns). See full videos in supplemental material

quality, we find that our model generates the most compelling human images, while other models tend to generate noisy (particularly Video-GAN) and blurry results due to their structural limitations. By examining the video sequences (provided in supplementary materials), we find that our model can generate natural and interpretable human motions. A key distinction is that we are able to produce large-scale and detailed motion. Another important observation is that, our results maintain high quality over the entire time interval, while the others' quality (especially prediction models) tend to degrade quickly over time.

In Fig. 9 we show the qualitative results for all three tasks on real-world video scenes from UCF-101 [32] to demonstrate our model's capability under real-world environments with background. As shown in the results, we successfully generate videos with high visual quality and interpretability. Additionally, we also test our model on real-world movie footages from the famous Forrest Gump scenes, as shown in Fig. 2. We generate a *Directing* action conducted by the little boy using the running scene as a reference.

5.2   Quantitative Results

Table 1 tabulates our quantitative evaluation results, "frame-IS" stands for Inception Score for frames, and "video-IS" stands for Inception Score for videos. While the ground truth (real) videos have the largest Inception Scores of both types, which matches our intuition, our generated videos have the highest scores among all the competing methods. This suggests that our model generates videos

Table 1. Frame and video inception score (IS)

Method	Real	VGAN [35]	Ours	PoseVAE [37]	PredNet [16]	MS-GAN [19]	Ours	cond-VGAN	Ours
frame-IS	**4.53 ± 0.01**	1.53 ± 0.04	**3.99 ± 0.02**	1.91 ± 0.01	2.60 ± 0.04	1.48 ± 0.01	**3.87 ± 0.02**	2.35 ± 0.02	**3.91 ± 0.02**
video-IS	**4.63 ± 0.09**	1.40 ± 0.16	**3.99 ± 0.18**	2.17 ± 0.11	2.94 ± 0.15	1.88 ± 0.10	**4.09 ± 0.15**	2.00 ± 0.06	**4.10 ± 0.07**

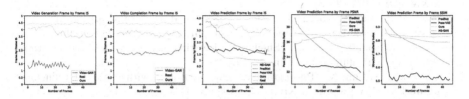

Fig. 10. Left three figures: frame-by-frame inception score for generation, completion and prediction, respectively. Right two figures: frame-by-frame PSNR and SSIM for prediction

that possess meaningful visual features closer to real videos in both image and video (temporal) domains, thus further indicating that our videos are more realistic. We also observe that other methods have much lower scores than ours, and VGAN [35] and MS-GAN [19] are even worse than PredNet [16]. All the statistics are consistent with our qualitative results.

Figure 10 (left three figures) shows a comparison of frame-by-frame Inception Score. We find that the ground truth videos maintain the highest scores at all time steps, and our results have considerably high scores closest to the ground truth quality. A more important observation is that, for the compared prediction models, PredNet [16] and MS-GAN [19], the scores tend to fall across time, indicating that the image quality is deteriorating over time. Although PoseVAE [37] does not decline, its overall image quality is much lower than ours. This observation is consistent with our qualitative evaluation. We also show in Fig. 10 (right two figures) the frame-by-frame PSNR and SSIM (though these are not encouraged). Our methods still outperform others by a large margin in longer timespan. This further illustrates our improvement over current state-of-the-arts.

6   Conclusion

We present a general generative model that addresses the problem of video generation, prediction and completion uniformly. By utilizing human pose as intermediate step with our novel generation strategy, we are able to generate large-scale human motion videos with longer duration. We are then able to solve the later two problems by constrained generation using our model. We find that our model can generate plausible human action videos both from scratch and under constraint, which surpasses current methods both quantitatively and visually.

Acknowledgement. This research is supported in part by Tencent Youtu.

References

1. Arjovsky, M., Chintala, S., Bottou, L.: Wasserstein GAN. arXiv e-prints, January 2017
2. Barratt, S., Sharma, R.: A note on the inception score. arXiv preprint arXiv:1801.01973 (2018)
3. Byrd, R.H., Lu, P., Nocedal, J., Zhu, C.: A limited memory algorithm for bound constrained optimization. SIAM J. Sci. Comput. **16**(5), 1190–1208 (1995)
4. Cao, Z., Simon, T., Wei, S.E., Sheikh, Y.: Realtime multi-person 2D pose estimation using part affinity fields. In: CVPR (2017)
5. Chen, Q., Koltun, V.: Photographic image synthesis with cascaded refinement networks. arXiv preprint arXiv:1707.09405 (2017)
6. Chen, Y., Shen, C., Wei, X., Liu, L., Yang, J.: Adversarial posenet: a structure-aware convolutional network for human pose estimation. CoRR abs/1705.00389 (2017). http://arxiv.org/abs/1705.00389
7. Dong, C., Loy, C.C., He, K., Tang, X.: Image super-resolution using deep convolutional networks. IEEE Trans. Pattern Anal. Mach. Intell. **38**(2), 295–307 (2016)
8. Gatys, L., Ecker, A.S., Bethge, M.: Texture synthesis using convolutional neural networks. In: Advances in Neural Information Processing Systems, pp. 262–270 (2015)
9. Gatys, L.A., Ecker, A.S., Bethge, M.: Image style transfer using convolutional neural networks. In: Proceedings of the IEEE Conference on Computer Vision and Pattern Recognition, pp. 2414–2423 (2016)
10. Goodfellow, I., et al.: Generative adversarial nets. In: NIPS, pp. 2672–2680 (2014). http://papers.nips.cc/paper/5423-generative-adversarial-nets.pdf
11. Gulrajani, I., Ahmed, F., Arjovsky, M., Dumoulin, V., Courville, A.C.: Improved training of Wasserstein GANS. CoRR abs/1704.00028 (2017). http://arxiv.org/abs/1704.00028
12. Ionescu, C., Papava, D., Olaru, V., Sminchisescu, C.: Human3.6M: large scale datasets and predictive methods for 3D human sensing in natural environments. IEEE Trans. Pattern Anal. Mach. Intell. **36**(7), 1325–1339 (2014)
13. Jia, J., Tai, Y.W., Wu, T.P., Tang, C.K.: Video repairing under variable illumination using cyclic motions. IEEE Trans. Pattern Anal. Mach. Intell. **28**(5), 832–839 (2006)
14. Johnson, J., Alahi, A., Fei-Fei, L.: Perceptual losses for real-time style transfer and super-resolution. In: Leibe, B., Matas, J., Sebe, N., Welling, M. (eds.) ECCV 2016. LNCS, vol. 9906, pp. 694–711. Springer, Cham (2016). https://doi.org/10.1007/978-3-319-46475-6_43
15. Li, C., Wand, M.: Combining Markov random fields and convolutional neural networks for image synthesis. In: Proceedings of the IEEE Conference on Computer Vision and Pattern Recognition, pp. 2479–2486 (2016)
16. Lotter, W., Kreiman, G., Cox, D.: Deep predictive coding networks for video prediction and unsupervised learning. arXiv preprint arXiv:1605.08104 (2016)
17. Ma, L., Jia, X., Sun, Q., Schiele, B., Tuytelaars, T., Van Gool, L.: Pose guided person image generation. arXiv preprint arXiv:1705.09368 (2017)
18. Marwah, T., Mittal, G., Balasubramanian, V.N.: Attentive semantic video generation using captions. In: 2017 IEEE International Conference on Computer Vision (ICCV), pp. 1435–1443. IEEE (2017)
19. Mathieu, M., Couprie, C., LeCun, Y.: Deep multi-scale video prediction beyond mean square error. CoRR abs/1511.05440 (2015). http://arxiv.org/abs/1511.05440

20. Mirza, M., Osindero, S.: Conditional generative adversarial nets. arXiv preprint arXiv:1411.1784 (2014)
21. Mordvintsev, A., Olah, C., Tyka, M.: Inceptionism: going deeper into neural networks. Google Research Blog, p. 14. Accessed 20 June 2015
22. Newell, A., Yang, K., Deng, J.: Stacked hourglass networks for human pose estimation. In: Leibe, B., Matas, J., Sebe, N., Welling, M. (eds.) ECCV 2016. LNCS, vol. 9912, pp. 483–499. Springer, Cham (2016). https://doi.org/10.1007/978-3-319-46484-8_29
23. Niklaus, S., Mai, L., Liu, F.: Video frame interpolation via adaptive separable convolution. arXiv preprint arXiv:1708.01692 (2017)
24. Odena, A., Dumoulin, V., Olah, C.: Deconvolution and checkerboard artifacts. Distill 1(10), e3 (2016)
25. Pérez, P., Gangnet, M., Blake, A.: Poisson image editing. In: ACM Transactions on graphics (TOG), vol. 22, pp. 313–318. ACM (2003)
26. Radford, A., Metz, L., Chintala, S.: Unsupervised representation learning with deep convolutional generative adversarial networks. arXiv preprint arXiv:1511.06434 (2015)
27. Ronneberger, O., Fischer, P., Brox, T.: U-net: Convolutional networks for biomedical image segmentation. CoRR abs/1505.04597 (2015). http://arxiv.org/abs/1505.04597
28. Salimans, T., et al.: Improved techniques for training GANS. In: Lee, D.D., Sugiyama, M., Luxburg, U.V., Guyon, I., Garnett, R. (eds.) Advances in Neural Information Processing Systems 29, pp. 2234–2242. Curran Associates, Inc. (2016). http://papers.nips.cc/paper/6125-improved-techniques-for-training-gans.pdf
29. Shi, W., et al.: Real-time single image and video super-resolution using an efficient sub-pixel convolutional neural network. In: Proceedings of the IEEE Conference on Computer Vision and Pattern Recognition, pp. 1874–1883 (2016)
30. Simonyan, K., Zisserman, A.: Very deep convolutional networks for large-scale image recognition. CoRR abs/1409.1556 (2014)
31. Simonyan, K., Zisserman, A.: Two-stream convolutional networks for action recognition in videos. In: Advances in Neural Information Processing Systems, pp. 568–576 (2014)
32. Soomro, K., Zamir, A.R., Shah, M.: UCF101: a dataset of 101 human actions classes from videos in the wild. arXiv preprint arXiv:1212.0402 (2012)
33. Toshev, A., Szegedy, C.: Deeppose: human pose estimation via deep neural networks. In: Proceedings of the 2014 IEEE Conference on Computer Vision and Pattern Recognition, pp. 1653–1660. CVPR 2014. IEEE Computer Society, Washington, DC, USA (2014). https://doi.org/10.1109/CVPR.2014.214
34. Villegas, R., Yang, J., Zou, Y., Sohn, S., Lin, X., Lee, H.: Learning to generate long-term future via hierarchical prediction. In: International Conference on Machine Learning, pp. 3560–3569 (2017)
35. Vondrick, C., Pirsiavash, H., Torralba, A.: Generating videos with scene dynamics. In: Lee, D.D., Sugiyama, M., Luxburg, U.V., Guyon, I., Garnett, R. (eds.) Advances in Neural Information Processing Systems 29, pp. 613–621. Curran Associates, Inc. (2016). http://papers.nips.cc/paper/6194-generating-videos-with-scene-dynamics.pdf
36. Walker, J., Doersch, C., Gupta, A., Hebert, M.: An uncertain future: forecasting from static images using variational autoencoders. In: Leibe, B., Matas, J., Sebe, N., Welling, M. (eds.) ECCV 2016. LNCS, vol. 9911, pp. 835–851. Springer, Cham (2016). https://doi.org/10.1007/978-3-319-46478-7_51

37. Walker, J., Marino, K., Gupta, A., Hebert, M.: The pose knows: Video forecasting by generating pose futures. CoRR abs/1705.00053 (2017). http://arxiv.org/abs/1705.00053

38. Wang, L., et al.: Temporal segment networks: towards good practices for deep action recognition. In: Leibe, B., Matas, J., Sebe, N., Welling, M. (eds.) ECCV 2016. LNCS, vol. 9912, pp. 20–36. Springer, Cham (2016). https://doi.org/10.1007/978-3-319-46484-8_2

39. Wang, X., Gupta, A.: Generative image modeling using style and structure adversarial networks. In: Leibe, B., Matas, J., Sebe, N., Welling, M. (eds.) ECCV 2016. LNCS, vol. 9908, pp. 318–335. Springer, Cham (2016). https://doi.org/10.1007/978-3-319-46493-0_20

40. Wang, Z., Bovik, A.C., Sheikh, H.R., Simoncelli, E.P.: Image quality assessment: from error visibility to structural similarity. IEEE Trans. Image Process. 13(4), 600–612 (2004)

41. Wei, S.E., Ramakrishna, V., Kanade, T., Sheikh, Y.: Convolutional pose machines. In: CVPR (2016)

42. Wexler, Y., Shechtman, E., Irani, M.: Space-time completion of video. IEEE Trans. Pattern Anal. Mach. Intell. 29(3), 463–476 (2007). https://doi.org/10.1109/TPAMI.2007.60

43. Xue, T., Wu, J., Bouman, K., Freeman, B.: Visual dynamics: probabilistic future frame synthesis via cross convolutional networks. In: Advances in Neural Information Processing Systems, pp. 91–99 (2016)

44. Yan, Y., Xu, J., Ni, B., Yang, X.: Skeleton-aided articulated motion generation. arXiv preprint arXiv:1707.01058 (2017)

45. Yeh, R.A., Chen, C., Lim, T.Y., Schwing, A.G., Hasegawa-Johnson, M., Do, M.N.: Semantic image inpainting with deep generative models. In: CVPR (2017)

46. Zanfir, M., Popa, A.I., Zanfir, A., Sminchisescu, C.: Human appearance transfer

47. Zhang, R., Isola, P., Efros, A.A.: Colorful image colorization. In: Leibe, B., Matas, J., Sebe, N., Welling, M. (eds.) ECCV 2016. LNCS, vol. 9907, pp. 649–666. Springer, Cham (2016). https://doi.org/10.1007/978-3-319-46487-9_40

48. Zhu, J.-Y., Krähenbühl, P., Shechtman, E., Efros, A.A.: Generative visual manipulation on the natural image manifold. In: Leibe, B., Matas, J., Sebe, N., Welling, M. (eds.) ECCV 2016. LNCS, vol. 9909, pp. 597–613. Springer, Cham (2016). https://doi.org/10.1007/978-3-319-46454-1_36

Semantic Match Consistency
for Long-Term Visual Localization

Carl Toft[1], Erik Stenborg[1], Lars Hammarstrand[1], Lucas Brynte[1],
Marc Pollefeys[2,3], Torsten Sattler[2(✉)], and Fredrik Kahl[1]

[1] Department of Electrical Engineering, Chalmers University of Technology,
Gothenburg, Sweden
`{carl.toft,erik.stenborg,brynte,fredrik.kahl}@chalmers.se`
[2] Department of Computer Science, ETH Zürich, Zürich, Switzerland
`sattlert@inf.ethz.ch`
[3] Microsoft, Zürich, Switzerland

Abstract. Robust and accurate visual localization across large appearance variations due to changes in time of day, seasons, or changes of the environment is a challenging problem which is of importance to application areas such as navigation of autonomous robots. Traditional feature-based methods often struggle in these conditions due to the significant number of erroneous matches between the image and the 3D model. In this paper, we present a method for scoring the individual correspondences by exploiting semantic information about the query image and the scene. In this way, erroneous correspondences tend to get a low semantic consistency score, whereas correct correspondences tend to get a high score. By incorporating this information in a standard localization pipeline, we show that the localization performance can be significantly improved compared to the state-of-the-art, as evaluated on two challenging long-term localization benchmarks.

Keywords: Visual localization · Semantic segmentation
Camera pose estimation · Outlier rejection · Self-driving cars

1 Introduction

Visual localization, i.e., estimating the camera pose of a query image with respect to a scene model, is one of the core problems in computer vision. It plays a central role in a wide range of practical applications, such as Structure-from-Motion (SfM) [43], augmented reality [9], and robotics [31], where visual navigation for autonomous vehicles has recently been receiving considerable attention.

Electronic supplementary material The online version of this chapter (https://doi.org/10.1007/978-3-030-01216-8_24) contains supplementary material, which is available to authorized users.

V. Ferrari et al. (Eds.): ECCV 2018, LNCS 11206, pp. 391–408, 2018.
https://doi.org/10.1007/978-3-030-01216-8_24

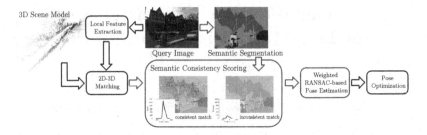

Fig. 1. Illustration of the visual localization approach proposed in this paper. We extend the standard localization pipeline (blue boxes) to include a semantic consistency score (red boxes). Our approach rates the consistency of each 2D-3D match and uses the score to prioritize more consistent matches during RANSAC-based pose estimation. (Color figure online)

Traditional approaches to the visual localization problem [27–29, 38, 40, 47, 58] rely on local feature descriptors to establish correspondences between 2D features found in a query image and 3D points in an SfM model of the scene. These 2D-3D matches are then used to estimate the camera pose of the query image by applying an n-point-pose solver, e.g., [23], inside a RANSAC loop [18]. Learning-based alternatives exist [6, 7, 21, 22, 51], but are either less accurate than feature-based approaches [40, 51] or struggle to handle larger scenes [7, 21, 37]. Feature-based approaches thus still represent the current state-of-the-art [37, 40, 51].

Existing feature-based methods for visual localization tend to work very well when the query image is taken under similar conditions as the database images used for creating the 3D model. However, feature matching performance suffers if the localization and mapping stages occur far apart in time [37], e.g., in different weather conditions, between day and night, or across different seasons. As feature detectors become less repeatable and feature descriptors less similar, localization pipelines struggle to find enough correct 2D-3D matches to facilitate successful pose estimation. One possible solution is to map the scene in as wide a range of different conditions as possible. Yet, 3D model construction and extensive data collection are costly, time-consuming, and tedious processes. At the same time, the resulting models consume a significant amount of memory. Developing localization algorithms that work well across a wide range of conditions, even if the 3D model is constructed using only a single condition, is thus desirable.

This paper presents a step towards robust algorithms for long-term visual localization through a novel strategy for robust inlier/outlier detection. The main insight is that semantic information can be used as a weak supervisory signal to distinguish between correct and incorrect correspondences: Given a semantic segmentation for each database image, we can assign a semantic label to each 3D point in the SfM model. Given a pose estimate for a query image, we can project the 3D points into a semantic segmentation of the query image. An estimate close to the correct pose should lead to a *semantically consistent* projection,

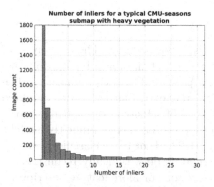
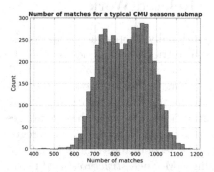

Fig. 2. For each ground truth camera pose, we have counted how many true inlier 2D-3D matches have been obtained at the matching stage (shown in the left figure). Note that in around 70% of the cases, there are less than 7 true inliers. For structure-based methods, typically 12 or more consistent 2D-3D matches are required to compute and verify a camera pose, cf. [27,28,36]. The right figure shows a histogram over the number of matches for the same submap from the CMU Seasons dataset [5,37].

where each point is projected to an image region with the same semantic label. Based on this idea, we assign each 2D-3D match a semantic consistency score, where high scores are assigned to matches more likely to be correct. We later use these scores to bias sampling during RANSAC-based pose estimation. See Fig. 1 for an overview. While conceptually simple, this strategy leads to dramatic improvements in terms of localization rate and pose accuracy in the long-term localization scenario. The reason is that, unlike existing methods, our approach takes advantage of unmatched 3D points, and consequently copes much better with situations in which only few correct matches can be found.

While the idea of using semantics for localization is not new, cf. [42,48], the challenge is to develop a computationally tractable framework that takes advantage of the available information. In detail, this paper makes the following contributions: (1) We present a new localization method that incorporates both standard feature matching and semantic information in a robust and efficient manner. At the center of our method is a novel semantic consistency check that allows us to rate the quality of individual 2D-3D matches. (2) We extensively evaluate and compare our method to the current state-of-the-art on two benchmarks for long-term visual localization. Our experimental results show significant improvements by incorporating semantics, particularly for challenging scenarios due to change of weather, seasonal, and lighting conditions.

The remainder of this paper is structured as follows: Section 2 reviews related work. Section 3 derives our semantic consistency score and shows how it can be incorporated into a state-of-the-art localization pipeline. Section 4 extensively evaluates our approach in the context of long-term localization.

2   Related Work

Traditionally, there are two approaches to visual localization: The first one uses image retrieval techniques to find the most relevant database images for each query image [1,11,24,39,41,49,56,57]. The pose of the query image is then approximated by the pose of the top-ranked retrieved image [11] or computed from the top-k ranking database images [40,56,59]. Instead of explicitly representing a scene by a database of images, another approach is to implicitly model a scene by a CNN trained for pose regression [21,22,51] or place classification [52].

The second approach is based on 3D scene models, typically reconstructed using SfM. Such *structure-based* methods assign one or more feature descriptors, e.g., SIFT [30] or LIFT [53], to each 3D point. For a given query image, 2D-3D correspondences are established using descriptor matching. These matches are then used to estimate the camera pose. Compared to image-retrieval approaches, structure-based methods tend to provide more accurate camera poses [40]. Yet, it is necessary that enough correct matches are found to not only estimate a pose, but also to verify that the pose is indeed correct, e.g., through inlier counting. As shown in Fig. 2 and [37], these conditions are often not satisfied when the query images are taken under significantly different conditions compared to the database images. Our approach extends structure-based methods by incorporating semantic scene understanding into the pose estimation stage.

Structure-based approaches for visual localization can be classified based on their efficiency and ability to handle more complex scenes. Approaches based on prioritized matching [12,28,36] focus on efficiency by terminating correspondence search once a fixed number of matches has been found. In order to handle more complex environments, robust structure-based approaches either relax the matching criteria [8,27,38,47,58] or restrict the search space [20,27,29,38]. The latter type of methods use image retrieval [20,38] or co-visibility information [27,29] to determine which parts of the scene are visible in a query image, potentially allowing them to disambiguate matches. The former type handles the larger amount of outliers resulting from a more relaxed matching stage through deterministic outlier filtering. To this end, they use geometric reasoning to determine how consistent each match is with all other matches [8,47,58]. Especially when the gravity direction is known, which is typically the case in practice (e.g., via sensors or vanishing points), such approaches can handle outlier ratios of 99% or more [47,58]. Our approach combines techniques from geometric outlier filtering [47,58] with reasoning based on scene semantics. This enables our method to better handle scenarios where it is hard to find correct 2D-3D matches.

An alternative to obtaining 2D-3D correspondences via explicit feature matching is to directly learn the matching function [6,7,10,33,45,50]. Such methods implicitly represent the 3D scene structure via a random forest or CNN that predicts a 3D scene coordinate for a given image patch [33]. While these methods can achieve a higher pose accuracy than feature-based approaches [7], they also have problems handling larger outdoor scenes to the extent that training might fail completely [7,37,42].

The idea of using semantic scene understanding as part of the visual localization process has gained popularity over the last few years. A common strategy is to include semantics in the matching stage of visual localization pipelines, either by detecting and matching objects [3,4,15,35,44,55] or by enhancing classical feature descriptors [2,25,46]. The latter type of approaches still mainly relies on the strength of the original descriptor as semantics only provide a weak additional signal. Thus, these approaches do not solve the problem of finding enough correct correspondences, which motivates our work. Recent work shows that directly learning a descriptor that encodes both 3D scene geometry and semantic information significantly improves matching performance [42]. Yet, this approach requires depth maps for each query image, e.g., from stereo, which are not necessarily available in the scenario we are considering.

In contrast to the previously discussed approaches, which aim at improving the matching stage in visual localization, our method focuses on the subsequent pose estimation stage. As such, most similar to ours is existing work on semantic hypothesis verification [14] and semantic pose refinement [48]. Given a hypothesis for the alignment of two SfM models, Cohen et al. [14] project the 3D points of one model into semantic segmentations of the images used to reconstruct the other model. They count the number of 3D points projecting into regions labelled as "sky" and select the alignment hypotheses with lowest number of such free-space violations. While Cohen et al. make hard decisions, our approach avoids them by converting our semantic consistency score into sampling probabilities for RANSAC. Our approach aims at improving pose hypothesis generation while Cohen et al. only rate given hypotheses. Given an initial camera pose hypothesis, Toft et al. [48] use semantics to obtain a refined pose estimate by improving the semantic consistency of projected 3D points and curve segments. Their approach could be used as a post-processing step for the poses estimated by our method.

3   Semantic Match Consistency for Visual Localization

As outlined above, long-term localization is a hard problem due to the difficulty of establishing reliable correspondences. Our approach follows a standard feature-based pipeline and is illustrated in Fig. 1. Our central contribution is a novel semantic consistency score that is used to determine which matches are likely to be correct. Building on top of existing work on geometric outlier filtering [47,58], we generate a set of pose hypotheses for each 2D-3D correspondence established during the descriptor matching stage. These poses are then used to measure the semantic consistency of each match. We then use the consistency scores to bias sampling inside RANSAC towards semantically consistent matches, allowing RANSAC to focus more on matches more likely to be correct.

Specifically, for each pose hypothesis generated by a given 2D-3D match, we project the visible 3D structure into the corresponding camera. Since each 3D point is endowed with a semantic label, it is possible to compare the observed semantic label in the query image with the label assigned to the 3D point. The semantic inlier count for that pose is given by the number of 3D points that

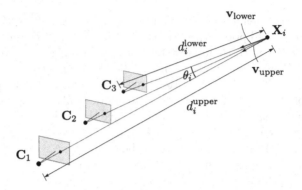

Fig. 3. Example triangulation of a point during the 3D reconstruction of the point cloud. The example shows a 3D point triangulated from three observations. The quantities θ_i, d_i^{lower} and d_i^{upper} as defined in the text are shown. The vector $\boldsymbol{v}_i$ for this point is the unit vector in the middle between $\boldsymbol{v}^{\text{lower}}$ and $\boldsymbol{v}^{\text{upper}}$.

project into pixels whose semantic class agrees with that of the point. The semantic consistency for the 2D-3D correspondence is then defined as the maximum semantic inlier count over all hypotheses generated by that correspondence.

Our approach offers a clear advantage over existing outlier filtering strategies [8,47,58]: Rather than being restricted to the 2D-3D correspondences found during the matching stage, the semantic consistency score allows us to also use unmatched 3D points when rating the 2D-3D matches. As a result, our approach is better able to handle scenarios in which it is hard to find many correct matches.

In this section, we present our proposed localization method based on semantic consistency in detail. We first introduce necessary notation. Section 3.1 explains the pose hypothesis generation stage. Our semantic consistency score is then described in Sect. 3.2. Finally, Sect. 3.3 summarizes the complete pipeline.

Notation. We compute the camera pose of a query image relative to a 3D point cloud that has been pre-computed using a regular Structure-from-Motion pipeline. The 3D map is defined as a set of 3D points

$$\mathcal{M} = \{(\boldsymbol{X}_i, c_i, \boldsymbol{f}_i, \boldsymbol{v}_i, \theta_i, d_i^{\text{lower}}, d_i^{\text{upper}})\}_{i=1}^N , \tag{1}$$

where N is the number of 3D points in the model. Each 3D point is defined by its 3D coordinates $\boldsymbol{X}_i$, its class label c_i (e.g., vegetation, road, etc.), visibility information, and its corresponding (mean) feature descriptor $\boldsymbol{f}_i$. We encode the visibility information of a point as follows (cf. Fig. 3): $\boldsymbol{v}_i$ is a unit vector pointing from the 3D point towards the mean direction from which the 3D point was seen during reconstruction. It is computed by determining the two most extreme viewpoints from which the point was triangulated ($\boldsymbol{v}_{\text{lower}}$ and $\boldsymbol{v}_{\text{upper}}$ in the figure) and choosing the direction half-way between them. The angle θ_i is the angle between the two vectors. The quantities d_i^{lower} and d_i^{upper} denote the

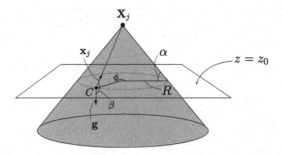

Fig. 4. If the gravity direction is known in the camera's coordinate system, a single 2D-3D match $x_j \leftrightarrow X_j$ constrains the camera center to lie on a cone with X_j at the vertex, and whose axis is parallel to the gravity direction. If the camera height is also known, the camera center must lie on a circle (shown in red). (Color figure online)

minimum and maximum distances, respectively, from which the 3D point was observed during SfM. Note that all this information is readily provided by SfM.

The semantic class labels are found by performing a pixelwise semantic labelling of all database images. For a 3D point in the SfM model, we assign its label c_i to the semantic class it was most frequently observed in.

3.1 Generating Camera Pose Hypotheses

In order to determine the semantic consistency of a single 2D-3D match $x_j \leftrightarrow X_j$, we compute a set of plausible camera poses for this match. We thereby follow the setup used by geometric outlier filters [47,58] and assume that the gravity direction g in the local camera coordinates of the query image is known. This assumption is not restrictive as the gravity direction can typically be estimated very reliably from sensors or from vanishing points. In the experiments, the gravity direction in local camera coordinates was extracted from the ground truth camera pose.

Knowing the intrinsic camera calibration and the point position X_j, the correspondence can be used to restrict the set of plausible camera poses under which X_j exactly projects to x_j [47,58]: The camera center must lie on a circular cone with X_j at its vertex (cf. Fig. 4). To see this, let the position of the camera center be C and the coordinates of X_j be $(x_j, y_j, z_j)^T$. In a slight abuse of notation, let x_j be the normalized viewing direction corresponding to the matching 2D feature. Since the gravity vector g in local camera coordinates is known, we can measure the angle β between the gravity direction and the line that joins C and X_j as $\beta = \arccos(g^T x_j)$. Assuming that the gravity direction in the 3D model coincides with the z-axis, the angle between the line joining C and X_j and the xy − plane then is

$$\alpha = \arccos(g^T x_j) - \pi/2 \ . \tag{2}$$

The set of points C such that the angle between the xy − plane and the line joining C and X_j equals α is a cone with X_j as the vertex. Note that the

---

Algorithm 1. Semantic consistency score calculation for single correspondence

```
 1: procedure CALCULATESCORE(x_j, X_j, g, z_0, M)
 2:     maxScore ← 0
 3:     α ← arccos(g^T x_j) − π/2                               ▷ Angle of cone
 4:     R ← |z_j − z_0|/| tan α|              ▷ Radius of circle of possible camera poses
 5:     for φ ∈ {0°, 1°, . . . , 359°} do
 6:         score ← 0
 7:         Calculate camera center C(φ) using φ
 8:         Calculate projection matrix P(φ) using R, C(φ)
 9:         for X_k ∈ M do
10:             u ← P(φ)X_k                           ▷ Project 3D point into query image
11:             if C(φ) ∈ V_k and I_semantic(u) = c_k then
12:                 score ← score + 1            ▷ Point is visible and semantically consistent
13:         if score > maxScore then
14:             maxScore ← score
15:             C_best ← C(φ)
16:     return (maxScore, C_best)
```

---

cone's position and opening angle are fully determined by g and the correspondence $x_j \leftrightarrow X_j$. Also note that the camera rotation is fully determined at each point of the cone [58]: two of the rotational degrees of freedom are fixed by the known gravity direction and the last degree is fixed by requiring that the viewing direction of x_j points to X_j. As a result, two degrees-of-freedom remain for the camera pose, corresponding to a position on the cone's surface.

Often, the camera height z_0 can be roughly estimated from the typical depth of the 3D point in the SfM model[1]. Knowing the camera height removes one degree of freedom. As a result, the camera must lie on the circle with radius R given by $R = |z_j − z_0|/| \tan α|$, which lies in the plane $z = z_0$, and whose center point is the point (x_j, y_j, z_0) [58]. For a single correspondence $x_j \leftrightarrow X_j$, we thus generate a set of plausible camera poses by varying an angle $φ$ that defines positions on this circle (cf. Fig. 4).

3.2   Measuring Semantic Match Consistency

Given a 2D-3D match $x_j \leftrightarrow X_j$ and its corresponding set of camera pose hypotheses (obtained by discretizing the circle into evenly spaced points), we next compute a *semantic consistency score* as described in Algorithm 1.

For a camera pose hypothesis corresponding to an angle $φ$, we project the semantically labelled 3D points from the SfM model into a semantic segmentation of the query image. We then count the number of 3D points that project to a pixel whose semantic class matches that of the 3D point. For each pose on the circle, we thus find the number of 3D points that agree with the semantic labelling of the query image. The semantic consistency score for a match $x_j \leftrightarrow X_j$ is then defined as the maximum number of semantic inliers while sweeping the angle $φ$. Note that we project all 3D points in the model, not only the correspondences found via descriptor matching. This means that the calculation of the consistency score is not dependent of the quality of the correspondences.

---

[1] This strategy is used in the experiments to estimate the camera heights.

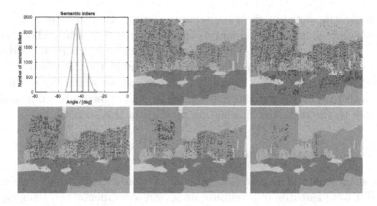

Fig. 5. An example for sweeping over the angle ϕ for a single correct 2D-3D match. The upper left figure shows the number of semantic inliers as a function of ϕ. The five images with projected points correspond to the red lines in the top left and are shown in order from left to right. The upper right image corresponds to the angle that yielded the largest number of semantic inliers. (Color figure online)

Since we are using all 3D points in a model, we need to explicitly handle occlusions: a 3D point is not necessarily visible in the image even though it projects inside the image area for a given camera pose. We do so by defining a visibility volume for each 3D point from the corresponding visibility information v_i, θ_i, d_i^{lower} and d_i^{upper}. The volume for the ith point is defined as

$$\mathcal{V}_i = \left\{ \boldsymbol{X} \in \mathbf{R}^3 : d_i^{\text{lower}} < ||\boldsymbol{X} - \boldsymbol{X}_i|| < d_i^{\text{upper}}||, \angle(\boldsymbol{X} - \boldsymbol{X}_i, \boldsymbol{v}_i) < \theta_i \right\} \ . \quad (3)$$

A 3D point is only considered visible from a camera pose with with its center at C if $C \in \mathcal{V}_i$. The intuition is that a 3D point only contributes to the semantic score if it is viewed from approximately the same distance and direction as the 3D point was seen from when it was triangulated during SfM. This is not too much of a restriction since local features are not completely invariant to changes in viewpoint, i.e., features naturally do not match anymore if a query image is taken too far away from the closest database image.

To further speed up the semantic scoring, we limit the set of labelled points that are projected into the image. For a 2D-3D match, only those 3D points inside a cylinder with radius R whose axis aligns with the gravity direction and goes through the 3D point $\boldsymbol{X}_j$ are considered.

Discussion. Intuitively, if a match $\boldsymbol{x}_j \leftrightarrow \boldsymbol{X}_j$ is correct, we expect the number of semantic inliers to be large for values of ϕ that correspond to camera poses close to the ground truth pose, and small for values of ϕ that yield poses distant to the ground truth pose. An example of this behavior is shown in Fig. 5. On the other hand, if a match is an outlier, we would expect only a small number of semantic inliers for all values of ϕ (cf. Fig. 1).

Naturally, the distribution of the number of semantic inliers over the angle ϕ and the absolute value of the semantic consistency score depend on how "semantically interesting"a scene is. As shown in Fig. 2, the case where many different classes are observed leads to a clear and high peak in the distribution. If only a single class is visible, e.g., "building", we can expect a more uniform distribution, both for correct and incorrect matches. As shown later, our approach degenerates to the standard localization pipeline in this scenario.

3.3   Full Localization Pipeline

Figure 1 shows our full localization pipeline: Given a query image, we extract local (SIFT [30]) features and compute its semantic segmentation. Using approximate nearest neighbor search, we compute 2D-3D matches between the query features and the 3D model points. We follow common practice and use Lowe's ratio test to filter out ambiguous matches [30]. Similar to work on geometric outlier filtering [8,47,58], we use a rather relaxed threshold of 0.9 for the ratio test to avoid rejecting correct matches. Next, we apply our proposed approach to compute a semantic consistency score per 2D-3D match (cf. Algorithm 1). For each correspondence, an estimate of the camera height z_0 is obtained by checking where the database trajectory (whose poses and camera heights are available) intersects the cone of possible poses. Lastly, we apply an n-point-pose solver inside a RANSAC loop for pose estimation, using 10'000 iterations.

We use the consistency scores to adapt RANSAC's sampling scheme. More precisely, we normalize each score by the sum of the scores of all matches. We interpret this normalized score as a probability p_j and use it to bias RANSAC's sampling, i.e., RANSAC selects a match $x_j \leftrightarrow X_j$ with probability p_j. This can thus be seen as a "soft" version of outlier rejection: instead of explicitly removing correspondences that seem to be outliers, it just becomes unlikely that they are sampled inside RANSAC. This strategy guarantees that our approach gracefully degenerates to a standard pipeline in semantically ambiguous scenes.

4   Experimental Evaluation

In this section we present experimental evaluations of the proposed algorithm on two challenging benchmark datasets for long-term visual localization. The datasets used are the *CMU Seasons* and *RobotCar Seasons* datasets from [37].

CMU Seasons. The dataset is based on the CMU Visual Localization dataset [5]. It consists of 7,159 database images that can be used for map building, and 75,335 query images for evaluation. The images are collected from two sideways facing cameras mounted on a car while traversing the same route in Pittsburgh on 12 different occasions over the course of a year. It captures many different environmental conditions, including overcast weather, direct sunlight, snow, and trees with and without foliage. The route contains urban and suburban areas, as well as parks mostly dominated by vegetation. All images are accompanied by accurate six degrees-of-freedom ground truth poses [37].

CMU Seasons is a very challenging dataset due to the large variations in appearance of the environment over time. Especially challenging are the areas dominated by vegetation, since these regions change drastically in appearance under different lighting conditions and in different seasons.

We used the Dilation10 network [54] trained on the Cityscapes dataset [16] to obtain the semantic segmentations. The classes used to label the 3D points were: sky, building, vegetation, road, sidewalk, pole and terrain/grass.

RobotCar Seasons. The dataset is based on a subset of the Oxford RobotCar dataset [32]. It was collected using a car-mounted camera rig consisting of 3 cameras facing to the left, right and rear of the car. The dataset consists of 26,121 database images taken at 8,707 positions, and 11,934 query images captured at 3,978 positions. All images are from a mostly urban setting in Oxford, UK, but they cover a wide variety of environmental conditions, including varying light conditions at day and night, seasonal changes from summer to winter, and various weather conditions such as sun, rain, and snow. All images have a reference pose associated with them. The average reference pose error is estimated to be below 0.10 m in position and 0.5° in orientation [37].

The most challenging images of this dataset are the night images. They both exhibit a big change in lighting, but also, due to longer exposure times, contain significant motion blur.

For the RobotCar dataset, semantic segmentations were obtained using the PSPNet network [60], trained jointly on the Cityscapes [16] and Mapillary Vistas [34] datasets[2]. Additionally, 69 daytime and 13 nighttime images from the RobotCar dataset [32] were manually annotated by us, and incorporated into the training, in order to alleviate generalization issues. The classes used to label the 3D points were: sky, building, vegetation, road, sidewalk, pole and terrain/grass.

Evaluation Protocol. We follow the evaluation protocol from [37], i.e., we report the percentage of query images for which the estimated pose differs by at most X m and $Y°$ from their ground truth pose. As in [37], we use three different threshold combinations, namely (0.25 m, 2°), (0.5 m, 5°), and (5 m, 10°).

4.1 Ablation Study

In this section we present an ablation study of our approach on both datasets.

The baseline is a standard, unweighted RANSAC procedure that samples each 2D-3D match with the same probability. We combine this RANSAC variant, denoted as *unweighted*, with two pose solvers: the first is a standard 3-point

---

[2] Starting from a network pretrained on Cityscapes, joint training was carried out by regarding 4 Cityscapes samples, 4 Mapillary Vistas samples and 1 RobotCar sample in each iteration. Mapillary Vistas labels were mapped to Cityscapes labels by us.

Table 1. Ablation study of our approach on the CMU Seasons dataset

Method / Setting m deg	Urban 0.25 / 0.5 / 5 2 / 5 / 10	Suburban 0.25 / 0.5 / 5 2 / 5 / 10	Park 0.25 / 0.5 / 5 2 / 5 / 10
Weighted, P3P	75.2 / 82.1 / 87.7	44.6 / 53.9 / 63.5	30.4 / 37.8 / 48.0
Unweighted, P3P	42.5 / 50.0 / 64.5	11.5 / 16.8 / 30.1	9.3 / 13.1 / 24.2
Weighted, P2P	**81.7 / 88.0 / 92.3**	**55.4 / 65.5 / 73.1**	**39.5 / 47.5 / 58.2**
Unweighted, P2P	72.9 / 80.0 / 87.0	41.3 / 50.8 / 61.8	29.7 / 37.0 / 49.1

Table 2. Ablation study of our approach on the RobotCar Seasons dataset

Method / Setting m deg	all day 0.25 / 0.5 / 5 2 / 5 / 10	all night 0.25 / 0.5 / 5 2 / 5 / 10
Weighted, P3P	**50.6 / 79.8 / 95.1**	7.6 / 21.5 / 45.4
Unweighted, P3P	47.0 / 74.8 / 91.9	0.5 / 4.2 / 16.0
Weighted, P2P	35.4 / 73.2 / 93.4	**13.0 / 34.1 / 63.1**
Unweighted, P2P	34.1 / 71.3 / 93.3	5.1 / 20.8 / 46.8

solver [19] (P3P) since the intrinsic calibration is known for all query images. The second solver is a 2-point solver [26] (P2P) that uses the known gravity direction. We compare both baselines against our proposed *weighted* RANSAC variant that uses our semantic consistency scores to estimate a sampling probability for each 2D-3D match. Again, we combine our approach with both pose solvers.

Tables 1 and 2 show the results of our ablation study. As can be seen, using our proposed semantic consistency scores (*weighted*) leads to clear and significant improvements in localization performance for all scenes and solvers on the CMU dataset. On the RobotCar dataset, we similar observe a significant improvement when measuring semantic consistency, with the exception of using the P2P solver during daytime. Interestingly, the P2P solver outperforms the P3P solver on both datasets using both RANSAC variants, with the exception of the daytime query images of the Oxford RobotCar dataset. The reason for this is likely due to sensitivity of the P2P solver to small noise in the ground truth vertical direction.

4.2   Comparison with State-of-the-Art

After demonstrating the benefit of our proposed semantic consistency scoring, we compare our localization pipeline against state-of-the-art approaches on both datasets, using the results reported in [37]. More concretely, we compare against ActiveSearch (AS) [36] and the City-Scale Localization (CSL) [47] methods, which represent the state-of-the-art in efficient and scalable localization, respectively. In addition, we compare against two image retrieval-based baselines, namely DenseVLAD [49] and NetVLAD [1], when their results are available in [37]. We omitted results for the methods LocalSfM, DenseSfM, ActiveSearch+Generalized Camera, and FABMAP [17] present in [37], since these use either a sequence of images (the latter two), costly SfM approaches

Table 3. Comparison of our approach, using semantic consistency scoring and the P3P pose solver, with state-of-the-art approaches on the CMU Seasons dataset

Method / Setting m deg	Urban 0.25 / 0.5 / 5 2 / 5 / 10	Suburban 0.25 / 0.5 / 5 2 / 5 / 10	Park 0.25 / 0.5 / 5 2 / 5 / 10
ActiveSearch [36]	55.2 / 60.3 / 65.1	20.7 / 25.9 / 29.9	12.7 / 16.3 / 20.8
CSL [47]	36.7 / 42.0 / 53.1	8.6 / 11.7 / 21.1	7.0 / 9.6 / 17.0
DenseVLAD [49]	22.2 / 48.7 / 92.8	9.6 / 26.6 / **85.2**	10.3 / 27.0 / **77.0**
NetVLAD [1]	17.4 / 40.3 / **93.2**	7.7 / 20.1 / 80.5	5.6 / 15.7 / 65.8
PROSAC P3P [13]	56.7 / 64.0 / 74.2	30.6 / 38.3 / 49.1	20.0 / 25.4 / 35.1
Single-match P3P	59.3 / 66.8 / 76.2	24.6 / 32.4 / 44.6	16.8 / 22.2 / 32.6
Sem. rank. (**ours**)	**75.2 / 82.1 / 87.7**	**44.6 / 53.9 / 63.5**	**30.4 / 37.8** / 48.0

Table 4. Comparison of our approach, using semantic consistency scoring and the P3P pose solver, with state-of-the-art approaches on the RobotCar Seasons dataset

Method / Setting m deg	all day 0.25 / 0.5 / 5 2 / 5 / 10	all night 0.25 / 0.5 / 5 2 / 5 / 10
ActiveSearch [36]	35.6 / 67.9 / 90.4	0.9 / 2.1 / 4.3
CSL [47]	45.3 / 73.5 / 90.1	0.6 / 2.6 / 7.2
PROSAC P3P [13]	50.4 / 79.1 / 96.4	3.9 / 14.1 / 34.4
Single-match P3P	**50.7** / 79.3 / **97.2**	2.5 / 6.4 / 16.7
Sem. rank. (**ours**)	50.6 / **79.8** / 95.1	**7.6 / 21.5 / 45.4**

coupled with a strong location prior (the former two), or use ground truth information (the former three), and are thus not directly comparable. For a fair comparison with AS and CSL, we use the variant of our localization pipeline that uses semantic consistency scoring and the P3P solver.

Tables 3 and 4 show the results of our comparison. As can be seen, our approach significantly outperforms both AS and CSL, especially in the high-precision regime. Especially the comparison with CSL is interesting as our pose generation stage is based on its geometric outlier filtering strategy. The clear improvements over CSL validate our idea of incorporating scene semantics into the pose estimation stage in general and the idea of using non-matching 3D points to score matches in particular.

On the CMU dataset, both DenseVLAD and NetVLAD can localize more query images in the coarse-precision regime (5 m, 10°). Both approaches represent images using a compact image-level descriptor and approximate the pose of the query image using the pose of the top-retrieved database image. Both methods do not use any feature matching between images. As shown in Fig. 6, this allows DenseVLAD and NetVLAD to handle scenarios with very strong appearance changes in which feature matching completely fails. Note that both DenseVLAD or NetVLAD could be used as a fallback option for our approach.

Database image   Query image   Segmented image

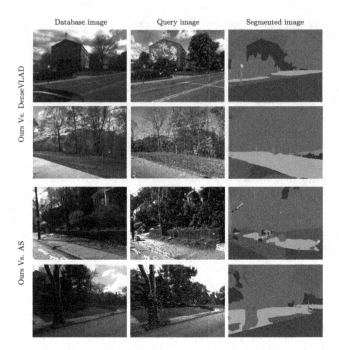

Fig. 6. Illustrations of the result of our method on the CMU Seasons dataset. Rows 1 and 3 show query images that our method successfully localizes (error < .25 m) while DenseVLAD and AS fail (error > 10 m) and rows 2 and 4 the vice versa. Green boxes indicate true correspondences, while gray circles indicate false correspondences. White/red crosses indicate correctly/incorrectly detected inliers, respectively. (Color figure online)

Interestingly, the P3P RANSAC baseline outperforms AS and CSL in several instances. This is likely due to differing feature matching strategies and different numbers of RANSAC iterations. Active Search uses a very strict ratio test, which causes problems in challenging scenes. CSL was evaluated on CMU Seasons by keeping all detected features (no ratio test), resulting in several thousand matches per image. CSL may have yielded better results with a ratio test.

In addition, we also compare our approach to two methods based on P3P RANSAC. The first is PROSAC [13], a RANSAC variant that uses a deterministic sampling strategy, where correspondences deemed more likely to be correct are given higher priority during sampling. In our experiments, the quality measure used was the Euclidean distance between the descriptors of the observed 2D point and the corresponding matched 3D point.

The second RANSAC variant employs a very simple single-match semantic outlier rejection strategy: all 2D-3D matches for which the semantic labels of the 2D feature and 3D point do not match are discarded before pose estimation.

As can be seen in Tables 3 and 4, all three methods perform similarly well on the relatively easy daytime queries of the RobotCar Seasons dataset. However, our approach significantly outperforms the other two methods under all other conditions. This clearly validates our idea of semantic consistency scoring.

5 Conclusion

In this paper, we have presented a method for soft outlier filtering by using the semantic content of a query image. Our method ranks the 2D-3D matches found by feature-based localization pipelines depending on how well they agree with the scene semantics. Provided that the gravity direction and camera height are (roughly) known, the camera is constrained to lie on a circle for a given match. Traversing this circle and projecting the semantically labelled scene geometry into the query image, we calculate a semantic consistency score for this match based on the fit between the projected and observed semantic labels. The scores are then used to bias sampling during RANSAC-based pose estimation.

Experiments on two challenging benchmarks for long-term visual localization show that our approach outperforms state-of-the-art methods. This validates our idea of using scene semantics to distinguish correct and wrong matches and shows the usefulness of semantic information in the context of visual localization.

Acknowledgements. This work was partially supported by the Wallenberg AI, Autonomous Systems and Software Program (WASP) funded by the Knut and Alice Wallenberg Foundation, the Swedish Research Council (grant no. 2016-04445), the Swedish Foundation for Strategic Research (Semantic Mapping and Visual Navigation for Smart Robots), and Vinnova/FFI (Perceptron, grant no. 2017-01942).

References

1. Arandjelović, R., Gronat, P., Torii, A., Pajdla, T., Sivic, J.: NetVLAD: CNN architecture for weakly supervised place recognition. In: CVPR (2016)
2. Arandjelović, R., Zisserman, A.: Visual vocabulary with a semantic twist. In: Cremers, D., Reid, I., Saito, H., Yang, M.-H. (eds.) ACCV 2014. LNCS, vol. 9003, pp. 178–195. Springer, Cham (2015). https://doi.org/10.1007/978-3-319-16865-4_12
3. Ardeshir, S., Zamir, A.R., Torroella, A., Shah, M.: GIS-assisted object detection and geospatial localization. In: Fleet, D., Pajdla, T., Schiele, B., Tuytelaars, T. (eds.) ECCV 2014. LNCS, vol. 8694, pp. 602–617. Springer, Cham (2014). https://doi.org/10.1007/978-3-319-10599-4_39
4. Atanasov, N., Zhu, M., Daniilidis, K., Pappas, G.J.: Localization from semantic observations via the matrix permanent. IJRR **35**(1–3), 73–99 (2016)
5. Badino, H., Huber, D., Kanade, T.: Visual topometric localization. In: IV (2011)
6. Brachmann, E., Krull, A., Nowozin, S., Shotton, J., Michel, F., Gumhold, S., Rother, C.: DSAC - differentiable RANSAC for camera localization. In: CVPR (2017)
7. Brachmann, E., Rother, C.: Learning less is more - 6D camera localization via 3D surface regression. In: CVPR (2018)
8. Camposeco, F., Sattler, T., Cohen, A., Geiger, A., Pollefeys, M.: Toroidal constraints for two-point localization under high outlier ratios. In: CVPR (2017)

9. Castle, R.O., Klein, G., Murray, D.W.: Video-rate localization in multiple maps for wearable augmented reality. In: ISWC (2008)

10. Cavallari, T., Golodetz, S., Lord, N.A., Valentin, J., Di Stefano, L., Torr, P.H.S.: On-the-fly adaptation of regression forests for online camera relocalisation. In: CVPR (2017)

11. Chen, D.M., Baatz, G., Köser, K., Tsai, S.S., Vedantham, R., Pylvänäinen, T., Roimela, K., Chen, X., Bach, J., Pollefeys, M., Girod, B., Grzeszczuk, R.: City-scale landmark identification on mobile devices. In: CVPR (2011)

12. Choudhary, S., Narayanan, P.J.: Visibility probability structure from SfM datasets and applications. In: Fitzgibbon, A., Lazebnik, S., Perona, P., Sato, Y., Schmid, C. (eds.) ECCV 2012. LNCS, vol. 7576, pp. 130–143. Springer, Heidelberg (2012). https://doi.org/10.1007/978-3-642-33715-4_10

13. Chum, O., Matas, J.: Matching with PROSAC - progressive sample consensus. In: CVPR (2005)

14. Cohen, A., Sattler, T., Pollefeys, M.: Merging the unmatchable: stitching visually disconnected SfM models. In: ICCV (2015)

15. Cohen, A., Schönberger, J.L., Speciale, P., Sattler, T., Frahm, J.-M., Pollefeys, M.: Indoor-outdoor 3D reconstruction alignment. In: Leibe, B., Matas, J., Sebe, N., Welling, M. (eds.) ECCV 2016. LNCS, vol. 9907, pp. 285–300. Springer, Cham (2016). https://doi.org/10.1007/978-3-319-46487-9_18

16. Cordts, M., Omran, M., Ramos, S., Rehfeld, T., Enzweiler, M., Benenson, R., Franke, U., Roth, S., Schiele, B.: The cityscapes dataset for semantic urban scene understanding. In: CVPR (2016)

17. Cummins, M., Newman, P.: Appearance-only SLAM at large scale with FAB-MAP 2.0. IJRR **30**(9), 1100–1123 (2011)

18. Fischler, M., Bolles, R.: Random sampling consensus: a paradigm for model fitting with application to image analysis and automated cartography. Commun. ACM **24**, 381–395 (1981)

19. Haralick, R., Lee, C.N., Ottenberg, K., Nölle, M.: Review and analysis of solutions of the three point perspective pose estimation problem. IJCV **13**(3), 331–356 (1994)

20. Irschara, A., Zach, C., Frahm, J.M., Bischof, H.: From structure-from-motion point clouds to fast location recognition. In: CVPR (2009)

21. Kendall, A., Cipolla, R.: Geometric loss functions for camera pose regression with deep learning. In: CVPR (2017)

22. Kendall, A., Grimes, M., Cipolla, R.: PoseNet: a convolutional network for real-time 6-DOF camera relocalization. In: ICCV (2015)

23. Kneip, L., Scaramuzza, D., Siegwart, R.: A novel parametrization of the perspective-three-point problem for a direct computation of absolute camera position and orientation. In: CVPR (2011)

24. Knopp, J., Sivic, J., Pajdla, T.: Avoiding confusing features in place recognition. In: Daniilidis, K., Maragos, P., Paragios, N. (eds.) ECCV 2010. LNCS, vol. 6311, pp. 748–761. Springer, Heidelberg (2010). https://doi.org/10.1007/978-3-642-15549-9_54

25. Kobyshev, N., Riemenschneider, H., Gool, L.V.: Matching features correctly through semantic understanding. In: 3DV (2014)

26. Kukelova, Z., Bujnak, M., Pajdla, T.: Closed-form solutions to minimal absolute pose problems with known vertical direction. In: Kimmel, R., Klette, R., Sugimoto, A. (eds.) ACCV 2010. LNCS, vol. 6493, pp. 216–229. Springer, Heidelberg (2011). https://doi.org/10.1007/978-3-642-19309-5_17

27. Li, Y., Snavely, N., Huttenlocher, D., Fua, P.: Worldwide pose estimation using 3D point clouds. In: Fitzgibbon, A., Lazebnik, S., Perona, P., Sato, Y., Schmid, C. (eds.) ECCV 2012. LNCS, vol. 7572, pp. 15–29. Springer, Heidelberg (2012). https://doi.org/10.1007/978-3-642-33718-5_2

28. Li, Y., Snavely, N., Huttenlocher, D.P.: Location recognition using prioritized feature matching. In: Daniilidis, K., Maragos, P., Paragios, N. (eds.) ECCV 2010. LNCS, vol. 6312, pp. 791–804. Springer, Heidelberg (2010). https://doi.org/10.1007/978-3-642-15552-9_57

29. Liu, L., Li, H., Dai, Y.: Efficient global 2D–3D matching for camera localization in a large-scale 3D map. In: ICCV (2017)

30. Lowe, D.: Distinctive image features from scale-invariant keypoints. IJCV **60**(2), 91–110 (2004)

31. Lynen, S., Sattler, T., Bosse, M., Hesch, J., Pollefeys, M., Siegwart, R.: Get out of my lab: large-scale, real-time visual-inertial localization. In: RSS (2015)

32. Maddern, W., Pascoe, G., Linegar, C., Newman, P.: 1 year, 1000km: the Oxford RobotCar dataset. IJRR **36**(1), 3–15 (2017)

33. Massiceti, D., Krull, A., Brachmann, E., Rother, C., Torr, P.H.: Random forests versus neural networks - what's best for camera relocalization? In: ICRA (2017)

34. Neuhold, G., Ollmann, T., Rota Bulò, S., Kontschieder, P.: The mapillary vistas dataset for semantic understanding of street scenes. In: ICCV (2017). https://www.mapillary.com/dataset/vistas

35. Salas-Moreno, R.F., Newcombe, R.A., Strasdat, H., Kelly, P.H.J., Davison, A.J.: SLAM++: simultaneous localisation and mapping at the level of objects. In: CVPR (2013)

36. Sattler, T., Leibe, B., Kobbelt, L.: Efficient & effective prioritized matching for large-scale image-based localization. PAMI **39**(9), 1744–1756 (2017)

37. Sattler, T., Maddern, W., Toft, C., Torii, A., Hammarstrand, L., Stenborg, E., Safari, D., Okutomi, M., Pollefeys, M., Sivic, J., Kahl, F., Pajdla, T.: Benchmarking 6DOF outdoor visual localization in changing conditions. In: CVPR (2018)

38. Sattler, T., Havlena, M., Radenovic, F., Schindler, K., Pollefeys, M.: Hyperpoints and fine vocabularies for large-scale location recognition. In: ICCV (2015)

39. Sattler, T., Havlena, M., Schindler, K., Pollefeys, M.: Large-scale location recognition and the geometric burstiness problem. In: CVPR (2016)

40. Sattler, T., Torii, A., Sivic, J., Pollefeys, M., Taira, H., Okutomi, M., Pajdla, T.: Are large-scale 3D models really necessary for accurate visual localization? In: CVPR (2017)

41. Schindler, G., Brown, M., Szeliski, R.: City-scale location recognition. In: CVPR (2007)

42. Schönberger, J.L., Pollefeys, M., Geiger, A., Sattler, T.: Semantic visual localization. In: CVPR (2018)

43. Schönberger, J.L., Frahm, J.M.: Structure-from-motion revisited. In: CVPR (2016)

44. Schreiber, M., Knöppel, C., Franke, U.: LaneLoc: lane marking based localization using highly accurate maps. In: IV (2013)

45. Shotton, J., Glocker, B., Zach, C., Izadi, S., Criminisi, A., Fitzgibbon, A.: Scene coordinate regression forests for camera relocalization in RGB-D images. In: CVPR (2013)

46. Singh, G., Košecká, J.: Semantically guided geo-location and modeling in urban environments. In: Zamir, A.R.R., Hakeem, A., Van Van Gool, L., Shah, M., Szeliski, R. (eds.) Large-Scale Visual Geo-Localization. ACVPR, pp. 101–120. Springer, Cham (2016). https://doi.org/10.1007/978-3-319-25781-5_6

47. Svärm, L., Enqvist, O., Kahl, F., Oskarsson, M.: City-scale localization for cameras with known vertical direction. PAMI **39**(7), 1455–1461 (2017)
48. Toft, C., Olsson, C., Kahl, F.: Long-term 3D localization and pose from semantic labellings. In: ICCV Workshops (2017)
49. Torii, A., Arandjelović, R., Sivic, J., Okutomi, M., Pajdla, T.: 24/7 place recognition by view synthesis. In: CVPR (2015)
50. Valentin, J., Nießner, M., Shotton, J., Fitzgibbon, A., Izadi, S., Torr, P.: Exploiting uncertainty in regression forests for accurate camera relocalization. In: CVPR (2015)
51. Walch, F., Hazirbas, C., Leal-Taixé, L., Sattler, T., Hilsenbeck, S., Cremers, D.: Image-based localization using LSTMs for structured feature correlation. In: ICCV (2017)
52. Weyand, T., Kostrikov, I., Philbin, J.: PlaNet - photo geolocation with convolutional neural networks. In: Leibe, B., Matas, J., Sebe, N., Welling, M. (eds.) ECCV 2016. LNCS, vol. 9912, pp. 37–55. Springer, Cham (2016). https://doi.org/10.1007/978-3-319-46484-8_3
53. Yi, K.M., Trulls, E., Lepetit, V., Fua, P.: LIFT: learned invariant feature transform. In: Leibe, B., Matas, J., Sebe, N., Welling, M. (eds.) ECCV 2016. LNCS, vol. 9910, pp. 467–483. Springer, Cham (2016). https://doi.org/10.1007/978-3-319-46466-4_28
54. Yu, F., Koltun, V.: Multi-scale context aggregation by dilated convolutions. In: ICLR (2016)
55. Yu, F., Xiao, J., Funkhouser, T.A.: Semantic alignment of LiDAR data at city scale. In: CVPR (2015)
56. Zamir, A.R., Shah, M.: Accurate image localization based on google maps street view. In: Daniilidis, K., Maragos, P., Paragios, N. (eds.) ECCV 2010. LNCS, vol. 6314, pp. 255–268. Springer, Heidelberg (2010). https://doi.org/10.1007/978-3-642-15561-1_19
57. Zamir, A.R., Shah, M.: Image geo-localization based on multiplenearest neighbor feature matching using generalized graphs. PAMI **36**(8), 1546–1558 (2014)
58. Zeisl, B., Sattler, T., Pollefeys, M.: Camera pose voting for large-scale image-based localization. In: ICCV (2015)
59. Zhang, W., Kosecka, J.: Image based localization in urban environments. In: 3DPVT (2006)
60. Zhao, H., Shi, J., Qi, X., Wang, X., Jia, J.: Pyramid scene parsing network. In: CVPR (2017)

Deep Generative Models for Weakly-Supervised Multi-Label Classification

Hong-Min Chu[1], Chih-Kuan Yeh[2], and Yu-Chiang Frank Wang[1(✉)]

[1] College of EECS, National Taiwan University, Taipei, Taiwan
{r04922031,ycwang}@ntu.edu.tw
[2] Machine Learning Department, Carnegie Mellon University, Pittsburgh, USA
cjyeh@cs.cmu.edu

Abstract. In order to train learning models for multi-label classification (MLC), it is typically desirable to have a large amount of fully annotated multi-label data. Since such annotation process is in general costly, we focus on the learning task of weakly-supervised multi-label classification (WS-MLC). In this paper, we tackle WS-MLC by learning deep generative models for describing the collected data. In particular, we introduce a sequential network architecture for constructing our generative model with the ability to approximate observed data posterior distributions. We show that how information of training data with missing labels or unlabeled ones can be exploited, which allows us to learn multi-label classifiers via scalable variational inferences. Empirical studies on various scales of datasets demonstrate the effectiveness of our proposed model, which performs favorably against state-of-the-art MLC algorithms.

Keywords: Multi-label classification · Generative models
Semi-supervised learning · Weakly-supervised learning

1 Introduction

Multi-label classification (MLC) solves the problem of assigning multiple labels to a single input instance, which has been seen in a variety of applications in the fields of machine learning, computer vision, data mining, and bio-informatics [2,9,28].

Like most classification algorithms, one typically needs a large number of data with ground truth labels, so that the associated MLC model can be learned with satisfactory performance. However, for the task of MLC, collecting fully annotated data would take extensive efforts and costs. How to alleviate the above limitation for designing effective MLC models becomes a challenging yet practical task. To be more specific, it would be desirable to train MLC models using

Electronic supplementary material The online version of this chapter (https://doi.org/10.1007/978-3-030-01216-8_25) contains supplementary material, which is available to authorized users.

© Springer Nature Switzerland AG 2018
V. Ferrari et al. (Eds.): ECCV 2018, LNCS 11206, pp. 409–425, 2018.
https://doi.org/10.1007/978-3-030-01216-8_25

training data with only *partial* labels, or even some training data with *empty* label sets observed. Thus, learning MLC models under the above settings can be formalized as a weakly-supervised setting. The differences between weakly-supervised MLC and related MLC settings are summarized in Table 1. The goal of this paper is to present an effective weakly-supervised MLC (WS-MLC) model by advancing deep learning techniques.

A number of MLC approaches which utilize partially labeled data exist (i.e., some training data are only with partial ground truth label information observed) [13,31,32,35]. As a representative work, [31] handles missing labels by imposing a label smoothness regularization during the learning of their model. However, this type of approaches cannot easily leverage rich information from unlabeled training data, which might not be desirable in practical scenarios in which a majority of collected training data are totally unlabeled.

To address the above challenging (semi-supervised) MLC problems, graph-based [37] approaches are proposed [5,14,18,20,33]. While they exhibit impressive abilities in handling unlabeled data, take label propagation based algorithms [5,18,20] for example, they only work under the transductive setting but not the inductive setting. That is, prediction can only be made for the presented unlabeled data but *not* for future test inputs. Another family of manifold regularization based algorithms [14,33], while applicable for inductive settings, are highly sensitive to graph structures and the associated distance measurements.

Deep generative models, on the other hand, have recently been widely applied to solving semi-supervised learning tasks [16,24]. Take [16] as an example, it described a deep generative model for single-label data, and applied variational inference for semi-supervised learning via observing both labeled and unlabeled data. Nevertheless, despite the compelling probabilistic interpretation of observed data, existing works mainly apply deep generative models for single label learning tasks. While generative approaches for MLC have been investigated in literature [13,23,29], existing solutions typically require training data to be fully or at least partially labeled. In other words, they cannot be easily extended to solving semi-supervised MLC or even WS-MLC tasks.

Table 1. Different settings for multi-label classification.

Setting	Fully-labeled data	Partially-labeled data	Unlabeled data
Supervised MLC	✓	✗	✗
Semi-supervised MLC	✓	✗	✓
MLC with missing label	✓	✓	✗
WS-MLC (Our work)	✓	✓	✓

In this paper, we tackle the challenging WS-MLC, which includes both semi-supervised MLC and MLC with missing labels as *special cases* as illustrated in Table 1. We achieve so by advancing novel deep generative models [16,17]. Inspired by [8,21,22,30], we approach WS-MLC by viewing MLC as a *sequential prediction* problem. We propose a *deep sequential generative model* to describe the multi-label data for WS-MLC with a unified probabilistic framework. In our proposed model, we present a *deep sequential classification model* for both prediction and approximation of posterior inference, and derive efficient learning algorithms with variational inference for addressing WS-MLC with promising performances.

The contributions of this paper are highlighted as follows:

- To the best of our knowledge, we are the first to advance deep generative models to tackle WS-MLC problems.
- We propose a probabilistic framework which integrates sequential prediction and generation processes with an efficient optimization procedure, so that information from unlabeled data or data with partially missing labels can be exploited.
- Our framework results in interpretable MLC models in weakly-supervised settings, and performs favorably against recent MLC approaches on multiple datasets.

2   Related Works

Multi-label classification (MLC) is among active research topics and benefits a variety of real-world applications [2,7,9]. Earlier studies of MLC algorithms typically utilize linear models as the building block [22,26,28]. Binary relevance [28], as a well-known example, trains a set of independent linear classifiers for each label.

In recent years, approaches based on deep neural networks (DNN) [10,21, 30,34] attract the attention of researchers in related fields. For example, [30] proposes to learn a linear embedding function, with label correlations modeled with a chain structure by recurrent neural networks (RNN). [21] further investigates different exploitation of RNN to perform MLC. On the other hand, [34] proposes to learn nonlinear embedding via deep canonical correlation analysis, while it decodes outputs labels with co-occurrence information preserved. Nevertheless, despite the success in applying DNN for MLC, training DNNs typically requires a large amount of labeled data, whose annotation process generally requires extensive manual efforts.

Weakly-supervised MLC (WS-MLC) is a practical setup that aims to learn MLC models from the dataset containing *fully-labeled* plus *partially-labeled* and/or *unlabeled* training data. As noted above, WS setting is particularly appealing regarding MLC tasks, as the cost to fullying annotate multi-label data is generally much more expensive than that for single-label data. MLC algorithms designed for dealing with partially-labeled data (or data with missing labels) exist [31,32,35]. For example, [32] formulates the problem of MLC with partially-labeled data as a convex quadratic optimization problems. [31] handles the missing labels by imposing a label smoothness regularization. Unfortunately, both [32] and [31] work only under transductive setting, i.e., the data to be predicted need to be presented during learning. While inductive MLC algorithms with missing labels are available [35], their incapability of exploiting information unlabeled data still makes them less desirable for practical scenarios.

Semi-supervised MLC algorithms which leverage information from both fully-labeled and unlabeled data have also been studied [5,14,18,20,33]. The majority of such methods focus on graph-based techniques to utilize the unlabeled data. Several graph-based algorithms consider label propagation techniques [5,18,20]. [18] is a representative example which designs a dynamic propagation proce-dures that explicitly considers the label correlation based on k-nearest-neighbors graph. Other graph-based algorithms exploit the information of unlabeled data by manifold regularization [14,33]. For example, [14] imposes manifold regular-ization during the learning of MLC models by enforcing similar predictions for both labeled and unlabeled data that is also similar in feature space. Neverthe-less, most label propagation based algorithms also require a transductive setting, limiting their applicability to real-wolrd scenarios. Manifold regularization based approaches are mainly inductive. However, the performance of these approaches critically depends on the predefined graph structures. Moreover, all the above semi-supervised MLC algorithms fail to generalize to handle data with partially observed labels.

We note that, generative leaning algorithms for semi-supervised single-label classification can be found in recent literature [1,16]. Focusing on the task of MLC, several generative approaches have also been investigated [13,23]. For example, [23] focuses on the mining of multi-labeled text data, where the data generative process is formulated based on Latent Dirichlet Analysis. Neverthe-less, the above algorithms are not designed to handle tarining data with missing labels or unlabeled training data, and thus cannot be easily extended to WS-MLC. In the next section, we will introduce our proposed deep generative model for WS-MLC.

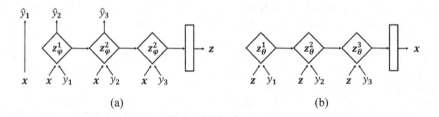

Fig. 1. Architectures of (a) encoder ϕ and (b) decoder θ in our DSGM. The former sequentially encodes the input data and their labels into each stochastic variable $\mathbf{z}_\phi^k$, and predicts the following label $\hat{y}_k$ of the k-th label conditioned on $\mathbf{x}$ and $y_1, \cdots, y_{k-1}$. The latter decodes $\mathbf{z}$ to $\mathbf{x}$ by sequentially incorporating each label y_k into stochastic variables $\mathbf{z}_\theta^k$. Note that we take three labels y_1, y_2 and y_3 for illustration purposes.

3   Our Proposed Method

3.1   Problem Formulation

In multi-label classification (MLC), we denote $\mathbf{x} \in \mathbb{R}^d$ as an instance with $\mathbf{y} \in \{0,1\}^K$ as the corresponding label vector (i.e., $\mathbf{y}[k] = 1$ if the instance is associated with the k-th label (out of K labels), otherwise $\mathbf{y}[k] = 0$). For weakly-supervised MLC (WS-MLC), we observe a training dataset $\mathcal{D} = \mathcal{D}_\ell \cup \mathcal{D}_o \cup \mathcal{D}_u$, where $\mathcal{D}_\ell = \{(\mathbf{x}_i, \mathbf{y}_i)\}_{i=1}^{N_\ell}$ denotes fully-labeled N_ℓ instances, $\mathcal{D}_o = \{(\mathbf{x}_j, \mathbf{y}_j^o)\}_{j=1}^{N_o}$ is the partially-labeled dataset with N_o instances, and $\mathcal{D}_u = \{\tilde{\mathbf{x}}_m\}_{m=1}^{N_u}$ is the unlabeled one with N_u instances. We use $\mathbf{y}^o$ to indicates the partially labeled vector (see detailed settings in experiments). For the sake of simplicity, we omit the subscripts i, j and m if possible in the remaining of this paper. And, we use the term "weakly-labeled" when referring to a subset of training data that is either partially-labeled or unlabeled.

Now, given a training set $\mathcal{D}$, the goal of WS-MLC is to learn a classification model so that the multi-label vector $\hat{\mathbf{y}}$ of an *unseen* instance $\hat{\mathbf{x}}$ can be predicted. In WS-MLC, the size of fully-labeled dataset is typically much smaller than that of weakly-labeled dataset. Therefore, an effective WS-MLC algorithm to exploit the information from both $\mathcal{D}_o$ and $\mathcal{D}_u$ would be desirable, so that improved MLC performance can be expected.

3.2   Deep Sequential Generative Models for WS-MLC

Inspired by recent advances in deep generative models (particularly those for semi-supervised learning [16,17]) and the use of sequential learning models for MLC [8,21,22,30], we propose a novel **Deep Sequential Generative Model** (DSGM) to tackle the challenging problem of WS-MLC. As illustrated in Fig. 1, our DGSM can be viewed as an extension of conditional variational autoencoder (CVAE) [25] with sequential layers of stochastic variables $\{\mathbf{z}_\phi^k\}_{k=1}^K$ and $\{\mathbf{z}_\theta^k\}_{k=1}^K$ decided by each label y_k. In particular, our DGSM consists of sequential generative models which aims at describing the generation of multi-label data, followed by a deep classification model for MLC. This classification stage would jointly perform classifcation and approximated posterior inference, and the derivation of the learning objective based on variational inference (VI), so that multi-label prediction in such a weakly-supervised learning setting can be achieved. It is worth pointing out that, from the encoder-decoder perspective, Fig. 1a and b illustrates the framework of our classification and generative models, respectively. In the following subsections, we will detail the functionality and design for the above models.

Sequential Generative Models for Multi-label Classification. To address WS-MLC using sequential generative models, we assume that each instance $\mathbf{x}$ is generated from $\mathbf{y}$ with an additional latent variable $\mathbf{z}$. Without the loss of generality and following most exisint generative models [16,17], we further assume that

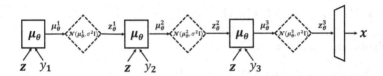

Fig. 2. Illustration of our sequential generative process using decoder θ. This process sequentially takes the latent variable $\mathbf{z}$ (from encoder ϕ), stochastic variables $\mathbf{z}_\theta^k$, and labels y_k for recovering input $\mathbf{x}$. Note that $\boldsymbol{\mu}_\theta(\cdot|\cdot)$ determines the mean of Gaussian distribution that generates each $\mathbf{z}_\theta^k$.

$p(\mathbf{z}) = \mathcal{N}(\mathbf{z}|0, \mathbf{I})$, and have factorization of $p(\mathbf{y})$ as $p(\mathbf{y}) = \prod_{k=1}^{K} \mathtt{Bern}(y_k|\gamma_k)$, where y_k is the k-th label of $\mathbf{y}$ and γ_k is the parameter of Bernoulli distribution for y_k. We note that, one might consider a more representative prior based on the factorization of $p(\mathbf{y}) = p(y_1)\cdot\prod_{k=2}^{K} p(y_k|y_1,\ldots,y_{k-1})$. For simplicity, we consider the generation of different labels to be independent, and such an alternative prior is sufficiently satisfactory as confirmed later by our experiments. And, following the setting of [16], the priors $p(\mathbf{y})$ and $p(\mathbf{z})$ are set to be marginally independent.

Inspired by recent sequential methods for MLC [8,21,22,30], our propose model also aims at leveraging information from multiple observed labels in a sequential manner during the learning process. More specifically, we choose to describe $p_\theta(\mathbf{x}|\mathbf{y}, \mathbf{z})$, i.e., generation of multi-label data $\mathbf{x}$, as a *sequential generative process* with an additional set of intermediate stochastic variables $\{\mathbf{z}_\theta^k\}_{k=1}^{K}$ as shown in Fig. 2. To be more precise, this generative process is formulated as follows:

$$
\begin{aligned}
p_\theta(\mathbf{x}|\mathbf{y}, \mathbf{z}) &= g(\mathbf{x}|\mathbf{z}_\theta^K; \boldsymbol{\theta}); \\
\mathbf{z}_\theta^k &\sim \mathcal{N}(\boldsymbol{\mu}_\theta(\mathbf{z}_\theta^{k-1}, y_k, \mathbf{z}), \sigma^2 \mathbf{I}); \ 1 \le k \le K \\
\mathbf{z}_\theta^0 &= 0,
\end{aligned}
\tag{1}
$$

where $g(\cdot|\cdot; \boldsymbol{\theta})$ is a likelihood function with parameters determined by non-linear transformation of $\boldsymbol{\theta}^K$. For example, Gaussian distribution can be utilized for $g(\cdot|\cdot)$ to describe the features with continuous values. In our framework, such a sequential generation process is realized by recurrent neural networks (RNN). That is, $\boldsymbol{\mu}_\theta(\cdot, \cdot, \cdot)$ outputs the mean vector from the non-linear transformation of $\mathbf{z}$, $\mathbf{z}_\theta^{k-1}$ and y_k, which is implemented as the RNN cell that shares the model parameters across all labels y_k.

With the above generative model $p_\theta(\mathbf{x}|\mathbf{y}, \mathbf{z})$, we are able to learn the model parameters θ by maximizing the marginal likelihood of $p_\theta(\mathbf{x}, \mathbf{y})$ (from fully-labeled data), $p_\theta(\mathbf{x}, \mathbf{y}^o)$ (from partially-labeled data), and/or $p_\theta(\tilde{\mathbf{x}})$ (from unlabeled data). In other words, we are able to obtain θ by solving

$$
\arg\max_{\theta} \sum_{(\mathbf{x}, \mathbf{y}) \in \mathcal{D}_\ell} \log p_\theta(\mathbf{x}, \mathbf{y}) + \sum_{(\mathbf{x}, \mathbf{y}^o) \in \mathcal{D}_o} \log p_\theta(\mathbf{x}, \mathbf{y}^o) + \sum_{\tilde{\mathbf{x}} \in \mathcal{D}_u} \log p_\theta(\tilde{\mathbf{x}}). \tag{2}
$$

To perform MLC with a given $\mathbf{x}$, classification can be achieved by $p_\theta(\mathbf{y}|\mathbf{x}) \propto p_\theta(\mathbf{x}|\mathbf{y})p(\mathbf{y})$ with model parameter $\boldsymbol{\theta}$.

Sequential Classification Model for Variational Inference of DSGM.
Unfortunately, learning (i.e., exact inference) of $\boldsymbol{\theta}$ by solving (2) is computationally prohibitive due to the need to compute intractable integral when applying Bayes rules. To enable an efficient approximated inference of $\boldsymbol{\theta}$, we design a novel learning algorithm based on the principle of variational inference [4,17]. In particular, we propose a *deep sequential classification model* for posterior inference approximation. We then derive the variational lower bound and the corresponding optimization procedure accordingly.

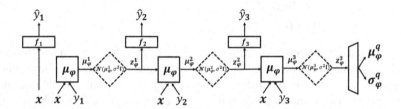

Fig. 3. Illustration of our sequential classification architecture ϕ in DSGM, which sequentially encodes input $\mathbf{x}$ and labels y_k into stochastic variables $\mathbf{z}_\phi^k$, with prediction layers f_k for determining label outputs $\hat{y}_k$.

We now discuss the design of our sequential classification model for the variational inference of $\boldsymbol{\theta}$. The key ingredient of variational inference is to introduce a fixed form distribution $q_\phi(\cdot|\cdot)$, so that the posterior inference from observed variables to the latent ones can be achieved via $q_\phi(\cdot|\cdot)$ instead of using $p_\theta(\cdot|\cdot)$ which is in practice intractable. In the case of learning with fully-labeled training data, we seek to infer $\mathbf{z}$ from $(\mathbf{x}, \mathbf{y})$ directly. For dealing with weakly-labeled data, unobserved labels are viewed as latent variables, which need to be inferred from $\mathbf{x}$ and the observed labels (if available).

With the above observation and motivation, the goal of $q_\phi(\cdot|\cdot)$ is to achieve the following approximation of posterior inference:

$$q_\phi(\mathbf{z}|\mathbf{x}, \mathbf{y}) \approx p_\theta(\mathbf{z}|\mathbf{x}, \mathbf{y}); \ \forall(\mathbf{x}, \mathbf{y}) \in \mathcal{D}_\ell$$
$$q_\phi(\mathbf{y}^\mathbf{m}, \mathbf{z}|\mathbf{x}, \mathbf{y}^\mathbf{o}) \approx p_\theta(\mathbf{y}^\mathbf{m}, \mathbf{z}|\mathbf{x}, \mathbf{y}^\mathbf{o}); \ \forall(\mathbf{x}, \mathbf{y}^\mathbf{o}) \in \mathcal{D}_o$$
$$q_\phi(\mathbf{y}, \mathbf{z}|\tilde{\mathbf{x}}) \approx p_\theta(\mathbf{y}, \mathbf{z}|\tilde{\mathbf{x}}); \ \forall(\tilde{\mathbf{x}}) \in \mathcal{D}_u,$$

where we have partially-labeled data $(\mathbf{x}, \mathbf{y}^\mathbf{o}) \in \mathcal{D}_o$ in which $\mathbf{y}^\mathbf{m}$ indicates the label vectors with missing ground truth. It is worth noting that, $q(\mathbf{y}, \mathbf{z}|\tilde{\mathbf{x}})$ essentially performs *classification as inference* for unlabeled data, and will be applied as the classification model for the testing stage. Inspired by [8,21,22,30] which approach MLC by solving the task of label sequence prediction, and to meet the sequential nature of our proposed generative process, our *deep sequential classification model* would serve as $q_\phi(\cdot|\cdot)$ for addressing WS-MLC (see Fig. 3 for illustration).

We now elaborate the architecture of our sequential classification model $q_\phi(\cdot|\cdot)$, and explain in details on how to perform posterior inference given either fully-labeled, partially-labeled or unlabeled data via a set of intermediate latent variables $\{\mathbf{z}_\phi^k\}_{k=1}^K$.

For labeled data, the sequential posterior inference $q_\phi(\mathbf{z}|\mathbf{x}, \mathbf{y})$ is performed as follows:

$$q_\phi(\mathbf{z}|\mathbf{y}, \mathbf{x}) = \mathcal{N}(\mathbf{z}|\boldsymbol{\mu}_\phi^q(\mathbf{z}_\phi^K), \boldsymbol{\sigma}_\phi^q(\mathbf{z}_\phi^K)); \tag{3}$$

$$\mathbf{z}_\phi^k \sim \mathcal{N}(\boldsymbol{\mu}_\phi(\mathbf{z}_\phi^{k-1}, \mathbf{x}, y_k), \sigma^2\mathbf{I}), \ 1 \leq k \leq K; \tag{4}$$

$$\hat{y}_k \sim \mathrm{Bern}(f_\phi^k(\mathbf{z}_\phi^{k-1})), \ 2 \leq k \leq K \tag{5}$$

$$\hat{y}_1 \sim \mathrm{Bern}(f_\phi^1(\mathbf{x})); \tag{6}$$

$$\mathbf{z}_\phi^0 = \mathbf{0},$$

where $\hat{y}_k$ denotes the prediction of k-th label. Here $\boldsymbol{\mu}_\phi^q(\cdot)$ and $\boldsymbol{\sigma}_\phi^q(\cdot)$ are the deterministic functions that calculate the mean vector and diagonal covariance matrix for $q_\phi(\mathbf{z}|\mathbf{x}, \mathbf{y})$, respectively. On the other hand, $f_\phi^k(\cdot, \cdot)$ determines the parameter of Bernouli distribution for prediction of $\hat{y}_k$. The main intuition behind such a design of $q_\phi(\cdot|\cdot)$ is to encode $\mathbf{z}_\phi^k$ with the information from $(\mathbf{x}, y_1, \ldots, y_k)$. Such encoding allows us to resemble the following factorization by predicting each $\hat{y}_{k+1}$ with $\mathbf{z}_\phi^k$:

$$q_\phi(\mathbf{y}|\mathbf{x}) = q_\phi(y_1|\mathbf{x}) \prod_{k=2}^K q_\phi(y_k|\mathbf{x}, y_1, \ldots, y_{k-1}).$$

We see that, $\mathbf{z}_\phi^K$ with such relation would encode information from all observed variables, and thus can be directly used to determine $\mathbf{z}$ from $\mathbf{x}$ and $\mathbf{y}$.

For partially-labeled data in WS-MLC, we adopt the same posterior inference procedure as (3)–(6) except that we now consider the meanfield variational family $q_\phi(\mathbf{y}^m, \mathbf{z}|\mathbf{x}, \mathbf{y}^o) = q_\phi(\mathbf{z}|\mathbf{x}, \mathbf{y}^o)q_\phi(\mathbf{y}^m|\mathbf{x}, \mathbf{y}^o)$. Nevertheless, despite the factorized probability representation, information from *all labels* should still be exploited to infer $\mathbf{z}$, which is achieved by utilizing the predicted label $\hat{y}_k$ instead (in the case where y_k is missing). To be more precise, we modify (4) to calculate $\mathbf{z}_\phi^k$ by.

$$\mathbf{z}_\phi^k \sim \begin{cases} \mathcal{N}(\boldsymbol{\mu}_\phi(\mathbf{z}_\phi^{k-1}, \mathbf{x}, y_k), \sigma^2\mathbf{I}), \ \text{if } y_k \in \mathbf{y}^o \\ \mathcal{N}(\boldsymbol{\mu}_\phi(\mathbf{z}_\phi^{k-1}, \mathbf{x}, \hat{y}_k), \sigma^2\mathbf{I}), \ \text{if } y_k \notin \mathbf{y}^o, \end{cases} \tag{7}$$

where $\hat{y}_k \in \{0, 1\}$ is a binary sample based on the predicted probability that $y_k = 1$ via (5). With such modification, our sequential classification model is able to infer $\mathbf{z}$ with information from all labels even if some are unobserved.

As for unlabeled data in WS-MLC, we also utilize the meanfiled variational family $q_\phi(\mathbf{y}, \mathbf{z}|\tilde{\mathbf{x}}) = q_\phi(\mathbf{z}|\tilde{\mathbf{x}})q_\phi(\mathbf{y}|\tilde{\mathbf{x}})$. By realizing that unlabeled data is the data with all label missing, we perform posterior sequential posterior inference in exactly the same way as that for partially-labeled data. In this case, (7) would degenerate to the case with each $y_k \notin \mathbf{y}^o$.

Finally, we implement the above sequntial posterior inference with $q_\phi(\cdot|\cdot)$ via RNN, as depicted in Fig. 3. That is, $\boldsymbol{\mu}_\phi(\cdot, \cdot, \cdot)$ used in both (4) and (7) is realized as an RNN cell, which is the same as those in our sequential generative model.

Objective for Variational Lower Bound. In this subsection, we discuss how we derive the objective of the lower bound for variational inference. Note that the calculation of $q_\phi(\mathbf{z}|\mathbf{x}, \mathbf{y})$ requires the integral over the samples of $\{\mathbf{z}_\phi^k\}_{k=1}^K$ even if $\mathbf{x}$ and $\mathbf{y}$ are known. This would be undesirable for the derivation of the variational lower bound, as such integrals cannot be analytically calculated.

By applying location-scale transform of Gaussian distributions, one would be able to determine the exact parameters of distribution $q_\phi(\mathbf{z}|\mathbf{x}, \mathbf{y})$ (i.e., mean and covariance) by introducing a set of random variables $\{\epsilon_\phi^k\}_{k=1}^K$. Thus, (4) can be rewritten as

$$\mathbf{z}_\phi^k = \boldsymbol{\mu}_\phi(\mathbf{z}_\phi^{k-1}, \mathbf{x}, y_k) + \sigma^2 \epsilon_\phi^k; \ 1 \le k \le K, \tag{8}$$

where each $\epsilon_\phi^k \sim \mathcal{N}(0, \mathbf{I})$ is an independent sample of standard Gaussian distribution. Consequently, one can derive the variational lower bound by taking

$$\mathbb{E}_{\epsilon_\phi^1, \ldots, \epsilon_\phi^K}[\mathcal{KL}(q_\phi(\mathbf{z}|\mathbf{x}, \mathbf{y}, \epsilon_\phi^1, \ldots, \epsilon_\phi^K) \, \| \, p_\theta(\mathbf{z}|\mathbf{x}, \mathbf{y}))]$$

as a starting point, where $q_\phi(\mathbf{z}|\mathbf{x}, \mathbf{y}, \epsilon_\phi^1, \ldots, \epsilon_\phi^K)$ denotes the fixed distribution given the sampled value of $\{\epsilon_\phi^k\}_{k=1}^K$.

Based on location-transform techniques of $p_\theta(\mathbf{x}|\mathbf{y}, \mathbf{z}) = \mathbb{E}_{\epsilon_\theta}[p_\theta(\mathbf{x}|\mathbf{y}, \mathbf{z}, \epsilon_\theta)]$, where $\epsilon_\theta = \{\epsilon_\theta^k\}_{k=1}^K$ is another set of independent samples from standard Gaussian distribution in addition to $\{\epsilon_\phi^k\}_{k=1}^K$ for $q_\phi(\cdot|\cdot)$, the lower bound for the labeled data $(\mathbf{x}, \mathbf{y}) \in \mathcal{D}_\ell$ can now be expressed as $\log p_\theta(\mathbf{x}, \mathbf{y}) \ge \mathbb{E}_{\epsilon_\phi}[-\mathcal{L}(\mathbf{x}, \mathbf{y}, \epsilon_\phi)]$, where $\epsilon_\phi = \{\epsilon_\phi^k\}_{k=1}^K$. Finally, by Jensen's inequality (for concave functions), we have

$$\begin{aligned}-\mathcal{L}(\mathbf{x}, \mathbf{y}, \epsilon_\phi) = {}& \log p(\mathbf{y}) + \mathbb{E}_{q_\phi(\mathbf{z}|\mathbf{x}, \mathbf{y}, \epsilon_\phi)}[\mathbb{E}_{\epsilon_\theta}[\log p_\theta(\mathbf{x}|\mathbf{y}, \mathbf{z}, \epsilon_\theta)]] \\ & - \mathcal{KL}(q_\phi(\mathbf{z}|\mathbf{x}, \mathbf{y}, \epsilon_\phi) \| p(\mathbf{z})).\end{aligned} \tag{9}$$

In order to deal with partially-labeled data $(\mathbf{x}, \mathbf{y}^\mathrm{o}) \in \mathcal{D}_o$, we need both $q_\phi(\mathbf{y}^\mathrm{m}|\mathbf{x}, \mathbf{y}^\mathrm{o})$ and $q_\phi(\mathbf{z}|\mathbf{x}, \mathbf{y}^\mathrm{o})$ for deriving the associated variational lower bound objective. However, as noted above, the sequential posterior inference with $q_\phi(\cdot, \cdot)$ using (7) involves sampling for unobserved labels. Even with the technique of location-scale transform on $\{\mathbf{z}_\phi^k\}_{k=1}^K$, oue still needs to marginalize out the sampling regarding $\mathbf{y}^\mathrm{m}$ to obtain $q_\phi(\mathbf{y}^\mathrm{m}|\mathbf{x}, \mathbf{y}^\mathrm{o})$ and $q_\phi(\mathbf{z}|\mathbf{x}, \mathbf{y}^\mathrm{o})$. To alleviate this problem, we choose to rewrite (7) as

$$\mathbf{z}_\phi^k = \begin{cases} \boldsymbol{\mu}_\phi(\mathbf{z}_\phi^{k-1}, \mathbf{x}, y_k) + \sigma^2 \epsilon_\phi^k, & \text{if } y_k \in \mathbf{y}^\mathrm{o} \\ [\![\alpha_k \ge p_k]\!] \boldsymbol{\mu}_\phi(\mathbf{z}_\phi^{k-1}, \mathbf{x}, 0) + [\![\alpha_k < p_k]\!] \boldsymbol{\mu}_\phi(\mathbf{z}_\phi^{k-1}, \mathbf{x}, 1) + \sigma^2 \epsilon_\phi^k, & \text{if } y_k \notin \mathbf{y}^\mathrm{o} \end{cases} \tag{10}$$

where $\alpha_k \sim U(0, 1)$, $\epsilon_k \sim \mathcal{N}(0, \mathbf{I})$, $[\![\cdot]\!]$ is the indicator function and p_k is the probability that $y_k = 1$ from (5) and (6). We see that (10) is effectively a reparameterization of sampling of $\mathbf{z}_\phi^k$ with $\boldsymbol{\alpha} = \{\alpha_k\}_{k=1}^K$ and $\epsilon_\phi = \{\epsilon_\phi^k\}_{k=1}^K$, which allows exact determinination of $q_\phi(\mathbf{y}^\mathrm{m}|\mathbf{x}, \mathbf{y}^\mathrm{o})$ and $q_\phi(\mathbf{z}|\mathbf{x}, \mathbf{y}^\mathrm{o})$ with a set of (α, ϵ_ϕ). With this observation, we have the lower bound objective for partially-labeled data as $\log p_\theta(\tilde{\mathbf{x}}) \geq \mathbb{E}_{\alpha,\epsilon_\phi}[-\mathcal{M}(\mathbf{x}, \mathbf{y}^\circ, \alpha, \epsilon_\phi)]$, where

$$
\begin{aligned}
-\mathcal{M}(\mathbf{x}, \mathbf{y}^\circ, \alpha, \epsilon_\phi) &= \mathbb{E}_{q_\phi(\mathbf{y}^m|\mathbf{x},\mathbf{y}^\circ,\alpha,\epsilon_\phi)}[\log p(\mathbf{y})] \\
&+ \mathbb{E}_{q_\phi(\mathbf{z}|\mathbf{x},\alpha,\mathbf{y}^\circ,\epsilon_\psi)}[\mathbb{E}_{q_\phi(\mathbf{y}^m|\mathbf{x},\alpha,\mathbf{y}^\circ,\epsilon_\phi)}[\mathbb{E}_{\epsilon_\theta}[\log p_\theta(\mathbf{x}|\mathbf{y}, \mathbf{z}, \epsilon_\theta)]]] \\
&- \mathcal{KL}(q_\phi(\mathbf{z}|\mathbf{x}, \alpha, \mathbf{y}^\circ, \epsilon_\phi)\|p(\mathbf{z})) + \mathcal{H}(q_\phi(\mathbf{y}^m|\mathbf{x}, \alpha, \mathbf{y}^\circ, \epsilon_\phi))
\end{aligned} \tag{11}
$$

where $\mathcal{H}(\cdot)$ is the entropy function by again realizing that the meanfield assumption still holds even with α, ϵ included due to the design of $q_\phi(\cdot, \cdot)$.

Finally, as for observation of unlabeled data $\tilde{\mathbf{x}} \in \mathcal{D}_u$, the variational lower bound can be derived similarly to that of partially-labeled data by realizing that the reparameterization of $\{\mathbf{z}_\phi^k\}_{k=1}^K$ using (10) degenerates to the case with each $y_k \notin \mathbf{y}^\circ$. Consequently, the lower bound objective for unlabeled data can be expressed as $\log p_\theta(\tilde{\mathbf{x}}) \geq \mathbb{E}_{\alpha,\epsilon_\phi}[-\mathcal{U}(\tilde{\mathbf{x}}, \epsilon_\phi)]$, where

$$
\begin{aligned}
-\mathcal{U}(\tilde{\mathbf{x}}, \alpha, \epsilon_\phi) &= \mathbb{E}_{q_\phi(\mathbf{y}|\mathbf{x},\alpha,\epsilon_\phi)}[\log p(y)] \\
&+ \mathbb{E}_{q_\phi(\mathbf{z}|\mathbf{x},\alpha,\epsilon_\phi)}[\mathbb{E}_{q_\phi(\mathbf{y}|\mathbf{x},\alpha,\epsilon_\phi)}[\mathbb{E}_{\epsilon_\theta}[\log p_\theta(\mathbf{x}|\mathbf{y}, \mathbf{z}, \alpha, \epsilon_\theta)]]] \\
&- \mathcal{KL}(q_\phi(\mathbf{z}|\mathbf{x}, \alpha, \epsilon_\phi)\|p(\mathbf{z})) + \mathcal{H}(q_\phi(\mathbf{y}|\tilde{\mathbf{x}}, \alpha, \epsilon_\phi)).
\end{aligned} \tag{12}
$$

With (9), (11) and (12), we now obtain the lower bound objective of marginal likelihood regarding the data with weakly labels. As suggested in [16], it is preferable to have the classifier directly perform label prediction. Thus, we further augment the derived lower bound objective with a discriminative loss on the observed labels for fully-labeled and partial labeled data, resulting in the following final minimization objective:

$$
\begin{aligned}
&\sum_{(\mathbf{x},\mathbf{y})\in\mathcal{D}_\ell} \mathbb{E}_{\epsilon_\phi}[\mathcal{L}(\mathbf{x}, \mathbf{y}, \epsilon_\phi) - \log q_\phi(\mathbf{y}|\mathbf{x}, \epsilon_\phi)] \\
&+ \sum_{(\mathbf{x},\mathbf{y}^\circ)\in\mathcal{D}_o} \mathbb{E}_{\epsilon_\alpha,\phi}[\mathcal{M}(\mathbf{x}, \mathbf{y}, \alpha, \epsilon_\phi) - \log q_\phi(\mathbf{y}^\circ|\mathbf{x}, \alpha, \epsilon_\phi)] \\
&+ \sum_{\tilde{\mathbf{x}}\in\mathcal{D}_u} \mathbb{E}_{\alpha,\epsilon_\phi}[\mathcal{U}(\tilde{\mathbf{x}}, \alpha, \epsilon_\phi)].
\end{aligned} \tag{13}
$$

With the set-up of the above objectives, the resulting $q_\phi(\mathbf{y}|\mathbf{x}, \alpha, \epsilon_\phi)$ will be used to recognize future unseen test data. For testing, we determine the binary prediction of each label $\hat{y}_k$ by directly thresholding the predicted probability with threshold of 0.5 (which is implemented by setting all $\alpha_k = 0.5$).

Learning of DSGM. We now detail the learning and optimization of our DGSM with the objective functions introduced above. For the loss of labeled data in (9), the KL-divergence term can be analytically computed for any ϵ_ϕ as both $q_\phi(\mathbf{z}|\cdot)$ and $p(\mathbf{z})$ are Gaussian distributions. For the part $\mathbb{E}_{q_\phi(\mathbf{z}|\cdot)}[\mathbb{E}_{\epsilon_\theta}[\log p_\theta(\mathbf{x}|\mathbf{y}, \mathbf{z}, \epsilon_\theta)]]$ of the loss function, the gradient can be efficiently estimated using the reparameterization trick on $q_\phi(\mathbf{z}|\cdot)$ [17] and a single sample of ϵ_θ. Since the gradient of the outer expectation $\mathbb{E}_{\epsilon_\theta}[\cdot]$ in (13) for the loss of fully-labeled data can be efficiently estimated using a single sample of ϵ_θ, we advance techniques of stochastic gradient descent (SGD) for optimizing our network parameters (θ, ϕ) using fully-labeled data.

For the loss of partially-labeled data in (11), we apply aforementioned techniques with a sample of α for gradient estimation. However, other optimization issues need to be addressed. First, we need to calculate the expectation $\mathbb{E}_{q_\phi(\mathbf{y}^m|\mathbf{x},\mathbf{y}^o,\cdot)} \log p_\theta(\mathbf{x}|\cdot)$ with respect to the predicted probability of missing labels $\mathbf{y}^o$ given $(\mathbf{x}, \mathbf{y}^o)$ (note that we omit ϵ_θ and ϵ_ϕ for presentation simplicity). The other issue is that, we need to handle the discontinuous indicator function in (7).

Regarding the calculation of $\mathbb{E}_{q_\phi(\mathbf{y}^m|\mathbf{x},\mathbf{y}^o,\cdot)}[\log p_\theta(\mathbf{x}|\cdot)]$, explicitly marginalizing out $q_\phi(\mathbf{y}^m|\mathbf{x}, \mathbf{y}^o, \cdot)$ is a possible solution. However, it would take $\mathcal{O}(2^{|\mathbf{y}^m|})$ time due to the need to examine each combination of missing labels, making it computationally prohibitive when the number of missing labels is large. To resolve the issue, we reparameterize the expectation to have the form

$$\mathbb{E}_\beta[\log p_\theta(\mathbf{x}|\cdot, \boldsymbol{\beta}, q_\phi(\mathbf{y}^m|\mathbf{x}, \mathbf{y}^o, \cdot)))],$$

where $\boldsymbol{\beta} = \{\beta_k\}_{k=1}^K$, $\beta_k \sim U(0,1)$ by rewriting the sampling of $\mathbf{z}_\theta^k$ in (1) as

$$\mathbf{z}_\theta^k = \begin{cases} \mu_\theta(\mathbf{z}_\theta^{k-1}, y_k, \mathbf{z}) + \sigma^2 \epsilon_\theta^k, & \text{if } y_k \notin \mathbf{y}^m \\ [\![\beta_k \geq p_k]\!]\mu_\theta(\mathbf{z}_\theta^{k-1}, 0, \mathbf{z}) + [\![\beta_k < p_k]\!]\mu_\theta(\mathbf{z}_\theta^{k-1}, 1, \mathbf{z}) + \sigma^2 \epsilon_\theta^k, & \text{if } y_k \in \mathbf{y}^m. \end{cases}$$

$$(14)$$

where p_k is the predicted probability that $y_k = 1$. It can be seen that, the above reparameterization is analogous to that of sampling $\mathbf{z}_\phi^k$ with (7) for the sequential posterior inference with $q_\phi \cdot |\cdot$. This allows us to efficiently estimate the gradient of the expectation $\mathbb{E}_{q_\phi(\mathbf{y}^m|\mathbf{x},\mathbf{y}^o,\cdot)} \log p_\theta(\mathbf{x}|\cdot)$ with an extra single sample of $\boldsymbol{\beta}$.

As for dealing with the discontinuity of the indicator function, we adopt the straight-through estimator (STE) in [3] for addressing this problem. More precisely, we calculate the loss in (11) in the forward pass using the normal indicator function, and replace the indicator function with identity function during the backward pass to calculate the gradient. The use of STE leads to promising performance as noted in [3].

For calculating the loss term of unlabeled data, we apply the same techniques and reparameterizing $\mathbf{z}_\theta^k$ with (14) by observing that (14) degenerates to the case with each $y_k \in \mathbf{y}^m$ for unlabeled data.

With the above explanation and derivations, we are able to efficiently obtain the estimation of gradient with respect to (13) for both fully-labeled and weakly-labeled data. As a result, the final discriminative classifier $q_\phi(\mathbf{y}|\mathbf{x})$ in our DSGM can be learned by updating (θ, ϕ) with SGD techniques.

3.3   Discussions

Finally, we discuss the connection and difference between our proposed DSGM and recent models for related learning tasks.

The use of deep generative models for semi-supervised mutli-class classification (not MLC) has been recently studied in [16]. In particular, [16] jointly trains their classification network $q_\phi(y|\mathbf{x})$, inference network $q_\phi(\mathbf{z}|\mathbf{x}, y)$, and generative network $p_\theta(\mathbf{x}|\mathbf{z}, y)$ by optimizing the variational lower bound for likelihood of observed labeled and unlabeled data. However, applying the models of [16] for (semi-supervised) MLC requires explicit examination of all 2^K possible label combinations when calculating the lower bound objective for unlabeled data. This is quite computationally infeasible especially when K is large. In contrast, the sequential architectures and the corresponding optimization procedure in our proposed DSGM provides linear dependency of K, which is in practice more applicable for semi-supervised or weakly-supervsied MLC tasks.

On the other hand, formulating MLC as a sequential label prediction has been studied in recent literature [8,21,22,30]. For example, [21,30] advances RNNs to sequentially predict the labels while implicitly observing their dependency. While the use of sequential label prediction has been widely investigated with promising performances, existing models cannot be easily extended to handle partially-labeled and unlabeled data (i.e., WS-MLC tasks). Such robustness is particularly introduced into our DSGM. As confirmed later by the experiments, our DSGM performs favorably against state-of-the-art deep MLC models in such challenging settings.

4   Experiments

4.1   Experiment Settings

To evaluate the performance of our proposed DSGM for WS-MLC, we consider the following datasets: *iaprtc12, espgame, mirflickr, NUS-WIDE,* and *MSCOCO*. The first three datasets are image recognition datasets used in [11], where 1000-dimensional of bag-of-words features based on SIFT. *NUS-WIDE* [7] and *MSCOCO* [19] are two other large scale datasets typically used for evaluation of image annotation. We summarize the key statistics of the above datasets in the appendix. For all datasets, we discard the instances with no positive labels as done in [10]. For *NUS-WIDE* and *MSCOCO*, we use the bottom four convolutional layers of a ResNet-152 [12] trained on Imagenet without fine-tuning to extract 2048-dimensional feature vectors in order to utilize both the high-level and low-level information of raw images.

In our DSGM architecture, we use gated-recurrent unit [6] as the recurrent cells to model $\boldsymbol{\mu}_\phi$ and $\boldsymbol{\mu}_\theta$. The dimensions of latent variables $\{\mathbf{z}_\theta^k\}_{k=1}^K$ and $\{\mathbf{z}_\phi^k\}_{k=1}^K$ are set to 128, while the dimension of $\mathbf{z}$ is fixed as 64. The variance σ^2 of $\{\mathbf{z}_\theta^k\}_{k=1}^K$ and $\{\mathbf{z}_\phi^k\}_{k=1}^K$ is set to 0.005. When applying DSGM for WS-MLC, we reduce the dimension of feature vector $\mathbf{x}$ to 512 by a linear transformation, which is parameterized as a fully connected layer without activation. Following [21,30], the label order for sequential learning/prediction is set from the most frequent one to the rarest one (see such suggestions in [21]). Nevertheless, in our experiment, we do not observe significant differences between the choices

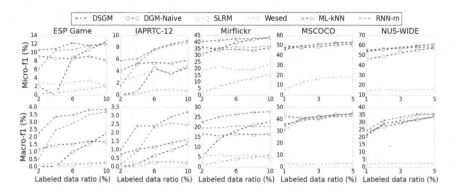

Fig. 4. Performance comparisons in terms of Micro-f1 and Macro-f1 for datasets with varying labeled data ratios.

of different label orders. To perform stochastic gradient descent for optimization, we exploit Adam [15] with a fixed learning rate of 0.003, and the batch size is fixed to 100. Note that for the experiment of semi-supervised MLC, we pretrai our DSGM with only labeled data for 100 epochs for faster convergence. Finally, both Micro-f1 and Macro-f1 are considered as evaluation metrics [27].

4.2 Comparisons with Semi-Supervised MLC Algorithms

We first evaluate our DSGM on the task of semi-supervised MLC (SS-MLC), where the dataset contains both fully-labeled and unlabeled data. Two state-of-the-arts SS-MLC algorithms are considered: Semi-supervised Low-rank Mapping (SLRM) [14] and Weakly Semi-supervised Deep Learning (Wesed) [33] (with its inductive setting viewed as a semi-supervised setting). In addition, we consider a naïve extension of state-of-the-art deep generative approach for semi-supervised multi-class classification (SS-MCC) [16], DGM-Naïve (detailed in supplementary). For completeness, we also include two well-known or state-of-the-art supervised MLC algorithms, ML-kNN [36] and RNN-m [21]. We follow [14,33] to set the hyper parameters for SLRM and Wesed, and fix $k = 5$ for ML-kNN. For RNN-m, we use the same RNN cell and the feature transformation as those in our DSGM, and set the learning rate as 0.001. The training details of DGM-Naïve are discussed in the supplementary material. For each dataset, we randomly split into two subsets with equal sizes for training and testing. The average results of five random splits are presented.

The comparison results are shown in Fig. 4, where the horizontal axis represents the ratio of labeled data with respect to the entire training set. Note that experiments of SLRM are not conducted on two large-scale datasets *NUS-WIDE* and *MSCOCO*, as SLRM requires pairwise information between training instances. From Fig. 4, we see that our DSGM achieved improved results when comparing to the state-of-the-art SS-MLC methods of SLRM and Wesed, as well as the extension of the recent generative SS-MCC approach, DGM-Naïve.

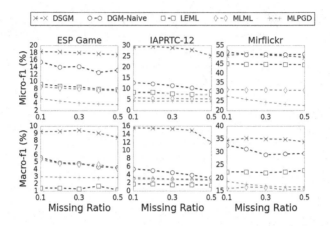

Fig. 5. Micro-f1 and Macro-f1 with different missing label ratios.

We note that, for large-scale datasets of *NUS-WIDE* and *MSCOCO*, supervised MLC method of ML-kNN and RNN-m achieved comparable results as ours did. The above empirical results support our exploitation of unlabeled data for MLC tasks.

Further inspection on Fig. 4 reveals that the use of more powerful features (i.e., those calculated by Resnet 152) generally resulted in favorable performances (e.g., DGM-Naïve, ML-kNN, RNN-m, and ours). On the other hand, when it comes to the datasets *iaprtc12*, *espgame* and *mirflickr* using low-level features, our DSGM clearly outperformed DGM-Naïve, ML-kNN and RNN-m in most of the cases. Moreover, we observe that DSGM remarkably performed against DGM-Naïve on the above three datasets especially when the labeled data ratio becomes smaller. This demonstrates the effectiveness of our sequential architecture in exploiting unlabeled data for MLC.

4.3   Comparisons with Algorithms for MLC with Missing Labels

Next, we compare our proposed model with state-of-the-art MLC algorithms for WS-MLC, particularly the observation of partially-labeled data, or data with missing labels. The methods to be compared to include LEML [35], Multi-label Learning with Missing Labels (MLML) [31], and ML-PGD (Multi-label Learning with Missing Labels Using Mixed Graph) [32]. We also modify DSGM-Naïve to handle data missing label data for comparison of state-of-the-art deep generative approach in such settings. The scenario of missing labels is simulated by randomly dropping the ground truth labels, with ratio varying from 10% to 50%.

Figure 5 illustrates and compares the performances, where the horizontal axis indicates the missing ratio. The results from Fig. 5 demonstrate that our algorithm performed against state-of-the-art algorithms, and confirmed the robustness of our methods for different MLC tasks (i.e., SS-MLC and MLC with missing labels). With a closer inspection between the results of DSGM and DGM-Naïve, we see that while DGM-Naïve reported promising and satisfactory results, DSGM in general still remarkably outperformed DGM-Naïve. This reflects the importance and the advantage of our sequential architecture which integrate generative models and discriminative classifiers for WS-MLC.

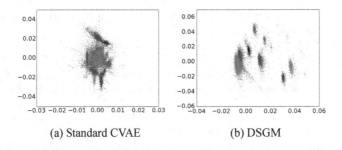

(a) Standard CVAE   (b) DSGM

Fig. 6. Visualization of the derived latent vectors on *mirflickr* for standard CVAE and DSGM.

4.4 Qualitative Studies

Finally, we provide qualitative studies regarding our sequential architecture of generative models. Specifically, we train a standard Conditional Variational Auto Encoder (CVAE) [25] and the sequential generative models of DSGM on *mirflickr* using the first 10 labels with the dimension of $\mathbf{z}$ set to 2. This allows us to visualize the inferred latent vectors for each instance $\mathbf{x}$. We plot the derived latent vectors of each $\mathbf{x}$ corresponding to the 10 most common label combinations in Fig. 6, which reflects label correlation information. The 10 most common combinations cover over 95% of instances, and each latent vector is colored based on its associated label combination in Fig. 6.

From the visualization results shown in Fig. 6, it is clear that our proposed sequential generative model resulted in more representative latent vectors when comparing to those of CVAE. From this figure, we see that our model better represents and describes the relationship between data with different labels. This also supports the use of our proposed deep generative model of multi-labeled data in the weakly-supervised setting.

5   Conclusion

We proposed a deep generative model, DSGM for solving WS-MLC problems. DSGM integrates a unique deep sequential generative model to descrbe multi-label data as well as a novel deep sequential classification model for both posterior inference and classification. The variational lower bound is derived for the learning of our sequential generative model together with an efficient optimization procedure. Experiment results confirmed the superiority of our proposed DSGM over state-of-the-art semi-supervised MLC approaches, and those designed to handle MLC with missing labels. We further demonstrated that DSGM would be more effective than naïve utilization of deep generative models regarding WS-MLC, i.e., SS-MLC and MLC with missing labels.

References

1. Adams, R.P., Ghahramani, Z.: Archipelago: nonparametric Bayesian semi-supervised learning. In: ICML 2019, pp. 1–8 (2009)
2. Bello, J.P., Chew, E., Turnbull, D.: Multilabel classification of music into emotions. In: ICMIR 2008, pp. 325–330 (2008)
3. Bengio, Y., Léonard, N., Courville, A.C.: Estimating or propagating gradients through stochastic neurons for conditional computation. CoRR abs/1308.3432 (2013)
4. Blei, D.M., Kucukelbir, A., McAuliffe, J.D.: Variational inference: a review for statisticians. CoRR abs/1601.00670 (2016)
5. Chen, G., Song, Y., Wang, F., Zhang, C.: Semi-supervised multi-label learning by solving a sylvester equation. In: SDM 2008, pp. 410–419 (2008)
6. Cho, K., van Merrienboer, B., Bahdanau, D., Bengio, Y.: On the properties of neural machine translation: encoder-decoder approaches. In: SSST@EMNLP 2014, pp. 103–111 (2014)
7. Chua, T., Tang, J., Hong, R., Li, H., Luo, Z., Zheng, Y.: NUS-WIDE: a real-world web image database from national university of Singapore. In: CIVR 2009 (2009)
8. Dembczynski, K., Cheng, W., Hüllermeier, E.: Bayes optimal multilabel classification via probabilistic classifier chains. In: ICML, pp. 279–286 (2010)
9. Elisseeff, A., Weston, J.: A kernel method for multilabelled classification. In: NIPS 2001 (2001)
10. Gong, Y., Jia, Y., Leung, T., Toshev, A., Ioffe, S.: Deep convolutional ranking for multilabel image annotation. CoRR abs/1312.4894 (2013)
11. Guillaumin, M., Mensink, T., Verbeek, J.J., Schmid, C.: TagProp: discriminative metric learning in nearest neighbor models for image auto-annotation. In: ICCV, pp. 309–316 (2009)
12. He, K., Zhang, X., Ren, S., Sun, J.: Deep residual learning for image recognition. In: CVPR, pp. 770–778 (2016)
13. Jain, V., Modhe, N., Rai, P.: Scalable generative models for multi-label learning with missing labels. In: ICML 2017, pp. 1636–1644 (2017)
14. Jing, L., Yang, L., Yu, J., Ng, M.K.: Semi-supervised low-rank mapping learning for multi-label classification. In: CVPR 2015, pp. 1483–1491 (2015)
15. Kingma, D.P., Ba, J.: Adam: a method for stochastic optimization. CoRR abs/1412.6980 (2014)
16. Kingma, D.P., Mohamed, S., Rezende, D.J., Welling, M.: Semi-supervised learning with deep generative models. In: NIPS 2014, pp. 3581–3589 (2014)
17. Kingma, D.P., Welling, M.: Auto-encoding variational bayes. CoRR abs/1312.6114 (2013)
18. Lin, G., Liao, K., Sun, B., Chen, Y., Zhao, F.: Dynamic graph fusion label propagation for semi-supervised multi-modality classification. Pattern Recognit. 68, 14–23 (2017)
19. Lin, T., et al.: Microsoft COCO: common objects in context. In: ECCV, pp. 740–755 (2014)

20. de Lucena, D.C.G., Prudêncio, R.B.C.: Semi-supervised multi-label k-Nearest neighbors classification algorithms. In: BRCIS 2015, pp. 49–54 (2015)
21. Nam, J., Loza Mencía, E., Kim, H.J., Fürnkranz, J.: Maximizing subset accuracy with recurrent neural networks in multi-label classification. In: NIPS 2017, pp. 5419–5429 (2017)
22. Read, J., Pfahringer, B., Holmes, G., Frank, E.: Classifier chains for multi-label classification. Mach. Learn. 85(3), 333–359 (2011)
23. Rubin, T.N., Chambers, A., Smyth, P., Steyvers, M.: Statistical topic models for multi-label document classification. Mach. Learn. 88(1–2), 157–208 (2012)
24. Salimans, T., Goodfellow, I.J., Zaremba, W., Cheung, V., Radford, A., Chen, X.: Improved techniques for training GANs. CoRR abs/1606.03498 (2016)
25. Sohn, K., Lee, H., Yan, X.: Learning structured output representation using deep conditional generative models. In: NIPS 2015, pp. 3483–3491 (2015)
26. Tai, F., Lin, H.: Multilabel classification with principal label space transformation. Neural Comput. 24(9), 2508–2542 (2012)
27. Tang, L., Rajan, S., Narayanan, V.K.: Large scale multi-label classification via metalabeler. In: WWW 2009, pp. 211–220 (2009)
28. Tsoumakas, G., Katakis, I., Vlahavas, I.P.: Mining multi-label data. In: Maimon, O., Rokach, L. (eds.) Data Mining and Knowledge Discovery Handbook, 2nd edn, pp. 667–685. Springer, Boston (2010). https://doi.org/10.1007/978-0-387-09823-4_34
29. Wang, H., Huang, M., Zhu, X.: A generative probabilistic model for multi-label classification. In: ICDM 2008, pp. 628–637 (2008)
30. Wang, J., Yang, Y., Mao, J., Huang, Z., Huang, C., Xu, W.: CNN-RNN: a unified framework for multi-label image classification. In: CVPR 2016, pp. 2285–2294 (2016)
31. Wu, B., Liu, Z., Wang, S., Hu, B., Ji, Q.: Multi-label learning with missing labels. In: ICPR 2014, pp. 1964–1968 (2014)
32. Wu, B., Lyu, S., Ghanem, B.: ML-MG: multi-label learning with missing labels using a mixed graph. In: ICCV 2015, pp. 4157–4165 (2015)
33. Wu, F., et al.: Weakly semi-supervised deep learning for multi-label image annotation. IEEE Trans. Big Data 1(3), 109–122 (2015)
34. Yeh, C., Wu, W., Ko, W., Wang, Y.F.: Learning deep latent space for multi-label classification. In: AAAI 2017, pp. 2838–2844 (2017)
35. Yu, H., Jain, P., Kar, P., Dhillon, I.S.: Large-scale multi-label learning with missing labels. In: ICML 2014, pp. 593–601 (2014)
36. Zhang, M., Zhou, Z.: ML-KNN: a lazy learning approach to multi-label learning. Pattern Recognit. 40(7), 2038–2048 (2007)
37. Zhu, X., Goldberg, A.B.: Introduction to Semi-Supervised Learning. Synthesis Lectures on Artificial Intelligence and Machine Learning. Morgan & Claypool Publishers, San Rafael (2009)

Efficient 6-DoF Tracking of Handheld Objects from an Egocentric Viewpoint

Rohit Pandey[✉], Pavel Pidlypenskyi, Shuoran Yang,
and Christine Kaeser-Chen

Google Inc., Mountain View, USA
rohitpandey@google.com, podlipensky@google.com, shuorany@google.com,
christinech@google.com

Abstract. Virtual and augmented reality technologies have seen significant growth in the past few years. A key component of such systems is the ability to track the pose of head mounted displays and controllers in 3D space. We tackle the problem of efficient 6-DoF tracking of a handheld controller from egocentric camera perspectives. We collected the HMD Controller dataset which consist of over 540,000 stereo image pairs labelled with the full 6-DoF pose of the handheld controller. Our proposed SSD-AF-Stereo3D model achieves a mean average error of 33.5 mm in 3D keypoint prediction and is used in conjunction with an IMU sensor on the controller to enable 6-DoF tracking. We also present results on approaches for model based full 6-DoF tracking. All our models operate under the strict constraints of real time mobile CPU inference.

Keywords: Virtual reality · 6DoF dataset · Handheld object tracking
MobileNet · SSD · Pose estimation

1 Introduction

In the past few years, virtual reality (VR) systems have seen an increased demand. These devices are typically in the form of a head mounted display (HMD) for rendering the virtual scene, and single or dual handheld controllers for interaction. The HMD and controllers need to be tracked in position and orientation to create an immersive experience. The tracking can either be 3 degrees of freedom (DoF) including only orientation (roll, pitch and yaw) or 6-DoF which includes position in 3D space as well.

More realistic experiences can be created with 6-DoF tracking but it often requires additional hardware. VR headsets like the HTC Vive use external IR cameras and markers for tracking, restricting the system to be only operational in limited space. Newer mobile 6-DoF headsets can achieve similar results with inside out tracking. Such headsets have one or more outward facing cameras attached to the headset. By applying localization algorithms such as SLAM on

---

R. Pandey and P. Pidlypenskyi—Equal contribution.

© Springer Nature Switzerland AG 2018
V. Ferrari et al. (Eds.): ECCV 2018, LNCS 11206, pp. 426–441, 2018.
https://doi.org/10.1007/978-3-030-01216-8_26

camera images, we can compute the headset's 6-DoF position with respect to the environment.

Meanwhile, tracking handheld controllers in 6-DoF for mobile HMD remains a difficult problem. Controllers tend to move faster than headsets, have a much larger movement range, and may be occluded by users' own bodies. Existing solutions rely on either additional sensing hardware, e.g. electromagnetic sensors in Sixense systems, or additional visual markers as in Sony PS VR systems. The former solution can be costly, and the latter suffers from reliability issues when markers are occluded.

In this work, we explore image-based markerless 6-DoF tracking of handheld controllers. Our key observation is that users' hands and arms provide excellent context for where the controller is in the image, and are robust cues even when the controller itself might be occluded. To simplify the system, we use the same cameras for headset 6-DoF pose tracking on mobile HMDs as our input. In our experiments, they are a pair of stereo monochrome fisheye cameras. We do not require additional markers or hardware beyond a standard IMU based controller. We believe this can enable extremely small and cheap clicker-like controllers, and eventually lead into purely hand based interaction.

1.1 Contributions

Our main contributions in this work are:

1. An approach to automatically label 6-DoF poses of handheld objects in camera space.
2. The HMD Controller dataset[1], the largest-to-date markerless object 6-DoF dataset. This dataset contains 547,446 stereo image pairs with the 6-DoF pose of a handheld controller. We provide timestamped 6-DoF pose of a handheld controller for each image. The dataset contains images for 20 different users performing 13 different movement patterns under varying lighting conditions. Our dataset will be publicly available prior to the conference.
3. Neural network models to enable 3-DoF and 6-DoF tracking of handheld objects with mobile CPU compute constraints.

2 Related Work

There are a few existing datasets of handheld objects for the task of object recognition. The Small Hand-held Object Recognition Test (SHORT) [21] dataset has images taken from hand-held or wearable cameras. The dataset collected in [14] uses RGBD data instead. The Text-IVu dataset [2] contains handheld objects with text on them for text recognition. None of these datasets contain pose information of handheld objects.

On the other hand, researchers have also collected datasets specifically for object 6-DoF pose estimation. Datasets like the ones presented in [8] and [23]

---

[1] https://sites.google.com/view/hmd-controller-dataset.

provide full 6D object pose as well as the 3D models for most object categories, but do not deal with handheld objects. It is worth noting that having 3D models of the objects can improve pose estimation accuracy, but is infeasible in our case where the hand shape and manner of holding the object vary across users.

Our work is closely related to hand pose estimation from an egocentric perspective. The EgoHands dataset [1] consists of videos taken from a Google Glass of social interactions between people. It contains pixel level segmentation of the hands, but no information on handheld objects. The SynthHands dataset [18] consists of real captured hand motion retargeted to a virtual hand with natural backgrounds and interactions with different objects. The BigHand2.2M benchmark dataset [26] is a large dataset which uses 6D magnetic sensors and inverse kinematics to automatically obtain 21 joints hand pose annotations on depth maps. The First-Person Hand Action Benchmark dataset [4] provides RGB-D video sequences of the locations of 21 joints on the hand as well as the 6-DoF pose of the object the hand is interacting with. The joint locations are captured using visible magnetic sensors on the hand.

We base our models on the SSD [15] architecture due to its computational efficiency and superior performance compared to other single shot object detection approaches like YOLO [20]. Some of the key factors for the improved accuracy of SSD come from using separate filters for different aspect ratios. They are applied to feature maps at different feature extractor layers to perform detection at multiple scales. The computational efficiency comes from the fact that it is a single stage approach that does detection and recognition in one go instead of two stage approaches like Faster RCNN [6] and Mask RCNN [7] that do detection in the first stage followed by recognition in the second.

A few recent work have extended object detection approaches to 3D and 6D in a manner similar to ours. Mousavian *et al.* [17] regress box orientation and dimensions for 3D bounding box prediction on the KITTI [5] and Pascal 3D+ [25] datasets. Kehl *et al.* [12] and Poirson *et al.* [19] have formulated object pose estimation as a classification problem of discrete pose candidates, and tackled the problem using variants of SSD. Other approaches like [16] treat pose estimation as a regression problem, and used a combination of a CNN based feature network and an object specific pose network to regress 3D pose directly.

3   HMD Controller Dataset

The HMD Controller dataset consists of over 540,000 stereo monochrome fisheye image pairs of 20 participants performing 13 different movement patterns with the controller in their right hand. We collect the 6-DoF pose (position and orientation in 3D space) of the handheld controller. For each image pair sample, we provide:

- Timestamp synchrnoized 6-DoF pose of the tip of the controller in left camera's coordinate frame;
- Timestamp synchronized 6-DoF pose of the cameras with respect to a static environment;
- Intrinsics and extrinsics of the camera pair.

3.1 Device Setup and Calibration

To collect precise groundtruth for 6-DoF pose of the controller we use the Vicon motion capture system [24], which can track retroreflective markers with static infrared cameras set up in the capture space. We attach constellation of Vicon markers to both the headset and the controller. The markers on the headset are outside the field of view of cameras. The markers on the controller are placed in a way that they would be occluded by human hand most of the time, and not visible in camera images. We asked users to perform predefined set of motions. As there was still risk to have certain poses where markers were visible, we had three versions of controllers with Vicon markers attached to different places (Fig. 1). Users were asked to repeat the same motion with each version of the controller.

Fig. 1. Different versions of Vicon attachments to controller.

Table 1. RMSE in hand-eye calibrations.

	Orientation (degree)	Position (mm)
Headset	0.349	6.693
Controller	0.032	0.658

Vicon system provides 6-DoF pose tracking at 500 Hz. The pose of the marker constellation on the back of the controller CB with respect to the Vicon room origin V (initialized in an one-off room calibration stage) is provided at every update. We denote this as T_V^{CB}.

As we have different marker constellations, we need to compute the pose of one canonical keypoint on the controller to be able to merge data captured in different sessions. We choose the tip of the controller CT as the canonical keypoint, as it best reflects users' intention for spatial interaction in VR. We further define the local coordinate space centered at controller tip to be axis-aligned with the physical controller. We denote the transformation between this canonical coordinate space and the camera space as T_{Cam}^{CT}.

The computation of T_{Cam}^{CT} depends on the tracking of headset in vicon space. We track the headset by introducing an additional Vicon trackable constellation H which is mounted rigidly on the headset. At every frame we receive updates on the pose of H in Vicon tracking space. We denote this as T_V^H. The headset-mounted constellation has a rigid transformation from the camera. This can be computed as a hand-eye calibration problem [3] in robotics.

We compute the rigid transformation of T_{Cam}^H with offline hand-eye calibration procedures. We also compute T_{CB}^{CT} offline, with temporarily mounting a tracking marker at the controller tip and record the Vicon poses of CB and CT:

$$T_{CB}^{CT} = T_V^{CB^{-1}} \cdot T_V^{CT}. \tag{1}$$

After T_{CB}^{CT} is computed for each controller configuration, we remove the marker on the tip of the controller for user data collection in order not to introduce visible markers to images.

Another important calibration step is time alignment between Vicon clock and headset camera clock. The alignment is done based on angular velocity calculated based on trajectory provided by Vicon and cameras handeye calibration [3]. This allows us to find camera frame and corresponding 6-DoF pose of the controller.

During data collection, we can compute synchronized 6-DoF pose of the tip of the controller in left camera space as follows:

$$T_{Cam}^{CT} = T_H^{Cam^{-1}} \cdot T_V^{H^{-1}} \cdot T_V^{CB} \cdot T_{CB}^{CT}. \tag{2}$$

Each of the calibration steps described above introduced some error, we estimate root mean squared errors (RMSE) for hand-eye calibration in Table 1. This represents the level of noise in groundtruth labels of our dataset.

3.2   Dataset Cleaning

We investigated two potential issues with samples in our dataset: frames with missing or incorrect 6-DoF poses, and frames with visible tracking markers.

To remove frames with missing or incorrect 6-DoF poses, we filter our dataset with the following criteria:

1. Controller position is restricted to be within 1 m away from the camera. All our dataset participants have arm length less than 1 m.
2. We can detect missing Vicon tracking frames with the Vicon system. We discard image frames with no corresponding Vicon poses. We also note that it takes approximately 0.6 s for Vicon to fully re-initialize. Poses produced during the reinitialization stage tends to be erroneous. Therefore we discard 20 subsequent camera frames after tracking is lost as well.
3. Incorrect 6-DoF labels due to Vicon tracking errors are more difficult to filter automatically. Figure 2 provides a few examples of imprecise pose labels. We use an active learning scheme for filtering such frames, where we apply our trained models on the dataset to detect potential incorrectly labeled frames. In our experiments, we detect frames with pose prediction error larger than 3 cm. We then manually scan the set of frames and remove invalid labels.

We provide timestamps for each image in our cleaned dataset, so that one can track discontinuity in frames.

Another potential issue with our dataset is accidental exposure of Vicon tracking markers in images. Since users are encouraged to move freely when completing a motion pattern, it is always possible that tracking markers are visible to head-mounted cameras.

We use the integrated gradient method [22] to analyze effects of visible markers in the training dataset. Interestingly, we observe that our train models do not pick up markers as visual cues. In Fig. 3, we show an sample input image with clearly visible markers. Pixels that contributed most to model prediction on this image does not include pixels of the marker. We believe this is due to the small number of frames with visible markers and the small size of markers in the grayscale image - each marker is approximately 2.5 pixels wide on average in training images. Therefore, our final dataset does not explicitly filter out frames with visible markers.

Fig. 2. Examples of Vicon tracking failures and incorrect 6-DoF poses.

Fig. 3. Input image with visible markers and pixels that contributed most to prediction.

3.3 Bounding Box and Label Assignment

Many objection detection models such as SSD [15] require 2D bounding boxes and labels as input. Since the controller to be tracked is largely occluded by hand, we instead compute the bounding box for the hand holding the controller. We observe that we can approximate users' thumb position with the controller tip position CT.

To compute the 3D bounding cube of users' hand in camera space, we have:

$$P_{Cam}^{c_i} = T_{Cam}^{CT} \cdot P_{CT}^{c_i} \quad \text{for } x = 1, \ldots, 8 \tag{3}$$

where c_i denotes the 8 corners of the bounding cube, and $P_{CT}^{c_i}$ denotes the location of the corners in local controller space CT. In our experiments, we set $P_{CT}^{c_i}$ to be the permutation of $\{\{-0.03, 0.05\}, \{-0.05, 0.01\}, \{-0.01, 0.10\}\}$ (in meters). The bounding box size reflects typical human hand size, and the location reflects the shape of the right hand viewed from the controller tip's local space.

Finally we compute the 2D hand bounding box by projecting the 3D bounding cube into the image space using camera intrinsics. We choose the smallest axis-aligned 2D bounding box that contains all projected bounding cube corners. All hand bounding boxes are automatically associated with the label for right hand. During model training, we add another label for background to all unmatched anchors.

Note that with using the full hand as object bounding box, we have transferred our problem to be hand detection and keypoint localization in image space. Hands and arms provide excellent context for controller pose even when the controller is not observable visually. Hands and arms also have more high-level features for neural networks to pick up on. This is a key to our solution of markerless controller tracking.

3.4 Dataset Statistics

After dataset cleaning, we obtained a final set with 547,446 frames. Figure 4 shows sample frames with visualized groundtruth pose annotations. Figures 5, 6 and 7 shows pose distribution in our dataset in image space, xyz space and orientation space.

Fig. 4. Sample images with visualized 6-DoF groundtruth annotation.

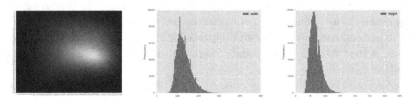

Fig. 5. *Left to right*: heatmap of pixels occupied by user hand and controller; histogram of 2D bounding box width; histogram of 2D bounding box height.

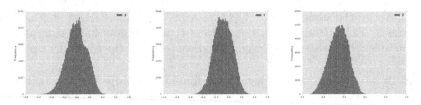

Fig. 6. *Left to right*: histograms of coordinates in x, y and z directions in meters.

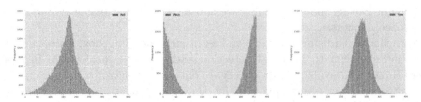

Fig. 7. *Left to right*: histograms of roll, pitch and yaw in degrees.

Groundtruth pose distribution in our dataset aligns with the space of natural human arm movement. We instructed all participants to use their right hands to operate the controller, therefore there are more samples in the right half of the image. We could easily flip the image vertically and use them as samples for building left hand models.

4   Additional Fields Multibox Detector

We define an extensible model architecture based on Single Shot Multibox Detector (SSD) [15] for egocentric hand detection and 6-DoF keypoint tracking experiments. Our model **SSD-AF** supports adding arbitrary number of **A**dditional **F**ields to the output of each box prediction. Such additional fields can be used to encode both regression and classification targets, for the cases of pose regression models and binning models respectively.

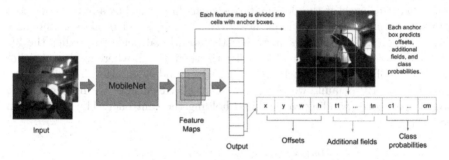

Fig. 8. MobileNet-SSD-AF architecture: we use MobileNet as the feature extractor network, and SSD with additional field output for detection and classification.

We choose an object detection approach based on SSD for our task because it has been shown to achieve good speed and accuracy tradeoff [11]. Additionally, SSD and similar approaches like YOLO [20] perform detection and classification simultaneously and thus tend to be more computationally efficient compared to two stage object detectors like Faster RCNN [6]. The SSD architecture also uses multi-scale feature maps from the feature extractor network to enable detection at different scales.

The classic form of the SSD architecture is a fully convolutional neural network that produces a fixed size collection of bounding boxes and class scores for the presence of an object within the box. This is followed by a non-maximum suppression step that chooses one or more boxes with the highest class scores. The output collection of boxes are represented as offsets to a set of heuristically chosen default boxes (similar to anchor boxes in [6]) of varying size and aspect ratio. For each default box we have:

$$output = [x_i, y_i, w_i, h_i, c_{i1}, \ldots, c_{im}] \text{ for default box } i \in \{1, \ldots, n\} \quad (4)$$

where x_i, y_i, w_i, h_i represents the offsets, c_{ij} represents class probability for class j, and n is the total number of matched boxes.

During training, target offset and class probabilities are assigned to default boxes whose overlap with groundtruth bounding boxes is above a given threshold. The loss calculated between the output and target vectors has two part: localization loss for the bounding box offsets, and classification loss for associated class confidences. The total loss is the weighted sum of the losses for the matched boxes and given by,

$$
\begin{aligned}
Loss = \frac{1}{n}[&L_{loc}(\langle x, y, w, h \rangle_i^{pred}, \langle x, y, w, h \rangle_i^{gt}, x_i) \\
&+ \alpha L_{conf}(c_{ij}^{pred}, c_{ij}^{gt}, x_i)] \quad \forall i \in \{1, \ldots, n\}, j \in \{1, \ldots, m\}
\end{aligned}
\tag{5}
$$

x_i is an indicator variable representing whether the i-th default box was matched to a ground truth box.

In order to predict 6-DoF pose along with the bounding boxes, we make the following modifications to the SSD architecture. We attach selected additional fields to each of the default boxes such that each box's output now has 4 offsets (x, y, w, h), k additional fields $(t_1, t_2, \ldots, t_k)$ and m class confidences $(c_1, c_2, \ldots, c_m)$. For example, if we use the additional fields to predict the 2D keypoint corresponding to the controller tip then $k = 2$, where as if we predict the full 6-DoF pose with position in xyz space and orientation in quaternions then $k = 7$. By default, we use $m = 1$ for all cases since we have only one object class corresponding to the hand holding the controller. The total loss in SSD-AF is,

$$
\begin{aligned}
Loss = \frac{1}{n}[&L_{loc}(\langle x, y, w, h \rangle_i^{pred}, \langle x, y, w, h \rangle_i^{gt}, x_i) \\
&+ \alpha L_{conf}(c_{ij}^{pred}, c_{ij}^{gt}, x_i) + \beta L_{fields}(t_{il}^{pred}, t_{il}^{gt}, x_i)] \\
&\forall i \in \{1, \ldots, n\}, j \in \{1, \ldots, m\}, l \in \{1, \ldots, k\}
\end{aligned}
\tag{6}
$$

Note that additional fields can vary depending on whether the model predicts regression targets such as 2D keypoint, 3D keypoint or full 6-DoF pose of the controller tip, or classification targets such as discretized bins of angular rotation. Additional field loss L_{fields} is set according to the type of target. Additionally, each additional field can be encoded with respect to the default box coordinates, just as in case of the bounding box coordinates which are encoded as offsets with respect to the default box.

We use MobileNet [10] as the feature extractor network for SSD-AF. Our final model architecture is shown in Fig. 8.

5   Experiments

5.1   Experiment Setup

We split the HMD Controller dataset into a training and evaluation set based on users. In total we use 508,690 samples for training and 38,756 samples for testing. All metrics below are reported on the testing set.

Our models are implemented using Python and Tensorflow. The input images are downsized from their original resolution of 640×480 to 320×240. The images are preprocessed by normalization to a $[0, 1]$ range, and random contrast and brightness perturbation is applied during training. We use a MobileNet with depth multipler 0.25 as our feature extractor. The ground truth target vector is generated by assigning anchors that have greater than 50% IOU with the groundtruth boxes. We use Smooth L1 loss [6] for localization and additional fields and binary cross entropy for classification. We set the loss weights α and β to be 1.0 in all our experiments.

The network is trained using stochastic gradient descent with ADAM optimizer [13]. As a post-processing step, we perform non-maximum suppression on the output boxes to pick the box with the highest class probability score. The final output consists of the coordinates of the output box with the corresponding additional fields and class confidences.

5.2   Metrics

We derive our metrics based on those defined in [9]. For a sample in our testing set, we denote the groundtruth 2D bounding box with B^{gt}, and a candidate 2D box as B^{pred}. We denote class probability of the object in the candidate box being users' right hand holding the controller as c^{pred}. Conversely, the probability of candidate box being in background class is $1 - c^{pred}$.

Detection Metrics: We use mean average precision (mAP) as our main metric for detection. The following algorithm is used to determine whether B^{pred} is a true positive TP, false positive FP, true negative TN, or false negative FN:

$$B^{pred} \text{ is } \begin{cases} TN, & \text{if } B^{gt} \text{ does not exist and } c^{pred} < t_c \\ TP, & \text{if } B^{gt} \text{ exists and } c^{pred} > t_c \text{ and } IOU_{(B^{GT}, B^{pred})} > t_{IOU} \\ FN, & \text{if } B^{gt} \text{ exists and } c^{pred} < t_c \\ FP, & \text{otherwise} \end{cases}$$

where t_c is a selected threshold on class probability, and t_{IOU} is a selected threshold on the value of intersection over union (IOU) between the groundtruth box and candidate box. In our results below, we set t_c to be 0.0001. Unless stated otherwise, we set t_{IOU} to be 0.05, which maps to a maximum of 92.4 millimeter in position error. Finally precision is given by $tp/(tp + fp)$.

For models which predicts orientation in discrete bins, we also evaluate the mAP of bin classification. mAP in bin classification is only computed on the true positives.

Pose Metrics: For regression targets, we calculate the mean average error (MAE) and root mean-squared error (RMSE) between the groundtruth and predicted values. We report keypoint errors in image space coordinate u, v in pixels, and in camera space coordinate x, y, z in meters. For experiments which has orientation as a regression target, we report orientation errors in camera space in degrees.

5.3   3D Position Estimation

First we present results on 3D pose estimation with SSD-AF. Our best model for this task **SSD-AF-Stereo3D** uses a stacked stereo image pair as input to the network and predicts boxes with 6 additional fields representing the 3D position of the controller tip in both cameras $(t_u^1, t_v^1, t_z^1, t_u^2, t_v^2, t_z^2)$. Let the 3D position of the object keypoint be $P_{Cam}^o = (P_x^o, P_y^o, P_z^o)$, and the projected keypoint be u_o, v_o in image space. We encode the offset of u_o, v_o with respect to the anchor box as t_u and t_v, and P_z^o with respect to the box height as t_z. We have:

$$t_u = (u_o - x_a)/w_a, \quad t_v = (v_o - y_a)/h_a, \quad t_z = P_z^o/h_a \qquad (7)$$

where x_a, y_a represent the default box a's center and w_a, h_a represent its width and height.

We show the qualitative results of our SSD-AF-Stereo3D model in Fig. 9.

Fig. 9. Prediction results of SSD-AF-Stereo3D on sample test set images. Groundtruth 3D position is visualized on the left half of each image, and predicted position is visualized on the right. The size of the overlay circle is inversely proportional to P_z^o. Our model performs within centimeter accuracy despite extremely challenging lighting conditions and complex situations such as user holding the controller with both hands.

Quantitatively, we compare our model with two other baseline model:

- **SSD-AF-2D:** Model input is one of the stereo images. Additional fields output are (t_u, t_v).
- **SSD-AF-3D:** Model input is one of the stereo images. Additional fields output are (t_u, t_v, t_z).

The evaluation results for bounding box and class prediction are shown in Table 2, and the results for 2D, 3D and 6-DoF tracking are shown in Table 3. It can be seen that the precision of the models are generally high, indicating good bounding box prediction performance. SSD-AF-Stereo3D achieved the best bounding box precision of 0.9534. It also achieves the lowest UV prediction MAE

Table 2. Detection mAP of 3D position models.

Model	mAP @0.05IOU	mAP @0.25IOU	mAP @0.5IOU
SSD-AF-2D	0.9140	0.8469	0.5180
SSD-AF-3D	0.9380	0.8761	0.5131
SSD-AF-Stereo3D	**0.9534**	**0.9533**	**0.7767**

Table 3. Pose prediction errors and latency: Position errors is measured in pixels in uv space, and in meters in xyz space. Mobile latency is measured in milliseconds on a Pixel 2 mobile phone using only 1 big CPU core, and on a desktop Titan X GPU. Note that we can run SSD-AF-2D on both images in the stereo pair, and triangulate with camera extrinsics to compute the 3D pose. This would effectively double the runtime.

Model	Position (uv)		Position (xyz)		Latency (ms)	
	MAE	RMSE	MAE	RMSE	Mobile	Titan X
SSD-AF-2D	12.41	30.01	-	-	30.140	6.378
SSD-AF-3D	10.23	24.38	0.0493	0.0937	30.649	6.303
SSD-AF-Stereo3D	**8.45**	**23.25**	**0.0335**	**0.0776**	31.768	6.512

of 8.45 pixels and 3D keypoint prediction MAE of 33.5 mm. Additionally, this model can run on one big mobile CPU at 30 fps.

The higher uv prediction performance of the SSD-AF-3D model compared to the SSD-AF-2D model indicates that adding t_z to the target helps bounding box and 2D keypoint prediction as well. Our observation is aligned with the theory that adding additional supervised information helps neural networks learn.

SSD-AF-Stereo3D model performs the best indicates that the model is able to infer positional information better using both stereo images as input. Interestingly, we also observed that models that use stereo input but only predict (t_u, t_v, t_z) in one of the images (instead of both) do not out-perform single image models such as SSD-AF-3D.

5.4 Orientation and 6-DoF Prediction

Second we also present results on orientation and 6-DoF pose estimation with SSD-AF. Recent notable work on 6-DoF pose estimation typically uses one of two methods: regression or discrete binning. Regression models such as in [16] predicts object poses directly. Orientation can be represented in either Euler angles or quaternions for regression. Discrete binning model such as in [19] splits the possible 6-DoF space into a number of discrete bins, or *Views* as in [12]. Pose estimation then becomes a classification problem of assigning the correct viewspace bin to the sample.

We implemented both approaches with SSD-AF model:

- **SSD-AF-Stereo6D-Quat:** This model takes a stacked stereo pair as input and predict boxes with 14 additional fields that represent the full 6 DoF pose

$(t_u, t_v, t_z, qx, qy, qz, qw)$ of the controller in both images. qx, qy, qz, qw is the quaternion representation of orientation.

- **SSD-AF-Stereo6D-Euler:** This model is similar to the one above besides that orientation is represented by 3 values α, β, γ in pitch, yaw, roll direction in Euler angle.
- **SSD-AF-Binned:** Instead of regression target, this model outputs b additional fields in class probabilities $(tc_1, \ldots, tc_b)$. tc_i corresponds to the i-th orientation bin. In our experiments, we split the full orientation space equally into bins.
- **SSD-AF-3D-Binned:** Similar to above but also predicts (t_u, t_v, t_z) in addition to orientation bins.
- **SSD-AF-3D-AxisBinned:** Similar to above but orientation is binned per axis.

Additionally, we also test the **SSD-AF-MultiplePoint** model, which outputs additional fields (t_u, t_v, t_z) for 4 keypoints for each image in the stereo pair, yielding a total of 24 additional fields. The additional keypoints are chosen to correspond to other keypoints on the controller which are not co-planar. We compute orientation from the 4 keypoints by fitting a plane to the predicted keypoints and computing the orientation of the plane in camera space.

The results of these experiments are shown in Tables 4 and 5.

Table 4. MAE of orientation prediction models. Errors are measured in radians.

Model	Orientation MAE			Position MAE
	Yaw	Pitch	Roll	xyz
SSD-AF-Stereo3D	-	-	-	**0.0335**
SSD-AF-Stereo6D-Quat	0.3666	1.4790	0.6653	0.0521
SSD-AF-Stereo6D-Euler	0.3630	1.5840	0.7334	0.0448
SSD-AF-MultiplePoint	0.3711	1.108	1.203	0.0452
SSD-AF-3D-AxisBinned (20×3 bins)	**0.1231**	**0.8594**	**0.5256**	0.0503

Table 5. Classification mAP of bining models.

Model	Orientation Bins mAP	Position MAE
SSD-AF-Binned (27 bins)	0.6538	-
SSD-AF-Binned (512 bins)	0.3627	-
SSD-AF-3D-Binned (27 bins)	0.6412	0.04760
SSD-AF-3D-Binned (512 bins)	0.3801	0.07167
SSD-AF-3D-AxisBinned-Yaw (20 bins)	0.4480	0.05124
SSD-AF-3D-AxisBinned-Pitch (20 bins)	0.3592	0.04975
SSD-AF-3D-AxisBinned-Roll (20 bins)	0.5532	0.04413

SSD-AF-3D-AxisBinned performs the best across the board with the lowest numbers in all three directions. Note that this model predicts orientation around only one of these directions at a time instead of simultaneously as in the case of the others. In general, binning models perform better than regression models on orientation. Our models with 512 bins achieves binning precision 38%, which is much higher than chance.

Among regression models, the quaternion encoding of SSD-AF-Stereo6D-Quat performs slightly better than the Euler angle encoding of SSD-AF-Stereo6D-Euler. This observation is different from results in [16]. SSD-AF-MultiplePoint outperforms SSD-AF-Stereo6D models in the pitch direction, but fails short in the roll direction.

Finally, all 6-DoF models perform slightly worse on 3D position prediction compared to SSD-AF-Stereo3D. We conjecture that this is due to our mobile friendly models running out of capacity for predicting both the position and rotation.

6   Conclusion and Future Work

We have presented approaches for efficient 6-DoF tracking of handheld controllers on mobile VR/AR headsets. Our methods use stereo cameras on the headset, and IMU on 3-DoF controllers as input. The HMD Controller dataset collected for this work consists of over 540,000 stereo pairs of fisheye images with markerless 6-DoF annotation of the controller pose. The 6-DoF annotation is automatically collected with a Vicon motion capture system and has sub-millimeter accuracy. Our dataset covers a diverse user base and challenging environments. To the best of our knowledge this is the largest dataset of its kind.

We have demonstrated that our SSD-AF-Stereo3D model achieves a low positional error of 33.5 mm in 3D keypoint tracking on our dataset. It can run on a single mobile CPU core at 30 frames per second. We have also presented results on end-to-end 6-DoF pose prediction under strict computational constraints.

Our future work includes improving orientation prediction results. We believe our models can be further improved by encoding orientation to be invariant to default box locations. Objects with the same orientation may have different appearance in different parts of the image due to camera projection. Instead of asking the network to learn the projection, we can explore using projection-adjusted orientation as groundtruth, such that objects with the same appearance always correspond to the same orientation label.

Another interesting research direction is to apply temporal and contextual information to our models. Currently all our models predict object poses on a frame-by-frame basis. Adding temporal filtering or using a RNN could significantly speed up tracking. Motion priors for different types of interaction can also be added to further improve tracking quality.

References

1. Bambach, S., Lee, S., Crandall, D.J., Yu, C.: Lending a hand: detecting hands and recognizing activities in complex egocentric interactions. In: IEEE International Conference on Computer Vision (ICCV) (2015)
2. Beck, C., Broun, A., Mirmehdi, M., Pipe, T., Melhuish, C.: Text line aggregation. In: The 3rd International Conference on Pattern Recognition Applications and Methods (2014)
3. Chou, J.C., Kamel, M.: Finding the position and orientation of a sensor on a robot manipulator using quaternions. Int. J. Robot. Res. **10**(3), 240–254 (1991)
4. Garcia-Hernando, G., Yuan, S., Baek, S., Kim, T.K.: First-person hand action benchmark with RGB-D videos and 3D hand pose annotations. arXiv preprint arXiv:1704.02463 (2017)
5. Geiger, A., Lenz, P., Urtasun, R.: Are we ready for autonomous driving? The KITTI vision benchmark suite. In: IEEE Conference on Computer Vision and Pattern Recognition (CVPR) (2012)
6. Girshick, R.: Fast R-CNN. In: IEEE International Conference on Computer Vision (ICCV) (2015)
7. He, K., Gkioxari, G., Dollár, P., Girshick, R.: Mask R-CNN. arXiv preprint arXiv:1703.06870 (2017)
8. Hinterstoisser, S., et al.: Model based training, detection and pose estimation of texture-less 3D objects in heavily cluttered scenes. In: Lee, K.M., Matsushita, Y., Rehg, J.M., Hu, Z. (eds.) ACCV 2012. LNCS, vol. 7724, pp. 548–562. Springer, Heidelberg (2013). https://doi.org/10.1007/978-3-642-37331-2_42
9. Hodaň, T., Matas, J., Obdržálek, Š.: On evaluation of 6D object pose estimation. In: Hua, G., Jégou, H. (eds.) ECCV 2016. LNCS, vol. 9915, pp. 606–619. Springer, Cham (2016). https://doi.org/10.1007/978-3-319-49409-8_52
10. Howard, A.G., et al.: MobileNets: efficient convolutional neural networks for mobile vision applications. arXiv preprint arXiv:1704.04861 (2017)
11. Huang, J., et al.: Speed/accuracy trade-offs for modern convolutional object detectors. In: IEEE Conference on Computer Vision and Pattern Recognition (CVPR) (2017)
12. Kehl, W., Manhardt, F., Tombari, F., Ilic, S., Navab, N.: SSD-6D: making RGB-based 3D detection and 6D pose estimation great again. In: IEEE Conference on Computer Vision and Pattern Recognition (CVPR) (2017)
13. Kingma, D., Ba, J.: Adam: a method for stochastic optimization. arXiv preprint arXiv:1412.6980 (2014)
14. Liu, S., Wang, S., Wu, L., Jiang, S.: Multiple feature fusion based hand-held object recognition with RGB-D data. In: International Conference on Internet Multimedia Computing and Service (2014)
15. Liu, W., et al.: SSD: single shot multibox detector. In: Leibe, B., Matas, J., Sebe, N., Welling, M. (eds.) ECCV 2016. LNCS, vol. 9905, pp. 21–37. Springer, Cham (2016). https://doi.org/10.1007/978-3-319-46448-0_2
16. Mahendran, S., Ali, H., Vidal, R.: 3D pose regression using convolutional neural networks. In: IEEE International Conference on Computer Vision (ICCV) (2017)
17. Mousavian, A., Anguelov, D., Flynn, J., Košecká, J.: 3D bounding box estimation using deep learning and geometry. In: IEEE Conference on Computer Vision and Pattern Recognition (CVPR) (2017)
18. Mueller, F., Mehta, D., Sotnychenko, O., Sridhar, S., Casas, D., Theobalt, C.: Real-time hand tracking under occlusion from an egocentric RGB-D sensor. In: IEEE International Conference on Computer Vision (ICCV) (2017)

19. Poirson, P., Ammirato, P., Fu, C.Y., Liu, W., Kosecka, J., Berg, A.C.: Fast single shot detection and pose estimation. In: IEEE International Conference on 3D Vision (3DV) (2016)
20. Redmon, J., Divvala, S., Girshick, R., Farhadi, A.: You only look once: unified, real-time object detection. In: IEEE Conference on Computer Vision and Pattern Recognition (CVPR) (2016)
21. Rivera-Rubio, J., Idrees, S., Alexiou, I., Hadjilucas, L., Bharath, A.A.: Small handheld object recognition test. In: IEEE Winter Conference on Applications of Computer Vision (WACV) (2014)
22. Sundararajan, M., Taly, A., Yan, Q.: Axiomatic attribution for deep networks. arXiv preprint arXiv:1703.01365 (2017)
23. Tejani, A., Tang, D., Kouskouridas, R., Kim, T.-K.: Latent-class hough forests for 3D object detection and pose estimation. In: Fleet, D., Pajdla, T., Schiele, B., Tuytelaars, T. (eds.) ECCV 2014. LNCS, vol. 8694, pp. 462–477. Springer, Cham (2014). https://doi.org/10.1007/978-3-319-10599-4_30
24. VICON: Vicon motion capture software. https://www.vicon.com/products/software/tracker. Accessed 13 Mar 2018
25. Xiang, Y., Mottaghi, R., Savarese, S.: Beyond PASCAL: a benchmark for 3D object detection in the wild. In: IEEE Winter Conference on Applications of Computer Vision (WACV) (2014)
26. Yuan, S., Ye, Q., Stenger, B., Jain, S., Kim, T.K.: BigHand2. 2M benchmark: hand pose dataset and state of the art analysis. arXiv preprint arXiv:1704.02612 (2017)

ForestHash: Semantic Hashing with Shallow Random Forests and Tiny Convolutional Networks

Qiang Qiu[1]([⊠]), José Lezama[2], Alex Bronstein[3], and Guillermo Sapiro[1]

[1] Duke University, Durham, USA
[2] Universidad de la República, Montevideo, Uruguay
[3] Technion-Israel Institute of Technology, Haifa, Israel
qiang.qiu@duke.edu

Abstract. In this paper, we introduce a random forest semantic hashing scheme that embeds tiny convolutional neural networks (CNN) into shallow random forests. A binary hash code for a data point is obtained by a set of decision trees, setting '1' for the visited tree leaf, and '0' for the rest. We propose to first randomly group arriving classes at each tree split node into two groups, obtaining a significantly simplified two-class classification problem that can be a handled with a light-weight CNN weak learner. Code uniqueness is achieved via the random class grouping, whilst code consistency is achieved using a low-rank loss in the CNN weak learners that encourages intra-class compactness for the two random class groups. Finally, we introduce an information-theoretic approach for aggregating codes of individual trees into a single hash code, producing a near-optimal unique hash for each class. The proposed approach significantly outperforms state-of-the-art hashing methods for image retrieval tasks on large-scale public datasets, and is comparable to image classification methods while utilizing a more compact, efficient and scalable representation. This work proposes a principled and robust procedure to train and deploy in parallel an ensemble of light-weight CNNs, instead of simply going deeper.

1 Introduction

In view of the recent huge interest in image classification and object recognition problems and the spectacular success of deep learning and random forests in solving these tasks, modest efforts are being invested into the related, and often more difficult, problems of image and multimodal content-based retrieval, and, more generally, similarity assessment in very large-scale databases. These problems, arising as primitives in many computer vision tasks, are becoming increasingly important in the era of exponentially increasing information. Semantic and similarity-preserving hashing methods have recently received considerable attention for addressing such a need, in part due to their significant memory and computational advantage over other representations. These methods learn to embed data points into a space of binary strings; thus producing compact

© Springer Nature Switzerland AG 2018
V. Ferrari et al. (Eds.): ECCV 2018, LNCS 11206, pp. 442–459, 2018.
https://doi.org/10.1007/978-3-030-01216-8_27

representations with constant or sub-linear search time; this is critical and one of the few options for low-cost truly big data. Such an embedding can be considered as a hashing function on the data, which translates the underlying similarity into the collision probability of the hash or, more generally, into the similarity of the codes under the Hamming metric. Examples of recent similarity-preserving hashing methods include Locality-Sensitive Hashing (LSH) [1] and its kernelized version (KLSH) [2], Spectral Hashing (SH) [3], Sparse Hash [4], Kernel-based Supervised Hashing (KSH) [5], Anchor Graph Hashing (AGH) [6], Self-Taught Hashing (STH) [7], and Deep Supervised Hashing (DSH) [8].

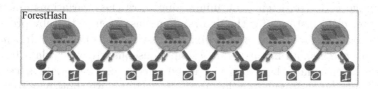

Fig. 1. ForestHash embeds tiny convolutional neural networks (CNN) into shallow random forests. ForestHash consists of shallow random trees in a forest, usually of depth 2 or 3. At each tree split node, arriving classes are randomly partitioned into two groups for a significantly simplified two-class classification problem, which can be sufficiently handled by a light-weight CNN weak learner, usually of 2 to 4 layers. We set '1' for the visited tree leaf, and '0' for the rest. By simultaneously pushing each data point through M trees of the depth d, we obtain $M(2^{d-1})$-bit hash codes. The random grouping of the classes enables code uniqueness by enforcing that each class shares code with different classes in different trees. The non-conventional low-rank loss adopted for CNN weak learners encourages code consistency by minimizing intra-class variations and maximizing inter-class distance for the two random class groups. The obtained ForestHash codes serve as efficient and compact image representation for both image retrieval and classification.

Due to the profound similarity between the problems of semantic hashing and that of binary classification, numerous classification techniques have been adapted to the former task. For example, multiple state-of-the-art supervised hashing techniques like ANN Hashing [9], SparseHash [4], HDML [10] and DSH [7] are based on deep learning methodologies. Besides deep learning, random forest [11,12] is another popular classification technique that has recently shown great success for a large variety of classification tasks, such as pose estimation [13] and object recognition [14]. However, to the best of our knowledge, random forests have not been used so far to construct semantic hashing schemes, and therefore do not enjoy the advantages of such compact and efficient codes. This is mainly because acting as hashing functions, a random forest fails to preserve the underlying similarity due to the inconsistency of hash codes generated in each tree for the same class data; it also lacks a principled way of aggregating hash codes produced by individual trees into a single longer code.

In this paper, we propose the *ForestHash* scheme. As shown in Fig. 1, the proposed ForestHash is designed to provide consistent and unique hashes to images from the same semantic class, by embedding tiny convolutional neural networks (CNN) into shallow random forests. We start with a simple hashing scheme, where random trees in a forest act as hashing functions by setting '1' for the visited tree leaf, and '0' for the rest. To enable such hashing scheme, we first introduce random class grouping to randomly partition arriving classes into two groups at each tree split node. The class random grouping enables code uniqueness by enforcing each class to share code with different classes in different trees, and also produces a significantly reduced two-class problem being sufficiently handled by a light-weight CNN.

We further adopt a non-conventional low-rank loss for CNN weak learners to encourage code consistency by minimizing intra-class variations and maximizing inter-class distance for the two random class groups, thereby preserving similarity. The low-rank loss is based on the assumption that high-dimensional data often have a small intrinsic dimension. Consequently, when data from the same low-dimensional subspace are arranged as columns of a single matrix, this matrix should be approximately low-rank. In Sect. 2.3, we show how to learn a linear transformation of subspaces using the matrix nuclear norm as the optimization criterion. We discuss both experimentally and theoretically that such learned transformation simultaneously minimizes intra-class variation and maximizes inter-class separation. We further show that kernelization or deep learning can be used to handle intricate data that do not necessarily admit a linear model.

Finally, the proposed information-theoretic aggregation scheme provides a principled way to combine hashes from each independently trained random tree in the forest. The aggregation process discussed in Sect. 2.4 is performed efficiently in a greedy way, which still achieves a near-optimal solution due to submodularity of the mutual information criterion being optimized. We discuss both unsupervised and supervised hash aggregation.

In Sect. 3, we show a comprehensive experimental evaluation of the proposed representation scheme, demonstrating that it significantly outperforms state-of-the-art hashing methods for large-scale image and multi-modal retrieval tasks.

2 Forest Hashing

We first discuss a simple random forest hashing scheme, where independently trained random trees act as hashing functions by setting '1' for the visited tree leaf, and '0' for the rest. We also show that hashes from a forest often fail to preserve the desired intra-class similarity.

2.1 A Toy Hashing Scheme

Random forest [11,12] is an ensemble of binary *decision trees*, where each tree consists of hierarchically connected *split* (internal) nodes and *leaf* (terminal) nodes. Each split node corresponds to a *weak learner*, and evaluates each arriving data point sending it to the left or right child based on the weak learner binary outputs. Each leaf node stores the statistics of the data points that arrived to it during training. During testing, each decision tree returns a class posterior probability for a test sample, and the forest output is often defined as the average (or otherwise aggregated distribution) of the tree posteriors.

Following the random forest literature [12], in this paper, we specify a maximum tree depth d to limit the size of a tree, which is different from algorithms like C4.5 [15] that grow the tree relying on other termination criteria; we also avoid post-training operations such as tree pruning. Thus, a tree of depth d consists of 2^{d-1} tree leaf nodes, indexed in the breadth-first order.

During training, we can introduce randomness into the forest through a combination of random set sampling and randomized node optimization, thereby avoiding duplicate trees. As discussed in [11,12], training each tree with a different randomly selected set decreases the risk of overfitting, improves the generalization of classification forests, and significantly reduces the training time. When given more than two classes, we introduce node randomness by *randomly* partitioning the classes arriving at each binary split node into two categories.

A toy pedagogic hashing scheme is constructed as follows: Each data point is pushed through a tree until reaching the corresponding leaf node. We simply set '1' for leaf nodes visited, and '0' for the rest. By ordering those bits in a predefined node order, e.g., the breadth-first order, we obtain a (2^{d-1})-bit hash code, always containing exactly one 1. In a random forest consisting of M trees of the depth d, each point is simultaneously pushed through all trees to obtain M (2^{d-1})-bit hash codes.

This hashing scheme has several obvious characteristics and advantages: First, both the training and the hashing processes can be done in parallel to achieve high computational efficiency on modern parallel CPU or GPU hardware. Second, multiple hash codes obtained from a forest, each from an independently trained tree, have the potential to inherit the boosting effect of the random forest, i.e., increasing the number of trees increases accuracy (sublinearly) [12]. Finally, the scheme guarantees 1-sparsity for hash codes from each tree.

However, hashes from a forest fail to preserve the underlying data similarity. In classification, for which the forest was originally designed, an ensemble posterior is obtained by averaging from a large number of trees, thus boosting the classification accuracy [11], and no confident class posteriors are required for individual trees. This has several negative consequences for constructing a suitable hash function. First, a forest often distributes same class samples over multiple leave nodes in a tree, thus, no consistent codes are assigned to each class. Second, for the same reason, samples of different classes can follow the same path, therefore a forest does not guarantee a unique code for each class. Moreover, it is not obvious how to combine hashes from different trees given a target code length.

The inconsistency of the hash codes becomes more severe when increasing the tree depth, as more leaf nodes are available to distribute the same class samples. This problem can not be solved by simply increasing the number of trees for longer total bit length. For example, if 4-bit inconsistency is allowed for a 64-bit hash code, the Hamming ball already contains $C_{64}^4 = 635,376$ codes. A principled way is required to combine hashes from each tree. One can choose to combine hashes from different trees simply through concatenating, averaging and thresholding, or voting. However, the principles behind those heuristics are not obvious, and we might loose control on code length, sparsity, and even binarity.

In what follows, we address these two problems. First, we propose the random class grouping scheme, followed with near-optimal code aggregation, to enforce code uniqueness for each class. Second, we adopt a non-conventional low-rank loss for weak learners to encourage code consistency.

2.2   Random Class Grouping

A random class grouping scheme is first introduced to randomly partition arriving classes into two groups at each tree split node. Random class grouping serves two main purposes: First, a multi-class problem is significantly reduced to a two-class classification problem at each split node, which can be sufficiently handled by a very light-weight CNN weak learner. Second, random class grouping enforces each class to share its code with different classes in different trees, which allows the information-theoretic aggregation developed in the sequel to later produce a near-optimal unique hash code for each class.

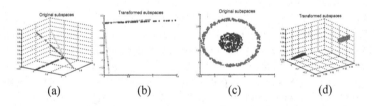

(a)	(b)	(c)	(d)

Fig. 2. Synthetic two-class examples illustrating the properties of the learned low-rank transformation. (a), (c) are transformed to (b), (d), respectively. In (a), two classes are defined as {blue, cyan} and {yellow, red}. An RBF kernel is applied to transform (c) to (d) (Color figure online)

2.3   Low-Rank Loss

A non-conventional low-rank loss is adopted for weak learners, e.g., a light-weight CNN learner, in a forest. Consider s-dimensional data points belonging to two classes after random class grouping, which for simplicity are denoted as positive and negative. We stack the points as columns of the matrices $\mathbf{X}^+$ and $\mathbf{X}^-$, respectively. Let $||\mathbf{A}||_*$ denote the *nuclear norm* of the matrix $\mathbf{A}$, i.e., the sum of its singular values. The nuclear norm is known to be the convex envelope of matrix rank over the unit ball of matrices [16]. The following result in [17] helps motivate our per-node classifier:

Lemma 1. *Let* **A** *and* **B** *be matrices of the same row dimensions, and* [**A, B**] *denote their column-wise concatenation. Then,* $||[\mathbf{A}, \mathbf{B}]||_* \leq ||\mathbf{A}||_* + ||\mathbf{B}||_*$*, with equality holding if the column spaces of* **A** *and* **B** *are orthogonal.*

At each tree split node, we propose to learn a weight matrix **W** minimizing the following low-rank loss function.

$$\min_{\mathbf{W}} ||\mathbf{W}\mathbf{X}^+||_* + ||\mathbf{W}\mathbf{X}^-||_* - ||\mathbf{W}[\mathbf{X}^+, \mathbf{X}^-]||_*, \tag{1}$$

Based on Lemma 1, the loss function (1) reaches its minimum 0 if the column spaces of the two classes become orthogonal after applying the learned transformation **W**. Equivalently, (1) reaches the minimum 0 if the subspaces of the two classes are maximally opened up after transformation, i.e., the smallest principal angle between the subspaces equals $\frac{\pi}{2}$. Simultaneously, minimizing the first two nuclear norm terms in (1) helps reduce the variation within classes. Synthetic examples presented in Fig. 2 illustrate the properties of the learned transformation. The trivial solution **W** = 0 can be avoided through a good initialization, e.g., the identity matrix [17].

Splitting Functions. With random class grouping, we have a two-class classification problem at each split node. We stack the training data points from each class as columns of the matrices $\mathbf{X}^+$ and $\mathbf{X}^-$, respectively.

During training, at the i-th split node, we denote the arriving training samples as $\mathbf{X}^+$ and $\mathbf{X}^-$. After a weight matrix **W** is successfully learned by minimizing (1), it is reasonable to assume that each of the classes will belong to a low-dimensional subspace, the distance from which can be used to classify previously unseen points. We use k-SVD [18] to learn a pair of dictionaries $\mathbf{D}^\pm$, for each of the two classes, by minimizing

$$\min_{\mathbf{D}_\pm, \mathbf{Z}^\pm} ||\mathbf{W}\mathbf{X}^\pm - \mathbf{D}^\pm\mathbf{Z}^\pm|| \text{ s.t. } ||\mathbf{z}^\pm||_0 \leq l, \tag{2}$$

where the ℓ_0 pseudonorm $||\mathbf{z}^\pm||_0$ counts the number of non-zero elements in each column of $\mathbf{Z}^\pm$, and l controls the subspace dimension.

At testing, given a data point **x**, the splitting function is evaluated by first projecting **x** onto both dictionaries and evaluating the projection errors

$$e^\pm(\mathbf{x}) = \arg\min_{\mathbf{z}^\pm} ||\mathbf{D}^\pm\mathbf{z}^\pm - \mathbf{W}\mathbf{x}||_2 = ||\mathbf{P}^\pm\mathbf{x}||_2, \tag{3}$$

where $\mathbf{P}^\pm = \mathbf{D}^\pm(\mathbf{D}^{\pm\mathrm{T}}\mathbf{D}^\pm)^{-1}\mathbf{D}^{\pm\mathrm{T}}\mathbf{W}$ are the $n \times n$ projection matrices. The point is sent to the left subtree if $e^-(\mathbf{x}) < e^+(\mathbf{x})$, and to the right subtree otherwise. In practice, we only store the projection matrices $\mathbf{P}^\pm$ at each split node. Note that similar splitting functions report success in a classification context with much deeper trees in [19].

Optimization. To optimize the low-rank loss function (1) using gradient descent, the subgradient of the nuclear norm of a matrix can be computed as follows: Let $\mathbf{A} = \mathbf{U}\boldsymbol{\Sigma}\mathbf{V}^\mathrm{T}$ be the SVD decomposition of the matrix A. Let $\hat{\mathbf{U}}$

and $\hat{\mathbf{V}}$ be the columns of $\mathbf{U}$ and $\mathbf{V}$ corresponding to eigenvalues larger than a predefined threshold. Following [17,20], the subgradient of the nuclear norm can be evaluated in a simplified form as

$$\partial\|\mathbf{A}\|_* = \hat{\mathbf{U}}\hat{\mathbf{V}}^{\mathrm{T}}$$

Note that (1) is a D.C. (difference of convex functions) program; and the minimization is guaranteed to converge to a local minimum (or a stationary point), with the D.C. procedure detailed in [21,22].

Kernelization. A sufficient number of tree splits could potentially handle nonlinearity in data for classification. In this work, only very limited number of splits is preferred in each tree, e.g., depth 1 to 3, to encourage short codes, which is insufficient in modeling data non-linearity well. Moreover, if we rely on tree splits in modeling non-linearity, we may still obtain less confident class posteriors as explained. The low-rank loss in (1) is particularly effective when data approximately lie in linear subspaces [17]. To improve the ability of handling more generic data, an effective way is to map data points into an inner product space prior to optimize for low-rank loss.

Given a data point $\mathbf{y}$, we create a nonlinear map $\mathcal{K}(\mathbf{x}) = (\kappa(\mathbf{x}, \mathbf{x}_1); \ldots; \kappa(\mathbf{x}, \mathbf{x}_n))$ by computing the inner product between $\mathbf{x}$ and a fixed set of n points $\{\mathbf{x}_1, \ldots, \mathbf{x}_n\}$ randomly drawn from the training set. The inner products are computed via the kernel function, $\kappa(\mathbf{x}, \mathbf{x}_i) = \varphi(\mathbf{x})'\varphi(\mathbf{x}_i)$, which has to satisfy the Mercer conditions; note that no explicit representation for φ is required. Examples of kernel functions include polynomial kernels $\kappa(\mathbf{y}, \mathbf{x}_i) = (\mathbf{x}'\mathbf{x}_i + p)^q$ (with p and q being constants), and radial basis function (RBF) kernels $\kappa(\mathbf{x}, \mathbf{x}_i) = \exp(-\frac{\|\mathbf{x}-\mathbf{x}_i\|_2^2}{2\sigma^2})$ with variance σ^2. Given the data points $\mathbf{X}$, the set of mapped data is denoted as $\mathcal{K}(\mathbf{X}) \subseteq \mathbb{R}^n$. We now learn a weight matrix $\mathbf{W}$ minimizing,

$$\min_{\mathbf{W}}\|\mathbf{W}\mathcal{K}(\mathbf{X}^+)\|_* + \|\mathbf{W}\mathcal{K}(\mathbf{X}^-)\|_* - \|\mathbf{W}[\mathcal{K}(\mathbf{X}^+), \mathcal{K}(\mathbf{X}^-)]\|_*, \qquad (4)$$

Deep Networks. While kernelization shows a simple yet effective non-linear mapping, we present a CNN-based weak learner now as the ultimate way in handling intricate data. With the gradient descent optimization discussed above, it is possible to implement the following function

$$L = \|\mathbf{\Phi}(\mathbf{X}^+)\|_* + \|\mathbf{\Phi}(\mathbf{X}^-)\|_* - \|[\mathbf{\Phi}(\mathbf{X}^+), \mathbf{\Phi}(\mathbf{X}^-)]\|_*, \qquad (5)$$

as a low-rank loss layer for general deep networks, where $\mathbf{\Phi}$ denotes the mapping from a deep network. From our experimental experience, the low-rank loss reports comparable performance as the standard softmax loss, while being used standalone as a classification loss for small classification problems. However, together with softmax, we observed consistent classification performance improvements over most popular CNN architectures and challenging datasets. As in Fig. 3, with low-rank loss, the intra-class variations among features are collapsed and inter-class features are orthogonal [23]. Such property is particularly beneficial at each tree split node.

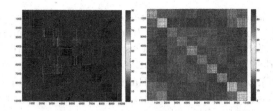

Fig. 3. Angles between the deep features learned for the validation set of CIFAR-10 using VGG-16. (Left) with additional low-rank loss. (Right) with the standard softmax loss. With low-rank loss, the intra-class variations among features are collapsed and inter-class features are orthogonal, which are particularly preferred at each tree split node.

2.4   Information-Theoretic Code Aggregation

After training each random tree with the low-rank loss learner to produce consistent hashes for similar data points, we propose an information-theoretic approach to aggregate hashes across trees into a unique code for each data class. As labels are usually unavailable or only available for a small subset of data, unsupervised aggregation allows exploiting all available data. We also explain how labels, if available, can be further incorporated for supervised hash aggregation. Note that the code aggregation step is only learned once during training, no cost at testing.

Unsupervised Aggregation. Consider a random forest consisting of M trees of depth d; the hash codes obtained for N training samples are denoted as $\mathcal{B} = \{\mathbf{B}_i\}_{i=1}^{M}$, with the $\mathbf{B}_i \in \{0,1\}^{(2^{d-1}) \times N}$ being the codes generated from the i-th tree, henceforth denoted as *code blocks*. Given the target hash code length L, our objective is to select k code blocks $\mathbf{B}^*$, $k \leq L/(2^{d-1})$, maximizing the mutual information between the selected and the remaining codes,

$$\mathbf{B}^* = \arg \max_{\mathbf{B}:|\mathbf{B}|=k} I(\mathbf{B}; \mathcal{B}\backslash\mathbf{B}). \tag{6}$$

A set function is said to be *submodular* if it has a diminishing return property, i.e., adding an element to a smaller set helps more than adding it to a larger set.

Lemma 2. $I(\mathbf{B}; \mathcal{B}\backslash\mathbf{B})$ *is submodular.*

The general problem of maximizing submodular functions is NP-hard, by reduction from the max-cover problem. However, motivated by the sensor placement strategy in [24], we propose a very simple greedy algorithm to approximate the solution of (6). We start with $B = \emptyset$, and iteratively choose the next best code block $\mathbf{b}^*$ from $\mathcal{B}\backslash\mathbf{B}$ which provides a maximum increase in mutual information, i.e.,

$$\arg \max_{b^* \in \mathcal{B}\backslash\mathbf{B}} I(\mathbf{B} \cup \mathbf{b}^*; \mathcal{B}\backslash(\mathbf{B} \cup \mathbf{b}^*)) - I(\mathbf{B}; \mathcal{B}\backslash\mathbf{B})$$
$$= \arg \max_{b^* \in \mathcal{B}\backslash\mathbf{B}} H(\mathbf{b}^*|\mathbf{B}) - H(\mathbf{b}^*|\mathcal{B}\backslash(\mathbf{B} \cup \mathbf{b}^*)), \tag{7}$$

where $H(\mathbf{b}^*|\mathbf{B})$ denotes the conditional entropy. Intuitively, the first term $H(\mathbf{b}^*|\mathbf{B})$ forces $\mathbf{b}^*$ to be most different from the already selected codes $\mathbf{B}$, and the second term $-H(\mathbf{b}^*|\mathcal{B}\backslash(\mathbf{B}\cup\mathbf{b}^*))$ forces $\mathbf{b}^*$ to be most representative among the remaining codes. By defining a covariance matrix with the ij-th entry equal to $\exp(-\frac{d_{\mathbb{H}}(\mathbf{B}_i,\mathbf{B}_j)}{N})$, with $d_{\mathbb{H}}$ being the Hamming distance, (7) can be efficiently evaluated in a closed form as detailed in [24]. It has been proved in [24,25] that the above greedy algorithm gives a polynomial-time approximation that is within $(1 - 1/e)$ of the optimum, where e is the Napier's constant. Based on similar arguments as those in [24], the near-optimality of our approach can be guaranteed if the forest size $|\mathcal{B}|$ is sufficiently larger than $2k$.

Supervised Aggregation. When the class labels C are available for the N training samples, an upper bound on the Bayes error over hashing codes $\mathbf{B}$ is given by $\frac{1}{2}(H(C) - I(\mathbf{B};C))$ [26]. This bound is minimized when $I(\mathbf{B};C)$ is maximized. Thus, discriminative hash codes can be obtained by maximizing

$$\arg\max_{\mathbf{B}:|\mathbf{B}|=k} I(\mathbf{B};C). \tag{8}$$

Similarly to the unsupervised case, we maximize (8) using a greedy algorithm initialized with $\mathbf{B} = \emptyset$ and iteratively choosing the next best code block $\mathbf{b}^*$ from $\mathcal{B}\backslash\mathbf{B}$ which provides a maximum mutual information increase, i.e.,

$$\arg\max_{\mathbf{b}^*\in\mathcal{B}\backslash\mathbf{B}} I(\mathbf{B}\cup\mathbf{b}^*;C) - I(\mathbf{B};C), \tag{9}$$

where $I(\mathbf{B};C)$ is evaluated as $I(\mathbf{B};C) = H(\mathbf{B}) - \sum_{c=1}^p p(c)H(\mathbf{B}|c)$. Entropy measures here involve computation of probability density functions $p(\mathbf{B})$ and $p(\mathbf{B}|c)$, which can both be efficiently computed by counting the frequency of unique codes in $\mathbf{B}$. Note that the number of unique codes is usually very small due to the learned transformation step.

Semi-supervised Aggregation. The above two aggregation models can be simply unified as

$$\arg\max_{\mathbf{b}^*\in\mathcal{B}\backslash\mathbf{B}} [I(\mathbf{B}\cup\mathbf{b}^*;\mathcal{B}\backslash(\mathbf{B}\cup\mathbf{b}^*)) - I(\mathbf{B};\mathcal{B}\backslash\mathbf{B})]$$
$$+ \lambda[I(\mathbf{B}\cup\mathbf{b}^*;C) - I(\mathbf{B};C)]. \tag{10}$$

The two terms here can be evaluated using different samples to exploit all labeled and unlabeled data. The parameter λ in (10) is suggested to be estimated as the ratio between the maximal information gained from a code block to each respective criteria, i.e., $\lambda = \frac{\max_i I(\mathbf{B}_i;\mathcal{B}\backslash\mathbf{B}_i)}{\max_i I(\mathbf{B}_i;C)}$. Exploiting the diminishing return property, only the first greedily selected code block based on (7) and (9) need to be evaluated, which leads to an efficient process for finding λ. Selecting using only semantic information gives a hash model that is less robust, e.g., overfits to training data, than a model also concerning the actual code representation. As shown in the experiments, both unsupervised and supervised aggregation approaches promote unique codes for each class, with further improvements when both are unified.

Table 1. Network structures of light-weight CNN learners.

CNN2		
1	Conv+ReLU+MaxPool	$5 \times 5 \times 3 \times 64$
2	Conv+ReLU+MaxPool	$5 \times 5 \times 64 \times 32$
3	FC	Output: 256
CNN4		
1	Conv+ReLU+MaxPool	$5 \times 5 \times 3 \times 64$
2	Conv+ReLU+MaxPool	$5 \times 5 \times 64 \times 64$
3	Conv+ReLU+MaxPool	$5 \times 5 \times 64 \times 64$
4	Conv+ReLU+MaxPool	$5 \times 5 \times 64 \times 64$
5	FC	Output: 256

Table 2. Retrieval performance (mAP) of different hashing methods on CIFAR-10. All methods use the 32×32 RGB images as input.

Method	12-bit	24-bit	36-bit	48-bit
LSH [1]	0.13	0.14	0.14	0.15
SH [3]	0.13	0.13	0.14	0.13
ITQ [30]	0.11	0.11	0.11	0.12
CCA-ITQ [30]	0.17	0.20	0.21	0.22
MLH [31]	0.18	0.20	0.21	0.21
BRE [32]	0.16	0.16	0.17	0.17
KSH [5]	0.29	0.37	0.40	0.42
CNNH [33]	0.54	0.56	0.56	0.56
DLBHC [34]	0.55	0.58	0.58	0.59
DNNH [35]	0.57	0.59	0.59	0.59
DSH [8]	0.62	0.65	0.66	0.68
ForestHash-CNN2	0.61	0.75	0.78	0.80
ForestHash-CNN4	0.70	0.80	0.82	0.84
ForestHash-VGG16	**0.76**	**0.82**	**0.86**	**0.89**

2.5   Multimodal Hashing

We can further extend ForestHash as a multimodal similarity learning approach. It is often challenging to enable similarity assessment across modalities, for example, searching a corpus consisting of audio, video, and text using queries from one of the modalities. The ForestHash framework can be easily extended for hashing data from multiple modalities into a single space.

At training, when multimodal data arrives at a tree split node, we simply enforce the same random class partition for all modalities, and learn for each modality a dictionary pair independently using the shared class partition. During

Table 3. Error rates (%) on CIFAR-10 image classification benchmark. ForestHash performs at the level of other state-of-the-art image classification techniques while utilizing a very compact 128-bit only representation.

Method	Depth	Params	CIFAR-10
Network in network [36]	-	-	10.41
All-CNN [37]	-	-	9.08
Deeply supervised net [38]	-	-	9.69
FractalNet [39]	21	38.6M	10.18
ResNet ([40])	110	1.7M	13.63
ResNet with stochastic depth [40]	110	1.7M	11.66
ResNet (pre-activation)[41]	164	1.7M	11.26
	1001	10.2M	10.56
ForestHash CNN2 128-bit	2 ($\times$ 64)	0.58M ($\times$ 64)	20.3
ForestHash CNN4 128-bit	4 ($\times$ 64)	0.38M ($\times$ 64)	16.47
ForestHash VGG16 128-bit	16 ($\times$ 64)	20.1M ($\times$ 64)	11.03

training, only the splitting function of one dominant (usually most discriminant) modality is evaluated for each arriving data point; during testing, based on the modality of an arriving point, the corresponding splitting function acts independently. As shown in Sect. 3, ForestHash significantly outperforms state-of-the-art hashing approaches on cross-modality multimedia retrieval tasks.

3   Experimental Evaluation

We present an experimental evaluation of ForestHash on image retrieval tasks using standard hashing benchmarks: the CIFAR-10 image dataset [27], the MNIST image dataset [28], and the Wikipedia image and document dataset [29]. CIFAR-10 is a challenging dataset of 60,000 32×32 labeled color images with 10 different object categories, and each class contains 6,000 samples. MNIST consists of 8-bit grayscale handwritten digit images of "0" to "9" with 7,000 examples per class, and a total of 70,000 images.

As discussed in Sect. 2.3, a low-rank weak learner at each tree split node is allowed in various implementations. Without particular specification, a 256-dimensional RBF kernelization is assumed. We use the CNN suffix when using a light-weight CNN as weak learner. Table 1 shows two network structures of light-weight CNN learners, CNN2 and CNN4, adopted in experiments. Unless otherwise specified, 128 trees are trained and semi-supervised aggregation are used (with only training data).

Note that a shallow tree is preferred; and a deeper tree ($d \geq 8$) becomes less preferred for (fast) retrieval, and loses the robustness gained from randomness. A tree of depth 2 is assumed by default in this section. In practice, the

Table 4. Retrieval performance (%) of different hashing methods (48-bit codes) on CIFAR-10 using reduced training. The methods on the top two groups use GIST features. For reference, the bottom group shows the performance of ForestHash with CNN features extracted from the 32×32 RGB images.

Method	Radius = 0		Radius $\leq$ 2	
	Precision	Recall	Precision	Recall
SH [3]	5.90	0.01	21.00	0.25
KSH [5]	8.50	0.07	21.41	0.66
AGH1 [6]	29.48	0.21	30.55	0.41
AGH2 [6]	29.92	0.24	30.13	0.58
SparseHash [4]	16.65	0.05	32.69	1.81
ForestHash (rand)	31.37	2.74	32.25	4.90
ForestHash (unsup)	34.02	3.65	34.55	6.40
ForestHash (sup)	33.86	3.33	34.02	5.21
ForestHash (semi)	**34.05**	**4.12**	33.73	**7.29**
ForestHash CNN4-softmax	22.72	0.33	34.27	1.52
ForestHash CNN2-softmax	23.00	0.42	32.13	1.56
ForestHash CNN4	28.66	0.86	**38.60**	2.88
ForestHash CNN2	29.30	1.78	38.29	4.68

Table 5. 36-bit retrieval performance (%) on MNIST (rejection hamming radius 0) using different training set sizes. Test time is the average binary encoding time in microseconds (μs).

	Test time (μs)	6,000 samples per class			100 samples per class			30 samples per class		
		Train time (s)	Prec.	Rec.	Train time (s)	Prec.	Rec.	Train time (s)	Prec.	Rec.
HDML [10]	10	93780	92.94	60.44	1505	62.52	2.19	458	24.28	0.21
FastHash [42]	115	865	84.70	76.60	213	73.32	33.04	151	57.08	11.77
TSH [43]	411	164325	86.30	3.17	21.08	74.00	5.19	2.83	56.86	3.94
ForestHash	57	24.20	86.53	46.30	4.19	84.98	45.00	1.43	79.38	42.27
ForestHash CNN2	13	81.6	**97.99**	**95.99**	7	**94.24**	**74.02**	2.69	**89.56**	**46.36**

choice of tree depth also depends of the target code length and the level of parallelism supported, as each hash tree can be trained and deployed independently in parallel.

3.1   Image Retrieval

We first adopt a CIFAR-10 protocol popular among many deep-learning based hashing methods, e.g., DSH [8], where the official CIFAR-10 train/test split is

Table 6. Mean average precision (mAP in %) in percent of Hamming ranking on MNIST.

	ForestHash CNN2	ForestHash	USPLH [44]	SH [3]	KLSH [2]	SIKH [45]	AGH1 [6]	AGH2 [6]
24 bits	**99.63**	82.99	46.99	26.99	25.55	19.47	49.97	67.38
48 bits	**99.68**	86.09	49.30	24.53	30.49	19.72	39.71	64.10

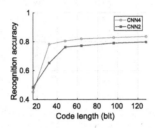

Fig. 4. The forest boosting effect using ForestHash codes. ForestHash shows a principled and robust procedure to train and deploy in parallel an ensemble of light-weight CNNs, instead of simply going deeper.

used; namely, 50,000 images are used as the training and the gallery, and 10,000 images as the query. Table 2 reports the retrieval performance comparisons with multiple hashing methods[1]. ForestHash with a simplest two-layer learner CNN2 in Table 1 already significantly outperforms state-of-the-art methods. Given such large size of training set, retrieval performance increases using more complex network structures as learners, e.g., CNN4 or VGG16 over CNN2.

The superior retrieval performance of the ForestHash codes in Table 2 can be easily explained by both the low-rank loss properties in Fig. 3 and the boosting effect of the random forest in Fig. 4. ForestHash shows a principled and robust procedure to train and deploy in parallel an ensemble of light-weight CNNs, instead of simply going deeper. As shown in Table 3, ForestHash performs at the level of other state-of-the-art image classification techniques, e.g., ResNet, while utilizing a 128-bit only representation.

We further experiment with CIFAR-10 using reduced size of training with both handcrafted feature and deep features. We adopt the same setup as in [4,5] for the image retrieval experiments: we only used 200 images from each class for training; and for testing, a disjoint test set of 1,000 images are evenly sampled from ten classes, to query the remaining 59,000 images. Images are used as inputs

Table 7. Cross-modality image retrieval using text queries on the Wiki dataset (mAP in %).

ForestHash (64-bit)	ForestHash (36-bit)	CM-SSH [46]	CM [29]	SM [29]	SCM [29]	MM-NN [9]	CM-NN [9]
50.8	45.5	18.4	19.6	22.3	22.6	27.4	25.8

---

[1] Results are taken from the respective papers.

for ForestHash with CNN learners, and 384-dimensional GIST descriptors are used for other compared methods, including ForestHash with an RBF kernel.

Table 4 summarizes the retrieval performance of various methods on CIFAR-10 at reduced training using the mean precision and recall for Hamming radius 0 and 2 hash look-up. For the compared methods SH, KSH, AGH1 and AGH2, we use the code provided by the authors; while for SparseHash, we reproduce the results from [4]. SH is unsupervised, while the rest of the hashing schemes are all supervised. We report the performance of ForestHash using the random, unsupervised, supervised, and semi-supervised hash aggregation schemes, respectively. We observe that the proposed information-theoretic code aggregation provides an effective way to combine hashes from different trees, and showing further benefits to unify both unsupervised and supervised aggregation. We also observe that using softmax loss only for CNN learners leads to performance degradation. At reduced training, more complex learner structures show no obvious advantage. In general, the proposed ForestHash shows significantly higher precision and recall compared to other methods.

The supervised hashing methods HDML [10], TSH [43], and FastHash [42] report excellent performance, where HDML is a deep learning based hashing method, and FastHash is a boosted trees based method. We adopt the experimental setting from [10], i.e., a 60 K training set and a disjoint 10 K query set split on the MNIST data. Each hashing method is assessed by the retrieval precision and recall at radius 0. As shown in Table 5, using all 60 K training samples, ForestHash with an RBF kernel shows comparable performance as HDML and FastHash, and better than TSH. ForestHash with a two-layer CNN significantly outperform all compared methods. We further assume labels are only available for a small subset of data, which is often the case for a retrieval system. When the number of labeled samples reduces to 100 and 30 per class respectively (instead of 6,000), the retrieval performance of other deep learning and boosted tree-based hashing degrades dramatically, as those methods require a dense training set to learn a rich set of parameters. Due to the subspace assumption behind the low-rank loss, which are known to be robust in the regime with few labeled training examples per class [47], ForestHash significantly outperforms state-of-the-art methods for such reduced training cases. Note that the training and hashing time of ForestHash reported here is the time for one tree, in order to emphasize the fact that different trees are trained and deployed independently and can easily be done in parallel.

More experiments were conducted on MNIST following [6], enabling the comparison with more hashing methods for which we have no implementation accessible. We split the MNIST dataset into a training set containing 69,000 samples and a disjoint query set of 1,000 samples. Table 6 reports the Hamming ranking performance measured by the Mean Average Precision (mAP) (performance of other methods is reproduced from [6]). For both code lengths, the proposed ForestHash significantly outperforms other hashing methods.

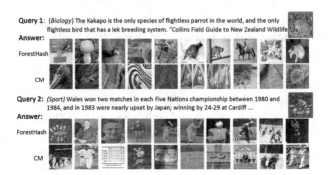

Fig. 5. Two examples of text queries and the top-10 images retrieved by ForestHash and CM [29]. Note that only text information are used to compose each query, and images are retrieved from the same category of the query text.

3.2   Cross-Modality Retrieval

We performed a cross-modality retrieval experiment following [9,29] on the Wikipedia dataset. The purpose is to demonstrate that ForestHash natively supports cross-modality, though not being designed for. The Wikipedia dataset contains a total of 2866 documents. These are article-image pairs, annotated with a label from 10 semantic classes. To enable a fair comparison, we adopted the provided features for both images and text from [29]. Table 7 shows the mean average precision scores for the cross-modality image retrieval using text queries. The proposed ForestHash significantly outperforms state-of-the-art hashing approaches on cross-modality multimedia retrieval tasks. Note that MM-NN and CM-NN [9] in Table 7 are both deep learning motivated hashing methods. Two examples of cross-modality text queries and the top-10 images retrieved are shown in Fig. 5, using ForestHash and CM [29]. Note that only text information is used to compose a query, and ForestHash retrieves images from the same category of the query text. ForestHash significantly outperforms CM with codes at least 10× shorter.

4   Conclusion

Considering the importance of compact and computationally efficient codes, we introduced a random forest semantic hashing scheme, extending random forest beyond classification and for large-scale multimodal retrieval of incommensurable data. The proposed scheme consists of a forest with random class grouping, low-rank loss, and an information-theoretic code aggregation scheme. Using the matrix nuclear norm as the optimization criterion, the low-rank loss simultaneously reduces variations within the classes and increases separations between the classes. Thus, hash consistency (similarity) among similar samples is enforced in a random tree. The information-theoretic code aggregation scheme provides a nearly optimal way to combine hashes generated from different trees, producing a unique code for each sample category, and is applicable in training regimes ranging from totally unsupervised to fully supervised. Note that the proposed framework combines in a fundamental fashion kernel methods, random forests, CNNs, and hashing. Our method shows exceptional effectiveness in preserving similarity in hashes, and significantly outperforms state-of-the-art hashing methods in large-scale single- and multi-modal retrieval tasks.

Acknowledgements. Work partially supported by AFOSR, ARO, NGA, NSF, ONR. José Lezama was supported by ANII (Uruguay) grant PD_NAC_2015_1_108550.

References

1. Gionis, A., Indyk, P., Motwani, R.: Similarity search in high dimensions via hashing. In: Proceedings of International Conference on Very Large Data Bases (1999)
2. Kulis, B., Grauman, K.: Kernelized locality-sensitive hashing for scalable image search. In: Proceedings of International Conference on Computer vision (2009)
3. Weiss, Y., Torralba, A., Fergus, R.: Spectral hashing. In: Advances in Neural Information Processing Systems (2009)
4. Masci, J., Bronstein, A.M., Bronstein, M.M., Sprechmann, P., Sapiro, G.: Sparse similarity-preserving hashing. In: International Conference on Learning Representations, Banff, Canada, April 2014
5. Liu, W., Wang, J., Ji, R., Jiang, Y., Chang, S.: Supervised hashing with Kernels. In: Proceedings of the IEEE Computer Society Conference on Computer Vision and Pattern Recognition, June 2012
6. Liu, W., Wang, J., Chang, S.: Hashing with graphs. In: International Conference on Machine Learning (2011)
7. Zhang, D., Wang, J., Cai, D., Lu, J.: Self-taught hashing for fast similarity search. In: Proceedings of International Conference on Research and Development in Information Retrieval (2010)
8. Liu, H., Wang, R., Shan, S., Chen, X.: Deep supervised hashing for fast image retrieval. In: Proceedings of IEEE Computer Society Conference on Computer Vision and Pattern Recognition (2016)
9. Masci, J., Bronstein, M.M., Bronstein, A.M., Schmidhuber, J.: Multimodal similarity-preserving hashing. IEEE Trans. Patt. Anal. Mach. Intell. **36**(4), 824–830 (2014)
10. Norouzi, M., Fleet, D.J., Salakhutdinov, R.: Hamming distance metric learning. In: Advances in Neural Information Processing Systems (2012)
11. Breiman, L.: Random forests. Mach. Learn. **45**(1), 5–32 (2001)
12. Criminisi, A., Shotton, J.: Decision Forests for Computer Vision and Medical Image Analysis. Springer, London (2013). https://doi.org/10.1007/978-1-4471-4929-3
13. Shotton, J.: Efficient human pose estimation from single depth images. IEEE Trans. Patt. Anal. Mach. Intell. **35**(12), 2821–2840 (2013)
14. Gall, J., Lempitsky, V.: Class-specific HOUGH forests for object detection. In: Proceedings of IEEE Computer Society Conference on Computer Vision and Pattern Recognition (2009)
15. Quinlan, J.R.: C4.5: Programs for Machine Learning. Morgan Kaufmann Publishers Inc., Burlington (1993)
16. Fazel, M.: Matrix Rank Minimization with Applications. Ph.D Thesis, Stanford University (2002)

17. Qiu, Q., Sapiro, G.: Learning transformations for clustering and classification. J. Mach. Learn. Res. **16**, 187–225 (2015)
18. Aharon, M., Elad, M., Bruckstein, A.: K-SVD: an algorithm for designing over-complete dictionaries for sparse representation. IEEE Trans. Sig. Process. **54**(11), 4311–4322 (2006)
19. Qiu, Q., Sapiro, G.: Learning transformations for classification forests. In: ICLR (2014)
20. Watson, G.A.: Characterization of the subdifferential of some matrix norms. Linear Algebra Appl. **170**, 1039–1053 (1992)
21. Sriperumbudur, B.K., Lanckriet, G.R.G.: A proof of convergence of the concave-convex procedure using Zangwill's theory. Neural Comput. **24**(6), 1391–1407 (2012)
22. Yuille, A.L., Rangarajan, A.: The concave-convex procedure. Neural Comput. **4**, 915–936 (2003)
23. Lezama, J., Qiu, Q., Musé, P., Sapiro, G.: Olé: orthogonal low-rank embedding, a plug and play geometric loss for deep learning. In: Proceedings of IEEE Computer Society Conference on Computer Vision and Pattern Recognition (2018)
24. Krause, A., Singh, A., Guestrin, C.: Near-optimal sensor placements in Gaussian processes: theory, efficient algorithms and empirical studies. J. Mach. Learn. Res. **9**, 235–284 (2008)
25. Nemhauser, G., Wolsey, L., Fisher, M.: An analysis of approximations for maximizing submodular set functions. Math. Program. **14**(1), 265–294 (1978)
26. Hellman, M.E., Raviv, J.: Probability of error, equivocation, and the Chernoff bound. IEEE Trans. Inf. Theory **16**, 368–372 (1979)
27. Krizhevsky, A.: Learning multiple layers of features from tiny images. Technical report (2009)
28. Lecun, Y., Bottou, L., Bengio, Y., Haffner, P.: Gradient-based learning applied to document recognition. Proc. IEEE **86**(11), 2278–2324 (1998)
29. Rasiwasia, N., et al.: A new approach to cross-modal multimedia retrieval. In: Proceedings of the International Conference on Multimedia (2010)
30. Gong, Y., Lazebnik, S.: Iterative quantization: a procrustean approach to learning binary codes. In: Proceedings of IEEE Computer Society Conference on Computer Vision and Pattern Recognition (2011)
31. Norouzi, M., Fleet, D.J.: Minimal loss hashing for compact binary codes. In: International Conference on Machine Learning (2011)
32. Kulis, B., Darrell, T.: Learning to hash with binary reconstructive embeddings. In: Advances in Neural Information Processing Systems (2009)
33. Xia, R., Pan, Y., Lai, H., Liu, C., Yan, S.: Supervised hashing for image retrieval via image representation learning. In: Proceedings of the Twenty-Eighth AAAI Conference on Artificial Intelligence (2014)
34. Lin, K., Yang, H.F., Hsiao, J.H., Chen, C.S.: Deep learning of binary hash codes for fast image retrieval. In: 2015 IEEE Conference on Computer Vision and Pattern Recognition Workshops (CVPRW) (2015)
35. Lai, H., Pan, Y., Liu, Y., Yan, S.: Simultaneous feature learning and hash coding with deep neural networks. In: Proceedings of the IEEE Computer Society Conference on Computer Vision and Pattern Recognition (2015)
36. Lin, M., Chen, Q., Yan, S.: Network In Network. In: ICLR (2014)
37. Springenberg, J.T., Dosovitskiy, A., Brox, T., Riedmiller, M.A.: Striving for simplicity: The all convolutional net. CoRR abs/1412.6806 (2014)
38. Lee, C., Xie, S., Gallagher, P.W., Zhang, Z., Tu, Z.: Deeply-supervised nets. In: AISTATS (2015)

39. Larsson, G., Maire, M., Shakhnarovich, G.: Fractalnet: ultra-deep neural networks without residuals. In: ICLR (2017)
40. Huang, G., Sun, Y., Liu, Z., Sedra, D., Weinberger, K.Q.: Deep networks with stochastic depth. In: Leibe, B., Matas, J., Sebe, N., Welling, M. (eds.) ECCV 2016. LNCS, vol. 9908, pp. 646–661. Springer, Cham (2016). https://doi.org/10. 1007/978-3-319-46493-0_39
41. He, K., Zhang, X., Ren, S., Sun, J.: Identity mappings in deep residual networks. In: Leibe, B., Matas, J., Sebe, N., Welling, M. (eds.) ECCV 2016. LNCS, vol. 9908, pp. 630–645. Springer, Cham (2016). https://doi.org/10.1007/978-3-319-46493-0_38
42. Lin, G., Shen, C., Shi, Q., van den Hengel, A., Suter, D.: Fast supervised hashing with decision trees for high-dimensional data. In: Proceedings of the IEEE Computer Society Conference on Computer Vision and Pattern Recognition (2014)
43. Lin, G., Shen, C., Suter, D., van den Hengel, A.: A general two-step approach to learning-based hashing. In: Proceedings of the International Conference on Computer vision (2013)
44. Wang, J., Kumar, S., Chang, S.F.: Sequential projection learning for hashing with compact codes. In: International Conference on Machine Learning, Haifa, Israel (2010)
45. Raginsky, M., Lazebnik, S.: Locality-sensitive binary codes from shift-invariant kernels. In: Advances in Neural Information Processing Systems (2010)
46. Bronstein, M., Bronstein, A., Michel, F., Paragios, N.: Data fusion through cross-modality metric learning using similarity-sensitive hashing. In: Proceedings of the IEEE Computer Society Conference on Computer Vision and Pattern Recognition, June 2010
47. Bengio, Y., Courville, A., Vincent, P.: Representation learning: a review and new perspectives. IEEE Trans. Patt. Anal. Mach. Intell. **35**(8), 1798–1828 (2013)

Local Orthogonal-Group Testing

Ahmet Iscen[(✉)] and Ondřej Chum

Visual Recognition Group, Faculty of EE, Czech Technical University in Prague,
Prague, Czech Republic
ahmet.iscen@cmp.felk.cvut.cz

Abstract. This work addresses approximate nearest neighbor search applied in the domain of large-scale image retrieval. Within the group testing framework we propose an efficient off-line construction of the search structures. The linear-time complexity orthogonal grouping increases the probability that at most one element from each group is matching to a given query. Non-maxima suppression with each group efficiently reduces the number of false positive results at no extra cost. Unlike in other well-performing approaches, all processing is local, fast, and suitable to process data in batches and in parallel. We experimentally show that the proposed method achieves search accuracy of the exhaustive search with significant reduction in the search complexity. The method can be naturally combined with existing embedding methods.

Keywords: Approximate nearest neighbours · Group testing
Image retrieval

1 Introduction

In this paper, we are interested in approximate nearest neighbor search, specifically in large-scale image search. First, since the seminal paper of Sivic and Zisserman [1], the image similarity was based on the bag-of-words approach [2–6]. Efficient image retrieval was performed via inverted file structure [7]. Later, high dimensional non-sparse descriptors were introduced by VLAD [8] and Fisher vectors [9,10]. Nowadays, image search is dominated by CNN descriptors [11–15], which also use high dimensional non-sparse vectors to represent images. Image similarity is typically measured by cosine similarity of the descriptors, or equivalently by an Euclidean distance of ℓ_2 normalized vectors. Efficient search in this case is performed by (approximate) nearest neighbor search.

A number of methods exist for efficient search in high dimensional data, using a variety of approaches such as partitioning and embedding. In partitioning, the descriptor space is subdivided and only a small fraction of the data is actually

Electronic supplementary material The online version of this chapter (https://doi.org/10.1007/978-3-030-01216-8_28) contains supplementary material, which is available to authorized users.

© Springer Nature Switzerland AG 2018
V. Ferrari et al. (Eds.): ECCV 2018, LNCS 11206, pp. 460–476, 2018.
https://doi.org/10.1007/978-3-030-01216-8_28

considered for possible nearest neighbors, majority of the data is filtered out. These approaches include kd-tree and forests [16], k-means tree [17], LSH [18–20]. Embedding approaches find a mapping from the original descriptor space to some other (typically of lower dimension or binary) space, where the distance, or the ordering by the distance, can be very efficiently approximated. As an example of the embedding methods we mention LSH [18–20] and other compact binary coding methods [21–24], product quantization [25] and methods derived from it [26,27]. Commonly, a combination of partitioning and embedding, such as PQ-IVFADC [25], is adopted. More recent works use neural networks to learn embeddings in a supervised manner [28,29].

An alternative to these approaches are methods based on group testing. Group testing was first used in World War II by the US army [30]. Due to limited resources, the US army did not want to test each individual soldier for an STD; instead they combined several blood samples into a single mixture, and tested the mixtures. If the test was negative, the associated individuals were deemed sound. If the test was positive, then all the recruits that contributed to this mixture were tested individually. Since the percentage of infected soldiers was low, this procedure dramatically reduced the number of tests needed to screen the population of soldiers.

In approximate nearest neighbor search, the individual blood samples are replaced with vectors, that are grouped into memory units. Each memory unit is represented by a vector, that is constructed from dataset vectors in the unit – different means of construction can be used [31], the simplest being a sum. In adaptive group testing [31–33], memory vectors are used for efficient pre-filtering of candidates. For the candidates, the exact similarity is then computed from the original vectors. To avoid storing the original vectors, methods of non-adaptive group testing were developed. Roughly, each input vector is stored in multiple memory units. The similarity of input vectors to the query is then estimated from a number of relevant memory units.

In this paper, we are interested in non-adaptive group testing. The contribution of the paper is twofold: local processing of the dataset when constructing the search structure and novel grouping of the vectors that introduces additional constraints used in the scoring stage. The proposed method matches the quality of the dictionary learning methods [34] that benefit from timely offline learning on the whole dataset, while preserving indexing efficiency of the basic group testing methods [32]. The process of encoding and search is outlined in Fig. 1.

Local Processing. The construction of the memory units and related decoding structures is linear in the size of the dataset. In order to encode the input data, the method (unlike [34]) does not need to see the whole dataset at once. This property makes it efficient in a streaming scenario, where the dataset is gradually increased in batches.

Vector Grouping. The group testing methods are efficient when the positive elements to be retrieved (syphilis infected individuals) are sparse in the dataset (population). By a simple and efficient greedy algorithm of selecting the vectors into groups, we try to minimize the chances that more than one element encoded in a single memory vector is positive. In the decoding stage, such a construction allows to suppress false positive responses. We call this process *correction*.

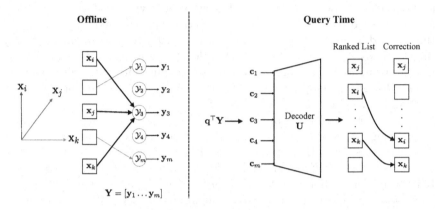

Fig. 1. The input data are represented by vectors $\mathbf{x}_1 \ldots \mathbf{x}_k$, By a greedy linear algorithm, vectors that are close to orthogonal are grouped into memory units $\mathcal{Y}_i$ represented by memory vectors $\mathbf{y}_i$. Sparse decoder matrix $\mathbf{U}$ captures the structure of the group assignment, and is also constructed in the off-line stage. At query time, responses of the memory vectors to the query q are evaluated and used to decode an estimate of the individual input vector similarities. A non-maxima suppression within each memory unit, called correction, is applied to filter out possible false positives. In this particular example, $\mathbf{x}_i$ and $\mathbf{x}_k$ were suppressed as they share $\mathcal{Y}_3$ with higher ranked $\mathbf{x}_j$.

The rest of the paper is structured as follows. The problem is mathematically formulated and current approaches are reviewed in Sect. 2. The proposed method is described in Sect. 3. Thorough experimental evaluation is presented in Sect. 4.

2   Problem Statement

In this section we detail the group testing setup and its applications in similarity search and image retrieval.

2.1   Adaptive Group Testing

Group testing was introduced in similarity search by Shi et al. [32]. Assume that the dataset has N d-dimensional vectors $\{\mathbf{x}_i\}_{i=1}^{N}$. The entire dataset is denoted by the $d \times N$ matrix $\mathbf{X} = [\mathbf{x}_1, \ldots, \mathbf{x}_N]$. Each vector $\mathbf{x}_i$ is ℓ_2-normalized such that $\|\mathbf{x}_i\| = 1$, $1 \leq i \leq N$. The similarity measure between a query $\mathbf{q}$ and a dataset vector $\mathbf{x}_i$ is computed by the scalar product $s_i = \mathbf{x}_i^\top \mathbf{q}$.

The goal of group testing is to infer the similarities s_i efficiently through M ($M \ll N$) group measurements and a decoder. It has three stages. The encoding stage first assigns vectors to groups. Shi et al. [32] define the encoding matrix $\mathbf{G}$ as a $M \times N$ matrix which keeps group assignments, such that $\mathbf{G}_{ji} = 1$ if $\mathbf{x}_i$

belongs to jth group. $\mathbf{G}$ is populated such that each vector is randomly assigned to m groups and each group has exactly n vectors:

$$M = \frac{mN}{n}. \tag{1}$$

Then the group vectors are created based on their assignments:

$$\mathbf{Y} = \mathbf{X}\mathbf{G}^\top. \tag{2}$$

This is equivalent to summing all image vectors assigned to a group:

$$\mathbf{y}_j = \sum_{\mathbf{x} \in \mathcal{Y}_j} \mathbf{x}, \tag{3}$$

where $\mathcal{Y}_j = \{\mathbf{x}_1, \ldots, \mathbf{x}_n\}$ is the set of n vectors from $\mathbf{X}$ assigned to jth group, for $j = 1, \ldots, M$.

The group measurement and decoding stages are performed during the query time. For a given query, the M group measurements are computed

$$\mathbf{c} = \mathbf{q}^\top \mathbf{Y}, \tag{4}$$

and pass them to a decoder to approximate N image similarities:

$$\hat{\mathbf{s}} = \mathbf{c}\mathbf{U} = \mathbf{q}^\top \mathbf{Y}\mathbf{U}. \tag{5}$$

The authors consider $\mathbf{U} = \mathbf{G}^\top$ in their work with an extra back-propagation step. In summary, when a new query is given, they (i) compute its similarities with group vectors (4), (ii) estimate the image vector similarities (5), (iii) perform a back propagation where the exact similarities with top ranked image vectors are computed, (iv) rank the images according to their similarity.

Iscen et al. [31] use a different setup but a similar idea. They assign each image vector to a single group (called memory units), thereby reducing the number of groups. Furthermore, the properties of randomly assigned memory units are theoretically analyzed. Assume that memory unit $\mathcal{Y}_j = \{\mathbf{x}_1, \ldots, \mathbf{x}_n\}$ stores n dataset vectors. Query $\mathbf{q}$ is related to $\mathbf{x}_1$, such that $\mathbf{q} = \alpha \mathbf{x}_1 + \beta \mathbf{Z}$ where α is the similarity between $\mathbf{q}$ and $\mathbf{x}_1$, and $\mathbf{Z}$ is a random vector orthogonal to $\mathbf{x}_1$ and $\|\mathbf{Z}\| = 1$. When sum aggregation (3) is used to create a group representative vector (called *memory vector*) $\mathbf{y}_j$ from $\mathcal{Y}_j$, the inner product between $\mathbf{q}$ and $\mathbf{y}_j$ becomes

$$\mathbf{y}_j^\top \mathbf{q} = \mathbf{x}_1^\top \mathbf{q} + \alpha \sum_{\mathbf{x}_i \in \mathcal{Y}_j \backslash \mathbf{x}_1} \mathbf{x}_i^\top \mathbf{x}_1 + \beta \sum_{\mathbf{x}_i \in \mathcal{Y}_j \backslash \mathbf{x}_1} \mathbf{x}_i^\top \mathbf{Z}, \tag{6}$$

where $\mathcal{Y}_j \backslash \mathbf{x}_1$ denotes all vectors in $\mathcal{Y}_j$ except $\mathbf{x}_1$.

The main source of noise for (6) comes from the middle term, which is basically the interference between $\mathbf{x}_1$ and the other $\mathbf{x}_i$ in $\mathcal{Y}_j$. In an attempt to eliminate this noise, a construction of the memory vectors by computing the pseudo-inverse of all vectors assigned to the group is proposed in [31]:

$$\mathbf{y}_j = ([\mathbf{x} \in \mathcal{Y}_j]^+)^\top \mathbf{1}_n, \tag{7}$$

where + denotes *Moore-Penrose pseudo-inverse* [35]. This construction is shown to perform better than the sum construction both theoretically and empirically under some mild conditions. At the final stage, they also re-rank all vectors of the highest scoring groups by computing their true similarity with the query vector.

Both methods indeed perform what is called *adaptive group testing* composed of two steps. The first step computes similarities with group representatives. These indicate which vector similarities are worth being investigated. The second step is a verification process computing the true similarities for these candidate vectors. Even though this strategy gives very accurate results with high efficiency, it requires group representatives as well as all database vectors to be kept in memory for the second adaptive step.

2.2 Non-adaptive Group Testing

A more modern view on group testing, called *non-adaptive group testing*, was adopted in other computer science related fields thanks to the advancements made in compressed sensing [36–40]. This approach argues that the identification of the infected individuals is possible just from the results of the group tests realized in the first step. There is no need of a second verification step.

A more recent dictionary learning based approach [34] applies non-adaptive group testing to similarity search. Group testing is defined as an optimization problem, where group vectors $\mathbf{Y}$ and the decoder $\mathbf{U}$ are optimized jointly. Unlike previous approaches [32], there are no assignment or construction constraints. The only constraint is to have a sparse $\mathbf{U}$ to reduce the number of vector multiplications during the query time. The solution is found by a dictionary learning optimization algorithm which yields a sparse decoding matrix $\mathbf{U}$:

$$\underset{\mathbf{Y},\mathbf{U}}{\text{minimize}} \quad \frac{1}{2}\|\mathbf{X} - \mathbf{YU}\|_F^2 + \lambda\|\mathbf{U}\|_1$$
$$\text{subject to} \quad \|\mathbf{y}_k\|_2 \leq 1 \text{ for all } 0 \leq k < M. \tag{8}$$

This method has a good search efficiency in terms of complexity and memory footprint, without compromising the search accuracy. Original database vectors need not be stored in the memory anymore since there is no need for re-ranking with original similarities. Nevertheless, its main weakness is its offline complexity. The solution to (8) requires the entire dataset to be available, which means that it needs to be recomputed as new data becomes available. Additionally, complexity of solving (8) grows dramatically as N and M increases, limiting its scalability for very large-scale scenarios.

3   Our Method

This section describes our contributions to group testing in this paper. Our framework groups orthogonal vectors together, which allows to have an efficient correction step without computing the true similarities of dataset vectors. Both, the encoder and decoder are learned locally from a subset of the dataset. We use the terminology introduced by [31] throughout the paper. Groups are called memory units, and group representatives are called memory vectors.

3.1   Orthogonal Memory Units

Random assignment [32] of the input vector to memory units is a basic assignment strategy: m permutations of $\{1, \ldots, N\}$ denoted by $\{\pi_k\}_{k=1}^m$ are drawn at random. For the k-th permutation, the vectors whose indices are $\pi_k((\ell - 1)n + 1), \ldots, \pi_k(\ell n)$, $\ell \in \{1, \ldots, N/n\}$, are grouped into one memory unit, assuming that n divides N. Random assignment is a convenient choice for large-scale datasets or streaming data due to its low complexity and locality. Other alternatives, such as assigning data based on k-means clustering [31] or kd-tree partitioning [33] show that grouping similar vectors together improve efficiency for adaptive group testing. However, these methods have a potentially expensive extra processing step and a verification step with re-ranking with true similarities is needed.

Our method heads the opposite direction. We propose to create a memory unit so that it contains mutually orthogonal vectors. The reason for such a construction is twofold, first minimizing the interference [31] between the vectors stored in a memory unit (6) and increasing the chances that there is only a single matching vector to a query in each memory unit. As we will show later, this property allows us to correct false positives and significantly improve the retrieval accuracy.

Instead of grouping m random vectors (selected via random permutation) as in [32], a random chunk of km vectors (again via random permutation) is selected. Within a chunk (considering only vectors from that chunk), k memory units of m vectors are constructed by a greedy approach. The memory units are initialized with m randomly selected vectors. In each iteration of the algorithm, each of the k memory units is greedily extended by one vector, that is "the most orthogonal" to the vectors already assigned to that particular memory unit[1].

Due to the greedy nature of the algorithm, the assignment is not globally optimal. Obtaining the globally optimal assignment is intractable. Our experiments show that in practice the group assignments are sufficiently independent: sum [32] and pseudo-inverse memory vector construction for orthogonal memory units are equally good.

The time complexity of the orthogonal assignment is the same as the time complexity of the random assignment, and the algorithm is fast in practice. This makes the algorithm an efficient option for large-scale scenarios. Since it works on small chunks of the dataset independently, it easily handles additional (streaming) data and is easily parallelized (unlike [34]).

---

[1] Matlab source code provided in supplementary material.

3.2   Local Decoder

After the assignment proposed in Sect. 3.1, M memory vectors are constructed with pseudo-inverse (7) and stored in a $d \times M$ matrix $\mathbf{Y} = [\mathbf{y}_1, \ldots, \mathbf{y}_M]$. During the query time, the goal is to approximate similarity of the query vector $\mathbf{q}$ and each individual input vector $\mathbf{x}_i$. This is achieved through a decoder matrix $\mathbf{U}$, so that

$$\mathbf{q}^\top \mathbf{X} \approx (\mathbf{q}^\top \mathbf{Y})\, \mathbf{U}.$$

Shi et al. [32], propose multiple decoding schemes for a given query. The first proposal is to take the pseudo-inverse of the sparse encoder $\mathbf{G}$ (see Sect. 2.1): $\mathbf{U} = \mathbf{G}^+$. This is a costly operation which involves computing and storing the dense pseudo-inverse of $\mathbf{G}$ in the query time. Thus, they use a simpler sparse decoder

$$\mathbf{U} = \mathbf{G}^\top \tag{9}$$

and an extra back-propagation step.

In the dictionary learning approach of Iscen et al. [34], group vectors $\mathbf{Y}$ and decoding matrix $\mathbf{U}$ are estimated by a joint optimization (8), which is extremely time demanding. Nevertheless, once the group vectors are constructed and fixed, the decoder matrix $\mathbf{U}$ is estimated by each column $\mathbf{u}_i$ independently by solving the system of linear equations

$$\mathbf{x}_i = \mathbf{Y} \mathbf{u}_i. \tag{10}$$

For efficiency reasons, it is important that $\mathbf{u}_i$ are sparse vectors. Let $\mathcal{S}(i)$ be the set of indices of the non-zero elements in $\mathbf{u}_i$. For a given $\mathcal{S}(i)$, the solution is found by solving a system of $\|\mathcal{S}(i)\|$ linear equations

$$\mathbf{x}_i = \mathbf{Y}_{\mathcal{S}(i)} \mathbf{u}_{i,\mathcal{S}(i)}, \tag{11}$$

where $\mathbf{Y}_{\mathcal{S}(i)}$ are the columns of $\mathbf{Y}$ whose indices are stored in $\mathcal{S}(i)$ and $\mathbf{u}_{i,\mathcal{S}(i)}$ is a vector composed of elements of $\mathbf{u}_i$ with indices $\mathcal{S}(i)$.

We propose to construct the set of indices $\mathcal{S}(i)$ based on the groupings of the input vectors into the memory units. Consider the bipartite graph B illustrated in Fig. 2. In this graph, one type of nodes corresponds to the input vectors, the other type corresponds to memory units. There is an edge between two nodes if the corresponding input vector is a member of the memory unit. It is natural to attempt to decode input vector $\mathbf{x}_i$ with memory units that vector is assigned to. We call this 0-order local decoder. For this decoder, the $\mathcal{S}_0(i)$ contains indices of memory units connected by a single edge to $\mathbf{x}_i$ in graph B, as illustrated in Fig. 2 left. Note that this construction has the same set of non-zero elements as the construction of Shi et al. [32], Eq. (9), however the weights estimated by (11) will differ from $\mathbf{G}^\top$.

Memory vectors with indices $\mathcal{S}_0(i)$, contain other input vectors than $\mathbf{x}_i$. These vectors influence the estimate of $\mathbf{q}^\top \mathbf{x}_i$. Using the same reasoning as before, we propose to select indices $\mathcal{S}_1(i)$ of the memory units that contain any input vector $\mathbf{x}_j$ assigned to any memory unit with indices $\mathcal{S}_0(i)$. We call this selection 1-order

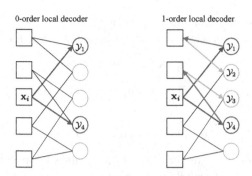

Fig. 2. Left: An illustration of 0-order local decoder for $\mathbf{x}_i$. $\mathcal{S}_0(i)$ contains indices of memory units that $\mathbf{x}_i$ is assigned to. **Right:** An illustration of 1-order local decoder for $\mathbf{x}_i$. $\mathcal{S}_1(i)$ contains indices of the memory units that contain any input vector $\mathbf{x}_j$ assigned to any memory unit with indices $\mathcal{S}_0(i)$.

local decoder, set $\mathcal{S}_1(i)$ contains indices of memory units connected by up to three edges to $\mathbf{x}_i$ in graph B, as illustrated in Fig. 2 right.

The proposed selection of the non-zero entries of the decoder $\mathbf{U}$ efficiently picks relevant memory vectors to be used during the estimation of $\mathbf{q}^\top \mathbf{x}_i$ for each $\mathbf{x}_i$ in time complexity that is independent of the size of the input data. This construction is local, does not require the presence of all memory vectors in the memory and thus is suitable for batch processing and parallelization.

Sparse Decoder. To sparsify the decoder matrix $\mathbf{U}$ further, we propose to add ℓ_1-norm regularization into (11):

$$\underset{\mathbf{u}_i}{\text{minimize}} \quad \frac{1}{2} \left\| \mathbf{x}_i - \mathbf{Y}_{\mathcal{S}(i)} \mathbf{u}_{i,\mathcal{S}(i)} \right\|_2^2 + \lambda \| \mathbf{u}_{i,\mathcal{S}(i)} \|_1 \tag{12}$$

In practice, we use a greedy algorithm called Orthogonal Matching Pursuit (OMP) [41,42]. OMP allows to choose the exact number of non-zero elements (instead of setting the parameter λ) in the solution so that the complexity of the decoder $\mathbf{U}$ is directly adjusted. All the local properties of the decoder construction are preserved.

Cascade Decoder. The decoder $\mathbf{U}$ can be decomposed into two matrices $\mathbf{U} = \mathbf{U}^0 + \mathbf{U}^1$. Let $\mathbf{c} = \mathbf{q}^\top \mathbf{Y}$, the decoder is then written as:

$$\mathbf{q}^\top \mathbf{X} \approx \mathbf{c}\mathbf{U}^0 + \mathbf{c}\mathbf{U}^1. \tag{13}$$

Since the estimated columns $\mathbf{u}_i$ of $\mathbf{U}$ contain a few significant elements (with high absolute value), some of them typically corresponding to $\mathcal{S}_0(i)$, and a larger number of less significant elements, the columns $\mathbf{u}_i^0$ of $\mathbf{U}^0$ are very sparse and contain the most significant entries, while the columns $\mathbf{u}_i^1$ of $\mathbf{U}^1$ contain the remaining elements of $\mathbf{u}_i$. The decomposition is then used in a cascade, first a short list of elements is efficiently obtained by using a rough approximation

$$\mathbf{q}^\top \mathbf{X} \approx \hat{\mathbf{s}}^0 = \mathbf{cU}^0. \tag{14}$$

Only for the shortlist $\mathcal{R}$, the finer estimate of the similarity (13) is performed as

$$\mathbf{q}^\top \mathbf{x}_i \approx \hat{\mathbf{s}}^0 + \mathbf{cu}_i^1 \quad i \in \mathcal{R}.$$

This process reduces the number of operations since $\mathbf{U}^0$ is much sparser than $\mathbf{U}$ and $|\mathcal{R}| \ll N$. The trade-off between the search accuracy and efficiency is controlled by the sparsity of $\mathbf{U}^0$. The memory requirements are increased only marginally, depending on the used representation of sparse matrices.

Synergy with Embedding Methods. In this section, we discuss the combination of the proposed method with embedding methods, in particular product quantization (PQ) [25]. In order to further reduce the memory footprint and the number of operations, the memory vectors $\mathbf{y}_i$ stored in $\mathbf{y}$ can be compressed by PQ. Approximating $\mathbf{q}^\top \mathbf{y}_i$ by asymmetric product quantizer is equivalent to actually evaluating $\mathbf{q}^\top \hat{\mathbf{y}}_i$, where $\hat{\mathbf{y}}_i$ is a quantized version of $\mathbf{y}_i$. Due to the local properties of the proposed algorithm, the decoder $\mathbf{U}$ can be construed from $\hat{\mathbf{Y}} = [\hat{\mathbf{y}}_1, \ldots, \hat{\mathbf{y}}_M]$ without any additional cost.

3.3   Decoder Correction

The search results are affected by inaccuracy of the similarity $\hat{\mathbf{s}} \approx \mathbf{q}^\top \mathbf{X}$ estimate (5). The estimate $\hat{\mathbf{s}}$ can be used as a pre-filtering, true similarities can be computed for highly ranked vectors and these scores can be back-propagated to update other scores, as proposed by Shi et al. [32]. This was shown to improve the search accuracy, but requires all dataset vectors to be accessible in the memory during query time. While such an approach reduces the complexity of the search (compared to the exhaustive search), it increases the memory footprint requirements.

Based on the orthogonal memory unit grouping, we propose a simple and efficient correction scheme, which completely avoids the utilization of the input vectors and their true similarities. Due to the orthogonality assignment, we make an assumption that there is at most one matching vector per memory unit to a query. In other words, if multiple vectors from the same memory unit score high in the ranked list, it is highly likely that only one is matching and the rest are false positives. We propose non-maxima suppression per memory unit. In practice, in a single pass through the ranked results, each top ranked (so far non-suppressed) result $\mathbf{x}_i$ suppresses all other vectors that appear in any of the memory vectors together with $\mathbf{x}_i$.

Experimentally, we show that the orthogonality of the vectors is essential for the correction to work. This correction scheme improves the search accuracy, especially for memory units composed of smaller number n of vectors.

4   Experiments

In this section, we experimentally verify the proposed method (all its components) in a large-scale image retrieval scenario. We first show the benefit of the orthogonal grouping and correction compared to random grouping. We define the following variants for our experiments. **LO-GT** is memory vectors with orthogonal assignment (Sect. 3.1) and local decoder (Sect. 3.2). **LO-GT*** additionally has the correction step (Sect. 3.3). Their random counterparts are **RND** and **RND***. Memory vectors from memory units are created with the pseudo-inverse construction (7) for all cases.

4.1   Experimental Setup

Datasets. We use two well-known large-scale image retrieval benchmarks in our experiments: Oxford105k and Paris106k. They contain about 105k and 106k images respectively. They are formed by adding 100k distractor images from Flickr [2] to Oxford Buildings [2] and Paris [3] datasets. We also perform a larger-scale experiment in revisited $\mathcal{R}$Oxford $+\mathcal{R}$1M [43], which consists of new 1M challenging distractor set. We evaluate using the Medium setup. Following the standard evaluation, the search performance is measured by mean average precision (mAP).

Image Representation. We use state-of-the-art image descriptors extracted from a ResNet101 network fine-tuned for image retrieval [15]. Each descriptor is extracted from 3 different image scales using GeM pooling, and combined into a single descriptor as in [43]. Each descriptor has $d = 2048$ dimensionality.

Complexity Analysis. Following the existing work [34], efficiency is reported by measuring the complexity ratio. This metric is based on the total number of scalar operations during the search. It is computed as $\rho = (Md + s)/dN$, where M is the total number of memory vectors, d is the dimensionality, s is the number of non-zero elements in the decoder $\mathbf{U}$, and N is the number of images in the dataset. Smaller ρ means more efficient search. Since our method does not require any image vectors to be loaded in the memory, ρ also relates to the gain in memory footprint compared to the exhaustive search. The only exception is the cascade decoder, where some of the columns of $\mathbf{U}^1$ are not touched.

4.2   Retrieval Performance

We now compare our orthogonal assignment with random assignment in a retrieval scenario. Various components of group testing, such as group size n, decoder order l and sparsity of $\mathbf{U}$ are analyzed. All the experiments in this subsection are performed on the Oxford105k dataset.

Group Size n. To keep the overall complexity fixed in this experiment, that is keeping sizes of $\mathbf{Y}$ and $\mathbf{U}$ constant, we set $m/n = M/N = 1/10$. Increasing the group size n also increases the number m of memory units each database vector

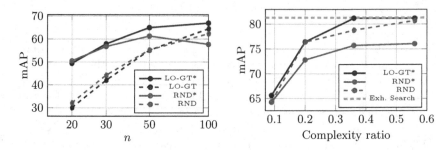

Fig. 3. Left: Impact of different n for $m = n/10$ and 0-order decoder on Oxford105k dataset. **Right:** Complexity ration vs. retrieval quality for $l = 1$-order decoding, $n = 50$, complexity ratio varies by changing $m = 2 \ldots 5$.

is assigned to. Figure 3 shows the mAP with the 0-order decoder for different values of n, comparing the proposed methods with the random grouping. For this settings, LO-GT without the decoder correction does not bring any significant improvement compared to random grouping. Using the decoder correction (LO-GT*) performs significantly better than the random grouping. As shown in the same figure, the correction actually degrades the performance of random grouping after certain complexity. This shows the benefit of our orthogonal grouping approach, which allows the correction process by assuming that there is only a single matching vector in the dataset.

Performance of the 1-Order Decoder. The 1-order decoder, non-sparse in this experiment, gives significantly better performance compared to 0-order decoder with higher complexity and memory footprint. In this experiment, we fix $n = 50$ and show the mAP and complexity (ρ) for varying m in Fig. 3. Our proposed method LO-GT* achieves the same mAP as exhaustive search with at the complexity ratio of $\rho = 0.36$ (corresponding to $m = 4$), outperforming the random variants.

Sparse decoder is obtained by adding a sparsity constraint on the solution of $\mathbf{U}$ (12). We show the impact of such sparsity constraint in Fig. 4. Orthogonal Matching Pursuit algorithm is used to adjust the number of non-zeros (L) on each column of $\mathbf{U}$. Smaller values L leads to a sparser solution, hence lower complexity ratio. It is shown that we achieve better accuracy than the random variants for all values of L. Setting $L = 300$ gives us the same accuracy as the exhaustive search. This corresponds to the complexity ratio of 0.23. As the complexity of the decoder increases, the benefit of the correction is less pronounced. At the same time LO-GT without correction, *i.e.* due to better estimates of the similarity, significantly outperforms both random grouping variants.

Cascade decoder is the decomposition of the decoder $\mathbf{U}$ in two matrices $\mathbf{U} = \mathbf{U}^0 + \mathbf{U}^1$ (Sect. 3.2). In this experiment, $n = 50$, $m = 4$ and the sparse decoder $\mathbf{U}$ with $L = 300$ from the previous experiment is decomposed it into two matrices. Each column of $\mathbf{U}^0$ is populated with the most significant entries

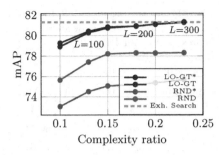 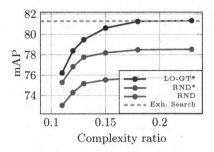

Fig. 4. Left: Search accuracy for sparse $\mathbf{U}$ of 1-order decoder. L is the number of non-zeros in each column of $\mathbf{U}$. **Right:** Impact of cascade decoder. Complexity ratio is varied by changing $p = 50\% \ldots 100\%$. $\mathbf{U}^0$ is populated with the most significant entries carrying p percent of the column energy. Rest of non-zero entries are assigned to $\mathbf{U}_1$.

carrying p percent of the column energy. Remaining non-zero entries are assigned to $\mathbf{U}_1$. Figure 4 shows the outcome of this approach. Different complexity ratio is obtained by changing $p = 50\% \ldots 100\%$. It is shown that the cascade decoder reduces the complexity ratio even further without harming the search accuracy.

Actual search time is measured as seconds instead of complexity ratio. In a single-thread CPU, exhaustive search in Oxford105k dataset takes 0.198 s per query on average. Our search time (when the complexity ratio is 0.18) in the same environment is 0.054 s per query. That's a ratio of 0.27, but we would like to note that we use a simple Matlab implementation which is not optimized for this task.

4.3 Comparison with Other Methods

We compare our method against the existing group testing techniques in the literature [32,34]. Two of our comparisons are made against the two variants of the group testing framework proposed by Shi et al. [32]. The first variant involves computing the full pseudo-inverse of the assignment graph $\mathbf{G}$. Since the resulting matrix is a large dense matrix, this variant is not efficient and is only included to serve as a baseline. We also compare against the back-propagation variant proposed by Shi et al. [32], where the scores are updated based on the true distance computations with dataset vectors. This variant is more efficient but requires higher memory footprint than the exhaustive search. All dataset vectors, in addition to memory vectors, need to be available in the memory.

We also compare against the dictionary learning solution proposed by Iscen et al. [34]. This method also has two variants. The first case involves using the entire the dataset to learn group vectors. Offline processing of this variant is not efficient for practical large-scale applications. Optimization problem (8) takes a long time to learn the group vectors. Alternatively, coresets [44,45] are proposed to reduce the indexing time. Coresets are representative data points sampled from the dataset. Number of coresets is set to $N/5$.

Table 1. Comparison of our method and existing group testing methods. Index time (in minutes) is the time it takes to create group vectors and the decoder. We set $M = 8408$ for all methods. We set the size of coresets $N/5$ for DL [34].

			Oxford105k		Paris106k	
	Complexity	Memory	Index time	mAP	Index time	mAP
Baseline	1.00	1.00	-	81.3	-	83.4
GT [32] pinv	4.20	4.20	<1	63.9	<1	56.5
GT [32] w/bp.	0.36	1.36	<1	73.4	<1	73.6
DL [34] w/cset	0.18	0.18	273	81.4	288	85.2
DL [34]	0.11	0.11	435	86.8	492	86.2
Ours, $l = 1$	0.18	0.23	4	81.3	4	83.7

Table 1 shows the comparison between our method and prior art in group testing algorithms. Timings are reported on a server with 32 cores. For every variant we set $M = 8408$, which corresponds to $n = 50$ and $m = 4$ for [32] and the proposed method. Note that DL has higher mAP but this comes at a significant offline cost. Finding group vectors with DL [34] involves solving an expensive optimization problem. It also requires entire dataset to be loaded in the memory at once, limiting its scalability for very large N. Furthermore, it is shown that the offline complexity of DL increases exponentially as N increases [34]. Therefore, this method is scalable only if the size of the dataset is reduced with coresets. Search accuracy is lower in that case, but the offline indexing time is still significantly higher than our method.

Batch Processing. We evaluate the search performance in a scenario where the data becomes available in batches over time. We divide the Oxford1M dataset randomly into b batches of equal size and create memory vectors $\mathbf{Y}_b$ and the decoding matrix $\mathbf{U}_b$ separately for each batch. After processing all the batches, we concatenate all $\mathbf{Y}_b$ and $\mathbf{U}_b$ and perform the search. Figure 5 shows the mAP for different number of batches. It can be observed that the search accuracy of DL [34] degrades significantly as the data are divided in more batches. This can be explained by the nature of this method, the fewer data are used in the global optimization, the less efficient search. The indexing time of DL is extremely high. Indexing the whole dataset in one go is not tractable, and for $b = 10$ it takes about 50 hours. On the contrary, our method can handle any scenario where matching vectors become available over time. This clearly shonws in Fig. 5, where the performance of our method is stable regardless of b.

Comparison with Partitioning. Finally, we compare our framework against the well-known FLANN toolbox [16]. We use the "autotuned" setting of FLANN, setting the target precision to 0.95. The average speed-up ratio after 5 runs is 1.45, which corresponds to a complexity ratio of 0.69. Compared to that, our method is able to achieve the baseline mAP performance with only 0.2 complexity ratio and memory footprint.

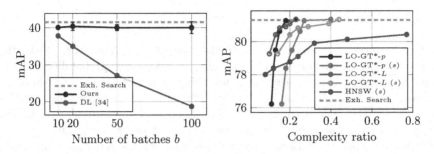

Fig. 5. Left: The mAP of the indexing structure constructed sequentially. $\mathcal{R}$Oxford + $\mathcal{R}$1M is divided into b batches and $\mathbf{Y}_b$ and $\mathbf{U}_b$ is created separately for each batch. We run our method multiple times and show the standard variation in vertical bars. **Right:** Comparison between our methods and HNSW [46] in Oxford105k. Curves with the complexity ratio based on measured run-time are denoted by (s), otherwise measured by the number of scalar operations.

Comparison with Graph-Based Indexing. Finally, we compare our method against a popular graph-based method by Malkov and Yashunin [46]. We use the implementation provided in FAISS toolbox [47]. To report the complexity ratio, a ratio of approximate-search time using the HNSW index to an exhaustive-search time, both on a single-thread CPU, is computed. A comparison of mAP on Oxford105k for different complexity ratios is shown in Fig. 5 (right plot). Two variants of the proposed method are shown: sparse 1-order decoder and cascade decoder $\mathbf{U}_0 + \mathbf{U}_1$ (as in Fig. 4), where the complexity is controlled by parameter L and p respectively. Additionally, we also report complexity ratio measured as a ratio of approximate-search and exhaustive-search times (as in HNSW). The plot shows that our method clearly outperforms HNSW. Furthermore, our framework requires significantly smaller memory footprint.

Combination with PQ. As described in Sect. 3.2, our method is compatible with existing embedding techniques, such as product quantization (PQ) [25]. We compress 2048D memory vectors into c bytes. Table 2 shows the mAP for different c. Note that learning $\mathbf{U}$ from compressed $\hat{\mathbf{Y}}$ (denoted by $\mathbf{U}^{pq}$ in the table) is important in this case. If $\mathbf{U}$ is learned from non-compressed $\mathbf{Y}$, then mAP is significantly degraded.

Table 2. Combination of PQ and our method. Each memory vector is compressed into c bytes.

Decoder	c		
	256	32	16
$\mathbf{U}$ from $\mathbf{Y}$	77.7	52.2	44.8
$\mathbf{U}^{pq}$ from $\hat{\mathbf{Y}}$	79.2	70.5	62.3

5   Conclusions

We have proposed two contributions to the group testing framework. First, the linear-time complexity orthogonal grouping increases the probability that at most one element from each group is matching to a given query. Non-maxima suppression with each group efficiently reduces the number of false positive results at no extra cost. Second, unlike in other similarly performing approaches, such as dictionary learning [34], all processing is local, orders of magnitude faster, and suitable to process data in batches and in parallel. We experimentally show, that for any choice of the efficiency, the proposed method significantly outperforms previously used random grouping. Finally, the proposed method achieves search accuracy of the exhaustive search with significant reduction in the search complexity.

Acknowledgments. The authors were supported by MSMT LL1303 ERC-CZ grant and the OP VVV funded project CZ.02.1.01/0.0/0.0/16_019/0000765 "Research Center for Informatics".

References

1. Sivic, J., Zisserman, A.: Video Google: a text retrieval approach to object matching in videos. In: ICCV (2003)
2. Philbin, J., Chum, O., Isard, M., Sivic, J., Zisserman, A.: Object retrieval with large vocabularies and fast spatial matching. In: CVPR, June 2007
3. Philbin, J., Chum, O., Isard, M., Sivic, J., Zisserman, A.: Lost in quantization: improving particular object retrieval in large scale image databases. In: CVPR, June 2008
4. Jégou, H., Douze, M., Schmid, C.: Improving bag-of-features for large scale image search. IJCV **87**(3), 316–336 (2010)
5. Jégou, H., Schmid, C., Harzallah, H., Verbeek, J.: Accurate image search using the contextual dissimilarity measure. IEEE Trans. PAMI **32**(1), 2–11 (2010)
6. van Gemert, J.C., Veenman, C., Smeulders, A.W., Geusebroek, J.: Visual word ambiguity. IEEE Trans. PAMI **32**(7), 1271–1283 (2010)
7. Babenko, A., Lempitsky, V.: The inverted multi-index. In: CVPR, June 2012
8. Jégou, H., Douze, M., Schmid, C., Pérez, P.: Aggregating local descriptors into a compact image representation. In: CVPR, June 2010
9. Perronnin, F., Dance, C.R.: Fisher kernels on visual vocabularies for image categorization. In: CVPR, June 2007
10. Perronnin, F., Sánchez, J., Mensink, T.: Improving the fisher kernel for large-scale image classification. In: Daniilidis, K., Maragos, P., Paragios, N. (eds.) ECCV 2010. LNCS, vol. 6314, pp. 143–156. Springer, Heidelberg (2010). https://doi.org/10.1007/978-3-642-15561-1_11
11. Babenko, A., Slesarev, A., Chigorin, A., Lempitsky, V.: Neural codes for image retrieval. In: Fleet, D., Pajdla, T., Schiele, B., Tuytelaars, T. (eds.) ECCV 2014. LNCS, vol. 8689, pp. 584–599. Springer, Cham (2014). https://doi.org/10.1007/978-3-319-10590-1_38
12. Tolias, G., Sicre, R., Jégou, H.: Particular object retrieval with integral max-pooling of CNN activations. In: ICLR (2016)

13. Gordo, A., Almazán, J., Revaud, J., Larlus, D.: Deep image retrieval: learning global representations for image search. In: Leibe, B., Matas, J., Sebe, N., Welling, M. (eds.) ECCV 2016. LNCS, vol. 9910, pp. 241–257. Springer, Cham (2016). https://doi.org/10.1007/978-3-319-46466-4_15

14. Radenović, F., Tolias, G., Chum, O.: CNN image retrieval learns from BoW: unsupervised fine-tuning with hard examples. In: Leibe, B., Matas, J., Sebe, N., Welling, M. (eds.) ECCV 2016. LNCS, vol. 9905, pp. 3–20. Springer, Cham (2016). https://doi.org/10.1007/978-3-319-46448-0_1

15. Radenović, F., Tolias, G., Chum, O.: Fine-tuning CNN image retrieval with no human annotation. arXiv preprint arXiv:1711.02512 (2017)

16. Muja, M., Lowe, D.G.: Scalable nearest neighbor algorithms for high dimensional data. IEEE Trans. PAMI **36**, 2227–2240 (2014)

17. Nistér, D., Stewénius, H.: Scalable recognition with a vocabulary tree. In: CVPR, pp. 2161–2168, June 2006

18. Indyk, P., Motwani, R.: Approximate nearest neighbors: towards removing the curse of dimensionality. In: STOC, pp. 604–613 (1998)

19. Gionis, A., Indyk, P., Motwani, R.: Similarity search in high dimension via hashing. In: VLDB, pp. 518–529 (1999)

20. Datar, M., Immorlica, N., Indyk, P., Mirrokni, V.: Locality-sensitive hashing scheme based on p-stable distributions. In: Proceedings of the Symposium on Computational Geometry (2004)

21. Lv, Q., Charikar, M., Li, K.: Image similarity search with compact data structures. In: CIKM, pp. 208–217, November 2004

22. Norouzi, M., Punjani, A., Fleet, D.J.: Fast search in hamming space with multi-index hashing. In: CVPR (2012)

23. Weiss, Y., Torralba, A., Fergus, R.: Spectral hashing. In: NIPS, December 2009

24. Raginsky, M., Lazebnik, S.: Locality-sensitive binary codes from shift-invariant kernels. In: NIPS (2010)

25. Jégou, H., Douze, M., Schmid, C.: Product quantization for nearest neighbor search. IEEE Trans. PAMI **33**(1), 117–128 (2011)

26. Ge, T., He, K., Ke, Q., Sun, J.: Optimized product quantization for approximate nearest neighbor search. In: CVPR, June 2013

27. Kalantidis, Y., Avrithis, Y.: Locally optimized product quantization for approximate nearest neighbor search. In: CVPR, (2014)

28. Jain, H., Zepeda, J., Pérez, P., Gribonval, R.: Subic: a supervised, structured binary code for image search. In: ICCV (2017)

29. Jain, H., Zepeda, J., Pérez, P., Gribonval, R.: Learning a complete image indexing pipeline (2018)

30. Dorfman, R.: The detection of defective members of large populations. The Ann. Math. Stat. **14**(4), 436–440 (1943)

31. Iscen, A., Furon, T., Gripon, V., Rabbat, M., Jégou, H.: Memory vectors for similarity search in high-dimensional spaces. IEEE Trans. Big Data **4**(1), 65–77 (2018)

32. Shi, M., Furon, T., Jégou, H.: A group testing framework for similarity search in high-dimensional spaces. In: ACM Multimedia, November 2014

33. Iscen, A., Amsaleg, L., Furon, T.: Scaling group testing similarity search. In: ACM ICMR (2016)

34. Iscen, A., Rabbat, M., Furon, T.: Efficient large-scale similarity search using matrix factorization. In: CVPR (2016)

35. Rao, C.R., Mitra, S.K.: Generalized inverse of a matrix and its applications. In: Proceedings of the Sixth Berkeley Symposium on Mathematical Statistics and Probability: Theory of Statistics, vol. 1 (1972)

36. Aldridge, M., Baldassini, L., Johnson, O.: Group testing algorithms: bounds and simulations. IEEE Trans. Inform Theory **60**, 3671–3687 (2014)
37. Bickson, D., Baron, D., Ihler, A., Avissar, H., Dolev, D.: Fault identification via nonparametric belief propagation. IEEE Trans. Signal Process. **59**(6), 2602–2613 (2011)
38. Cheraghchi, M., Hormati, A., Karbasi, A., Vetterli, M.: Compressed sensing with probabilistic measurements: a group testing solution. In: 47th Annual Allerton Conference on Communication, Control, and Computing (2009)
39. Gilbert, A., Indyk, P.: Sparse recovery using sparse matrices. Proc. IEEE **98**(6), 937–947 (2010)
40. Sejdinovic, D., Johnson, O.: Note on noisy group testing: asymptotic bounds and belief propagation reconstruction. In: 48th Annual Allerton Conference on Communication, Control, and Computing (2010)
41. Pati, Y.C., Rezaiifar, R., Krishnaprasad, P.: Orthogonal matching pursuit: recursive function approximation with applications to wavelet decomposition. In: ASILOMAR, pp. 40–44 (1993)
42. Davis, G.M., Mallat, S.G., Zhang, Z.: Adaptive time-frequency decompositions with matching pursuit. In: SPIE's International Symposium on Optical Engineering and Photonics in Aerospace Sensing, pp. 402–413 (1994)
43. Radenović, F., Iscen, A., Tolias, G., Avrithis, Y., Chum, O.: Revisiting oxford and paris: large-scale image retrieval benchmarking. In: CVPR (2018)
44. Agarwal, P.K., Har-Peled, S., Varadarajan, K.R.: Approximating extent measures of points. J. ACM **51**(4), 606–635 (2004)
45. Feldman, D., Feigin, M., Sochen, N.: Learning big (image) data via coresets for dictionaries. J. Math. Imaging Vis. **46**(3), 276–291 (2013)
46. Johnson, J., Douze, M., Jégou, H.: Billion-scale similarity search with GPUs. arXiv preprint arXiv:1702.08734 (2017)
47. Malkov, Y.A., Yashunin, D.: Efficient and robust approximate nearest neighbor search using hierarchical navigable small world graphs. arXiv preprint arXiv:1603.09320 (2016)

Rolling Shutter Pose and Ego-Motion Estimation Using Shape-from-Template

Yizhen Lao$^{(\boxtimes)}$, Omar Ait-Aider, and Adrien Bartoli

Institut Pascal, Université Clermont Auvergne/CNRS, Clermont-Ferrand, France
lyz91822@gmail.com, omar.ait-aider@uca.fr, adrien.bartoli@gmail.com

Abstract. We propose a new method for the absolute camera pose problem (PnP) which handles Rolling Shutter (RS) effects. Unlike all existing methods which perform 3D-2D registration after augmenting the Global Shutter (GS) projection model with the velocity parameters under various kinematic models, we propose to use local differential constraints. These are established by drawing an analogy with Shape-from-Template (SfT). The main idea consists in considering that RS distortions due to camera ego-motion during image acquisition can be interpreted as virtual deformations of a template captured by a GS camera. Once the virtual deformations have been recovered using SfT, the camera pose and ego-motion are computed by registering the deformed scene on the original template. This 3D-3D registration involves a 3D cost function based on the Euclidean point distance, more physically meaningful than the reprojection error or the algebraic distance based cost functions used in previous work. Results on both synthetic and real data show that the proposed method outperforms existing RS pose estimation techniques in terms of accuracy and stability of performance in various configurations.

Keywords: Rolling Shutter · Pose estimation · Shape-from-Template

1 Introduction

Many modern CMOS cameras are equipped with Rolling Shutter (RS) sensors which are relatively low-cost and electronically advantageous compared to Global Shutter (GS) ones. However, in RS acquisition mode, the pixel rows are exposed sequentially from the top to the bottom of the image. Therefore, images captured by moving RS cameras produce distortions (e.g. wobble, skew), which defeat the classical GS geometric models in 3D computer vision. Thus, new methods adapted to RS cameras are strongly desired. Recently, many methods have been designed to fit RS camera applications such as object pose calculation [1–3], 3D reconstruction from stereo rigs [3–5], bundle adjustment [6,7], relative pose estimation [8], dense matching [4,9] and degeneracy understanding [10,11].

Camera pose estimation (PnP) is the problem of calculating the pose of a calibrated camera from n 3D-2D correspondences. Camera pose estimation is important and extensively used in Simultaneous Localization And Mapping (SLAM)

© Springer Nature Switzerland AG 2018
V. Ferrari et al. (Eds.): ECCV 2018, LNCS 11206, pp. 477–492, 2018.
https://doi.org/10.1007/978-3-030-01216-8_29

for robotics, object or camera localization and Augmented Reality (AR). Most existing works focus on solving the minimal problem based on the GS model [12–15] with at least three point matches. Given such a minimal solution, RANSAC and non-linear optimization are two frameworks to further improve robustness and accuracy [16]. However, estimating the RS camera pose with the GS model does not give satisfactory results [17].

A few works focus on RS camera pose estimation [17–19]. These all try to extend GS-based PnP solutions by incorporating camera ego-motion in the projection model. In contrast, we provide a completely new perspective in RS projection and propose a novel solution to estimate RS camera pose and ego-motion simultaneously (**RS-PEnP**).

Our solution is based on an analogy with Shape-from-Template (SfT). This is the problem of reconstructing the shape of a deformable surface from a 3D template and a single image [20]. We show that theoretically RS image distortions caused by camera ego-motion can be expressed as virtual deformations of 3D shapes captured by a GS camera. Thus, the idea is to first retrieve virtual shape deformations using SfT, and then to re-interpret these deformations as RS effects by estimating camera ego-motion thanks to a new 3D-3D registration technique. By transforming the RS PnP problem into a 3D-3D registration problem, we show that our RS-PEnP solution is more robust and stable than existing works [17] because the constraints to be minimized are more physically meaningful and are all expressed in the same metric dimension.

1.1   Related Work and Motivations

One of the key issues in solving RS geometric problems is incorporating feasible camera ego-motion into projection models. Saurer et al. [18] propose a minimal solver to estimate RS camera pose based on the translation-only model with at least 5 3D-2D correspondences. However, this solution is limited to specific scenarios, such as a forward moving vehicle. It is not feasible for the majority of applications such as a hand-held camera, a drone or a moving robot, where ego-rotation contributes significantly to RS effects [7,21]. Albl et al. [19] propose another minimal solver, which requires at least 5 3D-2D matches too. It is based on a uniform ego-motion model. Nevertheless, it also requires the assistance of inertial measurement units (IMUs), which makes the algorithm dependent on additional sensors. Albl et al. also propose a minimal and non-iterative solution to the RS-PEnP problem called R6P [17], which can achieve higher accuracy than the standard P3P [12] by using an approximate doubly-linearized model. The approximation requires that the rotation between camera and world frames is small. Therefore, all 3D points need to be rotated first to satisfy the double-linearization assumption based on a rough estimation from IMU measurements or P3P. This pre-processing step makes R6P suffer from dependencies on additional sensors or the risk that P3P gives a non satisfactory rough estimate. Besides, R6P gives up to 20 feasible solutions and no flawless recipe is provided to choose the right one, which may lead to unstable performances.

Magerand et al. [22] present a polynomial projection model for RS cameras and propose the constrained global optimization of its parameters by means of a semidefinite programming problem obtained from the generalized problem of moments method. Contrarily to other methods, their optimization does not require an initialization and can be considered for automatic feature matching in a RANSAC framework. Unfortunately, the resolution is left to an automatic but computationally expensive solver.

In summary, a new efficient and stable solution to estimate the pose and ego-motion of an RS camera under general motion, without the need for other sensors, is still absent from the literature. Such a solution is highly required by many potential applications.

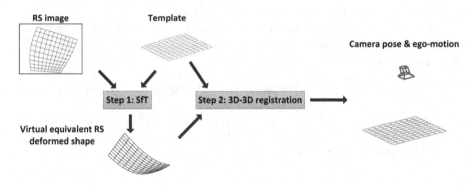

Fig. 1. An overview of the proposed pose and ego-motion estimation method: *Step 1:* Given an RS image and a known 3D template, we reconstruct the virtually deformed shape using SfT. *Step 2:* By performing 3D-3D registration between the virtually deformed shape and the template, RS camera pose and ego-motion are obtained simultaneously.

1.2   Contribution and Paper Organization

The main contributions of this paper are:

• We show and prove for the first time that RS effects can be explained by the GS-based projection of a virtually deformed shape. Thus, we show the analogy between the SfT and RS-PEnP problems.

• We propose a novel RS-PEnP method, illustrated in Fig. 1, which first recovers the virtual template deformation using SfT and then computes the pose and velocity parameters using 3D-3D registration.

We first introduce the RS projection model and the formulation of the RS camera pose problem in Sect. 2. Then we give a brief introduction to the SfT problem in Sect. 3. The links between the SfT and RS-PEnP problems are analyzed in Sect. 4. In Sect. 5, we show how to retrieve RS camera pose and ego-motion by using 3D-3D registration. The evaluation of the proposed method and conclusions are presented in Sects. 6 and 7.

2 The RS Pose and Ego-Motion Problem

2.1 The RS Projection Model

In the static case, an RS camera is equivalent to a GS one. It follows a classical pinhole camera projection model defined by the intrinsic parameters matrix $\mathbf{K}$, rotation $\mathbf{R} \in SO(3)$ and translation $\mathbf{t} \in \mathbb{R}^3$ between world and camera coordinate systems [23]:

$$\mathbf{q}_i = \Pi^{GS}(\mathbf{K}[\mathbf{R} \quad \mathbf{t}]\widetilde{\mathbf{P}}_i) = \Pi^{GS}(\mathbf{K}\mathbf{Q}_i) \tag{1}$$

where Π^{GS} is the GS projection operator defined as $\Pi^{GS}([X \ Y \ Z]^\top) = \frac{1}{Z}[X \ Y]^\top$, $\widetilde{\mathbf{P}}_i$ are the homogeneous coordinates of a 3D point $\mathbf{P}_i = [X_i, Y_i, Z_i]^\top$ in world coordinates, transformed by camera pose into camera coordinates as $\mathbf{Q}_i$. Finally, $\mathbf{q}_i = [u_i, v_i]^\top$ is its projection in the image.

For a moving RS camera, during frame exposure, each row will be captured in turn and thus with a different pose, yielding a new projection operator Π^{RS}. Thus, Eq. (1) becomes:

$$\mathbf{q}_i = \Pi^{RS}(\mathbf{K}\mathbf{Q}_i) = \Pi^{GS}(\mathbf{K}\mathbf{Q}_i^{RS}) = \Pi^{GS}(\mathbf{K}[\mathbf{R}(v_i) \quad \mathbf{t}(v_i)]\widetilde{\mathbf{P}}_i) \tag{2}$$

where $\mathbf{R}(v_i)$ and $\mathbf{t}(v_i)$ define the camera pose when the image row of index v_i is acquired. Therefore, a static 3D point $\mathbf{P}_i$ in world coordinates is transformed into $\mathbf{Q}_i^{RS}$, instead of $\mathbf{Q}_i$, in camera coordinates.

2.2 RS Pose and Ego-Motion Estimation (RS-PEnP)

Except [24], all existing methods for RS are based on augmenting the projection model by the rotational and translational velocity parameters during image acquisition. Considering that the scanning time for one frame is generally very short, different kinematic models are considered in order to express $\mathbf{R}(v_i)$ and $\mathbf{t}(v_i)$. Unfortunately, these additional parameters bring non-linearity in the projection model. A compromise should then be found between the accuracy of the kinematic model and the possibility to find an elegant and efficient solution for the RS-PEnP problem. A realistic simplified model is the uniform motion during each image acquisition (i.e. constant translational and rotational speed).

3 Shape-from-Template

SfT refers to the task of template-based monocular 3D reconstruction, which estimates the 3D shape of a deformable surface by using different physic-based deformation rules [20,25]. Figure 2 illustrates the geometric modeling of SfT. A 3D template $\tau \subset \mathbb{R}^3$ transforms to the deformed shape $S \subset \mathbb{R}^3$ by a 3D deformation $\Psi \in C^1(\tau, \mathbb{R}^3)$. If $\Omega \subset \mathbb{R}^2$ is a 2D space obtained by flattening a 3D template τ, thus, an unknown deformed embedding $\varphi \subset C^1(\Omega, \mathbb{R}^3)$ maps a 2D point $\mathbf{p} \in \Omega$ to $\mathbf{Q} \in S$. Finally, $\mathbf{Q}$ can be projected onto an image point $\mathbf{q} \in I$ by a known GS-based projection function Π^{GS}. The known transformation between

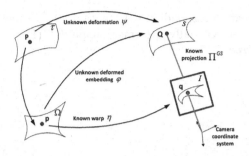

Fig. 2. Geometric modeling of SfT.

Ω and I is denoted as η. It is obtained from 3D-2D point correspondences using Bsplines as in [26]. The goal of SfT is to obtain the deformed surface S given $\mathbf{p}$, $\mathbf{q}$ and the first order derivatives of the optical flow at $\mathbf{p}$, namely $\frac{\partial \eta}{\partial p}(\mathbf{p})$.

The deformation constraints used to solve SfT can be categorized as:

• Isometric deformation. The geodesic distances are preserved by the deformation [20,25–28]. This assumption commonly holds for paper, cloth and volumetric objects.

• Conformal deformation. The isometric constraint can be relaxed to conformal deformation, which preserves angles and possibly handles isotropic extensible surfaces such as a balloon [20].

• Elastic deformation. Linear [29,30] or non-linear [31] elastic deformations are used to constrain extensible surfaces. Elastic SfT does not have local solution, in contrast to isometric SfT, and requires boundary condition to be available, as a set of known 3D surface points.

4   Moving Object Under RS or Deformed Template Under GS?

4.1   An Equivalence Between RS Projection and Surface Deformation

The main idea in this paper is that distortions in RS images caused by camera ego-motion can be expressed as the virtual deformation of a 3D shape captured by a GS camera. We first model the GS projection of a known 3D shape after a deformation Ψ:

$$\mathbf{m}_i = \Pi^{GS}(\mathbf{K}\Psi(\mathbf{P}_i)) \tag{3}$$

If we define the deformation as $\Psi^{RS}(\mathbf{P}_i) = \mathbf{R}(v_i)\mathbf{P}_i + \mathbf{t}(v_i)$, Eq. (3) becomes similar to Eq. (2):

$$\mathbf{m}_i = \Pi^{GS}(\mathbf{K}\Psi^{RS}(\mathbf{P}_i)) = \Pi^{GS}(\mathbf{K}(\mathbf{R}(v_i)\mathbf{P}_i + \mathbf{t}(v_i))) = \Pi^{RS}(\mathbf{K}\mathbf{Q}_i) \tag{4}$$

Equation (4) and Fig. 3 show that 3D shapes observed by a moving an RS camera are equivalent to corresponding deformed 3D shapes filmed by a GS camera.

We name this virtual corresponding deformation Ψ^{RS} as the ***equivalent RS deformation*** and the virtually deformed shape $\Psi^{RS}(\mathbf{P}_i)$ as the ***equivalent RS deformed shape***.

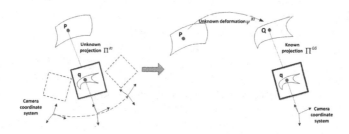

Fig. 3. Equivalence between the RS projection of a rigid object and a GS projection of a virtually deformed template.

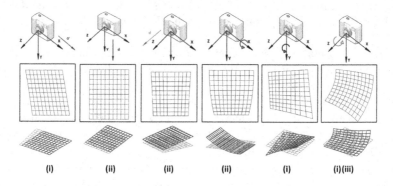

Fig. 4. The 3D template shapes (green) captured by a RS camera under different atomic ego-motions (first row) yield distorted RS images (second row). The exact same images are also obtained as the projection of the corresponding virtually deformed 3D shapes (blue) into a GS camera (third row). The type of corresponding virtual deformations are also given, see main text for details. (Color figure online)

4.2   Reconstruction of the Virtual RS Deformed Shape

After showing the link between the RS-PEnP and SfT problems, we focus on how to reconstruct the equivalent RS deformed shape by using SfT. Since the assumption on the physical properties of the template plays a crucial role in solving the SfT problem we should determine which one of the deformation constraints can best describe the equivalent RS deformation.

Any RS ego-motion can be regarded as a combination of six atomic ego-motions: translation along the X ($\mathbf{d}_x$), Y ($\mathbf{d}_y$), Z ($\mathbf{d}_z$) axes and rotation about the X ($\boldsymbol{\omega}_x$), Y ($\boldsymbol{\omega}_y$), Z ($\boldsymbol{\omega}_z$) axes. Figure 4 shows RS images and equivalent RS deformed shapes produced by different types of RS ego-motions. Albl et al. [19] and Rengarajan et al. [32] illustrated four different types of RS effects (2D deformations) produced by camera ego-motion. Differently, we focus on virtual 3D deformations instead. Figure 4 also shows that the corresponding virtual deformations caused by different camera ego-motions can be summarized into three types, by assuming a vertical scanning direction of the 3D template:

(i) Horizontal wobble: Translation along the x-axis, rotation along the y-axis and z-axis create surface wobble along the horizontal direction (perpendicular to the scan direction). In such cases, the distances are preserved only along the horizontal direction while the angles change during the deformation.

(ii) Vertical shrinking/extension: Translation along the y-axis or rotation along the x-axis produce a similar effect, which shrinks or extends the 3D shape along the scan direction (vertical). This deformation preserves the distances along the horizontal direction but changes the angles. Thus, unlike an elastic deformation, stretching the surface in the vertical direction will not introduce a compression in the horizontal direction.

(iii) Vertical wobble: Beside horizontal wobble, rotation along the z-axis also leads to wobble in the vertical direction. The distances along the horizontal direction remain unchanged while the angles vary dynamically.

It is important to notice that the virtual deformations do not follow any classical physics-based SfT surface models such as isometry, conformity or elasticity: isometric surface deformation preserves the distances along all directions while the equivalent RS distortion only preserves the distances along the horizontal direction. The conformal deformation is a relaxation of the isometric model, which allows local isotropic scaling and preserves the angles during deformation. However, it cannot describe how the virtual deformation angles change. The elastic surface stretches in one direction and generally produces extension in the orthogonal direction. In contrast, no shrinking or extension occurs along the horizontal direction during the equivalent RS deformation.

We focus on reconstructing the equivalent RS deformed shape based on the isometric and conformal deformations for the following reasons:

• The isometric constraint holds along the horizontal direction on the 3D shapes. Since the image acquisition time is commonly short, the effects of extension and compression of the 3D shape are limited, which makes the isometric model work in practice. Alternatively, the conformal model can reconstruct extensible 3D shapes [20]. Thus, the conformal model as a relaxation of the isometric model can be theoretically considered a better approximation to the equivalent RS deformation.

• A complex equivalent RS deformed shape will be produced if an RS camera is under general ego-motion, which is the composition of six types of atomic ego-motions. Therefore, different surface patches on the shape could be under different 3D deformations. Importantly, the isometric and conformal SfT solutions we used from [20] exploit **local** differential constraints and recover the local deformation around each point on the shape independently. The assumption we implicitly make is thus that the camera projection is GS in each neighbourhood. This turns out to be a very mild and valid assumption in practice.

• Analytical solutions to SfT using the isometric and conformal models are reported in [20], which are therefore faster and show the potential to form real-time applications [27]. In contrast, the existing solutions to the elastic model are made slower [29,30] and require boundary conditions unavailable in RS-PEnP.

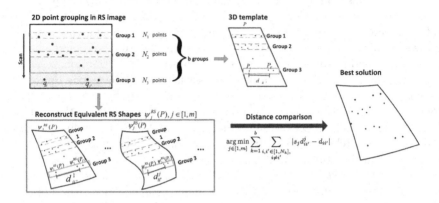

Fig. 5. Choosing the best equivalent RS shape from conformal SfT.

Isometric Deformation. Bartoli et al. showed that only one solution exists to isometric surface reconstitution from a single view and proposed the first analytical algorithm [20]. A stable solution framework for isometric SfT has been proposed later [28]. Thanks to the existing isometric algorithms, we can stably and efficiently obtain a single reconstruction of equivalent RS deformed shape $\Psi^{RS}(\mathbf{P}_i)$.

Conformal Deformation. Contrarily to the isometric case, conformal-based SfT theoretically yields a small, discrete set of solutions (at least two) and a global scale ambiguity [20]. Thus, we obtain multiple reconstructed equivalent RS deformed shapes by using the analytical SfT method under the conformal constraint. However, only one reconstruction is close to the real equivalent RS deformed shape $\Psi^{RS}(\mathbf{P}_i)$. Therefore, we pick up the most practically reasonable reconstruction based on distance preservation along the horizontal direction. We assume that a total of m reconstructed shapes $\{\Psi_j^{RS}(\mathbf{P}), \quad j = 1, 2..., m\}$ are obtained. As shown in Fig. 5 the 2D points located close to each other in the scanning direction in the image are segmented into b groups $\mathbb{G}_k, k \in [1, b]$ of N_k points. In the experiments, we group two 2D points into the same group if their difference of row index is lower than a threshold (experimentally set as 5 pixels). Then, we calculate a global scale factor s_j of each reconstructed equivalent RS deformed shape to the template by using $s_j := \frac{2}{n(n-1)} \sum_{i,i' \in [1,n], i \neq i'} d_{ii'} / d_{ii'}^j$, where $d_{ii'}$ is the euclidean distance between 3D points $\mathbf{P}_i$ and $\mathbf{P}_{i'}$ and $d_{ii'}^j$ is the euclidean distance of the corresponding reconstructed 3D points $\Psi_j^{RS}(\mathbf{P}_i)$ and $\Psi_j^{RS}(\mathbf{P}_{i'})$. We choose $i, i' \in [1, n]$ randomly and calculate the average value. Finally, we choose the reconstruction $\Psi_j^{RS}(\mathbf{P})$ with the smallest sum of distance differences along the horizontal direction between each equivalent RS deformed shapes ${}^x d_{ii'}^j$ and known 3D template ${}^x d_{ii'}$ as the best solution:

$$\arg\min_{j\in[1,m]} \sum_{k=1}^{b} \sum_{\substack{i,i'\in[1,N_k],\\ i\neq i'}} |s_j {}^x d_{ii'}^j - {}^x d_{ii'}| \tag{5}$$

5 Camera Pose and Ego-Motion Computation

5.1 Kinematic Model and RS Projection

Since the acquisition time of a frame is commonly short, one can generally assume a uniform kinematic model (with constant translational and rotational veloci-ties). Moreover, by considering small rotation angles, we obtain the so-called linearized model, which has been used in many applications [8,10,17,22].

By using the linearized RS ego-motion model, the rotation $\mathbf{R}(v_i)$ and trans-lation $\mathbf{t}(v_i)$ of the ith row in Eq. (2) become:

$$\begin{aligned} \mathbf{R}(v_i) &= (\mathbf{I} + [\omega]_\times v_i)\mathbf{R}_0 \\ \mathbf{t}(v_i) &= \mathbf{t}_0 + \mathbf{d}v_i \end{aligned} \tag{6}$$

where $\mathbf{R}_0$ and $\mathbf{t}_0$ are the rotation and the translation of the first row, which we set as the reference pose for the frame, $\mathbf{d}$ and $\boldsymbol{\omega} = [\omega_1, \omega_2, \omega_3]^\top$ are the trans-lational and rotational velocities respectively. Thus, the rotation during acquisi-tion can be defined by Rodrigues's formula as $\mathbf{a}\mathbf{a}^\top(1 - \cos(v_i\omega)) + \mathbf{I}\cos(v_i\omega) + [\mathbf{a}]_\times \sin(v_i\omega)$, where $\omega = |\boldsymbol{\omega}|$, $\mathbf{a} = \boldsymbol{\omega}/\omega$. With the assumption of short acquisition time, Rodrigues's formula can be simplified as $\mathbf{I} + v_i[\boldsymbol{\omega}]_\times$ by using the first order Taylor expansion, where $[\boldsymbol{\omega}]_\times$ is the skew-symmetric matrix of $\boldsymbol{\omega}$.

5.2 3D-3D Registration

After obtaining the equivalent RS shape $\Psi^{RS}(\mathbf{P})$, we register the virtually deformed shape to the known 3D template $\mathbf{P}$ using the RS ego-motion model. By iteratively minimizing the distance errors between the known 3D template and the reconstructed equivalent RS shape, we can obtain the camera pose and ego-motion parameters simultaneously:

$$\arg\min_{\mathbf{R}_0, \mathbf{t}_0, \boldsymbol{\omega}, \mathbf{d}} \sum_{i=1}^{n} \|\mathbf{R}(v_i)\mathbf{P}_i + \mathbf{t}(v_i) - \Psi^{RS}(\mathbf{P}_i)\| \tag{7}$$

where $\mathbf{R}_0$ and $\mathbf{t}_0$ are initialized using a classical PnP method [12]. Actually, we slightly abused the term 'registration' to mean that the 3D points of the virtually deformed surface are fitted with the corresponding 3D points of the template. This can be seen as a registration where the recovered parameters are not a mere rigid transformation but a local motion with constant velocity. The ego-motion parameters $(\boldsymbol{\omega}, \mathbf{d})$ are initialized by the following two steps: (1)

Group image points into sets of vertically close points (so that the RS effect can be neglected) and run P3P for each set. (2) Initialize $\mathbf{d}$ and $\boldsymbol{\omega}$ by computing the relative translation and rotation between groups and dividing by the scan time. Alternatively, we can operate in the same procedure by grouping the points of the deformed surface into subsets of close 3D points, which are registered by 3D point transformations [33]. However, in many practical situations, it is more convenient and more efficient to set the initial values of $\mathbf{d}$ and $\boldsymbol{\omega}$ to 0, which in our experiments always allowed convergence toward the correct solution.

6   Experiments

In our experiments, the analytical isometric solution [28][1] (**AnIRS**) and analytical conformal solution (**AnCRS**) [20](see footnote 1) are used to reconstruct the equivalent RS deformed shape of both synthetic and real planar and non planar templates under isometric and conformal constraints respectively. The Levenberg-Marquardt algorithm is used in the non-linear pose and ego-motion estimation from Eq. (7).

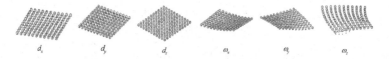

Fig. 6. Reconstructed equivalent RS deformed shapes by **AnIRS** (magenta points) and **AnCRS** (green crosses) compared to ground truth structure (blue circles) under six types of camera ego-motion. (Color figure online)

6.1   Synthetic Data

We simulated a calibrated pin-hole camera with 640×480 px resolution and 320 px focal length. The camera was located randomly on a sphere with a radius of 20 units and was pointing to a simulated surface (10×10 units) with varying average scanning angles from 0 to $90°$. We randomly drew n points on the surface to form the 3D template. Random Gaussian noise with standard deviation σ was also added to the 2D projected points $\mathbf{q}$.

Recovering the Equivalent RS Deformed Shape. We first evaluate the reconstruction accuracy of **AnIRS** and **AnCRS** on the equivalent RS deformed shape. Since the types of deformation depend on the type of RS ego-motion, we measure the mean and standard deviation of distances between the reconstructed 3D points and the corresponding points on the 3D template under six atomic ego-motion types (Sect. 4.2). For each motion type, we run 200 trials to obtain statistics. We varied the number of 3D-2D matches from 10 to 121 and used a noise level $\sigma = 1$ px. At each trial, the ego-motion speed was randomly set as follows: translational speed varying from 0 to 3 units/frame and rotational speed varying from 0 to $20°$/frame.

---

[1] http://igt.ip.uca.fr/~ab/Research.

Table 1. Mean ($|e_I|$, $|e_C|$) and standard deviation (σ_I, σ_C) of reconstruction errors (expressed in units) of the equivalent RS deformed shape by **AnIRS** and **AnCRS** under six types of camera ego-motion.

	d_x	d_y	d_z	ω_x	ω_y	ω_z
$|e_I|$	0.0130283	0.0113629	**0.0001183**	0.0023273	0.0020031	0.1338190
$|e_C|$	**0.0040963**	**0.0052104**	0.0009037	**0.0000921**	**0.0008493**	**0.0008417**
σ_I	0.0001810	0.0000943	**0.0000014**	0.0000834	0.0007209	0.0393570
σ_C	**0.0000318**	**0.0000529**	0.0000310	**0.0000206**	**0.0003639**	**0.0001201**

The results in Fig. 6 show that both **AnIRS** and **AnCRS** provide stable and high accuracy results for the equivalent RS deformed shape reconstruction. The quantitative evaluation in Table 1 demonstrates that **AnCRS** generally performs better than **AnIRS**. Specifically, it indicates that the advantages of **AnCRS** are significant in the cases of ego-rotation along the x or z-axis. The only exception is in translation along the z-axis, where the equivalent RS deformation is with relatively smaller extension/shrinking than other types. Thus, **AnIRS** gives better results than **AnCRS**. However, all observations confirm our analysis in Sect. 4.2 that conformal surfaces can better model the extensibility of equivalent RS deformation generally.

Pose Estimation. We compared **AnIRS** and **AnCRS** in camera pose estimation with both the GS PnP solution **GS-PnP**[2] [13] and the RS-PEnP solution **RS-PnP**[3] which uses R6P [17]. Since the ground truth of camera poses are known, we measured the absolute error of rotation (deg) and translation (units).

• *Accuracy vs ego-motion speed.* We fixed the number of 3D-2D matches to 60 and noise level to $\sigma = 1$ px. We increased the translational speed and rotational speed from 0 to 3 units/frame and 20°/frame gradually. At each configuration, we run 100 trials with random velocity directions and measured the average pose errors. The results in Fig. 7(a,b) show that both **AnIRS** and **AnCRS** provide significantly more accurate estimates of camera orientation and translation with all ego-rotation configurations (ω_x, ω_y and ω_z) compared to **GS-PnP** and **RS-PnP**. Under three ego-translations, **AnIRS** and **AnCRS** show an obvious superiority in camera rotation estimation, and perform slightly better in camera translation estimation than **RS-PnP**. As expected, GS-based **GS-PnP** fails in pose estimation once the ego-motion is strong. In contrast, **RS-PnP** achieves better results in translation than **GS-PnP**, but both of them provide an inaccurate estimate for camera rotation to the same extent.

• *Accuracy vs image noise.* In this experiment, we evaluated the robustness of the four solutions against different noise levels. Thus, we fixed the camera with translational and rotational speed at 1 unit/frame and 5°/frame. Random noise

---

[2] estimateWorldCameraPose function in MATLAB.

[3] http://cmp.felk.cvut.cz/~alblcene/r6p.

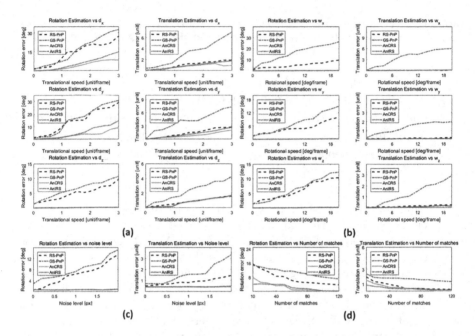

Fig. 7. Pose estimation errors for **AnIRS**, **AnCRS**, the GS **GS-PnP** and **RS-PnP** under different ego-translations (a), ego-rotations (b), image noise levels (c) and number of matches (d).

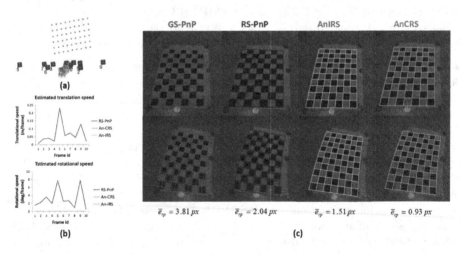

Fig. 8. Visual comparison of reprojected object boundaries by different camera pose and ego-motion estimates. e_{rp} is the reprojection error of the 3D marker points.

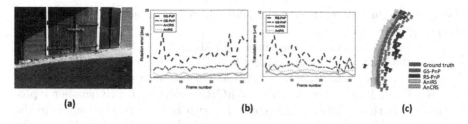

Fig. 9. Results of pose registration with real RS video: (a) An example of input RS image. (b) Rotation and translation errors of each frame. (c) Estimated trajectories by **GS-PnP**, **RS-PnP**, **AnIRS** and **AnCRS** compared to ground truth.

with levels varying from 0 to 2 px were added to the 60 image points. The results in Fig. 7(c) show that both **AnIRS** and **AnCRS** are robust to the increasing image noise. In contrast, **GS-PnP** and **RS-PnP** are relatively sensitive to image noise.

- *Accuracy vs number of matches.* The number of 3D-2D matches has a great impact on the PnP problem. Therefore, we evaluated the performance of the proposed method with different numbers of 3D-2D matches. The camera was fixed with translational and rotational speed at 1 unit/frame and 5°/frame. The image noise level was set to 1 px. Then we increased the number of matches from 10 to 120. The results in Fig. 7(d) show that the estimation accuracy of all four methods increases with the number of matches. However **AnIRS** and **AnCRS** provides better results in both rotation and translation estimation compared to **GS-PnP** and **RS-PnP**.

6.2   Real Data

Augmented Reality with an RS Video. The four methods have been further evaluated by using real RS images. A planar marker providing 64 3D-2D matches was captured by a hand-held logitech webcam. Strong RS effects are present on the recorded video due to the quick arbitrary camera ego-motion. This scenario can occur in many AR applications. After obtaining the camera pose and ego-motion, the boundaries of the calibration board were reprojected into the RS image. As shown in Fig. 8(c), if the poses and ego-motions are accurately recovered, the reprojected matrix boundaries can perfectly fit the planar marker. In addition to visual checking, the mean value of reprojection errors of 3D marker points of each frame were used as a quantitative measurement.

In the first frame, all four methods obtained acceptable reprojected matrix boundaries due to the small RS effects. However, finding more inliers does not ensure retrieving the true pose and ego-motion, as **RS-PnP** yields 20 geometrically feasible solutions and it is challenging to pick the 'true' one. For example, Fig. 8(a) shows the estimated pose in our AR dataset, where only static camera frames (without ego-motion) were picked. Figure 8(b) shows that R6P gives distributed locations and huge ego-motion up to 5 m/frame, while P3P and our method give similar poses.

In the second frame, with the camera quickly moving, **RS-PnP** and The GS-based method **GS-PnP** provide unstable estimates of camera pose. In contrast, both proposed methods **AnIRS** and **AnCRS** significantly outperform **GS-PnP** and **RS-PnP**. It is noteworthy that **AnCRS** achieves slightly smaller reprojection errors than **AnIRS**. This coincides with the observations made in the synthetic experiments and confirms the theoretical analysis of Sect. 4.2 that the conformal constraint is more suitable to explain the equivalent RS deformations.

Pose registration with real RS video. We tested the four methods for pose registration of an SfM reconstruction. The public dataset [7] was used, which was captured by both RS and GS cameras installed on a rig. The 3D points were obtained by performing SfM with the GS images. 3D-2D correspondences can be obtained by matching RS images to GS images. The results are presented in Fig. 9. The proposed methods **AnIRS** and **AnCRS** give clearly more accurate estimates than **GS-PnP** and **RS-PnP** for most frames.

Running Time. The experiments were conducted on an i5 CPU at 2.8 GHz with 4G RAM. On average, it took around 2.8 s for **AnIRS** (0.1 s for isometric reconstruction and 2.7 s for 3D-3D registration) and 14.6 s for **AnCRS** (10.6 s for conformal reconstruction and 4 s for 3D-3D registration). Since the proposed method was implemented in MATLAB, an improvement can be expected when using C++ and GPU acceleration, as shown in [27].

7   Conclusion

We have proposed a novel method which addresses the RS-PEnP problem from a new angle: using SfT. By analyzing the link between the SfT and RS-PEnP problems we have shown that RS effects can be explained by the GS projection of a virtually deformed shape. As a result the RS-PEnP problem is transformed into a 3D-3D registration problem. Experimental results have shown that the proposed methods outperform existing RS-PEnP techniques in terms of accuracy and stability. We interpret this improved accuracy as the result of transforming the problem from a 3D-2D registration into a 3D-3D registration problem. This has enabled us to use 3D point-distances instead of the re-projection errors, which carry more physical meaning and make the error terms homogeneous. A possible extension of our work is to derive the exact differential properties of equivalent RS deformation.

Acknowledgement. This work has been sponsored by the French government research program "Investissements d'Avenir" through the IDEX-ISITE initiative 16-IDEX-0001 (CAP 20-25), the IMobS3 Laboratory of Excellence (ANR-10-LABX-16-01) and the RobotEx Equipment of Excellence (ANR-10-EQPX-44). This research was also financed by the European Union through the Regional Competitiveness and Employment program -2014-2020- (ERDF - AURA region) and by the AURA region. This research has received funding from the EUs FP7 through the ERC research grant 307483 FLEXABLE.

References

1. Frank, E., Hall, M.: A simple approach to ordinal classification. In: De Raedt, L., Flach, P. (eds.) ECML 2001. LNCS (LNAI), vol. 2167, pp. 145–156. Springer, Heidelberg (2001). https://doi.org/10.1007/3-540-44795-4_13
2. Ait-Aider, O., Bartoli, A., Andreff, N.: Kinematics from lines in a single rolling shutter image. In: 2007 IEEE Conference on Computer Vision and Pattern Recognition, pp. 1–6. IEEE (2007)
3. Ait-Aider, O., Berry, F.: Structure and kinematics triangulation with a rolling shutter stereo rig. In: Proceedings of the IEEE International Conference on Computer Vision (ICCV), pp. 1835–1840 (2009)
4. Saurer, O., Pollefeys, M., Hee Lee, G.: Sparse to dense 3D reconstruction from rolling shutter images. In: The IEEE Conference on Computer Vision and Pattern Recognition (CVPR), June 2016
5. Saurer, O., Koser, K., Bouguet, J.Y., Pollefeys, M.: Rolling shutter stereo. In: 2013 IEEE International Conference on Computer Vision (ICCV) (2013)
6. Hedborg, J., Ringaby, E., Forssén, P.E., Felsberg, M.: Structure and motion estimation from rolling shutter video. In: Computer Vision Workshops (ICCV Workshops) (2011)
7. Hedborg, J., Forssen, P.E., Felsberg, M., Ringaby, E.: Rolling shutter bundle adjustment. In: Computer Vision and Pattern Recognition (CVPR) (2012)
8. Dai, Y., Li, H., Kneip, L.: Rolling shutter camera relative pose: generalized epipolar geometry. In: Proceedings of the IEEE Conference on Computer Vision and Pattern Recognition, pp. 4132–4140 (2016)
9. Kim, J.H., Cadena, C., Reid, I.: Direct semi-dense slam for rolling shutter cameras. In: 2016 IEEE International Conference on Robotics and Automation (ICRA), pp. 1308–1315, May 2016
10. Albl, C., Sugimoto, A., Pajdla, T.: Degeneracies in rolling shutter SfM. In: Leibe, B., Matas, J., Sebe, N., Welling, M. (eds.) ECCV 2016. LNCS, vol. 9909, pp. 36–51. Springer, Cham (2016). https://doi.org/10.1007/978-3-319-46454-1_3
11. Ito, E., Okatani, T.: Self-calibration-based approach to critical motion sequences of rolling-shutter structure from motion. In: 2017 IEEE Conference on Computer Vision and Pattern Recognition (CVPR) (2017)
12. Haralick, R.M., Lee, D., Ottenburg, K., Nolle, M.: Analysis and solutions of the three point perspective pose estimation problem. In: IEEE Computer Society Conference on Computer Vision and Pattern Recognition, 1991. Proceedings CVPR 1991, pp. 592–598. IEEE (1991)
13. Gao, X.S., Hou, X.R., Tang, J., Cheng, H.F.: Complete solution classification for the perspective-three-point problem. IEEE Trans. Pattern Anal. Mach. Intell. 25(8), 930–943 (2003)
14. Wu, Y., Hu, Z.: PnP problem revisited. J. Math. Imaging Vis. 24(1), 131–141 (2006)
15. Quan, L., Lan, Z.: Linear n-point camera pose determination. IEEE Trans. Pattern Anal. Mach. Intell. 21(8), 774–780 (1999)
16. Leng, D., Sun, W.: 2009 Finding all the solutions of PnP problem. In: IEEE International Workshop on Imaging Systems and Techniques, IST 2009, pp. 348–352. IEEE (2009)
17. Albl, C., Kukelova, Z., Pajdla, T.: R6P-rolling shutter absolute camera pose. In: Proceedings of the IEEE Conference on Computer Vision and Pattern Recognition, pp. 2292–2300 (2015)

18. Saurer, O., Pollefeys, M., Lee, G.H.: A minimal solution to the rolling shutter pose estimation problem. In: 2015 IEEE/RSJ International Conference on Intelligent Robots and Systems (IROS), pp. 1328–1334. IEEE (2015)
19. Albl, C., Kukelova, Z., Pajdla, T.: Rolling shutter absolute pose problem with known vertical direction. In: Proceedings of the IEEE Conference on Computer Vision and Pattern Recognition, pp. 3355–3363 (2016)
20. Bartoli, A., Gérard, Y., Chadebecq, F., Collins, T., Pizarro, D.: Shape-from-template. IEEE Trans. Pattern Anal. Mach. Intell. **37**(10), 2099–2118 (2015)
21. Duchamp, G., Ait-Aider, O., Royer, E., Lavest, J.M.: A rolling shutter compliant method for localisation and reconstruction. In: VISAPP (3), pp. 277–284 (2015)
22. Magerand, L., Bartoli, A., Ait-Aider, O., Pizarro, D.: Global optimization of object pose and motion from a single rolling shutter image with automatic 2D-3D matching. In: Fitzgibbon, A., Lazebnik, S., Perona, P., Sato, Y., Schmid, C. (eds.) ECCV 2012. LNCS, vol. 7572, pp. 456–469. Springer, Heidelberg (2012). https://doi.org/10.1007/978-3-642-33718-5_33
23. Hartley, R., Zisserman, A.: Multiple View Geometry in Computer Vision. Cambridge University Press, Cambridge (2003)
24. Magerand, L., Bartoli, A.: A generic rolling shutter camera model and its application to dynamic pose estimation. In: International Symposium on 3D Data Processing, Visualization and Transmission (2010)
25. Salzmann, M., Fua, P.: Linear local models for monocular reconstruction of deformable surfaces. IEEE Trans. Pattern Anal. Mach. Intell. **33**(5), 931–944 (2011)
26. Brunet, F., Bartoli, A., Hartley, R.I.: Monocular template-based 3D surface reconstruction: convex inextensible and nonconvex isometric methods. Comput. Vis. Image Underst. **125**, 138–154 (2014)
27. Collins, T., Bartoli, A.: [POSTER] Realtime shape-from-template: system and applications. In: 2015 IEEE International Symposium on Mixed and Augmented Reality (ISMAR), pp. 116–119. IEEE (2015)
28. Chhatkuli, A., Pizarro, D., Bartoli, A., Collins, T.: A stable analytical framework for isometric shape-from-template by surface integration. IEEE Trans. Pattern Anal. Mach. Intell. **39**(5), 833–850 (2017)
29. Malti, A., Bartoli, A., Hartley, R.: A linear least-squares solution to elastic shape-from-template. In: Proceedings of the IEEE Conference on Computer Vision and Pattern Recognition, pp. 1629–1637 (2015)
30. Malti, A., Herzet, C.: Elastic shape-from-template with spatially sparse deforming forces. In: Proceedings of the IEEE Conference on Computer Vision and Pattern Recognition, pp. 3337–3345 (2017)
31. Haouchine, N., Dequidt, J., Berger, M.O., Cotin, S.: Single view augmentation of 3D elastic objects. In: 2014 IEEE International Symposium on Mixed and Augmented Reality (ISMAR), pp. 229–236. IEEE (2014)
32. Rengarajan, V., Balaji, Y., Rajagopalan, A.: Unrolling the shutter: CNN to correct motion distortions. In: Proceedings of the IEEE Conference on Computer Vision and Pattern Recognition, pp. 2291–2299 (2017)
33. Horn, B.K., Hilden, H.M., Negahdaripour, S.: Closed-form solution of absolute orientation using orthonormal matrices. JOSA A **5**(7), 1127–1135 (1988)

Unveiling the Power of Deep Tracking

Goutam Bhat[1(✉)], Joakim Johnander[1,2], Martin Danelljan[1],
Fahad Shahbaz Khan[1,3], and Michael Felsberg[1]

[1] CVL, Department of Electrical Engineering, Linköping University,
Linköping, Sweden
goutam.bhat@liu.se
[2] Zenuity, Gothenburg, Sweden
[3] Inception Institute of Artificial Intelligence, Abu Dhabi, UAE

Abstract. In the field of generic object tracking numerous attempts
have been made to exploit deep features. Despite all expectations, deep
trackers are yet to reach an outstanding level of performance compared
to methods solely based on handcrafted features. In this paper, we investigate this key issue and propose an approach to unlock the true potential
of deep features for tracking. We systematically study the characteristics
of both deep and shallow features, and their relation to tracking accuracy
and robustness. We identify the limited data and low spatial resolution as
the main challenges, and propose strategies to counter these issues when
integrating deep features for tracking. Furthermore, we propose a novel
adaptive fusion approach that leverages the complementary properties
of deep and shallow features to improve both robustness *and* accuracy.
Extensive experiments are performed on four challenging datasets. On
VOT2017, our approach significantly outperforms the top performing
tracker from the challenge with a relative gain of 17% in EAO.

1 Introduction

Generic object tracking is the problem of estimating the trajectory of a target in
a video, given only its initial state. The problem is particularly difficult, primarily
due to the limited training data available to learn an appearance model of the
target *online*. Existing methods rely on rich feature representations to address
this fundamental challenge. While handcrafted features have long been employed
for this task, recent focus has been shifted towards deep features. The advantages
of deep features being their ability to encode high-level information, invariant
to complex appearance changes and clutter.

Despite the outstanding success of deep learning in a variety of computer
vision tasks, its impact in generic object tracking has been limited. In fact,
trackers based on handcrafted features [1,7,8,22,37] still provide competitive
results, even outperforming many deep trackers on standard benchmarks [16,36].

Electronic supplementary material The online version of this chapter (https://
doi.org/10.1007/978-3-030-01216-8_30) contains supplementary material, which is
available to authorized users.

V. Ferrari et al. (Eds.): ECCV 2018, LNCS 11206, pp. 493–509, 2018.
https://doi.org/10.1007/978-3-030-01216-8_30

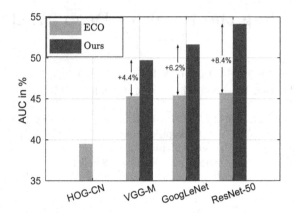

Fig. 1. Tracking performance on the Need for Speed dataset [12] when using deep features extracted from different networks. In all cases, we employ the same shallow representation, consisting of HOG and Color Names. The baseline ECO [7] does not benefit from more powerful network architectures, e.g. ResNet. Instead, our approach is able to exploit more powerful representations, achieving a consistent gain going from handcrafted features towards more powerful network architectures.

Moreover, contrary to the trend in image classification, object trackers do not tend to benefit from deeper and more sophisticated network architectures (see Fig. 1). In this work, we investigate the reasons behind the limited success of deep networks in visual object tracking.

We distinguish two key challenges generally encountered when integrating deep features into visual tracking models. Firstly, compared to traditional hand-crafted approaches, it is well known that deep models are data-hungry. This becomes a major obstacle in the visual tracking scenario, where training data is extremely scarce and a robust model must be learned from a single labeled frame. Even though pre-trained deep networks are frequently employed, the target model must learn the discriminative activations possessing invariance towards *unseen* appearance changes.

The second challenge for deep features is accurate target prediction. Not only is precise target localization crucial for tracking performance, it also affects the learning of the model since new frames are annotated by the tracker itself. As a result, inaccurate predictions may lead to model drift and eventual tracking failure. Deep convolutional layers generally trade spatial resolution for increased high-level invariance to account for appearance changes. Consequently, many trackers complement the deep representation with shallow-level activations [11, 23] or handcrafted features [7] for improved localization accuracy. This raises the question of how to optimally fuse the fundamentally different properties of shallow and deep features in order to achieve both accuracy *and* robustness.

Contributions: In this paper, we analyze the influential characteristics of deep and shallow features for visual tracking. This is performed by (i) systematically studying the impact of a variety of data augmentation techniques and (ii) investigating the accuracy-robustness trade-off in the discriminative learning of the target model. Our findings suggest that extensive data augmentation leads to a remarkable performance boost for the deep-feature-based model while often harming its shallow counterpart. Furthermore, we find that the deep model should be trained for robustness, while the shallow model should emphasize accurate target localization. These results indicate that the deep and shallow models should be trained *independently* and fused at a later stage. As our second contribution, we propose a novel fusion strategy to combine the deep and shallow predictions in order to exploit their complementary characteristics. This is obtained by introducing a quality measure for the predicted state, taking both accuracy and robustness into account.

Experiments are performed on five challenging benchmarks: Need for Speed, VOT2017, Temple128, UAV123 and OTB-2015. Our results clearly demonstrate that the proposed approach provides a significant improvement over the baseline tracker. Further, our approach sets a new state-of-the-art on all four tracking datasets. On the VOT2017 benchmark, our approach achieves an EAO score of 0.378, surpassing the competition winners (0.323) with a relative gain of 17%.

2 Related Work

Deep learning has pervaded many areas of computer vision. While these techniques have also been investigated for visual tracking, it has been with limited success. The SINT method [30] learns a similarity measure offline on a video dataset, and localizes the target using the initial labeled sample. Another approach is to directly regress the relative target location given an input patch [14,33]. Li et al. [18] tackle the tracking problem in an end-to-end fashion by training a classifier online. The FCNT [34] employs both pre-trained deep features and an online trained model. MDNet [26] further pre-trains a model offline using a multi-domain procedure. Following the end-to-end philosophy, recent works [28,31] have investigated integrating Discriminative Correlation Filters (DCF) [3,10] as a computational block in a deep network. The work of [31] integrate DCF into the Siamese framework [2]. Further, [28] employs DCF as a one-layer CNN for end-to-end training.

Other DCF methods focus on integrating convolutional features from a fixed pre-trained deep network [6,7,9,11,23,27,38]. Ma et al. [23] propose a hierarchical ensemble method of independent DCF trackers to combine multiple convolutional layers. Qi et al. [27] learn a correlation filter per feature map, and combine the individual predictions with a modified Hedge algorithm. The MCPF tracker proposed by Zhang et al. [38] combines the deep DCF with a particle filter. Danelljan et al. [11] propose the continuous convolution operator tracker (C-COT) to efficiently integrate multi-resolution shallow and deep feature maps. The subsequent ECO tracker [7] improves the C-COT tracker in terms of performance and efficiency. In this work we adopt the ECO tracking framework due to its versatility and popularity: in the most recent edition of VOT2017 [16], five of the top 10 trackers were based on either ECO or its predecessor C-COT.

3   Analyzing Deep Features for Tracking

Deep learning has brought remarkable performance improvements in many computer vision areas, such as object classification, detection and semantic segmentation. However, its impact is yet to be *fully* realized in the context of generic visual object tracking. In this section, we analyze the causes behind the below-expected performance of deep trackers and propose strategies to address them.

3.1   Motivation

In our quest to seek a better understanding of deep features for tracking, we investigate their properties in relation to the well studied shallow features. One of the well known issues of deep learning is the need for large amounts of labeled training data. Still, thousands of training samples are required to *fine-tune* a pre-trained deep network for a new task. Such amount of data is however not available in the visual tracking scenario, where initially only a single labeled frame is provided. This poses a major challenge when learning deep-feature-based models for visual tracking.

To maximally exploit the available training data, deep learning methods generally employ data augmentation strategies. Yet, data augmentation is seldom used in visual tracking. In fact, the pioneering work of Bolme et al. [3] utilized augmented gray-scale image samples to train a discriminative tracking model. Since then, state-of-the-art deep DCF tracking methods have ignored data augmentation as a strategy for acquiring additional training data. In Sect. 3.3 we therefore perform a thorough investigation of data augmentation techniques with the aim of better understanding deep features for tracking.

Another challenge when integrating deep features is their low spatial resolution, hampering accurate localization of the target. Object trackers based on low-level handcrafted features are primarily trained for accurate target localization to avoid long-term drift. However, this might not be the optimal strategy for deep features which exhibit fundamentally different properties. Deep features generally capture high-level semantics while being invariant to, e.g., small translations and scale changes. From this perspective it may be beneficial to train the deep model to emphasize robustness rather than accuracy. This motivates us to analyze the accuracy/robustness trade-off involved in the model learning, to gain more knowledge about the properties of deep and shallow features. This analysis is performed in Sect. 3.4.

3.2   Methodology

To obtain a clearer understanding of deep and shallow features, we aim to isolate their impact on the overall tracking performance. The analysis is therefore performed with a baseline tracker that exclusively employs either shallow or deep features. This exclusive treatment allows us to directly measure the impact of, e.g., data augmentation on both shallow and deep features separately.

We use the recently introduced ECO tracker [7] as a baseline, due to its state-of-the-art performance. For shallow features, we employ a combination of Histogram of Oriented Gradients (HOG) [5] and Color Names (CN) [35], as it has been used in numerous tracking approaches [7,10,15,19,21]. For the deep representation, we first restrict our analysis to ResNet-50, using the activations from the fourth convolutional block. Generalization to other networks is further presented in Sect. 5.4. The entire analysis is performed on the OTB-2015 [36] dataset.

3.3   Data Augmentation

Data augmentation is a standard strategy to alleviate problems with limited training data. It can lead to a better generalization of the learned model for unseen data. However, data augmentation can also lead to lower accuracy in the context of visual tracking due to increased invariance of the model to small translations or scale changes. Therefore, it is unclear whether data augmentation is helpful in the case of tracking.

We separately investigate the impact of different data augmentation techniques on both shallow as well as deep features. We consider the following data augmentation techniques:

Flip: The sample is horizontally flipped.
Rotation: Rotation from a fixed set of 12 angles ranging from $-60°$ to $60°$.
Shift: Shift of n pixels both horizontally and vertically prior to feature extraction. The resulting feature map is shifted back n/s pixels where s is the stride of the feature extraction.
Blur: Blur with a Gaussian filter. This is expected to simulate motion blur and scale variations, which are both commonly encountered in tracking scenarios.
Dropout: Channel-wise dropout of the sample. This is performed by randomly setting 20% of the feature channels to zero. As usual, the remaining feature channels are amplified in order to preserve the sample energy.

Figure 2a shows the impact of data augmentation on tracking performance (in AUC score [36]). It can be seen that the deep features consistently benefit from data augmentation. All augmentations, except for 'shift', give over 1% improvement in tracking performance. The maximum improvement is obtained using 'blur' augmentation, where a gain of 4% is obtained over the baseline, which employs no data augmentation. Meanwhile, shallow features do not benefit from data augmentation. This surprising difference in behavior of deep and shallow features can be explained by their opposing properties. Deep features capture higher level semantic information that is invariant to the applied augmentations like 'flip', and can thus gain from the increased training data. On the other hand, the shallow features capture low-level information that is hampered by augmentations like 'flip' or 'blur'. The use of data augmentation thus harms the training in this case.

3.4   Robustness/Accuracy Trade-Off

When comparing the performance of trackers, there are two important criteria: accuracy and robustness. The former is the measure of *how accurately* the target is localized during tracking. Robustness, on the other hand, is the tracker's resilience to failures in challenging scenarios and its ability to recover. In other words, robustness is a measure of *how often* the target is successfully localized. Generally, both accuracy and robustness are of importance, and a satisfactory trade-off between these properties is sought since they are weakly correlated [17]. This trade-off can be controlled in the construction and training of the tracker.

In a discriminative tracking framework, the appearance model can be learned to emphasize the accuracy criterion by only extracting positive samples very close to the target location. That is, only very accurate locations are treated as positive samples of the target appearance. Instead, increasing the region from which target samples are extracted allows for more positive training data. This has the potential of promoting the generalization and robustness of the model, but can also result in poor discriminative power when the variations in the target samples become too large.

We analyze the effect of training the tracking model for various degrees of accuracy-robustness trade-off when using either shallow or deep features. In DCF-based trackers, such as the baseline ECO, the size of the region from which positive training samples are extracted is controlled by the width of the label score function. ECO employs a Gaussian function for this task, with standard deviation proportional to the target size with a factor of σ. We analyze different values of σ for both shallow and deep features. Figure 2b shows the results

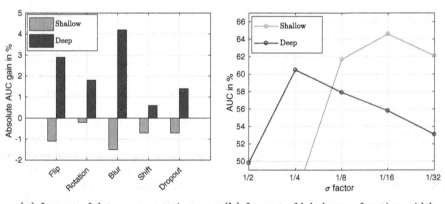

(a) Impact of data augmentation   (b) Impact of label score function width

Fig. 2. Impact of data augmentation (a) and label score function width (b) on shallow (blue) and deep (red) features on OTB-2015. The results are reported as area-under-the-curve (AUC). While deep features significantly benefit from data augmentation, the results deteriorate for shallow features. Similarly, a sharp label function is beneficial for the shallow features, whereas the deep features benefit from a wide label function. (Color figure online)

Table 1. Impact of data augmentation (denoted Aug) and wider label score function (denoted σ) on deep features. Results are shown in terms of AUC score on the OTB-2015 dataset. Both data augmentation and wider label scores provide significant improvement. The best result is obtained when employing both techniques.

	ResNet	ResNet+Aug	ResNet+σ	ResNet+Aug+σ
AUC	56.2	61.5	60.5	**62.0**

of this experiment. We observe that the deep features are utilized best when trained with higher value of σ, with $\sigma = \frac{1}{4}$ giving the best results. This behavior can be attributed to the invariance property of the deep features. Since they are invariant to small translations, training deep features to get higher accuracy might lead to a suboptimal model. The shallow features on the other hand, perform best when trained with a low σ and give inferior results when trained with a higher σ. This is due to the fact that the shallow features capture low level, higher resolution features, and hence are well suited to give high accuracy. Furthermore, due to their large variance to small transformations, the model is unable to handle the larger number of positive training samples implied by a higher σ, resulting in poor performance.

3.5   Observations

The aforementioned results from Sects. 3.3 and 3.4 show that the deep model significantly improves by the use of data augmentation *and* by training for increased robustness instead of accuracy. We further evaluate the combined effects of data augmentation and higher σ on the deep model. Table 1 shows the results on the OTB-2015 dataset in terms of the AUC measure. The baseline tracker (left) does not employ data augmentation and uses the default value $\sigma = \frac{1}{12}$. Combining all the data augmentation techniques evaluated in Sect. 3.3 provides an improvement of 5.3% in AUC over the baseline. Training with a σ-parameter of $\frac{1}{4}$ further improves the results by 0.5%. Thus our analysis indicates the benefit of using both data augmentation as well as a wider label function when training the deep-feature-based model.

Results from Sects. 3.3 and 3.4 thus highlight the complementary properties of deep and shallow features. Their corresponding models need to be trained differently, in terms of data and annotations, in order to best exploit their true potential. We therefore argue that the shallow and deep models should be trained independently. However, this raises the question of how to fuse these models in order to leverage their complementary properties, which we address in the next section.

4   Adaptive Fusion of Model Predictions

As previously discussed, the deep and shallow models possess different characteristics regarding accuracy and robustness. This is demonstrated in Fig. 3, showing detection scores from the shallow and deep models for an example frame. We propose a novel adaptive fusion approach that aims at fully exploiting their complementary nature, based on a quality measure described in Sect. 4.1. In Sect. 4.2 we show how to infer the deep and shallow weights and obtain the final target prediction.

4.1   Prediction Quality Measure

Our aim is to find a quality measure for the target prediction, given the detection score y over the search region of the image. We see the score y as a function over the image coordinates, where $y(t) \in \mathbb{R}$ is the target prediction score at location $t \in \mathbb{R}^2$. We require that the quality measure rewards both the accuracy and robustness of the target prediction. The former is related to the *sharpness* of the detection score around the prediction. A sharper peak indicates more accurate localization capability. The robustness of the prediction is derived from the margin to distractor peaks. If the margin is small, the prediction is ambiguous. On the other hand, a large margin indicates that the confidence of the prediction is significantly higher than at other candidate locations.

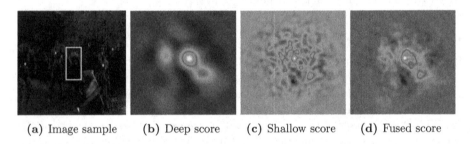

(a) Image sample   (b) Deep score   (c) Shallow score   (d) Fused score

Fig. 3. Visualization of the detection scores produced by the deep and shallow models for a sample frame (a). The deep score (b) contains a robust mode with high confidence, but it only allows for coarse localization. Meanwhile, the shallow score (c) has sharp peaks enabling accurate localization, but also contains distractor modes. Our approach fuses these scores by adaptively finding the optimal weights for each model, producing a sharp and unambiguous score function (d).

We propose the minimal weighted confidence margin as a quality measure of a candidate target prediction t^*,

$$\xi_{t^*}\{y\} = \min_t \frac{y(t^*) - y(t)}{\Delta(t - t^*)}. \tag{1}$$

The confidence margin in the numerator is computed as the difference between the confidence score $y(t^*)$ at the candidate prediction t^* and the score $y(t)$ at a location t. The margin is weighted by the distance between t^* and the location t, computed by a distance measure $\Delta : \mathbb{R}^2 \to [0,1]$ satisfying $\Delta(0) = 0$ and

$\lim_{|\tau|\to\infty} \Delta(\tau) = 1$. We also assume Δ to be twice continuously differentiable and have a positive definite Hessian at $\tau = 0$. For our purpose, we use

$$\Delta(\tau) = 1 - e^{-\frac{\kappa}{2}|\tau|^2}. \tag{2}$$

Here, κ is a parameter controlling the rate of transition $\Delta(\tau) \to 1$ when $|\tau|$ is increasing. As we will see, κ has a direct interpretation related to the behavior of the quality measure (1) close to the target prediction $t \approx t^*$. From the definition (1) it follows that $\xi_{t^*}\{y\} \geq 0$ if and only if $y(t^*)$ is a global maximum of y.

To verify that the proposed quality measure (1) has the desired properties of promoting both accuracy and robustness, we analyze the cases (a) where t is far from the prediction t^* and (b) when $t \to t^*$. In the former case, we obtain $|t - t^*| \gg 0$ implying that $\Delta(t - t^*) \approx 1$. In this case, we have that

$$\xi_{t^*}\{y\} \leq \frac{y(t^*) - y(t)}{\Delta(t - t^*)} \approx y(t^*) - y(t), \quad \text{whenever } |t - t^*| \gg 0. \tag{3}$$

As a result, the quality measure $\xi_{t^*}\{y\}$ is approximately bounded by the score-difference to the most significant distractor peak $y(t)$ outside the immediate neighborhood of the prediction t^*. Hence, a large quality measure $\xi_{t^*}\{y\}$ ensures that there are no distractors making the prediction ambiguous. Conversely, if there exists a secondary detection peak $y(t)$ with a similar score $y(t) \approx y(t^*)$, then the quality of the prediction is low $\xi_{t^*}\{y\} \approx 0$.

In the other case we study how the measure (1) promotes an accurate prediction by analyzing the limit $t \to t^*$. We assume that the detection score function y is defined over a continuous domain $\Omega \subset \mathbb{R}^2$ and is twice continuously differentiable. This assumption is still valid for discrete scores y by applying suitable interpolation. The ECO framework in fact outputs scores with a direct continuous interpretation, parametrized by its Fourier coefficients. In any case, we assume the prediction t^* to be a local maximum of y. We denote the gradient and Hessian of y at t as $\nabla y(t)$ and $\mathbf{H}y(t)$ respectively. Since t^* is a local maximum we conclude $\nabla y(t^*) = 0$ and $0 \geq \lambda_1^* \geq \lambda_2^*$, where λ_1^*, λ_2^* are the eigenvalues of $\mathbf{H}y(t^*)$. Using (2), we obtain the result[1]

$$\xi_{t^*}\{y\} \leq \frac{|\lambda_1^*|}{\kappa}. \tag{4}$$

Note that the eigenvalue $|\lambda_1^*|$ represents the minimum curvature of the score function y at the peak t^*. Thus, $|\lambda_1^*|$ is a measure of the *sharpness* of the peak t^*. The quality bound (4) is proportional to the sharpness $|\lambda_1^*|$. A high quality value $\xi_{t^*}\{y\}$ therefore ensures that the peak is distinctive, while a flat peak will result on a low quality value. The parameter κ controls the trade-off between the promotion of robustness and accuracy of the prediction. From (4) it follows that κ represents the sharpness $|\lambda_1^*|$ that yields a quality of at most $\xi_{t^*}\{y\} = 1$.

Our approach can be generalized to scale transformations and other higher-dimensional state spaces by extending t to the entire state vector. In this paper,

---

[1] See the supplementary material for a derivation.

we employ 2-dimensional translation and 1-dimensional scale transformations. In the next section, we show that (1) can be used for jointly finding the prediction t^* and the optimal importance weights for the shallow and deep scores.

4.2 Target Prediction

We present a fusion approach based on the quality measure (1), that combines the deep and shallow model predictions to find the optimal state. Let y_d and y_s denote the scores based on deep and shallow features respectively. The fused score is obtained as a weighted combination of the two scores

$$y_\beta(t) = \beta_d y_d(t) + \beta_s y_s(t), \tag{5}$$

where $\beta = (\beta_d, \beta_s)$ are the weights for the deep and shallow scores, respectively. Our aim is to jointly estimate the score weights β and the target state t^* that maximize the quality measure (1). This is achieved by minimizing the loss

$$\text{minimize:} \quad L_{t^*}(\beta) = -\xi_{t^*}\{y_\beta\} + \mu\left(\beta_d^2 + \beta_s^2\right) \tag{6a}$$

$$\text{subject to:} \quad \beta_d + \beta_s = 1, \quad \beta_d \geq 0, \quad \beta_s \geq 0. \tag{6b}$$

Note that we have added a regularization term, controlled by the parameter μ, penalizing large deviations in the weights. The score weights themselves are constrained to be non-negative and sum up to one.

To optimize (6), we introduce a slack variable $\xi = \xi_{t^*}\{y_\beta\}$, resulting in the equivalent minimization problem

$$\text{minimize:} \quad L_{t^*}(\xi, \beta) = -\xi + \mu\left(\beta_d^2 + \beta_s^2\right) \tag{7a}$$

$$\text{subject to:} \quad \beta_d + \beta_s = 1, \quad \beta_d \geq 0, \quad \beta_s \geq 0 \tag{7b}$$

$$y_\beta(t^*) - \xi\Delta(t^* - t) \geq y_\beta(t), \quad \forall t \in \Omega. \tag{7c}$$

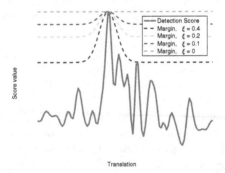

Fig. 4. An illustration of our fusion approach, based on solving the optimization problem (7). A one-dimensional detection score $y_\beta(t)$ (blue curve) is plotted for a particular choice of model weights β, with the candidate state t^* corresponding to the global maximum. The left-hand side of (7c) (dashed curves) is plotted for different values of the slack variable ξ, representing the margin. We find the maximum value of ξ satisfying the inequality (7c), which in this case is $\xi = 0.4$.

A visualization of this reformulated problem and the constraint (7c) is shown in Fig. 4. For any fixed state t^*, (7) corresponds to a Quadratic Programming (QP) problem, which can be solved using standard techniques. In practice, we sample a finite set of candidate states Ω based on local maxima from the deep and shallow scores. Subsequently, (7) is optimized for each state $t^* \in \Omega$ by solving a three-parameter QP problem, adding minimal computational overhead. We then select the candidate state t^* with lowest overall loss (7a) as our final prediction.

5   Experiments

5.1   Implementation Details

Our tracker is implemented in Matlab using MatConvNet [32]. Based on the analysis in Sect. 3.4, we select $\sigma_d = 1/4$ and $\sigma_s = 1/16$ for deep and shallow label functions respectively, when training the models. As concluded in Sect. 3.3, we employ the proposed data augmentation techniques only for deep features. For the fusion method presented in Sect. 4, the regularization parameter μ in (6) is set to 0.15. We set the κ parameter in the distance measure (2) to be inversely proportional to the target size with a factor of 8. All parameters were set using a *separate* validation set, described in the next section. We then use the same set of parameters for all datasets, throughout all experiments.

5.2   Evaluation Methodology

We evaluate our method on four challenging benchmarks: the recently introduced Need For Speed (NFS) [12], VOT2017 [16], UAV123 [24], and Temple128 [20]. NFS consists of 100 high frame rate (240 fps) videos as well as their 30 fps versions. We use the 30 fps version of the dataset for our experiments. Mean overlap precision (OP) and area-under-the-curve (AUC) scores are used as evaluation measures. The OP score is computed as the percentage of frames in a video where the intersection-over-union (IOU) overlap with the ground-truth exceeds a certain threshold. The mean OP over all videos is plotted over the range of IOU thresholds $[0, 1]$ to get the success plot. The area under this plot gives the AUC score. We refer to [36] for details. Due to the stochastic nature of the dropout augmentation, we run our tracker 10 times on each sequence and report average scores to robustly estimate the performance on *all* datasets. Details about VOT2017, UAV123 and Temple128 are provided in Sect. 5.5.

Validation Set: We use a subset of the popular OTB-2015 dataset [36] as our validation set for tuning all hyperparameters. The OTB-2015 dataset has been commonly used for evaluation by the tracking community. However, the dataset has saturated in recent years with several trackers [7, 26] achieving over 90% OP score at threshold 0.5 due to the majority of relatively easy videos. Instead, we are primarily interested in advancing tracking performance in the challenging and unsolved cases, where deep features are of importance. We therefore construct a subset of hard videos from OTB-2015 to form our validation set, termed OTB-H. To find the *hardest* videos in OTB-2015, we consider the per-video results of four deep-feature-based trackers with top overall performance on the dataset: ECO [7], C-COT [11], MDNet [26], and TCNN [25]. We first select sequences for which the average IOU is less than 0.6 for at least two of the four trackers. We further remove sequences overlapping with the VOT2017 dataset. The resulting OTB-H contains 23 sequences, which we use as the validation set when setting all the parameters. The remaining 73 easier videos form the OTB-E dataset that we use in our ablative studies as a test set along with NFS dataset.

5.3   Ablative Study

We first investigate the impact of the observations from Sect. 3 in a tracking framework employing both deep and shallow features. To independently evaluate our contributions, we fuse the model predictions as in (5) with fixed weights β. By varying these weights, we can further analyze the contribution of the deep and shallow models to the final tracking accuracy and robustness. We employ the widely used PASCAL criterion as an indicator of robustness. It measures the percentage of successfully tracked frames using an IOU threshold of 0.5, equivalent to OP at 0.5. Furthermore, we consider a localization to be *accurate* if its IOU is higher than 0.75, since this is the upper half $[0.75, 1]$ of the IOU range $[0.5, 1]$ representing successfully tracked frames.

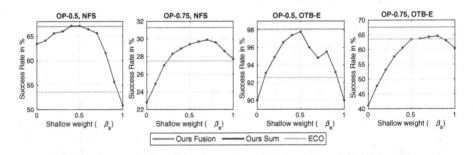

Fig. 5. Analysis of tracking robustness and accuracy using the OP scores at IOU thresholds of 0.5 and 0.75 respectively on the NFS and OTB-E datasets. We plot the performance of our approach using sum-fusion with fixed weights (red) for a range of different shallow weights β_s. These results are also compared with the baseline ECO (orange) and our adaptive fusion (blue). For a wide range of β_s values, our sum-fusion approach outperforms the baseline ECO in robustness on both datasets. Our adaptive fusion achieves the best performance both in terms of accuracy *and* robustness. (Color figure online)

Figure 5 plots the accuracy and robustness indicators, as described above, on NFS and OTB-E for different values of the shallow model weight β_s. In all cases, the deep weight is set to $\beta_d = 1 - \beta_s$. We also show the performance of the baseline

ECO, using the *same* set of deep and shallow features. We observe that our tracker with a fixed sum-fusion outperforms the baseline ECO for a wide range of weights β_s. This demonstrates the importance of employing specifically tailored training procedures for deep and shallow features, as observed in Sect. 3.5.

Despite the above improvements obtained by our analysis of deep and shallow features, we note that optimal robustness and accuracy are mutually exclusive, and cannot be obtained even by careful selection of the weight parameter β_s. While shallow features (large β_s) are beneficial for accuracy, deep features (small β_s) are crucial for robustness. Figure 5 also shows the results of our proposed adaptive fusion approach (Sect. 4), where the model weights β are dynamically computed in each frame. Compared to using a sum-fusion with fixed weights, our adaptive approach achieves improved accuracy *without* sacrificing robustness. Figure 6 shows a qualitative example of our adaptive fusion approach.

5.4 Generalization to Other Networks

With the advent of deep learning, numerous network architectures have been proposed in recent years. Here, we investigate the generalization capabilities of our findings across different deep networks. Table 2 shows the performance of the

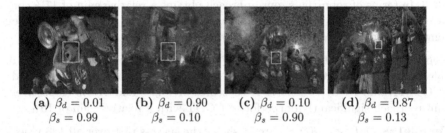

(a) $\beta_d = 0.01$ (b) $\beta_d = 0.90$ (c) $\beta_d = 0.10$ (d) $\beta_d = 0.87$
$\beta_s = 0.99$ $\beta_s = 0.10$ $\beta_s = 0.90$ $\beta_s = 0.13$

Fig. 6. Qualitative example of our fusion approach. The adaptively computed model weights β_d, β_s are shown for four frames from the *Soccer* sequence. The shallow model is prominent early in the sequence (a), before any significant appearance change. Later, when encountered with occlusions, clutter and out-of-plane rotations (b, d), our fusion emphasizes the deep model due to its superior robustness. In (c), where the target undergoes scale changes, our fusion exploits the shallow model for better accuracy.

Table 2. Generalization of our tracker across different network architectures. Results are shown in terms of AUC scores on the NFS and OTB-E dataset. The baseline ECO fails to exploit the power of more sophisticated architectures. Instead, our approach provides consistent gains over ECO when moving towards more advanced networks.

	VGG-M		GoogLeNet		ResNet-50	
	OTB-E	NFS	OTB-E	NFS	OTB-E	NFS
ECO	74.8	45.3	74.4	45.4	74.3	45.7
Ours	74.2	49.7	76.0	51.6	78.0	54.1

proposed method and baseline ECO on three popular architectures: VGG-M [4], GoogLeNet [29], and ResNet-50 [13]. The results are reported in terms of AUC scores on NFS and OTB-E datasets. ECO fails to exploit more sophisticated deeper architectures: GoogLeNet and ResNet. In case of ResNet, our approach achieves a significant gain of 3.7% and 8.4% on OTB-E and NFS datasets respectively. These results show that our analysis in Sect. 3 and the fusion approach proposed in Sect. 4 generalizes across different network architectures.

5.5   State-of-the-Art

Here, we compare our tracker with state-of-the-art methods on four challenging tracking datasets. Further details are provided in the supplementary material.

VOT2017 Dataset [16]: On VOT2017, containing 60 videos, tracking performance is evaluated both in terms of accuracy (average overlap during successful tracking) and robustness (failure rate). The Expected Average Overlap (EAO) measure, which merges both accuracy and robustness, is then used to obtain the overall ranking. The evaluation metrics are computed as an average over 15 runs (see [16] for further details). The results in Table 3 are presented in terms of EAO, robustness, and accuracy. Our approach significantly outperforms the top ranked method LSART with a relative gain of 17%, achieving an EAO score of 0.378. In terms of robustness, our approach obtains a relative gain of 17% compared to LSART. Furthermore, we achieve the best results in terms of accuracy, demonstrating the overall effectiveness of our approach.

Need For Speed Dataset [12]: Figure 7a shows the success plot over all the 100 videos. The AUC scores are reported in the legend. Among previous methods, CCOT [11] and ECO [7] achieve AUC scores of 49.2% and 47.0% respectively. Our approach significantly outperforms CCOT with a relative gain of 10%.

Temple128 Dataset [20]: Figure 7b shows the success plot over all 128 videos. Among the existing methods, ECO achieves an AUC score of 60.5%. Our approach outperforms ECO with an AUC score of 62.2%.

UAV123 Dataset [24]: This dataset consists of 123 aerial tracking videos captured from a UAV platform. Figure 7c shows the success plot. Among the existing methods, ECO achieves an AUC score of 53.7%. Our approach outperforms ECO by setting a new state-of-the-art, with an AUC of 55.0%.

Table 3. Comparison with the state-of-the-art in terms of expected average overlap (EAO), robustness (failure rate), and accuracy on the VOT2017 benchmark. We compare with the top-10 trackers in the competition. Our tracker obtains a significant relative gain of 17% in EAO, compared to the top-ranked method (LSART).

	MCPF	SiamDCF	CSRDCF	CCOT	MCCT	Gnet	ECO	CFCF	CFWCR	LSART	Ours
EAO	0.248	0.249	0.256	0.267	0.270	0.274	0.280	0.286	0.303	0.323	0.378
Robustness	0.427	0.473	0.356	0.318	0.323	0.276	0.276	0.281	0.267	0.218	0.182
Accuracy	0.510	0.500	0.491	0.494	0.525	0.502	0.483	0.509	0.484	0.493	0.532

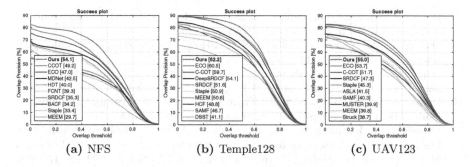

Fig. 7. Success plots on the NFS (a), Temple128 (b), and UAV123 (c) datasets. Our tracker significantly outperforms the state-of-the-art on all datasets.

6 Conclusions

We perform a systematic analysis to identify key causes behind the below-expected performance of deep features for visual tracking. Our analysis shows that individually tailoring the training for shallow and deep features is crucial to obtain both high robustness and accuracy. We further propose a novel fusion strategy to combine the deep and shallow appearance models leveraging their complementary characteristics. Experiments are performed on four challenging datasets. Our experimental results clearly demonstrate the effectiveness of the proposed approach, leading to state-of-the-art performance on all datasets.

Acknowledgments. This work was supported by the Swedish Foundation for Strategic Research (SymbiCloud), Swedish Research Council (EMC², starting grant 2016-05543), CENIIT grant (18.14), Swedish National Infrastructure for Computing, and Wallenberg AI, Autonomous Systems and Software Program.

References

1. Bertinetto, L., Valmadre, J., Golodetz, S., Miksik, O., Torr, P.H.S.: Staple: complementary learners for real-time tracking. In: CVPR (2016)
2. Bertinetto, L., Valmadre, J., Henriques, J.F., Vedaldi, A., Torr, P.H.S.: Fully-convolutional siamese networks for object tracking. In: Hua, G., Jégou, H. (eds.) ECCV 2016. LNCS, vol. 9914, pp. 850–865. Springer, Cham (2016). https://doi.org/10.1007/978-3-319-48881-3_56
3. Bolme, D.S., Beveridge, J.R., Draper, B.A., Lui, Y.M.: Visual object tracking using adaptive correlation filters. In: CVPR (2010)
4. Chatfield, K., Simonyan, K., Vedaldi, A., Zisserman, A.: Return of the devil in the details: delving deep into convolutional nets. arXiv preprint arXiv:1405.3531 (2014)
5. Dalal, N., Triggs, B.: Histograms of oriented gradients for human detection. In: CVPR (2005)
6. Danelljan, M., Bhat, G., Gladh, S., Khan, F.S., Felsberg, M.: Deep motion and appearance cues for visual tracking. Pattern Recogn. Lett. (2018). https://doi.org/10.1016/j.patrec.2018.03.009

7. Danelljan, M., Bhat, G., Shahbaz Khan, F., Felsberg, M.: ECO: efficient convolution operators for tracking. In: CVPR (2017)
8. Danelljan, M., Häger, G., Khan, F.S., Felsberg, M.: Discriminative scale space tracking. TPAMI **39**(8), 1561–1575 (2017)
9. Danelljan, M., Häger, G., Shahbaz Khan, F., Felsberg, M.: Convolutional features for correlation filter based visual tracking. In: ICCV Workshop (2015)
10. Danelljan, M., Häger, G., Shahbaz Khan, F., Felsberg, M.: Learning spatially regularized correlation filters for visual tracking. In: ICCV (2015)
11. Danelljan, M., Robinson, A., Shahbaz Khan, F., Felsberg, M.: Beyond correlation filters: learning continuous convolution operators for visual tracking. In: Leibe, B., Matas, J., Sebe, N., Welling, M. (eds.) ECCV 2016. LNCS, vol. 9909, pp. 472–488. Springer, Cham (2016). https://doi.org/10.1007/978-3-319-46454-1_29
12. Galoogahi, H.K., Fagg, A., Huang, C., Ramanan, D., Lucey, S.: Need for speed: a benchmark for higher frame rate object tracking. In: 2017 IEEE International Conference on Computer Vision (ICCV), pp. 1134–1143. IEEE (2017)
13. He, K., Zhang, X., Ren, S., Sun, J.: Deep residual learning for image recognition. In: Proceedings of the IEEE Conference on Computer Vision and Pattern Recognition, pp. 770–778 (2016)
14. Held, D., Thrun, S., Savarese, S.: Learning to track at 100 FPS with deep regression networks. In: Leibe, B., Matas, J., Sebe, N., Welling, M. (eds.) ECCV 2016. LNCS, vol. 9905, pp. 749–765. Springer, Cham (2016). https://doi.org/10.1007/978-3-319-46448-0_45
15. Hong, Z., Chen, Z., Wang, C., Mei, X., Prokhorov, D., Tao, D.: Multi-store tracker (muster): a cognitive psychology inspired approach to object tracking. In: Proceedings of the IEEE Conference on Computer Vision and Pattern Recognition, pp. 749–758 (2015)
16. Kristan, M., et al.: The visual object tracking VOT2017 challenge results. In: ICCV Workshop (2017)
17. Kristan, M., et al.: A novel performance evaluation methodology for single-target trackers. TPAMI **38**(11), 2137–2155 (2016)
18. Li, H., Li, Y., Porikli, F.: DeepTrack: learning discriminative feature representations by convolutional neural networks for visual tracking. In: BMVC (2014)
19. Li, Y., Zhu, J.: A scale adaptive kernel correlation filter tracker with feature integration. In: Agapito, L., Bronstein, M.M., Rother, C. (eds.) ECCV 2014. LNCS, vol. 8926, pp. 254–265. Springer, Cham (2015). https://doi.org/10.1007/978-3-319-16181-5_18
20. Liang, P., Blasch, E., Ling, H.: Encoding color information for visual tracking: algorithms and benchmark. TIP **24**(12), 5630–5644 (2015)
21. Lukežič, A., Vojíř, T., Čehovin, L., Matas, J., Kristan, M.: Discriminative correlation filter with channel and spatial reliability. arXiv preprint arXiv:1611.08461 (2016)
22. Lukežič, A., Vojíř, T., Zajc, L.Č., Matas, J., Kristan, M.: Discriminative correlation filter tracker with channel and spatial reliability. IJCV **126**(7), 671–688 (2018)
23. Ma, C., Huang, J.B., Yang, X., Yang, M.H.: Hierarchical convolutional features for visual tracking. In: ICCV (2015)
24. Mueller, M., Smith, N., Ghanem, B.: A benchmark and simulator for UAV tracking. In: Leibe, B., Matas, J., Sebe, N., Welling, M. (eds.) ECCV 2016. LNCS, vol. 9905, pp. 445–461. Springer, Cham (2016). https://doi.org/10.1007/978-3-319-46448-0_27
25. Nam, H., Baek, M., Han, B.: Modeling and propagating CNNs in a tree structure for visual tracking. CoRR abs/1608.07242 (2016)

26. Nam, H., Han, B.: Learning multi-domain convolutional neural networks for visual tracking. In: CVPR (2016)
27. Qi, Y., et al.: Hedged deep tracking. In: CVPR (2016)
28. Song, Y., Ma, C., Gong, L., Zhang, J., Lau, R., Yang, M.H.: CREST: convolutional residual learning for visual tracking. In: ICCV (2017)
29. Szegedy, C., et al.: Going deeper with convolutions. In: CVPR (2015)
30. Tao, R., Gavves, E., Smeulders, A.W.M.: Siamese instance search for tracking. In: CVPR (2016)
31. Valmadre, J., Bertinetto, L., Henriques, J.F., Vedaldi, A., Torr, P.H.S.: End-to-end representation learning for correlation filter based tracking. In: CVPR (2017)
32. Vedaldi, A., Lenc, K.: MatConvNet - convolutional neural networks for MATLAB. CoRR abs/1412.4564 (2014)
33. Wang, C., Galoogahi, H.K., Lin, C., Lucey, S.: Deep-LK for efficient adaptive object tracking. In: ICRA (2018)
34. Wang, L., Ouyang, W., Wang, X., Lu, H.: Visual tracking with fully convolutional networks. In: ICCV (2015)
35. van de Weijer, J., Schmid, C., Verbeek, J.J., Larlus, D.: Learning color names for real-world applications. TIP 18(7), 1512–1524 (2009)
36. Wu, Y., Lim, J., Yang, M.H.: Object tracking benchmark. TPAMI 37(9), 1834–1848 (2015)
37. Zhang, J., Ma, S., Sclaroff, S.: MEEM: robust tracking via multiple experts using entropy minimization. In: Fleet, D., Pajdla, T., Schiele, B., Tuytelaars, T. (eds.) ECCV 2014. LNCS, vol. 8694, pp. 188–203. Springer, Cham (2014). https://doi.org/10.1007/978-3-319-10599-4_13
38. Zhang, T., Xu, C., Yang, M.H.: Multi-task correlation particle filter for robust object tracking. In: CVPR (2017)

Recurrent Fusion Network for Image Captioning

Wenhao Jiang[1(✉)], Lin Ma[1], Yu-Gang Jiang[2], Wei Liu[1], and Tong Zhang[1]

[1] Tencent AI Lab, Shenzhen, China
cswhjiang@gmail.com, forest.linma@gmail.com, wl2223@columbia.edu,
tongzhang@tongzhang-ml.org
[2] Fudan University, Shanghai, China
ygj@fudan.edu.cn

Abstract. Recently, much advance has been made in image captioning, and an encoder-decoder framework has been adopted by all the state-of-the-art models. Under this framework, an input image is encoded by a convolutional neural network (CNN) and then translated into natural language with a recurrent neural network (RNN). The existing models counting on this framework employ only one kind of CNNs, *e.g.*, ResNet or Inception-X, which describes the image contents from only one specific view point. Thus, the semantic meaning of the input image cannot be comprehensively understood, which restricts improving the performance. In this paper, to exploit the complementary information from multiple encoders, we propose a novel recurrent fusion network (RFNet) for the image captioning task. The fusion process in our model can exploit the interactions among the outputs of the image encoders and generate new compact and informative representations for the decoder. Experiments on the MSCOCO dataset demonstrate the effectiveness of our proposed RFNet, which sets a new state-of-the-art for image captioning.

Keywords: Image captioning · Encoder-decoder framework
Recurrent fusion network (RFNet)

1 Introduction

Captioning [1–7], a task to describe images/videos with natural sentences automatically, has been an active research topic in computer vision and machine learning. Generating natural descriptions of images is very useful in practice. For example, it can improve the quality of image retrieval by discovering salient contents and help visually impaired people understand image contents.

Even though a great success has been achieved in object recognition [8,9], describing images with natural sentences is still a very challenging task. Image

Electronic supplementary material The online version of this chapter (https://doi.org/10.1007/978-3-030-01216-8_31) contains supplementary material, which is available to authorized users.

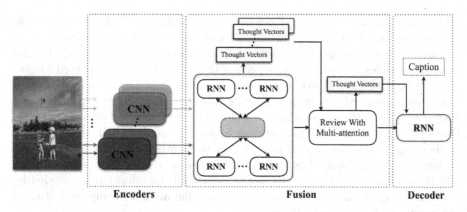

Fig. 1. The framework of our RFNet. Multiple CNNs are employed as encoders and a recurrent fusion procedure is inserted after the encoders to form better representations for the decoder. The fusion procedure consists of two stages. The first stage exploits interactions among the representations from multiple CNNs to generate multiple sets of thought vectors. The second stage performs multi-attention on the sets of thought vectors from the first stage and generates a new set of thought vectors for the decoder.

captioning models need to have a thorough understanding of the input image and capture the complicated relationships among objects. Moreover, they also need to capture the interactions between images and languages and thereby translate image representations into natural sentences.

The encoder-decoder framework, with its advance in machine translation [10,11], has demonstrated promising performance for image captioning [7,12,13]. This framework consists of two parts, namely an encoder and a decoder. The encoder is usually a convolutional neural network (CNN), while decoder is a recurrent neural network (RNN). The encoder is used to extract image representations, based on which the decoder is used to generate the corresponding captions. Usually, a pre-trained CNN for image classification is leveraged to extract image representations.

All existing models employ only one encoder, so the performance heavily depends on the expressive ability of the deployed CNN. Fortunately, there are quite a few well-established CNNs, e.g., ResNet [14], Inception-X [15,16], etc. It is natural to improve the image captioning models by extracting diverse representations with multiple encoders, which play a complementary role in fully depicting and characterizing the image semantic meaning. However, to the best of our knowledge, there are no models considering to exploit the complementary behaviors of multiple encoders for image captioning.

In this paper, to exploit complementary information from multiple encoders, we propose a recurrent fusion network (RFNet) for image captioning. Our framework, as illustrated in Fig. 1, introduces a fusion procedure between the encoders and decoder. The multiple CNNs, served as encoders, can provide diverse and more comprehensive descriptions of the input image. The fusion procedure performs a given number of RNN steps and outputs the hidden states as thought vectors. Our fusion procedure consists of two stages. The first stage contains multiple components and each component processes the information from one encoder. The interactions among the components are captured to generate thought vectors. Hence, each component can communicate with the other components and extract complementary information from them. The second stage compresses the outputs of the first stage into one set of thought vectors. During this procedure, the interactions among the sets of thought vectors are further exploited, thus, useful information is absorbed into the final thought vectors, which will be used as input of the attention model in the decoder. The intuition behind our proposed RFNet is to fuse all the information encoded by multiple encoders and produce thought vectors that are more comprehensive and representative than the original ones.

2 Related Works

2.1 Encoder-Decoder Methods for Image Captioning

Recently, inspired by advance in machine translation, the encoder-decoder framework [10,17] has also been introduced to image captioning [18]. In this framework, a CNN pre-trained on an image classification task is used as the encoder, while a RNN is used as the decoder to translate the information from the encoder into natural sentences. This framework is simple and elegant, and several extensions have been proposed. In [12], an attention mechanism was introduced. The model with this attention mechanism could determine which subregions should be focused on automatically at each time step. In [19], ReviewNet was proposed. The review steps can learn the annotation vectors and initial states for the decoder, which are more representative than those generated by the encoder directly. In [20], a guiding network which models attribute properties of input images was introduced for the decoder. In [21], the authors observed that the decoder does not need visual attendance when predicting non-visual words, and hence proposed an adaptive attention model that attends to the image or to the visual sentinel automatically at each time step.

Besides, several approaches that introduce useful information into this framework have been proposed to improve the image captioning performance. In [22], the word occurrence prediction was treated as a multi-label classification problem. And a region-based multi-label classification framework was proposed to extract visually semantic information. This prediction is then used to initialize a memory cell of a long short-term memory (LSTM) model. Yao *et al.* improved this procedure and discussed different approaches to incorporate word occurrence predictions into the decoder [23].

Recently, in order to optimize the non-differentiable evaluation metrics directly, policy-gradient methods for reinforcement learning are employed to train the encoder-decoder framework. In [24], the cross entropy loss was replaced with CIDEr [25]. The system was then trained with the REINFORCE algorithm [26], which significantly improves the performance. Such a training strategy can be leveraged to improve the performance of all existing models under the encoder-decoder framework.

2.2 Encoder-Decoder Framework with Multiple Encoders or Decoders

In [27], multi-task learning (MTL) was combined with sequence-to-sequence learning with multiple encoders or decoders. In the multi-task sequence-to-sequence learning, the encoders or decoders are shared among different tasks. The goal of [27] is to transfer knowledge among tasks to improve the performance. For example, the tasks of translation and image captioning can be formulated together as a model with only one decoder. The decoder is shared between both basks and responsible for translating from both image and source language. Both tasks can benefit from each other. A similar structure was also exploited in [28] to perform multi-lingual translation. In this paper, we propose a model to combine representations from multiple encoders for the decoder. In [27,28], the inputs of the encoders are different. But in our model, they are the same. Our goal is to leverage complementary information from different encoders to form better representations for the decoder.

2.3 Ensemble and Fusion Learning

Our RFNet also relates to information fusion, multi-view learning [29], and ensemble learning [30]. Each representation extracted from an individual image CNN can be regarded as an individual view depicting the input image. Combining different representations with diversity is a well-known technique to improve the performance. The combination process can occur at the input, intermediate, and output stage of the target model. For the input fusion, the most simple way is to concatenate all the representations and use the concatenation as input of the target model. This method usually leads to limited improvements. For the output fusion, the results of base learners for individual views are combined to form the final results. The common ensemble technique in image captioning is regarded as an output fusion technique, combining the output of the decoder at each time step [18,19,24]. For the intermediate fusion, the representations from different views are preprocessed by exploiting the relationships among them to form input for the target model. Our method can be regarded as a kind of intermediate fusion methods.

3 Background

To provide a clear description of our method, we present a short review of the encoder-decoder framework for image captioning in this section.

3.1   Encoder

Under the encoder-decoder framework for image captioning, a CNN pre-trained for an image classification task is usually employed as the encoder to extract the global representation and subregion representations of the input image. The global representation is usually the output of a fully connected layer and sub-region representations are usually the outputs of a convolutional layer. The extracted global representation and subregion representations are denoted as $\mathbf{a}_0$ and $A = \{\mathbf{a}_1, \ldots, \mathbf{a}_k\}$, respectively, where k denotes the subregion number.

3.2   Decoder

Given the image representations $\mathbf{a}_0$ and A, a decoder, which is usually a gated recurrent unit (GRU) [31] or long short-term memory (LSTM) [32], is employed to translate an input image into a natural sentence. In this paper, we use LSTM equipped with an attention mechanism as the basic unit of the decoder.

Recall that an LSTM with an attention mechanism is a function that outputs the results based on the current hidden state, current input, and context vector. The context vector is the weighted sum of elements from A, with the weights determined by an attention model. We adopt the same LSTM used in [12] and express the LSTM unit with the attention strategy as follows:

$$\begin{pmatrix} \mathbf{i}_t \\ \mathbf{f}_t \\ \mathbf{o}_t \\ \mathbf{g}_t \end{pmatrix} = \begin{pmatrix} \sigma \\ \sigma \\ \sigma \\ \tanh \end{pmatrix} \mathbf{T} \begin{pmatrix} \mathbf{H}_t \\ \mathbf{z}_{t-1} \end{pmatrix}, \tag{1}$$

$$\mathbf{c}_t = \mathbf{f}_t \odot \mathbf{c}_{t-1} + \mathbf{i}_t \odot \mathbf{g}_t, \tag{2}$$

$$\mathbf{h}_t = \mathbf{o}_t \odot \tanh(\mathbf{c}_t), \tag{3}$$

where $\mathbf{i}_t$, $\mathbf{f}_t$, $\mathbf{c}_t$, $\mathbf{o}_t$, and $\mathbf{h}_t$ are input gate, forget gate, memory cell, output gate, and hidden state of the LSTM, respectively. Here,

$$\mathbf{H}_t = \begin{bmatrix} \mathbf{x}_t \\ \mathbf{h}_{t-1} \end{bmatrix} \tag{4}$$

is the concatenation of input $\mathbf{x}_t$ of the time step t and hidden state $\mathbf{h}_{t-1}$, $\mathbf{T}$ is a linear transformation operator. $\mathbf{z}_t$ is the context vector, which is the output of attention model $f_{\mathrm{att}}(A, \mathbf{h}_{t-1})$. Specifically,

$$e_{ti} = \mathrm{sim}(\mathbf{a}_i, \mathbf{h}_{t-1}), \quad \alpha_{ti} = \frac{\exp(e_{ti})}{\sum_{j=1}^{k} \exp(e_{tj})}, \quad \text{and } \mathbf{z}_t = \sum_{i=1}^{k} \alpha_{ti} \mathbf{a}_i,$$

where $\mathrm{sim}(\mathbf{a}_i, \mathbf{h}_t)$ is a function to measure the similarity between $\mathbf{a}_i$ and $\mathbf{h}_t$, which is usually realized by a multilayer perceptron (MLP). In this paper, we use the shorthand notation

$$[\mathbf{h}_t, \mathbf{c}_t] = \mathrm{LSTM}(\mathbf{H}_t, f_{\mathrm{att}}(A, \mathbf{h}_{t-1})) \tag{5}$$

for the above equations.

The purpose of image captioning is to generate a caption $\mathcal{C} = (y_1, y_2, \cdots, y_N)$ for one given image $\mathcal{I}$. The objective adopted is usually to minimize a negative log-likelihood:

$$\mathcal{L} = -\log\, p(\mathcal{C}|\mathcal{I}) = -\sum_{t=0}^{N-1} \log p(y_{t+1}|y_t), \tag{6}$$

where $p(y_{t+1}|y_t) = \text{Softmax}(\mathbf{W}\mathbf{h}_t)$ and $\mathbf{h}_t$ is computed by setting $\mathbf{x}_t = \mathbf{E}\mathbf{y}_t$. Here, $\mathbf{W}$ is a matrix for linear transformation and y_0 is the sign for the start of sentences. $\mathbf{E}\mathbf{y}_t$ denotes the distributed representation of the word $\mathbf{y}_t$, in which $\mathbf{y}_t$ is the one-hot representation for word y_t and $\mathbf{E}$ is the word embedding matrix.

4 Our Method

In this section, we propose our recurrent fusion network (RFNet) for image captioning. The fusion process in RFNet consists of two stages. The first stage combines the representations from multiple encoders to form multiple sets of thought vectors, which will be compressed into one set of thought vectors in the second stage. The goal of our model is to generate more representative thought vectors for the decoder. Two special designs are adopted: (1) employing inter-actions among components in the first stage; (2) reviewing the thought vectors from the previous stage in the second stage. We will describe the details of our RFNet in this section and analyze our design in the experimental results section.

4.1 The Architecture

In our model, M CNNs serve as the encoders. The global representation and subregion representations extracted from the m-th CNN are denoted as $\mathbf{a}_0^{(m)}$ and $A^{(m)} = \{\mathbf{a}_1^{(m)}, \ldots, \mathbf{a}_{k_m}^{(m)}\}$, respectively.

The framework of our proposed RFNet is illustrated in Fig. 2. The fusion procedure of RFNet consists of two stages, specifically fusion stage I and II. Both stages perform a number of RNN steps with attention mechanisms and output hidden states as the thought vectors. The numbers of steps in stage I and II are denoted as T_1 and T_2, respectively. The hidden states from stage I and II are regarded as the thought vectors. The thought vectors of stage I will be used as the input of the attention model of stage II. The hidden states and memory cells after the last step of fusion stage I are aggregated to form the initial hidden state and the memory cell for fusion stage II. The thought vectors generated by stage II will be used in the decoder. RFNet is designed to capture the interactions among the components in stage I, and extract useful information and compress the M sets of thought vectors to generate more compact and informative ones in stage II. The details will be described in the following subsections.

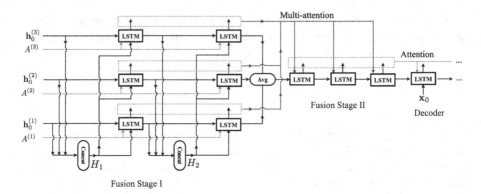

Fig. 2. An example with $M = 3$, $T_1 = 2$, and $T_2 = 3$ for illustrating our proposed RFNet (encoders are omitted). The fusion stage I contains M review components. The input of each review component at each time step is the concatenation of hidden states from all components at the previous time step. Each review component outputs the hidden state as a thought vector. The fusion stage II is a review component that performs the multi-attention mechanism on the multiple sets of thought vectors from fusion stage I. The parameters of LSTM units in the fusion procedure are all different. The purple rectangles indicate the sets of thought vectors. Moreover, in order to make it clear, the discriminative supervision is not presented.

4.2   Fusion Stage I

Fusion stage I takes M sets of annotation vectors as inputs and generates M sets of thought vectors, which will be aggregated into one set of thought vectors in fusion stage II. This stage contains M review components. In order to capture the interactions among the review components, each review component need to know what has been generated by all the components at the previous time step.

We denote the hidden state and memory cell of the m-th review component after time step t as $\mathbf{h}_t^{(m)}$ and $\mathbf{c}_t^{(m)}$. Their initial values $\mathbf{h}_0^{(m)}$ and $\mathbf{c}_0^{(m)}$ are initialized by

$$\mathbf{h}_0^{(m)} = \mathbf{c}_0^{(m)} = \mathbf{W}_0^{(m)} \mathbf{a}_0^{(m)}, \tag{7}$$

where $\mathbf{W}_0^{(m)} \in \mathbb{R}^{s \times d_m}$, s is the size of LSTM hidden state and d_m is the size of $\mathbf{a}_0^{(m)}$. At time step t, the hidden states of the m-th review component are computed as

$$\left[\mathbf{h}_t^{(m)}, \mathbf{c}_t^{(m)}\right] = \text{LSTM}_t^{(m)} \left(\mathbf{H}_t, f_{\text{att-fusion-I}}^{(m,t)}\left(A^{(m)}, \mathbf{h}_{t-1}^{(m)}\right)\right), \tag{8}$$

where

$$\mathbf{H}_t = \begin{bmatrix} \mathbf{h}_{t-1}^{(1)} \\ \vdots \\ \mathbf{h}_{t-1}^{(M)} \end{bmatrix} \tag{9}$$

is the concatenation of hidden states of all review components at the previous time step, $f_{\text{att-fusion-I}}^{(m,t)}(\cdot,\cdot)$ is the attention model for the m-th review component, and $\text{LSTM}_t^{(m)}(\cdot,\cdot)$ is the LSTM unit used by the m-th review component at time step t. Stage I can be regarded as a grid LSTM [33] with independent attention mechanisms. In our model, the LSTM unit $\text{LSTM}_t^{(m)}(\cdot,\cdot)$ can be different for different t and m. Hence, $M \times T_1$ LSTMs are used in fusion stage I. The set of thought vectors generated from the m-th component is denoted as:

$$B^{(m)} = \left\{ \mathbf{h}_1^{(m)}, \mathbf{h}_2^{(m)}, \cdots, \mathbf{h}_{T_1}^{(m)} \right\}. \tag{10}$$

In fusion stage I, the interactions among review components are realized via Eq. (9). The vector $\mathbf{H}_t$ contains the hidden states of all the components after time step $t-1$ and is shared as input among them. Hence, each component is aware of the states of the other components and thus can absorb complementary information from $\mathbf{H}_t$. This hidden state sharing mechanism provides a way for the review component to communicate with each other, which facilitates the generation of thought vectors.

4.3   Fusion Stage II

The hidden state and memory cell of fusion stage II are initialized with $\mathbf{h}_{T_1}^{(1)}, \cdots, \mathbf{h}_{T_1}^{(M)}$ and $\mathbf{c}_{T_1}^{(1)}, \cdots, \mathbf{c}_{T_1}^{(M)}$. We use averaging in our model:

$$\mathbf{h}_{T_1} = \frac{1}{M} \sum_{m=1}^{M} \mathbf{h}_{T_1}^{(m)}, \text{ and } \mathbf{c}_{T_1} = \frac{1}{M} \sum_{m=1}^{M} \mathbf{c}_{T_1}^{(m)}. \tag{11}$$

Fusion stage II combines M sets of thought vectors to form a new one using the multi-attention mechanism. At each time step, the concatenation of context vectors is calculated as:

$$\tilde{\mathbf{z}}_t = \begin{bmatrix} f_{\text{att-fusion-II}}^{(1,t)} \left(B^{(1)}, \mathbf{h}_{t-1} \right) \\ f_{\text{att-fusion-II}}^{(2,t)} \left(B^{(2)}, \mathbf{h}_{t-1} \right) \\ \vdots \\ f_{\text{att-fusion-II}}^{(M,t)} \left(B^{(M)}, \mathbf{h}_{t-1} \right) \end{bmatrix}, \tag{12}$$

where $f_{\text{att-fusion-II}}^{(m,t)}(\cdot,\cdot)$ is an attention model. Hence, this stage contains M independent attention models. They are all soft attention models, similar to [34]. With the context vector $\tilde{\mathbf{z}}_t$, the state transition is expressed as:

$$[\mathbf{h}_t, \mathbf{c}_t] = \text{LSTM}_t(\mathbf{h}_{t-1}, \tilde{\mathbf{z}}_t), \tag{13}$$

where LSTM_t is the LSTM unit at time step t. Please note that all the LSTM units in this stage are also different.

Fusion stage II can be regarded as review steps [19] with M independent attention models, which performs the attention mechanism on the thought vectors yielded in the first stage. It combines and compresses the outputs from stage

I and generates only one set of thought vectors. Hence, the generated thought vectors can provide more information for the decoder.

The hidden states of fusion stage II are collected to form the thought vector set:

$$C = \{\mathbf{h}_{T_1+1}, \cdots, \mathbf{h}_{T_1+T_2}\}, \tag{14}$$

which will be used as the input of the attention model in the decoder.

4.4 Decoder

The decoder translates the information generated by the fusion procedure into natural sentences. The initial hidden state and memory cell are inherited from the last step of fusion stage II directly. The decoder step in our model is the same as other encoder-decoder models, which is expressed as:

$$[\mathbf{h}_t, \mathbf{c}_t] = \text{LSTM}_{dec}(\mathbf{H}_t, f_{\text{att-dec}}(C, \mathbf{h}_{t-1})), \tag{15}$$

where $\text{LSTM}_{dec}(\cdot, \cdot)$ is the LSTM unit for all the decoder steps, $f_{\text{att-dec}}(\cdot, \cdot)$ is the corresponding attention model, $\mathbf{x}_t$ is the word embedding for the input word at the current time step, and

$$\mathbf{H}_t = \begin{bmatrix} \mathbf{x}_t \\ \mathbf{h}_{t-1} \end{bmatrix}. \tag{16}$$

4.5 Discriminative Supervision

We adopt the discriminative supervision in our model to further boost image captioning performance, which is similar to [19,35]. Given a set of thought vectors V, a matrix $\mathbf{V}$ is formed by selecting elements from V as column vectors. A score vector $\mathbf{s}$ of words is then calculated as

$$\mathbf{s} = \text{Row-Max-Pool}(\mathbf{WV}), \tag{17}$$

where $\mathbf{W}$ is a trainable linear transformation matrix and Row-Max-Pool$(\cdot)$ is a max pooling operator along the rows of the input matrix. The i-th element of $\mathbf{s}$ is denoted s_i, which represents the score for the i-th word. Adopting a multi-label margin loss, we obtain the loss function for discriminative supervision as:

$$\mathcal{L}_d(V) = \sum_{j \in \mathcal{W}} \sum_{i \notin \mathcal{W}} \max(0, 1 - (s_j - s_i)), \tag{18}$$

where $\mathcal{W}$ is the set of all frequent words in the current caption. In this paper, we only consider the 1,000 most frequent words in the captions of the training set.

By considering both the discriminative supervision loss in Eq. (18) and the captioning loss in Eq. (6), the complete loss function of our model is expressed as:

$$\mathcal{L}_{all} = \mathcal{L} + \frac{\lambda}{M+1} \left(\mathcal{L}_d(C) + \sum_{m=1}^{M} \mathcal{L}_d\left(B^{(m)}\right) \right), \tag{19}$$

where λ is a trade-off parameter, and $B^{(m)}$ and C are sets of thought vectors from fusion stages I and II.

5   Experimental Results

5.1   Dataset

The MSCOCO dataset[1] [36] is the largest benchmark dataset for the image captioning task, which contains 82,783, 40,504, and 40,775 images for training, validation, and test, respectively. This dataset is challenging, because most images contain multiple objects in the context of complex scenes. Each image in this dataset is associated with five captions annotated by human. For offline evaluation, we follow the conventional evaluation procedure [19,23,37], and employ the same data split as in [6], which contains 5,000 images for validation, 5,000 images for test, and 113,287 images for training. For online evaluation on the MSCOCO evaluation server, we add the testing set into the training set to form a larger training set.

For the captions, we discard all the non-alphabetic characters, transform all letters into lowercase, and tokenize the captions using white space. Moreover, all the words with the occurrences less than 5 times are replaced by the unknown token $<$UNK$>$. Thus a vocabulary consisting of 9,487 words is finally constructed.

5.2   Configurations and Settings

For the experiments, we use ResNet [14], DenseNet [38], Inception-V3 [15], Inception-V4, and Inception-ResNet-V2 [16] as encoders to extract 5 groups of representations. Each group of representations contains a global feature vector and a set of subregion feature vectors. The outputs of the last convolution layer (before pooling) are extracted as subregion features. For Inception-V3, the output of the last fully connected layer is used as the global feature vector. For the other CNNs, the means of subregion representations are regarded as the global feature vectors. The parameters for encoders are fixed during the training procedure. Since the reinforcement learning (RL) has become a common method to boost image captioning performance [24,39–42], we first train our model with cross entropy loss and fine-tune the trained model with CIDEr optimization using reinforcement learning [24]. The performance of models trained with both cross entropy loss and CIDEr optimization is reported and compared.

When training with cross entropy loss, the scheduled sampling [43], label-smoothing regularization (LSR) [15], dropout, and early stopping are adopted. For scheduled sampling, the probability of sampling a token from model is $\min(0.25, \frac{epoch}{100})$, where $epoch$ is the number of passes sweeping over training data. For LSR, the prior distribution over labels is uniform distribution and the smoothing parameter is set to 0.1. Dropout is only applied on the hidden states and the probability is set to 0.3 for all LSTM units. We terminate the

---

[1] http://mscoco.org/.

training procedure, if the evaluation measurement on validation set, specifically the CIDEr, reaches the maximum value. When training with RL [24], only dropout and early stopping are used.

The hidden state size is set as 512 for all LSTM units in our model. The parameters of LSTM are initialized with uniform distribution in $[-0.1, 0.1]$. The Adam [44] is applied to optimize the network with the learning rate setting as 5×10^{-4} and decaying every 3 epochs by a factor 0.8 when training with cross entropy loss. Each mini-batch contains 10 images. For RL training, the learning rate is fixed as 5×10^{-5}. For training with cross entropy, the weight of discriminative supervision λ is set to 10. And discriminative supervision is not used for training with reinforcement learning. To improve the performance, data augmentation is adopted. Both flipping and cropping strategies are used. We crop 90% of width and height at the four corners. Hence, $10\times$ images are used for training.

For sentence generation in testing stage, there are two common strategies. The first one is greedy search, which chooses the word with maximum probability at each time step and sets it as LSTM input for next time step until the end-of-sentence sign is emitted or the maximum length of sentence is reached. The second one is the beam search strategy which selects the top-k best sentences at each time step and considers them as the candidates to generate new top-k best sentences at the next time step. Usually beam search provides better performance for models trained with cross entropy loss. For model trained with RL, beam search and greedy search generate similar results. But greedy search is faster than beam search. Hence, for models trained with RL, we use greedy search to generate captions.

5.3   Performance and Analysis

We compare our proposed RFNet with the state-of-the-art approaches on image captioning, including Neural Image Caption (NIC) [18], Attribute LSTM [22], LSTM-A3 [23], Recurrent Image Captioner (RIC) [45], Recurrent Highway Network (RHN)[46], Soft Attention model [12], Attribute Attention model [48], Sentence Attention model [47], Review Net [19], Text Attention model [37], Att2in model [24], Adaptive model [21], and Up-Down model [42]. Please note that the encoder of Up-Down model is not a CNN pre-trained on ImageNet dataset [51]. It used Faster R-CNN trained on Visual Genome [52] to encode the input image.

Evaluation Metrics. Following the standard evaluation process, five types of metrics are used for performance comparisons, specifically the BLEU [53], METEOR [54], ROUGE-L [55], CIDEr [25], and SPICE [56]. These metrics measure the similarity between generated sentences and the ground truth sentences from specific viewpoints, e.g. n-gram occurrences, semantic contents. We use the official MSCOCO caption evaluation scripts[2] and the source code of SPICE[3] for the performance evaluation.

---

[2] https://github.com/tylin/coco-caption.
[3] https://github.com/peteanderson80/coco-caption.

Table 1. Performance comparisons on the test set of Karpathy's split [6]. All image captioning models are trained with the cross entropy loss. The results are obtained using beam search with beam size 3. $^\Sigma$ indicates an ensemble, † indicates a different data split, and $(-)$ indicates that the metric is not provided. All values are reported as percentage (%), with the highest value of each entry highlighted in boldface.

Model	BLEU-1	BLEU-2	BLEU-3	BLEU-4	METEOR	ROUGE-L	CIDEr	SPICE
Soft attention [12]	70.7	49.2	34.4	24.3	23.9	-	-	-
ReviewNet [19]	-	-	-	29.0	23.7	-	88.6	-
LSTM-A3 [23]	73.5	56.6	42.9	32.4	25.5	53.9	99.8	18.5
Text attention [37]	74.9	58.1	43.7	32.6	25.7	-	102.4	-
Attribute LSTM [22]	74.0	56.0	42.0	31.0	26.0	-	94.0	-
RIC [45]	73.4	53.5	38.5	29.9	25.4	-	-	-
RHN [46]	72.3	55.3	41.3	30.6	25.2	-	98.9	-
Adaptive [21]†	74.2	58.0	43.9	33.2	26.6	-	108.5	-
Att2in [24]	-	-	-	31.3	26.0	54.3	101.3	-
Up-down [42]	77.2	-	-	36.2	27.0	56.4	113.5	20.3
Sentence attention [47]$^\Sigma$	71.6	54.5	40.5	30.1	24.7	-	97.0	-
Attribute attention [48]$^\Sigma$	70.9	53.7	40.2	30.4	24.3	-	-	-
NIC [18]$^{\dagger\Sigma}$	-	-	-	32.1	25.7	-	99.8	-
Att2in [24]$^\Sigma$	-	-	-	32.8	26.7	55.1	106.5	-
ReviewNet [19]$^\Sigma$	76.7	60.9	47.3	36.6	27.4	56.8	113.4	20.3
RFNet	76.4	60.4	46.6	35.8	27.4	56.5	112.5	20.5
RFNet$^\Sigma$	**77.4**	**61.6**	**47.9**	**37.0**	**27.9**	**57.3**	**116.3**	**20.8**

Performance Comparisons. The performance of models trained with cross entropy loss is shown in Table 1, including the performance of single model and ensemble of models. First, it can be observed that our single model RFNet significantly outperformed the existing image captioning models, except the Up-Down model [42]. Our RFNet performed inferiorly to Up-Down in BLEU-1, BLEU-4, and CIDEr, while superiorly to Up-down in METEOR, ROUGGE-L, and SPICE. However, the encoder of Up-Down model was pre-trained on ImageNet dataset and fine-tuned on Visual Genome [52] dataset. The Visual Genome dataset is heavily annotated with objects, attributes and region descriptions and 51K images are extracted from MSCOCO dataset. Hence, the encoder of Up-Down model is trained with far more information than the CNNs trained on ImageNet. With the recurrent fusion strategy, RFNet can extract useful information from different encoders to remedy the lacking of information about objects and attributes in the representations.

Moreover, we can observe that our *single RFNet model* performed significantly better than other ensemble models, such as NIC, Att2in, and behaved comparably with ReviewNet$^\Sigma$ which is an ensemble of 40 ReviewNets (8 models for each CNNs). But RFNet$^\Sigma$, an ensemble of 4 RFNets, significantly outperformed all the ensemble models.

The performance comparisons with RL training are presented in Table 2. We compared RFNet with Att2all [24], Up-Down model [42], and ensemble of ReviewNets. For our method, the performance of single model and ensemble of 4 models are provided. We can see that our RFNet outperformed other methods.

Table 2. Performance comparisons on the test set of Karpathy's split [6]. All image captioning models are trained with the cross entropy loss. The results are obtained using beam search with beam size 3. Σ indicates an ensemble, $\dagger$ indicates a different data split, and $(-)$ indicates that the metric is not provided. All values are reported as percentage (%), with the highest value of each entry highlighted in boldface. The results are obtained using greedy search.

Models	BLEU-1	BLEU-2	BLEU-3	BLEU-4	METEOR	ROUGE-L	CIDEr	SPICE
Att2all [24]	-	-	-	34.2	26.7	55.7	114.0	-
Up-Down [42]	79.8	-	-	36.3	27.7	56.9	120.1	21.4
Att2all [24]$^\Sigma$	-	-	-	35.4	27.1	56.6	117.5	-
ReviewNet [19]$^\Sigma$	79.6	63.6	48.7	36.4	27.7	57.5	121.6	21.0
RFNet	79.1	63.1	48.4	36.5	27.7	57.3	121.9	21.2
RFNet$^\Sigma$	**80.4**	**64.7**	**50.0**	**37.9**	**28.3**	**58.3**	**125.7**	**21.7**

Table 3. Performance of different models on the MSCOCO evaluation server. All values are reported as percentage (%), with the highest value of each entry highlighted in boldface.

Methods	BLEU-1		BLEU-2		BLEU-3		BLEU-4		METEOR		ROUGE-L		CIDEr		SPICE	
	C5	C40	C5	C40	C5	C40	C5	C40	C5	C40	C5	C40	C5	C40	C5	C40
NIC [7]	71.3	89.5	54.2	80.2	40.7	69.4	30.9	58.7	25.4	34.6	53.0	68.2	94.3	94.6	18.2	63.6
Captivator [35]	71.5	90.7	54.3	81.9	40.7	71.0	30.8	60.1	24.8	33.9	52.6	68.0	93.1	93.7	18.0	60.9
M-RNN [49]	71.6	89.0	54.5	79.8	40.4	68.7	29.9	57.5	24.2	32.5	52.1	66.6	91.7	93.5	17.4	60.0
LRCN [50]	71.8	89.5	54.8	80.4	40.9	69.5	30.6	58.5	24.7	33.5	52.8	67.8	92.1	93.4	17.7	59.9
Hard-Attention [12]	70.5	88.1	52.8	77.9	38.3	65.8	27.7	53.7	24.1	32.2	51.6	65.4	86.5	89.3	17.2	59.8
ATT-FCN [48]	73.1	90.0	56.5	81.5	42.4	70.9	31.6	59.9	25.0	33.5	53.5	68.2	94.3	95.8	18.2	63.1
ReviewNet [19]	72.0	90.0	55.0	81.2	41.4	70.5	31.3	59.7	25.6	34.7	53.3	68.6	96.5	96.9	18.5	64.9
LSTM-A3 [23]	78.7	93.7	62.7	86.7	47.6	76.5	35.6	65.2	27.0	35.4	56.4	70.5	116.0	118.0	-	-
Adaptive [21]	74.8	92.0	58.4	84.5	44.4	74.4	33.6	63.7	26.4	35.9	55.0	70.5	104.2	105.9	19.7	67.3
PG-BCMR [41]	75.4	91.8	59.1	84.1	44.5	73.8	33.2	62.4	25.7	34.0	55.0	69.5	101.3	103.2	-	-
Att2all [24]	78.1	93.7	61.9	86.0	47.0	75.9	35.2	64.5	27.0	35.5	56.3	70.7	114.7	116.7	20.7	68.9
Up-Down [42]	80.2	**95.2**	64.1	88.8	49.1	79.4	36.9	68.5	27.6	36.7	57.1	72.4	117.9	120.5	21.5	71.5
RFNet	**80.4**	95.0	**64.9**	**89.3**	**50.1**	**80.1**	**38.0**	**69.2**	**28.2**	**37.2**	**58.2**	**73.1**	**122.9**	**125.1**	-	-

For online evaluation, we used the ensemble of 7 models and the comparisons are provided in Table 3. We can see that our RFNet still achieved the best performance. The C5 and C40 CIDEr scores were improved by 5.0 and 4.6, compared to the state-of-the-art Up-Down model [42].

Ablation Study of Fusions Stage I and II. To study the effects of the two fusion stages, we present the performance of the following models:

- **RFNet$_{-I}$** denotes RFNet without fusion stage I, with only the fusion stage II preserved. The global representations are concatenated to form one global representation and multi-attention mechanisms are performed on the subregion representation from the multiple encoders. The rest is the same with RFNet.
- **RFNet$_{-II}$** denotes RFNet without fusion stage II. Multiple attention models are employed in the decoder and the rest is the same as RFNet.

– **RFNet$_{-\text{inter}}$** denotes RFNet without the interactions in fusion stage I. Each
component in the fusion stage I is independent. Specifically, at each time step,
the input of the m-th component is just $\mathbf{h}_{t-1}^{(m)}$, and it is unaware of the hidden
states of the other components.

The CIDEr scores on the test set of the Karpathy's split are presented in
Table 4. We can see that both the two-stage structure and the interactions in
the first stage are important for our model. With the interactions, the quality of
thought vectors in the first stage can be improved. With the two-stage structure,
the thought vectors in the first stage can be refined and compressed into more
compact and informative set of thought vectors in the second stage. Therefore,
with the specifically designed recurrent fusion strategy, our proposed RFNet
provides the best performance.

Table 4. Ablation study of fusion stages I and II in our RFNet. The CIDEr scores are
obtained using beam search with beam size 3 on the test set of the Karpathy's split.

	RFNet$_{-\text{I}}$	RFNet$_{-\text{II}}$	RFNet$_{-\text{inter}}$	RFNet
CIDEr	108.9	111.5	112.1	112.5

Effects of Discriminative Supervision. We examined the effects of the discriminative supervision with different values of λ. First, it can be observed that
introducing discriminative supervision properly can help improve the captioning
performance, with 107.2 ($\lambda = 1$) and 107.3 ($\lambda = 10$) vs. 105.2 ($\lambda = 0$). However,
if λ is too large, *e.g.*, 100, the discriminative supervision will degrade the corresponding performance. Therefore, in this paper, λ is set as 10, which provided
the best performance (Table 5).

Table 5. CIDEr scores with different λ values on the test set. The captions are generated by greedy search.

λ	0	1	10	100
CIDEr	105.2	107.2	107.3	104.7

6 Conclusions

In this paper, we proposed a novel recurrent fusion network (RFNet), to exploit
complementary information of multiple image representations for image captioning. In the RFNet, a recurrent fusion procedure is inserted between the encoders
and the decoder. This recurrent fusion procedure consists of two stages, and each
stage can be regarded as a special RNN. In the first stage, each image representation is compressed into a set of thought vectors by absorbing complementary information from the other representations. The generated sets of thought

vectors are then compressed into another set of thought vectors in the second stage, which will be used as the input to the attention module of the decoder. The RFNet achieved leading performance on the MSCOCO evaluation server, which corroborates the effectiveness of our proposed network architecture.

References

1. Venugopalan, S., Rohrbach, M., Donahue, J., Mooney, R., Darrell, T., Saenko, K.: Sequence to sequence-video to text. In: Proceedings of the IEEE International Conference on Computer Vision, pp. 4534–4542 (2015)
2. Krishna, R., Hata, K., Ren, F., Fei-Fei, L., Niebles, J.C.: Dense-captioning events in videos. In: ICCV, pp. 706–715 (2017)
3. Chen, Y., Wang, S., Zhang, W., Huang, Q.: Less is more: picking informative frames for video captioning. arXiv preprint arXiv:1803.01457 (2018)
4. Wang, B., Ma, L., Zhang, W., Liu, W.: Reconstruction network for video captioning. In: Proceedings of the IEEE Conference on Computer Vision and Pattern Recognition, pp. 7622–7631 (2018)
5. Wang, J., Jiang, W., Ma, L., Liu, W., Xu, Y.: Bidirectional attentive fusion with context gating for dense video captioning. In: Proceedings of the IEEE Conference on Computer Vision and Pattern Recognition, pp. 7190–7198 (2018)
6. Karpathy, A., Fei-Fei, L.: Deep visual-semantic alignments for generating image descriptions. In: Proceedings of the IEEE conference on computer vision and pattern recognition, pp. 3128–3137 (2015)
7. Vinyals, O., Toshev, A., Bengio, S., Erhan, D.: Show and tell: lessons learned from the 2015 MSCOCO image captioning challenge. IEEE Trans. Pattern Anal. Mach. Intell. **39**(4), 652–663 (2017)
8. He, K., Zhang, X., Ren, S., Sun, J.: Spatial pyramid pooling in deep convolutional networks for visual recognition. In: Fleet, D., Pajdla, T., Schiele, B., Tuytelaars, T. (eds.) ECCV 2014. LNCS, vol. 8691, pp. 346–361. Springer, Cham (2014). https://doi.org/10.1007/978-3-319-10578-9_23
9. Krizhevsky, A., Sutskever, I., Hinton, G.E.: Imagenet classification with deep convolutional neural networks. In: Advances in neural information processing systems, pp. 1097–1105 (2012)
10. Cho, K., et al.: Learning phrase representations using RNN encoder-decoder for statistical machine translation. arXiv:1406.1078 (2014)
11. Bahdanau, D., Cho, K., Bengio, Y.: Neural machine translation by jointly learning to align and translate. In: ICLR 2015 (2014)
12. Xu, K., et al.: Show, attend and tell: Neural image caption generation with visual attention. In: ICML (2015)
13. Chen, X., Ma, L., Jiang, W., Yao, J., Liu, W.: Regularizing RNNs for caption generation by reconstructing the past with the present. In: The IEEE Conference on Computer Vision and Pattern Recognition (CVPR), June 2018
14. He, K., Zhang, X., Ren, S., Sun, J.: Deep residual learning for image recognition. In: Proceedings of the IEEE conference on computer vision and pattern recognition, pp. 770–778 (2016)
15. Szegedy, C., Vanhoucke, V., Ioffe, S., Shlens, J., Wojna, Z.: Rethinking the inception architecture for computer vision. In: CVPR (2016)
16. Szegedy, C., Ioffe, S., Vanhoucke, V., Alemi, A.A.: Inception-v4, inception-resnet and the impact of residual connections on learning. In: AAAI, pp. 4278–4284 (2017)

17. Sutskever, I., Vinyals, O., Le, Q.V.: Sequence to sequence learning with neural networks. In: Advances in Neural Information Processing Systems, pp. 3104–3112 (2014)
18. Vinyals, O., Toshev, A., Bengio, S., Erhan, D.: Show and tell: a neural image caption generator. In: CVPR, pp. 3156–3164 (2015)
19. Yang, Z., Yuan, Y., Wu, Y., Cohen, W.W., Salakhutdinov, R.R.: Review networks for caption generation. In: NIPS (2016)
20. Jiang, W., Ma, L., Chen, X., Zhang, H., Liu, W.: Learning to guide decoding for image captioning. In: The Thirty-Second AAAI Conference on Artificial Intelligence (2018)
21. Lu, J., Xiong, C., Parikh, D., Socher, R.: Knowing when to look: adaptive attention via a visual sentinel for image captioning. arXiv preprint arXiv:1612.01887 (2016)
22. Wu, Q., Shen, C., Liu, L., Dick, A., van den Hengel, A.: What value do explicit high level concepts have in vision to language problems? In: CVPR (2016)
23. Yao, T., Pan, Y., Li, Y., Qiu, Z., Mei, T.: Boosting image captioning with attributes. In: The IEEE International Conference on Computer Vision (ICCV), October 2017
24. Rennie, S.J., Marcheret, E., Mroueh, Y., Ross, J., Goel, V.: Self-critical sequence training for image captioning. In: The IEEE Conference on Computer Vision and Pattern Recognition (CVPR), July 2017
25. Vedantam, R., Lawrence Zitnick, C., Parikh, D.: Cider: consensus-based image description evaluation. In: CVPR (2015)
26. Williams, R.J.: Simple statistical gradient-following algorithms for connectionist reinforcement learning. Mach. Learn. 8(3–4), 229–256 (1992)
27. Luong, T., Le, Q.V., Sutskever, I., Vinyals, O., Kaiser, L.: Multi-task sequence to sequence learning. In: International Conference on Learning Representations (2016)
28. Firat, O., Cho, K., Bengio, Y.: Multi-way, multilingual neural machine translation with a shared attention mechanism. In: Proceedings of NAACL-HLT, pp. 866–875 (2016)
29. Xu, C., Tao, D., Xu, C.: A survey on multi-view learning. arXiv preprint arXiv:1304.5634 (2013)
30. Zhou, Z.H.: Ensemble Methods: Foundations and Algorithms. CRC Press, Boca Raton (2012)
31. Chung, J., Gulcehre, C., Cho, K., Bengio, Y.: Empirical evaluation of gated recurrent neural networks on sequence modeling. arXiv preprint arXiv:1412.3555 (2014)
32. Hochreiter, S., Schmidhuber, J.: Long short-term memory. Neural Comput. 9(8), 1735–1780 (1997)
33. Kalchbrenner, N., Danihelka, I., Graves, A.: Grid long short-term memory. arXiv preprint arXiv:1507.01526 (2015)
34. Xu, H., Saenko, K.: Ask, attend and answer: exploring question-guided spatial attention for visual question answering. In: Leibe, B., Matas, J., Sebe, N., Welling, M. (eds.) ECCV 2016. LNCS, vol. 9911, pp. 451–466. Springer, Cham (2016). https://doi.org/10.1007/978-3-319-46478-7_28
35. Fang, H., et al.: From captions to visual concepts and back. In: CVPR, pp. 1473–1482 (2015)
36. Lin, T.-Y., et al.: Microsoft COCO: Common Objects in Context. In: Fleet, D., Pajdla, T., Schiele, B., Tuytelaars, T. (eds.) ECCV 2014. LNCS, vol. 8693, pp. 740–755. Springer, Cham (2014). https://doi.org/10.1007/978-3-319-10602-1_48
37. Mun, J., Cho, M., Han, B.: Text-guided attention model for image captioning. In: AAAI (2017)

38. Huang, G., Liu, Z., van der Maaten, L., Weinberger, K.Q.: Densely connected convolutional networks. In: The IEEE Conference on Computer Vision and Pattern Recognition (CVPR), July 2017
39. Ranzato, M., Chopra, S., Auli, M., Zaremba, W.: Sequence level training with recurrent neural networks. ICLR-15 (2015)
40. Ren, Z., Wang, X., Zhang, N., Lv, X., Li, L.J.: Deep reinforcement learning-based image captioning with embedding reward. In: The IEEE Conference on Computer Vision and Pattern Recognition (CVPR), July 2017
41. Liu, S., Zhu, Z., Ye, N., Guadarrama, S., Murphy, K.: Improved image captioning via policy gradient optimization of spider. In: The IEEE International Conference on Computer Vision (ICCV), October 2017
42. Anderson, P., et al.: Bottom-up and top-down attention for image captioning and VQA. arXiv preprint arXiv:1707.07998 (2017)
43. Bengio, S., Vinyals, O., Jaitly, N., Shazeer, N.: Scheduled sampling for sequence prediction with recurrent neural networks. In: Advances in Neural Information Processing Systems, pp. 1171–1179 (2015)
44. Kingma, D., Ba, J.: Adam: a method for stochastic optimization. The International Conference on Learning Representations (ICLR) (2015)
45. Liu, H., Yang, Y., Shen, F., Duan, L., Shen, H.T.: Recurrent image captioner: describing images with spatial-invariant transformation and attention fieltering. arXiv:1612.04949 (2016)
46. Gu, J., Wang, G., Chen, T.: Recurrent highway networks with language CNN for image captioning. arXiv:1612.07086 (2016)
47. Zhou, L., Xu, C., Koch, P., Corso, J.J.: Watch what you just said: image captioning with text-conditional attention. arXiv:1606.04621 (2016)
48. You, Q., Jin, H., Wang, Z., Fang, C., Luo, J.: Image captioning with semantic attention. In: CVPR, pp. 4651–4659 (2016)
49. Mao, J., Xu, W., Yang, Y., Wang, J., Huang, Z., Yuille, A.: Deep captioning with multimodal recurrent neural networks (m-RNN). In: ICLR (2015)
50. Donahue, J., et al.: Long-term recurrent convolutional networks for visual recognition and description. In: Proceedings of the IEEE Conference on Computer Vision and Pattern Recognition, pp. 2625–2634 (2015)
51. Deng, J., Dong, W., Socher, R., Li, L.J., Li, K., Fei-Fei, L.: Imagenet: a large-scale hierarchical image database. In: 2009 IEEE Conference on Computer Vision and Pattern Recognition, CVPR 2009, pp. 248–255. IEEE (2009)
52. Krishna, R., et al.: Visual genome: connecting language and vision using crowd-sourced dense image annotations (2016)
53. Papineni, K., Roukos, S., Ward, T., Zhu, W.J.: BLEU: a method for automatic evaluation of machine translation. In: ACL (2002)
54. Banerjee, S., Lavie, A.: Meteor: an automatic metric for MT evaluation with improved correlation with human judgments. In: ACL workshop (2005)
55. Lin, C.Y.: Rouge: a package for automatic evaluation of summaries. In: ACL-04 Workshop (2004)
56. Anderson, P., Fernando, B., Johnson, M., Gould, S.: SPICE: semantic propositional image caption evaluation. In: Leibe, B., Matas, J., Sebe, N., Welling, M. (eds.) ECCV 2016. LNCS, vol. 9909, pp. 382–398. Springer, Cham (2016). https://doi.org/10.1007/978-3-319-46454-1_24

Good Line Cutting: Towards Accurate Pose Tracking of Line-Assisted VO/VSLAM

Yipu Zhao$^{(\boxtimes)}$ (iD) and Patricio A. Vela (iD)

Georgia Institute of Technology, Atlanta, GA 30332, USA
yipu.zhao@gatech.edu

Abstract. This paper tackles a problem in line-assisted VO/VSLAM: accurately solving the least squares pose optimization with unreliable 3D line input. The solution we present is *good line cutting*, which extracts the most-informative sub-segment from each 3D line for use within the pose optimization formulation. By studying the impact of line cutting towards the information gain of pose estimation in line-based least squares problem, we demonstrate the applicability of improving pose estimation accuracy with good line cutting. To that end, we describe an efficient algorithm that approximately approaches the joint optimization problem of good line cutting. The proposed algorithm is integrated into a state-of-the-art line-assisted VSLAM system. When evaluated in two target scenarios of line-assisted VO/VSLAM, low-texture and motion blur, the accuracy of pose tracking is improved, while the robustness is preserved.

Keywords: SLAM · Line feature · Least squares

1 Introduction

Visual Odometry (VO) and Visual SLAM (VSLAM) methods typically exploit point features as they are the simplest to describe and manage. A sensible alternative or addition is to consider lines given that edges are also fairly abundant in images; especially within man-made environments where sometimes the quantity of points may be lacking to the detriment of VO/VSLAM. The canonical examples being corridors and hallways, whose low-texture degrades the performance of point features methods. Under these circumstances, lines become more reliable constraints versus points.

Compared to points, additional benefits of lines is that their detection is less sensitive to the noise associated to video capturing, and that lines are trivially stable under a wide range of viewing angles [1,2]. Additionally, lines are more robust to motion blur [3]. Even with heavily blurred input image, one would

---

This work was supported, in part, by the National Science Foundation under Grant No. 1400256 and 1544857.

V. Ferrari et al. (Eds.): ECCV 2018, LNCS 11206, pp. 527–543, 2018.
https://doi.org/10.1007/978-3-030-01216-8_32

expect some lines that are parallel to the local direction of blur to remain track-able. That said, lines don't provide as strong a motion constraint as points, so incorporating whatever points exist within the scene is usually a good idea.

Rather than explicitly tracking points and lines, direct VO/VSLAM methods implicitly associate these strong features over time [4,5]. Direct SLAM optimizes the photometric error of sequential image registration over the space of possible pose changes between captured images. Since feature extraction is no longer needed, direct methods typically require less computational power. However, compared to feature-based methods, direct methods are more sensitive to several factors: image noise, geometric distortion, large displacement, lighting change, etc. Therefore, feature-based methods are more viable as SLAM solutions for robust and accurate pose tracking.

Adding line features to VO/VSLAM is not a trivial task. Significant progress has been made in line detection [6] and matching [7]. Yet triangulation of 3D lines still remains problematic. Triangulating a 3D line from 2D measurements requires more measurements and is more sensitive to measurement noise, com-pared to points. Lines are generally weak in constraining the correspondence along its direction of expansion. It is hard to establish reliable point-to-point correspondence between two lines (as segments), which degrades triangulation accuracy. In addition, lines are usually partially-occluded, which brings the chal-lenge of deciding the endpoint correspondence. Accurately solving line-based pose estimation requires resolving the low-reliability of triangulated 3D lines.

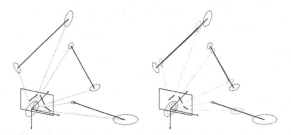

Fig. 1. A toy case illustrating the proposed good line cutting approach. **Left:** Giv-ing 3 line matchings with confidence ellipsoids (dashed line), the least squares pose estimation has high uncertainty. **Right:** Line-cutting applied to the line-based least squares problem. The cut line segments and their corresponding confidence ellipsoids are in red. The confidence ellipsoid of the new pose estimation improves. (Color figure online)

To reduce the impact of unreliable 3D lines, a common practice is to model the uncertainty of the 3D line, and weight the contribution of each line accord-ingly in pose optimization. The information matrix of the line residual [8–11] is one of such weighting terms. The residuals of uncertain lines get less weight so that the optimized pose is biased in favor of the certain lines. However, uncer-tainty of line residual does not immediately imply incorrect pose estimation (though there is some correlation): a certain line residual term might barely contribute to pose estimation, whereby it would make no sense to weight it highly. We posit that, in lieu of the uncertainty of line residual, the uncertainty of pose estimation should be assessed and exploited.

Another way to reduce uncertainty is to simply drop highly-uncertain lines when numerically constructing the pose optimization problem. However, line features are typically low in quantity (e.g. tens of lines). Too much information could be lost by dropping line features. Furthermore, there is a high risk of forming ill-conditioned optimization problem.

As opposed to line weighting and dropping, this paper aims to improve pose optimization through the concept of **good line cutting**. The goal of good line cutting is simple: for each 3D line, find the line segment that contributes the largest amount of information to pose estimation (a.k.a. a good line), and select only those informative segments to solve pose optimization. With line cutting, the conditioning of the optimization problem improves, leading to more accurate pose estimation than the original problem. An illustration of good line cutting can be found at Fig. 1. To the best of the authors' knowledge, this is the first paper discussing the role of line cutting in line-based pose optimization. The contributions of this paper are:

(1) Demonstration that good line cutting improves the overall conditioning of line-based pose optimization;
(2) An *efficient algorithm* for real-time applications that approaches the computationally more involved joint optimization solution to good line cutting; and
(3) Integration of proposed algorithm *into a state-of-the-art line-assisted VSLAM* system. When evaluated in two target scenarios (low-texture and motion blur), the proposed line cutting leads to accuracy improvements over line-weighting, while preserving the robustness of line-assisted pose tracking.

2   Related Work

This section first reviews related work on line-assisted VO/VSLAM, then examines the literature of feature selection(targeted for point features mostly), and discusses the connection between (point) feature selection and the proposed good line cutting method.

2.1   Line-Assisted VO/VSLAM

There has been continuous effort investigating line features in the SLAM community. In the early days of visual SLAM, lines are used to cope with large view change of monocular camera tracking [1,2]. In [1], the authors integrate lines into a point-based monocular Extended Kalman Filter SLAM (EKF-SLAM). Real-time pose tracking with lines only are demonstrated in [2] by using a Unscented Kalman Filter (UKF). Both methods model 3D lines as endpoint-pairs, project lines to image, then measure the residual. Alternatively, edges are extracted and utilized [3]. For the convenience of projection, a 12-DOF over-parameterization is used to model 3D edge. Again, the edge residual is measured after 3D-to-2D projection.

More recently, line-assisted VO/VSLAM are extended to 3D visual sensors, such as RGB-D sensor and stereo camera. In [8], a line-assisted RGB-D odometry system is proposed. It involves parameterizing the 3D lines as 3D endpoint-pairs and minimizing the endpoint residual in $SE(3)$. However, directly working in $SE(3)$ has the disadvantage of being sensitive to inaccurate depth measurements. With the progress in line detectors (e.g. LSD [6]) and descriptors (e.g. LBD [7]), growing attention has been paid towards stereo-base line VO/VSLAM, e.g. [11–13]. Though alternative parameterizations have been explored (e.g. Plücker coordinate [14], orthonormal representation [15]), most line-assisted VO/VSLAM continued to use the 3D endpoint-pair parametrization because it conveniently combines with the well-established point-based optimization. Pose estimation typically jointly minimizes the reprojection errors of both point and line matches. For line features, the endpoint-to-line distance is commonly used as the reprojection error term, i.e., *the line residual*. To cope with the 3D line uncertainty, a covariance matrix is maintained for each 3D line. Each line residual term is weighted by the inverse of the covariance matrix obtained by propagating the covariance from the 3D line to the endpoint-to-line distance.

Line features within monocular VO/VSLAM also gained attention recently [10,16,17]. The pipeline of [16] is similar to that of stereo pipelines. A more robust variant for the endpoint-to-line distance is defined in [9]. Line-assisted methods building from direct VO/VSLAM have also been developed [10,17]. Interestingly, neither of them use direct measurements (e.g. photometric error) for line terms in the joint optimization objective. Instead, the line residual is the least squares of endpoint-to-line distance, which is identical to other feature-based approaches.

Research into line-assisted VO/VSLAM is still ongoing. Among the systems described above, modules commonly employed are: (1) 3D lines parameterized as 3D endpoint-pairs; (2) endpoint-to-line distance and variants serve as the line residual; (3) in the optimization objective (pose only and joint), line residuals are weighted by some weighting matrix. The proposed good line cutting approach in this paper expands on these three modules.

2.2 Feature Selection

Feature selection has been part of VO/VSLAM for a long time. The goal of feature selection is to find subset of features with best value for pose estimation, so as to improve the efficiency and accuracy of VO/VSLAM. Two sources of information are typically used to guide the selection: image appearance and structural & motion information. Our work is a variant of the second one.

It is well-understood that covariance/information matrix captures the structural & motion information: it approximately represents the uncertainty/confident ellipsoid of pose estimation. Feature selection is effectively modeled as an optimization problem: the goal is to select a subset of features that minimize the covariance matrix (i.e. maximize the information matrix) under some metrics, e.g. information gain [18,19], entropy [20], covariance ratio [21], trace [22], minimum eigenvalue [23,24], and log-determinant [25].

The basic assumption of (point) feature selection is the availability of a large number of features (e.g. hundreds of points). In such case, the pose optimization problem will remain well-determined with only a subset of features. Since line features occur in low quantities, there is a high risk of forming an ill-conditioned optimization problem when a subset of lines are selected and utilized. Instead, identify the (sub-)segment of each line that contributes the largest amount of information so that all line segments get used for pose optimization. Doing so avoids the risk of ill-conditioning.

3   Least Squares Pose Optimization with Lines

In line-assisted VO/VSLAM, the goal of pose optimization is to estimate the pose x of calibrated camera(s) given a set of 3D features, i.e. points $\{P_i\}$ and lines $\{L_i\}$, and their corresponding 2D projections, i.e. points $\{p_i\}$ and lines $\{l_i\}$, in the image. As aligned with the current practice, endpoint-pairs are used to represent 3D lines $\{L_i\}$. Without loss of generality, the least squares objective of pose optimization with both point and lines can be written as,

$$\hat{x} = \arg\min\{\|p - h(x, P)\|^2 + \|l^T h(x, L)\|^2\} \tag{1}$$

where p and l are stacked matrices of 2D point measurements $\{p_i\}$ and 2D line coefficients $\{l_i\}$, respectively. P is the stacked matrix of 3D points $\{P_i\}$, while L is the stacked matrix of all endpoints from the 3D line set $\{L_i\}$. $h(x, P)$ consists of the pose transformation (decided by x) and pin-hole projection. Some researchers [16] suggest using the dual form of the line residual term in (1), which minimizes the distance between projection of 3D line and measured endpoint. Though we follow the definition of line residual as in (1) in this paper, the proposed good line cutting can be updated to the dual form easily. For simplicity, the least squares (1) is referred to as line-LSQ problem.

Solving the line-LSQ (1) often involves the first-order approximation of the non-linear measurement function. For instance, the endpoint-to-line distance $h(x, L)$ on image plane can be approximated as,

$$h(x, L) = h(x_0, L) + H_x(x - x_0) \tag{2}$$

so that the least squares of line residual term can be minimized with Gauss-Newton method, which iteratively updates the pose estimate:

$$\hat{x} = x_0 - (l^T H_x)^+ l^T (h(x_0, L)) \tag{3}$$

Accuracy of $\hat{x}$ is affected by two types of error in line features: 2D line measurement error and 3D line triangulation error. As mentioned earlier, 3D line triangulation is sensitive to noise and less-reliable than 3D point triangulation.

Therefore, here we only consider the error of 3D line endpoint L while assuming the 2D measurement l is accurate. Again, with the first-order approximation of $h(x_0, L)$ at the initial pose x_0 and triangulated 3D endpoint L_0, we may connect the pose optimization error ϵ_x and 3D line endpoint error ϵ_L,

$$\epsilon_x = (l^T H_x)^+ l^T H_L \epsilon_L = H^T \epsilon_L \tag{4}$$

where $H^T = (l^T H_x)^+ (l^T H_L)$. Here we intentionally ignore the error in point residual term. The reason is, when available, point features are known to be more accurate. Therefore, the main source of error in line-LSQ problem is from 3D line triangulation ϵ_L, which is propagated by factor H.

3.1   Information Matrix in Line-LSQ Problem

Common practice models the 3D endpoint-pair error ϵ_L as i.i.d. Gaussian under the proper parametrization, e.g. inverse-depth. With first-order approximation (4), we may write the pose information matrix Ω_x as,

$$\Omega_x = H^T \Omega_L H = \sum_i H_i^T \Omega_{L_i} H_i \tag{5}$$

where H_i is the corresponding row block in H for line L_i, and Ω_{L_i} is the information matrix of 3D endpoint-pair used to parametrize L_i. Notice that Ω_{L_i} is a block diagonal matrix under the i.i.d. assumption on 3D endpoint error. Set $\Omega_{L_i(0)}$, $\Omega_{L_i(1)}$ as the two diagonal blocks of Ω_{L_i}, and $H_i(0)$, $H_i(1)$ the corresponding row block in H_i, then (5) can be further broken down into:

$$\begin{aligned}\Omega_x &= \sum [H_i^T(0)\Omega_{L_i(0)}H_i(0) + H_i^T(1)\Omega_{L_i(1)}H_i(1)] \\ &= \sum H_i^T(\alpha_i)\Omega_{L_i(\alpha_i)}H_i(\alpha_i)\end{aligned} \tag{6}$$

where we extend the range of i from n lines to $2n$ endpoints, and set $[\alpha_i]$ as a $2n \times 1$ chessboard vector filled with 0 and 1.

As pointed out in the literature of point-feature selection [22–25], the spectral property of the pose information matrix has strong connection with the error of least squares pose optimization. For example, the worst-case error variance is quantified by the inverse of minimum eigenvalue of Ω_x [23,24]. Large min-eigenvalue of Ω_x is preferred to avoid fatal error in line-LSQ solving. Also, the volume of the confidence ellipsoid in pose estimation can be effectively measured with the log-determinant of Ω_x [25]. For accurately solving the line-LSQ problem, large log-determinant of Ω_x is pursued. In what follows, we quantify the spectral property of Ω_x with log-determinant, i.e. $\log \det(\Omega_x)$.

As mentioned early, line selection/dropping has a high risk of forming ill-conditioned line-LSQ problem. In what follows, we will describe an alternative method to improve $\log \det(\Omega_x)$, which is a better fit for line-LSQ problem.

4   Good Line Cutting in Line-LSQ Problem

4.1   Intuition of Good Line Cutting

Compared with points that are typically modeled as sizeless entity, lines are modeled to be able to extend along one certain dimension. For a 3D line L_i defined by endpoint-pair $L_i(0)$ and $L_i(1)$ in Euclidean space, the following equations hold for any intermediate 3D point $L_i(\alpha)$ that lies on L_i:

$$L_i(\alpha) = (1 - \alpha)L_i(0) + \alpha L_i(1)$$
$$\Omega_{L_i(\alpha)} = \Sigma_{L_i(\alpha)}^{-1} = \{(1 - \alpha)^2 \Sigma_{L_i(0)} + \alpha^2 \Sigma_{L_i(1)}\}^{-1},$$

where α is the interpolation ratio, and $\Sigma_{L_i(*)}$ is the covariance matrix of 3D point $L_i(*)$.

The covariance matrix of the intermediate 3D point, $\Sigma_{L_i(\alpha)}$, is **convex** to the interpolation ratio α, as both $\Sigma_{L_i(0)}$ and $\Sigma_{L_i(1)}$ are positive semi-definite. At some specific $\alpha_m \in [0,1]$, $\Sigma_{L_i(\alpha_m)}$ reaches a global minimum (and $\Omega_{L_i(\alpha_m)}$ a global maximum). In other word, at some intermediate 3D position $L_i(\alpha_m)$ (both endpoints included) the corresponding 3D uncertainty is minimized. The same conclusion holds when extending from a single 3D point to the 3D point-pair $\langle L_i(\alpha_1), L_i(\alpha_2) \rangle$ lying on the 3D line L_i: both 3D points share the least-uncertain position $L_i(\alpha_m)$. To minimize the amount of uncertainty introduced with 3D line endpoints, the 3D line L_i will shrink to a single 3D point!

However, the pose information Ω_x is not only dependent on endpoint information matrix $\Omega_{L_i(\alpha)}$, but also the Jacobian term $H_i(\alpha) = (l_i^T H_x(\alpha))^+ (l_i^T H_L(\alpha))$. Cutting 3D line into smaller segments will affect the corresponding Jacobian term as well. Intuitively, line cutting could hurt the spectral property of measurement Jacobian block $H_x(\alpha)$: if a 3D line gets cut to a single point, the corresponding measurement Jacobian will degenerate from rank-2 to rank-1, thereby losing one of the two constraints provided by the original 3D line matching.

Therefore, the objective of good line cutting can be written as follow,

$$[\alpha_i] = \arg\max \log \det(\Omega_x) \tag{7}$$
$$= \arg\max \log \det[\sum H_i^T(\alpha_i) \Omega_{L_i(\alpha_i)} H_i(\alpha_i) + \Omega_x^{pt}]$$

where we include a constant term Ω_x^{pt} to capture the information from point features, if applicable. Naturally, this objective can be solved with nonlinear optimization techniques.

4.2   Validation of Good Line Cutting

Before describing the optimization of (7), we would like to validate the idea of line cutting. One natural question towards line cutting with (7) being, is it possible that the Jacobian term $H_i^T(\alpha_i)$ has much stronger impact towards (7) than 3D uncertainty reduction, so that one should always use the **full-length of 3D line**? To address this question, we study the minimal case, **single line cutting**:

only one pair of cutting ratio $\langle \alpha_1, \alpha_2 \rangle$ can be changed, while the remaining $n - 1$ lines are not cut.

It is cumbersome to derive the function from line cut ratio α to Jacobian term $H_i(\alpha)$: it is highly non-linear, and the Jacobian term vary under different $SE(3)$ parameterizations of camera and 3D lines. Instead, a set of line-LSQ simulation are conducted to validate line cutting.

The testbed is developed based on the simulation framework of [26]. A set of 3D lines that form a cuboid are simulated, under homogeneous-points line (*HPL*) parameterization. To simulate the error in 3D line triangulation, the endpoints of 3D lines are perturbed with zero-mean Gaussians in inverse-depth space, as illustrated with blue lines in Fig. 2 left. For the 3D line in red, the optimal line cutting ratio, found through brute-force search, is plotted versus camera pose in Fig. 2 right. The boxplots indicate that cutting happens when the 3D line is orthogonal or parallel to the camera frame. In these cases, the measurement Jacobian of the red 3D line scales poorly with line length. Taking a smaller segment/point is preferred so as to introduce less noise into the least squares problem. According to Fig. 2, line cutting adapts to the information and uncertainty of the tracked lines based on the relative geometry.

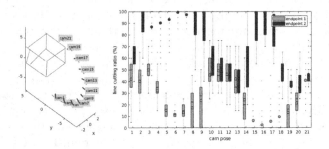

Fig. 2. Line cutting behavior under different camera poses. A pair $\langle 0, 100 \rangle$ indicates full line selection. Identical ratio pair, e.g. $\langle 45, 45 \rangle$ indicates cutting to a point. (Color figure online)

To visualize the outcomes of different line cutting ratios, we used brute-force sweep to generate the surface of $\log \det(\Omega_x)$ as a function of the line cutting ratio parameters. Three example surfaces are illustrated in Fig. 3. In the 1st example, global maximum of $\log \det(\Omega_x)$ is at $\langle \alpha_1 = 0, \alpha_2 = 1.0 \rangle$, which indicates the full-length of 3D line should be used. The 2nd one has global maximum at $\langle \alpha_1 = 0, \alpha_2 = 0.76 \rangle$, which encourages cutting out part of the line. In column 3, $\log \det(\Omega_x)$ is maximized at $\langle \alpha_1 = 0.52, \alpha_2 = 0.52 \rangle$, which means the original 3D line should be aggressively cut to a 3D point. To maximize pose information, line cutting is definitely preferred in some cases (e.g. Fig. 3 columns 2 and 3).

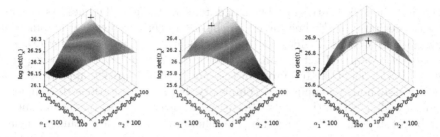

Fig. 3. Example surfaces of $\log \det(\Omega_x)$ in single line cutting set-up and *HPL* parameterization. The global maximum of $\log \det(\Omega_x)$ is marked with red cross. (Color figure online)

5 Efficient Line Cutting Algorithm

5.1 Single Line Cutting

To begin with, consider the single line cutting problem as simulated previously. Based on Fig. 3, we notice the mapping from $\langle \alpha_1, \alpha_2 \rangle$ to $\log \det(\Omega_x)$ is continuous, and concave within a certain neighborhood. Therefore, by doing gradient ascent in each of the concave regions, the global maximum of $\log \det(\Omega_x)$ is expected to be found. One possible triplet of initial pairs are: full-length $\langle \alpha_1 = 0, \alpha_2 = 1.0 \rangle$, 1st endpoint only $\langle \alpha_1 = 0, \alpha_2 = 0 \rangle$, and 2nd endpoint only $\langle \alpha_1 = 1.0, \alpha_2 = 1.0 \rangle$.

The effectiveness of the multi-start gradient ascent is demonstrated with 100-run repeated test. Two commonly used endpoint-pair parameterizations of 3D lines [26] are tested here: homogeneous-points line (*HPL*) and inverse-depth-points line (*IDL*). The error of endpoint estimation is simulated with i.i.d. Gaussian in inverse-depth space (standard deviation of 0.005 and 0.015 unit are used), and propagated to $SE(3)$ space. Five different sizes (6, 10, 15, 20 and 30) of 3D line set are tested. Under both *HPL* and *IDL* parametrization, we compare the best pair from the 3 gradient ascends with the brute-force result. The differences of line cutting ratios are smaller than 0.01 for over 99% of the cases. Therefore, single line cutting problem can be solved effectively using the outcomes from a combination of three gradient ascents.

5.2 Joint Line Cutting

Now extend the single line cutting to the complete problem of **joint line cutting**: how to find the line cutting ratios for all n 3D lines, so that the log det of pose information matrix generated from n line matchings is maximized?

Naturally, the joint line cutting objective (7) can be approached with nonlinear optimizers, e.g. interior-point [27], active-set [28]. Meanwhile, an alternative approach would be simple greedy heuristic: instead of optimizing the joint problem (or a smaller subproblem), simply searching for the local maximum for each

3D line as single line cutting problem, and iterating though all n lines. As demonstrated previously, single line cutting can be effectively solved with a combination of 3 gradient ascends. Besides, the 3 independent gradients ascends can execute in parallel. Compared with nonlinear joint optimization that typically requires $\mathcal{O}(\epsilon^{-c})$ iterations of the full problem (c some constant), greedy approach has a much well-bounded computation complexity. It takes n iterations to complete, while at each iteration the single line cutting is solved in $\mathcal{O}(m)$ (m the maximum number of steps in gradient ascend). The efficiency of joint line cutting is crucial, since only minimum overhead (e.g. milliseconds) shall be introduced to the real time pose tracking of targeted line-assisted VO/VSLAM applications.

The greedy algorithm for efficient joint line cutting is described in Algorithm 1. The component of pose information matrix from a full-length line L_i is denoted by $\Omega_x^i(0,1)$, while a line cut from $\langle \alpha_1, \alpha_2 \rangle$ is denoted by $\Omega_x^i(\alpha_1, \alpha_2)$. With the line-LSQ simulation platform, the effectiveness of greedy joint line cutting is demonstrated with 100-run repeated test. The Matlab implementations of interior-point [27], as well as three variants of active-set [28], are chosen to compare against the greedy algorithm. The results are presented as boxplots in Fig. 4. Under both 3D line parameterizations (*HPL* and *IDL*), greedy algorithm provides the largest increase of $\log\det(\Omega_x)$ (on average and in the worst case).

Algorithm 1. Efficient greedy algorithm for joint line cutting.

Data: 3D line set $\{L(i)\}_n$, 2D measurement set $\{l(i)\}_n$
Result: $\{\langle \alpha_1(i), \alpha_2(i) \rangle\}_n$
1   $\Omega_x = \sum \Omega_x^i(0,1)$;
2   **for** $i = 1 : n$ **do**
3      $\Omega_x^r = \Omega_x - \Omega_x^i(0,1)$;
4      $\langle \alpha_1(i), \alpha_2(i) \rangle = \arg\max\ \log\det(\Omega_x^i(\alpha_1, \alpha_2) + \Omega_x^r)$;
5      $\Omega_x = \Omega_x^r + \Omega_x^i(\alpha_1(i), \alpha_2(i))$;

---

6   Experiments on Line-Assisted VSLAM

This section evaluates the performance of the proposed line cutting approach. Two target scenarios of line-assisted VSLAM are set up for experiments: low-texture and motion blur.

We base the line cutting experiment on a state-of-the-art line-assisted VSLAM system, PL-SLAM [11]. As a stereo vision based system, it tracks both ORB [29] point features and LSD [6] line features between frames, and perform an on-manifold pose optimization with weighted residual terms of both feature types. One weakness of the original PL-SLAM[1] is that the point feature front-end is not as well tuned as other point-only VSLAM system, e.g. ORB-SLAM2 [30]. Two modifications were made by us in response: (1) replacing the

---

[1] https://github.com/rubengooj/pl-slam.

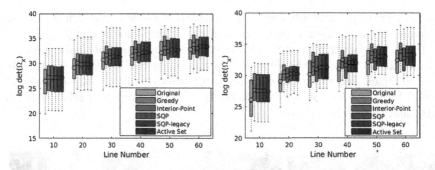

Fig. 4. Boxplots of joint line cutting with different approaches. **Left:** with *HPL* parametrization. **Right:** with *IDL* parametrization. Boxplots are presented in order: (1) original $\log \det(\Omega_x)$, (2) after line cutting with greedy approach, (3)–(6) after line cutting with nonlinear joint optimizers.

OpenCV ORB extractor with the ORB-SLAM2 implementation, which provides a larger number of (and well-distributed) point matchings than the original version; (2) changing the point feature matching strategy from global brute force search to local search (similar to ORB-SLAM2 implementation), which handles the increasing amount of point features efficiently.

The proposed good line cutting algorithm is integrated into the modified PL-SLAM in place of the original line-weighting scheme. It takes all feature matchings as input: lines are to be refined with line cutting, while points serve as constant terms in the line cutting objective. After line cutting, all features (points and cut lines) are sent to pose optimization. The loop closing module of PL-SLAM is turned off since the focus of this paper is real-time pose tracking.

For comprehensively evaluating the value of line cutting, five variants of the modified PL-SLAM are assessed: (1) point-only SLAM (P), (2) line-only SLAM (L), (3) line-only SLAM with line cutting ($L + Cut$), (4) point & line SLAM (PL), and (5) point & line SLAM with line cutting ($PL + Cut$). To better benchmarking the performance of point features, we also report the results of ORB-SLAM2[2] [30] (referred as *ORB2*) and *SVO2*[3] [4]. *SVO2* is a state-of-the-art direct VO system that supports stereo input. It tracks both image patches and edgelets. All systems above were running on an Intel i7 quadcore 4.20 GHz CPU (passmark score of 2583 per thread).

Accuracy of real-time pose tracking is evaluated with two relative metrics between ground truth track and SLAM estimated track: (1) **Relative Position Error(RPE)** [31], which captures the average drift of pose tracking in a short period of time; (2) **Relative Orientation Error(ROE)**, which captures the average orientation error of pose tracking with the same estimation pipeline as RPE. Both RPE and ROE are estimated with a fixed time window of 3 s.

---

[2] https://github.com/raulmur/ORB_SLAM2.
[3] http://rpg.ifi.uzh.ch/svo2.html.

Compared with the absolute metrics (e.g. RMSE of whole track), relative metrics are more suited for measuring the drift in real-time pose tracking [31].

Due to the fact that most SLAM systems have some level of randomness (e.g. feature extractor, multi-thread), all experiments in the following are repeated with 10 times. For those failed more than 2 times in 10 trials, we ignore the results due to the lack of consistency. For the rest, the average of relative metrics (RPE and ROE) are reported.

Fig. 5. Example frames of line cutting PL-SLAM running in challenging scenarios: (1) low-texture, (2) motion blur, (3) lighting change. Detected features are in green, while projected are in red. Notice the length of projected line being much shorter than the measurement, after line cutting. (Color figure online)

6.1   Low-Texture

To the authors' knowledge, no publicly available, low-texture stereo benchmark exists. To evaluate the proposed approach, we synthesized a low-texture stereo sequence with Gazebo. An example frame of the low-texture sequence is provided as the 1st plot in Fig. 5.

Relative errors are summarized in Table 1. After applying line cutting to line-assisted baseline (L and PL), the average relative errors are cut down by almost 40%, as highlighted in bold. The lowest tracking error (i.e. best accuracy) is achieved when combining point and line features, and cutting the lines with the proposed method ($PL + Cut$). Meanwhile, systems that only utilize point features perform poorly: point-only SLAM (P) has high ROE; ORB-SLAM2 ($ORB2$) failed to track. The direct approach $SVO2$ succeeded in tracking the whole low- texture sequence, but has the highest relative errors.

The evaluation results suggest that, line features are valuable for pose tracking in low-texture scenarios. However, simply using the full-length of lines for pose optimization may cause large tracking error. With the proposed line cutting, the accuracy of line-assisted pose tacking improves.

6.2   Motion Blur

Motion blur happens when the camera is moving too fast (e.g. on a flying vehicle) or when the scenario contains rapidly moving objects. Though the second case is also challenging for VO/VSLAM, it is beyond the scope of this work (as it

Table 1. Relative error on synthetic low-texture sequence

Metric	Approach						
	L	$L + Cut$	PL	$PL + Cut$	P	$ORB2$	$SVO2$
RPE(m/s)	0.246	**0.141**	0.242	**0.126***	0.222	-	0.372
ROE(deg/s)	4.78	**3.01**	3.83	**1.68***	5.13	-	8.83

violates the common assumption of static world). Here we focus on tracking the pose of a fast-moving camera, under different levels of motion blur.

The dataset chosen is the EuRoC MAV dataset [32]. It contains 11 sequences of stereo images recorded from a micro aerial vehicle. For each sequence, a precise ground-truth track is provided with external motion capture systems (Vicon & Leica MS50). Instead of running on all 11 sequences, only 6 fast-motion sequences recorded in a Vicon-equipped room (with high potential to exhibit motion blur) are used for motion blur evaluation. The RPEs are summarized in the upper half of Table 2. For each sequence, we compare the line-assisted baseline with the line cutting version, and highlight the better one in bold. Among all 7 methods evaluated here, the one that leads to the lowest error is marked with a star sign.

Compared with the line-assisted baselines (L and PL), the line cutting versions ($L + Cut$ and $PL + Cut$) clearly have lower level of RPEs on most sequences. The improvement is less significant on *V1-01-easy*, mostly due to the relative accurate line triangulation (the RPE of L is close to the lowest). Meanwhile, the performance of $ORB2$ is not as consistent: when tracking succeed, $ORB2$ has the lowest RPE among all 7 methods. However it failed to function reliably on the last 2 sequences. This is not surprising: when available, point features are known to be more accurate for pose tracking; they are just not as robust as lines under motion blur. Lastly, the direct $SVO2$ failed to track on 4 out of 6 sequences, similar to the results reported in [4] (failed on 3 out of 6). It is expected since direct approach are more sensitive to fast motion and lighting changes (e.g. the 3rd plot in Fig. 5) than feature-based ones.

The level of motion blur for the original EuRoC sequence is not severe: the shot of each camera is strictly controlled, and the vehicle is only doing fast motion at several moments during the entire sequence. To assess the performance under severe motion blur, we smooth the 6 Vicon sequences with a 5×5 box filter, and rerun all 7 VO/VSLAM methods on the blurred ones. Corresponding results are reported in the bottom half of Tables 2 and 3.

Under the severe motion blur, point-based approaches (P and $ORB2$) become much less accurate than before, while also easy to loss track. Meanwhile, the line-assisted approaches are more robust to the blur. More importantly, the accuracy of line-assisted approaches are clearly improved with line cutting: $PL + Cut$ reaches the lowest RPE on 3 sequences, while $L + Cut$ wins on another one. One exception is on *V2-01-easy blurred*, where PL is already accurate and line cutting leads to slight degeneracy. Last, $SVO2$ does slightly better than $PL + Cut$ on sequence *V2-03-dif blurred*, while has the highest RPE on other

5 sequences. One potential reason that $SVO2$ tracks on all 6 blurred sequences while failing on 4 original ones is that the blurring acts to pre-condition the direct objective (original highly non-smooth). The convergence rate of optimizing the direct objective improves and positively impacts the tracking rate.

Similarly, we also report the ROE in Table 3. The outcomes are consistent with the RPE outcomes and analysis. Compared to point features, line features

Table 2. Relative position(m/s) error on EuRoC sequences with fast motion

Sequence	Approach						
	L	L + Cut	PL	PL + Cut	P	ORB2	SVO2
V1-01-easy	0.044	**0.043**	0.048	0.048	0.058	0.041*	0.128
V1-02-med	0.135	**0.059**	0.046	**0.043**	0.072	0.034*	-
V1-03-dif	0.169	**0.133**	0.164	**0.156**	0.402	0.108*	-
V2-01-easy	0.100	**0.059**	0.042	**0.030**	0.053	0.011*	0.109
V2-02-med	0.126	**0.112***	0.179	**0.126**	-	-	-
V2-03-dif	0.483	**0.450**	0.431	**0.364***	-	-	-
V1-01-easy blurred	0.054	**0.047***	0.054	**0.052**	0.062	0.048	0.126
V1-02-med blurred	0.076	**0.068**	0.052	**0.049***	0.129	0.178	0.357
V1-03-dif blurred	0.233	**0.206**	-	**0.148***	-	-	0.277
V2-01-easy blurred	0.144	**0.054**	**0.034***	0.037	0.040	0.049	0.096
V2-02-med blurred	0.166	**0.138**	0.171	**0.127***	-	0.162	0.270
V2-03-dif blurred	-	-	-	**0.391**	-	-	0.289*

Table 3. Relative orientation(deg/s) error on EuRoC sequences with fast motion

Sequence	Approach						
	L	L + Cut	PL	PL + Cut	P	ORB2	SVO2
V1-01-easy	0.52	**0.49**	**0.61**	0.63	0.83	0.43*	4.23
V1-02-med	3.01	**1.52**	0.71	**0.64**	1.71	0.32*	-
V1-03-dif	4.99	**3.82**	**2.38**	2.85	9.58	1.96*	-
V2-01-easy	3.58	**2.56**	0.86	**0.77**	0.88	0.26*	4.49
V2-02-med	**2.14***	2.35	4.38	**3.47**	-	-	-
V2-03-dif	12.67	**11.77**	**10.77***	12.05	-	-	-
V1-01-easy blurred	0.80	**0.63***	0.77	**0.73**	0.95	0.66	4.24
V1-02-med blurred	1.69	**1.62**	0.84	**0.76***	3.08	2.63	8.63
V1-03-dif blurred	7.35	**6.65**	-	**3.17***	-	-	10.49
V2-01-easy blurred	2.94	**2.08**	**0.99**	1.07	0.92*	2.25	3.96
V2-02-med blurred	3.47	**2.67**	3.15	**2.62***	-	5.48	8.38
V2-03-dif blurred	-	-	-	**10.60**	-	-	8.58*

are robust to motion blur while preserving accurate position information. The proposed line cutting further improves the tracking accuracy of line-assisted VO/VSLAM.

Lastly, we briefly discuss the computation cost of line cutting. Since the baseline PL-SLAM does not maintain covariance matrix for each 3D line, we do so with a simple error model: (1) assume a constant i.i.d. Gaussian at the inverse-depth space of each 3D line endpoint; (2) propagate the endpoint covariance matrix from inverse-depth space of the previous frame to the Euclidean space of current frame. Then we run the greedy line cutting algorithm (Algorithm 1) with these covariance/information matrices. Most of compute time is spent on the iterative greedy algorithm. When averaged over the EuRoC sequences, the line cutting module takes 3 ms to process 60 lines per frame.

7   Conclusion and Future Work

This paper presents *good line cutting*, which deals with the uncertain 3D line measurements to be used in line-assisted VO/VSLAM. The goal of good line cutting is to find the (sub-)segment within each uncertain 3D line that contributes the most information towards pose estimation. By only utilizing those informative (sub-)segments, line-based least squares is solved more accurately. We also describe an efficient, greedy algorithm for the joint line cutting problem. With the efficient approximation, line cutting is integrated into a state-of-the-art line-assisted VSLAM system. When evaluated on two target scenarios of line-assisted VO/VSLAM(low-texture; motion blur), accuracy improvements are demonstrated, while robustness is preserved. In the future, we plan to extend line cutting to other 3D line parametrization, e.g. Plücker coordinates. The joint feature tuning problem, namely point selection & line cutting, is also worth exploring further.

References

1. Smith, P., Reid, I.D., Davison, A.J.: Real-time monocular SLAM with straight lines (2006)
2. Gee, A.P., Mayol-Cuevas, W.: Real-time model-based SLAM Using line segments. In: Bebis, G., et al. (eds.) ISVC 2006. LNCS, vol. 4292, pp. 354–363. Springer, Heidelberg (2006). https://doi.org/10.1007/11919629_37
3. Klein, G., Murray, D.: Improving the agility of keyframe-based SLAM. In: Forsyth, D., Torr, P., Zisserman, A. (eds.) ECCV 2008. LNCS, vol. 5303, pp. 802–815. Springer, Heidelberg (2008). https://doi.org/10.1007/978-3-540-88688-4_59
4. Forster, C., Zhang, Z., Gassner, M., Werlberger, M., Scaramuzza, D.: SVO: semidirect visual odometry for monocular and multicamera systems. IEEE Trans. Robot. **33**, 249–265 (2016)
5. Engel, J., Koltun, V., Cremers, D.: Direct sparse odometry. IEEE Trans. Pattern Anal. Mach. Intell. **40**(3), 611–625 (2018)
6. von Gioi, R.G., Jakubowicz, J., Morel, J.-M., Randall, G.: LSD: a line segment detector. Image Process. Line **2**, 35–55 (2012)

7. Zhang, L., Koch, R.: Line matching using appearance similarities and geometric constraints. In: Pinz, A., Pock, T., Bischof, H., Leberl, F. (eds.) DAGM/OAGM 2012. LNCS, vol. 7476, pp. 236–245. Springer, Heidelberg (2012). https://doi.org/10.1007/978-3-642-32717-9_24

8. Lu, Y., Song, D.: Robust RGB-D odometry using point and line features. In: IEEE International Conference on Computer Vision, pp. 3934–3942 (2015)

9. Vakhitov, A., Funke, J., Moreno-Noguer, F.: Accurate and linear time pose estimation from points and lines. In: Leibe, B., Matas, J., Sebe, N., Welling, M. (eds.) ECCV 2016. LNCS, vol. 9911, pp. 583–599. Springer, Cham (2016). https://doi.org/10.1007/978-3-319-46478-7_36

10. Yang, S., Scherer, S.: Direct monocular odometry using points and lines. In: IEEE International Conference on Robotics and Automation (ICRA), pp. 3871–3877. IEEE (2017)

11. Gomez-Ojeda, R., Moreno, F.-A., Scaramuzza, D., Gonzalez-Jimenez, J.: PL-SLAM: a stereo SLAM system through the combination of points and line segments. arXiv preprint arXiv:1705.09479 (2017)

12. Koletschka, T., Puig, L., Daniilidis, K.: MEVO: multi-environment stereo visual odometry. In: IEEE/RSJ International Conference on Intelligent Robots and Systems (IROS), pp. 4981–4988. IEEE (2014)

13. Gomez-Ojeda, R., Gonzalez-Jimenez, J.: Robust stereo visual odometry through a probabilistic combination of points and line segments. In: IEEE International Conference on Robotics and Automation (ICRA), pp. 2521–2526. IEEE (2016)

14. Přibyl, B., Zemčík, P., Čadík, M.: Camera pose estimation from lines using Plücker coordinates. In: British Machine Vision Conference (BMVC), pp. 1–12 (2015)

15. Zhang, G., Lee, J.H., Lim, J., Suh, I.H.: Building a 3-D line-based map using stereo slam. IEEE Trans. Robot. 31(6), 1364–1377 (2015)

16. Pumarola, A., Vakhitov, A., Agudo, A., Sanfeliu, A., Moreno-Noguer, F.: PL-SLAM: real-time monocular visual SLAM with points and lines. In: IEEE International Conference on Robotics and Automation (ICRA), pp. 4503–4508. IEEE (2017)

17. Gomez-Ojeda, R., Briales, J., Gonzalez-Jimenez, J.: PL-SVO: semi-direct monocular visual odometry by combining points and line segments. In: IEEE/RSJ International Conference on Intelligent Robots and Systems (IROS), pp. 4211–4216. IEEE (2016)

18. Davison, A.J.: Active search for real-time vision. In: IEEE International Conference on Computer Vision, vol. 1, pp. 66–73 (2005)

19. Kaess, M., Dellaert, F.: Covariance recovery from a square root information matrix for data association. Robot. Auton. Syst. 57(12), 1198–1210 (2009)

20. Zhang, S., Xie, L., Adams, M.D.: Entropy based feature selection scheme for real time simultaneous localization and map building. In: IEEE/RSJ International Conference on Intelligent Robots and Systems (IROS), pp. 1175–1180. IEEE (2005)

21. Cheein, F.A., Scaglia, G., di Sciasio, F., Carelli, R.: Feature selection criteria for real time EKF-SLAM algorithm. Int. J. Adv. Robot. Syst. 6(3), 21 (2009)

22. Lerner, R., Rivlin, E., Shimshoni, I.: Landmark selection for task-oriented navigation. IEEE Trans. Robot. 23(3), 494–505 (2007)

23. Zhang, G., Vela, P.A.: Optimally observable and minimal cardinality monocular SLAM. In: IEEE International Conference on Robotics and Automation (ICRA), pp. 5211–5218. IEEE (2015)

24. Zhang, G., Vela, P.A.: Good features to track for visual SLAM. In: IEEE Conference on Computer Vision and Pattern Recognition, pp. 1373–1382 (2015)

25. Carlone, L., Karaman, S.: Attention and anticipation in fast visual-inertial navigation. In: IEEE International Conference on Robotics and Automation (ICRA), pp. 3886–3893. IEEE (2017)

26. Sola, J., Vidal-Calleja, T., Civera, J., Montiel, J.M.M.: Impact of landmark parametrization on monocular EKF-SLAM with points and lines. Int. J. Comput. Vis. **97**(3), 339–368 (2012)

27. Waltz, R.A., Morales, J.L., Nocedal, J., Orban, D.: An interior algorithm for nonlinear optimization that combines line search and trust region steps. Math. Program. **107**(3), 391–408 (2006)

28. Powell, M.J.D.: A fast algorithm for nonlinearly constrained optimization calculations. In: Watson, G.A. (ed.) Numerical Analysis. LNM, vol. 630, pp. 144–157. Springer, Heidelberg (1978). https://doi.org/10.1007/BFb0067703

29. Rublee, E., Rabaud, V., Konolige, K., Bradski, G.: ORB: an efficient alternative to SIFT or SURF. In: IEEE International Conference on Computer Vision, pp. 2564–2571. IEEE (2011)

30. Mur-Artal, R., Montiel, J.M.M., Tardos, J.D.: ORB-SLAM: a versatile and accurate monocular slam system. IEEE Trans. Robot. **31**(5), 1147–1163 (2015)

31. Sturm, J., Burgard, W., Cremers, D.: Evaluating egomotion and structure-from-motion approaches using the TUM RGB-D benchmark. In: Workshop on Color-Depth Camera Fusion in Robotics IEEE/RJS International Conference on Intelligent Robot Systems (IROS), October 2012

32. Burri, M., et al.: The EuRoC micro aerial vehicle datasets. Int. J. Robot. Res. **35**, 1157–1163 (2016)

Composition Loss for Counting, Density Map Estimation and Localization in Dense Crowds

Haroon Idrees[1](✉), Muhmmad Tayyab[5], Kishan Athrey[5], Dong Zhang[2], Somaya Al-Maadeed[3], Nasir Rajpoot[4], and Mubarak Shah[5]

[1] Robotics Institute, Carnegie Mellon University, Pittsburgh, USA
hidrees@cs.cmu.edu
[2] NVIDIA Inc., Santa Clara, USA
[3] Computer Science Department, Faculty of Engineering,
Qatar University, Doha, Qatar
[4] Department of Computer Science, University of Warwick, Coventry, UK
[5] Center for Research in Computer Vision,
University of Central Florida, Orlando, USA

Abstract. With multiple crowd gatherings of millions of people every year in events ranging from pilgrimages to protests, concerts to marathons, and festivals to funerals; visual crowd analysis is emerging as a new frontier in computer vision. In particular, counting in highly dense crowds is a challenging problem with far-reaching applicability in crowd safety and management, as well as gauging political significance of protests and demonstrations. In this paper, we propose a novel approach that simultaneously solves the problems of counting, density map estimation and localization of people in a given dense crowd image. Our formulation is based on an important observation that the three problems are inherently related to each other making the loss function for optimizing a deep CNN decomposable. Since localization requires high-quality images and annotations, we introduce UCF-QNRF dataset that overcomes the shortcomings of previous datasets, and contains 1.25 million humans manually marked with dot annotations. Finally, we present evaluation measures and comparison with recent deep CNNs, including those developed specifically for crowd counting. Our approach significantly outperforms state-of-the-art on the new dataset, which is the most challenging dataset with the largest number of crowd annotations in the most diverse set of scenes.

Keywords: Crowd counting · Localization · Composition loss
Convolution Neural Networks

1 Introduction

Counting dense crowds is significant both from socio-political and safety perspective. At one end of the spectrum, there are large ritual gatherings such as during pilgrimages that typically have large crowds occurring in known and pre-defined

© Springer Nature Switzerland AG 2018
V. Ferrari et al. (Eds.): ECCV 2018, LNCS 11206, pp. 544–559, 2018.
https://doi.org/10.1007/978-3-030-01216-8_33

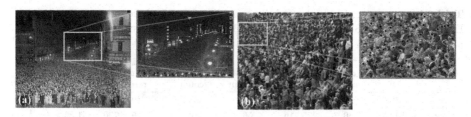

Fig. 1. This figure highlights the problems due to low resolution images from two existing dense crowd datasets: (a) shows a case where the annotations were not done on parts of the images as it is virtually impossible to distinguish heads of neighboring people, while (b) shows a case where some of the locations/counts are erroneous and therefore not suitable for localization. The UCF-QNRF dataset proposed in this paper overcomes such issues. (Color figure online)

locations. Although they generally have passive crowds coming together for peaceful purposes, disasters have known to occur, for instance, during Love Parade [9] and Hajj [1]. For active crowds, such as expressive mobs in demonstrations and protests, counting is important both from political and safety standpoint. It is very common for different sides to claim divergent numbers for crowd gathering, inclined towards their political standing on the concerned issue. Beyond subjectivity and preference for certain political or social outcomes, the disparate counting estimates from opposing parties have a basis in numerical cognition as well. In humans, the results on subitizing [21] suggest that once the number of observed objects increases beyond four, the brain switches from the exact Parallel Individuation System (PIS) to the inaccurate but scalable Approximate Number System (ANS) to count objects [11]. Thus, computer vision based crowd counting offers alternative fast and objective estimation of the number of people in such events. Furthermore, crowd counting is extendable to other domains, for instance, counting cells or bacteria from microscopic images [17,27], animal crowd estimates in wildlife sanctuaries [2], or estimating the number of vehicles at transportation hubs or traffic jams [19].

In this paper, we propose a novel approach to crowd counting, density map estimation and localization of people in a given crowd image. Our approach stems from the observation that these three problems are very interrelated - in fact, they can be decomposed with respect to each other. Counting provides an estimate of the number of people/objects without any information about their location. Density maps, which can be computed at multiple levels, provide weak information about location of each person. Localization does provide accurate location information, nevertheless, it is extremely difficult to estimate directly due to its very sparse nature. Therefore, we propose to estimate all three tasks simultaneously, while employing the fact that each is special case of another one. Density maps can be 'sharpened' till they approximate the localization map, whose integral should equal to the true count.

Furthermore, we introduce a new and the largest dataset to-date for training and evaluating **dense** crowd counting, density map estimation and localiza-

Table 1. Summary of statistics of different datasets. UCF_CC_50 (44 MB); World-Expo'10 (325 MB); ShanghaiTech_A (67 MB); and the proposed UCF-QNRF Dataset (4.33 GB).

Dataset	Number images	Number annotations	Average count	Maximum count	Average resolution	Average density
UCF_CC_50 [12]	50	63,974	1279	4633	2101 × 2888	2.02×10^{-4}
WorldExpo'10 [29]	3980	225,216	56	334	576 × 720	1.36×10^{-4}
ShanghaiTech_A [30]	482	241,677	501	3139	589 × 868	9.33×10^{-4}
UCF-QNRF	**1535**	**1,251,642**	**815**	**12865**	**2013 × 2902**	1.12×10^{-4}

tion methods, particularly suitable for training very deep Convolutional Neural Networks (CNNs). Though counting has traditionally been considered the primary focus of research, density map estimation and localization have significance and utility beyond counting. In particular, two applications are noteworthy: initialization/detection of people for tracking in dense crowds [13]; and rectifying counting errors from an automated computer vision algorithm. That is, a real user or analyst who desires to estimate the exact count for a real image *without any error*, the results of counting alone are insufficient. The single number for an entire image makes it difficult to assess the error or the source of the error. However, the localization can provide an initial set of dot locations of the individuals, the user then can quickly go through the image and remove the false positives and add the false negatives. The count using such an approach will be much more accurate and the user can get 100% precise count for the query image. This is particularly important when the number of image samples are few, and reliable counts are desired.

Prior to 2013, much of the work in crowd counting focused on low-density scenarios. For instance, UCSD dataset [4] contains 2,000 video frames with 49,885 annotated persons. The dataset is low density and low resolution compared to many recent datasets, where train and test splits belong to a single scene. World-Expo'10 dataset [29], contains 108 low-to-medium density scenes and overcomes the issue of diversity to some extent. UCF dataset [12] contains 50 different images with counts ranging between 96 and 4,633 per image. Each image has a different resolution, camera angle, and crowd density. Although it was the first dataset for dense crowd images, it has problems with annotations (Fig. 1) due to limited availability of high-resolution crowd images at the time. The ShanghaiTech crowd dataset [30] contains 1,198 annotated images with a total of 330,165 annotations. This dataset is divided into two parts: Part A contains 482 images and Part B with 716 images. The number of training images are 300 and 400 in both parts, respectively. Only the images in Part A contain high-density crowds, with 482 images and 250K annotations.

Table 1 summarizes the statistics of the multi-scene datasets for dense crowd counting. The proposed UCF-QNRF dataset has the most number of high-count crowd images and annotations, and a wider variety of scenes containing the most diverse set of viewpoints, densities and lighting variations. The resolution

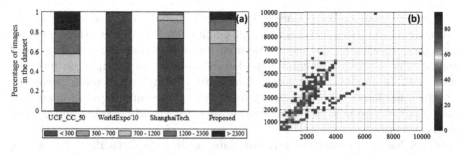

Fig. 2. (a) This graph shows the relative distribution of image counts among the four datasets. The proposed UCF-QNRF dataset has a fair number of images from all five count ranges. (b) This graph shows a 2D histogram of image resolution for all the images in the new dataset. The x-axis shows the number of rows, while y-axis is the number of columns. Each bin (500 × 500 pixels) is color-coded with the number of images that have the corresponding resolution. (Color figure online)

is large compared to WorldExpo'10 [29] and ShanghaiTech [30], as can be seen in Fig. 2(b). The average density, i.e., the number of people per pixel over all images is also the lowest, signifying high-quality large images. Lower per-pixel density is partly due to inclusion of background regions, where there are many high-density regions as well as zero-density regions. Part A of Shanghai dataset has high-count crowd images as well, however, they are severely cropped to contain crowds only. On the other hand, the new UCF-QNRF dataset contains buildings, vegetation, sky and roads as they are present in realistic scenarios captured in the wild. This makes this dataset more realistic as well as difficult. Similarly, Fig. 2(a) shows the diversity in counts among the datasets. The distribution of proposed dataset is similar to UCF_CC_50 [12], however, the new dataset is 30 and 20 times larger in terms of number of images and annotations, respectively, compared to UCF_CC_50 [12]. We hope the new dataset will significantly increase research activity in visual crowd analysis and will pave way for building deployable practical counting and localization systems for dense crowds.

The rest of the paper is organized as follows. In Sect. 2 we review related work, and present the proposed approach for simultaneous crowd counting, density map estimation and localization in Sect. 3. The process for collection and annotation of the UCF-QNRF dataset is covered in Sect. 4, while the three tasks and evaluation measures are motivated in Sect. 5. The experimental evaluation and comparison are presented in Sect. 6. We conclude with suggestions for future work in Sect. 7.

2   Related Work

Crowd counting is active an area of research with works tackling the three aspects of the problem: counting-by-regression [4,12,17,23,28], density map estimation [7,17,20,29,30] and localization [18,22].

Earlier regression-based approaches mapped global image features or a combination of local patch features to obtain counts [5, 6, 12, 15]. Since these methods only produce counts, they cannot be used for density map estimation or localization. The features were hand-crafted and in some cases multiple features were used [4, 12] to handle low resolution, perspective distortion and severe occlusion. On the other hand, CNNs inherently learn multiple feature maps automatically, and therefore are now being extensively used for crowd counting and density map estimation.

CNN based approaches for crowd counting include [2, 16, 19, 29, 30]. Zhang et al. [29] train a CNN alternatively to predict density map and count in a patch, and then average the density map for all the overlapping patches to obtain density map for the entire image. Lebanoff and Idrees [16] introduce a normalized variant of the Euclidean loss function in a deep network to achieve consistent counting performance across all densities. The authors in [30] use three column CNN, each with different filter sizes to capture responses at different scales. The count for the image is obtained by summing over the predicted density map. Sindagi and Patel [26] presented a CNN-based approach that incorporates global and local contextual information in an image to generate density maps. The global and local contexts are obtained by learning to classify the input image patches into various density levels, later fused with the output of a multi-column CNN to obtain the final density map. Similarly, in the approach by Sam et al. [24], image patches are relayed to the appropriate CNN using a switching mechanism learnt during training. The independent CNN regressors are designed to have different receptive fields while the switch classifier is trained to relay the crowd scene patch to the best CNN regressor.

For localization in crowded scenes, Rodriguez et al. [22] use density map as a regularizer during the detection. They optimize an objective function that prefers density map generated on detected locations to be similar to predicted density map [17]. This results in both better precision and recall. The density map is generated by placing a Gaussian kernel at the location of each detection. Ma et al. [18] first obtain density map using sliding window over the image through [17], and then use integer programming to localize objects on the density maps. Similarly, in the domain of medical imaging, Sirinukunwattana et al. [27] introduced spatially-constrained CNNs for detection and classification of cancer nuclei. In this paper, we present results and analysis for simultaneous crowd counting, density map estimation, and localization using Composition Loss on the proposed UCF-QNRF dataset.

3   Deep CNN with Composition Loss

In this section, we present the motivation for decomposing the loss of three interrelated problems of counting, density map estimation and localization, followed by details about the deep Convolutional Neural Network which can enable training and estimation of the three tasks simultaneously.

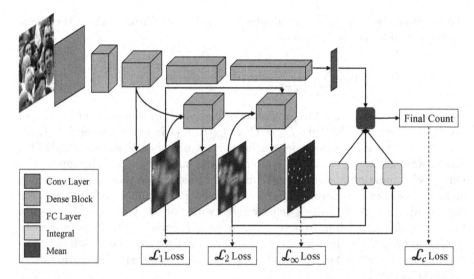

Fig. 3. The figure shows the proposed architecture for estimating count, density and localization maps simultaneously for a given patch in an image. At the top is the base DenseNet which regresses only the counts. The proposed Composition Loss is implemented through multiple dense blocks after branching off the base network. We also test the effect of additional constraint on the density and localization maps (shown with amber and orange blocks) such that the count after integral in each should also be consistent with the groundtruth count. (Color figure online)

3.1 Composition Loss

Let $\mathbf{x} = [x, y]$ denote a pixel location in a given image, and N be the number of people annotated with $\{\mathbf{x}_i : i = 1, 2, \ldots N\}$ as their respective locations. Dense crowds typically depict heads of people as they are the only parts least occluded and mostly visible. In localization maps, only a single pixel is activated, i.e., set to 1 per head, while all other pixels are set to 0. This makes localization maps extremely sparse and therefore difficult to train and estimate. We observe that successive computation of 'sharper' density maps which are relatively easier to train can aid in localization as well. Moreover, all three tasks should influence count, which is the integral over density or localization map. We use the Gaussian Kernel and adapt it for our problem of simultaneous solution for the three tasks.

Due to perspective effect and possibly variable density of the crowd, a single value of bandwidth, σ, cannot be used for the Gaussian kernel, as it might lead to well-defined separation between people close to the camera or in regions of low density, while excess blurring in other regions. Many images of dense crowds depict crowds in their entirety, making automatic perspective rectification difficult. Thus, we propose to define σ_i for each person i as the minimum of the ℓ_2 distance to its nearest neighbor in spatial domain of the image or some maximum threshold, τ. This ensures that the location information of each person is preserved precisely irrespective of default kernel bandwidth, τ. Thus, the adaptive Gaussian kernel is given by,

$$D(\mathbf{x},\ f(\cdot)) = \sum_{i=1}^{N} \frac{1}{\sqrt{2\pi}f(\sigma_i)}\exp\left(-\frac{(x-x_i)^2 + (y-y_i)^2}{2f(\sigma_i)^2}\right), \tag{1}$$

where the function f is used to produce a successive set of 'sharper' density maps. We define $f_k(\sigma) = \sigma^{1/k}$. Thus, $D_k = D(\mathbf{x}, f_k(\cdot))$. As can be seen when $k = 1$, D_k is a very smoothed-out density map using nearest-neighbor dependent bandwidth and τ, whereas as $k \longrightarrow \infty$, D_k approaches the binary localization map with a Dirac Delta function placed at each annotated pixel. Since each pixel has a unit area, the localization map assumes a unit value at the annotated location. For our experiments we used three density levels with last one being the localization map. It is also interesting to note that the various connections between density levels and base CNN also serve to provide intermediate supervision which aid in training the filters of base CNN towards counting and density estimation early on in the network.

Hypothetically, since integral over each estimated $\hat{D}_k$ yields a count for that density level, the final count can be obtained by taking the mean of counts from the density and localization maps as well as regression output from base CNN. This has two potential advantages: (1) the final count relies on multiple sources - each capturing count at a different scale. (2) During training the mean of four counts should equal the true count, which implicitly enforces an additional constraint that $\hat{D}_k$ should not only capture the density and localization information, but that each of their counts should also sum to the groundtruth count. For training, the loss function of density and localization maps is the mean square error between the predicted and ground truth maps, i.e. $L_k = \text{MSE}(\hat{D}_k, D_k)$, where $k = 1, 2$, and ∞, and regression loss, L_c, is Euclidean loss between predicted and groundtruth counts, while the final loss is defined as the weighted mean all four losses.

3.2   DenseNet with Composition Loss

We use DenseNet [10] as our base network. It consists of 4 Dense blocks where each block has a number of consecutive 1×1 and 3×3 convolutional layers. Each dense block (except for the last one) is followed by a Transition layer, which reduces the number of feature-maps by applying 1×1 convolutions followed by 2×2 average pooling with stride 2. In our experiments we used DenseNet-201 architecture. It has

Table 2. This table shows the filter dimensions and output of the three density layer blocks appended to the network in Fig. 3.

Layer	Output size	Filters
Density level 1	$512 \times 28 \times 28$	
	$1 \times 28 \times 28$	1×1 conv
Density level 2	$641 \times 28 \times 28$	$\begin{bmatrix} 1 \times 1 \text{ conv} \\ 3 \times 3 \text{ conv} \end{bmatrix} \times 4$
	$1 \times 28 \times 28$	1×1 conv
Density level ∞	$771 \times 28 \times 28$	$\begin{bmatrix} 1 \times 1 \text{ conv} \\ 3 \times 3 \text{ conv} \end{bmatrix} \times 4$
	$1 \times 28 \times 28$	1×1 conv

$\{6, 12, 48, 32\}$ sets of 1×1 and 3×3 convolutional layers in the four dense blocks, respectively.

For density map estimation and localization, we branch out from Dense-Block2 and feed it to our Density Network (see Table 2). The density network introduces 2 new dense blocks and three 1×1 convolutional layers. Each dense block has features computed at the previous step, concatenated with all the density levels predicted thus far as input, and learns features aimed at computing the current density/localization map. We used 1×1 convolutions to get the output density map from these features. Density Level 1 is computed directly from DenseBlock2 features.

We used Adam solver with a step learning rate in all our experiments. We used 0.001 as initial learning rate and reduce the learning rate by a factor of 2 after every 20 epochs. We trained the entire network for 70 epoch with a batch size of 16.

4   The UCF-QNRF Dataset

Dataset Collection. The images for the dataset were collected from three sources: Flickr, Web Search and the Hajj footage. The Hajj images were carefully selected so that there are multiple images that capture different locations, viewpoints, perspective effects and times of the day. For Flickr and Web Search, we manually generated the following queries: CROWD, HAJJ, SPECTATOR CROWD, PILGRIMAGE, PROTEST CROWD and CONCERT CROWD. These queries were then passed onto the Flickr and Google Image Search APIs. We selected desired number of images for each query to be 2000 for Flickr and 200 for Google Image Search. The search sorted all the results by RELEVANCE incorporating both titles and tags, and for Flickr we also ensured that only those images were downloaded for which original resolutions were permitted to be downloaded (through the URL_O specifier). The static links to all the images were extracted and saved for all the query terms, which were then downloaded using the respective APIs. The images were also checked for duplicates by computing image similarities followed by manual verification and discarding of duplicates.

Initial Pruning. The initial set of images were then manually checked for desirability. Many of the images were pruned due to one or more of the following reasons:

- Scenes that did not depict crowds at all or low-density crowds
- Objects or visualizations of objects other than humans
- Motion blur or low resolution
- Very high perspective effect that is camera height is similar to average human height
- Images with watermarks or those where text occupied more than 10% of the image.

In high-density crowd images, it is mostly the heads that are visible. However, people who appear far away from the camera become indistinguishable beyond a certain distance, which depends on crowd density, lighting as well as resolution of the camera sensor. During pruning, we kept those images where the heads were separable visually. Such images were annotated with the others, however, they were cropped afterwards to ensure that regions with problematic annotations or those with none at all due to difficulty in recognizing human heads were discarded.

We performed the entire annotation process in two stages. In the first stage, un-annotated images were given to the *annotators*, while in the second stage, the images were given to *verifiers* who corrected any mistakes or errors in annotations. There were 14 annotators and 4 verifiers, who clocked $1,300$ and $200\,h$ respectively. In total, the entire procedure involved $2,000$ human-hours spent through to its completion.

Statistics. The dataset has $1,535$ jpeg images with $1,251,642$ annotations. The train and test sets were created by sorting the images with respect to absolute counts, and selecting every 5th image into the test set. Thus, the training and test set consist of 1201 and 334 images, respectively. The distribution of images from [Flickr, Web, Hajj] for the train and test are [1078, 84, 39] and [306, 21, 7], respectively. In the dataset, the minimum and maximum counts are 49 and $12,865$, respectively, whereas the median and mean counts are 425 and 815.4, respectively.

5   Definition and Quantification of Tasks

In this section, we define the three tasks and the associated quantification measures.

Counting: The first task involves estimation of count for a crowd image i, given by c_i. Although this measure does not give any information about location or distribution of people in the image, this is still very useful for many applications, for instance, estimating size of an entire crowd spanning several square kilometers or miles. For the application of counting large crowds, Jacob's Method [14] due to Herbert Jacob is typically employed which involves dividing the area $\mathbf{A}$ into smaller sections, finding the average number of people or density $\mathbf{d}$ in each section, computing the mean density $\bar{\mathbf{d}}$ and extrapolating the results to entire region. However, with automated crowd counting, it is now possible to obtain counts and density for multiple images at different locations, thereby, permitting the more accurate integration of density over entire area covered by crowd. Moreover, counting through multiple aerial images requires cartographic tools to map the images onto the earth to compute ground areas. The density here is defined as the number of people in the image divided by ground area covered by the image. We propose to use the same evaluation measures as used in literature for this task: the Mean Absolute Error (C-MAE), Mean Squared Error (C-MSE) with the addition of Normalized Absolute Error (C-NAE).

Density Map Estimation amounts to computing per-pixel density at each location in the image, thus preserving spatial information about distribution of people. This is particularly relevant for safety and surveillance, since very high density at a particular location in the scene can be catastrophic [1]. This is different from counting since an image can have counts within safe limits, while containing regions that have very high density. This can happen due to the presence of empty regions in the image, such as walls and sky for mounted cameras; and roads, vehicles, buildings and forestation in aerial cameras. The metrics for evaluating density map estimation are similar to counting, except that they are per-pixel, i.e., the per-pixel Mean Absolute Error (DM-MAE) and Mean Squared Error (DM-MSE). Finally, we also propose to compute the 2D Histogram Intersection (DM-HI) distance after normalizing both the groundtruth and estimated density maps. This discards the effect of absolute counts and emphasizes the error in distribution of density compared to the groundtruth.

Localization: The ideal approach to crowd counting would be to detect all the people in an image and then count the number of detections. But since dense crowd images contain severe occlusions among individuals and fewer pixels per person for those away from the camera, this is not a feasible solution. This is why, most approaches to crowd counting bypass explicit detection and perform direct regression on input images. However, for many applications, the precise location of individuals is needed, for instance, to initialize a tracking algorithm in very high-density crowd videos.

To quantify the localization error, estimated locations are associated with the ground truth locations through 1–1 matching using greedy association, followed by computation of Precision and Recall at various distance thresholds $(1, 2, 3, \ldots, 100$ pixels$)$. The overall performance of the localization task is then computed through area under the Precision-Recall curve, L-AUC.

6   Experiments

Next, we present the results of experiments for the three tasks defined in Sect. 5.

6.1   Counting

For counting, we evaluated the new UCF-QNRF dataset using the proposed method which estimates counts, density maps and locations of people simultaneously with several state-of-the-art deep neural networks [3,8,10] as well as those specifically developed for crowd counting [24, 25,30]. To train the networks, we extracted patches of sizes 448, 224 and 112 pixels at random locations from each training image. While

Table 3. We show counting results obtained using state-of-the-art methods in comparison with the proposed approach. Methods with '*' regress counts without computing density maps.

Method	C-MAE	C-NAE	C-MSE
Idrees *et al.* [12]*	315	0.63	508
MCNN [30]	277	0.55	426
Encoder-Decoder [3]	270	0.56	478
CMTL [25]	252	0.54	514
SwitchCNN [24]	228	0.44	445
Resnet101 [8]*	190	0.50	277
Densenet201 [10]*	163	0.40	226
Proposed	**132**	**0.26**	**191**

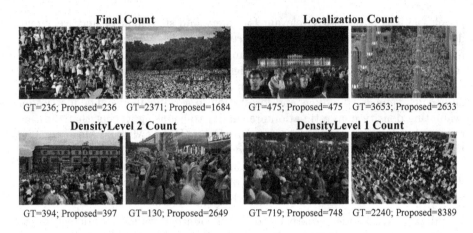

Fig. 4. This figure shows pairs of images where the left image in the pair has the lowest counting error while the right image has the highest counting error with respect to the four components of the Composition Loss.

deciding on image locations to extract patch from, we assigned higher probability of selection to image regions with higher count. We used mean square error of counts as the loss function. At test time, we divide the image into a grid of 224×224 pixel cells - zero-padding the image for dimensions not divisible by 224 - and evaluate each cell using the trained network. Final image count is given by aggregating the counts in all cells. Table 3 summarizes the results which shows the proposed network significantly outperforms the competing deep CNNs and crowd counting approaches. In Fig. 4, we show the images with the lowest and highest error in the test set, for counts obtained through different components of the Composition Loss.

6.2 Density Map Estimation

For density map estimation, we describe and compare the proposed approach with several methods that directly regress crowd density during training. Among the deep learning methods, MCNN [30] consists of three columns of convolution networks with different filter sizes to capture

Table 4. Results for density map estimation: we show results on histogram intersection (HI), obtained using existing state-of-the-art methods compared to the proposed approach.

Method	DM-MAE	DM-MSE	DM-HI	DM-SSIM
MCNN [30]	0.006670	0.0223	0.5354	0.7270
SwitchCNN [24]	0.005673	0.0263	0.5301	0.7518
CMTL [25]	0.005932	0.0244	0.5024	0.6019
Proposed	**0.00044**	**0.0017**	**0.9131**	**0.4068**

different head sizes and combines the output of all the columns to make a final density estimate. SwitchCNN [24] uses a similar three column network; however, it also employs a switching network that decides which column should exclusively handle the input patch. CMTL [25] employs a multi-task network that computes a high level prior over the image patch (crowd count classification) and density estimation. These networks are specifically designed for crowd density estimation and their results are reported in first three rows of Table 4. The results of proposed approach are shown in the bottom row of Table 4. The proposed approach outperforms existing approaches by an order of magnitude.

6.3   Localization

For the localization task, we adopt the same network configurations used for density map estimation to perform localization. To get the accurate head locations, we post-process the outputs by finding the local peaks/maximums based on a threshold, also known as non-maximal suppression. Once the peaks are found, we match the predicted location with the ground truth location using 1–1 matching, and compute precision and recall. We use different distance thresholds as the pixel distance, i.e., if the detection is within the a particular distance threshold of the groundtruth, it is treated as True Positive, otherwise it is a False Positive. Similarly, if there is no detection within a groundtruth location, it becomes a False Negative.

The results of localization are reported in Table 5. This table shows that DenseNet [10] and Encoder-Decoder [3] outperform ResNet [8] and MCNN [30], while the proposed approach is superior to all the compared methods. The performance on the localization task is dependent on post-processing, which can alter results. Therefore, finding optimal strategy for localization from neural network output or incorporating the post-processing into the network is an important direction for future research. We also show some qualitative results of localization in Fig. 5. The red dots represent the groundtruth while yellow circles are the locations estimated by the our approach.

6.4   Ablation Study

We performed an ablation study to validate the efficacy of composition loss introduced in this paper, as well as various choices in designing the network.

Table 5. This table shows the localization results averaged over four distance thresholds for different methods. We show Average Precision, Average Recall and AUC metrics.

Method	Av. Precision	Av. Recall	L-AUC
MCNN [30]	59.93%	63.50%	0.591
ResNet74 [8]	61.60%	66.90%	0.612
DenseNet63 [10]	70.19%	58.10%	0.637
Encoder-Decoder [3]	71.80%	62.98%	0.670
Proposed	**75.8%**	**59.75%**	**0.714**

Fig. 5. Two examples of localization using the proposed approach. Ground truth is depicted in red and predicted locations after threshold are shown in yellow. (Color figure online)

Table 6. This table shows the results of ablation study. D_∞ corresponds to the results of counting using localization map estimation, while D_2 and D_1 represent results from the two density maps, respectively.

Experiment	Count			D_∞			D_2			D_1		
	MAE	MSE	NAE	MAE	MSE	NAE	MAE	MSE	NAE	MAE	MSE	NAE
BaseNetwork	163	227	0.395	–	–	–	–	–	–	–	–	–
DenseBlock4	148	265	0.385	382	765	0.956	879	1235	3.892	2015	4529	4.295
DenseBlock3	144	236	0.363	295	687	0.721	805	1159	3.256	1273	2936	3.982
D_1 only	141	233	0.261	–	–	–	–	–	–	1706	2496	5.677
D_1 & D_2 only	137	208	0.251	–	–	–	691	1058	2.459	1887	3541	6.850
Concatenate	139	223	0.264	258	508	0.634	718	1096	3.570	1910	4983	6.574
Mean	150	341	0.271	405	710	1.135	1015	2099	2.916	1151	3170	3.283
Proposed	132	191	0.258	236	408	0.506	682	922	2.027	1629	3600	4.396

These results are shown in Table 6. Next, we describe and provide details for the experiment corresponding to each row in the table.

BaseNetwork: This row shows the results with base network of our choice, which is DenseNet201. A fully-connected layer is appended to the last layer of the network followed by a single neuron which outputs the count. The input patch size is 224 × 224.

DenseBlock4: This experiment studies the effect of connecting the Density Network (Table 2) containing the different density levels with DenseBlock4 of the base DenseNet instead of DenseBlock2. Since DenseBlock4 outputs feature maps of size 7 × 7, we therefore used deconvolution layer with stride 4 to upsample the features before feeding in to our Density Network.

DenseBlock3: This experiment is similar to **DenseBlock4**, except that we connect our Density Network to Denseblock3 of the base network. DenseBlock3 outputs feature maps which are 14×14 in spatial dimensions, whereas we intend to predict density maps of spatial dimension 28×28, so we upsample the feature maps by using deconvolution layer before feeding them to the proposed Density Network.

D_1 **only:** This row represents the results if we use Density Level 1 only in the Density Network along with regression of counts in the base network. The results are much worse compared to the proposed method which uses multiple levels in the Composition Loss.

D_1 **and** D_2 **only:** Similar to D_1 **only**, this row represents the results if we use Density Levels 1 and 2 and do not use the D_∞ in the Density Network. Incorporation of another density level improves results slightly in contrast to a single density level.

Concatenate: Here, we take the sum of the two density and one localization map to obtain 3 counts. We then concatenate these counts to the output of fully-connected layer of the base network to predict count from the single neuron. Thus, we leave to the optimization algorithm to find appropriate weights for these 3 values along with the rest of 1920 features of the fully-connected layer.

Mean: We also tested the effect of using equal weights for counts obtained from the base network and three density levels. We take sum of each density/localization map and take the mean of 4 values (2 density map sums, one localization sum, and one count from base network). We treat this mean value as final count output - both during training and testing. Thus, this imposes the constraint that not only the density and localization map correctly predict the location of people, but also their counts should be consistent with groundtruth counts irrespective of predicted locations.

Proposed: In this experiment, the Density Network is connected with the DenseBlock2 of base network, however, the Density Network simply outputs two density and one localization maps, none of which are connected to count output (see Fig. 3).

In summary, these results show that the Density Network contributes significantly to performance on the three tasks. It is better to branch out from the middle layers of the base network, nevertheless the idea of multiple connections back and forth from the base network and Density Network is an interesting direction for further research. Furthermore, enforcing counts from all sources to be equal to the groundtruth count slightly worsens the counting performance. Nevertheless, it does help in estimating better density and localization maps. Finally, the decrease in error rates from the right to left in Table 6 highlights the positive influence of the proposed Composition Loss.

7   Conclusion

This paper introduced a novel method to estimate counts, density maps and localization in dense crowd images. We showed that these three problems are interrelated, and can be decomposed with respect to each other through Composition Loss which can then be used to train a neural network. We solved the three tasks simultaneously with the counting performance benefiting from the density map estimation and localization as well. We also proposed the large-scale UCF-QNRF dataset for dense crowds suitable for the three tasks described in the paper. We provided details of the process of dataset collection and annotation, where we ensured that only high-resolution images were curated for the dataset. Finally, we presented extensive set of experiments using several recent deep architectures, and show how the proposed approach is able to achieve good performance through detailed ablation study. We hope the new dataset will prove useful for this type of research, with applications in safety and surveillance, design and expansion of public infrastructures, and gauging political significance of various crowd events.

Acknowledgment. This work was made possible in part by NPRP grant number NPRP 7-1711-1-312 from the Qatar National Research Fund (a member of Qatar Foundation). The statements made herein are solely the responsibility of the authors.

References

1. A history of hajj tragedies. The Guardian (2006). http://www.guardian.co.uk/world/2006/jan/13/saudiarabia. Accessed 1 July 2013
2. Arteta, C., Lempitsky, V., Zisserman, A.: Counting in the wild. In: Leibe, B., Matas, J., Sebe, N., Welling, M. (eds.) ECCV 2016. LNCS, vol. 9911, pp. 483–498. Springer, Cham (2016). https://doi.org/10.1007/978-3-319-46478-7_30
3. Badrinarayanan, V., Kendall, A., Cipolla, R.: SegNet: a deep convolutional encoder-decoder architecture for image segmentation. arXiv preprint arXiv:1511.00561 (2015)
4. Chan, A., Liang, Z., Vasconcelos, N.: Privacy preserving crowd monitoring: counting people without people models or tracking. In: CVPR (2008)
5. Chen, K., Loy, C., Gong, S., Xiang, T.: Feature mining for localised crowd counting. In: BMVC (2012)
6. Chen, K., Gong, S., Xiang, T., Change Loy, C.: Cumulative attribute space for age and crowd density estimation. In: Proceedings of the IEEE Conference on Computer Vision and Pattern Recognition, pp. 2467–2474 (2013)
7. Fiaschi, L., Köthe, U., Nair, R., Hamprecht, F.A.: Learning to count with regression forest and structured labels. In: 2012 21st International Conference on Pattern Recognition (ICPR). IEEE (2012)
8. He, K., Zhang, X., Ren, S., Sun, J.: Deep residual learning for image recognition. In: Proceedings of the IEEE Conference on Computer Vision and Pattern Recognition, pp. 770–778 (2016)
9. Helbing, D., Mukerji, P.: Crowd disasters as systemic failures: analysis of the love parade disaster. EPJ Data Sci. **1**(1), 1–40 (2012)
10. Huang, G., Liu, Z., Weinberger, K.Q., van der Maaten, L.: Densely connected convolutional networks. arXiv preprint arXiv:1608.06993 (2016)
11. Hyde, D.C.: Two systems of non-symbolic numerical cognition. Front. Hum. Neurosci. **5**, 150 (2011)

12. Idrees, H., Saleemi, I., Seibert, C., Shah, M.: Multi-source multi-scale counting in extremely dense crowd images. In: Proceedings of the IEEE Conference on Computer Vision and Pattern Recognition (2013)
13. Idrees, H., Warner, N., Shah, M.: Tracking in dense crowds using prominence and neighborhood motion concurrence. Image Vis. Comput. **32**(1), 14–26 (2014)
14. Jacobs, H.: To count a crowd. Columbia J. Rev. **6**, 36–40 (1967)
15. Kong, D., Gray, D., Tao, H.: A viewpoint invariant approach for crowd counting. In: 2006 18th International Conference on Pattern Recognition, ICPR 2006, vol. 3, pp. 1187–1190. IEEE (2006)
16. Lebanoff, L., Idrees, H.: Counting in dense crowds using deep learning (2015)
17. Lempitsky, V., Zisserman, A.: Learning to count objects in images. In: NIPS (2010)
18. Ma, Z., Yu, L., Chan, A.B.: Small instance detection by integer programming on object density maps. In: CVPR (2015)
19. Oñoro-Rubio, D., López-Sastre, R.J.: Towards perspective-free object counting with deep learning. In: Leibe, B., Matas, J., Sebe, N., Welling, M. (eds.) ECCV 2016. LNCS, vol. 9911, pp. 615–629. Springer, Cham (2016). https://doi.org/10.1007/978-3-319-46478-7_38
20. Pham, V.Q., Kozakaya, T., Yamaguchi, O., Okada, R.: COUNT forest: co-voting uncertain number of targets using random forest for crowd density estimation. In: Proceedings of the IEEE International Conference on Computer Vision (2015)
21. Piazza, M., Mechelli, A., Butterworth, B., Price, C.J.: Are subitizing and counting implemented as separate or functionally overlapping processes? Neuroimage **15**(2), 435–446 (2002)
22. Rodriguez, M., Sivic, J., Laptev, I., Audibert, J.Y.: Density-aware person detection and tracking in crowds. In: ICCV (2011)
23. Ryan, D., Denman, S., Fookes, C., Sridharan, S.: Crowd counting using multiple local features. In: 2009 Digital Image Computing: Techniques and Applications, DICTA 2009 (2009)
24. Sam, D.B., Surya, S., Babu, R.V.: Switching convolutional neural network for crowd counting. In: Proceedings of the IEEE Conference on Computer Vision and Pattern Recognition, vol. 1, no. 3, p. 6 (2017)
25. Sindagi, V.A., Patel, V.M.: CNN-based cascaded multi-task learning of high-level prior and density estimation for crowd counting. In: 2017 14th IEEE International Conference on Advanced Video and Signal Based Surveillance (AVSS), pp. 1–6. IEEE (2017)
26. Sindagi, V.A., Patel, V.M.: Generating high-quality crowd density maps using contextual pyramid CNNs. In: IEEE International Conference on Computer Vision (2017)
27. Sirinukunwattana, K., Raza, S.E.A., Tsang, Y.W., Snead, D.R., Cree, I.A., Rajpoot, N.M.: Locality sensitive deep learning for detection and classification of nuclei in routine colon cancer histology images. IEEE Trans. Med. Imaging **35**(5), 1196–1206 (2016)
28. Wang, C., Zhang, H., Yang, L., Liu, S., Cao, X.: Deep people counting in extremely dense crowds. In: Proceedings of the 23rd ACM International Conference on Multimedia. ACM (2015)
29. Zhang, C., Li, H., Wang, X., Yang, X.: Cross-scene crowd counting via deep convolutional neural networks. In: Proceedings of the IEEE Conference on Computer Vision and Pattern Recognition (2015)
30. Zhang, Y., Zhou, D., Chen, S., Gao, S., Ma, Y.: Single-image crowd counting via multi-column convolutional neural network. In: Proceedings of the IEEE Conference on Computer Vision and Pattern Recognition (2016)

Where Are the Blobs: Counting by Localization with Point Supervision

Issam H. Laradji[1,2(✉)], Negar Rostamzadeh[1], Pedro O. Pinheiro[1], David Vazquez[1], and Mark Schmidt[1,2]

[1] Element AI, Montreal, Canada
{negar,pedro,dvazquez}@elementai.com
[2] Department of Computer Science, University of British Columbia, Vancouver, Canada
{issamou,schmidtm}@cs.ubc.ca

Abstract. Object counting is an important task in computer vision due to its growing demand in applications such as surveillance, traffic monitoring, and counting everyday objects. State-of-the-art methods use regression-based optimization where they explicitly learn to count the objects of interest. These often perform better than detection-based methods that need to learn the more difficult task of predicting the location, size, and shape of each object. However, we propose a detection-based method that does not need to estimate the size and shape of the objects and that outperforms regression-based methods. Our contributions are three-fold: (1) we propose a novel loss function that encourages the network to output a single blob per object instance using point-level annotations only; (2) we design two methods for splitting large predicted blobs between object instances; and (3) we show that our method achieves new state-of-the-art results on several challenging datasets including the Pascal VOC and the Penguins dataset. Our method even outperforms those that use stronger supervision such as depth features, multi-point annotations, and bounding-box labels.

1 Introduction

Object counting is an important task in computer vision with many applications in surveillance systems [3,4], traffic monitoring [5,6], ecological surveys [1], and cell counting [7,8]. In traffic monitoring, counting methods can be used to track the number of moving cars, pedestrians, and parked cars. They can also be used to monitor the count of different species such as penguins, which is important for animal conservation. Furthermore, it has been used for counting objects present in everyday scenes in challenging datasets where the objects of interest come from a large number of classes such as the Pascal VOC dataset [2].

Many challenges are associated with object counting. Models need to learn the variability of the objects in terms of shape, size, pose, and appearance. Moreover, objects may appear at different angles and resolutions, and may be partially occluded (see Fig. 1). Also, the background, weather conditions, and

© Springer Nature Switzerland AG 2018
V. Ferrari et al. (Eds.): ECCV 2018, LNCS 11206, pp. 560–576, 2018.
https://doi.org/10.1007/978-3-030-01216-8_34

Fig. 1. Qualitative results on the Penguins [1] and PASCAL VOC datasets [2]. Our method explicitly learns to localize object instances using only point-level annotations. The trained model then outputs blobs where each unique color represents a predicted object of interest. Note that the predicted count is simply the number of predicted blobs. (Color figure online)

illuminations can vary widely across the scenes. Therefore, the model needs to be robust enough to recognize objects in the presence of these variations in order to perform efficient object counting.

Due to these challenges, regression-based models such as "glance" and object density estimators have consistently defined state-of-the-art results in object counting [9,10]. This is because their loss functions are directly optimized for predicting the object count. In contrast, detection-based methods need to optimize for the more difficult task of estimating the location, shape, and size of the object instances. Indeed, perfect detection implies perfect count as the count is simply the number of detected objects. However, models that learn to detect objects often lead to worse results for object counting [9]. For this reason, we look at an easier task than detection by focusing on the task of simply localizing object instances in the scene. Predicting the exact size and shape of the object instances is not necessary and usually poses a much more difficult optimization problem. Therefore, we propose a novel loss function that encourages the model to output instance regions such that each region contains a single object instance (i.e. a single point-level annotation). Similar to detection, the predicted count is the number of predicted instance regions (see Fig. 1). Our model only requires point supervision which is a weaker supervision than bounding-box, and per-pixel annotations used by most detection-based methods [11–13]. Consequently, we can train our model for most counting datasets as they often have point-level annotations.

This type of annotation is cheap to acquire as it requires lower human effort than bounding box and per-pixel annotations [14]. Point-level annotations provide a rough estimate of the object locations, but not their sizes nor shapes. Our counting method uses the provided point annotations to guide its attention to the object instances in the scenes in order to learn to localize them. As a result, our model has the flexibility to predict different sized regions for different object instances, which makes it suitable for counting objects that vary in size and shape. In contrast, state-of-the-art density-based estimators often assume a fixed object size (defined by the Gaussian kernel) or a constrained environment [6] which makes it difficult to count objects with different sizes and shapes.

Given only point-level annotations, our model uses a novel loss function that (i) enforces it to predict the semantic segmentation labels for each pixel in the image (similar to [14]) and (ii) encourages it to output a segmentation blob for each object instance. During the training phase, the model learns to split the blobs that contain more than one point annotation and to remove the blobs that contain no point-level annotations.

Our experiments show that our method achieves superior object counting results compared to state-of-the-art counting methods including those that use stronger supervision such as per-pixel labels. Our benchmark uses datasets representing different settings for object counting: Mall [15], UCSD [16], and ShangaiTech B [17] as crowd datasets; MIT Traffic [18], and Park lot [5] as surveillance datasets; Trancos [6] as a traffic monitoring dataset; and Penguins [1] as a population monitoring dataset. We also show counting results for the PASCAL VOC [2] dataset which consists of objects present in natural, 'everyday' images. We also study the effect of using different parts of the proposed loss function against counting and localization performance.

We summarize our contributions as follows: (1) we propose a novel loss function that encourages the network to output a single blob per object instance using point-level annotations only; (2) we design two methods for splitting large predicted blobs between object instances; and (3) we show that our method achieves new state-of-the-art results on several challenging datasets including the Pascal VOC and the Penguins dataset.

The rest of the paper is organized as follows: Sect. 2 presents related works on object counting; Sect. 3 describes the proposed approach; and Sect. 4 describes our experiments and results. Finally, we present the conclusion in Sect. 5.

2   Related Work

Object counting has received significant attention over the past years [8,9,19]. It can be roughly divided into three categories [20]: (1) counting by clustering, (2) counting by regression, and (3) counting by detection.

Early work in object counting use *clustering-based methods*. They are unsupervised approaches where objects are clustered based on features such as appearance and motion cues [19,21]. Rabaud and Belongie [19] proposed to use feature points which are detected by motion and appearance cues and are tracked through time using KLT [22]. The objects are then clustered based on similar features. Sebastian *et al.* [21] used an expectation-maximization method that cluster individuals in crowds based on head and shoulder features. These methods use basic features and often perform poorly for counting compared to deep learning approaches. Another drawback is that these methods only work for video sequences, rather than still images.

Counting by regression methods have defined state-of-the-art results in many benchmarks. They were shown to be faster and more accurate than other groups such as counting by detection. These methods include glance and density-based methods that explicitly learn how to count rather than optimize for a localization-based objective. Lempitsky *et al.* [8] proposed the first method that used object density to count people. They transform the point-level annotation matrix into a density map using a Gaussian kernel. Then, they train their model using a least-squares objective to predict the density map. One major challenge is determining the optimal size of the Gaussian kernel which highly depends on the object sizes. As a result, Zhang *et al.* [17] proposed a deep learning method that adjusted the kernel size using a perspective map. This assumes fixed camera images such as those used in surveillance applications. Onoro-Rubio *et al.* [10] extended this method by proposing a perspective-free multi-scale deep learning approach. However, this method cannot be used for counting everyday objects as their sizes vary widely across the scenes as it is highly sensitive to the kernel size.

A straight-forward method for counting by regression is 'glance' [9], which explicitly learns to count using image-level labels only. Glance methods are efficient if the object count is small [9]. Consequently, the authors proposed a grid-based counting method, denoted as "subitizing", in order to count a large number of objects in the image. This method uses glance to count objects at different non-overlapping regions of the image, independently. While glance is easy to train and only requires image-level annotation, the "subitizing" method requires a more complicated training procedure that needs full per-pixel annotation ground-truth.

Counting by detection methods first detect the objects of interest and then simply count the number of instances. Successful object detection methods rely on bounding boxes [11,12,23] and per-pixel labels [24–26] ground-truth. Perfect object detection implies perfect count. However, Chattopadhyay *et al.* [9] showed that Fast RCNN [27], a state-of-the-art object detection method, performs worse than glance and subitizing-based methods. This is because the detection task is challenging in that the model needs to learn the location, size, and shape of object instances that are possibly heavily occluded. While several works [8–10] suggest that counting by detection is infeasible for surveillance scenes where objects are often occluded, we show that learning a notion of localization can help the model improve counting.

Similar to our method is the line of work proposed by Arteta *et al.* [28–30]. They proposed a method that detects overlapping instances based on optimizing a tree-structured discrete graphical model. While their method showed promising detection results using point-level annotations only, it performed worse for counting than regression-based methods such as [8].

Our method is also similar to segmentation methods such as U-net [31] which learns to segment objects using a fully-convolutional neural network. Unlike our method, U-net requires the full per-pixel instance segmentation labels, whereas we use point-level annotations only.

3   Localization-Based Counting FCN

Our model is based on the fully convolutional neural network (FCN) proposed by Long *et al.* [24]. We extend their semantic segmentation loss to perform object counting and localization with point supervision. We denote the novel loss function as *localization-based counting loss* (LC) and, we refer to the proposed model as LC-FCN. Next, we describe the proposed loss function, the architecture of our model, and the prediction procedure.

3.1   The Proposed Loss Function

LC-FCN uses a novel loss function that consists of four distinct terms. The first two terms, the image-level and the point-level loss, enforces the model to predict the semantic segmentation labels for each pixel in the image. This is based on the weakly supervised semantic segmentation algorithm proposed by Bearman *et al.* [14]. These two terms alone are not suitable for object counting as the predicted blobs often group many object instances together (see the ablation studies in Sect. 4). The last two terms encourage the model to output a unique blob for each object instance and remove blobs that have no object instances. Note that LC-FCN only requires point-level annotations that indicate the locations of the objects rather than their sizes, and shapes.

Let T represent the point annotation ground-truth matrix which has label c at the location of each object (where c is the object class) and zero elsewhere. Our model uses a *softmax* function to output a matrix S where each entry S_{ic} is the probability that pixel i belongs to category c. The proposed loss function can be written as:

$$\mathcal{L}(S,T) = \underbrace{\mathcal{L}_I(S,T)}_{\text{Image-level loss}} + \underbrace{\mathcal{L}_P(S,T)}_{\text{Point-level loss}} + \underbrace{\mathcal{L}_S(S,T)}_{\text{Split-level loss}} + \underbrace{\mathcal{L}_F(S,T)}_{\text{False positive loss}} , \quad (1)$$

which we describe in detail next.

Image-Level Loss. Let C_e be the set of classes present in the image. For each class $c \in C_e$, $\mathcal{L}_I$ increases the probability that the model labels at least one pixel as class c. Also, let $C_{\neg e}$ be the set of classes not present in the image. For each class $c \in C_{\neg e}$, the loss decreases the probability that the model labels any pixel as class c. C_e and $C_{\neg e}$ can be obtained from the provided ground-truth point-level annotations. More formally, the image level loss is computed as follows:

$$\mathcal{L}_I(S,T) = -\frac{1}{|C_e|} \sum_{c \in C_e} \log(S_{t_c c}) - \frac{1}{|C_{\neg e}|} \sum_{c \in C_{\neg e}} \log(1 - S_{t_c c}) , \quad (2)$$

where $t_c = \text{argmax}_{i \in \mathcal{I}} S_{ic}$. For each category present in the image, at least one pixel should be labeled as that class. For classes that do not exist in the image, none of the pixels should belong to that class. Note that we assume that each image has at least one background pixel; therefore, the background class belongs to C_e.

Point-Level Loss. This term encourages the model to correctly label the small set of supervised pixels $\mathcal{I}_s$ contained in the ground-truth. $\mathcal{I}_s$ represents the locations of the object instances. This is formally defined as,

$$\mathcal{L}_P(S, T) = -\sum_{i \in \mathcal{I}_s} \log(S_{iT_i}) \, , \tag{3}$$

where T_i represents the true label of pixel i. Note that this loss ignores all the pixels that are not annotated.

Split-Level Loss. $\mathcal{L}_S$ discourages the model from predicting blobs that have two or more point-annotations. Therefore, if a blob has n point annotations, this loss enforces it to be split into n blobs, each corresponding to a unique object. These splits are made by first finding boundaries between object pairs. The model then learns to predict these boundaries as the background class. The model outputs a binary matrix $\mathcal{F}$ where pixel i is foreground if $\text{argmax}_k S_{ik} > 0$, and background, otherwise.

We apply the connected components algorithm proposed by [32] to find the blobs B in the foreground mask $\mathcal{F}$. We only consider the blobs with two or more ground truth point annotations $\bar{B}$. We propose two methods for splitting blobs (see Fig. 2),

1. *Line split method.* For each blob b in $\bar{B}$ we pair each point with its closest point resulting in a set of pairs b_P. For each pair $(p_i, p_j) \in b_P$ we use a scoring function to determine the best segment E that is perpendicular to the line between p_i and p_j. The segment lines are within the predicted blob and they intersect the blob boundaries. The scoring function $z(\cdot)$ for segment E is computed as,

$$z(E) = \frac{1}{|E|} \sum_{i \in E} S_{i0} \, , \tag{4}$$

which is the mean of the background probabilities belonging to segment E (where 0 is the background class). The best edge E_{best} is defined as the set of pixels representing the edge with the highest probability of being background among all the perpendicular lines. This determines the 'most likely' edge of separation between the two objects. Then we set T_b as the set of pixels representing the best edges generated by the line split method.

2. *Watershed split method.* This consists of global and local segmentation procedures. For the global segmentation, we apply the watershed segmentation algorithm [33] globally on the input image where we set the ground-truth point-annotations as the seeds. The segmentation is applied on the distance transform of the foreground probabilities, which results in k segments where k is the number of point-annotations in the image.

For the local segmentation procedure, we apply the watershed segmentation only within each blob b in $\bar{B}$ where we use the point-annotation ground-truth inside them as seeds. This adds more importance to splitting big blobs when computing the loss function. Finally, we define T_b as the set of pixels representing the boundaries determined by the local and global segmentation.

Predicted blobs   Line splits   Watershed splits

Fig. 2. Split methods. Comparison between the line split, and the watershed split. The loss function identifies the boundary splits (shown as yellow lines). Yellow blobs represent those with more than one object instance, and red blobs represent those that have no object instance. Green blobs are true positives. The squares represent the ground-truth point annotations. (Color figure online)

Figure 2 shows the split boundaries using the line split and the watershed split methods (as yellow lines). Given T_b, we compute the split loss as follows,

$$\mathcal{L}_S(S,T) = -\sum_{i \in T_b} \alpha_i \log(S_{i0}), \qquad (5)$$

where S_{i0} is the probability that pixel i belongs to the background class and α_i is the number of point-annotations in the blob in which pixel i lies. This encourages the model to focus on splitting blobs that have the most point-level annotations. The intuition behind this method is that learning to predict the boundaries between the object instances allows the model to distinguish between them. As a result, the penalty term encourages the model to output a single blob per object instance.

We emphasize that it is not necessary to get the right edges in order to accurately count. It is only necessary to make sure we have a positive region on each object and a negative region between objects. Other heuristics are possible to construct a negative region which could still be used in our framework. For example, fast label propagation methods proposed in [34,35] can be used to determine the boundaries between the objects in the image. Note that these 4 loss functions are only used during training. The framework does not split or remove false positive blobs at test time. The predictions are based purely on the blobs obtained from the probability matrix S.

False Positive Loss. $\mathcal{L}_F$ discourages the model from predicting a blob with no point annotations, in order to reduce the number of false positive predictions. The loss function is defined as

$$\mathcal{L}_F(S,T) = -\sum_{i \in B_{fp}} \log(S_{i0}), \qquad (6)$$

where B_{fp} is the set of pixels constituting the blobs predicted for each class (except the background class) that contain no ground-truth point annotations

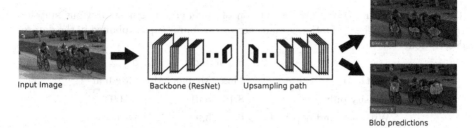

Input Image   Backbone (ResNet)   Upsampling path

Blob predictions

Fig. 3. Given an input image, our model first extracts features using a backbone architecture such as ResNet. The extracted features are then upsampled through the upsampling path to obtain blobs for the objects. In this example, the model predicts the blobs for persons and bikes for an image in the PASCAL VOC 2007 dataset.

(note that S_{i0} is the probability that pixel i belongs to the background class). All the predictions within B_{fp} are considered false positives (see the red blobs in Fig. 5). Therefore, optimizing this loss term results in less false positive predictions as shown in the qualitative results in Fig. 5. The experiments show that this loss term is extremely important for accurate object counting.

3.2 LC-FCN Architecture and Inference

LC-FCN can be any FCN architecture such as FCN8 architecture [24], Deeplab [36], Tiramisu [25], and PSPnet [26]. LC-FCN consists of a backbone that extracts the image features. The backbone is an Imagenet pretrained network such as VGG16 or ResNet-50 [37,38]. The image features are then upscaled using an upsampling path to output a score for each pixel i indicating the probability that it belongs to class c (see Fig. 3).

We predict the number of objects for class c through the following three steps: (i) the upsampling path outputs a matrix Z where each entry Z_{ic} is the probability that pixel i belongs to class c; then (ii) we generate a binary mask F, where pixel $F_{ic} = 1$ if $\arg\max_k Z_{ik} = c$, and 0 otherwise; lastly (iii) we apply the connected components algorithm [32] on F to get the blobs for each class c. The count is the number of predicted blobs (see Fig. 3).

4 Experiments

In this section we describe the evaluation metrics, the training procedure, and present the experimental results and discussion.

4.1 Setup

Evaluation Metric. For datasets with single-class objects, we report the mean absolute error (MAE) which measures the deviation of the predicted count p_i

Table 1. Penguins datasets. Evaluation of our method against previous state-of-the-art methods. The evaluation is made across the four setups explained in the dataset description.

Method	Separated		Mixed	
	Max	Median	Max	Median
Density-only [1]	8.11	5.01	9.81	7.09
With seg. and depth [1]	6.38	3.99	5.74	3.42
With seg and no depth [1]	5.77	3.41	5.35	3.26
Glance	6.08	5.49	1.84	2.14
LC-FCN8	**3.74**	**3.28**	1.62	1.80
LC-ResFCN	3.96	3.43	**1.50**	**1.69**

from the true count c_i, computed as $\frac{1}{N}\sum_i |p_i - c_i|$. MAE is a commonly used metric for evaluating object counting methods [39,40]. For datasets with multi-class objects, we report the mean root mean square error (mRMSE) as used in [9] for the PASCAL VOC 2007 dataset. We measure the localization performance using the average mean absolute error (GAME) as in [6]. Since our model predicts blobs instead of a density map, GAME might not be an accurate localization measure. Therefore, in Sect. 4.3 we use the F-Score metric to assess the localization performance of the predicted blobs against the point-level annotation ground-truth.

Training Procedure. We use the Adam [41] optimizer with a learning rate of 10^{-5} and weight decay of 5×10^{-5}. We use the provided validation set for early stopping only. During training, the model uses a batch size of 1 which can be an image of any size. We double our training set by applying the horizontal flip augmentation method on each image. Finally, we report the prediction results on the test set. We compare between three architectures: FCN8 [24]; ResFCN which is FCN8 that uses ResNet-50 as the backbone instead of VGG16; and PSPNet [26] with ResNet-101 as the backbone. We use the watershed split procedure in all our experiments.

4.2   Results and Discussion

Penguins Dataset [1]. The Penguins dataset comprises images of penguin colonies located in Antarctica. We use the two dataset splits as in [1]. In the 'separated' dataset split, the images in the training set come from different cameras than those in the test set. In the 'mixed' dataset split, the images in the training set come from the same cameras as those in the test set. In Table 1, the MAE is computed with respect to the Max and Median count (as there are multiple annotators). Our methods significantly outperform theirs in all of the four settings, although their methods use depth features and the multiple annotations

Table 2. Trancos dataset. Evaluation of our method against previous state-of-the-art methods, comparing the mean absolute error (MAE) and the grid average mean absolute error (GAME) as described in [6].

Method	MAE	GAME (1)	GAME (2)	GAME (3)
Lemptisky+SIFT [6]	13.76	16.72	20.72	24.36
Hydra CCNN [10]	10.99	13.75	16.69	19.32
FCN-MT [42]	5.31	-	-	-
FCN-HA [43]	4.21	-	-	-
CSRNet [44]	3.56	5.49	8.57	15.04
Glance	7.0	-	-	-
LC-FCN8	4.53	7.00	10.66	16.05
LC-ResFCN	**3.32**	5.2	7.92	12.57
LC-PSPNET	3.57	**4.98**	**7.42**	**11.67**

provided for each penguin. This suggests that LC-FCN can learn to distinguish between individual penguins despite the heavy occlusions and crowding.

Trancos Dataset [10]. The Trancos dataset comprises images taken from traffic surveillance cameras located along different roads. The task is to count the vehicles present in the regions of interest of the traffic scenes. Each vehicle is labeled with a single point annotation that represents its location in the image. We observe in Table 2 that our method achieves new state-of-the-art results for counting and localization. Note that $GAME(L)$ subdivides the image using a grid of 4^L non-overlapping regions, and the error is computed as the sum of the mean absolute errors in each of these subregions. For our method, the predicted count of a region is the number of predicted blob centers in that region. This provides a rough assessment of the localization performance. Compared to the methods in Table 2, LC-FCN does not require a perspective map nor a multi-scale approach to learn objects of different sizes. These results suggest that LC-FCN can accurately localize and count extremely overlapping vehicles.

Parking Lot [5]. The dataset comprises surveillance images taken at a parking lot in Curitiba, Brazil. We used the PUCPR subset of the dataset where the first 50% of the images was set as the training set and the last 50% as the test set. The last 20% of the training set was set as the validation set for early stopping. The ground truth consists of a bounding box for each parked car since this dataset is primarily used for the detection task. Therefore, we convert them into point-level annotations by taking the center of each bounding box. Table 5 shows that LC-FCN significantly outperforms Glance in MAE. LC-FCN8 achieves only 0.21 average miscount per image although many images contain more than 20 parked cars. This suggests that explicitly learning to localize parked cars can perform better in counting than methods that explicitly learn to count from

Table 3. PASCAL VOC. We compare against the methods proposed in [9]. Our model evaluates on the full test set, whereas the other methods take the mean of ten random samples of the test set evaluation.

Method	mRMSE	mRMSE-nz	m-relRMSE	m-relRMSE-nz
Glance-noft-2L [9]	0.50	1.83	0.27	0.73
Aso-sub-ft-3 × 3 [9]	0.42	1.65	0.21	0.68
Faster-RCNN [9]	0.50	1.92	0.26	0.85
LC-ResFCN	**0.31**	**1.20**	**0.17**	**0.61**
LC-PSPNet	0.35	1.32	0.20	0.70

Table 4. Crowd datasets MAE results.

Methods	UCSD	Mall	ShanghaiTech B
FCN-rLSTM [43]	1.54	-	-
MoCNN [45]	-	2.75	-
CNN-boosting [46]	1.10	2.01	-
M-CNN [17]	1.07	-	26.4
CP-CNN [47]	-	-	20.1
CSRNet [44]	1.16	-	**10.6**
LC-FCN8	1.51	2.42	13.14
LC-ResFCN	**0.99**	2.12	25.89
LC-PSPNet	1.01	**2.00**	21.61

Fig. 4. Predicted blobs on a ShanghaiTech B test image.

image-level labels (see Fig. 5 for qualitative results). Note that this is the first counting method being applied on this dataset.

MIT Traffic [3]. This dataset consists of surveillance videos taken from a single fixed camera. It has 20 videos, which are split into a training set (Videos 1–8), a validation set (Videos 0–10), and a test set (Videos 11–20). Each video frame is provided with a bounding box indicating each pedestrian. We convert them into point-level annotations by taking the center of each bounding box. Table 5 shows that our method significantly outperforms Glance, suggesting that learning a localization-based objective allows the model to ignore the background regions that do not contribute to the object count. As a result, LC-FCN is less likely to overfit on irrelevant features from the background. To the best of our knowledge, this is the first counting method being applied on this dataset.

Pascal VOC 2007 [2]. We use the standard training, validation, and test split as specified in [2]. We use the point-level annotation ground-truth provided by Bearman *et al.* [14] to train our LC-FCN methods. We evaluated against the count of the non-difficult instances of the Pascal VOC 2007 test set.

Table 3 compares the performance of LC-FCN with different methods proposed by [9]. We point the reader to [9] for a description of the evaluation metrics used in the table. We show that LC-FCN achieves new state-of-the-art results with respect to mRMSE. We see that LC-FCN outperforms methods that

Table 5. Quantitative results. Comparison of different parts of the proposed loss function for counting and localization performance.

Method	MIT Traffic		PKLot		Trancos		Penguins Separated	
	MAE	FS	MAE	FS	MAE	FS	MAE	FS
Glance	1.57	-	1.92	-	7.01	-	6.09	-
$\mathcal{L}_I + \mathcal{L}_P$	3.11	0.38	39.62	0.04	38.56	0.05	9.81	0.08
$\mathcal{L}_I + \mathcal{L}_P + \mathcal{L}_S$	1.62	0.76	9.06	0.83	6.76	0.56	4.92	0.53
$\mathcal{L}_I + \mathcal{L}_P + \mathcal{L}_F$	1.84	0.69	39.60	0.04	38.26	0.05	7.28	0.04
LC-ResFCN	1.26	**0.81**	10.16	0.84	**3.32**	0.68	3.96	0.63
LC-FCN8	**0.91**	0.69	**0.21**	**0.99**	4.53	**0.54**	**3.74**	**0.61**

explicitly learn to count although learning to localize objects of this dataset is a very challenging task. Further, LC-FCN uses weaker supervision than Aso-sub and Seq-sub as they require the full per-pixel labels to estimate the object count for different image regions.

Crowd Counting Datasets. Table 4 reports the MAE score of our method on 3 crowd datasets using the setup described in the survey paper [40]. For this experiment, we show our results using ResFCN as the backbone with the Watershed split method. We see that our method achieves competitive performance for crowd counting. Figure 4 shows the predicted blobs of our model on a test image of the ShanghaiTech B dataset. We see that our model predicts a blob on the face of each individual. This is expected since the ground-truth point-level annotations are marked on each person's face.

4.3 Ablation Studies

Localization Benchmark. Since robust localization is useful in many computer vision applications, we use the F-Score measure to directly assess the localization performance of our model. F-Score is a standard measure for detection as it considers both precision and recall, F-Score $= \frac{2TP}{2TP+FP+FN}$, where the number of true positives (TP) is the number of blobs that contain at least one point annotation; the number of false positives (FP) is the number of blobs that contain no point annotation; and the number of false negatives (FN) is the number of point annotations minus the number of true positives. Table 5 shows the localization results of our method on several datasets.

Loss Function Analysis. We assess the effect of each term of the loss function on counting and localization results. We start by looking at the results of a model trained with the image-level loss $\mathcal{L}_I$ and the point-level loss $\mathcal{L}_P$ only. These two terms were used for semantic segmentation using point annotations [14]. We observe in Fig. 5(b) that a model using these two terms results in a single blob

(a) Original Image   (b) $\mathcal{L}_I + \mathcal{L}_P$ (c) $\mathcal{L}_I + \mathcal{L}_P + \mathcal{L}_S$ (d) LC-FCN

■ True Positive   ■ False Positive   ■ More than one point annotation

Fig. 5. Qualitative results of LC-FCN trained with different terms of the proposed loss function. (a) Test images obtained from MIT Traffic, Parking Lot, Trancos, and Penguins. (b) Prediction results using only image-level and point-level loss terms. (c) Prediction results using image-level, point-level, and split-level loss terms. (d) Prediction results trained with the full proposed loss function. The green blobs and red blobs indicate true positive and false positive predictions, respectively. Yellow blobs represent those that contain more than one object instance. (Color figure online)

that groups many object instances together. Consequently, this performs poorly in terms of the mean absolute error and the F-Score (see Table 5). As a result, we introduced the split-level loss function $\mathcal{L}_S$ that encourages the model to predict blobs that do not contain more than one point-annotation. We see in Fig. 5(c) that a model using this additional loss term predicts several blobs as object instances rather than one large single blob. However, since $\mathcal{L}_I + \mathcal{L}_P + \mathcal{L}_S$ does not penalize the model from predicting blobs with no point annotations, it can often lead to many false positives. Therefore, we introduce the false positive loss $\mathcal{L}_F$ that discourages the model from predicting blobs with no point annotations. By adding this loss term to the optimization, LC-FCN achieves significant improvement as seen in the qualitative and quantitative results (see Fig. 5(d) and Table 5). Further, including only the split-level loss leads to predicting a huge number of small blobs, leading to many false positives which makes performance worse. Combining it with the false-positive loss avoids this issue which leads to a net improvement in performance. On the other hand, using only the false positive loss it tends to predict one huge blob.

Split method	Trancos	Penguins
LC-ResFCN (L)	4.77	1.89
LC-ResFCN (W)	3.34	0.95

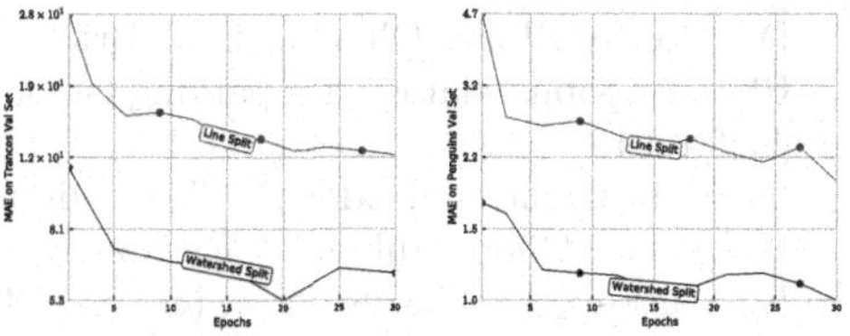

Fig. 6. Split Heuristics Analysis. Comparison between the watershed split method and the line split method against the validation MAE score.

Split Heuristics Analysis. In Fig. 6 we show that the watershed split achieves better MAE on Trancos and Penguins validation sets. Further, using the watershed split achieves much faster improvement on the validation set with respect to the number of epochs. This suggests that using proper heuristics to identify the negative regions is important, which leaves an open area for future work.

5   Conclusion

We propose LC-FCN, a fully-convolutional neural network, to address the problem of object counting using point-level annotations only. We propose a novel loss function that encourages the model to output a single blob for each object instance. Experimental results show that LC-FCN outperforms current state-of-the-art models on the PASCAL VOC 2007, Trancos, and Penguins datasets which contain objects that are heavily occluded. For future work, we plan to explore different FCN architectures and splitting methods that LC-FCN can use to efficiently split between overlapping objects that have complicated shapes and appearances.

Acknowledgements. We would like to thank the anonymous referees for their useful comments that significantly improved the paper. Issam Laradji is funded by the UBC Four-Year Doctoral Fellowships (4YF).

References

1. Arteta, C., Lempitsky, V., Zisserman, A.: Counting in the wild. In: Leibe, B., Matas, J., Sebe, N., Welling, M. (eds.) ECCV 2016. LNCS, vol. 9911, pp. 483–498. Springer, Cham (2016). https://doi.org/10.1007/978-3-319-46478-7_30
2. Everingham, M., Eslami, S.M., Gool, L., Williams, C.K., Winn, J., Zisserman, A.: The pascal visual object classes challenge: a retrospective. IJCV **111**, 98–136 (2015)
3. Wang, M., Wang, X.: Automatic adaptation of a generic pedestrian detector to a specific traffic scene. In: CVPR (2011)
4. Zen, G., Rostamzadeh, N., Staiano, J., Ricci, E., Sebe, N.: Enhanced semantic descriptors for functional scene categorization. In: ICPR (2012)

5. De Almeida, P.R., Oliveira, L.S., Britto Jr., A.S., Silva Jr., E.J., Koerich, A.L.: PKLot-a robust dataset for parking lot classification. Expert Syst. Appl. **42**, 4937–4949 (2015)
6. Guerrero-Gómez-Olmedo, R., Torre-Jiménez, B., López-Sastre, R., Maldonado-Bascón, S., Oñoro-Rubio, D.: Extremely overlapping vehicle counting. In: Paredes, R., Cardoso, J.S., Pardo, X.M. (eds.) IbPRIA 2015. LNCS, vol. 9117, pp. 423–431. Springer, Cham (2015). https://doi.org/10.1007/978-3-319-19390-8_48
7. Cohen, J.P., Boucher, G., Glastonbury, C.A., Lo, H.Z., Bengio, Y.: Count-ception: counting by fully convolutional redundant counting. In: ICCV Workshops (2017)
8. Lempitsky, V., Zisserman, A.: Learning to count objects in images. In: NIPS (2010)
9. Chattopadhyay, P., Vedantam, R., Selvaraju, R.R., Batra, D., Parikh, D.: Counting everyday objects in everyday scenes. In: CVPR (2017)
10. Oñoro-Rubio, D., López-Sastre, R.J.: Towards perspective-free object counting with deep learning. In: Leibe, B., Matas, J., Sebe, N., Welling, M. (eds.) ECCV 2016. LNCS, vol. 9911, pp. 615–629. Springer, Cham (2016). https://doi.org/10.1007/978-3-319-46478-7_38
11. Ren, S., He, K., Girshick, R., Sun, J.: Faster R-CNN: towards real-time object detection with region proposal networks. In: NIPS (2015)
12. Redmon, J., Divvala, S., Girshick, R., Farhadi, A.: You only look once: unified, real-time object detection. In: CVPR (2016)
13. Bai, M., Urtasun, R.: Deep watershed transform for instance segmentation. In: CVPR (2017)
14. Bearman, A., Russakovsky, O., Ferrari, V., Fei-Fei, L.: What's the point: semantic segmentation with point supervision. In: Leibe, B., Matas, J., Sebe, N., Welling, M. (eds.) ECCV 2016. LNCS, vol. 9911, pp. 549–565. Springer, Cham (2016). https://doi.org/10.1007/978-3-319-46478-7_34
15. Chen, K., Loy, C.C., Gong, S., Xiang, T.: Feature mining for localised crowd counting. In: BMVC (2012)
16. Chan, A.B., Liang, Z.S.J., Vasconcelos, N.: Privacy preserving crowd monitoring: counting people without people models or tracking. In: CVPR (2008)
17. Zhang, Y., Zhou, D., Chen, S., Gao, S., Ma, Y.: Single-image crowd counting via multi-column convolutional neural network. In: CVPR (2016)
18. Wang, X., Ma, X., Grimson, W.E.L.: Unsupervised activity perception in crowded and complicated scenes using hierarchical Bayesian models. PAMI **31**, 539–555 (2009)
19. Rabaud, V., Belongie, S.: Counting crowded moving objects. In: CVPR (2006)
20. Loy, C.C., Chen, K., Gong, S., Xiang, T.: Crowd counting and profiling: methodology and evaluation. In: Ali, S., Nishino, K., Manocha, D., Shah, M. (eds.) Modeling, Simulation and Visual Analysis of Crowds. TISVC, vol. 11, pp. 347–382. Springer, New York (2013). https://doi.org/10.1007/978-1-4614-8483-7_14
21. Tu, P., Sebastian, T., Doretto, G., Krahnstoever, N., Rittscher, J., Yu, T.: Unified crowd segmentation. In: Forsyth, D., Torr, P., Zisserman, A. (eds.) ECCV 2008. LNCS, vol. 5305, pp. 691–704. Springer, Heidelberg (2008). https://doi.org/10.1007/978-3-540-88693-8_51
22. Shi, J., Tomasi, C.: Good Features to Track. Cornell University, Ithaca (1993)
23. Liu, W., et al.: SSD: single shot multibox detector. In: Leibe, B., Matas, J., Sebe, N., Welling, M. (eds.) ECCV 2016. LNCS, vol. 9905, pp. 21–37. Springer, Cham (2016). https://doi.org/10.1007/978-3-319-46448-0_2
24. Long, J., Shelhamer, E., Darrell, T.: Fully convolutional networks for semantic segmentation. In: CVPR (2015)

25. Jégou, S., Drozdzal, M., Vazquez, D., Romero, A., Bengio, Y.: The one hundred layers tiramisu: fully convolutional densenets for semantic segmentation. In: CVPR (2017)
26. Zhao, H., Shi, J., Qi, X., Wang, X., Jia, J.: Pyramid scene parsing network. In: CVPR (2017)
27. Girshick, R.: Fast R-CNN. In: ICCV (2015)
28. Arteta, C., Lempitsky, V., Noble, J.A., Zisserman, A.: Learning to detect cells using non-overlapping extremal regions. In: Ayache, N., Delingette, H., Golland, P., Mori, K. (eds.) MICCAI 2012. LNCS, vol. 7510, pp. 348–356. Springer, Heidelberg (2012). https://doi.org/10.1007/978-3-642-33415-3_43
29. Arteta, C., Lempitsky, V., Noble, J.A., Zisserman, A.: Learning to detect partially overlapping instances. In: CVPR (2013)
30. Arteta, C., Lempitsky, V., Noble, J.A., Zisserman, A.: Detecting overlapping instances in microscopy images using extremal region trees. MIA **27**, 3–16 (2016)
31. Ronneberger, O., Fischer, P., Brox, T.: U-Net: convolutional networks for biomedical image segmentation. In: Navab, N., Hornegger, J., Wells, W.M., Frangi, A.F. (eds.) MICCAI 2015. LNCS, vol. 9351, pp. 234–241. Springer, Cham (2015). https://doi.org/10.1007/978-3-319-24574-4_28
32. Wu, K., Otoo, E., Shoshani, A.: Optimizing connected component labeling algorithms. In: Image Processing, Medical Imaging (2005)
33. Beucher, S., Meyer, F.: The morphological approach to segmentation: the watershed transformation. Opt. Eng.-N. Y.-Marcel Dekker Inc. **34**, 433 (1992)
34. Nutini, J., Laradji, I., Schmidt, M.: Let's make block coordinate descent go fast: faster greedy rules, message-passing, active-set complexity, and superlinear convergence. arXiv (2017)
35. Nutini, J., Sepehry, B., Laradji, I., Schmidt, M., Koepke, H., Virani, A.: Convergence rates for greedy Kaczmarz algorithms, and faster randomized Kaczmarz rules using the orthogonality graph. arXiv (2016)
36. Chen, L.C., Papandreou, G., Kokkinos, I., Murphy, K., Yuille, A.L.: DeepLab: semantic image segmentation with deep convolutional nets, atrous convolution, and fully connected CRFs. PAMI **40**, 834–848 (2018)
37. Simonyan, K., Zisserman, A.: Very deep convolutional networks for large-scale image recognition. In: ICLR (2015)
38. Deng, J., Dong, W., Socher, R., Li, L.J., Li, K., Fei-Fei, L.: ImageNet: a large-scale hierarchical image database. In: CVPR (2009)
39. Charles, R.M., Taylor, K.M., Curry, J.H.: Nonnegative matrix factorization applied to reordered pixels of single images based on patches to achieve structured nonnegative dictionaries. arXiv (2015)
40. Sindagi, V.A., Patel, V.M.: A survey of recent advances in CNN-based single image crowd counting and density estimation. Pattern Recognit. Lett. (2017)
41. Kingma, D.P., Ba, J.: Adam: a method for stochastic optimization. arXiv (2014)
42. Zhang, S., Wu, G., Costeira, J.P., Moura, J.M.: Understanding traffic density from large-scale web camera data. In: CVPR (2017)
43. Zhang, S., Wu, G., Costeira, J.P., Moura, J.M.: FCN-rLSTM: deep spatio-temporal neural networks for vehicle counting in city cameras. In: ICCV (2017)
44. Li, Y., Zhang, X., Chen, D.: CSRNET: dilated convolutional neural networks for understanding the highly congested scenes. In: CVPR (2018)
45. Kumagai, S., Hotta, K., Kurita, T.: Mixture of counting CNNs: adaptive integration of CNNs specialized to specific appearance for crowd counting. arXiv (2017)

46. Walach, E., Wolf, L.: Learning to count with CNN boosting. In: Leibe, B., Matas, J., Sebe, N., Welling, M. (eds.) ECCV 2016. LNCS, vol. 9906, pp. 660–676. Springer, Cham (2016). https://doi.org/10.1007/978-3-319-46475-6_41
47. Sindagi, V.A., Patel, V.M.: Generating high-quality crowd density maps using contextual pyramid CNNs. In: ICCV (2017)

Textual Explanations for Self-Driving Vehicles

Jinkyu Kim[1], Anna Rohrbach[1,2], Trevor Darrell[1], John Canny[1],
and Zeynep Akata[2,3]

[1] EECS, University of California, Berkeley, CA 94720, USA
[2] MPI for Informatics, Saarland Informatics Campus, 66123 Saarbrücken, Germany
[3] AMLab, University of Amsterdam, 1098 XH Amsterdam, The Netherlands
z.akata@uva.nl

Abstract. Deep neural perception and control networks have become
key components of self-driving vehicles. User acceptance is likely to benefit from easy-to-interpret textual explanations which allow end-users
to understand what triggered a particular behavior. Explanations may
be triggered by the neural controller, namely *introspective explanations*,
or informed by the neural controller's output, namely *rationalizations*.
We propose a new approach to introspective explanations which consists
of two parts. First, we use a visual (spatial) attention model to train
a convolutional network end-to-end from images to the vehicle control
commands, *i.e.*, acceleration and change of course. The controller's attention identifies image regions that potentially influence the network's output. Second, we use an attention-based video-to-text model to produce
textual explanations of model actions. The attention maps of controller
and explanation model are aligned so that explanations are grounded
in the parts of the scene that mattered to the controller. We explore
two approaches to attention alignment, strong- and weak-alignment.
Finally, we explore a version of our model that generates rationalizations,
and compare with introspective explanations on the same video segments. We evaluate these models on a novel driving dataset with ground-
truth human explanations, the Berkeley DeepDrive eXplanation (BDD-
X) dataset. Code is available at https://github.com/JinkyuKimUCB/
explainable-deep-driving.

Keywords: Explainable deep driving · BDD-X dataset

1 Introduction

Deep neural networks are an effective tool [3,26] to learn vehicle controllers for
self-driving cars in an end-to-end manner. Despite their effectiveness as function
estimators, DNNs are typically cryptic black-boxes. There are no explainable

Electronic supplementary material The online version of this chapter (https://
doi.org/10.1007/978-3-030-01216-8_35) contains supplementary material, which is
available to authorized users.

V. Ferrari et al. (Eds.): ECCV 2018, LNCS 11206, pp. 577–593, 2018.
https://doi.org/10.1007/978-3-030-01216-8_35

states or labels in such a network, and representations are fully distributed as sets of activations. Explainable models that make deep models more transparent are important for a number of reasons: (i) user acceptance – self-driving vehicles are a radical technology for users to accept, and require a very high level of trust, (ii) understanding and extrapolation of vehicle behavior – users ideally should be able to anticipate what the vehicle will do in most situations, (iii) effective communication – they help user communicate preferences to the vehicle and vice versa.

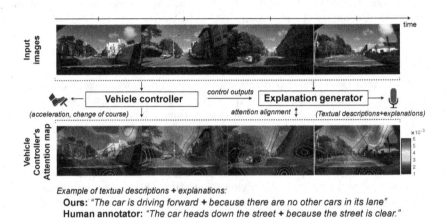

Example of textual descriptions + explanations:
Ours: *"The car is driving forward + because there are no other cars in its lane"*
Human annotator: *"The car heads down the street + because the street is clear."*

Fig. 1. Our model predicts vehicle's control commands, *i.e.*, an acceleration and a change of course, at each timestep, while an explanation model generates a natural language explanation of the rationales, *e.g.*, "The car is driving forward because there are no other cars in its lane", and a visual explanation in the form of attention – attended regions directly influence the textual explanation generation process. (color figure online)

Explanations can be either *rationalizations* – explanations that justify the system's behavior in a post-hoc manner, or *introspective explanations* – explanations that are based on the system's internal state. Introspective explanations represent *causal* relationships between the system's input and its behavior, and address all the goals above. Rationalizations can address acceptance, (i) above, but are less helpful with (ii) understanding the causal behavior of the model or (iii) communication which is grounded in the vehicle's internal state (known as theory of mind in human communication).

One way of generating introspective explanations is via visual attention [11, 27]. Visual attention filters out non-salient image regions, and image areas inside the attended region have potential causal effect on the output (those outside cannot). As shown in [11], additional salience filtering can be applied so that the attention map shows only regions that causally affect the output. Visual attention constrains the reasons for the controllers actions but does not *e.g.*, tie specific actions to specific input regions *e.g.*, "the vehicle slowed down because the light controlling the intersection is red". It is also likely to be less convenient for passengers to replay the attention map vs. a (typically on-demand) speech presentation of a textual explanation.

In this work, we focus on generating textual descriptions and explanations, such as the pair: "vehicle slows down" and "because it is approaching an intersection and the light is red" as in Fig. 1. Natural language has an advantage of being inherently understandable and does not require familiarity with the design of an intelligent system in order to provide useful information. In order to train such a model, we collect explanations from human annotators. Our explanation dataset is built on top of another large-scale driving dataset [26] collected from dashboard cameras in human driven vehicles. Annotators view the video dataset, compose descriptions of the vehicle's activity and explanations for the actions that the vehicle driver performed.

Obtaining training data for vehicle explanations is by itself a significant challenge. The ground truth explanations are in fact often rationalizations (generated by an observer rather than the driver), and there are additional challenges with acquiring driver data. But even more than that, it is currently impossible to obtain human explanations of *what the vehicle controller was thinking*, *i.e.*, a real ground truth. Nevertheless our experiments show that using *attention alignment* between controller and explanation models generally improves the quality of explanations, *i.e.*, generates explanations which better match the human rationalizations of the driving videos.

Our contributions are as follows. (1) We propose an introspective textual explanation model for self-driving cars to provide easy-to-interpret explanations for the behavior of a deep vehicle control network. (2) We integrate our explanation generator with the vehicle controller by aligning their attentions to ground the explanation, and compare two approaches: attention-aligned explanations and non-aligned rationalizations. (3) We generated a large-scale Berkeley Deep-Drive eXplanation (BDD-X) dataset with over 6,984 video clips annotated with driving descriptions, *e.g.*, "The car slows down" and explanations, *e.g.*, "because it is about to merge with the busy highway". Our dataset provides a new test-bed for measuring progress towards developing explainable models for self-driving cars.

2   Related Work

In this section, we review existing work on end-to-end learning for self-driving cars as well as work on visual explanation and justification.

End-to-End Learning for Self-Driving Cars: Most of vehicle controllers for self-driving cars can be divided in two types of approaches [5]: (1) a mediated perception-based approach and (2) an end-to-end learning approach. The mediated perception-based approach depends on recognizing human-designated features, such as lane markings, traffic lights, pedestrians or cars, which generally require demanding parameter tuning for a balanced performance [19]. Notable examples include [4,23], and [16].

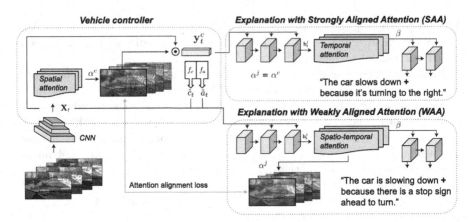

Fig. 2. Vehicle controller generates spatial attention maps α^c for each frame, predicts acceleration and change of course $(\hat{c}_t, \hat{a}_t)$ that condition the explanation. Explanation generator predicts temporal attention across frames (β) and a spatial attention in each frame (α^j). SAA uses α^c, WAA enforces a loss between α^j and α^c.

As for the end-to-end approaches, recent works [3,26] suggest that neural networks can be successfully applied to self-driving cars in an end-to-end manner. Most of these approaches use behavioral cloning that learns a driving policy as a supervised learning problem over observation-action pairs from human driving demonstrations. Among these, [3] present a deep neural vehicle controller network that directly maps a stream of dashcam images to steering controls, while [26] use a deep neural network that takes input raw pixels and prior vehicle states and predict vehicle's future motion. Despite their potential, the effectiveness of these approaches is limited by their inability to explain the rationale for the system's decisions, which makes their behavior opaque and uninterpretable. In this work, we propose an end-to-end trainable system for self driving cars that is able to justify its predictions visually via attention maps and textually via natural language.

Visual and Textual Explanations: The importance of explanations for an end-user has been studied from the psychological perspective [17,18], showing that humans use explanations as a guide for learning and understanding by building inferences and seeking propositions or judgments that enrich their prior knowledge. They usually seek for explanations to fill the requested gap depending on prior knowledge and goal in question.

In support of this trend, recently explainability has been growing as a field in computer vision and machine learning. Especially, there is a growing interest in introspective deep neural networks. [28] use deconvolution to visualize inner-layer activations of convolutional networks. [14] propose automatically-generated captions for textual explanations of images. [2] develop a richer notion of contribution of a pixel to the output. However, a difficulty with deconvolution-style approaches is the lack of formal measures of how the network output is affected by spatially-extended features (rather than pixels). Exceptions to this rule are attention-based approaches. [11] propose attention-based approach with causal filtering that removes spurious attention blobs. However, it is also important to be able to justify the decisions that were made and explain why they are reasonable in a human understandable manner, *i.e.*, a natural language. For an image classification problem, [7,8] used an LSTM [9] caption generation model that generates textual justifications for a CNN model. [21] combine attention-based model and a textual justification system to produce an interpretable model. To our knowledge, ours is the first attempt to justify the decisions of a real-time deep controller through a combination of attention and natural language explanations on a stream of images.

3   Explainable Driving Model

In this paper, we propose a driving model that explains how a driving decision was made both (i) by visualizing image regions where the decision maker attends to and (ii) by generating a textual description and explanation of what has triggered a particular driving decision, *e.g.*, "the car continues (description) because traffic flows freely (explanation)". As we summarize in Fig. 2, our model involves two parts: (1) a *Vehicle controller*, which is trained to learn human-demonstrated vehicle control commands, *e.g.*, an acceleration and a change of course; our controller uses a visual (spatial) attention mechanism that identifies potentially influential image regions for the network's output; (2) a *Textual explanation generator*, which generates textual descriptions and explanations controller behavior. The key to the approach is to align the attention maps.

Preprocessing. Our model is trained to predict two vehicle control commands, *i.e.*, an acceleration and a change of course. At each time t, an acceleration, a_t, is measured by taking the derivative of speed measurements, and a change of course, c_t, is computed by taking a difference between a current vehicle's course and a smoothed value by using simple exponential smoothing method [10]. We provide details in supplemental material. To reduce computational burden, we down-sample to 10 Hz and reduce the input dimensionality by resizing raw images to a $90 \times 160 \times 3$ image with nearest-neighbor scaling algorithm. Each image is then normalized by subtracting the mean from the raw input pixels and dividing by its standard deviation. This preprocessing is applied to the latest 4 frames, which are then stacked to produce the final input to the neural network.

Convolutional Feature Encoder. We use a convolutional neural network to encode the visual information into a set of visual feature vectors at time t, *i.e.*, convolutional feature cube $\mathbf{X}_t = \{\mathbf{x}_{t,1}, \mathbf{x}_{t,2}, \ldots, \mathbf{x}_{t,l}\}$ where $\mathbf{x}_{t,i} \in \mathcal{R}^d$ for $i \in \{1, 2, \ldots, l\}$ and l is the number of different spatial regions of the given input. Each feature vector contains a high-level description of objects present in a certain input region. This allows us to focus selectively on different regions of the given image by choosing a subset of these feature vectors. We use a five-layered convolutional network as in [3,11] and omit max-pooling layers to prevent spatial information loss [15]. The output is a three-dimensional feature cube $\mathbf{X}_t$ and the feature block has the size $w \times h \times d$ at each time t.

3.1   Vehicle Controller

Our vehicle controller is trained in an end-to-end manner. Given a stream of dashcam images and the vehicle's (current) sensor measurements, e.g., speed, the controller predicts the acceleration and the change of course at each timestep. We utilize a deterministic soft attention mechanism that is trainable by standard back-propagation methods. The soft attention mechanism applies attention weights multiplicatively to the features and additively pools the results through the maps π. Our model feeds the context vectors $\mathbf{y}_t^c$ produced by the controller map π^c to the controller LSTM:

$$\mathbf{y}_t^c = \pi^c(\{\alpha_{t,i}^c\}, \{\mathbf{x}_{t,i}\}) = \sum_{i=1}^{l} \alpha_{t,i}^c \mathbf{x}_{t,i} \tag{1}$$

where $i = \{1, 2, \ldots, l\}$. $\alpha_{t,i}^c$ is an attention weight map output by a spatial softmax and satisfies $\sum_i \alpha_{t,i}^c = 1$. These attention weights can be interpreted as the probability over l convolutional feature vectors. A location with a high attention weight is salient for the task (driving). The attention model $f_{\text{attn}}^c(\mathbf{X}_t, \mathbf{h}_{t-1}^c)$ is conditioned on the previous LSTM state $\mathbf{h}_{t-1}^c$, and the current feature vectors $\mathbf{X}_t$. It comprises a fully-connected layer and a spatial softmax to yield normalized $\{\alpha_{t,i}^c\}$.

The outputs of the vehicle controller are the vehicle's acceleration $\hat{a}_t$ and the change of course $\hat{c}_t$. To this end, we use additional multi-layer fully-connected blocks with ReLU non-linearities, denoted by $f_a(\mathbf{y}_t^c, \mathbf{h}_t^c)$ and $f_c(\mathbf{y}_t^c, \mathbf{h}_t^c)$. We also add the entropy H of the attention weight to the objective function:

$$\mathcal{L}_c = \sum_t \left((a_t - \hat{a}_t)^2 + (c_t - \hat{c}_t)^2 + \lambda_c H(\alpha_t^c) \right) \tag{2}$$

The entropy is computed on the attention map as though it were a probability distribution. Minimizing loss corresponds to minimizing entropy. Low entropy attention maps are sparse and emphasize relatively few regions. We use a hyperparameter λ_c to control the strength of the entropy regularization term.

3.2   Attention Alignments

The controller attention map provides input regions that the network attends to, and these regions have a direct influence on the network's output. Thus, to yield "introspective" explanation, we argue that the agent must attend to those areas. For example, if a vehicle controller predicts "acceleration" by detecting a green traffic light, the textual justification must mention this evidence, e.g., "because the light has turned green". Here, we explain two approaches to align the vehicle controller and the textual justifier such that they look at the same input regions.

Strongly Aligned Attention (SAA): A consecutive set of spatially attended input regions, each of which is encoded as a context vector $\mathbf{y}_t^c$ by the vehicle controller, can be directly used to generate a textual explanation (see Fig. 2, right-top). Thus, models share a single layer of an attention. As we detail in Sect. 3.3, our explanation module uses *temporal* attention with weights β to the controller context vectors $\{\mathbf{y}_t^j, t = 1, \ldots\}$ directly, and thus allows flexibility in output tokens relative to input samples.

Weakly Aligned Attention (WAA): Instead of directly using vehicle controller's attention, an explanation generator can have its own spatial attention network (see Fig. 2, right-bottom). A loss, *i.e.*, the Kullback-Leibler divergence (D_{KL}), between the two attention maps makes the explanation generator refer to the salient objects:

$$\mathcal{L}_a = \lambda_a \sum_t D_{\mathrm{KL}}(\alpha_t^c \| \alpha_t^j) = \lambda_a \sum_t \sum_{i=1}^{l} \alpha_{t,i}^c (\log \alpha_{t,i}^c - \log \alpha_{t,i}^j) \qquad (3)$$

where α^c and α^j are the attention maps generated by the vehicle controller and the explanation generator model, respectively. We use a hyperparameter λ_a to control the strength of the regularization term.

3.3   Textual Explanation Generator

Our textual explanation generator takes sequence of video frames of variable length and generates a variable-length description/explanation. Descriptions and explanations are typically part of the same sentence in the training data but are annotated with a separator. In training and testing we use a synthetic separator token `<sep>` between description and explanation, but treat them as a single sequence. The explanation LSTM predicts the description/explanation sequence and outputs per-word softmax probabilities.

The source of context vectors for the description generator depends on the type of alignment between attention maps. For weakly aligned attention or rationalizations, the explanation generator creates its own spatial attention map α^j at each time step t. This map includes a loss against the controller attention map for weakly-aligned attention, but has no such loss when generating rationalizations. The attention map α^j is applied to the CNN output yielding context vectors $\mathbf{y}_t^j$.

Our textual explanation generator explains the rationale behind the driving model, and thus we argue that a justifier needs the outputs from the vehicle motion predictor as an input. We concatenate a tuple $(\hat{a}_t, \hat{c}_t)$ with a spatially-attended context vector $\mathbf{y}_t^j$ and $\mathbf{y}_t^c$ respectively for weakly and strongly aligned attention approaches. This concatenated vector is then used to update the LSTM for a textual explanation generation.

The explanation module applies *temporal* attention with weights β to either the controller context vectors directly $\{\mathbf{y}_t^c, t = 1, \ldots\}$ (strong alignment), or to the explanation vectors $\{\mathbf{y}_t^j, t = 1, \ldots\}$ (weak alignment or rationalization). Such input sequence attention is common in sequence-to-sequence models and allows flexibility in output tokens relative to input samples [1]. The result of temporal attention application is (dropping the c or j superscripts on $\mathbf{y}$):

$$\mathbf{z}_k = \pi(\{\beta_{k,t}\}, \{\mathbf{y}_t\}) = \sum_{t=1}^{T} \beta_{k,t} \mathbf{y}_t \tag{4}$$

where $\sum_t \beta_{k,t} = 1$. The weight $\beta_{k,t}$ at each time k (for sentence generation) is computed by an attention model $f_{\text{attn}}^e(\{\mathbf{y}_t\}, \mathbf{h}_{k-1}^e)$, which is similar to the spatial attention as we explained in previous section (see supplemental material for details).

To summarize, we minimize the following negative log-likelihood (for training our justifier) as well as vehicle control estimation loss $\mathcal{L}_c$ and attention alignment loss $\mathcal{L}_a$:

$$\mathcal{L} = \mathcal{L}_c + \mathcal{L}_a - \sum_k \log p(\mathbf{o}_k | \mathbf{o}_{k-1}, h_k^e, \mathbf{z}_k) \tag{5}$$

4   Berkeley DeepDrive eXplanation Dataset (BDD-X)

In order to effectively generate and evaluate textual driving rationales we have collected textual justifications for a subset of the Berkeley Deep Drive (BDD) dataset [26]. This dataset contains videos, approximately 40 s in length, captured by a dashcam mounted behind the front mirror of the vehicle. Videos are mostly captured during urban driving in various weather conditions, featuring

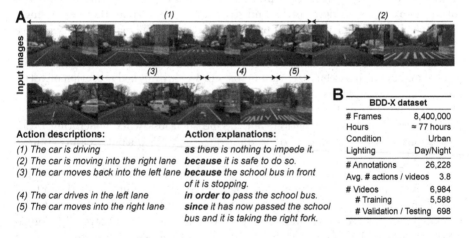

Action descriptions:

(1) The car is driving
(2) The car is moving into the right lane
(3) The car moves back into the left lane
(4) The car drives in the left lane
(5) The car moves into the right lane

Action explanations:

as there is nothing to impede it.
because it is safe to do so.
because the school bus in front of it is stopping.
in order to pass the school bus.
since it has now passed the school bus and it is taking the right fork.

BDD-X dataset	
# Frames	8,400,000
Hours	≈ 77 hours
Condition	Urban
Lighting	Day/Night
# Annotations	26,228
Avg. # actions / videos	3.8
# Videos	6,984
# Training	5,588
# Validation / Testing	698

Fig. 3. (A) Examples of input frames and corresponding human-annotated action description and justification of how a driving decision was made. For visualization, we sample frames at every two seconds. (B) BDD-X dataset details. Over 77 h of driving with time-stamped human annotations for action descriptions and justifications.

day and nighttime. The dataset also includes driving on other road types, such as residential roads (with and without lane markings), and contains all the typical driver's activities such as staying in a lane, turning, switching lanes, etc. Alongside the video data, the dataset provides a set of time-stamped sensor measurements, such as vehicle's velocity, course, and GPS location. For sensor logs unsynchronized with the time-stamps of video data, we use the estimates of the interpolated measurements.

In order to increase trust and reliability, the machine learning system underlying self driving cars should be able to explain why at a certain time they make certain decisions. Moreover, a car that justifies its decision through natural language would also be user friendly. Hence, we populate a subset of the BDD dataset with action description and justification for all the driving events along with their timestamps. We provide examples from our *Berkeley Deep Drive eXplanation (BDD-X)* dataset in Fig. 3(A).

Annotation. We provide a driving video and ask a human annotator in Amazon Mechanical Turk to imagine herself being a driving instructor. Note that we specifically select human annotators who are familiar with US driving rules. The annotator has to describe *what* the driver is doing (especially when the behavior changes) and *why*, from a point of view of a driving instructor. Each described action has to be accompanied with a start and end time-stamp. The annotator may stop the video, forward and backward through it while searching for the activities that are interesting and justifiable.

To ensure that the annotators provide us the driving rationales as well as descriptions, we require that they separately enter the *action description* and the *action justification*: e.g., *"The car is moving into the left lane"* and *"because the school bus in front of it is stopping."*. In our preliminary annotation studies, we found that giving separate annotation boxes is helpful for the annotator to understand the task and perform better.

Dataset Statistics. Our dataset (see Fig. 3(B)) is composed of over 77 h of driving within 6,984 videos. The videos are taken in diverse driving conditions, *e.g.*, day/night, highway/city/countryside, summer/winter etc. On an average of 40 s, each video contains around 3–4 actions, *e.g.*, speeding up, slowing down, turning right etc., all of which are annotated with a description and an explanation. Our dataset contains over $26K$ activities in over $8.4M$ frames. We introduce a training, a validation and a test set, containing 5,588, 698 and 698 videos, respectively.

Inter-human Agreement. Although we cannot have access to the internal thought process of the drivers, one can infer the reason behind their actions using the visual evidence of the scene. Besides, it would be challenging to setup the data collection process which enables drivers to report justifications for all their actions, if at all possible. We ensure the high quality of the collected annotations by relying on a pool of qualified workers (*i.e.*, they pass a qualification test) and selective manual inspection.

Further, we measure the inter-human agreement on a subset of 998 training videos, each of which has been annotated by two different workers. Our analysis is as follows. In 72% of videos the number of annotated intervals differs by less than 3. The average temporal IoU across annotators is 0.63 ($SD = 0.21$). When $IoU > 0.5$ the CIDEr score across action descriptions is 142.60, across action justifications it is 97.49 (random choice: 39.40/28.39, respectively). When $IoU > 0.5$ and action descriptions from two annotators are identical (165 clips[1]) the CIDEr score across justifications is 200.72, while a strong baseline, selecting a justification from a different video with the same action description, results in CIDEr score 136.72. These results show an agreement among annotators and relevance of collected action descriptions and justifications.

Coverage of Justifications. BDD-X dataset has over 26k annotations (77 h) collected from a substantial random subset of large-scale crowd-sourced driving video dataset, which consists of all the typical driver's activities during urban driving. The vocabulary of training action descriptions and justifications is 906 and 1,668 words respectively, suggesting that justifications are more diverse than descriptions. Some of the common actions are (frequency decreasing): moving forward, stopping, accelerating, slowing, turning, merging, veering, pulling [in]. Justifications cover most of the relevant concepts: traffic signs/lights, cars, lanes, crosswalks, passing, parking, pedestrians, waiting, blocking, safety etc.

5   Results and Discussion

Here, we first provide our training and evaluation details, then make a quantitative and qualitative analysis of our vehicle controller and our textual justifier.

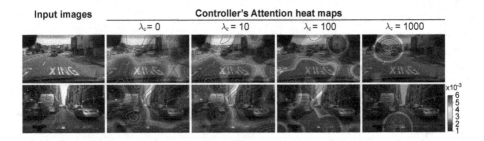

Fig. 4. Vehicle controller's attention maps in terms of four different entropy regularization coefficient $\lambda_c = \{0, 10, 100, 1000\}$. Red parts indicate where the model pays more attention. Higher value of λ_c makes the attention maps sparser. We observe that sparser attention maps improves the performance of generating textual explanations, while control performance is slightly degraded.

---

[1] The number of video intervals (not full videos), where the provided action descriptions (not explanations) are identical (common actions *e.g.*, "the car slows down").

Training and Evaluation Details. As the convolutional feature encoder, we use 5-layer CNN [3] that produces a $12\times20\times64$-dimensional convolutional feature cube from the last layer. The controller following the CNN has 5 fully connected layers (*i.e.*, #hidden dims: 1164, 100, 50, 10, respectively), which predict the acceleration and the change of course, and is trained end-to-end from scratch. Using other more expressive networks may give a performance boost over our base CNN configuration, but these explorations are out of our scope. Given the obtained convolutional feature cube, we first train our vehicle controller, and then the explanation generator (single layer LSTM unless stated otherwise) by freezing the control network. For training, we use Adam optimizer [12] and dropout [22] of 0.5 at hidden state connections and Xavier initialization [6]. The standard dataset is split as 80% (5,588 videos) as the training set, 10% (698 videos) as the test, and 10% (698 videos) as the validation set. Our model takes less than a day to train on a single NVIDIA Titan X GPU.

For evaluating the vehicle controller we use the mean absolute error (lower is better) and the distance correlation (higher is better) and for the justifier we use BLEU [20], METEOR [13], and CIDEr-D [24], as well as human evaluation. The former metrics are widely used for the evaluation of video and image captioning models automatically against ground truth.

5.1   Evaluating Vehicle Controller

We start by quantitatively comparing variants of our vehicle controller and the state of the art, which include variants of the work by Bojarski *et al.* [3] and Kim *et al.* [11] in Table 1. Note that these works differ from ours in that their output is the curvature of driving, while our model estimates continuous acceleration and the change of course values. Thus, their models have a single output, while ours estimate both control commands. In this experiment, we replaced their output layer with ours. For a fair comparison, we use an identical CNN for all models.

Table 1. Comparing variants of our vehicle controller with different values of the entropy regularization coefficient $\lambda_c=\{0, 10, 100, 1000\}$ and the state-of-the-art. High value of λ_c produces low entropy attention maps that are sparse and emphasize relatively few regions. [†]: Models use a single image frame as an input. The standard deviation is in braces. *Abbreviation:* FC (fully connected layer), P (prior inputs)

Model	λ_c	Mean of absolute error (MAE)		Mean of distance correlation	
		Acceleration (m/s^2)	Course (degree)	Acceleration (m/s^2)	Course (degree)
CNN+FC [3][†]	-	6.92 [7.50]	12.1 [19.7]	0.17 [0.15]	0.16 [0.14]
CNN+FC [3]+P	-	6.09 [7.73]	6.74 [14.9]	0.21 [0.18]	0.39 [0.33]
CNN+LSTM+Attention [11][†]	-	6.87 [7.44]	10.2 [18.4]	0.19 [0.16]	0.22 [0.18]
CNN+LSTM+Attention+P (Ours)	1000	5.02 [6.32]	6.94 [15.4]	0.65 [0.25]	0.43 [0.33]
CNN+LSTM+Attention+P (Ours)	100	2.68 [3.73]	6.17 [14.7]	0.78 [0.28]	0.43 [0.34]
CNN+LSTM+Attention+P (Ours)	10	2.33 [3.38]	6.10 [14.7]	0.81 [0.27]	0.46 [0.35]
CNN+LSTM+Attention+P (Ours)	0	**2.29 [3.33]**	**6.06 [14.7]**	**0.82 [0.26]**	**0.47 [0.35]**

In this experiment, each model estimates vehicle's acceleration and the change of course. Our vehicle controller predicts acceleration and the change of course, which generally requires prior knowledge of vehicle's current state, *i.e.*, speed and course, and navigational inputs, especially in urban driving. We observe that the use of the latest four consecutive frames and prior inputs (*i.e.*, vehicle's motion measurement and navigational information) improves the control prediction accuracy (see 3rd vs. 7th row), while the use of visual attention also provides improvements (see 1st vs. 3rd row). Specifically, our model without the entropy regularization term (last row) performs the best compared to CNN based approaches [3] and [11]. The improvement is especially pronounced for acceleration estimation.

In Fig. 4 we compare input images (first column) and corresponding attention maps for different entropy regularization coefficients $\lambda_c = \{0, 10, 100, 1000\}$. Red is high attention, blue is low. As we see, higher λ_c lead to sparser maps. For better visualization, an attention map is overlaid by its contour lines and an input image.

Quantitatively, the controller performance (error and correlation) slightly degrade as λ_c increases and the attention maps become more sparse (see bottom four rows in Table 1). So there is some tension between sparse maps (which are more interpretable), and controller performance. An alternative to regularization, [11] use causal filtering over the controller's attention maps and achieve about 60% reduction in "hot" attention pixels. Causal filtering is desirable for the present work not only to improve sparseness but because after causal filtering, "hot" regions necessarily *do* have a causal effect on controller behavior, whereas unfiltered attention regions may not. We will explore it in future work.

5.2   Evaluating Textual Explanations

In this section, we evaluate textual explanations against the ground truth explanation using automatic evaluation measures, and also provide human evaluation followed by a qualitative analysis.

Automatic Evaluation. For state-of-the-art comparison, we implement the S2VT [25] and its variants. Note that in our implementation S2VT uses our CNN and does not use optical flow features. In Table 2, we report a summary of our experiment validating the quantitative effectiveness of our approach. Rows 5–10 show that best explanation results are generally obtained with weakly-aligned attention. Comparing with row 4, the introspective models all gave higher scores than the rationalization model for explanation generation. Description scores are more mixed, but most of the introspective model scores are higher. As we will see in the next section, our rationalization model focuses on visual saliencies, which is sometimes different from what controller actually "looks at". For example, in Fig. 5 (5th example), our controller sees the front vehicle and our introspective models generate explanations such as "because the car in front is moving slowly", while our rationalization model does not see the front vehicle and generates "because it's turning to the right".

Table 2. Comparing generated and ground truth (columns 6–8) descriptions (*e.g.*, "the car stops") and explanations (*e.g.*, "because the light is red"). We implement S2VT [25] and variants with spatial attention (SA) and temporal attention (TA) as a baseline. We tested two different attention alignment approaches, *i.e.*, WAA (weakly aligned attention) and SAA (strongly aligned attention), with different combinations of two regularization coefficients: $\lambda_a=\{0,10\}$ for the attention alignment and $\lambda_c=\{0,10,100\}$ for the vehicle controller. Rationalization baseline relies on our model (WAA approach) but has no attention alignment. Note that we report all values as a percentage.

Type	Model	Control inputs	λ_a	λ_c	Explanations (*e.g., "because the light is red"*)			Descriptions (*e.g., "the car stops"*)		
					BLEU-4	METEOR	CIDEr-D	BLEU-4	METEOR	CIDEr-D
	S2VT [25]	N	-	-	6.332	11.19	53.35	30.21	27.53	179.8
	S2VT [25]+SA	N	-	-	5.668	10.96	51.37	28.94	26.91	171.3
	S2VT [25]+SA+TA	N	-	-	5.847	10.91	52.74	27.11	26.41	157.0
Rationalization	Ours (no constraints)	Y	0	0	6.515	12.04	61.99	31.01	28.64	205.0
	Ours (with SAA)	Y	-	0	6.998	12.08	62.24	**32.44**	29.13	213.6
	Ours (with SAA)	Y	-	10	6.760	12.23	63.36	29.99	28.26	203.6
Introspective explanation	Ours (with SAA)	Y	-	100	7.074	12.23	66.09	31.84	29.11	214.8
	Ours (with WAA)	Y	10	0	6.967	12.14	64.19	32.24	29.00	**219.7**
	Ours (with WAA)	Y	10	10	6.951	**12.34**	68.56	30.40	28.57	206.6
	Ours (with WAA)	Y	10	100	**7.281**	12.24	**69.52**	32.34	**29.22**	215.8

As our training data are human observer annotations of driving videos, and they are not the explanations of drivers, they are post-hoc rationalizations. However, based on the visual evidence, (*e.g.*, the existence of a turn right sign explains why the driver has turned right even if we do not have access to the exact thought process of the driver), they reflect typical causes of human driver behavior. The data suggest that grounding the explanations in controller internal state helps produce explanations that better align with human third-party explanations. Biasing the explanations toward controller state (which the WAA and SAA models do) improves their plausibility from a human perspective, which is a good sign. We further analyze human preference in the evaluation below.

Human Evaluation. In our first human evaluation experiment the human judges are only shown the *descriptions*, while in the second experiment they only see the *explanations* (e.g. "*The car ... because < explanation >*"), to exclude the effect of explanations/descriptions on the ratings, respectively. We randomly select 250 video intervals and compare the Rationalization, WAA ($\lambda_a=10$, $\lambda_c=100$) and SAA ($\lambda_c=100$) predictions. The humans are asked to rate a description/explanation on the scale $\{1..4\}$ (1: correct and specific/detailed, 2: correct, 3: minor error, 4: major error). We collect ratings from 3 human judges for each task. Finally, we compute the majority vote, *i.e.*, at least 2 out of 3 judges should rate the description/explanation with a score 1 or 2.

Table 3. Human evaluation of the generated action descriptions and explanations for randomly chosen 250 video intervals. We measure the success rate where at least 2 human judges rate the generated description or explanation with a score 1 (correct and specific/detailed) or 2 (correct).

Type	Model	Control inputs	λ_a	λ_c	Correctness rate	
					Explanations	Descriptions
Rationalization	Ours (no constraints)	Y	0	0	64.0%	92.8%
Introspective	Ours (with SAA)	Y	-	100	62.4%	90.8%
explanation	Ours (with WAA)	Y	10	100	**66.0%**	**93.5%**

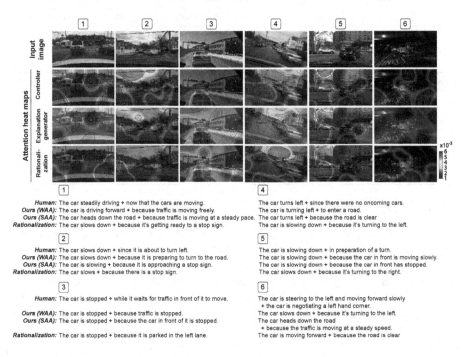

Fig. 5. Example descriptions and explanations generated by our model compared to human annotations. We provide (top row) input raw images and attention maps by (from the 2nd row) vehicle controller, textual explanation generator, and rationalization model (Note: $(\lambda_c, \lambda_a) = (100, 10)$ and the synthetic separator token is replaced by '+').

As shown in Table 3, our WAA model outperforms the other two, supporting the results above. Interestingly, Rationalization does better than SAA on this subset, according to humans. This is perhaps because the explanation in SAA relies on the exact same visual evidence as the controller, which may include counterfactually important regions (*i.e.*, there *could be* a stop sign here), but may confuse the explanation module.

Qualitative Analysis of Textual Justifier. As Fig. 5 shows, our proposed textual explanation model generates plausible descriptions and explanations, while our model also provides attention visualization of their evidence. In the first example of Fig. 5, controller sees neighboring vehicles and lane markings, while explanation model generates "the car is driving forward (description)" and "because traffic is moving freely (explanation)". In Fig. 5, we also provide other examples that cover common driving situations, such as driving forward (1st example), slowing/stopping (2nd, 3rd, and 5th), and turning (4th and 6th). We also observe that our explanations have significant diversity, *e.g.*, they provide various reasons for stopping: red lights, stop signs, and traffic. We provide more diverse examples as supplemental materials.

6 Conclusion

We described an end-to-end explainable driving model for self-driving cars by incorporating a grounded introspective explanation model. We showed that (i) incorporation of an attention mechanism and prior inputs improves vehicle control prediction accuracy compared to baselines, (ii) our grounded (introspective) model generates accurate human understandable textual descriptions and explanations for driving behaviors, (iii) attention alignment is shown to be effective at combining the vehicle controller and the justification model, and (iv) our BDD-X dataset allows us to train and automatically evaluate our interpretable justification model by comparing with human annotations.

Recent work [11] suggests that causal filtering over attention heat maps can achieve a useful reduction in explanation complexity by removing spurious blobs, which do not significantly affect the output. Causal filtering idea would be worth exploring to obtain causal attention heat maps, which can provide the causal ground of reasoning. Furthermore, it would be beneficial to incorporate stronger perception pipeline, e.g. object detectors, to introduce more "grounded" visual representations and further improve the quality and diversity of the generated explanations. Besides, incorporating driver's eye gaze into our explanation model for mimicking driver's behavior, would be an interesting potential future direction.

Acknowledgements. This work was supported by DARPA XAI program and Berkeley DeepDrive.

References

1. Bahdanau, D., Cho, K., Bengio, Y.: Neural machine translation by jointly learning to align and translate. In: Conference on Learning Representations (2014)
2. Bojarski, M., et al.: VisualBackProp: visualizing CNNs for autonomous driving. CoRR, vol. abs/1611.05418 (2016)
3. Bojarski, M., et al.: End to end learning for self-driving cars. CoRR abs/1604.07316 (2016)

4. Buehler, M., Iagnemma, K., Singh, S.: The DARPA Urban Challenge: Autonomous Vehicles in City Traffic. Springer, Heidelberg (2009). https://doi.org/10.1007/978-3-642-03991-1

5. Chen, C., Seff, A., Kornhauser, A., Xiao, J.: Deepdriving: learning affordance for direct perception in autonomous driving. In: 2015 IEEE International Conference on Computer Vision (ICCV), pp. 2722–2730. IEEE (2015)

6. Glorot, X., Bengio, Y.: Understanding the difficulty of training deep feedforward neural networks. In: Aistats, vol. 9, pp. 249–256 (2010)

7. Hendricks, L.A., Akata, Z., Rohrbach, M., Donahue, J., Schiele, B., Darrell, T.: Generating visual explanations. In: Leibe, B., Matas, J., Sebe, N., Welling, M. (eds.) ECCV 2016. LNCS, vol. 9908, pp. 3–19. Springer, Cham (2016). https://doi.org/10.1007/978-3-319-46493-0_1

8. Hendricks, L.A., Hu, R., Darrell, T., Akata, Z.: Grounding visual explanations. In: European Conference on Computer Vision (ECCV) (2018)

9. Hochreiter, S., Schmidhuber, J.: LSTM can solve hard long time lag problems. In: Advances in Neural Information Processing Systems, pp. 473–479 (1997)

10. Hyndman, R., Koehler, A.B., Ord, J.K., Snyder, R.D.: Forecasting with Exponential Smoothing: the State Space Approach. Springer, Heidelberg (2008). https://doi.org/10.1007/978-3-540-71918-2

11. Kim, J., Canny, J.: Interpretable learning for self-driving cars by visualizing causal attention. In: Proceedings of the IEEE International Conference on Computer Vision, pp. 2942–2950 (2017)

12. Kinga, D., Adam, J.B.: A method for stochastic optimization. In: International Conference on Learning Representations (ICLR) (2015)

13. Lavie, A., Agarwal, A.: Meteor: an automatic metric for MT evaluation with improved correlation with human judgments. In: Proceedings of the EMNLP 2011 Workshop on Statistical Machine Translation, pp. 65–72 (2005)

14. LeCun, Y., Bengio, Y., Hinton, G.: Deep learning. Nature **521**(7553), 436–444 (2015)

15. Lee, H., Grosse, R., Ranganath, R., Ng, A.Y.: Convolutional deep belief networks for scalable unsupervised learning of hierarchical representations. In: ICML, pp. 609–616. ACM (2009)

16. Levinson, J., et al.: Towards fully autonomous driving: systems and algorithms. In: Intelligent Vehicles Symposium (IV), pp. 163–168. IEEE (2011)

17. Lombrozo, T.: Explanation and abductive inference. In: The Oxford Handbook of Thinking And Reasoning (2012)

18. Lombrozo, T.: The structure and function of explanations. Trends Cogn. Sci. **10**(10), 464–470 (2006)

19. Paden, B., Čáp, M., Yong, S.Z., Yershov, D., Frazzoli, E.: A survey of motion planning and control techniques for self-driving urban vehicles. IEEE Trans. Intell. Veh. **1**(1), 33–55 (2016)

20. Papineni, K., Roukos, S., Ward, T., Zhu, W.J.: BLEU: a method for automatic evaluation of machine translation. In: Proceedings of the 40th Annual Meeting on Association for Computational Linguistics, pp. 311–318. Association for Computational Linguistics (2002)

21. Park, D.H., Hendricks, L.A., Akata, Z., Schiele, B., Darrell, T., Rohrbach, M.: Multimodal explanations: justifying decisions and pointing to the evidence. In: Proceedings of the IEEE Conference on Computer Vision and Pattern Recognition (CVPR) (2018)

22. Srivastava, N., Hinton, G.E., Krizhevsky, A., Sutskever, I., Salakhutdinov, R.: Dropout: a simple way to prevent neural networks from overfitting. J. Mach. Learn. Res. **15**(1), 1929–1958 (2014)
23. Urmson, C.: Autonomous driving in urban environments: boss and the urban challenge. J. Field Robot. **25**(8), 425–466 (2008)
24. Vedantam, R., Lawrence Zitnick, C., Parikh, D.: Cider: consensus-based image description evaluation. In: Proceedings of the IEEE Conference on Computer Vision and Pattern Recognition, pp. 4566–4575 (2015)
25. Venugopalan, S., Rohrbach, M., Donahue, J., Mooney, R., Darrell, T., Saenko, K.: Sequence to sequence-video to text. In: Proceedings of the IEEE International Conference on Computer Vision, pp. 4534–4542 (2015)
26. Xu, H., Gao, Y., Yu, F., Darrell, T.: End-to-end learning of driving models from large-scale video datasets. In: Proceedings of the IEEE Conference on Computer Vision and Pattern Recognition, pp. 2174–2182 (2017)
27. Xu, K., et al.: Show, attend and tell: neural image caption generation with visual attention. In: International Conference on Machine Learning, pp. 2048–2057 (2015)
28. Zeiler, M.D., Fergus, R.: Visualizing and understanding convolutional networks. In: Fleet, D., Pajdla, T., Schiele, B., Tuytelaars, T. (eds.) ECCV 2014. LNCS, vol. 8689, pp. 818–833. Springer, Cham (2014). https://doi.org/10.1007/978-3-319-10590-1_53

Contemplating Visual Emotions: Understanding and Overcoming Dataset Bias

Rameswar Panda[1]($\boxtimes$), Jianming Zhang[2], Haoxiang Li[3], Joon-Young Lee[2], Xin Lu[2], and Amit K. Roy-Chowdhury[1]

[1] Department of ECE, UC Riverside, Riverside, USA
rpand002@ucr.edu, amitrc@ece.ucr.edu
[2] Adobe Research, San Jose, USA
{jianmzha,jolee,xinl}@adobe.com
[3] Aibee, Palo Alto, USA
hxli@aibee.com

Abstract. While machine learning approaches to visual emotion recognition offer great promise, current methods consider training and testing models on small scale datasets covering limited visual emotion concepts. Our analysis identifies an important but long overlooked issue of existing visual emotion benchmarks in the form of dataset biases. We design a series of tests to show and measure how such dataset biases obstruct learning a generalizable emotion recognition model. Based on our analysis, we propose a webly supervised approach by leveraging a large quantity of stock image data. Our approach uses a simple yet effective curriculum guided training strategy for learning discriminative emotion features. We discover that the models learned using our large scale stock image dataset exhibit significantly better generalization ability than the existing datasets without the manual collection of even a single label. Moreover, visual representation learned using our approach holds a lot of promise across a variety of tasks on different image and video datasets.

Keywords: Emotion recognition · Webly supervised learning

1 Introduction

Recently, algorithms for object recognition and related tasks have become sufficiently proficient that new vision tasks beyond objects can now be pursued. One such task is to *recognize emotions expressed by images* which has gained momentum in last couple of years in both academia and industries [4,30,40,43,62,63]. Teaching machines to recognize diverse emotions is a very challenging problem with great application potential.

Electronic supplementary material The online version of this chapter (https://doi.org/10.1007/978-3-030-01216-8_36) contains supplementary material, which is available to authorized users.

V. Ferrari et al. (Eds.): ECCV 2018, LNCS 11206, pp. 594–612, 2018.
https://doi.org/10.1007/978-3-030-01216-8_36

Fig. 1. (a) An example image of an amusement park with negative emotion (sadness) (Source: Google Images). (b)-(c) Nearest neighbor images extracted from "amusement" and "sadness" category in the Deep Emotion dataset [63], which show a strong data bias. We use the pool5 features from our ResNet-50 trained on Deep Emotion dataset to extract these nearest neighbor images.

Let us consider the image shown in Fig. 1a. Can you recognize the basic emotion expressed by this image? Practically, this should not be a difficult task as a quick glance can well reveal that the overall emotional impact of the image is negative (i.e., sadness) (9 out of 10 students in our lab made it correct!). In fact, this is the image of a Six Flags theme park at New Orleans which has been closed since Hurricane Katrina struck the state of Louisiana in August 2005.[1]

Intrigued, we decided to perform a toy experiment using Convolutional Neural Networks (CNNs) to recognize emotions. A ResNet-50 [22] model that we trained on the current largest Deep Emotion dataset [63] predicts an emotion of "amusement/joy" with 99.9% confidence from the image in Fig. 1a. Why is this happening? Our initial investigation with the nearest neighbour images in Fig. 1.b/c shows that the dataset bias appears to be the main culprit. Specifically, the Deep Emotion dataset [63] suffers from two types of biases. The first is the positive set bias, which makes the *amusement* category in the dataset full of photos of amusement parks (see Fig. 1b). This is due to the lack of diversity in visual concepts when collecting the source images. The second is the negative set bias, where the rest of the dataset does not well represent the rest of the world, i.e., no images of sad park in the dataset (see Fig. 1c).

In this paper, instead of focusing on beating the latest benchmark numbers on the latest dataset, we take a step back and pose an important question: *how well do the existing datasets stack up overall in the emerging field of visual emotion recognition?* We first conduct a series of tests including a novel correlation analysis between emotion and object/scene categories to analyze the presence of bias in existing benchmarks. We then present a number of possible remedies, mainly proposing a new weakly-labeled large-scale emotion dataset collected from a stock website and a simple yet effective curriculum guided training strategy for learning discriminative features. Our systematic analysis, which is first in emotion recognition, will provide insights to the researchers working in this area to focus on the right training/testing protocols and more broadly simulate discussions in the community regarding this very important but largely neglected

---

[1] The image is taken from Google Images with the search keyword *sad amusement park*. Source: https://goo.gl/AUwoPZ.

issue of dataset bias in emotion recognition. We also hope our efforts in releasing several emotion benchmarks in this work will open up avenues for facilitating progress in this emerging area of computer vision.[2]

The key takeaways from this paper can be summarized as follows:

- **Existing visual emotion datasets appear to have significant bias.** We conduct extensive studies and experiments for analyzing emotion recognition datasets (Sect. 3). Our analysis reveals the presence of significant biases in current benchmark datasets and calls for rethinking the current methodology for training and testing emotion recognition models.
- **Learning with large amounts of web data helps to alleviate (at least minimize) the effect of dataset bias.** We show that models learned using large-scale stock data exhibit significantly better generalization ability while testing on new unseen datasets (Sect. 5.1). We further propose a simple yet effective curriculum guided training strategy (Sect. 4) for learning discriminative emotion features that achieves state-of-the-art performance on various tasks across different image and video datasets (Sect. 5.2). For example, we show improved performance (~3% in top-5 mAP) of a state-of-the-art video summarization algorithm [41] by just plugging in our emotion features.
- **New Datasets.** We introduce multiple image emotion datasets collected from different sources for model training and testing. Our stock image dataset is one of the largest in the area of visual emotion analysis containing about 268,000 high quality stock photos across 25 fine-grained emotion categories.

2   Related Work

Emotion Wheels. Various types of emotion wheels have been studied in psychology, e.g., Ekman's emotions [13] and Plutchik's emotions [45]. Our work is based on the popular Parrott's wheel of emotions [42] which organizes emotions in the form of a tree with primary, secondary and tertiary emotions. This hierarchical grouping is more interpretable and can potentially help to learn a better recognition model by leveraging the structure.

Image Emotion Recognition. A number of prior works studying visual emotion recognition focus on analyzing facial expressions [7,12,12,14–16,31,47]. Specifically, these works mainly predict emotions for images that involve a clear background with people as the primary subject. Predicting emotions from user-generated videos [27,29,60], social media images [56,57,60] and artistic photos [1,65] are also some recent trends in emotion recognition. While these approaches have obtained reasonable performance on such controlled emotion datasets, they have not yet considered predicting emotions from natural images as discussed in this paper. Most related to our work along the direction of recognizing emotions from natural images are the works of [30,38,43,63] which predict

---
[2] All our datasets, models and supplementary material are publicly available on our project page: https://rpand002.github.io/emotion.html.

emotions from images crawled from Flickr and Instagram. As an example, the authors in [63] learn a CNN model to recognize emotions in natural images and performs reasonably well on the Deep Emotion dataset [63]. However, it requires expensive human annotation and is difficult to scale up to cover the diverse emotion concepts. Instead, we focus on webly supervised learning of CNNs which can potentially avoid (at least minimize) the dataset design biases by utilizing vast amount of weakly labeled data from diverse concepts.

Webly Supervised Learning. There is a continued interest in the vision community on learning recognition models directly from web data since images on the web can cover a wide variety of visual concepts and, more importantly, can be used to learn computational models without using instance-level human annotations [5,10,17,18,28,32,35–37,49]. While the existing works have shown advantages of using web data by either manually cleaning the data or developing a specific mechanism for reducing the noise level, we demonstrate that noisy web data can be surprisingly effective with a curriculum guided learning strategy for recognizing fine-grained emotions from natural images.

Curriculum Learning. Our work is related to curriculum learning [2,11,19, 33,44,64] that learns a model by gradually including easy to complex samples in training so as to increase the entropy of training samples. However, unlike these prior works that typically focus on the evolution of the input training data, our approach focuses on the evolution of the output domain, i.e., evolution of emotion categories from being easy to difficult in prediction.

Hierarchical Recognition. Category hierarchies have been successfully leveraged in several recognition tasks: image classification [3,8,20,34,58,61], object detection [9,39], image annotation [52], and concept learning [24] (see [46] for an overview). CNN based methods [48,55,58,61] have also used class hierarchy for large scale image classification. Unlike these methods that mostly use clean manually labeled datasets to learn the hierarchy, we adopt an emotion hierarchy from psychology [42] to guide the learning with noisy web data. Our basic idea is that the emotion hierarchy can provide guidance for learning more difficult tasks in a sequential manner and also provide regularization for label noises.

3   Understanding Bias in Emotion Datasets

Goal. Our main goal in this section is to identify, show and measure dataset bias in existing emotion recognition datasets using a series of tests.

Datasets. We pick three representative datasets including one newly created by us: (1) Deep Sentiment [62] dataset containing 1269 images from Twitter, (2) the current largest Deep Emotion dataset [63], (3) our Emotion-6 dataset

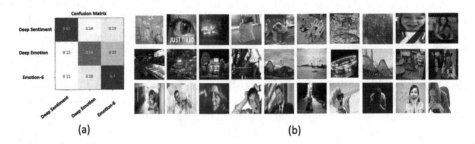

Fig. 2. (a) Confusion matrix, (b) From top to bottom, depicted are examples of high confident correct predictions from Deep Sentiment, Deep Emotion and Emotion-6 datasets respectively.

Table 1. Binary Cross-Dataset Generalization. Diagonal numbers refer to training and testing on same dataset while non-diagonal numbers refer to training on one dataset and testing on others. % Drop refers to the performance drop across the diagonal and the average of non-digonal numbers.

Train on	Test on			
	Deep sentiment	Deep emotion	Emotion-6	% Drop
Deep sentiment	78.74	68.38	49.76	**24.98**
Deep emotion	61.41	84.81	69.22	**22.99**
Emotion-6	54.33	64.28	77.72	**23.69**

of 8350 images (*anger*: 1604, *fear*: 1280, *joy*: 1964, *love*: 724, *sadness*: 2221, *surprise*: 557) labeled by five human subjects from intially 150 K images collected from Google and Flickr (see supp). Our main motivation on creating Emotion-6 dataset is to repeat the standard data collection/annotation protocol used by existing works [62,63] and see how well it performs regarding the dataset biases.

Test 1. Name That Dataset Game. With the aim of getting an initial idea on the relation among different datasets, we start our analysis by running *Name That Dataset Game* as in [51]. We randomly sample 500 images from the training portions of each of the three datasets and train a 3-class linear classifier over the ResNet-50 features. We then test on 100 random images from each of the test sets and observe that the classifier is reasonably good at telling different datasets apart, giving 63.67% performance. The distinct diagonal in confusion matrix (Fig. 2a) shows that these datasets possesses an unique signature leading to the presence of bias. For example, visually examining the high confidence correct predictions from the test set in Fig. 2b indicates that Deep Emotion dataset has a strong preference for outdoor scenes mostly focusing on parks (2nd row), while Emotion-6 tend to be biased toward images where a single object is centered with a clean background and a canonical viewpoint (3rd row).

Test 2. Binary Cross-Dataset Generalization. Given all three datasets, we train a ResNet-50 classifier to show cross-dataset generalization i.e., training on one dataset while testing on the other. For both Deep Emotion and Emotion-6, we randomly sample 80% of images for training and keep rest 20% for testing, while on Deep Sentiment, we use 90% of images for the training and keep the rest for testing, as in [62]. Since, exact emotion categories can vary from one dataset to another, we report binary classification accuracies (positive vs negative) which are computed by tranforming the predicted labels to two basic emotion categories, following Parrott's emotional grouping [42]. We call this *Binary Cross-Dataset Generalization Test*, as it asks the CNN model to predict the most trivial basic emotion category from an image. If a model cannot generalize well in this simple test, it will not work on more fine-grained emotion categories. Moreover, the binary generalization test only involves minimum post-processing of the model predictions, so it can evaluate different datasets more fairly.

Table 1 shows a summary of results. From Table 1, the following observations can be made: (1) As expected, training and testing on the same dataset provides the best performance on all cases (marked in red). (2) Training on one dataset and testing on the other shows a significant drop in accuracy, for instance, the classifier trained on Deep Emotion dataset shows a average drop of 22.99% in accuracy while testing on other two datasets. Why is this happening? Our observations suggest that the answer lies in the emotion dataset itself: it's size is relatively small, which results in the positive set bias due to the lack of diversity in visual concepts. As a result, models learned using such data essentially memorize all it's idiosyncrasies and lose the ability to generalize.

Test 3. Quantifying Negative Bias. We choose three common emotion categories across Deep Emotion and Emotion-6 datasets (*anger, fear* and *sadness*) to measure negative set bias in different datasets. For each dataset, we train a binary classifier (e.g., anger vs non-anger) on its own set of positive and negative instances while for testing, the positives come from that dataset, but the negatives come from other datasets. We train the classifiers on 500 positive and 2000 negative images randomly selected from each dataset. Then for testing, we use 200 positive and 4000 negative images from other datasets.

Table 2 summarizes the results. For both datasets, we observe a significant decrease in performance (maximum of about 25% for Deep Emotion dataset on *sadness* emotion), suggesting that some of the new negative samples coming from other datasets are confused with positive examples. This indicates that rest of the dataset does not well represent the rest of the visual world leading to overconfident, and not very discriminative, classifiers.

Test 4. Correlation Analysis with Object/Scene Categories. Given existing object/scene recognition models, the objective of this test is to see how well emotions are correlated with object/scene categories and whether analyzing the correlations can help to identify the presence of bias in emotion datasets. We use ResNet-50 pre-trained on ImageNet and ResNet-152 pre-trained on

Table 2. Quantifying Negative Bias. Self refers to testing on the original test set while Others refer to the testing on a set where positives come from the original dataset but negatives come from the other. % Drop refers to the performance drop across the self and others. Values in Others represent the average numbers. WEBEmo refers to our released dataset that we will discuss in next section.

Task	−ve set:	+ve set:		
		Deep emotion	Emotion-6	WEBEmo
Anger vs Non-anger	Self/Others/% Drop	90.64/78.98/**12.86**	92.40/83.56/**9.57**	83.90/83.37/**0.63**
Fear vs Non-fear	Self/Others/% Drop	85.95/80.77/**6.05**	81.14/76.02/**2.56**	82.97/84.79/**−2.19**
Sadness vs Non-sadness	Self/Others/% Drop	81.90/61.35/**25.09**	89.20/82.07/**7.99**	89.89/90.55/**−0.73**

Places365 as object and scene recognition models respectively. We start our analysis by predicting object/scene categories from images of three common emotion categories used in previous task. We then select top 200 most occurring object/scene categories from each emotion class and compute the conditional entropy of each object/scene category across positive and negative set of a specific emotion. Mathematically, given an object/scene category c and emotion category e, we compute the conditional entropy as $\mathcal{H}(Y|X = c) = -\sum_{y \in \{e_p, e_n\}} p(y|X = c)\log p(y|X = c)$, where e_p and e_n represent the positive and negative set of emotion e respectively (e.g., anger and non-anger). More number of object/scene categories with zero conditional entropy will most likely lead to a biased dataset as it shows the presence of these object/scene categories in either positive or negative set of an emotion resulting in an unbalanced representation of the visual world (Fig. 1).

Figure 3 shows the distribution of object/scene categories w.r.t conditional entropy for both Deep Emotion and Emotion-6 datasets. While analyzing correlations between objects and *sadness* emotion in Fig. 3a, we observe that about 30% of object categories (zero conditional entropy) are only present in either sadness or non-sadness category and then further examining these categories, we find most of them will lead to a dataset bias (see supp). For example, objects like balloon, candy store and parachute are only present in negative set of *sadness*. Categories like balloon are strongly related to happiness, but still there should be a few negative balloon images such as sad balloon in the negative set.[3] Completely missing the negative balloon images will lead to dataset bias. Emotion-6 appears to be less biased compared to Deep Emotion but still it has 25% of object categories in the entropy range of [0,0.5]. Similarly, on analyzing scene categories for *anger* emotion in Fig. 3b, we see that both datasets are biased towards to specific scene categories, e.g., for Deep Emotion, about 55% of scene categories have zero conditional entropy while about 20% of categories have zero entropy in Emotion-6. More results are included in the supplementary.

Our main conclusions from these series of tests indicate that despite all three datasets being collected from Internet and labeled using a similar paradigm involving multiple humans, they appear to have strong bias which severely obstruct learning a generalizable recognition model.

---

[3] For example, see: https://tinyurl.com/yazvkjmv.

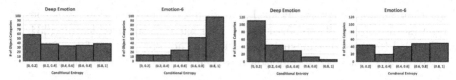

(a) Object Categories for *Sadness* Emotion   (b) Scene Categories for *Anger* emotion.

Fig. 3. Distribution of object/scene categories w.r.t conditional entropy. (a) objects in *sadness* emotion, (b) scenes in *anger* emotion. Both datasets show a strong presence of bias.

4   Curriculum Guided Webly Supervised Learning

Goal. The main goal of this section is to present possible remedies to the dataset bias issues described above, mainly proposing a large-scale web emotion database, called **WEBEmo** and an effective curriculum guided strategy for learning discriminative emotion features. Our basic idea is that we can potentially avoid (at least minimize) the effect of dataset design biases by exploiting vast amount of freely available web data covering a wide variety of emotion concepts.

Emotion Categories. Emotions can be grouped into different categories. Most prior works only consider a few independent emotion categories, e.g., Ekmas's six emotions [13] or Plutchik's eight emotion categories [45]. Instead, we opt for Parrott's hierarchical model of emotions [42] for two main advantages. First, by leveraging this hierarchy with associated lists of keywords, we are able to allieviate the search engine bias by diversifying the image search. Second, we are able to learn discriminative features by progressively solving different tasks.

Following [42], we design a three-level emotion hierarchy, starting from two basic categories (*positive* and *negative*) at level-1, six categories (*anger, fear, joy,*

Fig. 4. Sample images from our **WEBEmo** dataset across six secondary emotion categories. These images cover a wide range of visual concepts. Best viewed in color.

love, sadness, and *surprise*) at level-2 to 25 fine-grained emotion categories at level-3 (see Fig. 5 for all categories). Note that while data-driven learning [34,54] can be used for constructing such hierarchy, we chose to design it following prior psychological studies [42] as emotion has been well studied in psychology.

Retrieving Images from the Web. We use a stock website to retrieve web images and use those images without any additional manual labeling. Below, we provide a brief description of the dataset and refer to supplementary for details.

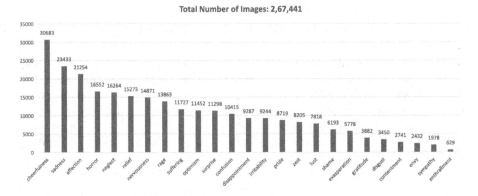

Fig. 5. Category-wise distribution of images in **WEBEmo** dataset. The are more than 30K images on *cheerfulness* category while only 629 images are there on *enthrallment* emotion category. Categories are sorted according to the number of images in corresponding category, from the highest (left) to the lowest (right). Best viewed in enlarged version.

To collect web images for emotion recognition, we follow [42] to assemble a list of keywords (shown in supp) for each 25 fine-grained emotions, focusing on diverse visual concepts (see Fig. 4). We then use the entire list of keywords to query a stock site and retrieve all the images (∼10,000) together with their tags returned for each query. In this way, we are able to collect about 300,000 weakly labeled images, i.e., labeled by the queries. We then remove images with non-English tags and also use captions with top-5 tags to remove duplicate images. After deduplication, we ended up with about 268,000 high-quality stock images. Figure 5 shows category-wise distribution of images in **WEBEmo** dataset. The total number of images in our **WEBEmo** dataset is about 12 times larger than the current largest Deep Emotion dataset [63].

Curriculum Guided Training. Our goal is to learn discriminative features for emotion recognition directly using our **WEBEmo** database. While it seems that one can directly train a CNN with such data, as in [32] for image classification, we found it is extremely hard to learn good features for our task, as emotions are intrinsically fine-grained, ambiguous, and web data is more prone to label noise. However, as shown in psychology [42], emotions are organized in a hierarchy starting from basic emotions like positive or negative to more fine-grained emotions like affection, contentment, optimism and exasperation, etc. Categorizing images to two basic emotions is an easier task compared to categorizing images to such fine-grained emotions. So, what we want is an approach that can learn visual representation in a sequential manner like we humans normally learn difficult tasks in an organized manner.

Inspired by curriculum learning [2] and the emotion wheel from psychology [42], we develop a curriculum guided strategy for learning discriminative features in a sequential manner. Our basic idea is to gradually inject the information to the learner (CNN) so that in the early stages of training, the coarse-scale properties of the data are captured while the finer-scale characteristics are learned in later stages. Moreover, since the amount of label noise is likely to be much less in coarse categories, it can produce regularization effect and enhance the generalization of the learned representations.

Let C be the set of fine-grained emotion categories ($= 25$ in our case) and $k \in \{1 \ldots K\}$ be the different stages of training. Assume $C_K = C$ is the fine-grained emotion categories that we want to predict; that is, our target is to arrive at the prediction of these emotion labels at the final stage of learning K. In our curriculum guided learning, we require a stage-to-stage emotional mapping operator $\mathcal{F}$ which projects C_k, the output labels at stage k, to a lower-dimensional C_{k-1} which is easier to predict compared to the prediction of C_k labels. We follow the Parrott's emotion grouping [42] as the mapping operator that groups C_K categories into six secondary and two primary level emotions as described earlier. Specifically, a CNN (pre-trained on ImageNet) is first fine-tuned with 2 basic emotions (positive/negative) at level-1 and then it serves to initialize a second one that discriminates six emotion categories at level-2 and the process is finally repeated for 25 fine-grained emotion categories at level-3.

5   Experiments

Goal. We perform rigorous experiments with the following two main objectives:

(a) How well our newly introduced **WEBEmo** dataset along with the curriculum guided learning help in reducing the dataset bias? (Sect. 5.1)
(b) How effective our visual representation learned using **WEBEmo** dataset in recognizing both image and video emotions? Do emotion features benefit other visual analysis tasks, say video summarization? (Sect. 5.2)

Implementation Details. All the networks are trained using the Caffe toolbox [25]. We choose ResNet-50 [22] as our default deep network and initialize from an ImageNet checkpoint while learning using web data [50]. During training, all input images are resized to 256×256 pixels and then randomly cropped to 224×224. We use batch normalization after all the convolutional layers and train using stochastic gradient descent with a minibatch size of 24, learning rate

Table 3. Cross-Dataset Generalization. "Self" refers to training and testing on same dataset and "Mean Others" refers to the mean performance on all others. Model trained using curriculum guided webly supervised learning generalizes well to other datasets.

Train on	Test on					
	Deep Sentiment	Deep Emotion	Emotion-6	WEBEmo	Self	Mean Others
Deep sentiment [62]	78.74	68.38	49.76	47.79	78.74	55.31
Deep Emotion [63]	61.41	84.81	69.22	59.95	84.81	63.52
Emotion-6 (Sect. 3)	54.33	64.28	77.72	64.30	77.72	62.30
WEBEmo (Ours)	68.50	71.42	78.38	81.41	81.41	**72.76**

of 0.01, momentum of 0.9 and weight decay of 0.0001. We reduce the learning rate to its $\frac{1}{10}$ while making transition in our curriculum guided training.

5.1   Revisiting Dataset Bias with Our Approach

Experiment 1: Quantifying Negative Bias. We use the same number of images (total 2500 for training and 4200 for testing) and follow the exact same testing protocol mentioned in Sect. 3: Test 2 to analyze negative bias on our **WEBEmo** dataset. Table 2 shows that classifiers trained on our dataset do not seem to be affected by a new external negative set across all three emotion categories (see right most column in Table 2). This is because **WEBEmo** dataset benefits from a large variability of negative examples and hence more comprehensively represent the visual world of emotions.

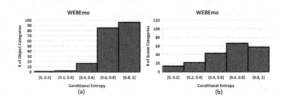

Fig. 6. Distribution of object/scene categories w.r.t conditional entropy on **WEBEmo** dataset. (a) objects in *sadness*, (b) scenes in *anger* emotion.

Experiment 2: Correlation Analysis with Object/Scene Categories. Figure 6 shows the correlation between emotion and object/scene categories in our **WEBEmo** dataset. As can be seen from Fig. 6a, less than 10% of object categories are within the entropy range [0,0.6] for *sadness* emotion leading to a much less biased dataset. This result is also consistent with the performance of the classifier trained for sadness vs non-sadness image classification in previous experiment (see Table 2). We also observe that more number of scene categories have entropy in the higher range (see Fig. 6b) showing that most of the scenes are well distributed across positive and negative emotion sets in our dataset. Note that the negative bias still persists regardless of the large size of our dataset

Table 4. Exploration study on different webly supervised learning strategies.

Methods	Deep sentiment	Deep emotion	Emotion-6	WEBEmo	Self	Mean others
Direct learning	62.20	67.48	74.73	76.65	76.65	68.13
Self-directed learning	64.56	68.76	76.15	78.69	78.69	69.82
Joint learning	66.71	69.08	75.36	78.27	78.27	70.38
Curriculum learning	68.50	71.42	78.38	81.41	81.41	**72.76**

covering a wide variety of concepts (some object/scene categories still have zero entropy). We can further minimize the bias by adding weakly labeled images associated with zero entropy categories such that both positive and negative set can have a balanced distribution. This experiment demonstrates that our correlation analysis can help to detect as well as reduce biases in datasets.

Experiment 3: Binary Cross-Dataset Generalization. Table 3 summarizes the results. We have the following key observations from Table 3: (1) Model trained using our **WEBEmo** dataset shows the best generalization ability compared to the models trained using manually labeled emotion datasets. We believe this is because learning by utilizing web data helps in minimizing the dataset biases by covering a wide variety of emotion concepts. (2) More interestingly, on Emotion-6 dataset, the model trained using our stock images even outperforms the model trained with images from the same Emotion-6 dataset (77.72% vs 78.38%). This is quite remarkable as our model has only been trained using the web images without any strong supervision.

Exploration Study. To better understand effectiveness of curriculum guided learning strategy, we analyze cross-dataset generalization performance by comparing with following methods: (1) Direct Learning – directly learning using the noisy web images of 25 fine-grained emotion categories, as in [28,32,63]; (2) Self-Directed Learning – start learning with a small clean set (500 images) and then progressively adapt the model by refining the noisy web data, as in [18,62]; (3) Joint Learning – simultaneously learning with all the tasks in a multi-task setting. For details please refer to our supplementary material. We have the following key observations from Table 4: (1) Performance of direct learning baseline is much worse compared to our curriculum guided learning. This is not surprising since emotions are highly complex and ambigious that directly learning models to categorize such finegrained details fails to learn discriminative features. (2) Self-directed learning shows better generalization compared to the direct learning but still suffers from the requirement of initial labeled data. (3) The joint learning baseline is more competitive since it learns a shared representation from multiple tasks. However, the curriculum guided learning still outperforms it in terms generalization across other datasets (70.38% vs 72.76%). We believe this is because by ordering training from easy to difficult in a sequential manner, it is able to learn more discriminative feature for recognizing complex emotions.

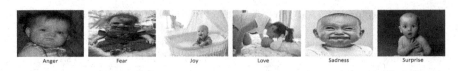

Fig. 7. Sample images from our challenging **UnBiasedEmo** test set. See supplementary file for more example images on different object/scenes. Best viewed in color.

Impact of Emotion Categories. We compare our three stage curriculum learning strategy (2-6-25) with a two stage one involving only six emotion categories (2-6). We found that the later produces inferior results, with an accuracy of 78.21% on the self test set and a mean accuracy of 70.05% on other two datasets, compared to 81.41% and 72.76% respectively by the three stage curriculum learning. Similarly, there is a drop of 2.31% in "self" test accuracy of the direct learning baseline while training with six emotion categories compared to the training with 25 emotion categories. In summary, we observe that the generalization ability of learned models increase with increased number of fine-grained emotion categories.

State-of-the-Art Results. Note that all the numbers presented in Table 3 represent the binary accuracies we achieved without using any ground truth training data from the testing dataset. By fine-tuning, our model achieves a state-of-the-art accuracy of 61.13% in classifying eight emotions on Deep Emotion dataset [63] and an accuracy of 54.90% on Emotion-6 dataset. Similarly, by utilizing training data from Deep Sentiment dataset, our model achieves an accuracy of 82.67% which is about 8% improvement over the prior work [62].

5.2 Analyzing Effectiveness of Our Learned Emotion Features

Experiment 1: Testing on Cross-Domain Unbiased Data. In this experiment, we introduce a new unbiased emotion test set, **UnBiasedEmo** of about 3000 images downloaded from Google to evaluate our learned models in recognizing very challenging emotions, e.g., different emotions with same object/scene

Table 5. Experimental results on our **UnBiasedEmo** test dataset. Features learned using curriculum learning outperforms all other basline features, including ImageNet.

Methods	Accuracy (%)
ImageNet	64.20
Direct learning	71.64
Self-directed learning	72.45
Joint learning	71.64
Curriculum learning	**74.27**

(see Fig. 7). Since source of this test set is different from our **WEBEmo** dataset, it helps us alleviate the dataset bias issue in evaluation, so we can compare the generalization ability of various learning strategies in a less biased manner. Note that developing a large-scale unbiased dataset containing hundred thousands of images like this is a very difficult task as it requires extensive effort and also provides poor scalability. For an example, we could only able to get 3045 emotional images across six emotion categories (same as Emotion-6 dataset) from a collection of about 60,000 images. More details on this unbiased dataset collection and annotations are included in the supplementary.

We use our learned models as feature extractors. We use 80% of the images for training and keep rest 20% for testing. Table 5 shows the classification accuracies achieved by the features learned using different methods. We have the following observations from Table 5: (1) Our curriculum learning strategy significantly outperforms all other baselines in recognizing fine-grained emotions from natural images. (2) Among the alternatives, self-directed learning baseline is the most competitive. However, our approach still outperforms it due to the fact that we use the emotion hierarchy to learn discriminative features by focusing tasks in a sequential manner. (3) Performance of ImageNet features is much worse compared to the features learned using our curriculum guided webly supervised learning (64.20% vs 74.27%). This is expected as ImageNet features are tailored towards object/scene classification while emotions are more fine-grained and can be orthogonal to object/scene category, as shown in Fig. 7.

We also investigate the quality of features learned using the current largest Deep Emotion dataset [63] in recognizing image emotions on this unbiased test set and found that it produces inferior results, with an accuracy of 68.88% compared to 74.27% by our curriculum guided webly-supervised learning strategy on the **WEBEmo** dataset. We believe this is because of the effective utilization of large scale web data covering a wide variety of emotion concepts.

Table 6. Experimental results on Image Advertisement dataset. Our curriculum learning model performs the best.

Methods	Accuracy (%)
ImageNet	23.42
Direct learning	25.43
Self-directed learning	24.92
Joint learning	26.18
Curriculum learning	**27.96**

Table 7. Experimental results on VideoStory-P14 dataset. Features learned using our proposed curriculum learning outperforms the knowledge transfer approach by a margin of about 4%.

Methods	Accuracy(%)
ImageNet	43.27
Direct learning	45.67
Self-directed learning	46.18
Joint learning	47.25
Knowledge transfer [59]	45.10
Curriculum learning	**49.22**

Experiment 2: Sentiment Analysis. We perform this experiment to verify the effectivenss of our features in recognizing sentiments from online advertisement images. We conduct experiments using Image Advertisement dataset [23]

consisting of 30,340 online ad images labeled with 30 sentiment categories (e.g., active, alarmed, feminine, etc, – see [23] for more details). We use the model weights as initialization and fine-tune the weights [23]. We use 2403 images for testing and rest for training as in [23]. We follow [23] and chose the most frequent sentiment as the ground-truth label for each advertisement image.

Table 6 shows results of different methods on predicting image sentiments on the Advertisement dataset. From Table 6, the following observations can be made: (1) Once again, our curriculum guided learning significantly outperforms all other baselines in predicting sentiments from online ad images. (2) We achieve an improvement of about 6% over the ImageNet baseline showing the advantage of our learned features in automatic ad understanding tasks.

Experiment 3: Video Emotion Recognition. The goal of this experiment is to evaluate quality of our features in recognizing emotions from user videos. We conduct experiments on VideoStory-P14 emotion dataset [59] consisting of 626 user videos across Plutchik's 14 emotion classes. We fine-tune the weights using video datasets and use 80%/20% of the videos in each category for training/testing. To produce predictions for an entire video, we average the frame-level predictions of 20 frames which are randomly selected from the video.

From Table 7, the following observations can be made: (1) We can see that all the models trained using **WEBEmo** dataset outperforms both ImageNet and transfer encoding features [59] indicating the generalizability of our learned features in recognizing video emotions. (2) We further observe that curriculum guided learning provides about 2% improvement over the joint learning baseline.

Experiment 4: Video Summarization. Our goal in this experiment is to see whether our learned features can benefit summarization algorithms in extracting high quality summaries from user videos. We believe this is possible since an accurate summary should keep emotional content conveyed by the original video.

We perform experiments on the CoSum dataset [6] containing 51 videos covering 10 topics from the SumMe benchmark [21]. We follow [6,41] and segment the videos into multiple non-uniform shots for processing. We first extract pool5 features from the network trained with curriculum learning on our **WEBEmo** dataset and then use temporal mean pooling to compute a single shot-level feature vector, following [41]. We follow the exact same parameter settings of [41] and compare the summarization results by only replacing the visual features.

By using our learned emotion features, the top-5 mAP score of the recent summarization method [41] improves by a margin of about 3% over the C3D features [53] (68.7% vs 71.2%). This improvement is attributed to the fact that good summary should be succinct but also provide good coverage of the original video's emotion content. This is an important finding in our work and we believe this can largely benefit researchers working in video summarization to consider the importance of emotion while generating good quality video summaries.

Additional Experiments in Supplementary. We analyze the effectivenss of our learned features in predicting communicative intents from persuasive images (e.g., politician photos) [26] and see that our approach outperforms all other baselines by a significant margin (∼8% improvement over ImageNet features). We also provide sample prediction results in the supplementary material.

6   Conclusion

In this paper, we have provided a thorough analysis of the existing emotion benchmarks and studied the problem of learning recognition models directly using web data without any human annotations. We introduced a new large-scale image emotion dataset containing about 268,000 high-quality images crawled from a stock website to train generalizable recognition models. We then proposed a simple actionable curriculum guided training strategy for learning discriminative emotion features that holds a lot of promise on a wide variety of visual emotion understanding tasks. Finally, we demonstrated that our learned emotion features can improve state-of-the-art methods for video summarization.

Acknowledgements. This work is partially supported by NSF grant 1724341 and gifts from Adobe. We thank Victor Hill of UCR CS for setting up the computing infrastructure used in this work.

References

1. Alameda-Pineda, X., Ricci, E., Yan, Y., Sebe, N.: Recognizing emotions from abstract paintings using non-linear matrix completion. In: CVPR (2016)
2. Bengio, Y., Louradour, J., Collobert, R., Weston, J.: Curriculum learning. In: ICML (2009)
3. Cesa-Bianchi, N., Gentile, C., Zaniboni, L.: Incremental algorithms for hierarchical classification. JMLR **7**, 31–54 (2006)
4. Chen, T., Borth, D., Darrell, T., Chang, S.F.: Deepsentibank: visual sentiment concept classification with deep convolutional neural networks. arXiv preprint arXiv:1410.8586 (2014)
5. Chen, X., Gupta, A.: Webly supervised learning of convolutional networks. In: ICCV (2015)
6. Chu, W.S., Song, Y., Jaimes, A.: Video co-summarization: video summarization by visual co-occurrence. In: CVPR (2015)
7. Chu, W.S., De la Torre, F., Cohn, J.F.: Selective transfer machine for personalized facial expression analysis. TPAMI **39**, 529–545 (2017)
8. Deng, J., Krause, J., Berg, A.C., Fei-Fei, L.: Hedging your bets: optimizing accuracy-specificity trade-offs in large scale visual recognition. In: CVPR (2012)
9. Deng, J., Satheesh, S., Berg, A.C., Li, F.: Fast and balanced: efficient label tree learning for large scale object recognition. In: NIPS (2011)
10. Divvala, S.K., Farhadi, A., Guestrin, C.: Learning everything about anything: webly-supervised visual concept learning. In: CVPR (2014)
11. Dong, Q., Gong, S., Zhu, X.: Multi-task curriculum transfer deep learning of clothing attributes. In: WACV (2017)

12. Du, S., Tao, Y., Martinez, A.M.: Compound facial expressions of emotion. In: Proceedings of the National Academy of Sciences (2014)
13. Ekman, P.: An argument for basic emotions. Cogn. Emot. **6**, 169–200 (1992)
14. Eleftheriadis, S., Rudovic, O., Pantic, M.: Discriminative shared Gaussian processes for multiview and view-invariant facial expression recognition. In: TIP (2015)
15. Eleftheriadis, S., Rudovic, O., Pantic, M.: Joint facial action unit detection and feature fusion: a multi-conditional learning approach. In: TIP (2016)
16. Fabian Benitez-Quiroz, C., Srinivasan, R., Martinez, A.M.: Emotionet: An accurate, real-time algorithm for the automatic annotation of a million facial expressions in the wild. In: CVPR (2016)
17. Gan, C., Sun, C., Duan, L., Gong, B.: Webly-supervised video recognition by mutually voting for relevant web images and web video frames. In: Leibe, B., Matas, J., Sebe, N., Welling, M. (eds.) ECCV 2016. LNCS, vol. 9907, pp. 849–866. Springer, Cham (2016). https://doi.org/10.1007/978-3-319-46487-9_52
18. Gan, C., Yao, T., Yang, K., Yang, Y., Mei, T.: You lead, we exceed: labor-free video concept learning by jointly exploiting web videos and images. In: CVPR (2016)
19. Gao, R., Grauman, K.: On-demand learning for deep image restoration. In: ICCV (2017)
20. Griffin, G., Perona, P.: Learning and using taxonomies for fast visual categorization. In: CVPR, pp. 1–8 (2008)
21. Gygli, M., Grabner, H., Riemenschneider, H., Van Gool, L.: Creating summaries from user videos. In: Fleet, D., Pajdla, T., Schiele, B., Tuytelaars, T. (eds.) ECCV 2014. LNCS, vol. 8695, pp. 505–520. Springer, Cham (2014). https://doi.org/10.1007/978-3-319-10584-0_33
22. He, K., Zhang, X., Ren, S., Sun, J.: Deep residual learning for image recognition. In: CVPR (2016)
23. Hussain, Z., et al.: Automatic understanding of image and video advertisements. In: CVPR (2017)
24. Jia, Y., Abbott, J.T., Austerweil, J.L., Griffiths, T., Darrell, T.: Visual concept learning: combining machine vision and Bayesian generalization on concept hierarchies. In: NIPS (2013)
25. Jia, Y., et al.: Caffe: convolutional architecture for fast feature embedding. In: MM (2014)
26. Joo, J., Li, W., Steen, F.F., Zhu, S.C.: Visual persuasion: inferring communicative intents of images. In: CVPR (2014)
27. Jou, B., Bhattacharya, S., Chang, S.F.: Predicting viewer perceived emotions in animated gifs. In: MM (2014)
28. Joulin, A., van der Maaten, L., Jabri, A., Vasilache, N.: Learning visual features from large weakly supervised data. In: Leibe, B., Matas, J., Sebe, N., Welling, M. (eds.) ECCV 2016. LNCS, vol. 9911, pp. 67–84. Springer, Cham (2016). https://doi.org/10.1007/978-3-319-46478-7_5
29. Kahou, S.E., et al.: Combining modality specific deep neural networks for emotion recognition in video. In: ICMI (2013)
30. Kim, H.R., Kim, S.J., Lee, I.K.: Building emotional machines: recognizing image emotions through deep neural networks. arXiv preprint arXiv:1705.07543 (2017)
31. Kosti, R., Alvarez, J.M., Recasens, A., Lapedriza, A.: Emotion recognition in context. In: CVPR (2017)
32. Krause, J., et al.: The unreasonable effectiveness of noisy data for fine-grained recognition. In: Leibe, B., Matas, J., Sebe, N., Welling, M. (eds.) ECCV 2016. LNCS, vol. 9907, pp. 301–320. Springer, Cham (2016). https://doi.org/10.1007/978-3-319-46487-9_19

33. Lee, Y.J., Grauman, K.: Learning the easy things first: self-paced visual category discovery. In: CVPR (2011)
34. Li, L.J., Wang, C., Lim, Y., Blei, D.M., Fei-Fei, L.: Building and using a semantivisual image hierarchy. In: CVPR (2010)
35. Li, W., Wang, L., Li, W., Agustsson, E., Van Gool, L.: Webvision database: visual learning and understanding from web data. arXiv preprint arXiv:1708.02862 (2017)
36. Liang, J., Jiang, L., Meng, D., Hauptmann, A.: Exploiting multi-modal curriculum in noisy web data for large-scale concept learning. arXiv preprint arXiv:1607.04780 (2016)
37. Liang, J., Jiang, L., Meng, D., Hauptmann, A.G.: Learning to detect concepts from webly-labeled video data. In: IJCAI (2016)
38. Machajdik, J., Hanbury, A.: Affective image classification using features inspired by psychology and art theory. In: MM (2010)
39. Marszalek, M., Schmid, C.: Semantic hierarchies for visual object recognition. In: CVPR (2007)
40. Ng, H.W., Nguyen, V.D., Vonikakis, V., Winkler, S.: Deep learning for emotion recognition on small datasets using transfer learning. In: ICMI (2015)
41. Panda, R., Roy-Chowdhury, A.K.: Collaborative summarization of topic-related videos. In: CVPR (2017)
42. Parrott, W.G.: Emotions in Social Psychology: Essential Readings. Psychology Press, Hove (2001)
43. Peng, K.C., Chen, T., Sadovnik, A., Gallagher, A.C.: A mixed bag of emotions: model, predict, and transfer emotion distributions. In: CVPR (2015)
44. Pentina, A., Sharmanska, V., Lampert, C.H.: Curriculum learning of multiple tasks. In: CVPR (2015)
45. Plutchik, R., Kellerman, H.: Emotion, Theory, Research, and Experience: Theory, Research and Experience. Academic Press, San Diego (1980)
46. Silla Jr., C.N., Freitas, A.A.: A survey of hierarchical classification across different application domains. Data Min. Knowl. Discov. 22, 31–72 (2011)
47. Soleymani, M., Asghari-Esfeden, S., Fu, Y., Pantic, M.: Analysis of EEG signals and facial expressions for continuous emotion detection. In: TAC (2016)
48. Srivastava, N., Salakhutdinov, R.R.: Discriminative transfer learning with tree-based priors. In: NIPS (2013)
49. Sukhbaatar, S., Fergus, R.: Learning from noisy labels with deep neural networks. arXiv preprint arXiv:1406.2080 (2014)
50. Sun, C., Shrivastava, A., Singh, S., Gupta, A.: Revisiting unreasonable effectiveness of data in deep learning era. In: ICCV (2017)
51. Torralba, A., Efros, A.A.: Unbiased look at dataset bias. In: CVPR (2011)
52. Tousch, A.M., Herbin, S., Audibert, J.Y.: Semantic hierarchies for image annotation: a survey. Pattern Recognit. 45, 333–345 (2012)
53. Tran, D., Bourdev, L., Fergus, R., Torresani, L., Paluri, M.: Learning spatiotemporal features with 3D convolutional networks. In: ICCV (2015)
54. Verma, N., Mahajan, D., Sellamanickam, S., Nair, V.: Learning hierarchical similarity metrics. In: CVPR (2012)
55. Wang, D., Shen, Z., Shao, J., Zhang, W., Xue, X., Zhang, Z.: Multiple granularity descriptors for fine-grained categorization. In: ICCV (2015)
56. Wang, X., Jia, J., Tang, J., Wu, B., Cai, L., Xie, L.: Modeling emotion influence in image social networks. TAC 6, 286–297 (2015)
57. Wu, B., Jia, J., Yang, Y., Zhao, P., Tang, J., Tian, Q.: Inferring emotional tags from social images with user demographics. TMM 19, 1670–1684 (2017)

58. Xiao, T., Zhang, J., Yang, K., Peng, Y., Zhang, Z.: Error-driven incremental learning in deep convolutional neural network for large-scale image classification. In: MM (2014)
59. Xu, B., Fu, Y., Jiang, Y.G., Li, B., Sigal, L.: Heterogeneous knowledge transfer in video emotion recognition, attribution and summarization. TAC **9**, 255–270 (2016)
60. Xu, B., Fu, Y., Jiang, Y.G., Li, B., Sigal, L.: Video emotion recognition with ferred deep feature encodings. In: ICMR (2016)
61. Yan, Z., et al.: HD-CNN: hierarchical deep convolutional neural networks for large scale visual recognition. In: ICCV (2015)
62. You, Q., Luo, J., Jin, H., Yang, J.: Robust image sentiment analysis using progressively trained and domain transferred deep networks. In: AAAI (2015)
63. You, Q., Luo, J., Jin, H., Yang, J.: Building a large scale dataset for image emotion recognition: the fine print and the benchmark. In: AAAI (2016)
64. Zhang, Y., David, P., Gong, B.: Curriculum domain adaptation for semantic segmentation of urban scenes. arXiv preprint arXiv:1707.09465 (2017)
65. Zhao, S., Gao, Y., Jiang, X., Yao, H., Chua, T.S., Sun, X.: Exploring principles-of-art features for image emotion recognition. In: MM (2014)

Deep Recursive HDRI: Inverse Tone Mapping Using Generative Adversarial Networks

Siyeong Lee, Gwon Hwan An, and Suk-Ju Kang[✉]

Department of Electronic Engineering, Sogang University, Seoul, South Korea
{siyeong,ghan,sjkang}@sogang.ac.kr

Abstract. High dynamic range images contain luminance information of the physical world and provide more realistic experience than conventional low dynamic range images. Because most images have a low dynamic range, recovering the lost dynamic range from a single low dynamic range image is still prevalent. We propose a novel method for restoring the lost dynamic range from a single low dynamic range image through a deep neural network. The proposed method is the first framework to create high dynamic range images based on the estimated multi-exposure stack using the conditional generative adversarial network structure. In this architecture, we train the network by setting an objective function that is a combination of $L1$ loss and generative adversarial network loss. In addition, this architecture has a simplified structure than the existing networks. In the experimental results, the proposed network generated a multi-exposure stack consisting of realistic images with varying exposure values while avoiding artifacts on public benchmarks, compared with the existing methods. In addition, both the multi-exposure stacks and high dynamic range images estimated by the proposed method are significantly similar to the ground truth than other state-of-the-art algorithms.

Keywords: High dynamic range imaging · Inverse tone mapping
Image restoration · Computational photography
Generative adversarial network · Deep learning

1 Introduction

Most single low dynamic range (LDR) images cannot capture light information for infinite levels owing to physical sensor limitations of a camera. For the too bright or dark area in the image, the boundary with surrounding objects does not appear. However, a high dynamic range (HDR) image containing various brightness information by acquiring and combining LDR images having different

Electronic supplementary material The online version of this chapter (https://doi.org/10.1007/978-3-030-01216-8_37) contains supplementary material, which is available to authorized users.

V. Ferrari et al. (Eds.): ECCV 2018, LNCS 11206, pp. 613–628, 2018.
https://doi.org/10.1007/978-3-030-01216-8_37

exposure levels does not encounter this problem. Owing to this property, interests on HDR imaging have been increasing in various fields. Unfortunately, creating an HDR image from multiple LDR images requires multiple shots, and HDR cameras are still unaffordable. As a result, alternative methods are needed to infer an HDR image from a single LDR image.

Generating an HDR image with only a single LDR image is referred to as an inverse tone mapping problem. This is an ill-posed problem, because a missing signal not appearing in a given image should be restored. Recently, studies have been conducted on an HDR image application using deep learning technique [1–3]. Endo *et al.* [1], Lee *et al.* [2], and Eilertsen *et al.* [3] successfully restored the lost dynamic range using deep learning. However, a disadvantage is that it requires additional training to generate additional LDR images or fails to restore some patterns.

Deep learning is a method of processing information by deriving a function that connects two domains that are difficult to find relation as a function approximator. Deep neural networks demonstrate noteworthy performance for real-world problems (image classification, image restoration, and image generation) that are difficult to be solved by the hand-crafted method. Deep learning, which has emerged in the field of supervised learning that requires labeled data during the learning process, has recently undergone a new turning with the stabilization of the generative adversarial network (GAN) structure [4–8].

We propose a novel method for inverse tone mapping using the GAN structure. This paper has the following three main contributions:

1. The GAN structure creates more realistic images than a network trained with a simple pixel-wise loss function because a discriminator represents a changeable loss that includes the global and local information in the input image during the training process. Thus, we use the structural advantages of the GAN to infer natural HDR images that extend the dynamic range of a given image.
2. We propose a novel network architecture that reconfigures the deep chain HDRI network structure [2], which is a state-of-art method for restoring the lost dynamic range. The reconfigured network can be significantly simplified in scale compared with the existing network, while the performance is maintained.
3. Unlike the conventional deep learning-based inverse tone mapping methods [1,2] that produce a fixed number of images with different exposure values, we represent the relationship between images with relative exposure values, which has the advantage of generating images with the wider dynamic range without the additional cost.

2   Related Works

Deep Learning-Based Inverse Tone Mapping. As with other image restoration problems, inverse tone mapping involves the issue of restoring the

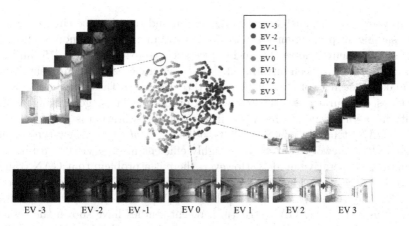

Fig. 1. Three-dimensional distribution for the image dataset with different exposure values in the image manifold space: for images labeled with the corresponding exposure value, we visualized the image space by three-dimensional reduction using t-distributed stochastic neighbor embedding [9]. Images having the same scene gradually change in the space. In addition, when the difference in the exposure value between the images is large, they are far from each other on the manifold. (Color figure online)

lost signal information. To solve this problem, the conventional hand-craft algorithms in this field deduce a function to infer the pixel luminance based on the lightness and relations between spatially adjacent pixels of a given image [10,11], create a pseudo multi-exposure image stack [12], or merge optimally exposed regions of LDR red/green/blue color components for generating an HDR image [13]. By contrast, methods using deep learning [1–3] are included in the example-based learning and successfully applied to restore the lost dynamic range of LDR images. In other words, these types of deep neural networks estimate a function mapping from the pixel brightness to the luminance from a given train set and generate HDR images of given LDR images. Endo *et al.*'s method [1] creates a multi-exposure stack for a given LDR image using a convolutional neural network (CNN) architecture which consists of three-dimensional convolutional layers. Similarly, Lee *et al.*'s method [2] constructs a multi-exposure image stack using a CNN-based network that is designed to generate images through a deeper network structure as the difference in exposure values between the input and the image to be generated increases. By contrast, Eilerstsen *et al.*'s method [3] determines a saturated region using a CNN-based network for an underexposed LDR image and produces the final HDR image by combining the given LDR image and estimated saturated region. These methods require further networks (or parameters) that generate additional images for creating the final HDR image with a wider dynamic range.

Deep Learning and Adversarial Network Architecture. Because AlexNet [14] has garnered considerable attention in image classification, deep learning is used in various fields, such as computer vision and signal processing, to demonstrate significant performance than conventional methods have not reached. For training deep neural networks, techniques such as residual block [15] and skip connection [16] have been introduced. These techniques smooth the weight space and make these networks easy to train [17]. Based on these methods, various structures of neural networks have been proposed. Thus, generating a high-quality image using neural networks in the image restoration is possible.

The GAN structure proposed by Goodfellow *et al.* [4] is a new type of neural network framework that enables highly efficient unsupervised learning than conventional generative models. However, there is a problem that GAN training is unstable. Hence, various types of min-max problems have been proposed for stable training recently: WGAN [18], LSGAN [19], and f-GAN [20]. In addition, by extending the basic GAN structure, recent studies have shown the remarkable success in the image-to-image translation for two different domains [6–8]. Ledig *et al.* [21] proposed a network, SRGAN, capable of recovering the high-frequency detail using the GAN structure and successfully restored the photo-realistic image through this network. Isola *et al.* [6] demonstrated that it can be successful in image-to-image translation using a simple combination of the modified conditional GAN loss [22] and $L1$ loss.

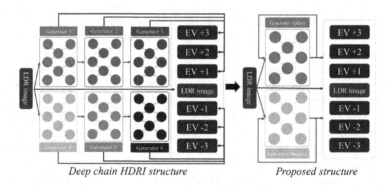

Deep chain HDRI structure   *Proposed structure*

Fig. 2. The structural relationship between a deep chain HDRI [2] and proposed network: the proposed network has a structure of folding sub-networks, which can be interpreted as a structure in which each network shares weight parameters.

3   Proposed Method

We first analyze the latest algorithms based on deep learning that focuses on the stack restoration and attempted to determine problems of these algorithms. As a solution, we propose novel neural networks by reconstructing a deep chain HDRI structure [2]. Figure 2 shows the overall structure of the proposed method.

3.1   Problems of Previous Stack-Based Inverse Tone Mapping Methods Using Deep Learning

The purpose of the inverse tone mapping algorithm to reconstruct the HDR image from the estimated multi-exposure stack is to generate images with different exposure values. When producing images with different exposure values, previous methods [1,2] generate LDR images with a uniform exposure differences T for a given input image (i.e., $T = 1$ or 0.7). In this case, generating $2M$ images with different exposure values from a given image requires $2M$ sub-networks, because each sub-network represents the relationship between input images and images with the difference of exposure value $i \times T$, for $i = \pm1, \pm2, \cdots, \pm M$. Hence, these methods have the disadvantage that the number of additional networks increases linearly to widen the dynamic range. In addition, different datasets and optimization process are needed to train additional networks. Moreover, these fail to restore some patterns by creating artifacts that do not exist. To solve this problem, we define two neural networks G^{plus} and G^{minus} considering the direction of change in the exposure value (plus or minus). In addition, these networks are constrained to generate images considering adjacent pixels using conditional GAN [22]. Then, using these networks, we infer images with relative exposure $+T$ and $-T$ for a given image.

3.2   Training Process Using an Adversarial Network Architecture

The conditional GAN based architecture that is constrained by input images produces higher-quality images than the basic GAN structure [6]. Therefore, we design the architecture conditioned on the exposure value of the given input using a conditional GAN structure. In other words, to convert to images with a relative exposure value $+T$ (or $-T$), we define a discriminator network D^{plus} (or D^{minus}) that outputs the probability to determine whether a given pair of images is real or fake.

The proposed architecture determines the optimal solution in the min-max problem of Eqs. (1) and (2):

$$G^{plus}, D^{plus} = \min_G \max_D \{ \mathbb{E}_{I^{EVi+1}, I^{EVi}}[log D(I^{EVi+1}, I^{EVi})] \tag{1}$$
$$+ \mathbb{E}_{I^{EVi}, z}[1 - log D(G(I^{EVi}, z), I^{EVi})] \},$$

$$G^{minus}, D^{minus} = \min_G \max_D \{ \mathbb{E}_{I^{EVi-1}, I^{EVi}}[log D(I^{EVi-1}, I^{EVi})]$$
$$+ \mathbb{E}_{I^{EVi}, z}[1 - log D(G(I^{EVi}, z), I^{EVi})] \}, \tag{2}$$

where I^{EVi} is an image with $EV\ i$, z is a random noise vector, and $\mathbb{E}$ is the expectation function. For D^{plus}, we set the pair (I^{EVi+1}, I^{EVi}) as a real and the pair $(G(I^{EVi}, z), I^{EVi})$ as a fake.

3.3 Structure of the Proposed Neural Network Architecture

We verified the specific network settings of the generator and discriminator through the supplementary document (Fig. 3).

Generator: U-Net [23] Structure. We adopt an encoder-decoder model as the generator structure. When the data goes to the next layer, the size of the feature map is reduced by one-half, vertically and horizontally, and conversely doubled. Then, the abstracted feature map is reassembled with the previous feature maps for creating the desired output through a structure that increases the width and height of the feature map. In this structure, we add skip-connections between encoder layers and decoder layers, so that the characteristics of low-level features are reflected in the output. The downsampling block consists of a convolutional layer, one batch normalization layer, and one parametric ReLU (PReLU) [24]. And, the upsampling block contains an upsampling layer, one convolutional layer, one batch normalization layer, and one PReLU. The upsampling layer doubles the feature map size using the nearest-neighbor interpolation. As with the deep chain HDRI, we used PReLU for the network inferring relative $EV + 1$ and MPReLU [2] for the opposite direction.

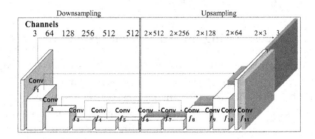

Fig. 3. Structure of proposed generators G^{plus}, G^{minus}.

Discriminator: Feature Matching. The neural network of the GAN structure is difficult to train [4,5,18–20]. In particular, the problem that the discriminator does not distinguish clearly between the real and fake leads to the difficulty in determining the desired solution in the min-max problem. To solve this problem, we use the method training the generator to match the similarity of features on an intermediate layer of the discriminator in the basic GAN [5]. Therefore, the proposed discriminator is similar to the Markovian discriminator structure [6,25]. This discriminator generates feature maps that consider the neighboring pixels in an input through convolutional layers. Hence, this network outputs the probability whether each patch in an input image is real or not. Unlike pixel-wise loss, the loss function expressed by the discriminator network represents the structured loss such as the structural similarity, feature matching, and conditional random field [26]. In other words, the loss produced by this discriminator allowed the generator to create natural images that reflect in the relationship between adjacent pixels. The proposed discriminator is composed of convolution blocks, including one convolution layer, one batch normalization layer, and one leaky ReLU layer [27]. The activation function of the last convolution block is a sigmoid function. In addition, there is no batch normalization layer for the first and last layers (Fig. 4).

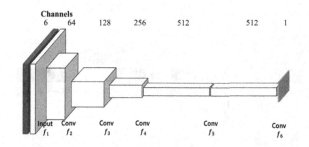

Fig. 4. Structure of proposed discriminators D^{plus}, D^{minus}.

3.4 Loss Functions

For G^{plus} and G^{minus}, we set an objective function that combined the following two losses for the training. We set the relative weights of each loss to $\lambda = 100$ through the experimental procedure. the final objective is:

$$G^{plus} = \arg\min_{G} L_{LSGAN}(G) + \lambda L_{L1}(G) \text{ for training pairs } (I^{EV1}, I) \text{ and } \quad (3)$$

$$G^{minus} = \arg\min_{G} L_{LSGAN}(G) + \lambda L_{L1}(G) \text{ for training pairs } (I^{EV-1}, I), \quad (4)$$

where I is an input image, I^{EV1} (or I^{EV-1}) is an image with the relative exposure difference 1 (or -1) for a given I.

GAN Loss. As the basic GAN structure [4] is unstable in the training process, we use LSGAN [19] to determine the optimal solution of the min-max problem. For an input image x, a reference image y, and random noise z,

$$L_{LSGAN}(D) = \frac{1}{2}\mathbb{E}_{x,y}[(D(y,x) - 1)^2] + \frac{1}{2}\mathbb{E}_{x,z}[(D(G(x,z),x))^2], \quad (5)$$

$$L_{LSGAN}(G) = \mathbb{E}_{x,z}[(D(G(x,z),x) - 1)^2], \quad (6)$$

where G and D are training networks. We divide the loss of the discriminator by half compared with the generator process to make the overall learning stable by delaying the training of the discriminator.

Content Loss. The pixel-wise mean absolute error (MAE) loss L_{L1} is defined as:

$$L_{L1}(G) = \mathbb{E}_{x,y,z}[\|y - G(x,z)\|_1]. \tag{7}$$

A method to calculate the pixel-wise difference between two images through $L2$ norm generates a blurred image relative to $L1$ norm for image restoration [28]. Therefore, we use $L1$ loss as a term of the objective function to recover low-frequency components.

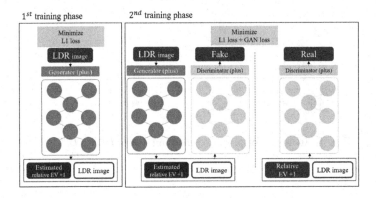

Fig. 5. The training process of proposed network architecture: we trained the generators to minimize $L1$ loss and defeat discriminator networks. The discriminator distinguishes the pair (reference, input) from the pair (estimated image, input) as the training progresses.

3.5 Optimization Process

The proposed architecture is trained through two steps, as shown in Fig. 5. In the first training phase, we used only $L1$ loss, and in the second training phase, we additionally used GAN loss. We set the two training phases epoch with the same ratio (1:1). In the second training phase, the discriminator and generator alternated one by one to minimize each objective function. We used the Adam optimizer [29] with 0.00005 of the learning rate, and momentum parameters were $\beta_1 = 0.5$ and $\beta_2 = 0.999$. We set the batch size to one. The dropout noise is added during training.

3.6 Inference

First, we generated images $\hat{I}^{EV1}$ and $\hat{I}^{EV-1}$ from the given LDR image, as shown in Fig. 6, using G^{plus}, G^{minus}. In the next phase, we obtained $\hat{I}^{EV2}$, $\hat{I}^{EV-2}$ by using $\hat{I}^{EV1}$ and $\hat{I}^{EV-1}$ as the input of G^{plus} and G^{minus}, respectively. We recursively repeated this process for creating a multi-exposure stack. Figure 6 shows an example of outputting the multi-exposure stack up to $EV \pm 3$.

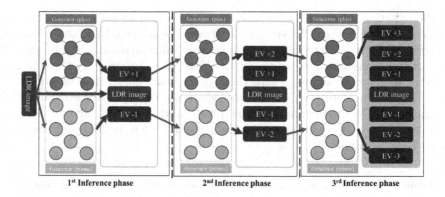

Fig. 6. The multi-exposure stack generation process of the proposed structure.

4   Experimental Results

For a dataset, we used 48 stacks of VDS dataset [2] for training, and other 48 stacks of VDS dataset and 41 stacks of HDREye dataset [30] for testing. VDS database is composed of images taken with Nikon 7000, and HDREye consists of images taken with Sony DSC-RX100 II, Sony NEX-5N, and Sony α6000. Both the VDS and HDREye datasets consists of seven images, each of which has uniformly different exposure levels. We set the unit exposure value T to exposure value one at $ISO - 100$ like the deep chain HDRI [2]. By using Debevec *et al.*'s algorithm [31], we synthesized the generated stack with a target HDR image, and we generated the tone-mapped images by using Reinhard *et al.*'s [32] and Kim and Kautz's methods [33] through HDR Toolbox [34]. For the image pair with the exposure value difference, we set the image with low exposure value as an input image and set the other image as a reference when training G^{plus}. (G^{minus} was done in the opposite way.) We randomly cropped the sub-images with the 256×256 pixel resolution from the training set, which contained adequate information about the entire image rather than patches, thereby providing 20,700 training pairs. We set epochs of the first and second phases to 10 for training.

First, to verify that the images were generated successfully, we compared them with the ground truths through the peak signal-to-noise ratios (PSNR), structural similarity (SSIM), and multi-scale SSIM (MS-SSIM) on test images with 512×512 pixel resolution. Second, we compared our method with the state-of-the-art algorithms using deep learning [1–3]. Finally, we confirmed the performance of the proposed method by testing the different loss functions with two cases: $L1$ loss and $L1 + GAN$ Loss.

4.1   Comparison Between the Ground Truth LDR and Inferred LDR Image Stacks

Table 1 and Fig. 7 show the several results and comparisons between estimated and ground truth stacks. In addition, we compared it to the deep chain HDRI method [2] that estimated a stack with the same unit exposure value $T = 1$. In the proposed method, the similarity between the inferred LDR and reference images was reduced as the difference of exposure value increased. This is because the artifacts were amplified as the input image passed recursively through the network to generate an image with the high exposure value. However, the proposed method used the GAN structure, where the discriminator evaluated the image quality by considering adjacent pixels, and generated inferred images, thereby increasing the similarity with the ground truth compared with the deep chain HDRI method.

Table 1. Comparison of the ground truth LDR and inferred LDR image stacks.

		PSNR(dB)		SSIM		MS-SSIM	
		m	σ	m	σ	m	σ
EV +3	Proposed	28.97	2.92	0.944	0.044	0.981	0.014
	[2]	28.18	2.77	0.953	0.065	0.983	0.015
EV +2	Proposed	29.43	2.85	0.952	0.039	0.986	0.010
	[2]	29.65	3.06	0.959	0.065	0.986	0.016
EV +1	Proposed	32.02	2.85	0.969	0.026	0.992	0.006
	[2]	31.90	3.43	0.969	0.039	0.992	0.008
EV −1	Proposed	31.22	3.69	0.951	0.031	0.986	0.09
	[2]	29.01	3.83	0.935	0.056	0.980	0.017
EV −2	Proposed	31.08	3.07	0.948	0.041	0.986	0.014
	[2]	26.72	4.54	0.952	0.029	0.974	0.021
EV −3	Proposed	29.15	4.75	0.910	0.061	0.966	0.025
	[2]	24.33	4.57	0.919	0.036	0.948	0.037

4.2   Comparisons with State-of-the-art Methods

For quantitative comparisons with the state-of-the-art methods, we compared PSNR, SSIM, and MS-SSIM with the ground truth for tone-mapped HDR images. Also, we used HDR-VDP-2 [35] based on the human visual system for evaluating the estimated HDR images. We set the input parameters of HDR-VDP-2 evaluation as follows: a 24-inch display, a viewing distance of 0.5 m, peak contrast of 0.0025, and gamma of 2.2. To establish a baseline, we reported the comparison with HDR images inferred by Masia *et al.*'s method [36] using the exponential expansion. Table 2 and Fig. 8 show the evaluation results. In addition, to verify the physics-based reconstruction, we performed to convert an LDR image of a color-checker into an HDR image. LDR and HDR image pairs including a color checker board [30] were used in the experiment. The results of the verification are shown in Fig. 9.

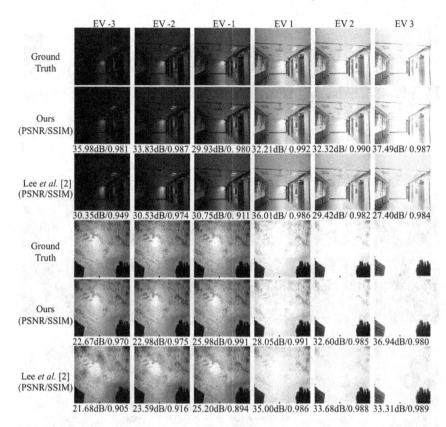

Fig. 7. Comparison of the ground truth LDR and inferred LDR image stacks.

The proposed method exhibited similar performance to the deep chain HDRI [2]. Moreover, the average PSNR of the tone-mapped images was 3 dB higher than that of Endo *et al.* [1], and the average of 10 dB was higher than Eilertsen *et al.* [3]. For HDREye dataset, which consists of images with different characteristics from the training set, the proposed method was almost better than other methods [1–3] in the HDR VDP Q-score. The reconstructed images of the proposed method were more similar to the ground truth than others in the overall tone and average brightness, as shown in Fig. 8. In addition, the dark and saturated regions of the input image were restored.

4.3 Comparison of the Different Loss Functions

To evaluate the effect of the GAN loss term, we compared images generated by the proposed method with training results using only $L1$ loss. When using only the $L1$ loss, we trained the network for 20 epochs. Table 3 presents the results of the quantitative comparison. For tone-mapped images by Reinhard's TMO [32], the average PSNR of the proposed method with $L1$ + GAN was

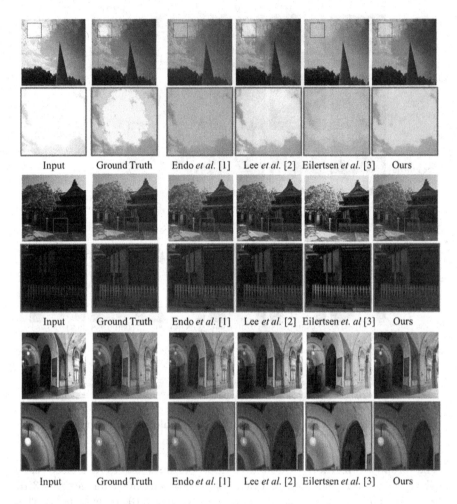

Fig. 8. Comparison of the ground truth HDR images with HDR images inferred by [1–3], and the proposed method (ours).

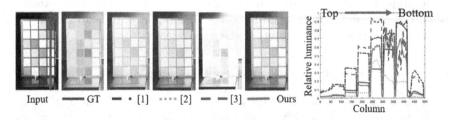

Fig. 9. Comparison of ground truth HDR with HDR images inferred by [1–3], and the proposed method (ours) about physical luminance.

Table 2. Comparison of the ground truth HDR images with HDR images inferred by [1–3,36] and ours. *Red* color indicates the best performance and *blue* color indicates the second best performance.

| | | PSNR (dB) | | PSNR (dB) | | VDP quality | |
| | | Reinhard's TMO | | Kim and Kautz's TMO | | Score | |
		m	σ	m	σ	m	σ
VDS	*Proposed*	*32.14*	3.53	*25.36*	4.11	*57.28*	5.17
	[1]	25.49	4.28	21.36	4.50	54.33	6.27
	[2]	*30.86*	3.36	*24.54*	4.01	*56.36*	4.41
	[3]	17.97	2.17	13.16	2.72	34.25	3.37
	[36]	20.13	2.21	10.74	2.16	51.24	5.67
HDREye	*Proposed*	*26.71*	2.78	*22.31*	3.20	*48.85*	4.91
	[1]	23.68	3.27	19.97	13.41	46.49	5.81
	[2]	*25.77*	2.44	*22.62*	3.39	*49.80*	5.97
	[3]	16.36	1.35	13.41	4.12	37.08	4.62
	[36]	17.18	1.89	9.89	1.94	45.74	5.69

2.27 dB higher than the other. For images generated by Kim and Kautz's TMO [33], the proposed method had an average PSNR of 1.29 dB higher. Figure 10 shows the tone-mapped HDR images generated by the proposed method using the Reinhard's TMO. The network trained by setting $L1$ loss as an objective function generated images that prominently contained artifacts. By contrast, the network architecture with GAN loss did not generate it.

Table 3. Average values of image quality metrics PSNR and VDP quality score on the testing dataset for different cost functions.

| | | PSNR (dB) | | PSNR (dB) | | VDP-quality | |
| | | Reinhard's TMO | | Kim and Kautz's TMO | | Score | |
		m	σ	m	σ	m	σ
VDS	$L1$	28.12	2.51	23.41	3.67	55.78	4.87
	$L1$+GAN	32.14	3.53	25.36	4.11	57.28	5.17
HDREye	$L1$	26.19	2.14	21.69	3.20	49.00	5.19
	$L1$+GAN	26.71	2.78	22.31	3.20	48.85	4.91

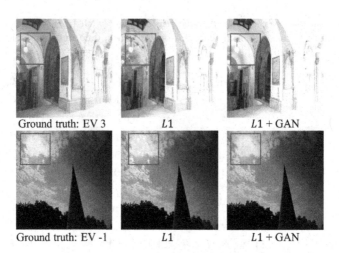

Fig. 10. Comparison of the ground truth HDR images with HDR images inferred by $L1$ and $L1$ + GAN. The proposed method generates fewer artifacts in the image than the network with $L1$.

5 Conclusion

We proposed the deep neural network architecture based on the GAN architecture to solve the inverse tone mapping problem, reconstructing missing signals from a single LDR image. Moreover, we trained this CNN-based neural network to infer the relation between relative exposure values using a conditional GAN structure. Therefore, the proposed method generated an HDR image recovered in a saturated (or dark) region of a given LDR image. This network differed from existing networks [1,2], in that it converted an LDR image into a non-linear LDR image corresponding to +1 or −1 exposure stops. This property led the architecture to generate images with varying exposure levels without additional networks and training process. In addition, we constructed a relatively simple network structure by changing the deep structure effect of deep chain HDRI into a recursive structure.

Acknowledgements. This research was supported by the National Research Foundation of Korea (NRF) grant funded by the Korea government (MSIT) (No. 2018R1D1A1B07048421) and Korea Electric Power Corporation. (Grant number R17XA05-28). We thank Yong Deok Ahn and members of the Sogang Vision and Display Lab. for helpful discussions.

References

1. Endo, Y., Kanamori, Y., Mitani, J.: Deep reverse tone mapping. ACM Trans. Graph. (TOG) **36**(6), 177 (2017)

2. Lee, S., An, G.H., Kang, S.J.: Deep chain HDRI: reconstructing a high dynamic range image from a single low dynamic range image. arXiv preprint arXiv:1801.06277 (2018)

3. Eilertsen, G., Kronander, J., Denes, G., Mantiuk, R.K., Unger, J.: HDR image reconstruction from a single exposure using deep CNNs. ACM Trans. Graph. (TOG) **36**(6), 178 (2017)

4. Goodfellow, I., et al.: Generative adversarial nets. In: Advances in Neural Information Processing Systems, pp. 2672–2680 (2014)

5. Salimans, T., Goodfellow, I., Zaremba, W., Cheung, V., Radford, A., Chen, X.: Improved techniques for training GANs. In: Advances in Neural Information Processing Systems, pp. 2234–2242 (2016)

6. Isola, P., Zhu, J.Y., Zhou, T., Efros, A.A.: Image-to-image translation with conditional adversarial networks

7. Zhu, J.Y., Park, T., Isola, P., Efros, A.A.: Unpaired image-to-image translation using cycle-consistent adversarial networks. arXiv preprint (2017)

8. Kim, T., Cha, M., Kim, H., Lee, J.K., Kim, J.: Learning to discover cross-domain relations with generative adversarial networks. arXiv preprint arXiv:1703.05192 (2017)

9. Maaten, L.V.D., Hinton, G.: Visualizing data using t-SNE. J. Mach. Learn. Res. **9**(Nov), 2579–2605 (2008)

10. Rempel, A.G.: Ldr2Hdr: on-the-fly reverse tone mapping of legacy video and photographs. ACM Trans. Graph. (TOG) **26**, 39 (2007)

11. Meylan, L., Daly, S., Süsstrunk, S.: The reproduction of specular highlights on high dynamic range displays. In: Color and Imaging Conference, vol. 2006, pp. 333–338. Society for Imaging Science and Technology (2006)

12. Wang, T.H., et al.: Pseudo-multiple-exposure-based tone fusion with local region adjustment. IEEE Trans. Multimed. **17**(4), 470–484 (2015)

13. Hirakawa, K., Simon, P.M.: Single-shot high dynamic range imaging with conventional camera hardware. In: 2011 IEEE International Conference on Computer Vision (ICCV), pp. 1339–1346. IEEE (2011)

14. Krizhevsky, A., Sutskever, I., Hinton, G.E.: ImageNet classification with deep convolutional neural networks. In: Advances in Neural Information Processing Systems, pp. 1097–1105 (2012)

15. He, K., Zhang, X., Ren, S., Sun, J.: Deep residual learning for image recognition. In: Proceedings of the IEEE Conference on Computer Vision and Pattern Recognition, pp. 770–778 (2016)

16. Mao, X.J., Shen, C., Yang, Y.B.: Image restoration using convolutional autoencoders with symmetric skip connections. arXiv preprint arXiv:1606.08921 (2016)

17. Li, H., Xu, Z., Taylor, G., Goldstein, T.: Visualizing the loss landscape of neural nets. arXiv preprint arXiv:1712.09913 (2017)

18. Arjovsky, M., Chintala, S., Bottou, L.: Wasserstein GAN. arXiv preprint arXiv:1701.07875 (2017)

19. Mao, X., Li, Q., Xie, H., Lau, R.Y., Wang, Z., Smolley, S.P.: Least squares generative adversarial networks. In: 2017 IEEE International Conference on Computer Vision (ICCV), pp. 2813–2821. IEEE (2017)

20. Nowozin, S., Cseke, B., Tomioka, R.: f-GAN: training generative neural samplers using variational divergence minimization. In: Advances in Neural Information Processing Systems, pp. 271–279 (2016)

21. Ledig, C., et al.: Photo-realistic single image super-resolution using a generative adversarial network. In: CVPR, vol. 2, p. 4 (2017)

22. Mirza, M., Osindero, S.: Conditional generative adversarial nets. arXiv preprint arXiv:1411.1784 (2014)
23. Ronneberger, O., Fischer, P., Brox, T.: U-net: convolutional networks for biomedical image segmentation. In: Navab, N., Hornegger, J., Wells, W.M., Frangi, A.F. (eds.) MICCAI 2015. LNCS, vol. 9351, pp. 234–241. Springer, Cham (2015). https://doi.org/10.1007/978-3-319-24574-4_28
24. He, K., Zhang, X., Ren, S., Sun, J.: Delving deep into rectifiers: surpassing human-level performance on ImageNet classification. In: Proceedings of the IEEE International Conference on Computer Vision, pp. 1026–1034 (2015)
25. Li, C., Wand, M.: Precomputed real-time texture synthesis with markovian generative adversarial networks. In: Leibe, B., Matas, J., Sebe, N., Welling, M. (eds.) ECCV 2016. LNCS, vol. 9907, pp. 702–716. Springer, Cham (2016). https://doi.org/10.1007/978-3-319-46487-9_43
26. Lafferty, J., McCallum, A., Pereira, F.C.: Conditional random fields: probabilistic models for segmenting and labeling sequence data (2001)
27. Maas, A.L., Hannun, A.Y., Ng, A.Y.: Rectifier nonlinearities improve neural network acoustic models
28. Zhao, H., Gallo, O., Frosio, I., Kautz, J.: Loss functions for image restoration with neural networks. IEEE Trans. Comput. Imaging **3**(1), 47–57 (2017)
29. Kingma, D., Ba, J.: Adam: a method for stochastic optimization. arXiv preprint arXiv:1412.6980 (2014)
30. Nemoto, H., Korshunov, P., Hanhart, P., Ebrahimi, T.: Visual attention in LDR and HDR images. In: 9th International Workshop on Video Processing and Quality Metrics for Consumer Electronics (VPQM), Number EPFL-CONF-203873 (2015)
31. Debevec, P.E., Malik, J.: Recovering high dynamic range radiance maps from photographs. In: ACM SIGGRAPH 2008 classes, p. 31. ACM (2008)
32. Reinhard, E., Stark, M., Shirley, P., Ferwerda, J.: Photographic tone reproduction for digital images. ACM Trans. Graph. (TOG) **21**(3), 267–276 (2002)
33. Kim, M.H., Kautz, J.: Consistent tone reproduction. In: Proceedings of the Tenth IASTED International Conference on Computer Graphics and Imaging (CGIM 2008), Innsbruck, Austria, pp. 152–159. IASTED/ACTA Press (2008)
34. Banterle, F., Artusi, A., Debattista, K., Chalmers, A.: Advanced High Dynamic Range Imaging. CRC Press, Boca Raton (2017)
35. Mantiuk, R., Kim, K.J., Rempel, A.G., Heidrich, W.: HDR-VDP-2: a calibrated visual metric for visibility and quality predictions in all luminance conditions. ACM Trans. Graph. (TOG) **30**, 40 (2011)
36. Masia, B., Agustin, S., Fleming, R.W., Sorkine, O., Gutierrez, D.: Evaluation of reverse tone mapping through varying exposure conditions. ACM Trans. Graph. (TOG) **28**(5), 160 (2009)

DeepKSPD: Learning Kernel-Matrix-Based SPD Representation For Fine-Grained Image Recognition

Melih Engin[1], Lei Wang[1]([⊠]), Luping Zhou[1,2], and Xinwang Liu[3]

[1] School of Computing and Information Technology, University of Wollongong,
Wollongong, NSW 2500, Australia
me648@uowmail.edu.au, leiw@uow.edu.au
[2] School of Electrical and Information Engineering, University of Sydney,
Sydney, NSW 2006, Australia
luping.zhou@sydney.edu.au
[3] School of Computer, National University of Defense Technology Changsha,
Hunan 410073, China
xinwangliu@nudt.edu.cn

Abstract. As a second-order pooled representation, covariance matrix has attracted much attention in visual recognition, and some pioneering works have recently integrated it into deep learning. A recent study shows that kernel matrix works considerably better than covariance matrix for this kind of representation, by modeling the higher-order, nonlinear relationship among pooled visual descriptors. Nevertheless, in that study neither the descriptors nor the kernel matrix is deeply learned. Worse, they are considered separately, hindering the pursuit of an optimal representation. To improve this situation, this work designs a deep network that jointly learns local descriptors and kernel-matrix-based pooled representation in an end-to-end manner. The derivatives for the mapping from a local descriptor set to this representation are derived to carry out backpropagation. More importantly, we introduce the Daleckiĭ-Kreĭn formula from Operator theory to give a concise and unified result on differentiating general functions defined on symmetric positive-definite (SPD) matrix, which shows its better numerical stability in conducting backpropagation compared with the existing method when handling the Riemannian geometry of SPD matrix. Experiments on fine-grained image benchmark datasets not only show the superiority of kernel-matrix-based SPD representation with deep local descriptors, but also verify the advantage of the proposed deep network in pursuing better SPD representations. Also, ablation study is provided to explain why and from where these improvements are attained.

Keywords: Kernel matrix · SPD representation · Deep learning
Fine-grained image recognition

Electronic supplementary material The online version of this chapter (https://doi.org/10.1007/978-3-030-01216-8_38) contains supplementary material, which is available to authorized users.

V. Ferrari et al. (Eds.): ECCV 2018, LNCS 11206, pp. 629–645, 2018.
https://doi.org/10.1007/978-3-030-01216-8_38

1 Introduction

To deal with image variations, modern visual recognition usually models the appearance of an image by a set of local descriptors. They evolve from early filter bank responses, through traditional local invariant features, to the activation feature maps of recent deep convolutional neural networks (CNNs). During the course, how to pool a set of local descriptors to obtain a global image representation has been a central issue, and many excellent methods have been proposed in the literature [1–4]. In the past few years, pooling a set of descriptors with covariance matrix has attracted increasing attention and shown promising results in object recognition [5], image set classification [6], and so on. It characterizes the pairwise correlation of descriptor components, and is generally called symmetric positive-definite (SPD) representation since covariance matrix is SPD. Also, this inspires the research on classification, clustering, and dimension reduction with respect to SPD representations [7–9]. In particular, several recent pioneering works integrate this covariance-matrix-based SPD representation into deep CNNs to jointly learn the covariance matrix with local visual descriptors. These works investigates multiple important issues on this deep learning framework, including the derivation of some matrix-based functions for backpropagation, the proper way to normalise covariance matrix, the help of second-order information to large-scale visual recognition, and so on. Together, they further demonstrate the great potential of this kind of representation [10–14].

The above works focus on covariance-matrix-based SPD representation. A recent progress on SPD representation is to model the nonlinear information in a set of descriptors [15–17]. Particularly, the work in [16] directly uses a kernel matrix to represent a descriptor set demonstrates its superiority. Given a set of d-dimensional descriptors, a $d \times d$ kernel matrix is computed with a predefined kernel function, where each entry is the kernel value between the realization of two descriptor components in this set. This method effectively models the nonlinear correlation among these descriptor components. The kernel function can be flexibly chosen to extract various nonlinear relationship, and the covariance matrix corresponds to the special case using a linear kernel. The resulting kernel-matrix-based SPD representation maintains the same size as its covariance-matrix-based counterpart, but produces considerable improvement on recognition performance.

Upon the existing literature, this work further improves the research on SPD representation from the following aspects. Firstly, different from its covariance counterpart, the kernel-matrix-based SPD representation in [16] has neither been developed upon deep local descriptors (instead, traditional descriptors like pixel intensities or Gabor filter responses are used only) nor been jointed learned with these descriptors via a deep learning framework. As a result, its potential has not been sufficiently explored for image recognition. The separated consideration of local descriptors and the kernel matrix in [16] prevents them from effectively negotiating with each other to obtain an optimal SPD representation for the ultimate goal of classification. Secondly, the incorporation of SPD representation, be it covariance-matrix-based or kernel-matrix-based, into deep networks complicates the backpropagation process. Also, to make the resulting SPD representation better work with the classifier, a matrix logarithm is usually employed to map the kernel matrix from Riemannian geometry to Euclidean geometry. Sometimes, matrix square rooting has also been used for this purpose. In the literature, the seminal work in [18] develops the backpropagation algorithm for matrix logarithm from the scratch. Although instructive and informative, it has been reported in the literature that this matrix backpropagation could have numerical stability issue when used to train the deep networks and some remedy has to be developed instead [12].

To address the first issue, this work builds the kernel-matrix-based SPD representation upon deep local descriptors and benchmarks it against the state-of-the-art image recognition methods. Moreover, we develop a deep network called DeepKSPD to jointly learn the deep local descriptors and the kernel-matrix-based SPD representation in an end-to-end training manner. Particularly, for the proposed DeepKSPD network, we highlight the layers designed to be different form the existing deep networks on covariance-matrix-based SPD representation and explain the necessity of these layers.

To address the second issue, we introduce the Daleckiĭ-Kreĭn formula in Operator theory [19,20] to the computer vision community, and utilise it to derive all the matrix derivatives involved in the mapping from a local descriptor set to the kernel-matrix-based SPD representation to fulfill the backpropagation algorithm for the proposed deep network. As shown, the Daleckiĭ-Kreĭn formula can provide us a more concise and unified result on the gradients of the functions on SPD matrices, regardless of whether matrix logarithm or matrix α-rooting are used as the normalisation method. We give theoretical proof to illustrate the relationship of this formula to the matrix backpropagation work [18], and show the discrepancy that leads to the numerical stability issue of [18].

Experimental study is conducted on multiple benchmark datasets, especially on fine-grained image recognition, to demonstrate the efficacy of the proposed DeepKSPD framework. Firstly, in contrast to the existing kernel-matrix-based representation built upon traditional local descriptors, we demonstrate the superiority of the kernel-matrix-based SPD representation using deep local descriptors. Secondly, we demonstrate the performance of the proposed DeepKSPD network in jointly learning local descriptors and the kernel-matrix-based SPD representation, with both normalisation methods of matrix logarithm and matrix α-rooting. Thirdly, ablation study is conducted to manifest the functions of the key layers in DeepKSPD, the improvement due to the kernel-matrix-based SPD representation, and the better numerical stability by using the gradients derived through the Daleckiĭ-Kreĭn formula. As will be seen, the proposed DeepKSPD network achieves the overall highest classification accuracy on the tested benchmark datasets, when compared with the related deep learning based methods.

2   Related Work

In the past decade, much work on covariance-matrix-based representation has been done in computer vision and machine learning, from a variety of perspective.

Also, the recent integration of this representation with deep learning keeps producing new research results. In the following, we focus on the important existing works that are closely related to the DeepKSPD proposed in this paper.

Let $X_{d \times n} = [x_1, x_2, \cdots, x_n]$ denote a data matrix, in which each column contains a local descriptor x_i ($x_i \in \mathcal{R}^d$), extracted from an image. The SPD representation traditionally computes a $d \times d$ covariance matrix over X as $\Sigma = \bar{X}\bar{X}^T$ (or simply XX^T), where $\bar{X}$ denotes the centered X. Originally, this covariance matrix is proposed as a region descriptor, for example, characterizing the covariance of the color intensities of pixels in an image patch. In the past several years, it has been employed as a promising second-order pooled image representation in visual recognition. One line of research on SPD representation models the nonlinear information in a set of descriptors. The work in [15] implicitly maps each descriptor x_i ($i = 1, 2, \cdots, n$) onto a kernel-induced feature space and computes a covariance matrix therein. Nevertheless, this results in a high (or even infinite) dimensional covariance matrix which is difficult to manipulate explicitly or computationally. Another work in [16] directly computes a kernel matrix K over X as follows. Let f_j denote the jth row of X, consisting of the n realizations of the jth component of x. The (i, j)th entry of K is calculated as $k(f_i, f_j)$, with a predefined kernel function k such as a Gaussian kernel. In this way, the nonlinear relationship among the d components can be extracted. The resulting kernel matrix K maintains the size of $d \times d$ and is more robust against the singularity issue caused by small sample. Covariance matrix is a special case in which k reduces to a linear kernel. As reported in [16], this kernel-matrix-based SPD representation considerably outperforms its covariance counterpart and the method in [15] on multiple visual recognition tasks.

Research on integrating the SPD representation *with* deep local descriptors or even *into* deep networks is still in its very early stage but has demonstrated both theoretical and practical values. In the recent work of Bilinear CNN [13,21], an outer product layer is applied to combine the activation features maps from two CNNs, and this produces clear improvement in fine-grained visual recognition. This outer product essentially leads to a covariance matrix (in the form of XX^T) when the two CNNs are set as the same. The work in [18] trains a deep network for image semantic segmentation by using the covariance-matrix-based SPD representation. It carefully derives the gradients of covariance matrix functions from the scratch to carry out backpropagation. Considering that SPD matrix induces a Riemannian geometry, various normalisation operations have been used in the literature to make the matrix work with the classifiers that usually assume a Euclidean geometry. Matrix logarithm normalisation, $\log(\cdot)$, has been commonly used [22], and it is also taken in in [18]. Recently, the work in [12] shows that matrix square-rooting normalisation can even do better than the matrix logarithm counterpart, when applied to covariance-matrix-based SPD representation for fine-grained image classification. The work in [10] further shows and analyses the effectiveness of matrix square-rooting normalisation on large-scale image classification. Due to the verified efficacy of SPD representation on visual recognition, more works are being developed in recent literature from a variety of perspectives. For example, instead of directly computing a kernel as usual, the authors of [17] utilises Taylor series to approximate a kernel function via explicit feature maps, which allows them to generalise the Bilinear CNN framework to consider higher-order feature interaction.

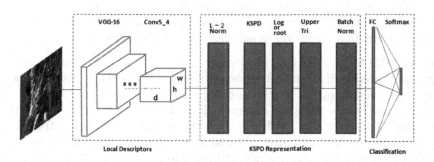

Fig. 1. The structure of the proposed DeepKSPD network

3 The Proposed Network DeepKSPD

DeepKSPD consists of three blocks, as shown in Fig. 1. The leftmost block maps an input image into a set of deep local descriptors via a convolutional neural network. The rightmost block includes the commonly used fully connected and softmax layers for classification. In between is our design of KSPD block, which contains the layers related to the kernel-matrix-based representation and the matrix normalisation operation. For example, the input of the KSPD block is the output of the last convolutional layer (conv5_3) of the VGG-16 network (other CNN networks can certainly be used). It consists of d activation feature maps of the size of $w \times h$. They will go through the L_2 normalization layer and the KSPD layer which computes the kernel values among the d maps. Following that is the matrix normalisation layer (say, matrix logarithm or square-rooting based) to handle the Riemannian geometry of SPD matrix. Finally, since the KSPD representation is a symmetric matrix, a layer extracting its upper triangular and diagonal entries is deployed next to avoid redundancy. Particularly, an L_2 normalization and a batch normalization layer (not confuse with the above matrix normalisation layer) are added at the two ends of the KSPD block, as further explained below. We find that they help the kernel-matrix-based SPD representation to produce better classification.

L_2 **Normalisation Layer.** As aforementioned, its input is the output of the last convolutional layer with the dimensions of $w \times h \times d$. L_2 normalisation is done within each *feature channel*. That is, each channel with the dimensions of $w \times h$ are normalised to have a unit norm. This makes feature vectors and image representation across a whole dataset comparable in terms of magnitude. Also, it helps to render the to-be-computed kernel values into their working range. This is essentially true when using the Gaussian RBF function which is exponential and bounded to $(0, 1]$. In this case, a poor initialisation of the Gaussian width θ (see Eq. (1)) could cause the kernel values in K too close to the boundary, making the backpropagation process inefficient. Also, it could decrease the discriminative capability of the learned SPD representation. With this L_2 normalisation layer, the proposed network becomes less sensitive to initialisation by restricting the feature vectors to a proper range and decreasing their variances.

Kernel SPD Layer. The local descriptors calculated from the L_2 normalisation layer are pooled with a kernel function to obtain a global image representation. The input consists of the d normalised activation feature maps of the size of $w \times h$. These feature maps are reshaped along the depth dimension d, and this gives the data matrix $X_{d \times n}$ with $n = w \times h$. Afterwards, the kernel matrix $K_{d \times d}$ is computed over X to pool the n deep local descriptors, capturing the pairwise nonlinear relationship among the d feature maps. Note that in this layer the Gaussian width θ in Eq. (1) will be jointly learned via backpropagation.

Matrix Function Layer. Following the KSPD layer, this framework performs matrix normalisation to handle the Riemannian geometry of SPD matrix, and this produces the matrix $H = f(K)$. Traditionally, the normalisation function f is chosen as matrix logarithm. Recent studies [10,12] report that matrix square rooting normalisation performs even better in majority of the cases. In our work, all the theoretical analysis assumes no specific normalisation operation and can handle any (continuously differentiable real) function f in backpropagation. In addition, Using the theoretical result provided in our work, we further generalize the existing matrix square-rooting normalisation to a matrix α-rooting normalisation, in which the power α is automatically learned via backpropagation instead of being fixed as 0.5. We also found that L_2 normalising the resulting matrix to have a unit norm allows a smoother convergence.

Batch Normalisation Layer. Batch normalisation layer is used as a post-processing step in our framework. During the forward propagation, each batch is normalised to have zero-mean and unit standard deviation. During the test, overall population statistics are used. In the literature, a layer alike has been used after convolutional layers to speed up convergence and reduce the sensitivity to initialisation. This batch normalisation layer in our framework functions in a similar way: it speeds up the convergence and allows a wider selection of an initial Gaussian width θ, in conjunction with the above L_2 normalisation layer, and helps to increase the overall classification accuracy subsequently. In the literature, the Bilinear CNN models use the setting of "element-wise signed square-rooting plus L_2 normalisation" after the image representation stage as the post-processing stage. Our investigation shows that the above batch normalisation setting works better with the proposed DeepKSPD framework and it is therefore taken in this paper.

4   End-to-end Training of DeepKSPD

4.1   Derivatives Between X and the kernel matrix K

Recall that $X_{d\times n}$ denotes a set of local descriptors. Considering that Gaussian RBF kernel is commonly used in the literature and that it is used in [16] to show the advantage of the kernel-matrix-based representation, we exemplify the proposed DeepKSPD with this kernel and derive the related gradients. Other kernels such as polynomial kernel can be dealt with in a similar way.

Let $I_{d\times d}$ and $1_{d\times d}$ denote an identity matrix and a matrix of 1s. Let $\circ$ denote the entry-wise product (Hadamard product) of two matrices, and $\exp[\cdot]$ denote an exponential function applied to a matrix in an entry-wise manner. In this way, the RBF kernel matrix K computed on X can be compactly expressed as

$$K = \exp\left[-\theta \cdot \left((I \circ XX^T)1 + 1^T(I \circ XX^T)^T - 2XX^T\right)\right], \qquad (1)$$

where θ is the Gaussian width. Let J be the objective function to be optimized by the DeepKSPD network. By temporarily assuming that the derivative $\frac{\partial J}{\partial K}$ has been known (will be resolved in the next section), we now work out the derivatives $\frac{\partial J}{\partial X}$ and $\frac{\partial J}{\partial \theta}$. J is a composition of functions applied to X and it can be rewritten as a function of each of the intermediate variables as follows.

$$J(X) = J_1(A) = J_2(E) = J_3(K), \qquad (2)$$

where A, E, and K are defined, respectively, as

$$A = XX^T, \quad E = \left((I \circ A)1 + 1^T(I \circ A)^T - 2A\right), \quad K = \exp[-\theta \cdot E]. \quad (3)$$

Following the rules for differentiation, the following relationship can be obtained

$$\delta A = (\delta X) X^T + X (\delta X)^T,$$

$$\delta E = (I \circ \delta A)1 + 1^T(I \circ \delta A)^T - 2\delta A, \quad \delta K = (-\theta K) \circ \delta E. \qquad (4)$$

It is known from the differentiation of a scalar-valued matrix function that

$$\delta J = \left\langle \text{vec}\left(\frac{\partial J_3}{\partial K}\right), \text{vec}(\delta K) \right\rangle = \text{trace}\left(\left(\frac{\partial J_3}{\partial K}\right)^T \delta K\right), \qquad (5)$$

where $\text{vec}(\cdot)$ denotes the vectorization of a matrix and $\langle \cdot, \cdot \rangle$ denotes the inner product. Combining this result with $\delta K = (-\theta K) \circ \delta E$ in Eq. (4) and using the identity that $\text{trace}(A^T(B \circ C)) = \text{trace}((B \circ A)^T C)$, we can obtain

$$\delta J = \text{trace}\left(\left(\frac{\partial J_3}{\partial K}\right)^T \delta K\right) = \text{trace}\left(\left(-\theta K \circ \frac{\partial J_3}{\partial K}\right)^T \delta E\right) = \text{trace}\left(\left(\frac{\partial J_2}{\partial E}\right)^T \delta E\right).$$

$$(6)$$

The last equality holds because from Eq. (2) we know that δJ can also be written as $\text{trace}\left(\left(\frac{\partial J_2}{\partial E}\right)^T \delta E\right)$. Noting that Eq. (6) is true for any δE, we obtain

$$\frac{\partial J_2}{\partial E} = (-\theta K) \circ \frac{\partial J_3}{\partial K}. \qquad (7)$$

Repeating the above process by using the relationship of δE and δA and that of δA and δX in Eq. (4), we can further have (proof is provided in the supplementary file)

$$\frac{\partial J_1}{\partial A} = I \circ \left(\left(\frac{\partial J_2}{\partial E} + \left(\frac{\partial J_2}{\partial E} \right)^T \right) \mathbf{1}^T \right) - 2 \frac{\partial J_2}{\partial E}; \quad \frac{\partial J}{\partial X} = \left(\frac{\partial J_1}{\partial A} + \left(\frac{\partial J_1}{\partial A} \right)^T \right) X. \tag{8}$$

In addition, the derivative $\frac{\partial J}{\partial \theta}$ can be obtained as

$$\frac{\partial J}{\partial \theta} = \text{trace} \left(\left(\frac{\partial J_3}{\partial K} \right)^T (-K \circ E) \right). \tag{9}$$

Therefore, when $\frac{\partial J_3}{\partial K}$ is available, we can work out $\frac{\partial J}{\partial X}$ and $\frac{\partial J}{\partial \theta}$ accordingly.

4.2   Derivatives of the Matrix Function on the Kernel Matrix K

Now, to obtain $\frac{\partial J_3}{\partial K}$ we deal with the matrix normalisation operation between K and J, which can be written as

$$J(X) = J_4(H) = J_4(f(K)). \tag{10}$$

Note that $\frac{\partial J_4}{\partial H}$ is ready to obtain because it only involves the classification layers like fully-connected layer, softmax regression and cross-entropy computation. The key issue is to obtain $\frac{\partial H}{\partial K}$. Now, we introduce the *Daleckiĭ-Kreĭn formula* [19] to give a concise and unified result on differentiating SPD matrix functions, of which both matrix logarithm and square-rooting normalisations are special cases.

Theorem 1 (pp. 60, [20]). *Let $\mathbb{M}_d$ be the set of $d \times d$ real symmetric matrices. Let I be an open interval and $\mathbb{M}_d(I)$ is the set of all real symmetric matrices whose eigenvalues belong to I. Let $C^1(I)$ be the space of continuously differentiable real functions on I. Every function f in $C^1(I)$ induces a differentiable map from A in $\mathbb{M}_d(I)$ to $f(A)$ in $\mathbb{M}_d$. Let $Df_A(\cdot)$ denote the derivative of $f(A)$ at A. It is a linear map from $\mathbb{M}_d$ to itself. When applied to $B \in \mathbb{M}_d$, $Df_A(\cdot)$ is given by the Daleckiĭ-Kreĭn formula as*

$$Df_A(B) = U \left(G \circ (U^T B U) \right) U^T, \tag{11}$$

where $A = U D U^T$ is the eigen-decomposition of A with $D = \text{diag}(\lambda_1, \cdots, \lambda_d)$, and $\circ$ is the entry-wise product. The entry of the matrix G is defined as

$$g_{ij} = \begin{cases} \frac{f(\lambda_i) - f(\lambda_j)}{\lambda_i - \lambda_j} & \text{if } \lambda_i \neq \lambda_j \\ f'(\lambda_i), & \text{otherwise.} \end{cases} \tag{12}$$

This theorem indicates that for a matrix function $f(\cdot)$ applied to $\boldsymbol{A}$, perturbing $\boldsymbol{A}$ by a small amount $\boldsymbol{B}$ will vary $f(\boldsymbol{A})$ by the quantity $Df_{\boldsymbol{A}}(\boldsymbol{B})$ in Eq. (11), where the variation is in the sense of the first-order approximation. Now we show how to derive the functional relationship between $\frac{\partial J_4}{\partial \boldsymbol{H}}$ and $\frac{\partial J_3}{\partial \boldsymbol{K}}$ based on Theorem 1. According to Eq. (2) and following the argument in Eq. (5),

$$\delta J = \operatorname{trace}\left(\left(\frac{\partial J_4}{\partial \boldsymbol{H}}\right)^T \delta \boldsymbol{H}\right) = \operatorname{trace}\left(\left(\frac{\partial J_3}{\partial \boldsymbol{K}}\right)^T \delta \boldsymbol{K}\right). \tag{13}$$

Applying the Daleckiĭ-Kreĭn formula, we can explicitly represent $\delta \boldsymbol{H}$ as

$$\delta \boldsymbol{H} = Df_K(\delta \boldsymbol{K}) = \boldsymbol{U}\left(\boldsymbol{G} \circ \left(\boldsymbol{U}^T \delta \boldsymbol{K} \boldsymbol{U}\right)\right)\boldsymbol{U}^T. \tag{14}$$

Replacing $\delta \boldsymbol{H}$ in Eq. (13) with this result and applying the properties of trace($\boldsymbol{A}^T \boldsymbol{B}$), the relationship of $\frac{\partial J_4}{\partial \boldsymbol{H}}$ and $\frac{\partial J_3}{\partial \boldsymbol{K}}$ can be derived similarly as in Eqs. (6) and (7):

$$\frac{\partial J_3}{\partial \boldsymbol{K}} = \boldsymbol{U}\left(\boldsymbol{G} \circ \left(\boldsymbol{U}^T \frac{\partial J_4}{\partial \boldsymbol{H}} \boldsymbol{U}\right)\right)\boldsymbol{U}^T. \tag{15}$$

where $\boldsymbol{U}$ and $\boldsymbol{G}$ are obtained from the eigen-decomposition of $\boldsymbol{K} = \boldsymbol{U}\boldsymbol{D}\boldsymbol{U}^T$. For matrix logarithm (or square-rooting) normalisation, g_{ij} in Eq. (12) is computed as $\frac{\log \lambda_i - \log \lambda_j}{\lambda_i - \lambda_j}$ (or $\frac{\sqrt{\lambda_i} - \sqrt{\lambda_j}}{\lambda_i - \lambda_j}$) when $i \neq j$, and λ_i^{-1} (or $\frac{1}{2\sqrt{\lambda_i}}$) otherwise.

The work in [18] derives the derivative of the matrix logarithm from the scratch with the basic facts of matrix differentiation, which is detailed and instructive. As previously mentioned, that work does not connect with the well-established Daleckiĭ-Kreĭn formula. Moreover, it is reported that the derivation in [18] could lead to numerical instability during training a deep model [12]. To solve this problem and clarify the link with the existing result in [18], we prove the following proposition (proof is provided in the supplementary file).

Proposition 1. *The functional relationship obtained in [18] shown in Eq. (16) (with the notation in this work for consistency) is equivalent to that in Eq. (15) obtained by this work.*

$$\frac{\partial J_3}{\partial \boldsymbol{K}} = \boldsymbol{U}\left\{\left(\tilde{\boldsymbol{G}} \circ \left(2\boldsymbol{U}^T \left(\frac{\partial J_4}{\partial \boldsymbol{H}}\right)_{sym} \boldsymbol{U} \log(\boldsymbol{D})\right)\right) + \left(\boldsymbol{D}^{-1}\left(\boldsymbol{U}^T \frac{\partial J_4}{\partial \boldsymbol{H}} \boldsymbol{U}\right)\right)_{diag}\right\}\boldsymbol{U}^T, \tag{16}$$

where $\boldsymbol{K} = \boldsymbol{U}\boldsymbol{D}\boldsymbol{U}^T$; $\tilde{g}_{ij} = (\lambda_i - \lambda_j)^{-1}$ when $i \neq j$ and zero otherwise; $\boldsymbol{A}_{diag}$ means the off-diagonal entries of $\boldsymbol{A}$ are all set to zeros; and $\boldsymbol{A}_{sym}$ is defined to represent $(\boldsymbol{A} + \boldsymbol{A}^T)/2$.

Connecting with the results in operator theory not only facilitates the access to the derivatives of general SPD matrix functions, but also provides us more insight on these functions that could be useful for future research.

4.3 Numerical Stability Issue of the Matrix Gradients

The numerical stability issue associated with the derivation in [18] is explained as follows. Recall that Eq. (16) is used in [18] to calculate the gradients of the matrix function $\partial J_3/\partial K$. In the matrix $\tilde{G}$, the elements are $\tilde{g}_{ij} = (\lambda_i - \lambda_j)^{-1}$ when $i \neq j$ and 0 when $i = j$ in Eq. (16). When two of the eigenvalues are too close to each other, due to the finite precision arithmetic, the λ_i will cancel λ_j and the $\tilde{g}_{ij}$ will become *infinity*. This causes problems in the backpropagation process, as reported by [12]. Using double precision is not enough to alleviate the problem. A few possible workarounds are: excluding the batches causing this problem or appending a small number ϵ to the term $\tilde{g}_{ij}$. However, both of these approaches cause considerable performance drop.

In our derivation with the Daleckiĭ-Kreĭn formula, this issue is resolved in Eq. (12), where g_{ij} is defined as $\frac{f(\lambda_i)-f(\lambda_j)}{\lambda_i-\lambda_j}$ if $\lambda_i \neq \lambda_j$ when $\lambda_i \neq \lambda_j$ and $f'(\lambda_i)$ otherwise. In this case, when λ_i is too close to λ_j, we can formulate the problem as $g_{ij} = \lim_{\lambda_i \to \lambda_j} \frac{f(\lambda_i)-f(\lambda_j)}{\lambda_i-\lambda_j}$, where λ_j is viewed as constant. Since this is a $\frac{0}{0}$ uncertainty, by applying L'Hôpitals rule we obtain that $g_{ij} = \lim_{\lambda_i \to \lambda_j} \frac{f(\lambda_i)-f(\lambda_j)}{\lambda_i-\lambda_j} = \lim_{\lambda_i \to \lambda_j} \frac{f'(\lambda_i)}{1} = f'(\lambda_j)$. In this way, the numerical stability in [18] is avoided. This theoretical analysis will be further supported by an experiment conducted later in this paper.

4.4 Generalise to Matrix α-rooting Normalisation

We are aware of the recent success of matrix square-rooting [10,12] used in deep learning structures to handle the Riemannian geometry of SPD matrices. In addition to highlighting that matrix square-rooting and matrix logarithm are two special cases of our derivation in Eq. (12), we further generalise the existing matrix square-rooting normalisation to a case that we call "matrix α-rooting" normalisation. It is defined as $f(\lambda) = \lambda^\alpha$ where α is a parameter to be jointly learned by our DeepKSPD framework, instead of being fixed as 0.5 in the matrix square-rooting normalisation. $\frac{\partial J_3}{\partial K}$ will still maintain as in Eq. (15) and the derivative with respect to the parameter α, $\frac{\partial J}{\partial \alpha}$, can be derived as:

$$\frac{\partial J}{\partial \alpha} = \text{trace}\left(\left(\frac{\partial J_4}{\partial H}\right)^T \left[U(\log(D) \circ D^\alpha)U^T\right]\right), \tag{17}$$

where U and D are the eigen-decomposition of K as previous. Note that this matrix α-rooting is still guaranteed to be numerically stable in backpropagation, as shown in Sect. 4.3. Its performance will also be experimentally verified later.

5 Experimental Result

We have two tasks: (i) test the performance of KSPD built upon deep local descriptors and (ii) test the performance of the proposed DeepKSPD network, on fine-grained image and scene recognition. Bounding boxes are not used in all datasets. Example images are in the supplementary file.

Datasets. Four benchmark data sets are tested. For scene recognition, the MIT Indoor data set has 67 classes with predefined 5600 training and 1340 test images. For fine-grained image recognition, three data sets of Cars [23], Birds [24], and Aircrafts [25] are tested. The Cars dataset has 16185 images from 196 classes; the Aircrafts contains 10200 images of 100 classes (variants). The Birds has 11788 samples of 200 bird species. *Note that in order to have a fair comparison with [13] and [12] on the Aircraft dataset, images are first resized 512×512 then a central 448×448 patch is cropped. This increases the classification accuracy by 2%–3%.*

Setting of Proposed Methods. For the first task, we propose a method called KSPD-VGG, which builds kernel-matrix-based SPD representation upon the deep local descriptors from VGG-19 pretrained on ImageNet. Specifically, the 512 feature maps (of size 27×27) of the last convolutional layer are reshaped to form 512 vectors with the dimensions of 729. These vectors are further used to compute the 512×512 kernel matrix $\boldsymbol{K}$. Then, the matrix logarithm is applied and the resulting KSPD representations of all images are further processed by PCA dimension reduction (to 4096 dimensions), standardization (to zero mean and unit standard deviation), and ℓ_2 normalization. A linear SVM classifier is employed to perform the classification.

For the second task, the proposed DeepKSPD network is trained and tested. DeepKSPD has three blocks (Fig. 1). In the local descriptor block, the network hyperparameters are set by following VGG-16. In the proposed KSPD block, no hyperparameter needs to be tuned, and θ and α will be automatically learned with their initial values set as 0.1 and 0.5, respectively, for all the experiments. We test both matrix logarithm (denoted as DeepKSPD-logm) and matrix α-rooting (denoted as DeepKSPD-rootm) normalisations. In the classification block, the size of FC layer is set as the number of classes for each data set. DeepKSPD is trained by Adaptive Moment Estimation (Adam) in mini-batch mode (with the batch-size of 20). A two-step training procedure [26] is applied as good performance is observed [21,26]. Specifically, we first train the last layer using softmax regression for 100 epochs, and fine-tune the whole system. The total training epochs are 70–100. We only use flipping in training time as data augmentation.

Methods in Comparison. We compare our KSPD-VGG and DeepKSPD with methods that are either comparable or competitive in the literature, as listed in the first column in Table 1, and are roughly grouped into three categories.

The first category can be deemed as feature extraction methods, to which KSPD-VGG belongs. This category also includes FV-SIFT [27], FC-VGG [18], FV-VGG [28], and COV-VGG (standing for covariance-matrix-based SPD representation). COV-VGG's setting is same as that of KSPD-VGG, except that a covariance matrix is constructed instead of a kernel matrix. Note that, we directly quote the results of FV-SIFT and FC-VGG from the literature, and provide our own implementation of FV-VGG, COV-VGG, and KSPD-VGG to ensure the same setting for fair comparison.

The second category includes six end-to-end learning methods. DeepKSPD-logm and DeepKSPD-rootm are the proposed methods. B-CNN denotes the bilinear CNN method [21] and Improved BCNN [12] is an extension of B-CNN where matrix square-rooting is applied. CBP [14] and LRBP [11] are both COV-based methods and KP [17] estimates Gaussian RBF features using Taylor series.

In the third category, additional methods previously reported on these data sets are quoted to extend the comparison and provide a whole picture.

Table 1. Comparison of methods

ACC (%)	MIT indoor	Cars	Aircraft	Birds	Average
Symbiotic Model [29]	–	78.0	72.5	–	–
FV-revisit [30]	–	82.7	80.7	–	–
FV-SIFT [27]	–	59.2	61.0	18.8	–
FC-VGG [21]	67.6	36.5	45.0	61.0	52.5
FV-VGG [28]	73.7	75.2	72.7	71.3	73.1
FV-VGG-ft [21]	–	85.7	78.7	74.7	73.1
COV-VGG	74.2	80.3	81.4	76	78.0
KSPD-VGG (**proposed**)	77.2	83.5	83.8	78.5	80.1
BCNN [13]	77.6	91.3	86.6	84.1	84.5
Improved BCNN [12]	–	92.0	88.5	85.8	–
CBP [14]	76.17	–	–	84.0	–
LRBP [11]	–	90.9	87.3	84.2	–
KP [17]	–	92.4	86.9	86.2	–
DeepKSPD-logm (**proposed**)	79.6	90.5	**91.5**	84.8	86.6
DeepKSPD-rootm (**proposed**)	**81.0**	**93.2**	91.0	**86.5**	**87.9**

Results and Discussion. From Table 1 we have the following observations. First, the proposed KSPD-VGG, DeepKSPD-logm, DeepKSPD-rootm demonstrate their effectiveness for visual recognition. On every dataset, the best performance is achieved by the proposed DeepKSPD. Moreover, DeepKSPD is superior to KSPD-VGG (up to 9.7 percentage points on Cars) and other competitive methods, demonstrating the essentials of the end-to-end learning of kernel-matrix-based representation. Among the two DeepKSPD methods, DeepKSPD-rootm performs better on MIT indoor, Cars, and Birds, while DeepKSPD-logm performs better on Aircraft. Overall, DeepKSPD-rootm wins over DeepKSPD-logm, which is consistent with the observation in [13] that matrix α-rooting seems to have some advantages in scaling the eigenvalues over matrix logarithm.

Second, KSPD-based methods consistently win COV-based ones (**or bilinear**) on all data sets, either based on feature extraction (KSPD-VGG vs

COV-VGG) or using end-to-end training (Deep KSPD vs other COV-based methods including B-CNN, improved B-CNN, CBP and LRBP). It is interesting to see that KP also shows promising performance by approximating kernel representation, which supports our arguments of employing kernel representation for visual recognition. However, this method neither directly learns kernel representation nor explicitly handles the Riemannian geometry of SPD matrix as our method. Instead, it approximates the kernel representation by Taylor expansion.

Third, the SPD representation (being it based on an outer product, covariance, or kernel matrix) outperforms Fisher vector representation in the given tasks. DeepKSPD also outperforms FV-VGG-ft obtained from fine-tuned VGG-16. The latter attained 78.7% on Aircraft, 74.7% on Birds, and 85.7% on Cars [21], which is worse than 81.0%, 86.5% and 93.2% achieved by DeepKSPD.

Fourth, in the literature, matrix logarithm normalisation has not been very successfully incorporated into deep CNNs up to our work due to numerical instability issue. Furthermore, it was dismissed due to poor results compared to matrix square-rooting. Our numerically stable gradients render the embedding of matrix logarithm into deep architecture possible. More importantly, we show that matrix logarithm is still relevant as it yields the best results on Aircraft dataset. Thus, matrix functions to handle the Riemannian geometry could be regarded as hyper-parameters and properly chosen via validation mechanism.

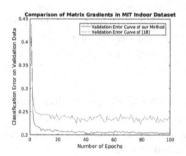

Table 2. DeepKSPD vs DeepCOV.

ACC (%)	MIT indoor	Cars	Aircraft	Birds
Improved BCNN [12]	–	92.0	88.5	85.8
DeepCOV-rootm	79.2	91.7	88.7	85.4
DeepKSPD-rootm	**81.0**	**93.2**	**91.0**	**86.5**

Fig. 2. On numerical stability.

Numerical Stability. Before ending the experiment part, we also conduct a test on the numerical stability of our formulation of matrix derivative. We investigate the performance of our DeepKSPD-logm on MIT indoor dataset with the derivative of matrix logarithm computed by [18] and our formulation, respectively. The result is shown in Fig. (2). As can be seen, our method achieves lower classification error consistently in all epochs. After 100 epochs of training, the classification error is 22.4% using our method, and 24% using the formulation in [18], well demonstrating the advantage of our derived unified solution.

6   Ablation Study

Different from the literature, our framework utilizes an L_2 normalisation layer before the pooling layer and a batch normalization layer after. Traditionally, these layers are not used in bilinear models. However, RBF kernel matrix has a very different nature than covariance matrix. As previously explained, its kernel values are bounded between 0 and 1. If one feature channel dominates the others in terms of the magnitude, it will cause numerical problems. A common way in machine learning to tackle this problem is to normalise feature channels o make them comparable in magnitude. We also adopt this approach and integrate L_2 normalisation as a layer into our framework before kernel pooling stage.

Post-processing is very important in SPD representations. In the literature, bilinear models [11,12,14,17,21] use element-wise signed rooting followed by L_2 normalisation layers, which contributes around **5.7%** [21] of the classification accuracy. In our framework, KSPD layer has a parameter θ which must be initialized properly. We found that batch normalisation layer, that is used to cope with poor initialization of convolutional layers, can be used for this task. Therefore, we replace element-wise signed square root with batch normalisation layer. In the table below, the experiments are conducted with DeepKSPD-rootm structure built on VGG-16 network.

According to Table 3 on average, batch normalization layer contributes to 2.56% of the performance; whereas, element-wise signed square root + L_2 normalisation processing increases performance about 1.45%. Furthermore, the convergence is around 3 times faster. Most importantly, our design choice allows a universal initial value (we choose 0.1) for the parameter θ for all the datasets. Note that we conduct a grid search for θ and report the best result in Table 3 for DeepKSPD-sqrt-L_2 and DeepKSPD-w/o BN.

In the Table 4 the initial and final values of α and θ are given. In the literature, [10,12] do a similar experiment with matrix rooting; however, the authors only do a grid search to find the best root. We provide derivatives for matrix rooting and update rooting power α with each iteration in our work.

As shown, α values do not deviate much from their initial values. However θ values end up in much different values from their starting point. Even when the initial θ is much lower than its final values, DeepKSPD performs excellent in each case; supporting our design choice to tackle the initialization problem.

6.1   Kernel Representation Versus Covariance Representation

Since DeepKSPD does not adopt the same network as bilinear methods, to show the benefits purely from kernelising, we test the covariance and the kernel representations when they share an identical network. For this purpose, we introduce another model called DeepCOV that is identical to DeepKSPD except that Deep-COV adopts covariance-based-matrix representation. We compare DeepCOV to DeepKSPD in Table 2. As shown, on all the datasets DeepKSPD outperforms DeepCOV. This is a clear demonstration of the superiority of kernelising local

Table 3. Comparison of post processing

ACC (%)	MIT indoor	Cars	Aircraft	Birds
DeepKSPD-sqrt-L_2	80.6	90.1	86.1	84.7
DeepKSPD-w/o BN	77.6	89.6	84.3	81.0
DeepKSPD-w BN	**81.0**	**93.2**	**91.0**	**86.5**

Table 4. Final Parameter Values

ACC (%)	MIT indoor	Cars	Aircraft	Birds
Initial θ	0.1	0.1	0.1	0.1
Initial α	0.5	0.5	0.5	0.5
Final θ	0.63	1.4	0.67	0.93
Final α	0.49	0.52	0.53	0.52

descriptors over the second-order pooling of them. Furthermore, DeepCOV performs almost identically to [12]. This indicates that the layers and strategies designed in our DeepKSPD cater well for the special characteristics of KSPD representation that are not necessarily presented in the bilinear models.

7 Conclusion

Motivated by the recent progress on SPD representation, we develop a deep neural network that jointly learns local descriptors and kernel-matrix-based SPD representation for fine-grained image recognition. The matrix derivatives required by the backpropagation process are derived and linked to the established literature on the theory of positive definite matrix. Experimental result on benchmark datasets demonstrates the improved performance of kernel-matrix-based SPD representation when built upon deep local descriptors and the superiority of the proposed DeepKSPD network.

References

1. Sivic, J., Zisserman, A.: Video Google: a text retrieval approach to object matching in videos. In: 9th IEEE International Conference on Computer Vision (ICCV 2003), pp. 1470–1477 (2003)
2. Wang, J., Yang, J., Yu, K., Lv, F., Huang, T.S., Gong, Y.: Locality-constrained linear coding for image classification. In: The Twenty-Third IEEE Conference on Computer Vision and Pattern Recognition, CVPR 2010, pp. 3360–3367 (2010)
3. Jegou, H., Douze, M., Schmid, C., Pérez, P.: Aggregating local descriptors into a compact image representation. In: The Twenty-Third IEEE Conference on Computer Vision and Pattern Recognition, CVPR 2010, pp. 3304–3311 (2010)
4. Sánchez, J., Perronnin, F., Mensink, T., Verbeek, J.J.: Image classification with the fisher vector: theory and practice. Int. J. Comput. Vis. **105**(3), 222–245 (2013)
5. Jayasumana, S., Hartley, R.I., Salzmann, M., Li, H., Harandi, M.T.: Kernel methods on the Riemannian manifold of symmetric positive definite matrices. In: 2013 IEEE Conference on Computer Vision and Pattern Recognition, pp. 73–80 (2013)
6. Wang, R., Guo, H., Davis, L.S., Dai, Q.: Covariance discriminative learning: a natural and efficient approach to image set classification. [7], pp. 2496–2503
7. IEEE Conference on Computer Vision and Pattern Recognition, Providence, RI, USA, 16–21 June 2012. IEEE Computer Society (2012)

8. Fleet, D.J., Pajdla, T., Schiele, B., Tuytelaars, T., (eds.): Computer Vision - ECCV 2014–13th European Conference, Zurich, Switzerland, 6–12 September 2014, Proceedings, Part II. Lecture Notes in Computer Science, vol. 8690. Springer, Cham (2014). https://doi.org/10.1007/978-3-319-10602-1

9. Bach, F.R., Blei, D.M., (eds.): Proceedings of the 32nd International Conference on Machine Learning, ICML 2015, Lille, France, 6–11 July 2015. JMLR Workshop and Conference Proceedings, vol. 37. JMLR.org (2015)

10. Li, P., Xie, J., Wang, Q., Zuo, W.: Is second-order information helpful for large-scale visual recognition? In: IEEE International Conference on Computer Vision, ICCV 2017, Venice, Italy, 22–29 October 2017, pp. 2089–2097 (2017)

11. Kong, S., Fowlkes, C.C.: Low-rank bilinear pooling for fine-grained classification. CoRR abs/1611.05109 (2016)

12. Lin, T.Y., Maji, S.: Improved bilinear pooling with CNNs. In: British Machine Vision Conference (BMVC)(2017)

13. Lin, T.Y., RoyChowdhury, A., Maji, S.: Bilinear CNNS for fine-grained visual recognition. IEEE Trans. Pattern Anal. Mach. Intell. **40**(6), 1309–1322 (2018)

14. Gao, Y., Beijbom, O., Zhang, N., Darrell, T.: Compact bilinear pooling. CoRR abs/1511.06062 (2015)

15. Harandi, M.T., Salzmann, M., Porikli, F.M.: Bregman divergences for infinite dimensional covariance matrices. In: 2014 IEEE Conference on Computer Vision and Pattern Recognition, CVPR 2014, pp. 1003–1010 (2014)

16. Wang, L., Zhang, J., Zhou, L., Tang, C., Li, W.: Beyond covariance: feature representation with nonlinear Kernel matrices. In: 2015 IEEE International Conference on Computer Vision, ICCV 2015, pp. 4570–4578 (2015)

17. Cui, Y., Zhou, F., Wang, J., Liu, X., Lin, Y., Belongie, S.: Kernel pooling for convolutional neural networks. In: Computer Vision and Pattern Recognition (CVPR), Honolulu, HI (2017)

18. Ionescu, C., Vantzos, O., Sminchisescu, C.: Matrix backpropagation for deep networks with structured layers. In: 2015 IEEE International Conference on Computer Vision, ICCV 2015, pp. 2965–2973 (2015)

19. Daleckiĭ, Y.L., Kreĭn, S.G.: Integration and differentiation of functions of hermitian operators and applications to the theory of perturbations. (Russian) Vorone. Gos. Univ. Trudy Sem. Funkcional. Anal. **1**(1), 81–105(1956). English translation is in book Thirteen Papers on Functional Analysis and Partial Differential Equations, American Mathematical Society Translations: Series 2, vol. 47 (1965)

20. Bhatia, R.: Positive Definite Matrices. Princeton University Press (2015)

21. Lin, T., Roy Chowdhury, A., Maji, S.: Bilinear CNN models for fine-grained visual recognition. In: 2015 IEEE International Conference on Computer Vision, ICCV 2015, pp. 1449–1457 (2015)

22. Arsigny, V., Fillard, P., Pennec, X., Ayache, N.: Log-euclidean metrics for fast and simple calculus on diffusion tensors. Mag. Reson. Med. **56**(2), 411–421 (2006)

23. Krause, J., Stark, M., Deng, J., Fei-Fei, L.: 3D object representations for fine-grained categorization. In: 4th International IEEE Workshop on 3D Representation and Recognition (3dRR-13), Sydney, Australia (2013)

24. Welinder, P., et al.: Caltech-UCSD Birds 200. Technical report CNS-TR-2010-001, California Institute of Technology (2010)

25. Maji, S., Rahtu, E., Kannala, J., Blaschko, M.B., Vedaldi, A.: Fine-grained visual classification of aircraft. CoRR abs/1306.5151 (2013)

26. Branson, S., Horn, G.V., Belongie, S., Perona, P.: Bird species categorization using pose normalized deep convolutional nets. In: British Machine Vision Conference (BMVC), Nottingham (2014)

27. Perronnin, F., Sánchez, J., Mensink, T.: Improving the Fisher Kernel for large-scale image classification. In: Daniilidis, K., Maragos, P., Paragios, N. (eds.) ECCV 2010. LNCS, vol. 6314, pp. 143–156. Springer, Heidelberg (2010). https://doi.org/10.1007/978-3-642-15561-1_11

28. Cimpoi, M., Maji, S., Vedaldi, A.: Deep filter banks for texture recognition and segmentation. In: IEEE Conference on Computer Vision and Pattern Recognition, CVPR 2015, pp. 3828–3836 (2015)

29. Chai, Y., Lempitsky, V., Zisserman, A.: Symbiotic segmentation and part localization for fine-grained categorization. In: IEEE International Conference on Computer Vision (2013)

30. Gosselin, P.H., Murray, N., Jégou, H., Perronnin, F.: Revisiting the Fisher vector for fine-grained classification. Pattern Recognit. Lett. **49**, 92–98 (2014)

Pairwise Relational Networks for Face Recognition

Bong-Nam Kang[1(✉)] ⓘ, Yonghyun Kim[2] ⓘ, and Daijin Kim[1,2] ⓘ

[1] Department of Creative IT Engineering, POSTECH, Pohang, Korea
{bnkang,dkim}@postech.ac.kr
[2] Department of Computer Science and Engineering, POSTECH, Pohang, Korea
gkyh0805@postech.ac.kr

Abstract. Existing face recognition using deep neural networks is difficult to know what kind of features are used to discriminate the identities of face images clearly. To investigate the effective features for face recognition, we propose a novel face recognition method, called a pairwise relational network (PRN), that obtains local appearance patches around landmark points on the feature map, and captures the pairwise relation between a pair of local appearance patches. The PRN is trained to capture unique and discriminative pairwise relations among different identities. Because the existence and meaning of pairwise relations should be identity dependent, we add a face identity state feature, which obtains from the long short-term memory (LSTM) units network with the sequential local appearance patches on the feature maps, to the PRN. To further improve accuracy of face recognition, we combined the global appearance representation with the pairwise relational feature. Experimental results on the LFW show that the PRN using only pairwise relations achieved 99.65% accuracy and the PRN using both pairwise relations and face identity state feature achieved 99.76% accuracy. On the YTF, both the PRN using only pairwise relations and the PRN using pairwise relations and the face identity state feature achieved the *state-of-the-art* (95.7% and 96.3%). The PRN also achieved comparable results to the *state-of-the-art* for both face verification and face identification tasks on the IJB-A, and the *state-of-the-art* on the IJB-B.

Keywords: Pairwise relational network · Relations · Face recognition

1 Introduction

Convolutional neural networks (CNNs) have achieved great success on computer vision community by improving the *state-of-the-art* in almost all of applications, especially in classification problems including object [12–14,20,22,29,33] scene [43,44], and so on. The key to success of CNNs is the availability of large scale of training data and the end-to-end learning framework. The most commonly used CNNs perform feature learning and prediction of label information by mapping the input raw data to deep embedded features which are commonly the output

© Springer Nature Switzerland AG 2018
V. Ferrari et al. (Eds.): ECCV 2018, LNCS 11206, pp. 646–663, 2018.
https://doi.org/10.1007/978-3-030-01216-8_39

of the last fully connected (FC) layer, and then predict labels using these deep embedded features. These approaches use the deep embedded features holistically for their applications, without knowing what part of the features is used and what it is meaning.

Face recognition in unconstrained environments is a very challenging problem in computer vision. Faces of the same identity can look very different when presented in different illuminations, facial poses, facial expressions, and occlusions. Such variations within the same identity could overwhelm the variations due to identity differences and make face recognition challenging. To solve these problems, many deep learning-based approaches have been proposed and achieved high accuracies of face recognition such as DeepFace [34], DeepID series [30–32,41], FaceNet [28], PIMNet [17], SphereFace [23], and ArcFace [10].

In face recognition tasks in unconstrained environments, the deeply learned and embedded features need to be not only separable but also discriminative. However, these features are learned implicitly for separable and distinct representations to classify among different identities without what part of the features is used, what part of the feature is meaningful, and what part of the features is separable and discriminative. Therefore, it is difficult to know what kind of features are used to discriminate the identities of face images clearly.

To overcome this limitation, we propose a novel face recognition method, called a pairwise relational network (PRN) to capture unique relations within same identity and discriminative relations among different identities. To capture relations, the PRN takes local appearance patches as input by ROI projection around landmark points on the feature map in a backbone CNN network. With these local appearance patches, the PRN is trained to capture unique pairwise relations between pairs of local appearance patches to determine facial part-relational structures and properties in face images. Because the existence and meaning of pairwise relations should be identity dependent, the PRN could condition its processing on a facial identity state feature. The facial identity state feature is learned from the long short-term memory (LSTM) units network with the sequential local appearance patches on the feature maps. To further improve accuracy of face recognition, we combined the global appearance representation with the local appearance representation (the relation features) (Fig. 1). More details of the proposed face recognition method are given in Sect. 2.

The main contributions of this paper can be summarized as follows:

- We propose a novel face recognition method using the pairwise relational network (PRN) which captures the unique and discriminative pairwise relations of local appearance patches on the feature maps to classify face images among different identities.
- We show that the proposed PRN is very useful to enhance the accuracy of both face verification and face identification.
- We present extensive experiments on the public available datasets such as Labeled Faces in the Wild (LFW), YouTube Faces (YTF), IARPA Janus Benchmark-A (IJB-A), and IARPA Janus Benchmark-B (IJB-B).

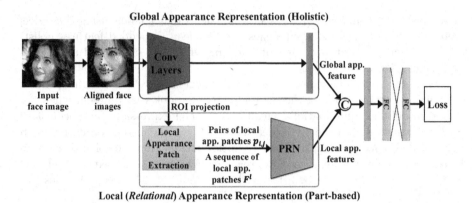

Fig. 1. Overview of the proposed face recognition method

The rest of this paper is as follows: in Sect. 2 we describe the proposed face recognition method including the base CNN architecture, face alignment, pairwise relational network, facial identity state feature, loss function used for training the proposed method, respectively; in Sect. 3 we present experimental results of the proposed method in comparison with the *state-of-the-art* on the public benchmark dataset and discussion; in Sect. 4 we draw a conclusion.

2   Proposed Methods

In this section, we describe our methods in detail including the base CNN model as backbone network for the global appearance representation, the face alignment method, the pairwise relational network, the pairwise relational network with face identity states, and the loss functions.

2.1   Base Convolutional Neural Network

We first describe the base CNN model. It is the backbone neural network to represent the global appearance representation and extract the local appearance patches to capture the relations (Fig. 1). The base CNN model consists of several 3-layer residual bottleneck blocks similar to the ResNet-101 [13]. The ResNet-101 has one convolution layer, one max pooling layer, 30 3-layer residual bottleneck blocks, one global average pooling (GAP) layer, one FC layer, and *softmax* loss layer. The ResNet-101 accepts a image with 224×224 resolution as input, and has 7×7 convolution filters with a stride of 2 in the first layer. In contrast, our base CNN model accepts a face image with 140×140 resolution as input, and has 5×5 convolution filters with a stride of 1 in the first layer (*conv1* in Table 1). Because of different input resolution, size of kernel filters, and stride, the output size in each intermediate layer is also different from the original ResNet-101. In the last layer, we use the GAP with 9×9 filter in each channel and the FC layer.

Table 1. Base convolutional neural network. The base CNN is similar to ResNet-101, but the dimensionality of input, the size of convolution filters, and the size of each output feature map are different from the original ResNet-101

Layer name	Output size	101-layer
conv1	140×140	5×5, 64
conv2_x	70×70	3×3 max pool, stride 2
		$\begin{bmatrix} 1 \times 1, 64 \\ 3 \times 3, 64 \\ 1 \times 1, 256 \end{bmatrix} \times 3$
conv3_x	35×35	$\begin{bmatrix} 1 \times 1, 128 \\ 3 \times 3, 128 \\ 1 \times 1, 512 \end{bmatrix} \times 4$
conv4_x	18×18	$\begin{bmatrix} 1 \times 1, 256 \\ 3 \times 3, 256 \\ 1 \times 1, 1024 \end{bmatrix} \times 23$
conv5_x	9×9	$\begin{bmatrix} 1 \times 1, 512 \\ 3 \times 3, 512 \\ 1 \times 1, 2048 \end{bmatrix} \times 3$
	1×1	Global average pool, 8630-d fc, *softmax*

The outputs of FC layer are fed into the *softmax* loss layer. More details of the base CNN architecture are given in Table 1.

To represent the global appearance representation $\boldsymbol{f}^g$, we use the $1 \times 1 \times 2048$ feature which is the output of the GAP in the base CNN (Table 1).

To represent the local appearance representation, we extract the local appearance patches $\boldsymbol{f}^l$ on the $9 \times 9 \times 2048$ feature maps (*conv5_3*) in the base CNN (Table 1) by ROI projection with facial landmark points. These $\boldsymbol{f}^l$ are used to capture and model pairwise relations between them. More details of the local appearance patches and relations are described in Sect. 2.3.

2.2   Face Alignment

In the base CNN model, the input layer accepts the RGB values of the face image pixels. We employ a face alignment method to align a face image into the canonical face image, then we adopt this aligned face image as input of our base CNN model.

The alignment procedures are as follows: (1) Use the DAN implementation of Kowalsky *et al.* by using multi-stage neural network [19] to detect 68 facial landmark points (Fig. 2b); (2) rotate the face in the image plane to make it upright based on the eye positions (Fig. 2c); (3) find a central point on the face by taking the mid-point between the leftmost and rightmost landmark points (the red point in Fig. 2d); (4) the center points of the eye and mouth (blue points

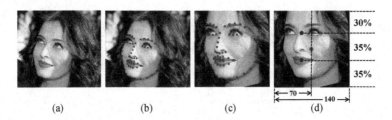

Fig. 2. A face alignment. The original image is shown in (a); (b) shows the detected 68 landmark points; (c) shows the aligned 68 landmark points in the aligned image plane; and (d) is the final aligned face image, where the red circle was used to center the face image along x-axis, and the blue circles denote the two points used for face cropping

in Fig. 2d) are found by averaging all the landmark points in the eye and mouth regions, respectively; (5) center the faces in the x-axis, based on the center point (red point); (6) fix the position along the y-axis by placing the eye center point at 30% from the top of the image and the mouth center point at 35% from the bottom of the image, respectively; (7) resize the image to a resolution of 140×140. Each pixel which value is in a range of $[0, 255]$ in the RGB color space is normalized by dividing 255 to be in a range of $[0, 1]$.

2.3   Pairwise Relational Network

The pairwise relational network (PRN) is a neural network and takes a set of local appearance patches on the feature maps as input and output a single feature vector as its relational feature for the face recognition task. The PRN captures unique pairwise relations between pairs of local appearance patches within the same identity and discriminative pairwise relations among different identities. In other words, the PRN captures the core common properties of faces within the same identity, while captures the discriminative properties of faces among different identities. Therefore, the PRN aims to determine pairwise-relational structures from pairs of local appearance patches in face images. The relation feature $r_{i,j}$ represents a latent relation of a pair of two local appearance patches, and can be written as follows:

$$r_{i,j} = \mathcal{G}_\theta \left(p_{i,j} \right), \tag{1}$$

where $\mathcal{G}_\theta$ is a multi-layer perceptron (MLP) and its parameters θ are learnable weights. $p_{i,j} = \{f_i^l, f_j^l\}$ is a pair of two local appearance patches (f_i^l and f_j^l) which are i-th and j-th local appearance patches corresponding to each facial landmark point, respectively. Each local appearance patches f_i^l is extracted by the ROI projection which projects a $m \times m$ region around i-th landmark point in the input image space to a $m^{'} \times m^{'}$ region on the feature map space. The same MLP operates on all possible parings of local appearance patches.

The permutation order of local appearance patches is a critical for the PRN, since without this invariance, the PRN would have to learn to operate on all

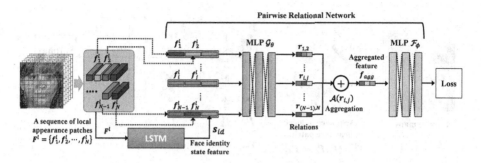

Fig. 3. Pairwise Relational Network (PRN). The PRN is a neural network module and takes a set of local appearance patches on the feature maps as input and outputs a single feature vector as its relational feature for the recognition task. The PRN captures unique pairwise relations between pairs of local appearance patches within the same identity and discriminative pairwise relations among different identities

possible permuted pairs of local appearance patches without explicit knowledge of the permutation invariance structure in the data. To incorporate this permutation invariance, we constrain the PRN with an aggregation function (Fig. 3):

$$f_{agg} = \mathcal{A}(r_{i,j}) = \sum_{\forall r_{i,j}} (r_{i,j}), \tag{2}$$

where f_{agg} is the aggregated relational feature, and $\mathcal{A}(\cdot)$ is the aggregation function which is summation of all pairwise relations among all possible pairing of the local appearance patches. Finally, a prediction $\tilde{r}$ of the PRN can be performed with:

$$\tilde{r} = \mathcal{F}_\phi \left(f_{agg} \right), \tag{3}$$

where $\mathcal{F}_\phi$ is a function with parameters ϕ, and are implemented by the MLP. Therefore, the final form of the PRN is a composite function as follows:

$$PRN(P) = \mathcal{F}_\phi \left(\mathcal{A} \left(\mathcal{G}_\theta \left(p_{i,j} \right) \right) \right), \tag{4}$$

where $P = \{p_{1,2}, \ldots, p_{i,j}, \ldots, p_{(N-1),N}\}$ is a set of all possible pairs of local appearance patches where N denotes the number of local patches on the feature maps.

To capture unique pairwise relations within same identity and discriminative pairwise relations among different identities, a pairwise relation should be identity dependent. So, we modify the PRN such that $\mathcal{G}_\theta$ could condition its processing on the identity information. To condition the identity information, we embed a face identity state feature s_{id} as the identity information in the PRN as follows:

$$PRN^+(P, s_{id}) = \mathcal{F}_\phi \left(\mathcal{A} \left(\mathcal{G}_\theta \left(p_{i,j}, s_{id} \right) \right) \right). \tag{5}$$

To get this s_{id}, we use the final state of a recurrent neural network composed of LSTM layers and two FC layers that process a sequence of total local appearance patches (Figs. 1 and 4).

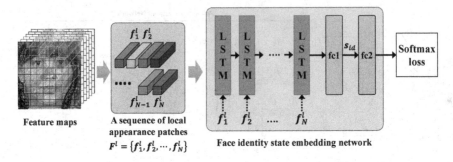

Fig. 4. Face identity state feature. A face on the feature maps is divided into 68 regions by ROI projection around 68 landmark points. A sequence of local appearance patches in these regions are used to encode the face identity state feature from LSTM networks

Face Identity State Feature. Pairwise relations should be identity dependent to capture unique and discriminative pairwise relations. Based on the feature maps which are the output of the *conv5_3* layer in the base CNN model, the face is divided into 68 local regions by ROI projection around 68 landmark points. In these local regions, we extract the local appearance patches to model the facial identity state feature s_{id}. Let f_i^l denote the local appearance patches of $m' \times m'$ i-th local region. To encode the facial identity state feature s_{id}, an LSTM-based network has been devised on top of a set of local appearance patches $F^l = \{f_1^l, \ldots, f_i^l, \ldots, f_N^l\}$ as followings:

$$s_{id} = \mathcal{E}_\psi(F^l),\tag{6}$$

where $\mathcal{E}_\psi(\cdot)$ is a neural network module which composed of the LSTM layers and two FC layers with learnable parameters ψ. We train $\mathcal{E}_\psi$ with *softmax* loss function (Fig. 4). The detailed configuration of $\mathcal{E}_\psi$ used in our proposed method will be presented in Sect. 3.1.

2.4   Loss Function

To learn the proposed PRN, we jointly use the triplet ratio loss L_t, pairwise loss L_p, and identity preserving loss L_{id} (*softmax*) to minimize distances between faces that have the same identity and to maximize distances between faces that are of different identities:

$$L = \lambda_1 L_t + \lambda_2 L_p + \lambda_3 L_{id}.\tag{7}$$

During training the PRN, we empirically set $\lambda_1 = 1$, $\lambda_2 = 0.5$, and $\lambda_3 = 1$.

Triplet Ratio Loss. Triplet ratio loss L_t is defined to maximize the ratio of distances between the positive pairs and the negative pairs in the triplets of faces. To maximize L_t, the Euclidean distances of positive pairs should be minimized and those of negative pairs should be maximized. Let $F(I) \in \mathbb{R}^d$, where I is the input facial image, denote the output of a network (the output of $\mathcal{F}_\phi$ in the PRN), the L_t is defined as follows:

$$L_t = \sum_{\forall T} \max \left(0, 1 - \frac{\|F(I_a) - F(I_n)\|_2}{\|F(I_a) - F(I_p)\|_2 + m} \right), \tag{8}$$

where $F(I_a)$ is the output of the network for an anchor face I_a, $F(I_p)$ is the output of the network for a positive face image I_p, and $F(I_n)$ is the output of the network for a negative face I_n in the triplets of faces T, respectively. m is a margin that defines a minimum ratio in Euclidean space. From recent work by Kang et $al.$ [17], they reported that an unbalanced range of distance measured between the pairs of data using only L_t during training; this result means that although the ratio of the distances is bounded in a certain range of values, the range of the absolute distances is not. To overcome this problem, they constrained L_t by adding the pairwise loss L_p.

Pairwise Loss. Pairwise loss L_p is defined to minimize the sum of the squared Euclidean distances between $F(I_a)$ for the anchor face I_a and $F(I_p)$ for the positive face I_p. These pairs I_a and I_p are in the triplets T.

$$L_p = \sum_{(I_a, I_p) \in T} \|F(I_a) - F(I_p)\|_2^2. \tag{9}$$

The joint training with L_t and L_p minimizes the absolute Euclidean distance between face images of a given pair in the triplets of facs T.

3   Experiments

The implementation details are given in Sect. 3.1. Then, we investigate the effectiveness of the PRN and the PRN with the face identity state feature in Sect. 3.2. In Sects. 3.3, 3.4, 3.5, and 3.6, we perform several experiments to verify the effectiveness of the proposed method on the public face benchmark datasets including LFW [15], YTF [38], IJB-A [18], and IJB-B [37].

3.1   Implementation Details

Training Data. We used the web-collected face dataset (VGGFace2 [3]). All of the faces in the VGGFace2 dataset and their landmark points are detected by the recently proposed face detector [42] and facial landmark point detector [19]. We used 68 landmark points for the face alignment and extraction of local appearance patches. When the detection of faces or facial landmark points is failed, we simply discard the image. Thus, we discarded $24,160$ face images from $6,561$ subjects. After removing these images without landmark points, it roughly goes to 3.1M images of $8,630$ unique persons. We generated a validation set by selecting randomly about 10% from each subject in refined dataset, and the remains are used as the training set. Therefore, the training set roughly has 2.8M face images and the validation set has $311,773$ face images, respectively.

Detailed Settings in the PRN. For pairwise relations between facial parts, we first extracted a set of local appearance patches $F^l = \{f^l_1, \ldots, f^l_i, \ldots, f^l_{68}\}$, $f^l_i \in \mathbb{R}^{1 \times 1 \times 2,048}$ from each local region (nearly 1×1 size of regions) around 68 landmark points by ROI projection on the $9 \times 9 \times 2,048$ feature maps (*conv5_3* in Table 1) in the backbone CNN model. Using this F^l, we make $2,278$ ($=$ $^{68}C_2$) possible pairs of local appearance patches. Then, we used three-layered MLP consisting of $1,000$ units per layer with batch normalization (BN) [16] and rectified linear units (ReLU) [25] non-linear activation functions for $\mathcal{G}_\theta$, and three-layered MLP consisting of $1,000$ units per layer with BN and ReLU non-linear activation functions for $\mathcal{F}_\phi$. To aggregate all of relations from $\mathcal{G}_\theta$, we used summation as an aggregation function. The PRN is jointly optimized by *triplet ratio* loss L_T, *pairwise* loss L_p, and *identity preserving* loss L_{id} (*softmax*) over the ground-truth identity labels using stochastic gradient descent (SGD) optimization method with learning rate 0.10. We used mini-batch size of 128 on four NVIDIA Titan X GPUs. During training the PRN, we froze the backbone CNN model to only update weights of the PRN model.

To capture unique and discriminative pairwise relations dependent on identity, the PRN should condition its processing on the face identity state feature s_{id}. For s_{id}, we use the LSTM-based recurrent network $\mathcal{E}_\psi$ over a sequence of the local appearance patches which is a set ordered by landmark points order from F^l. In other words, there is a sequence of 68 length per face. In $\mathcal{E}_\psi$, it consist of LSTM layers and two-layered MLP. Each of the LSTM layer has $2,048$ memory cells. The MLP consists of 256 and $8,630$ units per layer, respectively. The cross-entropy loss with *softmax* was used for training the $\mathcal{E}_\psi$ (Fig. 4).

Detailed Settings in the Model. We implemented the base CNN and the PRN models using the Keras framework [7] with TensorFlow [1] backend. For fair comparison in terms of the effects of each network module, we train three kinds of models (**model A**, **model B**, and **model C**) under the supervision of cross-entropy loss with *softmax*:

- **model A** is the baseline model which is the base CNN (Table 1).
- **model B** combining two different networks, one of which is the base CNN model (**model A**) and the other is the *PRN* (Eq. (4)), concatenates the output feature f^g of the GAP layer in **model A** as the global appearance representation and the output of the MLP $\mathcal{F}_\phi$ in the *PRN* without the face identity state feature s_{id} as the local appearance representation. f^g is the feature of size $1 \times 1 \times 2,048$ from each face image. The output of the MLP $\mathcal{F}_\phi$ in the *PRN* is the feature of size $1 \times 1 \times 1,000$. These two output features are concatenated into a single feature vector with $3,048$ size, then this concatenated feature vector is fed into the FC layer with $1,024$ units.
- **model C** is the combined model with the output of the base CNN model (**model A**) and the output of the PRN^+ (Eq. (5)) with the face identity state feature s_{id}. The output of **model A** in **model C** is the same of the output in **model B**. The size of the output in the PRN^+ is same as compared with the *PRN*, but output values are different.

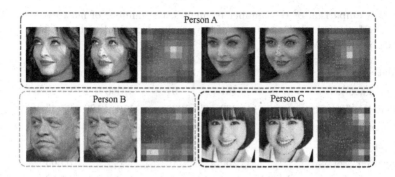

Fig. 5. Visualization of the localized facial parts

All of convolution layers and FC layers use BN and ReLU as nonlinear activation functions except for LSTM layers in $\mathcal{E}_\psi$.

3.2 Effects of the PRNs

To investigate the effectiveness of the PRN and the face identity state feature s_{id}, we performed experiments in terms of the accuracy of classification on the validation set during training. For these experiments, we trained two different network models, one of which is a network PRN (Eq. (4)) using only the PRN model, and the other is a network PRN^+ (Eq. (5)) using the PRN with the s_{id}. We achieved 94.2% and 96.7% accuracies of classification for PRN and PRN^+, respectively. From these evaluations, when using PRN^+, we observed that the face identity state feature s_{id} represents the identity property, and the pairwise relations should be dependent on an identity property of a face image. Therefore, these evaluations validate the effectiveness of using the PRN and the importance of the face identity state feature. We visualize the localized facial parts in Fig. 5, where *Col. 1*, *Col. 2*, and *Col. 3* of each identity are the aligned facial image, detected facial landmark points, and localized facial parts by ROI projection on the feature maps, respectively. We can see that the localized appearance representations are discriminative among different identities.

3.3 Experiments on the Labeled Faces in the Wild (LFW)

We evaluated the proposed method on the LFW dataset, which reveals the *state-of-the-art* of face verification in unconstrained environments. The LFW dataset is excellent benchmark dataset for face verification in image and contains 13,233 web crawling images with large variations in illuminations, occlusions, facial poses, and facial expressions, from 5,749 different identities. Our models such as **model A**, **model B**, and **model C** are trained on the roughly 2.8M outside training set (VGGFace2), with no people overlapping with subjects in the LFW. Following the test protocol of *unrestricted with labeled outside data* [21], we test on 6,000 face pairs by using a squared L_2 distance threshold to determine

Table 2. Comparison of the number of images, the number of networks, the dimensionality of feature, and the accuracy of the proposed method with the *state-of-the-art* methods on the LFW

Method	Images	Networks	Dimension	Accuracy (%)
DeepFace [34]	4M	9	$4,096 \times 4$	97.25
DeepID [30]	202,599	120	150×120	97.45
DeepID2+ [32]	300,000	25	150×120	99.47
DeepID3 [41]	300,000	50	300×100	99.52
FaceNet [28]	200M	1	128	99.63
Learning from scratch [40]	494,414	2	160×2	97.73
CenterFace [36]	0.7M	1	512	99.28
PIMNet$_{\text{TL-Joint Bayesian}}$ [17]	198,018	4	1,024	98.33
PIMNet$_{\text{fusion}}$ [17]	198,018	4	6	99.08
SphereFace [23]	494,414	1	1,024	99.42
ArcFace [10]	3.1M	1	512	99.78
model A (baseline, only $\boldsymbol{f}^g$)	2.8M	1	2,048	**99.6**
PRN	2.8M	1	1,000	**99.61**
PRN$^+$	2.8M	1	1,000	**99.69**
model B ($\boldsymbol{f}^g + PRN$)	2.8M	1	1,024	**99.65**
model C ($\boldsymbol{f}^g + PRN^+$)	2.8M	1	1,024	**99.76**

classification of *same* and *different*, and report the results in comparison with the *state-of-the-art* methods (Table 2).

From the experimental results (Table 2), we have the following observations. First, *PRN* itself provides slightly better accuracy than the baseline **model A** (the base CNN model, just uses $\boldsymbol{f}^g$) and PRN^+ outperforms **model B** which is jointly combined both $\boldsymbol{f}^g$ with PRN. Second, **model C** (jointly combined $\boldsymbol{f}^g$ with PRN^+) beats the baseline model **model A** by a significantly margin, improving the accuracy from 99.6% to 99.76%. This shows that combination of $\boldsymbol{f}^g$ and PRN^+ can notably increase the discriminative power of deeply learned features, and the effectiveness of the pairwise relations between facial local appearance parts (local appearance patches). Third, compared to **model B**, **model C** achieved better accuracy of verification (99.65% *vs.* 99.76%). This shows the importance of the face identity state feature to capture unique and discriminative pairwise relations in the designed PRN model. Last, compared to the *state-of-the-art* methods on the LFW, the proposed method **model C** is among the top-ranked approaches, outperforming most of the existing results (Table 2). This shows the importance and advantage of the proposed method.

3.4 Experiments on the YouTube Face Dataset (YTF)

We evaluated the proposed method on the YTF dataset, which reveals the *state-of-the-art* of face verification in unconstrained environments. The YTF dataset is excellent benchmark dataset for face verification in video and contains 3,425

Table 3. Comparison of the number of images, the number of networks, the dimensionality of feature, and the accuracy of the proposed method with the *state-of-the-art* methods on the YTF

Method	Images	Networks	Dimension	Accuracy (%)
DeepFace [34]	4M	9	$4,096 \times 4$	91.4
DeepID2+ [32]	300,000	25	150×120	93.2
FaceNet [28]	200M	1	128	95.1
Learning from scratch [40]	494,414	2	160×2	92.2
CenterFace [36]	0.7M	1	512	94.9
SphereFace [23]	494,414	1	1,024	95.0
NAN [39]	3M	1	128	95.7
model A (baseline, only f^g)	2.8M	1	2,048	**95.1**
PRN	2.8M	1	1,000	**95.3**
PRN$^+$	2.8M	1	1,000	**95.8**
model B ($f^g + PRN$)	2.8M	1	1,024	**95.7**
model C ($f^g + PRN^+$)	2.8M	1	1,024	**96.3**

videos with large variations in illuminations, facial pose, and facial expressions, from $1,595$ different identities, with an average of 2.15 videos per person. The length of video clip varies from 48 to $6,070$ frames and average of 181.3 frames. We follow the test protocol of *unrestricted with labeled outside data*. We test on $5,000$ video pairs and report the test results in comparison with the *state-of-the-art* methods (Table 3).

From the experimental results (Table 3), we have the following observations. First, *PRN* itself provides slightly better accuracy than the baseline **model A** (the base CNN model, just uses f^g) and PRN^+ outperforms **model B** which is jointly combined both f^g with PRN. Second, **model C** (jointly combined f^g with PRN^+) beats the baseline model **model A** by a significant margin, improving the accuracy from 95.1% to 96.3%. This shows that combination of f^g and PRN^+ can notably increase the discriminative power of deeply learned features, and the effectiveness of the pairwise relations between facial local appearance patches. Third, compared to **model B**, **model C** achieved better accuracy of verification (95.7% *v.s.* 96.3%). This shows the importance of the face identity state feature to capture unique pairwise relations in the designed PRN model. Last, compared to the *state-of-the-art* methods on the YTF, the proposed method **model C** is the *state-of-the-art* (96.3%), outperforming the existing results (Table 3). This shows the importance and advantage of the proposed method.

3.5 Experiments on the IARPA Janus Benchmark a (IJB-A)

We evaluated the proposed method on the IJB-A dataset [18] which contains face images and videos captured from unconstrained environments. It features full pose variation and wide variations in imaging conditions thus is very challenging.

Table 4. Comparison of performances of the proposed PRN method with the *state-of-the-art* on the IJB-A dataset. For verification, TAR *vs.* FAR are reported. For identification, TPIR *vs.* FPIR and the Rank-N accuracies are presented

Method	1:1 Verification TAR			1:N Identification TPIR				
	FAR=0.001	FAR=0.01	FAR=0.1	FPIR=0.01	FPIR=0.1	Rank-1	Rank-5	Rank-10
B-CNN [8]	-	-	-	0.143 ± 0.027	0.341 ± 0.032	0.588 ± 0.020	0.796 ± 0.017	-
LSFS [35]	0.514 ± 0.060	0.733 ± 0.034	0.895 ± 0.013	0.383 ± 0.063	0.613 ± 0.032	0.820 ± 0.024	0.929 ± 0.013	-
DCNN$_{manual}$+metric [6]	-	0.787 ± 0.043	0.947 ± 0.011	-	-	0.852 ± 0.018	0.937 ± 0.010	0.954 ± 0.007
Triplet Similarity [27]	0.590 ± 0.050	0.790 ± 0.030	0.945 ± 0.002	0.556 ± 0.065	0.754 ± 0.014	0.880 ± 0.015	0.95 ± 0.007	0.974 ± 0.005
Pose-Aware Models [24]	0.652 ± 0.037	0.826 ± 0.018	-	-	-	0.840 ± 0.012	0.925 ± 0.008	0.946 ± 0.005
Deep Multi-Pose [2]	-	0.876	0.954	0.52	0.75	0.846	0.927	0.947
DCNN$_{fusion}$ [5]	-	0.838 ± 0.042	0.967 ± 0.009	0.577 ± 0.094	0.790 ± 0.033	0.903 ± 0.012	0.965 ± 0.008	0.977 ± 0.007
Triplet Embedding [27]	0.813 ± 0.02	0.90 ± 0.01	0.964 ± 0.005	0.753 ± 0.03	0.863 ± 0.014	0.932 ± 0.01	-	0.977 ± 0.005
VGG-Face [26]	-	0.805 ± 0.030	-	0.461 ± 0.077	0.670 ± 0.031	0.913 ± 0.011	-	0.981 ± 0.005
Template Adaptation [9]	0.836 ± 0.027	0.939 ± 0.013	0.979 ± 0.004	0.774 ± 0.049	0.882 ± 0.016	0.928 ± 0.010	0.977 ± 0.004	0.986 ± 0.003
NAN [39]	0.881 ± 0.011	0.941 ± 0.008	0.978 ± 0.003	0.817 ± 0.041	0.917 ± 0.009	0.958 ± 0.005	0.980 ± 0.005	0.986 ± 0.003
VGGFace2 [3]	0.921 ± 0.014	0.968 ± 0.006	0.990 ± 0.002	0.883 ± 0.038	0.946 ± 0.004	0.982 ± 0.004	0.993 ± 0.002	0.994 ± 0.001
model A (baseline, only f^g)	0.895 ± 0.015	0.949 ± 0.008	0.980 ± 0.005	0.843 ± 0.035	0.923 ± 0.005	0.975 ± 0.005	0.992 ± 0.004	0.993 ± 0.001
model B ($f^g + PRN$)	0.901 ± 0.014	0.950 ± 0.006	0.985 ± 0.002	0.861 ± 0.038	0.931 ± 0.004	0.976 ± 0.003	0.992 ± 0.003	0.994 ± 0.003
model C ($f^g + PRN^+$)	0.919 ± 0.013	0.965 ± 0.004	0.988 ± 0.002	0.882 ± 0.038	0.941 ± 0.004	0.982 ± 0.004	0.992 ± 0.002	0.995 ± 0.001

It contains 500 subjects with 5,397 images and 2,042 videos in total, and 11.4 images and 4.2 videos per subject on average. We detect the faces using face detector [42] and landmark points using DAN landmark point detector [19], and then align the face image with our face alignment method explained in Sect. 2.2. In this dataset, each training and testing instance is called a 'template', which comprises 1 to 190 mixed still images and video frames. IJB-A dataset provides 10 split evaluations with two protocols (1:1 face verification and 1:N face identification). For face verification, we report the test results by using true accept rate (TAR) *vs.* false accept rate (FAR) (Table 4). For face identification, we report the results by using the true positive identification (TPIR) *vs.* false positive identification rate (FPIR) and Rank-N (Table 4). All measurements are based on a squared L_2 distance threshold.

From the experimental results (Table 4), we have the following observations. First, compared to **model A** (base CNN model), **model C** (jointly combined f^g with PRN^+) achieved a consistently superior accuracy (TAR and TPIR) on both 1:1 face verification and 1:N face identification. Second, compared to **model B** (jointly combined f^g with PRN), **model C** achieved also a consistently better accuracy (TAR and TPIR) on both 1:1 face verification and 1:N face identification. Last, more importantly, **model C** is trained from scratch and achieves comparable results to the *state-of-the-art* (VGGFace2 [3]) which is first pre-trained on the MS-Celeb-1M dataset [11], which contains roughly 10M face images, and then is fine-tuned on the VGGFace2 dataset. It shows that our proposed method can be further improved by training on the MS-Celeb-1M and our training dataset.

3.6 Experiments on the IARPA Janus Benchmark B (IJB-B)

We evaluated the proposed method on the IJB-B dataset [37] which contains face images and videos captured from unconstrained environments. The IJB-B dataset is an extension of the IJB-A, having 1,845 subjects with 21.8K still

Table 5. Comparison of performances of the proposed PRN method with the *state-of-the-art* on the IJB-B dataset. For verification, TAR *vs.* FAR are reported. For identification, TPIR *vs.* FPIR and the Rank-N accuracies are presented

Method	1:1 Verification TAR				1:N Identification TPIR				
	FAR=0.0001	FAR=0.0001	FAR=0.001	FAR=0.01	FPIR=0.01	FPIR=0.1	Rank-1	Rank-5	Rank-10
VGGFace2 [3]	0.671	0.800	0.0.888	0.949	0.746 ± 0.018	0.842 ± 0.022	0.912 ± 0.017	0.949 ± 0.010	0.962 ± 0.007
VGGFace2_ft [3]	0.705	0.831	0.908	0.956	0.763 ± 0.018	0.865 ± 0.018	0.914 ± 0.029	0.951 ± 0.013	0.961 ± 0.010
FPN [4]	-	0.832	0.916	0.965	-	-	0.911	0.953	0.975
model A (baseline, only f^g)	0.673	0.812	0.892	0.953	0.743 ± 0.019	0.851 ± 0.017	0.911 ± 0.017	0.950 ± 0.013	0.961 ± 0.010
model B (f^g + PRN)	0.692	0.829	0.910	0.956	0.773 ± 0.018	0.865 ± 0.018	0.913 ± 0.022	0.954 ± 0.010	0.965 ± 0.013
model C (f^g + PRN^+)	0.721	0.845	0.923	0.965	0.814 ± 0.017	0.907 ± 0.013	0.935 ± 0.015	0.965 ± 0.017	0.975 ± 0.007

images (including $11,754$ face and $10,044$ non-face) and 55K frames from $7,011$ videos, an average of 41 images per subject. Because images in this dataset are labeled with ground truth bounding boxes, we only detect landmark points using DAN [19], and then align face images with our face alignment method. Unlike the IJB-A, it does not contain any training splits. In particular, we use the 1:1 Baseline Verification protocol and 1:N Mixed Media Identification protocol for the IJB-B. For face verification, we report the test results by using TAR *vs.* FAR (Table 5). For face identification, we report the results by using TPIR *vs.* FPIR and Rank-N (Table 5). We compare our proposed methods with VGGFace2 [3] and FacePoseNet (FPN) [4]. All measurements are based on a squared L_2 distance threshold.

From the experimental results, we have the following observations. First, compared to **model A** (base CNN model, just uses f^g), **model C** (jointly combined f^g with PRN^+ as the local appearance representation) achieved a consistently superior accuracy (TAR and TPIR) on both 1:1 face verification and 1:N face identification. Second, compared to **model B** (jointly combined f^g with the PRN), **model C** achieved also a consistently better accuracy (TAR and TPIR) on both 1:1 face verification and 1:N face identification. Last, more importantly, **model C** achieved consistent improvement of TAR and TPIR on both 1:1 face verification and 1:N face identification, and achieved the *state-of-the-art* results on the IJB-B.

4 Conclusion

We proposed a novel face recognition method using the pairwise relational network (PRN) which takes local appearance patches around landmark points on the feature maps, and captures unique pairwise relations between a pair of local appearance patches. To capture unique and discriminative relations for face recognition, pairwise relations should be identity dependent. Therefore, the PRN conditioned its processing on the face identity state feature embedded by the LSTM based network using a sequential local appearance patches. To further improve accuracy of face recognition, we combined the global appearance representation with the PRN. Experiments verified the effectiveness and importance of our proposed PRN and the face identity state feature, which achieved 99.76%

accuracy on the LFW, the *state-of-the-art* accuracy (96.3%) on the YTF, comparable results to the *state-of-the-art* for both face verification and identification tasks on the IJB-A, and the *state-of-the-art* results on the IJB-B.

Acknowledgment. This research was supported by the MSIT, Korea, under the SW Starlab support program (IITP-2017-0-00897), and "ICT Consilience Creative program" (IITP-2018-2011-1-00783) supervised by the IITP.

References

1. Abadi, M., et al.: TensorFlow: large-scale machine learning on heterogeneous systems (2015). https://www.tensorflow.org/
2. AbdAlmageed, W., et al.: Face recognition using deep multi-pose representations. In: 2016 IEEE Winter Conference on Applications of Computer Vision (WACV), pp. 1–9, March 2016. https://doi.org/10.1109/WACV.2016.7477555
3. Cao, Q., Shen, L., Xie, W., Parkhi, O.M., Zisserman, A.: VGGFace2: a dataset for recognising faces across pose and age. CoRR abs/1710.08092 (2017). http://arxiv.org/abs/1710.08092
4. Chang, F.J., Tran, A.T., Hassner, T., Masi, I., Nevatia, R., Medioni, G.: Faceposenet: making a case for landmark-free face alignment. In: 2017 IEEE International Conference on Computer Vision Workshops (ICCVW), pp. 1599–1608, October 2017. https://doi.org/10.1109/ICCVW.2017.188
5. Chen, J.C., Patel, V.M., Chellappa, R.: Unconstrained face verification using deep CNN features. In: 2016 IEEE Winter Conference on Applications of Computer Vision (WACV), pp. 1–9, March 2016. https://doi.org/10.1109/WACV.2016.7477557
6. Chen, J.C., Ranjan, R., Kumar, A., Chen, C.H., Patel, V.M., Chellappa, R.: An end-to-end system for unconstrained face verification with deep convolutional neural networks. In: 2015 IEEE International Conference on Computer Vision Workshop (ICCVW), pp. 360–368, December 2015. https://doi.org/10.1109/ICCVW.2015.55
7. Chollet, F., et al.: Keras (2015). https://github.com/fchollet/keras
8. Chowdhury, A.R., Lin, T.Y., Maji, S., Learned-Miller, E.: One-to-many face recognition with bilinear cnns. In: 2016 IEEE Winter Conference on Applications of Computer Vision (WACV), pp. 1–9, March 2016. https://doi.org/10.1109/WACV.2016.7477593
9. Crosswhite, N., Byrne, J., Stauffer, C., Parkhi, O., Cao, Q., Zisserman, A.: Template adaptation for face verification and identification. In: 2017 12th IEEE International Conference on Automatic Face Gesture Recognition (FG 2017), pp. 1–8, May 2017. https://doi.org/10.1109/FG.2017.11
10. Deng, J., Guo, J., Zafeiriou, S.: ArcFace: additive angular margin loss for deep face recognition. arXiv e-prints, January 2018
11. Guo, Y., Zhang, L., Hu, Y., He, X., Gao, J.: MS-Celeb-1M: a dataset and benchmark for large-scale face recognition. In: Leibe, B., Matas, J., Sebe, N., Welling, M. (eds.) ECCV 2016. LNCS, vol. 9907, pp. 87–102. Springer, Cham (2016). https://doi.org/10.1007/978-3-319-46487-9_6
12. He, K., Zhang, X., Ren, S., Sun, J.: Delving deep into rectifiers: surpassing human-level performance on imagenet classification. In: 2015 IEEE International Conference on Computer Vision (ICCV), pp. 1026–1034, December 2015. https://doi.org/10.1109/ICCV.2015.123

13. He, K., Zhang, X., Ren, S., Sun, J.: Deep residual learning for image recognition. In: 2016 IEEE Conference on Computer Vision and Pattern Recognition (CVPR), pp. 770–778, June 2016. https://doi.org/10.1109/CVPR.2016.90

14. Huang, G., Liu, Z., Van Der Maaten, L., Weinberger, K.Q.: Densely connected convolutional networks. In: 2017 IEEE Conference on Computer Vision and Pattern Recognition (CVPR), pp. 2261–2269, July 2017. https://doi.org/10.1109/CVPR.2017.243

15. Huang, G.B., Ramesh, M., Berg, T., Learned-Miller, E.: Labeled faces in the wild: a database for studying face recognition in unconstrained environments. Technical report, 07–49, University of Massachusetts, Amherst, October 2007

16. Ioffe, S., Szegedy, C.: Batch normalization: accelerating deep network training by reducing internal covariate shift. In: Proceedings of the 32nd International Conference on Machine Learning, ICML 2015, Lille, France, 6–11 July 2015, pp. 448–456 (2015). http://jmlr.org/proceedings/papers/v37/ioffe15.html

17. Kang, B.N., Kim, Y., Kim, D.: Deep convolutional neural network using triplets of faces, deep ensemble, and score-level fusion for face recognition. In: 2017 IEEE Conference on Computer Vision and Pattern Recognition Workshops (CVPRW), pp. 611–618, July 2017. https://doi.org/10.1109/CVPRW.2017.89

18. Klare, B.F., et al.: Pushing the frontiers of unconstrained face detection and recognition: IARPA Janus benchmark A. In: 2015 IEEE Conference on Computer Vision and Pattern Recognition (CVPR), pp. 1931–1939, June 2015. https://doi.org/10.1109/CVPR.2015.7298803

19. Kowalski, M., Naruniec, J., Trzcinski, T.: Deep alignment network: a convolutional neural network for robust face alignment. In: 2017 IEEE Conference on Computer Vision and Pattern Recognition Workshops (CVPRW), pp. 2034–2043, July 2017. https://doi.org/10.1109/CVPRW.2017.254

20. Krizhevsky, A., Sutskever, I., Hinton, G.E.: Imagenet classification with deep convolutional neural networks. In: Proceedings of the 25th International Conference on Neural Information Processing Systems, NIPS 2012, vol. 1, pp. 1097–1105 (2012). http://dl.acm.org/citation.cfm?id=2999134.2999257

21. Learned-Miller, G.B.H.E.: Labeled faces in the wild: updates and new reporting procedures. Technical report, UM-CS-2014-003, University of Massachusetts, Amherst, May 2014

22. Liu, S., Deng, W.: Very deep convolutional neural network based image classification using small training sample size. In: 2015 3rd IAPR Asian Conference on Pattern Recognition (ACPR), pp. 730–734, November 2015. https://doi.org/10.1109/ACPR.2015.7486599

23. Liu, W., Wen, Y., Yu, Z., Li, M., Raj, B., Song, L.: Sphereface: deep hypersphere embedding for face recognition. In: 2017 IEEE Conference on Computer Vision and Pattern Recognition (CVPR), pp. 6738–6746, July 2017. https://doi.org/10.1109/CVPR.2017.713

24. Masi, I., Rawls, S., Medioni, G., Natarajan, P.: Pose-aware face recognition in the wild. In: 2016 IEEE Conference on Computer Vision and Pattern Recognition (CVPR), pp. 4838–4846, June 2016. https://doi.org/10.1109/CVPR.2016.523

25. Nair, V., Hinton, G.E.: Rectified linear units improve restricted Boltzmann machines. In: Proceedings of the 27th International Conference on International Conference on Machine Learning, ICML 2010, pp. 807–814 (2010). http://dl.acm.org/citation.cfm?id=3104322.3104425

26. Parkhi, O.M., Vedaldi, A., Zisserman, A.: Deep face recognition. In: Proceedings of the British Machine Vision Conference (BMVC), pp. 41.1–41.12, September 2015. https://doi.org/10.5244/C.29.41

27. Sankaranarayanan, S., Alavi, A., Castillo, C.D., Chellappa, R.: Triplet probabilistic embedding for face verification and clustering. In: 2016 IEEE 8th International Conference on Biometrics Theory, Applications and Systems (BTAS), pp. 1–8, September 2016. https://doi.org/10.1109/BTAS.2016.7791205
28. Schroff, F., Kalenichenko, D., Philbin, J.: FaceNet: a unified embedding for face recognition and clustering. In: 2015 IEEE Conference on Computer Vision and Pattern Recognition (CVPR), pp. 815–823, June 2015. https://doi.org/10.1109/CVPR.2015.7298682
29. Simonyan, K., Zisserman, A.: Very deep convolutional networks for large-scale image recognition. CoRR abs/1409.1556 (2014). http://arxiv.org/abs/1409.1556
30. Sun, Y., Wang, X., Tang, X.: Deep learning face representation from predicting 10,000 classes. In: 2014 IEEE Conference on Computer Vision and Pattern Recognition, pp. 1891–1898, June 2014. https://doi.org/10.1109/CVPR.2014.244
31. Sun, Y., Wang, X., Tang, X.: Deeply learned face representations are sparse, selective, and robust, pp. 2892–2900, June 2015. https://doi.org/10.1109/CVPR.2015.7298907
32. Sun, Y., Chen, Y., Wang, X., Tang, X.: Deep learning face representation by joint identification-verification, pp. 1988–1996 (2014). http://papers.nips.cc/paper/5416-deep-learning-face-representation-by-joint-identification-verification.pdf
33. Szegedy, C., et al.: Going deeper with convolutions. In: 2015 IEEE Conference on Computer Vision and Pattern Recognition (CVPR), pp. 1–9, June 2015. https://doi.org/10.1109/CVPR.2015.7298594
34. Taigman, Y., Yang, M., Ranzato, M., Wolf, L.: DeepFace: closing the gap to human-level performance in face verification. In: 2014 IEEE Conference on Computer Vision and Pattern Recognition, pp. 1701–1708, June 2014. https://doi.org/10.1109/CVPR.2014.220
35. Wang, D., Otto, C., Jain, A.K.: Face search at scale. IEEE Trans. Pattern Anal. Mach. Intell. 39(6), 1122–1136 (2017). https://doi.org/10.1109/TPAMI.2016.2582166
36. Wen, Y., Zhang, K., Li, Z., Qiao, Y.: A discriminative feature learning approach for deep face recognition. In: Leibe, B., Matas, J., Sebe, N., Welling, M. (eds.) ECCV 2016. LNCS, vol. 9911, pp. 499–515. Springer, Cham (2016). https://doi.org/10.1007/978-3-319-46478-7_31
37. Whitelam, C., et al.: IARPA Janus Benchmark-B face dataset. In: 2017 IEEE Conference on Computer Vision and Pattern Recognition Workshops (CVPRW), pp. 592–600 (2017). https://doi.org/10.1109/CVPRW.2017.87
38. Wolf, L., Hassner, T., Maoz, I.: Face recognition in unconstrained videos with matched background similarity. In: CVPR 2011, pp. 529–534, June 2011. https://doi.org/10.1109/CVPR.2011.5995566
39. Yang, J., et al.: Neural aggregation network for video face recognition. In: 2017 IEEE Conference on Computer Vision and Pattern Recognition (CVPR), pp. 5216–5225, July 2017. https://doi.org/10.1109/CVPR.2017.554
40. Yi, D., Lei, Z., Liao, S., Li, S.Z.: Learning face representation from scratch. CoRR abs/1411.7923 (2014). http://arxiv.org/abs/1411.7923
41. Sun, Y., Liang, D., Wang, X., Tang, X.: DeepID3: face recognition with very deep neural networks. CoRR abs/1502.00873 (2015). http://arxiv.org/abs/1502.00873
42. Yoon, J., Kim, D.: An accurate and real-time multi-view face detector using ORFS and doubly domain-partitioning classifier. J. Real-Time Image Process. (2018). https://doi.org/10.1007/s11554-018-0751-6

43. Zhou, B., Khosla, A., Lapedriza, À., Oliva, A., Torralba, A.: Object detectors emerge in deep scene CNNs. CoRR abs/1412.6856 (2014). http://arxiv.org/abs/1412.6856

44. Zhou, B., Lapedriza, A., Xiao, J., Torralba, A., Oliva, A.: Learning deep features for scene recognition using places database. In: Ghahramani, Z., Welling, M., Cortes, C., Lawrence, N.D., Weinberger, K.Q. (eds.) Advances in Neural Information Processing Systems 27, pp. 487–495. Curran Associates, Inc. (2014). http://papers.nips.cc/paper/5349-learning-deep-features-for-scene-recognition-using-places-database.pdf

Stereo Vision-Based Semantic 3D Object and Ego-Motion Tracking for Autonomous Driving

Peiliang Li[✉]⊙, Tong Qin⊙, and Shaojie Shen⊙

Hong Kong University of Science and Technology, Clear Water Bay, Hong Kong
{pliap,tong.qin,eeshaojie}@ust.hk

Abstract. We propose a stereo vision-based approach for tracking the camera ego-motion and 3D semantic objects in dynamic autonomous driving scenarios. Instead of directly regressing the 3D bounding box using end-to-end approaches, we propose to use the easy-to-labeled 2D detection and discrete viewpoint classification together with a light-weight semantic inference method to obtain rough 3D object measurements. Based on the object-aware-aided camera pose tracking which is robust in dynamic environments, in combination with our novel dynamic object bundle adjustment (BA) approach to fuse temporal sparse feature correspondences and the semantic 3D measurement model, we obtain 3D object pose, velocity and anchored dynamic point cloud estimation with instance accuracy and temporal consistency. The performance of our proposed method is demonstrated in diverse scenarios. Both the ego-motion estimation and object localization are compared with the state-of-of-the-art solutions.

Keywords: Semantic SLAM · 3D object localization
Visual Odometry

1 Introduction

Localizing dynamic objects and estimating the camera ego-motion in 3D space are crucial tasks for autonomous driving. Currently, these objectives are separately explored by end-to-end 3D object detection methods [1,2] and traditional visual SLAM approaches [3–5]. However, it is hard to directly employ these approaches for autonomous driving scenarios. For 3D object detection, there are two main problems: 1. end-to-end 3D regression approaches need lots of training data and require heavy workload to precisely label all the object boxes in 3D space and 2. the instance 3D detection produces frame-independent results, which are not consistent enough for continuous perception in autonomous driving. To overcome this, we propose a light-weight semantic 3D box inference method depending only on 2D object detection and discrete viewpoint classification (Sect. 4). Comparing with directly 3D regression, the 2D detection and

© Springer Nature Switzerland AG 2018
V. Ferrari et al. (Eds.): ECCV 2018, LNCS 11206, pp. 664–679, 2018.
https://doi.org/10.1007/978-3-030-01216-8_40

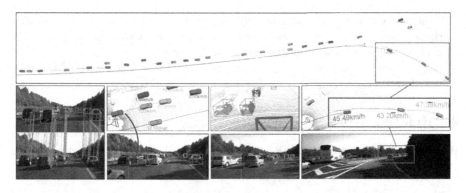

Fig. 1. Overview of our semantic 3D object and ego-motion tracking system. Top: 3D trajectories of ego-camera and all objects in the long travel history. Bottom: from left to right: stereo feature matching for each object (Sect. 5). An extreme car-truncated case where our system can still track the moving car accurately. Dynamic 3D sparse feature recovered by our object BA. Consistent movement and orientation estimation.

classification task are easy to train, and the training data can be easily labeled with only 2D images. However, the proposed 3D box inference is also frame-independent and conditional on the instance 2D detection accuracy. In another aspect, the well-known SLAM approaches can track the camera motion accurately due to precise feature geometry constraints. Inspired by this, we can similarly utilize the sparse feature correspondences for object relative motion constraining to enforce temporal consistency. However, the object instance pose cannot be obtained with pure feature measurement without semantic prior. To this end, due to the complementary nature of semantic and feature information, we integrate our instance semantic inference model and the temporal feature correlation into a tightly-coupled optimization framework which can continuously track the 3D objects and recover the dynamic sparse point cloud with instance accuracy and temporal consistency, which can be overviewed in Fig. 1. Benifitting from object-region-aware property, our system is able to estimate camera pose robustly without being affected by dynamic objects. Thanks to the temporal geometry constraints, we can track the objects continuously even for the extremely truncated case (see Fig. 1), where the object pose is hard for instance inference. Additionally, we employ a kinematics motion model for detected cars to ensure consistent orientation and motion estimation; it also serves as important smoothing for distant cars which have few feature observation. Depending only on a mature 2D detection and classification network [6], our system is capable of performing robust ego-motion estimation and 3D object tracking in diverse scenarios. The main contributions are summarized as follows:

– A light-weight 3D box inference method using only 2D object detection and the proposed viewpoint classification, which provides the object reprojection contour and occlusion mask for object feature extraction. It also serves as the semantic measurement model for the follow-up optimization.

- A novel dynamic object bundle adjustment approach which tightly couples the semantic and feature measurements to continuously track the object states with instance accuracy and temporal consistency.
- Demonstration over diverse scenarios to show the practicability of the proposed system.

2   Related Work

We review the related works in the context of semantic SLAM and learning-based 3D object detection from images.

Semantic SLAM. With the development of 2D object detection, several joint SLAM with semantic understanding works have sprung up, which we discuss in three categories. The first is semantic-aided localization: [7,8] focus on correcting the global scale of monocular Visual Odometry (VO) by incorporating object metric size of only one dimension into the estimation framework. Indoor with small objects and outdoor experiments are conducted respectively in these two works. [9] proposes an object data association method in a probabilistic formulation and shows its drift correcting ability when re-observing the previous objects. However, it omits the orientation of objects by treating the 2D bounding boxes as points. And in [10], the authors address the localization task from only object observation in a prior semantic map by computing a matrix permanent. The second is SLAM-aided object detection [11,12] and reconstruction [13,14]: [11] develops an 2D object recognition system which is robust to viewpoint changing with the assistance of camera localization, while [12] performs confidence-growing 3D objects detection using visual-inertial measurements. [13,14] reconstruct the dense surface of 3D object by fusing the point cloud from monocular and RGBD SLAM respectively. Finally, the third category is joint estimation for both camera and object poses: With pre-built bags of binary words, [15] localizes the objects in the datasets and correct the map scale in turns. In [16,17], the authors propose a semantic structure from motion (SfM) approach to jointly estimate camera, object with considering scene components interaction. However, neither of these methods shows the ability to solve dynamic objects, nor makes full use of 2D bounding box data (center, width, and height) and 3-dimensions object size. There are also some existing works [18–21] building the dense map and segmenting it with semantic labels. These works are beyond the scope of this paper, so we will not discuss them in details.

3D Object Detection. Inferring object pose from images by deep learning approaches provides an alternative way to localize 3D objects. [22,23] use the shape prior to reason 3D object pose, where the dense shape and wireframe models are used respectively. In [24], a voxel pattern is employed to detect 3D pose of objects with specific visibility patterns. Similarly to object proposal approaches in 2D detection [1,6] generates 3D proposals by utilizing depth information calculated from stereo images, while [2] exploits the ground plane assumption and

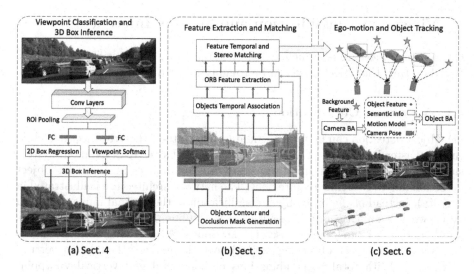

Fig. 2. Our whole semantic tracking system architecture.

additional segmentation features to produce 3D candidates; R-CNN is then used for candidates scoring and object recognition. Such high-dimension features used for proposal generating or model fitting are computationally complex for both training and deploying. Instead of directly generating 3D boxes, [25] regresses object orientation and dimensions in separate stages; then the 2D-3D box geometry constraints are used to calculate the 3D object pose, while purely depending on instance 2D box limits its performance in object-truncated cases.

In this work, we study the pros and cons of existing works and propose an integrated perception solution for autonomous driving that makes full use of the instance semantic prior and precise feature spatial-temporal correspondences to achieve robust and continuous state estimation for both the ego-camera and static or dynamic objects in diverse environments.

3   Overview

Our semantic tracking system has three main modules, as illustrated in Fig. 2. The first module performs 2D object detection and viewpoint classification (Sect. 4), where the objects poses are roughly inferred based on the constraints between 2D box edges and 3D box vertexes. The second module is feature extraction and matching (Sect. 5). It projects all the inferred 3D boxes to the 2D image to get the objects contour and occlusion masks. Guided feature matching is then applied to get robust feature associations for both stereo and temporal images. In the third module (Sect. 6), we integrate all the semantic information, feature measurements into a tightly-coupled optimization approach. A kinematics model is additionally applied to cars to get consistent motion estimation.

4   Viewpoint Classification and 3D Box Inference

Our semantic measurement includes the 2D object box and classified viewpoints. Based on this, the object pose can be roughly inferred instantly in close-form.

4.1   Viewpoint Classification

2D Object detection can be implemented by the state-of-the-art object detectors such as Faster R-CNN [6], YOLO [26], etc. We use Faster R-CNN in our system since it performs well on small objects. Only left images are used for object detection due to real-time requirement. The network architecture is illustrated in Fig. 2(a). Instead of the pure object classification in the original implementation of [6], we add sub-categories classification in the final FC layers, which denotes object horizontal and vertical discrete viewpoints. As Fig. 3a shown, We divide the continuous object observing angle into eight horizontal and two vertical viewpoints. With total 16 combinations of horizontal and vertical viewpoint classification, we can generate associations between edges in the 2D box and vertexes in the 3D box based on the assumption that the reprojection of the 3D bounding box will tightly fit the 2D bounding box. These associations provide essential condition to build the four edge-vertex constraints for 3D box inference (Sect. 4.2) and formulate our semantic measurement model (Sect. 6.2).

Comparing with direct 3D regression, the well-developed 2D detection and classification networks are more robust over diverse scenarios. The proposed viewpoint classification task is easy to train and have high accuracy, even for small and extreme occluded objects.

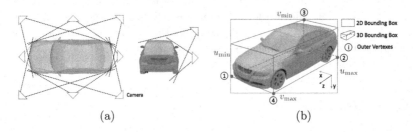

(a)   (b)

Fig. 3. (a) Presents all the horizontal and vertical viewpoints for our classification, their combinations are enough to cover all the observation cases in autonomous scenarios. (b) Illustrates the 3D car in a specific viewpoint, where the object frame, four vertexes corresponding to four 2D box edges are denoted respectively.

4.2   3D Box Inference Based on Viewpoint

Given the 2D box described by four edges in normalized image plane $[u_{min}, v_{min}, u_{max}, v_{max}]$ and classified viewpoint, we aim to infer the object pose based on four constriants between 2D box edges and 3D box vertexes, which is inspired by [25]. A 3D bounding box can be represented by its center position $\mathbf{p} = [p_x, p_y, p_z]^T$ and horizontal orientation θ respecting to camera frame and the dimensions prior $\mathbf{d} = [d_x, d_y, d_z]^T$. For example, in such a viewpoint presented in Fig. 3b from one of 16 combinations in Fig. 3a (denoted as red), four vertexes are projected to the 2D edges, the corresponding constraints can be formulated as:

$$\begin{cases} u_{\min} = \pi\left(\mathbf{p} + \mathbf{R}_\theta \mathbf{C}_1 \mathbf{d}\right)_u, \ u_{\max} = \pi\left(\mathbf{p} + \mathbf{R}_\theta \mathbf{C}_2 \mathbf{d}\right)_u, \\ v_{\min} = \pi\left(\mathbf{p} + \mathbf{R}_\theta \mathbf{C}_3 \mathbf{d}\right)_v, \ v_{\max} = \pi\left(\mathbf{p} + \mathbf{R}_\theta \mathbf{C}_4 \mathbf{d}\right)_v, \end{cases} \quad (1)$$

where π is a 3D projection warp function which defined as $\pi(\mathbf{p}) = [p_x/p_z, p_y/p_z]^T$, and $(\cdot)_u$ represents the u coordinate in the normalized image plane. We use $\mathbf{R}_\theta$ to denote the rotation parameterized by horizontal orientation θ from the object frame to the camera frame. $\mathbf{C}_{1:4}$ are four diagonal selection matrixes to describe the relations between the object center to the four selected vertexes, which can be determined after we get the classified viewpoint without ambiguous. From the object frame defined in Fig. 3b, it's easy to see that:

$$\mathbf{C}_{1:4} = \begin{bmatrix} 0.5 & 0 & 0 \\ 0 & 0.5 & 0 \\ 0 & 0 & 0.5 \end{bmatrix}, \begin{bmatrix} -0.5 & 0 & 0 \\ 0 & 0.5 & 0 \\ 0 & 0 & -0.5 \end{bmatrix}, \begin{bmatrix} 0.5 & 0 & 0 \\ 0 & -0.5 & 0 \\ 0 & 0 & -0.5 \end{bmatrix}, \begin{bmatrix} -0.5 & 0 & 0 \\ 0 & 0.5 & 0 \\ 0 & 0 & 0.5 \end{bmatrix}. \quad (2)$$

With these four equations, the 4 DoF object pose can be solved intuitively given the dimensions prior. This solving process has very trivial time consuming comparing with [25] which exhaustive tests all the valid edge-vertex configurations.

We convert the complex 3D object detection problem into 2D detection, viewpoint classification, and straightforward closed-form calculation. Admittedly, the solved pose is an approximated estimation which is conditioned on the instance "tightness" of the 2D bounding box and the object dimension prior. Also for some top view cases, the reprojection of the 3D box does not strictly fit the 2D box, which can be observed from the top edge in Fig. 3b. However, for the almost horizontal or slight looking-down viewpoints in autonomous driving scenarios, this assumption can be held reasonably. Note that our instance pose inference is only for generating object projection contour and occlusion mask for the feature extraction (Sect. 5) and serves as an initial value for the follow-up maximum-a-posteriori (MAP) estimation, where the 3D object trajectory will be further optimized by sliding window based feature correlation and object point cloud alignment.

5   Feature Extraction and Matching

We project the inferred 3D object boxes (Sect. 4.2) to the stereo images to generate a valid 2D contour. As Fig. 2(b) illustrates, we use different colors mask to represent visible part of each object (gray for the background). For occlusion objects, we mask the occluded part as invisible according to objects 2D overlap and 3D depth relations. For truncated objects which have less than four valid edges measurements thus cannot be inferred by the method in Sect. 4.2, we directly project the 2D box detected in the left image to the right image. We extract ORB features [27] for both the left and right image in the visible area for each object and the background.

Stereo matching is performed by epipolar line searching. The depth range of object features are known from the inferred object pose, so we limit the search area to a small range to achieve robust feature matching. For temporal matching, we first associate objects for successive frames by 2D box similarity score voting. The similarity score is weighted by the center distance and shape similarity of the 2D boxes between successive images after compensating the camera rotation. The object is treated as lost if its maximum similarity score with all the objects in the previous frame is less than a threshold. We note that there are more sophisticated association schemes such as probabilistic data association [9], but it is more suitable for avoiding the hard decision when re-visiting the static object scene than for the highly dynamic and no-repetitive scene for autonomous driving. We subsequently match ORB features for the associated objects and background with the previous frame. Outliers are rejected by RANSAC with local fundamental matrix test for each object and background independently.

6   Ego-Motion and Object Tracking

Beginning with the notation definition, we use $\mathbf{s}_k^t = \{\mathbf{b}_{kl}^t, \mathbf{b}_{kr}^t, l_k, \mathbf{C}_{k1:4}^t\}$ to denote the semantic measurement of the kth object at time t, where $\mathbf{b}_{kl}^t, \mathbf{b}_{kr}^t$ are the observations of the left-top and the right-bottom coordinates of the 2D bounding box respectively, l_k is the object class label and $\mathbf{C}_{k1:4}^t$ are four selection matrixes defined in Sect. 4.2. For measurements of sparse feature which is anchored to one object or the background, we use ${}^n\mathbf{z}_k^t = \{{}^n\mathbf{z}_{kl}^t, {}^n\mathbf{z}_{kr}^t\}$ to denote the stereo observations of the nth feature on the kth object at time t ($k = 0$ for the static background), where ${}^n\mathbf{z}_{kl}^t, {}^n\mathbf{z}_{kr}^t$ are feature coordinates in the normalized left and right image plane respectively. The states of the ego-camera and the kth object are represented as ${}^w\mathbf{x}_c^t = \{{}^w\mathbf{p}_c^t, {}^w\mathbf{R}_c^t\}$, ${}^w\mathbf{x}_{ok}^t = \{{}^w\mathbf{p}_{ok}^t, \mathbf{d}_k, {}^w\theta_{ok}^t, v_{ok}^t, \delta_{ok}^t\}$ respectively, where we use ${}^w(\cdot)$, $(\cdot)_c$ and $(\cdot)_o$ to denote the world, camera and object frame. ${}^w\mathbf{p}$ represents the position in the world frame. For objects orientation, we only model the horizontal rotation ${}^w\theta_{ok}^t$ instead of $\mathbb{SO}(3)$ rotation ${}^w\mathbf{R}_c^t$ for the ego-camera. $\mathbf{d}_k$ is the time-invariant dimensions of the kth object, and v_{ok}^t, δ_{ok}^t are the speed and steering angle, which are only estimated for cars. For conciseness, we visualize the measurements and states in Fig. 4 at the time t.

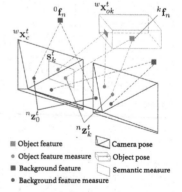

Fig. 4. Notation visualization.

Considering a general autonomous driving scene, we aim to continuously estimate the ego-motion of the onboard camera from time 0 to T: ${}^w\mathcal{X}_c = \{{}^w\mathbf{x}_c^t\}_{t=0:T}$, and track the K_t number of 3D objects: ${}^w\mathcal{X}_o = \{{}^w\mathbf{x}_{ok}\}_{k=1:K_t}$, ${}^w\mathbf{x}_{ok} =$

$\{^w\mathbf{x}_{ok}^t\}_{t=0:T}$, and recover the 3D position of the dynamic sparse features: $\mathcal{F} = \{^k\mathbf{f}\}_{k=0:K_t}$, $^k\mathbf{f} = \{^k\mathbf{f}_n\}_{n=0:N_k}$, (note that here we use $^k(\cdot)$ to denote the kth object frame, in which the features are relatively static, $k = 0$ for background world, in which the features are globally static), given the semantic measurements: $\mathcal{S} = \{\mathbf{s}_k\}_{k=1:K_t}$, $\mathbf{s}_k = \{\mathbf{s}_k^t\}_{t=0:T}$ and sparse feature observations anchored to the kth object: $\mathcal{Z} = \{\mathbf{z}_k\}_{k=0:K_t}$, $\mathbf{z}_k = \{^n\mathbf{z}_k\}_{n=0:N_k}$. $^n\mathbf{z}_k = \{^n\mathbf{z}_k^t\}_{t=0:T}$. We formulate our semantic objects and camera ego-motion tracking from the probabilistic model to a nonlinear optimization problem.

6.1 Ego-Motion Tracking

Given the static background feature observation, the ego-motion can be solved via maximum likelihood estimation (MLE):

$$^w\mathcal{X}_c, {}^0\mathbf{f} = \arg\max_{^w\mathcal{X}_c, {}^0\mathbf{f}} \prod_{n=0}^{N_0} \prod_{t=0}^{T} p(^n\mathbf{z}_0^t|^w\mathbf{x}_c^t, {}^0\mathbf{f}_n, {}^w\mathbf{x}_c^0) \tag{3}$$

$$= \arg\max_{^w\mathcal{X}_c, {}^0\mathbf{f}} \sum_{n=0}^{N_0} \sum_{t=0}^{T} \log p(^n\mathbf{z}_0^t|^w\mathbf{x}_c^t, {}^0\mathbf{f}_n, {}^w\mathbf{x}_c^0) \tag{4}$$

$$= \arg\min_{^w\mathcal{X}_c, {}^0\mathbf{f}} \sum_{n=0}^{N_0} \sum_{t=0}^{T} \left\| r_\mathcal{Z}(^n\mathbf{z}_0^t, {}^w\mathbf{x}_c^t, {}^0\mathbf{f}_n) \right\|_{0\Sigma_n^t}^2 . \tag{5}$$

This is the typical SLAM or SfM approach. The camera pose and background point cloud are estimated conditionally on the first state. As Eq. 3 shows, the log probability of measurement residual is proportional to its Mahalanobis norm $\|\mathbf{r}\|_\Sigma^2 = \mathbf{r}^T\Sigma^{-1}\mathbf{r}$. Then the MLE is converted to a nonlinear least square problem, this process is also known as Bundle Adjustment (BA).

6.2 Semantic Object Tracking

After we solve the camera pose, the object state at each time t can be solved based on the dimension prior and the instance semantic measurements (Sect. 4.2). We assume the object is a rigid body, which means the feature anchored to it is fixed respecting to the object frame. Therefore, the temporal states of the object are correlated if we have continuous object feature observations. States of different objects are conditionally independent given the camera pose, so we can track all the objects in parallel and independently. For the kth object, we have the dimension prior distribution $p(\mathbf{d}_k)$ for each class label. We assume the detection results and feature measurements for each object at each time are independent and Gaussian distributed. According to Bayes' rule, we have the following maximum-a-posteriori (MAP) estimation:

$$^{w}\mathbf{x}_{ok}, {}^{k}\mathbf{f} = \arg\max_{^{w}\mathbf{x}_{ok}, {}^{k}\mathbf{f}} p(^{w}\mathbf{x}_{ok}, {}^{k}\mathbf{f} \mid {}^{w}\mathbf{x}_{c}, \mathbf{z}_{k}, \mathbf{s}_{k}) \tag{6}$$

$$= \arg\max_{^{w}\mathbf{x}_{ok}, {}^{k}\mathbf{f}} p(\mathbf{z}_{k}, \mathbf{s}_{k} \mid {}^{w}\mathbf{x}_{c}, {}^{w}\mathbf{x}_{ok}, {}^{k}\mathbf{f}) p(\mathbf{d}_{k}) \tag{7}$$

$$= \arg\max_{^{w}\mathbf{x}_{ok}, {}^{k}\mathbf{f}} p(\mathbf{z}_{k} \mid {}^{w}\mathbf{x}_{c}, {}^{w}\mathbf{x}_{ok}, {}^{k}\mathbf{f}) p(\mathbf{s}_{k} \mid {}^{w}\mathbf{x}_{c}, {}^{w}\mathbf{x}_{ok}) p(\mathbf{d}_{k}) \tag{8}$$

$$= \arg\max_{^{w}\mathbf{x}_{ok}, {}^{k}\mathbf{f}} \prod_{t=0}^{T} \prod_{n=0}^{N_{k}} p(^{n}\mathbf{z}_{k}^{t} \mid {}^{w}\mathbf{x}_{c}^{t}, {}^{w}\mathbf{x}_{ok}^{t}, {}^{k}\mathbf{f}_{n}) p(\mathbf{s}_{k}^{t} \mid {}^{w}\mathbf{x}_{c}^{t}, {}^{w}\mathbf{x}_{ok}^{t}) p(^{w}\mathbf{x}_{ok}^{t-1} \mid {}^{w}\mathbf{x}_{ok}^{t}) p(\mathbf{d}_{k}). \tag{9}$$

Similar to Eq. 3, we convert the MAP to a nonlinear optimization problem:

$$^{w}\mathbf{x}_{ok}, {}^{k}\mathbf{f} = \arg\min_{^{w}\mathbf{x}_{ok}, {}^{k}\mathbf{f}} \left\{ \sum_{t=0}^{T} \sum_{n=0}^{N_{k}} \left\| r_{\mathcal{Z}}(^{n}\mathbf{z}_{k}^{t}, {}^{w}\mathbf{x}_{c}^{t}, {}^{w}\mathbf{x}_{ok}^{t}, {}^{k}\mathbf{f}_{n}) \right\|_{k \Sigma_{n}^{t}}^{2} + \left\| r_{\mathcal{P}}(d_{k}^{l}, \mathbf{d}_{k}) \right\|_{\Sigma^{l}}^{2} \right.$$
$$\left. + \sum_{t=1}^{T} \left\| r_{\mathcal{M}}(^{w}\mathbf{x}_{ok}^{t}, {}^{w}\mathbf{x}_{ok}^{t-1}) \right\|_{\Sigma_{k}^{t}}^{2} + \sum_{t=0}^{T} \left\| r_{\mathcal{S}}(\mathbf{s}_{k}^{t}, {}^{w}\mathbf{x}_{c}^{t}, {}^{w}\mathbf{x}_{ok}^{t}) \right\|_{\Sigma_{k}^{t}}^{2} \right\}, \tag{10}$$

where we use $r_{\mathcal{Z}}$, $r_{\mathcal{P}}$, $r_{\mathcal{M}}$, and $r_{\mathcal{S}}$ to denote the residual of the feature reprojection, dimension prior, object motion model, and semantic bounding box reprojection respectively. Σ is the corresponding covariance matrix for each measurement. We formulate our 3D object tracking problem into a dynamic object BA approach which makes fully exploit object dimension and motion prior and enforces temporal consistency. Maximum a posteriori estimation can be achieved by minimizing the sum of the Mahalanobis norm of all the residuals.

Sparse Feature Observation. We extend the projective geometry between static features and camera pose to dynamic features and object pose. Based on anchored relative static features respecting to the object frame, the object poses which share feature observations can be connected by a factor graph. For each feature observation, the residual can be represented by the reprojection error of predicted feature position and the actual feature observations on the left and right image:

$$r_{\mathcal{Z}}(^{n}\mathbf{z}_{k}^{t}, {}^{w}\mathbf{x}_{c}^{t}, {}^{w}\mathbf{x}_{ok}^{t}, {}^{k}\mathbf{f}_{n}) \tag{11}$$

$$= \begin{bmatrix} \pi\left(h^{-1}(^{w}\mathbf{x}_{c}^{t}, h(^{w}\mathbf{x}_{ok}^{t}, {}^{k}\mathbf{f}_{n}))\right) - {}^{n}\mathbf{z}_{kl}^{t} \\ \pi\left(h(^{r}\mathbf{x}_{l}, h^{-1}(^{w}\mathbf{x}_{c}^{t}, h(^{w}\mathbf{x}_{ok}^{t}, {}^{k}\mathbf{f}_{n})))\right) - {}^{n}\mathbf{z}_{kr}^{t} \end{bmatrix}, \tag{12}$$

where we use $h(\mathbf{x}, p)$ to denote applying a 3D rigid body transform $\mathbf{x}$ to a point p. For example, $h\left(^{w}\mathbf{x}_{ok}^{t}, {}^{k}\mathbf{f}_{n}\right)$ transforms the nth feature point ${}^{k}\mathbf{f}_{n}$ from the object frame to the world frame, $h^{-1}(\mathbf{x}, p)$ is the corresponding inverse transform. ${}^{r}\mathbf{x}_{l}$ denotes the extrinsic transform of the stereo camera, which is calibrated offline.

Semantic 3D Object Measurement. Benefiting from the viewpoint classification, we can know the relations between edges of the 2D bounding box and vertexes of the 3D bounding box. Assume the 2D bounding box is tightly fitted to the object boundary, then each edge is intersected with a reprojected 3D vertex. These relations can be determined as four selection matrixes for each 2D edge. The semantic residual can be represented by the reprojection error of the predicted 3D box vertexes with the detected 2D box edges:

$$r_{\mathcal{S}}(\mathbf{s}_k^t, {}^w\mathbf{x}_c^t, {}^w\mathbf{x}_{ok}^t, \mathbf{d}_k) = \begin{bmatrix} \pi\left(h_{\mathbf{C}_1}\right)_u - (\mathbf{b}_{kl}^t)_u \\ \pi\left(h_{\mathbf{C}_2}\right)_u - (\mathbf{b}_{kr}^t)_u \\ \pi\left(h_{\mathbf{C}_3}\right)_v - (\mathbf{b}_{kl}^t)_v \\ \pi\left(h_{\mathbf{C}_4}\right)_v - (\mathbf{b}_{kr}^t)_v \end{bmatrix}, \tag{13}$$

$$h_{\mathbf{C}_i} = h^{-1}({}^w\mathbf{x}_c^t, h({}^w\mathbf{x}_{ok}^t, \mathbf{C}_i\mathbf{d}_k^l)), \tag{14}$$

where we use $h_{\mathbf{C}_i}$ to project a vertex specified by the corresponding selection mátrix $\mathbf{C}_i$ of the 3D bounding box to the camera plane. This factor builds the connection between the object pose and its dimensions instantly. Note that we only perform 2D detection on the left image due to the real-time requirement.

Vehicle Motion Model. To achieve consistent estimation of motion and orientation for the vehicle class, we employ the kinematics model introduced in [28]. The vehicle state at time t can be predicted with the state at $t - 1$:

$$ {}^w\hat{\mathbf{x}}_{ok}^t = \begin{bmatrix} {}^w\mathbf{p}_{ok}^t \\ {}^w\theta_{ok}^t \\ \delta_{ok}^t \\ v_{ok}^t \end{bmatrix} = \begin{bmatrix} \mathbf{I}_{3\times3}, & \mathbf{0}, & \mathbf{0}, & \Lambda \\ \mathbf{0}, & 1, & 0, & \frac{\tan(\delta)\Delta t}{L} \\ \mathbf{0}, & 0, & 1, & 0 \\ \mathbf{0}, & 0, & 0, & 1 \end{bmatrix} \begin{bmatrix} {}^w\mathbf{p}_{ok}^{t-1} \\ {}^w\theta_{ok}^{t-1} \\ \delta_{ok}^{t-1} \\ v_{ok}^{t-1} \end{bmatrix}, \Lambda = \begin{bmatrix} \cos(\theta)\Delta t \\ \sin(\theta)\Delta t \\ 0 \end{bmatrix}, \tag{15}$$

$$r_{\mathcal{M}}({}^w\mathbf{x}_{ok}^t, {}^w\mathbf{x}_{ok}^{t-1}) = {}^w\mathbf{x}_{ok}^t - {}^w\hat{\mathbf{x}}_{ok}^t, \tag{16}$$

where L is the length of the wheelbase, which can be parameterized by the dimensions. The orientation of the car is always parallel to the moving direction. We refer readers to [28] for more derivations. Thanks to this kinematics model, we can track the vehicle velocity and orientation continuously, which provides rich information for behavior and path planning for autonomous driving. For other class such as pedestrians, we directly use a simple constant-velocity model to enhance smoothness.

Point Cloud Alignment. After minimizing all the residuals, we obtain the MAP estimation of the object pose based on the dimension prior. However, the pose might be biased estimated due to object size difference (See Fig. 5). We therefore align the 3D box to the recovered point cloud, which is unbiased because of accurate stereo extrinsic calibration. We minimize the distance of all 3D points with their anchored 3D box surfaces:

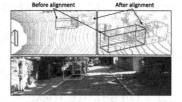

Fig. 5. Point cloud alignment.

$$^{w}\mathbf{x}_{ok}^{t} = \arg\min_{^{w}\mathbf{x}_{ok}} \sum_{n=0}^{N_k} d(^{w}\mathbf{x}_{ok}^{t}, {}^{k}\mathbf{f}_{n}), \tag{17}$$

where $d(^{w}\mathbf{x}_{ok}^{t}, {}^{k}\mathbf{f}_{n})$ denotes the distance of the kth feature with its corresponding observed surface. After all the above information is tightly fused together, we get consistent and accurate pose estimation for both the static and dynamic objects.

7   Experimental Results

We evaluate the performance of the proposed system on both KITTI [29, 30] and Cityscapes [31] dataset over diverse scenarios. The mature 2D detection and classification module has good generalization ability to run on unseen scenes, and the follow-up nonlinear optimization is data-independent. Our system is therefore able to perform consistent results on different datasets. The quantitative evaluation shows our semantic 3D object and ego-motion tracking system has better performance than the isolated state-of-the-art solutions.

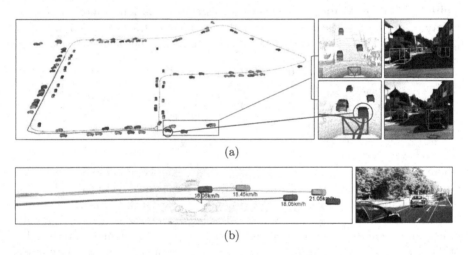

Fig. 6. Continuous tracking results over long trajectories. (a) shows a roughly 700 m close-loop trajectory including both static and dynamic cars. The right top and right bottom are enlarged start and end views respectively. The car in the blue circle is tracked over 200 m, the trajectory of which can be found in the left top view. (b) shows a scenario which mainly contains dynamic and truncated cars. The estimated trajectory, velocity and reprojected 2D image are presented in left and right respectively. Note that the LiDAR point cloud is only for reference in all the top views.

7.1   Qualitative Results over Diverse Scenarios

Firstly, we test the system on long challenging trajectories in KITTI dataset which contains 1240 × 376 stereo color and grayscale images captured at 10 Hz.

We perform 2D detection on left color images and extract 500 (for the background) and 100 (for the object) ORB features [27] on both left and right grayscale images. Figure 6a shows a 700 m close-loop trajectory which includes both static and dynamic cars. We use red cone and line to represent the camera pose and trajectory, and various color CAD models and lines to represent different cars and their trajectories, all the observed cars are visualized in the top view. Currently, our system performs object tracking in a memoryless manner, so the re-observed object will be treated as a new one, which can also be found in the enlarged start and end views in Fig. 6a. In Fig. 6b, the black car is continuously truncated over a long time, which is an unobservable case for instance 3D box inference (Sect. 4.2). However, we can still track its pose accurately due to temporal feature constraints and dynamic point cloud alignment.

We also demonstrate the system performance on different datasets over more scenarios which include concentrated cars, crossroads, and dynamic roads. All the reprojected images and the corresponding top views are shown in Fig. 7.

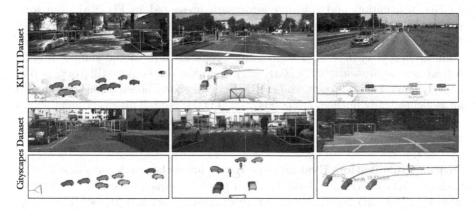

Fig. 7. Qualitative examples over diverse scenarios. From left to right: Concentrated cars. Crossroads which include both cars and pedestrians (note that we do not solve orientation for pedestrians), Dynamic cars. The top two rows are the results on the KITTI dataset, and the bottom two rows show the results on the Cityscapes dataset.

7.2   Quantitative Evaluation

Since there are no available integrated academic solutions for both ego-motion and dynamic objects tracking currently, we conduct quantitative evaluations for the camera and objects poses by comparing with the isolated state-of-the-art works: ORB-SLAM2 [4] and 3DOP [1].

Camera Pose Evaluation. Benefiting from the semantic prior, our system can perform robust camera estimation in dynamic environments. We evaluate the accuracy of camera odometry by comparing the relative pose error (RPE)

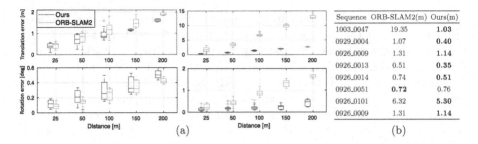

Sequence	ORB-SLAM2(m)	Ours(m)
1003_0047	19.35	**1.03**
0929_0004	1.07	**0.40**
0926_0009	1.31	**1.14**
0926_0013	0.51	**0.35**
0926_0014	0.74	**0.51**
0926_0051	**0.72**	0.76
0926_0101	6.32	**5.30**
0926_0009	1.31	**1.14**

Fig. 8. (a) RPEs comparison. Left and right are the results of 0929_0004 and 1003_0047 sequences from the KITTI raw dataset respectively. (b) RMSEs of ATE comparisons on ten long KITTI raw sequences.

[29] and RMSE of ATE (Absolute Trajectory Error) [32] with the ORB-SLAM2 [4] with stereo settings. Two sequences in KITTI raw dataset: 0929_0004 and 1003_0047 which include dynamic objects are used for RPEs comparison. The relative translation and rotation errors are presented in Fig. 8(a). Ten long sequences of KITTI raw dataset are additionally used to evaluate RMSEs of ATE, as detailed in Fig. 8(b). It can be seen that our estimation shows almost same accuracy with [4] in less dynamic scenarios due to the similar Bundle Adjustment approaches (0926_0051, etc.). However, our system still works well in high dynamic environments while ORB-SLAM2 shows non-trivial errors due to introducing many outliers (1003_0047, 0929_0004, etc.). This experiment shows that the semantic-aided object-aware property is essential for camera pose estimation, especially for dynamic autonomous driving scenarios.

Object Localization Evaluation. We evaluate the car localization performance on KITTI tracking dataset since it provides sequential stereo images with labeled objects 3D boxes. According to occlusion level and 2D box height, we divide all the detected objects into three regimes: easy, moderate and hard then evaluate them separately. To evaluate the localization accuracy of the proposed estimator, we collect objects average position error statistics. By setting series of Intersection-over-Unions (IoU) thresholds from 0 to 1, we calculate the true positive (TP) rate and the average error between estimated position of TPs and ground truth at each instance frame for each threshold. The average position error (in %) vs TP rate curves are shown in Fig. 9, where we use blue, red, yellow lines to represent statistics for easy, moderate and hard objects. It can be seen that the average error for half tuth positive objects is below 5%. For all the estimated results, the average

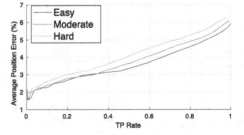

Fig. 9. Average position error vs TP rate results. We set 40 discrete IoU thresholds from 0 to 1, then count the TP rate and the average position error for the true positives for each IoU threshold.

position errors are 5.9%, 6.1% and 6.3% for easy, moderate and hard objects respectively.

To compare with baselines, we evaluate the Average Precision (AP) for bird's eye view boxes and 3D boxes by comparing with 3DOP [1], the state-of-the-art stereo based 3D object detection method. We set IoU thresholds to 0.25 and 0.5 for both bird's eye view and 3D boxes. Note that we use the oriented box overlap, so the object orientation is also implied evaluated in these two metrics. We use S, M, F, P to represent semantic measurement, motion model, feature observation, and point cloud alignment respectively. As listed in Table 1, the semantic measurement serves as the basis of the 3D object estimation. Adding feature observation increases the AP for easy (near) objects obviously due to large feature extraction area (same case for adding point clout alignment), while adding motion model helps the hard (far) objects since it "smooths" the non-trivial 2D detection noise for small objects. After integrating all these cues together, we obtain accurate 3D box estimation for both near and far objects. It can be seen that our integrated method shows more accurate results for all the AP in bird's eye view and 3D box with 0.25 IoU threshold. Due to the unregressed object size, our performance slightly worse than 3DOP in 3D box comparison of 0.5 IoU. However, we stress our method can efficiently track both static and dynamic 3D objects with temporal smoothness and motion consistency, which is essential for continuous perception and planning in autonomous driving.

Table 1. Average precision (in %) of bird's eye view and 3D boxes comparison.

Method	AP_{bv}(IoU = 0.25)			AP_{bv}(IoU = 0.5)			AP_{3d}(IoU = 0.25)			AP_{3d}(IoU = 0.5)			Time (ms)
	Easy	Mode	Hard	Easy	Mode	Hard	Easy	Mode	Hard	Easy	Mode	Hard	
S	63.12	56.37	53.18	33.12	28.91	27.77	58.78	52.42	48.82	25.68	21.70	21.02	120
S+M	66.27	63.81	58.84	41.08	38.90	34.84	62.97	60.70	55.28	34.18	30.98	27.32	121
S+F	76.23	70.18	66.18	48.82	43.07	39.80	73.35	66.86	62.66	38.93	33.43	30.46	170
S+F+M	77.87	74.48	70.85	46.96	44.39	42.23	73.32	71.06	67.30	40.50	36.28	34.59	171
S+F+M+P	**88.07**	**77.83**	**72.73**	**58.52**	**46.17**	**43.97**	**86.57**	**74.13**	**68.96**	48.51	37.13	34.54	173
3DOP	81.34	70.70	66.32	54.83	43.36	37.15	80.62	70.01	65.76	**53.73**	**42.27**	**35.87**	1200

8   Conclusions and Future Work

In this paper, we propose a 3D objects and ego-motion tracking system for autonomous driving. We integrate the instance semantic prior, sparse feature measurement and kinematics motion model into a tightly-coupled optimization framework. Our system can robustly estimate the camera pose without being affected by the dynamic objects and track the states and recover dynamic sparse features for each observed object continuously. Demonstrations over diverse scenarios and different datasets illustrate the practicability of the proposed system. Quantitative comparisons with state-of-the-art approaches show our accuracy for both camera estimation and objects localization.

In the future, we plan to improve the object temporal correlation by fully exploiting the dense visual information. Currently, the camera and objects tracking are implemented successively in our system. We are also going to model them into a fully-integrated optimization framework such that the estimation for both camera and dynamic objects can benefit from each other.

Acknowledgment. This work was supported by the Hong Kong Research Grants Council Early Career Scheme under project no. 26201616. The authors also thank Xiaozhi Chen for providing the 3DOP [1] results on the KITTI tracking dataset.

References

1. Chen, X., et al.: 3D object proposals for accurate object class detection. In: Advances in Neural Information Processing Systems, pp. 424–432 (2015)
2. Chen, X., Kundu, K., Zhang, Z., Ma, H., Fidler, S., Urtasun, R.: Monocular 3D object detection for autonomous driving. In: Proceedings of the IEEE Conference on Computer Vision and Pattern Recognition, pp. 2147–2156 (2016)
3. Qin, T., Li, P., Shen, S.: VINS-Mono: a robust and versatile monocular visual-inertial state estimator. arXiv preprint arXiv:1708.03852 (2017)
4. Mur-Artal, R., Tardós, J.D.: ORB-SLAM2: an open-source SLAM system for monocular, stereo and RGB-D cameras. IEEE Trans. Robot. **33**(5), 1255–1262 (2017)
5. Engel, J., Schöps, T., Cremers, D.: LSD-SLAM: large-scale direct monocular SLAM. In: Fleet, D., Pajdla, T., Schiele, B., Tuytelaars, T. (eds.) ECCV 2014. LNCS, vol. 8690, pp. 834–849. Springer, Cham (2014). https://doi.org/10.1007/978-3-319-10605-2_54
6. Ren, S., He, K., Girshick, R., Sun, J.: Faster R-CNN: towards real-time object detection with region proposal networks. In: Advances in Neural Information Processing Systems, pp. 91–99 (2015)
7. Frost, D.P., Kähler, O., Murray, D.W.: Object-aware bundle adjustment for correcting monocular scale drift. In: 2016 IEEE International Conference on Robotics and Automation (ICRA), pp. 4770–4776. IEEE (2016)
8. Sucar, E., Hayet, J.B.: Probabilistic global scale estimation for monoslam based on generic object detection. In: Computer Vision and Pattern Recognition Workshops (CVPRW) (2017)
9. Bowman, S.L., Atanasov, N., Daniilidis, K., Pappas, G.J.: Probabilistic data association for semantic slam. In: 2017 IEEE International Conference on Robotics and Automation (ICRA), pp. 1722–1729. IEEE (2017)
10. Atanasov, N., Zhu, M., Daniilidis, K., Pappas, G.J.: Semantic localization via the matrix permanent. In: Proceedings of Robotics: Science and Systems, vol. 2 (2014)
11. Pillai, S., Leonard, J.J.: Monocular slam supported object recognition. In: Proceedings of Robotics: Science and Systems, vol. 2 (2015)
12. Dong, J., Fei, X., Soatto, S.: Visual-inertial-semantic scene representation for 3-D object detection. arXiv preprint arXiv:1606.03968 (2016)
13. Civera, J., Gálvez-López, D., Riazuelo, L., Tardós, J.D., Montiel, J.: Towards semantic slam using a monocular camera. In: 2011 IEEE/RSJ International Conference on Intelligent Robots and Systems (IROS), pp. 1277–1284. IEEE (2011)
14. Salas-Moreno, R.F., Newcombe, R.A., Strasdat, H., Kelly, P.H., Davison, A.J.: Slam++: simultaneous localisation and mapping at the level of objects. In: 2013 IEEE Conference on Computer Vision and Pattern Recognition (CVPR), pp. 1352–1359. IEEE (2013)

15. Gálvez-López, D., Salas, M., Tardós, J.D., Montiel, J.: Real-time monocular object slam. Robot. Auton. Syst. **75**, 435–449 (2016)
16. Bao, S.Y., Savarese, S.: Semantic structure from motion. In: 2011 IEEE Conference on Computer Vision and Pattern Recognition (CVPR), pp. 2025–2032. IEEE (2011)
17. Bao, S.Y., Bagra, M., Chao, Y.W., Savarese, S.: Semantic structure from motion with points, regions, and objects. In: 2012 IEEE Conference on Computer Vision and Pattern Recognition (CVPR), pp. 2703–2710. IEEE (2012)
18. Kundu, A., Li, Y., Dellaert, F., Li, F., Rehg, J.M.: Joint semantic segmentation and 3D reconstruction from monocular video. In: Fleet, D., Pajdla, T., Schiele, B., Tuytelaars, T. (eds.) ECCV 2014. LNCS, vol. 8694, pp. 703–718. Springer, Cham (2014). https://doi.org/10.1007/978-3-319-10599-4_45
19. Vineet, V., et al.: Incremental dense semantic stereo fusion for large-scale semantic scene reconstruction. In: 2015 IEEE International Conference on Robotics and Automation (ICRA), pp. 75–82. IEEE (2015)
20. Li, X., Belaroussi, R.: Semi-dense 3D semantic mapping from monocular slam. arXiv preprint arXiv:1611.04144 (2016)
21. McCormac, J., Handa, A., Davison, A., Leutenegger, S.: Semanticfusion: Dense 3D semantic mapping with convolutional neural networks. In: 2017 IEEE International Conference on Robotics and Automation (ICRA), pp. 4628–4635. IEEE (2017)
22. Bao, S.Y., Chandraker, M., Lin, Y., Savarese, S.: Dense object reconstruction with semantic priors. In: 2013 IEEE Conference on Computer Vision and Pattern Recognition (CVPR), pp. 1264–1271. IEEE (2013)
23. Zia, M.Z., Stark, M., Schiele, B., Schindler, K.: Detailed 3D representations for object recognition and modeling. IEEE Trans. Pattern Anal. Mach. Intell. **35**(11), 2608–2623 (2013)
24. Xiang, Y., Choi, W., Lin, Y., Savarese, S.: Data-driven 3D voxel patterns for object category recognition. In: Proceedings of the IEEE Conference on Computer Vision and Pattern Recognition, pp. 1903–1911 (2015)
25. Mousavian, A., Anguelov, D., Flynn, J., Košecká, J.: 3D bounding box estimation using deep learning and geometry. In: 2017 IEEE Conference on Computer Vision and Pattern Recognition (CVPR), pp. 5632–5640. IEEE (2017)
26. Redmon, J., Divvala, S., Girshick, R., Farhadi, A.: You only look once: unified, real-time object detection. In: Proceedings of the IEEE Conference on Computer Vision and Pattern Recognition, pp. 779–788 (2016)
27. Rublee, E., Rabaud, V., Konolige, K., Bradski, G.: Orb: an efficient alternative to sift or surf. In: 2011 IEEE international conference on Computer Vision (ICCV), pp. 2564–2571. IEEE (2011)
28. Gu, T.: Improved trajectory planning for on-road self-driving vehicles via combined graph search, optimization and topology analysis. Ph.D. thesis, Carnegie Mellon University (2017)
29. Geiger, A., Lenz, P., Urtasun, R.: Are we ready for autonomous driving? The KITTI vision benchmark suite. In: Conference on Computer Vision and Pattern Recognition (CVPR) (2012)
30. Geiger, A., Lenz, P., Stiller, C., Urtasun, R.: Vision meets robotics: the KITTI dataset. Int. J. Robot. Res. (IJRR) (2013)
31. Cordts, M., et al.: The cityscapes dataset. In: CVPR Workshop on the Future of Datasets in Vision, vol, 1, March 2015
32. Sturm, J., Engelhard, N., Endres, F., Burgard, W., Cremers, D.: A benchmark for the evaluation of RGB-D slam systems. In: 2012 IEEE/RSJ International Conference on Intelligent Robots and Systems (IROS), pp. 573–580. IEEE (2012)

A+D Net: Training a Shadow Detector with Adversarial Shadow Attenuation

Hieu Le[1(✉)], Tomas F. Yago Vicente[1,2], Vu Nguyen[1], Minh Hoai[1], and Dimitris Samaras[1]

[1] Stony Brook University, Stony Brook, NY 11794, USA
{hle,tyagovicente,vhnguyen,minhhoai,samaras}@cs.stonybrook.edu
[2] Amazon/A9, Palo Alto, USA

Abstract. We propose a novel GAN-based framework for detecting shadows in images, in which a shadow detection network (D-Net) is trained together with a shadow attenuation network (A-Net) that generates adversarial training examples. The A-Net modifies the original training images constrained by a simplified physical shadow model and is focused on fooling the D-Net's shadow predictions. Hence, it is effectively augmenting the training data for D-Net with hard-to-predict cases. The D-Net is trained to predict shadows in both original images and generated images from the A-Net. Our experimental results show that the additional training data from A-Net significantly improves the shadow detection accuracy of D-Net. Our method outperforms the state-of-the-art methods on the most challenging shadow detection benchmark (SBU) and also obtains state-of-the-art results on a cross-dataset task, testing on UCF. Furthermore, the proposed method achieves accurate real-time shadow detection at 45 frames per second.

Keywords: Shadow detection · GAN · Data augmentation

1 Introduction

Shadows occur frequently in natural scenes, and can hamper many tasks such image segmentation, object tracking, and semantic labeling. Shadows are formed in complex physical interactions between light sources, geometry and materials of the objects in the scene. Information about the physical environment such as sparse 3D scene reconstructions [33], rough geometry estimates [22], and multiple images of the same scene under different illumination conditions [25] can aid shadow detection. Unfortunately, inferring the physical structure of a general scene from a single image is still a difficult problem.

Electronic supplementary material The online version of this chapter (https://doi.org/10.1007/978-3-030-01216-8_41) contains supplementary material, which is available to authorized users.

© Springer Nature Switzerland AG 2018
V. Ferrari et al. (Eds.): ECCV 2018, LNCS 11206, pp. 680–696, 2018.
https://doi.org/10.1007/978-3-030-01216-8_41

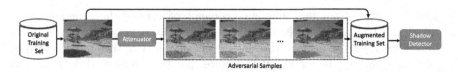

Fig. 1. Adversarial shadow attenuation. The attenuator takes an original shadow image and generates different adversarial shadow samples to train the shadow detector.

The difficulty of shadow detection is exacerbated when dealing with consumer-grade photographs and web images [15]. Such images often come from non-linear camera sensors, and present many compression and noise artifacts. In this case, it is better to train and use appearance-based classifiers [7,13,27,36] rather than relying on physical models of illumination [4,5]. Shadow classifiers, however, require annotated training data, and the performance of a classifier often correlates with the amount of training data. Unfortunately, annotated shadow data is expensive to collect and label. Only recently available training data has increased from a few hundred images [7,36] to a few thousands [30] thus enabling training more powerful shadow classifiers based on deep convolutional neural networks [20,30]. Nevertheless, even a few thousand images is a tiny amount compared to datasets that have driven progress in deep learning [2,16]. It is therefore safe to assume that the performance of deep learning shadow classifiers has not saturated yet, and it can be improved with more training data. Unfortunately, collecting and annotating shadow data is a laborious process. Even a lazy annotation approach [28] takes significant effort; the annotation step itself takes 20 s per image, not including data collection and cleansing efforts.

In this paper, instead of collecting additional data, we propose a method to increase the utility of available shadow data to the fullest extent. The main idea is to generate a set of augmented training images from a single shadow image by weakening the shadow area in the original training image. We refer to this process as shadow attenuation and we train a deep neural network to do so, called A-Net. This network modifies original shadow images so as to weaken the shadow effect, as illustrated in Fig. 1. The generated images serve as additional challenging training samples for a shadow detector D-Net. We present a novel framework, where the shadow attenuator and the shadow detector are trained jointly in an adversarial manner. The output of the attenuation model A-Net provides adversarial training samples with harder-to-detect shadow areas to improve the overall reliability of the detector D-Net.

Recent research also suggests that deep networks are highly sensitive to adversarial perturbations [19,26,34]. By jointly training A-Net and D-Net, we directly enhance the resistance of the detector D-Net to adversarial conditions and improve the generalization of the detector, following the recent trend [3,31,35].

Essentially, what is being proposed here is a data augmentation method for shadow detection. It is different from other data augmentation methods, and it does not suffer from two inherent problems of general data augmentation approaches, which are: (1) the augmented data might be very different from the real data, having no impact on the generalization ability of the trained classifier on real data, and (2) it is difficult to ensure that the augmented data samples have the same labels as the original data, and this leads to training label noise. A popular approach to address these problems is to constrain the augmented data samples to be close to the original data, e.g., setting an upper bound for the L_2 distance between the original sample and the generated sample. However, it is difficult to set the right bound; a big value would create label noise while a small value would produce augmented samples that are too similar to the original data, yielding no benefit. In this paper, we address these two problems in a principled way, specific to shadow detection. Our idea is to use a physics model of shadows and illumination to guide the data generation process and to estimate the probability of having label noise.

Note that we aim to attenuate the shadow areas, not to remove them. Shadow removal is an important problem, but training a good shadow removal network would require many training pairs of corresponding shadow/shadow-free images, which are not available. Furthermore, completely removed shadows would correspond to having label noise, and this might hurt the performance of the detector.

Experimental results show that our shadow detector outperforms the state-of-the-art methods in the challenging shadow detection benchmark SBU [30] as well as on the cross-dataset task (training on SBU and testing on the UCF dataset [36]). Furthermore, our method is more efficient than many existing ones because it does not require a post-processing step such as patch averaging or conditional random field (CRF) smoothing. Our method detects shadows at 45 frames per second for 256×256 input images.

2 Related Work

Single image shadow detection is a well studied problem. Earlier work focused on physical modeling of illumination [4,5]. These methods render illumination invariant representations of the images where shadow detection is trivial. These methods, however, only work well for high quality images taken with narrow-band sensors [15]. Another early attempt to incorporate physics based constraints with rough geometry was the approach of Panagopoulos *et al.* [21] where the illumination environment is modeled as a mixture of von Mises-Fisher distributions [1] and the shadow pixels are segmented via a graphical model. Recently, data-driven approaches based on learning classifiers [8,11,13,27] from small annotated datasets [7,36] have shown more success. For instance, Vicente *et al.* [27,29] optimized a multi-kernel Least-Squares SVM based on leave-one-out estimates. This approach yielded accurate results on the UCF [36] and UIUC [7] datasets, but its underlying training procedure and optimization method cannot handle a large amount of training data.

To handle and benefit from a large amount of training data, recent shadow detection methods have been developed based on the stochastic gradient descent training of deep neural networks. Vicente *et al.* [30] proposed a stacked-CNN architecture, combining an image-level Fully Convolution Neural Network (FCN) with a patch-CNN. This approach achieved good detection results, but it is cumbersome as the Fully Connected Network (FCN) has to be trained before its predictions are used to train the patch-CNN. Similarly, testing was computationally expensive as it requires the FCN prediction followed by predictions of densely sampled patches covering the testing image. Recently, Nguyen *et al.* [20] presented scGAN, a method based on Generative Adversarial Networks (GANs) [6]. They proposed a parametric conditional GAN [17] framework, where the generator was trained to generate the shadow mask, conditioned on an input RGB patch and a sensitivity parameter. To obtain the final shadow mask for an input image, the generator must be run on multiple image patches at multiple scales and the outputs are averaged. Their method achieved good results on the SBU dataset, but the detection procedure was computationally expensive at test time. Our proposed method also uses adversarial training for shadow detection, but it is fundamentally different from scGAN. scGAN uses the generator to generate a binary *shadow mask* conditioned on the input image, while our method uses the generator to generate augmented training images in RGB space. Furthermore, while scGAN uses the discriminator as a regulator to encourage global consistency, the discriminator in our approach plays a more prominent role for shadow pixel classification. In contrast to scGAN, our method does not require post processing or output averaging, leading to real-time shadow detection. Another method that uses GAN for shadow detection is Stacked Conditional GAN [32]. This method, however, requires the availability of shadow-free images. Another recent approach [10] proposes to use contextual information for a better shadow detection. Contextual information is incorporated by having several spatial-directional recurrent neural networks. While this method yields excellent results on shadow detection benchmarks, it also requires running a CRF as a post-processing step.

We propose a method to improve shadow detection with augmented training examples, in sync with recent trends on data augmentation. For example, Zhang *et al.* [35] proposed a simple augmentation method by enriching the dataset with the linear combinations of pairs of examples and their labels to improve the generalization of the network and its resistance toward adversarial examples. Another approach that used adversarial examples for training a network was proposed by Shrivastava *et al.* [24]. They adversarially trained a Refiner network that inputs synthetic examples and outputs more realistic images. The refined examples can be used as additional training data. In a similar way, our proposed Attenuator (A-Net) takes original training images and generates realistic images with attenuated shadows that act as additional training examples for our shadow detector. The generation of adversarial examples is an integral part of the joint training process with the detector (D-Net), in contrast to [24] where the generated data is a preprocessing step to enrich the training set. The effects of the shadow Attenuator can also be seen as related to adversarial perturbations [18]: A-Net modifies the input images so as to fool the predictions of the shadow detector D-Net. Adversarial examples also can be used to improve the generalization of the network for domain adaptation [31] in which a conditional GAN is used to perform feature augmentation.

3   Adversarial Training and Attenuation

3.1   Framework Overview

We present a novel framework for shadow detection based on adversarial training and shadow attenuation. Our proposed model contains two jointly trained deep networks. Figure 2 illustrates the flow diagram of our framework. The shadow attenuation network, called Attenuator or A-Net, takes as input a shadow image and its corresponding shadow mask. Based on these inputs, the Attenuator generates a version of the input image where the shadows have been attenuated. Attenuation can be thought of as partial shadow removal. The image generated by the Attenuator is fed into a shadow detection network, called Detector or D-Net, which predicts the shadow areas. On each training iteration, D-Net also takes the original input image, and learns to predict the corresponding annotated ground-truth shadow mask.

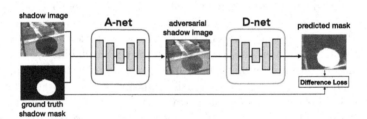

Fig. 2. Adversarial training of a shadow detector. A-Net takes a shadow image and its corresponding shadow mask as input, and generates an adversarial example by attenuating the shadow regions in the input image. The attenuated shadows are less discernible and therefore harder to detect. D-Net takes this image as input and aims to recover the original shadow mask.

A-Net is trained to attenuate shadow regions so as to fool the shadow detector. In particular, for pixels inside the provided shadow mask, A-Net manipulates the values of the pixels to disguise them as non-shadow pixels so that they cannot be recognized by D-Net. We further constrain the attenuation transformation using a loss that incorporates physics-inspired shadow domain knowledge. This enhances the quality of the generated pixels, improving the generalizability of the detector. At the same time, A-Net learns not to change the values or the pixels outside the shadow mask. We enforce this with a loss that penalizes the difference between the generated image and the input image on the area outside of the shadow mask (non-shadow pixels). The adversarial training process with all the aforementioned constraints and the back propagation error from the shadow detection network guides A-Net to perform shadow attenuation.

The detector network, D-Net, takes the adversarial examples generated by A-Net and predicts shadow masks. Shadow areas in the images generated by A-Net are generally harder to detect than in the input images, since A-Net is trained to attenuate the shadows to fool D-Net. As a result, D-Net is trained with challenging examples in addition to the original training examples. As D-Net improves its ability to detect shadows, A-Net also improves its ability to attenuate shadows to confound D-Net with tougher adversarial examples. This process strengthens the shadow detection ability of D-Net.

3.2   Physics-Based Shadow and Illumination Model

We use a physics-based illumination model to guide the data generation process and avoid label noise. We use the simplified illumination model used by Guo et al. [7,8] where, each pixel is lit by a combination of direct and environment lights: $I_i = (k_i L_d + L_e) R_i$, where I is an image and I_i denotes the color of the ith pixel of the image. R_i is the surface reflectance corresponding to the ith pixel. L_d and L_e are 3×1 vectors representing the colors and intensities of the direct light and the environment light (which models area sources and inter reflections), respectively. $k_i \in [0,1]$ is the shadowing factor that indicates how much of the direct light reaches the pixel i. k_i remains close to 0 for the umbra region of the shadow, while it gets increasingly close to 1 in the penumbra region. For pixels inside shadow-free areas $k_i = 1$. We can relate the original shadow region and its corresponding shadow-free version by the ratio:

$$\frac{I_i^{\text{shadow-free}}}{I_i^{\text{shadow}}} = \frac{L_d + L_e}{k_i L_d + L_e}.$$

By taking the ratio between the shadow-free and in-shadow values, we have eliminated the unknown reflectance factor. We assume that the direct light is constant over the scene depicted by the image, and the effects of the environment light are similar for all pixels. We incorporate this model into the training process of both A-Net and D-Net:

- **A-Net:** We design the *physics loss* to enforce the illumination ratios for pixels inside an attenuated shadow area to have a small variance.
- **D-Net:** We directly estimate the illumination ratio between the areas inside and outside the shadow mask to measure shadow strength in the attenuated images to avoid training label noise.

3.3   A-Net: Shadow Attenuator Network

The shadow attenuator network A-Net is trained to re-illuminate only the shadow areas so that they cannot be detected by the detector network D-Net. To obtain useful and realistic attenuated shadows, A-Net aims to fool D-Net while respecting a physical illumination model. Figure 3 shows the training process of A-Net, which attenuates shadow areas under the following constraints and

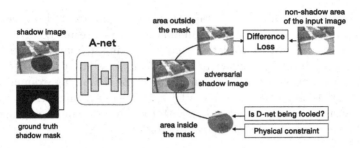

Fig. 3. A-Net. The area outside the shadow mask is constrained by the difference loss with respect to the input image. The area inside the shadow mask is constrained by the feedback from D-Net and the physics based constraint.

objectives: (1) Values of non-shadow pixels are preserved. (2) Shadow pixels are re-illuminated such that D-Net cannot recognize them as shadow pixels. (3) The resulting pixel transformation obeys physics-inspired illumination constraints.

These constraints and objectives can be incorporated in the training of A-Net by defining a proper loss function. Let I denote an input image, and $M(I)$ be the shadow mask of I. Let $A(I)$ denote the output of A-Net for the input pair of I and $M(I)$ (here we write $A(I)$ as the short form for $A(I, M(I))$). Let $D(I)$ denote the output of D-Net for an input image I, i.e. the predicted shadow mask. Ideally, the output should be 1 for shadow pixels and 0 otherwise. The objective of A-Net's training is to minimize a weighted combination of three losses:

$$\mathcal{L}_A(I) = \lambda_{nsd}\mathcal{L}_{nsd}(I) + \lambda_{sd}\mathcal{L}_{sd}(I) + \lambda_{ph}\mathcal{L}_{ph}(I), \tag{1}$$

where $\mathcal{L}_{nsd}$ is the loss that penalizes the modification of values for pixels outside the shadow mask $M(I)$ for the input image I: $\mathcal{L}_{nsd}(I) = \text{mean}_{i\notin M(I)} \|A(I)_i - I_i\|_1$. $\mathcal{L}_{sd}$ is the adversarial loss. It penalizes the correct recognition of D-Net for shadow pixels on the generated image, restricted to the area inside the training shadow mask $M(I)$: $\mathcal{L}_{sd}(I) = \text{mean}_{i\in M(I)}[D(A(I))_i]$. $\mathcal{L}_{ph}$ is a physics-inspired loss to ensure that the shadow area in the generated image is re-illuminated in a physically feasible way. Based on the illumination model described in Sect. 3.2, we want the ratio $\frac{A(I)_i}{I_i}$ to be similar for all pixels i inside a re-illuminated shadow area. We model this by adding a loss term for the variance of the log ratios

$$\mathcal{L}_{ph}(I) = \sum_{c\in\{R,G,B\}} \underset{i\in M(I)}{\text{Variance}} \left[\log(A(I)_i^c) - \log(I_i^c)\right].$$

where $(\cdot)^c$ denotes the pixel value in the color channel c of the RGB color image.

Figure 4 shows some examples of attenuated shadows that were generated by A-Net during the adversarial training process. The two original input images contain easy to detect shadows with strengths 3.46 and 2.63. The heuristic to measure these shadow strength values are described in Sect. 3.4. The outputs of A-Net given these input images and shadow masks are shown in columns (c, d, e),

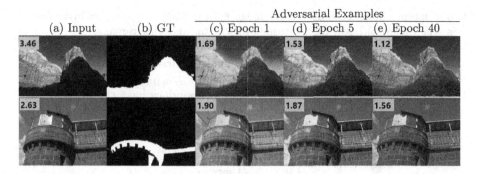

Fig. 4. Examples of attenuated shadows. (a) Input image. (b) Ground truth shadow mask. (c, d, e): adversarial examples with attenuated shadows generated by A-Net from epoch 1, 5, and 40 respectively. The corresponding *shadow strength* are shown as black text on the top-left corner of each image.

obtained at epochs 1, 5, and 40 during training. The shadows in the generated images become harder to detect as training progresses. Numerically, the shadow strength of the attenuated shadows decreases over time. Moreover, A-Net also learns to not change the non-shadow areas.

3.4   D-Net: Shadow Detector Network

The D-Net is central to our framework. It learns to detect shadows from adversarial examples generated by the A-Net as well as original training examples. On each training iteration, both the original input and the adversarially attenuated image are used to train D-Net. The learning objective for D-Net is to minimize the following loss function:

$$\mathcal{L}_D(I) = \lambda_{real}\,\|D(I) - M(I)\|_1 + \lambda_{adv}(A(I))\,\|D(A(I)) - M(I)\|_1, \qquad (2)$$

where λ_{real} and $\lambda_{adv}(A(I))$ control how much D-Net should learn from the real sample I and the adversarial example $A(I)$ respectively. $\lambda_{adv}(A(I))$ depends on how much the shadow in I has been attenuated. If $A(I)$ is the completely shadow-free version of I, $\lambda_{adv}(A(I))$ should ideally be zero. Otherwise, this loss function corresponds to having label noise as it requires the output of the shadow detector D-Net for the input $A(I)$ to be the same as the shadow mask $M(I)$, while $A(I)$ is a shadow-free image.

To determine if $A(I)$ is a shadow-free image, we derive a heuristic based on the illumination model described in Sect. 3.2. We first define two areas alongside the shadow boundary, denoted as $\mathcal{B}_{in}$ and $\mathcal{B}_{out}$, illustrated in Fig. 5. $\mathcal{B}_{out}$ (green) is the area right outside the boundary, computed by subtracting the shadow mask from its dilated version. The inside area $\mathcal{B}_{in}$ (red) is computed similarly with the eroded shadow mask. We define the *shadow strength* $k_{strength}$ as the ratio of average pixel intensities of the two boundary areas: $k_{strength}(A(I)) = \frac{\text{mean}_{i \in \mathcal{B}_{out}}[A(I)_i]}{\text{mean}_{i \in \mathcal{B}_{in}}[A(I)_i]}$. Figure 5 shows two examples of images with two different shadow strengths; an image with a darker shadow (relative to the non-shadow area) has a higher value of $k_{strength}$ and vice versa.

We use the shadow strength of the attenuated image to decide if D-Net should learn from the attenuated shadow image. Heuristically, the shadow might be completely removed if the shadow strength $k_{strength}$ is too close to 1, i.e., the two areas on the two sides of the shadow boundary have the same average intensities. Based on this heuristic, we set the weight for the adversarial example $A(I)$ as follows:

$$\lambda_{adv}(A(I)) = \begin{cases} \lambda_{adv}^0 & \text{if } k_{strength}(A(I)) > 1 + \epsilon \\ 0 & \text{otherwise,} \end{cases} \quad (3)$$

where λ_{adv}^0 is a tunable baseline factor for adversarial examples and ϵ is a small threshold which we empirically set to 0.05.

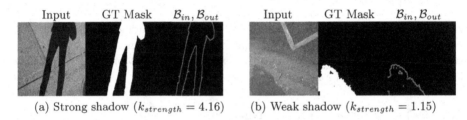

(a) Strong shadow ($k_{strength} = 4.16$)   (b) Weak shadow ($k_{strength} = 1.15$)

Fig. 5. Estimating the shadow strength. From the ground-truth shadow mask, we define two area $\mathcal{B}_{in}$ (red) and $\mathcal{B}_{out}$ (green) obtained by dilation and erosion of the shadow mask. The shadow strength $k_{strengh}$ is computed as the ratio between the average intensity of pixels in $\mathcal{B}_{out}$ over the average intensity of pixels in $\mathcal{B}_{in}$. (a) an image with very a strong dark shadow, $k_{strength} = 4.16$. (b) light shadow $k_{strength} = 1.15$. (Color figure online)

3.5   Network Architectures

Both A-Net and D-Net were developed based on the U-Net architecture [23]. Following [12], we created networks with seven skip-connection modules, each of which contains a sequence of Convolutional, BatchNorm, and Leaky-ReLu [9] layers. The A-Net input is a four channel image, which is the concatenation of the RGB image and the corresponding shadow mask. The A-Net output is a three channel RGB image. The input to D-Net is an RGB image, and the output is a single channel shadow mask.

4   Experiments and Results

We experiment on several public shadow datasets. One of them is the SBU Shadow dataset [30]. This dataset consists of pairs of RGB images and corresponding annotated shadow binary masks. The SBU dataset contains 4089 training images, and 638 testing images, and is currently the largest and most challenging shadow benchmark. We also perform cross-dataset experiments on the UCF testing set [36], which contains 110 images with corresponding shadow masks. We quantitatively evaluate shadow detection performance by comparing the testing ground-truth shadow masks with the prediction masks produced by D-Net. As is common practice in the shadow detection literature, we will use the Balanced Error Rate (BER) as the principal evaluation metric. The BER is defined as: $BER = 1 - \frac{1}{2}\left(\frac{TP}{TP+FN} + \frac{TN}{TN+FP}\right)$, where TP, TN, FP, FN are the total numbers of true positive, true negative, false positive, and false negative pixels respectively. Since natural images tend to overwhelmingly more non-shadow pixels, the BER is less biased than mean pixel accuracy. We also provide separate mean pixel error rates for the shadow and non-shadow classes.

Training and Implementation Details. We use stochastic gradient descent with the Adam solver [14] to train our model. We use mini batch SGD with batch size of 64. On each training iteration, we perform three forward passes consecutively: forward the input shadow image I to A-Net to get the adversarial example $A(I)$, then separately forward the adversarial image and shadow input image to D-Net. We alternate one parameter update step on D-Net with one update step on A-Net, as suggested by [6]. Before training and testing, we transform the images into log-space. We experimentally set our training parameters as: $(\lambda_{nsd}, \lambda_{sd}, \lambda_{ph}, \lambda_{real}, \lambda_{adv}^0) := (30, 1, 100, 0.8, 0.2)$. We implemented our framework on PyTorch. More details can be found at: www3.cs.stonybrook.edu/~cvl/projects/adnet/index.html.

4.1   Shadow Detection Evaluation

We evaluate the shadow detection performance of the proposed D-Net on the SBU and UCF datasets. To detect shadows in an image, we first resize the image to 256×256. We input this image to D-net to produce a shadow mask of size 256×256, which will be compared with the ground-truth shadow mask for evaluation (in the original size).

In Table 1, we compare the performance of our method with the state-of-the-art methods Stacked-CNN [30], scGAN [20], ST-CGAN [32], and DSC [10]. We also consider a variant of D-Net, trained without the attenuated shadow images from A-Net. All methods are trained on the SBU training set. Performance is reported in terms of BER, as well as shadow and non-shadow error rates. Note that DSC [10] only reported BER numbers on the SBU dataset and its cross-domain results were obtained on testing data that is different from the commonly used UCF test dataset (as proposed by [36]).

On the SBU test set, our detector (D-Net) outperforms the previous state-of-the-art methods. Compared to the Stacked-CNN we obtain a 51% error reduction. Compared to scGAN and ST-CGAN, D-Net brings a 41% error reduction and a 33% error reduction respectively. D-Net outperforms DSC by 0.2% BER, even though it is significantly simpler. D-Net is fully convolutional, without the need of for running recurrent neural networks and CRF post processing.

For the cross-dataset experiments, the detectors are trained on the SBU training set, but they are evaluated on the test set of the UCF dataset [36]. These datasets are disjoint; while SBU covers a wide range of scenes, UCF focuses on images where dark shadows as well dark albedo objects are present. Again, we compare our method with the previous state-of-the-art methods: Stacked-CNN [30], scGAN [20], and ST-CGAN [32]. In terms of BER, our proposed D-Net yields significant error reductions of 18% and 16% with respect to scGAN and ST-CGAN, respectively. The performance gap between D-Net trained with and without attenuated shadow images is very significant, highlighting the benefits of having attenuated shadow examples for training.

Table 1. Evaluation of shadow detection methods on the SBU Shadow dataset [30] and for cross-dataset detection on UCF [36]. All methods are trained on the SBU training data. Both Balanced Error Rate (BER) and per class error rates are shown. DSC [10] only reported BER numbers, and used a different UCF test dataset, so cross-domain performance cannot be compared. Best performances is printed in bold.

Method	Evaluated on SBU testset [30]			Evaluated on UCF testset [36]		
	BER	Shadow	Non shad.	BER	Shadow	Non shad.
stacked-CNN [30]	11.0	9.6	12.5	13.0	9.0	17.1
scGAN [20]	9.1	7.8	10.4	11.5	7.7	15.3
ST-CGAN [32]	8.1	**3.7**	12.5	11.2	**5.0**	17.5
DSC [10]	5.6	–	–	–	–	–
D-Net (w/o A-Net)	8.8	8.1	9.3	11.8	8.9	14.7
D-Net (with A-Net)	**5.4**	5.3	**5.5**	**9.4**	7.0	**11.8**

4.2   Qualitative Results

In Fig. 6(i) and (ii), we show shadow detection results on the SBU dataset. The columns show input images, ground truth shadow masks, and D-Net outputs, respectively. In Fig. 6(i), we see how the D-Net correctly predicts shadows on different types of scenes such as desert, mountain, snow, and under different weather conditions from sunny to cloudy and overcast. In Fig. 6(ii), notice how the D-Net accurately predicts shadows in close-ups as well as long-range shots, and in aerial images. Figure 7 shows qualitative comparisons with the shadow detection results of scGAN [20]. In general, D-Net produces more accurate shadows with sharper boundaries.

4.3   Failure Cases

Some failure cases of our method are shown in Fig. 8. Many are due to dark albedo material regions being incorrectly classified as shadows. We also investigate the locations of wrongly classified pixels to understand the causes of failure.

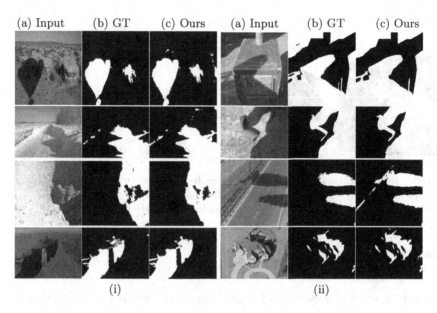

(a) Input   (b) GT   (c) Ours   (a) Input   (b) GT   (c) Ours

(i)   (ii)

Fig. 6. Shadow detection results. Our proposed method accurately detects shadows on: (i) different scenes, and illumination conditions; (ii) close-ups and long-range shots, as well as aerial images.

(a) Input   (b) GT   (c) scGAN   (d) Ours

Fig. 7. Comparison of shadow detection on SBU dataset. Qualitative comparison between our method and the state-of-the-art method scGAN [20]. (a) Input image. (b) Ground-truth shadow mask. (c) Predicted shadow mask by scGAN [20]. (d) Predicted shadow mask by our method.

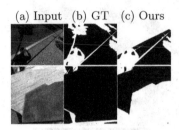

(a) Input   (b) GT   (c) Ours

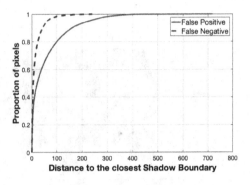

Fig. 8. Failed shadow detection examples. Failure cases of our method due to non-shadow dark albedo regions. (a) Input image. (b) Ground-truth mask. (c) Predicted shadow mask by our method.

Fig. 9. Cumulative curve of the distance of wrongly predicted pixels to the closest shadow boundary on the SBU testing set.

Figure 9 shows the proportion of wrongly predicted pixels with respect to their distances to the closest ground-truth shadow boundary on the SBU testing set. A large portion of missed shadow pixels is within a small distance to a boundary. Specifically, 65% of false negative cases are within 10 pixels of a shadow boundary. This means the shadow pixels missed by our method are probably either around the shadow boundaries or inside very small shadow regions. Meanwhile a large portion of false positive prediction is far away from a shadow boundary. This is perhaps due to the misclassifications of dark objects as shadows.

4.4   Ablation Study and Parameter Analysis

We conducted experiments to analyze the impact of the physics-based loss (L_{ph}) and the weight function λ_{adv} in our framework. We trained our model with two additional scenarios for comparison: (1) without the physics-based loss and without the weight function λ_{adv}, and (2) with the physics-based loss but without the weight function λ_{adv}. We denote these two configurations as $(-L_{ph}, -\lambda_{adv})$ and $(+L_{ph}, -\lambda_{adv})$ respectively. Table 2 shows the shadow detection results of the models trained with these modified conditions. We tested the models, trained on SBU, on both the UCF and SBU testing sets. As can be seen from Table 2, dropping the weight function λ_{adv} increased error rates slightly, while dropping the physics-based loss drastically increased error rates. In Fig. 10, we compare adversarial examples generated by the model trained with and without the physics-based loss. Incorporating this loss produces images with more realistic attenuated shadows. Thus, the produced examples aid the training of the shadow detector D-Net. In our experiments, at the 50th training epoch, approximately 6% of all images generated by A-Net, were not used based on λ_{adv}.

Table 2. Ablation study. Comparison of shadow detection results of our framework with and without inclusion of the physics based loss L_{ph}. Detection performance significantly profits from incorporating the physics based loss L_{ph} into the training process: 20% reduction of BER in SBU [30] testing set, and 27% error reduction in UCF [36] (cross-dataset task)

Method	Evaluated on SBU testset			Evaluated on UCF testset		
	BER	Shadow	Non shad.	BER	Shadow	Non shad.
D-Net $(+L_{ph}, +\lambda_{adv})$	**5.4**	**5.3**	5.5	**9.4**	**7.0**	**11.8**
D-Net $(+L_{ph}, -\lambda_{adv})$	5.7	6.2	**5.2**	9.9	7.3	12.5
D-Net $(-L_{ph}, -\lambda_{adv})$	7.1	7.6	6.7	13.6	15.9	11.3

| (a) Input | (b) Result w/o L_{ph} | (c) Result w/ L_{ph} |

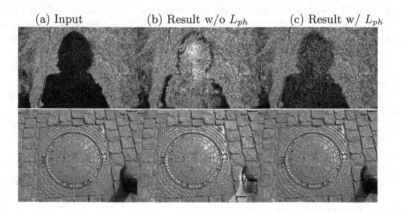

Fig. 10. Examples of adversarial examples generated with and without physics. (a) Input image I. (b) Adversarial example generated by A-Net trained without physics based loss. (c) Adversarial example generated by A-Net trained with physics based loss.

We conducted experiments to study the effect of the parameters of our framework. We started from the parameter settings reported in Sect. 4. When we chose $\lambda_{sd} = 10$, D-Net achieved 6.5% BER. As λ_{sd} increases, A-Net attenuates the shadow more dramatically but also tends to change the non-shadow part, generating lower quality images in general. In the second experiment, we rescaled the ratio between the real and adversarial images being input to D-Net. When we chose $\lambda_{adv}^0 = 0.5$ and $\lambda_{real} = 0.5$, D-Net achieved 7.0% BER.

5   Summary

In this paper, we have presented a novel framework for adversarial training of a shadow detector using shadow attenuation. We have shown experimentally how our model is able to effectively learn from both real shadow training examples as well as adversarial examples. Our trained model outperforms the previous state-of-art shadow detectors in two benchmark datasets, demonstrating the effectiveness and generalization ability of our model. Furthermore, to the best of our knowledge, this is the first shadow detector that can detect shadows accurately at real-time speed, 45 fps.

Acknowledgements. This work was supported by the Vietnam Education Foundation, a gift from Adobe, NSF grant CNS-1718014, the Partner University Fund, and the SUNY2020 Infrastructure Transportation Security Center. The authors would also like to thank NVIDIA for GPU donation.

References

1. Banerjee, A., Dhillon, I.S., Ghosh, J., Sra, S.: Clustering on the unit hypersphere using von Mises-Fisher distributions. J. Mach. Learn. Res. **6**, 1345–1382 (2005)
2. Deng, J., Dong, W., Socher, R., Li, L.J., Li, K., Fei-Fei, L.: ImageNet: a large-scale hierarchical image database. In: Proceedings of the IEEE Conference on Computer Vision and Pattern Recognition (2009)
3. Erraqabi, A., Baratin, A., Bengio, Y., Lacoste-Julien, S.: A3T: Adversarially augmented adversarial training. arXiv:1801.04055 (2018)
4. Finlayson, G., Hordley, S., Lu, C., Drew, M.: On the removal of shadows from images. IEEE Trans. Pattern Anal. Mach. Intell. **28**, 59–68 (2006)
5. Finlayson, G., Drew, M., Lu, C.: Entropy minimization for shadow removal. Int. J. Comput. Vis. **85**, 35–57 (2009)
6. Goodfellow, I.J., et al.: Generative adversarial networks. In: Advances in Neural Information Processing Systems (2014)
7. Guo, R., Dai, Q., Hoiem, D.: Single-image shadow detection and removal using paired regions. In: Proceedings of the IEEE Conference on Computer Vision and Pattern Recognition (2011)
8. Guo, R., Dai, Q., Hoiem, D.: Paired regions for shadow detection and removal. IEEE Trans. Pattern Anal. Mach. Intell. **35**, 2956–2967 (2012)
9. He, K., Zhang, X., Ren, S., Sun, J.: Delving deep into rectifiers: surpassing human-level performance on ImageNet classification. In: Proceedings of the International Conference on Computer Vision (2015)
10. Hu, X., Zhu, L., Fu, C.W., Qin, J., Heng, P.A.: Direction-aware spatial context features for shadow detection. In: Proceedings of the IEEE Conference on Computer Vision and Pattern Recognition (2018)
11. Huang, X., Hua, G., Tumblin, J., Williams, L.: What characterizes a shadow boundary under the sun and sky? In: Proceedings of the International Conference on Computer Vision (2011)
12. Isola, P., Zhu, J.Y., Zhou, T., Efros, A.A.: Image-to-image translation with conditional adversarial networks. In: Proceedings of the IEEE Conference on Computer Vision and Pattern Recognition (2017)
13. Khan, H., Bennamoun, M., Sohel, F., Togneri, R.: Automatic feature learning for robust shadow detection. In: Proceedings of the IEEE Conference on Computer Vision and Pattern Recognition (2014)
14. Kingma, D.P., Ba, J.: Adam: a method for stochastic optimization. In: Proceedings of the International Conference on Learning Representations (2015)
15. Lalonde, J.-F., Efros, A.A., Narasimhan, S.G.: Detecting ground shadows in outdoor consumer photographs. In: Daniilidis, K., Maragos, P., Paragios, N. (eds.) ECCV 2010. LNCS, vol. 6312, pp. 322–335. Springer, Heidelberg (2010). https://doi.org/10.1007/978-3-642-15552-9_24

16. Lin, T.-Y., et al.: Microsoft COCO: common objects in context. In: Fleet, D., Pajdla, T., Schiele, B., Tuytelaars, T. (eds.) ECCV 2014. LNCS, vol. 8693, pp. 740–755. Springer, Cham (2014). https://doi.org/10.1007/978-3-319-10602-1_48

17. Mirza, M., Osindero, S.: Conditional generative adversarial nets. arXiv preprint arXiv:1411.1784 (2014)

18. Moosavi-Dezfooli, S.M., Fawzi, A., Fawzi, O., Frossard, P.: Universal adversarial perturbations. In: Proceedings of the IEEE Conference on Computer Vision and Pattern Recognition (2017)

19. Moosavi-Dezfooli, S.M., Fawzi, A., Frossard, P.: DeepFool: a simple and accurate method to fool deep neural networks. In: Proceedings of the IEEE Conference on Computer Vision and Pattern Recognition (2016)

20. Nguyen, V., Vicente, T.F.Y., Zhao, M., Hoai, M., Samaras, D.: Shadow detection with conditional generative adversarial networks. In: Proceedings of the International Conference on Computer Vision (2017)

21. Panagopoulos, A., Samaras, D., Paragios, N.: Robust shadow and illumination estimation using a mixture model. In: Proceedings of the IEEE Conference on Computer Vision and Pattern Recognition (2009)

22. Panagopoulos, A., Wang, C., Samaras, D., Paragios, N.: Simultaneous cast shadows, illumination and geometry inference using hypergraphs. IEEE Trans. Pattern Anal. Mach. Intell. **35**, 437–449 (2013)

23. Ronneberger, O., Fischer, P., Brox, T.: U-Net: convolutional networks for biomedical image segmentation. In: Navab, N., Hornegger, J., Wells, W.M., Frangi, A.F. (eds.) MICCAI 2015. LNCS, vol. 9351, pp. 234–241. Springer, Cham (2015). https://doi.org/10.1007/978-3-319-24574-4_28

24. Shrivastava, A., Pfister, T., Tuzel, O., Susskind, J., Wang, W., Webb, R.: Learning from simulated and unsupervised images through adversarial training. In: Proceedings of the IEEE Conference on Computer Vision and Pattern Recognition (2016)

25. Sunkavalli, K., Matusik, W., Pfister, H., Rusinkiewicz, S.: Factored time-lapse video. In: Proceedings of the ACM SIGGRAPH Conference on Computer Graphics (2007)

26. Tramèr, F., Kurakin, A., Papernot, N., Goodfellow, I., Boneh, D., McDaniel, P.: Ensemble adversarial training: attacks and defenses. In: Proceedings of the International Conference on Learning Representations (2018)

27. Vicente, T.F.Y., Hoai, M., Samaras, D.: Leave-one-out kernel optimization for shadow detection. In: Proceedings of the International Conference on Computer Vision (2015)

28. Vicente, T.F.Y., Hoai, M., Samaras, D.: Noisy label recovery for shadow detection in unfamiliar domains. In: Proceedings of the IEEE Conference on Computer Vision and Pattern Recognition (2016)

29. Vicente, T.F.Y., Hoai, M., Samaras, D.: Leave-one-out kernel optimization for shadow detection and removal. IEEE Trans. Pattern Anal. Mach. Intell. **40**(3), 682–695 (2018)

30. Vicente, T.F.Y., Hou, L., Yu, C.-P., Hoai, M., Samaras, D.: Large-scale training of shadow detectors with noisily-annotated shadow examples. In: Leibe, B., Matas, J., Sebe, N., Welling, M. (eds.) ECCV 2016. LNCS, vol. 9910, pp. 816–832. Springer, Cham (2016). https://doi.org/10.1007/978-3-319-46466-4_49

31. Volpi, R., Morerio, P., Savarese, S., Murino, V.: Adversarial feature augmentation for unsupervised domain adaptation. In: Proceedings of the IEEE Conference on Computer Vision and Pattern Recognition (2018)

32. Wang, J., Li, X., Yang, J.: Stacked conditional generative adversarial networks for jointly learning shadow detection and shadow removal. In: Proceedings of the IEEE Conference on Computer Vision and Pattern Recognition (2018)
33. Wehrwein, S., Bala, K., Snavely, N.: Shadow detection and sun direction in photo collections. In: Proceedings of 3DV (2015)
34. Xie, C., Wang, J., Zhang, Z., Zhou, Y., Xie, L., Yuille, A.: Adversarial examples for semantic segmentation and object detection. In: Proceedings of the International Conference on Computer Vision (2017)
35. Zhang, H., Cisse, M., Dauphin, Y.N., Lopez-Paz, D.: mixup: beyond empirical risk minimization. In: Proceedings of the International Conference on Learning Representations (2018)
36. Zhu, J., Samuel, K., Masood, S., Tappen, M.: Learning to recognize shadows in monochromatic natural images. In: Proceedings of the IEEE Conference on Computer Vision and Pattern Recognition (2010)

Fast and Accurate Camera Covariance Computation for Large 3D Reconstruction

Michal Polic[1]([✉]) [iD], Wolfgang Förstner[2] [iD], and Tomas Pajdla[1] [iD]

[1] CIIRC, Czech Technical University in Prague, Prague, Czech Republic
{michal.polic,pajdla}@cvut.cz
[2] University of Bonn, Bonn, Germany
wfoerstn@uni-bonn.de,
http://www.ciirc.cvut.cz, http://www.ipb.uni-bonn.de

Abstract. Estimating uncertainty of camera parameters computed in Structure from Motion (SfM) is an important tool for evaluating the quality of the reconstruction and guiding the reconstruction process. Yet, the quality of the estimated parameters of large reconstructions has been rarely evaluated due to the computational challenges. We present a new algorithm which employs the sparsity of the uncertainty propagation and speeds the computation up about ten times w.r.t. previous approaches. Our computation is accurate and does not use any approximations. We can compute uncertainties of thousands of cameras in tens of seconds on a standard PC. We also demonstrate that our approach can be effectively used for reconstructions of any size by applying it to smaller sub-reconstructions.

Keywords: Uncertainty · Covariance propagation
Structure from motion · 3D reconstruction

1 Introduction

Three-dimensional reconstruction has a wide range of applications (e.g. virtual reality, robot navigation or self-driving cars), and therefore is an output of many algorithms such as Structure from Motion (SfM), Simultaneous location and mapping (SLAM) or Multi-view Stereo (MVS). Recent work in SfM and SLAM has demonstrated that the geometry of three-dimensional scene can be obtained from a large number of images [1,14,16]. Efficient non-linear refinement [2] of camera and point parameters has been developed to produce optimal reconstructions.

The uncertainty of detected points in images can be efficiently propagated in case of SLAM [16,28] into the uncertainty o three-dimensional scene parameters thanks to fixing the first camera pose and scale. In SfM framework, however, we are often allowing for gauge freedom [18], and therefore practical computation of the uncertainty [9] is mostly missing in the state of the art pipelines [23,30,32].

© Springer Nature Switzerland AG 2018
V. Ferrari et al. (Eds.): ECCV 2018, LNCS 11206, pp. 697–712, 2018.
https://doi.org/10.1007/978-3-030-01216-8_42

In SfM, reconstructions are in general obtained up to an unknown similarity transformation, i.e., a rotation, translation, and scale. The backward uncertainty propagation [13] (the propagation from detected feature points to parameters the of the reconstruction) requires the "inversion" of a Fischer information matrix, which is rank deficient [9,13] in this case. Naturally, we want to compute the uncertainty of the inner geometry [9] and ignore the infinite uncertainty of the free choice of the similarity transformation. This can be done by the Moore-Penrose (M-P) inversion of the Fisher information matrix [9,13,18]. However, the M-P inversion is a computationally challenging process. It has cubic time and quadratic memory complexity in the number of columns of the information matrix, i.e., the number of parameters.

Fast and numerically stable uncertainty propagation has numerous applications [26]. We could use it for selecting the next best view [10] from a large collection of images [1,14], for detecting wrongly added cameras to existing partial reconstructions, for improving fitting to the control points [21], and for filtering the mostly unconstrained cameras in the reconstruction to speed up the bundle adjustment [2] by reducing the size of the reconstruction. It would also help to improve the accuracy of the iterative closest point (ICP) algorithm [5], by using the precision of the camera poses, and to provide the uncertainty of the points in 3D [27].

2   Contribution

We present the first algorithm for uncertainty propagation from input feature points to camera parameters that works without any approximation of the natural form of the covariance matrix on thousands of cameras. It is about ten times faster than the state of the art algorithms [19,26]. Our approach builds on top of Gauss-Markov estimation with constraints by Rao [29]. The novelty is in a new method for nullspace computation in SfM. We introduce a fast sparse method, which is independent on a chosen parametrization of rotations. Further, we combine the fixation of gauge freedom by nullspace, from Förstner and Wrobel [9] and methods applied in SLAM, i.e., the block matrix inversion [6] and Woodbury matrix identity [12].

Our main contribution is a clear formulation of the nullspace construction, which is based on the similarity transformation between parameters of the reconstruction. Using the nullspace and the normal equation from [9], we correctly apply the block matrix inversion, which has been done only approximately before [26]. This brings an improvement in accuracy as well as in speed. We also demonstrate that our approach can be effectively used for reconstructions of any size by applying it to smaller sub-reconstructions. We show empirically that our approach is valid and practical.

Our algorithm is faster, more accurate and more stable than any previous method [19,26,27]. The output of our work is publicly available as source code which can be used as an external library in nonlinear optimization pipelines, like Ceres Solver [2] and reconstruction pipelines like [23,30,32]. The code, datasets, and detailed experiments will be available online https://michalpolic.github.io/usfm.github.io.

3   Related Work

The uncertainty propagation is a well known process [9,13,18,26]. Our goal is to propagate the uncertainties of input measurements, i.e. feature points in images, into the parameters of the reconstruction, e.g. poses of cameras and positions of points in 3D, by using the projection function [13]. For the purpose of uncertainty propagation, a non-linear projection function is in practice often replaced by its first order approximation using its Jacobian matrix [8,13]. For the propagation using higher order approximations of the projection function, as described in Förstner and Wrobel [9], higher order estimates of uncertainties of feature points are required. Unfortunately, these are difficult to estimate [9,25] reliably.

In the case of SfM, the uncertainty propagation is called the *backward propagation of non-linear function in over-parameterized case* [13] because of the projection function, which does not fully constrain the reconstruction parameters [22], i.e., the reconstruction can be shifted, rotated and scaled without any change of image projections.

We are primarily interested in estimating *inner geometry* , e.g. angles and ratios of distance, and its *inner precision* [9]. Inner precision is invariant to changes of gauge, i.e. to similarity transformations of the cameras and the scene [18]. A natural choice of the fixation of gauge, which leads to the inner uncertainty of inner geometry, is to fix seven degrees of freedom caused by the invariance of the projection function to the similarity transformation of space [9,13,18]. One way to do this is to use the Moore-Penrose (M-P) inversion [24] of the Fisher information matrix [9].

Recently, several works on speeding up the M-P inversion of the information matrix for SfM frameworks have appeared. Lhuillier and Perriollat [19] used the block matrix inversion of the Fisher information matrix. They performed M-P inversion of the Schur complement matrix [34] of the block related to point parameters and then projected the results to the space orthogonal to the similarity transformation constraints. This approach allowed working with much larger scenes because the square Schur complement matrix has the dimension equal to the number of camera parameters, which is at least six times the number of cameras, compared to the mere dimension of the square Fisher information matrix, which is just about three times the number of points.

However, it is not clear if the decomposition of Fisher information matrix holds for M-P inversion without fulfilling the rank additivity condition [33] and it was shown in [26] that approach [19] is not always accurate enough. Polic et al. [26] evaluated the state of the art solutions against more accurate results computed in high precision arithmetics, i.e. using 100 digits instead of 15 significant digits of double precision. They compared the influence of several fixations of the gauge on the output uncertainties and found that fixing three points that are far from each other together with a clever approximation of the inversion leads to a good approximation of the uncertainties.

The most related work is [29], which contains uncertainty formulation for Gauss-Markov model with constraints. We combine this result with our new approach for nullspace computation to fixing gauge freedom.

Finally, let us mention work on fast uncertainty propagation in SLAM. The difference between SfM and SLAM is that in SLAM we know, and fix, the first camera pose and the scale of the scene which makes the information matrix full rank. Thus one can use a fast Cholesky decomposition to invert a Schur complement matrix as well as other techniques for fast covariance computation [16,17]. Polok, Ila et al. [15,28] claim addressing uncertainty computation in SfM but actually assume full rank Fisher information matrix and hence do not deal with gauge freedom. In contrary, we solved here the full SfM problem which requires dealings with gauge freedom.

4   Problem Formulation

In this section, we describe basic notions in uncertainty propagation in SfM and provide the problem formulation.

The set of parameters of three-dimensional scene $\theta = \{P, X\}$ is composed from n cameras $P = \{P_1, P_2, \ldots, P_n\}$ and m points $X = \{X_1, X_2, \ldots, X_m\}$ in 3D. The i-th camera is a vector $P \in \mathbb{R}^8$, which consist of internal parameters (i.e. focal length $c_i \in \mathbb{R}$ and radial distortion $k_i \in \mathbb{R}$) and external parameters (i.e. rotation $r_i \in SO(3)$ and camera center $C_i \in \mathbb{R}^3$). Estimated parameters are labelled with the hat $\hat{\cdot}$.

We consider that the parameters $\hat{\theta}$ were estimated by a reconstruction pipeline using a vector of t observations $u \in \mathbb{R}^{2t}$. Each observation is a 2D point $u_{i,j} \in \mathbb{R}^2$ in the image i detected up to some uncertainty that is described by its covariance matrix $\Sigma_{u_{i,j}} = \Sigma_{\epsilon_{i,j}}$. It characterizes the Gaussian distribution assumed for the detection error $\epsilon_{i,j}$ and can be computed from the structure tensor [7] of the local neighbourhood of $u_{i,j}$ in the image i. The vector $\hat{u}_{i,j} = p(\hat{X}_j, \hat{P}_i)$ is a projection of point $\hat{X}_j$ into the image plane described by camera parameters $\hat{P}_i$. All pairs of indices (i, j) are in the index set S that determines which point is seen by which camera

$$\hat{u}_{i,j} = u_{i,j} - \epsilon_{i,j} \tag{1}$$

$$\hat{u}_{i,j} = p(\hat{X}_j, \hat{P}_i) \qquad \forall (i,j) \in S \tag{2}$$

Next, we define function $f(\hat{\theta})$ and vector ϵ as a composition of all projection functions $p(\hat{X}_j, \hat{P}_i)$ and related detection errors $\epsilon_{i,j}$

$$u = \hat{u} + \epsilon = f(\hat{\theta}) + \epsilon \tag{3}$$

This function is used in the non-linear least squares optimization (Bundle Adjustment [2])

$$\hat{\theta} = \arg \min_{\theta} \left\| f(\hat{\theta}) - u \right\|^2 \tag{4}$$

which minimises the sum of squared differences between the measured feature points and the projections of the reconstructed 3D points. We assume the Σ_u as a block diagonal matrix composed of $\Sigma_{u_{i,j}}$ blocks. The optimal estimate $\hat{\theta}$, minimising the Mahalanobis norm, is

$$\hat{\theta} = \arg\min_{\theta} r^\top(\hat{\theta})\Sigma_u^{-1} r(\hat{\theta}) \tag{5}$$

To find the formula for uncertainty propagation, the non-linear projection functions f can be linearized by the first order term of its Taylor expansion

$$f(\theta) \approx f(\hat{\theta}) + J_{\hat{\theta}}(\hat{\theta} - \theta) \tag{6}$$
$$f(\theta) \approx \hat{u} + J_{\hat{\theta}}\Delta\theta \tag{7}$$

which leads to the estimated correction of the parameters

$$\hat{\theta} = \theta + \arg\min_{\Delta\theta}(J_{\hat{\theta}}\Delta\theta + \hat{u} - u)^\top\Sigma_u^{-1}(J_{\hat{\theta}}\Delta\theta + \hat{u} - u) \tag{8}$$

Partial derivatives of the objective function must vanishing in the optimum

$$\frac{1}{2}\frac{\partial(r^\top(\theta)\Sigma_u^{-1}r(\theta))}{\partial\theta^\top} = J_{\hat{\theta}}^\top\Sigma_u^{-1}(J_{\hat{\theta}}\widehat{\Delta\theta} + \hat{u} - u) = J_{\hat{\theta}}^\top\Sigma_u^{-1}r(\hat{\theta}) = 0 \tag{9}$$

which defines the *normal equation system*

$$M\widehat{\Delta\theta} = m \tag{10}$$
$$M = J_{\hat{\theta}}^\top\Sigma_u^{-1}J_{\hat{\theta}}, \quad m = J_{\hat{\theta}}^\top\Sigma_u^{-1}(u - \hat{u}) \tag{11}$$

The normal equation system has seven degrees of freedom and therefore requires to fix seven parameters, called the gauge [18], namely a scale, a translation and a rotation. Any choice of fixing these parameters leads to a valid solution.

The natural choice of covariance, which is unique, has the zero uncertainty in the scale, the translation, and rotation of all cameras and scene points. It can be obtained by the M-P inversion of Fisher information matrix M or by Gauss-Markov Model with constraints [9]. If we assume a constraints $h(\hat{\theta}) = 0$, which fix the scene scale, translation and rotation, we can write their derivatives, i.e. the nullspace H, as

$$H^T\Delta\theta = 0 \qquad H = \frac{\partial h(\hat{\theta})}{\partial\hat{\theta}} \tag{12}$$

Using Lagrange multipliers λ, we are minimising the function

$$g(\Delta\theta, \lambda) = \frac{1}{2}(J_{\hat{\theta}}\Delta\theta + \hat{u} - u)^\top\Sigma_u^{-1}(J_{\hat{\theta}}\Delta\theta + \hat{u} - u) + \lambda^\top(H^T\Delta\theta) \tag{13}$$

that has partial derivative with respect λ equal to zero in the optimum (as in Eq. 9)

$$\frac{\partial g(\Delta\theta, \lambda)}{\partial\lambda} = H^T\Delta\theta = 0 \tag{14}$$

This constraints lead to the *extended normal equations*

$$\begin{bmatrix} M & H \\ H^\top & 0 \end{bmatrix} \begin{bmatrix} \hat{\theta} \\ \lambda \end{bmatrix} = \begin{bmatrix} J_{\hat{\theta}}^\top \Sigma_u^{-1}(\hat{u} - u) \\ 0 \end{bmatrix} \tag{15}$$

and allow us to compute the inversion instead of M-P inversion

$$\begin{bmatrix} \Sigma_{\hat{\theta}} & K \\ K^\top & T \end{bmatrix} = \begin{bmatrix} M & H \\ H^\top & 0 \end{bmatrix}^{-1} \tag{16}$$

5   Solution Method

We next describe how to compute the nullspace H and decompose the original Eq. 16 by a block matrix inversion. The proposed method assumes that the Jacobian of the projection function is provided numerically and provides the nullspace independently of the representation of the camera rotation.

5.1   The Nullspace of the Jacobian

The scene can be transformed by a similarity transformation[1]

$$^s\theta = {}^s\theta(\theta, q) \tag{17}$$

depending on seven parameters $q = [T, s, \mu]$ for translation, rotation, and scale without any change of the projection function $f(\theta) - f({}^s\theta(\theta, q)) = 0$. If we assume a difference similarity transformation, we obtain the total derivative

$$J_\theta \Delta\theta - (J_\theta \Delta\theta + J_\theta J_q \Delta q) = J_\theta J_q \Delta q = 0 \tag{18}$$

Since it needs to hold for any Δq, the matrix

$$H = \frac{\partial^s \theta}{\partial q} = J_q \tag{19}$$

is the nullspace of J_θ. Next, consider an order of parameters such that 3D point parameters follow the camera parameters

$$\hat{\theta} = \{P, X\} = \{P_1, \ldots P_n, X_1, \ldots X_m\} \tag{20}$$

The cameras have parameters ordered as $P_i = \{r_i, C_i, c_i, k_i\}$ and the projection function equals

$$p(\hat{X}_j, \hat{P}_i) = \Phi_i(c_i R(\hat{r}_i)(\hat{X}_j - \hat{C}_i)) \qquad \forall (i, j) \in S \tag{21}$$

where Φ_i projects vectors from $\mathbb{R}^3$ to $\mathbb{R}^2$ by (i) first dividing by the third coordinate, and (ii) then applying image distortion with parameters $\hat{P}_i$. Note that function Φ_i can be chosen quite freely, e.g. adding a tangential distortion or

---

[1] The variable $^s\theta$ is a function of θ and q.

encountering a rolling shutter projection model [3]. Using Eq. 17, we are getting for $\forall (i,j) \in S$

$$p(\hat{X}_j, \hat{P}_i) = p({}^s\hat{X}_j(q), {}^s\hat{P}_i(q)) \tag{22}$$

$$p(\hat{X}_j, \hat{P}_i) = \Phi_i(c_i \, {}^s R(\hat{r}_i, s)({}^s\hat{X}_j(q) - {}^s\hat{C}_i(q))) \tag{23}$$

$$p(\hat{X}_j, \hat{P}_i) = \Phi_i(c_i \, (R(\hat{r}_i)R(s)^{-1})\,((\mu R(s)\hat{X}_j + T) - (\mu R(s)\hat{C}_i + T))) \tag{24}$$

Note that for any parameters q, the projection remains unchanged. It can be checked by expanding the equation above. Eq. 24 is linear in T and μ. The differences of $\hat{X}_j$ and $\hat{C}_i$ are as follows

$$\Delta \hat{X}_j(\hat{X}_j, q) = \hat{X}_j - {}^s\hat{X}_j(q) = \hat{X}_j - (\mu R(s)\hat{X}_j + T) \tag{25}$$

$$\Delta \hat{C}_i(\hat{C}_i, q) = \hat{C}_i - {}^s\hat{C}_i(q) = \hat{C}_i - (\mu R(s)\hat{C}_i + T) \tag{26}$$

The Jacobian $J_{\hat{\theta}}$ and the nullspace H can be written as

$$J_{\hat{\theta}} = \frac{\partial f(\hat{\theta})}{\partial \hat{\theta}} = \begin{bmatrix} \frac{\partial p_1}{\partial \hat{P}_1} & \cdots & \frac{\partial p_1}{\partial \hat{P}_n} & \frac{\partial p_1}{\partial \hat{X}_1} & \cdots & \frac{\partial p_1}{\partial \hat{X}_m} \\ \vdots & & \vdots & \vdots & & \vdots \\ \frac{\partial p_t}{\partial \hat{P}_1} & \cdots & \frac{\partial p_t}{\partial \hat{P}_n} & \frac{\partial p_t}{\partial \hat{X}_1} & \cdots & \frac{\partial p_t}{\partial \hat{X}_m} \end{bmatrix}, \quad H = \begin{bmatrix} H_{\hat{P}_1}^T & H_{\hat{P}_1}^s & H_{\hat{P}_1}^\mu \\ \vdots & \vdots & \vdots \\ H_{\hat{P}_n}^T & H_{\hat{P}_n}^s & H_{\hat{P}_n}^\mu \\ H_{\hat{X}_1}^T & H_{\hat{X}_1}^s & H_{\hat{X}_1}^\mu \\ \vdots & \vdots & \vdots \\ H_{\hat{X}_m}^T & H_{\hat{X}_m}^s & H_{\hat{X}_m}^\mu \end{bmatrix} \tag{27}$$

where p_t is the tth observation, i.e. the pair $(i,j) \in S$. The columns of H are related to transformation parameters q. The rows are related to parameters $\hat{\theta}$. The derivatives of differences of scene parameters $\Delta \hat{P}_i = [\Delta \hat{r}_i, \Delta \hat{C}_i, \Delta \hat{c}_i, \Delta \hat{k}_i]$ and $\Delta \hat{X}_j$ with respect to the transformation parameters $q = [T, s, \mu]$ are exactly the blocks of the nullspace

$$H = \begin{bmatrix} \frac{\partial \Delta r_1}{\partial T} & \frac{\partial \Delta r_1}{\partial s} & \frac{\partial \Delta r_1}{\partial \mu} \\ \frac{\partial \Delta C_1}{\partial T} & \frac{\partial \Delta C_1}{\partial R(s)} & \frac{\partial \Delta C_1}{\partial \mu} \\ \frac{\partial \Delta c_1}{\partial T} & \frac{\partial \Delta c_1}{\partial R(s)} & \frac{\partial \Delta c_1}{\partial \mu} \\ \frac{\partial \Delta k_1}{\partial T} & \frac{\partial \Delta k_1}{\partial R(s)} & \frac{\partial \Delta k_1}{\partial \mu} \\ \frac{\partial T}{\partial T} & \frac{\partial R(s)}{\partial R(s)} & \frac{\partial \mu}{\partial \mu} \\ \vdots & \vdots & \vdots \\ \frac{\partial \Delta X_1}{\partial T} & \frac{\partial \Delta X_1}{\partial R(s)} & \frac{\partial \Delta X_1}{\partial \mu} \\ \vdots & \vdots & \vdots \\ \frac{\partial \Delta X_m}{\partial T} & \frac{\partial \Delta X_m}{\partial R(s)} & \frac{\partial \Delta X_m}{\partial \mu} \end{bmatrix} = \begin{bmatrix} 0_{3\times3} & H_{r_1} & 0_{3\times1} \\ I_{3\times3} & [C_1]_x & C_1 \\ 0_{1\times3} & 0_{1\times3} & 0 \\ 0_{1\times3} & 0_{1\times3} & 0 \\ \vdots & \vdots & \vdots \\ I_{3\times3} & [X_1]_x & X_1 \\ \vdots & \vdots & \vdots \\ I_{3\times3} & [X_m]_x & X_m \end{bmatrix} \tag{28}$$

where $[v]_x$ is the skew symmetric matrix such that $[v]_x\, y = v \times y$ for all $v, y \in \mathbb{R}^3$.

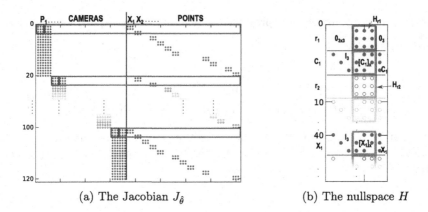

(a) The Jacobian $J_{\hat{\theta}}$ (b) The nullspace H

Fig. 1. The structure of the matrices $J_{\hat{\theta}}\, H$ for Cube dataset, for clarity, using 6 parameters for one camera $\hat{P}_i$(no focal length and lens distortion shown). The matrices $J_{\hat{r}}$ and $H_{\hat{r}}$ are composed from the red submatrices of J and H. The multiplication of green submatrices equals $-B$, see Eq. 31(Color figure online) .

Equation 24 is not linear in rotation s. To deal with any rotation representation, we can compute the values of $H_{\hat{r}_i}$ for all i using Eq. 18. The columns, which contain blocks $H_{\hat{r}_i}$, are orthogonal to the rest of the nullspace and to the Jacobian $J_{\hat{\theta}}$.

The system of equations $J_{\hat{\theta}}H = 0$ can be rewritten as

$$J_{\hat{r}}H_{\hat{r}} = B \tag{29}$$

where $J_{\hat{r}} \in \mathbb{R}^{3n \times 3n}$ is composed as a block-diagonal matrix from the red submatrices (see Fig. 1) of $J_{\hat{\theta}}$. The matrix $H_{\hat{r}} \in \mathbb{R}^{3n \times 3}$ is composed from red submatrices $H_{\hat{r}_i} \in \mathbb{R}^{3n \times 3}$ as

$$H_{\hat{r}} = \begin{bmatrix} H_{\hat{r}_1}^{\top} & \dots & H_{\hat{r}_n}^{\top} \end{bmatrix}^{\top} \tag{30}$$

The matrix $B \in \mathbb{R}^{3n \times 3}$ is composed of the green submatrices (see Fig. 1) of $J_{\hat{\theta}}$ multiplied by the minus green submatrices of H. The solution to this system is

$$H_{\hat{r}} = J_{\hat{r}}^{-1}B \tag{31}$$

where B is computed by a sparse multiplication, see Fig. 1. The inversion of $J_{\hat{r}}$ is the inversion of a sparse matrix with n blocks $\mathbb{R}^{3 \times 3}$ on the diagonal.

5.2 Uncertainty Propagation to Camera Parameters

The propagation of uncertainty is based on Eq. 16. The inversion of extended Fisher information matrix is first conditioned for better numerical accuracy as follows

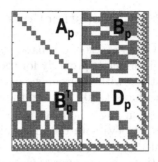

Fig. 2. The structure of the matrix Q_p for Cube dataset and $\hat{P}_i \in \mathbb{R}^6$.

$$\begin{bmatrix} \Sigma_{\hat{\theta}} & K \\ K^\top & T \end{bmatrix} = \begin{bmatrix} S_a & 0 \\ 0 & S_b \end{bmatrix} \left(\begin{bmatrix} S_a & 0 \\ 0 & S_b \end{bmatrix} \begin{bmatrix} M & H \\ H^\top & 0 \end{bmatrix} \begin{bmatrix} S_a & 0 \\ 0 & S_b \end{bmatrix} \right)^{-1} \begin{bmatrix} S_a & 0 \\ 0 & S_b \end{bmatrix} \tag{32}$$

$$\begin{bmatrix} \Sigma_{\hat{\theta}} & K \\ K^\top & T \end{bmatrix} = \begin{bmatrix} S_a & 0 \\ 0 & S_b \end{bmatrix} \begin{bmatrix} M_s & H_s \\ H_s^\top & 0 \end{bmatrix}^{-1} \begin{bmatrix} S_a & 0 \\ 0 & S_b \end{bmatrix} \tag{33}$$

$$\begin{bmatrix} \Sigma_{\hat{\theta}} & K \\ K^\top & T \end{bmatrix} = SQ^{-1}S \tag{34}$$

by diagonal matrices S_a, S_b which condition the columns of matrices J, H. Secondly, we permute the columns of Q to have point parameters followed by the camera parameters

$$\begin{bmatrix} \Sigma_{\hat{\theta}} & K \\ K^\top & T \end{bmatrix} = S\widetilde{P}(\widetilde{P}Q\widetilde{P})^{-1}\widetilde{P}S = S\widetilde{P}Q_p^{-1}\widetilde{P}S \tag{35}$$

where $\widetilde{P}$ is an appropriate permutation matrix. The matrix $Q_p = \widetilde{P}Q\widetilde{P}$ is a full rank matrix which can be decomposed and inverted using a block matrix inversion

$$Q_p^{-1} = \begin{bmatrix} A_p & B_p \\ B_p^\top & D_p \end{bmatrix}^{-1} = \begin{bmatrix} A_p^{-1} + A_p^{-1}BZ_p^{-1}B_p^\top A_p^{-1} & -A_p^{-1}BZ_p^{-1} \\ -Z_p^{-1}B_p^\top A_p^{-1} & Z_p^{-1} \end{bmatrix} \tag{36}$$

where Z_p is the symmetric Schur complement matrix of point parameters block A_p

$$Z_p^{-1} = (D_p - B_p^\top A_p^{-1}B_p)^{-1} \tag{37}$$

Matrix $A_p \in \mathbb{R}^{3m \times 3m}$ is a sparse symmetric block diagonal matrix with $\mathbb{R}^{3 \times 3}$ blocks on the diagonal, see Fig. 2. The covariances for camera parameters are computed using the inversion of Z_p with the size $\mathbb{R}^{(8n+7) \times (8n+7)}$ for our model of cameras (i.e., $P_i \in \mathbb{R}^8$)

$$\Sigma_{\hat{P}} = S_P Z_s S_P \tag{38}$$

where $Z_s \in \mathbb{R}^{8n \times 8n}$ is the left top submatrix of Z_p^{-1} and S_P is the corresponding sub-block of scale matrix S_a.

6   Uncertainty for Sub-reconstructions

The algorithm based on Gauss-Markov estimate with constraints, which is described in Sect. 5, works in principle properly for thousands of cameras. However, large-scale reconstructions with thousands cameras would require a large space, e.g. 131 GB for Rome dataset [20], to store the matrix Z_p for our camera model $\hat{P}_i \in \mathbb{R}^8$, and its inversion might be inaccurate due to rounding errors.

Fortunately, it is possible to evaluate the uncertainty of a camera $\hat{P}_i$ from only a partial sub-reconstruction comprising cameras and points in the vicinity of $\hat{C}_i$. Using sub-reconstructions, we can approximate the uncertainty computed from a complete reconstruction. The error of our approximation decreases with increasing size of a sub-reconstruction. If we add a camera to a reconstruction, we add at least four observations which influence the Fisher information matrix M_i as

$$M_{i+1} = M_i + M_\Delta \tag{39}$$

where the matrix M_Δ is the Fisher information matrix of the added observations. We can propagate this update using equations in Sect. 5 to the Schur complement matrix

$$Z_{i+1} = Z_i + Z_\Delta \tag{40}$$

which has full rank. Using Woodbury matrix identity

$$(Z_i + J_\Delta^\top \Sigma_\Delta J_\Delta)^{-1} = Z_i^{-1} - Z_i^{-1} J_\Delta^\top (I + J_\Delta Z_i J_\Delta^\top)^{-1} J_\Delta Z_i^{-1} \tag{41}$$

we can see that the positive definite covariance matrices are subtracted after adding some observations, i.e. the uncertainty decreases.

We show empirically that the error decreases with increasing the size of the reconstruction (see Fig. 3). We have found that for 100–150 neighbouring cameras, the error is usually small enough to be used in practice. Each evaluation of the sub-reconstruction produces an upper bound on the uncertainty for cameras involved in the sub-reconstruction. The accuracy of the upper bound depends on a particular decomposition of the complete reconstruction into sub-reconstructions. To get reliable results, it is useful to decompose the reconstruction several times and choose the covariance matrix with the smallest trace.

The theoretical proof of the quality of this approximation and selection of the optimal decomposition is an open question for future research.

7   Experimental Evaluation

We use synthetic as well as real datasets (Table 1) to test and compare the algorithms (Table 2) with respect the accuracy (Fig. 3) and speed (Fig. 4). The evaluations on sub-reconstructions are shown in Figs. 5, 6a, 6b. All experiments were performed on a single computer with one 2.6 GHz Intel Core i7-6700HQ with 32 GB RAM running a 64-bit Windows 10 operating system.

Compared algorithms are listed in Table 2. The standard way of computing the covariance matrix $\Sigma_{\hat{P}}$ is by using the M-P inversion of the information

Table 1. Summary of the datasets: N_P is the number of cameras, N_X is the number of points in 3D and N_u is the number of observations. Datasets 1 and 3 are synthetic, 2, 9 from COLMAP [30], and 4-8 from Bundler [31]

#	Dataset	N_P	N_X	N_u
1	Cube	6	15	60
2	Toy	10	60	200
3	Flat	30	100	1033
4	Daliborka	64	200	5205
5	Marianska	118	80 873	248 511
6	Dolnoslaskie	360	529 829	226 0026
7	Tower of London	530	65 768	508 579
8	Notre Dame	715	127 431	748 003
9	Seychelles	1400	407 193	2 098 201

matrix using the Singular Value Decomposition (SVD) with the last seven singular values set to zeros and inverting the rest of them as in [26]. There are many implementations of this procedure that differ in numerical stability and speed. We compared three of them. Algorithm 1 uses high precision number representation in Maple (runs 22 h on Daliborka dataset), Algorithm 2 denotes the implementation in Ceres [2], which uses Eigen library [11] internally (runs 25.9 min on Daliborka dataset) and Algorithm 3 is our Matlab implementation, which internally calls LAPACK library [4] (runs 0.45 s on Daliborka dataset). Further, we compared Lhuilier [19] and Polic [26] approaches, which approximate the uncertainty propagation, with our algorithm denoted as *Nullspace bounding uncertainty propagation* (NBUP).

Table 2. The summary of used algorithms

#	Algorithm
1.	M-P inversion of M using Maple (Kanatani [18]) (**Ground Truth**)
2.	M-P inversion of M using Ceres (Kanatani [18])
3.	M-P inversion of M using Matlab (Kanatani [18])
4.	M-P inversion of Schur complement matrix with correction term (Lhuillier [19])
5.	TE inversion of Schur complement matrix with three points fixed (Polic [27])
6.	**Nullspace bounding uncertainty propagation (NBUP)**

The accuracy of all algorithms is compared against the Ground Truth (GT) in Fig. 3. The evaluation is performed on the first four datasets which have reasonably small number of 3D points. The computation of GT for the fourth dataset took about 22 hours and larger datasets were uncomputable because of time and memory requirements. We decomposed information matrix using SVD, set exactly the last seven singular values to zero and inverted the rest of them. We also used 100 significant digits instead of 15 digits used by a double number representation. The GT computation follows approach from [26].

The covariance matrices for our camera model (comprising rotation, camera center, focal length and radial distortion) contain a large range of values. Some parameters, e.g. rotations represented by the Euler vector, are in units while other parameters, as the focal length, are in thousands of units. Moreover, the rotation is in all tested examples better constrained than the focal length. This fact leads to approximately mean absolute value in rotation part of the covariance matrix and approximately mean value for the focal length variance. Standard deviations for datasets 1–4 and are about for rotations and for focal lengths. To obtain comparable standard deviations for different parameters, we can divide the mean values of rotations by π and focal length by . We used the same approach for the comparison of the measured errors

$$err_{\hat{P}_i} = \frac{1}{64} \sum_{l=1}^{8} \sum_{m=1}^{8} \left(\sqrt{|\widetilde{\Sigma}_{\hat{P}_i(l,m)} - \widehat{\Sigma}_{\hat{P}_i(l,m)}|} \oslash O_{(l,m)} \right) \tag{42}$$

The error $err_{\hat{P}_i}$ shows the differences between GT covariance matrices $\widetilde{\Sigma}_{\hat{P}_i}$ and the computed ones $\widehat{\Sigma}_{\hat{P}_i}$. The matrix

$$O = \sqrt{E(|\hat{P}_i|)\, E(|\hat{P}_i|)^\top} \tag{43}$$

has dimension $O \in \mathbb{R}^{8 \times 8}$ and normalises the error to percentages of the absolute magnitude of the original units. Symbol $\oslash$ stands for element-wise division of matrices (i.e. $\bar{C} = \bar{A} \oslash \bar{B}$ equals $\bar{C}_{(i,j)} = \bar{A}_{(i,j)}/\bar{B}_{(i,j)}$ for $\forall (i,j)$).

Figure 3 shows the comparison of the mean of the errors for all cameras in the datasets. We see that our new method, NBUP, delivers the most accurate results on all datasets.

Speed of the algorithms is shown in Fig. 4. Note that the M-P inversion (i.e. Algorithm 1–3) cannot be evaluated on medium and larger datasets 5–9 because of memory requirements for storing dense matrix M. We see that our new method NBUP is faster than all other methods. Considerable speedup is obtained on datasets 7–9 where our NBUP method is about 8 times faster.

Uncertainty approximation on sub-reconstructions was tested on datasets 5–9. We decomposed reconstructions several times using a different number of cameras $\bar{k} = \{5, 10, 20, 40, 80, 160, 320\}$ inside smaller sub-reconstructions, and measured relative and absolute errors of approximated covariances for cameras parameters. Figure 6 shows the decrease of error for larger sub-reconstructions. There were 25 sub-reconstructions for each $\bar{k}_i$ with the set of neighbouring cameras randomly selected using the view graph. Note that Fig. 6a shows the mean of relative errors given by Eq. 42. Figure 6b shows that the absolute covariance

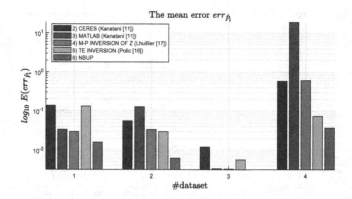

Fig. 3. The mean error $err_{\hat{P}_i}$ of all cameras $\hat{P}_i$ and Algorithm 2–6 on datasets 1–4. Note that the Algorithm 3, leading to the normal form of the covariance matrix, is numerically much more sensitive. It sometimes produces completely wrong results even for small reconstructions.

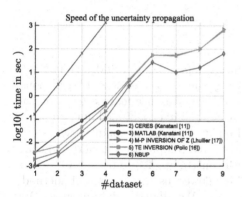

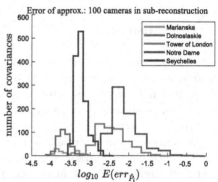

Fig. 4. The speed comparison. Full comparison against Algorithm 2, 3 was not possible because of the memory complexity. Algorithm 3 failed, see Fig. 3.

Fig. 5. The relative error for approximating camera covariances by one hundred of their neighbours from the view-graph.

error decreases significantly with increasing the number of cameras in a sub-reconstruction.

Figure 5 shows the error of the simplest approximation of covariances used in practice. For every camera, one hundred of its neighbours using view-graph were used to get a sub-reconstruction for evaluating the uncertainties. It produces upper bound estimates for the covariances for each camera from which we selected the smallest one, i.e. the covariance matrix with the smallest trace, and evaluate the mean of the relative error $err_{\hat{P}_i}$.

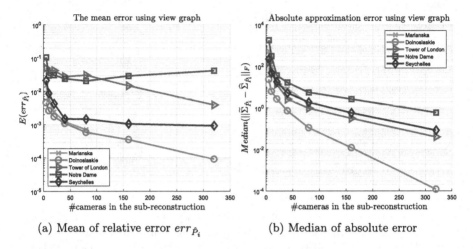

(a) Mean of relative error $err_{\hat{P}_i}$

(b) Median of absolute error

Fig. 6. The error of the uncertainty approximation using sub-reconstructions as a function of the number of cameras in the sub-reconstruction.

8   Conclusions

Current methods for evaluating of the uncertainty [19,26] in SfM rely 1) either on imposing the gauge constraints by using a few parameters as observations, which does not lead to the natural form of the covariance matrix, or 2) on the Moore-Penrose inversion [2], which cannot be used in case of medium and large-scale datasets because of cubic time and quadratic memory complexity.

We proposed a new method for the nullspace computation in SfM and combined it with Gauss Markov estimate with constraints [29] to obtain a full-rank matrix [9] allowing robust inversion. This allowed us to use efficient methods from SLAM such as block matrix inversion or Woodbury matrix identity. Our approach is the first one which allows a computation of natural form of the covariance matrix on scenes with more than thousand of cameras, e.g. 1400 cameras, with affordable computation time, e.g. 60 s, on a standard PC. Further, we show that using sub-reconstruction of roughly 100–300 cameras provides reliable estimates of the uncertainties for arbitrarily large scenes.

Acknowledgement. This work was supported by the European Regional Development Fund under the project IMPACT (reg. no. CZ.02.1.01/0.0/0.0/15_003/0000468), EU-H2020 project LADIO no. 731970, and by Grant Agency of the CTU in Prague projects SGS16/230/OHK3/3T/13, SGS18/104/OHK3/1T/37.

References

1. Agarwal, S., et al.: Building rome in a day. Commun. ACM **54**(10), 105–112 (2011)
2. Agarwal, S., et al.: Ceres solver. http://ceres-solver.org
3. Albl, C., Kukelova, Z., Pajdla, T.: R6P-rolling shutter absolute camera pose. In: Proceedings of the IEEE Conference on Computer Vision and Pattern Recognition, pp. 2292–2300 (2015)
4. Anderson, E., et al.: Lapack: a portable linear algebra library for high-performance computers. In: Proceedings of the 1990 ACM/IEEE Conference on Supercomputing, pp. 2–11. IEEE Computer Society Press (1990)
5. Besl, P.J., McKay, N.D.: Method for registration of 3-d shapes. In: Sensor Fusion IV: Control Paradigms and Data Structures, vol. 1611, pp. 586–607. International Society for Optics and Photonics (1992)
6. Eves, H.W.: Elementary Matrix Theory. Courier Corporation, North Chelmsford (1966)
7. Förstner, W.: Image Matching, chap. 16, vol. 2, pp. 289–379. Addison Wesley (1993)
8. Förstner, W.: Uncertainty and projective geometry. In: Corrochano, E.B. (ed.) Handbook of Geometric Computing. Springer, Heidelberg (2005). https://doi.org/10.1007/3-540-28247-5_15
9. Förstner, W., Wrobel, B.P.: Photogrammetric Computer Vision. Springer, Heidelberg (2016). https://doi.org/10.1007/978-3-319-11550-4
10. Frahm, J.-M., et al.: Building Rome on a cloudless day. In: Daniilidis, K., Maragos, P., Paragios, N. (eds.) ECCV 2010. LNCS, vol. 6314, pp. 368–381. Springer, Heidelberg (2010). https://doi.org/10.1007/978-3-642-15561-1_27
11. Guennebaud, G., et al.: Eigen v3.3 (2010). http://eigen.tuxfamily.org
12. Hager, W.W.: Updating the inverse of a matrix. SIAM Rev. **31**(2), 221–239 (1989)
13. Hartley, R., Zisserman, A.: Multiple View Geometry in Computer Vision. Cambridge University Press, Cambridge (2003)
14. Heinly, J., Schönberger, J.L., Dunn, E., Frahm, J.M.: Reconstructing the world* in six days *(as captured by the yahoo 100 million image dataset). In: Computer Vision and Pattern Recognition (CVPR) (2015)
15. Ila, V., Polok, L., Solony, M., Istenic, K.: Fast incremental bundle adjustment with covariance recovery. In: International Conference on 3D Vision (3DV), October 2017
16. Ila, V., Polok, L., Solony, M., Svoboda, P.: Slam++-a highly efficient and temporally scalable incremental slam framework. Int. J. Robot. Res. **36**(2), 210–230 (2017)
17. Kaess, M., Dellaert, F.: Covariance recovery from a square root information matrix for data association. Robot. Auton. Syst. **57**(12), 1198–1210 (2009)
18. Kanatani, K.I., Morris, D.D.: Gauges and gauge transformations for uncertainty description of geometric structure with indeterminacy. IEEE Trans. Inf. Theory **47**(5), 2017–2028 (2001)
19. Lhuillier, M., Perriollat, M.: Uncertainty ellipsoids calculations for complex 3D reconstructions. In: Proceedings 2006 IEEE International Conference on Robotics and Automation, ICRA 2006, pp. 3062–3069. IEEE (2006)
20. Li, Y., Snavely, N., Huttenlocher, D.P.: Location recognition using prioritized feature matching. In: Daniilidis, K., Maragos, P., Paragios, N. (eds.) ECCV 2010. LNCS, vol. 6312, pp. 791–804. Springer, Heidelberg (2010). https://doi.org/10.1007/978-3-642-15552-9_57

21. Maurer, M., Rumpler, M., Wendel, A., Hoppe, C., Irschara, A., Bischof, H.: Georeferenced 3D reconstruction: fusing public geographic data and aerial imagery. In: 2012 IEEE International Conference on Robotics and Automation (ICRA), pp. 3557–3558. IEEE (2012)
22. Morris, D.D.: Gauge freedoms and uncertainty modeling for 3D computer vision. Ph.D. thesis. Citeseer (2001)
23. Moulon, P., et al.: Openmvg. an open multiple view geometry library. https://github.com/openMVG/openMVG
24. Nashed, M.Z.: Generalized Inverses and Applications: Proceedings of an Advanced Seminar Sponsored by the Mathematics Research Center. The University of Wisconsin Madison, 8–10 October 1973, No. 32. Elsevier (2014)
25. Polic, M.: 3D scene analysis. http://cmp.felk.cvut.cz/~policmic
26. Polic, M., Pajdla, T.: Camera uncertainty computation in large 3D reconstruction. In: International Conference on 3D Vision (2017)
27. Polic, M., Pajdla, T.: Uncertainty computation in large 3D reconstruction. In: Sharma, P., Bianchi, F.M. (eds.) SCIA 2017. LNCS, vol. 10269, pp. 110–121. Springer, Cham (2017). https://doi.org/10.1007/978-3-319-59126-1_10
28. Polok, L., Ila, V., Smrz, P.: 3D reconstruction quality analysis and its acceleration on GPU clusters. In: 2016 24th European Signal Processing Conference (EUSIPCO), pp. 1108–1112, August 2016. https://doi.org/10.1109/EUSIPCO.2016.7760420
29. Rao, C.R., Statistiker, M.: Linear Statistical Inference and its Applications, vol. 2. Wiley, New York (1973)
30. Schönberger, J.L., Frahm, J.M.: Structure-from-motion revisited. In: IEEE Conference on Computer Vision and Pattern Recognition (CVPR) (2016)
31. Snavely, N., Seitz, S.M., Szeliski, R.: Photo tourism: exploring photo collections in 3D. ACM Trans. Graph. (TOG) **25**, 835–846 (2006)
32. Sweeney, C.: Theia multiview geometry library: Tutorial & reference. http://theia-sfm.org
33. Tian, Y.: The moore-penrose inverses of m × n block matrices and their applications. Linear Algebr. Appl. **283**(1), 35–60 (1998)
34. Zhang, F.: The Schur Complement and Its Applications. Springer, New York (2005). https://doi.org/10.1007/b105056

ECO: Efficient Convolutional Network for Online Video Understanding

Mohammadreza Zolfaghari$^{(\boxtimes)}$ (iD), Kamaljeet Singh, and Thomas Brox

University of Freiburg, Freiburg im Breisgau, Germany
{zolfagha,singhk,brox}@cs.uni-freiburg.de

Abstract. The state of the art in video understanding suffers from two problems: (1) The major part of reasoning is performed locally in the video, therefore, it misses important relationships within actions that span several seconds. (2) While there are local methods with fast per-frame processing, the processing of the whole video is not efficient and hampers fast video retrieval or online classification of long-term activities. In this paper, we introduce a network architecture (https://github.com/mzolfaghari/ECO-efficient-video-understanding) that takes long-term content into account and enables fast per-video processing at the same time. The architecture is based on merging long-term content already in the network rather than in a post-hoc fusion. Together with a sampling strategy, which exploits that neighboring frames are largely redundant, this yields high-quality action classification and video captioning at up to 230 videos per second, where each video can consist of a few hundred frames. The approach achieves competitive performance across all datasets while being 10× to 80× faster than state-of-the-art methods.

Keywords: Online video understanding · Real-time
Action recognition · Video captioning

1 Introduction

Video understanding and, specifically, action classification have benefited a lot from deep learning and the larger datasets that have been created in recent years. The new datasets, such as Kinetics [20], ActivityNet [13], and SomethingSomething [10] have contributed more diversity and realism to the field. Deep learning provides powerful classifiers at interactive frame rates, enabling applications like real-time action detection [30].

While action detection, which quickly decides on the present action within a short time window, is fast enough to run in real-time, activity understanding, which is concerned with longer-term activities that can span several seconds,

Electronic supplementary material The online version of this chapter (https://doi.org/10.1007/978-3-030-01216-8_43) contains supplementary material, which is available to authorized users.

© Springer Nature Switzerland AG 2018
V. Ferrari et al. (Eds.): ECCV 2018, LNCS 11206, pp. 713–730, 2018.
https://doi.org/10.1007/978-3-030-01216-8_43

requires the integration of the long-term context to achieve full accuracy. Several 3D CNN architectures have been proposed to capture temporal relations between frames, but they are computationally expensive and, thus, can cover only comparatively small windows rather than the entire video. Existing methods typically use some post-hoc integration of window-based scores, which is suboptimal for exploiting the temporal relationships between the windows.

In this paper, we introduce a straightforward, end-to-end trainable architecture that exploits two important principles to avoid the above-mentioned dilemma. Firstly, a good initial classification of an action can already be obtained from just a single frame. The temporal neighborhood of this frame comprises mostly redundant information and is almost useless for improving the belief about the present action[1]. Therefore, we process only a single frame of a temporal neighborhood efficiently with a 2D convolutional architecture in order to capture appearance features of such frame. Secondly, to capture the contextual relationships between distant frames, a simple aggregation of scores is insufficient. Therefore, we feed the feature representations of distant frames into a 3D network that learns the temporal context between these frames and so can improve significantly over the belief obtained from a single frame – especially for complex long-term activities. This principle is much related to the so-called early or late fusion used for combining the RGB stream and the optical flow stream in two-stream architectures [8]. However, this principle has been mostly ignored so far for aggregation over time and is not part of the state-of-the-art approaches.

Consequent implementation of these two principles together leads to a high classification accuracy without bells and whistles. The long temporal context of complex actions can be fully captured, whereas the fact that the method only looks at a very small fraction of all frames in the video leads to extremely fast processing of entire videos. This is very beneficial especially in video retrieval applications.

Additionally, this approach opens the possibility for online video understanding. In this paper, we also present a way to use our architecture in an online setting, where we provide a fast first guess on the action and refine it using the longer term context as a more complex activity establishes. In contrast to online action detection, which has been enabled recently [30], the approach provides not only fast reaction times, but also takes the longer term context into account.

We conducted experiments on various video understanding problems including action recognition and video captioning. Although we just use RGB images as input, we obtain on-par or favorable performance compared to state-of-the-art approaches on most datasets. The runtime-accuracy trade-off is superior on all datasets.

---

[1] An exception is the use of two frames for capturing motion, which could be achieved by optionally feeding optical flow together with the RGB image. In this paper, we only provide RGB images, but an extension with optical flow, e.g., a fast variant of FlowNet [16] would be straightforward.

2   Related Work

Video Classification with Deep Learning. Most recent works on video classification are based on deep learning [6,19,29,34,48]. To explore the temporal context of a video, 3D convolutional networks are on obvious option. Tran et al. [33] introduced a 3D architecture with 3D kernels to learn spatio-temporal features from a sequence of frames. In a later work, they studied the use of a Resnet architecture with 3D convolutions and showed the improvements over their earlier c3d architecture [34]. An alternative way to model the temporal relation between frames is by using recurrent networks [6,24,25]. Donahue et al. [6] employed a LSTM to integrate features from a CNN over time. However, the performance of recurrent networks on action recognition currently lags behind that of recent CNN-based methods, which may indicate that they do not sufficiently model long-term dynamics [24,25]. Recently, several works utilized 3D architectures for action recognition [5,35,39,48]. These approaches model the short-term temporal context of the input video based on a sliding window. At inference time, these methods must compute the average score over multiple windows, which is quite time consuming. For example, ARTNet [39] requires on average 250 samples to classify one video.

All these approaches do not sufficiently use the comprehensive information from the entire video during training and inference. Partial observation not only causes confusion in action prediction, but also requires an extra post-processing step to fuse scores. Extra feature/score aggregation reduces the speed of video processing and disables the method to work in a real-time setting.

Long-Term Representation Learning. To cope with the problem of partial observation, some methods increased the temporal resolution of the sliding window [4,36]. However, expanding the temporal length of the input has two major drawbacks. (1) It is computationally expensive, and (2) still fails to cover the visual information of the entire video, especially for longer videos.

Some works proposed encoding methods [26,28,42] to learn a video representation from samples. In these approaches, features are usually calculated for each frame independently and are aggregated across time to make a video-level representation. This ignores the relationship between the frames.

To capture long-term information, recent works [2,3,7,40] employed a sparse and global temporal sampling method to choose frames from the entire video during training. In the TSN model [40], as in the aggregation methods above, frames are processed independently at inference time and their scores are aggregated only in the end. Consequently, the performance in their experiments stays the same when they change the number of samples, which indicates that their model does not really benefit from the long-range temporal information.

Our work is different from these previous approaches in three main aspects: (1) Similar to TSN, we sample a fixed number of frames from the entire video to cover long-range temporal structure for understanding of video. In this way, the sampled frames span the entire video independent of the length of the video. (2) In contrast to TSN, we use a 3D-network to learn the relationship between the frames throughout the video. The network is trained end-to-end to learn this relationship. (3) The network directly provides video-level scores without post-hoc feature aggregation. Therefore, it can be run in online mode and in real-time even on small computing devices.

Video Captioning. Video captioning is a widely studied problem in computer vision [9,14,43,45]. Most approaches use a CNN pre-trained on image classification or action recognition to generate features [9,43,45]. These methods, like the video understanding methods described above, utilize a frame-based feature aggregation (e.g. Resnet or TSN) or a sliding window over the whole video (e.g. C3D) to generate video-level features. The features are then passed to a recurrent neural network (e.g. LSTM) to generate the video captions via a learned language model. The extracted visual features should represent both the temporal structure of the video and the static semantics of the scene. However, most approaches suffer from the problem that the temporal context is not properly extracted. With the network model in this work, we address this problem, and can consequently improve video captioning results.

Real-Time and Online Video Understanding. Deep learning accelerated image classification, but video classification remains challenging in terms of speed. A few works dealt with real-time video understanding [18,30,31,44]. EMV [44] introduced an approach for fast calculation of motion vectors. Despite this improvement, video processing is still slow. Kantorov [18] introduced a fast dense trajectory method. The other works used frame-based hand-crafted features for online action recognition [15,22]. Both accuracy and speed of feature extraction in these methods are far from that of deep learning methods. Soomro et al. [31] proposed an online action localization approach. Their model utilizes an expensive segmentation method which, therefore, cannot work in real-time. More recently, Singh et al. [30] proposed an online detection approach based on frame-level detections at 40 fps. We compare to the last two approaches in Sect. 5.

3   Long-Term Spatio-Temporal Architecture

The network architecture is shown in Fig. 1. A whole video with a variable number of frames is provided as input to the network. The video is split into N subsections S_i, $i = 1, ..., N$ of equal size, and in each subsection, exactly one frame is sampled randomly. Each of these frames is processed by a single 2D convolutional network (weight sharing), which yields a feature representation encoding the frame's appearance. By jointly processing frames from time segments that cover the whole video, we make sure that we capture the most relevant parts of an action over time and the relationship among these parts.

Randomly sampling the position of the frame is advantageous over always using the same position, because it leads to more diversity during training and makes the network adapt to variations in the instantiation of an action. Note that this kind of processing exploits all frames of the video during training to

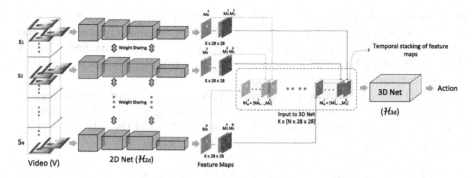

Fig. 1. Architecture overview of ECO Lite. Each video is split into N subsections of equal size. From each subsection a single frame is randomly sampled. The samples are processed by a regular 2D convolutional network to yield a representation for each sampled frame. These representations are stacked and fed into a 3D convolutional network, which classifies the action, taking into account the temporal relationship.

Fig. 2. (A) ECO Lite architecture as shown in more detail in Fig. 1. (B) Full ECO architecture with a parallel 2D and 3D stream.

model the variation. At the same time, the network must only process N frames at runtime, which makes the approach very fast. We also considered more clever partitioning strategies that take the content of the subsections into account. However, this comes with the drawback that each frame of the video must be processed at runtime to obtain the partitioning, and the actual improvement by such smarter partitioning is limited, since most of the variation is already captured by the random sampling during training.

Up to this point, the different frames in the video are processed independently. In order to learn how actions are made up of the different appearances of the scene over time, we stack the representations of all frames and feed them into a 3D convolutional network. This network yields the final action class label.

The architecture is very straightforward, and it is obvious that it can be trained efficiently end-to-end directly on the action class label and on large datasets. It is also an architecture that can be easily adapted to other video understanding tasks, as we show later in the video captioning Sect. 5.4.

3.1 ECO Lite and ECO Full

The 3D architecture in ECO Lite is optimized for learning relationships between the frames, but it tends to waste capacity in case of simple short-term actions that can be recognized just from the static image content. Therefore, we suggest an extension of the architecture by using a 2D network in parallel; see Fig. 2(B). For the simple actions, this 2D network architecture can simplify processing and ensure that the static image features receive the necessary importance, whereas the 3D network architecture takes care of the more complex actions that depend on the relationship between frames.

The 2D network receives feature maps of all samples and produces N feature representations. Afterwards, we apply average pooling to get a feature vector that is a representative for static scene semantics. We call the full architecture ECO and the simpler architecture in Fig. 2(A) ECO Lite.

3.2 Network Details

2D-Net: For the 2D network ($\mathcal{H}_{2D}$) that analyzes the single frames, we use the first part of the BN-Inception architecture (until inception-3c layer) [17]. Details are given in the supplemental material. It has 2D filters and pooling kernels with batch normalization. We chose this architecture due to its efficiency. The output of $\mathcal{H}_{2D}$ for each single frame consist of 96 feature maps with size of 28×28.

3D-Net: For the 3D network $\mathcal{H}_{3D}$ we adopt several layers of 3D-Resnet18 [34], which is an efficient architecture used in many video classification works [34, 39]. Details on the architecture are provided in the supplemental material. The output of $\mathcal{H}_{3D}$ is a one-hot vector for the different class labels.

2D-Net$_S$: In the ECO full design, we use 2D-Net_s in parallel with 3D-net to directly providing static visual semantics of video. For this network, we use the BN-Inception architecture from inception-4a layer until last pooling layer [17]. The last pooling layer will produce 1024 dimensional feature vector for each frame. We apply average pooling to generate video-level feature and then concatenate with features obtained from 3D-net.

3.3 Training Details

We train our networks using mini-batch SGD with Nesterov momentum and utilize dropout in each fully connected layer. We split each video into N segments and randomly select one frame from each segment. This sampling provides robustness to variations and enables the network to fully exploit all frames. In addition, we apply the data augmentation techniques introduced in [41]: we resize the input frames to 240×320 and employ fixed-corner cropping and scale jittering with horizontal flipping (temporal jittering provided by sampling). Afterwards, we run per-pixel mean subtraction and resize the cropped regions to 224×224.

The initial learning rate is 0.001 and decreases by a factor of 10 when validation error saturates for 4 epochs. We train the network with a momentum of 0.9, a weight decay of 0.0005, and mini-batches of size 32.

We initialize the weights of the 2D-Net weights with the BN-Inception architecture [17] pre-trained on Kinetics, as provided by [41]. In the same way, we use

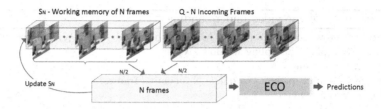

Fig. 3. Scheme of our sampling strategy for online video understanding. Half of the frames are sampled uniformly from the working memory in the previous time step, the other half from the queue (Q) of incoming frames.

the pre-trained model of 3D-Resnet-18, as provided by [39] for initializing the weights of our 3D-Net. Afterwards, we train ECO and ECO Lite on the Kinetics dataset for 10 epochs.

For other datasets, we finetune the above ECO/ECO Lite models on the new datasets. Due to the complexity of the Something-Something dataset, we finetune the network for 25 epochs reducing the learning rate every 10 epochs by a factor of 10. For the rest, we finetune for 4k iterations and the learning rate drops by a factor of 10 as soons as the validation loss saturates. The whole training process on UCF101 and HMDB51 takes around 3 h on one Tesla P100 GPU for the ECO architecture. We adjusted the dropout rate and the number of iterations based on the dataset size.

3.4 Test Time Inference

Most state-of-the-art methods run some post-processing on the network result. For instance, TSN and ARTNet [39,41], collect 25 independent frames/volumes per video, and for each frame/volume sample 10 regions by corner and center cropping, and their horizontal flipping. The final prediction is obtained by averaging the scores of all 250 samples. This kind of inference at test time is computationally expensive and thus unsuitable for real-time setting.

In contrast, our network produces action labels for the whole video directly without any additional aggregation. We sample N frames from the video, apply only center cropping then feed them directly to the network, which provides the prediction for the whole video with a single pass.

4 Online Video Understanding

Most works on video understanding process in batch mode, i.e., they assume that the whole video is available when processing starts. However, in several application scenarios, the video will be provided as a stream and the current belief is supposed to be available at any time. Such online processing is possible with a sliding window approach, yet this comes with restrictions regarding the size of the window, i.e., long-term context is missing, or with a very long delay.

Algorithm 1. Online video understanding

Input : Live video stream (V), ECO pretrained model (ECO_{NF}), Number of
            Samples =Sampling window (N)
Output: Predictions
Initialize an empty queue Q to queue N incoming frames;
Initialize working memory S_N ;
Initialize average predictions P_A;
while *new frames available from* V **do**
| Add frame f_i from V to queue Q;
| **if** $i \% N$ **then**
| | S_N := Sample 50% frames Q and 50% from S_N ;
| | Empty queue Q;
| | Feed S_N to model ECO_{NF} to get output probabilities P;
| | P_A := Average P and P_A ;
| | Output average predictions P_A;
| **end**
end

In this section, we show how ECO can be adapted to run very efficiently in online mode, too. The modification only affects the sampling part and keeps the network architecture unchanged. To this end, we partition the incoming video content into segments of N frames, where N is also the number of frames that go into the network. We use a working memory S_N, which always comprises the N samples that are fed to the network together with a time stamp. When a video starts, i.e., only N frames are available, all N frames are sampled densely and are stored in the working memory S_N. With each new time segment, N additional frames come in, and we replace half of the samples in S_N by samples from this time segment and update the prediction of the network; see Fig. 3. When we replace samples from S_N, we uniformly replace samples from previous time segments. This ensures that changes can be anticipated in real time, while the temporal context is taken into account and slowly fades out via the working memory. Details on the update of S_N are shown in Algorithm 1.

The online approach with ECO runs at 675 fps (and at 970 fps with ECO Lite) on a Tesla P100 GPU. In addition, the model is memory efficient by just keeping exactly N frames. This enables the implementation also on much smaller hardware, such as mobile devices. The video in the supplemental material shows the recorded performance of the online version of ECO in real-time.

5 Experiments

We evaluate our approach on different video understanding problems to show the generalization ability of approach. We evaluated the network architecture on the most common action classification datasets in order to compare its performance against the state-of-the-art approaches. This includes the older but still very popular datasets UCF101 [32] and HMDB51 [21], but also the more recent

Table 1. Comparison to the state-of-the-art on UCF101 and HMDB51 datasets (over all three splits), using just RGB modality.

Method	Pre-training	Dataset	
		UCF101 (%)	HMDB51 (%)
I3D [4]	ImageNet	84.5	49.8
TSN [41]	ImageNet	86.4	53.7
DTPP [47]	ImageNet	89.7	61.1
Res3D [34]	Sports-1M	85.8	54.9
TSN [41]	ImageNet + Kinetics	91.1	-
I3D [4]	ImageNet + Kinetics	**95.6**	**74.8**
ResNeXt-101 [12]	Kinetics	94.5	70.2
ARTNet [39]	Kinetics	93.5	67.6
T3D [5]	Kinetics	91.7	61.1
ECO_{En}	Kinetics	94.8	72.4

Table 2. Comparing performance of ECO with state-of-the-art methods on the Kinetics dataset.

Methods	Val (%)		Test (%)
	Top-1	Avg	Avg
ResNeXt-101 [12]	65.1	75.4	**78.4**
Res3D [34]	65.6	75.7	74.4
I3D-RGB [4]	–	–	78.2
ARTNet [39]	69.2	78.7	77.3
T3D [5]	62.2	–	71.5
ECO_{En}	**70.0**	**79.7**	76.3

Table 3. Comparison with state-of-the-arts on something-something dataset. Last row shows the results using both Flow and RGB.

Methods	Val (%)	Test (%)
I3D by [10]	-	27.23
M-TRN [46]	34.44	33.60
ECO_{En} Lite	**46.4**	**42.3**
ECO_{En} Lite $\begin{cases} RGB \\ Flow \end{cases}$	49.5	43.9

datasets Kinetics [20] and Something-Something [10]. Moreover, we applied the architecture to video captioning and tested it on the widely used Youtube2text dataset [11]. For all of these datasets, we use the standard evaluation protocol provided by the authors.

The comparison is restricted to approaches that take the raw RGB videos as input without further pre-processing, for instance, by providing optical flow or human pose. The term ECO_{NF} describes a network that gets N sampled frames as input. The term ECO_{En} refers to average scores obtained from an ensemble of networks with {16, 20, 24, 32} number of frames.

5.1   Benchmark Comparison on Action Classification

The results obtained with ECO on the different datasets are shown in Tables 1, 2, and 3 and compare them to the state of the art. For UCF-101, HMDB-51, and Kinetics, ECO outperforms all existing methods except I3D, which uses a much heavier network. On Something-Something, it outperforms the other methods with a large margin. This shows the strong performance of the comparatively simple and small ECO architecture.

Table 4. Runtime comparison with state-of-the-art approaches using Tesla P100 GPU on UCF101 and HMDB51 datasets (over all splits). For other approaches, we just consider one crop per sample to calculate the runtime. We reported runtime without considering I/O.

Method	Inference speed (VPS)	UCF101 (%)	HMDB51 (%)
Res3D [34]	<2	85.8	54.9
TSN [41]	21	87.7	51
EMV [44]	15.6	86.4	-
I3D [4]	0.9	95.6	74.8
ARTNet [39]	2.9	93.5	67.6
$ECO_{Lite-4F}$	**237.3**	87.4	58.1
ECO_{4F}	**163.4**	90.3	61.7
ECO_{12F}	**52.6**	92.4	68.3
ECO_{20F}	**32.9**	93.0	69.0
ECO_{24F}	**28.2**	93.6	68.4

Table 5. Accuracy and runtime of ECO and ECO Lite for different numbers of sampled frames. The reported runtime is without considering I/O.

Model	Sampled frames	Speed (VPS)		Accuracy (%)			
		Titan X	Tesla P100	UCF101	HMDB51	Kinetics	Someth
ECO	4	99.2	163.4	90.3	61.7	66.2	–
	8	49.5	81.5	91.7	65.6	67.8	39.6
	16	24.5	41.7	92.8	68.5	69.0	41.4
	32	12.3	20.8	93.3	68.7	67.8	–
ECO Lite	4	142.9	237.3	87.4	58.1	57.9	–
	8	71.1	115.9	90.2	63.3	–	38.7
	16	35.3	61.0	91.6	68.2	64.4	42.2
	32	18.2	30.2	93.1	68.3	–	41.3

5.2   Accuracy-Runtime Comparison

The advantages of the ECO architectures becomes even more prominent as we look at the accuracy-runtime trade-off shown in Table 4 and Fig. 4. The ECO architectures yield the same accuracy as other approaches at much faster rates.

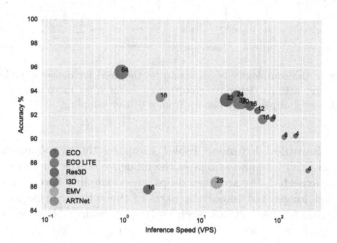

Fig. 4. Accuracy-runtime trade-off on UCF101 for various versions of ECO and other state-of-the-art approaches. ECO is much closer to the top right corner.

Fig. 5. Examples from the Something-Something dataset. In this dataset, the temporal context plays an even bigger role than on other datasets, since the same action is done with different objects, i.e., the appearance of the object or background gives almost no cues about the action.

Previous works typically measure the speed of an approach in frames per second (fps). Our model with ECO runs at 675 fps (and at 970 fps with ECO Lite) on a Tesla P100 GPU. However, this does not reflect the time needed to process a whole video. This becomes relevant for methods like TSN and ours, which do not look at every frame of the video, and motivates us to report *videos per second (vps)* to compare the speed of video understanding methods.

ECO can process videos at least an order of magnitude faster than the other approaches, making it an excellent architecture for video retrieval applications.

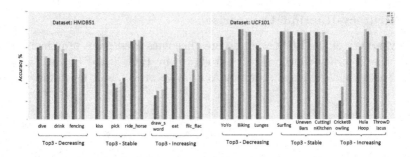

Fig. 6. Effect of the complexity of an action on the need for denser sampling. While simple short-term actions (leftmost group) even suffer from more samples, complex actions (rightmost group) clearly benefit from a denser sampling.

Number of Sampled Frames. Table 5 compares the two architecture variants ECO and ECO Lite and evaluates the influence on the number of sampled frames N. As expected, the accuracy drops when sampling fewer frames, as the subsections get longer and important parts of the action can be missed. This is especially true for fast actions, such as "throw discus". However, even with just 4 samples the accuracy of ECO is still much better than most approaches in literature, since ECO takes into account the relationship between these 4 instants in the video, even if they are far apart. Figure 6 even shows that for simple short-term actions, the performance decreases when using more samples. This is surprising on first glance, but could be explained by the better use of the network's capacity for simple actions when there are fewer channels being fed to the 3D network.

ECO Vs. ECO Lite. The full ECO architecture yields slightly better results than the plain ECO Lite architecture, but is also a little slower. The differences in accuracy and runtime between the two architectures can usually be compensated by using more or fewer samples. On the Something-Something dataset, where the temporal context plays a much bigger role than on other datasets (see Fig. 5), ECO Lite performs equally well as the full ECO architecture even with the same number of input samples, since the raw processing of single image cues has little relevance on this dataset.

5.3   Early Action Recognition in Online Mode

Figure 7 evaluates our approach in online mode and shows how many frames the method needs to achieve its full accuracy. We ran this experiment on the J-HMDB dataset due to the availability of results from other online methods on this dataset. Compared to these existing methods, ECO reaches a good accuracy faster and also saturates at a higher absolute accuracy.

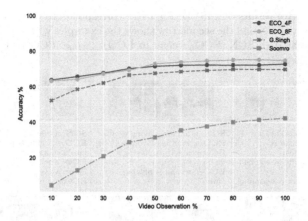

Fig. 7. Early action classification results of ECO in comparison to existing online methods [30,31] on the J-HMDB dataset. The online version of ECO yields a high accuracy already after seeing a short part of the video. Singh et al. [30] uses both RGB and optical flow.

Table 6. Captioning results on Youtube2Text (MSVD) dataset.

Methods	Metrics			
	B-3	B-4	METEOR	CIDEr
S2VT [38]	-	-	0.292	-
GRU-RCN [1]	-	0.479	0.311	0.678
h-RNN [43]	-	0.499	0.326	0.658
TDDF [45]	-	0.458	0.333	0.730
AF [14]	-	0.524	0.320	0.688
SCN-c3d [9]	0.587	0.482	0.330	0.692
SCN-resnet [9]	0.602	0.506	0.336	0.755
SCN-ensemble of 5 [9]	–	0.511	0.335	0.777
$ECO_{Lite-16F}$	0.601	0.504	0.339	0.833
ECO_{32F}	0.616	0.521	0.345	0.857
$ECO_{32F} + resnet$	**0.626**	**0.535**	**0.350**	**0.858**

5.4   Video Captioning

To show the wide applicability of the ECO architecture, we also combine it with a video captioning network. To this end, we use ECO pre-trained on Kinetics to analyze the video content and train the state-of-the-art Semantic Compositional Network [9] for captioning. We evaluated on the Youtube2Text (MSVD) dataset [11], which consists of 1,970 video clips with an average duration of 9 s and covers various types of videos, such as sports, landscapes, animals, cooking, and human activities. The dataset contains 80,839 sentences and each video is annotated with around 40 sentences.

Table 7. Qualitative results on MSVD. First row corresponds to the examples where ECO improved over SCN and the second row shows the examples where ECO decreased the quality compared to SCN. ECO_L refers to $ECO_{Lite-16F}$, ECO to ECO_{32F}, and ECO_R to $ECO_{32F+resnet}$.

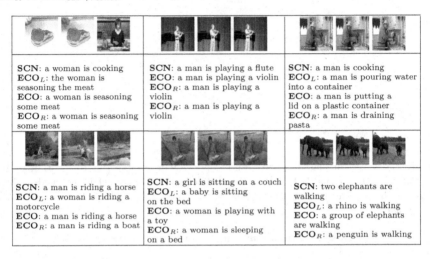

SCN: a woman is cooking ECO_L: the woman is seasoning the meat **ECO**: a woman is seasoning some meat ECO_R: a woman is seasoning some meat	**SCN**: a man is playing a flute **ECO**: a man is playing a violin ECO_R: a man is playing a violin ECO_R: a man is playing a violin	**SCN**: a man is cooking ECO_L: a man is pouring water into a container **ECO**: a man is putting a lid on a plastic container ECO_R: a man is draining pasta
SCN: a man is riding a horse ECO_L: a woman is riding a motorcycle **ECO**: a man is riding a horse ECO_R: a man is riding a boat	**SCN**: a girl is sitting on a couch ECO_L: a baby is sitting on the bed **ECO**: a woman is playing with a toy ECO_R: a woman is sleeping on a bed	**SCN**: two elephants are walking ECO_L: a rhino is walking **ECO**: a group of elephants are walking ECO_R: a penguin is walking

Table 6 shows that ECO compares favorably to previous approaches across all popular evaluation metrics (BLEU [27], METEOR [23], CIDEr [37]). Even ECO Lite is already on-par with a ResNet architecture pre-trained on ImageNet. Concatenating the features from ECO with those of ResNet improves results further. Qualitative examples that correspond to the improved numbers are shown in Table 7.

6   Conclusions

In this paper, we have presented a simple and very efficient network architecture that looks only at a small subset of frames from a video and learns to exploit the temporal context between these frames. This principle can be used in various video understanding tasks. We demonstrate excellent results on action classification, online action classification, and video captioning. The computational load and the memory footprint makes an implementation on mobile devices a viable future option. The approaches runs 10× to 80× faster than state-of-the-art methods.

Acknowledgements. We thank Facebook for providing us a GPU server with Tesla P100 processors for this research work.

References

1. Ballas, N., Yao, L., Pal, C., Courville, A.C.: Delving deeper into convolutional networks for learning video representations. In: ICLR (2016)
2. Bilen, H., Fernando, B., Gavves, E., Vedaldi, A.: Action recognition with dynamic image networks. IEEE Trans. Pattern Anal. Mach. Intell., 1 (2017). https://doi.org/10.1109/TPAMI.2017.2769085
3. Bilen, H., Fernando, B., Gavves, E., Vedaldi, A., Gould, S.: Dynamic image networks for action recognition. In: 2016 IEEE Conference on Computer Vision and Pattern Recognition (CVPR), pp. 3034–3042, June 2016. https://doi.org/10.1109/CVPR.2016.331
4. Carreira, J., Zisserman, A.: Quo vadis, action recognition? A new model and the kinetics dataset. CoRR abs/1705.07750 (2017). http://arxiv.org/abs/1705.07750
5. Diba, A., et al.: Temporal 3D ConvNets: new architecture and transfer learning for video classification. CoRR abs/1711.08200 (2017). http://arxiv.org/abs/1711.08200
6. Donahue, J., et al.: Long-term recurrent convolutional networks for visual recognition and description. In: CVPR (2015)
7. Feichtenhofer, C., Pinz, A., Wildes, R.P.: Spatiotemporal multiplier networks for video action recognition. In: 2017 IEEE Conference on Computer Vision and Pattern Recognition (CVPR), pp. 7445–7454, July 2017. https://doi.org/10.1109/CVPR.2017.787
8. Feichtenhofer, C., Pinz, A., Zisserman, A.: Convolutional two-stream network fusion for video action recognition. CoRR abs/1604.06573 (2016). http://arxiv.org/abs/1604.06573
9. Gan, Z., et al.: Semantic compositional networks for visual captioning. In: CVPR (2017)
10. Goyal, R., et al.: The "something something" video database for learning and evaluating visual common sense. CoRR abs/1706.04261 (2017). http://arxiv.org/abs/1706.04261
11. Guadarrama, S., et al.: YouTube2Text: recognizing and describing arbitrary activities using semantic hierarchies and zero-shot recognition. In: 2013 IEEE International Conference on Computer Vision, pp. 2712–2719, December 2013. https://doi.org/10.1109/ICCV.2013.337
12. Hara, K., Kataoka, H., Satoh, Y.: Can spatiotemporal 3D CNNs retrace the history of 2D CNNs and ImageNet? CoRR abs/1711.09577 (2017). http://arxiv.org/abs/1711.09577
13. Heilbron, F.C., Escorcia, V., Ghanem, B., Niebles, J.C.: ActivityNet: a large-scale video benchmark for human activity understanding. In: CVPR, pp. 961–970. IEEE Computer Society (2015). http://dblp.uni-trier.de/db/conf/cvpr/cvpr2015.html#HeilbronEGN15
14. Hori, C., et al.: Attention-based multimodal fusion for video description. In: 2017 IEEE International Conference on Computer Vision (ICCV), pp. 4203–4212, October 2017. https://doi.org/10.1109/ICCV.2017.450
15. Hu, B., Yuan, J., Wu, Y.: Discriminative action states discovery for online action recognition. IEEE Signal Process. Lett. 23(10), 1374–1378 (2016). https://doi.org/10.1109/LSP.2016.2598878
16. Ilg, E., Mayer, N., Saikia, T., Keuper, M., Dosovitskiy, A., Brox, T.: FlowNet 2.0: evolution of optical flow estimation with deep networks. In: IEEE Conference on Computer Vision and Pattern Recognition (CVPR), July 2017. http://lmb.informatik.uni-freiburg.de//Publications/2017/IMKDB17

17. Ioffe, S., Szegedy, C.: Batch normalization: accelerating deep network training by reducing internal covariate shift. In: Proceedings of the 32nd International Conference on International Conference on Machine Learning - Volume 37, ICML 2015, pp. 448–456. JMLR.org (2015). http://dl.acm.org/citation.cfm?id=3045118. 3045167
18. Kantorov, V., Laptev, I.: Efficient feature extraction, encoding, and classification for action recognition. In: 2014 IEEE Conference on Computer Vision and Pattern Recognition, pp. 2593–2600, June 2014. https://doi.org/10.1109/CVPR.2014.332
19. Karpathy, A., Toderici, G., Shetty, S., Leung, T., Sukthankar, R., Fei-Fei, L.: Large-scale video classification with convolutional neural networks. In: Proceedings of the 2014 IEEE Conference on Computer Vision and Pattern Recognition, CVPR 2014, pp. 1725–1732. IEEE Computer Society, Washington (2014). https://doi.org/10.1109/CVPR.2014.223
20. Kay, W., et al.: The kinetics human action video dataset. CoRR abs/1705.06950 (2017). http://arxiv.org/abs/1705.06950
21. Kuehne, H., Jhuang, H., Garrote, E., Poggio, T., Serre, T.: HMDB: a large video database for human motion recognition. In: Proceedings of the International Conference on Computer Vision (ICCV) (2011)
22. Kviatkovsky, I., Rivlin, E., Shimshoni, I.: Online action recognition using covariance of shape and motion. Comput. Vis. Image Underst. 129(C), 15–26 (2014). https://doi.org/10.1016/j.cviu.2014.08.001
23. Lavie, A., Agarwal, A.: METEOR: An automatic metric for MT evaluation with high levels of correlation with human judgments. In: Proceedings of the Second Workshop on Statistical Machine Translation, StatMT 2007, pp. 228–231. Association for Computational Linguistics, Stroudsburg (2007). http://dl.acm.org/citation.cfm?id=1626355.1626389
24. Lev, G., Sadeh, G., Klein, B., Wolf, L.: RNN fisher vectors for action recognition and image annotation. In: Leibe, B., Matas, J., Sebe, N., Welling, M. (eds.) ECCV 2016. LNCS, vol. 9910, pp. 833–850. Springer, Cham (2016). https://doi.org/10.1007/978-3-319-46466-4_50
25. Li, Z., Gavrilyuk, K., Gavves, E., Jain, M., Snoek, C.G.: VideoLSTM convolves, attends and flows for action recognition. Comput. Vis. Image Underst. 166(C), 41–50 (2018). https://doi.org/10.1016/j.cviu.2017.10.011
26. Ng, J.Y.H., Hausknecht, M.J., Vijayanarasimhan, S., Vinyals, O., Monga, R., Toderici, G.: Beyond short snippets: deep networks for video classification. In: CVPR, pp. 4694–4702. IEEE Computer Society (2015). http://dblp.uni-trier.de/db/conf/cvpr/cvpr2015.html#NgHVVMT15
27. Papineni, K., Roukos, S., Ward, T., Zhu, W.J.: BLEU: a method for automatic evaluation of machine translation. In: Proceedings of the 40th Annual Meeting on Association for Computational Linguistics, ACL 2002, pp. 311–318. Association for Computational Linguistics, Stroudsburg (2002). https://doi.org/10.3115/1073083. 1073135
28. Qiu, Z., Yao, T., Mei, T.: Deep quantization: encoding convolutional activations with deep generative model. In: CVPR (2017)
29. Simonyan, K., Zisserman, A.: Two-stream convolutional networks for action recognition in videos. In: Proceedings of the 27th International Conference on Neural Information Processing Systems - Volume 1, NIPS 2014, pp. 568–576. MIT Press, Cambridge (2014). http://dl.acm.org/citation.cfm?id=2968826.2968890

30. Singh, G., Saha, S., Sapienza, M., Torr, P.H.S., Cuzzolin, F.: Online real-time multiple spatiotemporal action localisation and prediction. In: IEEE International Conference on Computer Vision, ICCV 2017, Venice, Italy, 22–29 October 2017, pp. 3657–3666 (2017). https://doi.org/10.1109/ICCV.2017.393

31. Soomro, K., Idrees, H., Shah, M.: Predicting the where and what of actors and actions through online action localization. In: The IEEE Conference on Computer Vision and Pattern Recognition (CVPR), June 2016

32. Soomro, K., Zamir, A.R., Shah, M.: UCF101: a dataset of 101 human actions classes from videos in the wild. CoRR abs/1212.0402 (2012). http://arxiv.org/abs/1212.0402

33. Tran, D., Bourdev, L.D., Fergus, R., Torresani, L., Paluri, M.: C3D: generic features for video analysis. CoRR abs/1412.0767 (2014). http://arxiv.org/abs/1412.0767

34. Tran, D., Ray, J., Shou, Z., Chang, S., Paluri, M.: ConvNet architecture search for spatiotemporal feature learning. CoRR abs/1708.05038 (2017). http://arxiv.org/abs/1708.05038

35. Tran, D., Wang, H., Torresani, L., Ray, J., LeCun, Y., Paluri, M.: A closer look at spatiotemporal convolutions for action recognition. CoRR abs/1711.11248 (2017). http://arxiv.org/abs/1711.11248

36. Varol, G., Laptev, I., Schmid, C.: Long-term temporal convolutions for action recognition. CoRR abs/1604.04494 (2016). http://arxiv.org/abs/1604.04494

37. Vedantam, R., Zitnick, C.L., Parikh, D.: CIDEr: consensus-based image description evaluation. In: CVPR, pp. 4566–4575. IEEE Computer Society (2015). http://dblp.uni-trier.de/db/conf/cvpr/cvpr2015.html#VedantamZP15

38. Venugopalan, S., Rohrbach, M., Donahue, J., Mooney, R., Darrell, T., Saenko, K.: Sequence to sequence - video to text. In: Proceedings of the IEEE International Conference on Computer Vision (ICCV) (2015)

39. Wang, L., Li, W., Li, W., Gool, L.V.: Appearance-and-relation networks for video classification. CoRR abs/1711.09125 (2017). http://arxiv.org/abs/1711.09125

40. Wang, L., et al.: Temporal segment networks for action recognition in videos. CoRR abs/1705.02953 (2017). http://arxiv.org/abs/1705.02953

41. Wang, L., et al.: Temporal segment networks: towards good practices for deep action recognition. In: Leibe, B., Matas, J., Sebe, N., Welling, M. (eds.) ECCV 2016. LNCS, vol. 9912, pp. 20–36. Springer, Cham (2016). https://doi.org/10.1007/978-3-319-46484-8_2

42. Xu, Z., Yang, Y., Hauptmann, A.G.: A discriminative CNN video representation for event detection. CoRR abs/1411.4006 (2014). http://arxiv.org/abs/1411.4006

43. Yu, H., Wang, J., Huang, Z., Yang, Y., Xu, W.: Video paragraph captioning using hierarchical recurrent neural networks. In: 2016 IEEE Conference on Computer Vision and Pattern Recognition (CVPR), pp. 4584–4593 (2016)

44. Zhang, B., Wang, L., Wang, Z., Qiao, Y., Wang, H.: Real-time action recognition with enhanced motion vector CNNs. CoRR abs/1604.07669 (2016). http://arxiv.org/abs/1604.07669

45. Zhang, X., Gao, K., Zhang, Y., Zhang, D., Li, J., Tian, Q.: Task-driven dynamic fusion: reducing ambiguity in video description. In: 2017 IEEE Conference on Computer Vision and Pattern Recognition (CVPR), pp. 6250–6258, July 2017. https://doi.org/10.1109/CVPR.2017.662

46. Zhou, B., Andonian, A., Torralba, A.: Temporal relational reasoning in videos. CoRR abs/1711.08496 (2017). http://arxiv.org/abs/1711.08496

47. Zhu, J., Zou, W., Zhu, Z., Li, L.: End-to-end video-level representation learning for action recognition. CoRR abs/1711.04161 (2017). http://arxiv.org/abs/1711.04161

48. Zolfaghari, M., Oliveira, G.L., Sedaghat, N., Brox, T.: Chained multi-stream networks exploiting pose, motion, and appearance for action classification and detection. In: IEEE International Conference on Computer Vision (ICCV) (2017). http://lmb.informatik.uni-freiburg.de/Publications/2017/ZOSB17a

Multi-Scale Structure-Aware Network for Human Pose Estimation

Lipeng Ke[1]([✉]), Ming-Ching Chang[2], Honggang Qi[1], and Siwei Lyu[2]

[1] University of Chinese Academy of Sciences, Beijing, China
kelipeng15@mails.ucas.ac.cn, hgqi@ucas.ac.cn
[2] University at Albany, State University of New York, New York City, NY, USA
{mchang2,slyu}@albany.edu

Abstract. We develop a robust multi-scale structure-aware neural network for human pose estimation. This method improves the recent deep conv-deconv hourglass models with four key improvements: (1) *multi-scale supervision* to strengthen contextual feature learning in matching body keypoints by combining feature heatmaps across scales, (2) *multi-scale regression network* at the end to globally optimize the structural matching of the multi-scale features, (3) *structure-aware loss* used in the intermediate supervision and at the regression to improve the matching of keypoints and respective neighbors to infer a higher-order matching configurations, and (4) a *keypoint masking training* scheme that can effectively fine-tune our network to robustly localize occluded keypoints via adjacent matches. Our method can effectively improve state-of-the-art pose estimation methods that suffer from difficulties in scale varieties, occlusions, and complex multi-person scenarios. This multi-scale supervision tightly integrates with the regression network to effectively *(i)* localize keypoints using the ensemble of multi-scale features, and *(ii)* infer global pose configuration by maximizing structural consistencies across multiple keypoints and scales. The keypoint masking training enhances these advantages to focus learning on hard occlusion samples. Our method achieves the leading position in the MPII challenge leaderboard among the state-of-the-art methods.

Keywords: Human pose estimation
Conv-deconv network · Multi-scale supervision

1 Introduction

Human pose estimation refers to the task of recognizing postures by localizing body keypoints (head, shoulders, elbows, wrists, knees, ankles, *etc.*) from images. We focus on the problem of single-person pose estimation from a single RGB image with the input of a rough bounding box of a person, while the pose and the activity of the person can be arbitrary. The task is challenging due to the large variability of human body appearances, lighting conditions, complex background and occlusions, body physique and posture structures of the activities performed

© Springer Nature Switzerland AG 2018
V. Ferrari et al. (Eds.): ECCV 2018, LNCS 11206, pp. 731–746, 2018.
https://doi.org/10.1007/978-3-030-01216-8_44

by the subject. The inference is further sophisticated when the case extends to multi-person scenarios.

Fig. 1. State-of-the-art pose estimation networks face difficulties in diverse activities and complex scenes, which can be organized into three challenges: (top row) large scale varieties of body keypoints in the scenes, (middle row) occluded body parts or keypoints, (bottom row) ambiguities in matching multiple adjacent keypoints in crowded scenes.

Human pose estimation has been studied extensively [15]. Traditional methods rely on hand-craft features [3,5,6,8,20]. With the prosperity of Deep Neural Networks (DNN), Convolutional Neural Networks (CNN) [10,19,22,24,25], in particular the *hourglass* models [17] and their variants [11,26] have demonstrated remarkable performance in human pose estimation. The repeated bottom-up and top-down processing within the hourglass modules can reliably extract posture features across scales and viewing variabilities, and thus effectively localize body keypoints for pose estimation.

Although great progress has been made, state-of-the-art DNN-based pose estimation methods still suffer from several problems (Fig. 1):

(1) **Scale Instability:** Slight perturbation of the input bounding box from the person detector (such as the SSD [14]) can cause abrupt changes in the pose estimation, due to the influence of such dominating scales. Such scale instability causes unreliable pose estimations, and even the latest hourglass methods ([11, 26]) tend to overfit body keypoints in a particular scale (out of all scales in the deconv pyramid), which results in a domination of a single scale. Current practice to handle this scale instability (*e.g.* widely used in the MPII pose estimation challenge [1]), is to repeatedly performing pose estimations in multiple trials of various scales, and output the result with the highest score. This clearly shows the lack of a consistent scale representation in limitations of the existing methods. This will be addressed in this work in Sects. 3.1 and 3.2.

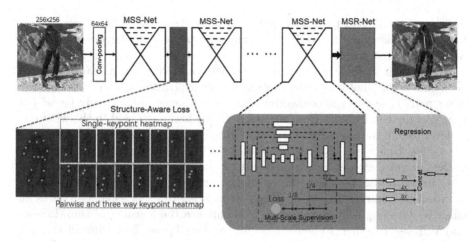

Fig. 2. The proposed network consists of three components: (i) multi-scale supervision network (MSS-net, Sect. 3.1), (ii) multi-scare regression network (MSR-net, Sect. 3.2), and (iii) intermediate supervision using the structure-aware loss (Sect. 3.3). The whole network pipeline is fine-tuned using the keypoint masking training scheme (Sect. 3.4).

(2) **Insufficient Structural Priors:** The second issue is how to effectively incorporate the structure of human body as priors in the deep network for pose estimation. Such priors can provide key information to solve challenges of pose estimation in real-world scenarios with complex multi-person activities and cluttered backgrounds, where body keypoint occlusions and matching ambiguities are the bottlenecks. In these challenge cases, accurate keypoint localization is not the only factor for successful pose estimation, as there will be questions on how best to associate the keypoints (invisible, or multiple visible ones among possibilities) to infer the global pose configuration. Known body structural priors can provide valuable cues to infer the locations of the hidden body parts from the visible ones. We propose to model the skeleton with an *intermediate structural loss* (Sect. 3.3) and through the use of a global regression network at the end (Sect. 3.2). We further develop a keypoint masking scheme to improve the training of our network on challenging cases of severely occluded keypoints (Sect. 3.4).

In this paper, we propose a holistic framework to effectively address the drawbacks in the existing state-of-art hourglass networks. Our method is based on two neural networks: the **multi-scale supervision network** (MSS-net) and the **multi-scale regression network** (MSR-net).

In MSS-net, a layer-wise loss term is added at each deconv layer to allow explicit supervision of scale-specific features in each layer of the network. This multi-scale supervision enables effective learning of multi-scale features that can better capture local contextual features of the body keypoints. In addition, coarse-to-fine deconvolution along the resolution pyramid also follows a paradigm similar to the *attention mechanism* to focus on and refine keypoint matches. The MSR-net takes output from multiple stacks of MSS-nets to perform a global keypoint regression by fusing multiple scales of keypoint heatmaps to determine the pose output.

In addition to the MSS-net and MSR-net which can jointly learn to match keypoints across multiple scales of features, we explicitly match connected keypoint pairs based on the connectivity and structure of human body parts. For example, the connectivity from the elbow to the lower-arm and to the wrist can be leveraged in the inference of an occluded wrist, when the elbow and lower-arm are visible. Hence, we add a *structure-aware loss* aims to improve the capacities of the current deep networks in modeling structural priors for pose estimation. This structure loss improves the estimations of occluded keypoints in complex or crowded scenarios. Lastly, our *keypoint masking training* scheme serves as an effective data augmentation approach to enhance the learning of the MSS-net and MSR-net together, to better recognize occluded poses from difficult training samples.

The main contributions of this paper can be summarized as follows:

- We introduce the **multi-scale supervision network** (MSS-net) together with the **multi-scale regression network** (MSR-net) to combine the rich multi-scale features to improve the robustness in keypoint localization by matching features across all scales.
- Both the MSS-net and MSR-net are designed using a **structure-aware loss** to explicitly learn the human skeletal structures from multi-scale features that can serve a strong prior in recovering occlusions in complex scenes.
- We propose a **keypoint masking training** scheme that can fine-tune our network pipeline by generating effective training samples to focus the training on difficult cases with keypoint occlusions and cluttered scenes. Figure 2 summarizes our multi-scale structure-aware network pipeline.

Experimental evaluations show that our method achieves state-of-the-art results on the MPII pose challenge benchmark.

2   Related Work

Image-based human pose estimation has many applications, for a comprehensive survey, see [15]. Early approaches such as the histogram of oriented gradients (HOG) and deformable parts model (DPM) rely on hand-craft features and graphical models [3,5,6,8,13,20]. These methods suffer from the limited representation capabilities and are not extensible to complex scenarios.

Pose estimation using deep neural networks (DNN) [10,19,22,24,25] has shown superior performance in recent years, due to the availability of larger training datasets and powerful GPUs. DeepPose developed by Toshev *et al.* [4] was an early attempt to directly estimate the postural keypoint positions from the observed image. Tompson *et al.* [22] adopted the *heatmap* representation of body keypoints to improve their localization during training. A Markov random field (MRF) inspired spatial model was used to estimate keypoint relationship.Chu *et al.* [10] proposed a transform kernel method to learn the inter-relationships between highly correlated keypoints using a bi-directional tree.

Recently, Wei *et al.* [25] used very deep sequential conv-deconv architecture with large receptive fields to directly perform pose matching on the heatmaps. They also enforced *intermediate supervision* between conv-deconv pairs to prevent gradient vanish, thus a very deep network became feasible, and the deeper network can learn the keypoints relationship with lager receptive field. The hourglass module proposed by Newell *et al.* [17] is an extension of Wei *et al.* with the addition of residual connections between the conv-deconv sub-modules. The *hourglass* module can effectively capture and combine features across scales. Chu *et al.* [11] adopted stacked hourglass networks to generate attention maps from features at multiple resolutions with various semantics. Yang *et al.* [26] designed a pyramid residual module (PRM) to enhance the deep CNN invariance across scales, by learning the convolutional filters on various feature scales.

State-of-the-art DNNs for pose estimation are still limited in the capability of modeling human body structural for effective keypoint matching. Existing methods rely on a brute-force approach by increasing network depth to implicitly enrich the keypoint relationship modeling capability. A major weakness in this regard is the ambiguities arising from the occlusions, clutter backgrounds, or multiple body parts in the scene. In the MPII pose benchmark [1], many methods [10,11,17,25,26] rely on repeating their pose estimation pipeline multiple times in various scales, in order to improve performance by a small margin using averaging of results. This indicates the lack of an effective solution to handle scale and structural priors in the modeling.

3   Method

Our multi-scale structure-aware network consists of two types of subnetworks: the *multi-scale supervision network* (MSS-net), which can be repeated for multiple stack, and the *multi-scale regression network* (MSR-net) at the end, see Fig. 2. Specifically, MSS-net is based on the conv-deconv hourglass module [17] trained with multi-scale loss supervision. The MSR-net performs a final pose structural regression by matching multi-scale keypoint heatmaps and their high-order associations. Both the MSS-net and the MSR-net share a common *structure-aware loss* function, which is designed to ensure effective multi-scale structural feature learning. The training of the whole pipeline is fine-tuned using the *keypoint masking training* scheme to focus on learning hard samples.

We describe two key observations that motivates the design of our method. First, the conv-deconv hourglass stacks capture rich features for keypoint detection across large variability in appearances and scales. However, such capability is very sensitive to a particular scale in the multi-scale pyramid, and lacks of a robust and consistent response across scales. This leads us to add explicit layer-wise supervisions to each of the deconv layer in the training of our MSS-net.

Secondly, the output of the MSS-net hourglass model is a set of heatmaps, and each heatmap corresponds to the location likelihood of each body keypoint

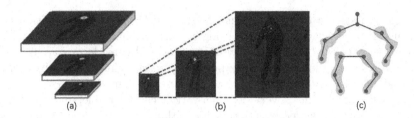

Fig. 3. In the multi-scale supervision network, the refinement of keypoint localization in up-sampling resolution works in analogy to the 'attention' mechanism used in the conventional resolution pyramid search. (a) shows the multi-scale heatmaps of the keypoint of the thorax. (b) shows the refinement of the keypoint heatmaps during the deconv up-sampling, where the location of the thorax is refined with increased accuracy. (c) shows our human skeletal graph with the visualization of keypoint connectivity links.

(elbows, wrists, ankles, knees, *etc.*). To train the MSS-net, the heatmaps are supervised against the ground-truth body keypoint heatmaps that are typically generated using 2D Gaussian blurring. At the testing of the MSS-net for pose estimation, the obtained heatmaps are mostly non-Gaussian, which variate according to the gesture of the subject. A key deficiency in the original hourglass model [17] is that each keypoint heatmap is estimated *independently*, such that the relationship between the keypoints are not considered. In other words, structural consistency among detected keypoints are not optimized.

To ensure structural consistency in the pose estimation pipeline, we introduce the *structure-aware loss* in between the MSS-net hourglass modules that serve as the purpose of intermediate supervision, to better capture the adjacency and associations among the body keypoints. The structure-aware loss is also used in the MSR-net at the end of the pipeline, to globally oversee all keypoint heatmaps across all scales. This way a globally consistent pose configuration can be inferred as the final output. The MSR-net regression not only matches individual body keypoints (first-order consistency), but also matches pairwise consistencies among adjacent keypoints (second-order consistency). To illustrate, the co-occurrence of a matching pair between a hand/leg *w.r.t.* the head/torso with high confidence should provide stronger hypothesis, in comparison to the separated, uncorrelated individual matches for the final pose inference. The MSR-net is trained to perform such optimization across all body keypoints, all scales of features, and all pairwise correlations in a joint regression.

3.1   Multi-Scale Supervision Network

The *multi-scale supervision network* (MSS-net) is designed to learn deep features across multiple scales. We perform multiple layer-wise supervision at each of the deconv layers of the MSS-net, where each layer corresponds to a certain scale. The gray box at the bottom of Fig. 2 depicts the MSS-net architecture.

Multi-scale supervision is performed by calculating the residual at each deconv layer using the corresponding down-sampled ground-truth heatmaps in the matching scale (*e.g.*, 1/2, 1/4, 1/8 down-sampling). Specifically, to make equal the feature map dimensions in order to compute the residual at the corresponding scale, we use an 1-by-1 convolutional kernel for dimension reduction, to convert the high-dimensional deconv feature maps into the desired number of features, where the number of reduced dimension matches the number of body keypoints (which is also the number of heatmaps). On the other hand, the ground-truth keypoint feature map is down-sampled to match the corresponding extracted keypoint heatmap at each scale to compute the residual.

The multi-scale supervision network localizes body keypoints in a way similar to the 'attention model' [27] used in the conventional resolution pyramid for image search. The activation areas in the low-res heatmap can provide guidance of the location refinement in the subsequent high-res layers, see Fig. 3.

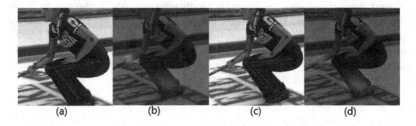

(a)   (b)   (c)   (d)

Fig. 4. Muti-scale keypoint regression to disambiguate multiple peaks in the keypoint heatmaps. (a–b) shows an example of (a) keypoint prediction and (b) heatmap from the MSS-net hourglass stacks, which will be fed into the MSR-net for regression. (c–d) shows (c) the output keypoint locations and (d) heatmap after regression. Observe that the heatmap peaks in (d) are more focused compared to (b).

We describe the loss function L_{MS} to train the multi-scale supervision network. The loss L_{MS} is defined by summing the L_2 loss from the heatmaps of all keypoints across all scales, similar to the multi-scale loss function in [17,25]. To detect the $N = 16$ keypoints (head, neck, pelvis, thorax, shoulders, elbows, wrists, knees, ankles, and hips), N heatmaps are generated after each conv-deconv stack. The loss at the i-th scale compares the predicted heatmaps of all keypoints against the ground-truth heatmaps at the matching scale:

$$L_{MS}^i = \frac{1}{N} \sum_{n=1}^{N} \sum_{x,y} \|P_n(x,y) - G_n(x,y)\|_2, \tag{1}$$

where $P_n(x,y)$ and $G_n(x,y)$ represent the predicted and the ground-truth confidence maps at the pixel location (x,y) for the n-th keypoint, respectively.

In standard dataset the ground-truth poses are provided as the keypoint locations. We follow the common practice for ground-truth heatmap generation as in Tompson *et al.* [23], where the n-th keypoint ground-truth heatmap $G_n(x, y)$ is generated using a 2D Gaussian centered at the keypoint location (x, y), with standard deviation of 1 pixel. Figure 2 (bottom left, first row) shows a few examples of the ground-truth heatmaps for a certain keypoints.

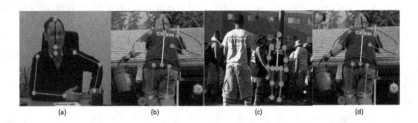

Fig. 5. Keypoint masking to simulate the hard training samples. (a) is a common case in human pose estimation, the keypoint (left-wrist) is occluded by an object, but it can be estimated from the limbs. (c) is another difficult case, where the nearby persons' keypoint can be mismatched to the target person. Thus there are two kind of keypoint masking, (b) is the background keypoint masking which crop a background patch and paste on a keypoint to simulate the keypoint invisible, (d) is the keypoint duplicate masking which crop a keypoint patch and paste on another keypoint to simulate multi-person or multi-peak keypoint heatmap.

3.2 Multi-Scale Regression Network

We use a *fully convolutional* multi-scale regression network (MSR-net) after the MSS-net conv-deconv stacks to globally refine the multi-scale keypoint heatmaps to improve the structural consistency of the estimated poses. The intuition is that the relative positions of arms and legs *w.r.t.* the head/torso provide useful action priors, which can be learned from the regression network by considering feature maps across all scales for pose refinement. The MSR-net takes the multi-scale heatmaps as input, and match them to the ground-truth keypoints at respective scales. This way the regression network can effectively combine heatmaps across all scales to refine the estimated poses.

The multi-scale regression network jointly optimizes the global body structure configuration via determining connectivity among body keypoints based on the mutli-scale features. This can be viewed as an extension to the work of the Convolutional Part Heatmap Regression [4], which only considers keypoint heatmap regression at the scale of the input image. The input image with the keypoint heatmaps can be seen as an attention method and provide larger resolution. In this case, the multi-scale regression network learns a scale-invariant and attention based structure model, thus provide better performance. Moreover, our multi-scale regression network optimizes the structure-aware loss, which matches individual keypoints as well as the higher-order association (pairs and triplets of keypoints) in estimating pose. The output from the multi-scale regression network is a comprehensive pose estimation that considers pose configurations across multiple feature scales, multiple keypoint associations, and high-order keypoint associations.

Figure 4 shows the efficacy of the multi-scale, high-order keypoint regression performed in the MSR-net. The MSR-net works hand-in-hand with the MSS-net to explicitly model the high-order relationship among body parts, such that posture structural consistency can be maintained and refined.

3.3   Structure-Aware Loss

It has been observed that deeper hourglass stacks lead to better pose estimation results [17]. As the depth of hourglass stacks increases, *gradient vanishing* becomes a critical issue in training the network, where *intermediate supervision* [11,17,25,26] is a common practice to alleviate gradient vanishing.

To this end, we design a structure-aware loss function following a graph to model the human skeletal structure. Specifically we introduced a *human skeletal graph* S (See Fig. 3(c) for a visualization of the human skeletal graph.) to define the structure-aware loss. Each node $S_n \in S$ represent a body keypoint of the human skeleton and its connected keypoints, $n \in \{1, ..., N\}$. The *structure-aware loss* at the i-th scale is formally defined as:

$$L_{SA}^i = \frac{1}{N} \sum_{n=1}^{N} ||P_n^i - G_n^i||_2 + \alpha \sum_{i=1}^{N} ||P_{S_n}^i - G_{S_n}^i||_2. \tag{2}$$

The first term is the multi-scale supervision loss L_{MS}^i in Eq. 1 that represents individual keypoint matching loss. The second term represents the structural matching loss, where P_{S_n} and G_{S_n} are the combination of the heatmaps from individual keypoint n and its neighbors in graph S. Hyperparameter α is a weighing parameter balancing the two terms.

Figure 2 (bottom left) shows a breakdown visualization of how our skeleton-guided structure-aware loss is calculated in traversing the keypoints and their relationships according to S. The top row in the sub-figure shows the intermediate loss defined on individual keypoints (*e.g.*, the right ankle, knee, hip, pelvis, thorax, head, wrist, elbow) as used in [17,25]. The bottom row shows our structure-aware loss defined for a set of connected keypoints.

We consider connected keypoints, *e.g.*, head-thorax, shoulder-elbow, wrist-elbow, hip-knee, hip-hip, knee-ankle, in the bottom sub-figure of Fig. 2. Because that the elbows and knees has additional physical connections (to the shoulders and wrists, and the hips and ankles, respectively), the structure-aware loss in these two joints are three-way to include a triplet of connected keypoints, *e.g.*, hip-knee-ankle, shoulder-elbow-wrist as in Fig. 2. In all cases, the list of structurally connected keypoints is empirically determined according to the human skeletal graph S, such that the loss can better capture the physical connectivity of the keypoints in the human body to obtain structural priors.

The structure-aware loss is used at two places in our network: (1) in-between the MSS-net stacks as a means of *intermediate supervision* to enforce structural consistency while localizing keypoints; and (2) in the MSR-net to find a globally consistent pose configuration.

3.4 Keypoint Masking Training

In the case of multi-person scenarios, more than one possible body keypoints can co-exist in the view. In occluded case, no keypoint can be visible observed. To tackle these challenging scenarios, we develop a novel *keypoint masking* data augmentation scheme to increase training data to fine-tune our networks.

Specifically, occlusion of key points is an aspect that strongly affects the performance of pose estimation methods. As shown in Fig. 5(a), the left wrist of the person is occluded by the mug, however the occluded wrist indeed can be estimated by visible connected keypoint (left elbow) o r the libs connecting wrist and elbow. Another difficult case is where there is another person nearby, *e.g.* in Fig. 5(c) that several people standing closely. In this case, the pose estimator may easily take the nearby person's keypoint as its own keypoint. One drawback of training the network using the original training set is that there usually exists insufficient amount of examples that contains the occlusion cases to train a deep network for accurate keypoint detection/localization. Conventional data augmentation method, such as the popular horizontally flipping, random crops and color jittering in classification, are not helpful in this case.

We propose a keypoint masking method to address this problem by copying and pasting body keypoint patches on the image for data augmentation. The main idea is to generate keypoint occluded training samples as well as the artificially inserted keypoints, such that the network can effectively improve its learning on these extreme cases. This data augmentation is easily doable from the known ground-truth keypoint annotations.

Specifically, we introduce two types of keypoint/occlusion sample generation methods: (1) As shown in Fig. 5(b), we copy a background patch and put it onto a keypoint to cover it, in order to simulate a keypoint occlusion. This kind of sample is useful for the learning of occlusion recovery. (2) As shown in Fig. 5 (d), we copy a body keypoint patches and put it onto a nearby background, in order to simulate the multiple existing keypoints, the case that mostly occurs in multi-person scenarios. Since this data augmentation results in multiple identical keypoint patches, the solution to a successful pose estimation must rely on some sort of structural inference or knowledge. It is thus especially beneficial to fine-tune to our global keypoint regression network.

Overall this keypoint masking strategy can effectively improve the focus of learning on challenge cases, where important body keypoints are purposely masked out or artificially placed at wrong locations. The effect of keypoint masking training in improving both (1) the detection and localization of occluded keypoints and (2) global structure recognition will be evaluated in Sect. 4.3.

4   Experiments and Analysis

We train and test our model on a workstation with 4 NVIDIA GTX 1080Ti GPUs and two public datasets – the MPII Human Pose Dataset and Challenge [1] and FLIC dataset [20]. The MPII dataset consists of images taken from a wide range of real-world activities with full-body pose annotations. It is considered as the "de facto" benchmark for state-of-the-art pose estimation evaluation. The MPII dataset includes around 25K images containing over 40K subjects with annotated body joints, where 28K subjects are used for training, and the remaining 12k are used for testing. The FLIC dataset consists of 5,003 selected images obtained from Hollywood movies. The images are annotated on the upper body, where the subjects are mostly facing the camera, thus there exists less keypoint occlusions.

Since the testing annotations for MPII are not available to the public, in our experiments, we perform training on a subset of the original training set, and perform hyper-parameter selection on a separated *validation set*, which contains around 3K subjects (that are in the original training set). We also report evaluation results that are reported from the MPII benchmark 4.2.

4.1   Implementation

Training is conducted on the respective datasets (MPII, FLIC) using the SGD optimizer for 300 epochs. In this work, we use 8 stacks of hourglass modules for both training and testing. The training processes can be decided into three stages: *(1)* MSS-Net training, *(2)* MSR-Net training, and *(3)* the joint training of the MSS-Net and MSR-Net with keypoint masking. We use the same data augmentation technique as in the original hourglass work [17] that includes rotation ($\pm$ 30 degrees), and scaling (.75 to 1.25) throughout the training process. Due to GPU memory limitation, the input images were cropped and rescaled to 256 $\times$ 256 pixels. For the first stage we train the MSS-Net for 150 epochs, with the initial learning rate to be 5e-4. The learn rate is reduced by a factor of 5 when the performance dose not improve after 8 epochs. We then train the MSR-Net for 75 epochs with the MSS-Net parameters fixed. Finally the whole network pipeline is trained for 75 epoch with keypoint masking fine-tuning.

Testing is performed on both the MPII and FLIC datasets. Since this work focuses on single-person pose estimation, and there often exists multiple subjects in the scene. We use a conditional testing method—We first test pose estimation in the original scale assuming the subject appears at the image center. We then check if the detected body keypoint confidence is lower then a specific threshold. If so, no successful human pose is found. We then perturb the putative person location, and repeat the pose finding, to see if a refined pose can be found. The keypoint confidence thresholds τ_c can be keypoint-dependent, and are empirically determined using the validation set. For the case multiple pose estimation test trials are performed, only the results with scores higher than a threshold τ_s are selected for the fusion of the pose output. The value of τ_s is also empirically determined from the validation set. We note that this testing refinement may reduce the testing performance of pose estimation, because the variation of the input (person bounding box) is also considered in the process.

4.2 Evaluation Results

Evaluation is conducted using the standard Percentage of Correct Keypoints (PCK) metric [21] which reports the percentage of keypoint detection falling within a normalized distance of the ground truth. For the FLIC evaluation, PCK is set to the percentage of disparities between the detected pose keypoints *w.r.t.* the ground-truth after a normalization against a fraction of the torso size. For the MPII evaluation, such disparities are normalized by a fraction of the head size, which is denoted as PCK^h.

FLIC: Table 1 summarizes the FLIC results, where our PCK reaches 99.2% for the elbow, and 97.3% for the wrist. Note that the elbows and wrists are the most difficult parts to localize in the FLIC dataset. Comparison with Newell *et al.* [17] demonstrates the improvement of our structure-aware design in the MSS-net and MSR-net in our method.

MPII: Table 2 summarizes the MPII evaluation results. Observe that our method achieves the *highest* total score (92.1) and state-of-the-art results across all keypoints on the MPII benchmark as well as the AUC score. In Fig. 6 we show several pose estimation results on the MPII dataset. In Fig. 7 we show some highly challenging examples with crowded scenes and severe occlusions. In this case, we run our pose estimation on the bounding box of each person, which is provided in the MPII dataset. Our method can extract complex poses for each targeted person, without confusing with other person's poses and in the presence of occlusions.

Table 1. Results on the FLIC dataset (PCK = 0.2)

	Elbow	Wrist
Tompson *et al.* CVPR'15 [22]	93.1	92.4
Wei *et al.* CVPR'16 [25]	97.8	95.0
Newell*et al.* ECCV'16 [17]	99.0	97.0
Our model	**99.2**	**97.3**

4.3 Component Analysis

We performed a series of ablation experiments to investigate the effect of individual components in our method. The ablation study is conducted on the validation set [23] of the MPII dataset. Note that our method can be reduced to the original hourglass model of Newell *et al.* [17] after all newly proposed features are taken

Table 2. Evaluation results on the MPII pose dataset ($PCK^h = 0.5$). Results were retrieved on 03/15/2018.

Our method	Head	Shoulder	Elbow	Wrist	Hip	Knee	Ankle	Total	AUC
	98.5	**96.8**	**92.7**	88.4	90.6	89.3	**86.3**	**92.1**	63.8
Chen et al. ICCV'17 [7]	98.1	96.5	92.5	**88.5**	90.2	**89.6**	86.0	91.9	61.6
Chou et al. arXiv'17 [9]	98.2	**96.8**	92.2	88.0	**91.3**	89.1	84.9	91.8	63.9
Chu CVPR'17 [11]	**98.5**	96.3	91.9	88.1	90.6	88.0	85.0	91.5	63.8
Luvizon et al. arXiv'17 [16]	98.1	96.6	92.0	87.5	90.6	88.0	82.7	91.2	63.9
Ning et al. TMM'17 [18]	98.1	96.3	92.2	87.8	90.6	87.6	82.7	91.2	63.6
Newell ECCV'16 [17]	98.2	96.3	91.2	87.1	90.1	87.4	83.6	90.9	62.9
Bulat ECCV'16 [4]	97.9	95.1	89.9	85.3	89.4	85.7	81.7	89.7	59.6
Wei CVPR'16 [25]	97.8	95.0	88.7	84.0	88.4	82.8	79.4	88.5	61.4
Insafutdinov ECCV'16 [12]	96.8	95.2	89.3	84.4	88.4	83.4	78.0	88.5	60.8
Belagiannis FG'17 [2]	97.7	95.0	88.2	83.0	87.9	82.6	78.4	88.1	58.8

out. Thus, we analysis each proposed network design, *i.e.*, the MSS-net, MSR-net, structure-aware loss, and keypoint masking, by comparing against Newell *et al.* with a baseline score of 87.1% at $PCK^h = 0.5$.

Multi-scale Supervision (MSS-net without structure-aware loss): We first evaluate the effect of the multi-scale supervision along. By adding the multi-scale supervision at the deconv layers of hourglass model [17], the PCK^h score improve from 87.1% to 87.6% and also with a significant computation reduction. This is because the original hourglass method [17] is tested with input images of multiple scales (6 scales in our experiment), while the evaluation of our multi-scale supervision network only need to be tested once in the original scale input. Our method does not require repeated runs and fusion of different scales as post-processing.

Multi-scale Regression (MSS-net and MSR-net without structure-aware loss): To justify the contribution of multi-scale regression, we evaluate the effect of the second stage of our training pipeline (*i.e.* the MSR-net after the MSS-net is trained, without keypoint masking fine-tuning). The PCK^h score here is 88.1% score, which is 0.4% improvement brought by the multi-scale regression.

Fig. 6. Example of pose estimation results on the MPII dataset using our method. (row 1) Examples with significant scale variations for keypoints. (row 2, 3) Examples with multiple persons. (row 4, 5) Examples with severe keypoint occlusions.

Fig. 7. Pose estimation results with our method on two very challenging images from the MPII dataset with crowded scene and severe occlusions. Our method can reliably recover complex poses for each targeted person.

Structure-aware Loss (MSS-net and MSR-net with structure-aware loss): The next in our ablation pipeline is to use structure-aware loss in the training of MSS-net and MSR-net, in comparison to the original loss defined in Eq. 1. The PCK^h score we obtained here is 88.3%, which is a 0.3% improvement brought by the use of structure-aware loss for training.

Keypoint Masking: After 75 epochs keypoint masking fine-tuning in the MSS-net and MSR-net pipeline with structure-aware loss, we achieve a 88.4% PCK^h score. The keypoint masking contributes 0.1% PCK^h improvement in this ablation study.

5   Conclusion

We describe an improved multi-scale structure-aware network for human pose estimation. The proposed multi-scale approach (multi-scale supervision and multi-scale regression) works hand-in-hand with the structure-aware loss design, to infer high-order structural matching of detected body keypoints, that can improve pose estimation in challenging cases of complex activities, heavy occlusions, multiple subjects and cluttered backgrounds. The proposed keypoint masking training can focus the learning of the network on difficult samples. Our method achieve the leading position in the MPII challenge leaderboard among the state-of-the-art methods. Ablation study shows the contribution and advantage of each proposed components.

References

1. Andriluka, M., Pishchulin, L., Gehler, P., Schiele, B.: 2D human pose estimation: new benchmark and state of the art analysis. In: CVPR, pp. 3686–3693 (2014)
2. Belagiannis, V., Zisserman, A.: Recurrent human pose estimation. In: FG, pp. 468–475 (2017)
3. Bourdev, L., Malik, J.: Poselets: body part detectors trained using 3D human pose annotations. In: ICCV, pp. 1365–1372 (2009)
4. Bulat, A., Tzimiropoulos, G.: Human pose estimation via convolutional part heatmap regression. In: Leibe, B., Matas, J., Sebe, N., Welling, M. (eds.) ECCV 2016. LNCS, vol. 9911, pp. 717–732. Springer, Cham (2016). https://doi.org/10.1007/978-3-319-46478-7_44
5. Chang, M., Qi, H., Wang, X., Cheng, H., Lyu, S.: Fast online upper body pose estimation from video. In: BMVC, pp. 104.1–104.12. Swansea (2015)
6. Charles, J., Pfister, T., Magee, D., Hogg, D., Zisserman, A.: Domain adaptation for upper body pose tracking in signed TV broadcasts. In: BMVC (2013)
7. Chen, Y., Shen, C., Wei, X.S., Liu, L., Yang, J.: Adversarial posenet: a structure-aware convolutional network for human pose estimation. In: 2017 IEEE International Conference on Computer Vision (ICCV), pp. 1221–1230 (2017)
8. Cherian, A., Mairal, J., Alahari, K., Schmid, C.: Mixing body-part sequences for human pose estimation. In: CVPR, pp. 2361–2368 (2014)
9. Chou, C., Chien, J., Chen, H.: Self adversarial training for human pose estimation. CoRR abs/1707.02439 (2017). http://arxiv.org/abs/1707.02439

10. Chu, X., Ouyang, W., Li, H., Wang, X.: Structured feature learning for pose estimation. In: CVPR, pp. 4715–4723 (2016)
11. Chu, X., Yang, W., Ouyang, W., Ma, C., Yuille, A.L., Wang, X.: Multi-context attention for human pose estimation. In: 2017 IEEE Conference on Computer Vision and Pattern Recognition (CVPR), pp. 5669–5678 (2017)
12. Insafutdinov, E., Pishchulin, L., Andres, B., Andriluka, M., Schiele, B.: DeeperCut: a deeper, stronger, and faster multi-person pose estimation model. In: Leibe, B., Matas, J., Sebe, N., Welling, M. (eds.) ECCV 2016. LNCS, vol. 9910, pp. 34–50. Springer, Cham (2016). https://doi.org/10.1007/978-3-319-46466-4_3
13. Lafferty, J.: Conditional random fields: probabilistic models for segmenting and labeling sequence data. In: ICML, pp. 282–289 (2001)
14. Liu, W., et al.: SSD: single shot multibox detector. In: ECCV (2016)
15. Liu, Z., Zhu, J., Bu, J., Chen, C.: A survey of human pose estimation. J. Vis. Commun. Image Represent. **32**, 10–19 (2015)
16. Luvizon, D.C., Tabia, H., Picard, D.: Human pose regression by combining indirect part detection and contextual information. CoRR abs/1710.02322 (2017). http://arxiv.org/abs/1710.02322
17. Newell, A., Yang, K., Deng, J.: Stacked hourglass networks for human pose estimation. In: Leibe, B., Matas, J., Sebe, N., Welling, M. (eds.) ECCV 2016. LNCS, vol. 9912, pp. 483–499. Springer, Cham (2016). https://doi.org/10.1007/978-3-319-46484-8_29
18. Ning, G., He, Z.: Dual path networks for multi-person human pose estimation. CoRR abs/1710.10192 (2017). http://arxiv.org/abs/1710.10192
19. Pfister, T., Charles, J., Zisserman, A.: Flowing ConvNets for human pose estimation in videos. In: ICCV, pp. 1913–1921 (2015)
20. Sapp, B., Taskar, B.: Multimodal decomposable models for human pose estimation. In: CVPR, pp. 3674–3681 (2013)
21. Tompson, J., Goroshin, R., Jain, A., Lecun, Y., Bregler, C.: Efficient object localization using convolutional networks. In: CVPR, pp. 648–656 (2015)
22. Tompson, J.J., Jain, A., LeCun, Y., Bregler, C.: Joint training of a convolutional network and a graphical model for human pose estimation. In: NIPS, vol. 27, pp. 1799–1807 (2014)
23. Tompson, J.J., Jain, A., LeCun, Y., Bregler, C.: Joint training of a convolutional network and a graphical model for human pose estimation. In: NIPS, pp. 1799–1807 (2014)
24. Toshev, A., Szegedy, C.: Deeppose: Human pose estimation via deep neural networks. In: CVPR, pp. 1653–1660 (2014)
25. Wei, S., Ramakrishna, V., Kanade, T., Sheikh, Y.: Convolutional pose machines. In: CVPR, pp. 4724–4732 (2016)
26. Yang, W., Li, S., Ouyang, W., Li, H., Wang, X.: Learning feature pyramids for human pose estimation. In: 2017 IEEE International Conference on Computer Vision (ICCV), pp. 1290–1299 (2017)
27. Zhao, B., Wu, X., Feng, J., Peng, Q., Yan, S.: Diversified visual attention networks for fine-grained object classification. IEEE Trans. Multimedia **19**(6), 1245–1256 (2017)

Diverse and Coherent Paragraph Generation from Images

Moitreya Chatterjee[✉] and Alexander G. Schwing

University of Illinois at Urbana-Champaign, Urbana, IL 61801, USA
metro.smiles@gmail.com, aschwing@illinois.edu

Abstract. Paragraph generation from images, which has gained popularity recently, is an important task for video summarization, editing, and support of the disabled. Traditional image captioning methods fall short on this front, since they aren't designed to generate long informative descriptions. Moreover, the vanilla approach of simply concatenating multiple short sentences, possibly synthesized from a classical image captioning system, doesn't embrace the intricacies of paragraphs: coherent sentences, globally consistent structure, and diversity. To address those challenges, we propose to augment paragraph generation techniques with "coherence vectors," "global topic vectors," and modeling of the inherent ambiguity of associating paragraphs with images, via a variational autoencoder formulation. We demonstrate the effectiveness of the developed approach on two datasets, outperforming existing state-of-the-art techniques on both.

Keywords: Captioning · Review generation
Variational autoencoders

1 Introduction

Daily, we effortlessly describe fun events to friends and family, showing them pictures to underline the main plot. The narrative ensures that our audience can follow along step by step and picture the missing pieces in their mind with ease. Key to filling in the missing pieces is a consistency in our narrative which generally follows the arrow of time.

While computer vision, natural language processing and artificial intelligence techniques, more generally, have made great progress in describing visual content via image or video captioning [5,11,18,29,38], the obtained result is often a single sentence of around 20 words, describing the main observation. Even if brevity caters to today's short attention span, 20 words are hardly enough to describe subtle interactions, let alone detailed plots of our experience. Those are much more meaningfully depicted in a paragraph of reasonable length.

Electronic supplementary material The online version of this chapter (https://doi.org/10.1007/978-3-030-01216-8_45) contains supplementary material, which is available to authorized users.

© Springer Nature Switzerland AG 2018
V. Ferrari et al. (Eds.): ECCV 2018, LNCS 11206, pp. 747–763, 2018.
https://doi.org/10.1007/978-3-030-01216-8_45

To this end, visual paragraph generation methods [17,22,26,47], which have been proposed very recently, provide a longer narrative which describes a given image or video. However, as argued initially, coherence between successive sentences of the narrative is a key necessity to effectively convey the plot of our experience. Importantly, models for many of the aforementioned methods provide no explicit mechanisms to ensure cross-sentence topic consistency. A notable exception is the work of Liang et al. [26].

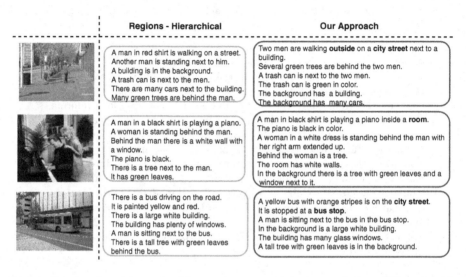

Fig. 1. Paragraphs generated with a prior state-of-the-art technique [22] and with our developed approach. Due to the introduced 'Coherence Vectors' we observe the generated paragraphs to be much more coherent than prior work [22] (Color figure online)

In particular, Liang et al. [26] propose to ensure consistency across sentence themes by training a standard paragraph generation module [22], coupled with an attention mechanism, under a Generative Adversarial Network (GAN) [13] setting which has an additional loss-term to enforce consistency. However, difficulties associated with training GANs [3] and no explicit coherence model, leave their method vulnerable to generating incoherent paragraphs.

Different from prior work, we explicitly focus on modeling the *diverse yet coherent possibilities* of successive sentences when generating a paragraph, while ensuring that the 'big picture' underlying the image does not get lost in the details. To this end, we develop a model that propagates, what we call "*Coherence Vectors*," which ensure cross-sentence topic smoothness, and a "*Global Topic Vector*," which captures the summarizing information about the image. Additionally, we observe improvements in the quality of the generated paragraphs, when our model is trained to incorporate diversity. Intuitively, the coherence vector embeds the theme of the most recently generated sentence. To ensure a smooth flow of the theme across sentences, we combine the coherence vector with the topic vector of the current sentence and a global topic vector. Figure 1 illustrates a sampling of a synthesized paragraph given an input image, using our method vis-à-vis prior work [22]. Notably, using our model, we observe a smooth transition between sentence themes, while capturing summarizing information about the image. For instance, generated paragraphs corresponding to the images in the first and the third rows in Fig. 1 indicate that the images have been captured in a 'city' setting.

Following prior work we quantitatively evaluate our approach on the standard Stanford Image-Paragraph dataset [22], demonstrating state-of-the-art performance. Furthermore, different from all existing methods, we showcase the generalizability of our model, evaluating the proposed approach by generating reviews from the "Office-Product" category of the Amazon product review dataset [30] and by showing significant gains over all baselines.

In the next section, we discuss prior relevant work before providing details of our proposed approach in Sect. 3. Section 4 presents empirical results. We finally conclude in Sect. 5, laying out avenues for future work.

2 Related Work

For a long time, associating language with visual content has been an important research topic [4,25,40]. Early techniques in this area associate linguistic 'tag-words' with visual data. Gradually, the focus shifted to generating entire sentences and paragraphs for visual data. For this, techniques from both natural language processing and computer vision are combined with the aim of building holistic AI systems that integrate naturally into common surroundings. Two tasks that spurred the growth of recent work in the language-vision area are *Image Captioning* [5,11,17,38,44], and *Visual Question Answering* [2,12,15,28,33–35,42,43,45]. More recently, image captioning approaches were extended to generate natural language descriptions at the level of paragraphs [17,22,26]. In the following, we review related work from the area of image captioning and visual paragraph generation in greater detail, and point out the distinction with our work.

Image Captioning: *Image Captioning* is the task of generating textual descriptions, given an input image. Classical methods for image captioning, are usually non-parametric. These methods build a pool of candidate captions from the training set of image-caption pairs, and at test time, a fitness function is used to retrieve the most compelling caption for a given input image [4,25,31]. However the computationally demanding nature of the matching process imposes a bottleneck when considering a set of descriptions of a reasonable size.

To address this problem, Recurrent Neural Network (RNN)-based approaches have come into vogue [1,10,18,29,38,39,44,46] lately. These approaches, typically, first use a Convolutional Neural Network (CNN) [24,36] to obtain an encoding of the given input image. This encoding is then fed to an RNN which samples a set of words (from a dictionary of words) that agree most with the image encoding. However, the captions generated through such techniques are short, spanning typically a single sentence of at most 20 words. Our approach differs from the aforementioned image captioning techniques, in that we generate a paragraph of multiple sentences rather than a short caption. Importantly, captioning techniques generally don't have to consider coherence across sentence themes, which is not true for paragraph generation approaches which we review next.

Visual Paragraph Generation: From a distance, the task of *Visual Paragraph Generation* resembles image captioning: given an image, generate a textual description of its content [22]. However, of importance for visual paragraph generation is the attention to detail in the textual description. In particular, the system is expected to generate a paragraph of sentences (typically 5 or 6 sentences per paragraph) describing the image in great detail. Moreover, in order for the paragraph to resemble natural language, there has to be a smooth transition across the themes of the sentences of the paragraph.

Early work in generating detailed captions, include an approach by Johnson *et al.* [17]. While generating compelling sentences individually, a focus on a theme of the story underlying a given image was missing. This problem was addressed by Krause *et al.* [22]. Their language model consists of a two-stage hierarchy of RNNs. The first RNN level generates sentence topics, given the visual representation of semantically salient regions in the image. The second RNN level translates this topic vector into a sentence. This model was further extended by Liang *et al.* [26] to encourage coherence amongst successive sentences. To this end, the language generation mechanism of Krause *et al.* [22], coupled with an attention mechanism, was trained in a Generative Adversarial Network (GAN) setting, where the discriminator is intended to encourage this coherence at training time. Dai *et al.* [8] also train a GAN for generating paragraphs. However, known difficulties of training GANs [3] pose challenges towards effectively implementing such systems. Xie *et al.* introduce regularization terms for ensuring diversity [41] which results in a constrained optimization problem that does not admit a closed form solution and is thus hard to implement. Different from these approaches [8, 26, 41], we demonstrate that a change of the generation mechanism is better suited to obtain coherent sentence structure within the paragraph. To this end we introduce *Coherence Vectors* which ensure a gradual transition of themes between sentences.

Additionally, different from prior work, we also incorporate a summary of the topic vectors to sensitize the model to the 'main plot' underlying the image. Furthermore, to capture the inherent ambiguity of generating paragraph from images, *i.e.*, multiple paragraphs can successfully describe an image, we cast our paragraph-generation model as a Variational Autoencoder (VAE) [7, 14, 16, 20], enabling our model to generate a set of diverse paragraphs, given an image.

3   Our Proposed Method for Paragraph Generation

As mentioned before, coherence of sampled sentences is important for automatic generation of human-like paragraphs from visual data, while not losing sight

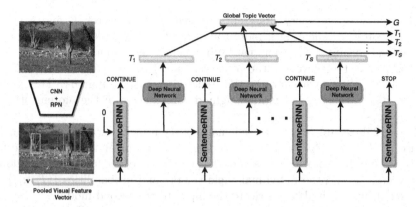

Fig. 2. Overview of the topic generation net of our proposed approach illustrating the construction of the individual and 'Global Topic Vector'.

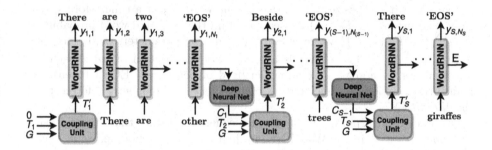

Fig. 3. Overview of the sentence generation net.

of the underlying 'big picture' story illustrated in the image. Further, another valuable element for an automated paragraph generation system is the diversity of the generated text. In the following we develop a framework which takes into account these properties. We first provide an overview of the approach in Sect. 3.1, before discussing our approach to generate coherent paragraphs in Sect. 3.2 and finally our technique to obtain diverse paragraphs in Sect. 3.3.

3.1 Overview

To generate a paragraph $y = (y_1, \ldots, y_S)$ consisting of S sentences y_i, $i \in \{1, \ldots, S\}$, each with N_i words $y_{i,j}$, $j \in \{1, \ldots, N_i\}$, for an image x, we use a deep net composed out of two modules which are coupled hierarchically: the *Topic Generation Net* and the *Sentence Generation Net*.

The *Topic Generation Net* illustrated in Fig. 2 seeks to extract a set of S topic vectors, $T_i \in \mathbb{R}^H \; \forall i \in \{1, \ldots, S\}$, given an appropriate visual representation of the input image x. The topic generation net is a parametric function which, recursively at every timestep, produces a topic vector T_i and a probability measure u_i indicating if more topics are to be generated. We implement this function using a recurrent net, subsequently also referred to as the *SentenceRNN*. We then leverage the topic vectors T_i to construct a *Global Topic Vector* $G \in \mathbb{R}^H$, which captures the underlying image summary. This global topic vector is constructed via a weighted combination of the aforementioned topic vectors T_i.

Figure 2 illustrates a detailed schematic of the topic generation net. Formally we use $(G, \{(T_i, u_i)\}_{i=1}^S) = \Gamma_{w_T}(x)$ to denote the input and output of the net $\Gamma_{w_T}(\cdot)$, where the vector w_T subsumes the parameters of the function. The global topic vector G, and the individual topic vectors and probabilities $\{(T_i, u_i)\}_{i=1}^S$ are the output which also constitute the input to the second module.

The second module of the developed approach, called the *Sentence Generation Net*, is illustrated in Fig. 3. Based on the output of the topic generation net, it is responsible for producing a paragraph y, one sentence y_i at a time.

Formally, the sentence generation module is also modeled as a parametric function which synthesizes a sentence y_i, one word $y_{i,j}$ at a time. More specifically, a recurrent net $\Gamma_{w_s}(\cdot, \cdot)$ is used to obtain the predicted word probabilities $\{p_{i,j}\}_{j=1}^{N_i} = \Gamma_{w_s}(T_i, G)$, where w_s subsumes all the parameters of the net, and $p_{i,j} \in [0,1]^V \; \forall j \in \{1, \ldots, N_i\}$ is a probability distribution over the set of V words in our vocabulary (including an 'End of Sentence' ('EOS') token). We realize the function, $\Gamma_{w_s}(\cdot, \cdot)$ using a recurrent net, subsequently referred to as the *WordRNN*.

In order to incorporate cross-sentence coherence, rather than directly using the topic vector T_i in the WordRNN, we first construct a modified topic vector T_i', which better captures the theme of the ith sentence. For every sentence i, we compute $T_i' \in \mathbb{R}^H$ via a *Coupling Unit*, by combining the topic vector T_i, the global topic vector G and a previous sentence representation C_{i-1}, called a *Coherence Vector*, which captures properties of the sentence generated at step $i-1$. Note that the synthesis of the first sentence begins by constructing T_1', which is obtained by coupling T_1 with the global topic vector G, and an all zero vector.

Visual Representation: To obtain an effective encoding of the input image, x, we follow Johnson *et al.* [17]. More specifically, a Convolutional Neural Network (CNN) (VGG-16 [36]) coupled with a Region Proposal Network (RPN) gives fixed-length feature vectors for every detection of a semantically salient region in the image. The obtained set of vectors $\{v_1, \ldots, v_M\}$ with $v_i \in \mathbb{R}^D$ each correspond to a region in the image. We subsequently pool these vectors into a single vector, $v \in \mathbb{R}^I$ – following the approach of Krause *et al.* [22]. This pooled representation contains relevant information from the different semantically salient regions in the image, which is supplied as input to our topic generation net. Subsequently, we use v and x interchangeably.

3.2   Coherent Paragraph Generation

The construction of coherent paragraphs adopts a two-step approach. In the first step, we derive a set of individual and a global topic-vector starting with the pooled representation of the image. This is followed by paragraph synthesis.

Topic Generation: The *Topic Generation Net* $(G, \{(T_i, u_i)\}_{i=1}^{S}) = \Gamma_{w_T}(x)$ constructs a set of relevant topics T_i for subsequent paragraph generation given an image x. Figure 2 provides a schematic of the proposed topic generation module. At first, the pooled visual representation of the image, v, is used as input for the *SentenceRNN*. The SentenceRNN is a single layer Gated Recurrent Unit (GRU) [6], parameterized by w_T. It takes an image representation v as input and produces a probability distribution u_i, over the labels 'CONTINUE' or 'STOP,' while its hidden state is used to produce the topic vector $T_i \in \mathbb{R}^H$ via a 2-layer densely connected deep neural network. A 'CONTINUE' label ($u_i > 0.5$), indicates that the recurrence should proceed for another time step, while a 'STOP' symbol terminates the recurrence.

However, automatic description of an image via paragraphs necessitates tying all the sentences of the paragraph to a 'big picture' underlying the scene. For example, in the first image in Fig. 1, the generated paragraph should ideally reflect that it is an image captured in a 'city' setting. To encourage this ability we construct a *Global Topic Vector* $G \in \mathbb{R}^H$ for a given input image (see Fig. 2).

Intuitively, we want this global topic vector to encode a holistic understanding of the image, by combining the aforementioned individual topic vectors as follows:

$$G = \sum_{i=1}^{n} \alpha_i T_i \quad \text{where} \quad \alpha_i = \frac{||T_i||_2}{\sum_i ||T_i||_2}. \tag{1}$$

Our intention is to facilitate representation of 'meta-concepts' (like 'city') as a weighted combination of its potential constituents (like 'car,' 'street,' 'men,' *etc.*). The synthesized global vector and the topic vectors are then propagated to the sentence generation net which predicts the words of the paragraph.

Sentence Generation: Given the individual topic vectors T_i and the global topic vector G, the *Sentence Generation Net* synthesizes sentences of the paragraph by computing word probabilities $\{p_{i,j}\}_{j=1}^{N_i} = \Gamma_{w_s}(T_i, G)$, conditioned on the previous set of synthesized words (see Fig. 3). One sentence is generated for each of the S individual topic vectors $T_1, \ldots, T_S$. Synthesis of the ith sentence commences by combining via the *Coupling Unit* the topic vector T_i, the global topic vector G, and the consistency ensuring *Coherence Vector* $C_{i-1} \in \mathbb{R}^H$.

The *Coupling Unit* produces a modified topic vector ($T_i' \in \mathbb{R}^H$), which is propagated to the *WordRNN* to synthesize the sentence. The WordRNN is a 2-layer GRU, which generates a sentence, y_i, one word at a time, conditioned on the previously synthesized words. The jth word of the ith sentence is obtained by selecting the word with the highest posterior probability, $p_{i,j}$, over the entries of the vocabulary V. A sentence is terminated when either the maximum word limit per sentence is reached or an 'EOS' token is predicted. In the following, we describe the mechanism for constructing the coherence vectors, and the coupling technique referenced above.

Coherence Vectors: An important element of human-like paragraphs is coherence between the themes of successive sentences, which ensures a smooth flow of the line of thought in a paragraph.

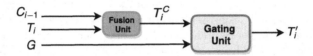

Fig. 4. The internal architecture of the 'Coupling Unit'.

As shown in Fig. 3, we encourage topic coherence across sentences by constructing *Coherence Vectors.* In the following we describe the process of building these vectors. In order to compute the coherence vector for the $(i-1)^{\text{th}}$ sentence, we extract the hidden layer representation $(\in \mathbb{R}^H)$ from the WordRNN, after having synthesized the last token of the $(i-1)^{\text{th}}$ sentence. This encoding carries information about the $(i-1)^{\text{th}}$ sentence, and if favorably coupled with the topic vector T_i of the ith sentence, encourages the theme of the ith sentence to be coherent with the previous one. However, for the aforementioned coupling to be successful, the hidden layer representation of the $(i-1)^{\text{th}}$ sentence still needs to be transformed to a representation that lies in the same space as the set of topic vectors. This transformation is achieved by propagating the final representation of the $(i-1)^{\text{th}}$ sentence through a 2-layer deep net of fully connected units, with the intermediate layer having H activations. We used Scaled Exponential Linear Unit (SeLU) activations [21] for all neurons of this deep net. The output of this network is what we refer to as 'Coherence Vector,' $C_{(i-1)}$.

Coupling Unit: Having obtained the coherence vector C_{i-1} from the $(i-1)^{\text{th}}$ sentence, a *Coupling Unit* combines it with the topic vector of the next sentence, T_i, and the global topic representation G. This process is illustrated in Fig. 4.

More specifically, we first combine C_{i-1} and T_i into a vector $T_i^C \in \mathbb{R}^H$ which is given by the solution to the following optimization problem:

$$T_i^C = \arg\min_{\hat{T}_i^C} \quad \alpha||T_i - \hat{T}_i^C||_2^2 + \beta||C_{i-1} - \hat{T}_i^C||_2^2 \quad \text{with} \quad \alpha, \beta \geq 0.$$

The solution, when α, β both are not equal to 0, is given by:

$$T_i^C = \frac{\alpha T_i + \beta C_{i-1}}{\alpha + \beta}.$$

We refer the interested reader to the supplementary for this derivation. Intuitively, this formulation encourages T_i^C to be 'similar' to both the coherence vector, C_{i-1} and the current topic vector, T_i – thereby aiding cross-sentence topic coherence. Moreover, the closed form solution of this formulation permits an efficient implementation as well.

The obtained vector T_i^C is then coupled with the global topic vector G, via a gating function. We implement this gating function using a single GRU layer with vector T_i^C as input and global topic vector G as its hidden state vector. The output of this GRU cell, T_i', is the final topic vector which is used to produce the ith sentence via the WordRNN.

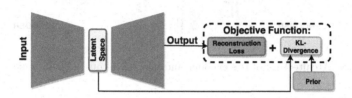

Fig. 5. General framework of our VAE formulation.

Loss Function and Training: Both Topic Generation Net and Sentence Generation Net are trained jointly end-to-end using labeled training data, which consists of pairs (x, y) of an image x and a corresponding paragraph y. If one image is associated with multiple paragraphs, we create a separate pair for each. Our training loss function $\ell_{\text{train}}(x, y)$ couples two cross-entropy losses: a binary cross-entropy sentence-level loss on the distribution u_i for the ith sentence $(\ell_{\text{s}}(u_i, \mathbb{1}_{i \leq S}))$, and a word-level loss, on the distribution $p_{i,j}$ for the jth word of the ith sentence $(\ell_{\text{w}}(p_{i,j}, y_{i,j}))$. Assuming S sentences in the ground-truth paragraph, with the ith sentence having N_i words, our loss function is given by:

$$\ell_{\text{train}}(x, y) = \lambda_s \sum_{i=1}^{S} \ell_{\text{s}}(u_i, \mathbb{1}_{i=S}) + \lambda_w \sum_{i=1}^{S} \sum_{j=1}^{N_i} \ell_{\text{w}}(p_{i,j}, y_{i,j}), \qquad (2)$$

where $\mathbb{1}_{\{\cdot\}}$ is the indicator function, λ_s, λ_w are the weights. Armed with this loss function our method is trained via the Adam optimizer [19] to update the parameters w_T and w_s.

3.3 Diverse Coherent Paragraph Generation

The aforementioned scheme for generating paragraphs lacks in one key aspect: it doesn't model the ambiguity inherent to a *diverse* set of paragraphs that fit a given image. In order to incorporate this element of diversity into our model, we cast the designed paragraph generation mechanism into a *Variational Autoencoder* (VAE) [20] formulation, a generic architecture of which is shown in Fig. 5. Note that we prefer a VAE formulation over other popular tools for modeling diversity, such as GANs, because of the following reasons: (1) GANs are known to suffer from training difficulties unlike VAEs [3]; (2) The intermediate sampling step in the generator of a GAN (for generating text) is not differentiable and thus one has to resort to Policy Gradient-based algorithms or Gumbel softmax, which makes the training procedure non-trivial. The details of our formulation follow.

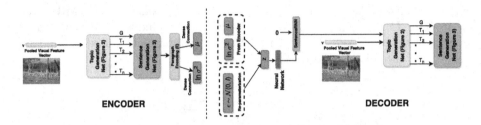

Fig. 6. Architecture of the encoder and decoder of our VAE formulation.

VAE Formulation: The goal of our VAE formulation is to model the log-likelihood of paragraphs y conditioned on images x, *i.e.*, $\ln p(y|x)$. To this end, a VAE assumes that the data, *i.e.*, in our case paragraphs, arise from a low-dimensional manifold space represented by samples z. Given a sample z, we reconstruct, *i.e.*, decode, a paragraph y by modeling $p_\theta(y|z, x)$ via a deep net. The ability to randomly sample from this latent space provides diversity. In the context of our task the decoder is the paragraph generation module described in Sect. 3.2, augmented by taking samples from the latent space as input. We subsequently denote the parameters of the paragraph generation module by $\theta = [w_T, w_s]$. To learn a meaningful manifold space we require the decoder's posterior $p_\theta(z|y, x)$. However computing the decoder's posterior $p_\theta(z|y, x)$ is known to be challenging [20]. Hence, we commonly approximate this distribution using another probability $q_\phi(z|y, x)$, which constitutes the encoder section of the model, parameterized by ϕ. Further, let $p(z)$ denote the prior distribution of samples in the latent space. Using the aforementioned distributions, the VAE formulation can be obtained from the following identity:

$$\ln p(y|x) - KL(q_\phi(z|y, x), p_\theta(z|y, x)) = \mathbb{E}_{q_\phi(z|y, x)}[\ln p_\theta(y|z, x)] - KL(q_\phi(z|y, x), p(z)),$$

where $KL(\cdot, \cdot)$ denotes the KL divergence between two distributions. Due to the non-negativity of the KL-divergence we immediately observe the right hand side to be a lower bound on the log-likelihood $\ln p(y|x)$ which can be maximized w.r.t. its parameters ϕ and θ. The first term on the right hand side optimizes the reconstruction loss, *i.e.*, the conditional likelihood of the decoded paragraph (for which we use the loss in Eq. 2), while the second term acts like a distributional regularizer (ensuring smoothness). Training this system end-to-end via backpropagation is hard because of the intermediate, non-differentiable, step of sampling z. This bottleneck is mitigated by introducing the *Re-parameterization Trick* [20]. The details of the encoder and decoder follow.

Encoder: The encoder architecture is shown in Fig. 6. Given the image x and a ground-truth paragraph y we encode the sample (x, y) by passing it through the topic and sentence generation nets. We then extract the hidden state vector ($E \in \mathbb{R}^H$) from the final WordRNN of the Sentence Generation net. This vector is passed through a 1-layer densely connected net, the output layer of which has $2H$ neurons. We assume the conditional distribution underlying the encoder, $q_\phi(z|y,x)$ to be a Gaussian, whose mean μ is the output of the first H neurons, while the remaining H neurons give a measure of the log-variance, *i.e.*, $\ln \sigma^2$.

Decoder: The decoding architecture is also shown in Fig. 6. While decoding, we draw a sample $z \sim \mathcal{N}(0, I)$ ($z \in \mathbb{R}^H$, for training: we additionally shift and scale it by: $z = \mu + \sigma\epsilon$, where $\epsilon \sim \mathcal{N}(0, I)$) and pass it to the SentenceRNN, via a single-layer neural net with I output neurons. The hidden state of this RNN is then forward propagated to the SentenceRNN unit, which also receives the pooled visual vector v. Afterwards, the decoding proceeds as discussed before.

4   Experimental Evaluations

Datasets: We first conduct experiments on the *Stanford image-paragraph dataset* [22], a standard in the area of visual paragraph generation. The dataset consists of 19,551 images from the Visual Genome [23] and MS COCO dataset [27]. These images are annotated with human-labeled paragraphs, 67.50 words long, with each sentence having 11.91 words, on average. The experimental protocol divides this dataset into 14,575 training, 2,487 validation, and 2,489 testing examples [22]. Further, in order to exhibit generalizability of our approach, different from prior work, we also undertake experiments on the much larger, *Amazon Product-Review dataset* ('Office-Products' category) [30] for the task of generating reviews. This is a dataset of images of common categories of office-products, such as printer, pens, *etc.* (see Fig. 7), crawled from amazon.com. There are 129,970 objects in total, each of which belongs to a category of office products. For every object, there is an associated image, captured in an uncluttered setting with sufficient illumination. Accompanying the image, are multiple reviews by users of the product. Further, each review is supplemented by a star rating, an integer between 1 (poor) and 5 (good). On an average there are 6.4 reviews per star rating per object. A review is 71.66 words long, with 13.52 words per sentence, on average. We randomly divide the dataset into 5,000 test, and 5,000 validation examples, while the remaining examples are used for training.

Baselines: We compare our approach to several recently introduced and our own custom designed baselines. Given an image, 'Image-Flat' directly synthesizes a paragraph, token-by-token, via a single RNN [18]. 'Regions-Hierarchical' on the other hand, generates a paragraph, sentence by sentence [22]. Liang *et al.* [26] essentially train the approach of Krause *et al.* [22] in a GAN setting ('RTT-GAN'), coupled with an attention mechanism. However, Liang *et al.* also report results on the Stanford image-paragraph dataset by using additional training data from the MS COCO dataset, which we refer to as 'RTT-GAN (Plus).' We also train our model in a GAN setting and indicate this baseline as 'Ours (GAN).' Additionally, we create baselines for our model without coherence vectors, essentially replacing them with a zero vector for every time-step. We refer to this baseline as 'Ours (NC).' In another setting, we only set the global topic vector to zero for every time-step. We refer to this baseline as 'Ours (NG).'

Evaluation Metrics: We report the performance of all models on 6 widely used language generation metrics: BLEU-{1, 2, 3, 4} [32], METEOR [9], and CIDEr [37]. While the BLEU scores largely measure just the n-gram precision, METEOR, and CIDEr are known to provide a more robust evaluation of language generation algorithms [37].

Implementation Details: For the Stanford dataset, we set the dimension of the pooled visual feature vector, v, to be 1024. For the Amazon dataset, however, we use a visual representation obtained from VGG-16 [36]. Since, these images are generally taken with just the principal object in view (see Fig. 7), a standard CNN suffices. We extract representations from the penultimate fully connected layer of the CNN, giving us a vector of 4,096 dimensions. Hence, we use a single-layer neural network to map this vector to the input vector of 1,024 dimensions. For both SentenceRNN and WordRNN, the GRUs have hidden layers (H) of 512 dimension. For the Amazon dataset, we condition the first SentenceRNN, with an H-dimensional embedding of the number of stars. We set λ_s, λ_w to be 5.0, and 1.0 respectively, the maximum number of sentences per paragraph, $S_{\max}$, to be 6, while the maximum number of words per sentence is set to be 30, for both datasets. In the coupling unit, α is set to 1.0, and β is set to 1.5 for the Stanford dataset, while for the Amazon dataset the corresponding values are 1.0 and 3.0. The learning rate of the model is set to 0.0001 for the first 5 epochs and is halved every 5 epochs after that, for both datasets. These hyper-parameters are chosen by optimizing the performance, based on the average of METEOR and CIDEr scores, on the validation set for both datasets. We use the same vocabulary as Krause *et al.* [22], for the Stanford dataset, while a vocabulary size of the 11,000 most frequent words is used for the Amazon dataset. Additional implementational details can be found on the project website[1]. For purposes of comparison, for the Amazon dataset, we run our implementation of all baselines, with their hyper-parameters picked based on a similar protocol, while for the Stanford dataset we report performance for prior approaches directly from [26].

Results: Tables 1 and 2 show the performance of our algorithm vis-à-vis other comparable baselines. Our model, especially when trained in the VAE setting, outperforms all other baselines (on all 6 metrics). Even the models trained under the regular (non-VAE) setup outperform most of the baselines and are comparable to the approach of Liang *et al.* [26], an existing state-of-the-art for this task. Our performance on the rigorous METEOR and CIDEr metrics, on both datasets, attest to our improved paragraph generation capability. The capacity to generate diverse paragraphs, using our VAE setup, pays off especially well on the Amazon dataset, since multiple reviews with the same star rating are associated with an object, creating an inherent ambiguity. Noticeably, our model is worse off in terms of performance, when trained under the GAN setting. This

---

[1] https://sites.google.com/site/metrosmiles/research/research-projects/capg_revg.

Table 1. Comparison of captioning performance on the stanford dataset

Method	BLEU-1	BLEU-2	BLEU-3	BLEU-4	METEOR	CIDEr
Image-flat [18]	34.04	19.95	12.2	7.71	12.82	11.06
Regions-hierarchical [22]	41.9	24.11	14.23	8.69	15.95	13.52
RTT-GAN [26]	41.99	24.86	14.89	9.03	17.12	16.87
RTT-GAN (Plus) [26]	42.06	25.35	14.92	9.21	18.39	20.36
Ours (NC)	42.03	24.84	14.47	8.82	16.89	16.42
Ours (NG)	42.05	25.05	14.59	8.96	17.26	18.23
Ours	42.12	25.18	14.74	9.05	17.81	19.95
Ours (with GAN)	42.04	24.96	14.53	8.95	17.21	18.05
Ours (with VAE)	**42.38**	**25.52**	**15.15**	**9.43**	**18.62**	**20.93**
Human (as in [22])	42.88	25.68	15.55	9.66	19.22	28.55

Table 2. Comparison of captioning performance on the amazon dataset

Method	BLEU-1	BLEU-2	BLEU-3	BLEU-4	METEOR	CIDEr
Image-flat [18]	40.31	30.63	25.32	15.64	10.97	9.63
Regions-hierarchical [22]	45.74	34.8	27.54	16.67	14.23	12.02
RTT-GAN [26]	45.93	36.42	28.28	17.26	16.29	15.67
Ours (NC)	45.85	35.97	27.96	16.98	15.86	15.39
Ours (NG)	45.88	36.33	28.15	17.17	16.04	15.54
Ours	46.01	36.86	28.73	17.45	16.58	16.05
Ours (with GAN)	45.86	36.25	28.07	17.06	15.98	15.43
Ours (with VAE)	**46.32**	**37.45**	**29.42**	**18.01**	**17.64**	**17.17**

observation is along the lines of prior work [8]. We surmise that this results from the difficulty of training GANs [3] in conjunction with the fact that the GAN-based setup isn't trained directly with maximum-likelihood.

Qualitative Results: Figure 7 presents a sampling of our generated paragraphs. The first example in the figure (the first row) shows that our model can generate coherent paragraphs, while capturing meta-concepts like 'car-park' or 'parking lot,' from images with complex scenes. Regions-Hierarchical [22] faces challenges to incorporate these 'meta-concepts' into the generated paragraphs. For several of the instances in the Amazon dataset (such as the images in the third and fourth rows), both our method and Regions-Hierarchical [22] successfully detect the principal object in the image. We speculate that this is due to easy object recognition for images of the Amazon dataset, and to a lesser extent due to an improved paragraph generation algorithm. Additionally in the VAE setting, we are able to generate two distinctly different paragraphs with the same set of inputs, just by sampling a different z each time (the two rightmost columns in Fig. 7), permitting our results to be diverse. Moreover, for the Amazon dataset (third and fourth rows in Fig. 7) we see that our model learns to synthesize 'sentiment' words depending on the number of input stars. We present additional visualizations in the supplementary material.

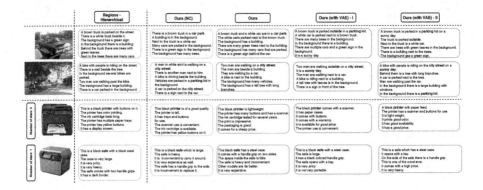

Fig. 7. Paragraphs generated under different settings with our developed approach, vis-à-vis regions-hierarchical [22]. The first, and second images are from the Stanford dataset, while the third and fourth images are from the amazon dataset.

Ablation Study: In one setting, we judge the importance of coherence vectors, by just using the global vector and setting the coherence vectors to 0, in the sentence generation net. The results for this setting ('Ours (NC)') are shown in Tables 1 and 2, while qualitative results are shown in Fig. 7. These numbers reveal that just by incorporating the global topic vector it is feasible to generate reasonably good paragraphs. However, incorporating coherence vectors makes the synthesized paragraphs more human-like. A look at the second column of Fig. 7 shows that even without coherence vectors we are able to detect the central underlying image theme, like 'car-park' but the sentences seem to exhibit sharp topic transition, quite like the Regions-Hierarchical [22] approach. We rectify this by introducing coherence vectors.

In another setting, we set the global topic vector to 0, at every time-step, while retaining the coherence vectors. The performance in this setting is indicated by 'Ours (NG)' in Tables 1 and 2. The results suggest that incorporating the coherence vectors is much more critical for improved paragraph generation.

5   Conclusions and Future Work

In this work, we developed 'coherence vectors' which explicitly ensure consistency of themes between generated sentences during paragraph generation. Additionally, the 'global topic vector' was designed to capture the underlying main plot of an image. We demonstrated the efficacy of the proposed technique on two datasets, showing that our model when trained with effective autoencoding techniques can achieve state-of-the-art performance for both caption and review generation tasks. In the future we plan to extend our technique for the task of generation of even longer narratives, such as stories.

Acknowledgments. This material is based upon work supported in part by the National Science Foundation under Grant No. 1718221, Samsung, and 3M. We thank NVIDIA for providing the GPUs used for this research.

References

1. Aneja, J., Deshpande, A., Schwing, A.G.: Convolutional image captioning. In: Proceedings CVPR (2018)
2. Antol, S., et al.: VQA: visual question answering. In: Proceedings ICCV (2015)
3. Arjovsky, M., Chintala, S., Bottou, L.: Wasserstein GAN. arXiv preprint 2017
4. Chatterjee, M., Leuski, A.: A novel statistical approach for image and video retrieval and its adaption for active learning. In: Proceedings ACM Multimedia (2015)
5. Chen, X., Lawrence Zitnick, C.: Mind's eye: a recurrent visual representation for image caption generation. In: Proceedings CVPR (2015)
6. Chung, J., Gulcehre, C., Cho, K., Bengio, Y.: Empirical evaluation of gated recurrent neural networks on sequence modeling. arXiv preprint 2014
7. Chung, J., Kastner, K., Dinh, L., Goel, K., Courville, A.C., Bengio, Y.: A recurrent latent variable model for sequential data. In: Proceedings NIPS (2015)
8. Dai, B., Fidler, S., Urtasun, R., Lin, D.: Towards diverse and natural image descriptions via a conditional GAN. arXiv preprint 2017
9. Denkowski, M., Lavie, A.: Meteor Universal: language specific translation evaluation for any target language. In: Proceedings Ninth Workshop on Statistical Machine Translation (2014)
10. Deshpande, A., Aneja, J., Wang, L., Schwing, A.G., Forsyth, D.A.: Diverse and controllable image captioning with part-of-speech guidance (2018). https://arxiv.org/abs/1805.12589
11. Donahue, J., et al: Long-term recurrent convolutional networks for visual recognition and description. In: Proceedings CVPR (2015)
12. Gao, H., Mao, J., Zhou, J., Huang, Z., Wang, L., Xu, W.: Are you talking to a machine? Dataset and methods for multilingual image question. In: Proceedings NIPS (2015)
13. Goodfellow, I., et al.: Generative adversarial nets. In: Proceedings NIPS (2014)
14. Gregor, K., Danihelka, I., Graves, A., Rezende, D.J., Wierstra, D.: Draw: a recurrent neural network for image generation. arXiv preprint 2015
15. Jain, U., Lazebnik, S., Schwing, A.G.: Two can play this game: visual dialog with discriminative question generation and answering. In: Proceedings CVPR (2018)
16. Jain, U., Zhang, Z., Schwing, A.: Creativity: generating diverse questions using variational autoencoders. In: Proceedings CVPR (2017)
17. Johnson, J., Karpathy, A., Fei-Fei, L.: DenseCap: fully convolutional localization networks for dense captioning. In: Proceedings CVPR (2016)
18. Karpathy, A., Fei-Fei, L.: Deep visual-semantic alignments for generating image descriptions. In: Proceedings CVPR (2015)
19. Kingma, D.P., Ba, J.: Adam: a method for stochastic optimization. arXiv preprint 2014

20. Kingma, D.P., Welling, M.: Auto-encoding variational bayes. arXiv preprint 2013
21. Klambauer, G., Unterthiner, T., Mayr, A., Hochreiter, S.: Self-normalizing neural networks. In: Proceedings NIPS (2017)
22. Krause, J., Johnson, J., Krishna, R., Fei-Fei, L.: A hierarchical approach for generating descriptive image paragraphs. In: Proceedings CVPR (2017)
23. Krishna, R.: Visual genome: connecting language and vision using crowdsourced dense image annotations. IJCV **123**(1), 32–73 (2017)
24. Krizhevsky, A., Sutskever, I., Hinton, G.E.: ImageNet classification with deep convolutional neural networks. In: Proceedings NIPS (2012)
25. Lavrenko, V., Manmatha, R., Jeon, J.: A model for learning the semantics of pictures. In: Proceedings NIPS (2004)
26. Liang, X., Hu, Z., Zhang, H., Gan, C., Xing, E.P.: Recurrent topic-transition GAN for visual paragraph generation. In: Proceedings ICCV (2017)
27. Lin, T.-Y., Maire, M., Belongie, S., Hays, J., Perona, P., Ramanan, D., Dollár, P., Zitnick, C.L.: Microsoft COCO: common objects in context. In: Fleet, D., Pajdla, T., Schiele, B., Tuytelaars, T. (eds.) ECCV 2014. LNCS, vol. 8693, pp. 740–755. Springer, Cham (2014). https://doi.org/10.1007/978-3-319-10602-1_48
28. Malinowski, M., Rohrbach, M., Fritz, M.: Ask your neurons: a neural-based approach to answering questions about images. In: Proceedings ICCV (2015)
29. Mao, J., Xu, W., Yang, Y., Wang, J., Huang, Z., Yuille, A.: Deep captioning with multimodal recurrent neural networks (m-RNN). arXiv preprint 2014
30. McAuley, J., Targett, C., Shi, Q., Van Den Hengel, A.: Image-based recommendations on styles and substitutes. In: Proceedings ACM SIGIR (2015)
31. Pan, J.Y., Yang, H.J., Duygulu, P., Faloutsos, C.: Automatic image captioning. In: Proceedings ICME (2004)
32. Papineni, K., Roukos, S., Ward, T., Zhu, W.J.: BLEU: a method for automatic evaluation of machine translation. In: Proceedings ACL (2002)
33. Ren, M., Kiros, R., Zemel, R.: Exploring models and data for image question answering. In: Proceedings NIPS (2015)
34. Schwartz, I., Schwing, A.G., Hazan, T.: High-order attention models for visual question answering. In: Proceedings NIPS (2017)
35. Shih, K.J., Singh, S., Hoiem, D.: Where to look: focus regions for visual question answering. In: Proceedings CVPR (2016)
36. Simonyan, K., Zisserman, A.: Very deep convolutional networks for large-scale image recognition. arXiv preprint 2014
37. Vedantam, R., Lawrence Zitnick, C., Parikh, D.: CIDEr: consensus-based image description evaluation. In: Proceedings CVPR (2015)
38. Vinyals, O., Toshev, A., Bengio, S., Erhan, D.: Show and tell: a neural image caption generator. In: Proceedings CVPR (2015)
39. Wang, L., Schwing, A.G., Lazebnik, S.: Diverse and accurate image description using a variational auto-encoder with an additive gaussian encoding space. In: Proceedings NIPS (2017)
40. Xiao, Y., Chua, T.-S., Lee, C.-H.: Fusion of region and image-based techniques for automatic image annotation. In: Cham, T.-J., Cai, J., Dorai, C., Rajan, D., Chua, T.-S., Chia, L.-T. (eds.) MMM 2007. LNCS, vol. 4351, pp. 247–258. Springer, Heidelberg (2006). https://doi.org/10.1007/978-3-540-69423-6_25
41. Xie, P.: Diversity-promoting and large-scale machine learning for healthcare (2018). http://www.cs.cmu.edu/~pengtaox/thesis_proposal_pengtaoxie.pdf. Accessed 25 July 2018
42. Xiong, C., Merity, S., Socher, R.: Dynamic memory networks for visual and textual question answering. In: Proceedings ICML (2016)

43. Xu, H., Saenko, K.: Ask, attend and answer: exploring question-guided spatial attention for visual question answering. In: Leibe, B., Matas, J., Sebe, N., Welling, M. (eds.) ECCV 2016. LNCS, vol. 9911, pp. 451–466. Springer, Cham (2016). https://doi.org/10.1007/978-3-319-46478-7_28
44. Xu, K., et al.: Show, attend and tell: neural image caption generation with visual attention. In: Proceedings ICML (2015)
45. Yang, Z., He, X., Gao, J., Deng, L., Smola, A.: Stacked attention networks for image question answering. In: Proceedings CVPR (2016)
46. You, Q., Jin, H., Wang, Z., Fang, C., Luo, J.: Image captioning with semantic attention. In: Proceedings CVPR (2016)
47. Yu, H., Wang, J., Huang, Z., Yang, Y., Xu, W.: Video paragraph captioning using hierarchical recurrent neural networks. In: Proceedings CVPR (2016)

From Face Recognition to Models of Identity: A Bayesian Approach to Learning About Unknown Identities from Unsupervised Data

Daniel Coelho de Castro[1]([✉]) and Sebastian Nowozin[2]

[1] Imperial College London, London, UK
dc315@imperial.ac.uk
[2] Microsoft Research, Cambridge, UK
Sebastian.Nowozin@microsoft.com

Abstract. Current face recognition systems robustly recognize identities across a wide variety of imaging conditions. In these systems recognition is performed via classification into known identities obtained from supervised identity annotations. There are two problems with this current paradigm: (1) current systems are unable to benefit from unlabelled data which may be available in large quantities; and (2) current systems equate successful recognition with labelling a given input image. Humans, on the other hand, regularly perform identification of individuals completely unsupervised, recognising the identity of someone they have seen before even without being able to name that individual. How can we go beyond the current classification paradigm towards a more human understanding of identities? We propose an integrated Bayesian model that coherently reasons about the observed images, identities, partial knowledge about names, and the situational context of each observation. While our model achieves good recognition performance against known identities, it can also discover new identities from unsupervised data and learns to associate identities with different contexts depending on which identities tend to be observed together. In addition, the proposed semi-supervised component is able to handle not only acquaintances, whose names are known, but also unlabelled familiar faces and complete strangers in a unified framework.

1 Introduction

For the following discussion, we decompose the usual face identification task into two sub-problems: *recognition* and *tagging*. Here we understand recognition as

---

D. C. de Castro—Work done during an internship at Microsoft Research.

Electronic supplementary material The online version of this chapter (https:// doi.org/10.1007/978-3-030-01216-8_46) contains supplementary material, which is available to authorized users.

V. Ferrari et al. (Eds.): ECCV 2018, LNCS 11206, pp. 764–780, 2018.
https://doi.org/10.1007/978-3-030-01216-8_46

the unsupervised task of matching an observed face to a cluster of previously seen faces with similar appearance (disregarding variations in pose, illumination etc.), which we refer to as an *identity*. Humans routinely operate at this level of abstraction to recognise familiar faces: even when people's names are not known, we can still tell them apart. Tagging, on the other hand, refers to putting names to faces, i.e. associating string literals to known identities.

Humans tend to create an inductive mental model of facial appearance for each person we meet, which we then query at new encounters to be able to recognise them. This is opposed to a transductive approach, attempting to match faces to specific instances from a memorised gallery of past face observations— which is how identification systems are often implemented [16].

An alternative way to represent faces, aligned with our inductive recognition, is via *generative* face models, which explicitly separate latent identity content, tied across all pictures of a same individual, from nuisance factors such as pose, expression and illumination [15,18,21]. While mostly limited to linear projections from pixel space (or mixtures thereof), the probabilistic framework applied in these works allowed tackling a variety of face recognition tasks, such as closed- and open-set identification, verification and clustering.

A further important aspect of social interactions is that, as an individual continues to observe faces every day, they encounter some people much more often than others, and the total number of distinct identities ever met tends to increase virtually without bounds. Additionally, we argue that human face recognition does not happen in an isolated environment, but situational contexts (e.g. 'home', 'work', 'gym') constitute strong cues for the groups of people a person expects to meet (Fig. 1b).

With regards to tagging, in daily life we very rarely obtain named face observations: acquaintances normally introduce themselves only once, and not repeatedly whenever they are in our field of view. In other words, humans are naturally

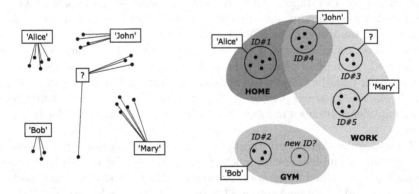

(a) Standard face recognition   (b) Context-aware model of identities

Fig. 1. Face recognition settings. Points represent face observations and boxes are name labels.

capable of semi-supervised learning, generalising sparse name annotations to all observations of the corresponding individuals, while additionally reconciling naming conflicts due to noise and uncertainty.

In contrast, standard computational face identification is *fully supervised* (see Fig. 1a), relying on vast labelled databases of high-quality images [1]. Although many supervised methods achieve astonishing accuracy on challenging benchmarks (e.g. [25,26]) and are successfully employed in practical biometric applications, this setting has arguably limited analogy to human social experience.

Expanding on the generative perspective, we introduce a unified Bayesian model which reflects all the above considerations on identity distributions, context-awareness and labelling (Fig. 1b). Our nonparametric identity model effectively represents an unbounded population of identities, while taking contextual co-occurrence relations into account and exploiting modern deep face representations to overcome limitations of previous linear generative models. Our main contributions in this work are twofold:

1. We propose an unsupervised face recognition model which can explicitly reason about people it has never seen; and
2. We attach to it a novel robust label model enabling it to predict names by learning from both named and unnamed faces.

Related Work. Other face recognition methods (even those formulated in a Bayesian framework) [9,17,27,32,33], often limit themselves to point estimates of parameters and predictions, occasionally including ad-hoc confidence metrics. A distinct advantage of our approach is that it is probabilistic end-to-end, and thus naturally provides predictions with principled, quantifiable uncertainties. Moreover, we employ modern Bayesian modelling tools—namely hierarchical nonparametrics—which enable dynamically adapting model complexity while faithfully reflecting the real-world assumptions laid out above.

Secondly, although automatic face tagging is a very common task, each problem setting can impose wildly different assumptions and constraints. Typical application domains involve the annotation of personal photo galleries [3,12,32,33], multimedia (e.g. TV) [17,27] or security/surveillance [16]. Our work focuses on egocentric human-like face recognition, a setting which seems largely unexplored, as most of the work using first-person footage appears to revolve around other tasks like object and activity recognition, face detection, and tracking [4]. As we explained previously, the dynamic, *online* nature of first-person social experience brings a number of specific modelling challenges for face recognition.

Finally, while there is substantial prior work on using contexts to assist face recognition, we emphasize that much (perhaps most) of it is effectively complementary to our unified framework. Notions of *global* context such as timestamp, geolocation and image background [3,9,30,33] can readily be used to inform our current context model (Sect. 2.1). In addition, we can naturally augment the proposed face model (Sect. 2.3) to leverage further *individual* context features, e.g. clothing and speech [3,17,27,33]. Integration of these additional factors opens exciting avenues for future research.

2   A Model of Identities

In this section, we describe in isolation each of the building blocks of the proposed approach to facial identity recognition: the context model, the identity model and the face model. We assume data is collected in the form of camera *frames* (either photographs or a video stills), numbered 1 to M, and faces are cropped with some face detection system and grouped by frame number indicators, $f_n \in \{1, \ldots, M\}$. The diagram in Fig. 2 illustrates the full proposed graphical model, including the label model detailed in Sect. 3.

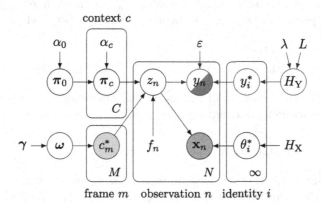

Fig. 2. Overview of the proposed generative model, encompassing the **context model**, **identity model, face model** and **label model**. Unfilled nodes represent latent variables, shaded nodes are observed, the half-shaded node is observed only for a subset of the indices and uncircled nodes denote fixed hyperparameters. π_0 and $(\pi_c)_{c=1}^{C}$ are the global and context-wise identity probabilities, ω denotes the context probabilities, $(c_m^*)_{m=1}^{M}$ are the frame-wise context labels, indexed by the frame numbers $(f_n)_{n=1}^{N}$, $(z_n)_{n=1}^{N}$ are the latent identity indicators, $(\mathbf{x}_n)_{n=1}^{N}$ are the face observations and $(y_n)_{n=1}^{N}$ are the respective name annotations, $(\theta_i^*)_{i=1}^{\infty}$ are the parameters of the face model and $(y_i^*)_{i=1}^{\infty}$ are the identities' name labels. See text for descriptions of the remaining symbols.

2.1   Context Model

In our identity recognition scenario, we imagine the user moving between contexts throughout the day (e.g. home–work–gym...). Since humans naturally use situational context as a strong prior on the groups of people we expect to encounter in each situation, we incorporate context-awareness in our model of identities to mimic human-like face recognition.

The context model we propose involves a categorical variable $c_n \in \{1, \ldots, C\}$ for each observation, where C is some fixed number of distinct contexts.[1] Crucially, we assume that all observations in frame m, $\mathcal{F}_m = \{n : f_n = m\}$, share the same context, c_m^* (i.e. $\forall n, c_n = c_{f_n}^*$).

---

[1] See footnote 4.

We define the identity indicators to be independent given the context of the corresponding frames (see Sect. 2.2, below). However, since the contexts are tied by frame, marginalising over the contexts captures identity co-occurrence relations. In turn, these allow the model to make more confident predictions about people who tend to be seen together in the same environment.

This formalisation of contexts as discrete semantic labels is closely related to the place recognition model in [30], used there to disambiguate predictions for object detection. It has also been demonstrated that explicit incorporation of a context variable can greatly improve clustering with mixture models [19].

Finally, we assume the context indicators c_m^* are independently distributed according to probabilities $\boldsymbol{\omega}$, which themselves follow a Dirichlet prior:

$$\boldsymbol{\omega} \sim \mathrm{Dir}(\boldsymbol{\gamma}) \tag{1}$$
$$c_m^* \mid \boldsymbol{\omega} \sim \mathrm{Cat}(\boldsymbol{\omega}), \qquad\qquad m = 1, \ldots, M, \tag{2}$$

where M is the total number of frames. In our simulation experiments, we use a symmetric Dirichlet prior, setting $\boldsymbol{\gamma} = (\gamma_0/C, \ldots, \gamma_0/C)$.

2.2   Identity Model

In the daily-life scenario described in Sect. 1, an increasing number of unique identities will tend to appear as more faces are observed. This number is expected to grow much more slowly than the number of observations, and can be considered unbounded in practice (we do not expect a user to run out of new people to meet). Moreover, we can expect some people to be encountered much more often than others. Since a Dirichlet process (DP) [10] displays properties that mirror all of the above phenomena [28], it is a sound choice for modelling the distribution of identities.

Furthermore, the assumption that all people can potentially be encountered in any context, but with different probabilities, is perfectly captured by a hierarchical Dirichlet process (HDP) [29]. Making use of the context model, we define one DP *per context* c, each with concentration parameter α_c and sharing the same *global* DP as a base measure.[2] This hierarchical construction thus produces context-specific distributions over a common set of identities.

We consider that each of the N face detections is associated to a latent identity indicator variable, z_n. We can write the generative process as

$$\boldsymbol{\pi}_0 \sim \mathrm{GEM}(\alpha_0) \tag{3}$$
$$\boldsymbol{\pi}_c \mid \boldsymbol{\pi}_0 \sim \mathrm{DP}(\alpha_c, \boldsymbol{\pi}_0), \qquad\qquad c = 1, \ldots, C \tag{4}$$
$$z_n \mid f_n = m, \mathbf{c}^*, (\boldsymbol{\pi}_c)_c \sim \mathrm{Cat}(\boldsymbol{\pi}_{c_m^*}), \qquad\qquad n = 1, \ldots, N, \tag{5}$$

---

[2] One could further allow an unbounded number of latent contexts by incorporating a nonparametric context distribution, resulting in a structure akin to the nested DP [5,23] or the dual DP described in [31]. More details in the online supplement, Sect. A.

where GEM(α_0) is the DP stick-breaking distribution, $\pi_{0i} = \beta_i \prod_{j=1}^{i-1}(1 - \beta_j)$, with $\beta_i \sim \text{Beta}(1, \alpha_0)$ and $i = 1, \dots, \infty$. Here, π_0 is the global identity distribution and $(\pi_c)_{c=1}^{C}$ are the context-specific identity distributions.

Although the full generative model involves infinite-dimensional objects, DP-based models present simple finite-dimensional marginals. In particular, the posterior predictive probability of encountering a known identity i is

$$p(z_{N+1} = i \mid c_{N+1} = c, \mathbf{z}, \mathbf{c}^*, \pi_0) = \frac{\alpha_c \pi_{0i} + N_{ci}}{\alpha_c + N_{c\cdot}}, \tag{6}$$

where N_{ci} is the number of observations assigned to context c and identity i and $N_{c\cdot}$ is the total number of observations in context c.

Finally, such a nonparametric model is well suited for an open-set identification task, as it can elegantly estimate the prior probability of encountering an unknown identity:

$$p(z_{N+1} = I + 1 \mid c_{N+1} = c, \mathbf{z}, \mathbf{c}^*, \pi_0) = \frac{\alpha_c \pi_0'}{\alpha_c + N_{c\cdot}}, \tag{7}$$

where I is the current number of distinct known identities and $\pi_0' = \sum_{i=I+1}^{\infty} \pi_{0i}$ denotes the global probability of sampling a new identity.

2.3   Face Model

In face recognition applications, it is typically more convenient and meaningful to extract a compact representation of face features than to work directly in a high-dimensional pixel space.

We assume that the observed features of the nth face, $\mathbf{x}_n$, arise from a parametric family of distributions, F_X. The parameters of this distribution, θ_i^*, drawn from a prior, H_X, are unique for each identity and are shared across all face feature observations of the same person:

$$\theta_i^* \sim H_X, \qquad\qquad i = 1, \dots, \infty \tag{8}$$
$$\mathbf{x}_n \mid z_n, \boldsymbol{\theta}^* \sim F_X(\theta_{z_n}^*), \qquad\qquad n = 1, \dots, N. \tag{9}$$

As a consequence, the marginal distribution of faces is given by a *mixture model*: $p(\mathbf{x}_n \mid c_n = c, \boldsymbol{\theta}^*, \pi_c) = \sum_{i=1}^{\infty} \pi_{ci} F_X(\mathbf{x}_n \mid \theta_i^*)$.

In the experiments reported in this paper, we used the 128-dimensional embeddings produced by OpenFace, a publicly available, state-of-the-art neural network for face recognition [2], implementing FaceNet's architecture and methodology [25]. In practice, this could easily be swapped for other face embeddings (e.g. DeepFace [26]) without affecting the remainder of the model. We chose isotropic Gaussian mixture components for the face features (F_X), with an empirical Gaussian–inverse gamma prior for their means and variances (H_X).

3   Robust Semi-supervised Label Model

We expect to work with only a small number of labelled observations manually provided by the user. Since the final goal is to identify any observed face, our probabilistic model needs to incorporate a semi-supervised aspect, generalising the sparse given labels to unlabelled instances. Throughout this section, the terms 'identity' and 'cluster' will be used interchangeably.

One of the cornerstones of semi-supervised learning (SSL) is the premise that clustered items tend to belong to the same class [8, Sect. 1.2.2]. Building on this *cluster assumption*, mixture models, such as ours, have been successfully applied to SSL tasks [6]. We illustrate in Fig. 3 our proposed label model detailed below, comparing it qualitatively to nearest-neighbour classification on a toy example.

With the motivation above, we attach a label variable (a *name*) to each cluster (identity), here denoted y_i^*. This notation suggests that there is a single true label $\tilde{y}_n = y_{z_n}^*$ for each observation n, analogously to the observation parameters: $\theta_n = \theta_{z_n}^*$. Finally, the observed labels, y_n, are potentially corrupted through some noise process, F_Y. Let $\mathcal{L}$ denote the set of indices of the labelled data. The complete generative process is presented below:

$$H_Y \sim \mathrm{DP}(\lambda, L) \tag{10}$$

$$y_i^* \mid H_Y \sim H_Y, \qquad\qquad i = 1, \ldots, \infty \tag{11}$$

$$y_n \mid z_n, \mathbf{y}^* \sim F_Y(y_{z_n}^*), \qquad\qquad n \in \mathcal{L}. \tag{12}$$

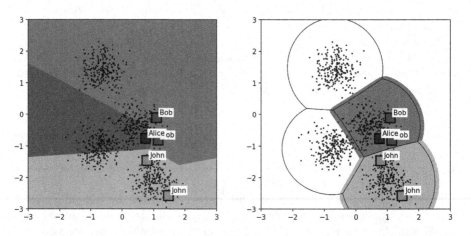

Fig. 3. Hard label predictions of the proposed semi-supervised label model (right) and nearest-neighbour classification (left). Points represent unlabelled face observations, squares are labelled and the black contours on the right show identity boundaries. The proposed label model produces more *natural* boundaries, assigning the 'unknown' label (white) to unlabelled clusters and regions distant from any observed cluster, while also accommodating label noise ('Bob' → 'Alice') without the spurious boundaries introduced by NN.

As mentioned previously, a related model for mixture model-based SSL with noisy labels was proposed in [6]. Instead of considering an explicit noise model for the class labels, the authors of that work model directly the conditional label distribution for each cluster. Our setting here is more general: we assume not only an unbounded number of clusters, but also of possible labels.

3.1   Label Prior

We assume that the number of distinct labels will tend to increase without bounds as more data is observed. Therefore, we adopt a further nonparametric prior on the cluster-wide labels:

$$H_Y \sim \mathrm{DP}(\lambda, L), \tag{13}$$

where L is some base probability distribution over the countable but unbounded label space (e.g. strings).[3] We briefly discuss the choice of L further below.

All concrete knowledge we have about the random label prior H_Y comes from the set of observed labels, $\mathbf{y}_\mathcal{L}$. Crucially, if we marginalise out H_Y, the predictive label distribution is simply [28]

$$y^*_{I+1} \mid \mathbf{y}^* \sim \frac{1}{\lambda + I}\left(\lambda L + \sum_{\ell \in \mathcal{Y}} J_\ell \delta_\ell\right), \tag{14}$$

which we will denote $\widehat{H_Y}(y^*_{I+1} \mid \mathbf{y}^*)$. Here, $\mathcal{Y}$ is the set of distinct known labels among $\mathbf{y}_\mathcal{L}$ and $J_\ell = |\{i : y^*_i = \ell\}|$, the number of components with label ℓ (note that $\sum_\ell J_\ell = I$).

In addition to allowing multiple clusters to have repeated labels, this formulation allows us to reason about *unseen* labels. For instance, some of the learned clusters may have no labelled training points assigned to them, and the true (unobserved) labels of those clusters may never have been encountered among the training labels. Another situation in which unseen labels come into play is with points away from any clusters, for which the identity model would allocate a new cluster with high probability. In both cases, this model gives us a principled estimate of the probability of assigning a special 'unknown' label.

The base measure L may be defined over a rudimentary language model. For this work, we adopted a geometric/negative binomial model for the string length $|\ell|$, with characters drawn uniformly from an alphabet of size K:

$$L_{\phi,K}(\ell) = \mathrm{Geom}(|\ell|; \tfrac{1}{\phi})\,\mathrm{Unif}(\ell; K^{|\ell|}) = \frac{1}{\phi - 1}\left(\frac{\phi - 1}{\phi K}\right)^{|\ell|}, \tag{15}$$

where ϕ is the expected string length.

---

[3] One could instead consider a Pitman–Yor process if power-law behaviour seems more appropriate than the DP's exponential tails [20].

3.2 Label Likelihood

In the simplest case, we could consider $F_Y(\cdot) = \delta.$, i.e. noiseless labels. Although straightforward to interpret and implement, this could make inference highly unstable whenever there would be conflicting labels for an identity. Moreover, in our application, the labels would be provided by a human user who may not have perfect knowledge of the target person's true name or its spelling, for example.

Therefore, we incorporate a label noise model, which can gracefully handle conflicts and mislabelling. We assume observed labels are noisy completely at random (NCAR) [11, Sect. II-C], with a fixed error rate ε:[4]

$$\widehat{F_Y}(\ell \mid y_i^*; \mathbf{y}^*) = \begin{cases} 1 - \varepsilon, & \ell = y_i^* \\ \varepsilon \frac{\widehat{H_Y}(\ell \mid \mathbf{y}^*)}{1 - \widehat{H_Y}(y_i^* \mid \mathbf{y}^*)}, & \ell \neq y_i^* \end{cases} . \tag{16}$$

Intuitively, an observed label, y_n, agrees with its identity's assigned label, $y_{z_n}^*$, with probability $1 - \varepsilon$. Otherwise, it is assumed to come from a modified label distribution, in which we restrict and renormalise $\widehat{H_Y}$ to exclude $y_{z_n}^*$. Here we use $\widehat{H_Y}$ in the error distribution instead of L to reflect that a user is likely to mistake a person's name for another known name, rather than for a completely random string.

3.3 Label Prediction

For label prediction, we are only concerned with the true, noiseless labels, $\tilde{y}_n$. The predictive distribution for a single new sample is given by

$$\begin{aligned} p(\tilde{y}_{N+1} = \ell \mid \mathbf{x}_{N+1}, \mathbf{z}, \mathbf{c}^*, \mathbf{y}^*, \boldsymbol{\theta}^*, \boldsymbol{\pi}_0) \\ = \sum_{i \leq I : y_i^* = \ell} p(z_{N+1} = i \mid \mathbf{x}_{N+1}, \mathbf{z}, \mathbf{c}^*, \boldsymbol{\theta}^*, \boldsymbol{\pi}_0) \\ + \widehat{H_Y}(y_{I+1}^* = \ell \mid \mathbf{y}^*)\, p(z_{N+1} = I+1 \mid \mathbf{x}_{N+1}, \mathbf{z}, \mathbf{c}^*, \boldsymbol{\theta}^*, \boldsymbol{\pi}_0). \end{aligned} \tag{17}$$

The sum in the first term is the probability of the sample being assigned to any of the existing identities that have label ℓ, while the last term is the probability of instantiating a new identity with that label.

4   Evaluation

One of the main strengths of the proposed model is that it creates a single rich representation of the known world, which can then be queried from various angles to obtain distinct insights. In this spirit, we designed three experimental setups to assess different properties of the model: detecting whether a person has

---

[4] The 'true' label likelihood $F_Y(\ell \mid y_i^*)$ is random due to its dependence on the unobserved prior H_Y. We thus define $\widehat{F_Y}$ as its posterior expectation given the known identity labels $\mathbf{y}^*$. See supplementary material, Sect. B, for details.

been seen before (outlier detection), recognising faces as different identities in a sequence of frames (clustering, unsupervised) and correctly naming observed faces by generalising sparse user annotations (semi-supervised learning).

In all experiments, we used celebrity photographs from the Labelled Faces in the Wild (LFW) database [13].[5] We have implemented inference via Gibbs Markov chain Monte Carlo (MCMC) sampling, whose conditional distributions can be found in the supplementary material (Sect. C), and we run multiple chains with randomised initial conditions to better estimate the variability in the posterior distribution. For all metrics evaluated on our model, we report the estimated 95% highest posterior density (HPD) credible intervals over pooled samples from 8 independent Gibbs chains, unless stated otherwise.

4.1 Experiment 1: Unknown Person Detection

In our first set of experiments, we study the model's ability to determine whether or not a person has been seen before. This key feature of the proposed model is evaluated based on the probability of an observed face not corresponding to any of the known identities, as given by Eq. (7). In order to evaluate purely the detection of unrecognised faces, we constrained the model to a single context ($C = 1$) and set aside the label model ($\mathcal{L} = \emptyset$).

This task is closely related to outlier/anomaly detection. In particular, our proposed approach mirrors one of its common formulations, involving a mixture of a 'normal' distribution, typically fitted to some training data, and a flatter 'anomalous' distribution[6] [7, Sect. 7.1.3].

We selected the 19 celebrities with at least 40 pictures available in LFW and randomly split them in two groups: 10 known and 9 unknown people. We used 27 images of each of the *known* people as training data and a disjoint test set of 13 images of each of the *known* and *unknown* people. We therefore have a binary classification setting with well-balanced classes at test time. Here, we ran our Gibbs sampler for 500 steps, discarding the first 100 burn-in iterations and thinning by a factor of 10, resulting in 320 pooled samples.

In Fig. 4a, we visualise the agreements between maximum *a posteriori* (MAP) identity predictions for test images:

$$\hat{z}_n = \arg\max_i p(z_n = i \mid \mathbf{x}_n, \mathbf{z}, \mathbf{c}^*, \boldsymbol{\pi}_0, \boldsymbol{\theta}^*), \tag{18}$$

where i ranges from 1 to $I + 1$, the latter indicating an *unknown* identity, absent from the training set, and n indexes the test instances. Despite occasional ambiguous cases, the proposed model seems able to consistently group together all unknown faces, while successfully distinguishing between known identities.

As a simple baseline detector for comparison, we consider a threshold on the distance to the nearest neighbour (NN) in the face feature space [7, Sect. 5.1]. We also evaluate the decision function of a one-class SVM [24], using an RBF kernel

---

[5] Available at: http://vis-www.cs.umass.edu/lfw/.

[6] The predictive distribution of $\mathbf{x}_n$ for new identities is a wide Student's t.

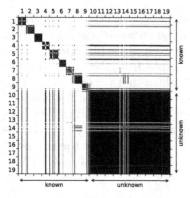
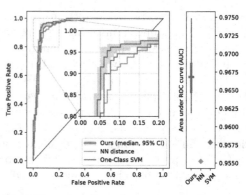

(a) Association matrix, counting agreements in the MAP identity predictions (including *unknown*). Ticks delimit ground-truth identities.

(b) ROC analysis for unknown person detection compared with baselines. AUC is shown with median and 50% and 95% HPD intervals.

Fig. 4. Results of the unknown person detection experiment on test images

with $\gamma = 10$, chosen via leave-one-person-out cross-validation on the training set (roughly equivalent to thresholding the training data's kernel density estimate with bandwidth $1/\sqrt{2\gamma} \approx 0.22$). We compare the effectiveness of both detection approaches using ROC curve analysis.

Figure 4b shows that, while all methods are highly effective at detecting unknown faces, scoring 95%+ AUC, ours consistently outperforms, by a small margin, both the NN baseline and the purpose-designed one-class SVM. Taking the MAP prediction, our model achieves [92.3%, 94.3%] detection accuracy.

4.2   Experiment 2: Identity Discovery

We then investigate the clustering properties of the model in a purely unsupervised setting, when only context is provided. We evaluate the consistency of the estimated partitions of images into identities with the ground truth in terms of the adjusted Rand index [14,22].

Using simulations, besides having an endless source of data with ground-truth context and identity labels, we have full control over several important aspects of experimental setup, such as sequence lengths, rates of encounters, numbers of distinct contexts and people and amount of provided labels. Below we describe the simulation algorithm used in our experiments and illustrated in Fig. 5.

In our experiments we aim to simulate two important aspects of real-world identity recognition settings: 1. *Context*: knowing the context (e.g. location or time) makes it more likely for us to observe a particular subset of people; and 2. *Temporal consistency*: identities will not appear and disappear at random but instead be present for a longer duration.

To reproduce contexts, we simulate a single session of a user meeting new people. To this end we first create a number of fixed contexts and then assign identities uniformly at random to each context. For these experiments, we defined three contexts: 'home', 'work' and 'gym'. At any time, the user knows its own context and over time transitions between contexts. Independently at each frame, the user may switch context with a small probability.

To simulate temporal consistency, each person in the current context enters and leaves the camera frame as an independent binary Markov chain. As shown in Fig. 5 this naturally produces grouped observations. The image that is observed for each 'detected' face is sampled from the person's pictures available in the database. We sample these images without replacement and in cycles, to avoid observing the same image consecutively.

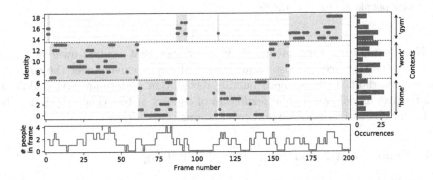

Fig. 5. The simulation used in Experiment 2, showing identities coming in and out of the camera frame. Identities are shown grouped by their context (far right), and shading indicates identities present in the user's current context.

For this set of experiments, we consider three practical scenarios:

- *Online:* data is processed on a frame-by-frame basis, i.e. we extend the training set after each frame and run the Gibbs sampler for 10 full iterations
- *Batch:* same as above, but enqueue data for 20 frames before extending the training set and updating the model for 200 steps
- *Offline:* assume entire sequence is available at once and iterate for 1000 steps.

In the interest of fairness, the number of steps for each protocol was selected to give them roughly the same overall computation budget (ca. 200 000 framewise steps). In addition, we also study the impact on recognition performance of disabling the context model, by setting $C = 1$ and $c_m^* = 1, \forall m$.

We show the results of this experiment in Fig. 6. Clearly it is expected that, as more identities are met over time, the problem grows more challenging and clustering performance tends to decrease. Another general observation is that online processing produced much lower variance than batch or offline in both cases. The incremental availability of training data therefore seems to lead to more coherent states of the model.

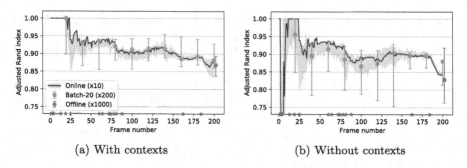

(a) With contexts   (b) Without contexts

Fig. 6. Identity clustering consistency. Markers on the horizontal axis ($\star$) indicate when new people are met for the first time.

Now, comparing Figs. 6a and b, it is evident that context-awareness not only reduces variance but also shows marginal improvements over the context-oblivious variant. Thus, without hurting recognition performance, the addition of a context model enables the *prediction* of context at test time, which may be useful for downstream user-experience systems.

4.3   Experiment 3: Semi-supervised Labelling

In our final set of experiments, we aimed to validate the application of the proposed label model for semi-supervised learning with sparse labels.

In the context of face identification, we may define three groups of people:

- *Acquainted:* known identity with known name
- *Familiar:* known identity with unknown name
- *Stranger:* unknown identity

We thus selected the 34 LFW celebrities with more than 30 pictures, and split them roughly equally in these three categories at random. From the *acquainted* and *familiar* groups, we randomly picked 15 of their images for training and 15 for testing, and we used 15 pictures of each *stranger* at test time only. We evaluated the label prediction accuracy as we varied the number of labelled training images provided for each acquaintance, from 1 to 15.

For baseline comparison, we evaluate nearest-neighbour classification (NN) and label propagation (LP) [34], a similarity graph-based semi-supervised algorithm. We computed the LP edge weights with the same kernel as the SVM in Sect. 4.1. Recall that the face embedding network was trained with a triplet loss to explicitly optimise Euclidean distances for classification [2]. As both NN and LP are distance-based, they are therefore expected to hold an advantage over our model for classifying labelled identities.

Figure 7a shows the label prediction results for the labelled identities (acquaintances). In this setting, NN and LP performed nearly identically and

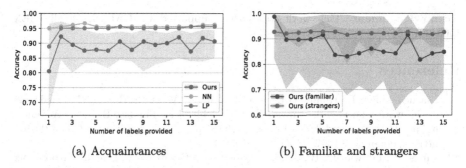

(a) Acquaintances   (b) Familiar and strangers

Fig. 7. Label prediction accuracy. Note that NN and LP effectively have null accuracy for the *familiar* and *strangers* groups, as they cannot predict 'unknown'.

slightly better than ours, likely due to the favourable embedding structure. Moreover, all methods predictably become more accurate as more supervision is introduced in the training data.

More importantly, the key distinctive capabilities of our model are demonstrated in Fig. 7b. As already discussed in Sect. 4.1, the proposed model is capable of detecting complete strangers, and here we see that it correctly predicts that their name is unknown. Furthermore, our model can acknowledge that familiar faces belong to different people, whose names may not be known. Neither of these functionalities is provided by the baselines, as they are limited to the closed-set identification task.

5   Conclusion

In this work, we introduced a fully Bayesian treatment of the face identification problem. Each component of our proposed approach was motivated from human intuition about face recognition and tagging in daily social interactions. Our principled identity model can contemplate an unbounded population of identities, accounting for context-specific probabilities of meeting them.

We demonstrated that the proposed identity model can accurately detect when a face is unfamiliar, and is able to incrementally learn to differentiate between new people as they are met in a streaming data scenario. Lastly, we verified that our approach to dealing with sparse name annotations can handle not only acquaintances, whose names are known, but also familiar faces and complete strangers in a unified manner—a functionality unavailable in conventional (semi-) supervised identification methods.

Here we considered a fully supervised context structure. As mentioned in Sect. 1, one could imagine an unsupervised approach involving global visual or non-visual signals to drive context inference (e.g. global image features, time or GPS coordinates), in addition to extensions to the face model with individual context information (e.g. clothing, speech). Yet another interesting research direction is to explicitly consider time dependence, e.g. by endowing the sequence of latent contexts with a hidden Markov model-like structure [30].

778   D. C. de Castro and S. Nowozin

Acknowledgement. This work was partly supported by CAPES, Brazil (BEX 1500/2015-05).

References

1. Learned-Miller, E., Huang, G.B., RoyChowdhury, A., Li, H., Hua, G.: Labeled faces in the wild: a survey. In: Kawulok, M., Celebi, M.E., Smolka, B. (eds.) Advances in Face Detection and Facial Image Analysis, pp. 189–248. Springer, Cham (2016). https://doi.org/10.1007/978-3-319-25958-1_8
2. Amos, B., Ludwiczuk, B., Satyanarayanan, M.: OpenFace: A general-purpose face recognition library with mobile applications. Technical report, CMU-CS-16-118, CMU School of Computer Science (2016)
3. Anguelov, D., Lee, K.C., Gökturk, S.B., Sumengen, B.: Contextual identity recognition in personal photo albums. In: CVPR 2007, pp. 1–7 (2007). https://doi.org/10.1109/CVPR.2007.383057
4. Betancourt, A., Morerio, P., Regazzoni, C.S., Rauterberg, M.: The evolution of first person vision methods: a survey. IEEE Trans. Circ. Syst. Video Technol. **25**(5), 744–760 (2015). https://doi.org/10.1109/TCSVT.2015.2409731
5. Blei, D.M., Griffiths, T.L., Jordan, M.I.: The nested Chinese restaurant process and Bayesian nonparametric inference of topic hierarchies. J. ACM **57**(2) (2010). https://doi.org/10.1145/1667053.1667056
6. Bouveyron, C., Girard, S.: Robust supervised classification with mixture models: learning from data with uncertain labels. Pattern Recogn. **42**(11), 2649–2658 (2009). https://doi.org/10.1016/j.patcog.2009.03.027
7. Chandola, V., Banerjee, A., Kumar, V.: Anomaly detection: a survey. ACM Comput. Surv. **41**(3), 1–58 (2009). https://doi.org/10.1145/1541880.1541882
8. Chapelle, O., Schölkopf, B., Zien, A. (eds.): Semi-supervised Learning. MIT Press, Cambridge (2006)
9. Choi, J.Y., De Neve, W., Ro, Y.M., Plataniotis, K.: Automatic face annotation in personal photo collections using context-based unsupervised clustering and face information fusion. IEEE Trans. Circ. Syst. Video Technol. **20**(10), 1292–1309 (2010). https://doi.org/10.1109/TCSVT.2010.2058470
10. Ferguson, T.S.: A Bayesian analysis of some nonparametric problems. Ann. Stat. **1**(2), 209–230 (1973). http://www.jstor.org/stable/2958008
11. Frénay, B., Verleysen, M.: Classification in the presence of label noise: a survey. IEEE Trans. Neural Netw. Learn. Syst. **25**(5), 845–869 (2014). https://doi.org/10.1109/TNNLS.2013.2292894
12. Gallagher, A.C., Chen, T.: Using context to recognize people in consumer images. IPSJ Trans. Comput. Vis. Appl. **1**, 115–126 (2009). https://doi.org/10.2197/ipsjtcva.1.115
13. Huang, G.B., Ramesh, M., Berg, T., Learned-Miller, E.: Labeled faces in the wild: a database for studying face recognition in unconstrained environments. Technical report, University of Massachusetts Amherst (2007)
14. Hubert, L., Arabie, P.: Comparing partitions. J. Classif. **2**(1), 193–218 (1985). https://doi.org/10.1007/BF01908075
15. Ioffe, S.: Probabilistic linear discriminant analysis. In: Leonardis, A., Bischof, H., Pinz, A. (eds.) ECCV 2006. LNCS, vol. 3954, pp. 531–542. Springer, Heidelberg (2006). https://doi.org/10.1007/11744085_41
16. Jafri, R., Arabnia, H.R.: A survey of face recognition techniques. J. Inf. Process. Syst. **5**(2), 41–68 (2009). https://doi.org/10.3745/JIPS.2009.5.2.041

17. Le, N., et al.: Towards large scale multimedia indexing: a case study on person discovery in broadcast news. In: CBMI 2017, pp. 18:1–18:6. ACM (2017). https://doi.org/10.1145/3095713.3095732

18. Li, P., Fu, Y., Mohammed, U., Elder, J.H., Prince, S.J.D.: Probabilistic models for inference about identity. IEEE Trans. Pattern Anal. Mach. Intell. **34**(1), 144–157 (2012). https://doi.org/10.1109/TPAMI.2011.104

19. Perdikis, S., Leeb, R., Chavarriaga, R., Millán, J.d.R.: Context-aware learning for finite mixture models (2015). http://arxiv.org/abs/1507.08272

20. Pitman, J., Yor, M.: The two-parameter Poisson-Dirichlet distribution derived from a stable subordinator. Ann. Probab. **25**(2), 855–900 (1997). http://www.jstor.org/stable/2959614

21. Prince, S.J., Elder, J.H.: Probabilistic linear discriminant analysis for inferences about identity. In: Proceedings of the 11th IEEE International Conference on Computer Vision (ICCV 2007). IEEE (2007). https://doi.org/10.1109/ICCV.2007.4409052

22. Rand, W.M.: Objective criteria for the evaluation of clustering methods. J. Am. Stat. Assoc. **66**(336), 846–850 (1971). https://doi.org/10.1080/01621459.1971.10482356

23. Rodríguez, A., Dunson, D.B., Gelfand, A.E.: The nested Dirichlet process. J. Am. Stat. Assoc. **103**(483), 1131–1154 (2008). https://doi.org/10.1198/016214508000000553

24. Schölkopf, B., Platt, J.C., Shawe-Taylor, J., Smola, A.J., Williamson, R.C.: Estimating the support of a high-dimensional distribution. Neural Comput. **13**(7), 1443–1471 (2001). https://doi.org/10.1162/089976601750264965

25. Schroff, F., Kalenichenko, D., Philbin, J.: FaceNet: a unified embedding for face recognition and clustering. In: Proceedings of the 2015 IEEE Conference on Computer Vision and Pattern Recognition (CVPR 2015), pp. 815–823. IEEE, June 2015. https://doi.org/10.1109/CVPR.2015.7298682

26. Taigman, Y., Yang, M., Ranzato, M., Wolf, L.: DeepFace: closing the gap to human-level performance in face verification. In: Proceedings of the 2014 IEEE Conference on Computer Vision and Pattern Recognition (CVPR 2014), pp. 1701–1708. IEEE, June 2014. https://doi.org/10.1109/CVPR.2014.220

27. Tapaswi, M., Bäuml, M., Stiefelhagen, R.: "Knock! Knock! Who is it?" Probabilistic person identification in TV-series. In: CVPR 2012, pp. 2658–2665 (2012). https://doi.org/10.1109/CVPR.2012.6247986

28. Teh, Y.W.: Dirichlet process. In: Sammut, C., Webb, G.I. (eds.) Encyclopedia of Machine Learning, pp. 280–287. Springer, Boston (2010). https://doi.org/10.1007/978-0-387-30164-8_219

29. Teh, Y.W., Jordan, M.I., Beal, M.J., Blei, D.M.: Hierarchical Dirichlet processes. J. Am. Stat. Assoc. **101**(476), 1566–1581 (2006). https://doi.org/10.1198/016214506000000302

30. Torralba, A., Murphy, K.P., Freeman, W.T., Rubin, M.A.: Context-based vision system for place and object recognition. In: Proceedings Ninth IEEE International Conference on Computer Vision (ICCV 2003), vol. 1, pp. 273–280 (2003). https://doi.org/10.1109/ICCV.2003.1238354

31. Wang, X., Ma, X., Grimson, W.E.L.: Unsupervised activity perception in crowded and complicated scenes using hierarchical bayesian models. IEEE Trans. Pattern Anal. Mach. Intell. **31**(3), 539–555 (2009). https://doi.org/10.1109/TPAMI.2008.87

32. Zhang, L., Chen, L., Li, M.; Zhang, H.: Automated annotation of human faces in family albums. In: MULTIMEDIA 2003, pp. 355–358. ACM Press (2003). https://doi.org/10.1145/957013.957090
33. Zhao, M., Teo, Y.W., Liu, S., Chua, T.-S., Jain, R.: Automatic person annotation of family photo album. In: Sundaram, H., Naphade, M., Smith, J.R., Rui, Y. (eds.) CIVR 2006. LNCS, vol. 4071, pp. 163–172. Springer, Heidelberg (2006). https://doi.org/10.1007/11788034_17
34. Zhu, X., Ghahramani, Z.: Learning from labeled and unlabeled data with label propagation. Technical report, CMU-CALD-02-107, Carnegie Mellon University (2002)

Author Index

Printed in the United States
By Bookmasters